# THE BARBOUR COLLECTION OF CONNECTICUT TOWN VITAL RECORDS

# THE BARBOUR COLLECTION OF CONNECTICUT TOWN VITAL RECORDS

COLCHESTER 1699–1850

COLEBROOK 1779–1810

COLUMBIA 1804–1852

CORNWALL 1740–1854

*Compiled by*

Lorraine Cook White

Genealogical Publishing Co., Inc.
Baltimore, Maryland

Second printing, 2003
Library of Congress Catalogue Card Number 96-76803
International Standard Book Number 0-8063-1521-0
*Made in the United States of America*

# THE BARBOUR COLLECTION OF CONNECTICUT TOWN VITAL RECORDS

COLCHESTER 1699–1850

COLEBROOK 1779–1810

COLUMBIA 1804–1852

CORNWALL 1740–1854

*Compiled by*

Lorraine Cook White

Genealogical Publishing Co., Inc.
Baltimore, Maryland

Second printing, 2003
Library of Congress Catalogue Card Number 96-76803
International Standard Book Number 0-8063-1521-0
*Made in the United States of America*

# INTRODUCTION

As early as 1640 the Connecticut Court of Election ordered all magistrates to keep a record of the marriages they performed. In 1644 the registration of births and marriages became the official responsibility of town clerks and registrars, with deaths added to their duties in 1650. From 1660 until the close of the Revolutionary War these vital records of birth, marriage, and death were generally well kept, but then for a period of about two generations until the mid-nineteenth century, the faithful recording of vital records declined in some towns.

General Lucius Barnes Barbour was the Connecticut Examiner of Public Records from 1911 to 1934 and in that capacity directed a project in which the vital records kept by the towns up to about 1850 were copied and abstracted. Barbour previously had directed the publication of the Bolton and Vernon vital records for the Connecticut Historical Society. For this new project he hired several individuals who were experienced in copying old records and familiar with the old script.

Barbour presented the completed transcriptions of town vital records to the Connecticut State Library where the information was typed onto printed forms. The form sheets were then cut, producing twelve small slips from each sheet. The slips for most towns were then alphabetized and the information was then typed a second time on large sheets of rag paper, which were subsequently bound into separate volumes for each town. The slips for all towns were then interfiled, forming a statewide alphabetized slip index for most surviving town vital records.

The dates of coverage vary from town to town, and of course the records of some towns are more complete than others. There are many cases in which an entry may appear two or three times, apparently because that entry was entered by one or more persons. Altogether the entire Barbour Collection--one of the great genealogical manuscript collections and one of the last to be published--covers 137 towns and comprises 14,333 typed pages.

# INTRODUCTION

# TABLE OF CONTENTS

# ABBREVIATIONS

ae.------------age
b. ------------born, both
bd.------------buried
B. G.---------Burying Ground
d. ------------died, day, or daughter
decd.---------deceased
f.--------------father
h.--------------hour
J. P.-----------Justice of Peace
m.-------------married or month
res.------------resident
s.--------------son
st.-------------stillborn
w. -----------wife
wid.----------widow
wk.-----------week
y. ------------year

# THE BARBOUR COLLECTION OF CONNECTICUT TOWN VITAL RECORDS

# COLCHESTER VITAL RECORDS
# 1699 - 1850

| | Vol. | Page |
|---|---|---|
| **ABEL**, Lydia, m. David **KILLBORN**, Nov. 5, 1767 | 1 | 88 |
| Sophia, b. May 16, 1800, of Colchester, m. Enoch **BULKELEY**, of Salem, Mar. 18, 1824, by Rev. W[illia]m Palmer, at the house of Hezekiah Abell, Jr. | 2 | 164 |
| **ACKLEY**, [see also **OCKLEY**], Fanny, m. Joseph **BECKWITH**, June 1, 1818 | 2 | 248 |
| Hannah, m. John **LORD**, Dec. 25, 1718 | L-1 | 450 |
| Joseph S., of Haddam, m. Laura **MINER**, of East Haddam, Sept. 7, 1851, by Rev. Geo[rge] W. Brewster | 2 | 152 |
| Lewis, s. [Nicolas & Sarah], b. Jan. 5, 1758 | 1 | 115 |
| Lydia, m. Theodore **WATROUS**, Apr. 1, 1827, by Samuel A. Peters, J. P. | 2 | 194 |
| Margaret C., m. Henry A. **COOK**, b. of East Haddam, Feb. 22, 1854, by Geo[rge] W. Pendleton | 3 | 60 |
| Nicholas, s. [Nicolas & Sarah], b. June 2, 1762 | 1 | 115 |
| Nicolas, m. Sarah **WILSON**, [ ] | 1 | 115 |
| **ADAMS, ADDAMS**, Abigaiell, [d. Thomas], b. Mar. 3, 1717/8 | L-1 | 399 |
| Abigail, [d. Daniel & Deborah], b. Mar. 25, 1754 | 1 | 53 |
| Albert Lorenzo, [s. Joseph L. & Fanny], b. Dec. 19, 1838 | 2 | 173 |
| Albert Lorenzo, s. [Joseph L. & Fanny], b. Dec. 19, 1838 | 3 | 7 |
| Andrew, [s. John & Ruth], b. Oct. 2, 1728 | L-1 | 452 |
| Ann Maria, m. Jedediah S. **MORGAN**, b. of Colchester, Oct. 19, 1845, by Rev. Pierpoint Brockett | 3 | 24 |
| Augustus, s. [Benjamin, Jr. & Mary], b. Sept. 23, 1794 | 2 | 115 |
| Benjamin, m. Mary **LO[O]MIS**, Nov. 25, 1719 | L-1 | 399 |
| Benjamin, [s. Benjamin & Mary], b. Apr. 8, 1721 | L-1 | 399 |
| Benjamin, m. Eunice **ROCKWELL**, Nov. 6, 1752 | 1 | 55 |
| Benjamin, d. Mar. 11, 1755 | 1 | 55 |
| Benjamin, [s. Benjamin & Mary], b. July 13, 1764 | 1 | 55 |
| Benjamin, Sr., d. May 13, 1796 | 1 | 55 |
| Benjamin, [s. Benjamin W. & Hannah], b. July 9, 1834 | 2 | 253 |
| Benjamin, b. in Colchester, honorably discharged as a musician, ae 28, y., June 16, 1865, at Richmond, Va., from 1st Lt. Constant G. Stranton's Company (6), 21st Reg. Conn. Inf. Vol., having served 3 yrs. | 3 | 66 |
| Benjamin, m. Mary **WHITCOMB** [ ] | 1 | 55 |
| Benjamin, Jr., m. Mary **WILLIAMS**, [ ] | 2 | 115 |
| Benjamin Williams, s. [Benjamin, Jr. & Mary], b. Apr. 4, 1792 | 2 | 115 |
| Caroline, d. [Benjamin, Jr. & Mary], b. Feb. 7, 1806 | 2 | 115 |
| Cynthia Lorinda, d. [David N. & Temperance], b. May 31, | | |

| | Vol. | Page |
|---|---|---|
| **ADAMS, ADDAMS**, (cont.) | | |
| 1831 | 2 | 153 |
| Daniel, s. John, Jr., b. Feb. 12, 1711 | TM-1 | 197 |
| Daniell, [s. John, Jr.], b. Feb. 12, 1711 | L-3 | 197 |
| Daniel, m. Deborah **CARRIER**, Dec. 1, 1751 | 1 | 53 |
| David, [s. John & Ruth], b. Dec. 13, 1719 | L-1 | 452 |
| David, m. Margery **WILLIAMS**, Feb. 1, 1738/9 | 1 | 134 |
| David, s. [David & Margery], b. Mar. 20, 1740; d. Feb. 28, 1743/4 | 1 | 134 |
| David, d. Aug. 10, 1754 | 1 | 134 |
| David, [s. Benjamin & Mary], b. Feb. 24, 1766 | 1 | 55 |
| David, m. Rachel **WILLIAMS**, Feb. 24, 1790 | 2 | 116 |
| David N., m. Temperance **BIGELOW**, b. of Colchester, Jan. 21, 1821, by John Bigelow, J. P., at the house of John Bigelow | 2 | 153 |
| David Williams, s. [David & Rachel], b. Mar. 5, 1797 | 2 | 116 |
| Deborah, [d. Daniel & Deborah], b. Sept. 29, 1752 | 1 | 53 |
| Electa, d. [David & Rachel], b. Apr. 4, 1799 | 2 | 116 |
| Electa, m. Aristobulas **CARRIER**, Nov. 30, 1819, by John Bigelow, J. P. | 2 | 244 |
| Elihu Bigelow, s. [Davis N. & Temperance], b. Jan. 14, 1822 | 2 | 153 |
| Elijah, [s. Thomas], b. May 30, 1724 | L-1 | 399 |
| Elijah, s. [Benjamin], b. Sept. 4, 1811 | 2 | 253 |
| Elisha, [s. Thomas], b. Sept. 28, 1732 | L-1 | 399 |
| Eliza, d. [Benjamin, Jr. & Mary], b. Apr. 14, 1801 | 2 | 115 |
| Eliza, m. Joseph **DAY**, b. of Colchester, May 24, 1824, by Jacob Seales, V. D. M., at the house of Capt. Benjamin Addams | 2 | 178 |
| Elizabeth, [d. Thomas], b. Nov. 3, 1720 | L-1 | 399 |
| Elizabeth, [d. John & Ruth], b. Dec. 21, 1730 | L-1 | 452 |
| Elizabeth, m. Elijah **WILLIAMS**, Dec. 20, 1750 | 1 | 134 |
| Elizabeth, d. [David & Margery], b. Apr. 5, 1754 | 1 | 134 |
| Elizabeth, wid. of Samuel, d. Nov. 18, 1801 | 2 | 83 |
| Elizabeth Ripley, d. [John & Elizabeth], b. July 7, 1805 | 2 | 64 |
| Elizabeth Ripley, d. [John & Elizabeth], b. July 7, 1805 | 2 | 102 |
| Eunice, [d. Benjamin & Eunice], b. Sept. 25, 1755 | 1 | 55 |
| Eunice, d. [David & Rachel], b. Apr. 26, 1795 | 2 | 116 |
| Eunice, of Colchester, m. Benjamin G. **GOFF**, of Ashtabula County, Denmark Township, at present residing in Montville, Aug. 21, 1825, by John Bigelow, J. P., at the house of David Adams | 2 | 181 |
| Eunice, w. Benjamin, d. [ ] | 1 | 55 |
| Hannah, m. Phillip **CAUERLEE**, Dec. 20, 1713 | L-1 | 654 |
| Hannah, [d. Thomas], b. July 4, 1722 | L-1 | 399 |
| Hannah, [d. John & Ruth], b. Oct. 5, 1733 | L-1 | 452 |
| Hannah, [d. Daniel & Deborah], b. Nov. 29, 1755 | 1 | 53 |
| Hannah, of Stonington, m. Jonathan **RATHBURN**, Nov. 23, 1789 | 2 | 49 |

| | Vol. | Page |
|---|---|---|
| **ADAMS, ADDAMS**, (cont.) | | |
| Harriet Hannah, d. [John & Elizabeth], b. Jan. 14, 1809 | 2 | 64 |
| Henry Packer, s. [Joseph L. & Fanny], b. July 25, 1841 | 3 | 7 |
| Huldah, d. [John & Sarah], b. Jan. 28, 1769 | 1 | 120 |
| Israel David, s. [David N. & Temperance], b. Mar. 21. 1828 | 2 | 153 |
| John, m. Ruth **LO[O]MIS**, June 20, 1708 | L-1 | 452 |
| John, s. John, Jr., b. Aug. 21, 1709 | L-3 | 197 |
| John, s. John, Jr., b. Aug. 21, 1709 | TM-1 | 197 |
| John, 1st, d. Nov. 22, 1732, in Colchester | TPR | 109 |
| John, m. Sarah **SKINNER**, May 1, 1755 | 1 | 120 |
| John, s. [John & Sarah], b. May 9, 1760 | 1 | 120 |
| John Gelsten, s. [David N. & Temperance], b. Mar. 9, 1826 | 2 | 153 |
| Joseph, [s. John & Ruth], b. Aug. 26, 1717 | L-1 | 452 |
| Joseph Lorenzo, s. [David & Rachel], b. Sept. 1, 1806 | 2 | 116 |
| Joseph N., of Canterbury, m. Rachel M **LEE**, of Colchester, Nov. 25, 1849, by Rev. A. F. Park | 3 | 43 |
| Joseph Williams, s. [David N. & Temperance], b. Dec. 1, 1823 | 2 | 153 |
| Laura, d. [Benjamin, Jr. & Mary], b. Apr. 27, 1797 | 2 | 115 |
| Laura J., of Colchester, m. Richard H. **DOWNE**, of Westbrook, Conn., Sept. 21, 1852, by G. W. Pendleton | 3 | 53 |
| Laura Jane, d. [Benjamin W. & Hannah], b. Aug. 27, 1826 | 2 | 253 |
| Lois, [d. Benjamin & Eunice], b. Oct. 10, 1757 | 1 | 55 |
| Lois, m. John **ISHAM**, 3d, b. of Colchester, Nov. 19, 1778 | 2 | 51 |
| Lois, d. [Benjamin], b. Nov. 26, 1808 | 2 | 253 |
| Lois, of Colchester, m. John **OLMSTEAD**, of East Haddam, Apr. 9, 1844, by Rev. S. D. Jewett, Westchester | 3 | 14 |
| Lydia, [d. Thomas], b. July 16, 1729 | L-1 | 399 |
| Lydia, d. [John & Sarah], b. June 4, 1756 | 1 | 120 |
| Marcy, w. Samuel, d. Jan. 31, 1777 | 2 | 21 |
| Margary, [d. David & Margery], b. July 30, 1744 | 1 | 134 |
| Margery, w. David, d. May 24, 1754 | 1 | 134 |
| Margery, m. Judah **SAXTON**,Jan. 5, 1762 | 1 | 13 |
| Marthah, twin with Mary, [d. Thomas], b. Mar. 17, 1727 | L-1 | 399 |
| Mary, m. Andrew **CARRIER**, Jan. 11, 1704/5 | L-3 | 193 |
| Mary, m. Andrew **CARRIER**, Jan. 11, 1704/5 | TM-1 | 193 |
| Mary, [d. John & Ruth], b. July 9, 1726 | L-1 | 452 |
| Mary, twin with Marthah, [d. Thomas], b. Mar. 17, 1727 | L-1 | 399 |
| Mary, m. Benj[amin] **BLUSH**, May 3, 1744 | 1 | 137 |
| Mary, d. [David & Margery], b. Mar. [ ], 1747 | 1 | 134 |
| Mary, [d. Benjamin & Eunice], b. Aug. 3, 1753 | 1 | 55 |
| Mary, m. Samuel **ISHAM**, Jan. 18, 1775 | 2 | 95 |
| Mary, d. [Benjamin, Jr. & Mary], b. Apr. 3, 1789 | 2 | 115 |
| Mary W., m. Henry C. **DIXON**, b. of Colchester, Jan. 24, 1831, by Rev. Joseph Harvey | 2 | 229 |
| Mary Whitcombe, d. [David & Rachel], b. May 20, 1801 | 2 | 116 |
| Mary Williams, [d. Benjamin W. & Hannah], b. Jan. 28, 1840 | 2 | 253 |
| Mehetable N., m. George C. H. **CHAMPLAIN**, b. of | | |

| | Vol. | Page |
|---|---|---|
| **ADAMS, ADDAMS**, (cont.) | | |
| Colchester, Oct. 27, 1850, by Rev. Geo[rge] W. Pendleton | 3 | 47 |
| Mehitable Warner, d. [Benjamin W. & Hannah], b. Jan. 2, 1830 | 2 | 253 |
| Rachell, [d. John & Ruth], b. Sept. 1, 1732 | L-1 | 452 |
| Rachel, d. [David & Margery], b. Mar. 20, 1751 | 1 | 134 |
| Rachel, d. [David & Rachel], b. Jan. 28, 1793 | 2 | 116 |
| Rachel, w. David, d. Jan. 10, 1841 | 2 | 116 |
| Rachel Lucinda, d. [Joseph L. & Fanny], b. Oct. 13, 1843 | 3 | 7 |
| Richard S., of Richmond, Va., m. Martha **ISHAM**, of Colchester, Dec. 5, 1833, by Rev. Lyman Strong | 2 | 260 |
| Ripley Perkins, s. John & Elizabeth, b. Jan. 11, 1804 | 2 | 64 |
| Rosetta Philena, [d. Joseph L. & Fanny], b. Dec. 22, 1837 | 2 | 173 |
| Rossetta Philena, d. [Joseph L. & Fanny], b. Dec. 22, 1837 | 3 | 7 |
| Ruth, [d. John & Ruth], b. Jan. 28, 1715/16 | L-1 | 452 |
| Ruth, m. Andrew **CARRIER**, Jr., Dec. 27, 1733 | TPR | 111 |
| Ruth, [d. Samuel & Mindwell], b. Mar. 12, 1742 | 1 | 102 |
| Ruth, [d. Daniel & Deborah], b. Aug. 15, 1759 | 1 | 53 |
| Ruth, m. Joseph **CARRIER**, Dec. 14, 1762 | 1 | 77 |
| Ruth Philena, d. [David & Rachel], b. Sept. 26, 1803 | 2 | 116 |
| Samuell, [s. John & Ruth], b. Jan. 26, 1713/14 | L-1 | 452 |
| Samuel, m. Mindwell **ROWLEY**, Apr. 15, 1740 | 1 | 102 |
| Samuel, m. Mercy **BATE**, Mar. 23, 1749/50 | 1 | 102 |
| Samuel, m. Elizabeth **CONE**, wid., May 22, 1777 | 2 | 21 |
| Samuel, d. July 22, 1794 | 2 | 83 |
| Samuel, m. Marcy **BATES**, [ ] | 2 | 21 |
| Sarah, d. Thomas, b. Feb. 1, 1716/17 | L-1 | 399 |
| Sarah, [d. Daniel & Deborah], b. Sept. 8, 1757 | 1 | 53 |
| Thomas, [s. Thomas], b. Aug. 30, 1719 | L-1 | 399 |
| Wait, [d. Benjamin & Eunice], b. Apr. 30, 1760 | 1 | 55 |
| Welcome K., of Canterbury, m. Charity E. **SWIFT**, of Colchester, Mar. 16, 1841, by Rev. Joel R. Arnold | 2 | 231 |
| William, s. [Benjamin, Jr. & Mary], b. Sept. 16, 1803 | 2 | 115 |
| William, s. [John & Elizabeth], b. Jan. 25, 1807 | 2 | 64 |
| **ALCOTT**, Eunice, m. Daniel **MORGAN**, Nov. 10, 1748 | 1 | 164 |
| **ALGER**, Sarah, of Lyme, m. John **SCHOLFIELD**, [ ] | 1 | 114 |
| Stephen, m. Mary **CHASE**, b. of Colchester, Nov. 11, 1833, by Rev. Joseph Harvey | 2 | 259 |
| **ALLEN**, [see also **ALLYN**], Mary, m. Elijah **LOOMIS**, Feb. 22, 1807 | 2 | 118 |
| **ALLYN**, [see also **ALLEN**], Lydia, m. Jonas **CLELAND**, b. of Colchester, Dec. 17, 1772 | 2 | 5 |
| **ALVORD, ALVORDS**, Alex, s. [Obell & Catharine], b. Aug. 6, 1767 | 1 | 127 |
| Alex, s. [Obed & Katharine], b. Aug. 6, 1767 | 2 | 23 |
| Asahel, s. Alexander, b. June 7, 1755 | 1 | 107 |
| E. D., of California, m. A. Jane **BROWN**, of Colchester, Mar. | | |

| | Vol. | Page |
|---|---|---|
| **ALVORD, ALVORDS**, (cont.0 | | |
| 1, 1854, by Geo[rge] W. Pendleton | 3 | 61 |
| Elijah, s. [Obed & Katharine], b. June 12, 1770 | 2 | 23 |
| Elisha, s. [Obed & Katharine], b. Apr. 5, 1785 | 2 | 23 |
| Eunice, d. [Alexander], d. June 26, 1754 | 1 | 107 |
| Eunice, d. [Obed & Katharine], b. Mar. 15, 1778 | 2 | 23 |
| Henry, of Bolton, m. Mary W. **GILLETT**, of Colchester, May 12, 1846, by Rev. Joel R. Arnold | 3 | 28 |
| Lucy, d. [Obed & Katharine], b. May 15, 1780 | 2 | 23 |
| Lydia, d. [Obed & Katharine], b. June 3, 1788 | 2 | 23 |
| Obed, m. Katharine **JOHNSON**, Jan. [ ], 1767 | 2 | 23 |
| Obed, m. Catharine **JOHNSON**, Jan. 4, 1767 (Written "Obell") | 1 | 127 |
| Obed, s. [Obed & Katharine], b. Sept. 21, 1782 | 2 | 23 |
| Rachel, d. [Obed & Katharine], b. Nov 19, 1772 | 2 | 23 |
| Sarah, d. [Obed & Katharine], b. May 23, 1775 | 2 | 23 |
| Semor, s. [Obed & Katharine], b. Apr. 7, 1793; d. May 12, 1793 | 2 | 23 |
| **ANDERSON**, William, m. Rebeckah **GLASS**, July 19, 1764 | 1 | 141 |
| **ANDREWS**, Joel, of Dedham, Mass., m. R. C. **SCOVILLE**, of Colchester, Mar. 29, 1843, by Rev. Joel R. Arnold | 3 | 3 |
| John, of Clinton, m. Mary Ann **BROWN**, of Colchester, Sept. 17, 1844, by Rev. Rob[er]t C. Mills | 3 | 17 |
| Roxillana, d. Thankfull **CROCKER**, b. July 24, 1758 | 1 | 32 |
| **ANDROS**, Ralph, m. Lavina **BROOKS**, Nov. 26, 1828, by Salmon Cone, V. D. M. | 2 | 208 |
| **APES**, Griswold, m. Sophia Emily **QUASH**, b. of Colchester, Sept. 13, 1835, by Rev. Lyman Strong | 2 | 279 |
| **AQUITFIELD**, [see under **QUITERFIELD**] | | |
| **ARADIEU**, Joanna, late of Germany, but now residing in Colchester, m. Moletz **BEEAMANN**, Apr. 20, 1853, by Erastus Dickinson | 3 | 55 |
| **ARMSTRONG**, Artemisia, of Colchester, m. Orcamell **JOHNSON**, of Bozrah, Mar. 20, 1822, at Isaiah Armstrong's by Rev. William Palmer | 2 | 144 |
| Caroline C., m. Charles **SMITH**, of Ellington, May 15, 1850, by Rev. George W. Pendleton | 3 | 3 |
| Leonard T., of Bozrah, m. Lois L. **SPICER**, of Lebanon, Sept. 30, 1822, by Rev. William Palmer, at the house of [Rev. William Palmer] | 2 | 155 |
| Lucinda, of Colchester, m. Jared **HURLBUTT**, of Hartford, Dec. 31, 1848, by Rev. P. Brockett | 3 | 38 |
| **ARNOLD**, Bethiah C., m. Erastus **CLARK**, b. of Bozrah, Aug. 19, 1822, by Rev. William Palmer, at the subscriber's house | 2 | 137 |
| George W., m. Lucy A. **BISSELL**, b. of Colchester, Sept. 10, 1840, by Rev. Daniel G. Sprague | 2 | 110 |
| Mary, of East Haddam, m. Oliver **BROWN**, of Colchester, May 24, 1770; d. Feb. 17, 1821, ae 74 | 2 | 67 |

| | Vol. | Page |
|---|---|---|
| **ARNOLD**, (cont.) | | |
| Mary B., of Haddam, m. Warren S. **WILLIAMS**, of Chatham, Oct. 18, 1842, by Rev. Joel R. Arnold | 2 | 206 |
| William E., of Haddam, m. Lucretia **DAY**, of Colchester, Oct. 11, 1829, by Rev. Joseph Harvey | 2 | 215 |
| **ASHLEY**, Henry, of Colchester, m. Mary J. **BIGELOW**, of Marlborough, Conn., Mar. 28, 1843, by Rev. Joel R. Arnold | 3 | 3 |
| **ASPINWALL**, Lewis, of Albany, m. Maria **MURFEY**, of Colchester, May 9, 1831, by Rev. Lyman Strong | 2 | 231 |
| **ATWATER**, Jason, Rev., of Middlebury, m. Clarissa M. **STRONG**, of Colchester, May 4, 1837, by Rev. Lyman Strong | 2 | 106 |
| **ATWELL**, Hannah A., m. Horace C. **CORNELL**, Oct. 28, 1839, by Rev. Hiram P. Arms, Norwich | 2 | 84 |
| **AUSTIN**, John, of Canterbury, m. Laura **STAPLES**, of Colchester, Oct. 21, 1832, by Rev. Lyman Strong | 2 | 239 |
| **AVERY**, Abigail, m. Jonathan **RATHBON**, Jr., Nov. 8, 1744 | 1 | 108 |
| Abigail, of Groton, m. Nehemiah **SMITH**, of Colchester, May 3, 1758 | 1 | 39 |
| Eleazer, d. Nov. 11, 1844, ae 73 | 3 | 18 |
| Julia S., of Colchester, m. Myron N. **MORRIS**, of Warren, Jan. 10, 1838, by Rev. Joel R. Arnold | 2 | 296 |
| Lucy, m. Peter **BULKELEY**, Jan. 13, 1742/3 | 1 | 142 |
| Margaret, w. John J., d. Nov. 6, 1843, ae 68 (Was first wife of the late Daniel **TAYLOR**) | 2 | 90 |
| Mary Angelina, m. Morton **TAINTOR**, Sept. 19, 1833, by Rev. Lyman Strong | 2 | 257 |
| Mary H., of Colchester, m. Israel B. **BIGELOW**, of Selma, Ala., Nov. 2, 1837, by Rev. Andrew M. Smith | 2 | 178 |
| Nancy E., of Colchester, m. Edmund B. **KELLOGG**, of Hartford, Sept. 11, 1838, by Rev. Joel R. Arnold | 2 | 232 |
| Orrin W., m. Matilda H. **LEFFINGWELL**, b. of Colchester, Feb. 25, 1844, by Rev. Joel R. Arnold | 3 | 10 |
| Rachel, w. Eleazer, d. July 25, 1843, ae 60 y. 5 m. | 2 | 64 |
| Rachel, w. Eleazer, d. July 25, 1843, ae 60 y. 6 m. 8 d. | 3 | 18 |
| William C., of Windham, m. Harriet **BREWSTER**, of Colchester, Sept. 25, 1853, by Rev. Anthony Palmer | 3 | 59 |
| **AYRES**, Abigail, d. Apr. 24, 1827 | 2 | 67 |
| Phebe, m. Rufus **RILEY**, Mar. 27, 1836, by Benj[ami]n Trumbull, J. P. | 2 | 284 |
| **BABBITT, BABBETT**, Dorcas, m. Rosel **BEEBE**, Mar. 7, 1763 | 1 | 10 |
| Dorcas, m. Rosel **BEEBE**, Mar. 5, 1763 | 1 | 87 |
| **BABCOCK**, Charles, of East Haddam, m. Elizabeth A. **GILLETT**, of Colchester, May 21, 1837, by Rev. Joel R. Arnold | 2 | 225 |
| Joseph, of Windham, m. Lucinda **LOOMIS**, of Colchester, Mar. 25, 1824, by Rev. Joseph Seales, at the house of Samuel Loomis | 2 | 163 |

| | Vol. | Page |
|---|---|---|
| **BABCOCK**, (cont.) | | |
| Lydia, of Hebron, m. James N. **POTTER**, of Colchester, Mar. 27, 1850, at Hebron, by Rev. George W. Pendleton | 3 | 1 |
| Mary Ann, m. Albert D. **NATHAN**, May 7, 1833, by Rev. Joseph Harvey | 2 | 254 |
| Sally, m. Gershom **BULKELEY**, Oct. 12, 1809 | 2 | 148 |
| **BACKUS**, Bethiah, m. William E. **GILLETT**, b. of Colchester, May 9, 1848, by Rev. J. R. Arnold | 3 | 35 |
| **BACON**, Abigail, w. Pairpoint, d. Mar. 8, 1800, ae 75 | 1 | 153 |
| Abigail, w. Peirpoint, d. Mar. 8, 1800, ae 75 | 2 | 16 |
| Adeline, m. Harvey **HYDE**, b. of Colchester, (colored), Dec. 16, 1829, by Samuel A. Peters, J. P. | 2 | 216 |
| Pairpoint, m. Abigail **NEWTON**, Mar. 21, 1751 | 1 | 153 |
| Peirpoint, m. Abigail **NEWTON**, Mar. 21, 1751; d. Dec. 30, 1800, ae 75 | 2 | 16 |
| Peerpoint had slaves: Cato, b. July 23, 1778; Anne, b. June 4, 1781; Roman, b. Dec. 8, 1783, d. Mar. 29, 1787; Candace, b. Oct. 24, 1786; Anna, b. Apr. 8, 1787; Frank, b. May 15, 1792; Mehetable, d. Zilpha, b. May 3, 1795 | 2 | 47 |
| Pairpoint, d. Dec. 30, 1800, ae 75 | 1 | 153 |
| **BAILEY**, [see under **BAYLEY**] | | |
| **BAKER**, Abishai A., of Montville, m. Mary G. **KEENEY**, of Colchester, May 24, 1829, by Salmon Cone, V. D. M. | 2 | 213 |
| Annis, d. [Asa & Comfort], b. Feb. 15, 1794 | 2 | 72 |
| Ansel, s. [Asa & Comfort], b. Apr. 15, 1802 | 2 | 72 |
| Anson, s. [Asa & Comfort], b. Sept. 17, 1792 | 2 | 72 |
| Asa, m. Comfort **KINNE**, Feb. 9, 1780, at Preston | 2 | 72 |
| Lena, d. [Asa & Comfort], b. Jan. 6, 1784, at Colchester; d. July 16, 1787 | 2 | 72 |
| Sarah Jane, m. Thomas Gross **LOMBARD**, Jan. 9, 1859, by Rev. L. Curtis | 3 | 65 |
| Thankfull, d. [Asa & Comfort], b. Jan. 6, 1781, at Preston; d. Nov. 9, 1785 | 2 | 72 |
| W[illia]m, m. Hannah **WELLS**, Jan. 31, 1782 | 2 | 32 |
| -----, s. [Asa & Comfort], b. Jan. 5, 1790; d. same day | 2 | 72 |
| **BALCH**, Ahimdaz, of Salem, m. Elizabeth **LEE**, of Colchester, Nov. 28, 1833, by Rev. Lyman Strong | 2 | 260 |
| Fanny, b. June 21, 1801; m. Jabez **WEST**, Feb. 19, 1824 | 2 | 250 |
| Mary, b. May 15, 1809, in Mansfield, Conn., m. Lucius G. **STANDISH**, Sept. 7, 1834, by Rev. Lyman Strong | 2 | 159 |
| Mary, of Colchester, m. Lucius G. **STANDISH**, of Bozrah, Sept. 7, 1834, by Rev. Lyman Strong | 2 | 269 |
| **BALCOM**, Emma, of Windham, m. Job **ELLSWORTH**, of Colchester, May 8, 1853, by Erastus Dickinson | 3 | 55 |
| **BALDWIN**, Eunice, of Norwich, m. John **ISHAM**, 2d, of Colchester, Nov. 7, 1764 | 2 | 14 |
| Eunice, of Norwich, m. John **STRONG**, of Colchester, Nov. | | |

| | Vol. | Page |
|---|---|---|
| **BALDWIN**, (cont.) | | |
| 7, 1764 | 1 | 76 |
| **BALIS**, Robert, m. Mary **JONES**, Apr. 15, 1798 | 2 | 78 |
| **BANISTER**, Rebecca, m. John **CARRIER**, Jr., Jan. 13, 1730/31 | TPR | 110 |
| **BANNING**, Charlotte, m. Phinehas **DOWD**, Oct. 30, 1842, by Giles Shattuck, J. P. | 2 | 280 |
| Edwin, m. Emily **WELLS**, Aug. 28, 1828, by Rev. Tubal Wakefield | 2 | 205 |
| George R., of East Haddam, m. Catharine C. **KEENEY**, of Colchester, Oct. 27, 1851, by Rev. George W. Pendleton | 2 | 220 |
| Rossetta, m. Jonathan D. **STEPHENS**, Oct. 30, 1842, by Giles Shattuck, J. P. | 2 | 281 |
| Selden W., of East Haddam, m. Fanny **KEENEY**, of Colchester, June 4, 1845, by Rev. Joel R. Arnold | 3 | 22 |
| **BARBER**, Ellen, m. Gilbert **BUTTON**, b. of Colchester, Dec. 22, 1850, by Rev. Albert F. Park | 2 | 69 |
| Mary, of Hebron, m. Solomon **JUDD**, of Colchester, Nov. 26, 1789 | 2 | 71 |
| William M., m. Julia R. **CHAPMAN**, b. of Hebron, Sept. 24, 1844, by Rev. Rob[er]t C. Mills | 3 | 17 |
| **BARNES, BARNS**, Hannah, of Colchester, m. George **JOHNSON**, of Montgomery, N. Y., Feb. 29, 1824, by Salmon Cone, V. D. M. | 2 | 113 |
| Sarah, m. Thomas **DAY**, June [ ], 1722 | 1 | 140 |
| **BARNEY**, Daniel, [s. John & Martha], b. Mar. 16, 1771 | 1 | 39 |
| Ely, [s. John & Martha], b. Mar. 11, 1773 | 1 | 39 |
| Harry, [s. John & Martha], b. Feb. 6, 1780, in Norwich | 1 | 39 |
| John, m. Martha **FOOT**, Dec. 8, 1768 | 1 | 39 |
| John, [s. John & Martha], b. Nov. 13, 1769 | 1 | 39 |
| **BARROWS**, Brutus, of Groton, m. Julia A. **WEST**, of Colchester, Sept. 21, 1836, by Rev. Andrew M. Smith | 2 | 290 |
| H. D., of Ohio City, Ohio, m. Elizabeth **WILLIAMS**, of Colchester, Jan. 1, 1840, by Rev. Joel R. Arnold | 2 | 118 |
| **BARTHOLOMEW**, Abiel L., of Saybrook, m. Sarah **GUSTIN**, of Colchester, Mar. 20, 1821, by Salmon Cone, V. D. M. | 2 | 142 |
| Catherine Anna, d. [Abiel L. & Sarah], b. Jan. 18, 1836 | 2 | 142 |
| Edward Sheffield, s. [Abiel L. & Sarah], b. July 8, 1822 | 2 | 142 |
| Margarette C., d. [Abiel L. & Sarah], b. Apr. 15, 1830 | 2 | 142 |
| Sarah Alleythina, d. [Abiel L. & Sarah], b. Oct. 12, 1824 | 2 | 142 |
| Sarah E., d. [Abiel L. & Sarah], b. Apr. 19, 1832 | 2 | 142 |
| Walter G., s. [Abiel L. & Sarah], b. June 26, 1826 | 2 | 142 |
| William A., s. [Abiel L. & Sarah], b. Mar. 18, 1828 | 2 | 142 |
| **BARTLETT**, Experience, m. Peleg **CHAMBERLIN**, May 8, 1735 | 1 | 143 |
| John M., m. Harriet A. **RIDER**, b. of Colchester, Mar. 11, 1849, by Rev. F. W. Bill | 3 | 39 |
| Laura, m. Timothy **DIMOCK**, b. of Lebanon, Oct. 29, 1838, by Rev. Lyman Strong | 2 | 229 |
| **BASSETT, BASSET***, Phebe, m. Hiram G. **BUELL**, b. of | | |

| | Vol. | Page |
|---|---|---|
| **BASSETT, BASSET***, (cont.) | | |
| Colchester, Sept. 10, 1839, by Rev. Lyman Strong | | |
| *BISSELL | 2 | 98 |
| Phillip, negro, m. Betsey **JAMSON**, May 14, 1741 | 1 | 144 |
| **BATES, BATE**, Abigail, m. Nath[anie]ll **SAXTON**, Nov. 24, 1741 | 1 | 139 |
| Ann, d. [James], b. Dec. 27, 1741 | 1 | 104 |
| Anna, m. John **BIGELOW**, Jr., Oct. 22, 1736 | 1 | 126 |
| Anna, d. James, b. Dec. 27, 1740 | 1 | 143 |
| Dorothy, [d. James], b. May 6, 1746 | 1 | 104 |
| Dorothy, d. [James], b. Aug. 2, 1746 | 1 | 143 |
| Ephraim, [s. James], b. May 7, 1744 | 1 | 104 |
| Ephraim, [s. James], b. May 8, 1744 | 1 | 143 |
| Eunice, m. James **MARSHALL**, of Colchester, Nov. 20, 1740 | 1 | 138 |
| James, m. [ ] | 1 | 104 |
| Marcy, m. Samuel **ADAMS**, [ ]; d. Jan. 31, 1777 | 2 | 21 |
| Mercy, m. Samuel **ADAMS**, Mar. 23, 1749/50 | 1 | 102 |
| Oliver, [s. James], b. June 15, 1748 | 1 | 104 |
| Sarah, m. John **BIGELOW**, Feb. 2, 1737/8 | 1 | 126 |
| Sarah, [d. James], b. July 15, 1750 | 1 | 104 |
| Timothy, s. James, b. Aug. 17, 1739 | 1 | 143 |
| Timothy, [s. James], b. Aug. 27, 1740 | 1 | 104 |
| Zachariah, s. [James], b. June 15, 1742 | 1 | 104 |
| Zachariah, s. [James], b. June 15, 1742 | 1 | 143 |
| **BATTIE**, Ellen M., of Litchfield, m. Albert S. **OTIS**, of Colchester, May 14, 1853, by Rev. Lyman Strong | 3 | 55 |
| **BAYLEY**, Amy, b. May 17, 1738, of Lebanon, m. Ezra **CLARK**, Feb. 3, 1757 | 2 | 92 |
| Joshua, m. Ann **FOOT**, Apr. 6, 1758 | 1 | 57 |
| **BEACH**, Ebenezer, s. John & Ann, b. Feb. 17, 1732/3; d. Apr. 5, 1734 | TPR | 109 |
| **BEADLE, BEEDLE**, Abigail, [d. Benjamin & Martha], b. Oct. 20, 1772 | 1 | 2 |
| Abigail, d. [Benjamin & Mary], b. Oct. 20, 1772 | 2 | 39 |
| Benjamin, m. Mary **MUNN**, Feb. 6, 1766 | 2 | 39 |
| Benjamin, [s. Benjamin & Martha], b. June 1, 1766 | 1 | 2 |
| Benjamin, s. [Benjamin & Mary], b. June 1, 1766 | 2 | 39 |
| Benjamin, m. Sybil **GILLETT**, Oct. 21, 1781 | 2 | 39 |
| Benjamin, m. Rhoda **HINCKLEY**, of Lebanon, Mar. 4, 1789 | 2 | 39 |
| Benjamin, m. Martha **MAN**, [ ] (Probably "**MUN**") | 1 | 2 |
| Chauncey, s. [Benjamin & Rhoda], b. June 25, 1791 | 2 | 39 |
| David, [s. Benjamin & Martha], b. June 8, 1767 | 1 | 2 |
| David, s. [Benjamin & Mary], b. June 8, 1767 | 2 | 39 |
| Flavel, s. [Benjamin & Sybel], b. Mar. 13, 1788 | 2 | 39 |
| Hael, s. [Benjamin & Rhoda], b. Jan. 23, 1793 (Perhaps "Joel"?) | 2 | 39 |
| Harvey, twin with Henry, s. [Benjamin & Sybil], b. Aug. 15, 1782 | 2 | 39 |
| Henry, twin with Harvey, s. [Benjamin & Sybil], b. | | |

| | Vol. | Page |
|---|---|---|
| **BEADLE, BEEDLE**, (cont.) | | |
| Aug. 15, 1782 | 2 | 39 |
| Hoel, s. [Benjamin & Rhoda], b. Jan. 23, 1793 (Perhaps Hael of Joel) | 2 | 39 |
| Homer, twin with Horace, s. [Benjamin & Sybel], b. Nov. 21, 1785 | 2 | 39 |
| Horace, twin with Homer, s. [Benjamin & Sybel], b. Nov. 21, 1785 | 2 | 39 |
| James, [s. Benjamin & Martha], b. Feb. 5, 1776 | 1 | 2 |
| James, s. [Benjamin & Mary], b. Feb. 5, 1776 | 2 | 39 |
| Joel, see under Hael and Hoel | | |
| Jonathan, [s. Benjamin & Martha], b. Dec. 22, 1770 | 1 | 2 |
| Jonathan, s. [Benjamin & Mary], b. Dec. 22, 1770 | 2 | 39 |
| Mary, d. Benjamin & Martha, b. Dec. 24, 1768 | 1 | 2 |
| Mary, d. [Benjamin & Mary], b. Dec. 24, 1768 | 2 | 39 |
| Mary, [w. Benjamin], d. Jan. 31, 1781 | 2 | 39 |
| Rhoda, d. [Benjamin & Rhoda], b. Nov. 15, 1789 | 2 | 39 |
| Sally, d. [Benjamin & Rhoda], b. Nov. 8, 1794 | 2 | 39 |
| Sybel, d. [Benjamin & Sybil], b. Aug. 25, 1784 | 2 | 39 |
| Sybil, [w. Benjamin], d. Jan. 11, 1789 | 2 | 39 |
| **BECKWITH**, Abigail, m. Anthony **RATHBONE**, b. of Colchester, Dec. 26, 1821, by Rev. William Palmer | 2 | 79 |
| Betsey, d. [Isaac & Phebe], b. Apr. 30, 1788 | 2 | 131 |
| Charles, s. [Joseph & Fanny], b. Oct. 5, 1829 | 2 | 248 |
| Charles A., of Colchester, m.Susan A. **CRUM**, of Bozrah, Dec. 30, 1849, by Rev. Lyman Strong | 3 | 44 |
| Dorcas, of Lyme, m. Nathan **NILES**, of Colchester, Nov. about the middle, 1774 | 1 | 144 |
| Elisha, s. [Isaac & Phebe], b. Apr. 15, 1794 | 2 | 131 |
| Elisha, of Waterford, m. Betsey **EDES**, of Colchester, Nov.8, 1836, by Amhurst D. Scoville, J. P. | 2 | 291 |
| Elisha, m. Hannah **QUASH**, b. of Colchester, Jan. 4, 1846, by Rev. M. P. Alderman | 3 | 26 |
| Elizabeth, d. [Joseph & Fanny], b. Sept. 5, 1820 | 2 | 248 |
| Eunice, d. [Isaac & Phebe], b. Sept. 16, 1787 | 2 | 131 |
| Hannah, d. [Stephen & Hannah], b. Aug. 11, 1753 | 1 | 148 |
| Isaac, m. Phebe **BECKWITH**, Nov. [ ], 1781, at Lyme | 2 | 131 |
| Isaac, s. [Isaac & Phebe], b. July 28, 1790 | 2 | 131 |
| Jane, of Lebanon, m. Dennis **MALLONEY**, Oct. 3, 1850, at my house, by Avery Morgan, J. P. | 2 | 111 |
| Joseph, m. Fanny **ACKLEY**, June 1, 1818 | 2 | 248 |
| Lois, d. [Isaac & Phebe], b. Sept. 26, 1797 | 2 | 131 |
| Nancy, b. June 30, 1793; m. Gurdon **SHAYLOR**, Dec. 25, 1813; d. Apr. 17, 1833, ae 40 | 2 | 259 |
| Phebe, m. Isaac **BECKWITH**, Nov. [ ], 1781, at Lyme | 2 | 131 |
| Phebe, d. [Isaac & Phebe], b. Dec. 27, 1793 | 2 | 131 |
| Prudence, m. Jesse **ROWLEY**, b. of Colchester, Oct. 2, 1842, by A. R. Pratt, J. P. | 2 | 271 |

| | Vol. | Page |
|---|---|---|
| **BECKWITH**, (cont.) | | |
| Ransom, of Colchester, m. Sally **TURNER**, of Montville, Apr. 6, 1824, by Salmon Cone, V. D. M. | 2 | 165 |
| Sally, d. [Isaac & Phebe], b. Jan. 29, 1785 | 2 | 131 |
| Samuel, s. [Isaac & Phebe], b. Apr. 26, 1799 | 2 | 131 |
| Sarah M., m. Asa J. **CHAMPLAIN**, b. of Colchester, Aug. 28, 1842, by Rev. Augustus Bolles | 3 | 40 |
| Stephen, m. Lydia **DANNIELS**, July 24, 1766 | 1 | 80 |
| Stephen, [m.] Hannah **NEWTON**, [ ] | 1 | 148 |
| Thankfull, m. Jesse **LEWIS**, Oct. 19, 1820, by W[illia]m Palmer, at the house of [William Palmer] | 2 | 154 |
| William R., m. May **BROOKS**, b. of Colchester, Oct. 2, 1842, by N. R. Park, J. P. | 2 | 270 |
| **BEEBE, BEBEE**, Anne, m. Ezra **CLARK**, Feb. 2, 1757 | 1 | 118 |
| Asa, m. Lydia **DAY**, Aug. 4, 1763 | 1 | 96 |
| Asa, [s. Asa & Lydia], b. May 2, 1764 | 1 | 96 |
| Comfort, [d. Rosel & Dorcas], b. Mar. 13, 1765 | 1 | 87 |
| Dudley, [s. Asa & Lydia], b. May 15, 1779 | 1 | 96 |
| Elizabeth, [d. Samuel & Esther], b. May 2, 1763. After the death of her mother, was bp. by the name of Esther | 1 | 78 |
| Elizabeth, of East Haddam, m. Timothy **JUDD**, of Colchester, Sept. 26, 1775 | 2 | 10 |
| Esther, w. Samuel, d. Dec. 31, 1770 | 1 | 78 |
| Esther, m. Jonathan **KEENEY**, Aug. 5, 1792 | 2 | 74 |
| Esther, see also Elizabeth | 1 | 78 |
| Harding, [s. Asa & Lydia], b. Apr. 30, 1783 | 1 | 96 |
| Hesekiah, [s. John], b. Sept. 26, 1729 | L-3 | 9 |
| James C., m. Elizabeth A. **RAND**, b. of Middletown, Dec. 9, 1838, by Rev. Lyman Strong | 2 | 235 |
| Jerusha, m. Young **FULLER**, Apr. 23, 1730 | L-3 | 456 |
| John, s. John, b. Dec. 5, 1727 | L-3 | 9 |
| Lucinda, [d. Asa & Lydia], b. Aug. 10, 1776 | 1 | 96 |
| Lucy B., m. Erastus **CONE**, b. of East Haddam, Sept. 23, 1828, by Salmon Cone, V. D. M. | 2 | 207 |
| Lydia, [d. Asa & Lydia], b. Oct. 26, 1767 | 1 | 96 |
| Mary E., of Colchester, m. Franklin **EMMONS**, of East Haddam, Sept. 7, 1840, by Rev. Daniel G. Sprague | 2 | 210 |
| Nathaniel, [s. Samuel & Esther], b. Nov. 25, 1756 | 1 | 78 |
| Oliver, [s. Asa & Lydia], b. Jan. 31, 1782 | 1 | 96 |
| Paphirus, [s. Asa & Lydia], b. Sept. 10, 1780 | 1 | 96 |
| Peter, [s. Samuel & Esther], b. Oct. 23, 1759 | 1 | 78 |
| Phebe, m. Samuel **JUDD**, Nov. 10, 1776 | 2 | 27 |
| Richard, [s. Rosel & Dorcas], b. Sept. 14, 1763 | 1 | 87 |
| Roecina, [d. Asa & Lydia], b. Jan. 10, 1778 | 1 | 96 |
| Rosel, m. Dorcas **BABBITT**, Mar. 5, 1763 | 1 | 87 |
| Rosel, m. Dorcas **BABBETT**, Mar. 7, 1763 | 1 | 10 |
| Sally, m. William **STARK**, Feb. 16, 1793 | 2 | 55 |
| Samuel, [s. Richard & Thankfull], b. June 5, 1733 | 1 | 57 |

| | Vol. | Page |
|---|---|---|
| **BEEBE, BEBEE**, (cont.) | | |
| Samuel, m. Esther **SKINNER**, Jan. [ ], 1756 | 1 | 78 |
| Sarra, m. Joseph **PUMERY**, Aug. 2, 1727; d. Sept. 3, 1728 | L-1 | 399 |
| Thankfull, m. Jesse **CRAW**, b. of East Windsor, Feb. 28, 1760; b. Feb. 1, 1739, in Colchester; d. Jan. 11, 1777 | 2 | 62 |
| Thankful, m. John **BIGELOW**, Aug. 5, 1773 | 2 | 1 |
| Thankful, m. Elisha **BIGELOW**, Aug. 5, 1773 | 2 | 55 |
| Wilbur, [s. Asa & Lydia], b. Sept. 4, 1771 | 1 | 96 |
| **BEERS**, Eliphalet, m. Amanda **BROWN**, b. of Chatham, Oct. 12, 1835, by Giles Shattuck, J. P. | 2 | 280 |
| **BELKNAP**, Perley, of Middletown, m. Katherine **GUSTIN**, of Colchester, Dec. 2, 1821, by Salmon Cone, V. D. M. | 2 | 108 |
| **BEMAN, BEEAMANN**, Moletz, m. Joanna **ARADIEU**, late of Germany, but now residing in Colchester, Apr. 20, 1853, by Erastus Dickinson | 3 | 55 |
| Sarah, of Colchester, m. Roswell **JEFFREY**, of Lyme, Feb. 18, 1827, by Samuel A. Peters, J. P. | 2 | 193 |
| **BENJAMIN**, Barbara, w. Stephen, d. Mar. 14, 1846, ae 67 | 2 | 27 |
| Eliza, m. Martin **RATHBUN**, b. of Colchester, Nov. 18, 1829, by Asa Willcox, Elder | 2 | 218 |
| Elvia, d. [Stephen & Barbara], b. Feb. 18, 1802 | 2 | 27 |
| Emily, d. [Stephen & Barbara], b. Mar. 1, 1817 | 2 | 27 |
| Emily C., of Colchester, m. Henry W. **RATHBUN**, of Salem, Apr. 17, 1838, by Rev. Andrew M. Smith | 2 | 195 |
| Esther, d. [Stephen & Barbara], b. May 9, 1804 | 2 | 27 |
| Harriet E., of Colchester, m. Gilbert B. **DARROW**, of East Lyme, Feb. 2, 1852, by Rev. George W. Pendleton | 3 | 50 |
| Henrietta, d. [Stephen & Barbara], b. Apr. 1, 1815 | 2 | 27 |
| Henrietta, of Colchester, m. Charles A. **SWIFT**, of Windham, Apr. 17, 1838, by Rev. Andrew M. Smith | 2 | 195 |
| Lucy, d. [Stephen & Barbara], b. June 12, 1806 | 2 | 27 |
| Lucy, m. Charles **LAMPHERE**, b. of Colchester, Nov. 15, 1824, by Rev. William Palmer, at Wid. Benjamin's, Norwich | 2 | 172 |
| Mary Raymond, d. [Stephen & Barbara], b. May 8, 1807; d. Oct. 3, 1818 | 2 | 27 |
| Stephen, m. Barbara **PHILLIPS**, Mar. 7, 1799; d. June 2, 1821 | 2 | 27 |
| Stephen Park, s. [Stephen & Barbara], b. Mar. 3, 1800 | 2 | 27 |
| Susan E., m. John T. P. **TREAT**, Sept. 18, 1854, by Rev. Selah B. Treat | 3 | 64 |
| **BENNETT**, Daniel, [s. Daniel & Abigail], b. Apr. 23, 1770 | 1 | 44 |
| Lucy, [d. Daniel & Abigail], b. Mar. 11, 1768 | 1 | 44 |
| Samuel F., of Hampton, m. Harriet G. **SPALDING**, of Colchester, Apr. 12, 1841, by Rev. Daniel G. Sprague | 2 | 212 |
| **BESSEL**, [see also **BISSELL**], Mary, m. Nathaniel **GILBERT**, Feb. 8, 1720/21 | L-1 | 447 |
| **BIDWELL**, Halsey F., of Norwich, m. Louisa B. **HAMMOND**, of | | |

| | Vol. | Page |
|---|---|---|
| **BIDWELL**, (cont.) | | |
| Colchester, Nov. 1, 1846, by Rev. P. Brockett | 3 | 29 |
| **BIGELOW, BIGLO, BIGLOE, BIGLOO**, Aaron, s. [Azariah & Margaret], b. June 8, 1768 | 1 | 128 |
| Aaron, s. [Elisha & Deborah], b. June 19, 1769 | 1 | 125 |
| Aaron, s. [Elisha & Deborah], b. June 19, 1769 | 2 | 55 |
| Aaron, s. [Joel & Lucretia], b. May 19, 1796 | 2 | 53 |
| Abby Jane, d. [Asa & Lydia], b. Sept. 16, 1804 | 2 | 78 |
| Abby Jane, m. Daniel **SAFFORD**, Dec. 24, 1828; d. July 17, 1830, in Boston | 2 | 78 |
| Abigaiell, [d. Isaac], b. Apr. 13, 1723 | L-3 | 199 |
| Abigail, d. Isaac, b. Apr. 13, 1723 | TM-1 | 199 |
| Abigail, [d. Isaac & Abigail], b. Jan. 1, 1734/5 | L-3 | 454 |
| Abigail, m. Daniel **PRATT**, Jr., Mar. 24, 1755 | 1 | 133 |
| Abner, s. [Azariah & Margaret], b. Apr. 22, 1770 | 1 | 128 |
| Addi, (a son) [Isaac & Abigail], b. Oct. 18, 1757 | L-3 | 454 |
| Alice, d. [Jonathan & Bettey], b. Mar. 21, 1766 | 2 | 72 |
| Alice, d. [Jonathan & Bettey], b. June 13, 1776 | 2 | 72 |
| Amasa, [s. David & Editha], b. Sept. 3, 1733 | L-3 | 455 |
| Amasa, m. Jemima **STRONG**, Dec. 13, 1754 | 1 | 11 |
| Amasa, [s. Amasa & Jemima], b. Jan. 1, 1769 | 1 | 11 |
| Amasai, [s. Isaac & Abigail], b. Dec. 28, 1741; d. Jan. 18, [1742] | L-3 | 454 |
| Amasai, [s. Isaac & Abigail], b. Feb. 11, 1755 | L-3 | 454 |
| And[rew], s. Bond & Sarah], d. Dec. 25, 178[ ] | 2 | 15 |
| Ann, [d. Isaac & Abigail], b. Mar. 7, 1736 | L-3 | 454 |
| Ann E., m. Nathaniel **STRONG**, b. of Colchester, Dec. 31, 1844, by Rev. Robert C. Mills | 3 | 18 |
| Ann Eliza, m. William T. **TURNER**, May 24, 1826, by Salmon Cone, V. D. M. | 2 | 187 |
| Ann Elizabeth, d. [Asa & Lydia], b. June 18, 1802 | 2 | 78 |
| Anna, [w. John, Jr.], d. Sept. 22, 1737 | 1 | 126 |
| Anna, [d. John & Sarah], b. Nov. 13, 1738 | 1 | 126 |
| Asa, [s. John & Sarah], b. Sept. 3, 1720 | L-1 | 654 |
| Asa, m. Dorothy **OTIS**, Dec. 13, 1737 | 1 | 138 |
| Asa. s. [Asa & Dorothy], b. Oct. 31, 1738; d. Sept. 18, 1754 | 1 | 138 |
| Asa, d. Oct. 9, 1754 | 1 | 138 |
| Asa, 2d, s. [Asa & Dorothy], b. May 12, 1755 | 1 | 138 |
| Asa, [s. John, Jr. & Hannah], b. Feb. 2, 1775 | 1 | 76 |
| Asa, m. Lydia **NEWTON**, Feb. 5, 1783; d. July 28, 1830, ae 75 | 2 | 78 |
| Asa, s. [Asa & Lydia], b. Oct. 10, 1794 | 2 | 78 |
| Asa Remock, s. [Guy & Sarah Ann], b. Mar. 28, 1828; d. Apr. 29, 1829 | 2 | 125 |
| Asa Remick, s. [Guy & Sarah Ann], b. Jan. 17, 1830 | 2 | 125 |
| Austin, s. [Joel & Lucretia], b. Feb. 13, 1792 | 2 | 53 |
| Azariah, [s. David & Editha], b. Dec. 26, 1741 | L-3 | 455 |
| Azariah, m. Margaret **FOOT**, Mar. 26, 1767 | 1 | 128 |

| | Vol. | Page |
|---|---|---|
| **BIGELOW, BIGLO, BIGLOE, BIGLOO,** (cont.) | | |
| Benet, s. [Elisha & Mary], b. May 18, 1755 | 2 | 55 |
| Betty, d. [Asa & Dorothy], b. Feb. 8, 1749; d. Jan. 28, 1751/2 | 1 | 138 |
| Bettey, d. [Asa & Dorothy], b. Mar. 21, 1753 | 1 | 138 |
| Betty, [d. Jonathan & Elizabeth], b. June [ ], 1768 | 1 | 38 |
| Betty, d. [Jonathan & Bettey], b. June 14, 1768 | 2 | 72 |
| Bettey, d. [Elisha & Thankful], b. May 9, 1786 | 2 | 55 |
| Bettey, d. [James & Anna], b. Sept. 1, 1789 | 2 | 72 |
| Bond, m. Sarah **PURPLE**, Apr. 21, 1772 | 2 | 15 |
| Charity, [d. Amasa & Jemima], b. Mar. 6, 1765 | 1 | 11 |
| Clarissa, d. [Asa & Lydia], b. Mar. 2, 1797 | 2 | 78 |
| Cynthia, twin with Sophia, d. [Elisha & Thankful], b. Aug. 1, 1783 | 2 | 55 |
| Cynthia, d. [John, Jr. & Temperance], b. Dec. 15, 1800 | 2 | 143 |
| Cynthia, of Colchester, m. Daniel **BULKELEY**, of Virginia, Aug. 1, 1830, by Rev. Alvan Ackley | 2 | 223 |
| Daniel, [s. David & Editha], b. May 25, 1738 | L-3 | 455 |
| Daniel, m. Mary **BRAINARD**, Jan. 8, 1761 | 1 | 22 |
| Daniel, [s. Daniel & Mary], b. Oct. 22, 1766 | 1 | 22 |
| David, m. Editha **DAY**, Dec. 11, 1729 | L-3 | 455 |
| David, [s. David & Editha], b. May 7, 1732 | L-3 | 455 |
| David, m. Marcy **LEWIS**, Jan. 21, 1747 | L-3 | 455 |
| David, s. [Bond & Sarah], b. Jan. 6, 1775 | 2 | 15 |
| David S., of Colchester, m. Abby M. **USHER**, of Chatham, Nov. 9, 1852, by Rev. S. D. Jewett | 3 | 54 |
| Deborah, d. [Elisha & Deborah], b. Oct. 13, 1766 | 1 | 125 |
| Deborah, d. [Elisha & Deborah], b. Oct. 13, 1766 | 2 | 55 |
| Deborah, w. Elisha, d. Jan. 21, 1773 | 1 | 126 |
| Deborah, w. Elisha, d. Jan. 21, 1773 | 2 | 55 |
| Delight, [d. Asa & Dorothy], b. Feb. 25, 1751; d. Sept. 28, 1754 | 1 | 138 |
| Delight, d. [Jonathan & Bettey], b. Dec. 24, 1759 | 2 | 72 |
| Dimmis, [d. John, Jr. & Hannah], b. July 16, 1762 | 1 | 76 |
| Dorothy, d. [Asa & Dorothy], b. Sept. 2, 1742 | 1 | 138 |
| Dorothy, [d. Jonathan & Elizabeth], b. Feb. 3, 1761 | 1 | 38 |
| Dorothy, d. [Jonathan & Bettey], b. Feb. 3, 1762 | 2 | 72 |
| Dorothy, m. Isaac **DAY**, Oct. 12, 1762 | 1 | 115 |
| Ebenezer Lathrop, s. [Joel & Lucretia], b. Dec. 6, 1806 | 2 | 53 |
| Editha, [d. David & Editha], b. Mar. 16, 1744 | L-3 | 455 |
| Editha, w. David, d. Jan. 19, 1746 | L-3 | 455 |
| Edetha, [d. Amasa & Jemima], b. Jan. 9, 1759 | 1 | 11 |
| Elcey, [d. Jonathan & Elizabeth], b. Mar. 21, 1766 | 1 | 38 |
| Eli, [s. David & Editha], b. Aug. 25, 1739; d. Aug. 10, 1751 | L-3 | 455 |
| Eli, [s. Amasa & Jemima], b. May 29, 1756 | 1 | 11 |
| Elihu, s. [John, Jr. & Temperance], b. Sept. 5, 1792 | 2 | 143 |
| Elisha, s. Sergt. Isaac, b. Apr. 14, 1731 | L-3 | 458 |
| Elisha, m. Mary **KILLBORN**, May 21, 1751 | 1 | 125 |
| Elisha, m. Mary **KILLBORN**, May 21, 1751 | 2 | 55 |

| | Vol. | Page |
|---|---|---|
| **BIGELOW, BIGLO, BIGLOE, BIGLOO,** (cont.) | | |
| Elisha, s. [Elisha & Mary], b. Jan. 17, 1752 | 1 | 125 |
| Elisha, s. [Elisha & Mary], b. Jan. 17, 1752 | 2 | 55 |
| Elisha, [s. John, Jr. & Hannah], b. Feb. 4, 1761 | 1 | 76 |
| Elisha, m. Deborah **CHA[P]MAN**, of East Haddam, Oct. 2, 1765 | 1 | 125 |
| Elisha, m. Deborah **CHAPMAN**, Oct. 2, 1765 | 2 | 55 |
| Elisha, m. Thankful **BEEBE**, Aug. 5, 1773 | 2 | 55 |
| Elisha, Jr., m. Welthan **GORTON**, Dec. 16, 1773 | 2 | 28 |
| Elisha, s. [Elisha, Jr. & Welthan], b. Feb. 5, 1775 | 2 | 28 |
| Elisha, s. [John, Jr. & Temperance], b. Sept. 5, 1792 | 2 | 62 |
| Eliza Ann, d. [John, Jr.], b. July 9, 1820 | 2 | 247 |
| Eliza Ann, m. Loren **FLOOD**, Aug. 29, 1835, by Rev. Joseph Harvey | 2 | 281 |
| Elizabeth, [d. Jonathan & Elizabeth], b. Dec. 23, 1759 | 1 | 38 |
| Emma, d. [Jonathan & Bettey], b. June 30, 1773 | 2 | 72 |
| Enoch, [s. Daniel & Mary], b. Nov. 15, 1770; d. Nov. 29, 1775 | 1 | 22 |
| Epaphroditus, [s. Daniel & Mary], b. Aug. 14, 1775; d. Feb. 2, 1778 | 1 | 22 |
| Eph[rai]m, s. [John & Sarah], b. Aug. 21, 1740 | 1 | 126 |
| Ephraim, of Colchester, m. Mary **WATERS**, of Hebron, Feb. 23, 1769 | 2 | 4 |
| Ephraim Bate[s], s. [Ephriam & Mary], b. May 19, 1772 | 2 | 4 |
| Erastus, of Troy, m. Maria **BURGESS**, of Colchester, Dec. 18, 1826, by Salmon Cone, V. D. M. | 2 | 191 |
| Eunice, d. [John, Jr. & Temperance], b. Mar. 1, 1805 | 2 | 143 |
| Ezra, [s. David & Editha], b. Apr. 10, 1736 | L-3 | 455 |
| Ezra, m. Hannah **STRONG**, Sept. 1, 1755 | 1 | 12 |
| Ezra, [s. Ezra & Hannah], b. June 15, 1757 | 1 | 12 |
| Frances A., of Colchester, m. Hiram D. **ROSE**, of East Haddam, Apr. 30, 1837, by Joshua B. Rogers, J. P. | 2 | 192 |
| George Newton, s. [Asa & Lydia], b. Apr. 4, 1799 | 2 | 78 |
| Guy, s. [Asa & Lydia], b. Aug. 21, 1785 | 2 | 78 |
| Guy, 2d, of Colchester, m. Nancy **HURD**, of East Haddam, Oct. 13, 1822, by John Bigelow, J. P., at James Bigelow's | 2 | 158 |
| Guy, m. Sarah Ann **WAITE**, Mar. 8, 1827 | 2 | 78 |
| Guy, m. Sarah Ann **WAITE**, Mar. 8, 1827 | 2 | 125 |
| Hannah, w. John, d. Mar. 31, 1709 | L-1 | 654 |
| Hannah, [d. Isaac], b. Oct. 2, 1721 | L-3 | 199 |
| Hannah, d. Isaac, b. Oct. 2, 1721 | TM-1 | 199 |
| Hannah, [d. David & Editha], b. Nov. 11, 1730 | L-3 | 455 |
| Hannah, m. Roger **CLARK**, Apr. [ ], 1746 | 1 | 94 |
| Hannah, [d. John & Sarah], b. Oct. 31, 1747 | 1 | 126 |
| Hannah, [d. Ezra & Hannah], b. Apr. 10, 1759 | 1 | 12 |
| Hannah, d. [Elisha & Deborah], b. Feb. 10, 1763 | 1 | 125 |
| Hannah, d. [Elisha & Deborah], b. Feb. 10, 1768 | 2 | 55 |

| | Vol. | Page |
|---|---|---|
| **BIGELOW, BIGLO, BIGLOE, BIGLOO,** (cont.) | | |
| Hannah, [d. John, Jr. & Hannah], b. Oct. 22, 1771 | 1 | 76 |
| Hannah, m. Elijah **STAPLES**, Jr., b. of Colchester, Sept. 22, 1778 | 2 | 23 |
| Henry, s. [Azariah & Margaret], b. June 28, 1772; d. Oct. 8, 1775 | 1 | 128 |
| Henry, 2d, [s. Azariah & Margaret], [b.] Feb. 20, 1778 | 1 | 128 |
| Henry Albert, s. [John, Jr.], b. Nov. 7, 1830 | 2 | 247 |
| Henry Waite, s. [Guy & Sarah Ann], b. July 15, 1836; d. Feb. 22, 1838 | 2 | 125 |
| Henry Waite, s. [Guy & Sarah Ann], b. Feb. 1, 1838 | 2 | 125 |
| Ira, [s. Ezra & Hannah], b. May 19, 1763 | 1 | 12 |
| Isa[a]ck, s. Isaac, b. May 4, 1713 | L-3 | 199 |
| Isaac, s. Isaac, b. May 4, 1713 | TM-1 | 199 |
| Isaac, m. Abigail **SKINNER**, Mar. 14, 1734 | L-3 | 454 |
| Isaac, [s. Isaac & Abigail], b. Nov. 17, 1737 | L-3 | 454 |
| Isaac, of Colchester, m. Mary **CHAMBERLAIN**, of East Haddam, Apr. 5, 1759 | 1 | 24 |
| Isaac, s. Elisha & Deborah, b. Jan. 23, 1771 | 1 | 126 |
| Isaac, s. [Elisha & Deborah], b. Jan. 23, 1771 | 2 | 55 |
| Israel B., of Selma, Ala., m. Mary H. **AVERY**, of Colchester, Nov. 2, 1837, by Rev. Andrew M. Smith | 2 | 178 |
| Israel Benoni, [s. John, Jr. & Temperance], b. Sept. 26, 1809 | 2 | 143 |
| Ithimer, [s. John, Jr. & Hannah], b. Jan. 18, 1764; d. Oct. 1, 1775 | 1 | 76 |
| J. Bond, s. [Elisha & Mary], b. May 18, 1755 | 1 | 125 |
| Jarius, s. [Bond & Sarah], b. June 9, 1784 (Jairus) | 2 | 15 |
| James, [s. Jonathan & Elizabeth], b. Mar. 16, 1764 | 1 | 38 |
| James, s. [Jonathan & Bettey], b. Mar. 16, 1764 | 2 | 72 |
| James, m. Anna **DAY**, Nov. 13, 1783 | 2 | 72 |
| Jared, s. [Bond & Sarah], b. Apr. 21, 1778 | 2 | 15 |
| Jemima, [d. Amasa & Jemima], b. May 27, 1763 | 1 | 11 |
| Jerusha, [d. Isaac & Abigail], b. Mar. 8, 1748/9 | L-3 | 454 |
| Jesse, s. [Azariah & Margaret], b. Jan. 29, 1775; d. Nov. 10, 1778 | 1 | 128 |
| Jesse, 2d, s. Azariah, b. May 18, 1780 | 1 | 128 |
| Joel, s. [Elisha & Mary], b. Jan. 9, 1761 | 1 | 125 |
| Joel, s. [Elisha & Mary], b. Jan. 9, 1761 | 2 | 55 |
| Joel, b. Jan. 9, 1761; m. Lucretia **LATHROP**, June 29, 1786; d. Feb. 12, 1849, ae 88 | 2 | 53 |
| Joel, [s. Aaron], b. Apr. 8, 1827 | 3 | 33 |
| John, s. John [& Hannah], b. Mar. 25, 1709 | L-1 | 654 |
| John, m. Sarah **BIGELOW**, Nov. 4, 1709 | L-1 | 654 |
| John, Jr., m. Anna **BATE[S]**, Oct. 22, 1736 | 1 | 126 |
| John, s. John & Anna, b. Sept. 2, 1737 | 1 | 126 |
| John, m. Sarah **BATE[S]**, Feb. 2, 1737/8 | 1 | 126 |
| John, 3d, m. Hannah **DOUGLASS**, June 10, 1759 | 1 | 21 |
| John, Jr., m. Hannah **DOUGLASS**, July 10, 1759 | 1 | 76 |

| | Vol. | Page |
|---|---|---|
| **BIGELOW, BIGLO, BIGLOE, BIGLOO,** (cont.) | | |
| John, [s. John, 3d & Hannah], b. Dec. 8, 1767 | 1 | 21 |
| John, [s. John, Jr. & Hannah], b. Dec. 8, 1767 | 1 | 76 |
| John, Sr., Lieut., d. Mar. 8, 1770, ae 94 | 1 | 83 |
| John, m. Thankful **BEEBE**, Aug. 5, 1773 | 2 | 1 |
| John, Jr., m. Temperance **SPENCER**, of Saybrook, Sept. 29, 1791 | 2 | 62 |
| John, Jr., m. Temperance **SPENCER**, Sept. 29, 1791 | 2 | 143 |
| John, formerly John, Jr., [d.] Feb. 24, 1812 | 1 | 76 |
| John, s. [Joel & Lucretia], b. July 27, 1787; d. Oct. 13, 1822, ae 35 | 2 | 53 |
| John Spencer, s. [John, Jr. & Temperance], b. Mar 14, 1807 | 2 | 143 |
| Jonathan, [s. John & Sarah], b. May 21, 1714 | L-1 | 654 |
| Jonathan, s. [Asa & Dorothy], b. Aug. 10, 1740 | 1 | 138 |
| Jonathan, m. Elizabeth **OTIS**, May 24, 1759 | 1 | 38 |
| Jonathan, m. Bettey **OTIS**, May 24, 1759, "according to Mr. Little's record" | 2 | 72 |
| Jonathan, s. [Jonathan & Bettey], b. Aug. 11, 1775 | 2 | 72 |
| Jonathan Edwards, s. [Guy & Sarah Ann], b. Oct. 8, 1834 | 2 | 125 |
| Joseph, s. [Elisha, Jr. & Welthan], b. Oct. 22, 1776 | 2 | 28 |
| Josiah, [s. Ezra & Hannah], b. May 5, 1765 | 1 | 12 |
| Lemuel, [s. John, Jr. & Hannah], b. Oct. 16, 1769; d. Sept. 9, 1775 | 1 | 76 |
| Loiza, d. [Asa & Lydia], b. July 19, 1792; d. June 11, 1806 | 2 | 78 |
| Lovina, [d. Ezra & Hannah], b. May 10, 1761 | 1 | 12 |
| Lucretia, [w. Joel], d. Feb. 16, 1851, ae 88 | 2 | 53 |
| Lucy, [d. Amasa & Jemima], b. Feb. 13, 1767 | 1 | 11 |
| Lucy, d. [Elisha & Thankful], b. Aug. 30, 1779 | 2 | 55 |
| Lucy, d. [Bond & Sarah], b. Mar. 3, 178[ ] | 2 | 15 |
| Lucy, d. [John, Jr. & Temperance], b. Sept. 10, 1798 | 2 | 143 |
| Lucy, of Colchester, m. William **GELSTON**, Jr., of East Haddam, Oct. 21, 1821, at the house of John Bigelow, by Rev. Simeon Dickinson | 2 | 129 |
| Lidia, [d. Isaac], b. Apr. 22, 1729 | L-3 | 199 |
| Lydia, d. Isaac, b. Apr. 22, 1729 | TM-1 | 199 |
| Lydia, d. [John & Sarah], b. Aug. 31, 1743 | 1 | 126 |
| Lydia, [d. Isaac & Abigail], b. May 2, 1745 | L-3 | 454 |
| Lydia, d. [Elisha & Mary], b. Dec. 12, 1762 | 1 | 125 |
| Lydia, d. [Elisha & Mary], b. Dec. 12, 1762 | 2 | 55 |
| Lydia, [d. John, Jr. & Hannah], b. Mar. 22, 1766 | 1 | 76 |
| Lydia, [d. John, Jr. & Hannah], d. Sept. 16, 1775 | 1 | 76 |
| Lydia, [d. John, Jr. & Hannah], b. May 20, 1776 | 1 | 76 |
| Lydia, d. [Asa & Lydia], b. Nov. 9, 1783; d. Oct. 21, 1788 | 2 | 78 |
| Lydia, m. Stephen **ROSSITER**, Apr. 21, 1784 | 2 | 59 |
| Lydia, 2d, d. [Asa & Lydia], b. Nov. 2, 1789 | 2 | 78 |
| Lydia, d. of Asa & Lydia, m. Justin **EDWARDS**, Sept. 17, 1817 | 2 | 78 |

| | Vol. | Page |
|---|---|---|
| **BIGELOW, BIGLO, BIGLOE, BIGLOO**, (cont.) | | |
| Lydia, w. Asa, d. July 31, 1844, ae 85 | 2 | 78 |
| Marcy, d. Isaac, b. July 23, 1711; d. about 3 m. after | L-3 | 199 |
| Marcy, [d. Isaac], b. Feb. 4, 1715 | L-3 | 199 |
| Mercy, d. Isaac, b. Feb. 4, 1715 | TM-1 | 199 |
| Marcy, [d. David & Marcy], b. Nov. 23, 1753 | L-3 | 455 |
| Marcy, m. Joseph **LOVELAND**, Nov. 12, 177[ ] | 2 | 2 |
| Margarett, [d. Isaac & Abigail], b. Aug. 2, 1747 | L-3 | 454 |
| Margarett, d. Isaac, Jr., b. Aug. 2, 1747 | 1 | 147 |
| Martha E., [d. Aaron], b. Oct. 19, 1828 | 3 | 33 |
| Mary, d. Isaac, b. July 23, 1711 | TM-1 | 199 |
| Mary, [d. Isaac], b. July 31, 1719 | L-3 | 199 |
| Mary, d. Isaac, b. July 31, 1719 | TM-1 | 199 |
| Mary, [d. Isaac & Abigail], b. Feb. 2, 1743 | L-3 | 454 |
| Mary, [d. John & Sarah], b. Dec. 10, 1749 | 1 | 126 |
| Mary, d. [Elisha & Mary], b. May 19, 1757 | 1 | 125 |
| Mary, d. [Elisha & Mary], b. May 19, 1757 | 2 | 55 |
| Mary, w. Elisha, d. Jan. 11, 1765 | 1 | 125 |
| Mary, w. Elisha, d. Jan. 11, 1765 | 2 | 55 |
| Mary, d. [Ephraim & Mary], b. May 31, 1770 | 2 | 4 |
| Mary, wid. of Isaac, Sr., & Mother to Elisha, d. July 9, 1775, ae 82 | 2 | 55 |
| Mary, w. Daniel, d. July 6, 1777 | 1 | 22 |
| Mary, d. [John, Jr. & Temperance], b. Jan. 6, 1803 | 2 | 143 |
| Mary, of Colchester, m. Elijah **SPENCER**, of Lyme, Sept. 12, 1824, by Rev. Simeon Dickinson | 2 | 169 |
| Mary Brainard, [d. Daniel & Mary[, b. June 11, 1777 | 1 | 22 |
| Mary E., m. Wakefield **GALE**, Sept. 18, 1828, by Salmon Cone, V. D. M. | 2 | 206 |
| Mary J., of Marlborough, Conn., m. Henry **ASHLEY**, of Colchester, Mar. 28, 1843, by Rev. Joel R. Arnold | 3 | 3 |
| Mary Louisa, d. [Asa & Lydia], b. Nov. 29, 1806 | 2 | 78 |
| Molle, d. [Elisha & Mary], b. Aug. 28, 1753 | 1 | 125 |
| Molly, d. [Elisha & Mary], b. Aug. 28, 1753 | 2 | 55 |
| Molly, m. Abner **CHAPMAN**, Jr., Mar. 31, 1781 | 2 | 53 |
| Moses, [s. David & Marcy], b. Oct. 4, 1750; d. Dec. 23, 1750 | L-3 | 455 |
| Nancy, d. [James & Anna], b. Mar. 20, 1784 | 2 | 72 |
| Nancy, m. John **WATROUS**, Mar. 30, 1809 | 2 | 245 |
| Nancy M., of Colchester, m. Ichabod L. **SKINNER**, of Independence, Ohio, May 19, 1824, by J. Seales, V. D. M., at the home of Stephen Bigelow | 2 | 178 |
| Noah, s. [Elisha & Mary], b. Feb. 7, 1759 | 1 | 125 |
| Noah, s. [Elisha & Mary], b. Feb. 7, 1759 | 2 | 55 |
| Oliver, [s. John, Jr. & Hannah], b. Dec. 23, 1759 | 1 | 76 |
| Oliver, [s. John, 3d, & Hannah], b. Dec. 23, 17[ ] | 1 | 21 |
| Olynda, d. [Elisha & Thankful], b. July 31, 1781 | 2 | 55 |
| Orimel, [s. Daniel & Mary], b. Oct. 19, 1768 | 1 | 22 |
| Oramel, m. Lydia **LOOMIS**, b. of Colchester, Feb. 9, 1834, | | |

| | Vol. | Page |
|---|---|---|
| **BIGELOW, BIGLO, BIGLOE, BIGLOO**, (cont.) | | |
| by Rev. Joseph Harvey | 2 | 263 |
| Otis, s. [Asa & Dorothy], b. Jan. 4, 1746/7 | 1 | 138 |
| Phebe, d. [Joel & Lucretia], b. Sept. 16, 1789 | 2 | 53 |
| Rhoda, d. [Timothy & Rhoda], b. Aug. 20, 1765 | 1 | 111 |
| Robert, s. [Elisha & Deborah], b. Jan. 19, 1773; d. Jan. 28, 1773 | 1 | 126 |
| Robert, s. [Elisha & Deborah], b. Jan. 19, 1773; d. Jan. 28, 1773 | 2 | 55 |
| Rubey, [d. Isaac & Abigail], b. Dec. 14, 1750 | L-3 | 454 |
| Ruby, [d. Isaac & Abigail], d. June 5, 1759 | L-3 | 454 |
| Sally, d. [Asa & Lydia], b. May 8, 1787 | 2 | 78 |
| Sally, d. of Asa & Lydia, m. Jared **REID**, Nov. 27, 1823; d. Feb. 12, 1845, in Tiverton, R. I. | 2 | 78 |
| Samuel, s. Isaac, b. Dec. 21, 1724 | TM-1 | 199 |
| Samuell, [s. Isaac], b. Dec. 21, 1724 | L-3 | 199 |
| Samuel, [s. Isaac & Abigail], b. Nov. 1, 1752 | L-3 | 454 |
| Samuel, s. [John & Thankful], b. May 19, 1774 | 2 | 1 |
| Samuell, s. [Elisha & Thankful], b. May 19, 1774; d. Mar. 28, 1775 | 2 | 55 |
| Samuel, 2d, s. [Elisha & Thankful], b. Nov. 19, 1775; d. Feb. 2, 1778 | 2 | 55 |
| Sam[ue]ll, s. [Bond & Sarah], b. Oct. 15, 1780 | 2 | 15 |
| Sarah, m. John **BIGELOW**, Nov. 4, 1709 | L-1 | 654 |
| Sarah, [d. John & Sarah], b. July 17, 1712 | L-1 | 654 |
| Sarah, [d. Isaac], b. June 27, 1727 | L-3 | 199 |
| Sarah, d. Isaac, b. June 27, 1727; d. 3 m. after | TM-1 | 199 |
| Sarah, d. [Asa & Dorothy], b. Nov. 13, 1744 | 1 | 138 |
| Sarah, m. Noah **SKINNER**, June 10, 1746 | 1 | 150 |
| Sarah, [d. John & Sarah], b. Oct. 10, 1750 | 1 | 126 |
| Sarah, m. Elias **RANSOM**, Nov. 19, 1761 | 1 | 94 |
| Sarah, of Colchester, m. Rev. Jared **REID**, of Reading, Mass., Nov. 27, 1823, by Salmon Cone, V. D. M. | 2 | 160 |
| Sarah Ann, m. Edward N. **CLARK**, b. of Colchester, Aug. 26, 1845, by Rev. S. D. Jewett, Westchester | 3 | 23 |
| Sarah Tudor, d. [Jonathan & Bettey], b. Mar. 2, 1771 | 2 | 72 |
| Sherman, s. [James & Anna], b. Jan. 7, 1793 | 2 | 72 |
| Sophia, twin with Cynthia, d. [Elisha & Thankful], b. Aug. 1, 1783 | 2 | 55 |
| Stephen, [s. David & Marcy], b. Oct. 27, 1747; d. Sept. 13, 1748 | L-3 | 455 |
| Stephen, [s. David & Marcy], b. June 5, 1749; d. Aug. 5, 1751 | L-3 | 455 |
| Stephen, [s. Daniel & Mary], b. Jan. 18, 1762 | 1 | 22 |
| Susan Lydia, d. [Guy & Sarah Ann], b. July 10, 1831; d. Apr. 7, 1832 | 2 | 125 |
| Temperance, d. [John, Jr. & Temperance], b. Sept. 13, 1794; d. Feb. 29, 1796 | 2 | 143 |

| | Vol. | Page |
|---|---|---|
| **BIGELOW, BIGLO, BIGLOE, BIGLOO**, (cont.) | | |
| Temperance, 2d, d. [John, Jr. & Temperance], b. Aug. 29, 1796 | 2 | 143 |
| Temperance, m. David N. **ADAMS**, b. of Colchester, Jan. 21, 1821, by John Bigelow, J. P., at the house of John Bigelow | 2 | 153 |
| Thankful, d. [Elisha & Thankful], b. Apr. 7, 1777 | 2 | 55 |
| Timothy, [s. Isaac & Abigail], b. Nov. 18, 1739 | L-3 | 454 |
| Timothy, [s. Amasa & Jemima], b. Feb. 4, 1761 | 1 | 11 |
| Timothy, m. Rhoda **WILLIAMS**, Dec. 2, 1762 | 1 | 111 |
| Waltha, d. [Elisha, Jr. & Welthan], b. Sept. 26, 1778; d. Oct. 20, 1778 | 2 | 28 |
| Waltha, 2d, d. [Elisha, Jr. & Welthan], b. Nov. 14, 1779 | 2 | 28 |
| Zelotes, [d. Daniel & Mary], b. Aug. 17, 1764 | 1 | 22 |
| -----, s. [Timothy & Rhoda], b. Oct. [ ], 1763, st. b. | 1 | 111 |
| -----, s. [Guy & Sarah Ann], b. Apr. 15, 1833; d. same day | 2 | 125 |
| -----, d., 2d child, [James & Anna], b. [ ]; d. 9th day of her age | 2 | 72 |
| **BILL**, Abil, s. [Pelegg & Jerusha], b. May 6, 1758 | 1 | 108 |
| Amos, m. Jerusha **GILLETT**, Feb. 3, 1757 | 1 | 54 |
| Betty, [d. Amos & Jerusha], b. Feb. 24, 1759 | 1 | 54 |
| Caroline M., m. Elias L. **WILLIAMS**, b. of Lebanon, Mar. 17, 1846, by Rev. Lyman Strong | 3 | 27 |
| Fanny, of Colchester, m. Julius **CHAPMAN**, of Griswold, Conn., Oct. 15, 1850, by Rev. Geo[rge] W. Pendleton | 3 | 46 |
| Jerusha, d. [Pelegg & Jerusha], b. June 18, 1756; d. Jan. 23, 1757 | 1 | 108 |
| Jerusha, [d. Amos & Jerusha], b. Jan. 12, 1758 | 1 | 54 |
| Jonathan, s. Edward & Zerviah, b. May 5, 1733 | TPR | 110 |
| Keziah, m. David **PRATT**, July 17, 1760 | 1 | 112 |
| Lydia A., of Colchester, m. George **YEMMONS**, of Columbia, Conn., Apr. 25, 1852, by Rev. George W. Pendleton | 3 | 51 |
| Lydia, A., of Colchester, m. George **YEOMAN**, of Columbia, Apr. 25, 1852, by Geo[rge] W. Pendleton | 3 | 52 |
| Nancy, of Colchester, m. Cyrus **CHAPMAN**, of Griswold, Conn., Oct. 15, 1850, by Rev. Geo[rge] W. Pendleton | 3 | 46 |
| Pelegg, m. Jerusha **SKINNER**, Jan. 1, 1755 | 1 | 108 |
| W[illia]m H., of Norwich, m. Elizabeth C. **FOOTE**, of Colchester, Jan. 1, 1845, by Rev. Robert Allyn | 3 | 19 |
| **BILLINGS, BILLING**, Betsey, of Montville, m. Amasa **RANSOM**, Jr., Sept. 13, 1810 | 2 | 138 |
| Charles, m. Salomi **HURD**, Feb. 10, 1828, by Zachariah Olmstead, J. P. | 2 | 201 |
| Elisha Chapman, s. [Zebulon & Margaret], b. July 20, 1804 | 2 | 129 |
| Mary Ann, of Salem, m. Primus **HYDE**, of East Haddam, b. colored, Oct. 30, 1822, by Samuel A. Peters, J. P. | 2 | 71 |
| Rhoda, d. [Zebulon & Margaret], b. June 24, 1809 | 2 | 129 |

| | Vol. | Page |
|---|---|---|
| **BILLINGS, BILLING**, (cont.) | | |
| Rhoda S., m. George W. **TREADWAY**, b. of Salem, Conn., Apr. 19, 1840, by Rev. Joel R. Arnold | 2 | 228 |
| Thomas, m. Hannah **HYDE**, Nov. 19, 1826, by Amherst D. Scoville, J. P. | 2 | 190 |
| Zebulon, s. William & Cyrene, b. Aug. 4, 1776 | 2 | 129 |
| Zebulon, m. Margaret **TARBELL**, Aug. 9, 1798 | 2 | 129 |
| **BINGHAM**, George D., of Colchester, m. Jane A. **BROWN**, of Columbia, Dec. 9, 1851, by Rev. E. Dickinson | 3 | 48 |
| **BIRGE**, Hiram F., of Genessee, N. Y., m. Anna A. **CONE**, of Colchestser, Apr. 16, 1849, by Rev. Joel R. Arnold | 3 | 39 |
| Lydia, m. Samuel **BROWN**, June [ ], 1779 | 2 | 245 |
| **BISHOP**, Mary, m. David **MINOR**, [ ] | 2 | 112 |
| **BISSELL**, [see also **BESSEL**], Daniel, Rev. of Charlestown, Mass., m. Mehetable **WYLLYS**, d. of Samuel & Ruth, of Hartford, & had d. Mabel, who m. Rev. John **HUBBARD**, of Jamaica, L. I. | 2 | 310 |
| Hezekiah, of Hebron, m. Mary J. **CONE**, of Colchester, Apr. 29, 1847, by Rev. P. Brockett | 3 | 32 |
| Louisa E., m. Solomon T. **GILLETT**, Oct. 18, 1832 | 2 | 270 |
| Lucy A., m. George W. **ARNOLD**, b. of Colchester, Sept. 10, 1840, by Rev. Daniel G. Sprague | 2 | 110 |
| Mabel, see under Mabel **HUBBARD** | 2 | 310 |
| Phebe, m. Hiram G. **BUELL**, both of Colchester, Sept. 10, 1839 (Handwritten in original manuscript) | | |
| **BLACKMAN**, Churchill, of Coventry, m. Mary **WAY**, of Colchester, Dec. 5, 1830, by Rev. Lyman Strong | 2 | 227 |
| Mary A., of Coventry, Conn., m. Josiah S. **FULLER**, of Andova, Conn., Jan. 25, 1847, by Rev. M. P. Alderman | 3 | 32 |
| **BLISH, BLUSH**, Alice, of East Haddam, m. Daniel **WILLIAMS**, Jr., of Colchester, May 9, 1834, by Amhurst D. Scoville, J. P. | 2 | 265 |
| Amia, [d. Benjamin?], d. Oct. [ ], 1752 | 1 | 153 |
| Anna, [d. Tristam & Anne Fuller], b. Nov. [ ], 1719; d. in the 18th year of her age | 1 | 142 |
| An[n]ah, d. [Benj[amin] & Mary], b. Aug. 30, 1751 | 1 | 137 |
| Benjamin, s. [Tristam & Anne Fuller], b. June 6, 1718 | 1 | 142 |
| Benj[amin], m. Mary **ADAMS**, May 3, 1744 | 1 | 137 |
| Benjamin, d. Aug. 21, 1752 | 1 | 137 |
| Benj[amin], [s. Benjamin?], d. Aug. 21, 1752 | 1 | 153 |
| Benjamin, s. [Benj[amin] & Mary], b. Feb. 11, 1753 | 1 | 137 |
| Daniel, s. Benj[amin] & Mary], b. Dec. 17, 1747; d. July 21, 1752 | 1 | 137 |
| Daniel, s. Benj[amin], d. July 21, 1752 | 1 | 153 |
| David, [s. Tristam & Anne Fuller], b. [ ], 1732 | 1 | 142 |
| Harriet M., m. Lucius **BRECKENRIDGE**, Aug. 23, 1841, by Rev. Augustus Bolles | 2 | 267 |
| Jeremiah, s. [Benj[amin] & Mary], b. Aug. 12, 1745 | 1 | 137 |

| | Vol. | Page |
|---|---|---|
| **BLISH, BLUSH,** (cont.) | | |
| John, [s. Tristam & Anne Fuller], b. [ ], 1727 | 1 | 142 |
| John Henry, s. [Reuben & Dimis], b. May 23, 1802 | 2 | 106 |
| Joseph, s. [Tristam & Anne Fuller], b. Dec. 1, 1729 | 1 | 142 |
| Lois, m. Joseph **ISHAM,** 3d, Sept. 9, 1790; d. Feb. 14, 1841, ae 71 | 2 | 62 |
| Mary, [d. Tristam & Anne Fuller], b. Mar. 2, 1736 | 1 | 142 |
| Patience, [d. Tristam & Anne Fuller], b. Feb. 2, 1730 | 1 | 142 |
| Rachel, [d. Benj[amin] & Mary], b. Mar. 12, 1748/9; d. July 27, 1752 | 1 | 137 |
| Rachel, d. July 27, 1752 | 1 | 153 |
| Reuben, m. Demis **WRIGHT,** Sept. [ ], 1800 | 2 | 106 |
| Sarah, d. [Benj[amin] & Mary], d. Oct. [ ], 1752 | 1 | 137 |
| Sylvanus, [s. Tristam & Anne Fuller], b. Oct. [ ], 1721 | 1 | 142 |
| Thankfull, [d. Tristam & Anne Fuller], b. Sept. [ ], 1725 | 1 | 142 |
| **BLISS,** Abigail, of Lebanon, m. David **COLE,** of Colchester, Feb. 9, 1762 | 1 | 120 |
| Asa, [s. Silvanus & Esther], b. July 9, 1761 | 1 | 23 |
| Daniel, [s. Silvanus & Esther], b. Dec. 17, 1757 | 1 | 23 |
| Elifall, of New London, m. Elisha **SCOVELL,** of Colchester, Feb. 19, 1756 | 1 | 21 |
| Elizabeth, m. Joshua **JONES,** [ ], 1740 | 1 | 106 |
| Esther, [d. Silvanus & Esther], b. Jan. 22, 1755 | 1 | 23 |
| Ezra, [s. Silvanus & Esther], b. Apr. 16, 1759 | 1 | 23 |
| Joseph, m. Elizabeth **SKINNER,** Mar. 22, 1753 | 1 | 29 |
| Lewis S., m. Harriet L. **CHAPMAN,** Sept. 27, 1841, by Rev. Daniel G. Sprague, Westchester | 2 | 235 |
| Lydia, [d. Joseph & Elizabeth], b. Mar. 28, 1754 | 1 | 29 |
| Lydia, d. [Henry & Mary], b. Oct. 6, 1761 | TPR | 112 |
| Mary, m. Joseph **SKINNER,** Apr. [ ], 1756 | 1 | 116 |
| [Mary], w. Henry, of Lebanon, wid. of Capt. John **HOPSON,** d. Mar. 31, 1761(?) | TPR | 112 |
| Rachel, [d. Silvanus & Esther], b. Nov. 22, 1752 | 1 | 23 |
| Reuben, [s. Silvanus & Esther], b. Oct. 16, 1763 | 1 | 23 |
| Silvanus, m. Esther **DAY,** Nov. [ ], 1751 | 1 | 23 |
| **BLODGETT,** Warren M., Jr., m. Elizabeth **BUTTON,** b. of Colchester, May 18, 1851, by Rev. George W. Pendleton | 2 | 80 |
| **BLUSH,** [see under **BLISH**] | | |
| **BLY,** Pattis P., of Ludlow, Mass., m. Frederic A. **WHEELER,** of Columbia, Mar. 14, 1841, at the house of Rev. J. R. Arnold, in Colchester, by Rev. Hiram Bell | 2 | 229 |
| **BOGUE, BOGE,** Aaron, of East Haddam, m. Susannah **SHAYLOR,** of Colchester, Apr. 1, 1824, by Rev. Jacob Seales, at the home of Rev. Jacob Seales | 2 | 163 |
| Clauda, [d. Jeremiah & Dorcas], b. Jan. 14, 1768 | 1 | 90 |
| Edwin, of East Haddam, m. Roxy **JACKSON,** of Colchester, June 4, 1829, by Salmon Cone, V. D. M. | 2 | 213 |
| Edwin, of Colchester, m. Eunice M. **WELLS,** of Marlboro, | | |

| | Vol. | Page |
|---|---|---|
| **BOGUE, BOGE,** (cont.) | | |
| Jan. 11, 1852, by Octavus Emmons, J. P. | 3 | 49 |
| Elisha, [s. Jeremiah & Dorcas], b. July 26, 1775 | 1 | 90 |
| Jeremiah, m. Dorcas **BURTT**, June 5, 1755 | 1 | 90 |
| Prudence, [d. Jeremiah & Dorcas], b. Sept. 30, 1758 | 1 | 90 |
| Sophia, m. Abel D. **STEVENS**, b. of Colchester, Sept. 21, 1834, by Rev. Joseph Harvey | 2 | 271 |
| Tabitha, [d. Jeremiah & Dorcas], b. Oct. 20, 1764 | 1 | 90 |
| **BOHAN, BOHANE**, Jesse, s. Molly **CHEESEBROUGH**, b. Jan. 30, 1794 (mulatto) | 2 | 48 |
| Reuben, s. Molly **CHEESEBROUGH**, b. Sept. 17, 1792 (mulatto) | 2 | 48 |
| Sally, m. James **FREEMAN**, Apr. 6, 1819 | 2 | 94 |
| **BOLLES**, Augustus, Rev., m. Esther **WHEELER**, b. of Colchester, Feb. 27, 1842, by Rev. J. R. Arnold | 2 | 231 |
| **BOOTH**, Almira, d. [William & Polly], b. Oct. 29, 1795 | 2 | 83 |
| Anne, [d. William & Hannah], b. Apr. 7, 1761 | 1 | 54 |
| Catharine, m. Jonathan **KEENEY**, of Long Island, N. Y., Jan. 3, 1767; d. May 26, 1790 | 2 | 74 |
| Versalle, m. Asahel **NEWTON**, Feb. 19, 1784 | 2 | 89 |
| William, m. Hannah **CHAMBERLAIN**, Jan. 31, 1760 | 1 | 54 |
| William, m. Polly **CHURCH**, May 15, 1794 | 2 | 83 |
| **BOWEN**, Lewis, m. Sophia **NIXON**, Apr. 18, 1821, by Salmon Cone, V. D. M. | 2 | 297 |
| **BRADFORD**, John Merit, s. [Merit & Lucy], b. Jan. 22, 1823 | 2 | 109 |
| Merit, of Canterbury, m. Lucy **FOOT**, of Colchester, Feb. 28, 1821, by Salmon Cone, V. D. M. | 2 | 109 |
| Merit, d. Jan. 28, 1846, in Newburg, N. Y. | 2 | 109 |
| **BRADLEY**, J. Lyman, M. D., of Manchester, Conn., m. Adaline C. **SLAYTON**, of Woodstock, Vt., Nov. 28, 1850, by Rev. Albert F. Park | 3 | 47 |
| Reuben, of Russell, Mass., m. Nancy S. **WORTHINGTON**, of Colchester, Apr. 13, 1823, by Salmon Cone, V.D.M. | 2 | 137 |
| **BRAGAW**, Isaac, of Newark, N. J., m. Elizabeth M. **WAY**, of Colchester, May 12, 1841, by Rev. Joel R. Arnold | 2 | 205 |
| **BRAGG**, Emeline, b. May [ ], 1830, in Liverpool, Eng.; d. Mar. 11, 1851, in Hebron, ae 20 y. 9 m. | 2 | 67 |
| **BRAINARD, BRAINERD**, Abigail L., of Colchester, m. Samuel A. **BRAINARD**, of Hamilton, N. Y., Sept. 26, 1832, by Rev. Joseph Harvey | 2 | 238 |
| Abigail Lucinda, d. [William & Patience], b. Sept. 27, 1807 | 2 | 211 |
| Albert, s. [Amaziah & Huldah], b. June 26, 1832 | 2 | 162 |
| Amasa Skinner, s. [Nathaniel F. & Lucy B.], b. Apr. 30, 1835 | 2 | 264 |
| Amaziah, m. Huldah **FOOTE**, b. of Colchester, Mar. 29, 1824, by Rev. Jacob Seales, at the house of Nathaniel Foot; d. Apr. 1, 1841, ae 61 | 2 | 162 |
| Ansel, Jr., of Haddam, m. Sarah **DAY**, of Colchester, Dec. 14, 1826, by Rev. David B. Ripley, Marlborough | 2 | 192 |

| | Vol. | Page |
|---|---|---|
| **BRAINARD, BRAINERD**, (cont.) | | |
| Arnold, s. [Nathaniel F. & Lucy B.], b. Oct. 16, 1837; d. Mar. 9, 1838 | 2 | 264 |
| Asa, s. [William & Patience], b. Dec. 24, 1816 | 2 | 211 |
| Clarissa L., m. Stephen B. **DAY**, b. of Colchester, Nov. 27, 1834, by Rev. Joseph Harvey | 2 | 274 |
| Clarissa Loomis, d. [William & Patience], b. July 19, 1814 | 2 | 211 |
| Dorothy, m. Oren **STAPLES**, Dec. 1, 1819 | 2 | 249 |
| Elijah, s. [William & Lucy], b. Mar. 23, 17[ ] | 2 | 14 |
| Elisabeth, [d. Stephen & Susannah], b. Dec. 17, 1733 | TPR | 111 |
| Ezra, s. [William & Lucy], b. Feb. 11, 17[ ] | 2 | 14 |
| Hannah, d. Stephen & Susannah, b. Nov. 2, 1737 | 1 | 126 |
| Hannah, d. [William & Lucy], b. May [ ], 178[ ] | 2 | 14 |
| Harriet Atwood, d. [William & Patience], b. Sept. 23, 1819 | 2 | 211 |
| Huldah, [s. Amaziah], d. Aug. 9, 1881, ae 79 y. 9 m. | 2 | 162 |
| Irena, d.[William & Lucy], b. Aug. 12, 1782 | 2 | 14 |
| Isaiah, s. [William & Lucy], b. June 12, 17[ ] | 2 | 14 |
| Jerusha, d. [William & Patience], b. Aug. 31, 1800 | 2 | 211 |
| Jerusha, of Colchester, m. Alfred **KELLOGG**, of Chatham, May 6, 1823, by Rev. Jacob Seales | 2 | 146 |
| Joseph, s. [Nathaniel F. & Lucy B.], b. Oct. 11, 1841; d. July 6, 1844 | 2 | 264 |
| Leveret, s. [Amaziah & Huldah], b. Feb. 13, 1828 | 2 | 162 |
| Lucy, d. [William & Lucy], b. Apr. 22, 17[ ] | 2 | 14 |
| Lucy Abigail, d. [Amaziah & Huldah], b. June 26, 1832 | 2 | 162 |
| Lucy D., of Colchester, m. William **BRAINARD**, of East Haddam, Sept. 16, 1824, by Jacob Seales, V. D. M., at the house of Capt. William Brainard | 2 | 170 |
| Lucy Day, d. [William & Patience], b. Nov. 4, 1804 | 2 | 211 |
| Margaret Foote, d. [William & Patience], b. July 6, 1812 | 2 | 211 |
| Mary, d. Stephen, b. Feb. 15, 1739/40 | 1 | 131 |
| Mary, m. Daniel **BIGELOW**, Jan. 8, 1761 | 1 | 22 |
| Mary, d. [William & Lucy], b. Feb. 23, 179[ ] | 2 | 14 |
| Mehetable, of East Haddam, m. Timothy **WRIGHT**, of Colchester, July 3, 1735 | 1 | 120 |
| Nathaniel F., m. Lucy B. **STAPLES**, b. of Colchester, Mar. 25, 1834, by Rev. Joseph Harvey | 2 | 264 |
| Nathaniel Foote, s. [William & Patience], b. Aug. 20, 1802 | 2 | 211 |
| Rebeccka, m. John **ROWLEY**, Sept. 4, 1752 | 1 | 104 |
| Roxa Meroa, d. [William & Patience], b. Mar. 23, 1824 | 2 | 211 |
| Samuel A., of Hamilton, N. Y., m. Abigail L. **BRAINARD**, of Colchester, Sept. 26, 1832, by Rev. Joseph Harvey | 2 | 238 |
| Samuel N., m. Charlotte F. **WILLIAMS**, b. of Colchester, June 9, 1853, by Rev. S. D. Jewett, Westchester | 3 | 56 |
| Samuel Newell, s. [William & Patience], b. Apr. 14, 1822 | 2 | 211 |
| Sarah, d. [Stephen], b. Apr. 30, 1744 | 1 | 131 |
| Sarah, d. Stephen, b. Apr. 30, 1744 | 1 | 143 |
| Sarah, m. Judah **LEWIS**, Feb. 4, 1762 | 1 | 165 |

| | Vol. | Page |
|---|---|---|
| **BRAINARD, BRAINERD**, (cont.) | | |
| Stephen, m. Susannah **GATES**, Dec. 24, 1730 | TPR | 111 |
| Stephen, s. Stephen, b. Mar. 24, 1741/2 | 1 | 131 |
| Susannah, [d. Stephen & Susannah], b. Sept. 24, 1731 | TPR | 111 |
| Susannah, m. Joseph **DAY**, Jr., Nov. 13, 1754 | 1 | 99 |
| Susannah, m. Joseph **STAPLES**, Dec. 8, 1808; d. Apr. 21, 1848, ae 60 | 2 | 114 |
| Tiddia, of Chatham, m. Charles B. **LANDFEAR**, of East Haddam, Sept. 29, 1846, by Rev. S. D. Jewett | 3 | 29 |
| Truin, m. Nehemiah **GATES**, Apr. 25, 1754 | 1 | 23 |
| William, [s. Stephen], b. Aug. 16, 1746 | 1 | 131 |
| William, m. Patience **FOOTE**, Oct. 31, 1799, by Justin Day. Recorded Jan. 31, 1829 | 2 | 211 |
| William, m. Lucy **DAY**, Dec. 31, 17[ ] | 2 | 14 |
| William, s. [William & Lucy], b. Oct. 23, 17[ ] | 2 | 14 |
| William, s. [William & Patience], b. Feb. 23, 1810 | 2 | 211 |
| William, of East Haddam, m. Lucy D. **BRAINARD**, of Colchester, Sept. 16, 1824, by Jacob Seales, V. D. M. at the house of Capt. William Brainard | 2 | 170 |
| William, Jr., m. Eliza **CARRIER**, b. of Colchester, July 13, 1837, by Rev. Ja[me]s Abell | 2 | 133 |
| William, Sr., d. Mar. 18, 1844 | 2 | 211 |
| ----rin, s. [William & Lucy], b. June 11, 178[ ] | 2 | 14 |
| **BRANNON**, John, of Rockville, Conn., m. Emily J. **MAINE**, of Colchester, Apr. 1, 1851, by Rev. G. W. Pendleton | 3 | 48 |
| **BRECKENRIDGE**, Lucius, m. Harriet M. **BLISH**, Aug. 23, 1841, by Rev. Augustus Bolles | 2 | 267 |
| **BREED**, Anna, m. Rev. Salmon **CONE**, Dec. 29, 1802; d. [ ], in Middletown | 2 | 69 |
| Hannah, of Stonington, m. Peter **BULKELEY**, Jr., of Colchester, Mar. 9, 1768 | 1 | 82 |
| John, m. Lucy **BULKELEY**, May 13, 1773; d. May 2, 1803 | 2 | 42 |
| Lucy, w. John, d. Dec. 30, 1821 | 2 | 42 |
| **BREWSTER**, Harriet, of Colchester, m. William C. **AVERY**, of Windham, Sept. 25, 1853, by Rev. Anthony Palmer | 3 | 59 |
| **BRIDGES**, Anna, d. [Edmund & Anne], b. Aug. 24, 1798 | 2 | 90 |
| Anne, w. Edmund, d. Feb. 23, 1842, ae 80, at Genessee, N. Y. | 2 | 90 |
| Aurelia A., m. John C. **SHEPARD**, b. of Colchester, Apr. 5, 1842, by Rev. Joel R. Arnold | 2 | 287 |
| Aurelia Ann, d. [Samuel & Content], b. Nov. 20, 1809 | 2 | 157 |
| Edmund, m. Anne **FOOT**, Mar. 20, 1784; d. Sept. 11, 1816, ae 53, at Genessee, N. Y. | 2 | 90 |
| Edmond, s. [Edmund & Anne], b. Nov. 14, 1791 | 2 | 90 |
| Edwin Newton, s. [Samuel & Content], b. July 14, 1798 | 2 | 157 |
| Esther, m. Russel[l] **KELLOGG**, [ ], 1777 | 2 | 91 |
| Jeremiah, s. [Edmund & Anne], b. Dec. 19, 1785 | 2 | 90 |
| Jonathan, [s. Samuel & Anne], b. Oct. 12, 1753 | 1 | 49 |
| Margaret, m. Charles **WORTHINGTON**, Apr. 23, 1797 | 2 | 248 |

| | Vol. | Page |
|---|---|---|
| **BRIDGES**, (cont.) | | |
| Marshua, s. [Edmund & Anne], b. Nov. 27, 1789 | 2 | 90 |
| Manerva, d. [Edmund & Anne], b. Dec. 9, 1795 | 2 | 90 |
| Noah W., m. Dorothy **OTIS**, Aug. 19, 1822, by Salmon Cone, V. D. M. | 2 | 157 |
| Noah Wells, s. [Samuel & Content], b. Apr. 11, 1800 | 2 | 157 |
| Orra O., of Colchester, m. Robert May **BROOKE**, of Easton, Penn., Oct. 9, 1827, by Salmon Cone, V. D. M. | 2 | 198 |
| Orra Olivia, d. [Samuel & Content], b. Mar. 24, 1808 | 2 | 157 |
| Samuel, m. Anna **FOOT**, Sept. 10, 1752 | 1 | 49 |
| Samuel, b. June 20, 1763; m. Content **NEWTON**, May 10, 1797; d. Nov. 28, 1837, ae 74. Recorded Feb. 7, 1851 | 2 | 157 |
| Samuel, s. [Edmund & Anne], b. Jan. 27, 1787 | 2 | 90 |
| Samuel Augustus, s. [Samuel & Content], b. Jan. 27, 1802 | 2 | 157 |
| Uzziel, s. [Edmund & Anne], b. Nov. 22, 1800 | 2 | 90 |
| Uzziel, of Genessee, N. Y., m. Ann R. **WELLS**, of Colchester, Nov. 24, 1845, by Rev. Joel R. Arnold | 3 | 26 |
| William, s. [Edmund & Anne], b. Jan. 6, 1793 | 2 | 90 |
| **BRIGGS**, Elizabeth, d. [Philip], b. July 12, 1828 | 2 | 100 |
| Elizabeth, m. Colchester, m. Robert B. **SHERMAN**, of Lebanon, Dec. 22, 1844, by Rev. Joel R. Arnold | 3 | 19 |
| Grace S., of Colchester, m. William S. **LATHROP**, of Lebanon, Jan. 24, 1847, by Rev. Joel R. Arnold | 3 | 30 |
| Harriet G., of Colchester, m. John H. **NORTHAM**, of Hebron, Nov. 24, 1844, by Rev. Joel R. Arnold | 3 | 18 |
| Louisa A., of Colchester, m. Timothy **DIMOCK**, of Norwich, Jan. 8, 1843, by Rev. Joel R. Arnold | 3 | 1 |
| Maria, w. Willard, d. Jan. 26, 1849, ae 57 | 2 | 61 |
| Phillip, of Lebanon, m. Grace **CHAMBERLAIN**, of Colchester, Aug. 20, 1820 | 2 | 298 |
| **BRIM**, A. G., of Chatham, m. Laura **DAY**, of Westchester, Nov. 24, 1847, by Rev. S. D. Jewett | 3 | 34 |
| **BROOKS, BROOKE**, Dennis, of Chatham, m. Betsey **WANTON**, of Colchester, Mar. 18, 1832, at her dwelling house in Colchester, by John Bigelow, J. P. | 2 | 237 |
| Elizabeth, of Colchester, m. Francis M. **FINCK**, of Ithaca, N. Y., May 25, 1853, by Rev. Lyman Strong | 3 | 56 |
| Hannah, m. Darius **CLARK**, [ ], 1774; d. Sept. 10, 1777 | 2 | 8 |
| Lavina, m. Ralph **ANDROS**, Nov. 26, 1828, by Salmon Cone, V. D. M. | 2 | 208 |
| May, m. William R. **BECKWITH**, b. of Colchester, Oct. 2, 1842, by N. R. Park, J. P. | 2 | 270 |
| Robert May, of Easton, Penn., m. Orra O. **BRIDGES**, of Colchester, Oct. 9, 1827, by Salmon Cone, V. D. M. | 2 | 198 |
| **BROTHERHOOD**, Phebe L., of Colchester, m. Joseph W. **SPENCER**, of East Haddam, Sept. 28, 1828, by Rev. Joseph Harvey | 2 | 207 |
| **BROWN**, A. Jane, of Colchester, m. E. D. **ALVORD**, of | | |

| | Vol. | Page |
|---|---|---|
| **BROWN**, (cont.) | | |
| California, Mar. 1, 1854, by Geo[rge] W. Pendleton | 3 | 61 |
| Abby Jane, d. [Charles & Mary], b. Sept. 4, 1826 | 2 | 58 |
| Abby Jane, of Colchester, m. William **STRICKLAND**, of New York, Aug. 20, 1851, by Rev. George W. Pendleton | 2 | 58 |
| Abel, s. [Ephraim & Ama], b. Apr. 27, 1788 | 2 | 52 |
| Abigail, d. [David & Abigail], b. Jan. 3, 1739/40 | 1 | 130 |
| Abijah, s. [Edward & Hannah], b. Sept. 10, 1758 | 1 | 149 |
| Abner, [s. Samuell & Mary], b. Mar. 25, 1730 | TPR | 110 |
| Alfred, s. [Samuel & Lydia], b. Apr. [ ], 1787 | 2 | 245 |
| Alice, d. [Oliver & Mary], b. July 17, 1774 | 2 | 67 |
| Alice, m. Abel **RATHBURN**, Jr. [ ] | 2 | 132 |
| Amanda, m. Eliphalet **BEERS**, b. of Chatham, Oct. 12, 1835, by Giles Shattuck, J. P. | 2 | 280 |
| Amasa, [s. George & Elizabeth], b. Feb. 26, 1750/51 | 1 | 56 |
| Amos, [s. Samuell], b. Dec. 1, 1730 | L-3 | 8 |
| Anna, d. [Oliver & Mary], b. Oct. 11, 1772 | 2 | 67 |
| Asahel, s. [Oliver & Mary], b. Oct. 18, 1770; d. Dec. 31, 1774 | 2 | 67 |
| Asahel, 2d, s. [Oliver & Mary], b. Mar. 20, 1781; d. Feb. 9, 1859, in Norwich | 2 | 67 |
| Bettsey, d. [Oliver & Mary], b. Aug. 23, 1789 | 2 | 67 |
| Caleb, [s. Elisha & Elydia], b. Aug. 3, 1759 | 1 | 44 |
| Caroline, m. Ralph **RANDALL**, May 4, 1826, by Rev. Tubal Wakefield | 2 | 189 |
| Cephas Cone, s. [Elisha & Lina], b. Apr. 29, 1808 | 2 | 116 |
| Charles, of Colchester, m. Lucy **CLARK**, of Salem, Apr. 23, 1848, by Samuel A. Kellogg, J. P. | 3 | 35 |
| Charles, m. Mary **BROWN**, [ ] | 2 | 58 |
| Charles Henry, s. [Charles & Mary], b. Dec. 6, 1828 | 2 | 58 |
| Charles W., of East Haddam, m. Debett **THOMPSON**, of Colchester, Jan. 4, 1843, by Rev. Abraham Holway | 3 | 5 |
| Charlotte M., m. Samuel C. **LOOMIS**, b. of Marlboro, Oct. 16, 1839, by Rev. Lyman Strong | 2 | 149 |
| Chloe, [d. George & Elizabeth], b. June 30, 1734/5 | 1 | 56 |
| Clarissa Elizabeth, d. [Richard & Betsey], b. Dec. 10, 1826 | 2 | 184 |
| Clarissa S., m. Daniel **STRONG**, b. of Colchester, Feb. 26, 1834, by Rev. Lyman Strong | 2 | 263 |
| Daniell, s. Samuell & Elizabeth Col[l]ings, b. June 12, 1714 | L-3 | 198 |
| Daniel, s. Sam[ue]l & Elizabeth Collins, b. June 12, 1714 | TM-1 | 198 |
| Daniel, s. [Samuel & Lydia], b. Aug. [ ], 1790; d. Mar. [ ], 1800 | 2 | 245 |
| Darius, [s. George & Elizabeth], b. Apr. 24, 1733 | 1 | 56 |
| Dauid, [s. Samuell & Presilla], b. Mar. 29, 1716 | L-3 | 198 |
| David, s. Sarah, b. Mar. 29, 1716 | TM-1 | 198 |
| David, s. [David & Abigail], b. July 22, 1744 | 1 | 130 |
| David, m. Nancy **DART**, Apr. 17, 1851, by Rev. Henry B. Whittington | 2 | 81 |

| | Vol. | Page |
|---|---|---|
| **BROWN**, (cont.) | | |
| David, m. Abigail **MILLS**, [ ] | 1 | 130 |
| Delia, m. Enoch **BROWN**, Sept. [ ], 1814 | 2 | 67 |
| Dimis, d. [Ephraim & Ama], b. May 19, 1786 | 2 | 52 |
| Edward, m. Hannah **THOMAS**, Feb. 7, 1745 | 1 | 149 |
| Edwin T., of Herkimer, N. Y., m. Adaline **CONE**, of Colchester, Sept. 13, 1848, by Rev. F. W. Bill | 3 | 36 |
| Eli, s. [Edward & Hannah], b. Nov. 1, 1761; d. Apr. 12, 1762 | 1 | 149 |
| Elijah, s. [Samuel & Lydia], b. Aug. 21, 1784 | 2 | 245 |
| Elisha, [s. David & Abigai], b. Nov. 14, 1751 | 1 | 130 |
| Elisha, m. Elydia **PENDLETON**, Apr. 12, 1758 | 1 | 44 |
| Elisha, s. [Samuel & Lydia], b. Nov. [ ], 1782 | 2 | 245 |
| Elisha, m. Lina **CONE**, Apr. 1, 1807 | 2 | 116 |
| Elizabeth, [d. John & Marah], b. Dec. 20, 1710 | L-1 | 444 |
| Elizabeth, w. Samuell, d. July 2, 1714 | L-3 | 198 |
| Elizabeth, w. Sam[ue]l, d. July 2, 1714 | TM-1 | 198 |
| Elizabeth, [d. Samuell], b. Nov. 16, 1720 | L-3 | 196 |
| Elizabeth, d. Sam[ue]l, b. Nov. 16, 1720 | TM-1 | 196 |
| Elizabeth, [d. George & Elizabeth], b. June 7, 1730/31 | 1 | 56 |
| Elizabeth, d. [Edward & Hannah], b. Dec. 1, 1755; d. Dec. 25, 1755 | 1 | 149 |
| Elizabeth, of Chatham, m. George **SAXTON**, Feb. 12, 1782 | 2 | 71 |
| Elizabeth Charity, d. [Edward & Hannah], b. Mar. 1, 1757 | 1 | 149 |
| Ellen M., m. Gurdon **ROGERS**, b. of Colchester, [Dec.] 28, 1850, by Rev. S. D. Jewett | 2 | 101 |
| Enoch, s. [Oliver & Mary], b. Feb. 28, 1786 | 2 | 67 |
| Enoch, m. Delia **BROWN**, Sept. [ ], 1814 | 2 | 67 |
| Ephraim, m. Ama **HARDEN**, Sept. 4, 1783 | 2 | 52 |
| Ephraim, s. [Ephraim & Ama], b. June 19, 1784 | 2 | 52 |
| Erastus, s. [Samuel & Lydia], b. Mar. [ ], 1793; d. Jan. [ ], 1815 | 2 | 245 |
| Erastus C., m. Hannah M. **SMITH**, June 6, 1847, by Rev. A. Gleason | 3 | 32 |
| Esther, m. Griswold **HOLMES**, b. of Colchester, Dec. 17, 1837, by Roderick Gardiner, J. P. | 2 | 295 |
| Eunice, [d. Samuel, 2d], b. Apr. 12, 1742 | 1 | 107 |
| Ezra, [s. George & Elizabeth], b. Aug. 29, 1744 | 1 | 56 |
| Francis, m. Stephen **GARDINER**, Jr., June 6, 1760 | 1 | 86 |
| Frances, d. [Charles & Mary], b. Apr. 4, 1822 | 2 | 58 |
| Francis, of Colchester, m. Nathan **WILLIAMS**, of East Haddam, Apr. 30, 1838, by Joshua B. Rodges, J. P. | 2 | 259 |
| Frances A., m. Giles **LILLIS**, b. of Colchester, July 28, 1856, by Rev. W[illia]m O. Cady | 2 | 151 |
| George, m. Elizabeth **WELLS**, Apr. 12, 1730 | 1 | 56 |
| George, d. Feb. 5, 1761 | 1 | 56 |
| George, s. [Ephraim & Ama], b. Apr. 12, 1790 | 2 | 52 |
| Hannah, m. Shubaiell **ROWLEE**, May 8, 1709 | L-3 | 193 |
| Hannah, m. Shubael **ROWLEE**, May 8, 1709 | TM-1 | 193 |

| | Vol. | Page |
|---|---|---|
| **BROWN**, (cont.) | | |
| Hannah, [d. John & Marah], b. June 26, 1717 | L-1 | 444 |
| Hannah, d. William, b. Jan. 25, 1718 | L-1 | 447 |
| Hannah, [d. George & Elizabeth], b. Oct. 28, 1738 | 1 | 56 |
| Hannah, d. [Edward & Hannah], b. Dec. 7, 1750 | 1 | 149 |
| Hannah, m. Lebbeus **HILLS**, Nov. 5, 1760 | 1 | 22 |
| Hannah, [d. Josiah & Lucy], b. Sept. 11, 1773 | 1 | 44 |
| Hannah, d. [Charles & Mary], b. Mar. 29, 1823 | 2 | 58 |
| Harriet W. P., [d. Ezekiel W. & Sally Parsons], d. Oct. 26, 1907, ae 78 y. 7 m., in New York City | 2 | 156 |
| Henry, of Colchester, m. Eliza **STODDARD**, of Ithaca, N. Y., July 7, 1852 | 3 | 51 |
| Isaiah, s. [Edward & Hannah], b. Dec. 8, 1752 | 1 | 149 |
| Jeames, d. May 8, 1704 | L-3 | 194 |
| James, d. May 8, 1704 | TM-1 | 194 |
| James, m. Anne **WICKWIRE**, Oct. 14, 1714 | L-1 | 799 |
| James, [s. James & Anne], b. Sept. 7, 1715 | L-1 | 799 |
| James Ransom, s. [Charles & Mary], b. Oct. 6, 1830 | 2 | 58 |
| Jane A., of Columbia, m. George D. **BINGHAM**, of Colchester, Dec. 9, 1851, by Rev. E. Dickinson | 3 | 48 |
| Jared, m. Nancy **THATCHER**, Mar. 20, 1828, by Avery Morgan, J. P. | 2 | 202 |
| Jedediah, [s. John & Marah], b. Mar. 21, 1729 | L-1 | 444 |
| Jesse, [s. George & Elizabeth], b. Feb. 2, 1746/7 | 1 | 56 |
| Joanna, d. [Ephraim & Ama], b. Aug. 17, 1792 | 2 | 52 |
| John, m. Marah **CHANDLER**, Mar. 20, 1710 | L-1 | 444 |
| John, [s. John & Marah], b. Apr. 4, 1715 | L-1 | 444 |
| John, m. Sarah **HAR[R]IS**, Aug. 13, 1724 | L-1 | 445 |
| John, [s. John & Sarah], b. Sept. 11, 1727 | L-1 | 445 |
| John, [s. Edward & Hannah], b. Jan. 10, 1748/9 | 1 | 149 |
| John, s. [Charles & Mary], b. July 5, 1824 | 2 | 58 |
| John G., m. Mary **LOOMIS**, b. of Colchester, Jan. 13, 1831, by Rev. Joseph Harvey | 2 | 228 |
| John T., m. Mary A. **LAMPHERE**, b. of Colchester, May 14, 1854, by Rev. Anthony Palmer | 3 | 62 |
| Jonah, [s. Josiah & Lucy], b. Oct. 28, 1767 | 1 | 44 |
| Jonathan, s. [David & Abigail], b. Feb. 25, 1746/7 | 1 | 130 |
| Joseph O., of New York, m. Harriet W. **PARSONS**, of Colchester, June 21, 1853, by Rev. Erastus Dickinson | 3 | 57 |
| Josiah, [s. Edward & Hannah], b. Aug. 1, 1747 | 1 | 149 |
| Josiah, m. Lucy **SKINNER**, [ ], 1766 | 1 | 44 |
| Kasiah, d. Thomas, b. Sept. 22, 1707 | L-3 | 196 |
| Kasiah, d. Tho[ma]s, b. Sept. 22, 1707 | TM-1 | 196 |
| Kesiah, [s. Samuell], b. Dec. 5, 1728 | L-3 | 8 |
| Laura A., of Columbia, Conn., m. George H. **COLEMAN**, of Hebron, May 5, 1850, by Albert F. Park, Minister | 3 | 1 |
| Lina, m. James **SEXTON**, Oct. 11, 1846, by Rev. S. D. Jewett | 3 | 29 |

| | Vol. | Page |
|---|---|---|
| **BROWN**, (cont.) | | |
| Linden, m. Olive **CONE**, Jan. 9, 1825, by Salmon Cone, V. D. M. | 2 | 174 |
| Lois, [d. Samuel 2d], b. Mar. 12, 1740 | 1 | 107 |
| Lucy, [d. Josiah & Lucy], b. Nov. 4, 1769 | 1 | 44 |
| Lucy, d. [Oliver & Mary], b. Jan. 31, 1779 | 2 | 67 |
| Lucy, m. Asa **RATHBURN**, [ ]; d. Jan. 4, 1824, ae 45 | 2 | 132 |
| Lydia, [d. George & Elizabeth], b. Aug. 27, 1736 | 1 | 56 |
| Lydia, d. [Samuel & Lydia], b. Aug. [ ], 1796 | 2 | 245 |
| Lydia, w. Samuel, d. Oct. [ ], 1799 | 2 | 245 |
| Lydia, m. Reuben **WATROUS**, Jan. 1, 1812 | 2 | 117 |
| Mary, m. John **CARRIER**, July 22, 1722 | L-1 | 449 |
| Mary, m. Daniell **SKIN[N]ER**, Mar. 21, 1728 | L-1 | 447 |
| Mary, [d. Samuell & Mary], b. Feb. 13, 1732 | TPR | 110 |
| Mary, d. [David & Abigail], b. May 6, 1749 | 1 | 130 |
| Mary, w. Oliver, d. Feb. 17, 1821, ae 74 | 2 | 67 |
| Mary, m. Charles **BROWN**, [ ] | 2 | 58 |
| Mary, [m.] John **CARRIER**, [ ] | 1 | 128 |
| Mary Amelia, d. [Samuel & Lucy], b. Jan. 30, 1839 | 3 | 8 |
| Mary Ann, d. [Charles & Mary], b. Jan. 1, 1820 | 2 | 58 |
| Mary Ann, of Colchester, m. John **ANDREWS**, of Clinton, Sept. 17, 1844, by Rev. Rob[er]t C. Mills | 3 | 17 |
| Mercy, m. Samuel **BROWN**, Aug. 13, 1724 | L-1 | 444 |
| Molle, d. [Edward & Hannah], b. Apr. 9, 1754 | 1 | 149 |
| Nancy, m. Daniel **WELCH**, Jr., Aug. 24, 1788 | 2 | 65 |
| Naomi, d. [David & Abigail], b. May 12, 1742 | 1 | 130 |
| Nehemiah, [s. John & Marah], b. Sept. 26, 1726 | L-1 | 444 |
| Oliver, [s. George & Elizabeth], b. Sept. 21, 1748 | 1 | 56 |
| Oliver, of Colchester, m. Mary **ARNOLD**, of East Haddam, May 24, 1770; d. May 23, 1823, ae 75 | 2 | 67 |
| Persis, [d. Samuel, 2d], b. Feb. 2, 1738/9 | 1 | 107 |
| Polly, d. [Oliver & Mary], b. Nov. 1, 1776 | 2 | 67 |
| Rebecca, m. Moses **FULLER**, [ ] | 1 | 139 |
| Richard, m. Betsey **FREEMAN**, Jan. 26, 1826, by Salmon Cone, V. D. M. | 2 | 184 |
| Russel[l], s. [Oliver & Mary], b. July 15, 1783 | 2 | 67 |
| Ruth, [d. Samuell[], b. Nov. 2, 1726 | L-3 | 8 |
| Samuell, s. Thankfull, b. Dec. 5, 1703 | L-3 | 194 |
| Samuel, s. Thankfull, b. Dec. 5, 1703 | TM-1 | 194 |
| Samuell, m. Elisabeth **COLLINS**, May 12, 1713 | L-3 | 196 |
| Samuel, m. Elizabeth **COLLINS**, May 12, 1713 | TM-1 | 197 |
| Samuell, m. Presilla **KENT**, Apr. 11, 1715 | L-3 | 198 |
| Samuel, m. Priscilla **KENT**, Apr. 11, 1715 | TM-1 | 198 |
| Samuell, s. Samuell, b. Dec. 12, 1718; d. Oct. 5, 1719 | L-3 | 196 |
| Samuel, s. Sam[ue]l, b. Dec. 12, 1718; d. Oct. 5, 1719 | TM-1 | 196 |
| Samuell, [s. Samuell], b. Mar. 10, 1723 | L-3 | 196 |
| Samuel, s. Sam[ue]l, b. Mar. 10, 1723 | TM-1 | 196 |
| Samuell, m. Mercy **BROWN**, Aug. 13, 1724 | L-1 | 444 |

| | Vol. | Page |
|---|---|---|
| **BROWN**, (cont.) | | |
| Samuell, m. Mary **DUNHAM**, Aug. 6, 1729 | TPR | 110 |
| Samuell, [s. Samuell & Mary], b. Aug. 17, 1729(?) | TPR | 110 |
| Samuel, m. Lydia **BIRGE**, June [ ], 1779 | 2 | 245 |
| Samuel, m. Wid. Dolly **DAY**, June [ ], 1800 | 2 | 245 |
| Sarah, [d. John & Marah], b. Jan. 6, 1719/20 | L-1 | 444 |
| Sarah, [d. John & Sarah], b. June 20, 1725 | L-1 | 445 |
| Sarah, [d. Samuel, 2d], b. Feb. 1, 1736/7 | 1 | 107 |
| Sarah, w. [Thomas], d. Feb. 9, 1829, ae 72 | 2 | 147 |
| Sarah Elizabeth, d. [Samuel & Lucy], b. Aug. 12, 1841 | 3 | 8 |
| Sarah C., m. Lyman **LEFFINGWELL**, Aug. 20, 1833, by Rev. Joseph Harvey | 2 | 256 |
| Sarah Chapman, d. [Elisha & Lina], b. May 17, 1813 | 2 | 116 |
| Stanton, s. [Charles & Mary], b. Nov. 10, 1832 | 2 | 58 |
| Thankfull, m. Richard **CAR[R]IER**, July 29, 1707 | L-3 | 198 |
| Thankfull, m. Richard **CARRIER**, July 29, 1707 | TM-1 | 198 |
| Thomas, Sr., d. Apr. 18, 1717 | L-3 | 197 |
| Thomas, Sr., d. Apr. 18, 1717 | TM-1 | 197 |
| Thomas, s. Samuell, b. Nov. 9, 1724 | L-3 | 8 |
| Thomas, d. Apr. 7, 1819, ae 67 | 2 | 147 |
| Timothy, [s. John & Marah], b. Dec. 3, 1721 | L-1 | 444 |
| William, [s. William], b. Oct. 7, 1720 | L-1 | 447 |
| William, s. [Samuel, 2d], b. Dec. 30, 1734 | 1 | 107 |
| William, s. [Edward & Hannah], b. Feb. 23, 1745/6 | 1 | 149 |
| ----, child of [George & Elizabeth], b. Sept. 9, 1740; d. [Sept.] 28, 1740 | 1 | 56 |
| ----, child of [George & Elizabeth], b. Feb. 10, 1742/3 | 1 | 56 |
| ----, s. [Edward & Hannah], b. Apr. 2, 1760; d. Apr. 3, 1760 | 1 | 149 |
| ----, d. [Oliver & Mary], b. Sept. [ ], 1791; d. same day | 2 | 67 |
| **BROWNELL**, Charles E., of East Haddam, m. Abigail T. **LOOMIS**, Nov. 25, 1852, by Rev. S. D. Jewett, at Westchester | 3 | 54 |
| **BRUMLEY**, George W., of Bozrah, m. Maria **WATROUS**, of Colchester, Sept. 7, 1845, by Rev. M. P. Alderman | 3 | 24 |
| **BUCK**, Franklin, of Lisbon, m. Sophronia **FREEMAN**, of Colchester, Dec. 13, 1824, by Salmon Cone, V. D. M. (See also **TUCK**) | 2 | 173 |
| **BUCKINGHAM**, Joseph A., of New London, m. Abby E. **WICKWIRE**, of Colchester, Sept. 24, 1848, by Rev. P. Brockett | 3 | 36 |
| **BUDD**, Hannah, m. John **LOOMIS**,Jr. June 13, 1790 | 2 | 78 |
| **BUDENTON**, Lucy, m. Bildad **WATERMAN**, Apr. 18, 1765 | 1 | 81 |
| **BUEL, BUELL**, Almy A., d. [Talcot L. & Mary G.], b. Apr. 24, 1830 | 2 | 167 |
| Caroline M., of Chatham, m. Nehemiah **TRACY**, of Colchester, May 5, 1833 | 2 | 247 |
| David, Jr., of New Haven, m. Sarah Ann **GILLETT**, of Colchester, Nov. 25, 1847, by Rev. Joel R. Arnold | 3 | 33 |

| | Vol. | Page |
|---|---|---|
| **BUEL, BUELL**, (cont.) | | |
| David C., s. [Joseph & Marcy], b. Dec. 7, 1803 | 2 | 246 |
| David C., m. Mary O. **DAY**, Feb. 1, 1829, by Rev. Joseph Harvey | 2 | 209 |
| Eunice, m. Daniel J. **NORTON**, Mar. 28, 1832, by Rev. S. D. Jewett | 3 | 50 |
| Eunice B., d. [Talcot L. & Mary G.], b. Oct. 24, 1832 | 2 | 167 |
| Francis A., s. [Joseph & Marcy], b. June 27, 1817 | 2 | 246 |
| Francis A., of Colchester, m. Julius **SHEPHARD**, of Coventry, Sept. 10, 1839, by Rev. Lyman Strong | 2 | 123 |
| Frances C., of Colchester, m. Alfred **SPENCER**, of Sheffield, Conn., Mar. 26, 1846, by Rev. Joel R. Arnold | 3 | 27 |
| Francis N., s. [Joseph & Marcy], b. July 2, 1815; d. Sept. 14, 1816 | 2 | 246 |
| Hannah, m. Jared **FOOT**, Oct. 18, 1753 | 1 | 150 |
| Harriet E., d. [Talcot L. & Mary G.], b. Apr. 19, 1828; d. May 6, 1901 | 2 | 167 |
| Harriet E., m. W[illia]m G. **CARRIER**, b. of Westchester, June 27, 1852, by W. O. Cady | 3 | 51 |
| Harriet R., d. [Joseph & Marcy], b. Jan. 3, 1806 | 2 | 246 |
| Harriet R., of Colchester, m. Euphrastus **CARRIER**, of Penn., Mar. 13, 1828, by Rev. Joseph Harvey | 2 | 202 |
| Hiram G., s. [Joseph & Marcy], b. Aug. 4, 1813 | 2 | 246 |
| Hiram G., m. Phebe **BASSETT*** (crossed out), b. of Colchester, Sept.10, 1839, by Rev. Lyman Strong (***BISSELL** handwritten in margin of original manuscript) | 2 | 98 |
| Horatio N., s. [Talcot L. & Mary G.], b. Mar. 6, 1825 | 2 | 167 |
| John R., s. [Joseph & Marcy], b. May 23, 1809 | 2 | 246 |
| Joseph, b. July 14, 1775; m. Marcy **CARRIER**, Nov. 4, 1795 | 2 | 246 |
| Joseph N., s. [Joseph & Marcy], b. May 11, 1811 | 2 | 246 |
| Joseph N., m. Susan L. **LEE**, b. of Colchester, Aug. 18, 1835, by Rev. Joseph Harvey | 2 | 278 |
| Joshua B., s. [Joseph & Marcy], b. Oct. 2, 1807 | 2 | 246 |
| Lucy M., d. [Joseph & Marcy], b. Mar. 21, 1800 | 2 | 246 |
| Lucy M., m. Charles **WATROUS**, b. of Colchester, Nov. 1, 1821, by Rev. Jacob Seales | 2 | 147 |
| Oliver, m. Judith **TILDEN**, Dec. 15, 1768 | 1 | 83 |
| Robert, of Hartford, m. Laura **WAY**, of Colchester, Sept. 27, 1830, by Rev. Lyman Strong | 2 | 225 |
| Sarah, m. Theodore **LORD**, June 11, 1772 | 1 | 107 |
| Sarah, m. Theodore **LORD**, June 11, 1772 | 2 | 11 |
| Talcott L., s. [Joseph & Marcy], b. Aug. 9, 1797 | 2 | 246 |
| Talcot[t] L., m. Mary G. **CARRIER**, Aug. 1, 1824, by Jacob Seales, V. D. M., at the house of Col. Uriah Carrier | 2 | 167 |
| Talcott Loveland, m. Dorothy **STAPLES**, b. of Colchester (Westchester), June 26, 1838, by Rev. Joel R. Arnold | 2 | 276 |

| | Vol. | Page |
|---|---|---|
| **BUGBEY**, Eleanor, m. Joseph **LEVETT**, Feb. 6, 1739/40 | 1 | 141 |
| **BULKELEY, BULKLEY**, Abigail, m. Ephraim **LITTLE**, Nov. 5, 1755 | 1 | 122 |
| Abigail, see also Abigail **LITTLE** | 2 | 310 |
| Amelia Josephine Maria, d. [Gershom & Sally], b. May 15, 1815 | 2 | 148 |
| Ann, d. [Gershom & Abigail], b. May 11, 1753 | 1 | 132 |
| Ann, m. Asa **SWAN**, May 29, 1771 | 2 | 5 |
| Ann Eliza, m. George **SMITH**, b. of Colchester, Nov. 16, 1834, by Rev. Lyman Strong | 2 | 272 |
| Anna, [d. Charles & Anne], b. Apr. 14, 1747 | 1 | 88 |
| Anna, of New London, m. Eliphalet **BULKELEY**, of Colchester, Sept. 16, 1767 | 2 | 77 |
| Anna, [d. Joshua & Louis], b. Oct. 18, 1770; d. July 5, 1776, in her 6th year | 1 | 29 |
| Anna, d. [David & Sally], b. June 26, 1808 | 2 | 67 |
| Asa, s. [roger & Jerusha], b. Apr. 24, 1774 | 2 | 50 |
| Asa, m. Sophia **LO[O]MIS**, Nov. 11, 1796 | 2 | 75 |
| Augustus Washington, s. [George & Sophia], b. Oct. 18, 1805 | 2 | 107 |
| Aurelia, d. [George & Sophia], b. Oct. 12, 1810 | 2 | 107 |
| Benjamin, s. [Oliver & Sophia], b. June 13, 1806; d. Jan. 22, 1819 | 2 | 75 |
| Benjamin R., m. Lois **WORTHINGTON**, [ ] | 2 | 149 |
| Benjamin Root, s. [Roger & Jerusha], b. Aug. 25, 1772; d. Oct. 25, 1776 | 2 | 50 |
| Benjamin Root, [s. Roger & Jerusha], b. Sept. 2, 1776 | 2 | 50 |
| Betsey F., d. [Oliver & Sophia], b. Apr. 27, 1816 | 2 | 75 |
| Calvin Foot, s. [Oliver & Sophia], b. Oct. 19, 1811 | 2 | 75 |
| Caroline, d. [George & Sophia], b. Nov. 4, 1807 | 2 | 107 |
| Celinda L., of Colchester, m. Dr. Alanson **PORTER**, of Williamstown, Oct. 5, 1823, by Salmon Cone, V. D. M. | 2 | 140 |
| Charles, [s. Rev. John], b. Dec. 26, 1710 | L-3 | 197 |
| Charles, s. John, b. Dec. 26, 1710 | TM-1 | 197 |
| Charles, of Colchester, m. Anne **LATTIMER**, of New London, Oct. 8, 1741 | 1 | 88 |
| Charles, s. [John & Abigail], b. May 22, 1752 | 1 | 133 |
| Charles, [s. Charles & Anne], b. Dec. 19, 1753 | 1 | 88 |
| Charles, s. [Peter & Susannah], b. Dec. 17, 1763 | 1 | 142 |
| Charles, m. Eunice **WATROUS**, [ ] | 2 | 78 |
| Charles Edwin, m. Mary **ISHAM**, June 4, 1827, by Salmon Cone, V. D. M. | 2 | 196 |
| Charles Edwin, s. [Charles Edwin & Mary], b. May 4, 1829 | 2 | 196 |
| Charlotte, d. [Charles & Eunice], b. May 17, 1790 | 2 | 78 |
| Chauncey, s. [Oliver & Sarah], b. Oct. 24, 1741 | 1 | 141 |
| Clarissa P., m. John T. **BULKELEY**, Feb. 22, 1830, by Salmon Cone, V. D. M. | 2 | 219 |
| Clarissa Pamelia, d. [Elijah & Pamelia], b. May 8, 1809 | 2 | 91 |
| Dan, s. [John & Judeth], b. Mar. 20, 1784 | 1 | 115 |

| | Vol. | Page |
|---|---|---|
| **BULKELEY, BULKLEY**, (cont.) | | |
| Dan[ie]ll, s. [Gershom & Abigail], b. May 13, 1744 | 1 | 132 |
| Daniel, of Colchester, m. Dorothy **OLMSTEAD**, of East Haddam, Aug. 16, 1764 | 1 | 38 |
| Dan[ie]ll, [s. Daniel & Dorothy], b. Aug. 19, 1766 | 1 | 38 |
| Daniel, s. [Oliver & Sophia], b. May 16, 1800 | 2 | 75 |
| Daniel, Capt., d. July 20, 1810 | 1 | 38 |
| Daniel, of Virginia, m. Cynthia **BIGELOW**, of Colchester, Aug. 1, 1830, by Rev. Alvan Ackley | 2 | 223 |
| David, s. [Gershom & Abigail], b. July 18, 1749 | 1 | 132 |
| David, b. Sept. 24, 1780; m. Sally **CHAPMAN**, Dec. 26, 1805, by Rev. Elijah Parsons, East Haddam. Recorded July 3, 1822; d. June 11, 1835, ae 55 | 2 | 67 |
| David Henry, s. [David & Sally], b. Sept. 19, 1806 | 2 | 67 |
| Dorothy, [d. Rev. John], b. Feb. 28, 1706 | L-3 | 197 |
| Dorothy, [d. John], b. Feb. 28, 1706 | TM-1 | 197 |
| Dorothy, [d. Daniel & Dorothy], b. Oct. 8, 1774; d. Nov. 17, 1776 | 1 | 38 |
| Dorothy, 2d, [d. Daniel & Dorothy], b. July 11, 1780 | 1 | 38 |
| Dorothy L., d. [Oliver & Sophia], b. May 28, 1814 | 2 | 75 |
| Elijah, s. [John & Judeth], b. Jan. 29, 1766 | 1 | 115 |
| Elijah, m. Pamelia **LOOMIS**, Apr. 22, 1787; d. July 31, 1842, ae 76 | 2 | 91 |
| Eliphalet, s. [John & Mary], b. Aug. 8, 1746 | 1 | 133 |
| Eliphalet, of Colchester, m. Anna **BULKELEY**, of New London, Sept. 16, 1767 | 2 | 77 |
| Eliphalet, s. [Eliphalet & Anna], b. Apr. 22, 1782 | 2 | 77 |
| Eliphalet A., m. Lydia S. **MORGAN**, Jan. 31, 1830, by Salmon Cone, V. D. M. | 2 | 218 |
| Eliza, d. [Asa & Sophia], b. Apr. 30, 1798 | 2 | 75 |
| Emeline N., m. Pomroy **HALL**, b. of Colchester, Oct. 5, 1823, by Salmon Cone, V. D. M. | 2 | 99 |
| Enoch, b. Dec. 31, 1801, of Salem, m. Sophia **ABEL**, of Colchester, Mar. 18, 1824, by Rev. W[illia]m Palmer, at Hez[ekiah] Abell's, Jr.; d. Mar. 19, 1847, ae 45 | 2 | 164 |
| Enoch Bolles, [s. Enoch & Sophia], b. Apr. 12, 1829; d. Oct. 11, 1838 | 2 | 164 |
| Epaphroditas, twin with Henry, s. [William & Polly], b. June 16, 1791; d. Jan. 26, 1817 | 2 | 50 |
| Eunice, d. [Gershom & Abigail], b. May 14, 1747 | 1 | 132 |
| Eunice, m. Elisha **LORD**, May 25, 1769; d. Apr. 2, 1796 | 2 | 33 |
| Eunice, [d. Daniel & Dorothy], b. Apr. 4, 1772 | 1 | 38 |
| Eunice, m. Roger **FOOT**, May 26, 1790; d. Jan. 22, 1846, ae 74 | 2 | 51 |
| Eunice, m. John **WELLS**, 3d. [ ] | 2 | 147 |
| Eunice E., [d. Enoch & Sophia], b. Nov. 27, 1836 | 2 | 164 |
| Fanny, d. [Eliphalet & Anna], b. Apr. 6, 1787 | 1 | 77 |
| Frances, s. [Charles & Eunice], b. July 27, 1787 | 2 | 78 |

| | Vol. | Page |
|---|---|---|
| **BULKELEY, BULKLEY**, (cont.) | | |
| Frances Harriet, d. [Benjamin R. & Lois], b. June 10, 1805; d. Sept. 7, 1806 | 2 | 149 |
| Frances Jane, d. [David & Sally], b. Mar. 27, 1819 | 2 | 67 |
| Frances Jane, of Colchester, m. Henry **WELLS**, of New Haven, Apr. 15, 1841, by Rev. Augustus Bolles | 2 | 191 |
| Frederick, m. Lydia **LATTEMORE**, Apr. 16, 1795 | 2 | 86 |
| Frederick, s. [Frederick & Lydia], b. Feb. 26, 1796 | 2 | 86 |
| Frederick, [s. Enoch & Sophia], b. Oct. 17, 1835; d. Feb. 17, 1836 | 2 | 164 |
| Gad, s. [John & Judeth], b. Feb. 20, 1779 | 1 | 115 |
| George, s. [Roger & Jerusha], b. Mar. 8 1780 | 2 | 50 |
| George, m. Sophia **BULKELEY**, Dec. 31, 1804; d. May 9, 1811 | 2 | 107 |
| George Chapman, s. [David & Sally], b. Sept. 9, 1812 | 2 | 67 |
| Ge[r]shom, [s. Rev. John], b. Feb. 4, 1708/9 | L-3 | 197 |
| Gershom, s. John, b. Feb. 4, 1708/9 | TM-1 | 197 |
| Gershom, m. Abigail **ROB[B]INS**, Nov. 27, 1733 | L-3 | 452 |
| Gershom, m. Abigail **ROB[B]INS**, Nov. 28, 1733 | 1 | 132 |
| Gershom, s. [John & Judeth], b. Oct. 3, 1763 | 1 | 115 |
| Gershom, Capt., had slaves Jack & Prince, twin s. Pegg, b. Apr. 13, 1783 | 2 | 47 |
| Gershom, s. [Roger & Jerusha], b. Nov. 1, 1783; d. Oct. 4, 1785 | 2 | 50 |
| Gershom, s. [Roger & Jerusha], b. May 14, 1788 | 2 | 50 |
| Gershom, m. Sally **BABCOCK**, Oct. 12, 1809 | 2 | 148 |
| Girdin, [s. Joshua & Lois], b. July 1, 1764; d. June 26, 1776, ae 12 | 1 | 29 |
| Gurdon, s. [John & Judeth], b. Mar. 15, 1777 | 1 | 115 |
| Hannah, [d. Peter, Jr. & Hannah], b. Aug. 25, 1775 | 1 | 82 |
| Hannah, d. of Peter, m. Daniel **CLARK**, Feb. 18, 1795; d. July 12, 1796 (?) | 2 | 65 |
| Hannah, m. Stephen **WEBSTER**, Feb. 1, 1829, by Rev. Joseph Harvey, of Westchester | 2 | 210 |
| Harriet, [d. John & Judeth], b. Jan. 22, 1787 | 1 | 115 |
| Harriet, [w. Joshua, 2d], d. May 25, 1808 | 2 | 113 |
| Harriet E., [d. Enoch & Sophia], b. May 1, 1838 | 2 | 164 |
| Henry, twin with Epaphroditas], s. [William & Polly], b. June 16, 1791 | 2 | 50 |
| Henry A., [s. Enoch & Sophia], b. Sept. 19, 1833 | 2 | 164 |
| Horatio Deming, s. [Gershom & Sally], b. Dec. 8, 1810; d. Sept. 28, 1823 | 2 | 148 |
| Ichabod, [s. Daniel & Dorothy], b. Sept. 23, 1769 | 1 | 38 |
| Irene, twin with Joseph, d. [Rev. John], b. Feb. 10, 1721/2; d. [Feb.] 20, [1721/2] | L-3 | 197 |
| Irene, twin with Joseph, d. [John], b. Feb. 10, 1721/2; d. [Feb.] 20, [1721/2 | TM-1 | 197 |
| Israel, s. [Peter & Susannah], b. Jan. 22, 1762 | 1 | 142 |

| | Vol. | Page |
|---|---|---|
| **BULKELEY, BULKLEY**, (cont.) | | |
| James, s. [Peter & Susannah], b. Sept. 7, 1757 | 1 | 142 |
| James, s. [Frederick & Lydia], b. Sept 13, 1798 | 2 | 86 |
| Jerusha, [w. Roger], d. July 27, 1788 | 2 | 50 |
| Jerusha, d. [Asa & Sophia], b. Jan. 26, 1800 | 2 | 75 |
| Jirah, s. [David & Sally], b. July 16, 1810 | 2 | 67 |
| John, [s. Rev. John], b. Apr 19, 1705 | L-3 | 197 |
| John, [s. John], b. Apr. 19, 1705 | TM-1 | 197 |
| John, Rev., 1st minister of Colchester, d. June 9, 1731 | L-3 | 456 |
| John, s. [Gershom & Abigail], b. Aug. 23, 1738 | 1 | 132 |
| John, m. Mary **GARDINER**, Oct. 29, 1738 | 1 | 133 |
| John, m. Mary **GARDINER**, Oct. [ ], 1738 | 1 | 130 |
| John, s. John & Mary], b. May 20, 1742; d. Nov. 13, 1742 | 1 | 133 |
| John, [s. Charles & Anne], b. Oct. 7, 1744 | 1 | 88 |
| John, m. Abigail **HASTINGS**, Apr. 16, 1751 | 1 | 133 |
| John, Col., d. July 21, 1753 | 1 | 133 |
| John, m. Judeth **WORTHINGTON**, Jan. 11, 1759 | 1 | 115 |
| John, s. [John & Judeth], b. Oct. 7, 1759 | 1 | 115 |
| John Adams, s. [Asa & Sophia], b. Feb. 1, 1802 | 2 | 75 |
| John Charles, s. [Eliphalet & Anna], b. Aug. 8, 1772 | 2 | 77 |
| John T., m. Clarissa P. **BULKELEY**, Feb. 22, 1830, by Salmon Cone, V. D. M. | 2 | 219 |
| John W., s. [Elijah & Pamelia], b. Jan. 22, 1788; d. Mar. 12, 1850 | 2 | 91 |
| Jonathan, s. [Elipahlet & Anna], b. July 8, 1777 | 2 | 77 |
| Joseph, twin with Irene, s. [Rev. John], b. Feb. 10, 1721/2; d. [Feb.] 25, 1721/2 | L-3 | 197 |
| Joseph, twin with Irene, s. [John], b. Feb. 10, 1721/2; d. [Feb.] 25, [1721/2] | TM-1 | 197 |
| Joseph, s. [Oliver & Sarah], b. Jan. 9, 1740 | 1 | 141 |
| Josephine M., [d. Enoch & Sophia], b. Oct. 31, 1842; d. Jan. 20, 1843 | 2 | 164 |
| Joshua, b. Feb. 24, 1741 | 1 | 29 |
| Joshua, s. [Gershom & Abigail], b. Feb. 24, 1741 | 1 | 132 |
| Joshua, m. Lois **DAY**, Nov. 19, 1761 | 1 | 29 |
| Joshua, [s. Daniel & Dorothy], b. June 5, 1778 | 1 | 38 |
| Joshua had slave Joel, s. Job, b. Mar. 1, 1796; Asher, s. Job, b. Dec. 25, 1793 | 2 | 325 |
| Joshua, 2d, m. Harriet **OLMSTEAD**, Mar. 18, 1806 | 2 | 113 |
| Joshua, s. [Oliver & Sophia], b. June 27, 1819 | 2 | 75 |
| Joshua, d. Jan. 22, 1821, ae 80 | 1 | 29 |
| Joshua Bobbins*, s. [John & Judeth], b. Nov. 2, 1771 (Probably "Robbins") | 1 | 115 |
| Joshua Robbins, m. Sarah **TAINTOR**, Sept. 7, 1793 | 2 | 68 |
| Judeth, d. [John & Judeth], b. Jan. 30, 1775 | 1 | 115 |
| Juliana, d. [Eliphalet & Anna], b. May 9, 1789 | 2 | 77 |
| Letinda, d. [Elijah & Pamelia], b. Aug. 23, 1793 (Perhaps "Selinda") | 2 | 91 |

| | Vol. | Page |
|---|---|---|
| **BULKELEY, BULKLEY,** (cont.) | | |
| Lois, d. [Oliver & Sophia], b. Aug. 9, 1803 | 2 | 75 |
| Lois, w. Joshua, d. July 8, 1812, ae 68 | 1 | 29 |
| Lois, [w. Benjamin R.], d. Dec. 26, 1818 | 2 | 149 |
| Lois, m. Eliphalet **LORD**, Nov. 9, 1826, by Salmon Cone, V. D. M. | 2 | 190 |
| Lucee, [d. Rev. John], b. Jan. 29, 1719/20 | L-3 | 197 |
| Lucy, d. John, b. Jan. 29, 1719/20 | TM-1 | 197 |
| Lucy, m. Epaphras **LORD**, Nov. 25, 1742 | 1 | 143 |
| Lucy, d. [John & Mary], b. Aug. 2, 1749 | 1 | 133 |
| Lucy, d. [Peter & Lucy], b. Aug. 4, 1749 | 1 | 142 |
| Lucy, w. Peter, d. Aug. 21, 1754 | 1 | 142 |
| Lucy, m. John **BREED**, May 13, 1773; d. Dec. 30, 1821 | 2 | 42 |
| Lucy, [d. Peter, Jr. & Hannah], b. Mar. 9, 1778 | 1 | 82 |
| Lucy, d. [Oliver & Sophia], b. May 21, 1824 | 2 | 75 |
| Lydia, d. [John & Mary], b. Oct. 21, 1739 | 1 | 133 |
| Lydia, [d. William & Lydia], b. Jan. 7, 1768 | 1 | 80 |
| Lydia, d. [John & Judeth], b. Apr. 25, 1781 | 1 | 115 |
| Lydia, d. [Frederick & Lydia], b. June 26, 1799 | 2 | 86 |
| Lydia, d. [John & Mary], b. Oct. [ ] | 1 | 130 |
| Lydia Ann, d. [Eliphalet & Anna], b. May 18, 1768 | 2 | 77 |
| Lydia Ann, m. Daniel **WATROUS**, [ ] | 2 | 100 |
| Marianna, [d. Enoch & Sophia], b. May 13, 1827 | 2 | 164 |
| Mary, d. [John & Mary], b. May 22, 1741; d. June 1, 1741 | 1 | 133 |
| Mary, d. [John & Mary], b. Nov. 15, 1743 | 1 | 133 |
| Mary, w. Col. John, d. Jan. 24, 1749/50 | 1 | 133 |
| Mary, d. [William & Polly], b. July 13, 1793 | 2 | 50 |
| Mary, m. Roger **BULKELEY**, Nov. 13, 1808 | 2 | 50 |
| Mary Addams, d. [Eliphalet & Anna], b. June 25, 1770 | 2 | 77 |
| Nabby, d. [John & Judeth], b. Dec. 30, 1769 | 1 | 115 |
| Nabby, m. Roger **TAINTOR**, Dec. 6, 1789 | 2 | 60 |
| Noah, s. [Oliver & Sarah], b. June 20, 1744 | 1 | 141 |
| Noah, d. Apr. 16, 1776 | 2 | 38 |
| Oleuer, [s. Rev. John], b. July 29, 1717 | L-3 | 197 |
| Oliver, s. John, b. July 29, 1717 | TM-1 | 197 |
| Oliver, [s. Daniel & Dorothy], b. Jan. 24, 1776 | 1 | 38 |
| Oliver, m. Sophia **FOOT**, Nov. 2, 1797; d. Dec. 23, 1837, ae 62 | 2 | 75 |
| Oliver, s. [Oliver & Sophia], b. Jan. 4, 1802; d. June 7, 1813 | 2 | 75 |
| Oliver, m. Sarah, d. Lt. Noah & Sarah **(WYATT) WELLS**,[ ] | 1 | 141 |
| Orlando, s. [Eliphalet & Anna], b. Jan. 19, 1793 | 2 | 77 |
| Patience, [d. Rev. John], b. Mar. 21, 1715 | L-3 | 197 |
| Patience, d. John, b. Mar. 21, 1715 | TM-1 | 197 |
| Patience, m. Ichabod **LORD**, Dec. 14, 1743 | 1 | 133 |
| Patience, [d. Charles & Anne], b. Apr. 23, 1749 | 1 | 88 |
| Patience, d. [Eliphalet & Anna], b. Dec. 17, 1774; d. July 7, 1777 | 2 | 77 |
| Pattie, d. [Eliphalet & Anna], b. Apr. 30, 1780 | 2 | 77 |

| | Vol. | Page |
|---|---|---|
| **BULKELEY, BULKLEY,** (cont.) | | |
| Peter, [s. Rev. John], b. Nov. 21, 1712 | L-3 | 197 |
| Peter, s. John, b. Nov. 21, 1712 | TM-1 | 197 |
| Peter, m. Lucy **AVERY**, Jan. 13, 1742/3 | 1 | 142 |
| Peter, s. [Peter & Lucy], b. Feb. 3, 1743/4 | 1 | 142 |
| Peter, m. Susannah **NEWTON**, Dec. 16, 1756 | 1 | 142 |
| Peter, Jr., of Colchester, m. Hannah **BREED**, of Stonington, Mar. 9, 1768 | 1 | 82 |
| Peter, [s. Peter, Jr. & Hannah], b. July 22, 1770 | 1 | 82 |
| Peter, d. Mar. 8, 1798 | 2 | 93 |
| Polly, d. [John & Judeth], b. Feb. 2, 1774 | 1 | 115 |
| Polly, m. Joseph **WORTHINGTON**, Sept. 10, 1791 | 2 | 63 |
| Prentice, [s. Peter, Jr. & Hannah], b. June 11, 1772 | 1 | 82 |
| Rhoda, [w. Roger], d. June 15, 1807 | 2 | 50 |
| Richard, s. [Elijah & Pamelia], b. Dec. 26, 1789 | 2 | 91 |
| Richard, s. [David & Sally], b. Feb. 17, 1824; d. Feb. 3, 1826 | 2 | 67 |
| Roger, s. [Gershom & Abigail], b. Sept. 14, 1751 | 1 | 132 |
| Roger, m. Jerusha **ROOT**, May 28, 1772 | 2 | 50 |
| Roger, s. [Roger & Jerusha], b. May 4, 1778; d. Sept. 22, 1785 | 2 | 50 |
| Roger, s. [Roger & Jerusha], b. May 6, 1786 | 2 | 50 |
| Roger, m. Mary **BULKELEY**, Nov. 13, 1808; d. Aug. 1, 1819 | 2 | 50 |
| Roger, m. Rhoda **KELLOGG**, [ ] | 2 | 50 |
| Sally, m. Hosea **FOOTE**, Nov. 6, 1798; d. June 20, 1817, ae 49 | 2 | 127 |
| Sally Maria, d. [David & Sally], b. Apr. 11, 1815 | 2 | 67 |
| Salmon Cone, s. [Oliver & Sophia], b. Feb. 23, 1810 | 2 | 75 |
| Sarah, d. Rev. John, b. Apr. 8, 1702 | L-3 | 197 |
| Sarah, d. Rev. John, b. Apr. 8, 1702 | TM-1 | 197 |
| Sarah, d. [Gershom & Abigail], b. Jan. 10, 1735 | 1 | 132 |
| Sarah, [d. Gershom & Abigail], b. Nov. 10, 1735 | L-3 | 452 |
| Sarah, d. [Oliver & Sarah], b. Dec. 4, 1745 | 1 | 141 |
| Sarah, m. John **TAINTOR**, Nov. 23, 1758 | 1 | 182 |
| Sarah, m. Joseph **ISHAM**, Jr., Jan. 17, 1765 | 1 | 144 |
| Sarah, d. [John & Sarah], b. Aug. 22, 1773 | 1 | 182 |
| Sarah, [d. Joshua & Lois], b. Oct. 9, 1779; m. Dr. Howell **ROGERS**, [ ]; d. Feb. 14, 1821, ae 42 | 1 | 29 |
| Sarah, b. Oct. 9, 1779; m. Dr. Ho[w]el[l] **ROGERS**, Oct. 9, 1796; d. Feb. 14, 1821, ae 42 | 2 | 84 |
| Sarah, [d. Enoch & Sophia], b. July 15, 1840; d. Jan. 28, 1843 | 2 | 164 |
| Sarah, w. Oliver, was d. of Lt. Noah **WELLS** | 1 | 141 |
| Sarah Chauncey, d. [Eliphalet & Anna], b. July 24, 1784 | 2 | 77 |
| Sarah M., [d. Enoch & Sophia], b. May 22, 1845; d. Mar. 31, 1850 | 2 | 164 |
| Sarah Maria, of Colchester, m. William N. **NILES**, of New Haven, Feb. 7, 1836, by Rev. Lyman Strong | 2 | 283 |
| Selinda, see under Letinda | 2 | 91 |

| | Vol. | Page |
|---|---|---|
| **BULKELEY, BULKLEY**, (cont.) | | |
| Silas D., m. Mary **DART**, b. of Colchester, Dec. 10, 1837, by Rev. Andrew M. Smith | 2 | 296 |
| Sophia, m. George **BULKELEY**, Dec. 31, 1804 | 2 | 107 |
| Sophia, d. [Oliver & Sophia], b. Jan. 2, 1808 | 2 | 75 |
| Sophia Jane, [d. Enoch & Sophia], b. Mar. 19, 1825 | 2 | 164 |
| Sophia Jane, m. Elihu **CLARK**, b. of Colchester, Jan. 22, 1851, by Rev. G. W. Pendleton | 2 | 108 |
| Sophia Maria, d. [Elijah & Pamelia], b. Nov. 15, 1811 | 2 | 91 |
| Susannah, d. [Peter & Susannah], b. Nov. 23, 1759 | 1 | 142 |
| Ursula Emeline, d. [Elijah & Pamelia], b. Sept. 12, 1806 | 2 | 91 |
| William, s. [Peter & Lucy], b. May 20, 1746 | 1 | 142 |
| William, s. [John & Judeth], b. Aug. 30, 1761 | 1 | 115 |
| William, m. Lydia **KELLOGG**, May 27, 1767 | 1 | 80 |
| William, m. Polly **CHAMPION**, Dec. 18, 1788; d. May 1, 1801 | 2 | 50 |
| William B. R., s. [Benjamin R. & Lois], b. July 12, 1809 | 2 | 149 |
| William E., s. [Oliver & Sophia], b. Oct. 4, 1798 | 2 | 75 |
| William E., m. Mary **TAYLOR**, June 8, 1826, by Salmon Cone, V. D. M. | 2 | 187 |
| William Edward, s. [Benjamin R. & Lois], b. Aug. 19, 1802; d. Aug. 31, 1802 | 2 | 149 |
| -----, d. [Rev. John], b. May 6, 1704; d. about 3 hrs. after birth | L-3 | 197 |
| -----, d. [John], b. May 6, 1704; d. 3 hrs. after birth | TM-1 | 197 |
| -----, [s. Daniel & Dorothy], b. Feb. 23, 1765; d. Feb. 23, 1765 | 1 | 38 |
| -----, s. [Benjamin R. & Lois], b. Apr. 12, 1811; d. same day | 2 | 149 |
| -----, d. [Benjamin R. & Lois], b. May 12, 1812; d. same day | 2 | 149 |
| **BUNCE**, Julia Ann, d. Hannah, colored, b. Oct. 31, 1815 | 2 | 326 |
| **BURCHAM**, James T., m. Arphelia L. **EMMONS**, Nov. 28, 1833, by Rev. Joseph Harvey | 2 | 261 |
| James Thomas, s. [James], b. Nov. 28, 1810 | 2 | 107 |
| Joseph, s. [James], b. Feb. 20, 1813 | 2 | 107 |
| **BURCHARD**, Phebe, of Norwich, m. Jacob **WORTHINGTON**, of Colchester, May 29, 1760 | 1 | 113 |
| Rebeckah, of East Windsor, m. Jonathan **LESTER**, of Colchester | 2 | 80 |
| **BURDETT**, Elvia B., m. Eliphalet S. **JONES**, Mar. 18, 1830, by Salmon Cone, V. D. M. | 2 | 220 |
| **BURGESS**, Maria, of Colchester, m. Erastus **BIGELOW**, of Troy, Dec. 18, 1826, by Salmon Cone, V. D. M. | 2 | 191 |
| **BURKE**, John, s. [William & Lettice], b. Dec. 24, 1780 | 2 | 54 |
| Joseph, s. [William & Lettice], b. Nov. 11, 1792 | 2 | 54 |
| Mary, d. [William & Lettice], b. July 3, 1784 | 2 | 54 |
| Sarah, d. [William & Lettice], b. July 8, 1787 | 2 | 54 |
| Thomas, s. [William & Lettice], b. Jan. 28, 1790 | 2 | 54 |
| William, m. Lettice **MINARD**, Apr. 11, 1778 | 2 | 54 |

| | Vol. | Page |
|---|---|---|
| **BURKE**, (cont.) | | |
| William, s. [William & Lettice], b. Aug. 23, 1782 | 2 | 54 |
| **BURNHAM, BURNAM**, Abigail, m. Phinehas **SABIN**, Apr. 22, 1756 | 1 | 94 |
| Asena, m. Bliss **ROGERS**, Sept. 6, 1818, by John Bigelow, J. P. | 2 | 151 |
| Benjamin, m. Catharine **TRUMBLE**, about 13 or 14 y. ago, by Epaphras **LORD**, J. P. Certificate dated Jan. 5, 1784 | 2 | 36 |
| Hannah, alias **INGRAHAM**, m. James R. **MILLER**, Oct. 17, 1824, by Samuel A. Peters, J. P. | 2 | 171 |
| Joseph T., of Hebron, m. Sarah B. **ISHAM**, Feb. 26, 1839, by Rev. Joel R. Arnold | 2 | 282 |
| Mary S., of Colchester, m. George W. **TAYLER**, of New London, Aug. 17, 1845, by Rev. Lyman Strong | 3 | 23 |
| William. of Colchester, m. Catharine **HURD**, of East Haddam, Sept. 5, 1824, by Jacob Seales, V. D. M. | 2 | 169 |
| **BURR**, Catie Isham, d. [Henry & Lucretia], b. Mar. 21, 1840 | 2 | 205 |
| Daniel A., of Haddam, m. Emily B. **SPENCER**, of Colchester, Oct. 15, 1849, by Rev. Albert F. Park | 3 | 42 |
| Henry, m. Lucretia **ISHAM**, Aug. 5, 1828, by Salmon Cone, V. D. M. | 2 | 205 |
| Henry, s. [Henry & Lucretia], b. Oct. 18, 1829 | 2 | 205 |
| Henry W., ae 23, m. Sarah Y. **THOMAS**, ae 22, b. of Colchester, June 21, 1853, by Rev. J. A. Copp | 3 | 59 |
| Horace H., s. [Henry & Lucretia], b. June 14, 1832 | 2 | 205 |
| Laura E., d. [Henry & Lucretia], b. Jan. 1, 1843 | 2 | 205 |
| **BURTT**, Dorcas, m. Jeremiah **BOGE**, June 5, 1755 | 1 | 90 |
| **BUSH**, Angelina, m. James L. **MAYNARD**, b. of Norwich, Jan. 6, 1850, by Rev. Lyman Strong | 3 | 45 |
| **BUTLER**, Dinah, m. Abner **CHAPMAN**, Mar. 10, 1749 | 1 | 153 |
| Elesebeth, m. Daniell **CLARK**, Dec. 4, 1704 | L-3 | 195 |
| Elizabeth, m. Daniel **CLARK**, Dec. 14, 1704 | TM-1 | 195 |
| Mabell, m. Ebenezer **KELLOGG**, July 6, 1706 | L-3 | 194 |
| Mabel, m. Ebenezer **KELLOGG**, July 6, 1706 | TM-1 | 194 |
| Mary, d. Mar. 19, 1715 | L-3 | 197 |
| Mary, d. Mar. 19, 1715 | TM-1 | 197 |
| Prudence, m. Ira **FILLMORE**, b. of Colchester, June 15, 1851, by Rev. W[illia]m O. Cady | 2 | 153 |
| **BUTTON**, Clarissa, of Colchester, m. John **TAYLOR**, of Lebanon, Apr. 1, 1850, by Griswold E. Morgan, J. P. | 3 | 40 |
| Elizabeth, m. Warren **BLEDGETT**, Jr., b. of Colchester, May 18, 1851, by Rev. George W. Pendleton | 2 | 80 |
| Emma, of Colchester, m. Samuel **JACOBS**, of Mansfield, Conn., Sept. 24, 1848, by Rev. F. W. Bill | 3 | 37 |
| Gilbert, m. Ellen **BARBER**, b. of Colchester, Dec. 22, 1850, by Rev. Albert F. Park | 2 | 69 |
| Joseph, of Montville, m. Clarissa **HANCOCK**, of Colchester, Apr. 9, 1849, by Griswold E. Morgan, J. P. Lebanon | 3 | 40 |

| | Vol. | Page |
|---|---|---|
| **BUTTON**, (cont.) | | |
| Nelson, m. Marion B. **PEIRCE**, b. of Colchester, Oct. 12, 1851, by Rev. Roger Allison | 2 | 71 |
| **CADWELL**, Jerusha, of Hartford, m. Nathaniel **FOOT**, 3d, Mar. 28, 1769 | 1 | 96 |
| **CADY**, John W., of Worcester, m. Electa **SHAILOR**, of Colchester, Apr. 21, 1845, by Rev. Pierpoint Brockett | 3 | 21 |
| **CAHOON**, Mary, m. Benjamin **RATHBUN**, Nov. 11, 1742 | 1 | 89 |
| **CALKINS**, Hannah, [d. Aquilla], b. Aug. 19, 1754; d. Nov. 13, 1754 | 1 | 46 |
| **CAMP**, Eliza P., of Durham, m. Ormi G. **CARRIER**, of East Haddam, [Jan.] 8, 1834, by Rev. S. D. Jewett, Westchester | 3 | 60 |
| **CANICE**, Sarah, m. Hiram **DANIELS**, b. of Colchester, Sept. 20, 1835, by Joshua b. Rogers, J. P. | 2 | 280 |
| **CARDWELL**, Sybel, m. William **TEW**, b. of Salem, Mar. 14, 1833, by Rev. Lyman Strong | 2 | 242 |
| **CARRIER, CARIER**, [see also **CURRIER**], Aaron, s. [Samuel & Rebecca], b. Nov. 14, 1781 | 2 | 33 |
| Aaron, s. [Samuel], b. Nov. 14, 1781 | 2 | 43 |
| Abby Jane, d. [Oren & Prudence R.], b. Nov. 22, 1824 | 2 | 166 |
| Abby Jane, m. William O. **STAPLES**, Apr. 8, 1844 | 2 | 249 |
| Abiall, d. [John & Mary], b. May 7, 1723 | L-1 | 449 |
| Abigail, d. [Samuel & Rebecca], b. July 10, 1771 | 2 | 33 |
| Abigail, d. [Samuel], b. July 10, 1771 | 2 | 43 |
| Abigail, m. Zenas **COLEMAN**, b. of Colchster, Oct. 19, 1774 | 2 | 17 |
| Albert Alonzo, s. [Aristobulas & Electa], b. Aug. 19, 1826 | 2 | 244 |
| Alfred, s. [Joseph], b. Apr. 3, 1789 | 2 | 5 |
| Amasa, s. [Joseph, Jr. & Lois], b. Mar. 25, 1792 | 2 | 40 |
| Ammaziah, s. [Amos & Phebe], b. July 17, 1754 | 1 | 102 |
| Ammi, s. [Joseph, Jr. & Lois], b. Dec. 5, 1799 | 2 | 40 |
| Ammi, of Marlborough, m. Mary **PRATT**, of Colchester, Jan. 9, 1825, by Jacob Seales, V. D. M. | 2 | 175 |
| Amos, s. Richard, [& Thankfull], b. July 3, 1722 | L-3 | 198 |
| Amos, s. Richard, b. July 3, 1722 | TM-1 | 198 |
| Amos, m. Phebe **KNEELAND**, June 6, 1745 | 1 | 102 |
| Amos, m. Phebe **NELAND**, June 6, 1745 | 1 | 145 |
| Amos, [s. Amos & Phebe], b. Apr. 18, 1748 | 1 | 102 |
| Andrew, m. Mary **ADDAMS**, Jan. 11, 1704/5 | L-3 | 193 |
| Andrew, m. Mary **ADDAMS**, Jan. 11, 1704/5 | TM-1 | 193 |
| Andrew, [s. Andrew & Mary], b. Feb. 2, 1705/6 | L-3 | 193 |
| Andrew, [s. J[oh]n, Jr. & Rebecca], b. Jan. 13, 1731/2; d. Jan. 24, 1736/7 | TPR | 110 |
| Andrew, Jr., m. Ruth **ADDAMS**, Dec. 27, 1733 | TPR | 111 |
| Andrew, [s. Andrew, Jr. & Ruth], b. Nov. 9, 1734 | TPR | 111 |
| Andrew, m. Rebecca **ROCKWELL**, Oct. 27, 1735 | TPR | 111 |
| And[re]w, s. John & Rebecca, b. Apr. 28, 1740 | 1 | 141 |
| Andrew, d. July 22, 1749 | 1 | 108 |

| | Vol. | Page |
|---|---|---|
| **CARRIER, CARIER,** (cont. | | |
| Andrew, s. [Samuel & Rebecca], b. Dec. 8, 1769 | 2 | 33 |
| Andrew, s. [Samuel], b. Dec. 8, 1769 | 2 | 43 |
| Andrew, Sr., d. Dec. 6, 1776 | 2 | 32 |
| Andrew, m. Phebe **WICKWARE**, Feb. 24, 1792 | 2 | 76 |
| Andrew, m. Anna **GELLETT**, Mar. 22, 1814 | 2 | 112 |
| Andrew E., m. Mary A. **MARKS**, b. of Colchester, May 11, 1842, by Rev. Daniel G. Sprague | 2 | 215 |
| Andrew Ely, s. [Andrew & Anna], b. July 2, 1816 | 2 | 112 |
| Ariadne, s. [Aristobulas & Electa], b. Feb. 24, 1829; d. Nov. 17, 1906, ae 68 y. 6 m., at N. Westchester, Conn. | 2 | 244 |
| Aristobulas, s. [Samuel], b. Aug. 11, 1790 | 2 | 244 |
| Aristobulas, m. Electa **ADAMS**, Nov. 30, 1819, by John Bigelow, J. P. | 2 | 244 |
| Bathe Minerva, d. [Andrew & Anna], b. Sept. 11, 1814 | 2 | 112 |
| Benjamin, [s. Andrew & Mary], b. Sept. 17, 1713 | L-3 | 193 |
| Benjamin, s. Andrew [& Mary], b. Sept. 17, 1713 | TM-1 | 193 |
| Benjamin, m. Elisabeth **KNEELAND**, Feb. 6, 1734/5 | L-3 | 454 |
| Benjamin, m. Elizabeth **KNEELAND**, Feb. 6, 1734/5 | 1 | 106 |
| Benjamin, s. Benjamin [& Elizabeth], b. Feb. 22, 1738/9 | 1 | 106 |
| Betsey, d. [Ebenezer & Clarissa], b. Aug. 30, 1796 | 2 | 84 |
| Caleb, s. Thomas, b. Oct. 17, 1715 | L-1 | 449 |
| Calista Abby, d. [Erastus & Nancy M.], b. Apr. 15, 1848 | 3 | 1 |
| Clarace, d. [Thomas & Lydia], b. Mar. 28, 1778 | 2 | 35 |
| Clarissa A., d. [Ozen & Emily], b. May 9, 1820 | 2 | 128 |
| Clarissa A., m. Ira W. **HOLMES**, b. of Colchester, Sept. 18, 1843, by Rev. Robert C. Mills | 3 | 6 |
| C[y]prien, d. [Uriah & Mary], b. Aug. 12, 1778 | 2 | 26 |
| David, [s. Thomas & Mary], b. Oct. 6, 1770 | 1 | 80 |
| David, s. [Joseph], b. May 12, 1776 | 2 | 5 |
| Deborah, d. [Thomas & Deborah], b. Apr. 25, 1742 | 1 | 131 |
| Deborah, m. Daniel **ADDAMS**, Dec. 1, 1751 | 1 | 53 |
| Deborah, d. [Joseph], b. Dec. 26, 1778 | 2 | 5 |
| Dolly, d. [Joseph], b. May 27, 1781 | 2 | 5 |
| Ebenezer, s. [Thomas & Deborah], b. Feb. 16, 1744/5 | 1 | 131 |
| Ebenezer, [s. Joseph & Deborah], b. Apr. 11, 1772; d. Feb. 20, 1773 | 1 | 77 |
| Ebenezer, 2d, [s. Joseph & Deborah], b. June 28, 1774 | 1 | 77 |
| Ebenezer, s. [Thomas & Mary], b. May 20, 1787 | 2 | 35 |
| Ebenezer, m. Clarissa **DAY**, Apr. 14, 1795 | 2 | 84 |
| Edwin Tracy, s. [Oren & Prudence], b. Aug. 11, 1837 | 2 | 166 |
| Electa, twin with Erastus, d. [Andrew & Anna], b. May 2, 1818 | 2 | 112 |
| Electa, of Colchester, m. Austin **HULING**, of Marlboro, Feb. 9, 1840, by Rev. Daniel G. Sprague | 2 | 133 |
| Eli, s. [Samuel & Rebecca], b. Jan. 13, 1767 | 2 | 33 |
| Elijah, [s. Benjamin & Elizabeth], b. May 15, 1743; | | |

| | Vol. | Page |
|---|---|---|
| **CARRIER, CARIER**, (cont.) | | |
| d. June 26, 1748 | 1 | 106 |
| Eliser, s. [Samuel], b. Jan. 13, 1767 | 2 | 43 |
| Eliza, m. William **BRAINARD**, Jr., b. of Colchester, July 13, 1837, by Rev. Ja[me]s Abell | 2 | 133 |
| Elisabeth, w. Richard, d. Mar. 6, 1704 | L-3 | 198 |
| Elizabeth, w. Richard, d. Mar. 6, 1704 | TM-1 | 198 |
| Elisabeth, [d. Timothy & Frances], b. Jan. 18, 1730/31; d. Aug. 26, 1731 | TPR | 111 |
| Elisabeth, [d. Timothy & Frances], b. Dec. 22, 1733/4 | TPR | 111 |
| Elisabeth, d. Benjamin & Elisabeth, b. Nov. 25, 1735 | L-3 | 452 |
| Elizabeth, d. [Benjamin & Elizabeth], b. Nov. 25, 1754 | 1 | 106 |
| Elizabeth, [d. Jeremiah & Elizabeth], b. July 9, 1759 | 1 | 21 |
| Ellen Jerome, d. [Oren & Prudence R.], b. July 8, 1830 | 2 | 166 |
| Emily, d. [Ozen & Emily], b. Dec. 25, 1829; d. Feb. 22, 1831 | 2 | 128 |
| Emily, d. [Ozen & Emily], b. Mar. 23, 1834 | 2 | 128 |
| Emma Sophronia, d. [Oren & Prudence R.], b. Apr. [ ], 1840 | 2 | 166 |
| Epaphroditus, s. [Lavina], b. Jan. 25, 1781; d. July 1, 1784 | 2 | 40 |
| Erastus, s. [Joseph], b. Apr. 14, 1784 | 2 | 5 |
| Erastus, twin with Electa, s. [Andrew & Anna], b. May 2, 1818 | 2 | 112 |
| Erastus, m. Nancy M. **GILLETT**, b. of Colchester, Feb. 9, 1843, by Rev. J. R. Arnold | 3 | 1 |
| Eunice, [d. Jeremiah & Elizabeth], b. Jan. 30, 1754 | 1 | 21 |
| Eunice, d. [Samuel], b. Mar. 7, 1774 | 2 | 43 |
| Eunice, d. [Samuel & Rebecca], b. Mar. 17, 1774 | 2 | 33 |
| Euphrastus, of Penn., m. Harriet R. **BUELL**, of Colchester, Mar. 13, 1828, by Rev. Joseph Harvey | 2 | 202 |
| Frances Lorenzo, s. [Aristobulas & Electa], b. Dec. 11, 1821 | 2 | 244 |
| Francis T., d. [Ozen & Emily], b. July 7, 1841 | 2 | 128 |
| George, s. [Ozen & Emily], b. Feb. 21, 1827 | 2 | 128 |
| George, m. Nancy **JOHNSON**, b. of Colchester, Jan. 11, 1852, by Rev. Geo[rge] W. Pendleton | 3 | 49 |
| George Ely, s. [Andrew E. & Mary A.], b. June 12, 1843 | 2 | 215 |
| Green, s. [John & Rebecca], b. Oct. 7, 1742 | 1 | 141 |
| Hannah, [d. Richard & Thankfull], b. May 1, 1708 | L-3 | 198 |
| Hannah, d. Richard [& Thankfull], b. May 1, 1708 | TM-1 | 198 |
| Hannah E., [d. Seth K. & Lydia], b. Dec. 4, 1820 | 2 | 255 |
| Hannah E., m. Hiram A. **DANIELS**, July 14, 1844, by Rev. Rob[er]t C. Mills | 3 | 15 |
| Henry Blish, s. [Oren & Prudence R.], b. June 16, 1827 | 2 | 166 |
| Huldah, [d. Jeremiah & Elizabeth], b. Feb. 13, 1762 | 1 | 21 |
| Isaac, [s. Thomas], b. July 5, 1718 | L-1 | 449 |
| Isaac, [s. Andrew & Rebecca], b. Apr. 21, 1744 | TPR | 111 |
| Isaac, [s. Thomas & Mary], b. Jan. 16, 1773 | 1 | 80 |
| Israell, [s. Andrew & Rebecca], b. Mar. 12, 1741/42 | TPR | 111 |
| Jeremiah, m. Elizabeth **ROBBINS**, Nov. 20, 1751 | 1 | 21 |
| Jeremiah, [s. Jeremiah & Elizabeth], b. Apr. 19, 1761 | 1 | 21 |

| | Vol. | Page |
|---|---|---|
| **CARRIER, CARIER**, (cont.) | | |
| Jerusha, d. [Joseph], b. Sept. 21, 1791 | 2 | 5 |
| Jerusha, [d. Seth K. & Lydia], b. Mar. 6, 1809 | 2 | 255 |
| John, [s. Andrew & Mary], b. June 14, 1707 | L-3 | 193 |
| John, s. Andrew [& Mary], b. June 14, 1707 | TM-1 | 193 |
| John, m. Mary **BROWN**, July 22, 1722 | L-1 | 449 |
| J[oh]n, Jr. m. Rebecca **BANISTER**, Jan. 13, 1730/31 | TPR | 110 |
| John, s. [John & Mary], b. July 13, 1737 | 1 | 128 |
| John, s. [Thomas & Deborah], b. July 21, 1746 | 1 | 131 |
| John, [m.] Mary **BROWN**, [ ] | 1 | 128 |
| Joseph, [s. Andrew & Rebecca], b. Mar. 3, 1738 | TPR | 111 |
| Joseph, [s. Jeremiah & Elizabeth], b. Aug. 21, 1752 | 1 | 21 |
| Joseph, m. Ruth **ADAM**, Dec. 14, 1762 | 1 | 77 |
| Joseph, [s. Joseph & Ruth], b. Aug. 4, 1766 | 1 | 77 |
| Joseph, m. Deborah **KNE[E]LAND**, Sept. [ ], 1771 | 1 | 77 |
| Joseph, Jr., m. Lois **DAY**, Jan. 8, 1789 | 2 | 40 |
| Josiah, [s. Benjamin & Elizabeth], b. Jan. 18, 1740/41 | 1 | 106 |
| Josiah, s. [Thomas & Lydia], b. July 15, 1780 | 2 | 35 |
| Julia, m. Timothy **WATROUS**, Dec. 25, 1826 | 2 | 246 |
| Lois, d. [Joseph, Jr. & Lois], b. Dec. 16, 1793 | 2 | 40 |
| Loren Loomis, s. [Oren & Emily], b. Feb. 19, 1832 | 2 | 128 |
| Lucy, [d. Thomas & Mary], b. Dec. 25, 1766 | 1 | 80 |
| Lucy, d. [Joseph, Jr. & Lois], b. Feb. 24, 1798 | 2 | 40 |
| Luther Marks, s. [Andrew E. & Mary A.], b. Dec. 12, 1845 | 2 | 215 |
| Lydia, d. [Thomas & Lydia], b. Sept. 30, 1782 | 2 | 35 |
| Lydia, [w. Thomas], d. June 1, 1784 | 2 | 35 |
| Marcy, b. May 15, 1776; m. Joseph **BUELL**, Nov. 4, 1795 | 2 | 246 |
| Margary, d. [Thomas & Mary], b. Nov. 19, 1792 | 2 | 35 |
| Mary, [d. Andrew & Mary], b. Apr. 19, 1708 | L-3 | 193 |
| Mary, d. Andrew [& Mary], b. Apr. 19, 1708 | TM-1 | 193 |
| Mary, [d. John & Mary], b. Dec. 26, 1727 | L-1 | 449 |
| Mary, [d. J[oh]n, Jr. & Rebecca], b. Dec. 7, 1733; d. Jan. 18, 1736/7 | TPR | 110 |
| Mary, d. [John & Rebecca], b. Feb. 7, 1738 | 1 | 141 |
| Mary, d. [Thomas & Mary], b. Aug. 20, 1743 | 1 | 132 |
| Mary, d. [Thomas & Deborah], b. Dec. 15, 1743 | 1 | 131 |
| Mary, w. Andrew, d. Sept. 23, 1748 | 1 | 108 |
| Mary, [d. Benjamin & Elizabeth], b. July 15, 1749 | 1 | 106 |
| Mary, [d. Jeremiah & Elizabeth], b. Mar. 26, 1765 | 1 | 21 |
| Mary, d. [Thomas & Mary], b. Mar. 28, 1786 | 2 | 35 |
| Mary, [d. Seth K. & Lydia], b. Dec. 13, 1811; d. Nov. 18, 1831 | 2 | 255 |
| Mary, d. [Andrew & Anna], b. Mar. 25, 1820; d. Jan. 25, 1908, ae 88 | 2 | 112 |
| Mary Buell, d. [Oren & Prudence R.], b. Nov. 6, 1835 | 2 | 166 |
| Mary G., m. Talcot L. **BUELL**, Aug. 1, 1824, by Jacob Seales, V. D. M., at the house of Col. Uriah Carrier | 2 | 167 |
| Mary Isham, d. [Oren & Emily], b. Apr. 24, 1838 | 2 | 128 |

| | Vol. | Page |
|---|---|---|
| **CARRIER, CARIER,** (cont.) | | |
| Matilda, d. [Samuel], b. Aug. 12, 1794 | 2 | 244 |
| Matilda, m. Elias **LOOMIS**, [ ] | 2 | 249 |
| Mahitabell, [d. Richard], b. Apr. 16, 1702 | L-3 | 198 |
| Mehetable, d. Richard, b. Apr. 16, 1702 | TM-1 | 198 |
| Mehetable, d. [Amos & Phebe], b. Feb. 9, 1756 | 1 | 102 |
| Mercy, d. [Andrew & Anna], b. June 26, 1822; d. Mar. 23, 1908, ae 85 y. 8 m. | 2 | 112 |
| Nancy Fidelia, d. [Erastus & Nancy M.], b. Apr. 6, 1846 | 3 | 1 |
| Olive, [d. Thomas & Mary], b. May 21, 1763 | 1 | 80 |
| Oliver, s. [Samuel & Rebecca], b. Aug. 4, 1784 | 2 | 33 |
| Oliver, [s. Seth K. & Lydia], b. Jan. 16, 1814 | 2 | 255 |
| Oren, m. Prudence R. **CHAPMAN**, b. of Colchester, Apr. 18, 1824, by Rev. Jacob Seales, at the house of David Loomis | 2 | 166 |
| Oren, m. Hope B. **COON**, [May] 26, 1844, by Rev. S. D. Jewett | 3 | 14 |
| Omri G., of East Haddam, m. Eliza P. **CAMP**, of Durham, [Jan.] 8, 1834, by Rev. S. D. Jewett, Westchester | 3 | 60 |
| Omri Gates, s. [Oren & Prudence], b. Oct. 22, 1831 | 2 | 166 |
| Phebe A., m. Leander **HOLDRICH**, Jan. 22, 1837, by Giles Shattuck, J. P. | 2 | 293 |
| Phebe Ann, d. [Andrew & Anna], b. Mar. 5, 1815 | 2 | 112 |
| Phillip, [s. Benjamin & Elizabeth], b. June 20, 1745 | 1 | 106 |
| Prudence, d. John & Mary, b. Mar. 22, 1731; d. Mar. 22, 1731 | L-3 | 458 |
| Prudence Robbins, d. [Oren & Prudence], b. Nov. 30, 1833 | 2 | 166 |
| Rachell, [s. Thomas], b. Sept. 15, 1720 | L-1 | 449 |
| Rachel, d. [Benjamin & Elizabeth], b. Sept. 6, 1747; d. Sept. 13, 1752 | 1 | 106 |
| Rachel, [d. Amos & Phebe], b. Nov. 4, 1750 | 1 | 102 |
| Rachel, [d. Benjamin & Elizabeth], b. Aug. 3, 1752 | 1 | 106 |
| Rachell, [s. Jeremiah & Elizabeth], b. Aug. 13, 1757 | 1 | 21 |
| Ralph, m. Patty **WATERS**, Aug. 30, 1819 | 2 | 130 |
| Ralph Robbins, s. [Ralph & Patty], b. Nov. 29, 1820 | 2 | 130 |
| Ralph T., s. [Ozen & Emily], b. Jan. 7, 1822 | 2 | 128 |
| Rebecca, d. [Samuel], b. Nov. 3, 1792 | 2 | 244 |
| Remembrance, d. Richard, b. Apr. 14, 1715 | L-3 | 197 |
| Remembrance, d. Richard, b. Apr. 14, 1715 | TM-1 | 197 |
| Richard, m. Thankfull **BROWN**, July 29, 1707 | L-3 | 198 |
| Richard, m. Thankfull **BROWN**, July 29, 1707 | TM-1 | 198 |
| Richard, d. Nov. 17, 1749 | 1 | 150 |
| Richard W., m. Lucretia **WATROUS**, b. of Colchester, June 30, 1844, by Rev. Lyman Strong | 3 | 14 |
| Richard Watrous, s. [Ralph & Patty], b. Sept. 1, 1822 | 2 | 130 |
| Roderick, s. [Seth K. & Lydia], b. Feb. 5, 1807 | 2 | 255 |
| Ruth, w. [Andrew, Jr.], d. Nov. 16, 1734 | TPR | 111 |
| Ruth, [d. Andrew & Rebecca], b. Aug. 14, 1736 | TPR | 111 |
| Ruth, [d. Joseph & Ruth], b. July 4, 1768 | 1 | 77 |

| | Vol. | Page |
|---|---|---|
| **CARRIER, CARIER**, (cont.) | | |
| Ruth, w. Joseph, d. Feb. 5, 1771 | 1 | 77 |
| Ruth, d. [Joseph, Jr. & Lois], b. Sept. 25, 1795 | 2 | 40 |
| Samuel, [s. Andrew & Rebecca], b. Jan. 6, 1739/40 | TPR | 111 |
| Samuel, m. [ ], Dec. 16, 1763 | 2 | 43 |
| Samuel, [s. Joseph & Ruth], b. Mar. 8, 1764; d. May 22, 1764 | 1 | 77 |
| Samuel, [s. Joseph & Ruth], b. May 14, 1765; d. July 22, 1765 | 1 | 77 |
| Samuel, m. Rebecca **SEARS**, Dec. 16, 1765 | 2 | 33 |
| Sam[ue]ll, s. [Samuel & Rebecca], b. Oct. 16, 1768 | 2 | 33 |
| Samuel, s. [Samuel], b. Oct. 16, 1768 | 2 | 43 |
| Samuel, [s. Joseph & Ruth], b. Jan. 25, 1771 | 1 | 77 |
| Samuel, s. [Joseph], d. Sept. 21, 1774 | 2 | 5 |
| Samuel, m. [ ], Nov. 26, 1788 | 2 | 244 |
| Samuel, d. Sept. 5, 1839, ae 70 | 2 | 244 |
| Sarah, [d. Richard], b. Apr. 13, 1701 | L-3 | 198 |
| Sarah, d. Richard, b. Apr. 13, 1701 | TM-1 | 198 |
| Sarah, m. John **CHAPMAN**, Sept. 7, 1707 | L-1 | 448 |
| Sarah, d. Richard, d. Sept. 27, 1717 | L-3 | 197 |
| Sarah, d. Rich[ar]d. d. Sept. 27, 1717 | TM-1 | 197 |
| Sarah, d. [Joseph, Jr. & Lois], b. Oct. 19, 1789; d. Aug. 20, 1794 | 2 | 40 |
| Sarah, d. [Joseph], b. Apr. 3, 1796 | 2 | 5 |
| Sarah, d. [Seth K. & Lydia], b. Oct. 14, 1805 | 2 | 255 |
| Sarah, m. Hiram **DANIELS**, Sept. 20, 1835; d. Jan. 31, 1850, ae 44 | 2 | 67 |
| Sieble, [d. John & Mary], b. Nov. 28, 1725 | L-1 | 449 |
| Simeon Sereno, s. [Aristobulas & Electa], b. Feb. 24, 1829 | 2 | 244 |
| Tabitha, d. [Samuel & Rebecca], b. Nov. 24, 1772 | 2 | 33 |
| Tabitha, d. [Samuel], b. Nov. 24, 1772 | 2 | 43 |
| Thankful[l], d. Richard, d. Apr. 29, 1711 | L-3 | 199 |
| Thankfull, d. Richard, b. Apr. 29, 1711 | TM-1 | 199 |
| Thankfull, [d. Timothy & Frances], b. Aug. 5, 1732 | TPR | 111 |
| Thankfull, [d. Amos & Phebe], b. Mar. 28, 1746 | 1 | 102 |
| Thankful, [d. Thomas & Mary], b. Feb. 20, 1765 | 1 | 80 |
| Thomas, [s. Andrew & Mary], b. June 20, 1711 | L-3 | 193 |
| Thomas, s. Andrew [& Mary], b. June 20, 1711 | TM-1 | 193 |
| Thomas, s. Thomas, m. Mary **PETERS**, Feb. 25, 1740/41 | 1 | 106 |
| Thomas, d. May 16, 1735, ae about 108, or 109 y. | L-3 | 454 |
| Thomas, m. Mary **PETERS**, Feb. 25, 1740/41 | 1 | 132 |
| Thomas, s. of Andrew, m. Deborah **DAY**, Apr. 9, 1741 | 1 | 131 |
| Thomas, s. [Thomas & Mary], b. Dec. 24, 1741 | 1 | 106 |
| Thomas, s. [Thomas & Mary], b. Dec. [ ], 1741 | 1 | 132 |
| Thomas, m. Mary **WATON**, July 21, 1762 | 1 | 80 |
| Thomas, [s. Thomas & Mary], b. Nov. 9, 1768 | 1 | 80 |
| Thomas, m. Lydia **INGHAM**, June 13, 1776 | 2 | 35 |
| Thomas, m. Mary **MARSHALL**, Dec. 6, 1784 | 2 | 35 |
| Timothy, s. Richard, b. July 22, 1699 | L-3 | 198 |

| | Vol. | Page |
|---|---|---|
| **CARRIER CARIER**, (cont.) | | |
| Timothy, s. Richard, b. July 22, 1699 | TM_1 | 198 |
| Timothy, m. Frances **CRIPIN**, Feb. 26, 1729/30 | L-3 | 6 |
| Timothy, m. Frances **CRIPPEN**, Feb. 26, 1729/30 | TPR | 111 |
| Timo[thy], s. [Samuel & Rebecca], b. Apr. 7, 1777 | 2 | 33 |
| Timothy, s. [Samuel], b. Apr. 7, 1777 | 2 | 43 |
| Timothy, d. Feb. 4, 1836, ae 59 | 2 | 244 |
| Titus, [s. John & Mary], b. Aug. 23, 1733 | L-1 | 449 |
| Uriah, s. John, b. Aug. 21, 1756; m. Mary **GATES**, July 10, 1777 | 2 | 26 |
| Uriah, s. [Oren & Emily], b. Jan. 4, 1825 | 2 | 128 |
| W[illia]m G., m. Harriet E. **BUELL**, b. of Westchester, June 27, 1852, by W. O. Cady | 3 | 51 |
| William Griswold, s. [Ralph & Patty], b. July 11, 1825 | 2 | 130 |
| William M., [s. Seth K. & Lydia], b. Sept. 20, 1816 | 2 | 255 |
| William M., m. Phebe L. **SPENCER**, May 12, 1850, by D. Trumbull | 3 | 3 |
| **CARROLL**, Jane G., m. Samuel A. **KELLOGG**, b. of Colchester, May 19, 1845, by Rev. Joel R. Arnold | 3 | 22 |
| **CARTER**, Aaron, [s. Aaron & Rachel], b. Feb. 25, 1766 | 1 | 75 |
| Asaph, [s. Aaron & Rachel], b. May 10, 1772 | 1 | 75 |
| Eleazer, m. Eunice **KELLOGG**, Jan. 16, 1777 | 2 | 16 |
| Eunice, d. [Eleazer & Eunice], b. Dec. 11, 1779 | 2 | 16 |
| Ezra, of Colchester, m. Huldah **MERVIN**, of Lyme, Nov. 3, 1768 | 1 | 96 |
| Jerusha, m. Asa **FOOT**, Apr. 26, 1752 | 1 | 149 |
| Jerusha, d. [Eleazer & Eunice], b. June 14, 1778; d. July 18, 1803 | 2 | 16 |
| Jerusha, d. May 9, 1781 | 2 | 16 |
| Lucretia, m. Theodore **FOSTER**, b. of Colchester, Mar. 30, [1845], by Rev. Robert Allyn | 3 | 21 |
| Mary, d. Ezra, b. Aug. 9, 1745 | 1 | 148 |
| Ned, m. Sybel [ ], Feb. 9, 1769, by Ichabod Allyn | 1 | 27 |
| Rachel, [d. Aaron & Rachel], b. Mar. 10, 1769 | 1 | 75 |
| Sarah, of Stonington, m. Samuel **TENNANT**, of Colchester, June 8, 1753 | 1 | 45 |
| -----, Sr., d. July 19, 1744 | 2 | 16 |
| -----, twin sons, [Eleazer & Eunice], b. Aug. 18, 1777; d. Aug. 18, 1777 | 2 | 16 |
| **CARVER**, George, of Hebron, m. Olive **SHALER**, of Colchester, July 21, 1839, by Rev. Andrew M. Smith | 2 | 106 |
| **CASE**, Asa, s. [Roger & Molly], b. Oct. 24, 1772 | 1 | 117 |
| Ezra M., of Hartford, m. Ellen E. **WEST**, of Colchester, Sept. 25, 1850, by Rev. Lyman Strong | 2 | 111 |
| Jerusha, d. [Roger & Molly], b. Jan. 3, 1777 | 1 | 117 |
| Molly, d. [Roger & Molly], b. May 15, 1775 | 1 | 117 |
| Noah Owen, s. [Roger & Molly], b. Dec. 5, 1773 | 1 | 117 |
| Roger, m. Molly **OWEN**, [ ], 1772 | 1 | 117 |

| | Vol. | Page |
|---|---|---|
| **CAVERLEY, CAVERLY, CAUERLEE**, Ann, d. [John & Mary], b. Jan. 31, 1769 | 1 | 100 |
| Hannah, d. [John & Mary], b. May 30, 1754 | 1 | 100 |
| Hannah, m. Joshua **HAUL**, Apr. 8, 1773; d. May 23, 1794, ae 40 | 2 | 6 |
| Hannah, w. Phillip, Sr., d. Aug. 16, 1775 | 2 | 15 |
| Hannah, w. Philip, d. Aug. 16, 1775 | 2 | 93 |
| John, s. Phillip & Hannah, b. Nov. 24, 1731 | TPR | 109 |
| John, of Colchester, m. Mary **SWAN**, of Stonington, Mar. 15, 1753 | 1 | 100 |
| John, s. [John & Mary], b. Oct. 10, 1759 | 1 | 100 |
| John, m. Elizabeth **CHESTER**, May 24, 1804 | 1 | 100 |
| John, Capt., d. Aug. 23, 1825, ae 95 | 1 | 100 |
| Mary, d. [John & Mary], b. Feb. 29, 1756 | 1 | 100 |
| Mary, w. John, d. Aug. 17, 1803 | 1 | 100 |
| Molly, m. Elias **PALMER**, Jr., Apr. 12, 1781 | 2 | 47 |
| Phillip, m. Hannah **ADDAMS**, Dec. 20, 1713 | L-1 | 654 |
| Phillip, (s.) [Phillip & Hannah], d. June 19, 1739 | TPR | 109 |
| Phillip, s. Phillip, d. June 19, 1739 | 1 | 105 |
| Philip, s. [John & Mary], b. Jan. 6, 1763 | 1 | 100 |
| Philip, d. Jan. 10, 1777 | 2 | 93 |
| Phillip, Sr., d. Jan. 16, 1778, ae 91 | 2 | 15 |
| **CHAMBERLAIN, CHAMBERLIN**, Aaron, [s. Joseph, Jr. & Hannah], b. Aug. 4, 1745 (?); d. Feb. 22, 1746/7 | 1 | 147 |
| Aaron, [s. Job & Deidama], b. Jan. 19, 1758 | 1 | 31 |
| Aaron, m. Catharine **WATERS**, Sept. 8, 1785 | 2 | 40 |
| Abigail, d. [Erastus & Lydia], b. Sept. 16, 1792 | 2 | 44 |
| Alice, m. Daniel **LO[O]MIS**, Jr., Feb. 25, 1756 | 1 | 87 |
| Anson, s. [Nathaniel, Jr. & Rh[o]da], b. Feb. 28, 1789 | 2 | 73 |
| Benjamin, m. Hannah **WYATT**, Dec. 14, 1731* *(1727 handwritten in original manuscript) | L-3 | 455 |
| Benjamin, [s. Ben[jamin], b. Dec. 27, 1731; d. [Dec.] 28, [1731] | L-3 | 455 |
| Betsey, d. [Erastus & Lydia], b. Dec. 29, 1790 | 2 | 44 |
| Catharine, [w. Aaron], d. Apr. 22, 1786 | 2 | 40 |
| Clarissa, m. John **KELLOGG**, 3d, Feb. 18, 1823, by Samuel Cone, V. D. M. | 2 | 86 |
| Daniell, [s. Daniell], b. Nov. 2, 1727 | L-1 | 446 |
| Daniel, [s. Daniel], b. Nov. 2, 1727 | TPR | 111 |
| Deborah, m. Benjamin **HATCH**, Dec. 7, 1769 | 1 | 89 |
| Diadama, m. Joseph **SHEPARDSON**, Oct. 13, 1793 | 2 | 80 |
| Eleazer, [s. Peleg & Experience], b. Aug. 14, 1737 | 1 | 143 |
| Elijah, s. [Nathaniel, Jr. & Rh[o]da], b. Apr. 2, 1787 | 2 | 73 |
| Eliphalet, m. Lucy **KELLOGG**, May 26, 1768 | 1 | 82 |
| Elisha, s. [John, Jr. & Lydia], b. May 19, 1759; d. Feb. 18, 1761 | 1 | 147 |
| Elisha, 2d, s. [John, Jr. & Lydia], b. Feb. 23, 1765 | 1 | 147 |
| Elizabeth, m. John **WEL[L]ES**, Sept. 8, 1715 | L-1 | 450 |

| | Vol. | Page |
|---|---|---|
| **CHAMBERLAIN, CHAMBERLIN**, (cont.) | | |
| Elisabeth, d. Daniel, b Mar. 18, 1720 | TPR | 110 |
| Elizabeth, m. Amasa **JONES**, July 12, 1749 | 1 | 150 |
| Elizabeth G., of Colchester, m. Stephen M. **FOWLER**, of Lebanon, Oct. 20, 1844, by Rev. Joel R. Arnold | 3 | 17 |
| Emery, s. [Nathaniel, Jr. & Rh[o]da], b. Dec. 28, 1790 | 2 | 73 |
| Erastus, m. Lydia **HOPSON**, Nov. 23, 1788 | 2 | 44 |
| Easter, d. Daniell, b. Oct. 18, 1722 | L-1 | 445 |
| Easter, d. Daniell, b. Oct. 18, 1722 | L-1 | 446 |
| Esther, [d. Daniel], b. Oct. 18, 1722 | TPR | 110 |
| Experience, d. [Peleg & Experience], b. Mar. 5, 1748/9 | 1 | 143 |
| Experience, w. [Peleg], d. Mar. 21, 1748/9 | 1 | 143 |
| Fre[e]dom, s. Joseph, b. Apr. 15, 1705 | L-1 | 448 |
| Grace, of Colchester, m. Phillip **BRIGGS**, of Lebanon, Aug. 20, 1820 | 2 | 298 |
| Hannah, m. William **BOOTH**, Jan. 31, 1760 | 1 | 54 |
| Irene, m. Israel **LOOMIS**, Nov. 5, 1763 | 1 | 87 |
| Jairus, [d. Job & Deidama], b. Aug. 25, 1765 | 1 | 31 |
| Jerusha, m. Charles **FOOT**, Oct. [ ], 1750 | 1 | 137 |
| Job, [s. Joseph], b. Feb. 8, 1725/6 | L-3 | 7 |
| Job, of Colchester, m. Deidama **DUNHAM**, of Hebron, Apr. 27, 1756 | 1 | 31 |
| Joel, m. Lydia **CHAPMAN**, Nov. 1, 1756 | 1 | 16 |
| Joel, [s. Joel & Lydia], b. July 1, 1759 | 1 | 16 |
| John, [s. Joseph], b. Jan. 31, 1707/8 | L-1 | 448 |
| John, [s. William & Sarah], b. Jan. 10, 1715/16 | L-1 | 445 |
| John, [s. William & Sarah], b. Jan. 10, 1715/16 | L-1 | 799 |
| John, Jr., m. Lydia **WELLS**, Mar. 16, 1758 | 1 | 147 |
| Jonathan, [s. Joseph], b. July 1, 1729; d. Sept. 30, 1729, ae 3 m. | L-3 | 7 |
| Jonathan, [s. Joseph], b. Feb. 22, 1729/30; d. Mar. 3, [1729/30] | L-3 | 7 |
| Jonathan, [s. Peleg & Experience], b. Feb. 3, 1745/6 | 1 | 143 |
| Joseph, [s. Joseph], b. Apr. 11, 1724 | L-3 | 7 |
| Joseph, Jr., m. Hannah **GILLETT**, July 15, 1738 | 1 | 147 |
| Lois, [d. Joel & Lydia], b. Feb. 15, 1757; d. Sept. 22, 1757 | 1 | 16 |
| Louisa, [d. Job & Deidama], b. Jan. 10, 1760 | 1 | 31 |
| Lidia, d. Joseph, b. Oct. 20, 1721 | L-3 | 7 |
| Lidiah, w. Joseph, d. Mar. 3, 1730 | L-3 | 7 |
| Lydia, d. [John, Jr. & Lydia], b. Apr. 3, 1761; d. May 14, 1761 | 1 | 147 |
| Lydia, 2d, d. [John, Jr. & Lydia], b. Mar. 14, 1762 | 1 | 147 |
| Marcy, [d. William & Sarah], b. [ ] | L-1 | 445 |
| Mary, of East Haddam, m. Isaac **BIGELOW**, of Colchester, Apr. 5, 1759 | 1 | 24 |
| Mary, m. Stephen **SKINNER**, Apr. 27, 1786 | 2 | 59 |
| Mary, of Colchester, m. Chauncey **GOTT**, of Hebron, Apr. 27, 1825, by Samuel A. Peters, J. P. | 2 | 177 |

| | Vol. | Page |
|---|---|---|
| **CHAMBERLAIN, CHAMBERLIN**, (cont.) | | |
| Mary, [d. William & Sarah], b. [ ] | L-1 | 445 |
| Mahetable, [d. Daniell], b. Apr. 9, 1725 | L-1 | 446 |
| Mehetibell, [d. Daniel], b. Apr. 9, 1725 | TPR | 110 |
| Mercy, [d. Joseph, Jr. & Hannah], b. Jan. 15, 1742/3 | 1 | 147 |
| Mercy, m. James **McCRACKEN**, Apr. 19, 1787 | 2 | 93 |
| Molly, d. [William], b. June 25, 1772 | 2 | 3 |
| Nathan, [s. Peleg & Experience], b. Apr. 19, 1741 | 1 | 143 |
| Nathaniel, Jr., m. Rh[o]da **DEWEY**, of Lebanon, Dec. 30, 1784 | 2 | 73 |
| Peleg, [s. William & Sarah], b. Nov. 25, 1713 | L-1 | 445 |
| Peleg, [s. William & Sarah], b. Nov. 28, 1713 | L-1 | 799 |
| Peleg, m. Experience **BARTLETT**, May 8, 1735 | 1 | 143 |
| Peleg, s. [Peleg & Experience], b. May 12, 1736 | 1 | 143 |
| Ralph, s. [Nathaniel, Jr. & Rh[o]da], b. June 16, 1794 | 2 | 73 |
| Rebecca, d. [Joseph & Hannah], b. Apr. 27, 1739 | 1 | 147 |
| Rhoda, m. Elias **WORTHINGTON**, Sept. 19, 1744 | 1 | 102 |
| Richard, [s. Daniel], b. July 5, 1730 | TPR | 111 |
| Roderick, s. [Erastus & Lydia], b. Aug. 31, 1789 | 2 | 44 |
| Roxanna, of Colchester, m. Samuel R. **JONES**, of Henron, Oct. 16, 1832, by Rev. Lyman Strong | 2 | 234 |
| Samuel, [s. Peleg & Experience], b. Sept. 9, 1743 | 1 | 143 |
| Sarah, m. Ephreaim **FOOT**, June [ ], 1708 | L-1 | 453 |
| Sarah, m. Josiah **FOOT**, Dec. 7, 1738 | 1 | 35 |
| Sarah, [d. Joseph, Jr. & Hannah], b. Mar. 29, 1748/9 | 1 | 147 |
| Sarah, m. John **WELLS**, Oct. 1, 1770 | 2 | 82 |
| Sarah, [d. William & Sarah], b. [ ] | L-1 | 445 |
| Sarah D., of Colchester, m. William E. **JONES**, of Hebron, Sept. 9, 1832, by Rev. Lyman Strong | 2 | 237 |
| Tabitha, m. Gardiner **WHEELER**, of Tolland, Sept. 10, 1837, by Rev. Joel R. Arnold | 2 | 113 |
| Timothy, [s. Job & Deidama], b Dec. 28, 1761 | 1 | 31 |
| William, m. Sarah **DAY**, Jan. 4, 1710 | L-1 | 445 |
| William, m. Sarah **DAY**, Jan. 4, 1710/11 | L-1 | 799 |
| William, [s. William & Sarah], b. Jan. 22, 1711/12 | L-1 | 445 |
| William, [s. William & Sarah], b. Jan. 22, 1711/12 | L-1 | 799 |
| William, [s. Daniell], b. Mar. 10, 1733 | TPR | 111 |
| William, m. Mary **DAY**, May 22, 1758 | 1 | 35 |
| William, of Colchester, m. [ ] **WEST**, of Lebanon, [ ] | 2 | 3 |
| Wyat[t], s. Ben[jamin], b. Oct. 12, 1728 | L-3 | 455 |
| ----, [d. Benjamin], b. Oct. 10, 1730; d. [Oct.] 19, 1730 | L-3 | 455 |
| **CHAMPION**, Abigail, d. [Henry, Jr. & Abigail], b. Jan. 17, 1787 | 2 | 30 |
| Abigail, m. David **DEMING**, Sept. 17, 1804 | 2 | 97 |
| Abigail, w. Henry, Jr., d. Apr. 19, 1818 | 2 | 30 |
| Aristarcus, twin with Aristobalus, s. [Henry, Jr. & Abigail], b. Oct. 23, 1784 | 2 | 30 |
| Aristobulus, twin with Aristarcus, s. [Henry, Jr. & Abigail], b. Oct. 23, 1784; d. Feb. 3, 1786 | 2 | 30 |

| | Vol. | Page |
|---|---|---|
| **CHAMPION**, (cont.) | | |
| Deborah, d. [Henry & Deborah], b. May 3, 1753 | 1 | 119 |
| Deborah, w. Henry, d. Mar. 17, 1789 | 1 | 119 |
| Dorothy, d. [Henry & Deborah], b. Oct. 29, 1759 | 1 | 119 |
| Elisa, twin with William, d. [Henry, Jr. & Abigail], b. July 19, 1797 | 2 | 30 |
| Elizabeth, twin with Mary, d. [Henry & Deborah], b. Sept. 11, 1762 | 1 | 119 |
| Epaphroditus, [s. Henry & Deborah], d. July 13, 1752 | 1 | 119 |
| Epaphroditus, s. [Henry & Deborah], b. Apr. 6, 1756 | 1 | 119 |
| Esther, d. [Henry & Deborah], b. May 8, 1766 | 1 | 119 |
| Harriet, d. [Henry, Jr. & Abigail], b. May 2, 1789 | 2 | 30 |
| Henry, s. [Henry & Deborah], b. Mar. 16, 1751 | 1 | 119 |
| Henry, Jr., m. Abigail **CLINKER**, Oct. 10, 1781 | 2 | 30 |
| Henry, s. [Henry & Abigail], b. Aug. 6, 1782 | 2 | 30 |
| Henry, m. Sarah **LEWIS**, Nov. 24, 1791 | 1 | 119 |
| Henry, d. July 23, 1797 | 1 | 119 |
| Henry, Jr., m. Ruth Kimberley **ROBBINS**, [ ] | 2 | 101 |
| Maria, d. [Henry, Jr. & Abigail], b. Nov. 19, 1791 | 2 | 30 |
| Mary, twin with Elizabeth, d. [Henry & Deborah], b. Sept. 11, 1762 | 1 | 119 |
| Polly, m. William **BULKELEY**, Dec. 18, 1788 | 2 | 50 |
| Robert Henry, s. [Henry, Jr. & Ruth Kimberley], b. June 5, 1804; d. Feb. 5, 1805 | 2 | 101 |
| William, twin with Elisa, s. [Henry, Jr. & Abigail], b. July 19, 1797; d. Apr. [ ], 1798 | 2 | 30 |
| **CHAMPLAIN**, Asa J., m. Sarah M. **BECKWITH**, b. of Colchester, Aug. 28, 1842, by Rev. Augustus Bolles | 3 | 40 |
| Emily, m. Joseph L. **GILLETT**, b. of Colchester, May 8, 1850, by Rev. Lyman Strong | 3 | 4 |
| George C. H., m. Mehetable N. **ADAMS**, b. of Colchester, Oct. 27, 1850, by Rev. Geo[rge] W. Pendleton | 3 | 47 |
| Latham H., m. Hannah **WHITNEY**, b. of Colchester, Jan. 4, 1853, by Rev. G. W. Pendleton | 3 | 54 |
| Martha Ann, m. Edwin P. **WILLIAMS**, June 28, 1840, by Rev. Augustus Bolles | 2 | 104 |
| Thomas, of Lebanon, m. Marion A. **MERRILL**, of Colchester, Mar. 21, 1852, by Rev. S. M. Minor | 3 | 50 |
| **CHANDLER**, Lucy, m. Stephen **OTIS**, Feb. 9, 1762 | 1 | 163 |
| Marah, m. John **BROWN**, Mar. 20, 1710 | L-1 | 444 |
| Zerviah, of Lebanon, m. Hubbell **WELLS**, of Colchester, May 20, 1754 | 1 | 140 |
| **CHAPIN**, Samuel N., of Goshen, m. Emily S. **GILLETT**, of Colchester, June 17, 1834, by Rev. Lyman Strong | 2 | 267 |
| **CHAPMAN, CHAMAN**, Abagaiell, [d. William], b. June 28, 1720 | L-3 | 3 |
| Abigaiell, [d. Ecabod & Abigaiell], b. Mar. 10, 1724 | L-1 | 452 |
| Abigail, m. Joshua **KNIGHT**, Dec. 9, 1742 | 1 | 138 |

| | Vol. | Page |
|---|---|---|
| **CHAPMAN, CHAMAN**, (cont.) | | |
| Abner, [s. John & Sarah], b. Mar. 5, 1722 | L-1 | 448 |
| Abner, m. Dinah **BUTLER**, Mar. 10, 1749 | 1 | 153 |
| Abner, s. [Abner & Dinah], b. Aug. 6, 1757 | 1 | 153 |
| Abner, Jr., m. Molly **BIGELOW**, Mar. 31, 1781 | 2 | 53 |
| Alice, m. Edmond **CLARK**, Mar. 2, 1806 (See also Ellas) | 2 | 120 |
| Amasa, [s. Thomas & Lydia], b. Aug. 9, 1767; d. Apr. 13, 1771 | 1 | 79 |
| Ann, [d. Ecabod & Abigaiell], b. Feb. 27, 1726/7 | L-1 | 452 |
| Ann, d. [Abner & Dinah], b. May 8, 1750 | 1 | 153 |
| Ann, m. William **TUBELL**, Mar. [ ], 1772 | 2 | 83 |
| Anna, [d. Thomas & Lydia], b. Mar. 24, 1769 | 1 | 79 |
| Anna, d. [Noah], b. Oct. 22, 1776; d. Dec. 13, 1777 | 2 | 27 |
| Asa, s. Abner & Dinah], b. Oct. 7, 1769 | 1 | 153 |
| Barnabus, [s. Daniell & Retern], b. Mar. 28, 1728 | L-1 | 399 |
| Barnabas, [s. Daniel & Katharine], b. Mar. 18, 1728 | TPR | 112 |
| Bethiah, m. John **CHAPMAN**, Apr. 10, 1740 | TPR | 109 |
| Bethiah, [d. John & Bethiah], b. Feb. 27, 1743 | TPR | 019 |
| Bethiah, m. Josiah **CRIDENTON**, May 5, 1762 | 1 | 114 |
| Butler, s. [Abner & Dinah], b. Aug. 3, 1753; d. Nov. 8, 1757 | 1 | 153 |
| Charlotte, d. [Abner & Dinah], b. June 6, 1764 | 1 | 153 |
| Cyrus, of Griswold, Conn., m. Nancy **BILL**, of Colchester, Oct. 15, 1850, by Rev. Geo[rge] W. Pendleton | 3 | 46 |
| Daniell, m. Ketern **WINTWORTH**, Mar. 22, 1713 (Ketern?) | L-1 | 399 |
| Daniel, m. Katharine **WENTWORTH**, Mar. 22, 1713 | TPR | 112 |
| Daniell, [s. Daniell & Retern], b. Apr. 10, 1722 | L-1 | 399 |
| Daniel, [s. Daniel & Katharine], b. Apr. 10, 1722 | TPR | 112 |
| David, of Chatham, m. Sally **SHAYLOR**, of Colchester, Apr. 1, 1824, by Rev. Jacob Seales, at the home of Rev. Jacob Seales | 2 | 164 |
| Deborah, of East Haddam, m. Elisha **BIGELOW**, Oct. 2, 1765 | 1 | 125 |
| Deborah, m. Elisha **BIGELOW**, Oct. 2, 1765; d. Jan. 21, 1773 | 2 | 55 |
| Delight, [d. John & Sarah], b. Oct. 16, 1728 | L-1 | 448 |
| Delight, b. Oct. 16, 1728; m. Asahel **NEWTON**, had s. Asahel **NEWTON**, b. June 1, 1758 | 1 | 21 |
| Dinah, w. [Abner], d. Dec. [ ], 1780 | 1 | 153 |
| Ebenezer, [s. William], b. Mar. 22, 1724 | L-3 | 3 |
| Elias, [s. Daniell & Retern], b. Jan. 14, 1725/6 | L-1 | 399 |
| Elias, [s. Daniel & Katharine], b. Jan. 14, 1725/6 | TPR | 112 |
| Eliphalet, [s. Noah & Esther], b. May 19, 1765 | 1 | 22 |
| Eliphalet, s. [Noah], b. May 19, 1765 | 2 | 27 |
| Elisha, [s. Ecabod & Abigaiel], b. Dec. 13, 1735 | L-1 | 452 |
| Elisha, m. Lydia **WATERMAN**, May 29, 1760 | 1 | 56 |
| Ellas, [d. Gideon & Lucretia], b. Mar. 20, 1763 (see also Alice) | 1 | 51 |
| Elizabeth A., m. George **LANGDON**, Sept. 3, 1851, by | | |

| | Vol. | Page |
|---|---|---|
| **CHAPMAN, CHAMAN**, (cont.) | | |
| Rev. J. A. Copp | 3 | 48 |
| Elizabeth C., of East Haddam, m. Ira M. **CLARK**, of Colchester, Mar. 12, 1844, by Rev. Lyman Strong | 3 | 11 |
| Esther, d. [Noah], b. July 20, 1773 | 2 | 27 |
| Esther W., b. June 28, 1792, in East Haddam; m. George **WAY**, Aug. 14, 1820 | 2 | 84 |
| Eunice, [d. Daniel & Katharine], b. Apr. 28, 1737 | TPR | 112 |
| Faroziena, m. Asa **CONE**, May 1, 1820, in East Haddam | 2 | 257 |
| Gideon, [s. John & Sarah], b. July 26, 1726 | L-1 | 448 |
| Gideon, of Colchester, m. Lucretia **CHAPMAN**, of New London, Dec. 6, 1751 | 1 | 51 |
| Gideon, [s. Gideon & Lucretia], b. Oct. 1, 1756 | 1 | 51 |
| Harriet L., m. Lewis S. **BLISS**, Sept. 27, 1841, by Rev. Daniel G. Sprague, Westchester | 2 | 235 |
| Ecabod, m. Abigaiell **CLOTHER**, July 4, 1723 | L-1 | 452 |
| Ichabod, [s. Ecabod & Abigaiell], b. Sept. 28, 1732 | L-1 | 452 |
| Ira, s. [Noah], b. Apr. 15, 1780 | 2 | 27 |
| Irene, [d. Ecabod & Abigaiell], b. Feb. 2, 1724/5 | L-1 | 452 |
| Irene, [d. Ecabod & Abigaiell], b. May 4, 1729 | L-1 | 452 |
| Isham, s. [Abner & Diana], b. Oct. 5, 1759 | 1 | 153 |
| James, [s. John & Sarah], b. Jan. 31, 1719/20 | L-1 | 448 |
| Jeane, [d. John & Sarah], b. Oct. 15, 1708 (Jane?) | L-1 | 448 |
| Jason, [s. John & Sarah], b. Dec. 7, 1716 | L-1 | 448 |
| Jason, twin with Thomas, [s. John & Bethiah], b. Feb. 20, 1749 | TPR | 109 |
| Jason, s. [Noah], b. Feb. 26, 1763 | 2 | 27 |
| Jason, [s. Noah & Esther], b. [ ], at New London | 1 | 22 |
| Jeremiah, [s. Daniel & Katharine], b. Apr. 12, 1733 | TPR | 112 |
| Jerusha, d. Sarah, b. Dec. 20, 1768; d. Dec. 9, 1784 | 1 | 15 |
| Jerusha Hard, d. [John], d. Dec. 9, 1784 | 2 | 12 |
| John, m. Sarah **CAR[R]IER**, Sept. 7, 1707 | L-1 | 448 |
| John, [s. John & Sarah], b. Jan. 10, 1714/15 | L-1 | 448 |
| John, m. Bethiah **CHAPMAN**, Apr. 10, 1740 | TPR | 109 |
| John, Jr., d. Nov. 20, 1745, ae 60 | 1 | 146 |
| John, [s. John & Bethiah], b. Apr. 6, 1747 | TPR | 109 |
| John, [s. Noah], b. Feb. 12, 1761 | 2 | 27 |
| John, [s. Noah & Esther], b. [ ], at New London | 1 | 22 |
| Jonathan, s. [Abner & Dinah], b. Feb. 22, 1755 | 1 | 153 |
| Juda, [s. Gideon & Lucretia], b. Oct. 8, 1754 | 1 | 51 |
| Julia R., m. William M. **BARBER**, b. of Hebron, Sept. 24, 1844, by Rev. Rob[er]t C. Mills | 3 | 17 |
| Julius, of Griswold, Conn., m. Fanny **BILL**, of Colchester, Oct. 15, 1850, by Rev. Geo[rge] W. Pendleton | 3 | 46 |
| Ketem, [d. Daniell & Retem], b. Dec. 23, 1715 (Arnold Copy has the name "Retem" | L-1 | 399 |
| Katharine, [d. Daniel & Katharine], b. Dec. 23, 1715 | TPR | 112 |
| Leander, m. Emily E. **LANPHERE**, May 18, 1851, by Rev. | | |

| | Vol. | Page |
|---|---|---|
| **CHAPMAN, CHAMAN,** (cont.) | | |
| George W. Pendleton | 2 | 80 |
| Leenora A., of Colchester, m. Frances H. **DOLBEAR**, of Natchez, Miss., Aug. 29, 1836, by Rev. Lyman Strong | 2 | 287 |
| Lucretia, of New London, m. Gideon **CHAPMAN**, of Colchester, Dec. 6, 1751 | 1 | 51 |
| Lucretia, [d. Gideon & Lucretia], b. Nov. 26, 1752; d. [ ] | 1 | 51 |
| Luse, [d. John & Sarah], b. Nov. 8, 1712 | L-1 | 448 |
| Lucy, m. Nathan **CHAPMAN**, Jan. 26, 1758 | 1 | 51 |
| Lydia, m. Ephraim **WELLS**, Jr., Feb. 2, 1726/7 | 1 | 135 |
| Lydia, [d. Ecabod & Abigaiell], b. Sept. 15, 1738 | L-1 | 452 |
| Lydia, m. Joel **CHAMBERLAIN**, Nov. 1, 1756 | 1 | 16 |
| Lydia, d. [Noah], b. Mar. 27, 1768 | 2 | 27 |
| Lydia, of Colchester, m. Erastus **EVERGASON**, of Bozrah, May 9, 1852, by F. W. Bill | 3 | 51 |
| Marcy m. William **CHAPMAN**, Dec. 19, 1728 | L-3 | 3 |
| Marthah, [d. Daniell & Retem], b. July 2, 1717 | L-1 | 399 |
| Martha, [d. Daniel & Katharine], b. July 2, 1717 | TPR | 112 |
| Mary, [d. William], b. Jan. 20, 1717/18 | L-3 | 3 |
| Mary, [d. Gideon & Lucretia], b. Mar. 30, 1761 | 1 | 51 |
| Mary, . m. Peter **GRAVES**, Jr., May 17, 1764 | 1 | 103 |
| Mercy, [d. Daniel & Katharine], b. Apr. 14, 1735 | TPR | 112 |
| Nathan, m. Lucy **CHAPMAN**, Jan. 26, 1758 | 1 | 51 |
| Nathan, [s. Gideon & Lucretia], b. Oct. 18, 1765 | 1 | 51 |
| Noah, [s. Gideon & Lucretia], b. Feb. 3, 1759 | 1 | 51 |
| Noah, s. [Noah], b. Sept. 21, 1770; d. Oct. 28, 1777 | 2 | 27 |
| Noah, m. Esther **PLACE**, [ ], at New London | 1 | 22 |
| Obadiah, s. [Abner & Dinah], b. Apr. 6, 1762 | 1 | 153 |
| Paul, [s. Daniell & Retem], b. Apr. 12, 1714 | L-1 | 399 |
| Paul, [s. Daniel & Katharine], b. Apr. 12, 1714 | TPR | 112 |
| Paul, [s. Daniel & Katharine], d. Sept. 28, 1738 | TPR | 112 |
| Prudence R., m. Oren **CARRIER**, b. of Colchester, Apr. 18, 1824, by Rev. Jacob Seales, at the house of David Loomis | 2 | 166 |
| Rhode, [d. Abner & Dinah], b. Jan. 29, 1752 | 1 | 153 |
| Rhoda, [d. John & Bethiah], b. Sept. 20, 1754; d. Apr. 20, 1765 | TPR | 109 |
| Rossel, [s. John & Bethiah], b. May 17, 1751 | TPR | 109 |
| Russell, m. Celinda B. **PORTER**, Feb. 22, 1830, by Salmon Cone, V. D. M. | 2 | 219 |
| Sally, b. May 13, 1782; m. David **BULKELEY**, Dec. 26, 1805, by Rev. Elijah Parsons, East Haddam. Recorded July 3, 1822 | 2 | 67 |
| Sarah, [d. John & Sarah], b. Apr. 25, 1710 | L-1 | 448 |
| Sarah, [d. Daniell & Retem], b. June 1, 1720 | L-1 | 399 |
| Sarah, [d. Daniel & Katharine], b. June 1, 1720; d. Dec. 22, 1738 | TPR | 112 |
| Sarah, m. George **HOLMS**, Mar. 28, 1736/7 | 1 | 138 |

| | Vol. | Page |
|---|---|---|
| **CHAPMAN, CHAMAN,** (cont.) | | |
| Sarah, [d. John & Bethiah], b. May 13, 1745 | TPR | 109 |
| Sarah, wid. John, d. Dec. 7, 1772, ae 89 | 1 | 15 |
| Sarah Ausgood (Osgood?), d. John, d. Oct. 3, 1762 | 2 | 12 |
| Silas, [s. Daniel & Katharine], b. Apr. 8, 1724 | TPR | 112 |
| Silas, [s. Daniell & Retern], b. Apr. 18, 1724 | L-1 | 399 |
| Silena, m. Elisha **DODGE,** [ ], 1781 | 2 | 54 |
| Stephen N., m. Nancy B. **COOKE,** b. of Colchester, Oct. 6, 1850, by Rev., Geo[rge] W. Pendleton | 3 | 46 |
| Susan L., of Westchester, m. W[illiam] **WALBRIDGE,** of Portland, Sept. 21, 1845, by Rev. S. D. Jewett | 3 | 24 |
| Susan[n]ah, d. William, b. Feb. 28, 1715/16 | L-3 | 3 |
| Thomas, twin with Jason, [s. John & Bethiah], b. Feb. 20, 1749; d. Jan. 21, 1759 | TPR | 109 |
| Thomas, m. [ ], May 7, 1760 | 1 | 144 |
| Thomas, m. Lydia **HARDING,** Dec. 11, 1766 | 1 | 79 |
| William, m. Marcy **CHAPMAN,** Dec. 19, 1728 | L-3 | 3 |
| Ziporah, [d. John & Sarah], b. Apr. 22, 1724 | L-1 | 448 |
| ---, d. [Daniell & Retern], b. Apr. [ ], 1719, st. b. | L-1 | 399 |
| ---, d. [Daniel & Katharine], b. Apr. [ ], 1719, st. b. | TPR | 112 |
| ---, d. William [& Marcy], b. Jan. 3, 1730; d. Jan. 3, 1730 | L-3 | 3 |
| **CHAPPELL, CHAPEL,** Abijah, m. John **STRONG,** Feb. 5, 1723/4 | L-1 | 446 |
| Isaac D., of Lyme, m. Harriet **SWIFT,** of Colchester, Mar. 27, 1839, by Rev. Joel R. Arnold | 2 | 169 |
| Mary, m. Samuell **GILLET,** Jan. 30, 1718/19 | L-1 | 449 |
| Patience, m. Cornelious **FULLER,** Feb. 25, 1730 | L-3 | 9 |
| Piercy, m. Joseph **MAXFIELD,** Apr. 21, 1833, by Benj[amin] Trumbull, J. P. | 2 | 243 |
| **CHASE,** Charles A., m. Laura **WILLIAMS,** Sept. 2, 1827, by Salmon Cone, V. D. M. | 2 | 198 |
| Mary, m. Stephen **ALGER,** b. of Colchester, Nov. 11, 1833, by Rev. Joseph Harvey | 2 | 259 |
| Mary Ann, of Amherst, Mass., m. Albert **FOOTE,** of Colchester, Nov. 11, 1831, by Rev. W[illia]m O. Cady | 2 | 212 |
| **CHEENEY,** Olive, m. Noah **NEWTON,** Oct. 21, 1802 | 2 | 141 |
| **CHEESEBROUGH, CHEESEBOROUGH,** Molly, had s. Jesse **BOHAN,** b. Jan. 30, 1794, & Reuben **BOHAN,** b. Sept. 17, 1792 (Mulatto) | 2 | 48 |
| Polly, of Stonington, m. Elisha **FISH,** Dec. 2, 1804 | 2 | 98 |
| **CHESTER,** Albert, s. [Erastus & Lydia], b. Apr. 6, 1825 | 2 | 139 |
| Elizabeth, m. John **CAVERLEY,** May 24, 1804 | 1 | 100 |
| Elizabeth, d. [Erastus & Lydia], b. Jan. 8, 1813 | 2 | 139 |
| Erastus, m. Lydia **WILLIAMS,** Mar. 29, 1812 | 2 | 139 |
| Erastus, s. [Erastus & Lydia], b. Mar. 2, 1823 | 2 | 139 |
| Hezekiah Griswold, s. [Erastus & Lydia], b. Apr. 27, 1821 | 2 | 139 |
| Joseph, s. [Erastus & Lydia], b. Oct. 13, 1815 | 2 | 139 |
| Laura Maria, d. [Erastus & Lydia], b. Mar. 23, 1817 | 2 | 139 |

| | Vol. | Page |
|---|---|---|
| **CHESTER**, (cont.) | | |
| Mary, m. Moses **DODGE**, Nov. 13, 1755 | 1 | 145 |
| Mary Jane, d. [Erastus & Lydia], b. Aug. 6, 1819 | 2 | 139 |
| Sophia M., m. John T. **PETERS**, Sept. 1, 1824, by Salmon Cone, V. D. M. | 2 | 168 |
| **CHICK**, Joseph P., m. Cornelia **THOMPSON**, b. of Colchester, Feb. 17, 1851, by Rev. Lyman Strong | 3 | 1 |
| **CHITTENDEN**, [see also **CRIDENTON**], Alfred, of Killingworth, m. Lucretia L. **LOOMIS**, Mar. 23, 1851, by Rev. S. D. Jewett | 3 | 3 |
| **CHRISTOPHERS**, Jerusha, of New London, m. Dr. Thomas **SKINNER**, of Colchester, Apr. 2, 1788 | 2 | 68 |
| **CHURCH**, Anne, d. [Samuel & Phebe], b. Dec. 13, 1747 | 1 | 100 |
| Asa, s. [Samuel, Jr. & Sarah], b. July 26, 1775 | 2 | 81 |
| Daniel, s. [Samuel & Phebe], b. Jan. 26, 1760 | 1 | 100 |
| Daniel, s. [Samuel, Jr. & Sarah], b. Jan. 12, 1785 | 2 | 81 |
| Edward, s. [Samuel & Phebe], b. Oct. 30, 1756 | 1 | 100 |
| Elizabeth, m. William **SKINNER**, Aug. 31, 1767 | 1 | 113 |
| Hannah, d. [Samuel & Phebe], b. Mar. 10, 1749 | 1 | 100 |
| Hannah, d. [Samuel, Jr. & Sarah], b. Jan. 13, 1773 | 2 | 81 |
| John, s. [Samuel & Phebe], b. Nov. 16, 1754 | 1 | 100 |
| Lydia, d. [Samuel & Phebe], b. Aug. 20, 1746 | 1 | 100 |
| Lydia, d. [Samuel, Jr. & Sarah], b. Sept. 24, 1776 | 2 | 81 |
| Phebe, d. [Samuel & Phebe], b. Feb. 20, 1752 | 1 | 100 |
| Polly, m. William **BOOTH**, May 15, 1794 | 2 | 83 |
| Samuel, m. Phebe **FULLER**, June 17, 1744 | 1 | 100 |
| Samuel, s. [Samuel & Phebe], b. Aug. 12, 1745 | 1 | 100 |
| Samuel, Jr., m. Sarah **ROGERS**, Nov. 7, 1771; d. Dec. 22, 1790 | 2 | 81 |
| Samuel, s. [Samuel, Jr. & Sarah], b. May 9, 1774; d. July 30, 1804, at Troy | 2 | 81 |
| Samuel, of Montville, m. Dorcas Ann **HAZARD**, Nov. 8, 1825, by Samuel A. Peters, J. P. | 2 | 180 |
| Sarah, d. [Samuel, Jr. & Sarah], b. Sept. 9, 1781; d. Dec. 1795 | 2 | 81 |
| Sarah, [w. Samuel, Jr.], d. May 24, 1816 | 2 | 81 |
| **CLARK, CLARKE**, Alexander, [s. Daniell & Elesebeth], b. Nov. 6, 1717 | L-3 | 195 |
| Alexander, s. Daniel [& Elizabeth], b. Nov. 6, 1717 | TM-1 | 195 |
| Amasa, of East Haddam, m. Nancy S. **WHITE**, of Chatham, Sept. 26, 1847, by Rev. J. R. Arnold | 3 | 33 |
| Ann, m. Nathaniel **FOOT**, July 4, 1711 | L-1 | 799 |
| Ann, m. Nath[anie]l **FOOT**, July 4, 1711 | TM-1 | 198 |
| Ann, m. Nathaniell **FOOT**, July 4, 1711 | L-3 | 198 |
| Ann, [d. Daniel, Jr. & Hannah], b. Mar. 15, 1755 | 1 | 57 |
| Ann, d. [Uriah & Anne], b. Sept. 20, 1755; d. Feb. 15, 1758 | 1 | 142 |
| Asa, m. Sarah **HOPSON**, Dec. 4, 1755 | 1 | 42 |
| Ashbell, s. [Uriah & Anne], b. Jan. 5, 1758 | 1 | 142 |

| | Vol. | Page |
|---|---|---|
| **CLARK, CLARKE**, (cont.) | | |
| Betsey, d. [Gurdon & Eunice], b. Nov. 27, 1788 | 2 | 76 |
| Charles, s. [Zelotes & Eunice], b. Sept. 12, 1812 | 2 | 92 |
| Clarissa, [d. Titus & Betsey Kellogg], d. Feb. 24, 1903 | 2 | 256 |
| Daniell, m. Elesebeth **BUTLER**, Dec. 4, 1704 | L-3 | 195 |
| Daniel, m. Elizabeth **BUTLER**, Dec. 14, 1704 | TM-1 | 195 |
| Daniell, [s. Daniell & Elesebeth], b. Sept. 28, 1711 | L-3 | 195 |
| Daniel, s. Daniel [& Elizabeth], b Sept. 28, 1711 | TM-1 | 195 |
| Daniel, [s. Daniel, Jr. & Hannah], b. Mar. 11, 1747 | 1 | 57 |
| Daniel, [s. Daniel, Jr. & Hannah], b. May 21, 1750 | 1 | 57 |
| Daniel, [s. Daniel, Jr. & Hannah], b. Oct. 25, 1767 | 1 | 57 |
| Daniel, m. Hannah **BULKELEY**, d. of Peter, Feb. 18, 1795; d. | 2 | 65 |
| Daniel, Sr., d. Feb. 18, 1794 | 2 | 65 |
| Daniel, s. [Daniel & Hannah], b. July 8, 1796; d. July 25, 1797 | 2 | 65 |
| Daniel, Jr., m. Hannah **JONES**, [ ] | 1 | 57 |
| Daniel Williams, s. [Edmond & Alice], b. Oct. 24, 1824; d. Feb. 13, 1902, ae 77 | 2 | 120 |
| Darius, [s. Dan[ie]ll], b. Feb. 2, 1719/20 | L-3 | 195 |
| Darius, s. Daniel, b. Feb. 2, 1719/20 | TM-1 | 195 |
| Darius, m. Hannah **BROOKS**, [ ], 1774 | 2 | 8 |
| Darius, m. Bettey **DeWIT[T]**, Jan. 16, 1780 | 2 | 8 |
| David, [s. Daniel, Jr. & Hannah], b. Dec. 24, 1751 | 1 | 57 |
| Edmond, m. Alice **CHAPMAN**, Mar. 2, 1806; d. Feb. 12, 1841, ae 66 | 2 | 120 |
| Edward N., m. Sarah Ann **BIGELOW**, b. of Colchester, Aug. 26, 1845, by Rev. S. D. Jewett, Westchester | 3 | 23 |
| Elihu, [s. Noah & Sarah], b. Nov. 8, 1727 | L-1 | 447 |
| Elihu, s. [Zelotes & Eunice], b. Feb. 25, 1814 | 2 | 92 |
| Elihu, m. Sophia Jane **BULKELEY**, b. of Colchester, Jan. 22, 1851, by Rev. G. W. Pendleton | 2 | 108 |
| Elijah Olcott, s. [Edmond & Alice], b. Sept. 15, 1817 | 2 | 120 |
| Elisha, m. Elizabeth **KELLOGG**, May 9, 1750 | 1 | 3 |
| Elisha, [s. Elisha & Elizabeth], b. Sept. 7, 1755 | 1 | 3 |
| Elisabeth, [d. Daniell & Elesebeth], b. June 29, 1708 | L-3 | 195 |
| Elizabeth, d. Dan[ie]l [& Elizabeth], b. June 29, 1708 | TM-1 | 195 |
| Elizabeth, [d. Elisha & Elizabeth], b. Mar. 7, 1759; d. Aug. 9, 1759 | 1 | 3 |
| Elizabeth, [d. Elisha & Elizabeth], b. Feb. 10, 1763 | 1 | 3 |
| Elizabeth, [d. Daniel, Jr. & Hannah], b. June 15, 1763 | 1 | 57 |
| Elizabeth, d. [Zelotes & Eunice], b. Sept. 29, 1818 | 2 | 92 |
| Elizabeth, m. Russell **GILLETT**, b. of Colchester, Mar. 18, 1845, by Rev. Joel R. Arnold | 3 | 20 |
| Enos, s. [Ezra & Amy], b. June 12, 1769; d. Apr. 21, 1848, ae 79 | 2 | 92 |
| Ephraim, [s. Elisha & Elizabeth], b. Oct. 26, 1751; d. Dec. 15, 1757 | 1 | 3 |

| | Vol. | Page |
|---|---|---|
| **CLARK, CLARKE,** (cont.) | | |
| Erastus, m. Bethiah C. **ARNOLD**, b. of Bozrah, Aug. 19, 1822, by Rev. William Palmer, at the subscriber's house | 2 | 137 |
| Esther, [d. Noah & Sarah], b. Oct. 14, 1729 | L-1 | 447 |
| Esther, m. John **TAINTOR**, [ ], 1751 | 1 | 182 |
| Esther, d. [Ezra & Amy], b. Oct. 31, 1757 | 2 | 92 |
| Eunice, [d. Daniel, Jr. & Hannah], b. Feb. 13, 1753 | 1 | 57 |
| Eunice, w. [Noah], d. Jan. 10, 1755 | 1 | 144 |
| Eunice, twin with Ezra, d. [Ezra, 2d, & Eunice], b. Jan. 22, 1787 | 2 | 92 |
| Eunice, d. [Gurdon & Eunice], b. Aug. 10, 1799 | 2 | 76 |
| Eunice, m. Zelotes **CLARK**, Nov. [ ], 1811 | 2 | 92 |
| Eunice, [w. Gurdon], d. Nov. 8, 1848, ae 82 | 2 | 76 |
| Eunice, w. Ezra, d. Aug. 1, 1851, ae 84 y. 8 m. | 2 | 92 |
| Ezra, [s. Noah & Sarah], b. Nov. 8, 1725 | L-1 | 447 |
| Ezra, s. Noah & Sarah **TAINTOR**, b. Nov. 22, 1726; m. Amy **BAYLEY**, of Lebanon, Feb. 3, 1757 | 2 | 92 |
| Ezra, m. Anne **BEBEE**, Feb. 2, 1757 | 1 | 118 |
| Ezra, 2d, b. May 5, 1759; m. Eunice **FOOT**, Nov. 24, 1785; d. Feb. 9, 1826; ae 67 | 2 | 92 |
| Ezra, s. [Ezra & Amy], b. May 15, 1759 | 2 | 92 |
| Ezra, twin with Eunice, s. [Ezra, 2d, & Eunice], b. Jan. 22, 1787 | 2 | 92 |
| Frances Jane, d. [Zelotes & Eunice], b. June 4, 1816 | 2 | 92 |
| Frances Jane, m. Benjamin Fowler **OTIS**, b. of Colchester, Jan. 1, 1840, by Rev. Joel R. Arnold | 2 | 118 |
| George, s. [Ezra, 2d, & Eunice], b. June 13, 1791 | 2 | 92 |
| Gurdon, [s. Nath[anie]ll & Elizabeth], b. May 8, 1761 | 1 | 36 |
| Gurdon, m. Eunice **GILLET**, Nov. 8, 1788; d. Jan. 30, 1843, ae 82 | 2 | 76 |
| Hannah, [d. Daniell & Elesebeth], b. June 30, 1706 | L-3 | 195 |
| Hannah, d. Dan[ie]l [& Elizabeth], b. June 30, 1706 | TM-1 | 195 |
| Han[n]ah, m. Aaron **GILLET**, July 10, 1728 | L-1 | 444 |
| Hannah, [d. Daniel, Jr. & Hannah], b. June 6, 1748 | 1 | 57 |
| Hannah, d. [Noah & Eunice], b. Feb. 26, 1753 | 1 | 144 |
| Hannah, m. Simon **CONE**, Dec. 30, 1770 | 2 | 58 |
| Hannah, w. Roger, d. Apr. 5, 1771 | 1 | 94 |
| Hannah, w. Darius, d. Sept. 10, 1777 | 2 | 8 |
| Hannah, w. Daniel, [Sr.], d. July 12, 1796 | 2 | 65 |
| Helen M., of Colchester, m. Hobart C. **CULTER**, of Oxford, Mass., Nov. 19, 1840, by Rev. Lyman Strong | 2 | 97 |
| Hiram Chapman, s. [Edmond & Alice], b. Mar. 17, 1814 | 2 | 120 |
| Ira Clark, s. [Edmond & Alice], b. July 24, 1820 | 2 | 120 |
| Ira M., of Colchester, m. Elizabeth C. **CHAPMAN**, of East Haddam, Mar. 12, 1844, by Rev. Lyman Strong | 3 | 11 |
| James F., of Cleveland, Ohio, m. Eliza Ann **MURFEY**, of Colchester, Oct. 1, 1834, by Rev. Lyman Strong | 2 | 271 |
| Jeheil, [s. Asa & Sarah], b. May 29, 1756 | 1 | 42 |

| | Vol. | Page |
|---|---|---|
| **CLARK, CLARKE,** (cont.) | | |
| Jerusha, [d. Noah & Sarah], b. Feb. 28, 1724 | L-1 | 447 |
| Jerusha, m. Levi **WELLS**, May 3, 1759 | 1 | 104 |
| Jerusha, d. [Ezra, 2d, & Eunice], b. Apr. 16, 1789 | 2 | 92 |
| Johan[n]ah, [d. John], b. Feb.[ ], 1725/6; d. Nov. 5, 1729 | L-3 | 5 |
| Joanna, d. J[oh]n & Mindwell, b. July 4, 1731 | L-3 | 5 |
| John, [s. John], d. Sept. 22, 1728 | L-3 | 5 |
| Jonah, [s. Daniell & Elesebeth], b. Dec. 19, 1713 | L-3 | 195 |
| Jonah, s. Daniel [& Elizabeth], b. Dec. 19, 1713 | TM-1 | 195 |
| Jonah, m. Mary **KNIGHT**, Nov. 24, 1745 | 1 | 107 |
| Josiah, s. [Darius & Bettey], b. Mar. 25, 1781 | 2 | 8 |
| Josiah, d. Mar. 18, 1816, ae 35 | 2 | 107 |
| Judah, s. [Darius & Hannah], b. May 5, 1775 | 2 | 8 |
| Julia, d. [Gurdon & Eunice], b. Nov. 16, 1791; d. Feb. 21, 1793 | 2 | 76 |
| Laura Esther, d. [Edmond & Alice], b. Mar. 8, 1811 | 2 | 120 |
| Laura Esther, of Colchester, m. Oliver **SNOW**, of Suffield, Feb. 5, 1832, by Rev. Lyman Strong | 2 | 236 |
| Lucy, [d. Daniel, Jr. & Hannah], b. Mar. 18, 1757 | 1 | 57 |
| Lucy, [d. Asa & Sarah], b. Mar. 15, 1760 | 1 | 42 |
| Lucy, of Salem, m. Charles **BROWN**, of Colchester, Apr. 23, 1848, by Samuel A. Kellogg, J. P. | 3 | 35 |
| Lydia, [d. Daniel, Jr. & Hannah], b. Aug. 30, 1758 | 1 | 57 |
| M. G., Rev., m. Mary **GURLEY**, Nov. 8, 1841, by Rev. Augustus Bolles | 2 | 267 |
| Mabell, [d. Daniell & Elesebeth], b. Oct. 7, 1721 | L-3 | 195 |
| Mabel, d. Daniel [& Elizabeth], b. Oct. 7, 1721 | TM-1 | 195 |
| Mary, [d. Jonah & Mary], b. Sept. 18, 1746; d. Nov. 24, 1746 | 1 | 107 |
| Mary, w. Jonah, d. Sept. 30, 1746 | 1 | 107 |
| Mary, of Colchester, m. Edward H. **CUTLER**, of Oxford, Mass., Oct. 21, 1845, by Rev. Joel R. Arnold | 3 | 25 |
| Mehetable, m. Samuel **JUDD**, Nov. 13, 1771 | 2 | 1 |
| Molly, [d. Nath[anie]ll & Elizabeth], b. Aug. 12, 1759 | 1 | 36 |
| Molly, [d. Daniel, Jr. & Hannah], b. Aug. 31, 1764 | 1 | 57 |
| Nathaniell, [s. J[oh]n & Mindwell], b. Feb. 17, 1733/4 | L-3 | 5 |
| Nath[aniel]ll, m. Elizabeth **JONES**, Oct. 16, 1757 | 1 | 36 |
| Noah, m. Sarah **TAINTOR**, June 10, 1719 | L-1 | 447 |
| Noah, [s. Noah & Sarah], b. Aug. 24, 1722/3 | L-1 | 447 |
| Noah, m. Eunice **QUITFIELD**, Dec. 3, 1752 | 1 | 144 |
| Noah, d. Jan. 9, 1755 | 1 | 144 |
| Noah, s. [Ezra & Amy], b. Apr. 14, 1764 | 2 | 92 |
| Noah, d. July 29, 1851, ae 87 y., in Whitestown, N. Y. | 2 | 92 |
| Ralph, s. [Ezra & Amy], b. Oct. 31, 1766; d. Oct. 7, 1793 | 2 | 92 |
| Ralph, s. [Gurdon & Eunice], b. Apr. 7, 1794 | 2 | 76 |
| Ralph Bulkeley, s. [Edmond & Alice], b. Dec. 31, 1809 | 2 | 120 |
| Rebeckah, d. Dan[ie]ll, b. June 16, 1726 | L-3 | 195 |
| Rebeckah, d. Daniel, b. June 16, 1726 | TM-1 | 195 |
| Robert, s. [Daniel & Hannah], b. Aug. 23, 1798 | 2 | 65 |

| | Vol. | Page |
|---|---|---|
| **CLARK, CLARKE,** (cont.) | | |
| Roger, [s. Daniel] & Elesebeth], b. Dec. 24, 1715 | L-3 | 195 |
| Roger, s. Daniel [& Elizabeth], b. Dec. 24, 1715 | TM-1 | 195 |
| Roger, m. Hannah **BIGELOW**, Apr. [ ], 1746 | 1 | 94 |
| Russel[l], s. [William & Mary], b. Nov. 5, 1748 | 1 | 148 |
| Sabra, m. Hardein **TUCKER**, b. of Bozrah, Dec. 15, 1822, by Rev. William Palmer, at the house of [William Palmer] | 2 | 158 |
| Sally, d. [Ezra, 2d, & Eunice], b. Mar. 1, 1796 | 2 | 92 |
| Sally, m. Ezekiel W. **PARSONS**, b. of Colchester, June 17, 1822, by Salmon Cone, V. D. M. | 2 | 156 |
| Sarah, [d. Noah & Sarah], b. Feb. 19, 1719; d. [ ] | L-1 | 447 |
| Sarah, [d. Noah & Sarah], b. Mar. 9, 1721 | L-1 | 47 |
| Sarah, d. John, b. Aug. 13, 1723 | L-3 | 5 |
| Sarah, m. Joseph **KELLOGG**, Jan. 15, 1740/41 | 1 | 106 |
| Sarah, [d. Asa & Sarah], b. Apr. 17, 1758 | 1 | 42 |
| Sarah, [d. Daniel, Jr. & Hannah], b. June 3, 1760 | 1 | 57 |
| Sarah, d. [Ezra & Amy], b. Oct. 12, 1761; d. Sept. 28, 1781 | 2 | 92 |
| Silas, m. Hannah **TENNANT**, b. of Colchester, Nov. 21, 1823, by Daniel Waldo | 2 | 159 |
| Susan H., of Colchester, m. William H. **PALMER**, of Salem, Mar. 28, 1838, by Rev. Andrew M. Smith | 2 | 194 |
| Uriah, s. Daniel, b. Nov. 2, 1722 | TM-1 | 195 |
| Uriah, [s. Dan[ie]ll], b. Nov. 21, 1722 | L-3 | 195 |
| Uriah, m. Anne **KILLBORN**, Oct. 24, 1751 | 1 | 142 |
| Uriah, s. [Uriah & Anne], b. Sept. 2, 1753; d. Jan. 15, 1758 | 1 | 142 |
| Violetta, [d. Elisha & Elizabeth], b. Sept. 9, 1760 | 1 | 3 |
| William, m. Mary **PARSONS**, May 10, 1747 | 1 | 148 |
| William, s. [Ezra & Amy], b. June 14, 1772 | 2 | 92 |
| William F., of Chatham, m. Frances A. **WATROUS**, of Colchester, Sept. 14, 1851, by Rev. S. D. Jewitt | 2 | 139 |
| Zelotes, m. Eunice **CLARK**, Nov. [ ], 1811; d. May 2, 1837, ae 67 | 2 | 92 |
| Zuruiah, [d. Daniell & Elesebeth], b. Mar. 14, 1719 | L-3 | 195 |
| Zurviah, d. Dan[ie]l & Elizabeth, b. Mar. 14, 1719 | TM-1 | 195 |
| ----, s. [Daniell & Elesabeth], b. July 17, 1710; d. July 17, 1710 | L-3 | 195 |
| ----, s. Daniel [& Elizabeth], b. July 17, 1710; d. same day | TM-1 | 195 |
| ----, s. [Daniel & Hannah], b. Oct. 23. 1800 | 2 | 65 |
| **CLELAND**, Jonas, m. Lydia **ALLYN**, b. of Colchester, Dec. 17, 1772 | 2 | 5 |
| Jonas, s. [Jonas & Lydia], b. Aug. 4, 1773 | 2 | 5 |
| Salley, d. [Jonas & Lydia], b. Feb. 1, 1776 | 2 | 5 |
| **CLINKER**, Abigail, m. Henry **CHAMPION**, Jr., Oct. 10, 1781; d. Apr. 19, 1818 | 2 | 30 |
| **CLOTHER**, Abigaiell, d. John, b. Nov. 30, 1704 | L-1 | 453 |
| Abigaiell, m. Ecabod **CHAPMAN**, July 4, 1723 | L-1 | 452 |
| Ann, m. Joseph **FOOT**, Dec. 12, 1719 | L-1 | 444 |

| | Vol. | Page |
|---|---|---|
| **CLOTHER**, (cont.) | | |
| Ann, m. Hezekiah **KILBURN**, Dec. 25, 1728 | L-3 | 8 |
| Anne, [d. John], b. Mar. 8, 1711 | L-1 | 453 |
| Barbra, [d. John], b. Dec. 3, 1714 | L-1 | 453 |
| Elizabeth, [d. John], b. Nov. 29, 1716 | L-1 | 453 |
| John, [s. John], b. Jan. 3, 1707 | L-1 | 453 |
| Lucrese, [d. John ], b. June 20, 1720 | L-1 | 453 |
| Mary, [d. John], b. Sept. 10, 1717/18 | L-1 | 453 |
| Sarah, [d. John], b. Mar. 13, 1709 | L-1 | 453 |
| **COATS**, Lucy, of Colchester, m. James **FOSYTH**, of Groton, Feb. 16, 1804, by John R. Watrous, J. P. | 2 | 176 |
| **COBB**, Rebecca M., m. Eliphalet **FREEMAN**, b. of Colchester, Mar. 2, 1851, by Rev. Lyman Strong | 2 | 76 |
| **COGGESHALL**, Mary E., m. Hezekiah **RUDD**, Sept. 4, 1828, by Salmon Cone, V. D. M. | 2 | 206 |
| Rebecca C., m. Amherst D. **SCOVILLE**, Jan. 10, 1825, by Salmon Cone, V. D. M. | 2 | 175 |
| **COKE**, Godfrey, m. Barbara **KASER**, b. of Wertemburg, Germany, Apr. 25, 1854, by Erastus Dickinson | 3 | 61 |
| **COLE**, Anne, d. [David & Abigail], b. Apr. 2, 1765 | 1 | 120 |
| Bette, d. [David & Abigail], b. Dec. 10, 1762 | 1 | 120 |
| David, of Colchester, m. Abigail **BLISS**, of Lebanon, Feb. 9, 1762 | 1 | 120 |
| Nathaniel, s. Joshua & Mary, b. Jan. 31, 1734/5 | L-3 | 454 |
| **COLEMAN, COLMAN**, Abigail, d. [Zenas & Abigail, b. Dec. 24, 1776 | 2 | 17 |
| Acsah, d. [Zenas & Abigail], b. July 31, 1775; d. Feb. 24, 1776 | 2 | 17 |
| Asaph, s. [Noah & Mercy], b. Sept. 27, 1747 | 1 | 127 |
| Charles, s. [Daniel & Elizabeth], b. May 9, 1778 | 2 | 81 |
| Daniel, s. [Noah & Mercy], b. Apr. 17, 1741 | 1 | 127 |
| Daniel, m. Elizabeth **LITTLE**, Sept. 12 1771 | 2 | 81 |
| Daniel, s. [Daniel & Elizabeth], b. Nov. 3, 1774 | 2 | 81 |
| Ebenezer, m. Ruth **NIELES**, Mar. 11, 1704/5 | L-1 | 799 |
| Electa, d. [Daniel & Elizabeth], b. Aug. 4, 1773 | 2 | 81 |
| Elizabeth, d. [Daniel & Elizabeth], b. Dec. 26, 1776 | 2 | 81 |
| George H., of Hebron, m. Laura A. **BROWN**, of Columbia, Conn., May 5, 1850, by Albert F. Park, Minister | 3 | 1 |
| Hannah, m. Azariah **PRATT**, May 5, 1725 | L-1 | 654 |
| Hannah, w. Noah, d. July 14, 1752 | 1 | 48 |
| Jason, m. Betsey **WELLS**, Aug. 28, 1780, by Ichabod Allyn | 2 | 5 |
| John, s. Noah, b. June 28, 1708 | TM-1 | 193 |
| John, s. Joseph & Elizabeth, b. Apr. 16, 1731 | 1 | 43 |
| John, of Colchester, m. Hannah **GAY**, of Norwich, Nov. 28, 1751 | 1 | 27 |
| John, [s. John & Hannah], b. June 30, 1752 | 1 | 27 |
| Joseph, s. Noah, b. June 28, 1706 | L-3 | 193 |
| Joseph, d. Aug. 20, 1770 | 1 | 80 |

| | Vol. | Page |
|---|---|---|
| **COLEMAN, COLMAN**, (cont.) | | |
| Josiah A., b. in Colchester; Corp. of Capt. M. V. B. Tiffany's Co. E. 18th Reg. Conn. Vol.; enrolled July 25, 1862; discharged June 27, 1865, ae 37, at Harper's Ferry, Va. | 3 | 71 |
| Mary, [d. Ebenezer & Ruth], b. Apr. 8, 1718 | L-1 | 799 |
| Mahittabel, [d. Ebenezer & Ruth], b. July 14, 1713 | L-1 | 799 |
| Mercy, [d. Noah & Mercy], b. Feb. 25, 1731 | 1 | 127 |
| Mercy, m. Israel **GILLETT**, May 14, 1747 | 1 | 99 |
| Niels, [s. Ebenezer & Ruth], b. Feb. 20, 1706 | L-1 | 799 |
| Noah, d. Nov. 7, 1711 | L-3 | 193 |
| Noah, d. Nov. 7, 1711 | TM-1 | 193 |
| Noah, m. Mercy **WRIGHT**, Mar. 5, 1730 | L-3 | 6 |
| Noah, [s. Noah & Mercy], b. Jan. 2, 1736 | 1 | 127 |
| Noah, Sr., d. Sept. 9, 1770 | 2 | 81 |
| Ozias, [s. Noah & Mercy], b. Dec. 22, 1738 | 1 | 127 |
| Ruth, [d. Ebenezer & Ruth], b. June 20, 1709 | L-1 | 799 |
| Sybell, [d. Noah & Mercy], b. Nov. 5, 1733 | 1 | 127 |
| Sibbell, m. Benj[amin] **ROBERTS**, Mar. 14, 1754 | 1 | 129 |
| Zenas, s. [Noah & Mercy], b. Jan. 15, 1750/51 | 1 | 127 |
| Zenas, m. Abigail **CARRIER**, b. of Colchester, Oct. 19, 1774 | 2 | 17 |
| ----, s. [Daniel & Elizabeth], b. July 25, 1772; d. same day | 2 | 81 |
| ----, s. [Daniel & Elizabeth], b. Jan. 20, 1776; d. Feb. 24, [1776], ae 5 w. | 2 | 81 |
| **COLLINS**, Elisabeth, m. Samuell **BROWN**, May 12, 1713 | L-3 | 196 |
| Elizabeth, m. Samuel **BROWN**, May 12, 1713 | TM-1 | 197 |
| **COLYAR**, Sarah, m. Joseph **PRAT[T]**, July 22, 1697 | L-3 | 195 |
| Sarah, m. Joseph **PRATT**, July 22, 1697 | TM-1 | 195 |
| **COMSTOCK**, Almira, see under Nathaniel **COMSTOCK** | 3 | 67-68 |
| Ama, m. Amos **RANSOM**, Apr. 12, 1750 | 1 | 39 |
| Asahel O., of La Roy, N. Y., m. Fanny B. **WHEELER**, of Colchester, May 8, 1836, by Rev. Lyman Strong | 2 | 285 |
| Diadama, m. Charles **WORTHINGTON**, b. of Colchester, Mar. 9, 1834, by Rev. Lyman Strong | 2 | 248 |
| Emma D., of Colchester, m. Leonard **WHEELER**, of Avon, Aug. 31, 1836, by Rev. Andrew M. Smith | 2 | 290 |
| Nathaniel, m. Almira **FOX**, b. of Colchester, Apr. 1, 1840, by Rev. Joel R. Arnold | 2 | 214 |
| Nathaniel's will, dated Aug. 31, 1853, appraised May 12, 1856, in which he gives all his estate to his w. Almira | 3 | 67-68 |
| Sarah, of Lyme, m. Andrew C. **PHELPS**, of East Haddam, Mar. 23, 1835, by Rev. Lyman Strong | 2 | 274 |
| William P., m. Almantha B. **EDGATON**, b. of Colchester, Apr. 1, 1838, by Rev. Andrew M. Smith | 2 | 193 |
| -----, m. Abner **HILLS** | 1 | 79 |
| **CONE**, Abby H., d. [Asa & Faroziena], b. July 22, 1824 | 2 | 257 |
| Abigail, m. Elnathan **ROWLEY**, Dec. 26, 1723 | L-3 | 456 |
| Abigail, m. John **OLMSTEAD**, June 9, 1745 | 1 | 56 |

| | Vol. | Page |
|---|---|---|
| **CONE**, (cont.) | | |
| Abigail, d. [Simon & Hannah], b. Jan. 20, 1778 | 2 | 58 |
| Adaline, of Colchester, m. Edwin T. **BROWN**, of Herkimer, N. Y., Sept. 13, 1848, by Rev. F. W. Bill | 3 | 36 |
| Albert, s. [Rev. Salmon & Polly (Mary?), b. Apr. 5, 1799 | 2 | 69 |
| Alvenus, m. Hannah P. **TAYLOR**, Nov. 29, 1824, by Salmon Cone, V. D. M. | 2 | 173 |
| Ann A., d. [Asa & Faroziena], b. May 19, 1830 | 2 | 257 |
| Anna, w. Rev. Salmon, d. [ ], in Middletown | 2 | 69 |
| Anna A., of Colchester, m. Hiram F. **BIRGE**, of Genessee, N. Y., Apr. 16, 1849, by Rev. Joel R. Arnold | 3 | 39 |
| Asa, s. [Simon & Hannah], b. Feb. 25, 1773 | 2 | 58 |
| Asa, m. Faroziena **CHAPMAN**, May 1, 1820, in East Haddam | 2 | 257 |
| Cephus, m. Sarah **GATES**, Dec. 9, 1779 | 2 | 36 |
| Charles Clark, s. [Simon & Hannah], b. June 13, 1790 | 2 | 58 |
| Daniel C., m. Statura Y. **STILLMAN**, b. of East Haddam, Sept. 28, 1845, by Rev. M. P. Alderman | 3 | 25 |
| Deborah, of East Haddam, m. William **WILLIAMS**, of Colchester, Feb. 16, 1738 | 1 | 102 |
| Electra, d. [Cephus & Sarah], b. May 15, 1790 | 2 | 36 |
| Elizabeth, wid., m. Samuel **ADAMS**, May 22, 1777 | 2 | 21 |
| Erastus, m. Lucy B. **BEEBE**, b. of East Haddam, Sept. 23, 1828, by Salmon Cone, V. D. M. | 2 | 207 |
| Eunice, d. [Simon & Hannah], b. Jan. 6, 1776 | 2 | 58 |
| Frances Caroline, m. George **TAYLOR**, b. of Colchester, Feb. 2, 1832, by Salmon Cone, V. D. M. | 2 | 236 |
| Green, of Chatham, m. Abigail **PERRY**, of Colchester, Jan. 4, 1844, by Rev. Daniel G. Sprague | 3 | 8 |
| John Cook, s. [Simon & Hannah], b. Dec. 20, 1780 | 2 | 58 |
| Jonathan, s. [Cephus & Sarah], b. July 12, 1784 | 2 | 36 |
| Lina, d. [Cephus & Sarah], b. Oct. 26, 1786 | 2 | 36 |
| Lina, m. Elisha **BROWN**, Apr. 1, 1807 | 2 | 116 |
| Lucy, d. [Simon & Hannah], b. Jan. 30, 1788 | 2 | 58 |
| Mary, of East Haddam, m. Amos **JONES**, of Colchester, Dec. 27, 1759 | 1 | 155 |
| Mary, see also Polly | | |
| Mary J., d. [Asa & Faroziena], b. June 16, 1826 | 2 | 257 |
| Mary J., of Colchester, m. Hezekiah **BISSELL**, of Hebron, Apr. 29, 1847, by Rev. P. Brockett | 3 | 32 |
| Olive, d. [Simon & Hannah], b. Nov. 19, 1783 | 2 | 58 |
| Olive, m. Eli **WILLIAMS**, Dec. 9, 1823, by Salmon Cone, V. D. M. | 2 | 139 |
| Olive, m. Linden **BROWN**, Jan. 9, 1825, by Salmon Cone, V. D. M. | 2 | 174 |
| Polly, d. [Rev. Salmon & Polly (Mary?)], b. Feb. 27, 1793 | 2 | 69 |
| Polly (Mary?), w. Rev. Salmon, d. Mar. 2, 1802 | 2 | 69 |
| Salmon, Rev., m. Polly **PYNEO**, Jan. 25, 1792 | 2 | 69 |
| Salmon, Rev., m. Anna **BREED**, Dec. 29, 1802; d. May 24, | | |

| | Vol. | Page |
|---|---|---|
| **CONE**, (cont.) | | |
| 1834, ae 68; was pastor in the Congregational Church, 38 y. | 2 | 69 |
| Salmon Edward, s. [Rev. Salmon & Polly], b. Mar. 30, 1795 | 2 | 69 |
| Sarah, d. [Cephus & Sarah], b. Nov. 20, 1780 | 2 | 36 |
| Simon, m. Hannah **CLARK**, Dec. 30, 1770 | 2 | 58 |
| **CONGDOL**, Abigail, m. David **LOVERIDGE**, Sept. 15, 1771; d. July 29, 1796 | 2 | 69 |
| **COOK, COOKE**, Abby Jane, m. Henry A. **LATHAM**, b. of Colchester, Oct. 6, 1851, by Rev. Geo[rge] W. Pendleton | 3 | 46 |
| Betsey Lucretia, m. Marvin **MITCHELL**, July 6, 1828, by Salmon Cone, V. D. M. | 2 | 204 |
| Cyrus W., m. Sarah **FOOTE**, Mar. 9, 1851, by Rev. W[illia]m Worland, of Hebron | 3 | 47 |
| David Andrew, s. David & Elizabeth, b. Dec. 9, 1822 | 2 | 106 |
| Henry A., m. Margaret C. **ACKLEY**, b. of East Haddam, Feb. 22, 1854, by Geo[rge] W. Pendleton | 3 | 60 |
| Lora Ann, m. W[illia]m B. **LORD**, b. of Colchester, Dec. 31, 1844, by Rev. Robert Allyn | 3 | 19 |
| Nancy B., m. Stephen N. **CHAPMAN**, b. of Colchester, Oct. 6, 1850, by Rev. Geo[rge] W. Pendleton | 3 | 46 |
| Oliver, of Arlington, Vt., m. Thankfull T. **COOKE**, of Colchester, Apr. 12, 1835, by Rev. Benajah Cook, Jr., of Willimantic Falls, Ct. | 2 | 277 |
| Thankfull T., of Colchester, m. Oliver **COOK**, of Arlington, Vt., Apr. 12, 1835, by Rev. Benajah Cook, Jr., of Willimantic Falls, Ct. | 2 | 277 |
| **COON**, Hope B., m. Oren **CARRIER**, [May] 26, 1844, by Rev. S. D. Jewett | 3 | 14 |
| Laura C., of East Haddam, m. Henry **TAYLOR**, of Colchester, Mar. 9, 1843, by Rev. Rob[er]t C. Mills | 3 | 2 |
| **COPP**, Joseph A., Rev., of Sag Harbor, N. Y., m. Fedora F. **ISHAM**, of Colchester, July 13, 1836, by Rev. Joel R. Arnold | 2 | 287 |
| **CORBIN**, Eli S., of Chenango Co., N. Y., m. Abigail B. **TAINTOR**, of Colchester, June 5, 1843, by Rev. Joel R. Arnold | 3 | 6 |
| **COREY**, Roswell, of Plainfield, Conn., m. Wealthy Ann **HANCOCK**, of Colchester, July 27, 1851, by Rev. George W. Pendleton | 2 | 58 |
| **CORNELL**, Horace C., m. Hannah A. **ATWELL**, Oct. 28, 1839, by Rev. Hiram P. Arms, Norwich | 2 | 84 |
| **CORPS**, Susannah, m. John **WALLER**, b. of Colchester, Dec. [ ], 1759 | 1 | 28 |
| **COTTON**, Allen, of Hartford, m. Philothee L. **HARVEY**, of Colchester, June 3, 1823, by Rev. William Palmer, at the house of Mr. Harvey | 2 | 145 |
| **COUZZENS**, Hannah, m. Gideon **QUASH**, b. of Colchester, Dec. | | |

| | Vol. | Page |
|---|---|---|
| **COUZZENS**, (cont.) | | |
| 27, 1829, by Amhurst D. Scoville, J. P. | 2 | 217 |
| **COVELL**, Maltby, of Eastbury, m. Nancy **WATROUS**, of Colchester, Oct. 9, 1833, by Rev. Lyman Strong | 2 | 258 |
| **CRAGIN**, Edwin T., of New York, m. Ardelia E. **SPARROW**, of Colchester, May 31, 1853, by Erastus Dickinson, Minister (Perhaps **CROGIN**) | 3 | 56 |
| **CRANE**, Sally, of Colchester, m. Caleb **WADHAM**, of Pittsfield, Mass., Mar. 20, 1825, by Benjamin Trumbull, J. P. | 2 | 176 |
| **CRAW**, Amon, s. [Jesse & Thankfull], b. Dec. 24, 1761 | 2 | 62 |
| Asahel, s. [Jesse & Thankfull], b. Aug. 3, 1764; d. Jan. 3, 1791 | 2 | 62 |
| Jesse, b. Apr. 1, 1739, in East Windsor; m. Thankfull **BEEBE**, b. of East Windsor, Feb. 28, 1760 | 2 | 62 |
| Jesse, s. [Jesse & Thankfull], b. Mar. 21, 1776 | 2 | 62 |
| Jesse, m. Tabitha **POLLY**, Apr. 10, 1809; d. Feb. 21, 1820 | 2 | 62 |
| John, s. [Jesse & Thankfull], b. Nov. 29, 1773 | 2 | 62 |
| Richard, s. [Jesse & Thankfull], b. Nov. 9, 1770 | 2 | 62 |
| Thankfull, w. Jesse, d. Jan. 11, 1777 | 2 | 62 |
| **CRAY**, Amelia A., of Lebanon, m. Appleton R. **PARK**, of Colchester, Oct. 12, 1841; d. May 7, 1844, ae 30 | 3 | 13 |
| **CREMER**, Anne, m. Peter **MASON**, June 1, 1786, at Weathersfield | 2 | 80 |
| **CRIDENTON**, Bethiah, d. [Josiah & Bethiah], b. Jan. 4, 1766 | 1 | 114 |
| Esther, d. [Josiah & Bethiah], b. Mar. 23, 1768 | 1 | 114 |
| Josiah, m. Bethiah **CHAPMAN**, May 5, 1762 | 1 | 114 |
| Molly, d. [Josiah & Bethiah], b. Apr. 10, 1771 | 1 | 114 |
| R[h]oda, d. [Josiah & Bethiah], b. May 16, 1763 | 1 | 114 |
| **CRIPPEN, CRIPIN, CRIPEN**, Experience, m. John **LORD**, Dec. 26, 1724 | TPR | 111 |
| Frances, [d. Jabez & Thankfull], b. June 26, 1710 | TPR | 111 |
| Frances, m. Timothy **CAR[R]IER**, Feb. 26, 1729/30 | L-3 | 6 |
| Frances, m. Timothy **CARRIER**, Feb. 26, 1729/30 | TPR | 111 |
| Jabez, m. Thankfull **FULLER**, July 9, 1707 | TPR | 111 |
| Jabez, [s. Jabez & Thankfull], b. July 14, 1717 | TPR | 111 |
| John, [s. Jabez & Thankfull], b. Mar. 20, 1720 | TPR | 111 |
| Joseph, [s. Jabez & Thankfull, b. June 7, 1726 | TPR | 111 |
| Lydia, [d. Jabez & Thankfull], b. Mar. 17, 1713 | TPR | 111 |
| Lydia, m. Richard **QUITFIELD**, Mar. 1, 1732 | TPR | 110 |
| Mahitabell, [d. Jabez & Thankfull], b. July 6, 1722 | TPR | 111 |
| Samuel, [s. Jabez & Thankfull], b. July 7, 1724 | TPR | 111 |
| Susanna, [d. Jabez & Thankfull], b. May 21, 1708 | TPR | 111 |
| Thankfull, [d. Jabez & Thankfull], b. Apr. 2, 1728 | TPR | 111 |
| Thomas, [s. Jabez & Thankfull], b. May 15, 1715 | TPR | 111 |
| **CRITTENDEN**, [see under **CRIDENTON**] | | |
| **CROCKER**, Abby Lucretia, d. [Joseph & Deborah], b. Aug. 14, 1823 | 2 | 145 |
| Abigaiell, [d. James], b. Mar. 22, 1724 | L-3 | 7 |

| | Vol. | Page |
|---|---|---|
| **CROCKER**, (cont.) | | |
| Abigail, [d. Isaac & Elisabeth], b. Mar. 10, 1733 | L-3 | 451 |
| Abigail, m. John **WILLIAMS**, Feb. 25, 1744 | 1 | 52 |
| Amos, [s. Jonathan & Rachel], b. Oct. 25, 1757 | 1 | 49 |
| Anne, d. Isaac, d. Mar. 29, 1772 | 1 | 120 |
| Asa, s. [Tomothy & Neoma], b. Sept. 23, 1785 | 2 | 70 |
| Daniel, s. [James & Rhoda], b. Jan. 30, 1760 | 1 | 111 |
| David, [s. Jonathan & Rachel], b. Nov. 18, 1759 | 1 | 49 |
| Dorothy, d. [Simeon & Dorothy], b. [ ], 1762; d. Oct. 10, 1775 | 1 | 112 |
| Dorothy, d. [Simeon & Hannah], b. July 27, 1783 | 2 | 70 |
| Elijah, s. [Simeon & Hannah], b. Oct. 21, 1788 | 2 | 70 |
| Eliza Ann, d. [Joseph & Deborah], b. Aug. 30, 1825 | 2 | 145 |
| Ephraim, [s. James], b. Sept. 21, 1739 | L-3 | 7 |
| Ephraim, s. [Timothy & Neoma], b. Feb. 17, 1782 | 2 | 70 |
| Erastus, s. [Timothy & Neoma], b. Sept. 21, 1787 | 2 | 70 |
| Garshom, s. [Timothy & Neoma], b. Feb. 6, 1790 | 2 | 70 |
| Gurdon, s. [Joseph & Sarah], b. Oct. 27, 1766 | 1 | 123 |
| Hannah, [d. James], b. Jan. 17, 1726 | L-3 | 7 |
| Hannah, d. [Simeon & Hannah], b. Jan. 9, 1791 | 2 | 70 |
| Isaac, s. [Joseph & Sarah], b. Nov. 25, 1749 | 1 | 123 |
| Isaac, s. [Simeon & Dorothy], b. Aug. 28, 1755; d. Sept. 29, 1775 | 1 | 112 |
| Isaac, d. Aug. 8, 1769 | 1 | 120 |
| Isaac, s. [Simeon & Hannah], b. Sept. 25, 1780 | 2 | 70 |
| James, [s. James], b. Apr. 20, 1732 | L-3 | 7 |
| James, s. James, b. Apr. 20, 1732 | TPR | 109 |
| James, of Colchester, m. Rhoda **JOHNSON**, of Norwich, Feb. 23, 1757 | 1 | 111 |
| James, s. [James & Rhoda], b. Nov. 11, 1757 | 1 | 111 |
| Jonathan, [s. James], b. Mar. 16, 1730 | L-3 | 7 |
| Jonathan, m. Rachel **SKINNER**, Mar. 27, 1755 | 1 | 49 |
| Jonathan, [s. Jonathan & Rachel], b. Feb. 7, 1762 | 1 | 49 |
| Joseph, m. Sarah **LEWIS**, Nov. 10, 1748 | 1 | 123 |
| Joseph, s. [Joseph & Sarah], b. Dec. 7, 1771 | 1 | 123 |
| Joseph, m. Deborah **FULLER**, b. of Colchester, Apr. 27, 1823, by Jacob Seales, V. D. M. | 2 | 145 |
| Joseph, s. [Joseph & Deborah], b. Jan. 10, 1828 | 2 | 145 |
| Joseph, elder, d. July 17, 1828 | 2 | 145 |
| Levy, [s. James], b. May 11, 1728 | L-3 | 7 |
| Lydia, d. James, b. Jan. 14, 1735/6 | 1 | 126 |
| Lydia, [d. James], b. Jan. 14, 1735/6 | L-3 | 7 |
| Lydia, d. [Joseph & Sarah], b. May 3, 1756 | 1 | 123 |
| Martha, d. Isaac & Elisabeth, b. Mar. 3, 1731 | L-3 | 451 |
| Neomi, d. [Timothy & Neoma], b. May 23, 1792 | 2 | 70 |
| Neoma, w. Timothy, d. July 17, 1828 | 2 | 70 |
| Olive, [d. Jonathan & Rachel], b. Dec. 24, 1755 | 1 | 49 |
| Sarah, d. [Joseph & Sarah], b. May 9, 1752 | 1 | 123 |

| | Page | Page |
|---|---|---|
| **CROCKER**, (cont.) | | |
| Simion, s. James, b. Sept. 19, 1722 | L-3 | 7 |
| Simeon, m. Dorothy **WILLIAMS**, Mar. 7, 1751 | 1 | 112 |
| Simeon, s. [Simeon & Dorothy], b. Sept. 16, 1752; d. Feb. 13, 1778 | 1 | 112 |
| Simeon, m. Hannah **WILLIAMS**, Nov. 26, 1779 | 2 | 70 |
| Simeon, s. Simeon & Hannah, b. Feb. 16, 1785 | 2 | 70 |
| Stephen, of Waterford, m. Grace **DAYTON**, Nov. 6, 1825, by Benjamin Trumbull, J. P. | 2 | 179 |
| Thankfull, [d. James], b. Jan. 27, 1733/4 | L-3 | 7 |
| Thankful[l], [d. James], b. Jan. 27, 1733/4 | TPR | 109 |
| Thankfull had d. Roxillana **ANDREWS**, b. July 24, 1758 | 1 | 32 |
| Timothy, d. [Simeon & Dorothy], b. Mar. 12, 1758 | 1 | 112 |
| Timothy, m. Neoma **FOX**, Dec. 20, 1779 | 2 | 70 |
| William, s. [Simeon & Dorothy], b. June 8, 1760 | 1 | 112 |
| William, of Colchester, m. Lucretia **KORTRIGHT**, of New York, Nov. 5, 1826, by Salmon Cone, V. D. M. | 2 | 189 |
| Zilpha, d. [Joseph & Sarah], b. July 4, 1769 | 1 | 123 |
| -----, d. [Isaac & Elisabeth], b. Sept. 26, 1736, st. b. | L-3 | 451 |
| **CROFUT**, Calvin, of Hartford, m. Martha D. **MELLEN**, of Colchester, Aug. 17, 1845, by Rev. Lyman Strong | 3 | 23 |
| **CROGIN**, [see under **CRAGIN**] | | |
| **CROUCH**, Bettras, m. Asa **STRONG**, June 7, 1744 | 1 | 133 |
| **CROWLEY**, Nancy, of Colchester, m. Henry **GRIGGS**, of Middletown, Nov. 29, 1849, by Rev. Augustus Bolles | 3 | 43 |
| W[illia]m N., of Colchester, m. Cynthia **GRIGGS**, of Ashford, May 24, 1850, by Rev. Lyman Strong | 3 | 4 |
| **CRUMB, CRUM**, Cordelia, m. Alpheas B. **DYER**, b. of Westerly, R. I., Oct. 21, 1850, by Rev. Geo[rge] W. Pendleton, at Colchester | 3 | 47 |
| Susan A., of Bozrah, m. Charles A. **BECKWITH**, of Colchester, Dec. 30, 1849, by Rev. Lyman Strong | 3 | 44 |
| **CURRIER**, [see also **CARRIER**], Abigail, d. [Andrew], b. May 16, 1753 | 1 | 103 |
| David, [s. Andrew], b. Mar. [ ], 1746/7; d. Dec. 29, 1749 | 1 | 103 |
| David, s. [Andrew], b. Dec. 4, 1755 | 1 | 103 |
| Rebecca, [d. Andrew], b. Mar. 29, 1745/6 | 1 | 103 |
| Thomas, [s. Andrew], b. May 3, 1749; d. Jan. 3, 1749/50 | 1 | 103 |
| Thomas, s. [Andrew], b. Mar. 15, 1750 | 1 | 103 |
| **CURTIS, CURTISS**, Hervey G., of Egremont, Mass., m. Lois B. **ROGERS**, of Colchester, Apr. 11, 1838, by Rev. Joel R. Arnold | 2 | 241 |
| Lois B., d. [Dr. Ho[w]el[l] **ROGERS** & Sarah **ROGERS**], [d. June 30, 1843, ae 29 | 2 | 84 |
| Lois, B., d. June 30, 1843, ae 29 | 2 | 241 |
| Rachel, m. John **STRONG**, Sept. 26, 1765 | 1 | 75 |
| **CUSHMAN**, Elaura, of Stafford, m. Justus R. **SHAYLOR**, of Colchester, Dec. 8, 1850, by Rev. Albert F. Park | 3 | 64 |

| | Vol. | Page |
|---|---|---|
| **CUSHMAN**, (cont.) | | |
| Elvira, of Stafford, Ct., m. Justin R. **SHAYLOR**, of Colchester, Dec. 8, 1850, by Rev. Albert F. Park | 2 | 69 |
| **CUTLER**, Abigaiell, d. Jonathan, b. Aug. 28, 1711 | L-1 | 399 |
| Beach, s. Jonathan, b. July 4, 1716 | L-1 | 399 |
| Edward H., of Oxford, Mass., m. Mary **CLARK**, of Colchester, Oct. 21, 1845, by Rev. Joel R. Arnold | 3 | 25 |
| Hobart C., of Oxford, Mass., m. Helen M. **CLARK**, of Colchester, Nov. 19, 1840, by Rev. Lyman Strong | 2 | 97 |
| Jonathan, [s. Jonathan], b. Aug. 17, 1713 | L-1 | 399 |
| **DALEY, DALEE**, John, s. Joseph & Patience, b. Dec. 11, 1708 | L-3 | 453 |
| Rebec[c]ah, m. James **ROBERDS**, Nov. [ ], 1718 | L-1 | 451 |
| **DANIELS, DANNIELS**, Amasa, [s. Nehemiah & Elizabeth], b. Sept. 19, 1762 | 1 | 57 |
| Asenath, d. [Hiram & Sena], b. Apr. 13, 1824 | 2 | 67 |
| Asenath, w. Hiram, d. Apr. 17, 1835, ae 44 | 2 | 67 |
| Asenath, of Colchester, m. Francis A. **WILLIAMS**, of East Haddam, May 12, 1844, by Rev. Robe[r]t C. Mills | 3 | 13 |
| Charles T., of Colchester, m. Mary Ann **JONES**, of New Haven, Jan. 28, 1838, by Rev. Andrew M. Smith | 2 | 297 |
| Cynthia E., d. [Hiram & Sena], b. Oct. 8, 1828 | 2 | 67 |
| Cynthia E., m. Ransom B. **TAHBONE**, b. of Colchester, Nov. 20, 1849, by Rev. Geo[rge] W. Pendleton | 3 | 42 |
| Elizabeth E., d. [Hiram & Sena], b. Jan. 17, 1833; d. Oct. 1, 1838, ae 5 | 2 | 67 |
| Hiram, m. Sarah **CANICE**, b. of Colchester, Sept. 20, 1835, by Joshua B. Rogers, J. P. | 2 | 280 |
| Hiram, m. Sarah **CARRIER**, Sept. 20, 1835; d. July 31, 1845, ae 49 | 2 | 67 |
| Hiram, m. Sena **WILLIAMS**, [ ] | 2 | 67 |
| Hiram A., s. [Hiram & Sena], b. Nov. 24, 1821 | 2 | 67 |
| Hiram A., m. Hannah E. **CARRIER**, July 14, 1844, by Rev. Rob[er]t C. Mills | 3 | 15 |
| Jemima, [d. Jonathan], b. June 14, 1720 | L-1 | 446 |
| Joanna, d. [Hiram & Sena], b. Aug. 6, 1826 | 2 | 67 |
| Joanna, of Colchester, m. Henry G. **WILLIAMS**, of East Haddam, Feb. 28, 1847, by Rev. P. Brockett | 3 | 31 |
| Jonathan, [s. Nehemiah & Elizabeth], b. June 1, 1760 | 1 | 57 |
| Joseph W., s. [Hiram & Sena], b. Nov. 11, 1830 | 2 | 67 |
| Lemewell, s. Jonathan, b. Apr. 6, 1717 | L-1 | 446 |
| Lydia, m. Stephen **BECKWITH**, July 24, 1766 | 1 | 80 |
| Nehemiah, m. Elizabeth **WORTHINGTON**, Jan. [ ], 1744 | 1 | 57 |
| Rebeckah, m. Jeremiah **MARSHALL**, [ ] | 2 | 54 |
| Rhoda, [d. Nehemiah & Elizabeth], b. Apr. 17, 1744 | 1 | 57 |
| Sarah, w. Hiram, d. Jan. 31, 1850, ae 44 | 2 | 67 |
| **DARBEE**, Mary, m. Ebenezer **HAMBLIN**, Sept. 17, 1761 | 1 | 25 |
| **DARLEY**, Elizabeth Otis, d. James F. **OTIS**, & Elizabeth H. H. **OTIS**, d. May 24, 1874, ae 42 | 2 | 64 |

| | Vol. | Page |
|---|---|---|
| **DARROW**, Gilbert B., of East Lyme, m. Harriet E. **BENJAMIN**, of Colchester, Feb. 2, 1852, by Rev. George W. Pendleton | 3 | 50 |
| **DART**, Anna, w. [Caleb], d. Dec. 16, 1844, ae 74 | 2 | 42 |
| Caleb, d. Nov. 12, 1849, ae 76 | 2 | 42 |
| Henry, m. Margary **WILLIAMS**, b. of Colchester, Apr. 2, 1822, by Rev. William Palmer, at Mr. E. William's | 2 | 99 |
| Lucy T., m. John T. **OTIS**, Jr., b. of Colchester, Apr. 21, 1830, by Asa Willcox, Elder | 2 | 222 |
| Mary, m. Silas D. **BULKELEY**, b. of Colchester, Dec. 10, 1837, by Rev. Andrew M. Smith | 2 | 296 |
| Nancy, m. David **BROWN**, Apr. 17, 1851, by Rev. Henry B. Whittington | 2 | 81 |
| **DATHICK**, [see under **DETHICK**] | | |
| **DAVENPORT**, Andrew, s. [John & Mary E.], b. Aug. 29, 1816 | 2 | 140 |
| John, m. Mary E. **SKINNER**, May 10, 1814 | 2 | 140 |
| **DAVIS, DAUIS**, Easter, [d. Isaac], b. Apr. 20, 1720 | L-1 | 449 |
| Isaac, [s. Isaac], b. June 13, 1716 | L-1 | 449 |
| Jaell, [s. Isaac], b. May 4, 1718 | L-1 | 449 |
| Laura Ann, m. James **KELLOGG**, alias James **RICHARDS**, b. of Colchester, Sept. 1, 1822, (colored persons), by Samuel A. Peters, J. P. | 2 | 94 |
| Myles F., of Colchester, m. Hannah F. **MORGAN**, of New London, July 10, 1842, by A. R. Park, J. P. | 2 | 268 |
| Samuel, m. Ann E. **FREEMAN**, Jan. 18, 1826, by Benjamin Trumbull, J. P. | 2 | 184 |
| Sarah, d. Isaac, b. June 3, 1713 | L-1 | 449 |
| **DAWLEY**, [see also **DARLEY**], Elizabeth, [w. Peleg A.], d. [James F. **OTIS** & Elizabeth H. H. **OTIS**, d. May 24, 1874, at Colchester, ae 42 | 2 | 234 |
| Peleg A., of R. I., (Harrisville Coventry), m. Elizabeth Hammond **OTIS**, d. [James F. & Elizabeth H. H.], [ ] | 2 | 234 |
| **DAY**, Aaron, [s. Benjamin & Margaret], b. Sept. 14, 1740 | TPR | 110 |
| Abell, s. [Thomas & Mary], b. July 26, 1743; d. Dec. 23, 1736 | 1 | 140 |
| Abraham, [s. John], b. Mar. 17, 1712 | L-3 | 193 |
| Abraham, s. John, b. Mar. 17, 1712 | TM-1 | 193 |
| Abraham, m. Irena **FOOT**, Nov. 20, 1740 | 1 | 123 |
| Abraham, s. [Abraham & Irena], b. Sept. 20, 1747 | 1 | 123 |
| Adonijah, [s. Benjamin & Margaret], b. July 16, 1733 | TPR | 110 |
| Adonijah, m. Sarah **LOOMIS**, [ ], 1753 | 1 | 121 |
| Adonijah, s. [Adonijah & Sarah], b. Dec. 28, 1759 | 1 | 121 |
| Albert, [s. Charles & Anne], b. Mar. 16, 1803; d. Mar. 28, 1803 | 2 | 120 |
| Almyra, d. [Asa & Anne], b. Aug. 18, 1794 | 2 | 72 |
| Almira, of Colchester, m. Erastus **SHELDON**, of New Marlborough, Mass., Nov. 27, 1835, by Rev. Joseph Harvey | 2 | 282 |

| | Vol. | Page |
|---|---|---|
| **DAY**, (cont.) | | |
| Alvin, s. [Adonijah & Sarah], b. May 20, 1763 | 1 | 121 |
| Amasai, [s. Benjamin & Margaret], b. Apr. 21, 1742 | TPR | 110 |
| Amasa, s. [Justin & Matilda], b. May 12, 1808 | 2 | 102 |
| Ann, [d. Benjamin & Margaret], b. Feb. 27, 1730 | TPR | 110 |
| Ann, d. [Isaac & Ann], b. Nov. 7, 1742 | 1 | 115 |
| Ann, m. Joseph **SKINNER**, Sept. 30, 1762 | 1 | 75 |
| Ann, m. Joseph **SKINNER**, b. of Colchester, Sept. 30, 1762 | 2 | 8 |
| Ann, [d. Noah & Ann], b. Mar. 4, 1764 | 1 | 30 |
| Ann Eliza, d. [Isaac Henry & Sarah E.], b. Apr. 29, 1844 | 2 | 126 |
| Anna, m. James **BIGELOW**, Nov. 13, 1783 | 2 | 72 |
| Anna, d. [Asa & Anne], b. Jan. 28, 1791 | 2 | 72 |
| Anna Lovett, d. [Charles & Anne], b. July 31, 1801 | 2 | 120 |
| Anne, w. Isaac, d. June 22, 1760 | 1 | 115 |
| Artemus, s. [Charles & Anne], b. Dec. 11, 1812 | 2 | 120 |
| Asa, [s. Benjamin & Margaret], b. May 16, 1735; d. [May] 23, [1735] | TPR | 110 |
| Asa, [s. Benjamin & Margaret], b. June 1, 1836; d. [June] 13, [1736] | TPR | 110 |
| Asa, [s. Joseph & Esther], b. Mar. 13, 1743 | TPR | 110 |
| Asa, s. Joseph, d. Sept. 10, 1760 | 1 | 152 |
| Asa, [s. Joseph, Jr. & Susannah], b. Aug. 12, 1761 | 1 | 99 |
| Asa, m. Anne **MARVIN**, Apr. 25, 1790 | 2 | 72 |
| Asa, s. [Asa & Anne], b. Oct. 20, 1802 | 2 | 72 |
| Asenath, [d. Joseph, Jr. & Susannah], b. Apr. 2, 1759 | 1 | 99 |
| Asenath, m. Daniel **WILLIAMS**, Dec. 14, 1780 | 2 | 46 |
| Benjamin, [s. John], b. Feb. 7, 1703/4 | L-3 | 193 |
| Benjamin, s. John, b. Feb. 7, 1703/4 | TM-1 | 193 |
| Benjamin, m. Margaret **FOOT**, Mar. 6, 1729 | TPR | 110 |
| Benjamin, [s. Benjamin & Margaret], b. Sept. 13, 1731 | TPR | 110 |
| Catharine, d. [John & Katharine], b. Feb. 5, 1796 | 2 | 68 |
| Charles, s. [Adonijah & Sarah], b. Sept. 18, 1753 | 1 | 121 |
| Charles, s. [Isaac & Dorothy], b. July 14, 1763 | 1 | 115 |
| Charles, m. Anne **WORTHINGTON**, Jan. 17, 1796; d. Aug. 29, 1836, ae 73 | 2 | 120 |
| Charles Frederick, s. [Charles & Anne], b. Jan. 12, 1798 | 2 | 120 |
| Clarissa, m. Ebenezer **CARRIER**, Apr. 14, 1795 | 2 | 84 |
| Daniell, [s. John], b. Mar. 9, 1709 | L-3 | 193 |
| Daniel, s. John, b. Mar. 9, 1709 | TM-1 | 193 |
| Daniel, [s. Benjamin & Margaret], b. July 21, 1747 | TPR | 110 |
| Dauid, [s. John], b. July 18, 1710 | L-3 | 193 |
| David, s. John, b. July 18, 1710 | TM-1 | 193 |
| David, m. Hannah **LEWIS**, Dec. 12, 1734 *Hannah **KELLOGG** in "Day Genealogy (handwritten in margin of original manuscript) | TPR | 111 |
| David, [s. Benjamin & Margaret], b. Aug. 4, 1749 | TPR | 110 |
| Deborah, d. Thomas, d. Oct. 20, 1703 | L-3 | 196 |
| Deborah, d. Thomas, d. Oct. 20, 1703 | TM-1 | 196 |

| | Vol. | Page |
|---|---|---|
| **DAY**, (cont.) | | |
| Deborah, [d. Ebenezer & Sarah], b. Nov. 26, 1718 | L-1 | 446 |
| Deborah, m. Thomas **CARRIER**, s. of Andrew, Apr. 9, 1741 | 1 | 131 |
| Dolly, wid., m. Samuel **BROWN**, June [ ], 1800 | 2 | 245 |
| Dolly C., d. [Justin & Matilda], b. Sept. 16, 1813 | 2 | 102 |
| Dorothy O., m. Brainard D. **KELLOGG**, b. of Colchester, Mar. 13, 1834, by Rev. Joseph Harvey | 2 | 264 |
| Dudley, [s. Ephraim & Sarah], b. Dec. 1, 1764 | 1 | 12 |
| Ebenezer, m. Sarah **TIFFINE**, Feb. 3, 1717/18 | L-1 | 446 |
| Ebenezer, [s. Ebenezer & Sarah], b. July 28, 1726 | L-1 | 446 |
| Eaditha, [d. John], b. Sept. 10, 1705 | L-3 | 193 |
| Editha, m. David **BIGLOE**, Dec. 11, 1729 | L-3 | 455 |
| Editha, [d. Benjamin & Margaret], b. Jan. 5, 1752 | TPR | 110 |
| Editha, m. Elijah **WILLIAMS**, Jr., June 27, 1775 | 2 | 77 |
| Elenor Louisa, d. [Justin & Matilda], b. Feb. 18, 1804 | 2 | 102 |
| Eleanor Louisa, m. Ansel **HUNGERFORD**, of East Haddam, Feb. 19, 1833, by Rev. Joseph Harvey | 2 | 241 |
| Eli, [s. Joseph, Jr. & Susannah], b. Nov. 12, 1768 | 1 | 99 |
| Elijah, s. [Abraham & Irena], b. Dec. 1, 1754 | 1 | 123 |
| Elijah, of Colchester, m. Dorothy **OLMSTEAD**, of Chatham, Mar. 10, 1776 | 2 | 24 |
| Elijah, s. [Justin & Matilda], b. June 13, 1802 | 2 | 102 |
| Elijah Worthington, s. [Charles & Anne], b. Sept. 17, 1799 | 2 | 120 |
| Elisha, s. [Abraham & Irena], b. Jan. 30, 1749 | 1 | 123 |
| Elisha Marvin, s. [Asa & Anne], b. Jan. 25, 1807 | 2 | 72 |
| Eliza, w. [Thomas], d. Dec. 28, 1748 | 1 | 149 |
| Eliza Maria, d. [Charles & Anne], b. Sept. 21, 1804 | 2 | 120 |
| Elizabeth, m. John **HOPSON**, June 6, 1710 | L-1 | 799 |
| Elizabeth, d. [Asa & anne], b. July 30, 1800 | 2 | 72 |
| Elizabeth, m. William E. **TRACY**, b. of Colchester, Nov. 3, 1836, by Rev. Samuel J. Curtiss | 2 | 297 |
| Ephraim, s. [Abraham & Irena], b. July 10, 1741 | 1 | 123 |
| Ephraim, [m.] Sarah **STUKLEY**, [ ] | 1 | 12 |
| Erastus, s. [Charles & Anne], b. Nov. 13, 1810 | 2 | 120 |
| Erastus Sheldon, [s. Elihu M.], b. July 7, 1836 | 3 | 9 |
| Erial, s. [Adonijah & Sarah], b. July 20, 1768 | 1 | 121 |
| Easther, d. John, b. Sept. 10, 1705 | TM-1 | 193 |
| Esther, [d. Joseph & Esther], b. Mar. 12, 1733 | TPR | 110 |
| Esther, m. Silvanus **BLISS**, Nov. [ ], 1751 | 1 | 23 |
| Esther, [d. Joseph, Jr. & Susannah], b. Oct. 1, 1763 | 1 | 99 |
| Ezra, [s. Joseph & Esther], b. Jan. 18, 1730; d. July 23, [1730] | TPR | 110 |
| Ezra, [s. Joseph & Esther], b. July 20, 1740; d. Mar. 17, 1742 | TPR | 110 |
| Ezra, s. [Abraham & Irena], b. Apr. 22, 1743 | 1 | 123 |
| Fanny, d. [Elijah & Dorothy], b. Aug. 20, 1783 | 2 | 24 |
| Frances M., s. [Justin & Matilda], b. Apr. 16, 1820 | 2 | 102 |
| Frances M., of Colchester, m. Jared C. **KELLOGG**, of Ellington, Oct. 7, 1839, by Rev. Lyman Strong | 2 | 159 |
| Grace, [d. Joseph & Esther], b. Mar. 12, 1736 | TPR | 110 |

| | Vol. | Page |
|---|---|---|
| **DAY**, (cont.) | | |
| Grace, m. Adonijah **FOOT**, Oct. 24, 1754 | 1 | 122 |
| Guy Bigelow, s. [Charles & Anne], b. July 21, 1818 | 2 | 120 |
| Hannah, d. [Isaac & Ann], b. Aug. 26, 1756 | 1 | 115 |
| Ira, [s. Stephen & Dimis], b. May 5, 1767 | 1 | 98 |
| Irene, d. [Abraham & Irena], b. Mar. 7, 1757 | 1 | 123 |
| Irene, m. David **YOEMANS**, b. of Colchester, Jan. 7, 1774 | 2 | 16 |
| Isaac, [s. John], b. May 17, 1713 | L-3 | 193 |
| Isaac, s. John, b. May 17, 1713 | TM-1 | 193 |
| Isaac, m. Ann **FOOT**, July 3, 1740 | 1 | 115 |
| Isaac, s. [Isaac & Anne], b. Nov. 15, 1750 | 1 | 115 |
| Isaac, m. Dorothy **BIGELOW**, Oct. 12, 1762 | 1 | 115 |
| Isaac Henry, s. [Charles & Anne], b. Nov. 10, 1808 | 2 | 120 |
| Isaac Henry, b. Nov. 10, 1808; m. Sarah E. **WILLIAMS**, Oct. 10, 1842, in Chatham, Ct. | 2 | 126 |
| Israel, [s. Thomas & Mary], b. Jan. 25, 1739; d. July 10, 1740 | 1 | 140 |
| Jacob, s. [Isaac & Ann], b. Aug. 31, 1753 | 1 | 115 |
| Jane Maria, [d. Elihu M.], b. Mar. 19, 1842 | 3 | 9 |
| Jeremiah, [s. Thomas & Mary], b. Jan. 25, 1737 | 1 | 140 |
| Jerusha J., of Colchester, m. Ezekiel **ROOT**, of Haddam, Jan. 2, 1831, by Rev. Joseph Harvey | 2 | 228 |
| Jesse, s. Joseph, b. Jan. 16, 1748 | 1 | 152 |
| Jesse, [s. Joseph & Esther], b. Jan. 16, 1748 | TPR | 110 |
| John, Jr., m. Sarah **LO[O]MIS**, Aug. 20, 1725 | L-1 | 447 |
| John, s. Dea. John & Sarah, b. Nov. 20, 1738 | 1 | 134 |
| John, s. [Isaac & Ann], b. Dec. 14, 1748 | 1 | 115 |
| John, d. Nov. 4, 1752, N. S. | 1 | 115 |
| John, [s. Noah & Ann], b. May 6, 1762 | 1 | 30 |
| John, of Colchester, m. Katharine **JONES**, of Hebron, Dec. 20, 1792 | 2 | 68 |
| John, s. [Charles & Anne], b. May 16, 1815; d. Dec. 12, 1835, ae 20 y. 7 m. 4 d. | 2 | 120 |
| John Bailey, s. [Isaac Henry & Sarah E.], b. Sept. 23, 1847 | 2 | 126 |
| Jonathan, [s. Ebenezer & Sarah], b. Sept. 28, 1723 | L-1 | 446 |
| Jonathan, [s. Ebenezer & Sarah], d. Aug. 18, 1727 | L-1 | 446 |
| Jonathan, s. [Thomas & Mary], b. Aug. 7, 1729 | 1 | 140 |
| Jonathan, [s. Joseph, Jr. & Susannah], b. Jan. 6, 1772 | 1 | 99 |
| Joseph, s. John, b. Sept. 27, 1702 | L-3 | 193 |
| Joseph, s. John, b. Sept. 27, 1702 | TM-1 | 193 |
| Joseph, m. Esther **HUNGERFORD**, Apr. 1, 1729 | TPR | 110 |
| Joseph, [s. Joseph & Esther], b. May 6, 1731 | TPR | 110 |
| Joseph, Jr., m. Susannah **BRAINARD**, Nov. 13, 1754 | 1 | 99 |
| Joseph, twin with Rhoda, [s. Joseph, Jr. & Susannah], b. Aug. 2, 1756 | 1 | 99 |
| Joseph, s. [Asa & Anne], b. Nov. 28, 1792 | 2 | 72 |
| Joseph, m. Eliza **ADAMS**, b. of Colchester, May 24, 1824, by Jacob Seales, V. D. M., at the house of Capt. Benjamin Adams | 2 | 178 |

| | Vol. | Page |
|---|---|---|
| **DAY**, (cont.) | | |
| Justin, s. [Elijah & Dorothy], b. Apr. 2, 1781 | 2 | 24 |
| Justin, m. Matilda **DAY**, Nov. 5, 1800 | 2 | 102 |
| Justin, s. [Justin & Matilda], b. Dec. 26, 1815 | 2 | 102 |
| Justin E., m. Eliza m. **RANSOM**, Nov. 10, [ ], by Rev. Lyman Strong | 2 | 282 |
| Justin Edwin, s. [Charles & Anne], b. Oct. 4, 1806 | 2 | 120 |
| Laura, d. [Justin & Matilda], b. Oct. 16, 1822 | 2 | 102 |
| Laura, of Westchester, m. A. G. **BRIM**, of Chatham, Nov. 24, 1847, by Rev. S. D. Jewett | 3 | 34 |
| Levi, s. [Adonijah & Sarah], b. Mar. 14, 1765 | 1 | 121 |
| Lodena, [d. Stephen & Dimis], b. July 6, 1769 | 1 | 98 |
| Lois, b. Mar. 13, 1744 | 1 | 29 |
| Lois, m. Joshua **BULKLEY**, Nov. 19, 1761 | 1 | 29 |
| Lois, [d. Noah & Ann], b. Mar. 4, 1768 | 1 | 30 |
| Lois, m. Joseph **CARRIER**, Jr., Jan. 8, 1789 | 2 | 40 |
| Lucretia, of Colchester, m. William E. **ARNOLD**, of Haddam, Oct. 11, 1829, by Rev. Joseph Harvey | 2 | 215 |
| Lucy, d. [Abraham & Irena], b. May 14, 1752 | 1 | 123 |
| Lucy, d. [Adonijah & Sarah], b. June 12, 1756 | 1 | 121 |
| Lucy, m. William **BRAINARD**, Dec. 31, 17[ ] | 2 | 14 |
| Lydia, [d. Benjamin & Margaret], b. Apr. 21, 1744 | TPR | 110 |
| Lydia, m. Asa **BEEBE**, Aug. 4, 1763 | 1 | 96 |
| Lydia, d. [Adonijah & Sarah], b. Jan. 12, 1766 | 1 | 121 |
| Margaret, [d. Benjamin & Margaret], b. Oct. 27, 1737 | TPR | 110 |
| Margaret, d. [Adonijah & Sarah], b. Feb. 12, 1758 | 1 | 121 |
| Maria, d. [John & Katharine], b. Jan. 30, 1794 | 2 | 68 |
| Mary, m. Jonathan **NORTHAM**, Dec. 20, 1722 | L-1 | 452 |
| Mary, [d. Joseph & Esther], b. July 2, 1738 | TPR | 110 |
| Mary, d. [Isaac & Ann], b. Dec. 27, 1744 | 1 | 115 |
| Mary, w. John, d. Nov. 1, 1749 | 1 | 115 |
| Mary, m. William **CHAMBERLAIN**, May 22, 1758 | 1 | 35 |
| Mary, [d. Joseph, Jr. & Susannah], b. Oct. 14, 1765 | 1 | 99 |
| Mary, m. John **KELLOGG**, Dec. 26, 1791 | 2 | 56 |
| Mary Ann, d. [Joseph & Eliza], b. Feb. 14, 1827 | 2 | 178 |
| Mary Ann, of Colchester, m. Clark **PAYNE**, of Lebanon, Feb. 10, 1828, by Avery Morgan, J. P. | 2 | 200 |
| Mary O., m. David C. **BUELL**, Feb. 1, 1829, by Rev. Joseph Harvey | 2 | 209 |
| Mary Octavo, d. [Asa & Anne], b. Aug. 18, 1804 | 2 | 72 |
| Matilda, m. Justin **DAY**, Nov. 5, 1800 | 2 | 102 |
| Nancy, [d. Charles & Anne], b. Dec. 25, 1797; d. Feb. 6, 1797 | 2 | 120 |
| Nehemiah, s. [Abraham & Irena], b. Mar. 5, 1745 | 1 | 123 |
| Nehemiah, m. Dimmis **KILLBORN**, Aug. 21, 1766 | 1 | 119 |
| Noah, s. [Dea. John & Sarah], b. June 10, 1740 | 1 | 134 |
| Noah, m. Ann **LEWIS**, Dec. 6, 1759 | 1 | 30 |
| Noah, [s. Noah & Ann], b. May 27, 1766 | 1 | 30 |
| Oliver, s. [Abraham & Irena], b. Sept. 12, 1761 | 1 | 123 |

| | Vol. | Page |
|---|---|---|
| **DAY**, (cont.) | | |
| Oliver, s. [Adonijah & Sarah], b. Aug. 16, 1783 | 1 | 121 |
| Rachel, [s. Joseph & Esther], b. Nov. 22, 1745 | TPR | 110 |
| Rhoda, twin with Joseph, [d. Joseph, Jr. & Susannah], b. Aug. 2, 1756 | 1 | 99 |
| Rhoda, m. John **STAPLES**, Mar. 9, 1783 | 2 | 44 |
| Roderick, s. [Justin & Matilda], b. Nov. 16, 1817; d. Dec. 16, 1821 | 2 | 102 |
| Roderick, s. [Justin & Matilda], b. May 16, 1825 | 2 | 102 |
| Russel[l], s. Benj[amin], b. Sept. 16, 1756 | 1 | 115 |
| Sally M., d. [Justin & Matilda], b. Aug. 10, 1810 | 2 | 102 |
| Sally M., of Colchester, m. John J. **WORTHINGTON**, of East Haddam, May 6, 1830, by Rev. Joseph Harvey | 2 | 222 |
| Samuell, s. Thomas, b. Sept. 15, 1704 | L-3 | 196 |
| Samuel, s. Tho[ma]s, b. Sept. 15, 1704 | TM-1 | 196 |
| Samuel, s. [Isaac & Ann], b. Nov. 14, 1746 | 1 | 115 |
| Sarah, m. William **CHAMBERLIN**, Jan. 4, 1710 | L-1 | 445 |
| Sarah, m. William **CHAMBERLAIN**, Jan. 4, 1710/11 | L-1 | 799 |
| Sarah, [d. Ebenezer & Sarah], b. July 12, 1720 | L-1 | 446 |
| Sarah, [w. Thomas], d. Mar. 29, 1726 | 1 | 140 |
| Sarah, d. [Dea. John & Sarah], b. Mar. 12 1742 | 1 | 134 |
| Sarah, [d. Thomas & Mary], b. June 24, 1742 | 1 | 140 |
| Sarah, d. [Adonijah & Sarah], b. Feb. 9, 1755 | 1 | 121 |
| Sarah, d. [Abraham & Irena], b. Mar. 26, 1759 | 1 | 123 |
| Sarah, [d. Noah & Ann], b. Dec. 26, 1760 | 1 | 30 |
| Sarah, m. Charles **FOOT**, Jr., Dec. 17, 1778 | 2 | 31 |
| Sarah, m. Samuel **NORTHAM**, Jr., Apr. 8, 1779 | 2 | 25 |
| Sarah, of Colchester, m. Ansel **BRAINARD**, Jr., of Haddam, Dec. 14, 1826, by Rev. David B. Ripley, of Marlborough | 2 | 192 |
| Sarah Ann Janette, d. [Isaac Henry & Sarah E.], b. Aug. 14, 1850 | 2 | 126 |
| Silence, [d. Ebenezer & Sarah], b. June 1, 1728 | L-1 | 446 |
| Silence, m. Isaac **JONES**, Feb. 28, 1752 | 1 | 26 |
| Sparrow Williams, s. [Isaac Henry & Sarah E.], b. Feb. 22, 1846 | 2 | 126 |
| Stephen, s. [Dea. John & Sarah], b Feb. 20, 1746 | 1 | 134 |
| Stephen, m. Dimis **RANSOM**, Mar. 27, 1766 | 1 | 98 |
| Stephen, s. [Elijah & Dorothy], b. Aug. 26, 1779 | 2 | 24 |
| Stephen B., m. Clarissa L. **BRAINARD**, b. of Colchester, Nov. 27, 1834, by Rev. Joseph Harvey | 2 | 274 |
| Stephen Brainard, s. [Asa & Anne], b. Nov. 2, 1808 | 2 | 72 |
| Stephen Olmstead, s. [Justin & Matilda], b. Jan. 17, 1806 | 2 | 102 |
| Susan, [d. Elihu M.], b. June 3, 1834 | 3 | 9 |
| Susanna, [d. Joseph, Jr. & Susannah], b. Jan. 27, 1755 | 1 | 99 |
| Susanna, m. Elisha **KELLOGG**, June 9, 1776 | 2 | 65 |
| Susannah, d. [Asa & Anne], b. Sept. 14, 1798 | 2 | 72 |
| Tabitha, [d. Joseph, Jr. & Susannah], b. Apr. 12, 1774 | 1 | 99 |
| Tabitha, of Colchester, m. Warren **WEST**, of Chatham, Apr. | | |

| | Vol. | Page |
|---|---|---|
| **DAY**, (cont.) | | |
| 30, 1821, by Rev. Jacob Seales | 2 | 125 |
| Talitha, d. [Asa & Anne], b. June 21, 1796 | 2 | 72 |
| Tamor, d. [Thomas & Mary], b. Nov. 29, 1727 | 1 | 140 |
| Thomas, m. Sarah **BARNS**, June [ ], 1722 | 1 | 140 |
| Thomas, m. Mary **WELLS**, Feb. 2, 1727 | 1 | 140 |
| Thomas, d. Jan. 14, 1729 | 1 | 149 |
| -----, w. John, d. May 12, 1714 | L-3 | 196 |
| -----, w. John, d. May 12, 1714 | TM-1 | 192 |
| **DAYTON**, Grace, m. Stephen **CROCKER**, of Waterford, Nov. 6, 1825, by Benjamin Trumbull, J. P. | 2 | 179 |
| William, of Colchester, m. Mary **TUCK**, of Hebron, Apr. 7, 1833, by Amherst Scoville, J. P. | 2 | 242 |
| **DEAN, DEANE**, Benjamin D., of Fall River, Mass., m. Sarah T. **ROGERS**, of Colchester, d. of Dr. Howell **ROGERS**, Nov. 19, 1844, by Rev. Joel R. Arnold | 3 | 17 |
| Sarah T., d. [Dr. Ho[w]el[l] **ROGERS** & Sarah], d. Oct. 28, 1847, ae 30 | 2 | 84 |
| Seth, m. Ann **SKIN[N]ER**, Oct. 29, 1721 | L-1 | 444 |
| **DEMING, DEMMING**, Abigail Champion, d. [David & Abigail], b. June 18, 1810 | 2 | 97 |
| Alice, [d. Jonathan & Allice], b. Dec. 21, 1778 | 1 | 42 |
| Anna, d. [Henry & Anna], b. Sept. 4, 1772 | 2 | 9 |
| Betty, [d. Jonathan & Allice], b. Apr. 2, 1775 | 1 | 42 |
| Daniel, [s. Jonathan & Allice], b. Aug. 23, 1781 | 1 | 42 |
| David, [s. Jonathan & Allice], b. Dec. 8, 1768; d. Sept. 14, 1769 | 1 | 42 |
| David, [s. Jonathan & Allice], b. May 8, 1773; d. Oct. 6, 1775 | 1 | 42 |
| David, s. [Henry & Anna], b. Jan. 12, 1779 | 2 | 9 |
| David, m. Abigail **CHAMPION**, Sept. 17, 1804; d. June 6, 1827, ae 46 | 2 | 97 |
| Demia, d. Henry & Anna, b. July 22, 1774 | 1 | 165 |
| Dimmis, d. [Henry & Anna], b. July 22, 1774 | 2 | 9 |
| Harriet Tinker, d. [David & Abigail], b. Feb. 23, 1808; d. Sept. 5, 1810 | 2 | 97 |
| Henry, m. Anna **LORD**, Feb. 6, 1772 | 1 | 94 |
| Henry, m. Anna **LORD**, Feb. 6, 1772 | 2 | 9 |
| Henry, s. [Henry & Anna], b. Feb. 12, 1777 | 2 | 9 |
| Henry, s. [Henry], b. Feb. 12, [1777] | 2 | 13 |
| Henry, m. [ ] **LORD** | 2 | 13 |
| Henry Champion, s. [David & Abigail], b. May 23, 1815 | 2 | 97 |
| Jonathan, m. Allice **SKINNER**, Dec. 30, 1767 | 1 | 42 |
| Jonathan Amory, s. [David & Abigail], b. Oct. 19, 1812 | 2 | 97 |
| Lovina, d. [Henry & Anna], b. Oct. 23, 1781 | 2 | 9 |
| Mary, [d. Jonathan & Allice], b. Oct. 10, 1770; d. June 19, 1776 | 1 | 42 |
| Mary, 2d, [d. Jonathan & Allice], b. Sept. 3, 1777; d. Jan. 15, 1778 | 1 | 42 |

| | Vol. | Page |
|---|---|---|
| **DEMING, DEMMING**, (cont.) | | |
| Mary, d. [David & Abigail], b. Oct. 9, 1805 | 2 | 97 |
| Mary T., m. Rev. Thomas L. **SHIPMAN**, May 3, 1827, by Salmon Cone, V. D. M. | 2 | 195 |
| **DENNEO**, Lydia, m. Eliphalet **GILLETT**, Mar. 27, 1760 | 1 | 28 |
| **DERBY, DERBE**, Hannah, m. Elijah **STAPLES**, Oct. 20, 1744 | 1 | 95 |
| Moses, [s. John & Hannah], b. Oct. 1, 1759 | 1 | 23 |
| **DESTON**, George, of New London, m. Charlotte C. **LEE**, of Colchester, Aug. 1, 1842, by Rev. Joel R. Arnold | 2 | 283 |
| **DETHICK, DIRTHICK, DETHOCK, DATHICK**, Ab[i]aga[i]l, m. Guy **LOOMIS**, Aug. 28, 1799 | 2 | 80 |
| Amia, [d. John & Anne], b. Mar. 23, 1744 | 1 | 84 |
| Annanias, [s. John], b. Dec. 24, 1730 | TPR | 112 |
| Annanias, [s. John & Anne], b. Jan. 18, 1750 | 1 | 84 |
| Ananias, m. Mary Ann **WELCH**, Feb. 14, 1771 | 1 | 163 |
| Anna, d. Aug. 22, 1750 | 1 | 84 |
| Elisabeth, [d. John], b. Dec. 17, 1721 | TPR | 112 |
| Elizabeth, [d. John & Anne], b. Feb. 15, 1752; d. Oct. 17, 1756 | 1 | 84 |
| Ephraim, [s. John & Anne], b. Apr. 21, 1756 | 1 | 84 |
| Hannah, [d. John], b. June 29, 1733 | TPR | 112 |
| Hopestill, [d. John & Anne], b. Nov. 26, 1742 | 1 | 84 |
| James, s. [Ananias & Mary Ann], b. Aug. 10, 1773 | 1 | 163 |
| John, s. John, b. Mar. 10, 1719 | TPR | 112 |
| John, m. Anne **DODGE**, Dec. 22, 1741 | 1 | 84 |
| John, [s. John & Anne], b. July 18, 1754 | 1 | 84 |
| Mary, [d. John], b. Mar. 10, 1725 | TPR | 112 |
| Mary, [d. John & Anne], b. Aug. 9, 1758; d. Apr. 13, 1765 | 1 | 84 |
| Mary Ann, d. [Ananias & Mary Ann], b. Sept. 14, 1772; d. Mar. 19, 1773 | 1 | 163 |
| Naomi, [d. John], b. May 11, 1729 | TPR | 112 |
| Peter, [s. John & Anne], b. Jan. 13, 1748; d. Aug. 22, 1750 | 1 | 84 |
| Ruth, [d. John], b. July 16, 1734 | TPR | 112 |
| Sarah, [d. John], b. Mar. 5, 1727 | TPR | 112 |
| Susanna, [d. John], b. Dec. 17, 1723 | TPR | 112 |
| Susannah, [d. John & Anne], b. Mar. 28, 1746; d. Aug. 19, 1750 | 1 | 84 |
| **DEWEY**, Molly, of Lebanon, m. Solomon **SCOVELL**, [ ], in Lebanon; d. Sept. 13, 1829, ae 69 | 2 | 46 |
| Rh[o]da, of Lebanon, m. Nathaniel **CHAMBERLAIN**, Jr., Dec. 30, 1784 | 2 | 73 |
| -----, m. Thomas **DODGE**, Jr., Jan. 18, 1759 | 1 | 87 |
| **DEWIT[T]**, Bettey, m. Darius **CLARK**, Jan. 26, 1780 | 2 | 8 |
| **DIBBLE, DIBLE, DIBELL, DIBELLS**, Ann, [d. Ebenezar & An[n], b. June 27, 1708 | L-3 | 194 |
| Ann, d. Eben[eze]r [& Ann], b. June 27, 1708 | TM-1 | 194 |
| Ann, w. Ebenezer, d. July 22, 1708 | L-3 | 194 |
| Ann, w. Eben[eze]r, d. July 22, 1708 | TM-1 | 194 |

| | Vol. | Page |
|---|---|---|
| **DIBBLE, DIBLE, DIBELL, DIBELLS,** (cont.) | | |
| Ebenezar, m. An[n] **HOOTON**, Aug. 29, 1706 | L-3 | 194 |
| Ebenezer, m. Ann **HEATON**, Aug. 29, 1706 | TM-1 | 194 |
| Ebenezer, m. Mary **LEWESS**, Dec. 30, 1708 | L-3 | 194 |
| Ebenezer, m. Mary **LEWIS**, Dec. 30, 1708 | TM-1 | 194 |
| Elizabeth, d. Ebenezer [& Mary], b. Aug. 8, 1701 | L-3 | 194 |
| Elizabeth, d. Ebenezer [& Mary], b. Aug. 8, 1701 | TM-1 | 194 |
| Elizabeth, m. Georg[e] **SAXTON**, Nov. 21, 1723 | L-1 | 447 |
| Mary, w. Ebenezar, d. Sept. 24, 1703 | L-3 | 194 |
| Mary, w. Ebenezer, d. Sept. 24, 1703 | TM-1 | 194 |
| Mary, m. Joseph **PEPOON**, Dec. 12, 1717 | L-1 | 453 |
| Mary, w. Ebenezer, d. Mar. 5, 1736 | L-3 | 452 |
| **DICKINSON**, Sarah, of Colchester, m. Dea. Amasa **PALMER**, of Mansfield, Feb. 12, 1840, by Rev. Joel R. Arnold | 2 | 69 |
| **DICKSON**, [see under **DIXON**] | | |
| **DIMOCK**, Timothy, m. Laura **BARTLETT**, b. of Lebanon, Oct. 29, 1838, by Rev. Lyman Strong | 2 | 229 |
| Timothy, of Norwich, m. Louisa A. **BRIGGS**, of Colchester, Jan. 8, 1843, by Rev. Joel R. Arnold | 3 | 1 |
| **DIRTHICK**, [see under **DETHICK**] | | |
| **DIXON, DICKSON**, Grace, d. William & Rebecca, b. Mar. 12, 1721 | L-3 | 6 |
| Henry C., m. Mary W. **ADAMS**, b. of Colchester, Jan. 24, 1831, by Rev. Joseph Harvey | 2 | 229 |
| John, s. William [& Rebecca], b. Nov. 12, 1722 | L-3 | 6 |
| Margaret, [d. William & Rebecca], b. Aug. 18, 1727; d. Nov. 18, 1728 | L-3 | 6 |
| Rebec[c]ah, [d. William & Rebecca], b. Jan. 12, 1725 | L-3 | 6 |
| Silas E., of East Haddam, m. Harriet **LOOMIS**, of Colchester, May 7, 1834, by Rev. Joseph Harvey | 2 | 265 |
| Thomas, [s. William & Rebecca], b. May 3, 1733 | L-3 | 6 |
| Timothy, [s. William & Rebecca], b. May 5, 1730 | L-3 | 6 |
| William, [s. William & Rebecca], b. May 12, 1724 | L-3 | 6 |
| **DOANE**, Cornelius B., of Essex, m. Charlotte M. **NORTHAM**, of Colchester, [Sept.] 13, 1854, by Rev. S. D. Jewett | 3 | 63 |
| George E., of Saybrook, m. Abigail **FULLER**, of Colchester, Sept. 5, 1833, by Rev. Joseph Harvey | 2 | 259 |
| **DODGE**, Abigail, d. [David & Rebecca], b. Feb. 23, 1741 | 1 | 145 |
| Abigail, [d. Jonathan & Mercy], b. Aug. 18, 1759 | 1 | 37 |
| Abigail, m. William **WISE**, Oct. 23, 1760 | 1 | 54 |
| Abigail, [d. Nathan & Abigail], b. June 12, 1763 | 1 | 54 |
| Abigail, d. [Benjamin & Tabitha], b. Sept. 6, 1779 | 2 | 66 |
| Abigail, [d. Oliver & Abigail], b. Oct. 30, 1781 | 2 | 19 |
| Abimael, [s. Amos & Mary], b. Aug. 21, 1760 | 1 | 48 |
| Alex, s. [David & Rebecca], b. July 18, 1723 | 1 | 145 |
| Alexander, Jr., m. Susannah **WALLER**, wid., Jan. 2, 1764 | 1 | 28 |
| Alvin, [s. Jonathan, Jr. & Mary, Jr.], b. May 7, 1782 | 1 | 82 |
| Alpheus, s. Oliver & Abigail, b. Oct. 2, 1776 | 2 | 19 |

| | Vol. | Page |
|---|---|---|
| **DODGE**, (cont.) | | |
| Amasa, [s. Nathan & Abigail], b. Jan. 20, 1760; d. [ ], 1765 | 1 | 54 |
| Amos, s. [David & Rebecca], b. May 31, 1732 | 1 | 145 |
| Amos, of Colchester, m. Mary **HALL**, of New London, Jan. 27, 1756 | 1 | 48 |
| Amos, [s. Amos & Mary], b. Apr. 2, 1758 | 1 | 48 |
| Ann, d. [David & Rebecca], b. Mar. 22, 1743 | 1 | 145 |
| Anna, [d. Jonathan & Mercy], b. Sept. 14, 1761 | 1 | 37 |
| Anne, m. John **DETHOCK**, Dec. 22, 1741 | 1 | 84 |
| Anne, d. [George & Jemima], b. Apr. 9, 1770 | 1 | 153 |
| Anne, d. [Benjamin & Tabitha], b. Aug. 1, 1781 | 2 | 66 |
| Azube, d. [Moses & Mary], b. Apr. 10, 1761 | 1 | 145 |
| Bathsheba, [d. Daniel & Ruth], b. Nov. 9, 1764 | 1 | 85 |
| Benjamin, m. Tabitha **DODGE**, Mar. 19, 1773 | 2 | 66 |
| Betty, d. [George & Jemima], b. May 27, 1772 | 1 | 153 |
| Charles, [s. Amos & Mary], b. Aug. 1, 1756 | 1 | 48 |
| Delilah, m. Simeon **SHAW**, July 5, 1773 | 2 | 71 |
| Dan, s. [Elisha & Silena], b. May 16, 1788 | 2 | 54 |
| Daniel, s. [David & Rebecca], b. July 18, 1729 | 1 | 145 |
| Daniel, [s. Jonathan & Mercy], b. Jan. 23, 1752; d. Aug. 31, 1753 | 1 | 37 |
| Daniel, m. Ruth **WORDEN**, Apr. 11, 1756 | 1 | 85 |
| Daniel, [s. Jonathan & Mercy], b. July 19, 1757 | 1 | 37 |
| Daniel, Jr., of Colchester, m. Lucy **LATTIMER**, of Lyme, Dec. 2, 1779; b. July 19, 1757; d. Sept. 14, 1807, ae 50 | 2 | 57 |
| David, m. Rebecca **YEOMAN**, May 15, 1717 | 1 | 145 |
| David, s. [David & Rebecca], b. July 15, 1719 | 1 | 145 |
| David, [s. Amos & Mary], b. Oct. 27, 1767 | 1 | 48 |
| Edmund, s. [Oliver & Abigail], b. Dec. 22, 1777 | 2 | 19 |
| Elisha, [s. Nathan & Abigail], b. Aug. 21, 1756 | 1 | 54 |
| Elisha, s. [George & Jemima], b. Oct. 24, 1761 | 1 | 153 |
| Elisha, m. Silena **CHAPMAN**, [ ], 1781 | 2 | 54 |
| Elisha, s. [Elisha & Selena], b. Feb. 27, 1784 | 2 | 54 |
| Elizabeth, [d. John, 3d, & Tabitha], b. Aug. 15, 1755 | 1 | 83 |
| Elizabeth, d. [John, Jr. & Lydia], b. Feb. 12, 1756 | 1 | 153 |
| Elizabeth, [d. Daniel & Ruth], b. Jan. 9, 1768 | 1 | 85 |
| Elizabeth, d. [Benjamin & Tabitha], b. June 26, 1775 | 2 | 66 |
| Esther, [d. John, 3d, & Tabitha], b. Aug. 30, 1768 | 1 | 83 |
| Esther, d. [Benjamin & Tabitha], b. Oct. 2, 1790 | 2 | 66 |
| Eunice, [d. Thomas, Jr.], b. May 5, 1760 | 1 | 87 |
| Eunice, d. [George & Jemima], b. Oct. 16, 1774 | 1 | 153 |
| Frances, d. [Daniel, Jr. & Lucy], b. Mar. 4, 1784 | 2 | 57 |
| George, s. [David & Rebecca], b. Aug. 6, 1738 | 1 | 145 |
| George, m. Jemima **WISE**, Jan. 29, 1761 | 1 | 153 |
| George, s. [George & Jemima], b. June 20, 1776 | 1 | 153 |
| Grace, m. Lewis **LOVERIDGE**, Mar. 24, 1757 | 1 | 78 |
| Hannah, [d. Oliver & Sarah], b. Oct. 31, 1769; | 1 | 77 |

| | Vol. | Page |
|---|---|---|
| **DODGE**, (cont.) | | |
| d. Nov. 23, 1771 | 1 | 77 |
| Hannah, d. [Daniel & Ruth], b. Apr. 3, 1772 | 1 | 111 |
| Hannah, [d. Oliver & Abigail], b. July 25, 1774 | 1 | 77 |
| Huldah, [d. Daniel & Ruth], b. Feb. 14, 1760 | 1 | 85 |
| Israel, s. [John, Jr. & Lydia], b. Sept. 3, 1760 | 1 | 152 |
| Israel, s. [Benjamin & Tabitha], b. Dec. 2, 1776 | 2 | 66 |
| Jacob, twin with Tabitha, [s. John, 3d, & Tabitha], b. May 7, 1750 | 1 | 83 |
| Jarves, s. [Moses & Mary], b. Jan. 27, 1764 | 1 | 145 |
| Jemima, d. [George & Jemima], b. Oct. 20, 1766 | 1 | 153 |
| Jerusha, [d. John, 3d & Tabitha], b. May 1, 1761 | 1 | 83 |
| Jerusha, d. [George & Jemima], b. June 16, 1768 | 1 | 153 |
| Joel, s. [Benjamin & Tabitha], b. Aug. 6, 1784 | 2 | 66 |
| John, s. [David & Rebecca], b. Feb. 15, 1730 | 1 | 145 |
| John, Jr., m. Lydia **ROGERS**, Oct. 23, 1748 | 1 | 152 |
| John, 3d, m. Tabitha **DODGE**, Dec. 7, 1749 | 1 | 83 |
| John, s. [John, Jr. & Lydia], b. July 12, 1751 | 1 | 152 |
| Jonathan, s. [David & Rebecca], b. Aug. 3, 1721 | 1 | 145 |
| Jonathan, of Colchester, m. Mercy **WILLIAMS**, of New London, Nov. 7, 1744 | 1 | 37 |
| Jonathan, m. Mercy **WILLIAMS**, Nov. 7, 1744 | 1 | 140 |
| Jonathan, [s. Jonathan & Mercy], b. Sept. 26, 1747 | 1 | 37 |
| Jonathan, s. [Jonathan & Mercy], b. Sept. 26, 1747 | 1 | 140 |
| Jonathan, Jr., m. Mary **VENNER**, July 13, 1769 | 1 | 42 |
| Jonathan, Jr., m. Mary **WARNER**, 2d, July 13, 1769; d. Sept. 28, 1794 | 2 | 65 |
| Jonathan, Jr., m. Mary **WARNER**, Jr., July 13, 1770 | 1 | 82 |
| Jonathan, Sr., d. June 19, 1794 | 1 | 37 |
| Jonathan, s. [Daniel, Jr. & Lucy], b. Feb. 1, 1800 | 2 | 57 |
| Jonathan Sacket, [s. Jonathan, Jr. & Mary, Jr.], b. Oct. 17, 1777 | 1 | 82 |
| Jordan, s. [John, Jr. & Lydia], b. Aug. 6, 1749 | 1 | 152 |
| Josiah Rogers, s. [John, Jr. & Lydia], b. Sept. 28, 1762 | 1 | 152 |
| Judah, s. [Daniel & Ruth], b. Feb. 11, 1770 | 1 | 111 |
| Lebbeus, s. [Benjamin & Tabitha], b. Nov. 8, 1773 | 2 | 66 |
| Lemuel, s. [Moses & Mary], b. Sept. 14, 1758 | 1 | 145 |
| Lodeme, [d. John, 3d & Tabitha], b. Aug. 14, 1759 | 1 | 83 |
| Lois, d. [George & Jemima], b. Mar. 23, 1763 | 1 | 153 |
| Lucy, d. [Daniel, Jr. & Lucy], b. Mar. 11, 1782; d. Sept. 2, 1783 | 2 | 57 |
| Lydia, d. [John, Jr. & Lydia], b. May 18, 1758 | 1 | 152 |
| Lydia, d. [Elisha & Silena], b. Feb. 3, 1786 | 2 | 54 |
| Lynde, [d. Oliver & Abigail], b. Mar. 12, 1783 | 2 | 19 |
| Mark, s. [Daniel, Jr. & Lucy], b. June 3, 1791 | 2 | 57 |
| Mary, d. [David & Rebecca], b. Sept. 9, 1725 | 1 | 145 |
| Mary, [d. Jonathan & Mercy], b. Sept. 2, 1749 | 1 | 140 |
| Mary, [d. Jonathan & Mercy], b. Sept. 20, 1749 | 1 | 37 |

| | Vol. | Page |
|---|---|---|
| **DODGE**, (cont.) | | |
| Mary, [d. Jonathan & Mercy], b. Oct. 10, 1754 | 1 | 37 |
| Mary, [d. Jonathan, Jr. & Mary, Jr.], b. Oct. 20, 1771; d. Jan. 3, 1772 | 1 | 82 |
| Mary, d. [Jonathan, Jr. & Mary, 2d], b. Oct. 20, 1771; d. Jan. 8, 1772 | 2 | 65 |
| Mary, 2d. [d. Jonathan, 2d, & Mary, Jr.], b. Aug. 28, 1775 | 1 | 82 |
| Mehetable, [d. Alexander, Jr. & Susannah], b. Dec. 22, 1765 | 1 | 28 |
| Mercy, [d. Jonathan, Jr. & Mary, Jr.], b. Jan. 3, 1780 | 1 | 82 |
| Merebah, [d. John, 3d & Tabitha], b. Aug. 15, 1753 | 1 | 83 |
| Miriam, [d. John, 3d & Tabitha], b. Apr. 14, 1752 | 1 | 83 |
| Moses, s. [David & Rebecca], b. May 8, 1734 | 1 | 145 |
| Moses, m. Mary **CHESTER**, Nov. 13, 1755 | 1 | 145 |
| Moses, [s. Amos & Mary], b. June 4, 1762 | 1 | 48 |
| Nancy, d. [Daniel, Jr. & Lucy], b. Apr. 29, 1787 | 2 | 57 |
| Nancy, m. Elijah **LOOMIS**, Jan. 15, 1809, in Salem, Ct. | 2 | 118 |
| Nathan, s. [David & Rebecca], b. July 14, 1736 | 1 | 145 |
| Nathan, m. Abigail **GRAVES**, Oct. 10, 1755 | 1 | 54 |
| Nathan, [s. Nathan & Abigail], b. Oct. 21, 1765 | 1 | 54 |
| Olive, [d. Nathan & Abigaie], b. Oct. 14, 1758 | 1 | 54 |
| Oliver, [s. Jonathan & Mercy], b. Sept. 2, 1745 | 1 | 37 |
| Oliver, s. [Jonathan & Mercy], b. Sept. 2, 1745 | 1 | 140 |
| Oliver, m. Sarah **WILLIAMS**, Mar. 19, 1767 | 1 | 77 |
| Oliver, m. Abigail **HARRIS**, Nov. 1, 1773 | 1 | 77 |
| Oliver Williams, [s. Oliver & Abigail], b. Oct. 3, 1775 | 1 | 77 |
| Peter, s. [John, Jr. & Lydia], b. Nov. 16, 1753; d. Dec. 16, 1759 | 1 | 152 |
| Peter, [s. Daniel & Ruth], b. Jan. 8, 1757 | 1 | 85 |
| Rebeckah, [d. Daniel & Ruth], b. Feb. 4, 1762 | 1 | 85 |
| Rebeckah, d. [George & Jemima], b. Oct. 14, 1764 | 1 | 153 |
| Reuben, [s. John, 3d, & Tabitha], b. Dec. 6, 1763 | 1 | 83 |
| Russel[l], s. [Benjamin & Tabitha], b. Apr. 6, 1786 | 2 | 66 |
| Ruth, [d. Daniel & Ruth], b. Apr. 31, 1758 | 1 | 85 |
| Sabra, [d. Amos & Mary], b. Sept. 14, 1764 | 1 | 48 |
| Sally, d. [Daniel, Jr. & Lucy], b. June 22, 1795 | 2 | 57 |
| Sarah, d. [Moses & Mary], b. Aug. 15, 1756 | 1 | 145 |
| Sarah, [d. Jonathan & Mercy], b. June 3, 1764 | 1 | 37 |
| Sarah, [d. Thomas, Jr.], b. June 15, 1768 | 1 | 87 |
| Sarah, [d. Oliver & Sarah], b. [ ]; d. Dec. 8, 1772 | 1 | 77 |
| Sarah, [d. Jonathan, Jr. & Mary], b. Jan. 17, 1773 | 1 | 42 |
| Sarah, d. [Jonathan, Jr. & Mary, 2d], b. Jan. 17, 1773 | 2 | 65 |
| Sarah, w. Oliver, d. May 1, 1773 | 1 | 77 |
| Seth, [s. John, 3d, & Tabitha], b. July 24, 1765 | 1 | 83 |
| Silena, d. [Elisha & Silena], b. Dec. 16, 1781 | 2 | 54 |
| Silence, [d. Thomas, Jr.], b. Nov. [ ], 1761; d. Dec. 19, 1761 | 1 | 87 |
| Tabitha, m. John **DODGE**, 3d, Dec. 7, 1749 | 1 | 83 |
| Tabitha, twin with Jacob, [d. John, 3d, & Tabitha], b. May 7, 1750 | 1 | 83 |

| | Vol. | Page |
|---|---|---|
| **DODGE**, (cont.) | | |
| Tabitha, m. Benjamin **DODGE**, Mar. 19, 1773 | 2 | 66 |
| Thomas, Jr., m. [ ] **DEWEY**, Jan. 18, 1759 | 1 | 87 |
| Thomas, [s. Thomas, Jr.], b. Nov. 22, 1765 | 1 | 87 |
| Thomas, s. [Benjamin & Tabitha], b. July 11, 1788 | 2 | 66 |
| William, m. Anne **WALCH**, June 30, 1757 | 1 | 30 |
| **DOLBEAR**, Frances H., of Natchez, Miss., m. Leenora A. **CHAPMAN**, of Colchester, Aug. 29, 1836, by Rev. Lyman Strong | 2 | 287 |
| Samuel, Sr., father Samuel P., d. July 13, 1850, ae 70 | 2 | 193 |
| Samuel P., of Lebanon, m. Sophronia S. **GURLEY**, of Colchester, Apr. 9, 1838, by Rev. Andrew M. Smith; d. Apr. 10, 1842, ae 31 | 2 | 193 |
| **DOOLITTLE**, Patty, m. Solomon **GILLETT**, [ ] | 2 | 150 |
| Seth, of Wallingford, m. Betsey **HEALEY**, of Colchester, Apr. 2, 1826, by Am[h]erst D. Scoville, J. P. | 2 | 185 |
| **DOUGLASS, DUGLES**, Daniel, [s. John & Elisabeth], b. Oct. 15, 1735 | TPR | 109 |
| Elizabeth, [d. John & Elisabeth], b. Dec. 5, 1733 | TPR | 109 |
| Hannah, m. John **BIGELOW**, 3d, June 10, 1759 | 1 | 21 |
| Hannah, m. John **BIGELOW**, Jr., July 10, 1759 | 1 | 76 |
| John, m. Elizabeth **QUITERFIELD**, Jan. 27, 1728 | L-3 | 9 |
| John, s. John & Elisabeth, b. Oct. 12, 1731 | TPR | 109 |
| Mary, [d. John & Elizabeth], b. Nov. 29, 1729 | L-3 | 9 |
| Reuben P., m. Caroline **WATROUS**, b. of Colchester, Apr. 26, 1852, by Geo[rge], W. Pendleton | 3 | 51 |
| Reuben P., m. Caroline **WATROUS**, b. of Colchester, Apr. 26, 1852, by Geo[rge] W. Pendleton | 3 | 52 |
| **DOWD**, Phineas, m. Charlotte **BANNING**, Oct. 30, 1842, by Giles Shattuck, J. P. | 2 | 280 |
| **DOWNE**, Richard H., of Westbrook, Conn., m. Laura J. **ADAMS**, of Colchester, Sept. 21, 1852, by G. W. Pendleton | 3 | 53 |
| **DOWNER**, Bette, d. [Richard & Mercy], b. Oct. 21, 1752 | 1 | 148 |
| **DOWNES, DOWNS**, Hannah, m. James **NEWTON**, Jr., Oct. 14, 1742 | 1 | 137 |
| Sarah A., m. Isaac **HUBBARD**, of Philadelphia, May 5, 1836, by Rev. Lyman Strong | 2 | 284 |
| **DRINKWATER**, Elisha Clauvel **BLISH**, s. of Elizabeth, b. Apr. 18, 1817 | 2 | 77 |
| **DUNHAM**, Betsey, d. [Eleazer & Elizabeth], b. Apr. 7, 1763 | 2 | 42 |
| Deidama, of Hebron, m. Job **CHAMBERLAIN**, of Colchester, Apr. 27, 1756 | 1 | 31 |
| Eleazer, [s. William & Persis], b. Dec. 15, 1742 | 1 | 37 |
| Eleazer, s. [Eleazer & Elizabeth], b. Jan. 2, 1765 | 2 | 42 |
| Esther, [d. William & Persis], b. May 8, 1748 | 1 | 37 |
| Jonathan, [s. William & Persis], b. Jan. 20, 1745 | 1 | 37 |
| Mary, m. Samuell **BROWN**, Aug. 6, 1729 | TPR | 110 |
| Mary, [d. William & Persis], b. Mar. 17, 1754; d. May 13, | | |

| | Vol. | Page |
|---|---|---|
| **DUNHAM**, (cont.) | | |
| 1755 | 1 | 37 |
| Mahitable, m. John **WHITCOM[BE]**, Feb. 15, 1715/16 | L-1 | 444 |
| Obadiah, s. [Obediah & Lucy], b. Nov. 17, 1760 | 1 | 130 |
| Persis, m. William **DUNHAM**, Nov. 10, 1739 | 1 | 37 |
| Persis, [d. William & Persis], b. May 20, 1747 | 1 | 37 |
| Samuel, [s. William & Persis], b. Oct. 10, 1751 | 1 | 37 |
| William, m. Persis **DUNHAM**, Nov. 10, 1739 | 1 | 37 |
| William, [s. William & Persis], b. Sept. 6, 1740 | 1 | 37 |
| William, s. [Eleazer & Elizabeth], b. July 14, 1767 | 2 | 42 |
| **DUTTON**, Amaziah, [s. Timothy & Martha], b. Aug. 27, 1762 | 1 | 48 |
| Ambrose, m. Rhoda E. **OTIS**, Apr. 5, 1830, by Salmon Cone, V. D. M. | 2 | 221 |
| Ambrose, d. Oct. 28, 1841, ae 82 y. | 2 | 67 |
| Martha, [d. Timothy & Martha], b. Jan. 6, 1765 | 1 | 48 |
| Olive, [d. Timothy & Martha], b. Aug. 20, 1769 | 1 | 48 |
| Prudence, w. [Ambrose], d. May 29, 1850, ae 88 | 2 | 67 |
| Rhoda E., w. Ambrose, d. May 9, 1833, ae 26 | 2 | 221 |
| Rhoda Emeline, w. Ambrose, d. of [David & Anna Otis], d. May 9, 1833, in Easton Madison Co., N. Y. | 2 | 95 |
| Russell, m. Harriet **OTIS**, b. of Colchester, May 1, 1849, by Rev. J. R. Arnold | 3 | 41 |
| Timothy Bartholomew, [s. Timothy & Martha], b. June 15, 1774 | 1 | 48 |
| **DYER**, Alpheas B., m. Cordelia **CRUMB**, b. of Westerly, R. I., Oct. 21, 1850, by Rev. Geo[rge] W. Pendleton, at Colchester | 3 | 47 |
| **EATON**, James Howard, s. [James S. & Louisa H.], b. June 21, 1842 | 3 | 2 |
| **EDES**, Betsey, of Colchester, m. Elisha **BECKWITH**, of Waterford, Nov. 8, 1836, by Amhurst D. Scoville, J. P. | 2 | 291 |
| **EDGATON**, Almantha B., m. William P. **COMSTOCK**, b. of Colchester, Apr. 1, 1838, by Rev. Andrew M. Smith | 2 | 193 |
| **EDMUND**, James D., m. Mary E. **SHATTUCK**, Dec. 17, 1849, by Rev. S. D. Jewett, at Westchester | 3 | 45 |
| **EDWARDS**, Justin, m. Lydia **BIGELOW**, d. of Asa & Lydia, Sept. 17, 1817 | 2 | 78 |
| Ruth, b. July 6, 1789; m. Elias **HARVEY**, [ ], 1810 | 2 | 57 |
| **ELDERKIN**, Abby, of Windham, m. William **PERRY**, of Colchester, Nov. 13, 1827, by Salmon Cone, V. D. M. | 2 | 199 |
| George, of Lebanon, m. Esther **LATHAM**, of Colchester, July [ ], 1824, by Salmon Cone, V. D. M. | 2 | 167 |
| **ELLIS**, Elizabeth, d. [John], b. Aug. 6, [ ] | 1 | 58 |
| Erastus, s. [John], b. July 2, 1790 | 2 | 58 |
| Hannah, d. [John], b. Oct. 22, 1784 | 2 | 58 |
| John, s. [John], b. May 11, 1780 | 2 | 58 |
| John, m. [ ] **LORD** | 2 | 58 |
| Lydia, d. [John], b. July 19, 1773 | 2 | 58 |

| | Vol. | Page |
|---|---|---|
| **ELLIS**, (cont.) | | |
| Martha, d. [John], b. Dec. 6, 1774 | 2 | 58 |
| Mary, d. [John], b. Jan. 30, 1775 | 2 | 58 |
| Patience Prentice, d. [John], b. Feb. 14, 1782 | 2 | 58 |
| **ELLSWORTH**, Job, of Colchester, m. Emma **BALCOM**, of Windham, May 8, 1853, by Erastus Dickinson | 3 | 55 |
| Laura, w. Job, d. June 11, 1851, ae 52 | 2 | 67 |
| **ELY, ELEY**, Hephzibah, of Lyme, m. John **PRATT**, of Colchester, May 13, 1771 | 1 | 96 |
| Sarah, m. Jonathan **GILLET**, Jan. 3, 1717 | L-1 | 446 |
| **EMERSON**, Nancy T., of Westchester, m. David B. **WILLIAMS**, of East Haddam, July 4, 1850, in Westchester, by Rev. Stephen F. Lopee, of Hadlyme | 2 | 96 |
| **EMMONS**, Aaron E., m. Mary N. **KELLOGG**, Dec. 26, 1825, by Salmon Cone, V. D. M. | 2 | 182 |
| Albert H., m. Nancy **HOLDCOMB**, of Marlborough, Aug. 10, 1853, by Rev. S. D. Jewett | 3 | 57 |
| Albert Henry, s. [Octavus], b. Mar. 27, 1831 | 2 | 251 |
| Almira Melissa, d. [Octavus], b. Dec. 4, 1828 | 2 | 251 |
| Arphelia L., m. James T. **BURCHAM**, Nov. 28, 1833, by Rev. Joseph Harvey | 2 | 261 |
| Caroline, d. [Aaron E. & Mary N.], b. Sept. 1, 1838 | 2 | 182 |
| Elizabeth, d. [Aaron E. & Mary N.], b. Apr. 21, 1831 | 2 | 182 |
| Elizabeth, of West Chester, m. William **PHELPS**, of Marlborough, Dec. 24, 1850, by Rev. S. D. Hewett, in West Chester | 2 | 101 |
| Ellen, d. [Aaron E. & Mary N.], b. Dec. 1, 1834 | 2 | 182 |
| Emily, d. [Aaron E. & Mary N.], b. Feb. 1, 1829 | 2 | 182 |
| Franklin, of East Haddam, m. Mary E. **BEEBE**, of Colchester, Sept. 7, 1840, by Rev. Daniel G. Sprague | 2 | 210 |
| Henry, s. [Aaron E. & Mary N.], b. Apr. 13, 1827 | 2 | 182 |
| Horace, s. [Aaron E. & Mary N.], b. Jan. 4, 1833 | 2 | 182 |
| John, s. [Aaron E. & Mary N.], b. [ ] | 2 | 182 |
| Julius, s. [Aaron E. & Mary N.], b. Feb. 3, 1837; d. Aug. 16, 1837 | 2 | 182 |
| Justus, s. [Aaron E. & Mary N.], b. Dec. 8, 1840 | 2 | 182 |
| Lydia, m. R[e]uben **FOOT**, June 10, 1787 | 2 | 75 |
| Mary N., w. [Aaron E.], d. [ ] | 2 | 182 |
| Nancy, m. Robert C. **NORTHAM**, b. of Colchester, June 9, 1831, by Rev. Joseph Harvey | 2 | 232 |
| Nancy Jane, d. [Octavus], b. Dec. 8, 1830 | 2 | 251 |
| Nelson, s. [Aaron E. & Mary N.], b. Apr. 13, 1843 | 2 | 182 |
| Phebe E., of Colchester, m. John C. **SNOW**, of Chatham, Dec. 27, 1825, by Jacob Seales, V. D. M., at the house of Dyar Emmons | 2 | 183 |
| Thersa Ann, d. [Octavius], b. Feb. 28, 1833 | 2 | 251 |
| **ENSWORTH**, Lucy, w. Horace, & d. of William & Dimmis **WAY**, d. May 26, 1839, ae 26 | 2 | 151 |

| | Vol. | Page |
|---|---|---|
| **ESTABROOKS**, Jerusha, m. Robert **ROBBINS**, Dec. 5, 1781 | 2 | 82 |
| **EVANS, EVEANS**, Ira P., of Norwich, m. Elizabeth **PERKINS**, of Colchester, Sept. 27, 1842, by Rev. Joel R. Arnold | 2 | 294 |
| Mary Ann, m. Charles M. **QUASH**, b. of Colchester, Mar. 10, 1850, by Rev. Albert F. Park | 2 | 122 |
| William, of Colchester, Conn., m. Mary Ann **THOMPSON**, of Newark, N. Y., Aug. 23, 1843, by Rev. Joel R. Arnold | 3 | 6 |
| **EVERGASON**, Erastus, of Bozrah, m. Lydia **CHAPMAN**, of Colchester, May 9, 1852, by F. W. Bill | 3 | 51 |
| **FALLS**, Eunice, m. Gurdon **HAMILTON**, Mar. 30, 1807; d. Dec. 21, 1831, ae 55 | 2 | 134 |
| **FARWELL**, Asa, of Hartford, m. Eliza **ISHAM**, of Colchester, Oct. 19, 1825, by Salmon Cone, V. D. M. | 2 | 179 |
| **FENNER**, Sarah, m. Jonathan **FOOT**, May 25, 1748 | 1 | 152 |
| Sarah, m. Jonathan **FOOT**, May 25, 1749 | 1 | 130 |
| **FILLEY**, Daniel G., of New York, m. Harriet A. **WATROUS**, of Colchester, [Sept.] 13, 1854, by Rev. S. D. Jewett | 3 | 63 |
| **FILLMORE**, [see also **PHILOMORE**], Abby, w. Ira, d. Aug. 13, 1850, ae 49 | 2 | 153 |
| Ira, m. Prudence **BUTLER**, b. of Colchester, June 15, 1851, by Rev. W[illia]m O. Cady | 2 | 153 |
| Sophia, w. Ira, d. Feb. 5, 1847, ae 47 | 2 | 153 |
| **FINCH**, Henry, s. [Henry & Mary], b. July 26, 1794 | 2 | 61 |
| Henry, m. Mary [ ], from New Hampshire State | 2 | 61 |
| Maria, d. [Henry & Mary], b. Apr. 10, 1792 | 2 | 61 |
| **FINCK**, Francis M., of Ithaca, N. Y., m. Elizabeth **BROOKE**, of Colchester, May 25, 1853, by Rev. Lyman Strong | 3 | 56 |
| **FISH**, Elisha, m. Polly **CHEESEBOROUGH**, of Stonington, Dec. 2, 1804 | 2 | 98 |
| Emeline, m. Warren **TILLOTSON**, b. of Colchester, Sept. 2, 1838, by Rev. Andrew M. Smith | 2 | 180 |
| **FISK**, Lavinia F., m. Noah W. **POM[E]ROY**, Sept. 14, 1812 (Perhaps "**FISH**") | 2 | 137 |
| Mary, b. Jan. 11, 1783, in Bozrah; m. Ira **HOLMES**, Oct. 16, 1803 | 2 | 124 |
| **FLOOD**, Loren, m. Eliza Ann **BIGELOW**, Aug. 29, 1835, by Rev. Joseph Harvey | 2 | 281 |
| **FLOWER**, David, m. Fanny **WHIPPLE**, Nov. 23, 1825, by Salmon Cone, V. D. M. | 2 | 180 |
| **FOGG**, William, of Greenfield, Penn., m. Nabby **HAZARD**, of Colchester, Nov. 18, 1821, by Salmon Cone, V. D. M. | 2 | 326 |
| **FOOT, FOOTE**, Aaron, [s. Nath[anie]l, Jr. & Patience], b. Mar. 10, 1744 | 1 | 107 |
| Aaron, m. Mary **ISHAM**, Jan. 3, 1774; d. July 13, 1824 | 2 | 4 |
| Aaron, s. [Aaron & Mary], b. May 16, 1781 | 2 | 4 |
| Abigail, d. [Israel & Elizabeth], b. Mar. 13, 1757 | 1 | 151 |
| Abigail, m. Nathaniel **FOOT**, Jr., Jan. 31, 1791 | 1 | 96 |

| | Vol. | Page |
|---|---|---|
| **FOOT, FOOTE**, (cont.) | | |
| Abigail, d. [Joel & Abigail **ROBBINS**], b. Dec. 15, 1792 | 2 | 56 |
| Abigail, [d. Nathaniel, Jr. & Abigail], b. June 26, 1798 | 1 | 96 |
| Abigail, m. Alfred J. **LOOMIS**, b. of West Chester, Apr. 6, 1826, by Jacob Seales, V. D.M., at the house of Nathaniel Foote | 2 | 186 |
| Abigail **ROBBINS**, [w. Joel], d. Jan. 8, 1795 | 2 | 56 |
| Adonijah, m. Grace **DAY**, Oct. 24, 1754 | 1 | 122 |
| Addonijah, s. [Adonijah & Grace], b. Mar. 26, 1760 | 1 | 122 |
| Albert, of Colchester, m. Mary Ann **CHASE**, of Amherst, Mass., Nov. 11, 1831, by Rev. W[illia]m O. Cady | 2 | 212 |
| Alfred, s. [Stephen & Hannah], b. Dec. 8, 1787 | 2 | 56 |
| Allithear, [d. Josiah & Sarah], b. July 17, 1744 | 1 | 35 |
| Amasa, s. [Aaron & Mary], b. July 7, 179[ ] | 2 | 4 |
| Amasa, m. Lydia **TRACY**, Mar. 5, 1820 | 2 | 252 |
| Ambross, [s. Joseph & Ann], b. Apr. 3, 1723 | L-1 | 444 |
| Ambrose, m. Ann **FOOT**, Dec. 13, 1781 | 2 | 31 |
| Amelia, d. [Roger & Eunice], b. July 15, 1801 | 2 | 51 |
| Ann, d. [Nath[anie]ll & Ann], b. Aug. 25, 1715 | 1 | 117 |
| An[n], [d. Nathaniel & Ann], b. Aug. 26, 1715 | L-1 | 799 |
| Ann, w. [Nath[anie]ll], d. June 25, 1726 | 1 | 117 |
| Ann, [d. Nath[anie]l, Jr. & Patience], b. Aug. 1, 1739 | 1 | 107 |
| Ann, m. Isaac **DAY**, July 3, 1740 | 1 | 115 |
| Ann, d. [Daniel & Margarett], b. Apr. 11, 1754 | 1 | 134 |
| Ann, m. Joshua **BAYLEY**, Apr. 6, 1758 | 1 | 57 |
| Ann, m. Ambrose **FOOT**, Dec. 13, 1781 | 2 | 31 |
| Anna, m. Samuel **BRIDGES**, Sept. 10, 1752 | 1 | 49 |
| Anne, m. Edmund **BRIDGES**, Mar. 20, 1784; d. Feb. 23, 1842, ae 80, at Genessee, N. Y. | 2 | 90 |
| Asa, s. [Nath[anie]ll & Ann], b. May 4, 1726 | 1 | 117 |
| Asa, m. Jerusha **CARTER**, Apr. 26, 1752 | 1 | 149 |
| Asa, s. [Asa & Jerusha], b. May 1, 1753; d. [ ] | 1 | 149 |
| Asa, s. [Nath[anie]ll, Jr.], b. Jan. 31, 1785 | 2 | 29 |
| Asa, s. [Joel & Abigail Robbins], b. Apr. 26, 1791; d. Nov. 24, 1791 | 2 | 56 |
| Asa, s. [Joel & Rachel], b. Mar. 20, 1798 | 2 | 56 |
| Asa, d. May 11, 1799 | 1 | 149 |
| Betsey, m. James Harvey **PEASE**, b. of Colchester, Nov. 21, 1824, by Salmon Cone, V. D. M. | 2 | 171 |
| Betty, b. Jan. 17, 1752; m. Joseph **FOOT**, Apr. 3, 1777 | 2 | 183 |
| Betty, d. [Joseph & Betty], b. Jan. 24, 1780 | 2 | 183 |
| Calvin, s. [Joseph & Betty], b. Mar. 1, 1790 | 2 | 183 |
| Caroline, d. [Roger & Eunice], b. Sept. 7, 1806 | 2 | 51 |
| Carter, s. [Roger & Eunice], b. June 10, 1804 | 2 | 51 |
| Catharine, [d. Josiah], b. Apr. 13, 1733 | 1 | 128 |
| Catharine, m. Daniel **ISHAM**, July 14, 1756 | 1 | 148 |
| Charles, [s. Nathaniel & Ann], b. Dec. 16, 1718 | L-1 | 799 |
| Charles, [s. Nath[anie]ll & Ann], b. Dec. 26, 1718; | | |

| | Vol. | Page |
|---|---|---|
| **FOOT, FOOTE**, (cont.) | | |
| d. June 15, 1719 | 1 | 117 |
| Charles, 2d, s. [Nath[anie]ll & Ann], b. Nov. 10, 1723 | 1 | 117 |
| Charles, m. Jerusha **CHAMBERLAIN**, Oct. [ ], 1750 | 1 | 137 |
| Charles, s. [Charles & Jerusha], b. June 5, 1753 | 1 | 137 |
| Charles, Jr., m. Sarah **DAY**, Dec. 17, 1778 | 2 | 31 |
| Charles, s. [Charles, Jr. & Sarah], b. Feb. 4, 1781 | 2 | 31 |
| Charles had slave Judah, d. Hagor, b. Dec. 25, 1787; Beulah, d. Hager, b. Feb. 20, 1775. Entered Aug. 6, 1811 | 2 | 325 |
| Charles, d. Aug. 25, 1795 | 1 | 137 |
| Charles, s. [Jeremiah & Jerusha], b. Aug. 20, 1796 | 2 | 93 |
| Charles, s. [Roger & Eunice], b. July 1, 1817 | 2 | 51 |
| Charles, m. Esther **TAYLOR**, b. of Colchester, Nov. 22, 1820, by Salmon Cone, V. D. M. | 2 | 97 |
| C[h]loe, d. [Charles & Jerusha], b. June 5, 1764 | 1 | 137 |
| Clarissa Pamelia, d. [Jeremiah & Jerusha], b. May 26, 1800 | 2 | 93 |
| Dan, s. [Nath[anie]l, Jr. & Patience], b. Aug. 16, 1755 | 1 | 107 |
| Dan F., m. Eliza A. **FOOTE**, May 12, 1836, by Rev. Joel R. Arnold | 2 | 286 |
| Dan T., m. Lucretia **KELLOGG**, b. of Colchester, Jan. 31, 1841, by Rev. Lyman Strong | 2 | 286 |
| Dan Taylor, s. Joseph, Jr. & Clarissa, b. Feb. 27, 1808 | 2 | 96 |
| Daniell, [s. Nathaniel & Ann], b. Feb. 6, 1716/17 | L-1 | 799 |
| Daniel, s. [Nath[anie]ll & Ann], b. Feb. 6, 1716/17 | 1 | 117 |
| Daniel, m. Margarett **PARSONS**, June 9, 1743 | 1 | 134 |
| Daniel, s. [Daniel & Margarett], b. June 21, 1744 | 1 | 134 |
| Daniel, m. Mary **SKINNER**, July 31, 1766 | 1 | 134 |
| Daniel, s. [Stephen & Hannah], b. Sept. 23, 1789; d. Oct. 8, 1815, ae 26, in Westfield, Mass. | 2 | 56 |
| Dan[ie]l, s. [Aaron & Mary], b. Aug. 9, 179[ ] | 2 | 4 |
| Dan[iel], s. [Amasa & Lydia], b. Mar. 26, 1824 | 2 | 252 |
| David, [s. Josiah], b. Feb. 24, 1718 | 1 | 128 |
| David, s. [Jonathan & Sarah], b. Sept. 4, 1760 | 1 | 130 |
| David, s. [Asa & Jerusha], b. Oct. 5, 1760; d. Aug. 1, 1793 | 1 | 149 |
| David, [s. Nathaniel, Jr. & Abigail], b. Apr. 22, 1796 | 1 | 96 |
| David, s. [Roger & Eunice], b. Aug. 15, 1809 | 2 | 51 |
| David, m. Dorothy **SHATTUCK**, b. of Colchester, May 28, 1828, by Rev. Joseph Harvey | 2 | 203 |
| David, of Marlborough, m. Caroline B. **TAYLOR**, of Colchester, Apr. 17, 1831, by Rev. Lyman Strong | 2 | 230 |
| David Yoemans, s. [Noah B. & Sophia], b. Aug. 27, 1802 | 2 | 102 |
| Deborah, d. [Adonijah & Grace], b. Apr. 24, 1774 | 1 | 122 |
| Delight, [d. Josiah & Sarah], b. Aug. 11, 1741 | 1 | 35 |
| Dolly Olmstead, d. [Roger & Eunice], b. Mar. 3, 1797 | 2 | 51 |
| Dorothy, m. John **ISHAM**, Dec. 19, 1751 | 1 | 114 |
| Dorothy, d. [Aaron & Mary], b. Dec. 28, 1774 | 2 | 4 |
| Dorothy, m. James **OTIS**, Nov. 18, 1792; d. Feb. 24, 1849, | | |

| | Vol. | Page |
|---|---|---|
| **FOOT, FOOTE**, (cont.) | | |
| ae 74 | 2 | 64 |
| Dyer, s. [Aaron & Mary], b. July 29, 178[ ] | 2 | 4 |
| Dyar, s. [Amasa & Lydia], b. Nov. 24, 1830 | 2 | 252 |
| Ebenezer, s. [Daniel & Margarett], b. Apr. 12, 1756 | 1 | 134 |
| Edwin, s. [Joel & Rachel], b. Nov. 15, 1799 | 2 | 56 |
| Edwin Tracy, s. [Amasa & Lydia], b. Nov. 21, 1832 | 2 | 252 |
| Eli, s. [Daniel & Margarett], b. Oct. 30, 1747 | 1 | 134 |
| Eli, s. [Stephen & Hannah], b. May 7, 1793 | 2 | 56 |
| Elias, s. [Charles & Jerusha], b. Oct. 4, 1766 | 1 | 137 |
| Elisha, s. [Charles & Jerusha], b. Jan. 10, 1757 | 1 | 137 |
| Eliza, d. [Hosea & Sally], b. Mar. 20, 1807 | 2 | 127 |
| Eliza A., m. Dan F. **FOOTE**, May 12, 1836, by Rev. Joel R. Arnold | 2 | 286 |
| Eliza Lydia, d. [Noah B. & Sophia], b. Nov. 19, 1799 | 2 | 102 |
| Elizabeth, d. [Nath[anie]ll & Ann], b. Feb. 15, 1722 | 1 | 117 |
| Elizabeth, d. [Israel & Elizabeth], b. May 29, 1750 | 1 | 151 |
| Elizabeth, m. Rev. David **HUNTINGTON**, Nov. 5, 1778; d. Oct. 25, 1845, ae 95 y. 4 m. 15 d. | 2 | 18 |
| Elizabeth C., of Colchester, m. W[illia]m H. **BILL**, of Norwich, Jan. 1, 1845, by Rev. Robert Allyn | 3 | 19 |
| Emily, d. [Joel & Rachel], b. Apr. 25, 1805 | 2 | 56 |
| Enos, s. [Jeremiah & Jerusha], b. May 6, 1794 | 2 | 93 |
| Epaphroditus, s. [Adonijah & Grace], b. Sept. 14, 1769 | 1 | 122 |
| Ephreaim, m. Sarah **CHAMBERLIN**, June [ ], 1708 | L-1 | 453 |
| Ephreaim, [s. Ephreaim & Sarah], b. Apr. 27, 1716 | L-1 | 453 |
| Ephraim, d. June 10, 1765 | 1 | 121 |
| Ephraim, s. [Adonijah & Grace], b. Aug. 1, 1765 | 1 | 122 |
| Esther, [d. Nath[anie]l, Jr. & Patience], b. Apr. 13, 1748 | 1 | 107 |
| [E]uniss, m. Micaiell **TAINTOR**, Dec. 3, 1712 | L-1 | 451 |
| Eunice, [d. Josiah], b. Sept. 26, 1716 | 1 | 128 |
| Eunice, m. Josiah **TREADWAY**, May 13, 1735 | 1 | 94 |
| Eunice, d. [Charles & Jerusha], b. Mar. 13, 1759 | 1 | 137 |
| Eunice, b. Nov. 29, 1766; m. Ezra **CLARK**, 2d, Nov. 24, 1785; d. Aug. 1, 1851, ae 84 y. 8 m. | 2 | 92 |
| Eunice, m. William **HALL**, Aug. 12, 1787 | 2 | 73 |
| Eunice, d. [Roger & Eunice], b. May 12, 1791 | 2 | 51 |
| Eunice, w. Roger, d. Jan. 22, 1846, ae 74 | 2 | 51 |
| Eunice A., of Colchester, m. Lyman A. **LORING**, of Great Barrington, Mass., Nov. 28, 1849, by Rev. Alpheas Geer, of East Haddam | 3 | 43 |
| Ezra, s. [Asa & Jerusha], b. Aug. 22, 1759; d. [ ] | 1 | 149 |
| Ezra, s. [Roger & Eunice], b. Oct. 30, 1792; d. July 29, 1793 | 2 | 51 |
| Ezra, 2d, s. [Roger & Eunice], b. Jan. 7, 1795 | 2 | 51 |
| Fenner, s. [Jonathan & Sarah], b. Oct. 5, 1754 | 1 | 130 |
| Freelove, d. [Jonathan & Sarah], b. Mar. 11, 1749 | 1 | 152 |
| Freelove, d. [Jonathan & Sarah], b. Mar. 11, 1750 | 1 | 130 |
| Gad C., m. Mary **FOOTE**, Feb. 27, 1828, by Salmon Cone, | | |

| | Vol. | Page |
|---|---|---|
| **FOOT, FOOTE**, (cont.) | | |
| V. D. M. | 2 | 201 |
| George, s. [Joel & Rachel], b. Oct. 5, 1801; d. Oct. 7, 1801 | 2 | 56 |
| George, s. [Joel & Rachel], b. Nov. 22, 1802 | 2 | 56 |
| Grace, d. [Adonijah & Grace], b. Dec. 19, 1763 | 1 | 122 |
| Grace, w. Adonijah, d. Mar. 16, 1776 | 1 | 122 |
| Habbakah, [s. Josiah], b. Jan. 27, 1722/3 (Arnold Copy says "Hubbard") | 1 | 128 |
| Hannah, d. [Nath[anie]ll & Ann], b. Apr. 17, 1720 | 1 | 117 |
| Hannah, d. [Jared & Hannah], b. Nov. 19, 1754 | 1 | 150 |
| Hannah, m. Gibbons **MATHER**, Jan. 28, 1789 | 2 | 60 |
| Hannah, [w. Stephen], d. Jan. 20, 1848, ae 82 | 2 | 56 |
| Henry, of Great Barrington, Mass., m. Jane **FOOTE**, of Colchester, Oct. 27, 1842, by Rev. Alpheas Geer, of Hebron | 2 | 268 |
| Henry, m. Mary A. **LAMB**, b. of Colchester, Jan. 13, 1850, by Rev. Lyman Strong | 3 | 45 |
| Horace, s. [Roger & Eunice], b. Mar. 21, 1799 | 2 | 51 |
| Horace, m. Lucy A. **WEBSTER**, b. of Colchester, Oct. 10, 1849, by Rev. G. W. Pendleton | 3 | 42 |
| Hosea, m. Sally **BULKELEY**, Nov. 6, 1798 | 2 | 127 |
| Hosea, s. [Hosea & Sally], b. Apr. 23, 1800 | 2 | 127 |
| Hubbard, [s. Josiah], b. Jan. 27, 1722/3 (See Habbakah) | 1 | 128 |
| Huldah, [d. Nathaniel, 3d, & Jerusha], b. Dec. 15, 1769 | 1 | 96 |
| Huldah, [d. Nathaniel, Jr. & Abigail], b. Dec. 4, 1791 | 1 | 96 |
| Huldah, m. Amaziah **BRAINARD**, b. of Colchester, Mar. 29, 1824, by Rev. Jacob Seales, at the house of Nathaniel Foot; d. Aug. 9, 1881, ae 79 y. 9 m. | 2 | 162 |
| Irena, m. Abraham **DAY**, Nov. 20, 1740 | 1 | 123 |
| Isaac, [s. Daniel & Margarett], b. Jan. 4, 1744/5 | 1 | 134 |
| Isaac, [s. Daniel & Margarett], b. Jan. 4, 1745/6 | 1 | 134 |
| Isaac, m. Mary **KELLOGG**, May 31, 1768 | 1 | 137 |
| Israel, [s. Nathaniel & Ann], b. Oct. 16, 1713 | L-1 | 799 |
| Israel, s. [Nath[anie]ll & Ann], b. Oct. 16, 1713 | 1 | 117 |
| Israel, m. Elizabeth **KIMBERLEY**, Dec. 28, 1748 | 1 | 151 |
| Israel, s. [Israel & Elizabeth], b. Jan. 30, 1755 | 1 | 151 |
| Israel, Jr., m. Sarah **OTIS**, b. of Colchester, Nov. 5, 1778 | 2 | 20 |
| Israel, [s. Nathaniel, Jr. & Abigail], b. May 29, 1794 | 1 | 96 |
| Jane, of Colchester, m. Henry **FOOTE**, of Great Barrington, Mass., Oct. 27, 1842, by Rev. Alpheas Geer, of Hebron | 2 | 268 |
| Jared, s. [Nath[anie]ll & Mercy], b. Aug. 28, 1728 | 1 | 117 |
| Jared, m. Hannah **BUEL**, Oct. 18, 1753 | 1 | 150 |
| Jared, s. [Jared & Hannah], b. Apr. 5, 1763 | 1 | 150 |
| Jeremiah, [s. Joseph & Ann], b. Oct. 11, 1725 | L-1 | 444 |
| Jeremiah, m. Jerusha **TAYLOR**, Oct. 16, 1791 | 2 | 93 |
| Jeremiah, s. [Jeremiah & Jerusha], b. Aug. 3, 1792 | 2 | 93 |
| Jerusha, [d. Josiah & Sarah], b. June 4, 1739 | 1 | 35 |
| Jerusha, d. [Asa & Jerusha], b. Feb. 24, 1755;d. May 30, 1793 | 1 | 149 |

| | Vol. | Page |
|---|---|---|
| **FOOT, FOOTE**, (cont.) | | |
| Jerusha, d. [Charles & Jerusha], b. Mar. 2, 1755 | 1 | 137 |
| Jerusha, d. Nath[anie]ll, Jr., b. Apr. 3, 1781 | 2 | 29 |
| Jerusha, w. Charles, d. Apr. 10, 1782 | 1 | 137 |
| Jerusha, d. [Joel & Abigail Robbins], b. Jan. 4, 1789 | 2 | 56 |
| Jesse, s. Adonijah, b. Dec. 25, 1756 | 1 | 50 |
| Jesse, s. [Adonijah & Grace], b. Dec. 25, 1756 | 1 | 122 |
| Jirah Tracy, s. [Amasa & Lydia], b. Oct. 10, 1825 | 2 | 252 |
| Joel, s. [Asa & Jerusha], b. June 26, 1763 | 1 | 149 |
| Joel, m. Abigail Robbins **LORD**, Oct. 28, 1787 | 2 | 56 |
| Joel, m. Rachel **LORD**, of East Haddam, Nov. 15, 1795; d. July 12, 1846, ae 83 | 2 | 56 |
| John, [s. Josiah], b. Aug. 15, 1728 | 1 | 128 |
| John, s. [Daniel & Margarett], b. Feb. 17, 1760 | 1 | 134 |
| Jonathan, [s. Josiah], b. Mar. 23, 1715 | 1 | 128 |
| Jonathan, m. Sarah **FENNER**, May 25, 1748 | 1 | 152 |
| Jonathan, m. Sarah **FENNER**, May 25, 1749 | 1 | 130 |
| Jonathan, s. [Jonathan & Sarah], b. Mar. 30, 1752 | 1 | 130 |
| Joseph, m. Ann **CLOTHER**, Dec. 12, 1719 | L-1 | 444 |
| Joseph, [s. Josiah], b. May 12, 1721 | 1 | 128 |
| Joseph, b. Oct. 26, 1755; m. Betty **FOOT**, Apr. 3, 1777 | 2 | 183 |
| Joseph, s. [Joseph & Betty], b. Nov. 18, 1777;d. Jan. 10, 1814 | 2 | 183 |
| Josiah, [s. Josiah], b. July 28, 1713 | 1 | 128 |
| Josiah, m. Sarah **CHAMBERLAIN**, Dec. 7, 1738 | 1 | 35 |
| Julia, m. Julius **FREEMAN**, July 31, 1823, by Salmon Cone, V. D. M. | 2 | 139 |
| Justin, s. [Daniel & Margarett], b. July 31, 1762 | 1 | 134 |
| Linus, s. [Roger & Eunice], b. July 12, 1813 | 2 | 51 |
| Lois, d. [Charles & Jerusha], b. Apr. 22, 1751 | 1 | 137 |
| Lois, d. [Joseph & Betty], b. Nov. 5, 1785; d. Jan. 30, 1816 | 2 | 183 |
| Louis, m. Dan **WORTHINGTON**, [ ], 1772 | 2 | 7 |
| Louisa, d. [Aaron & Mary], b. June 18, 178[ ]; d. June 7, 178[ ] | 2 | 4 |
| Lucinda, d. [Nath[anie]ll, Jr.], b. Apr. 24, 1788 | 2 | 29 |
| Lucy, d. [Nath[anie]l, Jr. & Patience], b. July 28, 1750 | 1 | 107 |
| Lucy, d. [Jared & Hannah], b. Dec. 6, 1767 | 1 | 150 |
| Lucy, d. [Joseph & Betty], b. May 2, 1784; d. Oct. 13, 1784 | 2 | 183 |
| Lucy, 2d, d. [Joseph & Betty], b. Mar. 27, 1795 | 2 | 183 |
| Lucy, d. [Aaron & Mary], b. July 18, 179[ ] | 2 | 4 |
| Lucy, of Colchester, m. Merit **BRADFORD**, of Canterbury, Feb. 28, 1821, by Salmon Cone, V. D. M. | 2 | 109 |
| Lucy Maria, d. [Amasa & Lydia], b. May 1, 1822; d. July 14, 1894 | 2 | 252 |
| Lydia, d. [Ruben & Lydia], b. Dec. 27, 1792 | 2 | 75 |
| Margarit, [d. Ephreaim & Sarah], b. May 13, 1711 | L-1 | 453 |
| Margaret, m. Benjamin **DAY**, Mar. 6, 1729 | TPR | 110 |
| Margaret, [d. Nath[anie]l, Jr. & Patience], b. May 7, 1746 | 1 | 107 |
| Margaret, [d. Daniel & Margarett], b. May 31, 1749; | | |

| | Vol. | Page |
|---|---|---|
| **FOOT, FOOTE**, (cont.) | | |
| d. Dec. 14, 1751 | 1 | 134 |
| Margarett, [d. Daniel & Margarett], b. May 24, 1752 | 1 | 134 |
| Margaret, w. Daniel, d. July 6, 1765 | 1 | 134 |
| Margaret, m. Azariah **BIGELOW**, Mar. 26, 1767 | 1 | 128 |
| Margaret, d. [Aaron & Mary], b. Mar. 19, 1779 | 2 | 4 |
| Margaret, m. Daniel **TAYLOR**, Oct. 28, 1792; d. Nov. 6, 1843, ae 68 | 2 | 90 |
| Margaret Parsons, d. [Isaac & Mary], b. Dec. 29, 1771 | 1 | 137 |
| Marina, d. [Roger & Eunice], b. Jan. 16, 1812; d. Apr. 16, 1812 | 2 | 51 |
| Martha, [d. Daniel & Margarett], b. Jan. 27, 1750/51 | 1 | 134 |
| Martha, m. John **BARNEY**, Dec. 8, 1768 | 1 | 39 |
| Mary, [d. Josiah], b. May 22, 1726 | 1 | 128 |
| Mary, m. Jonas **WILDE**, Oct. 10, 1748 | 1 | 152 |
| Mary, d. [Israel & Elizabeth], b. Apr. 3, 1752 | 1 | 151 |
| Mary, d. [Nath[anie]l, Jr. & Patience], b. Jan. 8, 1753 | 1 | 107 |
| Mary, d. [Isaac & Mary], b. Feb. 27, 1769 | 1 | 137 |
| Mary, m. Stephen **SKINNER**, Oct. 17, 1775 | 2 | 9 |
| Mary, m. Stephen **SKINNER**, Oct. 17, 1775; d. Apr. 14, 1785, ae 33 | 2 | 59 |
| Mary, m. Nath[anie]ll **OTIS**, b. of Colchester, Nov. 5, 1778; d. Nov. 14, 1837, in New London | 2 | 18 |
| Mary, d. [Jeremiah & Jerusha], b. Apr. 21, 1806 | 2 | 93 |
| Mary, m. Gad C. **FOOTE**, Feb. 27, 1828, by Salmon Cone, V. D. M. | 2 | 201 |
| Mary, d. [David & Dorothy], b. Jan. 10, 1847 | 2 | 203 |
| Mercy, d. [Jared & Hannah], b. July 3, 1760 | 1 | 150 |
| Molly, d. [Aaron & Mary], b. Jan. 13, 1777 | 2 | 4 |
| Nath[anie]ll, s. Nath[anie]ll, b. Sept. 9, 1682 | 1 | 117 |
| Nathaniel, m. Ann **CLARK**, July 4, 1711 | L-1 | 799 |
| Nathaniell, m. Ann **CLARK**, July 4, 1711 | L-3 | 198 |
| Nath[anie]l, m. Ann **CLARK**, July 4, 1711 | TM-1 | 198 |
| Nath[anie]ll, m. Ann **PARK**, Sept.[ ], 1711 | 1 | 117 |
| Nathaniell, [s. Nathaniel & Ann], b. May 28, 1712 | L-1 | 799 |
| Nath[anie]ll, s. [Nath[anie]ll & Ann], b. May 28, 1712 | 1 | 117 |
| Nath[anie]ll, m. Mercy **HEECOCK**, wid. of Joseph, of Durham, Sept. 13, 1727 | 1 | 117 |
| Nath[anie]l, Jr., m. Patience **GATES**, Apr. 15, 1736 | 1 | 107 |
| Nath[anie]l, [s. Nath[anie]l, Jr. & Patience], b. Feb. 7, 1742 | 1 | 107 |
| Nathaniel, 3d, m. Jerusha **CADWELL**, of Hartford, Mar. 28, 1769 | 1 | 96 |
| Nath[anie]ll, d. Aug. 20, 1774, ae 92 | 1 | 117 |
| Nathaniel, Jr., m. Abigail **FOOT**, Jan. 31, 1791 | 1 | 96 |
| Nathaniel, d. Jan. 22, 1829 | 1 | 107 |
| Nathaniel, s. [David & Dorothy], b. Aug. 8, 1831 | 2 | 203 |
| Nathaniel, 3d, m. Patience **SKINNER**, [ ] | 1 | 96 |
| Noah, m. Esther **KELLOGG**, Apr. 18, 1768 | 1 | 143 |

| | Vol. | Page |
|---|---|---|
| **FOOT, FOOTE,** (cont.) | | |
| Noah B., m. Sophia **YOEMANS**, [ ] | 2 | 102 |
| Olive, m. Daniel **HUBBARD**, Sept. 26, 1805 | 2 | 108 |
| Patience, d. [Nath[anie]l, Jr. & Patience], b. June 17, 1737 | 1 | 107 |
| Patience, d. [Nath[anie]ll, Jr.], b. Feb. 1, 1783 | 2 | 29 |
| Patience, w. Nathaniel, d. Mar. 12, 1790 | 1 | 96 |
| Patience, m. William **BRAINARD**, Oct. 31, 1799, by Justin Day. Recorded Jan. 31, 1829 | 2 | 211 |
| Prudence, d. [Joseph & Betty], b. May 8, 1788 | 2 | 183 |
| Rachel, [s. Joel], d. Oct. 6, 1843, ae 73 | 2 | 56 |
| Rachel Lord, d. [Joel & Rachel], b. Jan. 25, 1809; d. May 5, 1809 | 2 | 56 |
| Ralph, of Colchester, m. Nancy **FREEMAN**, of Hebron, July 5, 1835, by Rev. W. F. Vail | 2 | 278 |
| Renny, s. [Jeremiah & Jerusha], b. Aug. 26, 1798 | 2 | 93 |
| Reuben, s. [Adonijah & Grace], b. Nov. 8, 1761 | 1 | 122 |
| R[e]uben, m. Lydia **EMMONS**, June 10, 1787 | 2 | 75 |
| Reuben M., of Great Barrington, Mass., m. Nancy M. **JOHNSON**, of Colchester, Nov. 29, 1849, by Rev. John Avery, of Exeter | 3 | 44 |
| Robbins, s. [Joel & Abigail Robbins], b. Jan. 4, 1795; d. Jan. 12, 1795 | 2 | 56 |
| Roger, s. [Asa & Jerusha], b. June 9, 1765 | 1 | 149 |
| Roger, b. June 9, 1765; m. Eunice **BULKELEY**, May 26, 1790; d. June 10, 1823 | 2 | 51 |
| Russell, s. [Charles & Jerusha], b. Dec. 29, 1769 | 1 | 137 |
| Sally, w. Hosea, d. June 20, 1817, ae 49 | 2 | 127 |
| Sally Isham, d. [Stephen & Hannah], b. May 4, 1791 | 2 | 56 |
| Salmon, s. [Joseph & Betty], b. Mar. 6, 1792 | 2 | 183 |
| Samuel Phillips Lord, s. [Joel & Rachel], b. Aug. 10, 1811; d. Sept. 30, 1812 | 2 | 56 |
| Sarah, [d. Ephreaim & Sarah], b. Oct. 20, 1713 | L-1 | 453 |
| Sarah, [d. Josiah], b. Jan. 28, 1730/31 | 1 | 128 |
| Sarah, [d. Josiah & Sarah], b. June 15, 1746; d. Nov. 7, 1747 | 1 | 35 |
| Sarah, 2d, [d. Josiah & Sarah], b. Apr. 11, 1748 | 1 | 35 |
| Sarah, d. [Jonathan & Sarah], b. Jan. 12, 1758 | 1 | 130 |
| Sarah, d. [Adonijah & Grace], b. Mar. 3, 1767 | 1 | 122 |
| Sarah, d. [Israel, Jr. & Sarah], b. Aug. 2, 1779 | 2 | 20 |
| Sarah, d. [Charles, Jr. & Sarah], b. Sept. 17, 1779 | 2 | 31 |
| Sarah, w. Israel, Jr., d. Oct. 1, 1781 | 2 | 20 |
| Sarah, m. Cyrus W. **COOKE**, Mar. 9, 1851, by Rev. W[illia]m Worland, of Hebron | 3 | 47 |
| Sarah A., of Colchester, m. Stephen **TRACY**, of Franklin, Feb. 25, 1824, by Rev. William Palmer, at the house of Solomon Scoville | 2 | 162 |
| Solomon B., m. Lucinda **RIDER**, b. of Colchester, June 27, 1847, by Rev. Seawell Lamberton | 3 | 33 |
| Solomon Bulkeley, s. [Hosea & Sally], b. Aug. 26, 1802 | 2 | 127 |

| | Vol. | Page |
|---|---|---|
| **FOOT, FOOTE**, (cont.) | | |
| Sophia, d. [Joseph & Betty], b. Mar. 24, 1781; d. Feb. 13, 1782 | 2 | 183 |
| Sophia, d. [Joseph & Betty], b. Oct. 21, 1782 | 2 | 183 |
| Sophia, m. Oliver **BULKELEY**, Nov. 2, 1797 | 2 | 75 |
| Sophia, d. [Hosea & Sally], b. Sept. 8, 1804 | 2 | 127 |
| Sophia J., of Colchester, m. Jedediah A. **POST**, of Hebron, May 31, 1843, by Rev. Henry Forbush | 3 | 5 |
| Stephen, s. [Daniel & Margarett], b. Jan. 10, 1758 | 1 | 134 |
| Stephen, of Colchester, m. Hannah **WATERMAN**, of Bozrah, Nov. 16, 1786; d. Mar. 26, 1843, ae 85 | 2 | 56 |
| Susanna Waterman, d. [Stephen & Hannah], b. Aug. 18, 1796 | 2 | 56 |
| Tabitha, d. [Adonijah & Grace], b. Mar. 16, 1776 | 1 | 122 |
| Walter, twin with We[a]lthy, [s. Joseph & Thankfull], b. May 12, 1755 | 1 | 44 |
| We[a]lthy, twin with Walter, [d. Joseph & Thankfull], b. May 12, 1755 | 1 | 44 |
| William, s. [Charles & Jerusha], b. Aug. 4, 1772 | 1 | 137 |
| William Henry, s. [Stephen & Hannah], b. Dec. 20, 1794 | 2 | 56 |
| William Lord, s. [Joel & Rachel], b. Mar. 27, 1807 | 2 | 56 |
| -----, twin s. Josiah & Sarah, b. Jan. [ ], 1751; d. Jan. [ ], 1751 | 1 | 35 |
| -----, st. b. [s. Josiah & Sarah], b. Jan. [ ], 1752 | 1 | 35 |
| -----, [s. Nathaniel, 3d, & Patience], d. Mar. 12, 1790 | 1 | 96 |
| **FORD**, Alma E., m. Alfred **OTIS**, b. of Colchester, Jan. 14, 1851, by Rev. Lyman Strong | 2 | 238 |
| Daniel, s. [Mathew, Jr. & Ruth], b. Feb. 16, 1737/8 | 1 | 129 |
| Lucius E., of Colchester, m. Ann J. **WESTCOTT**, of New Haven, Apr. 6, 1849, by Rev. G. W. Pendleton | 3 | 39 |
| Mat[t]hew, Jr., of Hebron, m. Ruth **PALMETER**, of Colchester, Mar. 29, 1737 | 1 | 129 |
| **FO[R]SYTH**, James, of Groton, m. Lucy **COATS**, of Colchester, Feb. 16, 1804, by John R. Watrous, J. P. | 2 | 176 |
| **FOSTER**, Mary Anne, [w. Theodore], d. Mar. 29, 1843, ae 25 | 2 | 66 |
| Sarah, d. Jeremiah, b. June 2, 1748 | 1 | 148 |
| Theodore, of Smithfield, R. I., m. Mary Anne **GRAVES**, of Colchester, Aug. 16, 1840, by Henry Worthington, J. P. | 2 | 66 |
| Theodore, m. Lucretia **CARTER**, b. of Colchester, Mar. 30, [1845], by Rev. Robert Allyn | 3 | 21 |
| William, of New Milford, Conn., m. Amanda **YEAPON**, of Colchester, July 8, 1849, by Augustus W. Lord, J. P. | 3 | 41 |
| **FOWLER**, Anna, of Lebanon, m. David **OTIS**, of Colchester, Nov. 25, 1802 | 2 | 95 |
| Stephen M., of Lebanon, m. Elizabeth G. **CHAMBERLAIN**, of Colchester, Oct. 20, 1844, by Rev. Joel R. Arnold | 3 | 17 |
| **FOX**, Almira, of East Haddam, m. Joseph **SMITH**, of Colchester, Mar. 29, 1824, by Salmon Cone, V. D. M. | 2 | 165 |

| | Vol. | Page |
|---|---|---|
| **FOX**, (cont.) | | |
| Almira, m. Nathaniel **COMSTOCK**, b. of Colchester, Apr. 1, 1840, by Rev. Joel R. Arnold | 2 | 214 |
| Anna, d. Isaac, d. Nov. 14, 1736 | 1 | 126 |
| Betsey, d. [John & Mehetable], b. May 20, 1789 | 2 | 58 |
| Daniel, s. [John & Mehetable], b. Nov. 5, 1778 | 2 | 58 |
| Deborah, of Norwich, m. James **SAXTON**, of Colchester, Nov. 17, 1770 | 1 | 37 |
| Deborah, of Norwich, m. James **SAXTON**, of Colchester, June 27, 1770 | 2 | 5 |
| Dimmis, d. [John & Mehetable], b. Apr. 20, 1787 | 2 | 58 |
| Elizabeth, m. Zephaniah **MITCHELL** , June 7, 1757 | 1 | 52 |
| Elizabeth, b. Oct. 31, 1770, m. Sala **JONES**, Sept. 28, 1793 | 2 | 87 |
| George, m. Eunice **PETTIS**, Mar. [ ], 1804 | 2 | 109 |
| Gesham, s. Isaac, b. Dec. 23, 1716 | L-1 | 654 |
| Gidian, [s. Isaac], b. Oct. 24, 1719 | L-1 | 654 |
| Jesse, d. Feb. 13, 1834, ae 80 | 2 | 193 |
| John, m. Mehetable **WELCH**, Dec. 9, 1777 | 2 | 58 |
| John, s. [John & Mehetable], b. Aug. 11, 1779 | 2 | 58 |
| Mehetable, d. [John & Mehetable], b. Dec. 6, 1782 | 2 | 58 |
| Neoma, m. Timothy **CROCKER**, Dec. 20, 1779; d. July 17, 1828 | 2 | 70 |
| Ransom, s. [John & Mehetable], b. June 5, 1785 | 2 | 58 |
| Ruth, w. [Jesse], d. Jan. 27, [ ], in Cleveland, Ohio, ae 83 | 2 | 193 |
| Sophia Ann, d. [George & Eunice], b. July 20, 1805 | 2 | 109 |
| **FRANCIS, FRANCES**, James H., Rev., of Middletown, m. A. J. **OTIS**, of Colchester, May 10, 1843, by Rev. Joel R. Arnold | 3 | 5 |
| Lucretia M., m. Charles M. **QUASH**, b. of Colchester, [ ], by Rev. Joel R. Arnold; d. Oct. 3, 1849, ae 29 | 2 | 122 |
| Richard R., of Lebanon, m. Lucy Ann **LITTLE**, of Colchester, Jan. 1, 1843, by Rev. Rob[er]t C. Mills | 2 | 262 |
| Samentha, of Colchester, m. Gilbert **SOLES**, of Lebanon, Apr. 1, 1842, by Rev. Rob[er]t C. Mills | 2 | 192 |
| **FREEMAN**, Ann E., m. Samuel **DAVIS**, Jan. 18, 1826, by Benjamin Trumbull, J. P. | 2 | 184 |
| Asenena, of Colchester, m. James **WILLIAMS**, of Hebron, Jan. 1, 1824, by Salmon Cone, V. D. M. | 2 | 161 |
| Betsey, m. Richard **BROWN**, Jan. 26, 1826, by Salmon Cone, V. D. M. | 2 | 184 |
| Caroline, m. George Leonard **HYDE**, colored, b. of Colchester, Dec. 26, 1843, by Rev. Augustus Bolles | 3 | 10 |
| Clarissa, m. James **QUASH**, Oct. 23, 1814; d. Oct. 4, 1819 | 2 | 110 |
| Dinah, d. Providence & Dinah, b., July 25, 1799, at Waterford | 2 | 326 |
| Eliphalet, m. Rebecca M. **COBB**, b. of Colchester, Mar. 2, 1851, by Rev. Lyman Strong | 2 | 76 |
| George W., of Colchester, m. Lucy Ann **THOMPSON**, of Windham, Nov. 23, 1841, by Rev. Joel R. Arnold | 2 | 121 |

| | Vol. | Page |
|---|---|---|
| **FREEMAN**, (cont.) | | |
| Gilbert, m. Mary **RANSOM**, b. of Colchester, June 15, 1845, by George Kay, J. P. | 3 | 20 |
| Harriet, m. Richard **SEYMOUR**, Apr. 20, 1828, by Salmon Cone, V. D. M. | 2 | 203 |
| James, m. Sally **BOHANE**, Apr. 6, 1819 | 2 | 94 |
| Julius, m. Julia **FOOTE**, July 31, 1823, by Salmon Cone, V. D. M. | 2 | 139 |
| Louisa, alias **TAYLOR**, m. Samuel **FREEMAN**, b. of Colchester, (colored), Dec. 17, 1829, by Samuel A. Peters, J. P. | 2 | 217 |
| Mary, d. [Providence & Betty], b. Nov. 10, 1809 | 2 | 326 |
| Nabby, d. [Providence & Betty], b. Dec. 10, 1806 | 2 | 326 |
| Nancy, of Hebron, m. Ralph **FOOTE**, of Colchester, July 5, 1835, by Rev. W. F. Vail | 2 | 278 |
| Polly, of Colchester, m. Aquilla **PROCTER**, of Killingly, May 17, 1829, by Salmon Cone, V. D. M. | 2 | 212 |
| Roxana, d. Providence, b. Feb. 22, 1817 | 2 | 94 |
| Sally, m. James **QUAS**, b. of Colchester, Sept. 17, 1821, by Salmon Cone, V. D. M. | 2 | 110 |
| Samuel, m. Louisa **TAYLOR**, alias **FREEMAN**, b. of Colchester, (colored), Dec. 17, 1829, by Samuel A. Peters, J. P. | 2 | 217 |
| Sophronia, of Colchester, m. Franklin **BUCK**, of Lisbon, Dec. 13, 1824, by Salmon Cone, V. D. M. | 2 | 173 |
| **FRINK**, Almira, m. Benj[ami]n **PHILOMORE**, b. of Lebanon, Nov. 11, 1823, at the house of the subscriber, by Rev. William Palmer | 2 | 104 |
| Lieucretiae, b. June 26, 1765 | 1 | 146 |
| Silas, m. Almira **MAYNARD**, Sept. 16, 1838, by Rev. Benjamin G. Goff | 2 | 111 |
| **FULLER**, A[a]ron, [s. Samuell], b. June 3, 1711 | L-3 | 198 |
| Aaron, s. Samuel, b. June 3, 1711 | TM-1 | 198 |
| Aaron, m. Ruth **SAWYER**, June 10, 1734 | 1 | 128 |
| Aaron, [s. Aaron], b. May 9, 1738 | 1 | 108 |
| Aaron, [s. Aaron & Ruth], b. May 11, 1738 | 1 | 128 |
| Abby, d. [Andrew], b. Jan. 10, 1810 | 2 | 71 |
| Abigaiell, [d. Edward & Elizabeth], b. Apr. 3, 1718 | L-1 | 799 |
| Abigail, of Colchester, m. George E. **DOANE**, of Saybrook, Sept. 5, 1833, by Rev. Joseph Harvey | 2 | 259 |
| Abner, [s. Samuell], b. Dec. 10, 1724 | L-3 | 198 |
| Abner, s. Sam[ue]l, b. Dec. 10, 1724 | TM-1 | 198 |
| Amos Jones, s. [Warren & Deborah Harvey], b. Nov. 2, 1797 | 2 | 130 |
| Ann, [d. Edward & Elizabeth], b. May 28, 1716 | L-1 | 799 |
| Ann, m. Lewis **LOVERIDGE**, Dec. 31, 1733 | 1 | 137 |
| Anne, m. Lewis **LOVERIDGE**, Dec. 31, 1733 | 1 | 78 |
| Asa, m. Esther **WILLIAMS**, Feb. 16, 1823, by Rev. Simeon Dickenson at the house of Mr. Daniel Williams | 2 | 82 |

| | Vol. | Page |
|---|---|---|
| **FULLER**, (cont.) | | |
| Asa Williams, s. [Asa & Esther], b. Feb. 13, 1826 | 2 | 82 |
| Bethiah, d. Timothy & Jane, b. May 22, 1742 | 1 | 144 |
| Clarissa, d. [Asa & Esther], b. Sept. 29, 1823 | 2 | 82 |
| Clarissa E., of Colchester, m. Joseph W. **TILDEN**, of Lebanon, Nov. 25, 1841, by Rev. Daniel G. Sprague, West Chester | 2 | 141 |
| Cornelious, m. Patience **CHAPPELL**, Feb. 25, 1730 | L-3 | 9 |
| Daniel, s. [Warren & Deborah Harvey], b. Apr. 1, 1801 | 2 | 130 |
| Daniel Andrew, s. [Asa & Esther], b. Nov. 10, 1832; d. Sept. 25, 1850, ae 18 | 2 | 82 |
| David, s. Edward & Elisa, b. Jan. 26, 1727 | L-3 | 458 |
| David, [s. Edward & Elizabeth], b. Jan. 28, 1728 | L-1 | 799 |
| Deborah, m. Joseph **CROCKER**, b. of Colchester, Apr. 27, 1823, by Jacob Seales, V. D. M. | 2 | 145 |
| Desire, [d. Samuell], b. Feb. 2, 1723 | L-3 | 198 |
| Desire, d. Sam[ue]l, b. Feb. 22, 1723 | TM-1 | 198 |
| Edward, m. Elizabeth **ROWLEE**, July 21, 1715 | L-1 | 799 |
| Edward, [s. Edward & Elisa], b. May 11, 1730 | L-3 | 458 |
| Edward, d. Jan. 7, 1731 | L-3 | 458 |
| Electa Jones, d. [Warren & Deborah Harvey], b. Dec. 9, 1803 | 2 | 130 |
| Eliza, m. Ezra **WOOD**, b. of Colchester, Jan. 12, 1834, by Artemas Worthington, J. P. | 2 | 262 |
| Eliza, of Colchester, m. Ebenezer **SELDEN**, of Lebanon, Mar. 25, 1841, by Rev. Lyman Strong | 2 | 236 |
| Elizabeth, w. Andrew, d. Oct. 6, 1850, ae 82 | 2 | 82 |
| Ellary, s. [Joseph], b. May 12, 1786 | 2 | 54 |
| [E]unice, [d. Edward & Elizabeth], b. May 12, 1726 | L-1 | 799 |
| George McKeene, s. [Stephen H.], b. Jan. 31, 1833 | 2 | 121 |
| Hannah, m. Josiah **STRONG**, Nov. 1, 1733 | 1 | 46 |
| Hannah, [d. Moses & Susannah], b. July 22, 1783 | 2 | 22 |
| Harriet, d. [Asa & Esther], b. Oct. 19, 1828 | 2 | 82 |
| Helen Mar, d. [Stephen H.], b. Apr. 9, 1830 | 2 | 121 |
| Henry, s. [Aaron & Ruth], b. Feb. 8, 1734/5 | 1 | 128 |
| Henry, s. Aaron, b. Jan. 8, 1736/7 | 1 | 108 |
| Israel, [s. Aaron], b. Nov. 9, 1743 | 1 | 108 |
| Jane, [d. Timothy & Jane], b. Sept. 26, 1744 | 1 | 144 |
| Joanna, d. [Timothy & Jane], b. Nov. 22, 1747 | 1 | 144 |
| John, s. Samuell, b. Nov. 3, 1704 | L-3 | 198 |
| John, s. Samuel, b. Nov. 3, 1704 | TM-1 | 198 |
| John, s. [Moses & Ruth], b. June 3, 1770 | 2 | 22 |
| Jonathan, of Colchester, m. Abigail **PERRY**, of Ashford, Apr. 23, 1761 | 1 | 153 |
| Joseph, s. [Moses & Ruth], b. Feb. 15, 1779 | 2 | 22 |
| Joseph, s. [Joseph], b. Aug. 12, 1782 | 2 | 54 |
| Joshua, [s. Young & Jerusha], b. Sept. 9, 1730 | L-3 | 456 |
| Josiah S., of Andova, Conn., m. Mary A. **BLACKMAN**, of Coventry, Conn., Jan. 25, 1847, by Rev. M. P. | | |

| | Vol. | Page |
|---|---|---|
| **FULLER**, (cont.) | | |
| Alderman | 3 | 32 |
| Judah, [s. Aaron], b. Feb. 9, 1745/6 | 1 | 108 |
| Lambert, s. [Joseph], b. June 7, 1788 | 2 | 54 |
| Lucy, m. Isaac **WILLIAMS**, June 22, 1752 | 1 | 35 |
| Mary, [d. Samuell], b. Feb. 28, 1721 | L-3 | 198 |
| Mary, d. Samuel, b. Feb. 28, 1721 | TM-1 | 198 |
| Mary, m. Joseph **SMITH**, Nov. 1, 1750 | 1 | 104 |
| Mahitable, [d. Samuell], b. Aug. 6, 1716 | L-3 | 198 |
| Mehitable, d. Samuel, b. Aug. 6, 1716 | TM-1 | 198 |
| Mercy, d. Samuel, b. June 27, 1718 (Marcy) | TM-1 | 198 |
| Marcy, [d. Samuell], b. June 27, 1718 | L-3 | 198 |
| Molly, d. [Moses & Ruth], b. July 18, 1776 | 2 | 22 |
| Moses, [s. Samuell], b. Jan. 30, 1708 | L-3 | 198 |
| Moses, s. Samuel, b. Jan. 30, 1708/9 | TM-1 | 198 |
| Moses, [s. Moses & Rebecca], b. June 6, 1740 | 1 | 139 |
| Moses, d. May 15, 1759 | 1 | 139 |
| Moses, m. Ruth **GROVER**, Apr. 11, 1768 | 2 | 22 |
| Moses, m. Susannah **TAYLOR**, Dec. 12, 1782 | 2 | 6 |
| Moses, m. Susannah **TAYLOR**, Dec. 12, 1782 | 2 | 22 |
| Moses, m. Rebecca **BROWN**, [ ] | 1 | 139 |
| Nora, d. Sam[ue]l, b. June [ ], 1727 | TM-1 | 198 |
| Febee (Phebe), [d. Edward & Elizabeth], b. Apr. 18, 1723 | L-1 | 799 |
| Phebe, m. Samuel **CHURCH**, June 17, 1744 | 1 | 100 |
| Polly, d. [Warren & Deborah Harvey], b. Aug. 10, 1799 | 2 | 130 |
| Rebecca, d. [Moses & Rebecca], b. Aug. 7, 1737 | 1 | 139 |
| Robert James, s. [Stephen H.], b. Apr. 18, 1827 | 2 | 121 |
| Roswell, [s. Aaron], b. Mar. 22, 1741 | 1 | 108 |
| Ruth, [d. Aaron], b. Nov. 15, 1747 | 1 | 108 |
| Ruth, d. [Moses & Ruth], b. Dec. 27, 1772 | 2 | 22 |
| Ruth, w. Moses, d. Mar. 10, 1782 | 2 | 6 |
| Ruth, [s. Moses], d. Mar. 10, 1782 | 2 | 22 |
| Samuell, [s. Samuell], b. Aug. [31], 1706 | L-3 | 198 |
| Samuel, s. Sam[ue]l, b. Aug. [31], 1706 | TM-1 | 198 |
| Samuel, s. [Moses & Ruth], b. Oct. 3, 1774 | 2 | 22 |
| Sarah, [d. Edward & Elizabeth], b. July 8, 1719 | L-1 | 799 |
| Sarah, m. John **GATES**, Apr. 19, 1722 | TPR | 111 |
| Silence, [d. Edward & Elizabeth], b. May 22, 1721 | L-1 | 799 |
| Solomon, s. [Moses & Ruth], b. Sept. 5, 1771 | 2 | 22 |
| Stephen Edward, s. [Stephen H.], b. Dec. 8, 1836 | 2 | 121 |
| Thankfull, m. Jabez **CRIPPEN**, July 9, 1707 | TPR | 111 |
| Warren, m. Deborah Harvey **JONES**, June 5, 1796 | 2 | 130 |
| Warren, s. [Warren & Deborah Harvey], b. Sept. 26, 1805 | 2 | 130 |
| William, s. [Moses & Susannah], b. July 22, 1783 | 2 | 6 |
| Young, m. Jerusha **BEBEE**, Apr. 23, 1730 | L-3 | 456 |
| -----, d. [Samuell], b. June [ ], 1727 | L-3 | 198 |
| **GALE, GALES**, Susannah, m. Robert **USHER**, May 23, 1765 | 1 | 11 |
| Wakefield, m. Mary E. **BIGELOW**, Sept. 18, 1828, by | | |

| | Vol. | Page |
|---|---|---|
| **GALE, GALES,** (cont.) | | |
| Salmon Cone, V. D. M. | 2 | 206 |
| **GALLAGER,** Anthony, m. Mary **HANCOCK,** Sept. 25, 1842, by Rev. Rob[er]t C. Mills | 2 | 230 |
| **GALLUP,** Ichabod, of Norwich, m. Sarah Maria **ISHAM,** of Colchester, Dec. 1, 1830, by Rev. Lyman Strong | 2 | 227 |
| **GALUSIAH,** Elizabeth, d. Daniell, b. Oct. 3, 1719 | L-1 | 449 |
| **GARDINER,** [see also **GARDNER**], Abigail, [d. Stephen, Jr. & Francis], b. Apr. 17, 1764 | 1 | 86 |
| Almy, [d. Stephen], b. Feb. 17, 1725 | 1 | 141 |
| Anson, m. Harriet **PALMER,** b. of Colchester, Mar. 30, 1851, by Rev. G. W. Pendleton | 3 | 48 |
| Bathsheba, m. John **WAY,** Jr., Jan. 15, 1756 | 1 | 24 |
| Desire, [d. Stephen, Jr. & Francis], b. July 6, 1762; d. Oct. 29, 1762, ae 3 m. 21 d. | 1 | 86 |
| Edwin B., of Norwich, m. Emily **STARK,** of Colchester, Apr. 16, 1848, by Rev. P. Brockett | 3 | 35 |
| Esther, [d. Stephen], b. Dec. 26, 1729 | 1 | 141 |
| Esther, [d. Stephen, Jr. & Francis], b. Aug. 24, 1767 | 1 | 86 |
| Frances, [s. Stephen], b. June 7, 1723 | 1 | 141 |
| Francis, [s. Stephen, Jr. & Francis], b. Dec. 21, 1760 | 1 | 86 |
| George, [s. William & Lucy], b. Mar. 23, 1772 | 1 | 86 |
| George, m. Phebe **LEWIS,** b. of Lebanon, Sept. 18, 1836, at Colchester, by Samuel A. Peters, J. P. | 2 | 289 |
| Hannah, [d. Stephen], b. Nov. 7, 1734 | 1 | 141 |
| Hannah, m. Thomas **JONES,** Apr. 5, 1753 | 1 | 35 |
| Jerusha, w. Jonathan, & mother of Jerusha **MORGAN,** w. of Avery **MORGAN,** d. Mar. 22, 1847, ae 86 | 2 | 254 |
| Jonathan, father of Jerusha **MORGAN,** w. of Avery **MORGAN,** d. May 6, 1847, ae 88 | 2 | 254 |
| Lovina, [d. Perserved & Anna], b. Mar. 27, 1764 | 1 | 56 |
| Lucy, d. [William, Jr. & Lucy], b. Dec. 21, 1774 | 1 | 141 |
| Lydia, [d. Stephen], b. Mar. 20, 1727 | 1 | 141 |
| Lydia, m. John **JENKINS,** Aug. 1, 1751. Removed to Wyoming Valley in 1769 | 1 | 104 |
| Margary, [d. Preserved & Anna], b. Nov. 20, 1765 | 1 | 56 |
| Mary, [d. Stephen], b. Dec. 20, 1737 | 1 | 141 |
| Mary, m. John **BULKELEY,** Oct. [ ], 1738 | 1 | 130 |
| Mary, m. John **BULKLEY,** Oct. 29, 1738 | 1 | 133 |
| Mary, m. Israel **JONES,** Mar. 8, 1759 | 1 | 86 |
| Preserved, m. Anna **WELLS,** May 19, 1763 | 1 | 56 |
| Sarah, [d. Stephen], b. Feb. 10, 1731 | 1 | 141 |
| Stephen, [s. Stephen], b. Mar. 27, 1735 | 1 | 141 |
| Stephen, Jr., m. Francis **BROWN,** June 6, 1760 | 1 | 86 |
| Stephen, [s. Stephen, Jr. & Francis], b. Jan. 29, 1766 | 1 | 86 |
| Thomas, [s. Stephen], b. Sept. 4, 1740 | 1 | 141 |
| William, m. [Lucy **LILLEY**], Dec. 22, 1768 | 1 | 86 |
| William, Jr., m. Lucy **LILLY,** Dec. 18, 1769 | 1 | 141 |

| | Vol. | Page |
|---|---|---|
| **GARDINER**, (cont.) | | |
| W[illia]m, [s. William & Lucy], b. Jan. 5, 1770 | 1 | 86 |
| William, s. [William, Jr. & Lucy], b. Jan. 5, 1770 | 1 | 141 |
| **GARDNER**, [see also **GARDINER**], Eunice W., of East Haddam, m. Harvey **GILLETT**, of Colchester, Mar. 26, 1839, by Rev. Andrew M. Smith | 2 | 29 |
| Mehetabel, [d. Stephen], b. Nov. 11, 1745 | 1 | 141 |
| Rhoda, of Bozrah, m. Abel **GATES**, Sept. [ ], 1788 | 2 | 80 |
| **GASTIN**, [see also **GUSTIN**], David, s. [Thomas, Jr. & Hannah], b. Oct. 11, 1747; d. Oct. 25, 1750 | 1 | 148 |
| Ebenezer, s. [Thomas, Jr. & Hannah], b. Nov. 6, 1762 | 1 | 148 |
| Edward, s. [Thomas, Jr. & Hannah], b. Apr. 13, 1758 | 1 | 148 |
| Elizabeth, d.. [Thomas, Jr. & Hannah], b. Aug. 7, 1760 | 1 | 148 |
| Ezra, s. [Thomas, Jr. & Hannah], b. Feb. 2, 1754 | 1 | 148 |
| Sarah, d. [Thomas, Jr. & Hannah], b. July 19, 1749 | 1 | 148 |
| Sarah, w. Dea. Thomas, d. Sept. 6, 1763 | 1 | 148 |
| Thomas, Jr., m. Hannah **GRISWOLD**, Dec. 11, 1746 | 1 | 148 |
| Thomas, s. [Thomas, Jr. & Hannah], b. Jan. 8, 1756 | 1 | 148 |
| Walter, s. [Thomas, Jr. & Hannah], b. Aug. 3, 1751 | 1 | 148 |
| **GATES**, Abel, s. [Thomas & Ruth], b. Oct. 6, 1768 | 1 | 125 |
| Abel, m. Rhoda **GARDNER**, of Bozrah, Sept. [ ], 1788; d. Dec. 11, 1850, ae 82 y., in Salem, Ct. | 2 | 80 |
| Abel, Capt., d. Dec. 11, 1850 | 1 | 125 |
| Abigaiell, [d. Josiah & Grace], b. Aug. 13, 1719 | L-1 | 451 |
| Abner, [s. Josiah, Jr. & Lydia], b. Aug. 4, 1769 | 1 | 52 |
| Amander, s. [Abel & Rhoda], b. Aug. 5, 1808 | 2 | 80 |
| Anna, d. Josiah, b. Dec. 31, 1734 | 1 | 141 |
| Anna, d. [Thomas & Ruth], b. May 6, 1755 | 1 | 125 |
| Asa, s. [Abel & Rhoda], b. July 6, 1806 | 2 | 80 |
| Augusta E., m. John Henry **WORTHINGTON**, b. of East Hampton, [Oct.] 11, 1834, by Rev. S. D. Jewett, at Colchester | 3 | 65 |
| Daniel, [s. Josiah, Jr. & Lydia], b. Feb. 28, 1767 | 1 | 52 |
| Deboro[h], d. [Jonathan & Susanna], b. July 21, 1750 | 1 | 137 |
| Electa, d. [Abel & Rhoda], b. June 18, 1790 | 2 | 80 |
| Electa, m. Alexander **MINARD**, Jan. 10, 1811 | 2 | 152 |
| Eli, s. [Abel & Rhoda], b. Jan. 31, 1798 | 2 | 80 |
| Elizabeth, [d. Josiah & Grace], b. May 8, 1729 | L-1 | 451 |
| Elizabeth, m. Nathan **SCOVEL**, Sept. 8, 1749 | 1 | 144 |
| Elizabeth, [d. Josiah, Jr. & Lydia], b. Jan. 17, 1756 | 1 | 52 |
| Elizabeth, d. [Samuel & Elizabeth], b. Sept. 7, 1761 | 1 | 145 |
| Enos, s. [Abel & Rhoda], b. Feb. 16, 1800 | 2 | 80 |
| Esther, [d. Josiah, Jr. & Lydia], b. Mar. 26, 1773 | 1 | 52 |
| Eve, [d. Josiah, Jr. & Lydia], b. July 28, 1771 | 1 | 52 |
| Ezra, [s. John & Sarah], b. July 20, 1736 | TPR | 111 |
| Ezra, m. Hannah **STEVENS**, June 23, 1756 | 1 | 47 |
| Ezra, [s. Ezra & Hannah], b. Aug. 30, 1758 | 1 | 47 |
| Freeman, s. [Samuel & Elizabeth], b. Oct. 13, 1765 | 1 | 145 |

| | Vol. | Page |
|---|---|---|
| **GATES**, (cont.) | | |
| Gardner, s. [Abel & Rhoda], b. May 12, 1796 | 2 | 80 |
| Grace, [d. Josiah & Grace], b. Oct. 8, 1725 | L-1 | 451 |
| Grace, [d. Josiah, Jr. & Lydia], b. Jan. 25, 1759 | 1 | 52 |
| Hannah, [d. Josiah & Grace], b. Sept. 5, 1721 | L-1 | 451 |
| Hannah, [d. Josiah, Jr. & Lydia], b. Feb. 7, 1761 | 1 | 52 |
| Jacob, [s. Ezra & Hannah], b. Nov. 22, 1756 | 1 | 47 |
| John, m. Sarah **FULLER**, Apr. 19, 1722 | TPR | 111 |
| John, [s. John & Sarah], b. Aug. 19 1728 | TPR | 111 |
| John, Jr., m. Rebeckah **SNOW**, Jan. 22, 1755 | 1 | 41 |
| John, s. [Abel & Rhoda], b. Mar. 19, 1792 | 2 | 80 |
| Jonathan, m. Susanna **OLMSTEAD**, July 16, 1747 | 1 | 137 |
| Jonathan, [s. John, Jr. & Rebeckah], b. Mar. 9, 1757 | 1 | 41 |
| Jonathan, d. June 1, 1771 | 1 | 137 |
| Josiah, m. Grace **RATHBON**, May 9, 1714 | L-1 | 451 |
| Josiah, [s. Josiah & Grace], b. Jan. 15, 1722/3 | L-1 | 451 |
| Josiah, Jr., m. Lydia **MARVIN**, Apr. 19, 1753 | 1 | 52 |
| Josiah, [s. Josiah, Jr. & Lydia], b. Dec. 18, 1754 | 1 | 52 |
| Laben, s. [Thomas & Ruth], b. July 23, 1753 | 1 | 125 |
| Lodema, d. [Thomas & Ruth], b. Nov. 18, 1766 | 1 | 125 |
| Lois, [d. Nehemiah & Truin], b. Sept. 16, 1756 | 1 | 23 |
| Lucy, d. [Abel & Rhoda], b. Feb. 14, 1802 | 2 | 80 |
| Lydia, [d. Josiah, Jr. & Lydia], b. Dec. 29, 1753 | 1 | 52 |
| Lydia, w. Josiah, d. June 10, 1775 | 1 | 52 |
| Martha, d. [Samuel & Elizabeh], b. June 19, 1763 | 1 | 145 |
| Marvin, [s. Josiah, Jr. & Lydia], b. Oct. 1, 1757 | 1 | 52 |
| Mary, [d. Josiah & Grace], b. July 3, 1715 | L-1 | 451 |
| Mary, [d. Nehemiah & Truin], b. Mar. 22, 1755 | 1 | 23 |
| Mary, m. Uriah **CARRIER**, July 10, 1777 | 2 | 26 |
| Mathias, [s. John & Sarah], b. Feb. 13, 1733/4 | TPR | 111 |
| Molley, m. Isaiah **RATHBUN**, Jan. 9, 1763 | 1 | 14 |
| Nehemiah, [s. John & Sarah], b. Apr. 17, 1730 | TPR | 111 |
| Nehemiah, m. Truin **BRAINARD**, Apr. 25, 1754 | 1 | 23 |
| Patience, m. Nath[anie]l **FOOT**, Jr., Apr. 15, 1736 | 1 | 107 |
| Phebe, [d. Josiah, Jr. & Lydia], b. Jan. 28, 1765 | 1 | 52 |
| Phebe, m. Alpheas **TREADWAY**, [ ] | 2 | 142 |
| Philura, d. [Thomas & Ruth], b. Sept. 4, 1770 | 1 | 125 |
| Reynold, [s. Josiah, Jr. & Lydia], b. Oct. 22, 1762 | 1 | 52 |
| Ruth, d. [Thomas & Ruth], b. Mar. 12, 1759 | 1 | 125 |
| Sam[ue]ll, [s. Josiah & Grace], b. Dec. 26, 1730 | L-1 | 451 |
| Samuel, m. Elizabeth **WATERMAN**, Jan. 5, 1757 | 1 | 145 |
| Samuel, s. [Samuel & Elizabeth], b. Nov. 18, 1757 | 1 | 145 |
| Sarah, [d. John & Sarah], b. Aug. 10, 1725 | TPR | 111 |
| Sarah, d. Josiah & Grace, b. Nov. 12, 1732 | TPR | 109 |
| Sarah, [d. John, Jr. & Rebeckah], b. Oct. 26, 1755 | 1 | 41 |
| Sarah, m. Ephraim **WELLS**, Feb. 10, 1763 | 1 | 127 |
| Sarah, m. Cephus **CONE**, Dec. 9, 1779 | 2 | 36 |
| Stephen, [s. Ezra & Hannah], b. Oct. 10, 1760 | 1 | 47 |

| | Vol. | Page |
|---|---|---|
| **GATES**, (cont.) | | |
| Susannah, m. Stephen **BRAINERD**, Dec. 24, 1730 | TPR | 111 |
| Susanna, d. [Jonathan & Susanna], b. Aug. 22, 1748 | 1 | 137 |
| Thomas, [s. Josiah & Grace], b. July 3, 1724 | L-1 | 451 |
| Thomas, m. Ruth **RANDALL**, Dec. 29, 1748 | 1 | 125 |
| Thomas, Dea., d. May 12, 1793 | 2 | 80 |
| Thomas, s. [Abel & Rhoda], b. Aug. 1, 1794 | 2 | 80 |
| William, s. [Abel & Rhoda], b. Mar. 31, 1804 | 2 | 80 |
| Zebulon Waterman, s. [Samuel & Elizabeth], b. Dec. 27, 1759 | 1 | 145 |
| ----, m. James **JONES**, [ ] | 1 | 147 |
| **GAY**, Hannah, of Norwich, m. John **COLMAN**, of Colchester, Nov. 28, 1751 | 1 | 27 |
| **GAYLORD**, Samuel W., of Bristol, m. Esther P. **LORD**, of Colchester, Feb. 16, 1839, by Rev. Andrew M. Smith | 2 | 109 |
| **GELSTON**, William, Jr., of East Haddam, m. Lucy **BIGELOW**, of Colchester, Oct. 21, 1821, at the house of John Bigelow, by Rev. Simeon Dickinson | 2 | 129 |
| **GILBERT**, Betsey, of Hebron, m. John **ISHAM**, 3d, of Colchester, Jan. 19, 1797 | 2 | 83 |
| Content, wid., m. William **RICHARDSON**, Mar. 2, 1778 | 2 | 20 |
| Lydia, d. Samuell, b. Sept. 4, 1707 | L-3 | 198 |
| Lydia, d. Samuel, b. Sept. 4, 1707 | TM-1 | 198 |
| Mary, [d. Nathaniel & Mary], b. Nov. 19, 1721 | L-1 | 447 |
| Mercy, [d. Samuell], b. Oct. 4, 1709 | L-3 | 198 |
| Mercy, d. Samuel, b. Oct. 4, 1709 | TM-1 | 198 |
| Nathaniel, m. Mary **BESSEL**, Feb. 8, 1720/21 | L-1 | 447 |
| Samuell, [s. Nathaniel & Mary], b. Jan. 31, 1723/4 | L-1 | 447 |
| Sophia, m. James M. **STANTON**, b. of Hebron, Apr. 23, 1835, by Rev. Lyman Strong | 2 | 277 |
| **GILLETT, GILLET, GILLITT, GELLETT**, Aaron, m. Han[n]ah **CLARK**, July 10, 1728 | L-1 | 444 |
| Aaron, d. Nov. 30, 1730, in Boston | TPR | 109 |
| Aaron, [s. Jonathan & Sarah], b. May 23, 1732 | L-3 | 456 |
| Aaron, m. Anna **PRATT**, Mar. 31, 1757 | 1 | 126 |
| Aaron, m. Anne **PRATT**, [ ]; d. June 14, 1786 | 2 | 42 |
| Aaron, s. [Aaron & Anna], b. Jan. 2, 1758; d. Aug. 16, 1758 | 1 | 126 |
| Aaron, s. [Aaron & Anna], b. Feb. 23, 1765 | 1 | 126 |
| Aaron, s. [Joseph, Jr. & Sarah], b. Aug. 8, 1800 | 2 | 76 |
| Aaron Griswold, s. [Solomon & Patty], b. Jan. 5, 1819 | 2 | 150 |
| Abel Bissell, s. [Solomon T. & Louisa E.], b. Sept. 7, 1834; d. Sept. 20, 1850, at Vernon | 2 | 270 |
| Abigail, d. [Joseph & Abigail], b. Dec. 28, 1759 | 1 | 110 |
| Abigail Rogers, d. [Jonathan & Betsey], b. July 21, 1808; d. Jan. 15, 1809 | 2 | 81 |
| Adonijah, [s. Samuell & Mary], b. May 30, 1724 | L-1 | 449 |
| Alphard, s. [Caleb & Civel], b. May 1, 1793 | 2 | 78 |
| Alvin, s. [Eliphalet & Lydia], b. June 29, 1774 | 2 | 45 |
| Amasa, [s. Israel & Mercy], b. Jan. 1, 1764 | 1 | 99 |

| | Vol. | Page |
|---|---|---|
| **GILLETT, GILLET, GILLITT, GELLETT,** (cont.) | | |
| Amos, s. [Jonathan & Huldah], b. Dec. 18, 1811 | 2 | 81 |
| Anna, d. [Aaron & Anna], b. May 9, 1759 | 1 | 126 |
| Anna, d. [Joseph & Abigail], b. Nov. 12, 1770 | 1 | 110 |
| Anna, m. Andrew **CARRIER**, Mar. 22, 1814 | 2 | 112 |
| Anne, m. Isaac **SKINNER**, Jr., May 14, 1778 | 2 | 13 |
| Anne, d. [Aaron & Anne], b. Apr. 5, 1781 | 2 | 42 |
| Asa, s. [Joseph, Jr. & Sarah], b. Dec. 5, 1793 | 2 | 76 |
| Asa Ely, s. [Samuel, 2d, & Nabby], b. Aug. 5, 1817 | 2 | 146 |
| Attaline, d. [Harvey & Eunice W.], b. Nov. 22, 1841 | 2 | 29 |
| Betsey, d. [Eliphalet & Lydia], b. June 11, 1780 | 2 | 45 |
| Betsey, [w. Jonathan], d. Mar. 12, 1810 | 2 | 81 |
| Betsey, d. [Jonathan & Huldah], b. Apr. 10, 1813 | 2 | 81 |
| Caleb, s. [Samuel], b. Sept. 3, 1739 | 1 | 130 |
| Caleb, [s. Eliphalet & Lydia], b. Nov. 12, 1762 | 1 | 28 |
| Caleb, s. [Eliphalet & Lydia], b. Nov. 12, 1762 | 2 | 45 |
| Caleb, of Colchester, m. Civel **HUNTINGTON**, of Hebron, Ct., Oct. 30, 1790; d. Apr. 14, 1830, ae 67 | 2 | 78 |
| Caleb Huntington, s. [Caleb & Civel], b. Mar. 7, 1800 | 2 | 78 |
| Charles, s. Josiah & Sarah, b. Oct. 22, 1728 | 1 | 135 |
| Charles, [s. Israel & Mercy], b. Aug. 8, 1761 | 1 | 99 |
| Charles Edwin, s. [Solomon & Patty], b. Oct. 23, 1823 | 2 | 150 |
| Civel, [w. Caleb], d. Jan. 20, 1841, ae 76 | 2 | 78 |
| Crimel, s. [Caleb & Civel], b. Feb. 28, 1802 | 2 | 78 |
| Daniell, [s. Josiah & Sarah], b. Feb. 2, 1714 | L-1 | 450 |
| Daniel Watrous, s. [Solomon L. & Mary J.], b. June 20, 1829 | 2 | 188 |
| Dauid, [s. Josiah & Sarah], b. June 30, 1719 | L-1 | 450 |
| David, d. Oct. 15, 1742 | 1 | 135 |
| Dimmis, [d. Nehemiah & Martha], b. Aug. 18, 1782 | 1 | 55 |
| Dimis Eliza, d. [Caleb & Civel], b. Apr. 30, 1805 | 2 | 78 |
| Elijah, [s. Nehemiah & Martha], b. Jan. 14, 1776 | 1 | 55 |
| Eli, s. [Aaron & Anna], b. May 14, 1767 | 1 | 126 |
| Ely, of Colchester, m. Phebe **HAUL**, of Lyme, Apr. 8, 1790; d. Dec. 11, 1846, ae 80 | 2 | 77 |
| Ely H., m. Mary **WILLIAMS**, b. of Colchester, Sept. 11, 1821, by Salmon Cone, V. D. M. | 2 | 143 |
| Ely Hall, s. [Ely & Phebe], b. Oct. 6, 1794 | 2 | 77 |
| Eliphalet, [s. Samuell & Mary], b. Nov. 1, 1726; d. Aug. 22, 1728 | L-1 | 449 |
| Eliphalet, s. Sam[ue]l & Abig[ai]l, b. Apr. 29, 1734 | L-1 | 449 |
| Eliphalet, m. Lydia **DENNEO**, Mar. 27, 1760 | 1 | 28 |
| Eliphalet, m. Lydia **PINEO**, of Lebanon, Mar. 27, 1760 | 2 | 45 |
| Eliphalet, s. [Eliphalet & Lydia], b. Nov. 19, 1768 | 2 | 45 |
| Eliphalet, s. [Caleb & Civel], b. Oct. 11, 1791 | 2 | 78 |
| Eliza, m. William **SILLIMAN**, of East Haddam, Nov. 7, 1827, by Salmon Cone, V. D. M. | 2 | 199 |
| Elizabeth, [d. Josiah & Sarah], b. Apr. 15, 1721 | L-1 | 450 |
| Elizabeth A., of Colchester, m. Charles **BABCOCK**, of | | |

| | Vol. | Page |
|---|---|---|
| **GILLETT, GILLET, GILLITT, GELLETT**, (cont.) | | |
| East Haddam, May 21, 1837, by Rev. Joel R. Arnold | 2 | 225 |
| Elizabeth Abby, d. [Samuel, 2d, & Nabby], b. Oct. 9, 1813 | 2 | 146 |
| Elizabeth Clark, d. [Harvey & Eunice W.], b. Apr. 27, 1848 | 2 | 29 |
| Elizabeth **KELLOGG**, d. [Solomon L. & Mary J.], b. Oct. 18, 1826; d. Oct. 10, 1829 | 2 | 188 |
| Emily S., of Colchester, m. Samuel N. **CHAPIN**, of Goshen, June 17, 1834, by Rev. Lyman Strong | 2 | 267 |
| Emma Louisa, d. [Ely H. & Mary], b. May 9, 1826 | 2 | 143 |
| Emma Louise, of Colchester, m. Stephen Holly **MATTHEWS**, of Oberlin, O., Aug. 10, 1852, by Erastus Dickinson | 3 | 52 |
| Esther, d. [Josiah & Sarah], b. Nov. 25, 1734 | 1 | 135 |
| Eunice, d. [Joseph & Abigai], b. Jan. 24, 1766 | 1 | 110 |
| Eunice, m. Gurdon **CLARK**, Nov. 8, 1788; d. Nov. 8, 1848, ae 82 | 2 | 76 |
| Ezra, s. [Joseph & Abigail], b. Aug. 23, 1769; d. Sept. 15, 1769 | 1 | 110 |
| Ezra, 2d, s. [Joseph & Abigail], b. Dec. 11, 1772 | 1 | 110 |
| Ezra Hall, s. [Ely H. & Mary], b. July 15, 1823 | 2 | 143 |
| Frances R., of Colchester, m. John R. **GRIFFING**, of East Haddam, July 3, 1851, by Rev. Lyman Strong | 2 | 109 |
| Frances R., d. [Samuel, 2d & Nabby], b. [ ] | 2 | 146 |
| Hannah, m. Joseph **CHAMBERLAIN**, Jr., July 15, 1738 | 1 | 147 |
| Hannah, m. Lemuel **STORES**, June 11, 1749 | 1 | 149 |
| Hannah, d. [Aaron & Anna], b. Apr. 20, 1771; d. Mar. 25, 1773 | 1 | 126 |
| Hannah, [d. Nehemiah & Martha], b. Jan. 6, 1779 | 1 | 55 |
| Harvey, s. [Joseph, Jr. & Sarah], b. Dec. 27, 1802 | 2 | 76 |
| Harvey, of Colchester, m. Eunice W. **GARDNER**, of East Haddam, Mar. 26, 1839, by Rev. Andrew M. Smith | 2 | 29 |
| Henry, s. [Caleb & Civel], b. May 10, 1797 | 2 | 78 |
| Huldah, d. [Jonathan & Huldah], b. Aug. 8, 1816 | 2 | 81 |
| Isreall, [s. Samuell & Mary], b. Feb. 10, 1721/2 | L-1 | 449 |
| Israel, m. Mercy **COLMAN**, May 14, 1747 | 1 | 99 |
| Israel, [s. Israel & Mercy], b. Mar. 30, 1748 | 1 | 99 |
| Jane, d. [Ely H. & Mary], b. June 19, 1834 | 2 | 143 |
| Jerusha, d. Samuel & Mary, b. Oct. 20, 1736 | 1 | 128 |
| Jerusha, m. Amos **BILL**, Feb. 3, 1757 | 1 | 54 |
| Jerusha Bartlett, d. [Harvey & Eunice W.], b. May 31, 1845 | 2 | 29 |
| Joanna, d. Jonathan, b. July 8, 1739 | 1 | 139 |
| Joanna, d. [Aaron & Anne], b. May 12, 1761; d. Apr. 24, 1763 | 1 | 126 |
| Joel Doolittle, s. [Solomon & Patty], b. Aug. 27, 1809 | 2 | 150 |
| John Albert, s. [Ely H. & Mary], b. Oct. 4, 1828 | 2 | 143 |
| Jonah, [s. Jonathan & Sarah], b. Apr. 10, 1730 | L-1 | 446 |
| Jonah, s. Jonathan & Sarah, d. Apr. 10, 1731 | L-3 | 456 |
| Jonathan, m. Sarah **ELEY**, Jan. 3, 1717 | L-1 | 446 |

| | Vol. | Page |
|---|---|---|
| **GILLETT, GILLET, GILLITT, GELLETT,** (cont.) | | |
| Jonathan, [s. Jonathan & Sarah], b. Mar. 22, 1720 | L-1 | 446 |
| Jonathan, 3d, m. Phebe **MARVIN**, Jan. 11, 1747 | 1 | 109 |
| Jonathan, s. [Jonathan, 3d, & Phebe], b. Dec. 17, 1753 | 1 | 109 |
| Jonathan, s. [Joseph & Abigail], b. Mar. 21, 1768 | 1 | 110 |
| Jonathan, m. Betsey **ROGERS**, Apr. 23, 1800 | 2 | 81 |
| Jonathan, m. Huldah **MARVIN**, Feb. 12, 1811; d. May 22, 1820, ae 53 | 2 | 81 |
| Jonathan Rogers, s. [Jonathan & Betsey], b. Feb. 16, 1801 | 2 | 81 |
| Joseph, [s. Jonathan & Sarah], b. Dec. 30, 1725 | L-1 | 446 |
| Joseph, m. Abigail **KELLOGG**, Dec. 8, 1757 | 1 | 110 |
| Joseph, s. [Joseph & Abigail], b. Aug. 29, 1758 | 1 | 110 |
| Joseph, Jr., m. Sarah **ROOT**, of Hebron, June 10, 1783; d. Apr. 29, 1838, ae 80 | 2 | 76 |
| Joseph, s. [Joseph, Jr. & Sarah], b. Apr. 17, 1789 | 2 | 76 |
| Joseph applied for freedom of negro slave Domini between the age of 25 and 45 y., May 26, 1800. Signed by John R. **WATROUS** & Roger **BULKELEY**, Selectmen, & Joseph **ISHAM**, J. P. Certificate signed by Joseph **GILLET**, Lucy **GILLET**, Uriah **GILLET**. | 2 | 87 |
| Joseph L., s. [Samuel, 2d, & Nabby], b. June 27, 1819 | 2 | 146 |
| Joseph L., m. Emily **CHAMPLAIN**, b. of Colchester, May 8, 1850, by Rev. Lyman Strong | 3 | 4 |
| Josiah, m. Sarah **PELLET**, Mar. 7, 1711 | L-1 | 450 |
| Josiah, [s. Josiah & Sarah], b. Nov. 11, 1712; d. Oct. 13, 1714 | L-1 | 450 |
| Josiah, [s. Josiah & Sarah], b. Dec. 7, 1715 | L-1 | 450 |
| Josiah, d. Oct. 14, 1742 | 1 | 135 |
| Joyce, [s. Eliphalet & Lydia], b. Oct. 9, 1764 | 1 | 28 |
| Joyce, d. [Eliphalet & Lydia], b. Oct. 9, 1764 | 2 | 45 |
| Laura, d. [Caleb & Civel], b. June 26, 1795; d. Sept. 14, 1839, ae 44 | 2 | 78 |
| Lois, [d. Nehemiah & Martha], b. Mar. 21, 1763; d. Oct. 5, 1785 | 1 | 55 |
| Louisa, d. [Solomon T. & Louisa E.], b. Dec. 28, 1835 | 2 | 270 |
| Lucy, d. [Joseph & Abigail], b. Apr. 12, 1764 | 1 | 110 |
| Lucy A., of Colchester, m. Jamin **STRONG**, of Bolton, Conn., Sept. 20, 1848, by Rev. F. W. Bill | 3 | 37 |
| Luna, d. [Eliphalet & Lydia], b. Oct. 5, 1772 | 2 | 45 |
| Lydia, [d. Israel & Mercy], b. Aug. 13, 1750 | 1 | 99 |
| Lydia, m. Nehemiah **GILLETT**, Sept. 13, 1757 | 1 | 55 |
| Lydia, [d. Nehemiah & Lydia], b. July 29, 1758 | 1 | 55 |
| Lydia, w. [Nehemiah], d. Aug. 7, 1758 | 1 | 55 |
| Lydia, d. [Eliphalet & Lydia], b. Nov. 12, 1770 | 2 | 45 |
| Marcy, d. [Aaron & Anne], b. Feb. 11, 1777 | 2 | 42 |
| Martha, [d. Nehemiah & Martha], b. Apr. 12, 1767 | 1 | 55 |
| Martha, w. [Nehemiah], d. July 21, 1827, ae 85 | 1 | 55 |
| Martha M., of Colchester, m. John **LOOMIS**, of Coventry, May 9, 1838, by Rev. Joel R. Arnold | 2 | 207 |

| | Vol. | Page |
|---|---|---|
| **GILLETT, GILLET, GILLITT, GELLETT,** (cont.) | | |
| Martha Matilda, d. [Solomon & Patty], b. May 26, 1812 | 2 | 150 |
| Martin, s. [Jonathan, 3d, & Phebe], b. July 19, 1752 | 1 | 109 |
| Mary, m. Nathaniell **SKIN[N]ER,** June 13, 1706 | L-3 | 194 |
| Mary, m. Nathaniel **SKINNER**, June 13, 1706 | TM-1 | 194 |
| Mary, [d. Jonathan & Sarah], b. Dec. 13, 1723 | L-1 | 446 |
| Mary, [d. Josiah & Sarah], b. Mar. 3, 1725; d. Apr. 17, [1725] | L-1 | 450 |
| Mary, [d. Samuell & Mary], b. Apr. 11, 1729 | L-1 | 449 |
| Mary, [d. Jonathan & Sarah], b. May 23, 1734 | L-3 | 456 |
| Mary, [d. Eliphalet & Lydia], b. May 17, 1761 | 1 | 28 |
| Mary, d. [Eliphalet & Lydia], b. May 17, 1761; d. Sept. 17, 1832 | 2 | 45 |
| Mary, d. [Joseph, Jr. & Sarah], b. Aug. 22, 1796 | 2 | 76 |
| Mary, of Colchester, m. Norman T. **WADHAMS**, of Goshen, Nov. 6, 1838, by Rev. Lyman Strong | 2 | 109 |
| Mary Ann, d. [Solomon & Patty], b. Apr. 3, 1807 | 2 | 150 |
| Mary Kellogg, d. [Jonathan & Betsey], b. Dec. 29, 1803; d. Mar. 11, 1809 | 2 | 81 |
| Mary W., of Colchester, m. Henry **ALVORD**, of Bolton, May 12, 1846, by Rev. Joel R. Arnold | 3 | 28 |
| Mary Williams, d. [Ely H. & Mary], b. Dec. 24, 1824 | 2 | 143 |
| Mercy, [d. Israel & Mercy], b. Oct. 14, 1758 | 1 | 99 |
| Mercy, d. [Aaron], b. Feb. 7, 1776 | 1 | 126 |
| Mercy, d. [Aaron & Anna], b. Feb. 2, 1796 | 1 | 126 |
| Meshalham, [s. Nehemiah & Martha], b. Dec. 12, 1769 | 1 | 55 |
| Molly, d. [Aaron & Anna], b. Mar. 30, 1763 | 1 | 126 |
| Nancy M., m. Erastus **CARRIER**, b. of Colchester, Feb. 9, 1843, by Rev. J. R. Arnold | 3 | 1 |
| Nancy M., d. [Samuel, 2d, & Nabby], b. [ ] | 2 | 146 |
| Nehemiah, [s. Jonathan & Sarah], b. Mar. 1, 1727/8 | L-1 | 446 |
| Nehemiah, m. Lydia **GILLETT**, Sept. 13, 1757 | 1 | 55 |
| Nehemiah, m. Martha **STORES**, Jan. 22, 1761 | 1 | 55 |
| Nehemiah, d. Aug. 25, 1814, ae 86 | 1 | 55 |
| Olive, [d. Nehemiah & Martha], b. Dec. 3, 1761 | 1 | 55 |
| Ozias, [s. Israel & Mercy], b. Mar. 4, 1756 | 1 | 99 |
| Patience, d. [Joseph, Jr. & Sarah], b. Dec. 23, 1786; d. Feb. 27, 1840, ae 52 | 2 | 76 |
| Phebe, d. [Ely & Phebe], b. Mar. 17, 1796 | 2 | 77 |
| Ralph, s. [Joseph & Abigail], b. June 4, 1777 | 1 | 110 |
| Reynnold, s. [Jonathan, 3d, & Phebe], b. Apr. 23, 1750 | 1 | 109 |
| Reynold, s. Jonathan, b. June 11, 1750 | 1 | 149 |
| Russel[l], s. [Aaron & Anna], b. Aug. 31, 1769 | 1 | 126 |
| Russell, s. [Solomon & Patty], b. Aug. 13, 1814 | 2 | 150 |
| Russell, m. Elizabeth **CLARKE**, b. of Colchester, Mar. 18, 1845, by Rev. Joel R. Arnold | 3 | 20 |
| Ruth, [d. Samuell & Mary], b. Dec. 17, 1731 | L-1 | 449 |
| Salmon Cone, s. [Ely H. & Mary], b. June 12, 1830 | 2 | 143 |

| | Vol. | Page |
|---|---|---|
| **GILLETT, GILLET, GILLITT, GELLETT,** (cont.) | | |
| Samuell, m. Mary **CHAPPELL**, Jan. 30, 1718/19 | L-1 | 449 |
| Samuell, [s. Samuell & Mary], b. Apr. 20, 1719 | L-1 | 449 |
| Samuel, s. [Eliphalet & Lydia], b. Nov. 18, 1766; d. Oct. 8, 1771 | 2 | 45 |
| Sam[ue]ll, s. [Joseph & Abigail], b. Aug. 25, 1779 | 1 | 110 |
| Samuel, 2d, m. Nabby **LORD**, Oct. 29, 1812; d. Aug. 9, 1842 | 2 | 146 |
| Samuel Selden, s. [Samuel, 2d, & Nabby], b. Dec. 31, 1815 | 2 | 146 |
| Sarah, [d. Josiah & Sarah], b. June 24, 1717 | L-1 | 450 |
| Sarah, [d. Jonathan & Sarah], b. Jan. 1, 1718 | L-1 | 446 |
| Sarah, d. [Jonathan, 3d, & Phebe], b. Oct. 24, 1748 | 1 | 109 |
| Sarah, d. [Joseph & Abigail], b. Aug. 28, 1762 | 1 | 110 |
| Sarah, d. [Joseph, Jr. & Sarah], b. Apr. 2, 1792 | 2 | 76 |
| Sarah, d. [Harvey & Eunice W.], b. Apr. 27, 1840 | 2 | 29 |
| Sarah, [w. Joseph, Jr.], d. Feb. 25, 1850, ae 87 | 2 | 76 |
| Sarah A., m. Alfred H. **OTIS**, Mar. 15, 1831, by Rev. Lyman Strong | 2 | 230 |
| Sarah Ann, d. [Ely & Phebe], b. July 7, 1809 | 2 | 77 |
| Sarah Ann, of Colchester, m. David **BUEL**, Jr., of New Haven, Nov. 25, 1847, by Rev. Joel R. Arnold | 3 | 33 |
| Solomon, s. Aaron, b. Aug. 10, 1773 | 1 | 126 |
| Solomon, s. [Aaron & Anne], b. Aug. 12, 1774 | 2 | 42 |
| Solomon, s. [Aaron & Anna], b. Aug. 10, 1798 | 1 | 126 |
| Solomon, m. Patty **DOOLITTLE**, [ ] | 2 | 150 |
| Solomon L., m. Mary J. **WATROUS**, July 24, 1826, by Salmon Cone, V. D. M. | 2 | 188 |
| Solomon Lewis, s. [Solomon & Patty], b. Sept. 20, 1803 | 2 | 150 |
| Solomon T., m. Louisa E. **BISSELL**, Oct. 18, 1832 | 2 | 270 |
| Solomon Tracy, s. [Caleb & Civel], b. June 23. 1807 | 2 | 78 |
| Storrs, [s. Nehemiah & Martha], b. Apr. 5, 1773; d. Oct. 5, 1828, ae 55 | 1 | 55 |
| Sibble, [d. Israel & Mercy], b. Oct. 4, 1753 | 1 | 99 |
| Sybil, m. Benjamin **BEADLE**, Oct. 21, 1781; d. Jan. 11, 1789 | 2 | 39 |
| Theod[o]tia, d. [Joseph, Jr. & Sarah], b. Dec. 5, 1784 | 2 | 76 |
| Timothy, [s. Josiah & Sarah], b. June 27, 1723 | L-1 | 450 |
| William E., m. Bethiah **BACKUS**, b. of Colchester, May 9, 1848, by Rev. J. R. Arnold | 3 | 35 |
| William Ely, s. [Ely H. & Mary], b. June 21, 1822 | 2 | 143 |
| Zerviah, d. [Joseph & Abigail], b. Mar. 18, 1775 | 1 | 110 |
| Zubea, [d. Nehemiah & Martha], b. Aug. 20, 1765; d. Oct. 1, 1785 | 1 | 55 |
| -----, s. [Joseph & Abigail], b. Aug. 22, 1761; d. Aug. 24, 1761 | 1 | 110 |
| -----, d. [Solomon & Patty], b. Jan. 28, 1806; d. same day | 2 | 150 |
| **GILMAN**, Caleb G., of New Hampshire, m. Catharine **JORDAN**, of Colchester, May 25, 1851, by Rev. George W. Pendleton | 2 | 102 |
| **GIMBLE**, John, b. in Germany, priv. of Capt. M. V. B. Tiffany's | | |

| | Vol. | Page |
|---|---|---|
| **GIMBLE**, (cont.) | | |
| Co. E., 18th Reg. Conn. Vol., enrolled July 25, 1862; honorably discharged June 27, 1865, ae 31, at Harper's Ferry, Va. | 3 | 69 |
| **GLASS**, Alex, [s. James & Rebecca], b. May 11, 1746 | 1 | 146 |
| Alex, [s. James], b. May 1, 1746 | 1 | 151 |
| Alexander, s. [James & Rebecca], b. May 1, 1746 | 1 | 104 |
| Alice, [d. James], b. Feb. 17, 1751 | 1 | 151 |
| Ellis, d. [James & Rebecca], b. Feb. 17, 1751 | 1 | 104 |
| James, m. Rebecca **ROBERTS**, Dec. 20, 1741 | 1 | 104 |
| James, m. Rebecca **ROBERTS**, Dec. 20, 1741 | 1 | 146 |
| James, s. [James & Rebecca], b. Jan. 28, 1748 | 1 | 104 |
| James, [s. James], b. Jan. 28, 1748 | 1 | 151 |
| Rebecca, d. [James & Rebecca], b. July 17, 1744 | 1 | 104 |
| Rebecca, [d. James & Rebecca], b. July 17, 1744 | 1 | 146 |
| Rebecca, [d. James], b. July 17, 1744 | 1 | 151 |
| Rebeckah, m. William **ANDERSON**, July 19, 1764 | 1 | 141 |
| Rufhes, s. [James & Rebecca], b. Apr. 22, 1757 | 1 | 104 |
| Sarah, d. [James & Rebecca], b. Nov. 1, 1742 | 1 | 146 |
| Sarah, [d. James], b. Nov. 1, 1742 | 1 | 151 |
| Sarah, d. [James & Rebecca], b. Nov. 1, 1742; d. Dec. 18, 1752 | 1 | 104 |
| **GLOSSENGER**, Julia A., m. Calvin D. **SHAYLOR**, b. of Colchester, Sept. 7, 1834, by Rev. Lyman Strong | 2 | 269 |
| **GLOVER**, Mary, m. Ebenezer **NORTHAM**, Jan. 15, 1718/19 | L-1 | 446 |
| **GODFREY**, John, [s. Susannah], b. Mar. 12, 1765 | 2 | 3 |
| Peter, [s. Susannah], b. July 15, 1767 | 2 | 3 |
| **GOFF**, Benjamin G., of Ashtabula County, Denmark Township, at present residing in Montville, m. Eunice **ADAMS**, of Colchester, Aug. 21, 1825, by John Bigelow, J. P, at the house of David Adams | 2 | 181 |
| Edmund, m. Elizabeth J. **MAPLES**, Mar. 16, 1845, by Rev. Benjamin G. Goff | 3 | 20 |
| **GOLD**, Sarah, d. John, b. Apr. 24, 1718 | L-1 | 449 |
| **GOODSPEED**, Elizabeth, [d. Nath[anie]ll & Elizabeth], b. May 24, 1766 | 1 | 32 |
| Hannah, [d. Nath[anie]ll & Elizabeth], b. Apr. 5, 1759 | 1 | 32 |
| Lydia, [d. Nath[anie]ll & Elizabeth], b. Jan. 19, 1763 | 1 | 32 |
| Nath[anie]ll, [s. Nath[anie]ll & Elizabeth], b. Sept. 12, 1764 | 1 | 32 |
| Rebecka, [d. Nath[anie]ll & Elizabeth], b. Mar. 21, 1755, in Barnstable | 1 | 32 |
| **GORTON**, Welthan, m. Elisha **BIGELOW**, Jr., Dec. 16, 1773 | 2 | 28 |
| **GOTT**, Chauncey, of Hebron, m. Mary **CHAMBERLAIN**, of Colchester, Apr. 27, 1825, by Samuel A. Peters, J. P. | 2 | 177 |
| Hazard, of Hebron, m. Rebecca **STRONG**, of Colchester, Mar. 20, 1821, by Salmon Cone, Minister | 2 | 154 |
| **GRANT**, Anna, of East Windsor, m. Walter **GUSTIN**, of Colchester, May 2, 1781, by Daniel Ellsworth, J. P., | | |

| | Vol. | Page |
|---|---|---|
| **GRANT**, (cont.) | | |
| East Windsor; d. Jan. 26, 1849 | 2 | 60 |
| **GRAVES, GREAVES**, Abagail, [d. Peter & Sarah], b. May 2, 1749 | 1 | 95 |
| Abigail, m. Nathan **DODGE**, Oct. 10, 1755 | 1 | 54 |
| Anna, d. [Peter, Jr. & Mary], b. Sept. 6, 1764 | 1 | 103 |
| Ariel, s. [Peter, Jr. & Mary], b. Jan. 21, 1767 | 1 | 103 |
| Asa, [s. Peter & Sarah], b. May 8, 1747 | 1 | 95 |
| Asa, m. Mercy **KELLOGG**, Mar. 2, 1786, d. May 21, 1800 | 2 | 55 |
| Asa, s. [Charles & Sally], b. Jan. 29, 1829 | 2 | 55 |
| Benjamin, d. Dec. 29, 1752 | 1 | 54 |
| Charles, s. [Asa & Mercy], b. June 30, 1788 | 2 | 55 |
| Charles, b. June 30, 1788; m. Sally **WHITE**, Oct. 6, 1811 | 2 | 55 |
| Clarissa, d. [Charles & Sally], b. Aug. 12, 1821 | 2 | 55 |
| Clarissa, m. Morgan **MOTT**, b. of Colchester, Jan. 31, 1847, by Rev. J. R. Arnold | 3 | 30 |
| David, s. [Charles & Sally], b. Nov. 19, 1812 | 2 | 55 |
| Deborah, [d. Peter & Sarah], b. May 14, 1754; d. Dec. 5, 1754 | 1 | 95 |
| Diademia, [d. Peter & Sarah], b. Jan. 3, 1759 | 1 | 95 |
| Elizer, [d. Peter & Sarah], b. Mar. 24, 1743; d. Nov. 24, 1760 | 1 | 95 |
| Eliza, d. [Charles & Sally], b. Jan. 24, 1816 | 2 | 55 |
| Eliza, m. William **GREENWOOD**, Jr., Apr. 23, 1835, by Benj[ami]n Trumbull, J. P. | 2 | 276 |
| Elizabeth, [d. Peter & Sarah], b. Oct. 29, 1751 | 1 | 95 |
| Hellen, of Colchester, m. Joseph **ROWLEY**, of East Haddam, Oct. 11, 1846, by Rev. P. Brockett | 3 | 28 |
| John, [s. Peter & Sarah], b. Apr. 12, 1756 | 1 | 95 |
| Lois, [d. Peter & Sarah], b. Aug. 20, 1763 | 1 | 95 |
| Lucy, d. [Asa & Mercy], b. Apr. 26, 1787; d. Mar. [ ], 1814, ae 27 | 2 | 55 |
| Lucy, d. [Charles & Sally], b. May 7, 1814 | 2 | 55 |
| Mary Ann, d. [Charles & Sally], b. Apr. 21, 1818; d. Mar. 29, 1843, ae 25 | 2 | 55 |
| Mary Anne, of Colchester, m. Theodore **FOSTER**, of Smithfield, R. I., Aug. 16, 1840, by Henry Worthington, J. P.; d. Mar. 29, 1843, ae 25 | 2 | 66 |
| Mercy, [w. Asa], d. Oct. 8, 1806 | 2 | 55 |
| Peter, m. Sarah **WEDGE**, July 1, 1742 | 1 | 95 |
| Peter, [s. Peter & Sarah], b. Nov. 3, 1744 | 1 | 95 |
| Peter, Jr., m. Mary **CHAPMAN**, May 17, 1764 | 1 | 103 |
| Sarah Jane, d. [Charles & Sally], b. Sept. 16, 1834; d. Sept. 15, 1850, ae 16 | 2 | 55 |
| William, s. [Charles & Sally], b. June 10, 1823 | 2 | 55 |
| **GRAY**, July Ann Tracy, d. [Gamaliel R. & Sally], b. July 22, 1810; d. Jan. 25, 1811 | 3 | 7 |
| Nehemiah Tracy, s. [Gamaliel R. & Sally], b. July 9, 1805 | 3 | 7 |
| Ralph Tracy, s. [Gamaliel R. & Sally], b. Dec. 26, 1799; d. July 18, 1823 | 3 | 7 |

| | Vol. | Page |
|---|---|---|
| **GRAY**, (cont.) | | |
| Susan E. Tracy, d. [Gamaliel R. & Sally], b. Oct. 20, 1803 | 3 | 7 |
| **GREENE**, Eliza Ann Maria, of Colchester, m. Hiram **HYDE**, of Norwich, Sept. 11, 1836, by Rev. Joel R. Arnold | 2 | 288 |
| **GREENWOOD**, William, Jr.,, m. Eliza **GRAVES**, Apr. 23, 1835, by Benj[ami]n Trumbull, J. P. | 2 | 276 |
| **GRIFFIN, GRIFFING**, John R., of East Haddam, m. Frances R. **GILLET**, of Colchester, July 3, 1851, by Rev. Lyman Strong | 2 | 109 |
| Sarah, m. David **TREADWAY**, May 8, 1766 | 1 | 79 |
| Walter, m. Betty **HARRIS**, b. of Colchester, Jan. 27, 1772 | 1 | 83 |
| **GRIGGS**, Cynthia, of Ashford, m. W[illia]m N. **CROWLEY**, of Colchester, May 24, 1850, by Rev. Lyman Strong | 3 | 4 |
| Henry, of Middletown, m. Nancy **CROWLEY**, of Colchester, Nov. 29, 1849, by Rev. Augustus Bolles | 3 | 43 |
| **GRISWOLD**, Hannah, m. Thomas **GASTIN**, Jr., Dec. 11, 1746 | 1 | 148 |
| Ursula, m. Ephraim **WELLS**, Mar. 3, 1800 | 2 | 103 |
| **GROT**, Elizabeth, m. George **SMITH**, b. of Colchester, June 5, 1854, by Erastus Dickinson | 3 | 62 |
| **GROVER**, Ruth, m. Moses **FULLER**, Apr. 11, 1768; d. Mar. 10, 1782 | 2 | 22 |
| **GURLEY**, Mary, m. Rev. M. G. **CLARK**, Nov. 8, 1841, by Rev. Augustus Bolles | 2 | 267 |
| Sophronia S., of Colchester, m. Samuel P. **DOLBEAR**, of Lebanon, Apr. 9, 1838, by Rev. Andrew M. Smith | 2 | 193 |
| **GURSTIN**, [see also **GASTIN** and **GUSTIN**], Thomas, m. Sarah **HOLM[E]S**, June 7, 1722 | L-1 | 799 |
| Thomas, s. Thomas & [Sarah], b. July 19, 1725 | L-1 | 799 |
| **GUSTIN**, [see also **GURSTIN** and **GASTIN**], Amanda H., d. [Walter & Anna], b. Aug. 21, 1801 | 2 | 60 |
| Anna, d. [Walter & Anna], b. Oct. 17, 1783 | 2 | 60 |
| Anna, [w. Walter], d. Jan. 26, 1849 | 2 | 60 |
| Cata, d. [Walter & Anna], b. Apr. 21, 1790 | 2 | 60 |
| Clarissa, [d. Walter & Anna], b. June 10, [1782]; d. Dec. 24, 1782 | 2 | 60 |
| Dan, s. [Walter & Anna], b. Jan. 30, 1788 | 2 | 60 |
| Edward, m. Weltha **MARTIN**, Jan. 21, 1778 | 2 | 32 |
| Jonathan Grant, s. [Walter & Anna], b. Feb. 20, 1794 | 2 | 60 |
| Katherine, of Colchester, m. Perley **BELKNAP**, of Middletown, Dec. 2, 1821, by Salmon Cone, V. D. M. | 2 | 108 |
| Mary, d. [Walter & Anna], b. June 22, 1796; d. Mar. 3, 1849, ae 53 | 2 | 60 |
| Phebe, d. [Walter & Anna], b. Nov. 25, 1785 | 2 | 60 |
| Philotheta, [d. Edward & Weltha], b. Apr. 4, 1779 | 2 | 32 |
| Sarah, m. David **TREADWAY**, Oct. 12, 1765 | 2 | 79 |
| Sarah, d. [Walter & Anna], b. Dec. 19, 1798 | 2 | 60 |
| Sarah, of Colchester, m. Abiel L. **BARTHOLOMEW**, of Saybrook, Mar. 20, 1821, by Salmon Cone, V. D. M. | 2 | 142 |

| | Vol. | Page |
|---|---|---|
| **GUSTIN**, (cont.) | | |
| Sophia, d. [Walter & Anna], b. May 23, 1792 | 2 | 60 |
| Thomas, s. [Edward & Weltha], b. Jan. 22, 1781 | 2 | 32 |
| Walter, of Colchester, m. Anna **GRANT**, of East Windsor, May 2, 1781, by Daniel Ellsworth, J. P., East Windsor; d. May 17, 1824, ae 75 | 2 | 60 |
| **HACKLEY**, Samuel, m. Arine **TILDEN**, Nov. 8, 1764 | 1 | 83 |
| **HALE**, Walter, of Glastonbury, m. Fanny **SMITH**, of Colchester, Nov. 14, 1836, by Rev. Andrew M. Smith | 2 | 292 |
| **HALL, HAUL**, Anne, d. [Joshua & Hannah], b. July 19, 1783 | 2 | 6 |
| Dudley, s. [Joshua & Hannah], b. Nov. 24, 1786 | 2 | 6 |
| Elam, of Somers, m. Laura W. **MORGAN**, of Colchester, Apr. 7, 1822, by Salmon Cone, V. D. M. | 2 | 141 |
| Ely, s. [William & Eunice], b. Apr. [ ], 1793 | 2 | 73 |
| Ezra, of Lyme, m. Elizabeth C. **KELLOGG**, of Colchester, Feb. 17, 1831, by Rev. Lyman Strong | 2 | 229 |
| Hannah, d. [Joshua & Hannah], b. Dec. 12, 1776 | 2 | 6 |
| Hannah, [w. Joseph], d. May 23, 1794, ae 40 | 2 | 6 |
| Henry, s. [Joshua & Hannah], b. May 4, 1789 | 2 | 6 |
| Jane Elizabeth, m. Daniel **KELLOGG**, b. of Colchester, May 28, 1850, by Henry M. Field | 3 | 45 |
| John, s. [Joshua & Hannah], b. Apr. 29, 1781 | 2 | 6 |
| Joshua, m. Hannah **CAVERLY**, Apr. 8, 1773; d. May 5, 1812, ae 71 | 2 | 6 |
| Joshua, s. [Joshua & Hannah], b. May 28, 1775 | 2 | 6 |
| Mary, of New London, m. Amos **DODGE**, of Colchester, Jan. 27, 1756 | 1 | 48 |
| Mary, d. [Joshua & Hannah], b. Feb. 14, 1779 | 2 | 6 |
| Mary Ann, d. Capt. Joshua, d. Dec. 7, 1819, ae 19 | 2 | 6 |
| Phebe, of Lyme, m. Ely **GILLET**, of Colchester, Apr. 8, 1790 | 2 | 77 |
| Polly, d. [William & Eunice], b. June 9, 1788 | 2 | 73 |
| Pom[e]roy, m. Emeline N. **BULKELEY**, b. of Colchester, Oct. 5, 1823, by Salmon Cone, V. D. M. | 2 | 99 |
| Stephen, m. Mary **KIMBALL**, b. of Colchester, Oct. 16, 1820, by Samuel A. Peters, J. P. | 2 | 153 |
| William, m. Eunice **FOOT**, Aug. 12, 1787 | 2 | 73 |
| Wyllys, s. [William & Eunice], b. Aug. 29, 1790 | 2 | 73 |
| **HAMILTON**, Avis, [d. James], b. Feb. 7, 1754 | 1 | 78 |
| Charity, [d. James], b. July 13, 1749 | 1 | 78 |
| Daniel, of Colchester, m. Sarah **PERKINS**, of Lyme, Sept. 6, 1759 | 1 | 20 |
| Daniel, [s. Daniel & Sarah], b. Apr. 23, 1760 | 1 | 20 |
| Daniel, d. June 22, 1761 | 1 | 20 |
| Daniel, s. [Gurdon & Eunice], b. Jan. 23, 1813 | 2 | 134 |
| Elizabeth, [d. James], b. Feb. 5, 1760 | 1 | 78 |
| Eunice, w. [Gurdon], d. Dec. 21, 1831, ae 55 | 2 | 134 |
| Freelove, [d. James], b. Oct. 29, 1740 | 1 | 78 |
| Freelove, of Colchester, m. John **WILLIAMS**, June 3, 1764 | 1 | 79 |

| | Vol. | Page |
|---|---|---|
| **HAMILTON**, (cont.) | | |
| Gurdin, [s. James], b. May 2, 1751 | 1 | 78 |
| Gurdon, m. Eunice **FALLS**, Mar. 30, 1807; d. Feb. 5, 1831, ae 80 | 2 | 134 |
| Gurdon Waterman, s. [Gurdon & Eunice], b. July 11, 1808 | 2 | 134 |
| Guy Wheeler, s. [Gurdon & Eunice], b. Nov. 22, 1819 | 2 | 134 |
| James, [s. James], b. Dec. 25, 1742 | 1 | 78 |
| John Rogers, s. [Gurdon & Eunice], b. Apr. 26, 1815 | 2 | 134 |
| Justin Gilbert, s. [Gurdon & Eunice], b. Apr. 8, 1811 | 2 | 134 |
| Laruhamy, child of [James], b. Dec. 29, 1744 | 1 | 78 |
| Lucretia, [d. James], b. Dec. 6, 1746 | 1 | 78 |
| Lucretia, m. Jehiel **JONES**, Sept. 19, 1765 | 1 | 86 |
| Sarah, [d. James], b. May 13, 1756; d. Oct. 30, 1748 *Error in record was hand printed in original manuscript | 1 | 78 |
| Sarah, m. Zebulon **WATERMAN**, Oct. 14, 1776 | 2 | 75 |
| *Vail, child of [James], b. May 29, 1762 *(Bail handwritten in margin of originall manuscript) | 1 | 78 |
| **HAMLIN, HAMBLIN**, Cornelius, m. Mary **MUDGE**, Dec. 5, 1732 | TPR | 111 |
| Cornelius, [s. Cornelius & Mary], b. Sept. 25, 1733 | TPR | 111 |
| Ebenezer, m. Mary **DARBEE**, Sept. 17, 1761 | 1 | 25 |
| Hopestill, m. Samuel **WATERS**, Nov. 6, 1751 | 1 | 24 |
| Lovice, [d. Ebenezer & Mary], b. Dec. 3, 1764 | 1 | 25 |
| Lydia, [d. Ebenezer & Mary], b. Aug. 9, 1762 | 1 | 25 |
| **HAMMOND**, Daniel Hubbard, s. [Joseph C & Abby J.], b. Nov. 20, 1832 | 2 | 233 |
| David Green, s. [Joseph C. & Abby J.], b. Mar 4, 1839; d. Sept. 28, 1839 | 2 | 233 |
| Elizabeth, d. [James F. or E. & Elizabeth H.], b. May 30, 1832; m. Peleg A. **DAWLEY**, of R. I., [Harrisville Coventry] | 2 | 234 |
| Elizabeth H., of Providence, R. I., m. James F. **OTIS**, of Colchester, Aug. 18, 1831, by Rev. W[illia]m Phillips, Providence | 2 | 234 |
| Elizabeth P., w. Julius S. [& d. Daniel & Olive **HUBBARD**], d. Nov. 5, 1835 | 2 | 108 |
| Elizabeth P., [w. Julius S.], d. Nov. 5, 1835, ae 29 | 2 | 195 |
| Joseph C., of Vernon, m. Abby J. **HUBBARD**, of Colchester, Sept. 28, 1831, by Rev. Lyman Strong | 2 | 233 |
| Joseph Churchill, s. [Joseph C. & Abby J.], b. Dec. 15, 1836 | 2 | 233 |
| Julius S., m. Elizabeth P. **HUBBARD**, May 6, 1827, by Salmon Cone | 2 | 195 |
| Louisa B., of Colchester, m. Halsey F. **BIDWELL**, of Norwich, Nov. 1, 1846, by Rev. P. Brockett | 3 | 29 |
| Mary, d. Sept. 10, 1851, ae 44 | 2 | 233 |
| -----, s. [Joseph C. & Abby J.], b. Dec. 16, 1835; d. Dec. 28, 1835 | 2 | 233 |
| **HANCOCK, HANDCOX**, Clarissa, of Colchester, m. Joseph | | |

| | Vol. | Page |
|---|---|---|
| **HANCOCK, HANDCOX,** (cont.) | | |
| **BUTTON**, of Montville, Apr. 9, 1849, by Griswold E. Morgan, J. P., Lebanon | 3 | 40 |
| James, m. Nancy **TAYLOR**, b. of Colchester, June 2, 1850, by Griswold E. Morgan, J. P. | 3 | 2 |
| Mary, m. Anthony **GALLAGER**, Sept. 25, 1842, by Rev. Rob[er]t C. Mills | 2 | 230 |
| Wealthy Ann, of Colchester, m. Roswell **COREY**, of Plainfield, Conn., July 27, 1851, by Rev. George W. Pendleton | 2 | 58 |
| **HARDEN**, [see also **HARDING**], Ama, m. Ephraim **BROWN**, Sept. 4, 1783 | 2 | 52 |
| **HARDING**, [see also **HARDEN**], Almy, d. Stephen, b. Mar. 6, 1744; d. June 6, 1762 | 1 | 150 |
| Benjamin, s. [Stephen], b. May 16, 1753 | 1 | 150 |
| Elisha, s. [Stephen], b. Aug. 6, 1763 | 1 | 150 |
| Esther, d. [Stephen], b. Apr. 13, 1759 | 1 | 150 |
| Israel, s. [Stephen], b. Apr. 18, 1757 | 1 | 150 |
| Jemima, [d. Stephen], b. Feb. 13, 1747 | 1 | 150 |
| Lydia, [d. Stephen], b. May 29, 1745 | 1 | 150 |
| Lydia, m. Thomas **CHAPMAN**, Dec. 11, 1766 | 1 | 79 |
| Micajah, s. [Stephen], b. Apr. 20, 1762 | 1 | 150 |
| Stateley, s. [Stephen], b. Mar. 27, 1755 | 1 | 150 |
| Stephen, [s. Stephen], b. Jan. 13, 1748/9 | 1 | 150 |
| Thomas, [s. Stephen], b. Apr. 13, 1751 | 1 | 150 |
| **HARRINGTON**, Jane, m. Boliver **WOODWORTH**, b. of Norwich, Apr. 20, 1846, by Rev. Pierpoint Brockett | 3 | 27 |
| **HARRIS**, Abigaill, [d. James], b. May 17, 1711 | L-1 | 452 |
| Abigail, m. Oliver **DODGE**, Nov. 1, 1773 | 1 | 77 |
| Alph, [s. James], b. Feb. 29, 1708; d. Aug. 30, 1708 | L-1 | 452 |
| Alph, [s. James], b. Aug. 31, 1716 | L-1 | 452 |
| Betty, m. Walter **GRIFFIN**, b. of Colchester, Jan. 27, 1772 | 1 | 83 |
| Deborah, m. Elijah **TREADWAY**, [ ] | 2 | 124 |
| Delight, [d. James], b. Oct. 17, 1720 | L-1 | 452 |
| Dorothy, d. [Nathaniel & Mary], b. Jan. 26, 1779 | 2 | 64 |
| Hannah, m. Isaac **ROWLEE**, May 30, 1717 | L-1 | 654 |
| Hannah, d. Evan & Mary, b. Aug. 22, 1732 | TPR | 109 |
| Hannah, d. [Nathaniel & Mary], b. Sept. 19, 1786 | 2 | 64 |
| James, [s. James], b. Jan. 26, 1699 | L-1 | 452 |
| James, s. James, b. Jan. 26, 1719 | L-1 | 446 |
| Joel, s. [Nathaniel & Mary], b. July 8, 1766 | 2 | 64 |
| Jonathan, [s. James], b. June 15, 1705 | L-1 | 452 |
| Jonathan, s. [Nathaniel & Mary], b. Aug. 21, 1788; d. Apr. 27, 1850, ae 62 y., in Salem, Conn. | 2 | 64 |
| Leb[b]eus, [s. James], b. Aug. 11, 1713 | L-1 | 452 |
| Lebbeus, s. [Nathaniel & Mary], b. Sept. 19, 1764 | 2 | 64 |
| Lois, d. [Nathaniel & Mary], b. July 1, 1768 | 2 | 64 |
| Lydia, d. [Nathaniel & Mary], b. Nov. 16, 1784 | 2 | 64 |

| | Vol. | Page |
|---|---|---|
| **HARRIS**, (cont.) | | |
| Lydia, m. Asa **RATHBURN**, Apr. [ ], 1825 | 2 | 132 |
| Mariah, d. [Nathaniel & Mary], b. Feb. 3, 1775 | 2 | 64 |
| Mary, [d. James], b. Nov. 1, 1702 | L-1 | 452 |
| Merebah, m. Seth **LATHROP**, Sept. 28, 1794 | 2 | 75 |
| Merebah, m. Seth **LATHROP**, Sept. 28, 1794 | 2 | 133 |
| Nathaniel, m. Mary **TOZER**, Feb. 1, 1764 | 2 | 64 |
| Nathaniel, s. [Nathaniel & Mary], b. Feb. 24, 1777 | 2 | 64 |
| Polly, d. [Nathaniel & Mary], b. Sept. 14, 1770 | 2 | 64 |
| Rachel, m. John **LO[O]MIS**, Dec. 18, 1760 | 1 | 152 |
| Rachel, d. [Nathaniel & Mary], b. Jan. 17, 1783 | 2 | 64 |
| Rachel Ann, of Colchester, m. Aaron T. **NILES**, of Middletown, July 21, 1827, by Rev. Joseph Harvey | 2 | 197 |
| Samuel, s. [Nathaniel & Mary], b. Dec. 10, 1780 | 2 | 64 |
| Sarah, [d. James], b. Sept. 27, 1697 | L-1 | 452 |
| Sarah, m. John **BROWN**, Aug. 13, 1724 | L-1 | 445 |
| Sarah, d. [Nathaniel & Mary], b. Sept. 10, 1772 | 2 | 64 |
| Tabitha, m. Jabez **ROWLE[Y]**, Feb. 20, 1724 | L-1 | 448 |
| **HARVEY**, Allen Lyman, s. [Elias & Ruth], b. Apr. 4, 1823 | 2 | 57 |
| Amos S., s. [Elias & Ruth], b. May 6, 1817; d. Aug. [ ], 1818 | 2 | 57 |
| Amos Stanton, 2d, s. [Elias & Ruth], b. Jan. 5, 1825 | 2 | 57 |
| Daniel B., s. [Elias & Ruth], b. Aug. 12, 1815, d. Jan. [ ], 1819 | 2 | 57 |
| Daniel B., of East Haddam, m. Attarista M. **HOLDRIDGE**, of Colchester, Jan. 11, 1841, by Rev. Lyman Strong | 2 | 243 |
| Daniel Babcock, 2d, s. [Elias & Ruth], b. June 16, 1819 | 2 | 57 |
| Elias, b. Apr. 11, 1775; m. Ruth **EDWARDS**, [ ], 1810 | 2 | 57 |
| Elias, Jr., b. Oct. 29, 1800, in Lebanon; m. Sally Maria **RANSOM**, Sept. 12, 1830, in Salem | 2 | 57 |
| Harriet Newell, d. [Elias, Jr. & Sally Maria], b. Nov. 19, 1843 | 2 | 57 |
| Henry William, s. [Elias & Ruth], b. Dec. 20, 1810 | 2 | 57 |
| Israel E., m. Harriet A. **UTTLEY**, b. of Colchester, Mar. 19, 1844, by Rev. Joel R. Arnold | 3 | 11 |
| John Ransom, s. [Elias, Jr. & Sally Maria], b. Nov. 22, 1836 | 2 | 57 |
| Lucinda, d. [Elias & Ruth], b. May 15, 1812; d. Nov. [ ], 1814 | 2 | 57 |
| Lucinda A., of Colchester, m. George W. **STANDISH**, of Bozrah, Feb. 14, 1850, by Rev. Albert F. Park | 3 | 12 |
| Lucinda Angeline, d. [Elias & Ruth], b. Feb. 3, 1827 | 2 | 57 |
| Lydia Newton, d. [Elias, Jr. & Sally Maria], b. Oct. 8, 1833 | 2 | 57 |
| Phebe, w. Elias, d. June [ ], 1809 | 2 | 57 |
| Philothee L., of Colchester, m. Allen **COTTON**, of Hartford, June 3, 1823, by Rev. William Palmer, at the house of Mr. Harvey | 2 | 145 |
| Ruth, d. [Elias & Ruth], b. Dec. 28, 1813; d. Nov. [ ], 1814 | 2 | 57 |
| Sally Maria, d. [Elias, Jr. & Sally Maria], b. Aug. 7, 1841 | 2 | 57 |
| William Erastus, s. [Elias, Jr. & Sally Maria], b. Oct. 30, 1846 | 2 | 57 |

| | Vol. | Page |
|---|---|---|
| **HARVEY**, (cont.) | | |
| William H., m. Margaret **JOHNSON**, b. of Colchester, Feb. 12, 1837, by Rev. Joel R. Arnold | 2 | 294 |
| **HASTINGS**, Abigail, m. John **BULKLEY**, Apr. 16, 1751 | 1 | 133 |
| Abigail, see Abigail **LITTLE** | 2 | 310 |
| **HATCH**, Benjamin, m. Deborah **CHAMBERLAIN**, Dec. 7, 1769 | 1 | 89 |
| **HAYNES**, David, of Lebanon, m. Amanda A. **TAYLOR**, of Colchester, Nov. 29, 1849, by Rev. John Avery, of Exeter | 3 | 44 |
| Ruth, d. John, 1st Gov. of Conn. Colony, m. Samuel **WYLLYS**, of Hartford, [ ] | 2 | 310 |
| **HAZARD**, Dorcas Ann, m. Samuel **CHURCH**, of Montville, Nov. 8, 1825, by Samuel A. Peters, J. P. | 2 | 180 |
| Nabby, of Colchester, m. William **FOGG**, of Greenfield, Penn., Nov. 18, 1821, by Salmon Cone, V. D. M. | 2 | 326 |
| **HEALEY**, Betsey, of Colchester, m. Seth **DOOLITTLE**, of Wallingford, Apr. 2, 1826, by Amerst D. Scoville, J. P. | 2 | 185 |
| **HEATON**, Ann, m. Ebenezer **DIBELL**, Aug. 29, 1706 | TM-1 | 194 |
| **HEWETT**, Eleanor, d. Sept. 18, 1846 | 3 | 15 |
| **HICKOCK, HEECOCK**, [see also **HITCHCOCK**], Mercy, wid. of Joseph, of Durham, m. [Nath[anie]ll **FOOT**], Sept. 13, 1727 | 1 | 117 |
| Sarah, m. Charles **KELLOGG**, Apr. 24, 1748 | 1 | 76 |
| **HICKS**, George, m. Elizabeth **MARTHER**, b. of Colchester, June 18, 1854, by Erastus Dickinson | 3 | 62 |
| **HILLS**, Abner, s. [Joseph & Temperance], b. Oct. 17, 1796 | 2 | 74 |
| Abner, m. [ ] **COMSTOCK**, [ ] | 1 | 79 |
| Asahel, [s. Lebbeus & Hannah], b. Jan. 29, 1766 | 1 | 22 |
| Elijah, m. Grace **MARRINER**, Mar. 17, 1768 | 1 | 87 |
| Elijah, [s. Elijah & Grace], b. Mar. 28, 1772 | 1 | 87 |
| Ellis, [d. Lebbeus & Hannah], b. Oct. 17, 1769 | 1 | 22 |
| Grace, [d. Elijah & Grace], b. Nov. 29, 1768 | 1 | 87 |
| Guy, [s. Samuel & Sarah], b. Feb. 2, 1764 | 1 | 28 |
| Hannah, [d. Lebbeus & Hannah], b. May 6, 1764 | 1 | 22 |
| Joseph, of Colchester, m. Temperance **WATERS**, of Hebron, Oct. 6, 1791 | 2 | 74 |
| Katharine, d. [Joseph & Temperance], b. Mar. 25, 1794 | 2 | 74 |
| Lebbeus, m. Hannah **BROWN**, Nov. 5, 1760 | 1 | 22 |
| Lebbeus, [s. Lebbeus & Hannah], b. Aug. 13, 1761 | 1 | 22 |
| Lucy, [d. Lebbeus & Hannah], b. Dec. 31, 1767 | 1 | 22 |
| Lucy, [d. Abner], b. May 19, 1771 | 1 | 79 |
| Margaret, m. William **WATERS**, Jan. 13, 1725 | L-1 | 449 |
| Margaret T., of Colchester, m. Julius T. **SMITH**, of Middle Haddam, Sept. 27, 1846, by Rev. P. Brockett | 3 | 28 |
| Rozel, [s. Lebbeus & Hannah], b. Feb. 18, 1763 | 1 | 22 |
| Samuel, [s. Samuel & Sarah], b. Aug. 14, 1761 | 1 | 28 |
| Samuel, m. Thankfull **ROWLEY**, Sept. 3, 1768 | 1 | 28 |
| Sarah, w. Samuel, d. May 31, 1766 | 1 | 28 |

| | Vol. | Page |
|---|---|---|
| **HILLS**, (cont.) | | |
| William Comstock, [s. Abner], b. Jan. 13, 1769 | 1 | 79 |
| Worthy, s. [Joseph & Temperance], b. Sept. 6, 1792 | 2 | 74 |
| ----, s. [Joseph & Temperance], b. July [ ], 1797; d. July [ ], 1797 | 2 | 74 |
| **HINCKLEY, HINKLEY**, Hannah, m. Daniel **JUDD**, Feb. 21, 1779 | 1 | 51 |
| Rhoda, of Lebanon, m. Benjamin **BEADLE**, Mar. 4, 1789 | 2 | 39 |
| **HITCHCOCK**, [see also **HICKOCK**], Eliakim, [s. John], b. Feb. 14, 1712/13 | L-3 | 193 |
| Eliakim, s. John, b. Feb. 14, 1712/13 | TM-1 | 193 |
| Elizabeth, d. John, b. May 3, 1708 | L-3 | 193 |
| Elesebeth, d. John, b. Mar. 23, 1708 | L-3 | 197 |
| Elizabeth, d. John, b. May 23, 1708 | TM-1 | 193 |
| Elizabeth, d. John, b. May 23, 1708 | TM-1 | 197 |
| Elizabeth, m. Daniell **SKIN[N]ER**, Dec. 22, 1727 | L-3 | 8 |
| Easter, [d. John], b. Sept. [ ], 1720 | L-3 | 193 |
| Esther, d. John, b. Sept. [ ], 1720 | TM-1 | 193 |
| Esther, m. Samuel **NORTHAM**, Nov. 21, 1754 | 1 | 131 |
| Hannah, [d. John], b. Oct. 29, 1717 | L-3 | 193 |
| Hannah, d. John, b. Oct. 29, 1717 | TM-1 | 193 |
| **HOLBROOK**, Mary, of Lebanon, m. John **NEWTON**, of Colchester, Dec. 27, 1756 | 1 | 115 |
| **HOLCOMB, HOLDCOMB**, Jane M., m. Hiram **SNOW**, b. of Colchester, Sept. 10, 1834, by Rev. Augustus Bolles | 3 | 63 |
| Nancy, of Marlborough, m. Albert H. **EMMONS**, Aug. 10, 1853, by Rev. S. D. Jewett | 3 | 57 |
| **HOLDRIDGE, HOLDRICH, HOLDREDGE**, Andrew L., Jr., d. Sept. 3, 1908, in Woburn, Mass., ae 62; b. in Colchester | 2 | 293 |
| Attarista M., of Colchester, m. Daniel B. **HARVEY**, of East Haddam, Jan. 11, 1841, by Rev. Lyman Strong | 2 | 243 |
| Bettey, [s. Israel], d. July 25, 1781 | 1 | 49 |
| Bridget M., d. Dec. 12, 1857 | 2 | 44 |
| Israel, m. Betty **NORTHAM**, Feb. 14, 1769 | 1 | 49 |
| Israel, [s. Israel & Betty], b. Nov. 7, 1769 | 1 | 49 |
| Leander, m. Phebe A. **CARRIER**, Jan. 22, 1837, by Giles Shattuck, J. P. | 2 | 293 |
| Lydia, m. Ambrose **STRONG**, Oct. 4, 1770 | 2 | 62 |
| **HOLMES, HOLMS**, Abigail, of Stonington, m. Rosel **SMITH**, of Colchester, Mar. 11, 1762 | 1 | 57 |
| Alexander, s. [Samuel & Lucy], b. Jan. 17, 1792 | 2 | 119 |
| Amasa W., s. [John & Anna], b. July 20, 1798; d. Nov. 23, 1839, ae 41, in Monroe County, Wis. | 2 | 82 |
| Ann, m. Rev. Joseph **LOVETT**, Apr. 3, 1734 | L-3 | 453 |
| Ann, d. John, b. June 1, 17[ ] | L-1 | 450 |
| Anna, w. John, d. Jan. 8, 1810, ae 51 | 2 | 82 |
| Augustus Selden, s. [Samuel & Lucy], b. May 18, 1810 | 2 | 119 |
| Betsey, d. [Samuel & Lucy], b. Dec. 28, 1793 | 2 | 119 |

| | Vol. | Page |
|---|---|---|
| **HOLMES, HOLMS,** (cont.) | | |
| Bettey, d. [John & Anna], b. Aug. 21, 1796 | 2 | 82 |
| Calvin, s. [Samuel & Lucy], b. Apr. 29, 1796 | 2 | 119 |
| Calvin B., s. [Ira & Mary], b. May 2, 1818 | 2 | 124 |
| Calvin B., of Colchester, m. Adaline E. **SANDERS**, of Hebron, May 19, 1844, by Rev. Rob[er]t C. Mills | 3 | 13 |
| Clarissa, d. [Samuel & Tabella], b. Mar. 10, 1786 | 2 | 60 |
| Clarissa Jane, d. [Ira W. & Clarissa A.], b. Sept. 6, 1849 | 3 | 6 |
| Curtis, s. [John & Anna], b. Mar. 17, 1794; d. Dec. 23, 1823, ae 29, in Lynchburg, Va. | 2 | 82 |
| Curtis K., s. [Ira & Mary], b. Mar. 5, 1824 | 2 | 124 |
| David, s. [Samuel & Lucy], b. Dec. 26, 1804; d. [ ] | 2 | 119 |
| Dimmis, d. [John & Anna], b. Dec. 13, 1786 | 2 | 82 |
| Dorothy, [d. John], b. Aug. 14, 1726 | L-1 | 450 |
| Elizabeth, m. Samuel **LO[O]MIS**, Dec. 12, 1717 | L-1 | 451 |
| Elizabeth, w. John, d. Dec. 14, 1726 | L-1 | 450 |
| Fanny, d. [Samuel & Lucy], b. Apr. 23, 1798 | 2 | 119 |
| Francis H., s. [Ira & Mary], b. Jan. 28, 1816 | 2 | 124 |
| George, m. Sarah **CHAPMAN**, Mar. 28, 1736/7 | 1 | 138 |
| George, m. Lydia **SHOLES**, [ ] | 2 | 131 |
| George Isham, s. [George & Lydia], b. June 8, 1802 | 2 | 131 |
| Griswold, m. Esther **BROWN**, b. of Colchester, Dec. 17, 1837, by Roderick Gardiner, J. P. | 2 | 295 |
| Harvey H., s. [Ira & Mary], b. Mar. 29, 1807; d. Oct. 17, 1824, in Lynchburg, Va., ae 17 | 2 | 124 |
| Henry, s. [Samuel & Tabella], b. Sept. 28, 1790 | 2 | 60 |
| Henry Green, s. [John & Anna], b. Sept. 8, 1800; d. Aug. 10, 1828, ae 28, in Salem, Conn. | 2 | 82 |
| Ira, s. [John & Anna], b. Oct. 12, 1780; d. June 29, 1825, ae 44 | 2 | 82 |
| Ira, b. Oct. 12, 1780, in Salem; m. Mary **FISK**, Oct. 16, 1803 | 2 | 124 |
| Ira, d. Jan. 29, 1825, ae 44 | 2 | 124 |
| Ira W., m. Clarissa A. **CARRIER**, b. of Colchester, Sept. 18, 1843, by Rev. Robert C. Mills | 3 | 6 |
| Ira Wilson, s. [Ira & Mary], b. Oct. 31, 1813 | 2 | 124 |
| James, s. [Samuel & Tabella], b. Dec. 9, 1771 | 2 | 60 |
| Jesse, s. John, b. May 14, 1748 | 1 | 43 |
| John, Lt., m. Ann **ROCKWELL**, Dec. 3, 1729 | L-3 | 8 |
| John, m. Anna **RATHBUN**, Sept. 1, 1775; d. July 12, 1823, in Salem, Conn. | 2 | 82 |
| John, s. [John & Anna], b. Aug. 4, 1784; d. Oct. 3, 1810, ae 26 | 2 | 82 |
| John, Patten, s. [Samuel & Lucy], b. Apr. 19, 1788 | 2 | 119 |
| John R., s. [Ira & Mary], b. Aug. 29, 1811 | 2 | 124 |
| Joseph Wightman, s. [George & Lydia], b. May 20, 1806 | 2 | 131 |
| Joshua, s. [John & Anna], b. Nov. 18, 1778; d. Feb. 21, 1790 | 2 | 82 |
| Joshua, 2d, s. [John & Anna], b. Dec. 25, 1791; d. May 24, 1845, ae 54, in Lynchburg, Va. | 2 | 82 |

| | Vol. | Page |
|---|---|---|
| **HOLMES, HOLMS**, (cont.) | | |
| Justin, s. [John & Anna], b. May 14, 1789; d. Nov. 30, 1796 | 2 | 82 |
| Lucy, d. [John & Anna], b. Sept. 20, 1782 | 2 | 82 |
| Lucy, [w. Samuel], d. [ ] | 2 | 119 |
| Lyman, s. [Samuel & Lucy], b. Nov. 1, 1806 | 2 | 119 |
| Mary, d. [George & Sarah], b. Feb. 22, 1737/8 | 1 | 138 |
| Mary, m. Hezekiah **KILLBORN**, Jr., Dec. 27, 1753 | 1 | 136 |
| Mary, m. John **RILEIGH**, Mar. 5, 1780 | 2 | 26 |
| Nancy, d. [John & Anna], b. Oct. 19, 1776; d. June 29, 1794 | 2 | 82 |
| Nathaniel F., s. [Ira & Mary], b. Feb. 21, 1805 | 2 | 124 |
| Polly, d. [Samuel & Tabella], b. Oct. 25, 1773 | 2 | 60 |
| Sallena, d. [George & Lydia], b. Sept. 13, 1804 | 2 | 131 |
| Sally, d. [Samuel & Tabella], b. May 19, 1770 | 2 | 60 |
| Samuel, b. Aug. 27, 1762; m. Lucy **POTTER**, [ ] | 2 | 119 |
| Samuel, m. Tabella **RATHBUN**, Feb. 1, 1770 | 2 | 60 |
| Samuel, s. [Samuel & Tabella], b. Oct. 2, 1779 | 2 | 60 |
| Samuel Marvin, s. [Samuel & Lucy], b. Oct. 14, 1800 | 2 | 119 |
| Sarah, m. Thomas **GURSTIN**, June 7, 1722 | L-1 | 799 |
| Sarah, d. [George & Sarah], b. Apr. 20, 1740 | 1 | 138 |
| Sarah, w. George, d. Apr. 24, 1740 | 1 | 138 |
| Seth, s. [Samuel & Tabella], b. July 29, 1775 | 2 | 60 |
| Sophia, d. [Samuel & Lucy], b. Jan. 2, 1790; d. Apr. [ ], 1845, ae 55 | 2 | 119 |
| William, s. [Samuel & Tabella], b. Dec. 10, 1781 | 2 | 60 |
| William, s. [Samuel & Lucy], b. Oct. 18, 1802 | 2 | 119 |
| William, [s. Samuel & Lucy], was drowned, [ ] | 2 | 119 |
| **HOLT**, Robert D., of Waterford, Ct., m. Ellen R. **PETERS**, of Colchester, June 8, 1851, by Rev. George W. Pendleton | 2 | 113 |
| **HOOK**, Ede, of Chatham, m. William **SHEPERSON**, Nov. 24, 1791 | 2 | 64 |
| Sarah, m. Silas **KELLOGG**, June 21, 1768 | 1 | 78 |
| **HOOTON**, [see also **HEATON**], An[n], m. Ebenezar, **DIBELL**, Aug. 29, 1706 | L-3 | 194 |
| **HOPSON**, Betty, [d. John & Mary], b. Feb. 16, 1735 | TPR | 112 |
| Elijah Worthington, s. [John & Mary], b. May 21, 1771 | 1 | 119 |
| Elizabeth, [d. John & Elizabeth], b. May 1, 1711 | L-1 | 799 |
| Hannah, [d. John & Mary], b. Sept. 29, 1747 | TPR | 112 |
| John, m. Sarah **NORTHAM**, Jan. [ ], 1704 | L-1 | 799 |
| John, [s. John & Sarah], b. Nov. 12, 1707 | L-1 | 799 |
| John, m. Elizabeth **DAY**, June 6, 1710 | L-1 | 799 |
| John, d. Feb. 22, 1714 | L-1 | 799 |
| John, m. Lydiah **KELLOGG**, May 28, 1730 | L-3 | 7 |
| John, m. Mary **KELLOGG**, May 28, 1730 | TPR | 112 |
| John, [s. John & Mary], b. Nov. 5, 1731; d. July 14, 1732 | TPR | 112 |
| John, [s. John & Mary], b. Jan. 29, 1734 | TPR | 112 |
| John, s. John & Lydia, ae 7 y., on Jan. 28, 1741, had "the fleshy part of his ear bitten off by a horse". Affidavit made by father on Apr. 16, 1741 | 1 | 155 |

| | Vol. | Page |
|---|---|---|
| **HOPSON**, (cont.) | | |
| John, Capt., d. Aug. 9, 1751, in 44th y. of his age | TPR | 112 |
| John, m. Mary **WORTHINGTON**, Apr. 19, 1759 | 1 | 119 |
| John, s. [John & Mary], b. July 11, 1764 | 1 | 119 |
| Lydia, [d. John & Mary], b. Aug. 20, 1739; d. July 6, 1740 | TPR | 112 |
| Lydia, [d. John & Mary], b. Oct. 24, 1741 | TPR | 112 |
| Lydia, d. [John & Mary], b. Nov. 14, 1761 | 1 | 119 |
| Lydia, m. Erastus **CHAMBERLAIN**, Nov. 23, 1788 | 2 | 44 |
| Mary, [s. John & Sarah], b. July 2, 1705 | L-1 | 799 |
| Mary, [d. John & Mary], b. Apr. 16, 1745 | TPR | 112 |
| Mary, w. [John], d. July 29, 1798 | 1 | 119 |
| Mary, see Mary **BLISS** | TPR | 112 |
| Molly, of Colchester, m. Elijah **METCALF**, of East Haddam, Sept. 23, 1762 | 1 | 131 |
| Molly, d. [John & Mary], b. May 4, 1768; d. Aug. 15, 1775 | 1 | 119 |
| Prudence, [d. John & Mary], b. Dec. 16, 1750 | TPR | 112 |
| Sarah, w. John, d. Mar. 16, 1708 | L-1 | 799 |
| Sarah, [d. John & Mary], b. Jan. 29, 1737 | TPR | 112 |
| Sarah, m. Asa **CLARK**, Dec. 4, 1755 | 1 | 42 |
| Theodocia, d. [John & Mary], b. Apr. 25, 1760 | 1 | 119 |
| **HORSFORD**, Anna, m. Samuel **LOOMIS**, 2d, Nov. 26, 1799 | 2 | 84 |
| Sarah, m. David **MILLER**, Sept. 19, 1759 | 1 | 94 |
| **HOSKETT**, Abigail, w. William **JAY**, of New York, & d. [Bartholomew & Hannah **SMITH**], d. May 28, 1841, ae 49, in New York | 2 | 110 |
| **HOSKIN**, Enoch, [s. Enoch & Mary], b. July 23, 1765 | 1 | 75 |
| Onner, [d. Enoch & Mary], b. Sept. 18, 1763 (Anna?) | 1 | 75 |
| **HOUGH**, Mary, d. [ ], d. Apr. 8, 1847, ae 22 | 2 | 1 |
| Uriah, s. [ ], d. Oct. 8, 1828, ae 2 | 2 | 1 |
| **HOUGHTON**, [see under **HOOTON**] | | |
| **HOUSE**, Benjamin C., of Coventry, m. Jerusha S. **SHEPARD**, of Colchester, Nov. 5, 1823, by Salmon Cone, V. D. M. | 2 | 135 |
| **HUBBARD**, Abby J., of Colchester, m. Joseph C. **HAMMOND**, of Vernon, Sept. 28, 1831, by Rev. Lyman Strong | 2 | 233 |
| Abby Jane, d. [Daniel & Olive], b. Feb. 20, 1810 | 2 | 108 |
| Daniel, m. Olive **FOOT**, Sept. 26, 1805; d. Oct. 2, 1811, ae 30 | 2 | 108 |
| Elizabeth P., m. Julius B. **HAMMOND**, May 6, 1827, by Salmon Cone; d. Nov. 5, 1835, ae 29 | 2 | 195 |
| Elizabeth Perkins, d. [Daniel & Olive], b. July 24, 1806; d. Nov. 5, 1835 | 2 | 108 |
| Isaac, of Philadelphia, m. Sarah A. **DOWNES**, May 5, 1836, by Rev. Lyman Strong | 2 | 284 |
| John, Rev., of Jamaica, L. I., d. Oct. 5, 1705, ae 28 | 2 | 310 |
| Mabel, wid. of Rev. John, of Jamaica, L. I., & only child of Rev. Daniel **BISSELL**, of Charlestown, Mass., & Mehetable (**WYLLYS**) **BISSELL**, m. Rev. Samuel **WOODBRIDGE**, Dec. 9, 1707 | 2 | 310 |

| | Vol. | Page |
|---|---|---|
| **HUBBARD**, (cont.) | | |
| Olive, m. Howell **ROGERS**, Sept. 10, 1821, by Salmon Cone, V. D. M. | 2 | 84 |
| **HULING**, Austin, of Marlboro, m. Electa **CARRIER**, of Colchester, Feb. 9, 1840, by Rev. Daniel G. Sprague | 2 | 133 |
| **HUNGERFORD**, Ansel, of East Haddam, m. Eleanor Louisa **DAY**, Feb. 19, 1833, by Rev. Joseph Harvey | 2 | 241 |
| Esther, m. Joseph **DAY**, Apr. 1, 1729 | TPM | 110 |
| Robert, Capt., of East Haddam, m. Huldah R. **SKINNER**, of Colchester, Dec. 28, 1820, by Rev. Jacob Seales | 2 | 101 |
| **HUNT**, Huldah, m. Timothy **PEPOON**, Dec. 7, 1752 | 1 | 153 |
| **HUNTINGTON**, Anna, d. [Rev. David & Elizabeth], b. Sept. 1, 1785 | 2 | 18 |
| Betty Kimberly, d. [Rev. David & Elizabeth], b. Aug. 8, 1779 | 2 | 18 |
| Civel, of Hebron, m. Caleb **GILLET**, of Colchester, Oct. 30, 1790; d. Jan. 20, 1841, ae 76 | 2 | 78 |
| Dan[iel], of Lebanon, m. Harriet **WELLS**, of Colchester, Oct. 28, 1830, by Rev. Lyman Strong | 2 | 225 |
| David, Rev., m. Elizabeth **FOOT**, Nov. 5, 1778; d. Apr. 12, 1812, ae 67, in N. Lyme | 2 | 18 |
| David, s. [Rev. David & Elizabeth], b. Mar. 1, 1784 | 2 | 18 |
| Elizabeth, w. Rev. David, d. Oct. 25, 1845, ae 95 y. 4 m. 15 d. | 2 | 18 |
| Israel Foot, s. [Rev. David & Elizabeth], b. Dec. 28, 1786 | 2 | 18 |
| Jerusha, m. John **WATROUS**, May 28, 1760 | 1 | 118 |
| John G., of Norwich, m. Mary **ISHAM**, of Colchester, Sept. 1, 1836, by Rev. Joel R. Arnold | 2 | 288 |
| Lois, d. [Rev. David & Elizabeth], b. May 29, 1790 | 2 | 18 |
| Simon, of Griswold, m. Sarah R. **WORTHINGTON**, of Colchester, Sept. 22, 1833, by Rev. Lyman Strong | 2 | 257 |
| **HUNTLEY**, Augustus, s. [Richard Harris & Rachel], b. Jan. 5, 1779 | 1 | 106 |
| Aurelia, d. [Richard Harris & Rachel], b. Jan. 13, 1777 | 1 | 106 |
| Carolina Matilda, d. [Richard Harris & Rachel], b. Mar. 20, 1775 | 1 | 106 |
| Charles, s. [Richard Harris & Rachel], b. Mar. 12, 1787 | 1 | 106 |
| Demerus, b. Apr. 30, 1785; m. Amos **OTIS**, May 11, 1842 | 2 | 73 |
| Irena, m. Justin **RATHBUN**, Nov. 20, 1826, by Amherst D. Scoville, J. P. | 2 | 191 |
| Nabby, d. [Richard Harris & Rachel], b. Feb. 21, 1784 | 1 | 106 |
| Philon, s. [Richard Harris & Rachel], b. Sept. 8, 1781 | 1 | 106 |
| Richard Harris, m. Rachel **LITTLE**, Mar. 17, 1768 | 1 | 106 |
| Richard Harris, s. [Richard Harris & Rachel], b. Dec. 7, 1768 | 1 | 106 |
| Syashes, s. [Richard Harris & Rachel], b. Dec. 8, 1770 | 1 | 106 |
| William C., s. [Richard Harris & Rachel], b. Mar. 1, 1773 | 1 | 106 |
| **HURD**, Ann, m. Justin Lewis, Nov. 27, 1823, by Salmon Cone, V. D. M. | 2 | 160 |
| Catharine, of East Haddam, m. William **BURNHAM**, of | | |

| | Vol. | Page |
|---|---|---|
| **HURD**, (cont.) | | |
| Colchester, Sept. 5, 1824, by Jacob Seales, V. D. M. | 2 | 169 |
| Joseph D., of East Haddam, m. Maria R. **WILLIAMS**, of Colchester, Mar. 17, 1850, at Westchester, by Rev. S. D. Jewett | 3 | 3 |
| Maria Matilda, of East Haddam, m. John **WEST**, of Colchester, Sept. 2, 1834, by Rev. Lyman Strong | 2 | 269 |
| Nancy, of East Haddam, m. Guy **BIGELOW**, 2d, of Colchester, Oct. 13, 1822, by John Bigelow, J. P., at James Bigelow's | 2 | 158 |
| Salomi, m. Charles **BILLINGS**, Feb. 10, 1828, by Zachariah Olmstead, J. P. | 2 | 201 |
| Sybel, b. Dec. 22, 1755 | 1 | 23 |
| **HURLBUTT**, Anne, d. [Asaph & Hannah], b. May 15, 1805 | 2 | 111 |
| Asaph, s. [Asaph & Hannah], b. Feb. 9, 1804 | 2 | 111 |
| Asaph, m. Hannah **STODDARD**, June 18, 1809, at Groton | 2 | 111 |
| Hannah, d. [Asaph & Hannah], b. Oct. 13, 1802 | 2 | 111 |
| Hannah, d. Feb. 27, 1809 (Probably 1st w. of Asaph) | 2 | 111 |
| Jared, of Hartford, m. Lucinda **ARMSTRONG**, of Colchester, Dec. 31, 1848, by Rev. P. Brockett | 3 | 38 |
| Ralph, s. [Asaph & Hannah], b. May 22, 1807 | 2 | 111 |
| Tabitha, d. [Asaph & Hannah], b. May 12, 1810 | 2 | 111 |
| **HUTCHINS**, Ransiel N., of Bolton, m. Harriet **WATROUS**, of Colchester, Apr. 10, 1834, by Rev. Lyman Strong | 2 | 266 |
| **HUTCHINSON**, Harvey, m. Susan C. **TRACY**, Nov. 4, 1830, by Rev. Joseph Harvey | 2 | 226 |
| **HYDE**, Eliza Ann, m. Henry Augustus **MORGAN**, b. of Colchester, Aug. 29, 1830, by Amherst D. Scoville, J. P. | 2 | 224 |
| George Leonard, m. Caroline **FREEMAN**, colored, b. of Colchester, Dec. 26, 1843, by Rev. Augustus Bolles | 3 | 10 |
| Hannah, m. Thomas **BILLINGS**, Nov. 19, 1826, by Amherst D. Scoville, J. P. | 2 | 190 |
| Harriet C., m. Augustus T. **RANSOM**, b. of Colchester, Nov. 27, 1850, by Rev. G. W. Pendleton | 2 | 185 |
| Harvey, m. Adeline **BACON**, b. of Colchester, (colored), Dec. 16, 1829, by Samuel A. Peters, J. P. | 2 | 216 |
| Hiram, of Norwich, m. Eliza Ann Maria **GREEN**, of Colchester, Sept. 11, 1836, by Rev. Joel R. Arnold | 2 | 288 |
| Marion, of Colchester, m. Edward **OLMSTEAD**, of New Haven, Dec. 30, 1851, by E. Dickinson | 3 | 49 |
| Primus, of East Haddam, m. Mary Ann **BILLING**, of Salem, b. colored, Oct. 30, 1822, by Samuel A. Peters, J. P. | 2 | 71 |
| **INGHAM**, Hannah, m. Israel **KELLOGG**, Jr., b. of Colchester, [ ], 1775 | 2 | 10 |
| Lydia, m. Thomas **CARRIER**, June 13, 1776; d. June 1, 1784 | 2 | 35 |
| Sene, of Saybrook, m. Sylvester **MUNGER**, Oct. 24, 1810, by Rev. Frederick W[illia]m Hotchkiss. Recorded Aug. 1, 1825, Saybrook | 2 | 181 |

| | Vol. | Page |
|---|---|---|
| **INGRAHAM**, Asahel, s. [Elknah & Mary], b. Mar. 25, 1781 | 2 | 28 |
| Bettey, d. [Joseph & Bettey], b. Sept. 2, 1774 | 1 | 139 |
| Elkanah, [s. Nathaniel & Sarah], b. July 22, 1757 | 1 | 55 |
| Elk[a]nah, m. Mary [ ], Mar. 2, 1780 | 2 | 28 |
| Hannah, d. [Elknah & Mary], b. Nov. 23, 1782 | 2 | 28 |
| Hannah, alias **BURNHAM**, m. James R. **MILLER**, Oct. 17, 1824, by Samuel A. Peters, J. P. | 2 | 171 |
| Harriet, m. Chauncey **MITCHELL**, May 7, 1825, by Zachariah Olmstead, J. P. | 2 | 177 |
| Jacob, m. Waitstill **INGRAHAM**, June 9, 1769 | 1 | 96 |
| Jacob, [s. Jacob & Waitstill], b. Mar. 27, 1770; d. July 1, 1770 | 1 | 96 |
| Jacob, 2d, [s. Jacob & Waitstill], b. [ ] 29, 1771; d. May 22, 1772 | 1 | 96 |
| Jared, d. Apr. 19, 1781 | 2 | 30 |
| Joel, of Chatham, m. Nancy **INGRAHAM**, of Westchester, Aug. 27, 1848, by Rev. S. D. Jewett | 3 | 37 |
| Joseph, m. Bettey **TAYLOR**, Nov. 24, 1773 | 1 | 139 |
| Nancy, of Westchester, m. Joel **INGRAHAM**, of Chatham, Aug. 27, 1848, by Rev. S. D. Jewett | 3 | 37 |
| Nathaniel, m. Sarah **PITTS**, Sept. 25 or 26, 1745 | 1 | 55 |
| Nath[anie]l, [s. Nathaniel & Sarah], b. May 20, 1747 | 1 | 55 |
| Nath[anie]ll, s. Nath[anie]ll, b. May 20, 1747 | 1 | 129 |
| Waitstill, m. Jacob **INGRAHAM**, June 9, 1769 | 1 | 96 |
| **IRISH**, Betsey, of Colchester, m. William W. **MORGAN**, of Hartford, May 18, 1834, by Rev. Daniel Waldo, of Lebanon | 2 | 266 |
| **ISHAM**, Abigail, d. Joseph & Susanna, b. May 21, 1732 | TPR | 111 |
| Abigail, d. [Daniel & Catharine], b. Apr. 11, 1773; d. Oct. 15, 1776 | 1 | 148 |
| Albert Baldwin, s. [John, 3d, & Betsey], b. July 13, 1805 | 2 | 83 |
| Alfred, s. [Joseph, Jr. & Sarah], b. Nov. 24, 1765; d. Oct. 12, 1768 | 1 | 144 |
| Alfred, s. [Joseph, Jr. & Sarah], b. Apr. 30, 1769 | 1 | 144 |
| Alfred, m. Clarissa **LOOMIS**, Dec. 18, 1796 | 2 | 84 |
| Ann, d. [Ralph & Laura], b. June 13, 1813 | 2 | 105 |
| Ann, of Colchester, m. Benjamin **SWAN**, Jr., of Woodstock, Vt., July 3, 1834, by Rev. Lyman Strong | 2 | 268 |
| Asa, s. [Daniel & Catharine], b. Dec. 8, 1769 | 1 | 148 |
| Asa Worthington, s. [Ralph & Laura], b. May 1, 1815; d. Oct. 11, 1824 | 2 | 105 |
| Augustus, s. [John, 3d & Betsey], b. Jan. 22, 1801 | 2 | 83 |
| Benjamin, s. [John, 3d & Lois], b. Sept. 28, 1779 | 2 | 21 |
| Catherine, d. [Ralph & Laura], b. June 14, 1819; d. Dec. 31, 1831 | 2 | 105 |
| Charles, s. [Samuel & Mary], b. Aug. 20, 1784 | 2 | 95 |
| Charles T., m. Mary A. **ROGERS**, Nov. 21, 1830, by Rev. Lyman Strong | 2 | 226 |

| | Vol. | Page |
|---|---|---|
| **ISHAM**, (cont.) | | |
| Charles Taintor, s. [Joseph], b. June 17, 1799 | 2 | 63 |
| Clarissa C., of Colchester, m. John G. **MIX**, of Hartford, Apr. 11, 1833, by Rev. Lyman Strong | 2 | 243 |
| Clarissa Champion, d. [John, 3d, & Betsey], b. Dec. 3, 1807 | 2 | 83 |
| Dan, s. [Joseph, 3d, & Lois], b. Oct. 23, 1791 | 2 | 62 |
| Daniel, m. Catharine **FOOT**, July 14, 1756 | 1 | 148 |
| Daniel, s. [Daniel & Catharine], b. Sept. 23, 1768 | 1 | 148 |
| David, s. [Daniel & Catharine], b. Oct. 23, 1759; d. Apr. 12, 1787 | 1 | 148 |
| David, s. [Joseph, Jr. & Sarah], b. Aug. 18, 1767; d. Aug. 31, 1767 | 1 | 144 |
| David, s. [Joseph, 3d, & Lois], b. June 9, 1793; d. Apr. 13, 1796 | 2 | 62 |
| Dorothy, d. [John & Dorothy], b. Oct. 19, 1770 | 1 | 114 |
| Edward, s. [Joseph, 3d, & Lois], b. July 14, 1799 | 2 | 62 |
| Eliza, d. [John, 3d, & Betsey], b. Nov. 6, 1797 | 2 | 83 |
| Eliza, of Colchester, m. Asa **FARWELL**, of Hartford, Oct. 19, 1825, by Salmon Cone, V. D. M. | 2 | 179 |
| Elizabeth, m. Benjamin **MORGAN**, Mar. 12, 1761 | 1 | 179 |
| Ellis, child of [Daniel & Catharine], b. Mar. 7, 1761 | 1 | 148 |
| Ephraim, s. [John & Dorothy], b. July 16, 1766 | 1 | 114 |
| Esther, w. [Hon. Joseph], d. Jan. 21, 1834, ae 78 | 2 | 63 |
| Ezra, s. [John & Dorothy], b. Mar. 5, 1773 | 1 | 114 |
| Fedora F., of Colchester, m. Rev. Joseph A. **COPP**, of Sag Harbor, N. Y., July 13, 1836, by Rev. Joel R. Arnold | 2 | 287 |
| Frances Fedora, d. [Ralph & Laura], b. Mar. 11, 1817 | 2 | 105 |
| Giles, s. [Samuel & Mary], b. Sept. 25, 1789 | 2 | 95 |
| Grisvanlet, [s. Joseph], b. Dec. 12, 1797 | 2 | 63 |
| Hannah, d. [John, 2d & Eunice], b. Sept. 4, 1765 | 2 | 14 |
| Harriet, d. [John, 3d, & Betsey], b. Apr. 2, 1820 | 2 | 83 |
| Harriet, m. Elijah C. **KELLOGG**, of Hartford, May 5, 1846, by Rev. Joel R. Arnold | 3 | 19 |
| Harry, s. [Joseph, 3d, & Lois], b. Jan. 4, 1803 | 2 | 62 |
| Jane, [d. Joseph & Susanna], b. Feb. 2, 1734 | TPR | 112 |
| Jira, s. Joseph, b. Sept. 10, 1740; d. Sept. 30, 1747 | 1 | 126 |
| John, s. [Joseph], b. May 7, 1742 | 1 | 126 |
| John, m. Dorothy **FOOT**, Dec. 19, 1751 | 1 | 114 |
| John, s. [John & Dorothy], b. June 20, 1757 | 1 | 114 |
| John, 2d, of Colchester, m. Eunice **BALDWIN**, of Norwich, Nov. 7, 1764; d. May 5, 1828, ae 86 y. wanting 19 days | 2 | 14 |
| John, s. [John, 2d, & Eunice], b. Feb. 24, 1774 | 2 | 14 |
| John, 2d, s. [John, 2d, & Eunice], b. Apr. 24, 1776 | 2 | 14 |
| John, 3d, m. Lois **ADAMS**, b. of Colchester, Nov. 19, 1778 | 2 | 21 |
| John, 3d, of Colchester, m. Betsey **GILBERT**, of Hebron, Jan. 19, 1797 | 2 | 83 |
| John Gilbert, s. [John, 3d, & Betsey], b. Mar. 11, 1799; | | |

| | Vol. | Page |
|---|---|---|
| **ISHAM**, (cont.) | | |
| d. Oct. 26, 1818 | 2 | 83 |
| Jonathan, s. [John & Dorothy], b. July 16, 1759 | 1 | 114 |
| Joseph, [s. Joseph & Susanna], b. Oct. 15, 1735 | TPR | 112 |
| Joseph, Jr., m. Sarah **BULKELEY**, Jan. 17, 1765 | 1 | 144 |
| Joseph, Jr., m. Esther **TAINTOR**, May 18, 1774 | 1 | 144 |
| Joseph, Jr., had slave Daphne, d. of Dinah, b. Nov. 20, 1788; & Lucy, d. Peg, b. Sept. 12, 1795 | 2 | 325 |
| Joseph, 3d, m. Lois **BLISH**, Sept. 9, 1790 | 2 | 62 |
| Joseph, twin with Lois, s. [Joseph, 3d, & Lois], b. Mar. 23, 1806 | 2 | 62 |
| Joseph, Hon., d. Nov. 1, 1810, ae 75 | 2 | 63 |
| Joseph Giles, s. [Ralph & Laura], b. Jan. 15, 1811 | 2 | 105 |
| Julia, d. [Alfred & Clarissa], b. Feb. 4, 1798 | 2 | 84 |
| Laura, w. Ralph, d. June 7, 1847, ae 61 | 2 | 105 |
| Laura E., m. John L. **WATROUS**, Oct. 20, 1824, by Salmon Cone, V. D. M. | 2 | 170 |
| Laura Esther, d. [Ralph & Laura], b. Jan. 29, 1805 | 2 | 105 |
| Lois, d. [John & Dorothy], b. July 8, 1761 | 1 | 114 |
| Lois, twin with Joseph, d. [Joseph, 3d, & Lois], b. Mar. 23, 1806 | 2 | 62 |
| Lois, w. Joseph, d. Feb. 14, 1841, ae 71 | 2 | 62 |
| Lucretia, d. [Ralph & Laura], b. Feb. 3, 1807 | 2 | 105 |
| Lucretia, m. Henry **BURR**, Aug. 5, 1828, by Salmon Cone, V. D. M. | 2 | 205 |
| Lucy, twin with Noah, d. [John & Dorothy], b. Apr. 4, 1764; d. Dec. 25, 1775 | 1 | 114 |
| Lucy, d. [Samuel & Mary], b. Sept. 22, 1780 | 2 | 95 |
| Martha, twin with Mary, d. [John, 3d, & Betsey], b. Feb. 16, 1815 | 2 | 83 |
| Martha, of Colchester, m. Richard S. **ADAMS**, of Richmond, Va., Dec. 5, 1833, by Rev. Lyman Strong | 2 | 260 |
| Mary, d. [Daniel & Catharine], b. July 3, 1757 | 1 | 148 |
| Mary, m. Aaron **FOOT**, Jan. 3, 1774 | 2 | 4 |
| Mary, d. [Samuel & Mary], b. Feb. 19, 1776 | 2 | 95 |
| Mary, d. [Joseph, 3d, & Lois], b. Sept. 12, 1801 | 2 | 62 |
| Mary, twin with Martha, d. [John, 3d, & Betsey], b. Feb. 16, 1815 | 2 | 83 |
| Mary, m. Charles Edwin **BULKELEY**, June 4, 1827, by Salmon Cone, V. D. M. | 2 | 196 |
| Mary, of Colchester, m. John G. **HUNTINGTON**, of Norwich, Sept. 1, 1836, by Rev. Joel R. Arnold | 2 | 288 |
| Molly, d. [John & Dorothy], b. Sept. 24, 1755 | 1 | 114 |
| Noah, twin with Lucy, s. [John & Dorothy], b. Apr. 4, 1764 | 1 | 114 |
| Ralph, s. [Joseph, Jr. & Esther], b. June 25, 1776 | 1 | 144 |
| Ralph, b. June 25, 1776; m. Laura **WORTHINGTON**, Mar. | | |

| | Vol. | Page |
|---|---|---|
| **ISHAM**, (cont.) | | |
| 29, 1804; d. Sept. 29, 1845, ae 69 | 2 | 105 |
| Ralph Henry, s. [Ralph & Laura], b. Feb. 17, 1809 | 2 | 105 |
| Ralph Henry, m. Anna Heywood **TRUMBULL**, b. of Colchester, June 12, 1838, by Rev. Joel R. Arnold | 2 | 264 |
| Sally, d. [Joseph, 3d, & Lois], b. Nov. 30, 1795 | 2 | 62 |
| Sally, d. [Joseph, Jr. & Esther], b. July 15, 1796 | 1 | 144 |
| Sally Maria, d. [John, 3d, & Betsey], b. Jan. 15, 1810 | 2 | 83 |
| Samuel, s. [John & Dorothy], b. Dec. 20, 1752 | 1 | 114 |
| Samuel, m. Mary **ADAMS**, Jan. 18, 1775 | 2 | 95 |
| Samuel Gilbert, s. [John, 3d , & Betsey], b. May 24, 1812 | 2 | 83 |
| Sarah, d. [John & Dorothy], b. July 31, 1754; d. [ ] | 1 | 114 |
| Sarah, d. [Daniel & Catharine], b. Feb. 9, 1771; d. Aug. 7, 1776 | 1 | 148 |
| Sarah, d. [Joseph, Jr. & Sarah], b. Nov. 23, 1771 | 1 | 144 |
| Sarah, w. Joseph, Jr., d. Feb. 9, 1773 | 1 | 144 |
| Sarah, d. [Samuel & Mary], b. Mar. 13, 1778 | 2 | 95 |
| Sarah B., m. Joseph T. **BURNHAM**, of Hebron, Feb. 26, 1839, by Rev. Joel R. Arnold | 2 | 282 |
| Sarah Maria, of Colchester, m. Ichabod **GALLUP**, of Norwich, Dec. 1, 1830, by Rev. Lyman Strong | 2 | 227 |
| Sarah T., of Colchester, m. Gardiner **SOUTHWORTH**, of Natchez, July 28, 1829, by Salmon Cone, V. D. M. | 2 | 214 |
| Susannah, d. Joseph, b. Feb. 14, 1737/8 | L-3 | 467 |
| Waitstill, d. [Samuel & Mary], b. Oct. 23, 1786 | 2 | 95 |
| William, s. [John, 3d, & Betsey], b. Mar. 10, 1803 | 2 | 83 |
| ---, d. [John, 2d, & Eunice], b. Aug. 23, 1767 | 2 | 14 |
| ---, s. [John, 2d, & Eunice], b. July 20, 1769; d. Oct. 14, 1775 | 2 | 14 |
| ---, d. [John, 2d, & Eunice], b. Oct. 12, 1771; d. Oct. 17, 1775 | 2 | 14 |
| **JACKSON**, , Anson W., of East Haddam, m. Emeline **WANTON**, of Colchester, Nov. 26, 1834, by Rev. Joseph Harvey | 2 | 273 |
| Roxy, of Colchester, m. Edwin **BOGUE**, of East Haddam, June 4, 1829, by Salmon Cone, V. D. M. | 2 | 213 |
| William, s. Roxana, b. July 22, 1822 | 2 | 326 |
| **JACOBS**, Samuel, of Mansfield, Conn., m. Emma **BUTTON**, of Colchester, Sept. 24, 1848, by Rev. F. W. Bill | 3 | 37 |
| **JAMSON**, Betsey, m. Phillip **BASSET**, negro, May 14, 1741 | 1 | 144 |
| **JANE**, Mary C., of "Glastonbury or Colchester", m. Samuel **LEWIS**, of Colchester, Dec. 18, 1825, at Daniel Cuff's house in Colchester, by John Bigelow, J. P. Bans published 8 d. before. | 2 | 185 |
| **JEFFREYS, JEFFREY, JEFFERIS**, Caleb, m. Hannah **PARSONS**, reputed d. of Jonathan, late of Northampton, Dec. 17, 1710 | L-3 | 198 |
| Caleb, m. Hannah **PARSONS**, Dec. 17, 1710 | TM-1 | 198 |
| Roswell, of Lyme, m. Sarah **BEMAN**, of Colchester, Feb. 18, 1827, by Samuel A. Peters, J. P. | 2 | 193 |
| **JENKINS**, Amy, d. [John & Lydia], b. Jan. 12, 1757 | 1 | 104 |

| | Vol. | Page |
|---|---|---|
| **JENKINS**, (cont.) | | |
| Benjamin, s. [John & Lydia], b. July 18, 1754 | 1 | 104 |
| John, m. Lydia **GARDINER**, Aug. 1, 1751; removed to Wyoming Valley in 1769 | 1 | 104 |
| John, s. [John & Lydia], b. Nov. 27, 1751 | 1 | 104 |
| Stephen, s. [John & Lydia], b. Feb. 22, 1753 | 1 | 104 |
| Thomas, s. [John & Lydia], b. Jan. 19, 1761 | 1 | 104 |
| Weekes, s. [John & Lydia], b. Jan. 18, 1767 | 1 | 104 |
| William, s. [John & Lydia], b. Oct. 30, 1764 | 1 | 104 |
| **JEPOON**, Mercy, m. Hezekiah **KNEELAND**, [ ] **PEPOON**?) | 1 | 106 |
| **JEWETT**, Deborah, of East Haddam, m. William **WELCH**, Jr., of Colchester, July 7, 1775 | 2 | 11 |
| **JINKS**, Ruby, m. Joseph **MAXFIELD**, Jan. 26, 1791 | 2 | 53 |
| **JOHNSON, JONSON**, Abigail, d. [John, Jr. & Anstress], b. Nov. 20, 1756 | 1 | 131 |
| Anstress, d. [John, Jr. & Anstress], b. Feb. 17, 1741/2 | 1 | 131 |
| Anstress, w. John, Jr., d. Oct. 27, 1761 | 1 | 131 |
| Catharine, m. Obell **ALVORD**, Jan. 4, 1767 | 1 | 127 |
| Christopher, d. Nov. 8, 1843 | 2 | 88 |
| Dauid, [s. John], b. Feb. 10, 1715/16 | L-3 | 194 |
| David, s. John, b. Feb. 10, 1715/16 | TM-1 | 194 |
| Dorothy, m. William **WILLIAMS**, Oct. 21, 1713 | L-1 | 451 |
| Elijah, [s. John], b. Sept. 20, 1718 | L-3 | 194 |
| Elijah, s. John, b. Sept. 20, 1718 | TM-1 | 195 |
| Elisha, [s. John], b. July 16, 1724 | L-3 | 194 |
| Elisha, s. John, b. July 16, 1724 | TM-1 | 195 |
| Elizabeth, [d. John], b. Feb. 17, 1720/21 | L-3 | 194 |
| Elizabeth, d. John, b. Feb. 17, 1720/21 | TM-1 | 195 |
| Ellenor, twin with Mary, d. [John, Jr. & Anstress], b. July 15, 1750; d. Sept. 14, 1757 | 1 | 131 |
| Eunice, d. [John, Jr. & Anstress], b. May 14, 1740 | 1 | 131 |
| George, of Montgomery, N. Y., m. Hannah **BARNES**, of Colchester, Feb. 29, 1824, by Salmon Cone, V. D. M. | 2 | 113 |
| Israel, [s. John, Jr. & Anstress], b. Sept. 25, 1739; d. Dec. 31, 1741 | 1 | 131 |
| Israel, twin with John, s. [John, Jr. & Anstress], b. June [ ], 1753; d. June [ ], 1753 | 1 | 131 |
| Israel, s. [John, Jr. & Anstress], b. Feb. 17, 1760 | 1 | 131 |
| John, s. John, b. Jan. 16, 1712/13 | L-3 | 194 |
| John, s. John, b. Jan. 16, 1712/13 | TM-1 | 194 |
| John, Jr., m. Anstress **NEWTON**, Jan. 6, 1736 | 1 | 131 |
| John, s. [John, Jr. & Anstress], b. May 30, 1737; d. Dec. 27, 1741 | 1 | 131 |
| John, twin with Israel, s. [John, Jr. & Anstress], b. June [ ], 1753; d. June [ ], 1753 | 1 | 131 |
| John, s. [John, Jr. & Anstress], b. May 12, 1754 | 1 | 131 |
| John, m. Ann **SMITH**, Sept. 6, 1764 | 1 | 131 |
| John, s. [Micael & Lucy], b. Feb. 18, 1776 | 2 | 6 |

| | Vol. | Page |
|---|---|---|
| **JOHNSON, JONSON**, (cont.) | | |
| John, m. Margarett J. **ROUTLEDGE**, b. of Colchester, Sept. 28, 1852, by Geo[rge] W. Pendleton | 3 | 53 |
| Katharine, m. Obed **ALVORD**, Jan. [ ], 1767 | 2 | 23 |
| Laura, b. Aug. 30, 1806; m. Sala **JONES**, Jr., Sept. 28, 1831 | 2 | 88 |
| Margaret, m. William H. **HARVEY**, b. of Colchester, Feb. 12, 1837, by Rev. Joel R. Arnold | 2 | 294 |
| Mary, [d. John, Jr. & Anstress], b. Dec. 27, 1745; d. [Dec.] 30, [1745] | 1 | 131 |
| Mary, twin with Ellenor, d. [John, Jr. & Anstress], b. July 15, 1750 | 1 | 131 |
| Nancy, m. George **CARRIER**, b. of Colchester, Jan. 11, 1852, by Rev. Geo[rge] W. Pendleton | 3 | 49 |
| Nancy M., of Colchester, m. Reuben M. **FOOTE**, of Great Barrington, Mass., Nov. 29, 1849, by Rev. John Avery, of Exeter | 3 | 44 |
| Orcamell, of Bozrah, m. Artemisia **ARMSTRONG**, of Colchester, Mar. 20, 1822, at Isaiah Armstrong's by Rev. William Palmer | 2 | 144 |
| Rhoda, of Norwich, m. James **CROCKER**, of Colchester, Feb. 23, 1757 | 1 | 111 |
| -----, of Norwich, m. Levi **PURPLE**, of East Haddam, Apr. 26, [1847], b. Rev. S. D. Jewett, Westchester | 3 | 32 |
| **JOHNSTON**, Edward, of Lebanon, m. Nancy M. **TAYLOR**, of Colchester, Nov. 26, 1846, by Rev. Joel R. Arnold | 3 | 30 |
| **JONES**, Abby Ann, d. [Sala, Jr. & Laura], b. July 19, 1836 | 2 | 88 |
| Abigail, [d. Daniell & Mary], b. May 1, 1732 | L-1 | 446 |
| Abijah, m. Sarah **PECK**, Jan. 5, 1769 | 1 | 81 |
| Abijah, [s. Jabez & Ann], b. July 5, 1750 | TPR | 109 |
| Abijah, [s. Abijah & Sarah], b. July 28, 1769 | 1 | 81 |
| Alect, s. [Amos, Jr. & Aurel], b. June 25, 1800 | 2 | 89 |
| Alfred, s. [Daniel & Abigail], b. May 2, 1801 | 2 | 117 |
| Alonzo, s. [Sala, Jr. & Laura], b. Feb. 11, 1834 | 2 | 88 |
| Althear, twin with Anne, [d. Joshua & Elizabeth], b. Feb. 22, 1744 | 1 | 106 |
| Amasa, m. Elizabeth **CHAMBERLAIN**, July 12, 1749 | 1 | 150 |
| Amasa, m. Hope **LORD**, Aug. 27, 1754 | 1 | 150 |
| Amasa, s. [Amasa & Hope], b. July 27, 1757 | 1 | 150 |
| Amasai, [s. Daniell & Mary], b. Oct. 2, 1726 | L-1 | 446 |
| Ambrose, [s. Abijah & Sarah], b. Oct. 12, 1771 | 1 | 81 |
| Amos, [s. Jabez & Ann], b. Jan. 2, 1734/5 | TPR | 109 |
| Amos, of Colchester, m. Mary **CONE**, of East Haddam, Dec. 27, 1759 | 1 | 155 |
| Amos, s. [Amos & Mary], b. Feb. 19, 1764 | 1 | 155 |
| Amos, Jr., m. Aurel **NEWTON**, Oct. 9, 1788 | 2 | 89 |
| Amos, s. [Amos, Jr. & Aurel], b. Feb. 19, 1798 | 2 | 89 |
| Amos Allen, s. [Sala, Jr. & Laura], b. June 25, 1840 | 2 | 88 |
| Anna, [d. Jabez & Ann], b. Oct. 5, 1736 | TPR | 109 |

| | Vol. | Page |
|---|---|---|
| **JONES**, (cont.) | | |
| Anna, m. Levi **WEBSTER**, b. of Colchester, [Mar.] 30, 1851, by Rev. S. D. Jewett | 2 | 73 |
| Anne, twin with Althear, [d. Joshua & Elizabeth], b. Feb. 22, 1744 | 1 | 106 |
| Anne, twin with Sarah, [d. Ariel & Dimmis], b. May 26, 1770 | 1 | 81 |
| Ariel, [s. Jabez & Ann], b. Sept. 28, 1745 | TPR | 109 |
| Ariel, m. Dimmis **KNIGHT**, Nov. 13, 1765 | 1 | 81 |
| Ariel, [s. Ariel & Dimmis], b. May 21, 1766 | 1 | 81 |
| Asa, [s. Isaac], b. Oct. 16, 1733 | L-3 | 6 |
| Asa, [s. Jabez & Ann], b. June 9, 1739 | TPR | 109 |
| Asa, s. [Asa & Sarah], b. July 18, 1762 | 1 | 110 |
| Asa. m. Sarah **TREADWAY**, [ ], 1762 | 1 | 110 |
| Asahel, [s. James], b. July 7, 1751 | 1 | 147 |
| Bela, s. [Daniel & Abigail], b. July 1, 1790 | 2 | 117 |
| Betsey, [d. Isaac & Silence], b. Aug. 7, 1757 | 1 | 26 |
| Celia Abby, d. [Daniel & Abigail], b. July 2, 1808; d. July 24, 1808 | 2 | 117 |
| Daniell, m. Mary **WORTHINGTON**, Oct. 13, 1720 | L-1 | 446 |
| Daniel, s. [Amasa & Elizabeth], b. May 28, 1752; d. Oct. 27, 1753 | 1 | 150 |
| Daniel, 2d, s. [Amasa & Hope], b. Aug. 28, 1755 | 1 | 150 |
| Daniel, s. [Amos & Mary], b. May 1, 1766 | 1 | 155 |
| Daniel, Capt., of Salem, Conn., d. July 20, 1849, ae 83 | 2 | 89 |
| Daniel, Capt., d. July 20, 1849, ae 83 | 2 | 117 |
| Daniel, m. Abigail **NEWTON**, [ ] | 2 | 117 |
| David, s. [Joshua & Elizabeth], b. Jan. 23, 1752 | 1 | 106 |
| Deborah Harvey, m. Warren **FULLER**, June 5, 1796 | 2 | 130 |
| Dimmis, [d. Ariel & Dimmis], b. June 12, 1768 | 1 | 81 |
| Diodate, of East Haddam, d. Mar. 23, 1849, ae 80 | 2 | 89 |
| Edmund, s. [Sala & Elizabeth], b. Apr. 18, 1796 | 2 | 87 |
| Electa, m. James **SAXTON**, Jr., Oct. 2, 1805; d. Aug. 4, 1846 | 2 | 126 |
| Elenor, [d. Hazael & Eleneor], b. June 16, 1767 | 1 | 81 |
| Elenor, m. William **MORGAN**, Jan. 31, 1787 | 2 | 55 |
| Eliab, s. [Amos, Jr. & Aurel], b. May 26, 1794 | 2 | 89 |
| Elijah, [s. Isaac & Hannah], b. Jan. 21, 1719/20 | L-1 | 453 |
| Eliphalet S., m. Elvia B. **BURDETT**, Mar. 18, 1830, by Salmon Cone, V. D. M. | 2 | 220 |
| Elizabeth, d. [Joshua & Elizabeth], b. Oct. 4, 1746 | 1 | 106 |
| Elizabeth, w. Amasa, d. Sept. 23, 1753 | 1 | 150 |
| Elizabeth, m. Nath[anie]ll **CLARK**, Oct. 16, 1757 | 1 | 36 |
| Elizabeth B., d. [Sala & Elizabeth], b. Sept. 12, 1799 | 2 | 87 |
| Esther, [d. Thomas & Hannah], b. Apr. 30, 1758; d. Nov. [ ], 1759 | 1 | 35 |
| Eunice, [d. Isaac], b. Mar 10, 1735 | L-3 | 6 |
| Esekiell, [s. Isaac], b. Mar. 22, 1729 | L-3 | 6 |
| Fanny Luella, d. [Daniel & Abigail], b. Jan. 1, 1796 | 2 | 117 |
| Francis, s. [Daniel & Abigail], b. Jan. 13, 1798 | 2 | 117 |

| | Vol. | Page |
|---|---|---|
| **JONES**, (cont.) | | |
| Grace, [d. James], b. June 25, 1754 | 1 | 147 |
| Hannah, [d. Isaac & Hannah], b. Mar. 12, 1721 | L-1 | 453 |
| Hannah, [d. Thomas & Hannah], b. Jan. 30, 1760 | 1 | 35 |
| Hannah, m. Daniel **CLARK**, Jr., [ ] | 1 | 57 |
| Hannah Church, d. Bethuel & Hannah, b. May 19, 1801 | 2 | 81 |
| Hazael, [s. Jabez & Anna], b. Jan. 6, 1742/3 | TPR | 109 |
| Hazael, m. Eleneor **MORGAN**, Mar. 7, 1765 | 1 | 81 |
| Henry M., of Huntington, L. I., m. Harriet M. **LATHAM**, of Colchester, July 7, 1845, by Rev. P. Brockett | 3 | 22 |
| Huldah, d. [Sala & Elizabeth], b. Aug. 24, 1801 | 2 | 87 |
| Irene, d. [James], b. Feb. 10, 1739 | 1 | 147 |
| Isaac, m. Hannah **WEL[L]ES**, July 11, 1717 | L-1 | 453 |
| Isaac, [s. Isaac & Hannah], b. June 19, 1722 | L-1 | 453 |
| Isaac, m. Silence **DAY**, Feb. 28, 1752 | 1 | 26 |
| Isaac, [s. Isaac & Silence], b. Mar. 8, 1755 | 1 | 26 |
| Israell, [s. Jabez & Ann], b. Jan. 7, 1737/8 | TPR | 109 |
| Israel, m. Mary **GARDINER**, Mar. 8, 1759 | 1 | 86 |
| Israel, s. [Daniel & Hannah], b. Dec. 8, 1765 | 1 | 130 |
| Israel Newton, s. [Daniel & Abigail], b. July 14, 1803 | 2 | 117 |
| Jabez, [s. Jabez & Ann], b. Jan. 14, 1733/4 | TPR | 109 |
| Jabez, Jr., m. Mary **WATERMAN**, Feb. 24, 1757 | 1 | 44 |
| Jabez, s. [Amos & Mary], b. Dec. 1, 1761 | 1 | 155 |
| Jabez, s. [Daniel & Abigail], b. Dec. 10, 1792 | 2 | 117 |
| James, s. [James], b. Apr. 30, 1741 | 1 | 147 |
| James, d. Sept. 8, 1755 | 1 | 147 |
| James, m. [ ] **GATES**, [ ] | 1 | 147 |
| Jehiel, [s. Jabez & Ann], b. Sept. 20, 1743 | TPR | 109 |
| Jehiel, m. Lucretia **HAMILTON**, Sept. 19, 1765 | 1 | 86 |
| Jehiel, [s. Jehiel & Lucretia], b. Dec. 8, 1765 | 1 | 86 |
| Jehu, [s. James], b. Dec. 7, 1748 | 1 | 147 |
| Joel, [s. Isaac & Hannah], b. Aug. 29, 1718 | L-1 | 453 |
| Jonathan, d. Dec. 11, 1770 | 1 | 54 |
| Joshua, m. Elizabeth **BLISS**, [ ], 1740 | 1 | 106 |
| Joshua, s. [Joshua & Elizabeth], b. Jan. 18, 1742; d. Oct. 28, 1749 | 1 | 106 |
| Joshua, s. [Joshua & Elizabeth], b. Aug. 15, 1754 | 1 | 106 |
| Josiah, [s. Isaac], b. Jan. 20, 1740/41 | L-3 | 6 |
| Julia Abby, d. [Daniel & Abigail], b. Mar. 31, 1805; d. Dec. 3, 1806 | 2 | 117 |
| Katharine, of Hebron, m. John **DAY**, of Colchester, Dec. 20, 1792 | 2 | 68 |
| Lemuel, [s. Isaac], b. Oct. 18, 1739 | L-3 | 6 |
| Leonard, s. [Amos, Jr. & Aurel], b. Jan. 1, 1796 | 2 | 89 |
| Louisa, d. [Daniel & Abigail], b. Oct. 27, 1794 | 2 | 117 |
| Lucy, d. [Amos, Jr. & Aurel], b. Apr. 2, 1791 | 2 | 89 |
| Luruhamah, [d. Jehiel & Lucretia], b. Jan. 12, 1768 | 1 | 86 |
| Lusenday, [d. Thomas & Hannah], b. Dec. 22, 1761 | 1 | 35 |

| | Vol. | Page |
|---|---|---|
| **JONES**, (cont.) | | |
| Luther, [s. Isaac & Silence], b. Aug. 7, 1753 | 1 | 26 |
| Lydia, [d. Isaac], b. Nov. 14, 1725 | L-3 | 6 |
| Lydia, m. Daniel **JUDD**, Mar. 14, 1751 | 1 | 51 |
| Lydia, [d. Thomas & Hannah], b. Nov. 2, 1754 | 1 | 35 |
| Mary, [d. Daniell & Mary], b. May 16, 1724 | L-1 | 446 |
| Mary, [d. Daniell & Mary], b. June 13, 1729 | L-1 | 446 |
| Mary, [d. Isaac], b. July 27, 1737 | L-3 | 6 |
| Mary, [d. James], b. Dec. 20, 1743 | 1 | 147 |
| Mary, m. Robert **BALIS**, Apr. 15, 1798 | 2 | 78 |
| Mary Ann, of New Haven, m. Charles T. **DANIELS**, of Colchester, Jan. 28, 1838, by Rev. Andrew M. Smith | 2 | 297 |
| Nathan, [s. Isaac], b. Dec. 30, 1731 | L-3 | 6 |
| Octa, d. [Amos, Jr. & Aurel], b. June 24, 1789 | 2 | 89 |
| Octava, d. [Sala & Elizabeth], b. Apr. 19, 1812 | 2 | 87 |
| Onda, d. [Sala & Elizabeth], b. Dec. 7, 1794 | 2 | 87 |
| Oren, s. [Sala & Elizabeth], b. Nov. 8, 1805; d. Feb. 28, 1808, ae 3 | 2 | 87 |
| Rhoda, d. [Amasa & Elizabeth], b. Oct. 4, 1750 | 1 | 150 |
| Rhoda, m. Aaron **KELLOGG**, Jr., July 3, 1766 | 1 | 80 |
| Salla, [d. Asa & Sarah], b. Mar. 6, 1766 | 1 | 110 |
| Sala, b. Mar. 19, 1771; m. Elizabeth **FOX**, Sept. 28, 1793; d. June 26, 1849, ae 78 | 2 | 87 |
| Sala, s. [Sala & Elizabeth], b. July 27, 1803 | 2 | 87 |
| Sala, Jr., b. July 27, 1803; m. Laura **JOHNSON**, Sept. 28, 1831 | 2 | 88 |
| Sam[ue]ll, s. Isaac, b. Apr. 22, 1724 | L-3 | 6 |
| Sam[ue]ll, [s. James], b. July 20, 1746 | 1 | 147 |
| Samuel R., of Hebron, m. Roxanna **CHAMBERLAIN**, of Colchester, Oct. 16, 1831, by Rev. Lyman Strong | 2 | 234 |
| Sarah, [d. Isaac], b. Feb. 16, 1736 | L-3 | 6 |
| Sarah, m. Newton **RANSOM**, Sept. 20, 1742 | 1 | 136 |
| Sarah, m. Newton **RANSOM**, Sept. 21, 1742 | 1 | 143 |
| Sarah, [d. Jabez & Ann], b. Jan. 7, 1746/7 | TPR | 109 |
| Sarah, d. [Joshua & Elizabeth], b. May 31, 1749 | 1 | 106 |
| Sarah, [d. Asa & Sarah], b. Dec. 30, 1764; d. Apr. 22, 1766 | 1 | 110 |
| Sarah, m. Alpheas **RANSOM**, Jan. 29, 1767 | 1 | 84 |
| Sarah, twin with Anne, [d. Ariel & Dimmis], b. May 26, 1770 | 1 | 81 |
| Sarah, [d. Abijah & Sarah], b. June [ ], 1774; d. Mar. 17, 1776 | 1 | 81 |
| Sarah Ann, d. [Sala & Elizabeth], b. July 23, 1809; d. Oct. 15, 1831 | 2 | 87 |
| Silas, of Salem, Conn., d. June 26, 1849, ae 78 | 2 | 89 |
| Thomas, s. Jabez & Ann, b. May 21, 1732 | TPR | 109 |
| Thomas, m. Hannah **GARDINER**, Apr. 5, 1753 | 1 | 35 |
| Weltha, [d. Joshua & Elizabeth], b. May 13, 1757 | 1 | 106 |
| William, [s. Isaac], b. Sept. 18, 1727 | L-3 | 6 |
| William E., of Hebron, m. Sarah D. **CHAMBERLAIN**, of | | |

| | Vol. | Page |
|---|---|---|
| **JONES**, (cont.) | | |
| Colchester, Sept. 9, 1832, by Rev. Lyman Strong | 2 | 237 |
| William Henry, s. [Sala, Jr. & Laura], b. June 24, 1843 | 2 | 88 |
| ----, d. [Amos & Mary], b. Dec. 27, 1760; d. Dec. 27, 1760 | 1 | 155 |
| **JORDAN, JURDEN**, Catharine, of Colchester, m. Caleb G. **GILMAN**, of New Hampshire, May 25, 1851, by Rev. George W. Pendleton | 2 | 102 |
| Mary, of Middletown, m. William **WATERS**, Jr., of Colchester, June 21, 1759 | 1 | 43 |
| **JOYNER**, Elizabeth, m. Samuel **STARK**, Oct. 7, 1742 | 1 | 147 |
| **JUDD**, Abigail, [d. Daniel & Lydia], b. Nov. 11, 1765 | 1 | 51 |
| Amasa, s. [Samuel & Mehetable], b. Nov. 5, 1788 | 2 | 1 |
| Ansel, s. [Samuel & Mehetable], b. Sept. 22, 1786 | 2 | 1 |
| Asa, s. [Samuel & Mehetable], b. Sept. 17, 1780 | 2 | 1 |
| Bettey, d. [Timothy & Elizabeth], b. Aug. 25, 1778 | 2 | 10 |
| Daniel, m. Lydia **JONES**, Mar. 14, 1751 | 1 | 51 |
| Daniel, [s. Daniel & Lydia], b. Oct. 13, 1751 | 1 | 51 |
| Daniel, m. Hannah **HINKLEY**, Feb. 21, 1779 | 1 | 51 |
| Daniel, d. Oct. 25, 1807 | 1 | 51 |
| Daniel Clark, s. [Samuel & Mehetable], b. Oct. 18, 1772 | 2 | 1 |
| Eli, s. [Samuel & Mehetable], b. Jan. 26, 1785; d. Feb. 13, 1789 | 2 | 1 |
| Emily A., of Colchester, m. Charles **TAYLOR**, of Great Barrington, Mass., June 3, 1823, by Salmon Crane, V. D. M. | 2 | 146 |
| Emily Alice, d. [Solomon & Mary], b. July 6, 1803 | 2 | 71 |
| Ephraim, [s. Daniel & Lydia], b. July 11, 1759 | 1 | 51 |
| Eunice, d. [Samuel & Mehetable], b. Nov. 24, 1778 | 2 | 1 |
| Isaac, s. [Samuel & Phebe], b. Mar. 20, 1779 | 2 | 27 |
| Jeheil, [s. Daniel & Lydia], b. Mar. 7, 1763 | 1 | 51 |
| Lydia, [d. Daniel & Lydia], b. Mar. 9, 1761 | 1 | 51 |
| Lydia, w. Daniel, d. Feb. 26, 1774 | 1 | 51 |
| Mabel, d. [Samuel & Mehetable], b. Oct. 23, 1782 | 2 | 1 |
| Mary, d. [Solomon & Mary], b. Oct. 24, 1793 | 2 | 71 |
| Mehetabel, d. [Samuel & Mehetable], b. May 30, 1775; d. May 23, 1777 | 2 | 1 |
| Patriarch, [s. Daniel & Lydia], b. Sept. 23, 1757; d. Oct. 8, 1771 | 1 | 51 |
| R[e]ubin, [s. Daniel & Lydia], b. Feb. 3, 1756 | 1 | 51 |
| Russel[l], s. [Samuel & Phebe], b. Dec. 3, 1780 | 2 | 27 |
| Samuel, [s. Daniel & Lydia], b. Aug. 1, 1754 | 1 | 51 |
| Samuel, m. Mehetable **CLARK**, Nov. 13, 1771 | 2 | 1 |
| Samuel, m. Phebe **BEEBE**, Nov. 10, 1776 | 2 | 27 |
| Samuel, s. [Samuel & Phebe], b. July 7, 1777 | 2 | 27 |
| Solomon, [s. Daniel & Lydia], b. Sept. 25, 1767 | 1 | 51 |
| Solomon, of Colchester, m. Mary **BARBER**, of Hebron, Nov. 26, 1789 | 2 | 71 |
| Solomon, s. [Solomon & Mary], b. May 29, 1791 | 2 | 71 |

| | Vol. | Page |
|---|---|---|
| **JUDD**, (cont.) | | |
| Statira, d. [Timothy & Elizabeth], b. Apr. 5, 1782 | 2 | 10 |
| Susannah, d. [Samuel & Mehetable], b. Sept. 10, 1792 | 2 | 1 |
| Timothy, [s. Daniel & Lydia], b. Feb. 8, 1753 | 1 | 51 |
| Timothy, of Colchester, m. Elizabeth **BEEBE**, of East Haddam, Sept. 26, 1775 | 2 | 10 |
| Timothy, s. [Timothy & Elizabeth], b. July 3, 1776 | 2 | 10 |
| **JURDEN, JURDAN**, [see under **JORDAN**] | | |
| **KASER**, Barbara, m. Godfrey **COKE**, b. of Wertemburg, Germany, Apr. 25, 1854, by Erastus Dickinson | 3 | 61 |
| **KEENEY**, Catharine C., of Colchester, m. George R. **BANNING**, of East Haddam, Oct. 27, 1851, by Rev. George W. Pendleton | 2 | 220 |
| Catharine, w. Jonathan, d. May 26, 1790 | 2 | 74 |
| Celinda Catharine, d. [William & Mary Ann], b. Apr. 18, 1834 | 2 | 220 |
| Elizabeth Ann, d. [William & Mary Ann], b. Jan. 1, 1837 | 2 | 220 |
| Hannah, d. [Jonathan & Catharine], b. Dec. 15, 1775, in Long Island | 2 | 74 |
| John, s. [Jonathan & Catharine], b. Apr. 29, 1786 | 2 | 74 |
| Jonathan, m. Catharine **BOOTH**, [b.] of Long Island, N. Y., Jan. 3, 1767 | 2 | 74 |
| Jonathan, s. [Jonathan & Catharine], b. Oct. 9, 1781; d. May 23, 1782 | 2 | 74 |
| Jonathan, m. Esther **BEEBE**, Aug. 5, 1792 | 2 | 74 |
| Mary G., of Colchester, m. Abishai A. **BAKER**, of Montville, May 24, 1829, by Salmon Cone, V. D. M. | 2 | 213 |
| Salenda, d. [Jonathan & Catharine], b. July 13, 1789 | 2 | 74 |
| William, s. [Jonathan & Catharine], b. Oct. 3, 1767, in Long Island | 2 | 74 |
| William, b. Feb. 20, 1799; m. Mary Ann **WILLIAMS**, Mar. 7, 1830, by Salmon Cone, V. D. M. | 2 | 220 |
| **KEITH**, Samuel, b. Aug. 2, 1781 | 2 | 46 |
| **KELLEY**, Charles Williams, [s. Eunice], b. June 11, 1811 | 2 | 23 |
| George Williams, s. [Eunice], b. June 10, 1816 | 2 | 23 |
| James Williams, s. [Eunice], b. Feb. 24, 1819 | 2 | 23 |
| **KELLOGG**, Aaron, m. Mary **LEWAYS**, July 10, 1740 | 1 | 130 |
| Aaron, s. [Aaron & Mary], b. Aug. 9, 1746 | 1 | 130 |
| Aaron, Jr., m. Rhoda **JONES**, July 3, 1766 | 1 | 80 |
| Abigaiell, [d. Ebenezer & Mabell], b. June 25, 1707 | L-3 | 194 |
| Abigail, d. Ebenezer [& Mabel], b. June 25, 1707 | TM-1 | 194 |
| Abigail, [d. Samuel & Abigail], b. Oct. 29, 1736 | L-3 | 451 |
| Abigail, d. [Ebenezer & Abigail], b. Jan. 27, 1754; d. Dec. 18, 1758 | 1 | 126 |
| Abigail, m. Joseph **GILLETT**, Dec. 8, 1757 | 1 | 110 |
| Abigail, 2d, d. [Ebenezer & Abigail], b. Dec. 29, 1758 | 1 | 126 |
| Abigail, [d. Israel & Abigail], b. Nov. 15, 1760 | 1 | 26 |
| Abigail, d. [Amos & Mary], b. Feb. 26, 1791 | 2 | 49 |

| | Vol. | Page |
|---|---|---|
| **KELLOGG**, (cont.) | | |
| Abigail, wid. of Samuel, d. Aug. 23, 1802 | 2 | 80 |
| Abner, m. Lydia **OTIS**, June 26, 1740 | 1 | 132 |
| Abner, d. Nov. 18, 1754 | 1 | 132 |
| Alfred, of Chatham, m. Jerusha **BRAINARD**, of Colchester, May 6, 1823, by Rev. Jacob Seales | 2 | 146 |
| Amasa, [s. Aaron, Jr. & Rhoda], b. Feb. 3, 1767 | 1 | 80 |
| Amos, [s. Israel & Abigail], b. Aug. 5, 1758 | 1 | 26 |
| Amos, m. Mary **PUM[E]ROY**, of Summers, June 28, 1781 | 2 | 49 |
| Amos, s. [Amos & Mary], b. June 5, 1782 | 2 | 49 |
| Ann, d. Nath[aniel]ll, Jr., b. Jan. 28, 1741/2 | 1 | 108 |
| Ann, [d. Samuel & Abigail], b. Nov. 30, 1742; d. July 9, 1758, in the 16th y. of her age | L-3 | 451 |
| Anna, d. [Joseph], b. Sept. 28, 1752, O. S. | 1 | 109 |
| Anna, d. [Russel & Esther], b. Dec. 24, 1798 | 2 | 91 |
| Asa, s. Nath[aniel]l, Jr., May 14, 1746; d. Dec. 19, 1746 | 1 | 108 |
| Asa, [s. Charles & Sarah], b. Jan. 21, 1749 | 1 | 76 |
| Bethiah, [d. Martin & Sarah], b. Oct. 24, 1762 | 1 | 36 |
| Betsey, d. [Titus & Betsey], b. Oct. 7, 1806 | 2 | 256 |
| Betsey, d. July 4, 1887 | 2 | 256 |
| Betsey, m. Titus **KELLOGG**, [ ] | 2 | 256 |
| Brainard D., m. Dorothy O. **DAY**, b. of Colchester, Mar. 13, 1834, by Rev. Joseph Harvey | 2 | 264 |
| Butler, s. [Ebenezer & Abigail], b. July 21, 1766 | 1 | 126 |
| Butler, m. Sally **TREADWAY**, Jan. 9, 1778 | 2 | 57 |
| Charles, [s. Nathaniel & Elizabeth], b. Sept. 17, 1726 | L-3 | 9 |
| Charles, [s. Nathaniell & Elizabeth], b. Sept. 17, 1726 | L-3 | 9 |
| Charles, m. Sarah **HICKOCK**, Apr. 24, 1748 | 1 | 76 |
| Charles, s. [Daniel & Elizabeth], b. Apr. 4, 1781; d. Feb. 6, 1786 | 2 | 80 |
| Charles, s. [Amos & Mary], b. Jan. 14, 1789 | 2 | 49 |
| Charles, s. [Russel & Esther], b. June 3, 1789 | 2 | 91 |
| Charles, 2d, s. [Daniel & Elizabeth], b. Nov. 6, 1791 | 2 | 80 |
| Clarissa, d. [Titus & Betsey], b. Oct. 2, 1817; d. Feb. 24, 1903 | 2 | 256 |
| Daniell, [s. Joseph & Abigaill], b. May 6, 1720 | L-1 | 445 |
| Daniel, [s. Samuel & Abigail], b. June 1, 1749 | L-3 | 451 |
| Daniel, s. [Aaron & Mary], b. Sept. 3, 1756 | 1 | 130 |
| Daniel, m. Elizabeth **WELLS**, Jan. 14, 1778 | 2 | 80 |
| Daniel, s. [Daniel & Elizabeth], b. Nov. 27, 1779 | 2 | 80 |
| Daniel, m. Jane Elizabeth **HALL**, b. of Colchester, May 28, 1850, by Henry M. Field | 3 | 45 |
| David, m. Eleanor **WILLIAMS**, of Lebanon, [ ], 1766 | 1 | 121 |
| Delight, d. [Abner & Lydia], b. Apr. 6, 1741 | 1 | 132 |
| Delight, [d. Nathaniel & Elizabeth], b. Oct. 5, 1734 | L-3 | 9 |
| Dianthy, d. [Israel, Jr. & Hannah], b. Sept. 27, 1777 | 2 | 10 |
| Ebenezer, m. Mabell **BUTLER**, July 6, 1706 | L-3 | 194 |
| Ebenezer, m. Mabel **BUTLER**, July 6, 1706 | TM-1 | 194 |
| Ebenezer, [s. Ebenezer & Mabell], b. Jan. 30, 1709/10 | L-3 | 194 |

| | Vol. | Page |
|---|---|---|
| **KELLOGG**, (cont.) | | |
| Ebenezer, s. Eben[eze]r [& Mabel], b. Jan. 30, 1709/10 | TM-1 | 194 |
| Eben[eze]r, d. Apr. 23, 1746 | 1 | 135 |
| Ebenezer, m. Abigail **ROWLEE**, May 10, 1752 | 1 | 126 |
| Ebenezer, s. Ebenezer [& Abigail], b. Mar. 16, 1756 | 1 | 126 |
| Editha, m. Joseph **PRAT[T]**, Mar. 2, 1727 | L-1 | 444 |
| Editha, m. Joseph **PRAT[T]**, Mar. 2, 1727 | L-3 | 6 |
| Edmund, of Colchester, m. Elizabeth **SKINNER**, of Conajaharrie, N. Y., Aug. 29, 1848, by Rev. S. D. Jewett, Westchester | 3 | 38 |
| Edmund B., of Hartford, m. Nancy E. **AVERY**, of Colchester, Sept. 11, 1838, by Rev. Joel R. Arnold | 2 | 232 |
| Elam, s. [Amos & Mary], b. Dec. 30, 1786 | 2 | 49 |
| Electa, d. [Israel, Jr. & Hannah], b. June 7, 1791 | 2 | 10 |
| Elijah, [s. Joseph & Abigaill], b. Jan. 15, 1728 | L-1 | 445 |
| Elijah C., of Hartford, m. Harriet **ISHAM**, May 5, 1846, by Rev. Joel R. Arnold | 3 | 19 |
| Elisha, s. [John & Mary], b. Nov. 15, 1775 | 1 | 129 |
| Elisha, m. Susanna **DAY**, June 9, 1776 | 2 | 65 |
| Elizabeth, [d. Ebenezer & Mabell], b. Sept. 25, 1712 | L-3 | 194 |
| Elizabeth, d. Eben[eze]r & Mabel], b. Sept. 25, 1712 | TM-1 | 194 |
| Elizabeth, [d. Nathaniell & Elizabeth], b. July 8, 1729 | L-3 | 9 |
| Elizabeth, m. Elisha **CLARK**, May 9, 1750 | 1 | 3 |
| Elizabeth, [d. Aaron, Jr. & Rhoda], b. Dec. 11, 1768 | 1 | 80 |
| Elizabeth, [w. Daniel], d. May 23, 1815 | 2 | 80 |
| Elizabeth C., of Colchester, m. Ezra **HALL**, of Lyme, Feb. 17, 1831, by Rev. Lyman Strong | 2 | 229 |
| Emma, of Colchester, m. Nelson B. **LOOMIS**, of Columbia, Jan. 11, 1848, by Rev. Joel R. Arnold | 3 | 34 |
| Erastus, s. [John & Mary], b. Oct. 22, 1792 | 2 | 56 |
| Easther, [d. Joseph], b. May 21, 1745 | 1 | 109 |
| Esther, m. Noah **FOOT**, Apr. 18, 1768 | 1 | 143 |
| Esther, d. [Russel & Esther], b. Aug. [ ], 1783; d. May [ ], 1784 | 2 | 91 |
| Esther, d. [Russel & Esther], b. Mar. 16, 1792 | 2 | 91 |
| [E]unice, m. Benjamin **QUITERFIELD**, July 11, 1728 | L-3 | 9 |
| Eunice, [d. Samuel & Abigail], b. Feb. 26, 1747 | L-3 | 451 |
| Eunice, m. Eleazer **CARTER**, Jan. 16, 1777 | 2 | 16 |
| Ezekiel, [s. Abner & Lydia], b. Sept. 17, 1748 | 1 | 132 |
| Ezra, [s. Nathaniell], b. Sept. 6, 1724 | L-3 | 199 |
| Ezra, s. Nath[anie]l, b. Sept. 6, 1724 | TM-1 | 199 |
| Ezra, s. [ Abner & Lydia], b. Sept. 5, 1754 | 1 | 132 |
| George W., of Belchertown, Mass., m. Lusina **WEST**, of Colchester, Dec. 1, 1845, by Rev. Joel R. Arnold | 3 | 26 |
| George W., m. Lydia Maria **PAYNE**, b. of Colchester, Feb. 7, 1853, by Rev. Erastus Dickinson | 3 | 53 |
| Hannah, [d. Samuel & Abigail], b. Sept. 30, 1740 | L-3 | 451 |
| Hannah, d. [John & Mary], b. Dec. 3, 1751 | 1 | 129 |

| | Vol. | Page |
|---|---|---|
| **KELLOGG**, (cont.) | | |
| Hannah, d. [Aaron & Mary], b. Mar. 17, 1754 | 1 | 130 |
| Hosea, s. [Russel & Esther], b. Dec. 24, 1795 | 2 | 91 |
| Israel, s. [John & Mary], b. May 31, 1746 | 1 | 129 |
| Israel, m. Abigail **NORTHAM**, Jan. 31, 1752 | 1 | 26 |
| Israel, [s. Israel & Abigail], b. May 18, 1756 | 1 | 26 |
| Israel, Jr., m. Hannah **INGHAM**, b. of Colchester, [ ], 1775 | 2 | 10 |
| Israel, s. [Israel, Jr. & Hannah], b. Aug. 2, 1782 | 2 | 10 |
| Israel, s. [Amos & Mary], b. Nov. 14, 1792 | 2 | 49 |
| James, alias James **RICHARDS**, m. Laura Ann **DAVIS**, b. of Colchester, Sept. 1, 1822, (colored persons), by Samuel A. Peters, J. P. | 2 | 94 |
| Jared C., of Ellington, m. Frances M. **DAY**, of Colchester, Oct. 7, 1839, by Rev. Lyman Strong | 2 | 159 |
| John, m. Mary **NEWTON**, Apr. 2, 1738 | 1 | 129 |
| John, s. [John & Mary], b. Dec. 20, 1743 | 1 | 129 |
| John, d. Jan. 22, 1762 | 1 | 129 |
| John, s. [Daniel & Elizabeth], b. Nov. 30, 1784 | 2 | 80 |
| John, m. Mary **DAY**, Dec. 26, 1791 | 2 | 56 |
| John, 3d, m. Clarissa **CHAMBERLAIN**, Feb. 18, 1823, by Samuel Cone, V. D. M. | 2 | 86 |
| John Samuel, s. [Samuel A. & Jane G.], b. Sept. 19, 1846 | 3 | 22 |
| Jonathan, m. Ann **NEWTON**, Jan. 3, 1710/11 | L-1 | 444 |
| Jonathan, [s. Jonathan & Ann], b. Sept. 18, 1712 | L-1 | 444 |
| Jonathan, Jr., m. Mary **NILES**, Jan. 1, 1735/6 | 1 | 127 |
| Jonathan, [s. Israel & Abigail], b. Oct. 10, 1754 | 1 | 26 |
| Jonathan, [s. Martin & Sarah], b. May 4, 1767 | 1 | 36 |
| Joseph, [s. Jonathan & Ann], b. June 6, 1714 | L-1 | 444 |
| Joseph, m. Abigaill **MILLER**, Oct. 23, 1717 | L-1 | 445 |
| Joseph, [s. Joseph & Abigaill], b. Aug. 8, 1718 | L-1 | 445 |
| Joseph, m. Sarah **CLARK**, Jan. 15, 1740/41 | 1 | 106 |
| Joseph, d. June 16, 1762 | 1 | 78 |
| Joseph, [s. Silas & Sarah], b. Dec. 2, 1770; d. Mar. 19, 1772 | 1 | 78 |
| Joseph Day, s. [Elisha & Susanna], b. Aug. 9, 1778 | 2 | 65 |
| Judah, s. [John & Mary ], b. Mar. 8, 1739 | 1 | 129 |
| Lois, d. [Israel, Jr. & Hannah], b. Nov. 24, 1775 | 2 | 10 |
| Lou, [d. Martin & Sarah], b. Feb. 4, 1770 | 1 | 36 |
| Lovina, d. [Aaron & Mary], b. Mar. 10, 1760 | 1 | 130 |
| Lucretia, m. Dan T. **FOOT**, b. of Colchester, Jan. 31, 1841, by Rev. Lyman Strong | 2 | 286 |
| Lucy, d. [Aaron & Mary], b. Mar. 21, 1741; d. Apr. 8, [1741] | 1 | 130 |
| Lucy, 2d, d. [Aaron & Mary], b. Feb. 19, 1742 | 1 | 130 |
| Lucy, m. Eliphalet **CHAMBERLAIN**, May 26, 1768 | 1 | 82 |
| Lydya, [d. Nathaniell], b. May 29, 1710 | L-3 | 199 |
| Lydia, d. [Nath[anie]ll], b. May 29, 1710 | TM-1 | 199 |
| Lydiah, m. John **HOPSON**, May 28, 1730 | L-3 | 7 |
| Lydia, d. [Abner & Lydia], b. Jan. 15, 1742/3 | 1 | 132 |
| Lydia, d. [Aaron & Mary], b. Feb. 23, 1749 | 1 | 130 |

| | Vol. | Page |
|---|---|---|
| **KELLOGG**, (cont.) | | |
| Lydia, d. [David & Eleanor], b. Oct. 4, 1766 | 1 | 121 |
| Lydia, m. William **BULKELEY**, May 27, 1767 | 1 | 80 |
| Lydia, d. [Israel, Jr. & Hannah], b. Sept. 28, 1786 | 2 | 10 |
| Mabel, d. [Ebenezer & Abigail], b. Aug. 3, 1763 | 1 | 126 |
| Marcy, [d. Joseph & Abigaill], b. May 20, 1723 | L-1 | 445 |
| Margarett, [d. Nathaniel & Elizabeth], b. Jan. 17, 1736/7 | L-3 | 9 |
| Margaret, w. Nath[anie]ll, d. Nov. 15, 1747 | 1 | 135 |
| Margaret, [d. Abner & Lydia], b. Jan. 16, 1751/2 | 1 | 132 |
| Margeree, [d. Jonathan & Ann], b. Aug. 10, 1716 | L-1 | 444 |
| Margery, d. [Jonathan, Jr. & Mary], b. Sept. 6, 1738 | 1 | 127 |
| Martha, [d. Jonathan, Jr. & Mary], b. Jan. [ ], 1740/41 | 1 | 127 |
| Martin, [s. Jonathan & Ann], b. Feb. 15, 1734/5 | L-1 | 444 |
| Martin, m. Sarah **TREADWAY**, Feb. 4, 1762 | 1 | 36 |
| Martin, [s. Martin & Sarah], b. Dec. 16, 1764 | 1 | 36 |
| Mary, [d. Ebenezer & Mabell, b. June 3, 1715 | L-3 | 194 |
| Mary, d. Eben[eze]r [& Mabel], b. June 3, 1715 | TM-1 | 194 |
| Mary, m. John **HOPSON**, May 28, 1730 | TPR | 112 |
| Mary, [d. Samuel & Abigail], b. Apr. 27, 1745, N. S. | L-3 | 451 |
| Mary, d. [John & Mary], b. Dec. 17, 1749 | 1 | 129 |
| Mary, d. [Aaron & Mary], b. Aug. 23, 1751 | 1 | 130 |
| Mary, m. Isaac **FOOT**, May 31, 1768 | 1 | 137 |
| Mary, d. [Israel, Jr. & Hannah], b. Sept. 19, 1779 | 2 | 10 |
| Mary N., m. Aaron E. **EMMONS**, Dec. 26, 1825, by Salmon Cone, V. D. M.; d. [ ] | 2 | 182 |
| Mercy, m. Rev. Judah **LEWIS**, Dec. 24, 1734 | L-3 | 9 |
| Mercy, d. [John & Mary], b. June 11, 1741 | 1 | 129 |
| Mercy, m. Asa **GRAVES**, Mar. 2, 1786; d. Oct. 8, 1806 | 2 | 55 |
| Mercy, m. William **OAKLEY**, Dec. 7, 1835, by Giles Shattuck, J. P. | 2 | 281 |
| Molly, [d. Silas & Sarah], b. Apr. 26, 1769 | 1 | 78 |
| Moses, [s. Joseph & Abigaill], b. [ ], 10, 1725 | L-1 | 445 |
| Nathaniell, s. Nathaniell, b. May 8, 1703 | L-3 | 199 |
| Nathaniel, s. Nath[anie]l, b. May 8, 1703 | TM-1 | 199 |
| Nathaniel, m. Elizabeth **WILLIAMS**, July [ ], 1725 | L-3 | 9 |
| Nathaniell, m. Elizabeth **WILLIAMS**, July 1, 1725 | L-3 | 9 |
| Nath[anie]ll, s. Nath[anie]ll, Jr., b. July 10, 1739 | 1 | 129 |
| Nath[anie]ll, Sergt., d. Aug. 22, 1757, ae 87 | 1 | 55 |
| Polly, d. [Amos & Mary], b. Feb. 2, 1785 | 2 | 49 |
| Prudence, [d. Ebenezer & Mabell], b. Dec. 24, 1717 | L-3 | 194 |
| Prudence, d. Eben[eze]r [& Mabel], b. Dec. 24, 1717 | TM-1 | 194 |
| Prudence, m. William **ROBERTS**, May 6, 1736 | 1 | 53 |
| Rachel C., of Colchester, m. Hiram **SMITH**, of Margaretta, Ohio, Oct. 17, 1838, by Rev. Joel R. Arnold | 2 | 118 |
| Rhoda, m. Roger **BULKELEY**, [ ]; d. June 15, 1807 | 2 | 50 |
| Russel[l], s. [David & Eleanor], b. June 1, 1770 | 1 | 121 |
| Russel[l], m. Esther **BRIDGES**, [ ], 1777 | 2 | 91 |
| Russel[l], s. [Russel & Esther], b. Oct. 27, 1786 | 2 | 91 |

| | Vol. | Page |
|---|---|---|
| **KENYON**, (cont.) | | |
| Israel, of Onondaga, N. Y., m. Dimis **STRONG**, of Colchester, Feb. 5, 1821, by Salmon Cone, V. D. M. | 2 | 123 |
| **KILLBORN, KILBURN**, Amasa, s. [Hezekiah, Jr. & Mary], b. Sept. 30, 1762 | 1 | 136 |
| Ann, [d. Hezekiah & Ann], b. Mar. 25, 1734 | L-3 | 8 |
| Anne, m. Uriah **CLARK**, Oct. 24, 1751 | 1 | 142 |
| Asa, [s. Hezekiah & Ann], b. Jan. 26, 1731/2 | L-3 | 8 |
| David, s. [Jonathan, Jr. & Mary], b. Nov. 13, 1744 | 1 | 105 |
| David, m. Lydia **ABEL**, Nov. 5, 1767 | 1 | 88 |
| David, [s. David & Lydia], b. June 25, 1770 | 1 | 88 |
| David, Jr., m. Lydia **WELLS**, Mar. 13, 1793 | 2 | 79 |
| David Wells, s. [David, Jr. & Lydia], b. July 7, 1800; d. Feb. 20, 1802 | 2 | 79 |
| Dimmis, m. Nehemiah **DAY**, Aug. 21, 1766 | 1 | 119 |
| Dimmis, [d. David & Lydia], b. May 26, 1777 | 1 | 88 |
| Elijah, d. Sept. 30, 1804 | 2 | 67 |
| Elizabeth, d. Jonathan, b. Oct. 15, 1713 | L-3 | 193 |
| Elizabeth, d. Jonathan, b. Oct. 15, 1713 | TM-1 | 193 |
| Elisabeth, m. John **QUITFIELD**, Dec. 7, 1733 | TPR | 110 |
| Elizabeth, m. Jacob **QUITFIELD**, Oct. 25, 1759 | 1 | 163 |
| Elizabeth, m. Jacob **QUITFIELD**, Oct. 25, 1759 | 2 | 12 |
| Elizabeth, [d. David & Lydia], b. Jan. 22, 1775; d. Aug. 6, 1784 | 1 | 88 |
| Elnida, d. [David, Jr. & Lydia], b. Apr. 17, 1796 | 2 | 79 |
| Hesekiah, [s. Jonathan], b. Nov. 2, 1708 | L-3 | 193 |
| Hezekiah, s. Jonathan, b. Nov. 2, 1708 | TM-1 | 193 |
| Hezekiah, m. Ann **CLOTHER**, Dec. 25, 1728 | L-3 | 8 |
| Hezekiah, [s. Hezekiah & Ann], b. Dec. 1, 1729 | L-3 | 8 |
| Hezekiah, Jr., m. Mary **HOLMS**, Dec. 27, 1753 | 1 | 136 |
| John, s. [Hezekiah, Jr. & Mary], b. Jan. 30, 1756 | 1 | 136 |
| John, [s. David & Lydia], b. Aug. 26, 1779 | 1 | 88 |
| Jonathan, s. Jonathan, b. June 8, 1707 | L-3 | 193 |
| Jonathan, s. Jonathan, b. Jan. 8, 1707 | TM-1 | 193 |
| Jonathan, Jr., m. Mary **SKINNER**, Oct. 20, 1734 | 1 | 105 |
| Jonathan, s. [Jonathan, Jr. & Mary], b. Mar. 19, 1737; d. May 15, 1737 | 1 | 105 |
| Jonathan, s. [Jonathan, Jr. & Mary], b. Apr. 12, 1742 | 1 | 105 |
| Jonathan, d. Oct. 14, 1785 | 2 | 6 |
| Joseph, s. [Hezekiah, Jr. & Mary], b. Mar. 2, 1758 | 1 | 136 |
| Lydia, d. [Jonathan, Jr. & Mary], b. Apr. 28, 1738; d. July 1, 1738 | 1 | 105 |
| Lydia, d. [Jonathan, Jr. & Mary], b. May 2, 1739 | 1 | 105 |
| Lydia, [d. David & Lydia], b. Apr. 4, 1768 | 1 | 88 |
| Lydia, d. [David, Jr. & Lydia], b. July 12, 1794 | 2 | 79 |
| Mary, d. [Jonathan, Jr. & Mary], b. Aug. 10, 1735 | 1 | 105 |
| Mary, m. Elisha **BIGELOW**, May 21, 1751 | 1 | 125 |
| Mary, m. Elisha **BIGELOW**, May 21, 1751; d. Jan. 11, 1765 | 2 | 55 |

**KELLOGG**, (cont.)

Samuell, d. Aug. 24, 1708
Samuel, d. Aug. 24, 1708 TM
Samuel, m. Abigail **STERLING**, Jan. 8, 1735/6 1
Samuel, [s. Samuel & Abigail], b. Dec. 20, 1738 I
Samuel, s. [Daniel & Elizabeth], b. Feb. 10, 1783
Samuel, d. July 31, 1783
Samuel, s. [Israel, Jr. & Hannah], b. Aug. 4, 1784; d. June 23, 1787
Samuel, 2d, s. [Israel, Jr. & Hannah], b. Dec. 30, 1788
Samuel had slaves Lydia, d. Jinne, b. Mar. 18, 1793; Jim, s. Jinne, b. Feb. [ ], 1791; Sias, s. Jinne, b. May 20, 1795 2
Samuel A., m. Jane G. **CARROLL**, b. of Colchester, May 19, 1845, by Rev. Joel R. Arnold 3
Sarah, d. Nath[anie]l, b. Dec. 27, 1706 TM-1
Sarah, [d. Nathaniell], b. Dec. 27, 1707 L-3
Sarah, m. Judah **LEWES**, Feb. 19, 1728/9 L-1
Sarah, m. Judah **LEWES**, Feb. 19, 1728/9 L-3
Sarah, [d. Nathaniell & Elizabeth], b. Feb. 22, 1731/2 L-3
Sarah, [d. Nathaniel & Elizabeth], b. Feb. 22, 1732 L-3
Sarah, [d. Joseph], b. Aug. 11, 1749 1
Sarah, [d. Silas & Sarah], b. July 11, 1772 1
Sarah, d. [Russel & Esther], b. Feb. 14, 1801 2
Sarah, of Colchester, m. Harvey **TALCOTT**, of Coventry, Apr. 17, 1822, by Solomon Cone, V. D. M. 2
Sarah Ann, alias **RICHARDS**, d. [James & Laura Ann], b. Feb. 2, 1823 (colored) 2
Seymour, s. [Titus & Betsey], b. Aug. 29, 1808 2
Silas, [s. Jonathan & Ann], b. Jan. 11, 1732/3 L-1
Silas, s. [Joseph & Sarah], b. Aug. 25, 1742 1
Silas, m. Sarah **HOOK**, June 21, 1768 1
Solomon, s. [Aaron & Mary], b. July 14, 1744 1
Stephen, [s. Jonathan & Ann], b. Mar. 15, 1724 L-1
Tabitha, d. [Elisha & Susanna], b. July 27, 1789 2
Tabitha, m. Jonathan **WILLIAMS**, Feb. 16, 1808 2
Theodey, d. [David & Eleanor], b. Sept. 24, 1768 1
Titus, m. Betsey **KELLOGG**, [ ] 2
William, s. Moses, b. Jan. 28, 1756 1 1
William, s. [Titus & Betsey], b. Sept. 20, 1811 2 2
-----, s. [Daniel & Elizabeth], b. Oct. 20, 1778; d. Dec. 25, 1778 2 8

**KENT**, Presilla, m. Samuell **BROWN**, Apr. 11, 1715 L-3 19
Priscilla, m. Samuel **BROWN**, Apr. 11, 1715 TM-1 19

**KENYON**, [see also **KINION**], Edwin, b. in Richmond; Corp. of Capt. J. E. Woodard's Co. F. 18th Reg. Conn. Inf. Vol. enrolled Aug. 11, 1862; dischardged June 27, 1865, at Harper's Ferry, Va., ae 18 3 70

| | Vol. | Page |
|---|---|---|
| **KILLBORN, KILBURN**, (cont.) | | |
| Mary, w. Jona[tha]n, d. Aug. 11, 1780 | 1 | 105 |
| Mary, [d. David & Lydia], b. Sept. 1, 1786 | 1 | 88 |
| Ralph, [s. David & Lydia], b. Nov. 12, 1781 | 1 | 88 |
| Sally, d. [David, Jr. & Lydia], b. Jan. 27, 1798 | 2 | 79 |
| Samuel, [s. David & Lydia], b. July 7, 1772 | 1 | 88 |
| Sarah, m. Thomas **WELLS**, Sept. 18, 1740 | 1 | 145 |
| Sarah, d. [Hezekiah, Jr. & Mary], b. Dec. 11, 1759 | 1 | 136 |
| Sarah, m. Amos **RANALL**, Mar. 27, 1776 | 2 | 69 |
| **KIMBALL**, Mary, m. Stephen **HALL**, b. of Colchester, Oct. 16, 1820, by Samuel A. Peters, J. P. | 2 | 153 |
| **KIMBERLEY**, Elizabeth, m. Israel **FOOT**, Dec. 28, 1748 | 1 | 151 |
| Ruth, m. Rev. Robert **ROBBINS**, Jan. 10, 1769; d. Apr. 13, 1769 | 2 | 82 |
| **KINION**, [see also **KENYON**], Abigaiel, [d. James], b. Oct. 8, 1724 | L-1 | 445 |
| Mary, d. James, b. Dec. 10, 1722 | L-1 | 445 |
| **KINNE**, Comfort, m. Asa **BAKER**, Feb. 9, 1780, at Preston | 2 | 72 |
| **KITERFIELD**, [see under **QUITERFIELD**] | | |
| **KITHOPHELL**, [see under **QUITERFIELD**] | | |
| **KNEELAND, NELAND, KNELAND**, Deborah, [d. Edward], b. Nov. 9, 1757 | 1 | 34 |
| Deborah, m. Joseph **CARRIER**, Sept. [ ], 1771 | 1 | 77 |
| Dolly Ruth, d. [Hezekiah & Mercy], b. Mar. 2, 1760 | 1 | 106 |
| Dorothy, d. [Hezekiah & Mercy], b. Dec. 3, 1753; d. Jan. 16, 1754 | 1 | 106 |
| Edward, [s. Edward], b. Sept. 30, 1768 | 1 | 34 |
| Elisabeth, m. Benjamin **CARRIER**, Feb. 6, 1734/5 | L-3 | 454 |
| Elizabeth, m. Benjamin **CARRIER**, Feb. 6, 1734/5 | 1 | 106 |
| Hezekiah, m. Mercy **JEPOON**, [ ] (**PEPOON**?) | 1 | 106 |
| Jabez, s. Benj[amin], b. Apr. 14, 1738; d. [Apr.] 27, [1738] | 1 | 127 |
| Lennad, s. [Hezekiah & Mercy], b. May 16, 1755 | 1 | 106 |
| Lizzie, d. [Hezekiah & Mercy], b. June 7, 1762; d. Apr. 10, 1767 | 1 | 106 |
| Lizzie, 2d, d. [Hezekiah & Mercy], b. Feb. 2, 1768 | 1 | 106 |
| Lucinda, d. [Hezekiah & Mercy], b. Oct. 6, 1764; d. June 8, 1766 | 1 | 106 |
| Lucinda, [d. Edward], b. Aug. 16, 1766 | 1 | 34 |
| Marcy, d. Hezekiah & [Mercy], b. Nov. 25, 1751 | 1 | 106 |
| Mehetable, w. [Benj[amin]], d. May 17, 1738 | 1 | 127 |
| Phebe, m. Amos **CARRIER**, June 6, 1745 | 1 | 102 |
| Phebe, m. Amos **CARRIER**, June 6, 1745 | 1 | 145 |
| Rachel, d. Hezekiah [& Mercy], b. Dec. 27, 1749 | 1 | 106 |
| Silvai, d. [Hezekiah & Mercy], b. Mar. 27, 1767; d. Apr. 9, 1767 | 1 | 106 |
| **KNIGHT**, Ann, d. [Joshua & Abigail], b. Nov. 1, 1743; d. Mar. 18, 1764 | 1 | 138 |
| Charles, s. [Joshua & Abigail], b. May 3, 1764 | 1 | 138 |

| | Vol. | Page |
|---|---|---|
| **KNIGHT**, (cont.) | | |
| Dimmis, d. [Joshua & Abigail], b. Oct. 15, 1745 | 1 | 138 |
| Dimmis, m. Ariel **JONES**, Nov. 13, 1765 | 1 | 81 |
| Elihu, s. [Joshua & Abigail], b. Mar. 4, 1761 | 1 | 138 |
| Joshua, [s. Samuel & Mary], b. June 20, 1721 | L-1 | 399 |
| Joshua, m. Abigail **CHAPMAN**, Dec. 9, 1742 | 1 | 138 |
| Lydia, [d. Samuel & Mary], b. June 26, 1730 | L-1 | 399 |
| Lydia, d. [Joshua & Abigail], b. May 5, 1758 | 1 | 138 |
| Mary, [d. Samuel & Mary], b. July 13, 1724 | L-1 | 399 |
| Mary, m. Jonah **CLARK**, Nov. 24, 1745 | 1 | 107 |
| Mary, d. [Joshua & Abigail], b. June 21, 1749 | 1 | 138 |
| Samuell, m. Mary **RANSOM**, Nov. 29, 1716 | L-1 | 399 |
| Samuel, s. [Joshua & Abigail], b. Apr. 4, 1755 | 1 | 138 |
| Sarah, d. [Joshua & Abigail], b. May 9, 1752 | 1 | 138 |
| **KNOWLES**, John P., m. Ann R. **NICHOLS**, Oct. 23, 1828, by Benjamin Trumbull, J. P. | 2 | 208 |
| **KNOWLTON**, Susannah, m. Azariah **MITCHELL**, May 11, 1762 | 1 | 41 |
| **[K]NOX**, Elizabeth, [d. John & Elizabeth], b. Mar. 28, 1726 | L-1 | 399 |
| John, m. Elizabeth **ROBERDS**, Apr. 20, 1720 | L-1 | 399 |
| **KORTRIGHT**, Lucretia, of New York, m. William **CROCKER**, of Colchester, Nov. 5, 1826, by Salmon Cone, V. D. M. | 2 | 189 |
| **LACEY**, Eleazer, of Middletown, m. Eliza F. **MARSH**, of Colchester, Sept. 24, 1834, by Rev. Lyman Strong | 2 | 270 |
| **LAMB**, Asa, m. Silence, [ ], of Groton | 2 | 71 |
| Henry F., m. Frances **McSHANE**, Mar. 12, 1818 | 2 | 145 |
| James, m. Abby R. **WELD**, b. of Colchester, Mar. 27, 1851, by Rev. George W. Pendleton | 2 | 270 |
| Lucy, m. Benjamin **PECK**, June 10, 1802 | 2 | 121 |
| Mary A., m. Henry **FOOTE**, b. of Colchester, Jan. 13, 1850, by Rev. Lyman Strong | 3 | 45 |
| Nancy, d. [Asa & Silence], b. Feb. 7, 1793, in Colchester | 2 | 71 |
| **LAMPHERE, LANPHERE, LANDFEAR, LAMPHEAR**, Charles, m. Lucy **BENJAMIN**, b. of Colchester, Nov. 15, 1824, by Rev. William Palmer, at wid. Benjamin's, Norwich | 2 | 172 |
| Charles B., of East Haddam, m. Tiddia **BRAINARD**, of Chatham, Sept. 29, 1846, by Rev. S. D. Jewett | 3 | 29 |
| Cynthia, of Colchester, m. Seth B. **WEST**, of Marlborough, Conn., June 28, 1852, by Geo[rge] W. Pendleton | 3 | 52 |
| Emily E., m. Leander **CHAPMAN**, May 18, 1851, by Rev. George W. Pendleton | 2 | 80 |
| Fanny, m. Isaiah **RATHBUN**, Mar. 9, 1764 | 1 | 14 |
| Mary A., m. John T. **BROWN**, b. of Colchester, May 14, 1854, by Rev. Anthony Palmer | 3 | 62 |
| **LANDON**, [see also **LANGDON**], Deborah, [d. Daniell], b. Feb. 16, 1725 | L-3 | 8 |
| Joshua, [s. Daniell], b. Apr. 13, 1729 | L-3 | 8 |
| Samuell, s. Daniell, b. Feb. 19, 1723 | L-1 | 446 |

| | Vol. | Page |
|---|---|---|
| **LANDON**, (cont.) | | |
| Samuell, s. Daniell, b. Feb. 19, 1723 | L-3 | 8 |
| William, [s. Daniell], b. Apr. 25, 1727 | L-3 | 8 |
| **LANGDON**, [see also **LANDON**], Elizabeth, [w. George], d. Dec. 8, 1909, at Plymouth, Conn., ae 80 | 3 | 48 |
| George, m. Elizabeth A. **CHAPMAN**, Sept. 3, 1851, by Rev. J. A. Copp | 3 | 48 |
| **LATHAM**, Almy, w. [Cary], d. Mar. 18, 1845, in Salem, ae 93 | 2 | 23 |
| Amos B., of Hebron, m. Caroline M. **LOOMIS**, of Colchester, Sept. 5, 1837, by Rev. W[illia]m F. Vaill | 2 | 101 |
| Amos S., Dea., d. Oct. 30, 1846, ae 49 | 2 | 23 |
| Cary, Jr., [s. Cary & Almy], d. Sept. 28, 1812, ae 40 | 2 | 23 |
| Cary, d. Aug. 23, 1823, ae 83; formerly of Groton | 2 | 23 |
| Esther, of Colchester, m. George **ELDERKIN**, of Lebanon, July, [ ], 1824, by Salmon Cone, V. D. M. | 2 | 167 |
| Esther, d. [Cary, Jr. & Esther], d. May 31, 1833, in Middletown, ae 31 | 2 | 23 |
| Esther, w. [Cary, Jr.] & 2d w. Rowland **PERRY**, d. Nov. 20, 1841, ae 65 | 2 | 23 |
| Hannah, m. Rowland **PERRY**, Jr., July 23, 1827, by Salmon Cone, V. D. M. | 2 | 197 |
| Hannah, d. [Cary, Jr. & Esther], d. Sept. 12, 1833, ae 34 | 2 | 23 |
| Harriet M., of Colchester, m. Henry M. **JONES**, of Huntington, L. I., July 7, 1845, by Rev. P. Brockett | 3 | 22 |
| Henry A., m. Abby Jane **COOKE**, b. of Colchester, Oct. 6, 1851, by Rev. Geo[rge] W. Pendleton | 3 | 46 |
| Israel, s. [Cary, Jr. & Esther], d. Nov. 14, 1812, ae 9 | 2 | 23 |
| William, s. [Cary, Jr. & Esther], d. Apr. 14, 1826, ae 30, in Tauqerier County, Va., of Typhus fever | 2 | 23 |
| **LATHROP**, Ebenezer, d. Oct. 22, 1806 | 2 | 75 |
| Lucretia, b. Apr. 14, 1763; m. Joel **BIGELOW**, June 29, 1786; d. Feb. 16, 1851, ae 88 | 2 | 53 |
| Mat[t]hew, s. Benj[amin], b. July 25, 1747 | 1 | 141 |
| Phebe, w. Eben[eze]r, d. Mar. 20, 1806 | 2 | 75 |
| Seth, m. Merebah **HARRIS**, Sept. 28, 1794; d. Feb. 23, 1849; ae 78 | 2 | 75 |
| Seth m. Merebah **HARRIS**, Sept. 28, 1794 | 2 | 133 |
| Seth E., of Salem, m. Caroline **WORTHINGTON**, of Colchester, Sept. 28, 1824, by Rev. William Jarvis | 2 | 168 |
| Seth Ebenezer, s. [Seth & Merebah], b. Jan. 6, 1797 | 2 | 75 |
| Seth Ebenezer, s. [Seth & Merebah], b. Jan. 6, 1797 | 2 | 133 |
| Walter, [s. Benjamin], b. Nov. 19, 1749 | 1 | 99 |
| William S., of Lebanon, m. Grace S. **BRIGGS**, of Colchester, Jan. 24, 1847, by Rev. Joel R. Arnold | 3 | 30 |
| **LATTIMORE, LATTEMORE**, Anne, of New London, m. Charles **BULKLEY**, of Colchester, Oct. 8, 1741 | 1 | 88 |
| Lucy, of Lyme, b. Dec. [ ], 1758; m. Daniel **DODGE**, Jr., of Colchester, Dec. 2, 1779; d. Apr. 7, 1832, ae 73 | 2 | 57 |

| | Vol. | Page |
|---|---|---|
| **LATTIMORE, LATTEMORE**, (cont.) | | |
| Lydia, m. Frederick **BULKELEY**, Apr. 16, 1795 | 2 | 86 |
| **LAVIT**, Anna, m. Elijah **WORTHINGTON**, Apr. 29, 1756 | 1 | 45 |
| **LEE**, Benjamin S., of Colchester, m. Harriet P. **MAINE**, of Lock, N. Y., Sept. 13, 1852, by Rev. E. H. Gillett | 3 | 53 |
| Charlotte C., of Colchester, m. George **DESTON**, of New London, Aug. 1, 1842, by Rev. Joel R. Arnold | 2 | 283 |
| Clarissa W., m. John **WAY**, Feb. 1, 1829, by Salmon Cone, V. D. M. | 2 | 209 |
| Elizabeth, of Colchester, m. Ahimdaz **BALCH**, of Salem, Nov. 28, 1833, by Rev. Lyman Strong | 2 | 260 |
| Ellen Maria, of Colchester, m. Seth Abram **WILLSON**, of Killingly, Sept. 21, 1853, by Rev. Erastus Dickinson | 3 | 58 |
| Frederick W., of Guilford, m. Rebeckah R. **STANNARD**, of Colchester, Dec. 9, 1832, by Rev. Lyman Strong | 2 | 240 |
| H. Nelson, of Essex, m. Caroline E. **MARSH**, of Colchester, Feb. 3, 1847, by Rev. Joel R. Arnold | 3 | 31 |
| John C., m. Eunice **PACKER**, d. of John, b. of Colchester, Nov. 30, 1848, by Rev. Augustus Bolles | 3 | 38 |
| Rachel M., of Colchester, m. Joseph N. **ADAMS**, of Canterbury, Nov. 25, 1849, by Rev. A. F. Park | 3 | 43 |
| Susan A., m. Joseph N. **BUELL**, b. of Colchester, Aug. 18, 1835, by Rev. Joseph Harvey | 2 | 278 |
| **LEFFINGWELL**, Almira, m. Justus W. **WILLIAMS**, b. of Colchester, Jan. 1, 1833, by Rev. Benjamin G. Goff | 2 | 240 |
| Cynthia B., d. [William], b. Jan. 5, 1831 | 2 | 119 |
| Joseph Lyman, s. [William], b. Feb. 17, 1833 | 2 | 119 |
| Lyman, m. Sarah C. **BROWN**, Aug. 20, 1833, by Rev. Joseph Harvey | 2 | 256 |
| Matilda H., m. Orrin W. **AVERY**, b. of Colchester, Feb. 25, 1844, by Rev. Joel R. Arnold | 3 | 10 |
| William, m. [ ] | 2 | 119 |
| **LESTER**, Anna, d. [Jonathan & Rebeckah], b. Dec. 27, 1784 | 2 | 80 |
| Jonathan, m. Mabel **WEBSTER**, Apr. 11, 1789 | 2 | 80 |
| Jonathan, of Colchester, m. Rebeckah **BURCHARD**, of East Windsor, [ ] | 2 | 80 |
| **LEVERIDGE**, [see also **LOVERIDGE**], David had negro servant Prince b. May 3, 1807 | 2 | 325 |
| **LEWIS, LEWES, LEWESS, LEWAYS, LOUIS**, Abigaill, [d. Thomas & Mary], b. Nov. 30, 1724 | L-1 | 446 |
| Abraham, [s. Samuel & Mary], b. Apr. 29, 1738 | L-3 | 456 |
| Ann, m. Noah **DAY**, Dec. 6, 1759 | 1 | 30 |
| Basset, s. Thomas & Mary, b. Oct. 27, 1732 | 1 | 127 |
| Benjamin, [s. Samuel & Mary], b. Mar. 29, 1733 | L-3 | 456 |
| Bethia, m. John **RANSOM**, Apr. 6, 1732 | TPR | 111 |
| Betty, d. [Daniel], b. Sept. 6, 1738 | 1 | 103 |
| Betty, m. James **RANSOM**, Dec. 15, 1757 | 1 | 55 |
| Dan[ie]ll, s. [Daniel], b. June 16, 1734 | 1 | 103 |

| | Vol. | Page |
|---|---|---|
| **LEWIS, LEWES, LEWESS, LEWAYS, LOUIS,** (cont.) | | |
| Daniel, s. [Thomas & Mary], b. Aug. 31, 1736 | 1 | 127 |
| Elizabeth, m. Nathan **WILLIAMS**, Sept. 16, 1725 | L-3 | 8 |
| Elisabeth, d. Samuel & Mary, b. June 22, 1731 | L-3 | 456 |
| Ephraim, [s. Rev. Judah & Mercy], b. Oct. 4, 1735 | L-3 | 9 |
| Ephraim, m. Lois **RANSOM**, Aug. 15, 1765 | 1 | 23 |
| Esther, [d. Thomas & Mary], b. Dec. 31, 1730 | L-1 | 446 |
| Fannie Pamelia, [d. Ephraim & Lois], b. Apr. 29, 1768 | 1 | 23 |
| Hannah, d. Benjamin, b. Apr. 7, 1717 | L-1 | 654 |
| Hannah, w. Benjamin, d. June 9, 1732 | TPR | 111 |
| Hannah, m. David **DAY**, Dec. 12, 1734 | TPR | 111 |
| Isaac, [s. Samuel & Mary], b. Feb. 14, 1738/9 | L-3 | 456 |
| Jesse, m. Thankfull **BECKWITH**, Oct. 19, 1820, by W[illia]m Palmer, at the house of [W[illia]m Palmer] | 2 | 154 |
| J[oh]n, [s. Samuel & Mary], b. June 16, 1734 | L-3 | 456 |
| John, [s. Daniel], b. June 6, 1741 | 1 | 103 |
| Judah, m. Sarah **KELLOGG**, Feb. 19, 1728/9 | L-1 | 399 |
| Judah, m. Sarah **KELLOG[G]**, Feb. 19, 1728/9 | L-3 | 9 |
| Judah, Rev., m. Mercy **KELLOG[G]**, Dec. 24, 1734 | L-3 | 9 |
| Judah, [s. Rev. Judah & Mercy], b. Mar. 14, 1738/9 | L-3 | 9 |
| Judah, Rev., d. Apr. 15, 1739 | L-3 | 9 |
| Judah, m. Sarah **BRAINARD**, Feb. 4, 1762 | 1 | 165 |
| Justin, m. Ann **HURD**, Nov. 27, 1823, by Salmon Cone, V. D. M. | 2 | 160 |
| Lois, w. Ephraim, d. Jan. 25, 1774 | 1 | 23 |
| Lydia, [d. Rev. Judah & Mercy], b. Mar. 14, 1736/7; d. Sept. 12, 1748 | L-3 | 9 |
| Lydia, d. [Judah & Sarah], b. Aug. 1, 1762 | 1 | 165 |
| Marcy, m. David **BIGELOW**, Jan. 21, 1747 | L-3 | 455 |
| Mary, m. Ebenezer **DIBELL**, Dec. 30, 1708 | L-3 | 194 |
| Mary, m. Ebenezer **DIBELL**, Dec. 30, 1708 | TM-1 | 194 |
| Mary, [d. Benjamin], b. June 17, 1720 | L-1 | 654 |
| Mary, [d. Thomas & Mary], b. Oct. [ ], 1728 | L-1 | 446 |
| Mary, m. Aaron **KELLOGG**, July 10, 1740 | 1 | 130 |
| Mary A., [w. William A.], d. Nov. 7, 1846, ae 30 | 2 | 160 |
| Mat[t]hew, s. [Thomas & Mary], b. July 3, 1734 | 1 | 127 |
| Phebe, m. George **GARDINER**, b. of Lebanon, Sept. 18, 1836, at Colchester, by Samuel A. Peters, J. P. | 2 | 289 |
| Samuell, [s. Samuel & Mary], b. Jan. 9, 1735/6 | L-3 | 456 |
| Samuel, of Colchester, m. Mary C. **JANE**, of "Glastonbury or Colchester", Dec. 18, 1825, at Daniel Cuff's house in Colchester, by John Bigelow, J. P. Bans published 8 d. before | 2 | 185 |
| Samuel Mather, [s. Ephraim & Lois], b. Mar. 20, 1766 | 1 | 23 |
| Sarah, [d. Thomas & Mary], b. Oct. 10, 1723 | L-1 | 446 |
| Sarah, [d. Judah & Sarah], b. Jan. 18, 1729/30 | L-3 | 9 |
| Sarah, m. Joseph **CROCKER**, Nov. 10, 1748 | 1 | 123 |
| Sarah, m. Henry **CHAMPION**, Nov. 24, 1791 | 1 | 119 |

| | Vol. | Page |
|---|---|---|
| **LEWIS, LEWES, LEWESS, LEWAYS, LOUIS,** (cont.) | | |
| Sarah B., m. Elijah **WORTHINGTON**, Jr., Sept. 8, 1791 | 2 | 63 |
| Sarah Ransom, [s. Ephraim & Lois], b. Mar. 5, 1770 | 1 | 23 |
| Shubaiel, [s. Thomas & Mary], b. Dec. 6, 1721 | L-1 | 446 |
| Sybell, d. Thomas & Mary, b. Aug. 31, 1738 | 1 | 105 |
| Theodolia, d. [Judah & Sarah], b. July 8, 1764 | 1 | .165 |
| Thomas, m. Mary **ROWLEE**, Feb. 25, 1720 | L-1 | 446 |
| Thomas, [s. Thomas & Mary], b. Oct. 14, 1726 | L-1 | 446 |
| William A., m. Mary A. **SHAILER**, June 6, 1841, by Rev. Augustus Bolles | 2 | 160 |
| **LILLEY, LILLY, LILLIE**, Giles, m. Frances A. **BROWN**, b. of Colchester, July 28, 1856, by Rev. W[illia]m O. Cady | 2 | 151 |
| Lucy, d. Gilbert & Lucy, b. Oct. 1, 1750 | 1 | 86 |
| Lucy, m. William **GARDINER**, Dec. 22, 1768 | 1 | 86 |
| Lucy, m. William **GARDINER**, Jr., Dec. 18, 1769 | 1 | 141 |
| **LITTLE**, Abigail, w. [Rev. Ephraim], d. June 24, 1786, ae 69 | 1 | 122 |
| Abigail, [d. ----**MARSH**, of Hadley, Mass., & w. Rev. was Ephraim **LITTLE**], d. June 24, 1786, in her 69th y. She formerly wid. of Dr. Waitstill **HASTINGS**, of Hatfield, Mass., & of Hon. John **BULKELEY**, of Colchester | 2 | 310 |
| Content, d. [Rev. Ephraim & Elizabeth], b. Aug. 11, 1740 | 1 | 122 |
| Content, d. [Rev. Ephraim & Elizabeth], b. Aug. 11, 1740 | 2 | 310 |
| Deodah, s. [Rev. Ephraim & Elizabeth], b. Sept. 10, 1750 | 1 | 122 |
| Diodate, s. [Rev. Ephraim & Elizabeth], b. Sept. 10, 1750 | 2 | 310 |
| Elizabeth, d. [Rev. Ephraim & Elizabeth], b. Jan. 26, 1739 | 1 | 122 |
| Elizabeth, d. [Rev. Ephraim & Elizabeth], b. Jan. 26, 1739 | 2 | 310 |
| Elizabeth, w. [Rev. Ephraim], d. Nov. 13, 1754, ae 40 | 1 | 122 |
| Elizabeth, [d. Rev. Samuel **WOODBRIDGE**, 1st minister at East Hartford, Ct., & w. Rev. Ephraim **LITTLE**], d. Nov. 13, 1754, ae 40 | 2 | 310 |
| Elizabeth, m. Daniel **COLEMAN**, Sept. 12, 1771 | 2 | 81 |
| Ephraim, Rev., m. Elizabeth **WOODBRIDGE**, Dec. 8, 1737 | 1 | 122 |
| Ephraim, [Rev., of Colchester, m. Elizabeth **WOODBRIDGE**, d. of Rev. Samuel **WOODBRIDGE**, 1st minister at East Hartford, Conn., Dec. 8, 1737 | 2 | 310 |
| Ephraim, Rev., m. Abigail **BULKELEY**, wid., of Maj. Charles [sic] Nov. 5, 1755. She was Abigail **MARSH**, of Hadley, Mass., & m. first to Dr. Waitstill **HASTINGS**, of Hatfield, Mass., & 2d to Hon. John **BULKELEY**, of Colchester. | 2 | 310 |
| Ephraim, s. [Rev. Ephraim & Elizabeth], b. June 18, 1742; d. Dec. 9, 1745 | 1 | 122 |
| Ephraim, 2d, s. [Rev. Ephraim & Elizabeth], b. Nov. 10, 1748 | 1 | 122 |
| Ephraim, 2d, s. [Rev. Ephraim & Elizabeth], b. Nov. 10, 1748 | 2 | 310 |
| Ephraim, s. [Rev. Ephraim & Elizabeth], b. June 18, 1742; d. Dec. 9, 1745 | 2 | 310 |
| Ephraim, m. Abigail **BULKELEY**, Nov. 5, 1755 | 1 | 122 |
| Ephraim, Rev., d. June 5, 1787, ae 80 | 1 | 122 |

| | Vol. | Page |
|---|---|---|
| **LITTLE**, (cont.) | | |
| Ephraim, Rev., d. June 5, 1787, in his 80th y. & the 55th y. of his ministry | 2 | 310 |
| Justin, s. [Ephraim & Abigail], b. Apr. 2, 1759 | 1 | 122 |
| Justin, s. [Rev. Ephraim & Abigail], b. Apr. 2, 1759 | 2 | 310 |
| Lucretia, d. [Rev. Ephraim & Elizabeth], b. Jan. 11, 1747 | 1 | 122 |
| Lucretia, d. [Rev. Ephraim & Elizabeth], b. Jan. 11, 1747 | 2 | 310 |
| Lucy Ann, of Colchester, m. Richard R. **FRANCIS**, of Lebanon, Jan. 1, 1843, by Rev. Rob[er]t C. Mills | 2 | 262 |
| Mable, d. [Rev. Ephraim & Elizabeth], b. June 7, 1744 | 1 | 122 |
| Mabel, d. [Rev. Ephraim & Elizabeth], b. June 7, 1744 | 2 | 310 |
| Mary, m. Pomp **RANSOM**, June 5, 1820, by Salmon Cone | 2 | 298 |
| Molle, d. [Rev. Ephraim & Elizabeth], b. Aug. 8, 1752 | 1 | 122 |
| Molly, s.[sic], Rev. Ephraim & Elizabeth, b. Aug. 8, 1752 | 2 | 310 |
| Rachel, m. Richard Harris **HUNTLEY**, Mar. 17, 1768 | 1 | 106 |
| Sophia, d. [Ephraim & Abigail], b. Aug. 14, 1756 | 1 | 122 |
| Sophia, d. [Rev. Ephraim & Abigail], b. Aug. 14, 1756 | 2 | 310 |
| Sophia, m. Asahel **RANSOM**, Jan. 15, 1778 | 2 | 51 |
| **LOMBARD**, Thomas Cross, m. Sarah Jane **BAKER**, Jan. 9, 1859, by Rev. L. Curtis | 3 | 65 |
| **LONG**, William, of Colchester, m. Mary **RILEY**, of East Hartford, Feb. 3, 1848, by Rev. Augustus Bolles | 3 | 34 |
| **LOOMIS, LOMIS, LOMAS**, Abagail, w. [Lieut. Azariah], d. Jan. 15, 1778 | 2 | 81 |
| Abigail Foote, d. [Alfred J. & Abigail], b. Feb. 11, 1827 | 2 | 186 |
| Abigail T., m. Charles E. **BROWNELL**, of East Haddam, Nov. 25, 1852, by Rev. S. D. Jewett, at Westchester | 3 | 54 |
| Alfred, s. [Guy & Abagal], b. July 7, 1802 | 2 | 80 |
| Alfred, s. [Alfred J. & Abigail], b. Nov. 2, 1829 | 2 | 186 |
| Alfred J., m. Abigail **FOOTE**, b. of West Chester, Apr. 6, 1826, by Jacob Seales, V. D. M., at the house of Nathaniel Foote | 2 | 186 |
| Alice, [d. Israel & Irene], b. Dec. 13, 1766; d. June 19, 1768 | 1 | 87 |
| Alice, d. [Samuel & Martha], b. Mar. 11, 1787; d. Mar. 13, 1790 | 2 | 24 |
| Alpheas, [s. Daniel, Jr. & Alice], b. Nov. 10, 1758 | 1 | 87 |
| Ama, d. [Samuel & Martha], b. Mar. 22, 1778 | 2 | 24 |
| Amasa, s. [Guy & Abagal], b. [ ] | 2 | 80 |
| Asa, s. [John, Jr. & Hannah], b. July 2, 1795 | 2 | 78 |
| Azariah, s. Dea. Samu[e]ll, b. May 2, 1700 | L-3 | 196 |
| Azariah, s. Dea. Sam[ue]l, b. May 2, 1700 (Arnold copy says "Lewis") | TM-1 | 196 |
| Asariah, m. Abigaiell **NEWTON**, Dec. 25, 1723; d. Feb. 9, 1758 | L-3 | 9 |
| Azariah, Lieut., d. Feb. 20, 1757 | 2 | 81 |
| Betsey, of Colchester, m. Ebenezer **STOWEL**, of Windham, Feb. 24, 1822, by Rev. Jacob Seales | 2 | 113 |
| Bettey, d. [John & Rachel], b. Mar. 15, 1757(?) (1767) | 1 | 152 |

| | Vol. | Page |
|---|---|---|
| **LOOMIS, LOMIS, LOMAS**, (cont.) | | |
| Caleb, [s. Dea. Samu[e]ll], b. Sept. 20, 1707 | L-3 | 196 |
| Caleb, s. Samuel, b. Sept. 20, 1707 (Arnold Copy says "Lewis") | TM-1 | 196 |
| Caleb, m. Joanah **SKIN[N]ER**, [Feb.] 28, 1728/9 | L-3 | 8 |
| Caleb, [s. Caleb & Joanah], b. Nov. 28, 1729 | L-3 | 8 |
| Caleb, Jr., m. [ ] **STRONG**, Aug. 31, 1755 | 1 | 40 |
| Caleb, [s. Caleb, Jr. ], b. Oct. 4, 1758 | 1 | 40 |
| Caleb, Jr., d. Jan. 28, 1774 | 1 | 40 |
| Caroline M., of Colchester, m. Amos B. **LATHAM**, of Hebron, Sept. 5, 1837, by Rev. W[illia]m F. Vaill | 2 | 101 |
| Caroline Matilda, d. [Elias & Matilda], b. Sept. 23, 1820 | 2 | 249 |
| Chauncey , of Lebanon, m. Mary **SHAYLOR**, of Colchester, Feb. 15, 1821, by Rev. Jacob Seales | 2 | 107 |
| Clarissa, m. Alfred **ISHAM**, Dec. 18, 1796 | 2 | 84 |
| Daniell, [s. Dea. Samu[e]ll], b. Feb. 20, 1708/9 | L-3 | 196 |
| Daniel, s. Samuel, b. Feb. 20, 1708/9 (Arnold copy says "Lewis") | TM-1 | 196 |
| Daniel, m. Hannah **WITHERELL**, Oct. 7, 1731 | L-3 | 456 |
| Daniel, [d. Daniel & Hannah], b. June 16, 1735 | L-3 | 456 |
| Daniel, Jr., m. Alice **CHAMBERLAIN**, Feb. 25, 1756 | 1 | 87 |
| Daniel, [s. Daniel, Jr. & Alice], b. June 5, 1761 | 1 | 87 |
| Daniel, s. [John, Jr. & Hannah], b. Oct. 4, 1797 | 2 | 78 |
| Dimis, [d. Asariah & Abigaiell], b. Sept. 5, 1724 | L-3 | 9 |
| Dimmis, d. [Azariah & Abigail], b. Sept. 20, 1724 | 1 | 139 |
| Dimmis, m. Dudley **WRIGHT**, Sept. 9, 1744 | 1 | 132 |
| Eley, d. [John & Rachel], b. Jan. 19, 1769 | 1 | 152 |
| Elias, s. [Guy & Abagal], b. Dec. 20, 1806 | 2 | 80 |
| Elias, m. Matilda **CARRIER**, [ ] | 2 | 249 |
| Elijah, m. Mary **ALLEN**, Feb. 22, 1807 | 2 | 118 |
| Elijah, m. Nancy **DODGE**, Jan. 15, 1809, in Salem, Ct.; d. Aug. 25, 1847, ae 68 | 2 | 118 |
| Elijah Griswold, s. [Guy & Abagal], b. [ ] | 2 | 80 |
| Elisabeth, [d. Dea. Samu[e]ll], b. Nov. 13, 1702 | L-3 | 196 |
| Elizabeth, d. Sam[ue]l, b. Nov. 13, 1702 (Arnold Copy has the name "Lewis) | TM-1 | 196 |
| Elizabeth, m. Daniell **WORTHINGTON**, Jan. 3, 1720/21 | L-1 | 448 |
| Ellis, [d. Daniel, Jr. & Alice], b. Sept. 1, 1768 (see also Alice) | 1 | 87 |
| Emily Harvey, d. [Alfred J. & Abigail], b. Mar. 20, 1837 | 2 | 186 |
| Feadom, [s. Daniel, Jr. & Alice], b. Nov. 10, 1765 | 1 | 87 |
| George Champion, s. [Alfred J. & Abigail], b. Jan. 30, 1835 | 2 | 186 |
| George Trumbull, of Bolton, m. Sally Maria **NORTHAM**, Sept. 14, 1836, by Rev. Joel R. Arnold | 2 | 289 |
| Guy, m. Abaga[i]l **DIRTHICK**, Aug. 28, 1799 | 2 | 80 |
| Guy Nelson, s. [Guy & Abagal], b. Dec. 14, 1811 | 2 | 80 |
| Hannah, [d. Daniel & Hannah], b. July 15, 1732 | L-3 | 456 |
| Hannah, m. James **WELLS**, Mar. 28, 1754 | 1 | 32 |

| | Vol. | Page |
|---|---|---|
| **LOOMIS, LOMIS, LOMAS,** (cont.) | | |
| Hannah, [d. Israel & Irene], b. Sept. 23, 1764; d. June 25, 1768 | 1 | 87 |
| Harriet, d. [Elias & Matilda], b. Nov. 17, 1815 | 2 | 249 |
| Harriet, of Colchester, m. Silas E. **DIXON**, of East Haddam, May 7, 1834, by Rev. Joseph Harvey | 2 | 265 |
| Harris, s. [John & Rachel], b. Sept. 9, 1770 | 1 | 152 |
| Israel, m. Irene **CHAMBERLAIN**, Nov. 5, 1763 | 1 | 87 |
| Israel, [s. Israel & Irene], b. Sept. 27, 1768 | 1 | 87 |
| Israel Foote, s. [Alfred J. & Abigail], b. Nov. 8, 1839 | 2 | 186 |
| Jacob, m. Hannah **TAYLOR**, Mar. 22, 1716 | L-1 | 447 |
| Jacob, [s. Caleb, Jr.], b. June 1, 1756 | 1 | 40 |
| Jacob, s. [John & Rachel], b. June 19, 1761 | 1 | 152 |
| Jane, [triplet with Janet & a female child], d. [Elias & Matilda], b. Jan. 24, 1833 | 2 | 249 |
| Jane Clarissa, d. [Alfred J. & Abigail], b. July 31, 1832 | 2 | 186 |
| Janet, triplet with Jane & a female child], d. [Elias & Matilda], b. Jan. 24, 1833; d. Dec. 11, 1851, ae 19 | 2 | 249 |
| Joanna, m. Weeks **WILLIAMS**, Dec. 20, 1750 | 1 | 142 |
| Joel, s. [John & Rachel, b. May 6, 1773 | 1 | 152 |
| Joel, s. [Caleb & Catharine], b. Apr. 1, 1822 | 2 | 250 |
| John, m. Rachel **HARRIS**, Dec. 18, 1760 | 1 | 152 |
| John, s. [John & Rachel], b. Apr. 7, 1763 | 1 | 152 |
| John, Jr., m. Hannah **BUDD**, June 13, 1790 | 2 | 78 |
| John, s. [John, Jr. & Hannah], b. Apr. 26, 1800 | 2 | 78 |
| John, of Coventry, m. Martha M. **GILLETT**, of Colchester, May 9, 1838, by Rev. Joel R. Arnold | 2 | 207 |
| Jonathan, s. [John, Jr. & Hannah], b. May 19, 1791 | 2 | 78 |
| Josiah, s. Zebediah, b. Dec. 22, 1726 (Perhaps "Josiah **TOMAS**") | 1 | 128 |
| Justin, s. [John, Jr. & Hannah], b. Apr. 11, 1793 | 2 | 78 |
| Lebbeus, [s. Daniel, Jr. & Alice], b. Feb. 23, 1757 | 1 | 87 |
| Lois, m. Lazarus **WATERS**, Dec. 11, 1760 | 1 | 44 |
| Loren W., m. Caroline L. **WILLIAMS**, b. of Colchester, Nov. 19, 1834, by Rev. Joseph Harvey | 2 | 273 |
| Louisa, d. [John, Jr. & Hannah], b. Sept. 15, 1802 | 2 | 78 |
| Louisa, d. [Caleb & Catharine], b. Mar. 10, 1821 | 2 | 250 |
| Lucinda, of Colchester, m. Joseph **BABCOCK**, of Windham, Mar. 25, 1824, by Rev. Joseph Seales, at the house of Samuel Loomis | 2 | 163 |
| Lucretia Hubbard, m. Matthew Griswold **WARNER**, Nov. 30, 1825, by Jacob Seales, V. D. M., at the house of David Loomis | 2 | 182 |
| Lucretia L., m. Alfred **CHITTENDEN**, of Killingworth, Mar. 23, 1851, by Rev. S. D. Jewett | 3 | 3 |
| Lydia, m. Mic[h]ael **TAINTOR**, Jr., Apr. 2, 1767 | 1 | 25 |
| Lydia, m. Oramel **BIGELOW**, b. of Colchester, Feb. 9, 1834, by Rev. Joseph Harvey | 2 | 263 |

| | Vol. | Page |
|---|---|---|
| **LOOMIS, LOMIS, LOMAS**, (cont.) | | |
| Lydia Lucretia, d. [Elias & Matilda], b. Oct. 30, 1828 | 2 | 249 |
| Lyman, s. [Caleb & Catharine], b. Apr. 4, 1831; d. Feb. 7, 1835, ae 4 | 2 | 250 |
| Lyman, s. [Caleb & Catharine], b. Nov. 18, 1836 | 2 | 250 |
| Maria Ann, d. [Elias & Matilda], b. May 2, 1830 | 2 | 249 |
| Martha, [w. Samuel], d. Sept. 26, 1839, ae 88 | 2 | 24 |
| Mary, m. Benjamin **ADDAMS**, Nov. 25, 1719 | L-1 | 399 |
| Mary, m. Judah **SCOVEL**, Jan. 27, 1771 | 2 | 76 |
| Mary, d. [Samuel, 2d, & Anna], b. Sept. 7, 1800 | 2 | 84 |
| Mary, [w. Elijah], d. Sept. 9, 1807 | 2 | 118 |
| Mary, m. John G. **BROWN**, b. of Colchester, Jan. 13, 1831, by Rev. Joseph Harvey | 2 | 228 |
| Mary Ann, d. [Elias & Matilda], b. Jan. 5, 1825 | 2 | 249 |
| Matilda, w. Elias, d. June 30, 1849, ae 55 | 2 | 249 |
| Mercy, [d. Daniel & Hannah], b. Aug. 18, 1733 | L-3 | 456 |
| Milton Lathrop, s. [Alfred J. & Abigail], b. July 16, 1842 | 2 | 186 |
| Nabby, d. [Guy & Abagal], b. July 25, 1800 | 2 | 80 |
| Nancy Jerusha, d. [Samuel, 2d, & Anna], b. July 19, 1801 | 2 | 84 |
| Nathaniel, m. Sarah **SKIN[N]ER**, Aug. 7, 1721 | L-1 | 449 |
| Nelson B., of Columbia, m. Emma **KELLOGG**, of Colchester, Jan. 11, 1848, by Rev. Joel R. Arnold | 3 | 34 |
| Parmelia, d. [Samuel & Martha], b. Oct. 22, 1771 | 1 | 152 |
| Parmelia, d. [Samuel & Martha], b. Oct. 22, 1771 | 2 | 2 |
| Pamelia, d. [Samuel & Martha], b. Oct. 22, 1771 | 2 | 24 |
| Pamelia, m. Elijah **BULKELEY**, Apr. 22, 1787 | 2 | 91 |
| Rachel, d. [John & Rachel], b. May 15, 1765 | 1 | 152 |
| Rachel, m. Oliver **WARNER**, Dec. 8, 1786 | 2 | 73 |
| Robert, s. [Caleb & Catharine], b. June 7, 1829 | 2 | 250 |
| Ruby, m. Enos **WILLIAMS**, Dec. 8, 1785 | 2 | 67 |
| Russel[l], [s. Daniel, Jr. & Alice], b. Sept. 1, 1763 | 1 | 87 |
| Ruth, m. John **ADDAMS**, June 20, 1708 | L-1 | 452 |
| Ruth, d. Nathaniell, b. Aug. 21, 1713 | L-1 | 654 |
| Samuell, m. Elizabeth **HOLMES**, Dec. 12, 1717 | L-1 | 451 |
| Samuel, [s. Caleb, Jr.], b. May 12, 1760 | 1 | 40 |
| Samuel, m. Martha **RANSOM**, Nov. 15, 1770 | 1 | 152 |
| Samuel, m. Martha **RANSOM**, Nov. 15, 1770; d. Nov. 4, 1814, ae 66, in Essex | 2 | 24 |
| Samuel, m. Martha **RANSOM**, Nov. 15, 1773 | 2 | 2 |
| Samuel, s. [Samuel & Martha], b. Mar. 26, 1776 | 2 | 24 |
| Samuel, 2d, m. Anna **HORSFORD**, Nov. 26, 1799 | 2 | 84 |
| Samuel C., m. Charlotte M. **BROWN**, b. of Marlboro, Oct. 16, 1839, by Rev. Lyman Strong | 2 | 149 |
| Samuel Carrier, s. [Elias & Matilda], b. Mar. 24, 1813 | 2 | 249 |
| Sarah, [d. Dea. Samu[e]ll], b. Mar. 7, 1705 | L-3 | 196 |
| Sarah, d. Sam[ue]l, b. Mar. 7, 1705 (Arnold Copy says "Lewis") | TM-1 | 196 |
| Sarah, [d. Nathaniel & Sarah], b. Sept. 15, 1722 | L-1 | 449 |

| | Vol. | Page |
|---|---|---|
| **LOOMIS, LOMIS, LOMAS,** (cont.) | | |
| Sarah, m. John **DAY**, Jr., Aug. 20, 1725 | L-1 | 447 |
| Sarah, [d. Zebediah], b. Dec. 4, 1738 (Perhaps Sarah **TOMAS**) | 1 | 128 |
| Sarah, m. Adonijah **DAY**, [ ], 1753 | 1 | 121 |
| Silence, d. [Azariah & Abigail], b. Jan. 6, 1737 | 1 | 139 |
| Silence, [d. Asariah & Abigaiell], b. Jan. 6, 1737 | L-3 | 9 |
| Sophia, d. [Samuel & Martha], b. Apr. 20, 1780 | 2 | 24 |
| Sophia, m. Asa **BULKELEY**, Nov. 11, 1796 | 2 | 75 |
| Sophia Esther, d. [Guy & Abagal], b. Oct. 14, 1809 | 2 | 80 |
| Thaddeus, [s. Daniel, Jr. & Alice], b. Aug. 8, 1760 | 1 | 87 |
| ----, [d. Caleb, Jr. ], b. Sept. 27, 1764 | 1 | 40 |
| ----, female, triplet with Jane & Janet, child of [Elias & Matilda], b. Jan. 24, 1833; d. Jan. 28, 1833 | 2 | 249 |
| **LORD**, Abigail, d. [Ichabod & Patience], b. Nov. 22, 1744 | 1 | 133 |
| Abigail, [d. Epaphras & Lucy], b. Jan. 3, 1761 | 1 | 143 |
| Abigail, d. [Theodore & Sarah], b. Nov. 10, 1790 | 2 | 11 |
| Abigail Robbins, d. [Elisha & Eunice], b. July 24, 1770 | 2 | 33 |
| Abigail Robbins, m. Joel **FOOT**, Oct. 28, 1787; d. Jan. 8, 1795 | 2 | 56 |
| Alfred, [s. Elisha & Eunice], b. Sept. 13, 1785 | 2 | 33 |
| Amasa, s. [Elisha & Eunice], b. Feb. 22, 1783 | 2 | 33 |
| Anna, d. [Ichabod & Patience], b. Sept. 19, 1753 | 1 | 133 |
| Anna, m. Henry **DEMING**, Feb. 6, 1772 | 1 | 94 |
| Anna, m. Henry **DEMING**, Feb. 6, 1772 | 2 | 9 |
| Anne, d. [Ezekiel], b. Mar 8, 1783 | 2 | 114 |
| Bulkeley, s. [Epaphras & Lucy], b. Jan. 15, 1751; d. Jan. 25, 1751 | 1 | 143 |
| Caroline, d. [Epaphras & Lucy], b. Mar. 2, 1758 | 1 | 143 |
| Daniel, s. [Ezekiel], b. Apr. 4, 1787 | 2 | 114 |
| David Miller, s. [Theodore & Sarah], b. July 25, 1773 | 2 | 11 |
| Dorothy, d. [Epaphras & Lucy], b. Apr. 27, 1746; d. May 26, 1752 | 1 | 143 |
| Dorothy, 2d, d. [Epaphras & Lucy], b. June 16, 1752; d. Apr. 16, 1753 | 1 | 143 |
| Dorothy, 3d, [d. Epaphras & Lucy], b. Sept. 16, 1753 | 1 | 143 |
| Eliphalet, m. Lois **BULKELEY**, Nov. 9, 1826, by Salmon Cone, V. D. M. | 2 | 190 |
| Elisha, s. [Epaphras & Lucy], b. Mar. 18, 1744/5 | 1 | 143 |
| Elisha, m. Eunice **BULKELEY**, May 25, 1769 | 2 | 33 |
| Elisha, twin with Eunice, s. [Elisha & Eunice], b. Oct. 12, 1773 | 2 | 33 |
| Elisha, m. Sarah **OLMSTEAD**, Nov. 12, 1797 | 2 | 33 |
| Elizabeth, d. [Ichabod & Patience], b. Oct. 7, 1751 | 1 | 133 |
| Elizabeth, d. [Theodore & Sarah], b. Feb. 21, 1780 | 2 | 11 |
| Epaphras, m. Lucy **BULKELEY**, Nov. 25, 1742 | 1 | 143 |
| Epaphras, s. [Epaphras & Lucy], b. Dec. 22, 1743 | 1 | 143 |
| Epapheus, Jr., (Epaphras), m. Patience **LORD**, Dec. 8, 1766 | 1 | 88 |

| | Vol. | Page |
|---|---|---|
| **LORD**, (cont.) | | |
| Epaphras, s. [Epaphras, Jr. & Patience], b. Jan. 23, 1772 | 2 | 43 |
| Epaphras had slave Candia who had d. Juda, b. July 26, 1793 | 2 | 48 |
| Epaphras, Jr., m. Patience **LORD**, [ ], 17[ ] | 2 | 43 |
| Esther P., of Colchester, m. Samuel W. **GAYLORD**, of Bristol, Feb. 16, 1839, by Rev. Andrew M. Smith | 2 | 109 |
| Eunice, d. [Epaphras & Lucy], b. July 26, 1756 | 1 | 143 |
| Eunice, twin with Elisha, d. [Elisha & Eunice], b. Oct. 12, 1773 | 2 | 33 |
| Eunice, d. [Theodore & Sarah], b. July 22, 1787 | 2 | 11 |
| Eunice, [w. Elisha], d. Apr. 2, 1796 | 2 | 93 |
| Experience, d. [Jonathan & Ruth], b. Feb. 14, 1749/50 | 1 | 109 |
| Ezekiel, [s. William & Tabitha], b. July 16, 1757 | 1 | 45 |
| Ezekiel, m. Sarah **WOODWELL**, Sept. 16, 1798 | 2 | 114 |
| Gardner, s. [Epaphras, Jr. & Patience], b. May 2, 1783 | 2 | 43 |
| George, s. [Epaphras, Jr. & Patience], b. Jan. 25, 1779 | 2 | 43 |
| Garshom, s. [Elisha & Eunice], b. Oct. 27, 1777 | 2 | 33 |
| Hannah, w. John, d. Mar. 3, 1722/3 | L-1 | 450 |
| Hope, m. Amasa **JONES**, Aug. 27, 1754 | 1 | 150 |
| Hope, [d. Epapheus, Jr. & Patience], b. Jan. 28, 1768 | 1 | 88 |
| Ichabod, m. Patience **BULKLEY**, Dec. 14, 1743 | 1 | 133 |
| Ichabod, s. [Epaphras & Lucy], b. June 12, 1762 | 1 | 143 |
| Ichabod, d. Dec. 18, 1762 | 1 | 133 |
| Jarvis, twin with Ogden, s. [Elisha & Eunice], b. Dec. 24, 1794; d. Sept. [ ], 1795 | 2 | 33 |
| Jerusha, [d. Epaphras & Lucy], b. Nov. 7, 1749 | 1 | 143 |
| Jerusha, d. [Ichabod & Patience], b. Feb. 5, 1755 | 1 | 133 |
| Jerusha, m. David **SKINNER**, Feb. 28, 1771 | 1 | 89 |
| Jerusha, m. David **SKINNER**, Mar. 1, 1771 | 2 | 41 |
| John, m. Hannah **ACKLEY**, Dec. 25, 1718 | L-1 | 450 |
| John, [s. John & Hannah], b. Mar. 3, 1722/3 | L-1 | 450 |
| John, m. Experience **CRIPPEN**, Dec. 26, 1724 | TPR | 111 |
| John, s. [Theodore & Sarah], b. Dec. 12, 1783; d. Dec. 26, 1783 | 2 | 11 |
| John Bulkely, s. [Epaphras & Lucy], b. Nov. 5, 1754 | 1 | 143 |
| Jonathan, [s. John & Experience], b. Oct. 3, 1726 | TPR | 111 |
| Jonathan, m. Ruth **ROGERS**, Nov. 20, 1746 | 1 | 109 |
| Joseph S., Rev., of Lyme, m. Harriet N. **PAINTER**, of Colchester, May 17, 1836, by J. A. Copp, M. G. | 2 | 285 |
| Lucinda, twin with Matilda, d. [Ezekiel], b. Apr. 1, 1797 | 2 | 114 |
| Luce, [d. Epaphras & Lucy], b. Aug. 26, 1748 | 1 | 143 |
| Lucy Bulkeley, d. [Elisha & Eunice], b. Aug. 16, 1775 | 2 | 33 |
| Lydia, d. [Ichabod & Patience], b. July 4, 1756; d. Jan. 18, 1759 | 1 | 133 |
| Lydia, [d. Epaphras & Lucy], b. Nov. 4, 1759 | 1 | 143 |
| Lydia, d. [Theodore & Sarah], b. May 11, 1785 | 2 | 11 |
| Lydia, d. [Ezekiel], b. June 23, 1789 | 2 | 114 |
| Mary, d. [Ichabod & Patience], b. May 12, 1748 | 1 | 133 |

| | Vol. | Page |
|---|---|---|
| **LORD**, (cont.) | | |
| Mary, d. [Epaphras, Jr. & Patience], b. Oct. 2, 1776 | 2 | 43 |
| Matilda, twin with Lucinda, d. [Ezekiel], b. Apr. 1, 1797 | 2 | 114 |
| Mehetable, m. Elias **PECK**, Jr., Mar. 2, 1808 | 2 | 122 |
| Nabby, m. Samuel **GILLETT**, 2d, Oct. 29, 1812 | 2 | 146 |
| Nath[anie]ll, s. [Jonathan & Ruth], b. Dec. 25, 1747 | 1 | 109 |
| Ogden, twin with Jarvis, s. [Elisha & Eunice], b. Dec. 24, 1794; d. Dec. 24, 1795 | 2 | 33 |
| Oliver, s. [Elisha & Eunice], b. May 6, 1792 | 2 | 33 |
| Patience, d. [Ichabod & Patience], b. Feb. 7, 1745/6 | 1 | 133 |
| Patience, m. Epapheus **LORD**, Jr., Dec. 8, 1766 | 1 | 88 |
| Patience, d. [Epaphras, Jr. & Patience], b. June 17, 1774 | 2 | 43 |
| Patience, m. Epaphras **LORD**, Jr., [ ], 17[ ] | 2 | 43 |
| Polly, d. [Theodore & Sarah], b. Jan. 14, 1789 | 2 | 11 |
| Rachel, d. [Theodore & Sarah], b. Oct. 23, 1788 | 2 | 11 |
| Rachel, of East Haddam, m. Joel **FOOT**, Nov. 15, 1795; d. Oct. 6, 1843, ae 73 | 2 | 56 |
| Ralph, s. [Elisha & Eunice], b. Mar. 6, 1790 | 2 | 33 |
| Rhoda, [d. William & Tabitha], b. July 16, 1751 | 1 | 45 |
| Rhoda, d. [Ezekiel], b. Aug. 23, 1791 | 2 | 114 |
| Russel[l], s. [Elisha & Eunice], b. June 3, 1780 | 2 | 33 |
| Sally, d. [Ezekiel], b. Sept. 3, 1794; d. June 5, 1803, ae 9 | 2 | 114 |
| Sarah, [d. John & Hannah], b. Apr. 17, 1721 | L-1 | 450 |
| Sarah, d. [Ichabod & Patience], b. Nov. 28, 1749 | 1 | 133 |
| Sarah, m. David **SKINNER**, b. of Colchester, Dec. 8, 1766 | 1 | 89 |
| Sarah, m. David **SKINNER**, Dec. 8, 1766; d. Aug. 31, 1769 | 2 | 41 |
| Sarah, d. [Theodore & Sarah], b. Dec. 28, 1775 | 2 | 11 |
| Sarah, d. [Epaphras, Jr. & Patience], b. Feb. 28, 1781 | 2 | 43 |
| Tabitha, [d. William & Tabitha], b. Jan. 30, 1749 | 1 | 45 |
| Theodore, m. Sarah **BUELL**, June 11, 1772 | 1 | 107 |
| Theodore, m. Sarah **BUEL[L]**, June 11, 1772 | 2 | 11 |
| Theodore, s. [Theodore & Sarah], b. Mar. 19, 1778 | 2 | 11 |
| Theodoret, [s. Epaphras & Lucy], b. May 18, 1747 | 1 | 143 |
| William, of Colchester, m. Tabitha **PORTER**, of Hebron, Mar. 21, 1745 | 1 | 45 |
| William, [s. William & Tabitha], b. Mar. 28, 1747 | 1 | 45 |
| William, s. [Ezekiel], b. May 2, 1785 | 2 | 114 |
| W[illia]m B., m. Lora Ann **COOK**, b. of Colchester, Dec. 31, 1844, by Rev. Robert Allyn | 3 | 19 |
| ----, w. Ezekiel, d. Apr. 16, 1797 | 2 | 114 |
| ----, m. Henry **DEMING**, [ ] | 2 | 13 |
| ----, m. John **ELLIS**, [ ] | 2 | 58 |
| **LORING**, Lyman A., of Great Barrington, Mass., m. Eunice A. **FOOTE**, of Colchester, Nov. 28, 1849, by Rev. Alpheas Geer, of East Haddam | 3 | 43 |
| **LOVEL**, Andrew, s. [Silas & Mary], b. May 3, 1748 | 1 | 144 |
| Mary, d. [Silas & Mary], b. May 27, 1746 | 1 | 144 |
| Silas, s. Silas & Mary, b. June 1, 1743 | 1 | 144 |

| | Vol. | Page |
|---|---|---|
| **LOVELAND**, Joseph, m. Marcy **BIGELOW**, Nov. 12, 177[ ] | 2 | 2 |
| Joseph, s. [Joseph & Marcy], b. July 18, 17[ ] | 2 | 2 |
| **LOVERIDGE**, [see also **LEVERIDGE**], Abigail, w. David, d. July 29, 1795 | 2 | 69 |
| Abner, [s. Lewis & Anne], b. Aug. 2, 1745 | 1 | 78 |
| Amasa, [s. Lewis & Grace], b. Dec. 3, 1762 | 1 | 78 |
| Anna, [d. Lewis & Anne], d. Sept. 20, 1756 | 1 | 78 |
| Anna, [d. Lewis & Grace], b. Mar. 15, 1760 | 1 | 78 |
| David, [s. Lewis & Anne], b. July 8, 1748 | 1 | 78 |
| David, m. Abigail **CONGDOL**, Sept. 15, 1771 | 2 | 69 |
| Edward, [s. Lewis & Anne], b. Oct. 8, 1734 | 1 | 78 |
| Edward, s. [Lewis & Ann], b. Oct. 8, 1734 | 1 | 137 |
| Edward, m. Mary **WELCH**, June 31 (?), 1762 | 1 | 81 |
| Eunice, [d. Lewis & Anne], b. Aug. 17, 1740 | 1 | 78 |
| Eunice, [d. Lewis & Ann], b. Aug. 17, 1740 | 1 | 137 |
| Grace, [d. Lewis & Grace], b. July 24, 1768 | 1 | 78 |
| John, [s. Lewis & Anne], b. Mar. 9, 1736 | 1 | 78 |
| John, s. [Lewis & Ann], b. Mar. 9, 1736 | 1 | 137 |
| Lewis, b. Jan. 4, 1711, "stated by himself" | 1 | 78 |
| Lewis, b. Jan. 4, 1711/12 | 1 | 137 |
| Lewis, m. Anne **FULLER**, Dec. 31, 1733 | 1 | 78 |
| Lewis, m. Ann **FULLER**, Dec. 31, 1733 | 1 | 137 |
| Lewis, m. Grace **DODGE**, Mar. 24, 1757 | 1 | 78 |
| Mary, [d. Edward & Mary], b. Aug. 14, 1765 | 1 | 81 |
| Noah, [s. Lewis & Grace], b. Sept. 27, 1764 | 1 | 78 |
| Sarah, [d. Edward & Mary], b. Apr. 11, 1768 | 1 | 81 |
| William,, [s. Lewis & Grace], b. May 28, 1761 | 1 | 78 |
| **LOVETT, LOVET**, Anna, d. Rev. Joseph & Anna, b Mar. 23, 1739 | 1 | 129 |
| Anna, w. Rev. Joseph, d. May 13, 1739 | 1 | 129 |
| Eleanor, d. [Joseph & Eleanor], b. Apr. 26, 1741 | 1 | 141 |
| Elizabeth, d. Rev. Joseph & Anna, b. Apr. 8, 1737 | 1 | 129 |
| Elizabeth, d. Nov. 1, 1750 | 1 | 129 |
| Joseph, Rev., m. Ann **HOLM[E]S**, Apr. 3, 1734 | L-3 | 453 |
| Joseph, m. Eleanor **BUGBEY**, Feb. 6, 1739/40 | 1 | 141 |
| Josephus, b. Sept. [9], 1747 | 1 | 129 |
| Molly, b. Nov. 19, 1749 | 1 | 129 |
| Samuel, [s. Rev. Joseph & Ann], b. Jan. 12, 1734/5 | L-3 | 453 |
| Samuel, s. Rev. Joseph, d. Jan. 10, 1754 | 1 | 129 |
| **LYMAN**, Lydia, of Lebanon, m. Elias **PECK**, Oct. 4, 1787 | 2 | 37 |
| **MACCOLL**, Hannah , m. Ambrose **NILES**, [ ] | 1 | 17 |
| **MACKALL**, Anna, [d. Ebenezer], b. Nov. 29, 1741 | 1 | 82 |
| Daniel, [s. Ebenezer], b. Sept. 7, 1743 | 1 | 82 |
| Ebenezer, [s. Ebenezer], b. Aug. 24, 1754 | 1 | 82 |
| Elisha, [s. Ebenezer], b. Mar. 14, 1749 | 1 | 82 |
| Jacob, [s. Ebenezer], b. May 21, 1747 | 1 | 82 |
| James, [s. Ebenezer], b. Dec. 9, 1758 | 1 | 82 |
| Lucy, [d. Ebenezer], b. Dec. 20, 1763 | 1 | 82 |

| | Vol. | Page |
|---|---|---|
| **MACKALL**, (cont.) | | |
| Rachel, [d. Ebenezer], b. Aug. 31, 1752 | 1 | 82 |
| Rebeckah, [d. Ebenezer], b. Aug. 21, 1756 | 1 | 82 |
| Sarah, [d. Ebenezer], b. Mar. 20, 1761 | 1 | 82 |
| **MAINE**, Emily J., of Colchester, m. John **BRANNON**, of Rockville, Conn., Apr. 1, 1851, by Rev. G. W. Pendleton | 3 | 48 |
| Harriet P., of Lock, N. Y., m. Benjamin S. **LEE**, of Colchester, Sept. 13, 1852, by Rev. E. H. Gillett | 3 | 53 |
| **MALLONEY**, Dennis, m. Jane **BECKWITH**, of Lebanon, Oct. 3, 1850, "at my house", by Avery Morgan, J. P. | 2 | 111 |
| **MANC**, Rosanna, m. Frederick **MAYLE**, b. of Wertemburg, Germany, Apr. 25, 1854, by Erastus Dickinson | 3 | 61 |
| **MANN**, [see also **MUNN**], Levi, of Hebron, m. Clarissa **STRONG**, of Colchester, Jan. 8, 1832, by Rev. Lyman Strong | 2 | 235 |
| **MAPLES**, Elizabeth J., m. Edmund **GOFF**, Mar. 16, 1845, by Rev. Benjamin G. Goff | 3 | 20 |
| **MARKS**, Mary A., m. Andrew E. **CARRIER**, b. of Colchestser, May 11, 1842, by Rev. Daniel G. Sprague | 2 | 215 |
| **MARRINER, MARINER**, Abigaiell, [d. William & Abigaiell], b. Mar. 4, 1724 | L-1 | 448 |
| Abigail, d. [Ezra or Asa & Mary], b. Dec. 6, 1771 | 2 | 3 |
| Asa, [s. William & Abigaiell], b. Oct. 9, 1732 | L-1 | 448 |
| Asa, s. William & Abigail, b. Oct. 9, 1732 | TPR | 110 |
| Asa, see also Ezra | | |
| Content, d. Sarah, b. Jan. 20, 1755 | 1 | 50 |
| Ebenezer, [s. William & Abigaiell], b. June 30, 1726 | L-1 | 448 |
| Ephraim, [s. William & Abigaiell], b. Sept. 26, 1735 | L-1 | 448 |
| Ezra or Asa, m. Mary **WELCH**, Apr. 17, 1770 | 2 | 3 |
| Grace, [d. William & Abigaiell], b. June 5, 1737 | L-1 | 448 |
| Grace, m. Elijah **HILLS**, Mar. 17, 1768 | 1 | 87 |
| Mary, d. [Ezra or Asa & Mary], b. May 25, 1774 | 2 | 3 |
| Rachell, twin with Sarah, [d. William & Abigaiell], b. June 14, 1729 | L-1 | 448 |
| Sarah, twin with Rachell, [s. William & Abigaiell], b. June 14, 1729 | L-1 | 448 |
| William, m. Abigaiell **WELLES**, Jan. 27, 1721/22 | L-1 | 448 |
| **MARSH**, Abigail, see Abigail **LITTLE** | 2 | 310 |
| Caroline E., of Colchester, m. H. Nelson **LEE**, of Essex, Feb. 3, 1847, by Rev. Joel R. Arnold | 3 | 31 |
| Dan[iel], d. July 26, 1828, ae 72 | 2 | 1 |
| Dan[iel], Jr. [s. Dan & Olive], d. June 28, 1849, ae 64 | 2 | 1 |
| Eliza F., of Colchester, m. Eleazer **LACEY**, of Middletown, Sept. 24, 1834, by Rev. Lyman Strong | 2 | 270 |
| Olive, w. [Dan], d. Mar. 2, 1848, ae 90 | 2 | 1 |
| **MARSHALL**, Abigail, d. [Jeremiah & Rebeckah], b. [ ] | 2 | 54 |
| Daniel, s. [Jeremiah & Rebeckah], b. [ ] | 2 | 54 |
| Dimmis, d. [Jeremiah & Rebeckah], b. [ ] | 2 | 54 |
| Holmes, s. [Jeremiah & Rebeckah], b. [ ] | 2 | 54 |

| | Vol. | Page |
|---|---|---|
| **MARSHALL**, (cont.) | | |
| Ire, s. [Jeremiah & Rebeckah], b. [ ] | 2 | 54 |
| Jacob, s. [Jeremiah & Rebeckah], b. [ ] | 2 | 54 |
| James, of Colchester, m. Eunice **BATE[S]**, Nov. 20, 1740 | 1 | 138 |
| James, s. [James & Eunice], b. Apr. 10, 1742; d. Aug. 16, 1742 | 1 | 138 |
| Jeremiah, m. Rebeckah **DANIELS**, [ ] | 2 | 54 |
| Jeremiah, s. [Jeremiah & Rebeckah], b. [ ] | 2 | 54 |
| John, s. [Jeremiah & Rebeckah], b. Aug. 30, 1765 | 2 | 54 |
| Mary, m. Thomas **CARRIER**, Dec. 6, 1784 | 2 | 35 |
| Rebeckah, d. [Jeremiah & Rebeckah], b. [ ] | 2 | 54 |
| Thomas, s. [Jeremiah & Rebeckah], b. Apr. 12, 1767 | 2 | 54 |
| **MARSY**, Simeon, Dr., of Conajoharie, Montgomery County, N. Y., m. Sarah **OTIS**, of Colchester, Oct. 31, 1822, by Salmon Cone, V. D. M. | 2 | 156 |
| **MARTIN**, Weltha, m. Edward **GUSTIN**, Jan. 21, 1778 | 2 | 32 |
| **MARVIN**, [see also **MERVIN**], A. J., of Colchester, m. Rev. A. **SCHOLFIELD**,, of Hamilton, N. Y., Apr. 3, 1844, by Rev. Joel R. Arnold | 3 | 12 |
| Anne, m. Asa **DAY**, Apr. 25, 1790 | 2 | 72 |
| Elizabeth R., of Colchester, m. Abishai **SCOFIELD**, of Peterboro, N. Y., Nov. 7, 1836, by Rev. Joel R. Arnold | 2 | 293 |
| Huldah, m. Jonathan **GILLET**, Feb. 12, 1811 | 2 | 81 |
| Lydia, m. Josiah **GATES**, Jr., Apr. 19, 1753 | 1 | 52 |
| Phebe, m. Jonathan **GILLETT**, 3d, Jan. 11, 1747 | 1 | 109 |
| Sophronia, of Hebron, m. David **NILES**, of Colchester, Dec. 29, 1833, by Rev. Lyman Strong | 2 | 261 |
| **MASON**, Betsey, d. [Peter & Anne], b. Aug. 28, 1788 | 2 | 80 |
| Harriet, d. [Peter & Anne], b. July 14, 1792 | 2 | 80 |
| Peter, m. Anne **CREMER**, June 1, 1786, at Weathersfield | 2 | 80 |
| Sally, d. [Peter & Anne], b. Aug. 20, 1790 | 2 | 80 |
| **MATHER, MARTHER**, Benjamin, Capt., [m.] Abigail **WORTHINGTON**, Mar. 14, 1763 | 1 | 61 |
| Elizabeth, of Saybrook, m. Benjamin **TRUMBULL**, of Colchester, Mar. 15, 1800 | 2 | 85 |
| Elizabeth, m. George **HICKS**, b. of Colchester, June 18, 1854, by Erastus Dickinson | 3 | 62 |
| Gibbons, m. Hannah **FOOT**, Jan. 28, 1789 | 2 | 60 |
| Gibbons Pierson, s. [Gibbons & Hannah], b. Dec. 7, 1791 | 2 | 60 |
| Henry DeWolf, s. [Gibbons & Hannah], b. July 3, 1794 | 2 | 60 |
| Hyram Foot, s. [Gibbons & Hannah], b. Feb. 13, 1796 | 2 | 60 |
| Ralph Colten, s. [Gibbons & Hannah], b. Dec. 9, 1798 | 2 | 60 |
| Rhoda, [d. Benjamin & Mary], b. Jan. 1, 1769 | 1 | 79 |
| William, [s. Capt. Benjamin & Abigail], b. Dec. 30, 1766 | 1 | 61 |
| ----, s. [Gibbons & Hannah], b. Apr. 13, 1801; d. same day | 2 | 60 |
| **MATTHEWS**, Stephen Holly, of Oberlin, O., m. Emma Louise **GILLET**, of Colchester, Aug. 10, 1852, by Erastus Dickinson | 3 | 52 |

| | Vol. | Page |
|---|---|---|
| **MAXFIELD**, Joseph, m. Ruby **JINKS**, Jan. 26, 1791 | 2 | 53 |
| Joseph, m. Piercy **CHAPPELL**, Apr. 21, 1833, by Benj[amin] Trumbull, J. P. | 2 | 243 |
| **MAYLE**, Frederick, m. Rosanna **MANC**, b. of Wertemburg, Germany, Apr. 25, 1854, by Erastus Dickinson | 3 | 51 |
| **MAYNARD**, Abby, of New London, m. Edwin B. **REYNOLDS**, of Colchester, June 14, 1853, by Rev. Erastus Dickinson | 3 | 57 |
| Almira, m. Silas **FRINK**, Sept. 16, 1838, by Rev. Benjamin G. Goff | 2 | 111 |
| James L., m. Angelina **BUSH**, b. of Norwich, Jan. 6, 1850, by Rev. Lyman Strong | 3 | 45 |
| **McCRACKEN**, Betsey, d. [James & Mercy], b. Aug. 18, 1795 | 2 | 93 |
| Betsey, of Salem, m. Renssalear **RATHBURN**, of Colchester, Apr. 13, 1823, at W[illia]m Palmer's, by Rev. William Palmer | 2 | 138 |
| Henry, s. [James & Mercy], b. Nov. 15, 1790 | 2 | 93 |
| James, m. Mercy **CHAMBERLAIN**, Apr. 19, 1787 | 2 | 93 |
| James, s. [James & Mercy], b. Nov. 9, 1787 | 2 | 93 |
| Jennet, d. [James & Mercy], b. Mar. 18, 1789 | 2 | 93 |
| Maria, d. [James & Mercy], b. Mar. 25, 1802 | 2 | 93 |
| **McINTIRE**, Henry L., of Mansfield, m. Maria G. **SEAMAN**, of Colchester, May 10, 1846, by Rev. P. Brockett | 3 | 27 |
| **McSHANE**, Frances, m. Henry F. **LAMB**, Mar. 12, 1818 | 2 | 145 |
| **MEACHAM, MEECHAM**, Mary, m. Elias **RANDALL**, Apr. 11, 1756 | 1 | 37 |
| Zeba, m. Elizabeth **PENDLETON**, Mar. 1, 1761 | 1 | 151 |
| **MELLEN**, Martha d., of Colchester, m. Calvin **CROFUT**, of Hartford, Aug. 17, 1845, by Rev. Lyman Strong | 3 | 23 |
| **MENTOR**, Abigail, [d. Richard & Elizabeth], b. Oct. 19, 1756; d. Nov. 9, 1756 | 1 | 33 |
| Christina, [d. Richard & Elizabeth], b. Mar. 31, 1741; d. Apr. 27, 1741 | 1 | 33 |
| Daniel, [s. Richard & Elizabeth], b. Aug. 13, 1743 | 1 | 33 |
| Elizabeth, [d. Richard & Elizabeth], b. May 27, 1738 | 1 | 33 |
| Elizabeth, w. Richard, d. Nov. 10, 1756 | 1 | 33 |
| Mercy, [d. Richard & Elizabeth], b. Aug. 9, 1747 | 1 | 33 |
| Richard, m. Elizabeth **ROBERTS**, Dec. 11, 1735 | 1 | 33 |
| Richard, m. Mary **WATERS**, Sept. 29, 1757 | 1 | 33 |
| Richard, d. [ ], 1773 | 1 | 33 |
| Silence, d. [Richard & Elizabeth], b. Oct. 6, 1751 | 1 | 33 |
| Simeon, [s. Richard & Mary], d. May 3, 1758 | 1 | 33 |
| Simon, [s. Richard & Elizabeth], b. Aug. 25, 1736 | 1 | 33 |
| **MERRILL**, Marion A., of Colchester, m. Thomas **CHAMPLAIN**, of Lebanon, Mar. 21, 1852, by Rev. S. M. Minor | 3 | 50 |
| **MERVIN**, [see also **MARVIN**], Huldah, of Lyme, m. Ezra **CARTER**, of Colchester, Nov. 3, 1768 | 1 | 96 |
| **METCALF**, Elijah, of East Haddam, m. Molly **HOPSON**, of Colchester, Sept. 23, 1762 | 1 | 131 |

| | Vol. | Page |
|---|---|---|
| **MILLER**, Abigaill, m. Joseph **KELLOGG**, Oct. 23, 1717 | L-1 | 445 |
| David, m. Sarah **HORSFORD**, Sept. 19, 1759 | 1 | 94 |
| James P., m. Hannah **INGRAHAM**, alias **BURNHAM**, Oct. 17, 1824, by Samuel A. Peters, J. P. | 2 | 171 |
| Mary Ann, of Colchester, m. John **SMITH**, of Somers, May 10, 1843, by Rev. Joel R. Arnold | 3 | 4 |
| **MILLS**, Abigail, m. David **BROWN**, [ ] | 1 | 130 |
| **MINARD**, Alexander, m. Electa **GATES**, June 10, 1811 | 2 | 152 |
| Dimmis, w. Nathan, d. Apr. 6, 1824, ae 37 | 2 | 82 |
| Electa, d. [Alexander & Electa], b. May 13, 1811 | 2 | 152 |
| Eliza Ann, d. [Alexander & Electa], b. Sept. 4, 1812 | 2 | 152 |
| Joshua Gates, s. [Alexander & Electa], b. Aug. 10, 1818 | 2 | 152 |
| Lettice, m. William **BURKE**, Apr. 11, 1778 | 2 | 54 |
| Orlando, s. [Alexander & Electa], b. Nov. 11, 1816 | 2 | 152 |
| **MINER, MINOR**, Ann, [d. John], b. May 14, 1739 | 1 | 103 |
| Christopher, s. [David & Mary], b. Oct. 5, 1800 | 2 | 112 |
| David, s. [David & Mary], b. Nov. 9, 1790 | 2 | 112 |
| David, m. Mary **BISHOP**, [ ] | 2 | 112 |
| Edward, s. [David & Mary], b. May 15, 1803 | 2 | 112 |
| Elizabeth A., of Glastenbury, m. Chauncey G. **PARISH**, of Hartford, Oct. 10, 1842, by Rev. Rob[er]t C. Mills | 2 | 260 |
| Esther, [d. John], b. July 24, 1735 | 1 | 103 |
| George, s. [David & Mary], b. June 16, 1793; d. Jan. 1, 1805 | 2 | 112 |
| Jonathan, s. [David & Mary], b. Oct. 3, 1788 | 2 | 112 |
| Laura, of East Haddam, m. Joseph S. **ACKLEY**, of Haddam, Sept. 7, 1851, by Rev. Geo[rge] W. Brewster | 2 | 152 |
| Nancy, d. [David & Mary], b. May 20, 1798 | 2 | 112 |
| Peregrine, s. [David & Mary], b. Nov. 11, 1795 | 2 | 112 |
| Rachel, [d. John], b. Apr. 22, 1737 | 1 | 103 |
| Thomas Bishop, s. [David & Mary], b. July 31, 1807 | 2 | 112 |
| **MITCHELL**, Asa, [s. Zephaniah & Elizabeth], b. Mar. 27, 1763 | 1 | 52 |
| Azariah, m. Susannah **KNOWLTON**, May 11, 1762 | 1 | 41 |
| Chauncey, m. Harriet **INGRAHAM**, May 7, 1825, by Zachariah Olmstead, J. P. | 2 | 177 |
| Isaac, [s. Zephaniah & Elizabeth], b. Sept. 11, 1767 | 1 | 52 |
| Joseph, [s. Azariah & Susannah], b. Oct. 3, 1762 | 1 | 41 |
| Laura A., m. Joseph **SNOW**, b. of Colchester, Jan. 8, 1854, by Rev. Anthony Palmer | 3 | 59 |
| Marvin, m. Betsey Lucretia **COOKE**, July 6, 1828, by Salmon Cone, V. D. M. | 2 | 204 |
| Rebeckah, [d. Zephaniah & Elizabeth], b. Mar. 27, 1758 | 1 | 52 |
| Susannah, [d. Azariah & Susannah], b. Sept. 10, 1768 | 1 | 41 |
| Zachariah, s. Lydia, b. [ ] | 2 | 71 |
| Zenas, [s. Azariah & Susannah], b. Dec. 8, 1763 | 1 | 41 |
| Zephaniah, m. Elizabeth **FOX**, June 7, 1757 | 1 | 52 |
| Zephaniah, [s. Zephaniah & Elizabeth], b. July 22, 1765 | 1 | 52 |
| ----, twin s. [Azariah & Susannah], b. Oct. 29, 1765; d. Oct. 29, 1765 | 1 | 41 |

| | Vol. | Page |
|---|---|---|
| **MITCHELL**, (cont.) | | |
| ----, d. [Lydia], b. June 19, 1793; d. same day | 2 | 71 |
| **MIX**, John G., of Hartford, m. Clarissa C. **ISHAM**, of Colchester, Apr. 11, 1833, by Rev. Lyman Strong | 2 | 243 |
| **MORGAN**, Abigail, m. James **MORGAN**, July 5, 1770 | 1 | 91 |
| Amos, m. Sarah **WELCH**, Nov. 9, 1769 | 1 | 91 |
| Amos, [s. Amos & Sarah], b. Nov. 13, 1771 | 1 | 91 |
| Ann, d. [Frederick & Caroline], b. July 21, 1829, at Ellington | 2 | 148 |
| Anna, d. [Daniel & Eunice], b. Apr. 10, 1752 | 1 | 164 |
| Anne, m. Elias **WORTHINGTON**, Jr., Oct. 24, 1771 | 1 | 84 |
| Benjamin, m. Elizabeth **ISHAM**, Mar. 12, 1761 | 1 | 179 |
| Betsey B., d. Amos & Elizabeth, b. Nov. 22, 1816 | 2 | 80 |
| Catharine, d. [Frederick & Caroline], b. Dec. 16, 1838 | 2 | 148 |
| Claracy, d. [Jonathan & Esther], b. Sept. 24, 1790 | 2 | 61 |
| Daniel, m. Eunice **ALCOTT**, Nov. 10, 1748 | 1 | 164 |
| Daniel, s. [Daniel & Eunice], b. Oct. 25, 1754 | 1 | 164 |
| Daniel, m. Irena **RATHBON**, Nov. 18, 1761 | 1 | 164 |
| David, m. Mary **WELLS**, Dec. 17, 1757 | 1 | 164 |
| Deliverance, [d. Samuel, Jr. & Deliverance], b. Aug. 15, 1771 | 1 | 91 |
| Dudley, [s. Samuel, Jr. & Deliverance], b. Mar. 11, 1773 | 1 | 91 |
| Edward Payson, s. [Frederick & Caroline], b. Feb. 21, 1834 | 2 | 148 |
| Eleneor, m. Hazael **JONES**, Mar. 7, 1765 | 1 | 81 |
| Elias, s. [Joshua & Wealthy], b. Oct. 22, 1783 | 2 | 61 |
| Elizabeth, w. Daniel, d. Sept. 25, 1747 | 1 | 164 |
| Elizabeth, [w. Benjamin], d. June 3, 1766 | 1 | 179 |
| Elizabeth B., of Colchester, m. George C. **WHITE**, of Bolton, Sept. 23, 1841, by Rev. Joel R. Arnold | 2 | 243 |
| Esther, d. [Jonathan & Esther], b. Mar. 8, 1785 | 2 | 61 |
| Eunice, w. Daniel, d. Mar. 23, 1757 | 1 | 164 |
| Francis Rose, s. [Frederick & Caroline], b. Sept. 10, 1842 | 2 | 148 |
| Frederick, s. [Jonathan & Esther], b. Oct. 7, 1788 | 2 | 61 |
| Frederick, m. Caroline **WATROUS**, May 20, 1823, by Salmon Cone, V. D. M. | 2 | 148 |
| Frederick, s. [Frederick & Caroline], b. May 17, 1827, at Middletown | 2 | 148 |
| George A., of Colchester, m. Ann D. **STRICKLAND**, of New London, Jan. 8, 1851, by Rev. Albert F. Park | 2 | 69 |
| Hannah, m. Joseph **TUBBS**, Apr. 31 (?), 1767 | 1 | 87 |
| Hannah F., of New London, m. Myles F. **DAVIS**, of Colchester, July 10, 1842, by A. R. Park, J. P. | 2 | 268 |
| Harry, s. [Joshua & Wealthy], b. July 15, 1786 | 2 | 61 |
| Harry, m. Lucy M. **PALMER**, Nov. 1, 1835, by Benj[ami]n Trumbull, J. P. | 2 | 279 |
| Henry Augustus, m. Eliza Ann **HYDE**, b. of Colchester, Aug. 29, 1830, by Amherst D. Scoville, J. P. | 2 | 224 |
| James, m. Abigail **MORGAN**, July 5, 1770 | 1 | 91 |
| Jedediah S., m. Ann Maria **ADAMS**, b. of Colchester, Oct. 19, 1845, by Rev. Pierpoint Brockett | 3 | 24 |

| | Vol. | Page |
|---|---|---|
| **MORGAN**, (cont.) | | |
| Jesse, s. Samuel, Sr. & Abigail, b. July 18, 1761 | 1 | 85 |
| John, s. [William & Elenor], b. Oct. 15, 1788 | 2 | 55 |
| John, s. Frederick & Caroline, b. Mar. 30, 1824 | 2 | 148 |
| Jonathan, s. [David & Mary], b. June 26, 1760 | 1 | 164 |
| Jonathan, m. Esther **PALMER**, June 22, 1784 | 2 | 61 |
| Joshua, s. [David & Mary], b. Sept. 14, 1758 | 1 | 164 |
| Joshua, m. Wealthy **PALMER**, June 3, 1779 | 2 | 61 |
| Joshua, s. [Joshua & Wealthy], b. Jan. 18, 1780 | 2 | 61 |
| Laura W., of Colchester, m. Elam **HALL**, of Somers, Apr. 7, 1822, by Salmon Cone, V. D. M. | 2 | 141 |
| Lydia, d. [Jonathan & Mary], d. Oct. 30, 1848, ae 43 | 2 | 61 |
| Lydia S., m. Eliphalet A. **BULKELEY**, Jan. 31, 1830, by Salmon Cone, V. D. M. | 2 | 218 |
| Mary, d. [Daniel & Eunice], b. Feb. 25, 1750 | 1 | 164 |
| Mary, w. Daniel, d. June 14, 1761 | 1 | 164 |
| Mary, [d. Samuel, Jr. & Deliverance], b. Nov. 7, 1774 | 1 | 91 |
| Mary, w. Jonathan, d. Dec. 1, 1848, ae 68 | 2 | 61 |
| Polly, d. [Joshua & Wealthy], b. Aug. 29, 1788 | 2 | 61 |
| Richard Henry, s. [Frederick & Caroline], b. Jan. 21, 1832 | 2 | 148 |
| Robert Dudley, s. [Frederick & Caroline], b. Mar. 15, 1836 | 2 | 148 |
| Samuel, Jr., m. Deliverance **RATHBURN**, Apr. 27, 1769 | 1 | 91 |
| Samuel, [s. Samuel, Jr. & Deliverance], b. Feb. 13, 1770 | 1 | 91 |
| Sarah, d. [Jonathan & Mary], d. Nov. 2, 1848, ae 35 | 2 | 61 |
| Theode, d. [David & Mary], d. Oct. 26, 1760 | 1 | 164 |
| Uriah, [s. James & Abigail], b. Feb. 4, 1776 | 1 | 91 |
| We[a]lthy, d. [Joshua & Wealthy], b. Jan. 17, 1782 | 2 | 61 |
| William, s. [Benjamin & Elizabeth], b. July 23, 1764 | 1 | 179 |
| William, [s. Amos & Sarah], b. May 10, 1770 | 1 | 91 |
| William, m. Elenor **JONES**, Jan. 31, 1787 | 2 | 55 |
| William W., of Hartford, m. Betsey **IRISH**, of Colchester, May 18, 1834, by Rev. Daniel Waldo, of Lebanon | 2 | 266 |
| Zerniah, m. Gurdon **TABER**, Jan. 23, 1839, by Benj[amin] Trumbull, J. P. | 2 | 97 |
| Zerniah Taylor, d. [Jonathan & Mary], d. June 21, 1848, ae 41 | 2 | 61 |
| **MORRIS**, Edward Livingstone, s. [Myron N. & Julia S.], b. Sept. 19, 1843 | 2 | 296 |
| Julia Louisa, d. [Myron N. & Julia S.], b. Apr. 3, 1840, in Mass. | 2 | 296 |
| Myron N., of Warren, m. Julia S. **AVERY**, of Colchester, Jan. 10, 1838, by Rev. Joel R. Arnold | 2 | 296 |
| **MORSE**, Clarissa, b. [ ] | 2 | 83 |
| **MOTT**, Morgan, m. Clarissa **GRAVES**, b. of Colchester, Jan. 31, 1847, by Rev. J. R. Arnold | 3 | 30 |
| **MUCKET**, Charles D., of East Haddam, m. Frances L. **SPENCER**, of Colchester, Feb. 17, 1847, by Rev. P. Brockett | 3 | 31 |
| **MUDGE**, Mary, m. Cornelius **HAMLIN**, Dec. 5, 1732 | TPR | 111 |
| **MUNGER**, Ebenezer Ingham, s. [Sylvester & Sene], b. Apr. 1, 1816 | 2 | 181 |

| | Vol. | Page |
|---|---|---|
| **MUNGER**, (cont.) | | |
| Elizabeth, d. [Sylvester & Sene], b. Mar. 5, 1818 | 2 | 181 |
| Henry Martin, s. [Sylvester & Sene], b. June 7, 1825 | 2 | 181 |
| Mary Cone, d. [Sylvester & Sene], b. Dec. 1, 1813 | 2 | 181 |
| Nelson Hotchkiss, s. [Sylvester & Sene], b. Dec. 1, 1813 | 2 | 181 |
| Stephen Ingham, s. [Sylvester & Sene], b. May 31, 1822 | 2 | 181 |
| Sylvester, m. Sene **INGHAM**, of Saybrook, Oct. 24, 1810, by Rev. Frederick W[illia]m Hotchkiss. Recorded Aug. 1, 1825, Saybrook | 2 | 181 |
| Sylvester Stonsbury, s. [Sylvester & Sene], b. June 3, 1820 | 2 | 181 |
| **MUNN, MUN, MAN**, Abigaiell, d. John*, b. Oct. 17, 1700 *(Probably James) | L-3 | 196 |
| Abigail, d. James, b. Oct. 17, 1700 | TM-1 | 196 |
| Abigail, [d. James, Jr. & Martha], b. Aug. 14, 1746 | 1 | 136 |
| Anna, [d. Isaiah & Abi], b. Nov. 3, 1779 | 1 | 95 |
| Benjamin, s. [James, Jr. & Martha], b. Jan. 29, 1754 | 1 | 136 |
| Bulah, d. [James, Jr. & Martha], b. Jan. 27, 1743/4 | 1 | 136 |
| Comfort, d. [James, Jr. & Martha], b. Feb. 3, 1751/2 | 1 | 136 |
| Elezier, [s. Isaiah & Abi], b. Nov. 20, 1769 | 1 | 95 |
| Hannah, [d. James & Mary], b. Mar. 26, 1706 | L-3 | 196 |
| Hannah, d. James, b. Mar. 26, 1706 | TM-1 | 196 |
| Hannah, d. [James, Jr. & Martha], b. Feb. 7, 1756 | 1 | 136 |
| Isaiah, s. [James, Jr. & Martha], b. May 11, 1740 | 1 | 136 |
| Isaiah, m. Abi **TIFFENEY**, Jan. 18, 1767 | 1 | 95 |
| Isaiah, [s. Isaiah & Abi], b. Aug. 30, 1767 | 1 | 95 |
| James, s. James & Mary, b. Feb. 2, 1703 | L-3 | 196 |
| James, s. James & Mary, b. Feb. 2, 1703 | TM-1 | 196 |
| James, Jr., m. Martha **SMITH**, Nov. 23, 1738 | 1 | 136 |
| James, d. Dec. 16, 1743, ae 87 | 1 | 135 |
| James, [s. James, Jr. & Martha], b. June 29, 1748 | 1 | 136 |
| Martha, [d. Isaiah & Abi], b. June 17, 1782 | 1 | 95 |
| Mary, d. [James, Jr. & Martha], b. Jan. 27, 1740/41 | 1 | 136 |
| Martha, m. Benjamin **BEEDLE**, [ ] (Mary) | 1 | 2 |
| Mary, m. Benjamin **BEADLE**, Feb. 6, 1766; d. Jan. 31, 1781 | 2 | 39 |
| Mary, [d. Isaiah & Abi], b. June 16, 1786 | 1 | 95 |
| R[e]uben, [s. Isaiah & Abi], b. Feb. 20, 1772 | 1 | 95 |
| Sarah, [d. James & Mary], b. June 28, 1708 | L-3 | 196 |
| Sarah, d. James, b. June 28, 1708 | TM-1 | 196 |
| Sarah, m. James **TRE[A]DWAY**, June 4, 1729 | L-3 | 8 |
| Sarah, [d. Isaiah & Abi], b. Mar. 31, 1775 | 1 | 95 |
| **MURFEY**, Eliza Ann, of Colchester, m. James F. **CLARKE**, of Cleveland, Ohio, Oct. 1, 1834, by Rev. Lyman Strong | 2 | 271 |
| Frances Cleveland, d. [John], b. Dec. 29, 1822 | 2 | 128 |
| Gardiner **BOWEN**, s. [John], b. Nov. 3, 1820 | 2 | 128 |
| Henry, s. [John], b. July 19, 1827 | 2 | 128 |
| John, Capt., d. Apr. 3, 1844, ae 68 | 2 | 128 |
| Maria, of Colchester, m. Lewis **ASPINWALL**, of Albany, May 9, 1831, by Rev. Lyman Strong | 2 | 231 |

| | Vol. | Page |
|---|---|---|
| **MURFEY**, (cont.) | | |
| Mary, d. [John], b. Sept. 7, 1829; d. Mar. 12, 1831 | 2 | 128 |
| Samuel Southworth, s. [John], b. Jan. 8, 1825 | 2 | 128 |
| **MURPHY**, [see under **MURFEY**] | | |
| **NATHAN**, Albert D., m. Mary Ann **BABCOCK**, May 7, 1833, by Rev. Joseph Harvey | 2 | 254 |
| **NEWHALL**, Mary, of Malden, m. Rev. Thomas **SKINNER**, of Colchester, July 9, 1740 | 1 | 138 |
| **NEWTON**, Abbey T., d. [Israel & Harriet], b. Oct. 11, 1821 | 2 | 166 |
| Abel, s. [John & Mary], b. June 9, 1763 | 1 | 115 |
| Abigaiell, [d. Isreall], b. Oct. 17, 1723 | L_1 | 654 |
| Abigaiell, m. Asariah **LO[O]MIS**, Dec. 25, 1723 | L-3 | 9 |
| Abigail, m. Pairpoint **BACON**, Mar. 21, 1751 | 1 | 153 |
| Abigail, m. Peirpoint **BACON**, Mar. 21, 1751; d. Mar. 8, 1800, ae 75 | 2 | 16 |
| Abigail, d. Israel, 2d, b. Apr. 6, 1768 | 2 | 15 |
| Abigail, m. Daniel **JONES**, [ ] | 2 | 117 |
| Alfred Cheeney, s. [Noah & Olive], b. Nov. 11, 1803 | 2 | 141 |
| Alice, d. James, b. Feb. 28, 1686 | L-1 | 451 |
| Alvin, [s. Asahel], b. [ ] ; d. [ ] | 1 | 85 |
| Ann, m. Jonathan **KELLOGG**, Jan. 3, 1710/11 | L-1 | 444 |
| Anne, [d. James], b. Apr. 13, 1692 | L-1 | 451 |
| Anson, s. [Asahel & Versalle], b. Feb. 3, 1798 | 2 | 89 |
| Ansess, d. Isreall, b. Jan. 1, 1716 | L-1 | 654 |
| Anstress, m. John **JOHNSON**, Jr., Jan. 6, 1736 | 1 | 131 |
| Asa, [s. Israel & Lois], b. Feb. 17, 1754 | 1 | 50 |
| Asa, m. Lydia **WORTHINGTON**, b. of Colchester, Jan. 23, 1777 | 2 | 88 |
| Asa, s. [Asa & Lydia], b. Oct. 3, 1782 | 2 | 88 |
| Asa had slave Rachel, d. Desire, negro, b. Oct. 3, 1789 | 2 | 94 |
| Asa, s. [Israel & Harriet], b. July 9, 1824 | 2 | 166 |
| Asahel, s. Delight **CHAPMAN**, b. June 1, 1758 | 1 | 21 |
| Asahel, m. [ ], Apr. 6, 1761 | 1 | 85 |
| Asahel, [s. Asahel], b. Oct. 7, 1763 | 1 | 85 |
| Asahel, m. Versalle **BOOTH**, Feb. 19, 1784 | 2 | 89 |
| Asahel, m. Delight **CHAPMAN**, [ ] | 1 | 21 |
| Aurel, m. Amos **JONES**, Jr., Oct. 9, 1788 | 2 | 89 |
| Bethiah, [d. Asahel], b. Aug. 17, 1765 | 1 | 85 |
| Charles Worthington, s. [Elias W. & Judith], b. Feb. 18, 1816 | 2 | 104 |
| Content, b. Aug. 10, 1775; m. Samuel **BRIDGES**, May 10, 1797. Recorded Feb. 7, 1851 | 2 | 157 |
| Dinah, [d. James & Susanah], b. Feb. 24, 1730 | L-1 | 399 |
| Dorothy, [d. James & Susanah], b. Feb. 25, 1717/8 | L-1 | 399 |
| Dudley, [s. Asahel], b. Apr. 10, 1780; d. July 7, 1862 | 1 | 85 |
| Eber, [s. Asahel], b. Oct. 1, 1771; d. May 28, 1850, buried in Allen, N. Y. | 1 | 85 |
| Elias, s. [Elijah & Lydia], b. Aug. 14, 1808; d. Sept. 29, 1817 | 2 | 115 |
| Elias W., s. [Asa & Lydia], b. Nov. 16, 1780 | 2 | 88 |

| | Vol. | Page |
|---|---|---|
| **NEWTON**, (cont.) | | |
| Elias W., m. Judith **WORTHINGTON**, Apr. 25, 1803 | 2 | 104 |
| Elijah, m. Lydia **THOMPSON**, Nov. 30, 1807, at Columbia | 2 | 115 |
| Elizabeth Worthington, d. [Elias W. & Judith], b. Nov. 8, 1808 | 2 | 104 |
| Emily A., d. [Elijah & Lydia], b. Mar. 21, 1821 | 2 | 115 |
| Erastus, s. [Asahel & Versalle], b. Feb. 22, 1795 | 2 | 89 |
| Eunice, [d. Israel & Lois], b. Jan. 2, 1756 | 1 | 50 |
| Eunice, m. Joel **WORTHINGTON**, Jan. 23, 1777; d. Aug. 16, 1846, ae 90 | 2 | 34 |
| Frances Caroline, d. [Elias W. & Judith], b. Apr. 27, 1804 | 2 | 104 |
| Hannah, [d. Isreall], b. June 28, 1721 | L-1 | 654 |
| Hannah, [d. Asahel], b. Jan. 17, 1762 | 1 | 85 |
| Hannah, [m.] Stephen **BECKWITH**, [ ] | 1 | 148 |
| Harvey, twin with Henry, s. [Asahel & Versalle], b. Nov. 15, 1800 | 2 | 89 |
| Henry, twin with Harvey, s. [Asahel & Versalle], b. Nov. 15, 1800 | 2 | 89 |
| Ira, [s. Asahel], b. Aug. 22, 1769 | 1 | 85 |
| Isaac, [s. Asahel], b. Sept. 17, 1767 | 1 | 85 |
| Isreall, [s. James], b. Mar. 5, 1694 | L-1 | 451 |
| Isreall had negro Kuff, m. Indian woman Sarah, Mar. [ ], 1716 | L-3 | 194 |
| Isreal had negro man Kuff m. Indian woman Sarah, Mar. [ ], 1716 | TM-1 | 194 |
| Isreal had negro Martha, d. Kuff & Sarah, b. Jan. 25, 1719 | L-3 | 194 |
| Isreal had negro Martha, d. Kuff & Sarah, b. Jan. 25, 1719 | TM-1 | 194 |
| Isreall, [s. James & Susanah], b. Feb. 17, 1725 | L-1 | 133 |
| Isreal, m. Lois **TREADWAY**, June 7, 1750 | 1 | 50 |
| Isreal, twin with Lois, s. [Isreal & Lois], b. Mar. 1, 1752; d. Aug. 28, 1753 | 1 | 50 |
| Israel had negro Lilley, d. Ama, b. Aug. 28, 1782 | 2 | 94 |
| Israel, s. [Asa & Lydia], b. Feb. 11, 1794 | 2 | 88 |
| Israel, d. July 9, 1804 | 1 | 50 |
| Israel, 2d, d. June 19, 1808 | 1 | 117 |
| Israel, m. Harriet **TURNER**, Jan. 14, 1819 | 2 | 166 |
| James, [s. James], b. Apr. 3, 1690 | L-1 | 451 |
| James, m. Susan[n]ah **WYAT[T]**, May 31, 1716 | L-1 | 399 |
| James, [s. James & Susannah], b. June 27, 1721 | L-1 | 399 |
| James, Jr., m. Hannah **DOWNS**, Oct. 14, 1742 | 1 | 137 |
| James, s. [John & Mary], b. Oct. 4, 1759 | 1 | 115 |
| Jerusha, w. Israel, 2d, d. Apr. 14, 1816 | 1 | 117 |
| Joel Worthington, s. [Asa & Lydia], b. May 29, 1799 | 2 | 88 |
| John, [s. James & Susanah], b. Sept. 30, 1719 | L-1 | 399 |
| John, of Colchester, m. Mary **HOLBROOK**, of Lebanon, Dec. 27, 1756 | 1 | 115 |
| John, s. [John & Mary], b. Apr. 8, 1758 | 1 | 115 |
| Josiah C., s. [Elijah & Lydia], b. May 14, 1816 | 2 | 115 |

| | Vol. | Page |
|---|---|---|
| **NEWTON**, (cont.) | | |
| Josiah C., m. Sarah **WEBSTER**, b. of Colchester, June 18, 1837, by Rev. Andrew M. Smith | 2 | 154 |
| Judeth Emeline, d. [Elias W. & Judith], b. Mar. 16, 1806 | 2 | 104 |
| Laura, d. [Elijah & Lydia], b. July 4, 1811; d. Oct. 28, 1826 | 2 | 115 |
| Laura Maria, d. [Asa & Lydia], b. Feb. 15, 1802 | 2 | 88 |
| Laura Maria, d. [Elias W. & Judith], b. Apr. 18, 1813 | 2 | 104 |
| Leodemiah, d. James, Jr. & Susannah, b. May 7, 1732 | TPR | 109 |
| Lois, twin with Israel, [d. Israel & Lois], b. Mar. 1, 1752; d. Aug. 20, 1753 | 1 | 50 |
| Louisa, d. [Asa & Lydia], b. Jan. 23, 1796 | 2 | 88 |
| Lydia, [d. Israel & Lois], b. Dec. 29, 1759 | 1 | 50 |
| Lydia, m. Asa **BIGELOW**, Feb. 5, 1783; d. July 31, 1844, ae 85 | 2 | 78 |
| Lydia, d. [Asa & Lydia], b. Jan. 21, 1788 | 2 | 88 |
| Lydia, [w. Elijah], d. June 27, 1827 | 2 | 115 |
| Lydia Louisa, d. [Elias W. & Judith], b. May 9, 1811 | 2 | 104 |
| Lydia Louisa, [d. Israel & Harriet], b. Nov. 28, 1831 | 2 | 166 |
| Lyman, [s. Israel & Harriet], b. Feb. 27, 1836 | 2 | 166 |
| Maria T., [d. Israel & Harriet], b. Aug. 9, 1827 | 2 | 166 |
| Maria T., m. John M. **PEDDINGHOUSE**, b. of Colchester, Sept. 14, 1852, by Erastus Dickinson | 3 | 53 |
| Mary, m. Jonathan **WELLS**, July 11, 1717 | L-1 | 452 |
| Mary, [d. Isreall], b. Mar. 1, 1719 | L-1 | 654 |
| Mary, m. John **KELLOGG**, Apr. 2, 1738 | 1 | 129 |
| Mary, d. [John & Mary], b. Aug. 6, 1761 | 1 | 115 |
| Mary Louisa, d. [Elias W. & Judith], b. June 20, 1818 | 2 | 104 |
| Matthew T., [s. Israel & Harriet], b. June 4, 1829; d. July 24, 1909, ae 80 | 2 | 166 |
| Nancy, d. [Asahel & Versalle], b. Apr. 9, 1792 | 2 | 89 |
| Noah, b. July 2, 1778 | 1 | 117 |
| Noah, m. Olive **CHEENEY**, Oct. 21, 1802 | 2 | 141 |
| Noah Wells, s. [Noah & Olive], b. Sept. 21, 1808 | 2 | 141 |
| Polly, d. [Asahel & Versalle], b. [ ] 6, 1789 | 2 | 89 |
| Rhoda, d. [Asa & Lydia], b. Jan. 28, 1785 | 2 | 88 |
| Sally, d. [Asa & Lydia], b. Apr. 2, 1791 | 2 | 88 |
| Sarah, [d. Israel & Lois], b. Oct. 6, 1757 | 1 | 50 |
| Sophia Ely, d. [Noah & Olive], b. Apr. 1, 1805 | 2 | 141 |
| Sophia M., d. [Elijah & Lydia], b. Jan. 27, 1819 | 2 | 115 |
| Susannah, [d. James, Jr. & Susannah], b. Mar. 15, 1735 | TPR | 109 |
| Susanna, w. James, d. July 26, 1747 | 1 | 109 |
| Susannah, m. Peter **BULKELEY**, Dec. 16, 1756 | 1 | 142 |
| Thomas, [s. James & Susanah], b. Aug. 4, 1728; d. Sept. 21, [1728] | L-1 | 399 |
| Versalle, d. [Asahel & Versalle], b. Aug. 16, 1784 | 2 | 89 |
| William, s. [Asahel & Versalle], b. Oct. 15, 1786 | 2 | 89 |
| -----, w. James. d. Aug. 4, 1756 | 1 | 101 |
| **NICHOLS**, Ann R., m. John P. **KNOWLES**, Oct. 23, 1828, | | |

| | Vol. | Page |
|---|---|---|
| **NICHOLS**, (cont.) | | |
| by Benjamin Trumbull, J. P. | 2 | 208 |
| Betty, of Colchester, m. Abel **PHELPS**, of Hebron, Feb. 8, 1821, by Salmon Cone, V. D. M. | 2 | 124 |
| **NILES, NIELES**, Aaron, s. [Nathan & Mary], b. Apr. 30, 1751 | 1 | 145 |
| Aaron T., of Middletown, m. Rachel Ann **HARRIS**, of Colchester, July 21, 1827, by Rev. Joseph Harvey | 2 | 197 |
| Abby Jane, d. [Noah D. & Sarah], b. Mar. 26, 1844 | 2 | 76 |
| Abigaiell, [d. John], b. Sept. 4, 1730 | L-3 | 7 |
| Ambrose, [s. John], b. Mar. 30, 1741 | 1 | 138 |
| Ambrose, m. Hannah **MACCOLL**, [ ] | 1 | 17 |
| Barnabus, [s. John], b. June 12, 1735 | 1 | 138 |
| Daniel, s. [Nathan & Mary], b. May 4, 1762; d. July 10, 1762 | 1 | 145 |
| Daniel, [s. Ambrose & Hannah], b. Feb. 9, 1769 | 1 | 17 |
| David, s. John, b. Feb. 9, 1733 | 1 | 138 |
| David, of Colchester, m. Sophronia **MARVIN**, of Hebron, Dec. 29, 1833, by Rev. Lyman Strong | 2 | 261 |
| Elihu, [s. Ambrose & Hannah], b. Apr. 25, 1765 | 1 | 17 |
| Elisha, s. [Nathan & Mary], b. Feb. 28, 1764 | 1 | 145 |
| Elizabeth, d. [Nathan & Mary], b. Aug. 22, 1743; d. June 4, 1748 | 1 | 145 |
| Ellen, d. [Noah D. & Sarah], b. Jan. 6, 1846 | 2 | 76 |
| Emeline, d. [Noah D. & Sarah], b. Mar. 31, 1842 | 2 | 76 |
| Hannah, w. John, Jr., d. Aug. 5, 1746 | 1 | 129 |
| Hannah, d. [Nathan & Mary], b. Dec. 7, 1747; d. Feb. 3, 1747/8 | 1 | 145 |
| Irene Elizabeth, d. [William N. & Sarah Maria], b. Oct. 4, 1837 | 2 | 283 |
| John, s. John, b. Mar. 25, 1718 | L-3 | 7 |
| John, [s. Ambrose & Hannah], b. Nov. 29, 1768 | 1 | 17 |
| John, s. [Nathan & Dorcas], b. Dec. 31, 1775 | 1 | 144 |
| John Nelson, s. [William N. & Sarah Maria], b. Sept. 10, 1845; d. Feb. 16, 1846, ae 5 m. 6 d. | 2 | 283 |
| Lidia, d. [Nathan & Mary], b. Aug. 16, 1753 | 1 | 145 |
| Lydia, d. [Nathan & Dorcas], b. Aug. 2, 1777 | 1 | 144 |
| Mary, [d. John], b. June 26, 1726 | L-3 | 7 |
| Mary, m. Jonathan **KELLOGG**, Jr., Jan. 1, 1735/6 | 1 | 127 |
| Mary, of Colchester, m. Dan[iel] **PORTER**, of Columbia, Nov. 4, 1848 | 2 | 282 |
| Mary, d. [Nathan & Mary], b. Feb. 25, 1748/9 | 1 | 145 |
| Nathan, s. John, b. Feb. 20, 1720 | L-3 | 7 |
| Nathan, [s. John], b. May 7, 1724 | L-3 | 7 |
| Nathan, m. Mary **SAXTON**, Oct. 28, 1742 | 1 | 145 |
| Nathan, s. [Nathan & Mary], b. Dec. 7, 1746; d. Jan. 27, 1746/7 | 1 | 145 |
| Nathan, s. [Nathan & Mary], b. Nov. 20, 1755 | 1 | 145 |
| Nathan, of Colchester, m. Dorcas **BECKWITH**, of Lyme, Nov. "about the middle", 1774 | 1 | 144 |

| | Vol. | Page |
|---|---|---|
| **NILES, NIELES,** (cont.) | | |
| Noah, s. [Nathan & Mary], b. Dec. 26, 1759 | 1 | 145 |
| Noah, s. [Nathan & Dorcas], b. May 8, 1779 | 1 | 144 |
| Noah D., m. Sarah **WATROUS**, b. of Colchester, Mar. 5, 1840, by Rev. Lyman Strong | 2 | 76 |
| Rachel, d. [Nathan & Mary],b. Aug. 9, 1745; d. June 14, 1748 | 1 | 145 |
| Rhoda, m. Henry **SMITH**, Aug. 19, 1820 | 2 | 152 |
| Ruth, m. Ebenezer **COLEMAN**, Mar. 11, 1704/5 | L-1 | 799 |
| Sam[ue]ll, [s. John], b. Mar. 13, 1722; d. Aug. [ ], 1726 | L-3 | 7 |
| Samuel, s. John, Jr. [& Hannah], b. July 28, 1746; d. Oct. 12, 1746 | 1 | 129 |
| Sarah, d. [Nathan & Mary], b. Dec. 24, 1757 | 1 | 145 |
| Sarah, m. John **WOODWORTH**, [ ], 1776 | 2 | 17 |
| Thomas, [s. John], b. Sept. 28, 1728 | L-3 | 7 |
| William N., of New Haven, m. Sarah Maria **BULKELEY**, of Colchester, Feb. 7, 1836, by Rev. Lyman Strong | 2 | 283 |
| William Nelson, d. Apr. 20, 1849, ae 39 | 2 | 283 |
| William Otis, s. [William N. & Sarah Maria], b. May 31, 1839 | 2 | 283 |
| **NIXON**, Sophia, m. Lewis **BOWEN**, Apr. 18, 1821, by Salmon Cone, V. D. M. | 2 | 297 |
| **NORCROSS**, Eunice B., of Colchester, m. Lewis **PRESCOTT**, of Medway, Mass., Oct. 9, 1853, by G. W. Pendleton | 3 | 58 |
| **NORTHAM**, Abigail, [d. John & Hannah], b. Aug. 23, 1731 | L-1 | 449 |
| Abigail, m. Israel **KELLOGG**, Jan. 31, 1752 | 1 | 26 |
| Ann, twin with Ruhama, [d. John & Hannah], b. Oct. 15, 1727 | L-1 | 449 |
| Ann, [d. Jonathan, Jr. & Anna Mack], b. June 15, 1759 | 1 | 99 |
| Anna, [d. John & Anna], b. July 18, 1760 | 1 | 27 |
| Asa. [s. Jonathan & Mary], b. Dec. 4, 1728 | L-1 | 452 |
| Asa, [s. John & Anna], b. Feb. 9, 1764 | 1 | 27 |
| Asa. s. [Jonathan, Jr. & Anna Mack], b. Oct. 27, 1766 | 1 | 99 |
| Betty, m. Israel **HOLDREDGE**, Feb. 14, 1769 | 1 | 49 |
| Charles, s. [Jonathan, Jr. & Anna Mack], b. July 18, 1768 | 1 | 99 |
| Charlotte M., of Colchester, m. Cornelius B. **DOANE**, of Essex, [Sept.] 13, 1854, by Rev. S. D. Jewett | 3 | 63 |
| David, s. [Samuel & Esther], b. Apr. 1, 1757 | 1 | 131 |
| Dorothy, [d. Jonathan & Mary], b. Mar. 17, 1727 | L-1 | 452 |
| Ebenezer, m. Mary **GLOVER**, Jan. 15, 1718/19 | L-1 | 446 |
| Ebenezer, s. Eben[ezer], b. June 22, 1721 | L-1 | 447 |
| Ebenezer, s. [Samuel & Esther], b. Aug. 21, 1760 | 1 | 131 |
| Eli, s. [Jonathan, Jr. & Anna Mack], b. June 2, 1770 | 1 | 99 |
| Elijah, [s. Eben], b. June 18, 1733 | L-1 | 447 |
| Elisebeth, m. William **ROBERDS**, July 20, 1705 | L-3 | 198 |
| Elizabeth, m. William **ROBERDS**, July 20, 1705 | TM-1 | 198 |
| Elizabeth, [d. John & Hannah], b. Apr. 20, 1729 | L-1 | 449 |
| Esther, d. [Samuel & Esther], b. Jan. 26, 1759 | 1 | 131 |
| Eunice, [d. Jonathan, Jr. & Anna Mack], b. Sept. 25, 1757 | 1 | 99 |
| Experience, twin with Katherine, [d. John & Hannah], b. Apr. 13, 1733 | L-1 | 449 |

| | Vol. | Page |
|---|---|---|
| **NORTHAM**, (cont.) | | |
| Grace, [d. Jonathan & Mary], b. Jan. 24, 1731 | L-1 | 452 |
| Hannah, [d. John & Hannah], b. June 6, 1722 | L-1 | 449 |
| Hannah, [d. John & Hannah], b. May 29, 1724 | L-1 | 449 |
| Joel, twin with Joseph, [s. John & Anna], b. Aug. 4, 1766 | 1 | 27 |
| John, m. Hannah **PUMERY**, May 9, 1721 | L-1 | 449 |
| J[oh]n, [s. John & Hannah], b. May 29, 1725 | L-1 | 449 |
| John, of Colchester, m. Anna **WHITE**, of Hebron, Nov. 10, 1757 | 1 | 27 |
| John, [s. John & Anna], b. Aug. 17, 1758 | 1 | 27 |
| John H., of Hebron, m. Harriet G. **BRIGGS**, of Colchester, Nov. 24, 1844, by Rev. Joel R. Arnold | 3 | 18 |
| Jonathan, m. Mary **DAY**, Dec. 20, 1722 | L-1 | 452 |
| Jonathan, [s. Jonathan & Mary], b. Aug. 29, 1725 | L-1 | 452 |
| Jonathan, Jr., m. Anna Mack **WILLIAMS**, Apr. 1, 1754 | 1 | 99 |
| Jonathan, [s. Jonathan, Jr. & Anna Mack], b. Apr. 10, 1756 | 1 | 99 |
| Joseph, twin with Joel, [s. John & Anna], b. Aug. 4, 1766; d. Oct. 3, 1767 | 1 | 27 |
| Katherine, twin with Experience, [d. John & Hannah], b. Apr. 13, 1733 | L-1 | 449 |
| Lois, d. [Jonathan, Jr. & Anna Mack], b. Feb. 4, 1763 | 1 | 99 |
| Lucy, d. [Jonathan, Jr. & Anna Mack], b. Oct. 31, 1764 | 1 | 99 |
| Luranah, [d. John & Hannah], b. May 25, 1723 | L-1 | 449 |
| Lurana, m. Noah **PUMERY**, Apr. 24, 1748 | 1 | 34 |
| Lidia, [d. Eben], b. Oct. 25, 1727 | L-1 | 447 |
| Mary, [d. Jonathan & Mary], b. Nov. 28, 1723 | L-1 | 452 |
| Mary, [d. Eben], b. Mar. 13, 1725 | L-1 | 447 |
| Mary, w. Ebenezer, d. June 5, 1756 | 1 | 48 |
| Mary, d. [Samuel & Esther], b. June 13, 1762 | 1 | 131 |
| Robert C., m. Nancy **EMMONS**, b. of Colchester, June 9, 1831, by Rev. Joseph Harvey | 2 | 232 |
| Ruhama, twin with Ann, [d. John & Hannah], b. Oct. 15, 1727 | L-1 | 449 |
| Russel[l], s. [Jonathan, Jr. & Anna Mack], b. Feb. 11, 1761 | 1 | 99 |
| Russel[l], s. [Samuel, Jr. & Sarah], b. Dec. 24, 1779 | 2 | 25 |
| Sally Maria, m. George Trumbull **LOOMIS**, of Bolton, Sept. 14, 1826, by Rev. Joel R. Arnold | 2 | 289 |
| Samuell, [s. Ebenezer & Mary], b. Oct. 29, 1720 | L-1 | 446 |
| Samuel, d. Nov. 12, 1726 | L-1 | 654 |
| Samuel, m. Esther **HITCHCOCK**, Nov. 21, 1754 | 1 | 131 |
| Samuel, [s. Jonathan, Jr. & Anna Mack], b. Jan. 25, 1755 | 1 | 99 |
| Samuel, Jr., m. Sarah **DAY**, Apr. 8, 1779 | 2 | 25 |
| Sarah, m. John **HOPSON**, Jan. [ ], 1704 | L-1 | 799 |
| Sarah, [d. John & Hannah], b. Aug. 6, 1726 | L-1 | 449 |
| Sibbel, m. Josiah **TAYLOR**, Nov. 4, 1761 | 1 | 52 |
| Timothy, [s. Eben], b. June 16, 1723 | L-1 | 447 |
| Timothy, s. [Samuel & Esther], b. July 13, 1755 | 1 | 131 |
| **NORTON**, Daniel J., m. Eunice **BUEL**, Mar. 28, 1832, by Rev. | | |

| | Vol. | Page |
|---|---|---|
| **NORTON**, (cont.) | | |
| S. D. Jewett | 3 | 50 |
| **OAKLEY**, William, m. Mercy **KELLOGG**, Dec. 7, 1835, by Giles Shattuck, J. P. | 2 | 281 |
| **OCKLEY**, [see also **ACKLEY**], Ruth, of Chatham, m. Samuel **SKINNER**, Oct. 19, 1786 | 2 | 67 |
| **OLMSTEAD**, Abby Ann, d. [Zephaniah & Elizabeth], b. May 27, 1805 | 2 | 157 |
| Abigail, [d. John & Abigail], b. Apr. 28, 1746; d. Nov. 11, 1749 | 1 | 56 |
| Albert, s. [Zephaniah & Elizabeth], b. Mar. 7, 1809; d. Aug. 7, 1835, ae 26 | 2 | 157 |
| Augustus, s. [Zephaniah & Elizabeth], b. Apr. 28, 1802; d. July 25, 1851, ae 49 | 2 | 157 |
| Catharine Gardiner, d. [Jonathan & Elizabeth C.], b. Dec. 4, 1839 | 3 | 9 |
| Dorothy, of East Haddam, m. Daniel **BULKLEY**, of Colchester, Aug. 16, 1764 | 1 | 38 |
| Dorothy, of Chatham, m. Elijah **DAY**, of Colchester, Mar. 10, 1776 | 2 | 24 |
| Edward, of New Haven, m. Marion **HYDE**, of Colchester, Dec. 30, 1851, by E. Dickinson | 3 | 49 |
| Elizabeth C., m. Edward C. **PARKHURST**, b. of Colchester, Oct. 11, 1842, by Rev. Daniel G. Sprague, of Westchester | 2 | 206 |
| Elizabeth Clark, d. [Zephaniah & Elizabeth], b. Mar. 16, 1815 | 2 | 157 |
| Harriet, m. Joshua **BULKELEY**, 2d, Mar. 18, 1806; d. May 25, 1808 | 2 | 113 |
| John, m. Abigail **CONE**, June 9, 1745 | 1 | 56 |
| John, [s. John & Abigail], b. Aug. 23, 1750 | 1 | 56 |
| John, of East Haddam, m. Lois **ADAMS**, of Colchester, Apr. 9, 1844, by Rev. S. D. Jewett, Westchester | 3 | 14 |
| Jonathan, s. [Zephaniah & Elizabeth], b. Jan. 2, 1807 | 2 | 157 |
| Maria, d. [Zephaniah & Elizabeth], b. Mar. 9, 1804 | 2 | 157 |
| Maria, of Colchester, m. Daniel **PECK**, of East Haddam, Nov. 5, 1832, by Rev. Joseph Harvey | 2 | 239 |
| Mary, [d. John & Abigail], b. Sept. 3, 1753 | 1 | 56 |
| Samuel, 2d, of East Haddam, m. Huldah **ROGERS**, of Colchester, Feb. 12, 1827, by Salmon Cone, V. D. M. | 2 | 192 |
| Sarah, [d. John & Abigail], b. July 26, 1756 | 1 | 56 |
| Sarah, m. Elisha **LORD**, Nov. 12, 1797 | 2 | 33 |
| Susanna, m. Jonathan **GATES**, July 16, 1747 | 1 | 137 |
| Susanna, [d. John & Abigail], b. July 10, 1748; d. Oct. 13, 1749 | 1 | 56 |
| William, s. [Zephaniah & Elizabeth], b. Jan. 5, 1821; d. June 6, 1851, ae 30 | 2 | 157 |
| W[illia]m E., s. [Jonathan & Elizabeth C.], b. [ ] | 3 | 9 |
| Zachariah, d. Dec. 26, 1831, ae 68 | 2 | 157 |

| | Vol. | Page |
|---|---|---|
| **OSBORN, OSBORNE**, Elijah, of Savannah, Ga., m. Sophronia Tyler **WOODARD**, of Glastonbury, Sept. 19, 1830, by Salmon Cone, V. D. M. | 2 | 224 |
| Elizabeth Frances, of Colchester, m. Charles Gustavus **TAYLOR**, of New York, Sept. 11, 1844, by Rev. Joel R. Arnold | 3 | 16 |
| **OTIS**, A. J., of Colchester, m. Rev. James H. **FRANCES**, of Middletown, May 10, 1843, by Rev. Joel R. Arnold | 3 | 5 |
| Abiel, s. [Nath[anie]ll & Mary], b. June 28, 1781 | 2 | 18 |
| Albert S., of Colchester, m. Ellen M. **BATTIE**, of Litchfield, May 14, 1853, by Rev. Lyman Strong | 3 | 55 |
| Alfred, s. [David & Anna], b. Mar. 4, 1804 | 2 | 95 |
| Alfred, m. Alma E. **FORD**, b. of Colchester, Jan. 14, 1851, by Rev. Lyman Strong | 2 | 238 |
| Alfred, m. Sophia Jane **WORTHINGTON**, Sept. 17, 1832, by Rev. Lyman Strong | 2 | 238 |
| Alfred H., m. Sarah A. **GILLETT**, Mar. 15, 1831, by Rev. Lyman Strong | 2 | 230 |
| Amos. s. [John & Prudence], b. Apr. 18, 1776 | 1 | 153 |
| Amos, b. Apr. 18, 1776; m. Demerus **HUNTLEY**, May 11, 1842 | 2 | 73 |
| Amos. s. [John T., Jr. & Lucy T.], b. Feb. 6, 1840 | 2 | 222 |
| Ann, d. [John & Prudence], b. Mar. 15, 1757 | 1 | 153 |
| Aruanna, s. [Stephen & Lucy], b. Jan. 6, 1763 | 1 | 163 |
| Asa, s. [Nath[anie]ll & Mary], b. Feb. 16, 1786 | 2 | 18 |
| Benjamin Fowler, s. [David & Anna], b. Nov. 20, 1811 | 2 | 95 |
| Benjamin Fowler, m. Frances Jane **CLARK**, b. of Colchester, Jan. 1, 1840, by Rev. Joel R. Arnold | 2 | 118 |
| Bettey, m. Jonathan **BIGELOW**, May 24, 1759, "according to Mr. Little's record" | 2 | 72 |
| Bettey, d. [Nath[anie]ll & Mary], b. Jan. 19, 1789 | 2 | 18 |
| Calvin, s. [Stephen & Lucy], b. Oct. 16, 1766 | 1 | 163 |
| Caroline, d. [Stephen & Lucy], b. Dec. 18, 1764 | 1 | 163 |
| Chandler, s. [Stephen & Lucy], b. Apr. 18, 1770 | 1 | 163 |
| Charles, s. [John & Prudence], b. Oct. 29, 1760 | 1 | 153 |
| Charles P., s. [John T., Jr. & Lucy T.], b. Nov. 6, 1837 | 2 | 222 |
| Charles Pum[e]roy, s. [John Thatcher & Louisa], b. Apr. 22, 1790; d. Jan. 7, 1837, ae 47 | 2 | 73 |
| Clarissa F., m. Otis **SKEELE**, of Chicopee, Mass., May 6, 1851, by Rev. Orin F. Otis, of Chepatchet, R. I. | 2 | 95 |
| Clarissa Fowler, d. [David & Anna], b. Aug. 17, 1805 | 2 | 95 |
| David, s. [John & Prudence], b. Aug. 20, 1773 | 1 | 153 |
| David, of Colchester, m. Anna **FOWLER**, of Lebanon, Nov. 25, 1802; d. May 13, 1847, ae 74 | 2 | 95 |
| Delight, [d. Nathaniel], b. Mar. 16, 1730 | L-1 | 445 |
| Delight, d. Nath[anie]l & Hannah, b. Mar. 23, 1731; d. July 20, 1740 | TPR | 108 |
| Desier, [s. Nathaniel], b. May 20, 1723 | L-1 | 445 |

| | Vol. | Page |
|---|---|---|
| **OTIS**, (cont.) | | |
| Dolly, d. [John Thatcher & Louisa], b. Aug. 13, 1798 | 2 | 73 |
| Dorothy, [d. Nathaniel], b. Apr. 16, 1721 | L-1 | 445 |
| Dorothy, m. Asa **BIGELOW**, Dec. 13, 1737 | 1 | 138 |
| Dorothy, m. Noah W. **BRIDGES**, Aug. 19, 1822, by Salmon Cone, V. D. M. | 2 | 157 |
| Dorothy, [w. James], d. Feb. 24, 1849, ae 74 | 2 | 64 |
| Elcy, d. [Stephen & Lucy], b. Sept. 12, 1768 | 1 | 163 |
| Elizabeth, m. Jonathan **BIGELOW**, May 24, 1759 | 1 | 38 |
| Elizabeth H. H., w. James F., d. Dec. 27, 1844, ae 83 | 2 | 64 |
| Eunice, d. [John & Prudence], b. Nov. 28, 1770 | 1 | 153 |
| Eunice, d. [John Thatcher & Louisa], b. Mar. 29, 1794; d. Dec. 30, 1814, ae 21 | 2 | 73 |
| Eunice, d. [John T., Jr. & Lucy T.], b. June 25, 1831 | 2 | 222 |
| Frances Sophia, d. [Alfred & Sophia Jane], b. Sept. 21, 1833 | 2 | 138 |
| Hannah, [d. Nathaniel], b. Feb. 29, 1717/18 | L-1 | 445 |
| Hannah, d. [John & Prudence], b. Feb. 24, 1751/2 | 1 | 153 |
| Hannah, d. June 12, 1752 | TPR | 109 |
| Harriet, d. [David & Anna], b. Mar. 22, 1814 | 2 | 95 |
| Harriet, d. [John T., Jr. & Lucy T.], b. May 18, 1833; d. Sept. 14, 1846, ae 13 | 2 | 222 |
| Harriet, m. Russell **DUTTON**, b. of Colchester, May 1, 1849, by Rev. J. R. Arnold | 3 | 41 |
| Horatio Nelson, s. [David & Anna], b. July 24, 1816 | 2 | 95 |
| Israel Taintor, s. [John Thatcher & Louisa], b. July 3, 1805 | 2 | 73 |
| James, s. [John & Prudence], b. June 6, 1767 | 1 | 153 |
| James, s. [Stephen & Lucy], b. Nov. 5, 1780 | 1 | 163 |
| James, m. Dorothy **FOOT**, Nov. 18, 1792; d. Mar. 2, 1845, ae 78 | 2 | 64 |
| James F., of Colchester, m. Elizabeth H. **HAMMOND**, of Providence, R. I., Aug. 18, 1831, by Rev. W[illia]m Phillips, Providence | 2 | 234 |
| James Foot, s. [James & Dorothy], b. Sept. 24, 1804; d. Apr. 5, 1846, ae 42 | 2 | 64 |
| John, [s. Nathaniel], b. Apr. 1, 1728 | L-1 | 445 |
| John, m. Prudence **TAINTOR**, Dec. 20, 1750 | 1 | 153 |
| John, s. [John T., Jr. & Lucy T.], b. Nov. 29, 1835 | 2 | 222 |
| John Nelson, s. [James & Dorothy], b. Apr. 28, 1809; d. Apr. [ ], 1812 | 2 | 64 |
| John T., Jr., m. Lucy T. **DART**, b. of Colchester, Apr. 21, 1830, by Asa Willcox, Elder | 2 | 222 |
| John Thatcher, s. [John & Prudence], b. Oct. 31, 1758 | 1 | 153 |
| John Thatcher, m. Louisa **PUM[E]ROY**, Sept. 29, 1782; d. Sept. 18, 1842, ae 84 | 2 | 73 |
| John Thatcher, s. [John Thatcher & Louisa], b. Aug. 4, 1786 | 2 | 73 |
| Joseph, s. [Stephen & Lucy], b. Feb. 5, 1782 | 1 | 163 |
| Laura Emeline, d. [Alfred & Sophia Jane], b. Oct. 14, 1836; d. Sept. 1, 1842, ae 5 y. 10 m. 16 d. | 2 | 238 |

| | Vol. | Page |
|---|---|---|
| **OTIS**, (cont.) | | |
| Louisa, d. [John Thatcher & Louisa], b. June 27, 1788 | 2 | 73 |
| Louisa, w. John Thatcher, d. Dec. 3, 1838, ae 77 | 2 | 73 |
| Lovisa, m. Denison **SMITH**, Nov. 8, 1815, by Salmon Cone | 2 | 84 |
| Lucretia, m. Richard **SKINNER**, Jr., Jan. 13, 1767 | 1 | 35 |
| Lucy, d. [Stephen & Lucy], b. Jan. 4, 1772 | 1 | 163 |
| Lydya, d. Nathaniel, b. Jan. 20, 1716/17 | L-1 | 445 |
| Lydia, m. Abner **KELLOGG**, June 26, 1740 | 1 | 132 |
| Marcy, [d. Nath[anie]l & Hannah], b. July 3, 1734 | TPR | 108 |
| Mary, d. [Nath[anie]ll & Mary], b. Aug. 25, 1779 | 2 | 18 |
| Mary, wid. Nathaniel, d. Nov. 14, 1837, in New London | 2 | 18 |
| Mary P., d. Charles P., b. Jan. 3, 1837; d. Feb. 22, 1893, ae 56, at the Faith Home for Incurables in Brooklyn, N. Y., bd. in Colchester | 2 | 73 |
| Mercy, [d. Nathaniel], b. July 3, 1734 | L-1 | 445 |
| Mercy, d. [John & Prudence], b. Sept. 17, 1764 | 1 | 153 |
| Nathaniel, [s. Nathaniel], b. Aug. 20, 1725 | L-1 | 445 |
| Nath[anie]ll, [s. Nath[anie]l & Hannah], b. Jan. 24, 1740/41 | TPR | 108 |
| Nath[anie]ll, s. [John & Prudence], b. June 19, 1753 | 1 | 153 |
| Natha[nie]ll, d. Apr. 15, 1771, in the 81st y. of his age | TPR | 109 |
| Nath[anie]ll, m. Mary **FOOT**, b. of Colchester, Nov. 5, 1778; d. Mar. 8, 1734 (sic), in New London (Probably 1834) | 2 | 18 |
| Nathaniel, s. [Stephen & Lucy], b. Nov. 26, 1778 | 1 | 163 |
| Orin, s. [David & Anna], b. May 8, 1810 | 2 | 95 |
| Prudence, d. [John & Prudence], b. Nov. 23, 1762 | 1 | 153 |
| Rhoda E., m. Ambrose **DUTTON**, Apr. 5, 1830, by Salmon Cone, V. D. M. | 2 | 221 |
| Rhoda Emeline, d. [David & Anna], b. July 27, 1807; d. May 9, 1833, in East Madison Co., N. Y. | 2 | 95 |
| Sarah, d. [John & Prudence], b. May 24, 1755 | 1 | 153 |
| Sarah, m. Israel **FOOT**, Jr., b. of Colchester, Nov. 5, 1778; d. Oct. 1, 1781 | 2 | 20 |
| Sarah, d. [John Thatcher & Louisa], b. May 9, 1784 | 2 | 73 |
| Sarah, wid. of James, d. Feb. 15, 1788 | 2 | 45 |
| Sarah, of Colchester, m. Dr. Simeon **MARSY**, of Conajoharie, Montgomery County, N. Y., Oct. 31, 1822, by Salmon Cone, V. D. M. | 2 | 156 |
| Sarah Rebecca, d. [David & Anna], b. July 21, 1823 | 2 | 95 |
| Seth, s. [Stephen & Lucy], b. June 24, 1777 | 1 | 163 |
| Sophia, w. Alfred, d. Oct. 7, 1849, ae 43 | 2 | 238 |
| Sophia Jane, w. Alfred, & d. [Henry & Sophia Worthington], d. Oct. 7, 1849, ae 43 | 2 | 172 |
| Stephen, m. Lucy **CHANDLER**, Feb. 9, 1762 | 1 | 163 |
| **OWEN**, Mary, m. Nathan **WARNER**, Mar. 21, 1751 | 1 | 80 |
| Molly, m. Roger **CASE**, [ ], 1772 | 1 | 117 |
| **PACKER**, Eliza M., m. John A. **PAYNE**, b. of Colchester, Sept. 14, 1853, by G. W. Pendleton | 3 | 58 |

| | Vol. | Page |
|---|---|---|
| **PACKER**, (cont.) | | |
| Eunice, d. John, m. John C. **LEE**, b. of Colchester, Nov. 30, 1848, by Rev. Augustus Bolles | 3 | 38 |
| Henry, m. Mary **RANDALL**, Apr. [ ], 1831, by Asa Wilcox, Elder | 2 | 235 |
| Henry, m. Susan A. **WRIGHT**, b. of Colchester, Apr. 1, 1835, by Rev. Lyman Strong | 2 | 275 |
| John, m. Eunice **RANDALL**, b. of Colchester, Mar. 15, 1829, at the house of Asa Randall, Jr., by Asa Willcox, Elder | 2 | 212 |
| **PACKWOOD**, Dimmis, m. William **WAY**, [ ]; d. Feb. 13, 1850, ae 70 | 2 | 151 |
| Dimmis Wright, d. [Joseph D. & Harriet], b. Feb. 8, 1841 | 2 | 214 |
| Harriet Smith, w. [Joseph D.], b. Nov. 17, 1803 | 2 | 214 |
| Harriet Smith, d. [Joseph D. & Harriet], b. May 13, 1835 | 2 | 214 |
| Joseph D., m. Harriet **SMITH**, Sept. 1, 1829, by Salmon Cone, V. D. M., b. Nov. 3, 1800 | 2 | 214 |
| Joseph Henry, s. [Joseph D. & Harriet], b. May 11, 1830; d. Mar. 29, 1834 | 2 | 214 |
| Mary, d. [Joseph D. & Harriet], b. Mar. 24, 1837; d. Oct. 27, 1837 | 2 | 214 |
| -----, d. [Joseph D. & Harriet], b. Dec. 1, 1845; d. Jan. 2, 1846 | 2 | 214 |
| **PAINTER**, Harriet N., of Colchester, m. Rev. Joseph S. **LORD**, of Lyme, May 17, 1836, by J. A. Copp, M. G. | 2 | 285 |
| **PALMER**, Amasa, Dea., of Mansfield, m. Sarah **DICKINSON**, of Colchester, Feb. 12, 1840, by Rev. Joel R. Arnold | 2 | 69 |
| Charles L., m. Violett C. **SMITH**, of Woodstock, Nov. 1, 1853, by Rev. Anthony Palmer | 3 | 60 |
| Elias, Jr., m. Molly **CAVERLY**, Apr. 12, 1781 | 2 | 74 |
| Elias, s. [Elias, Jr. & Molly], b. June 28, 1783 | 2 | 74 |
| Elias, m. Esther [ ] | 2 | 71 |
| Esther, m. Jonathan **MORGAN**, June 22, 1784 | 2 | 61 |
| Harriet, m. Anson **GARDINER**, b. of Colchester, Mar. 30, 1851, by Rev. G. W. Pendleton | 3 | 48 |
| John, of Colchester, m. Lucy **THOMAS**, of Lebanon, Feb. 10, 1791 | 2 | 66 |
| Joshua, s. [Elias & Esther], b. July 20, 1778 | 2 | 71 |
| Justin, s. [Elias, Jr. & Molly], b. Nov. 21, 1788 | 2 | 74 |
| Lucy, d. [John & Lucy], b. Oct. 22, 1791 | 2 | 86 |
| Lucy M., m. Henry **MORGAN**, Nov. 1, 1835, by Benj[ami]n Trumbull, J. P. | 2 | 279 |
| Phebe, m. Oliver **RANDALL**, b. of Colchester, Mar. 20, 1822, at Mr. Richard Palmer's, by Rev. William Palmer | 2 | 37 |
| Polly, d. [Elias, Jr. & Molly], b. Sept. 18, 1785; d. Aug. [ ], 1881, ae 96 y., in Frankfort, N. Y. | 2 | 74 |
| Teresa E., of East Haddam, m. Judah S. **TRACY**, of Colchester, (Westchester), May 9, 1842, by Rev. Lyman Strong | 2 | 293 |

| | Vol. | Page |
|---|---|---|
| **PALMER**, (cont.) | | |
| Thomas Randal[l], s. [Elias & Esther], b. Apr. 18, 1776 | 2 | 71 |
| Wealthy, m. Joshua **MORGAN**, June 3, 1779 | 2 | 61 |
| William H., of Salem, m. Susan H. **CLARK**, of Colchester, Mar. 28, 1838, by Rev. Andrew M. Smith | 2 | 194 |
| **PALMETER, PALMITER**, Charles, [s. Elnathan & Elisabeth], b. Feb. 15, 1751/2 | TPR | 112 |
| Ebenezer, [s. Ebenezer], b. May 10, 1723 | L-1 | 452 |
| Ebenezer, Jr., m. Mary **PALMITER**, May 5, 1748 | 1 | 103 |
| Elisabeth, [d. Elnathan & Elisabeth], b. Jan. 26, 1736/7 | TPR | 112 |
| Elisabeth, [d. Elnathan & Elisabeth], b. Dec. 11, 1741 | TPR | 112 |
| Elnathan, m. Elisabeth **SCOVELE**, Apr. 16, 1734 | TPR | 112 |
| Eunice, [d. Elnathan & Elisabeth], b. Apr. 11, 1739 | TPR | 112 |
| Hannah, d. Ebenezer, b. Aug. 22, 1720 | L-1 | 452 |
| Irene, [d. Elnathan & Elisabeth], b. May 28, 1745 | TPR | 112 |
| John, [s. Elnathan & Elisabeth], b. Jan. 7, 1747/8 | TPR | 112 |
| Josiah, s. [Ebenezer, Jr. & Mary], b. Nov. 24, 1749 | 1 | 103 |
| Mary, m. Ebenezer **PALMITER**, Jr., May 5, 1748 | 1 | 103 |
| Nathan, [s. Elnathan & Elisabeth], b. Mar. 9, 1749/50 | TPR | 112 |
| Ruth, of Colchester, m. Mat[t]hew **FORD**, Jr., of Hebron, Mar. 29, 1737 | 1 | 129 |
| Sarah, [d. Elnathan & Elisabeth], b. Mar. 18, 1734/5 | TPR | 112 |
| **PARISH**, Chauncey G., of Hartford, m. Elizabeth A. **MINER**, of Glastenbury, Oct. 10, 1842, by Rev. Rob[er]t C. Mills | 2 | 260 |
| **PARK**, Amelia A., w. [Appleton R.], d. May 7, 1844, ae 30 | 3 | 13 |
| Ann, m. Nath[anie]ll **FOOT**, Sept. [ ], 1711 | 1 | 117 |
| Anna W., d. Shubael & Abigail, b. Apr. 20, 1819 (Entry incorrect); b. May 10, 1818; d. Oct. 15, 1842 in Salem, Ct. | 2 | 141 |
| Appleton R., of Colchester, m. Amelia A. **CRAY**, of Lebanon, Oct. 12, 1841; d. Sept. 5, 1850, in Placerville, Cal., aged about 43 | 3 | 13 |
| Shubael, d. Dec. 9, 1846, ae 72, ae 72 y. 11 m. | 2 | 141 |
| **PARKHURST**, Edward C., m. Elizabeth C. **OLMSTEAD**, b. of Colchester, Oct. 11, 1842, by Rev. Daniel G. Sprague, Westchester | 2 | 206 |
| Elizabeth A., m. W[illia]m A. **WILLIAMS**, b. of Colchester, Apr. 3, 1843, by Rev. Daniel G. Sprague | 3 | 4 |
| Helen Elizabeth, d. [Edward C. & Elizabeth C.], July 29, 1843 | 2 | 206 |
| **PARSONS**, Caroline Sophia, d. [Ezekiel W. & Sally], b. Oct. 8, 1830 | 2 | 156 |
| Ezekiel W., m. Sally **CLARK**, b. of Colchester, June 17, 1822, by Salmon Cone, V. D. M. | 2 | 156 |
| Hannah, reputed d. of Jonathan, late of Northampton, m. Caleb **JEFFERIS**, Dec. 17, 1710 | L-3 | 198 |
| Hannah, m. Caleb **JEFFREYS**, Dec. 17, 1710 | TM-1 | 198 |
| Harriet W., of Colchester, m. Joseph O. **BROWN**, of New York, June 21, 1853, by Rev. Erastus Dickinson | 3 | 57 |

| | Vol. | Page |
|---|---|---|
| **PARSONS**, (cont.) | | |
| Harriet Williams, d. [Ezekiel W. & Sally], b. Mar. 3, 1829 | 2 | 156 |
| Margarett, m. Daniel **FOOT**, June 9, 1743 | 1 | 134 |
| Mary, m. William **CLARK**, May 10, 1747 | 1 | 148 |
| Mary Salter, d. [Ezekiel W. & Sally], b. Nov. 16, 1836 | 2 | 156 |
| ----, reputed d. Jonathan, late of Northampton, d. [ ] | TM-1 | 198 |
| **PATTEN**, Elizabeth Francis, d. [John & Elizabeth M.], b. Feb. 1, 1850 | 2 | 156 |
| John, b. Jan. 26, 1815, in Montville, Ct.; m. Elizabeth M. **WILLIAMS**, Feb. 3, 1846, in Salem, Conn. | 2 | 156 |
| Lucy Jane, d. [John & Elizabeth M.], b. Mar. 22, 1848, in Salem, Conn. | 2 | 156 |
| **PATTERSON**, William, d. Dec. [ ], 1769 | 1 | 85 |
| **PAYNE, PAIN**, Abby B., m. Sherwood B. **RANSOM**, b. of Colchester, Oct. 8, 1851, by Erastus Dickinson | 3 | 39 |
| Abigail, b. July 11, 1768; m. Frederick **SMITH**, Mar. 28, 1789; d. Nov. 14, 1832, ae 64 | 2 | 68 |
| Clark, of Lebanon, m. Mary Ann **DAY**, of Colchester, Feb. 10, 1828, by Avery Morgan, J. P. | 2 | 200 |
| John A., m. Eliza M. **PACKER**, b. of Colchester, Sept. 14, 1853, by G. W. Pendleton | 3 | 58 |
| Lydia Maria, m. George W. **KELLOGG**, b. of Colchester, Feb. 7, 1853, by Rev. Erastus Dickinson | 3 | 53 |
| Mary, d. Stephen & Deborah, b. Dec. 29, 1734 | TPR | 111 |
| **PEASE**, James Harvey, m. Betsey **FOOTE**, b. of Colchester, Nov. 21, 1824, by Salmon Cone, V. D. M. | 2 | 177 |
| John N., m. Emily E. **WEBSTER**, b. of Colchester, Apr. 14, 1835, by Rev. Lyman Strong | 2 | 276 |
| **PECK**, Benjamin, [s. Elias & Sarah], b. May 15, 1779 | 2 | 37 |
| Benjamin, m. Lucy **LAMB**, June 10, 1802 | 2 | 121 |
| Caroline, d. [Benjamin & Lucy], b. Sept. 4, 1815 | 2 | 121 |
| Clarissa, d. [Benjamin & Lucy], b. July 22, 1810 | 2 | 121 |
| Daniel, of East Haddam, m. Maria **OLMSTEAD**, of Colchester, Nov. 5, 1832, by Rev. Joseph Harvey | 2 | 239 |
| Elias, s. [Elias & Sarah], b. Oct. 9, 1784 | 2 | 37 |
| Elias, m. Lydia **LYMAN**, of Lebanon, Oct. 4, 1787 | 2 | 37 |
| Elias, Jr., m. Mehetable **LORD**, Mar. 2, 1808 | 2 | 122 |
| Elias Selden, s. [Elias, Jr. & Mehetable], b. Jan. 10, 1812 | 2 | 122 |
| Eliza, d. [Benjamin & Lucy], b. Aug. 10, 1804 | 2 | 121 |
| Elizabeth, [d. Elias & Sarah], b. Aug. 20, 1775 | 2 | 37 |
| Ezra, [s. Elias & Sarah], b. Dec. 12, 1781; d. Oct. 20, 1786 | 2 | 37 |
| Ezra Ely, s. [Benjamin & Lucy], b. Apr. 26, 1803 | 2 | 121 |
| Judah Lord, s. [Elias & Mehetable], b. May 15, 1809 | 2 | 122 |
| Lucy, d. [Benjamin & Lucy], b. Nov. 9, 1807 | 2 | 121 |
| Lydia, d. [Elias & Lydia], b. Aug. 27, 1789 | 2 | 37 |
| Mary, [d. Elias & Sarah], b. Apr. 25, 1777 | 2 | 37 |
| Rachel, d. [Elias & Lydia], b. June 14, 1791; d. Nov. 27, 1791 | 2 | 37 |
| Sarah, m. Abijah **JONES**, Jan. 5, 1769 | 1 | 81 |

| | Vol. | Page |
|---|---|---|
| **PECK**, (cont.) | | |
| Sarah, [d. Elias & Sarah], b. Jan. 1, 1774; d. Nov. 9, 1774 | 2 | 37 |
| Sarah, d. [Elias & Sarah], b. June 13, 1786 | 2 | 37 |
| Sarah, w. Elias, d. July 20, 1786 | 2 | 37 |
| Sarah Abigail, d. [Benjamin & Lucy], b. May 4, 1817 | 2 | 121 |
| Sophronia, d. [Benjamin & Lucy], b. Feb. 2, 1813 | 2 | 121 |
| William Henry, s. [Elias, Jr. & Mehetable], b. June 18, 1814 | 2 | 122 |
| **PEDDINGHOUSE**, John M., m. Maria T. **NEWTON**, b. of Colchester, Sept. 14, 1852, by Erastus Dickinson | 3 | 53 |
| **PELLET**, Sarah, m. Josiah **GILLETT**, Mar. 7, 1711 | L-1 | 450 |
| **PENDLETON**, Elizabeth, m. Zeba **MEECHAM**, Mar. 1, 1761 | 1 | 151 |
| Elydia, m. Elisha **BROWN**, Apr. 12, 1758 | 1 | 44 |
| **PEPOON**, [see also **JEPOON**], Elizabeth, [d. Joseph & Mary], b. Oct. 10, 1725 | L-1 | 453 |
| Jehiel, s. [Timothy & Huldah], b. Dec. 11, 1753 | 1 | 153 |
| Joseph, m. Mary **DIBELL**, Dec. 12, 1717 | L-1 | 453 |
| Joseph, [s. Joseph & Mary], b. May 20, 1719 | L-1 | 453 |
| Joseph, m. Mary **THOMAS**, Jan. 13, 1725 | L-1 | 453 |
| Joseph, [s. Joseph & his 1st w. Mary], d. Oct. 20, 1725 | L-1 | 453 |
| Joseph, d. Dec. 22, 1755 | 1 | 153 |
| Marcy, [d. Joseph & Mary], b. Sept. 25, 1727 | L-1 | 453 |
| Mary, [d. Joseph & Mary], b. Apr. 18, 1721 | L-1 | 453 |
| Mary, w. Joseph, d. Feb. 23, 1724 | L-1 | 453 |
| Mary, [d. Joseph & his 1st w. Mary], d. Oct. 23, 1725 | L-1 | 453 |
| Ruth, twin with Sarah, [d. Joseph & Mary], b. Dec. 30, 1728 | L-1 | 453 |
| Sarah, twin with Ruth, [d. Joseph & Mary], b. Dec. 30, 1728; d. Mar. 31, 1729 | L-1 | 453 |
| Silas, [s. Joseph & Mary], b. Jan. 5, 1722/3 | L-1 | 453 |
| Timothy, s. Joseph, b. Aug. 19, 1730 | L-1 | 654 |
| Timothy, m. Huldah **HUNT**, Dec. 7, 1752 | 1 | 153 |
| Timothy, s. [Timothy & Huldah], b. Sept. 27, 1755 | 1 | 153 |
| **PERKINS**, Elizabeth, of Colchester, m. Ira P. **EVEANS**, of Norwich, Sept. 27, 1842, by Rev. Joel R. Arnold | 2 | 294 |
| Sarah, of Lyme, m. Daniel **HAMILTON**, of Colchester, Sept. 6, 1759 | 1 | 20 |
| **PERRY**, Abigail, of Ashford, m. Jonathan **FULLER**, of Colchester, Apr. 23, 1761 | 1 | 153 |
| Abigail, of Colchester, m. Green **CONE**, of Chatham, Jan. 4, 1844, by Rev. Daniel G. Sprague | 3 | 8 |
| Esther, see Esther **LATHAM** | 2 | 23 |
| George, of Lebanon, m. Eliza **WELLS**, of Colchester, June 24, 1844, by Rev. Charles William Bradley | 3 | 16 |
| Katharine Hill, d. Dec. 15, 1896, at Lebanon | 2 | 74 |
| Rowland, Jr., m. Hannah **LATHAM**, July 23, 1827, by Salmon Cone, V. D. M. | 2 | 197 |
| William, of Colchester, m. Abby **ELDERKIN**, of Windham, Nov. 13, 1827, by Salmon Cone, V. D. M. | 2 | 199 |
| **PETERS**, Abigail O., d. [John T. & Sophia M.], b. Nov. 13, 1837 | 2 | 168 |

| | Vol. | Page |
|---|---|---|
| **PETERS**, (cont.) | | |
| Abigail Thompson, d. [Samuel A. & Orrel], b. May 12, 1807; d. Sept. 9, 1841, ae 34 | 2 | 86 |
| Deborah, [d. Joseph], b. May 4, 1753 | 1 | 14 |
| Ellen R., d. [John T. & Sophia M.], b. Sept. 27, 1825 | 2 | 168 |
| Ellen R., of Colchester, m. Robert D. **HOLT**, of Waterford, Ct., June 8, 1851, by Rev. George W. Pendleton | 2 | 113 |
| Henry, of Hebron, m. Emily **RUSSELL**, of Colchester, [Oct.] 15, 1843, by Rev. Rob[er]t C. Mills | 3 | 7 |
| John T., m. Sophia M. **CHESTER**, Sept. 1, 1824, by Salmon Cone, V. D. M. | 2 | 168 |
| John T., s. [John T. & Sophia M.], b. Aug. 13, 1831 | 2 | 168 |
| John Thompson, twin with Samuel Andrew, s. [Samuel A. & Orrel], b. Oct. 27, 1799 | 2 | 86 |
| Joseph, [s. Joseph], b. Jan. 5, 1756 | 1 | 14 |
| Mariah D., d. [John T. & Sophia M.], b. [ ], 1842; d. [ ], 1842 | 2 | 168 |
| Mary, m. Thomas **CARRIER**, Feb. 25, 1740/41 | 1 | 132 |
| Mary, m. Thomas **CARRIER**, s. Thomas, Feb. 25, 1740/41 | 1 | 106 |
| Mary S., d. [John T. & Sophia M.], b. July 15, 1840 | 2 | 168 |
| Orrel, w. Samuel A., d. May 20, 1836, ae 58 | 2 | 86 |
| Rebecca W., d. [John T. & Sophia M.], b. Sept. 13, 1829 | 2 | 168 |
| Samuel, s. Joseph, b. Dec. 9, 1750 | 1 | 150 |
| Samuel A., b. Jan. 17, 1770; m. Orrel **WYLES**, Jan. 17, 1799; d. Dec. 19, 1854, ae 84 y. 11 m. 2 d. | 2 | 86 |
| Samuel A., s. [John T. & Sophia M.], b. Aug. 15, 1827 | 2 | 168 |
| Samuel Andrew, twin with John Thompson, s. [Samuel A. & Orrel], b. Oct. 27, 1799; d. Sept. 9, 1806 | 2 | 86 |
| Sarah C., d. [John T. & Sophia M.], b. Nov. 7, 1833 | 2 | 168 |
| William Hugh, s. [John T. & Sophia M.], b. Nov. 2, 1844; d. Nov. 4, 1850 | 2 | 168 |
| **PETTIS**, Eunice, m. George **FOX**, Mar. [ ], 1804 | 2 | 109 |
| **PHELPS**, Abel, of Hebron, m. Betty **NICHOLS**, of Colchester, Feb. 8, 1821, by Salmon Cone, V. D. M. | 2 | 124 |
| Andrew C., of East Haddam, m. Sarah **COMSTOCK**, of Lyme, Mar. 23, 1835, by Rev. Lyman Strong | 2 | 274 |
| Ann, [d. Josiah], b. Feb. 8, 1708/9 | L-3 | 199 |
| Ann, d. Josiah, b. Feb. 8, 1708/9 | TM-1 | 199 |
| Daniell, s. Josiah, b. Dec. 17, 1704 | L-3 | 199 |
| Daniel, s. Josiah, b. Dec. 17, 1704 | TM-1 | 199 |
| Elizabeth, [d. Josiah], b. May 16, 1715 | L-3 | 199 |
| Elizabeth, d. Josiah, b. May 16, 1715 | TM-1 | 199 |
| Isaac, [s. Josiah], b. Feb. 1, 1710/11 | L-3 | 199 |
| Isaac, s. Josiah, b. Feb. 1, 1710/11 | TM-1 | 199 |
| Isaac, s. Josiah, d. Feb. 25, 1715/16 | L-1 | 654 |
| Josiah, [s. Josiah], b. Sept. [ ], 1717 | L-1 | 654 |
| Lydia, of Hebron, m. Job **STILES**, Jr., of Colchester, Mar. 30, 1758 | 1 | 22 |

| | Vol. | Page |
|---|---|---|
| **PHELPS**, (cont.) | | |
| Roger L., of Hebron, m. Elizabeth W. **STRONG**, of Colchester, May 29, 1834, by Rev. Lyman Strong | 2 | 267 |
| William, of Marlborough, m. Elizabeth **EMMONS**, of West Chester, Dec. 24, 1850, by Rev. S. D. Jewett, in West Chester | 2 | 101 |
| Zefeniah, [s. Josiah], b. Nov. 7, 1712 | L-3 | 199 |
| Zepheniah, s. Josiah, b. Nov. 7, 1712 | TM-1 | 199 |
| Zefaniah, [s. Josiah], d. Apr. 10, 1716 | L-1 | 654 |
| **PHILLIPS**, Barbara, m. Stephen **BENJAMIN**, Mar. 7, 1799; d. Mar. 14, 1846, ae 67 | 2 | 27 |
| **PHILOMORE**, [see also **FILLMORE**], Benj[ami]n, m. Almira **FRINK**, b. of Lebanon, Nov. 11, 1823, at the house of the subscriber, by Rev. William Palmer | 2 | 104 |
| **PIERCE, PEIRCE**, Alfred B., m. Harriet **WORTHINGTON**, b. of Colchester, May 25, 1831, by Rev. Lyman Strong | 2 | 231 |
| Emily, of Utica, N. Y., m. Otis **WHIPPLE**, Mar. 13, 1827, by Salmon Cone, V. D. M. | 2 | 193 |
| Emily, of Lebanon, m. Elias M. **WORTHINGTON**, of Colchester, Nov. 8, 1832 | 2 | 272 |
| Emily, m. Elias M. **WORTHINGTON**, Nov. 8, 1832 | 2 | 283 |
| Eunice S., of Colchester, m. Jesse F. **TAINTOR**, of Venice, Ohio, July 28, 1834, by Rev. Lyman Strong | 2 | 268 |
| Marion B., m. Nelson **BUTTON**, b. of Colchester, Oct. 12, 1851, by Rev. Roger Allison | 2 | 71 |
| **PINEO, PYNEO**, Lydia, of Lebanon, m. Eliphalet **GILLET**, Mar. 27, 1760 | 2 | 45 |
| Polly (Mary?), m. Rev. Salmon Cone, Jan. 25, 1792; d. Mar. 2, 1802 | 2 | 69 |
| **PITTS**, Sarah, m. Nathaniel **INGRAHAM**, Sept. 25, or 26, 1745 | 1 | 55 |
| **PLACE**, Esther, m. Noah **CHAPMAN**, [ ], at New London | 1 | 22 |
| **POHEAGIN**, Jenney, d. Marcy, Dec. 24, 1756 | 1 | 88 |
| **POLLY**, Tabitha, m. Jesse **CRAW**, Apr. 10, 1809 | 2 | 62 |
| **POMEROY, PUMERY, PUMROY**, Abigail, [d. Joseph, Jr. & Elisabeth], b. June 2, 1736 | L-3 | 458 |
| Charles, [s. Noah & Lurana], b. Apr. 22, 1749 | 1 | 34 |
| Daniell, [s. Noah & Elizabeth], b. Oct. 13, 1727 | L-1 | 444 |
| Elizabeth, m. Joshua **SMITH**, Jan. 11, 1750 | 1 | 132 |
| Hannah, m. John **NORTHAM**, May 9, 1721 | L-1 | 449 |
| Hannah, d. Joseph & Elisabeth, b. Apr. 28, 1734 | L-3 | 453 |
| Hannah, [d. Joseph, Jr. & Elisabeth], b. Apr. 28, 1734 | L-3 | 458 |
| Joseph, m. Sarra **BEEBE**, Aug. 2, 1727 | L-1 | 399 |
| Joseph, Jr., m. Elisabeth **RANDALL**, Dec. 25 1728 | L-3 | 458 |
| Joseph, [s. Joseph, Jr. & Elisabeth], b. Aug. 17, 1731 | L-3 | 458 |
| Larana, see also Lurana | | |
| Larana, m. Martin **WELLS**, [ ], 1767; d. May 12, 1818, ae 66 | 2 | 59 |
| Louisa, m. John Thatcher **OTIS**, Sept. 29, 1782; d. Dec. 3, | | |

| | Vol. | Page |
|---|---|---|
| **POMEROY, PUMERY, PUMROY**, (cont.) | | |
| 1838, ae 77 | 2 | 73 |
| Lovisa, [d. Noah & Lurana], b. Sept. 3, 1761 | 1 | 34 |
| Lurana, [d. Noah & Lurana], b. May 22, 1752 | 1 | 34 |
| Lurana, see also Larana | | |
| Mary, of Summors, m. Amos **KELLOGG**, June 28, 1781 | 2 | 49 |
| Noah, [s.] Joseph & Hannah, b. May 19, 1700 | L-1 | 450 |
| Noah, m. Elizabeth **STERLING**, Dec. 16, 1724 | L-1 | 444 |
| Noah, [s. Noah & Elizabeth], b. Oct. 8, 1725 | L-1 | 444 |
| Noah, m. Elizabeth **RANDALL**, Dec. 25, 1728 | L-3 | 7 |
| Noah, m. Lurana **NORTHAM**, Apr. 24, 1748 | 1 | 34 |
| Noah, [s. Noah & Lurana], b. Aug. 18, 1754 | 1 | 34 |
| Noah, Jr., m. Rhoda **WELLS**, Jan. 12, 1780; d. Sept. 17, 1798 | 2 | 96 |
| Noah W., m. Lavinia F. **FISK**, Sept. 14, 1812 (Perhaps "**FISH**"] | 2 | 137 |
| Noah Wells, s. [Noah, Jr. & Rhoda], b. Dec. 2, 1793 | 2 | 96 |
| Sarra, w. Joseph, d. Sept. 3, 1728 | L-1 | 399 |
| -----, d. Joseph, b. Feb. 29, [ ]; d. Dec. latter end, [ ] | L-3 | 7 |
| **PORTER**, Alanson, Dr., of Williamstown, m. Celinda L. **BULKELEY**, of Colchester, Oct. 5, 1823, by Salmon Cone, V. D. M. | 2 | 140 |
| Ann, m. Elisha **PRATT**, Feb. 27, 1735/6 | L-3 | 451 |
| Celinda B., m. Russell **CHAPMAN**, Feb. 22, 1830, by Salmon Cone, V. D. M. | 2 | 219 |
| Dan[iel], of Columbia, m. Mary **NILES**, of Colchester, Nov. 4, 1848 | 2 | 282 |
| Martha, m. Moses **ROWLEE**, Sept. [ ], 1707 | L-1 | 445 |
| Tabitha, of Hebron, m. William **LORD**, of Colchester, Mar. 21, 1745 | 1 | 45 |
| **POST**, Jedediah A., of Hebron, m. Sophia J. **FOOT**, of Colchester, May 31, 1843, by Rev. Henry Forbush | 3 | 5 |
| **POTTER**, James N., of Colchester, m. Lydia **BABCOCK**, of Hebron, Mar. 27, 1850, at Hebron, by Rev. George W. Pendleton | 3 | 1 |
| John A., m. Susan T. **WALBRIDGE**, b. of Bozrah, Apr. 4, 1852, by Rev. George W. Pendleton | 3 | 50 |
| Lucy, b. July 23, 1764; m. Samuel **HOLMES**, [ ]; d. | 2 | 119 |
| **PRATT, PRAT**, Abigaiel, [d. Joseph & Sarah], b. Nov. 30, 1702 | L-3 | 195 |
| Abigail, d. Joseph [& Sarah], b. Nov. 30, 1702 | TM-1 | 195 |
| Abigail, [d. Azariah & Hannah], b. Jan. 8, 1733/4 | L-1 | 654 |
| Abigail, d. [Daniel, Jr. & Abigail], b. Feb. 1, 1760 | 1 | 133 |
| Abigail, w. [Daniel], d. Apr. 8, 1791 | 1 | 136 |
| Abigail, 2d w. of Lt. Daniel], d. Apr. 8, 1791 | 2 | 80 |
| Abijah, s. [Daniel, Jr. & Abigail], b. Apr. 21, 1758 | 1 | 133 |
| Ann, [d. Daniell & Mary], b. Sept. 1, 1739 | 1 | 136 |
| Ann, d. [Elisha], b. Sept. 5, 1740 | 1 | 146 |
| Anna, m. Aaron **GILLETT**, Mar. 31, 1757 | 1 | 126 |
| Anne, [d. John & Hephzibah, b. Mar. 6, 1772; d. Feb. 9, 1778 | 1 | 96 |

| | Vol. | Page |
|---|---|---|
| **PRATT, PRAT**, (cont.) | | |
| Anne, [d. John & Hephzibah], b. Apr. 16, 1778 | 1 | 96 |
| Anne, m. Aaron **GILLET**, [ ] | 2 | 42 |
| Asariah, [s. Joseph & Sarah], b. Dec. 7, 1699 | L-3 | 195 |
| Azariah, s. Joseph [& Sarah], b. Dec. 7, 1699 | TM-1 | 195 |
| Azariah, m. Hannah **COLEMAN**, May 5, 1725 | L-1 | 654 |
| Azariah, [s. Azariah & Hannah], b. Feb. 25, 1729/30 | L-1 | 654 |
| Daniell, [s. Joseph & Sarah], b. May 26, 1710 | L-3 | 195 |
| Daniel, s. Joseph [& Sarah], b. May 26, 1710 | TM-1 | 196 |
| Daniell, m. Mary **SWIFT**, Oct. [ ], 1733 | 1 | 136 |
| Daniel, s. [Daniell & Mary], b. July 7, 1734 | 1 | 136 |
| Daniel, Jr., m. Abigail **BIGELOW**, Mar. 24, 1755 | 1 | 133 |
| Daniel, s. [Daniel, Jr. & Abigail], b. Aug. 22, 1756 | 1 | 133 |
| Daniel, m. Abigail **WHITE**, wid., July [ ], 1776 | 1 | 136 |
| Daniel, s. John, b. Mar. 1, 1780 | 2 | 15 |
| Daniel, d. Dec. 2, 1795, ae 86 | 1 | 136 |
| Daniel, Lieut., d. Dec. 2, 1795, ae 86 | 2 | 80 |
| David, [s. Elisha & Ann], b. Apr. 30, 1738 | L-3 | 451 |
| David, s. [Elisha], b. Apr. 30, 1738 | 1 | 146 |
| David, [s. John & Hephzibah], b. Mar. 1, 1780 | 1 | 96 |
| Dimmis, d. [Daniell & Mary], b. Feb. 5, 1750/1 | 1 | 136 |
| Eleanor, d. Azariah & Hannah, b. Feb. 12, 1738/9 | 1 | 126 |
| Eli, [s. John & Hephzibah], b. Oct. 4, 1782 | 1 | 96 |
| Elijah, m. Mary **WATERS**, Oct. 22, 1778 | 2 | 22 |
| Elisha, [s. Joseph & Sarah], b. Aug. 10, 1707 | L-3 | 195 |
| Elisha, s. Jos[eph & Sarah], b. Aug. 10, 1707 | TM-1 | 195 |
| Elisha, [s. Elisha & Ann], b. Jan. 25, 1735/6 | L-3 | 451 |
| Elisha, m. Ann **PORTER**, Feb. 27, 1735/6 | L-3 | 451 |
| Elisha, of Colchester, m. Mary **SPAF[F]ORD**, of Lebanon, May 3, 1758 | 1 | 155 |
| Elisha, s. [Elisha & Mary], b. Feb. 9, 1759; d. Mar. 22, 1759 | 1 | 155 |
| Elisha, 2d, s. [Elisha & Mary], b. May 26, 1760 | 1 | 155 |
| Elisha, s. [Daniel, Jr. & Abigail], b. Feb. 10, 1774 | 1 | 133 |
| Elizabeth, d. [Elisha & Mary], b. July 25, 1762 | 1 | 155 |
| Han[n]ah, m. Richard **SKIN[N[ER**, Nov. 24, 1708 | L-1 | 799 |
| Hannah, [d. Azariah & Hannah], b. June 8, 1726 | L-1 | 654 |
| Hepzibah, [d. John & Hephzibah], b. Aug. 23, 1774 | 1 | 96 |
| Isaac, s. [Daniel, Jr. & Abigail], b. Mar. 10, 1769 | 1 | 133 |
| Jared, s. [Elisha], b. Mar. 28, 1743/4 | 1 | 146 |
| Joel, s. [Elisha], b. Sept. 26, 1746 | 1 | 146 |
| John, [s. Daniell & Mary], b. Dec. 14, 1741 | 1 | 136 |
| John, of Colchester, m. Hephzibah **ELY**, of Lyme, May 13, 1771 | 1 | 96 |
| John, [s. John & Hephzibah], b. Apr. 19, 1776 | 1 | 96 |
| Joseph, m. Sarah **COLYER**, July 22, 1697 | L-3 | 195 |
| Joseph, m. Sarah **COLYER**, July 22, 1697 | TM-1 | 195 |
| Joseph, [s. Joseph & Sarah], b. June 30, 1698 | L-3 | 195 |
| Joseph, s. Joseph [& Sarah], b. June 30, 1698 | TM-1 | 195 |

| | Vol. | Page |
|---|---|---|
| **PRATT, PRAT**, (cont.) | | |
| Joseph, m. Editha **KELLOGG**, Mar. 2, 1727 | L-1 | 444 |
| Joseph, m. Editha **KELLOGG**, Mar. 2, 1727 | L-3 | 6 |
| Joseph, [s. Joseph & Editha], b. Aug. 2, 1732 | L-3 | 6 |
| Joseph, s. Joseph, Jr., b. Aug. 2, 1732 | TPR | 109 |
| Joshua, [s. Elisha], b. June 18, 1742 | 1 | 146 |
| Lois, [d. Joseph & Editha], b. Dec. 13, 1727 | L-1 | 444 |
| Lois, [d. Joseph & Editha], b. Dec. 13, 1727 | L-3 | 6 |
| Lucresee, [d. Azariah & Hannah], b. Feb. 8, 1727/8 | L-1 | 654 |
| Lydiah, [d. Joseph & Editha], b. Mar. 3, 1730 | L-3 | 6 |
| Lydia, [d. Elisha], b. May 27, 1751 | 1 | 146 |
| Lydia, d. [Daniel, Jr. & Abigail], b. Oct. 13, 1764 | 1 | 133 |
| Marcy, [d. Daniell & Mary], b. Oct. 17, 1738; d. June 3, 1741 | 1 | 136 |
| Marcy, d. [Daniell & Mary], b. Mar. 29, 1746 | 1 | 136 |
| Mary, [d. Daniell & Mary], b. Aug. 5, 1736; d. [ ] 10, 1741 | 1 | 136 |
| Mary, d. [Daniell & Mary], b. Jan. 14, 1743/4 | 1 | 136 |
| Mary, d. [Daniel, Jr. & Abigail], b. June 10, 1771 | 1 | 133 |
| Mary, [d. John & Hephzibah], b. Dec. 17, 1786 | 1 | 96 |
| Mary, of Colchester, m. Ammi **CARRIER**, of Marlborough, Jan. 9, 1825, by Jacob Seales, V. D. M. | 2 | 175 |
| Mary, w. [Daniell], d. [ ] | 1 | 136 |
| Mary Russ, d. [Elijah & Mary], b. Aug. 7, 1779 | 2 | 22 |
| Molly, d. [Daniel, Jr. & Abigail], b. Feb. 18, 1767; d. Feb. 5, 1771 | 1 | 133 |
| Peter, [s. Joseph & Editha], b. Feb. 8, 1734/5 | L-3 | 6 |
| Phebe, [d. John & Hephzibah], b. Nov. 23, 1784 | 1 | 96 |
| Rube, d. [Daniel, Jr. & Abigail], b. July 14, 1762 | 1 | 133 |
| Ruth, [d. Joseph & Sarah], b. Mar. 16, 1705/6 | L-3 | 195 |
| Ruth, d. Joseph [& Sarah], b. Mar. 16, 1705/6 | TM-1 | 195 |
| Ruth, d. [Daniell & Mary], b. Mar. 23, 1754 | 1 | 136 |
| Sarah, d. Jos[eph & Sarah], b. Aug. [ ], 1713 | TM-1 | 196 |
| Sarah, w. Sergt. Joseph, d. Nov. 20, 1730 | L-3 | 456 |
| Sarah, [d. Azariah & Hannah], b. Oct. 16, 1732 | L-1 | 654 |
| Sarah, m. Moses **YEOMANS**, June 11, 1738 | 1 | 139 |
| Zilpha, d. [Daniell & Mary], b. Oct. 11, 1756 | 1 | 136 |
| ----, [s. John & Hephzibah], b. Apr. 12, 1789; d. Apr. 15, 1789 | 1 | 96 |
| **PRESCOTT**, Lewis, of Medway, Mass., m. Eunice B. **NORCROSS**, of Colchester, Oct. 9, 1853, by G. W. Pendleton | 3 | 58 |
| **PROCTER**, Aquilla, of Killingly, m. Polly **FREEMAN**, of Colchester, May 17, 1829, by Salmon Cone, V. D. M. | 2 | 212 |
| **PUMERY, PUMROY**, [see under **POMEROY**] | | |
| **PURPLE**, Levi, of East Haddam, m. [ ] **JOHNSON**, of Norwich, Apr. 26, [1847], by Rev. S. D. Jewett, Westchester | 3 | 32 |
| Sarah, m. Bond **BIGELOW**, Apr. 21, 1772 | 2 | 15 |
| **QUAS**, Gideon, m. Alice **WATERS**, [ ] | 2 | 47 |

| | Vol. | Page |
|---|---|---|
| **QUAS**, (cont.) | | |
| James, s. [Gideon & Alice], b. June 8, 1794 | 2 | 47 |
| James, m. Sally **FREEMAN**, b. of Colchester, Sept. 17, 1821, by Salmon Cone, V. D. M. | 2 | 110 |
| Polly, d. [Gideon & Alice], b. June 25, 1796 | 2 | 47 |
| **QUASH**, Abby Ann, d. [James & Clarissa], b. Nov. 4, 1816 | 2 | 110 |
| Charles James, s. [Charles M. & Lucretia M.], b. Sept. 17, 1843 | 2 | 122 |
| Charles M., m. Mary Ann **EVANS**, b. of Colchester, Mar. 10, 1850, by Rev. Albert F. Park | 2 | 122 |
| Charles M., m. Lucretia M. **FRANCIS**, b. of Colchester, [ ], by Rev. Joel R. Arnold | 2 | 122 |
| Charles Mansfield, s. [James & Clarissa], b. Aug. 16, 1815 | 2 | 110 |
| Clarissa, [w. James], d. Oct. 4, 1819 | 2 | 110 |
| Gideon, m. Hannah **COUZZENS**, b. of Colchester, Dec. 27, 1829, by Amhurst D. Scoville, J. P. | 2 | 217 |
| Hannah, m. Elisha **BECKWITH**, b. of Colchester, Jan. 4, 1846, by Rev. M. P. Alderman | 3 | 26 |
| James, m. Clarissa **FREEMAN**, Oct. 23, 1814 | 2 | 110 |
| Joannah, d. [Charles M. & Lucretia M.], b. Mar. 2, 1848 | 2 | 122 |
| Lucretia M., [w. Charles M.], d. Oct. 3, 1849, ae 29 | 2 | 122 |
| Sophia Emily, d. [James & Clarissa], b. May 3, 1818 | 2 | 110 |
| Sophia Emily, m. Griswold **APES**, b. of Colchester, Sept. 13, 1835, by Rev. Lyman Strong | 2 | 279 |
| -----, s. Charles [M. & Mary Ann], b. [ ]; d. Oct. 22, 1851, aged about 2 d. | 2 | 122 |
| **QUASHEE**, Ruth, d. Cato & Pegg, b. Mar. 27, 1780 | 2 | 12 |
| Simon, s. [Cato & Pegg], b. Dec. 31, 1786 | 2 | 12 |
| Tamor, d. [Cato & Pegg], b. Apr. 15, 1782 | 2 | 12 |
| **QUITERFIELD, QUITFIELD, KITERFIELD, AQUITFIELD, QUITTIFIELD, KITHOPHELL**, Abner, [s., Richard & Lydia], b. Aug. 27, 1732 | TPR | 110 |
| Amasa, [s. John], d. July 7, 1741 | 1 | 133 |
| Amasai, [s. John & Elizabeth], b. Dec. 11, 1734 | TPR | 110 |
| Asa, [s. Benjamin & [E]unice], b. June 28, 1733 | L-3 | 9 |
| Asa, brother of Eunice **CLARK**, w. Noah **CLARK**, d. Mar. 5, 1755 | 1 | 144 |
| Benjamin, s. Clemenc, b. Apr. 11, 1704 | L-3 | 196 |
| Benjamin, s. Clement, b. Apr. 11, 1704 | TM-1 | 196 |
| Benjamin, m. [E]unice **KELLOGG**, July 11, 1728 | L-3 | 9 |
| Benjamin, [s. Benjamin & [E]unice], b. Apr. 22, 1729 | L-3 | 9 |
| Bettey, d. [Jacob & Elizabeth], b. July 21, 1768 | 2 | 12 |
| Colings, s. Clement, b. Nov. 9, 1720 | L-3 | 196 |
| Colings, s. Clement, b. Nov. 9, 1720 | TM-1 | 196 |
| Elizabeth, [d. Clemenc], b. June 3, 1709 | L-3 | 196 |
| Elizabeth, d. Clement, b. June 3, 1709 | TM-1 | 196 |
| Elizabeth, m. John **DUGLES**, Jan. 27, 1728 | L-3 | 9 |
| Erastus, s. [Jacob & Elizabeth], b. Mar. 24, 1776 | 2 | 12 |

| | Vol. | Page |
|---|---|---|
| **QUITERFIELD, QUITFIELD, KITERFIELD, AQUITFIELD, QUITTIFIELD, KITHOPHELL,** (cont.) | | |
| Eunice, [d. Benjamin & [E]unice], b. Feb. 26, 1730 | L-3 | 9 |
| Eunice, d. Benja[min] & Eunice, b. Feb. 26, 1730/31 | TPR | 108 |
| Eunice, m. Noah **CLARK**, Dec. 3, 1752 | 1 | 144 |
| Eunice, d. [Jacob & Elizabeth], b. Oct. 22, 1761 | 2 | 12 |
| Hannah, [d. Benjamin & [E]unice], b. Nov. 3, 1737; d. Dec. 10, 1738 | L-3 | 9 |
| Israell, [s. Benjamin & [E]unice], b. Aug. 28, 1735 | L-3 | 9 |
| Jacob, s. Benjamin & Eunice, b. Apr. 12, 1741 | 1 | 141 |
| Jacob, s. Benjamin & Eunice, b. Apr. 12, 1741; m. Elizabeth **KILLBORN**, Oct. 25, 1759; d. May 28, 1777 | 2 | 12 |
| Jacob, m. Elizabeth **KILLBORN**, Oct. 25, 1759 | 1 | 163 |
| Jacob, s. [Jacob & Elizabeth], b. Feb. 14, 1764; d. Mar. 14, 1766 | 2 | 12 |
| Jacob, 2d, s. [Jacob & Elizabeth], b. June 16, 1773; d. Sept. 27, 1776 | 2 | 12 |
| John, [s. Clemenc], b. Sept. 3, 1711 | L-3 | 196 |
| John, s. Clement, b. Sept. 3, 1711 | TM-1 | 196 |
| John, m. Elisabeth **KILBORN**, Dec. 7, 1733 | TPR | 110 |
| Lois, d. [Jacob & Elizabeth], b. Oct. 26, 1770 | 2 | 12 |
| Lucy, d. [Richard], b. Mar. 16, 1744 | 1 | 104 |
| Mary, [d. John], b. Feb. 7, 1743/4 | 1 | 133 |
| Mehetable, d. Richard, b. Mar. 26, 1739 | 1 | 104 |
| Mercy, [d. John], b. Nov. 16, 1741 | 1 | 133 |
| Rhoda, d. [Jacob & Elizabeth], b. Apr. 13, 1766 | 2 | 12 |
| Richard, [s. Clemenc], b. Sept. 27, 1706 | L-3 | 196 |
| Richard, s. [Clement], b. Sept. 27, 1706 | TM-1 | 196 |
| Richard, m. Lydia **CRIPEN**, Mar. 1, 1732 | TPR | 110 |
| Sarah, d. [John], b. Apr. 13, 1739 | 1 | 133 |
| -----, s. [Richard & Lydia], b. Dec. 22, 1733, st. b. | TPR | 110 |
| -----, s. [Jacob & Elizabeth], b. Aug. 14, 1760; d. Aug. 14, 1760 | 1 | 163 |
| **QUITLAND**, Thankfull, d. [Richard], b. May 15, 1741 | 1 | 132 |
| **RAND**, Elizabeth A., m. James C. **BEEBE**, b. of Middletown, Dec. 9, 1838, by Rev. Lyman Strong | 2 | 235 |
| Frederick P., of Hartford, m. Harriet **WAY**, of Colchester, Sept. 30, 1833, by Rev. Lyman Strong | 2 | 258 |
| **RANDALL, RANALL**, Amos, m. Sarah **KILLBORN**, Mar. 27, 1776 | 2 | 69 |
| Amos, s. [Amos & Sarah], b. June 4, 1778 | 2 | 69 |
| Asa, Jr., m. Mary **WILLIAMS**, b. of Colchester, Dec. 25, 1836, by Rev. Andrew M. Smith | 2 | 292 |
| Catharine, [d. Rufus & Margaret], b. Sept. 21, 1761 | 1 | 32 |
| Dauid, [s. Enos], b. Aug. 21, 1724 | L-1 | 452 |
| Eleanor, m. David **WYLES**, June [ ], 1775 | 2 | 68 |
| Elias, m. Mary **MEACHAM**, Apr. 11, 1756 | 1 | 37 |
| Elias, s. Benjamin, d. Mar. 20, 1799, ae 64 y. & 1/2 | 2 | 61 |

| | Vol. | Page |
|---|---|---|
| **RANDALL, RANALL,** (cont.) | | |
| Elizabeth, m. Noah **PUMERY**, Dec. 25, 1728 | L-3 | 7 |
| Elisabeth, m. Joseph **PUMERY**, Jr. Dec. 25, 1728 | L-3 | 458 |
| Esther, [d. Rufus & Margaret], b. Dec. 4, 1758 | 1 | 32 |
| Eunice, m. John **PACKER**, b. of Colchester, Mar. 15, 1829, at the house of Asa Randall, Jr., by Asa Willcox, Elder | 2 | 212 |
| George, of Salem, m. Almeda **THOMAS**, of Colchester, Jan. 30, 1853, by Rev. G. W. Pendleton | 3 | 54 |
| Hannah, d. Enos, b. Nov. 1, 1717 | L-1 | 452 |
| Henrietta, d. [Amos & Sarah], b. Oct. 13, 1791 | 2 | 69 |
| Humility, m. Amos **RATHBUN**, s. John, Feb. 12, 1758 | 1 | 107 |
| Joseph, [s. Enos], b. Aug. 5, 1721 | L-1 | 452 |
| Mary, m. John **TENNANT**, Feb. 28, 1760 | 1 | 179 |
| Mary, m. Henry **PACKER**, Apr. [ ], 1831, by Asa Wilcox, Elder | 2 | 235 |
| Nancy, d. [Amos & Sarah], b. Nov. 16, 1783 | 2 | 69 |
| Oliver, m. Phebe **PALMER**, b. of Colchester, Mar. 20, 1822, at Mr. Richard Palmer's, by Rev. William Palmer | 2 | 37 |
| Polly, d. [Amos & Sarah], b. Apr. 13, 1789 | 2 | 69 |
| Ralph, m. Caroline **BROWN**, May 4, 1826, by Rev. Tubal Wakefield | 2 | 189 |
| Rufus, of Colchester, m. Margaret **WHITMAN**, of Norwich, Dec. 6, 1757 | 1 | 32 |
| Russell, s. [Amos & Sarah], b. Sept. 19, 1786 | 2 | 69 |
| Ruth, m. Thomas **GATES**, Dec. 29, 1748 | 1 | 125 |
| Sally, d. [Amos & Sarah], b. [ ] 12, 1781 | 2 | 69 |
| **RANSOM**, Alce, [d. Robert], b. Sept. 6, 1719 | L-3 | 196 |
| Alice, d. Rob[er]t, b. Sept. 6, 1719 | TM-1 | 196 |
| Alice, [d. James & Sarah], b. Sept. 20, 1743 | 1 | 51 |
| Alice, [d. Amos & Anna], b. Oct. 29, 1765 | 1 | 39 |
| Ellice, [d. Peleg], b. Aug. [ ], 1768 | 1 | 88 |
| Alice, d. [Asahel & Sophia], b. Dec. 5, 1785 | 2 | 51 |
| Alpheas, m. Sarah **JONES**, Jan. 29, 1767 | 1 | 84 |
| Alpheas, [s. Alpheas & Sarah], b. Nov. 30, 1769 | 1 | 84 |
| Ama, [d. Amos & Ama], b. Feb. 15, 1755 | 1 | 39 |
| Amasa, [s. James & Sarah], b. Aug. 13, 1741 | 1 | 51 |
| Amasa, m. Betsey **BILLINGS**, of Montville, Sept. 13, 1810 (Jr.) | 2 | 138 |
| Amia, [d. Peleg], b. Apr. 19, 1750 | 1 | 88 |
| Amos, [s. Robert], b. Feb. 17, 1727 | L-3 | 196 |
| Amos, s. Robert, b. Feb. 17, 1727 | TM-1 | 196 |
| Amos, m. Ama **COMSTOCK**, Apr. 12, 1750 | 1 | 39 |
| Amos, [s. Amos & Ama], b. Dec. 4, 1760 | 1 | 39 |
| Amy, [d. Robert & Alice], b. Aug. 2, 1732 | TPR | 109 |
| Asahel, [s. James & Sarah], b. May 30, 1746 | 1 | 51 |
| Asahel, m. Sophia **LITTLE**, Jan. 15, 1778 | 2 | 51 |
| Asahel, s. [Asahel & Sophia], b. Feb. 13, 1784 | 2 | 51 |
| Augustus T., m. Harriet C. **HYDE**, b. of Colchester, Nov. | | |

| | Vol. | Page |
|---|---|---|
| **RANSOM**, (cont.) | | |
| 27, 1850, by Rev. G. W. Pendleton | 2 | 185 |
| Azaal, s. [Newton & Sarah], b. Jan. 3, 1756 | 1 | 143 |
| Bettey, [d. James & Betty], b. July 5, 1768 | 1 | 55 |
| Calvin, twin with Luther, [s. Newton & Sarah], b. June 19, 1758 | 1 | 143 |
| Daniel, [s. Peleg], b. July 2, 1766 | 1 | 88 |
| Dimis, m. Stephen **DAY**, Mar. 27, 1766 | 1 | 98 |
| Eleaner, d. [Newton & Sarah], b. June 22, 1750; d. Nov. 13, 1750 | 1 | 143 |
| Eleaner, 2d, d. [Newton & Sarah], b. [ ] | 1 | 143 |
| Elias, [s. James & Sarah], b. Feb. 17, 1736/7 | 1 | 51 |
| Elias, m. Sarah **BIGELOW**, Nov. 19, 1761 | 1 | 94 |
| Elias, [s. Elias & Sarah], b. Aug. 18, 1762 | 1 | 94 |
| Elijah, [s. James & Sarah], b. June 12, 1751 | 1 | 51 |
| Elisha, s. [Newton & Sarah], b. Dec. 24, 1753 | 1 | 143 |
| Eliza M., m. Justin E. **DAY**, Nov. 10, [ ], by Rev. Lyman Strong | 2 | 282 |
| Elisabeth, d. Robert & Alice, b. May 1, 1729 | TPR | 109 |
| Elizabeth, [d. Peleg], b. Feb. 5, 1747 | 1 | 88 |
| Ephraim, s. [Asahel & Sophia], b. [ ] | 2 | 51 |
| Ezekiel, s. [Newton & Sarah], b. Jan. 3, 1745; d. Nov. 14, 1760 | 1 | 143 |
| Ezekiel, 2d, s. [Newton & Sarah], b. Oct. 1, 1763 | 1 | 143 |
| Frances A., of Colchester, m. Henry G. **RANSOM**, of East Haddam, May 31, 1848, by Rev. J. R. Arnold | 3 | 36 |
| George, s. [Asahel & Sophia], b. Sept. 9, 1792 | 2 | 51 |
| Harris, [s. Peleg], b. Aug. 18, 1755 | 1 | 88 |
| Henry G., of East Haddam, m. Frances A. **RANSOM**, of Colchester, May 31, 1848, by Rev. J. R. Arnold | 3 | 36 |
| Ichabod, s. [Newton & Sarah], b. June 2, 1760 | 1 | 143 |
| Irenus, [s. James & Betty], b. May 5, 1766 | 1 | 55 |
| Israel, [s. James & Sarah], b. Oct. 26, 1753; d. June 4, 1758 | 1 | 51 |
| Israel, [s. James & Betty], b. July 21, 1760 | 1 | 55 |
| Jabez, s. [Newton & Sarah], b. Dec. 24, 1746 | 1 | 143 |
| James, [s. Robert], b. Mar. 13, 1713 | L-3 | 196 |
| James, s. Rob[er]t, b. Mar. 13, 1713 | TM-1 | 196 |
| James, m. Sarah **TREADWAY**, May 22, 1735 | 1 | 51 |
| James, [s. James & Sarah], b. Jan. 16, 1738/9 | 1 | 51 |
| James, m. Betty **LOUIS**, Dec. 15, 1757 | 1 | 55 |
| James, [s. James & Betty], b. Nov. 17, 1761 | 1 | 55 |
| James, d. Mar. 3, 1773 | 1 | 51 |
| Jerusha, [d. James & Betty], b. July 13, 1779 | 1 | 55 |
| Joel, [s. James & Betty], b. July 6, 1770 | 1 | 55 |
| John, s. Robert, b. Nov. 13, 1709 | L-3 | 196 |
| John, s. Robert, b. Nov. 13, 1709 | TM-1 | 196 |
| John, m. Bethia **LEWIS**, Apr. 6, 1732 | TPR | 111 |
| John, s. [Newton & Sarah], b. Nov. 11, 1748 | 1 | 143 |

| | Vol. | Page |
|---|---|---|
| **RANSOM**, (cont.) | | |
| Jonathan, [s. Elias & Sarah], b. Sept. 13, 1767 | 1 | 94 |
| Joshua, [s. Robert], b. May 3, 1715 | L-3 | 196 |
| Joshua, s. Rob[er]t, b. May 3, 1715 | TM-1 | 196 |
| Justin, s. [Asahel & Sophia], b. Apr. 8, 1780; d. Mar. 30, 1851, ae 71 | 2 | 51 |
| Loice, [d. James & Sarah], b. Aug. 16, 1748 | 1 | 51 |
| Lois, m. Ephraim **LEWIS**, Aug. 15, 1765 | 1 | 23 |
| Lois, [d. James & Betty], b. [ ] | 1 | 55 |
| Louisa, of Colchester, m. Roger **SOUTHWORTH**, of Mansfield, Jan. 21, 1834, by Rev. Lyman Strong | 2 | 262 |
| Lucretia, [d. Peleg], b. June 5, 1755 (?) | 1 | 88 |
| Lucretia W., m. John R. **WATROUS**, Mar. 30, 1829 | 2 | 41 |
| Lucy, [d. Alpheas & Sarah], b. Jan. 12, 1768 | 1 | 84 |
| Luther, twin with Calvin, [s. Newton & Sarah], b. June 19, 1758 | 1 | 143 |
| Lydia, [d. Elias & Sarah], b. Dec. 2, 1765 | 1 | 94 |
| Margaret, [d. Amos & Ama], b. Mar. 26, 1758 | 1 | 39 |
| Martha, [d. Amos & Ama], b. Apr. 19, 1751 | 1 | 39 |
| Martha, m. Samuel **LOMIS**, Nov. 15, 1770 | 1 | 152 |
| Martha, m. Samuel **LOMIS**, Nov. 15, 1770; d. Sept. 26, 1839, ae 88 | 2 | 24 |
| Martha, m. Samuel **LOMIS**, Nov. 15, 1773 | 2 | 2 |
| Mary, [d. Robert], b. Aug. 30, 1711 | L-3 | 196 |
| Mary, d. Rob[er]t, b. Aug. 30, 1711 | TM-1 | 196 |
| Mary, m. Samuel **KNIGHT**, Nov. 29, 1716 | L-1 | 399 |
| Mary, [d. Amos & Ama], b. Oct. 15, 1753 | 1 | 39 |
| Mary, m. Gilbert **FREEMAN**, b. of Colchester, June 15, 1845, by George Kay, J. P. | 3 | 20 |
| Miriam, [d. Peleg], b. Apr. 18, 1758 | 1 | 88 |
| Nath[anie]ll, [s. Amos & Ama], b. Sept. 15, 1763 | 1 | 39 |
| Nathaniel P., of Colchester, m. Sally **SPENCER**, of East Haddam, Dec. 12, 1799 | 2 | 73 |
| Newton, [s. Robert], b. Feb. 21, 1722 | L-3 | 196 |
| Newton, s. Rob[er]t, b. Feb. 21, 1722 | TM-1 | 196 |
| Newton, m. Sarah **JONES**, Sept. 20, 1742 | 1 | 136 |
| Newton, m. Sarah **JONES**, Sept. 21, 1742 | 1 | 143 |
| Newton, s. [Newton & Sarah], b. May 11, 1762 | 1 | 143 |
| Olive, [d. James & Betty], b. June 20, 1758 | 1 | 55 |
| Peleg, [s. Robert], b. Sept. 20, 1724 | L-3 | 196 |
| Peleg, s. Robert, b. Sept. 20, 1724 | TM-1 | 196 |
| Peleg, [s. Peleg], b. Nov. 10, 1753; d. Mar. 10, 1769 | 1 | 88 |
| Pomp, m. Mary **LITTLE**, June 5, 1820, by Salmon Cone; d. Feb. 2, 1841, aged about 44 | 2 | 298 |
| Rayzel, s. [Newton & Sarah], b. Dec. 8, 1751 | 1 | 143 |
| *Robert, m. Alice **NEWTON**, dau. of James. She was born Feb. 28, 1686 *(handwritten in original manuscript) | | |
| Robert, [s. Robert], b. Mar. 25, 1717 | L-3 | 196 |

| | Vol. | Page |
|---|---|---|
| **RANSOM**, (cont.) | | |
| Robert, s. Rob[er]t, b. Mar. 25, 1717 | TM-1 | 196 |
| Robert, [s. John & Bethia], b. Apr. 8, 1733 | TPR | 111 |
| Robert, s. [Newton & Sarah], b. Aug. 26, 1743; d. Jan. 23, 1761 | 1 | 143 |
| Robert, [s. Peleg], b. June 24, 1763 | 1 | 88 |
| Russell, [s. James & Betty], b. May 4, 1772; d. Feb. 28, 1788 | 1 | 55 |
| Sally Maria, b. Aug. 7, 1810, in Montville; m. Elias **HARVEY**, Jr., Sept. 12, 1830, in Salem | 2 | 57 |
| Sarah, [d. Peleg], b. Feb. 18, 1752 | 1 | 88 |
| Sarah, [d. James & Betty], b. Feb. 28, 1764 | 1 | 55 |
| Sarah, w. James, d. May 12, 1793 | 1 | 51 |
| Sherwood B., m. Abby B. **PAYNE**, b. of Colchester, Oct. 8, 1851, by Erastus Dickinson | 3 | 39 |
| Sophia, d. [Asahel & Sophia], b. July 29, 1782 | 2 | 51 |
| Sophia, m. Henry **WORTHINGTON**, Jan. 6, 1806, by Salmon Cone | 2 | 172 |
| Sophia Ann, m. Russel[l] **WAY**, b. of Colchester, Oct. 5, 1841, by Rev. Joel R. Arnold | 2 | 176 |
| Statira, d. [Asahel & Sophia], b. Mar. 4, 1788 | 2 | 51 |
| ----, [s. James & Betty], b. May 13, 1777; d. May 23, 1777 | 1 | 55 |
| **RATHBURN, RATHBUN, RATHBON, RATHBONE**, Abel, s. [John & Anna], b. Dec. 17, 1746 | 1 | 108 |
| Abel, d. May 27, 1804 | 2 | 15 |
| Abel, s. [Abel, Jr. & Alice], b. Apr. 8, 1808 | 2 | 132 |
| Abel, Jr., m. Alice **BROWN**, [ ] | 2 | 132 |
| Abram*, m. Harriet L. H. **ROGERS**, b. of Colchester, Oct. 16, 1836, by Rev. Andrew M. Smith; d. July 27, 1841, ae 37 (*Probably "Alvan") | 2 | 291 |
| Adam, s. [Jonathan & Hannah], b. July 11, 1792 | 2 | 49 |
| Alvan, s. [Asa & Lucy], b. Nov. 27, 1803; d. July 27, 1841, ae 38 | 2 | 132 |
| Alvan, s. [Abram* & Harriet L. H.], b. Nov. 7, 1839 (*Probably "Alvan") | 2 | 291 |
| Alvan, d. July 27, 1841, ae 37 | 2 | 291 |
| Alvan, see also Abram | | |
| Amos, s. [John & Anna], b. Mar. 5, 1738 | 1 | 108 |
| Amos, s. John, m. Humility **RANDALL**, Feb. 12, 1758 | 1 | 107 |
| Amos, s. [Asa & Lucy], b. [ ] | 2 | 132 |
| Anna, d. [John & Anna], b. July 2, 1745 | 1 | 108 |
| Anna, twin with Samuel, d. [Joshua & Sarah], b. Sept. 12, 1758 | 1 | 108 |
| Anna, m. John **HOLMES**, Sept. 1, 1775; d. Jan. 8, 1810, ae 51 | 2 | 82 |
| Ansel, m. Lodice **ROTH**, Mar. 11, 1810 | 2 | 98 |
| Anthony, m. Abigail **BECKWITH**, b. of Colchester, Dec. 26, 1821, by Rev. William Palmer | 2 | 79 |
| Asa, s. [Asa & Lucy], b. Oct. 3, 1800; d. Dec. 25, 1840, | 2 | 132 |

| | Vol. | Page |
|---|---|---|
| **RATHBURN, RATHBUN, RATHBON, RATHBONE**, (cont.) | | |
| ae 40 | 2 | 132 |
| Asa, m. Lydia **HARRIS**, Apr. [ ], 1825 | 2 | 132 |
| Asa, m. Lucy **BROWN**, [ ] | 2 | 132 |
| Ashley, [s. Isaiah & Molley], b. Oct. 4, 1763 | 1 | 14 |
| Benjamin, m. Mary **CAHOON**, Nov. 11, 1742 | 1 | 89 |
| Benjamin, [s. Benjamin & Mary], b. Oct. 29, 1745; d. Mar. 31, 1746 | 1 | 89 |
| Benjamin, 2d, [s. Benjamin & Mary], b. Jan. 2, 1747 | 1 | 89 |
| Betsey, [d. Isaiah & Fanny], b. July 13, 1766 | 1 | 14 |
| Christopher, s. [Jonathan & Hannah], b. Aug. 2, 1794 | 2 | 49 |
| Daniel, [s. Benjamin & Mary], b. July 8, 1743; d. Oct. 27, 1761 | 1 | 89 |
| Deliverance, [d. Benjamin & Mary], b. Dec. 24, 1749 | 1 | 89 |
| Deliverance, m. Samuel **MORGAN**, Jr., Apr. 27, 1769 | 1 | 91 |
| Demming, s. [Jonathan & Hannah], b. July 2, 1796 | 2 | 49 |
| Eleanor, d. [Jonathan, Jr. & Abigail], b. Mar. [ ], 1746/7 | 1 | 108 |
| Elizabeth, d. [Joshua & Sarah], b. June 9, 1747 | 1 | 108 |
| Enoch Arnold, s. [Abel, Jr. & Alice], b. Mar. 16, 1801 | 2 | 132 |
| Erastus, s. [Abel, Jr. & Alice], b. Apr. 8, 1799 | 2 | 132 |
| George W., s. [Asa & Lucy], b. Aug. 18, 1809 | 2 | 132 |
| Grace, m. Josiah **GATES**, May 9, 1714 | L-1 | 451 |
| Hannah, d. [Jonathan & Hannah], b. Oct. 5, 1802 | 2 | 49 |
| Harriet, d. [Abram* & Harriet L. H.], b. Feb. 8, 1838, in East Haddam (*Probably "Alvan") | 2 | 291 |
| Henry W., of Salem, m. Emily C. **BENJAMIN**, of Colchester, Apr. 17, 1838, by Rev. Andrew M. Smith | 2 | 195 |
| Hyram, s. [Jonathan & Hannah], b. Apr. 15, 1798 | 2 | 49 |
| Hubbard W., m. Abigail **SAXTON**, Feb. 10, 1808 | 2 | 133 |
| Irena, m. Daniel **MORGAN**, Nov. 18, 1761 | 1 | 164 |
| Isaiah, m. Molley **GATES**, Jan. 9, 1763 | 1 | 14 |
| Isaiah, m. Fanny **LAMPHEAR**, Mar. 9, 1764 | 1 | 14 |
| Job, [s. Benjamin & Mary], b. July 24, 1748 | 1 | 89 |
| John, s. Jonathan & Elizabeth, b. Jan. 1, 1715 | 1 | 108 |
| John, m. Anna **TENNANT**, Mar. 30, 1737 | 1 | 108 |
| John, s. [John & Anna], b. Apr. 28, 1742 | 1 | 108 |
| John, d. Nov. 27, 1755, ae 41 | 1 | 108 |
| John, s. [Amos & Humility], b. Dec. 9, 1758 | 1 | 107 |
| Jonathan, Jr., m. Abigail **AVERY**, Nov. 8, 1744 | 1 | 108 |
| Jonathan, Jr., d. Dec. 5, 1755, ae 29 | 1 | 125 |
| Jonathan, [s. Isaiah & Fanny], b. Jan. 6, 1765 | 1 | 14 |
| Jonathan, m. Hannah **ADAMS**, of Stonington, Nov. 23, 1789 | 2 | 49 |
| Jonathan, s. [Jonathan & Hannah], b. Mar. 10, 1791 | 2 | 49 |
| Jonathan, Jr., m. Irene **SCOVILLE**, [ ] | 1 | 125 |
| Joshua, m. Sarah **TENNANT**, Dec. 4, 1745 | 1 | 108 |
| Joshua, s. [Joshua & Sarah], b. May 7, 1751 | 1 | 108 |
| Justin, m. Irena **HUNTLEY**, Nov. 20, 1826, by Amherst D. Scoville, J. P. | 2 | 191 |

| | Vol. | Page |
|---|---|---|
| **RATHBURN, RATHBUN, RATHBON, RATHBONE**, (cont.) | | |
| Lucia Ann, d. [Abel, Jr. & Alice], b. Nov. 8, 1803 | 2 | 132 |
| Lucy, d. [Joshua & Sarah], b. Apr. 29, 1756 | 1 | 108 |
| Lucy A., m. Gershom B. **WORTHINGTON**, b. of Colchester, Sept. 18, 1831, by Rev. Lyman Strong | 2 | 233 |
| Lucy, w. Asa, d. Jan. 4, 1824, ae 45 | 2 | 132 |
| Lucy Ann, d. [Asa & Lucy], b. Oct. 13, 1807 | 2 | 132 |
| Martin, m. Eliza **BENJAMIN**, b. of Colchester, Nov. 18, 1829, by Asa Willcox, Elder | 2 | 218 |
| Mary Abby, d. [Hubbard W. & Abigail], b. Jan. 16, 1809 | 2 | 133 |
| Mercy, [d. Isaiah & Fanny], b. June 28, 1768 | 1 | 14 |
| Mercy, m. Asa **WILLCOX**, Nov. 28, 1791; d. Mar. 28, 1837, in Salem, Ct. | 2 | 135 |
| Molley, w. [Isaiah], d. Oct. 15, 1763 | 1 | 14 |
| Moses, s. [Joshua & Sarah], b. Nov. 12, 1754 | 1 | 108 |
| Nancy, d. Simeon & Avis, b. Sept. 25, 1778 | 2 | 63 |
| Ransom B., m. Cynthia E. **DANIELS**, b. of Colchester, Nov. 20, 1849, by Rev. Geo[rge] W. Pendleton | 3 | 42 |
| Renssalear, of Colchester, m. Betsey **McCRACKEN**, of Salem, Apr. 13, 1823, at W[illia]m Palmer's, by Rev. William Palmer | 2 | 138 |
| Russel[l], s. [Asa & Lucy], b. Sept. 27, 1802 | 2 | 132 |
| Samuel, twin with Anna, s. [Joshua & Sarah], b. Sept. 12, 1758 | 1 | 108 |
| Sarah, d. [Joshua & Sarah], b. Nov. 23, 1752 | 1 | 108 |
| Simeon, [s. Benjamin & Mary], b. May 2, 1751 | 1 | 89 |
| Tabella, m. Samuel **HOLMES**, Feb. 1, 1770 | 2 | 60 |
| Tabitha, d. [Joshua & Sarah], b. Aug. 4, 1749 | 1 | 108 |
| William, Sr., d. Apr. 1, 1766, ae 75 y. less 4 d. | 1 | 81 |
| William, s. [Jonathan & Hannah], b. Aug. 30, 1800 | 2 | 49 |
| **RAYMOND**, Lucretia, m. James **SEXTON**, b. of Colchester, Jan. 30, 1850, by Rev. Lyman Strong | 3 | 29 |
| **REID**, Bettey, m. Dudley **WORTHINGTON**, Oct. 12, 1814 | 2 | 74 |
| Jared, m. Sally **BIGELOW**, d. Asa & Lydia, Nov. 27, 1823 | 2 | 78 |
| Jared, Rev., of Reading, Mass., m. Sarah **BIGELOW**, of Colchester, Nov. 27, 1823, by Salmon Cone, V. D. M. | 2 | 160 |
| Sally, w. Jared, d. Feb. 12, 1845, in Tiverton, R. I. | 2 | 78 |
| **REXFORD**, William, m. Mary **STAPLES**, May 30, 1830, by Rev. Peter Griffing | 2 | 223 |
| **REYNOLDS**, Edwin B., of Colchester, m. Abby **MAYNARD**, of New London, June 14, 1853, by Rev. Erastus Dickinson | 3 | 57 |
| **RICE**, Ebe[neze]r D., of Marlborough, Mass., m. Phebe **SHAYLOR**, of Colchester, Oct. 25, 1829, by Rev. Joseph Harvey | 2 | 215 |
| **RICHARDS**, James, alias James **KELLOGG**, m. Laura Ann **DAVIS**, b. of Colchester, Sept. 1, 1822, (colored persons), by Samuel A. Peters, J. P. | 2 | 94 |
| Rebecca, m. Alanson B. **STANNARD**, b. of Colchester, | | |

| | Vol. | Page |
|---|---|---|
| **RICHARDS**, (cont.) | | |
| Nov. 14, 1821, by Salmon Cone, V. D. M. | 2 | 149 |
| **RICHARDSON**, William, m. Content **GILBERT**, wid., Mar. 2, 1778 | 2 | 20 |
| William, s. [William & Content], b. Feb. 5, 1779 | 2 | 20 |
| **RIDER**, Harriet A., m. John M. **BARTLETT**, b. of Colchester, Mar. 11, 1849, by Rev. F. W. Bill | 3 | 39 |
| Lucinda, m. Solomon B. **FOOTE**, b. of Colchester, June 27, 1847, by Rev. Seawell Lamberton | 3 | 33 |
| **RILEY, RILEIGH**, Huldah, m. [ ] **SKINNER**, May 3, 1792 | 2 | 13 |
| John, m. Mary **HOLMS**, Mar. 5, 1780 | 2 | 26 |
| Jonathan, s. [John & Mary], b. Mar. 8, 1781 | 2 | 26 |
| Mary, of East Hartford, m. William **LONG**, of Colchester, Feb. 3, 1848, by Rev. Augustus Bolles | 3 | 34 |
| Rufus, m. Phebe **AYRES**, Mar. 27, 1836, by Benj[ami]n Trumbull, J. P. | 2 | 284 |
| **ROBBINS, ROBINS**, Abigail, m. Gershom **BULKLEY**, Nov. 27, 1733 | L-3 | 452 |
| Abigail, m. Gershom **BULKELEY**, Nov. 28, 1733 | 1 | 132 |
| Amatus, s. [Robert & Jerusha], b. Oct. 1, 1789 | 2 | 82 |
| Bela, s. [Robert & Jerusha], b. Dec. 5, 1791; d. Sept. 13, 1831 | 2 | 82 |
| Elizabeth, m. Jeremiah **CARRIER**, Nov. 20, 1751 | 1 | 21 |
| Jerusha, d. [Robert & Jerusha], b. May 1, 1784 | 2 | 82 |
| Mandana, m. Revilo C. **USHER**, Apr. 4, 1827 | 2 | 122 |
| Mandana, of Colchester, m. Revilo **USHER**, of Chatham, Apr. 4, 1827, by Rev. Joseph Harvey | 2 | 194 |
| Meroe, twin with Ruth Kimberly, d. [Robert & Jerusha], b. Oct. 5, 1782; d. July 23, 1784 | 2 | 82 |
| Meroe, [d. Robert & Jerusha], b. Feb. 13, 1794 | 2 | 82 |
| Rebeckah, m. Gad **WORTHINGTON**, Sept. 25, 1774 | 2 | 7 |
| Robert, Rev., m. Ruth **KIMBERLEY**, Jan. 10, 1769 | 2 | 82 |
| Robert, m. Jerusha **ESTABROOKS**, Dec. 5, 1781; d. Jan. 22, 1804, ae 63 | 2 | 82 |
| Robert Chanay, s. [Robert & Jerusha], b. May 16, 1786 | 2 | 82 |
| Ruth, [w. Rev. Robert], d. Apr. 13, 1769 | 2 | 82 |
| Ruth Kimberly, twin with Meroe, d. [Robert & Jerusha], b. Oct. 5, 1782 | 2 | 82 |
| Ruth Kimberley, m. Henry **CHAMPION**, Jr. [ ] | 2 | 101 |
| Samuel Wells, s. [Robert & Jerusha], b. Dec. 4, 1787 | 2 | 82 |
| **ROBERTS, ROBERDS**, An[n], [d. William & Elisebeth], b. Mar. 8, 1707/8 | L-3 | 198 |
| Ann, d. William [& Elizabeth], b. Mar. 8, 1707/8 | TM-1 | 198 |
| Benj[amin], m. Sibbell **COLMAN**, Mar. 14, 1754 | 1 | 129 |
| Benjamin, s. [Benj[amin] & Sibbell], b. Nov. 21, 1754 | 1 | 129 |
| Cornelius, s. [Benj[amin] & Sibbell], b. July 29, 1760 | 1 | 129 |
| Dorcas, d. [Benj[amin] & Sibbell], b. June 10, 1756 | 1 | 129 |
| Edenah, [d. James & Rebecah], b. May 11, 1722 | L-1 | 451 |
| Elenah, [d. James & Rebecah], b. Jan. 9, 1727 | L-1 | 451 |

| | Vol. | Page |
|---|---|---|
| **ROBERTS, ROBERDS,** (cont.) | | |
| Elizabeth, m. John **[K]NOX,** Apr. 20, 1720 | L-1 | 399 |
| Elizabeth, w. William, d. Aug. 22, 1728 | L-3 | 198 |
| Elizabeth, w. Will[ia]m **ROBERDS,** d. Aug. 22, 1728 | TM-1 | 198 |
| Elizabeth, m. Richard **MENTOR,** Dec. 11, 1735 | 1 | 33 |
| George, s. [Benj[amin] & Sibbell], b. Apr. 16, 1765 | 1 | 129 |
| James, m. Rebecah **DAYLEE,** Nov. [ ], 1718 | L-1 | 451 |
| James, [s. James & Rebecah], b. Sept. 9, 1724 | L-1 | 451 |
| Jemima, m. Noah **SKINNER,** Nov. 9, [ ] | 2 | 13 |
| Jerusha, [d. William & Elisebeth], b. Jan. 31, 1713 | L-3 | 198 |
| Jerusha, d. W[illia]m & Elizabeth, b. Jan. 31, 1713 | TM-1 | 198 |
| Lemewell, [s. William & Elisebeth], b. Mar. 24, 1717 | L-3 | 198 |
| Mabel, [d. William & Prudence], b. Jan. 22, 1742 | 1 | 53 |
| Mabel, m. Asa **TREADWAY,** Dec. 27, 1759 | 1 | 82 |
| Mabel, m. Asa **TREADWAY,** [ ] | 2 | 53 |
| Mary, [d. William & Elisabeth], b. Apr. 1, 1721 | L-3 | 198 |
| Mary, d. Will[ia]m [& Elizebeth], b. Apr. 1, 1721 | TM-1 | 199 |
| Mary, d. W[illia]m, b. Apr. 30, 1721 | TM-1 | 199 |
| Noah, s. [Benj[amin] & Sibbell], b. Jan. 24, 1758 | 1 | 129 |
| Prudence, w. William, d. Nov. 3, 1791 | 2 | 5 |
| Rebec[c]ah, [d. James & Rebecah], b. Jan. 3, 1719/20 | L-1 | 451 |
| Rebecca, m. James **GLASS,** Dec. 20, 1741 | 1 | 104 |
| Rebecca, m. James **GLASS,** Dec. 20, 1741 | 1 | 146 |
| Sam[ue]ll, [s. William & Elisabeth], b. Feb. 8, 1705/6 | L-3 | 198 |
| Samuel, s. William [& Elizebeth], b. Feb. 8, 1705/6 | TM-1 | 198 |
| Samuel, s. Will[ia]m, b. Mar. 24, 1717 | TM-1 | 198 |
| Sarah, [d. William & Elisabeth], b. Sept. 13, 1710 | L-3 | 198 |
| Sarah, d. William [& Elizebeth], b. Sept. 13, 1710 | TM-1 | 198 |
| Sibbell, d. [Benj[amin] & Sibbell], b. Dec. 3, 1762 | 1 | 129 |
| William, m. Elisebeth **NORTHAM,** July 20, 1705 | L-3 | 198 |
| William, m. Elizabeth **NORTHAM,** July 20, 1705 | TM-1 | 198 |
| William, [s. William & Elisebeth], b. Mar. 4, 1715 | L-3 | 198 |
| William, s. W[illia]m [& Elizabeth], b. Mar. 4, 1715 | TM-1 | 198 |
| William, m. Prudence **KELLOGG,** May 6, 1736 | 1 | 53 |
| **ROCKWELL,** Ann, m. Lieut. John **HOLMES,** Dec. 3, 1729 | L-3 | 8 |
| Eunice, m. Benjamin **ADDAMS,** Nov. 6, 1752 | 1 | 55 |
| Josiah, s. [Josiah & Lucy], b. May 10, 1743 | 1 | 140 |
| Lucy, d. [Josiah & Lucy], b. July 19, 1745; d. July 21, [1745] | 1 | 140 |
| Lucy, d. [Josiah & Lucy], b. July 20, 1746 | 1 | 140 |
| Rebecca, m. Andrew **CARRIER,** Oct. 27, 1735 | TPR | 111 |
| **ROGERS,** Abby R., of Colchester, m. Cornelius D. **WELD,** of New York, Aug. 28, 1834, by Rev. Alpheas Geer, of Hebron | 2 | 270 |
| Abby Robbins, d. [Dr. Hoel & Sarah], b. Sept. 28, 1811 | 2 | 84 |
| Anna Bulkeley, d. [Dr. Hoel & Sarah], b. Dec. 14, 1802; d. Sept. 29, 1805 | 2 | 84 |
| Betsey, m. Jonathan **GELLETT,** Apr. 23, 1800; d. Mar. 12, 1810 | 2 | 81 |

| | Vol. | Page |
|---|---|---|
| **ROGERS**, (cont.) | | |
| Bliss, m. Asena **BURNAM**, Sept. 6, 1818, by John Bigelow, J. P. | 2 | 151 |
| Charles Howell, s. [Howell & Olive], b. July 24, 1826 | 2 | 84 |
| George Hammond, s. [Howell & Olive], b. Apr. 26, 1824 | 2 | 84 |
| Gilbert, Dea., of Waterford, m. Sarah **ROWE**, of Colchester, Mar. 7, 1842, by Rev. Augustus Bolles | 2 | 232 |
| Gurdon, m. Ellen M. **BROWN**, b. of Colchester, [Dec.] 28, 1850, by Rev. S. D. Jewett | 2 | 101 |
| Gurdon Bulkeley, s. [Dr. Hoel & Sarah], b. Mar. 28, 1798; d. May 24, 1820, ae 22 | 2 | 84 |
| Harriet L. H., m. Abram* **RATHBONE**, b. of Colchester, Oct. 16, 1836, by Rev. Andrew M. Smith (*Probably "Alvan") | 2 | 291 |
| Henry, s. [Joshua B. & Lucy B.], b. Jan. 25, 1839 | 2 | 241 |
| Howell, Dr., b. Oct. 22, 1774, in South Hampton, L. I.; m. Sally **BULKELEY**, Oct. 9, 1796; d. Sept. 5, 1851, ae 77 | 2 | 84 |
| Howell, m. Olive **HUBBARD**, Sept. 10, 1821, by Salmon Cone, V. D. M. | 2 | 84 |
| Huldah, of Colchester, m. Samuel **OLMSTEAD**, 2d, of East Haddam, Feb. 12, 1827, by Salmon Cone, V. D. M. | 2 | 192 |
| John Day, s. [Dr. Hoel & Sarah], b. Mar. 20, 1807 | 2 | 84 |
| John Howell, s. [Joshua B. & Lucy B.], b. July 1, 1836 | 2 | 241 |
| Joshua B., m. Lucy B. **WELLS**, Feb. 27, 1833, by Salmon Cone, V. D. M. | 2 | 241 |
| Joshua Bulkeley, s. [Dr. Hoel & Sarah], b. Feb. 27, 1804 | 2 | 84 |
| Lois B., of Colchester, m. Hervey G. **CURTISS**, of Egremont, Mass., Apr. 11, 1838, by Rev. Joel R. Arnold | 2 | 241 |
| Lois Bulkeley, d. [Dr. Hoel & Sarah], b. Feb. 27, 1814; d. June 30, 1843, ae 29 | 2 | 84 |
| Lorenda H ., d. [Bliss & Asena], b. Feb. 4, 1819 | 2 | 151 |
| Lucy B., w. T. B., d. Sept. 17, 1841, ae 34 | 2 | 147 |
| Lucy B., w. Joshua B., d. Sept. 17, 1841 | 2 | 241 |
| Lucy Breed, d. [Joshua B. & Lucy B.], b. June 15, 1841 | 2 | 241 |
| Lydia, m. John **DODGE**, Jr., Oct. 23, 1748 | 1 | 152 |
| Mary A., m. Charles T. **ISHAM**, Nov. 21, 1830, by Rev. Lyman Strong | 2 | 226 |
| Mary Ann Bulkeley, d. [Dr. Hoel & Sarah], b. Oct. 9, 1809 | 2 | 84 |
| Mary F., m. Joshua **TINKER**, Apr. 15, 1810 | 2 | 134 |
| Ruth, m. Jonathan **LORD**, Nov. 20, 1746 | 1 | 109 |
| Sarah, m. Samuel **CHURCH**, Jr., Nov. 7, 1771; d. May 24, 1816 | 2 | 81 |
| Sarah, w. Dr. Howell, d. Feb. 14, 1821, ae 42 | 1 | 29 |
| Sarah T., d. Dr. Howell **ROGERS**, of Colchester, m. Benjamin D. **DEAN**, of Fall River, Mass., Nov. 19, 1844, by Rev. Joel R. Arnold | 3 | 17 |
| Sarah Taintor, d. [Dr. Hoel & Sarah], b. Aug. 3, 1817 | 2 | 84 |

| | Vol. | Page |
|---|---|---|
| **ROGERS**, (cont.) | | |
| William Henry, s. [Howell & Olive], b. Nov. 9, 1822; d. Nov. 11, 1843, ae 21 | 2 | 84 |
| **ROOD**, Rufus, b. Mar. 25, 1818 | 2 | 294 |
| **ROOT**, Ezekiel, of Haddam, m. Jerusha J. **DAY**, of Colchester, Jan. 2, 1831, by Rev. Joseph Harvey | 2 | 228 |
| Jerusha, m. Roger **BULKELEY**, May 28, 1772; d. July 27, 1788 | 2 | 50 |
| Sarah, of Hebron, m. Joseph **GILLET**, Jr., June 10, 1783; d. Feb. 25, 1850, ae 87 | 2 | 76 |
| **ROSE**, Hiram D., of East Haddam, m. Frances A. **BIGELOW**, of Colchester, Apr. 30, 1837, at Joshua B. Rogers, J. P. | 2 | 192 |
| Parsons, of New York, m. Frances Augusta **WATROUS**, of Colchester, June 14, 1826, by Nath[anie]l T. Wheaton | 2 | 188 |
| **ROSSITER**, Almira, d. [Stephen & Lydia], b. Apr. 18, 1785 | 2 | 59 |
| Lydia, d. [Stephen & Lydia], b. Feb. 7, 1793 | 2 | 59 |
| Marrilla, d. [Stephen & Lydia], b. Oct. 10, 1796 | 2 | 59 |
| Orril, d. [Stephen & Lydia], b. Dec. 23, 1786 | 2 | 59 |
| Stephen, m. Lydia **BIGELOW**, Apr. 21, 1784 | 2 | 59 |
| Stephen, s. [Stephen & Lydia], b. Aug. 6, 1788 | 2 | 59 |
| **ROTH**, Lodice, m. Ansel **RATHBUN**, Mar. 11, 1810 | 2 | 98 |
| **ROWE**, Sarah, of Colchester, m. Dea. Gilbert **ROGERS**, of Waterford, Mar. 7, 1842, by Rev. Augustus Bolles | 2 | 232 |
| **ROWLEY, ROWLEE, ROWLE**, Abigail, [d. Elnathan & Abigail], b. May 7, 1725; d. Oct. 17, 1726 | L-3 | 456 |
| Abigail, [d. Elnathan & Abigail], b. Oct. 2, 1730 | L-3 | 456 |
| Abigail, w. Elnathan, d. Dec. 8, 1735 | L-3 | 456 |
| Abigail, m. Ebenezer **KELLOGG**, May 10, 1752 | 1 | 126 |
| Ann, [d. Moses & Martha], b. Apr. 5, 1716 | L-1 | 445 |
| Deborah, [d. John], b. Dec. 14, 1725 | L-3 | 6 |
| Dorothy, [d. Jabez & Tabitha], b. Apr. 28, 1741 | TPR | 110 |
| Elizabeth, [d. Shubaiell & Hannah], b. Oct. 3, 1714 | L-3 | 193 |
| Elizabeth, d. Shubael, b. Oct. 3, 1714 | TM-1 | 193 |
| Elizabeth, m. Edward **FULLER**, July 21, 1715 | L-1 | 799 |
| Elnathan, m. Abigail **CONE**, Dec. 26, 1723 | L-3 | 456 |
| Elnathan, m. Lidia **WELLS**, Oct. 3, 1736 | L-3 | 456 |
| Elnathan, s. [Jesse & Bathsheba], b. Mar. 25, 1775 | 2 | 19 |
| Ephraim, [s. Elnathan & Lidia], b. Oct. 17, 1737 | L-3 | 456 |
| Eunice, [d. Jabez & Tabitha], b. Apr. 3, 1735 | TPR | 110 |
| Experience, [d. Shubaiell & Hannah], b. Aug. 8, 1718 | L-3 | 193 |
| Experience, d. Shubael, b. Aug. 8, 1718 | TM-1 | 193 |
| Ezra, [s. Elnathan], b. Nov. 10, 1742 | 1 | 131 |
| Ezra, s. Elnathan, b. Nov. 10, 1742 | 1 | 142 |
| Hannah, [d. Shubaiell & Hannah], b. Mar. 10, 1712 | L-3 | 193 |
| Hannah, d. Shubael, b. Mar. 10, 1712 | TM-1 | 193 |
| Harris, [s. Isaac & Hannah], b. Aug. 1, 1721 | L-1 | 654 |
| Isaac, m. Hannah **HARRIS**, May 30, 1717 | L-1 | 654 |
| Isaac, [s. Isaac & Hannah], b. Sept. 8, 1725 | L-1 | 654 |

| | Vol. | Page |
|---|---|---|
| **ROWLEY, ROWLEE, ROWLE,** (cont.) | | |
| Israel, [s. Elnathan & Abigail], b. Feb. 20, 1732/3 | L-3 | 456 |
| Jabez, m. Tabitha **HARRIS**, Feb. 20, 1724 | L-1 | 448 |
| Jabez, [s. Jabez & Tabitha], b. Jan. 10, 1726 | L-1 | 448 |
| Jesse, [s. Elnathan & Abigail], b. May 8, 1728 | L-3 | 456 |
| Jesse, [s. Elnathan], d. May 31, 1746 | 1 | 131 |
| Jesse, [s. Elnathan], b. Sept. 17, 1750; d. Oct. 8, [1750] | 1 | 131 |
| Jesse, s. [Elnathan], b. Mar. 6, 1751/2 | 1 | 131 |
| Jesse, s. Elnathan, b. Mar. 6, 1752 | 2 | 19 |
| Jesse, s. [Jesse & Bathsheba], b. Oct. 13, 1779 | 2 | 19 |
| Jesse, m. Prudence **BECKWITH**, b. of Colchester, Oct. 2, 1842, by A. R. Pratt, J. P. | 2 | 271 |
| John, [s. John], b. July 7, 1727 | L-3 | 6 |
| John, s. [Joseph & Susannah], b. Feb. 9, 1744/5 | 1 | 140 |
| John, m. Rebeccka **BRAINARD**, Sept. 4, 1752 | 1 | 104 |
| John, Ensign, d. Jan. 23, 1763 | 1 | 105 |
| Joseph, s. [John & Rebeccka], b. June 15, 1753 | 1 | 104 |
| Joseph, s. [John, Jr.], b. Jan. 5, 1753; d. [ ], 1833 | 1 | 101 |
| Joseph, of East Haddam, m. Hellen **GRAVES**, of Colchester, Oct. 11, 1846, by Rev. P. Brockett | 3 | 28 |
| Lois, [d. Jabez & Tabitha], b. Nov. 14, 1731 | TPR | 110 |
| Lydia, [d. Jabez & Tabitha], b. June 27, 1739 | TPR | 110 |
| Lydia, [d. Elnathan], b. Aug. 12, 1745 | 1 | 131 |
| Lydia, w. Elnathan, d. May 4, 1762 | 1 | 142 |
| Lydia, d. [Jesse & Bathsheba], b. Feb. 6, 1777 | 2 | 19 |
| Lydia, [d. Elnathan & Lidia], b. [ ] | L-3 | 456 |
| Mabel, d. [Jesse & Bathsheba], b. Oct. 29, 1787 | 2 | 19 |
| Marcy, [d. Shubaiell & Hannah], b. Apr. 30, 1710 | L-3 | 193 |
| Martha, [d. Moses & Martha], b. Feb. 11, 1710/11 | L-1 | 445 |
| Mary, [d. Moses & Martha], b. Dec. 15, 1708 | L-1 | 445 |
| Mary, d. Shubael, Jr., b. Apr. 30, 1710 | TM-1 | 193 |
| Mary, m. Thomas **LEWIS**, Feb. 25, 1720 | L-1 | 446 |
| Mary, d. Joseph & Susannah, b. July 26, 1743 | 1 | 140 |
| Mary, d. [John & Rebeccka], b. Apr. 13, 1757 | 1 | 104 |
| Mat[t]hew, [s. Shubaiell & Hannah], b. Oct. 5, 1720 | L-3 | 193 |
| Matthew, s. Shubael, b. Oct. 5, 1720 | TM-1 | 193 |
| Mindwell, m. Samuel **ADAMS**, Apr. 15, 1740 | 1 | 102 |
| Mindwell, d. [John & Rebeccka], b. Feb. 28, 1755 | 1 | 104 |
| Moses, m. Martha **PORTER**, Sept. [ ], 1707 | L-1 | 445 |
| Moses, [s. Moses & Martha], b. Sept. 5, 1714 | L-1 | 445 |
| Nathan, [s. Jabez & Tabitha], b. Feb. 12, 1737 | TPR | 110 |
| Patience, [d.Shubaiell & Hannah], b. Aug. 16, 1723 | L-3 | 193 |
| Patience, d. Shubael, b. Aug. 16, 1723 | TM-1 | 193 |
| Patience, m. Richard **SKINNER**, Feb. 24, 1736/7 | 1 | 105 |
| Patience, m. Richard **SKINNER**, [ ] | 1 | 147 |
| Phinehas, [s. Jabez & Tabitha], b. Oct. 7, 1729 | TPR | 110 |
| Polly, d. [Jesse & Bathsheba], b. May 29, 1785 | 2 | 19 |
| Retern, [d. Isaac & Hannah], b. Aug. 26, 1719 | L-1 | 654 |

| | Vol. | Page |
|---|---|---|
| **ROWLEY, ROWLEE, ROWLE,** (cont.) | | |
| Ruth, [d. Elnathan], b. Mar. 31, 1747/8 | 1 | 131 |
| Sarah, d. John, b. Jan. [ ], 1722 | L-3 | 6 |
| Sarah, d. [Joseph & Susannah], b. Mar. 7, 1746/7 | 1 | 140 |
| Seth, [s. John], b. May 6, 1730 | L-3 | 6 |
| Seth, s. [John & Rebeccka], b. July 29, 1759 | 1 | 104 |
| Shubaiell, m. Hannah **BROWN**, May 8, 1709 | L-3 | 193 |
| Shubael, m. Hannah **BROWN**, May 9, 1709 | TM-1 | 193 |
| Shubaiell, d. Mar. 28, 1714 | L-3 | 197 |
| Shubael, d. Mar. 28, 1714 | TM-1 | 197 |
| Simeon, [s. Jabez & Tabitha], b. June 17, 1733 | TPR | 110 |
| Stephen, s. [Jesse & Bathsheba], b. Mar. 17, 1782 | 2 | 19 |
| Tabitha, [s. Jabez & Tabitha], b. Oct. 20, 1724 | L-1 | 448 |
| Thankfull, [d. Elnathan & Abigail], b. Dec. 3, 1735; d. Dec. 9, 1735 | L-3 | 456 |
| Thankful[l], d. Elnathan, b. Aug. 18, 1740 | 1 | 131 |
| Thankfull, m. Samuel **HILLS**, Sept. 3, 1768 | 1 | 28 |
| Thankful[l], [d. Elnathan & Lidia], b. [ ] | L-3 | 456 |
| Thomas, [s. Isaac & Hannah], b. Mar. 4, 1723 | L-1 | 654 |
| William, s. Jabez & Tabitha, b. Oct. 15, 1727 | TPR | 110 |
| -----, d. [Shubaiell & Hannah], b. Dec. 12, 1716; d. Jan. 10, [1717] | L-3 | 193 |
| -----, d. Shubael, b. Dec. 12, 1716; d. Jan. 10, [1717] | TM-1 | 193 |
| **RUDD**, Hezekiah, m. Mary E. **COGGESHALL**, Sept. 4, 1828, by Salmon Cone, V. D. M. | 2 | 206 |
| **RUSSELL**, Emily, of Colchester, m. Henry **PETERS**, of Hebron, [Oct.] 15, 1843, by Rev. Rob[er]t C. Mills | 3 | 7 |
| **[RUTLEDGE], ROUTLEDGE**, Margarett J., m. John **JOHNSON**, b. of Colchester, Sept. 28, 1852, by Geo[rge] W. Pendleton | 3 | 53 |
| **SABIN**, Adriel, [s. Phinehas & Abigail], b. May 24, 1762 | 1 | 94 |
| Eldad, [s. Phinehas & Abigail], b. June 7, 1764 | 1 | 94 |
| Jonathan, [s. Phinehas & Abigail], b. Feb. 26, 1757 | 1 | 94 |
| Phebe, [d. Phinehas & Abigail], b. Oct. 13, 1759 | 1 | 94 |
| Phinehas, m. Abigail **BURNHAM**, Apr. 22, 1756 | 1 | 94 |
| **SAFFORD**, Abby Jane, w. Daniel, d. July 17, 1830 | 2 | 78 |
| Daniel, m. Abby Jane **BIGELOW**, Dec. 24, 1828 | 2 | 78 |
| Daniel, m. Ann Eliza **TURNER**, June 25, 1833 | 2 | 78 |
| Daniel, of Boston, Mass., m. Ann Eliza **TURNER**, June 25, 1833 | 2 | 187 |
| **SALTER**, John W., Rev., of Bozrah, m. Eliza **TURNER**, of Colchester, Mar. 1, 1842, by Rev. Joel R. Arnold | 2 | 218 |
| **SANDERS**, Adaline E., of Hebron, m. Calvin B. **HOLMES**, of Colchester, May 19, 1844, by Rev. Rob[er]t C. Mills | 3 | 13 |
| **SANFORD**, Lucy Ann, w. Rollin, of Brooklyn, N. Y., & d. [Amasa & Nancy **WRIGHT**], d. Apr. 20, 1843, ae 27 | 2 | 25 |
| **SAUNDERS**, Leonard, m. Caroline M. **SHAYLOR**, b. of Colchester, Jan. 25, 1852, by Rev. G. W. Pendleton | 3 | 49 |

| | Vol. | Page |
|---|---|---|
| **SAWYER**, Ruth, m. Aaron **FULLER**, June 10, 1734 | 1 | 128 |
| **SAXTON, SEXTON**, Abby Ann, d. [James, Jr. & Electa], b. June 24, 1815; d. Apr. [ ], 1835 | 2 | 126 |
| Abigail, d. [Nath[anie]ll & Abigail], b. Oct. 5, 1745 | 1 | 139 |
| Abigail, d. [James & Deborah], b. Jan. 3, 1788 | 2 | 5 |
| Abigail, m. Hubbard W. **RATHBUN**, Feb. 10, 1808 | 2 | 133 |
| Amos Jones, s. [James, Jr. & Electa], b. May 12, 1806 | 2 | 126 |
| Amos Jones, s. [James, Jr. & Electa], b. May [ ], 1807 (Incorrect entry) | 2 | 126 |
| Anna, d. [Knight & Elizabeth], b. June 27, 1751 | 1 | 127 |
| Bela, s. [James, Jr. & Electa], b. Jan. 24, 1811 | 2 | 126 |
| Damares, d. [Nath[anie]ll & Abigail], b. Aug. 4, 1754 | 1 | 139 |
| Deborah, d. [James & Deborah], b. Jan. 22, 1775; d. Jan. 22, 1775 | 2 | 5 |
| Deborah, 2d, d. [James & Deborah], b. Oct. 6, 1778 | 2 | 5 |
| Electa, [w. James, Jr.], d. Aug. 4, 1846 | 2 | 126 |
| Elizabeth, [d. Georg[e] & Elizabeth], b. Jan. 11, 1724/5 | L-1 | 447 |
| Elizabeth, d. [Knight & Elizabeth], b. Aug. 15, 1738 | 1 | 127 |
| Elizabeth, d. [George & Elizabeth], b. Nov. 28, 1787 | 2 | 71 |
| Eunice, d. [Nath[anie]ll & Abigail], b. Nov. 18, 1751 | 1 | 139 |
| Eunice, d. [James & Deborah], b. Sept. 6, 1785 | 2 | 5 |
| Georg[e], m. Elizabeth **DIB[B]LE**, Nov. 21, 1723 | L-1 | 447 |
| George, m. Elizabeth **BROWN**, of Chatham, Feb. 12, 1782 | 2 | 71 |
| George, s. [George & Elizabeth], b. June 28, 1785 | 2 | 71 |
| Harriet, d. [George & Elizabeth], b. Sept. 10, 1792 | 2 | 71 |
| Israel, s. [Knight & Elizabeth], b. Jan. 29, 1757 | 1 | 127 |
| James, s. [Nath[anie]ll & Abigail], b. July 29, 1747 | 1 | 139 |
| James, of Colchester, m. Deborah **FOX**, of Norwich, June 27, 1770 | 2 | 5 |
| James, of Colchester, m. Deborah **FOX**, of Norwich, Nov. 17, 1770 | 1 | 37 |
| James, [s. James & Deborah], b. June 25, 1771 | 1 | 37 |
| James, s. [James & Deborah], b. Mar. 25, 1773; d. Sept. 21, 1775 | 2 | 5 |
| James, 2d, s. [James & Deborah], b. Aug. 11, 1780 | 2 | 5 |
| James, Jr., m. Electa **JONES**, Oct. 2, 1805 | 2 | 126 |
| James, m. Lina **BROWN**, Oct. 11, 1846, by Rev. S. D. Jewett | 3 | 29 |
| James, m. Lucretia **RAYMOND**, b. of Colchester, Jan. 30, 1850, by Rev. Lyman Strong | 3 | 29 |
| Jesse, s. [Nath[anie]ll & Abigail], b. May 8, 1743; d. Jan. 5, 1749 | 1 | 139 |
| Jesse, 2d, s. [Nath[anie]ll & Abigail], b. May 2, 1749 | 1 | 139 |
| Judah, s. [Knight & Elizabeth], b. July 20, 1742 | 1 | 127 |
| Judah, m. Margery **ADDAMS**, Jan. 5, 1762 | 1 | 13 |
| Judah, [s. Judah & Margery], b. July 16, 1765 | 1 | 13 |
| Justin, s. [George & Elizabeth], b. Apr. 22, 1790 | 2 | 71 |
| Knight, m. Elizabeth **SKINNER**, May 25, 1735 | 1 | 127 |
| Knight, s. [Knight & Elizabeth], b. May 31, 1736 | 1 | 127 |

| | Vol. | Page |
|---|---|---|
| **SAXTON, SEXTON**, (cont.) | | |
| Lidia, d. [Knight & Elizabeth], b. Oct. 15, 1746 | 1 | 127 |
| Margary, [d. Judah & Margery], b. May 14, 1763 | 1 | 13 |
| Mary, m. Nathan **NILES**, Oct. 28, 1742 | 1 | 145 |
| Mary, d. [Knight & Elizabeth], b. Aug. 27, 1753 | 1 | 127 |
| Nath[anie]ll, m. Abigail **BATE[S]**, Nov. 24, 1741 | 1 | 139 |
| Nathaniel, d. Feb. 17, 1767 | 1 | 139 |
| Nath[anie]ll, s. [James & Deborah], b. June 25, 1771; d. Sept. 15, 1775 | 2 | 5 |
| Nath[anie]ll, 2d, [s. James & Deborah], b. Aug. 6, 1776 | 2 | 5 |
| Noah, s. [Knight & Elizabeth], b. Sept. 5, 1740 | 1 | 127 |
| Noah, m. Ama **WORTHINGTON**, Apr. 7, 1762 | 1 | 88 |
| Noah, [s. Noah & Ama], b. Mar. 2, 1764 | 1 | 88 |
| Olive, d. [Nath[anie]ll & Abigail], b. Jan. 31, 1759 | 1 | 139 |
| Samuel, s. [Knight & Elizabeth], b. Jan. 29, 1749 | 1 | 127 |
| Sarah, d. [Knight & Elizabeth], b. Sept. 5, 1744 | 1 | 127 |
| Tallathey, d. [George & Elizabeth], b. Feb. 12, 1783 | 2 | 71 |
| William, s. [James, Jr. & Electa], b. Apr. 6, 1809 | 2 | 126 |
| **SCOFIELD, SCHOLFIELD**, [see also **SCOVILLE**], A., Rev., of Hamilton, N. Y., m. A. J. **MARVIN**, of Colchester, Apr. 3, 1844, by Rev. Joel R. Arnold | 3 | 12 |
| Abishai, of Peterboro, N. Y., m. Elizabeth R. **MARVIN**, of Colchester, Nov. 7, 1836, by Rev. Joel R. Arnold | 2 | 293 |
| Eleizer, s. [John & Sarah], b. July 12, 1754 | 1 | 114 |
| John, m. Sarah **ALGER**, of Lyme, [ ] | 1 | 114 |
| **SCOVILLE, SCOVELL, SCOVEL, SCOVIL, SCOVELE**, [see also **SCOFIELD**], Amherst D., m. Rebecca C. **COGGESHALL**, Jan. 10, 1825, by Salmon Cone, V.D.M. | 2 | 175 |
| Amherst David, s. [Solomon & Molly], b. Feb. 1, 1798 | 2 | 46 |
| Clarasa, d. [Judah & Mary], b. Feb. 21, 1783 | 2 | 76 |
| David, [s. Elisha & Elifall], b. Aug. 17, 1759 | 1 | 21 |
| Delight, d. John [& Sarah], b. Dec. 13, 1750 | 1 | 148 |
| Eleizer, s. [John & Sarah], b. July 12, 1754 | 1 | 148 |
| Elisha, of Colchester, m. Elifall **BLISS**, of New London, Feb. 19, 1756 | 1 | 21 |
| Elisabeth, m. Elnathan **PALMITER**, Apr. 16, 1734 | TPR | 112 |
| Eunice, d. [Judah & Mary], b. Dec. 27, 1785 | 2 | 76 |
| Franklin Jackson, s. [Amherst D. & Rebecca C.], b. Sept. 22, 1832 | 2 | 175 |
| Hannah, d. [Solomon & Molly], b. Jan. 1, 1788 | 2 | 46 |
| Henry Amherst, s. [Amherst D. & Rebecca C.], b. Apr. 5, 1826 | 2 | 175 |
| Irene, m. Jonathan **RATHBUN**, Jr., [ ] | 1 | 125 |
| Jerusha, d. [Nathan & Elizabeth], b. July 30, 1750 | 1 | 144 |
| Joanna, d. [Judah & Mary], b. Nov. 22, 1780 | 2 | 76 |
| Jonathan, [s. Elisha & Elifall], b. Mar. 6, 1757 | 1 | 21 |
| Judah, m. Mary **LOMIS**, Jan. 27, 1771 | 2 | 76 |

| | Vol. | Page |
|---|---|---|
| **SCOVILLE, SCOVELL, SCOVEL, SCOVIL, SCOVELE,** (cont.) | | |
| Lois, d. [Judah & Mary], b. Oct. 14, 1792 | 2 | 76 |
| Lucy, d. [Judah & Mary], b. Feb. 6, 1779 | 2 | 76 |
| Lydia, d. [Judah & Mary], b. Aug. 29, 1772 | 2 | 76 |
| Mary, d. [Judah & Mary], b. June 8, 1774 | 2 | 76 |
| Mirian, d. John & Sarah, b. Feb. 25, 1747/8 | 1 | 148 |
| Molly, [w. Solomon], d. Sept. 13, 1829, ae 69 | 2 | 46 |
| Nathan, m. Elizabeth **GATES**, Sept. 8, 1749 | 1 | 144 |
| Nathan, s. Nathan [& Elizabeth], b. May 8, 1757 | 1 | 144 |
| Polly, d. [Solomon & Molly], b. Sept. 24, 1785 | 2 | 46 |
| R. C., of Colchester, m. Joel **ANDREWS**, of Dedham, Mass., Mar. 29, 1843, by Rev. Joel R. Arnold | 3 | 3 |
| Sarah Ann, d. [Solomon & Molly], b. Feb. 13, 1791 | 2 | 46 |
| Solomon, m. Molly **DEWEY**, of Lebanon, [ ], in Lebanon; d. Dec. 1, 1832 | 2 | 46 |
| Zada, d. [Judah & Mary], b. July 9, 1788 | 2 | 76 |
| **SEALES**, Sarah Moulton, d. Jacob & [Nancy B.], b. Oct. 24, 1824 | 2 | 140 |
| Thomas Spencer, s. Jacob & Nancy B., b. Mar. 28, 1822 | 2 | 140 |
| **SEAMAN**, Maria G., of Colchester, m. Henry L. **McINTIRE**, of Mansfield, May 10, 1846, by Rev. P. Brockett | 3 | 27 |
| **SEARS**, Lucy, of East Haddam, m. John **WRIGHT**, of Colchester, Nov. 22, 1776;. d. Sept. 15, 1829, ae 77 | 2 | 25 |
| Rebecca, m. Samuel **CARRIER**, Dec. 16, 1765 | 2 | 33 |
| **SELDEN**, Ebenezer, of Lebanon, m. Eliza **FULLER**, of Colchester, Mar. 25, 1841, by Rev. Lyman Strong | 2 | 236 |
| **SEYMOUR**, Richard, m. Harriet **FREEMAN**, Apr. 20, 1828, by Salmon Cone, V. D. M. | 2 | 203 |
| **SHAILOR**, [see under **SHAYLOR**] | | |
| **SHATTUCK**, David Olcott, m. Lydia **WATROUS**, Mar. 1, 1824, at the house of Rev. Jacob Seales, in West Chester, by Rev. Jacob Seales | 2 | 126 |
| Dorothy, m. David **FOOTE**, b. of Colchester, May 28, 1828, by Rev. Joseph Harvey | 2 | 203 |
| Francis Elliot, s. [Giles & Nancy], b. Oct. 16, 1828 | 2 | 252 |
| Francis M., s. [Giles & Nancy], b. Sept. 28, 1822; d. July 22, 1827 | 2 | 252 |
| George, s. [Giles & Nancy], b. Nov. 26, 1836 | 2 | 252 |
| Giles, s. David, b. Jan. 24, 1798 | 2 | 252 |
| Mary, d. [Giles & Nancy], b. Dec. 21, 1822 | 2 | 252 |
| Mary E., m. James D. **EDMUND**, Dec. 17, 1849, by Rev. S. D. Jewett, at Westchester | 3 | 45 |
| **SHAW**, Delilah, m. Stephen **WEBSTER**, Aug. 3, 1790 | 2 | 26 |
| Fanny, d. [Simeon & Dalilah], b. July 29, 1784 | 2 | 71 |
| Simeon, m. Dalilah **DODGE**, July 5, 1773; d. Dec. 28, 1790 | 2 | 71 |
| William Johnson, s. [Simeon & Dalilah], b. [ ] | 2 | 71 |
| **SHAYLOR, SHAILOR, SHAYLER, SHALER**, Abby Jane, d. [Gurdon & Nancy], b. June 29, 1818 | 2 | 259 |
| Abby Jane, m. Thomas **UNDERWOOD**, b. of Colchesster, | | |

| | Vol. | Page |
|---|---|---|
| **SHAYLOR, SHAILOR, SHAYLER, SHALER,** (cont.) | | |
| Aug. 15, 1839, by Rev. Joel R. Andrews | 2 | 103 |
| Asa Calvin, s. [Abner], b. Nov. 27, 1817 | 2 | 251 |
| Calvin D., m. Julia A. **GLOSSENGER**, b. of Colchseter, Sept. 7, 1834, by Rev. Lyman Strong | 2 | 269 |
| Calvin Dudley, s. [Gurdon & Nancy], b. June 29, 1814 | 2 | 259 |
| Caroline M., m. Leonard **SAUNDERS**, b. of Colchester, Jan. 25, 1852, by Rev. G. W. Pendleton | 3 | 49 |
| Charles Kellogg, s. [Gurdon & Nancy], b. [ ] | 2 | 259 |
| Daniel C., [s. James], b. Aug. 5, 1830 | 2 | 254 |
| Electa, of Colchester, m. John W. **CADY**, of Worchester, Apr. 21, 1845, by Rev. Pierpoint Brockett | 3 | 21 |
| Elizabeth N., d. [Gurdon & Nancy], b. Nov. [ ], [ ] | 2 | 259 |
| Gurdon, b. July 19, 1794; m. Nancy **BECKWITH**, Dec. 25, 1813; d. Oct. 20, 1851, ae 57 | 2 | 259 |
| Henry, s. [Gurdon & Nancy], b. June [ ], 1831 | 2 | 259 |
| Huldah Ann, d. [James], b. Oct. 7, 1827 | 2 | 254 |
| Julia, d. [Gurdon & Nancy], b. Feb. 12, 1833 | 2 | 259 |
| Justin K., s. [Gurdon & Nancy], b. Mar. 20, 1824 | 2 | 259 |
| Justin R., of Colchester, m. Elvira **CUSHMAN**, of Stafford, Ct., Dec. 8, 1850, by Rev. Albert F. Park | 2 | 69 |
| Justus R., of Colchester, m. Elaura **CUSHMAN**, of Stafford, Dec. 8, 1850, by Rev. Albert F. Park | 3 | 64 |
| Mary, of Colchester, m. Chauncey **LOOMIS**, of Lebanon, Feb. 15, 1821, by Rev. Jacob Seales | 2 | 107 |
| Mary A., m. William A. **LEWIS**, June 6, 1841, by Rev. Augustus Bolles; d. Nov. 7, 1846, ae 30 | 2 | 160 |
| Mary Ann, d. [Gurdon & Nancy], b. Apr. 6, 1816 | 2 | 259 |
| Matilda, d. [Gurdon & Nancy], b. Sept. 4, 1822 | 2 | 259 |
| Mercy Maria, d. [Abner], b. Mar. 18, 1821; d. July 7, 1825 | 2 | 251 |
| Nancy, w. [Gurdon], d. Apr. 17, 1833, ae 40 | 2 | 259 |
| Olive, of Colchester, m. George **CARVER**, of Hebron, July 21, 1839, by Rev. Andrew M. Smith | 2 | 106 |
| Olive Carva, d. [Gurdon & Nancy], b. Mar. 30, 1820 | 2 | 259 |
| Phebe, of Colchester, m. Ebe[neze]r D. **RICE**, of Marlborough, Mass., Oct. 25, 1829, by Rev. Joseph Harvey | 2 | 215 |
| Sally, of Colchester, m. David **CHAPMAN**, of Chatham, Apr. 1, 1824, by Rev. Jacob Seales, at the home of Rev. Jacob Seales | 2 | 164 |
| Simon N., s. [James], b. July 2, 1825 | 2 | 254 |
| Susannah, of Colchester, m. Aaron **BOGUE**, of East Haddam, Apr. 1, 1824, by Rev. Jacob Seales, at the home of Rev. Jacob Seales | 2 | 163 |
| **SHELDON**, Erastus, of New Marlborough, Mass., m. Almira **DAY**, of Colchester, Nov. 27, 1835, by Rev. Joseph Harvey | 2 | 282 |
| **SHEPARD, SHEPERD, SHEPHARD**, Jerusha s., of Colchester, m. Benjamin C. **HOUSE**, of Coventry, Nov. 5, 1823, by | 2 | 135 |

| | Vol. | Page |
|---|---|---|
| **SHEPARD, SHEPERD, SHEPHARD**, (cont.) Salmon Cone, V. D. M. | 2 | 135 |
| John C., m. Aurelia A. **BRIDGES**, b. of Colchester, Apr. 5, 1842, by Rev. Joel R. Arnold | 2 | 287 |
| John C., m. Mary Ann **WATROUS**, b. of Colchester, Mar. 30, 1853, by Rev. S. D. Jewett | 3 | 55 |
| Julius, of Coventry, m. Francis A. **BUELL**, of Colchester, Sept. 10, 1839, by Rev. Lyman Strong | 2 | 123 |
| William, of Colchester, m. Eliza J. **SMITH**, of Salem, Mar. 23, 1835, by Rev. Lyman Strong | 2 | 275 |
| **SHEPARDSON, SHEPERSON,**, Diadama, d. [Joseph & Diadama], b. Mar. 28, 1797 | 2 | 80 |
| Edward, s. [Joseph & Diadama], b. May 23, 1799 | 2 | 80 |
| Joseph, m. Diadama **CHAMBERLAIN**, Oct. 13, 1793 | 2 | 80 |
| Joseph, s. [Joseph & Diadama], b. Nov. 19, 1794 | 2 | 80 |
| Lora, d. [William & Ede], b. Dec. 23, 1792 | 2 | 64 |
| Timothy Chamberlain, s. [Joseph & Diadama], b. June 6, 1802 | 2 | 80 |
| William, m. Ede **HOOK**, of Chatham, Nov. 24, 1791 | 2 | 64 |
| **SHERIDEN**, Mary, d. Edward & Mary, b. June 17, 1787 | 2 | 77 |
| **SHERMAN**, Robert B., of Lebanon, m. Elizabeth **BRIGGS**, of Colchester, Dec. 22, 1844, by Rev. Joel R. Arnold | 3 | 19 |
| **SHIPMAN**, Margary, of Colchester, m. John **TROWBRIDGE**, of Chatham, May 9, 1826, by Salmon Cone, V. D. M. | 2 | 186 |
| Thomas L., Rev., m. Mary T. **DEMING**, May 3, 1827, by Salmon Cone, V. D. M. | 2 | 195 |
| **SHOLES**, Lydia, m. George **HOLMES**, [ ] | 2 | 131 |
| **SILLIMAN**, William, of East Haddam, m. Eliza **GILLETT**, Nov. 7, 1827, by Salmon Cone, V. D. M. | 2 | 199 |
| **SKEELE**, Otis, of Chicopee, Mass., m. Clarissa F. **OTIS**, May 6, 1851, by Rev. Orin F. Otis, of Chepatchet, R. I. | 2 | 95 |
| **SKINNER, SKINER**, A[a]ron, [s. of John], b. June 14, 1713 | L-1 | 799 |
| Aaron, m. Eunice **TAINTOR**, Aug. 4, 1737 | 1 | 127 |
| Aaron, m. Eunice **TAINTOR**, Aug. 4, 1737 | TPR | 112 |
| Aaron, s. [Aaron & Eunice], b. July 12, 1740 | 1 | 127 |
| Aaron, m. Mehetable **WORTHINGTON**, Apr. 12, 1764 | 1 | 148 |
| Aaron, s. [Aaron & Mehetable], b. Jan. 13, 1765 | 1 | 148 |
| Aaron, [s. David & Jerusha], b. Mar. 22, 1779 | 1 | 89 |
| Aaron, s. [David & Jerusha], b. Mar. 22, 1779 | 2 | 41 |
| Abiah, d. [Joseph, 2d], b. July 29, 1746; d. Nov. 1, 1750 | 1 | 146 |
| Abiah, [d. Joseph, 2d], b. Jan. 26, 1750/51; d. Sept. 2, 1751 | 1 | 146 |
| Abigaiell, [d. Ebenezar], b. July 9, 1715 | L-3 | 195 |
| Abigail, d. Ebenezer, b. July 9, 1715 | TM-1 | 195 |
| Abigail, m. Isaac **BIGLOE**, Mar. 14, 1734 | L-3 | 454 |
| Abigail, d. [Richard & Patience], b. June 9, 1739; d. July 13, 1748 | 1 | 147 |
| Abigail, 2d, d. [Richard & Patience], b. Aug. 17, 1748 | 1 | 147 |
| Abraham, s. [Joseph, 2d], b. Sept. 10, 1748; d. June 4, 1747 | 1 | 146 |
| Alfred, twin with Amasa, s. [Stephen & Mary], b. Apr. 25, | | |

| | Vol. | Page |
|---|---|---|
| **SKINNER, SKINER**, (cont.) | | |
| 1781 | 2 | 9 |
| Alfred, twin with Amasa, s. [Stephen & Mary], b. Apr. 25, 1781 | 2 | 59 |
| Alice, d. [Rev. Thomas & Mary], b. Sept. 2, 1747 | 1 | 138 |
| Allice, m. Jonathan **DEMMING**, Dec. 30, 1767 | 1 | 42 |
| Amasa, twin with Alfred, s. [Stephen & Mary], b. Apr. 25, 1781 | 2 | 9 |
| Amasa, twin with Alfred, s. [Stephen & Mary], b. Apr. 25, 1781 | 2 | 59 |
| Amasa, s. [Aaron & Eunice], b. [ ] | 1 | 127 |
| An[n], [d. John], b. Oct. 1, 1700 | L-1 | 799 |
| Ann, [d. Ebenezar], b. Sept. 8, 1717 | L-3 | 195 |
| Ann, d. Ebenezer, b. Sept. 8, 1717 | TM-1 | 195 |
| Ann, m. Seth **DEAN**, Oct. 29, 1721 | L-1 | 444 |
| Ann, d. [John & Esther], b. May 14, 1739 | 1 | 143 |
| Ann, d. [Joseph & Elizabeth], b. Feb. 17, 1753; d. Aug. [ ], 1754 | 1 | 116 |
| Ann, [d. Joseph & Ann], b. Oct. 7, 1763 | 1 | 75 |
| Ann, d. [Joseph & Ann], b. Oct. 7, 1763 | 2 | 8 |
| Anna, m. Job **WHITCOMB**, Mar. 10, 1757 | 1 | 38 |
| Anne, w. Noah, d. Apr. 5, 1779 | 2 | 13 |
| Appleton, s. [Aaron & Mehetable], b. Jan. 5, 1773 | 1 | 148 |
| Asa, s. [Joseph, 2d], b. Feb. 11, 1744/5 | 1 | 146 |
| Asa, s. [Aaron & Mehetable], b. May 8, 1769 | 1 | 148 |
| Asahel, s. [Samuel & Ruth], b. Feb. 19, 1791 | 2 | 67 |
| Asahel, b. Feb. 28, 1791; m. Jerusha C. **TRACY**, Jan. 15, 1817; d. June 19, 1849, ae 58 | 2 | 105 |
| Benjamin, s. [Rev. Thomas & Mary], b. June 11, 1754 | 1 | 138 |
| Bethiah, d. [Joseph & Elizabeth], b. July [ ], 1736 | 1 | 116 |
| Betty Williams, d. [Joseph & Ann], b. Jan. 5, 1781 | 2 | 8 |
| Charles, [s. Aaron & Eunice], b. Jan. 3, 1748/9 | 1 | 127 |
| Charles, [s. David & Jerusha], b. Dec. 1, 1775; d. June 27, 1776 | 1 | 89 |
| Charles, s. [David & Jerusha], b. Dec. 1, 1775; d. June 27, 1776 | 2 | 41 |
| Charles, 2d, [s. David & Jerusha], b. Apr. 15, 1777 | 1 | 89 |
| Charles, 2d, s. [David & Jerusha], b. Apr. 25, 1777; d. Oct. [ ], 1791 | 2 | 41 |
| Charles, 3d, s. [David & Jerusha], b. Apr. 30, 1794 | 2 | 41 |
| Daniell, [s. John], b. Aug. 30, 1705 | L-1 | 799 |
| Daniell, m. Elizabeth **HITCHCOCK**, Dec. 22, 1727 | L-3 | 8 |
| Daniell, m. Mary **BROWN**, Mar. 21, 1728 | L-1 | 447 |
| Daniell, [s. Daniell & Elizabeth], b. Feb. last day, 1728/9 | L-3 | 8 |
| Daniel, s. [Joseph & Mary], b. May 29, 1758 | 1 | 116 |
| David, [s. Dea. Nath[anie]ll & Mary], b. Jan. 7, 1717; d. Jan. 31, [1717] | L-3 | 194 |
| David, [s. Nathaniel & Mary], b. Jan. 7, 1717; d. Jan. 31, | | |

| | Vol. | Page |
|---|---|---|
| **SKINNER, SKINER**, (cont.) | | |
| [1717] | TM-1 | 194 |
| David, [s. Dea. Nath[anie]ll & Mary], b. Nov. 6, 1719 | L-3 | 194 |
| David, [s. Nathaniel & Mary], b. Nov. 6, 1719 | TM-1 | 194 |
| David, s. [Aaron & Eunice], b. Dec. 22, 1743 | 1 | 127 |
| David, m. Sarah **LORD**, b. of Colchestser, Dec. 8, 1766 | 1 | 89 |
| David, m. Sarah **LORD**, Dec. 8, 1766 | 2 | 41 |
| David, [s. David & Sarah], b. Apr. 15, 1769 | 1 | 89 |
| David, s. [David & Sarah], b. Apr. 15, 1769 | 2 | 41 |
| David, m. Jerusha **LORD**, Feb. 28, 1771 | 1 | 89 |
| David, m. Jerusha **LORD**, Mar. 1, 1771 | 2 | 41 |
| David, s. [Stephen & Mary], b. Feb. 13, 1787 | 2 | 59 |
| David, Dea., had slaves Ira, s. Dinah, b. May 22, 1788; Peter, s. Dinah, b. Dec. 25, 1790 | 2 | 48 |
| Deborah, [d. Ebenezar], b. Aug. 24, 1710 | L-3 | 195 |
| Deborah, d. Ebenezer, b. Aug. 24, 1710 | TM-1 | 195 |
| Deborah, d. Eben[eze]r & Sarah, b. Feb. 23, 1735 | TPR | 111 |
| Deborah, d. [Richard & Patience], b. Sept. 8, 1741 | 1 | 105 |
| Deborah, d. Richard, b. Sept. 8, 1741 | 1 | 135 |
| Deborah, d. [Richard & Patience], b. Sept. 8, 1741 | 1 | 147 |
| Deborah, [d. Richard, Jr. & Lucretia], b. Oct. 2, 1767 | 1 | 35 |
| Dolly, d. [Joseph & Ann], b. Sept. 4, 1777 | 2 | 8 |
| Dorothy, twin with Elizabeth, d. [Joseph & Elizabeth], b. Oct. [ ], 1738 | 1 | 116 |
| Dorothy, m. Policarpas **SMITH**, Jan. 4, 1758 | 1 | 113 |
| Ebenezar, s. Ebenezar, b. Aug. 8, 1703 | L-3 | 195 |
| Ebenezer, s. Eben[eze]r, b. Aug. 8, 1703 | TM-1 | 195 |
| Ebenezer, m. Sarah **TAYLOR**, Mar. 17, 1725 | L-1 | 450 |
| Ebenezer, [s. Ebenezer & Sarah], b. May 14, 1729 | L-1 | 450 |
| Eli, b. July 30, 1760 | 1 | 127 |
| Eli, s. [Aaron & Eunice], b. [ ] | 1 | 127 |
| Elijah, [s. Daniell & Mary], b. Dec. 1, 1728 | L-1 | 447 |
| Elijah, [s. Daniell & Elizabeth], b. June 8, 1742 | L-3 | 8 |
| Elijah, m. Mercy **PRATT**, Nov. 20, 1766 | 1 | 103 |
| Elizabeth, [d. Ebenezer & Sarah], b. July 17, 1727 | L-1 | 450 |
| Elisabeth, [d. Daniell & Elizabeth], b. Mar. 22, 1733 | L-3 | 8 |
| Elizabeth, m. Knight **SAXTON**, May 25, 1735 | 1 | 127 |
| Elizabeth, twin with Dorothy, d. [Joseph & Elizabeth], b. Oct. [ ], 1738; d. Apr. 20, 1754 | 1 | 116 |
| Elizabeth, m. Joseph **BLISS**, Mar. 22, 1753 | 1 | 29 |
| Elizabeth, w. Joseph, d. Apr. 22, 1754 | 1 | 116 |
| Elizabeth, d. [William & Elizabeth], b. Sept. 16, 1768 | 1 | 113 |
| Elizabeth, [d. Richard, Jr. & Lucretia], b. Aug. 7, 1769 | 1 | 35 |
| Elizabeth, of Conajaharrie, N. Y., m. Edmund **KELLOGG**, of Colchester, Aug. 29, 1848, by Rev. S. D. Jewett, Westchester | 3 | 38 |
| Esther, d. [John & Esther], b. July 24, 1735 | 1 | 143 |
| Esther, m. Samuel **BEEBE**, Jan. [ ], 1756 | 1 | 78 |

| | Vol. | Page |
|---|---|---|
| **SKINNER, SKINER**, (cont.) | | |
| Eunice, d. Dea. Nath[anie]ll & Mary, b. Dec. 15, 1715 | L-3 | 194 |
| Eunice, d. Nath[anie]l & Mary, b. Dec. 15, 1715 | TM-1 | 194 |
| Eunice, d. [Aaron & Eunice], b. July 22, 1738 | 1 | 127 |
| Eunice, d. [Aaron & Mehetable], b. Feb. 25, 1771 | 1 | 148 |
| Eunice, d. [David & Jerusha], b. Aug. 3, 1788 | 2 | 41 |
| George Christophers, s. [Dr. Thomas & Jerusha], b. May 23, 1796 | 2 | 68 |
| Gidion, [s. Ebenezar], b. Oct. 19, 1712 | L-3 | 195 |
| Gideon, s. Ebenezer, b. Oct. 19, 1712 | TM-1 | 195 |
| Hannah, [d. Richard & Han[n]ah], b. Apr. 16, 1714 | L-1 | 799 |
| Hannah, [d. Daniell & Elizabeth], b. May 26, 1745 | L-3 | 8 |
| Hannah Church, d. [William & Elizabeth], b. Apr. 24, 1773 | 1 | 113 |
| Hannah Day, d. [Joseph & Ann], b. Jan. 24, 1776 | 2 | 8 |
| Henry, [s. David & Jerusah], b. June 22, 1781 | 1 | 89 |
| Henrey, s. [David & Jerusha], b. June 22, 1781 | 2 | 41 |
| Huldah R., of Colchester, m. Capt. Robert **HUNGERFORD**, of East Haddam, Dec. 28, 1820, by Rev. Jacob Seales | 2 | 101 |
| Ichabod L., of Independence, Ohio, m. Nancy M. **BIGELOW**, of Colchester, May 19, 1824, by J. Seales, V. D. M., at the home of Stephen Bigelow | 2 | 178 |
| Ichabod Lord, [s. David & Sarah], b. Sept. 2, 1767 | 1 | 89 |
| Ichabod Lord, s. [David & Sarah], b. Sept. 2, 1767 | 2 | 41 |
| Isaac, [s. Joseph & Ann], b. Dec. 7, 1764 | 1 | 75 |
| Isaac, s. [Joseph & Ann], b. Dec. 7, 1764 | 2 | 8 |
| Isaac, twin with Olive, s. [Noah & Sarah], b. Apr. 13, 1768 | 1 | 150 |
| Isaac, Jr., m. Anne **GELLETT**, May 14, 1778 | 2 | 13 |
| Israel, s. Ebenezer, Jr. & Sarah, b. Jan. 18, 1730/31 | L-3 | 455 |
| Israel, s. [Richard & Patience], b. June 31, 1757 | 1 | 147 |
| Jacob, s. [Joseph & Ann], b. Nov. 19, 1766 | 2 | 8 |
| Jared, [s. Aaron & Eunice], b. Nov. 18, 1751 | 1 | 127 |
| Jemima, d. [Noah & Sarah], b. Oct. 16, 1763; d, Jan, 16, 1791 | 1 | 150 |
| Jerusha, m. Pelegg **BILL**, Jan. 1, 1755 | 1 | 108 |
| Jerusha,[d. David & Jerusha],b. Oct. 28, 1773 | 1 | 89 |
| Jerusha, d. [David & Jerusha], b. Oct. 28, 1773 | 2 | 41 |
| Jerusha C., [w. Asahel], d. Feb. 15, 1851, ae 57 | 2 | 105 |
| Joanah, [d. John], b. Jan. 27, 1707 | L-1 | 799 |
| Joanna, [d. Dea. Nath[anie]ll & Mary], b. Mar. 19, 1727 | TPR | 109 |
| Joanah, m. Caleb **LO[O]MIS**, [Feb.] 28, 1728/9 | L-3 | 8 |
| John, [s. John], b. Aug. 30, 1703 | L-1 | 799 |
| John, s. Eben[eze]r, Jr. & Sarah], b. Feb. 23, 1732/3 | TPR | 109 |
| John, [s. Daniell & Elizabeth], b. Aug. 17, 1738 | L-3 | 8 |
| John, [s. Nathaniel, Jr.], b. Sept. 7, 1738 | L-3 | 455 |
| John, Dea., d. Aug. 27, 1740, ae 66 | 1 | 137 |
| John, s. [Richard & Patience], b. Aug. 19, 1751 | 1 | 147 |
| John, m. Tabitha **WORTHINGTON**, Nov. 9, 1758 | 1 | 38 |
| John, [s. John & Tabitha], b. June 6, 1760 | 1 | 38 |
| Jona[than], s. Dea. Nath[anie]ll & Mary, b. Aug. 15, 1721 | TPR | 109 |

| | Vol. | Page |
|---|---|---|
| **SKINNER, SKINER**, (cont.) | | |
| Joseph, [s. Ebenezar], b. Jan. 17, 1707/8 | L-3 | 195 |
| Joseph, s. Ebenezer, b. Jan. 17, 1707/8 | TM-1 | 195 |
| Joseph, [s. John], b. Oct. 7, 1710 | L-1 | 799 |
| Joseph, m. Elizabeth **WILLIAMS**, Nov. [ ], 1733 | 1 | 116 |
| Joseph, s. [Joseph & Elizabeth], b. [ ], 1734; d. Aug. [ ], 1738 | 1 | 116 |
| Joseph, 2d, s. [Joseph & Elizabeth], b. Mar. [ ], 1741 | 1 | 116 |
| Joseph, s. Joseph, 2d, b. Aug. 19, 1743 | 1 | 146 |
| Joseph, m. Mary **BLISS**, Apr. [ ], 1756 | 1 | 116 |
| Joseph, m. Ann **DAY**, Sept. 30, 1762 | 1 | 75 |
| Joseph, m. Ann **DAY**, b. of Colchester, Sept. 30, 1762 | 2 | 8 |
| Joseph, s. [Joseph & Ann], b. Sept. 21, 1768 | 2 | 8 |
| Josiah, [s. Dea. Nath[anie]ll & Mary], b. Apr. 30, 1724 | TPR | 109 |
| Justin, s. [Joseph & Ann], b. Apr. 14, 1779 | 2 | 8 |
| Justin, s. [Stephen & Mary], b. Dec. 29, 1790 | 2 | 59 |
| Lois, d. [Joseph & Mary], b. July [ ], 1756 | 1 | 116 |
| Lovina, d. [Aaron & Eunice], b. Mar. 7, 1757 | 1 | 127 |
| Lucretia, [d. Richard, Jr. & Lucretia], b. June 18, 1780 | 1 | 35 |
| Lucy, d. [Joseph & Elizabeth], b. June [ ], 1749 | 1 | 116 |
| Lucy, m. Josiah **BROWN**, [ ], 1766 | 1 | 44 |
| Lucy, d. [William & Elizabeth], b. Apr. 5, 1775 | 1 | 113 |
| Lucy, d. Israel, b. Mar. 20, 1779 | 2 | 29 |
| Lydia, [d. Ebenezer], b. Apr. 20, 1723 | L-3 | 196 |
| Lydia, d. Ebenezer, b. Apr. 20, 1723 | TM-1 | 196 |
| Lydia, [d. Daniell & Elizabeth], b. Oct. 15, 1747; d. June 26, 1753 | L-3 | 8 |
| Lydia, d. [Aaron & Eunice], b. Aug. 5, 1754 | 1 | 127 |
| Lydia, d. [Noah & Sarah], b. Sept. 8, 1761 | 1 | 150 |
| Lydia, d. [David & Jerusha], b. Apr. 9, 1792 | 2 | 41 |
| Margaritt, [d. Ebenezer], b. Dec. 28, 1725 | L-3 | 196 |
| Margaret, d. Ebenezer, b. Dec. 28, 1725 | TM-1 | 196 |
| Maria, d. [Dr. Thomas & Jerusha], b. Jan. 14, 1789; d. Jan. 8, 1792 | 2 | 68 |
| Mary, w. Dea. Thomas, d. Mar. 26, 1704 | L-3 | 197 |
| Mary, w. Dea. Thomas, d. Mar. 26, 1704 | TM-1 | 197 |
| Mary, [d. Nathaniell & Mary], b. July 10, 1709 | L-3 | 194 |
| Mary, d. Nathaniel [& Mary], b. July 10, 1709 | TM-1 | 194 |
| Mary, [d. Ebenezar], b. Sept. 18, 1719 | L-3 | 195 |
| Mary, d. Ebenezer, b. Sept. 18, 1719 | TM-1 | 195 |
| Mary, m. Jonathan **KILLBORN**, Jr., Oct. 20, 1734 | 1 | 105 |
| Mary, [d. Ebenezer & Sarah], b. Mar. 17, 1736/7 | L-1 | 450 |
| Mary, d. Ebenezer, b. Mar. 17, 1736/7 | TPR | 112 |
| Mary, d. [Rev. Thomas & Mary], b. Jan. 31, 1742/3 | 1 | 138 |
| Mary, w. Rev. Thomas, d. Nov. 29, 1745 | 1 | 138 |
| Mary, [d. Aaron & Eunice], b. Feb. 4, 1745/6 | 1 | 127 |
| Mary, d. [Noah & Sarah], b. May 30, 1759 | 1 | 150 |
| Mary, d. [Joseph & Mary], b. Nov. 3, 1761 | 1 | 116 |

| | Vol. | Page |
|---|---|---|
| **SKINNER, SKINER**, (cont.) | | |
| Mary, m. Daniel **FOOT**, July 31, 1766 | 1 | 134 |
| Mary, d. [Stephen & Mary], b. Aug. 26, 1776 | 2 | 9 |
| Mary, d. [Stephen & Mary],. b. Aug. 26, 1776 | 2 | 59 |
| Mary, w. Stephen, d. Apr. 14, 1785, ae 33 | 2 | 59 |
| Mary A., m. Jonathan O. **WILLIAMS**, Nov. 9, 1840, by Rev. Daniel G. Sprague, West Chester | 2 | 272 |
| Mary Ann, d. [Asahel & Jerusha C.], b. June 11, 1819 | 2 | 105 |
| Mary E., m. John **DAVENPORT**, May 10, 1814 | 2 | 140 |
| Mary Elizabeth, d. [Dr. Thomas & Jerusha], b. Mar. 23, 1794 | 2 | 68 |
| Mehetable, d. [Rev. Thomas & Mary], b. Jan. 10, 1749/50; d. Jan. 10, 1749/50 | 1 | 138 |
| Mehetable, 2d, d. [Rev. Thomas & Mary], b. Jan. 8, 1756 | 1 | 138 |
| Mehetable, d. [Aaron & Mehetable], b. Sept. 13, 1767 | 1 | 148 |
| Nathaniell, m. Mary **GILLET**, June 13, 1706 | L-3 | 194 |
| Nathaniel, m. Mary **GILLET**, June 13, 1706 | TM-1 | 194 |
| Nathaniell, [s. Nathaniell & Mary], b. July 10, 1707 | L-3 | 194 |
| Nathaniel, s. Nathaniel & [Mary], b. July 10, 1707 | TM-1 | 194 |
| Nathaniel, [s. Nath[aniel] & Mary], b. June 23, 1732 | L-3 | 455 |
| Noah, m. Sarah **BIGELOW**, June 10, 1746 | 1 | 150 |
| Noah, s. [Noah & Sarah], b. Feb. 29, 1748; d. Aug. 27, 1751 | 1 | 150 |
| Noah, s. [Noah & Sarah], b. Aug. 10, 1753 | 1 | 150 |
| Noah, m. Jemima **ROBERTS**, Nov. 9, [ ]; d. Jan. 16, 1791 | 2 | 13 |
| Olive, twin with Isaac, d. [Noah & Sarah], b. Apr. 13, 1768 | 1 | 150 |
| Oliver, s. [David & Jerusha], b. Aug. 16, 1783; d. Apr. 10, 1786 | 2 | 41 |
| Oliver, 2d, s. [David & Jerusha], b. June 2, 1786 | 2 | 41 |
| Otis, [s. Richard, Jr. & Lucretia], b. Mar. 26, 1773 | 1 | 35 |
| Patience, d. [Richard & Patience], b. Feb. 23, 1744; d. June 17, 1745 | 1 | 147 |
| Patience, 2d, d. [Richard & Patience], b. Apr. 20, 1755 | 1 | 147 |
| Patience, m. Nathaniel **FOOT**, 3d, [ ] | 1 | 96 |
| Rachel, d. [John & Esther], b. Apr. 22, 1737 | 1 | 113 |
| Rachel, m. Jonathan **CROCKER**, Mar. 27, 1755 | 1 | 49 |
| Rachel, d. [Rev. Thomas & Mary], b. Dec. 21, 1758 | 1 | 138 |
| Rachel, d. [Joseph & Mary], b. Oct. 5, 1770 | 1 | 116 |
| Rachel, m. William **TOWNSEND**, Oct. [ ], 1784 | 2 | 56 |
| Ralph, of Marlborough, m. Clarissa **STARK**, of Colchester, May 28, 1823, by Salmon Cone, V. D. M. | 2 | 136 |
| Ralph H., m. Dorothy R. **STAPLES**, Sept. 15, 1850, by Rev. S. D. Jewett | 3 | 2 |
| Ralph Henry, s. [Asahel & Jerusha C.], b. Jan. 2, 1827 | 2 | 105 |
| Rebecca, d. Nath[aniel] & Mary, b. Dec. 3, 1730 | L-3 | 455 |
| R[h]oda, d. [Joseph, 2d], b. Sept. 6, 1754 | 1 | 146 |
| Richard, m. Han[n]ah **PRAT[T]**, Nov. 24, 1708 | L-1 | 799 |
| Richard, m. Patience **ROWLEY**, Feb. 24, 1736/7 | 1 | 105 |
| Richard, s. [Richard & Patience], b. Dec. 23, 1737 | 1 | 105 |
| Richard, s. [Richard & Patience], b. Dec. 28, 1737; | | |

| | Vol. | Page |
|---|---|---|
| **SKINNER, SKINER**, (cont.) | | |
| d. Feb. 23, 1738 | 1 | 147 |
| Richard, 2d, s. [Richard & Patience], b. Feb. 16, 1746 | 1 | 147 |
| Richard, Jr., m. Lucretia **OTIS**, Jan. 13, 1767 | 1 | 35 |
| Richard, m. Patience **ROWLEY**, [ ] | 1 | 147 |
| Rubin, [s. Daniell & Elizabeth], b. Aug. 8, 1750 | L-3 | 8 |
| Rubin, s. [Joseph, 2d], b. July 15, 1752 | 1 | 146 |
| Sally B., m. Alanson **WILLIAMS**, Nov. 22, 1805 | 2 | 150 |
| Sally L., m. Ebenezer **STARR**, b. of Colchester, Oct. 20, 1845, by Rev. S. D. Jewett | 3 | 25 |
| Sally Lewis, d. [Asahel & Jerusha C.], b. Mar. 10, 1822 | 2 | 105 |
| Samuell, s. Nathaniel, Jr., b. Sept. 11, 1735 | L-3 | 455 |
| Samuel, s. [Noah & Sarah], b. July 8, 1755; d. Oct. 19, 1756 | 1 | 150 |
| Samuel, s. [Joseph & Mary], b. May 3, 1765 | 1 | 116 |
| Samuel, s. [Noah & Sarah], b. Oct. 16, 1765 | 1 | 150 |
| Samuel, m. Ruth **OCKLEY**, of Chatham, Oct. 19, 1786 | 2 | 67 |
| Sarah, d. John, b. July 17, 1697 | L-1 | 799 |
| Sarah, [d. Ebenezar], b. Aug. 6, 1705 | L-3 | 195 |
| Sarah, d. Eben[eze]r, b. Aug. 6, 1705 | TM-1 | 195 |
| Sarah, m. Nathaniel **LO[O]MIS**, Aug. 7, 1721 | L-1 | 449 |
| Sarah, [d. Ebenezer & Sarah], b. Jan. 10, 1725/6 | L-1 | 450 |
| Sarah, [d. Daniell & Elizabeth], b. Nov. 25, 1735 | L-3 | 8 |
| Sarah, d. [Joseph & Elizabeth], b. Mar. [ ], 1747 | 1 | 116 |
| Sarah, d. [Noah & Sarah], b. Nov. 22, 1750; d. Oct. 20, 1756 | 1 | 150 |
| Sarah, m. John **ADDAMS**, May 1, 1755 | 1 | 120 |
| Sarah, 2d, d. [Noah & Sarah], b. Aug. 18, 1757 | 1 | 150 |
| Sarah, w. David, d. Aug. 30, 1769 | 1 | 89 |
| Sarah, w. David, d. Aug. 31, 1769 | 2 | 41 |
| Sarah, [d. David & Jerusha], b. Jan. 28, 1772 | 1 | 89 |
| Sarah, d. [David & Jerusha], b. Jan. 28, 1772 | 2 | 41 |
| Sarah, m. Timothy **WATERS**, Feb. 24, 1779 | 2 | 61 |
| Sarah, d. [Samuel & Ruth], b. Sept. 3, 1787 | 2 | 67 |
| Sophia, d. [Stephen & Mary], b. Nov. 26, 1788 | 2 | 59 |
| Stephen, s. [Richard & Patience], b. Mar. 18, 1753 | 1 | 147 |
| Stephen, m. Mary **FOOT**, Oct. 17, 1775 | 2 | 9 |
| Stephen, m. Mary **FOOT**, Oct. 17, 1775 | 2 | 59 |
| Stephen, s. [Stephen & Mary], b. Mar. 20, 1779 | 2 | 9 |
| Stephen, s. [Stephen & Mary], b. Mar. 20, 1779 | 2 | 59 |
| Stephen, m. Mary **CHAMBERLAIN**, Apr. 27, 1786 | 2 | 59 |
| Thomas, [s. Nathaniell & Mary], b. Apr. 6, 1712 | L-3 | 194 |
| Thomas, s. Nath[anie]l & Mary], b. Apr. 6, 1712 | TM-1 | 194 |
| Thomas, Rev., of Colchester, m. Mary **NEWHALL**, of Malden, July 9, 1740 | 1 | 138 |
| Thomas, s. [Rev. Thomas & Mary], b. May 31, 1741 | 1 | 138 |
| Thomas, Rev., of Colchester, m. Mary **THOMSON**, of Belerica, Oct. 2, 1746 | 1 | 138 |
| Thomas, Rev., d. Oct. 10, 1762 | 1 | 138 |
| Thomas, dr., of Colchester, m. Jerusha **CHRISTOPHERS**, of | | |

| | Vol. | Page |
|---|---|---|
| **SKINNER, SKINER**, (cont.) | | |
| of New London, Apr. 2, 1788; d. Aug. 7, 1796 | 2 | 68 |
| Thomas Manwaring, s. [Dr. Thomas & Jerusha], b. June 7, 1791 | 2 | 68 |
| Thompson Joseph, s. [Rev. Thomas & Mary], b. May 24, 1752 | 1 | 138 |
| Timothy, s. Ebenezer, b. July 10, 1721 | L-3 | 196 |
| Timothy, s. Ebenezer, b. July 10, 1721 | TM-1 | 196 |
| Uriah, s. [Joseph & Mary], b. Dec. 29, 1759 | 1 | 116 |
| Waltha, d. [Israel], b. Apr. 13, 1781 | 2 | 29 |
| Warren, s. [Samuel & Ruth], b. Mar. 7, 1789 | 2 | 67 |
| William, s. [Joseph & Elizabeth], b. July [ ], 1743 | 1 | 116 |
| William, m. Elizabeth **CHURCH**, Aug. 31, 1767 | 1 | 113 |
| Zerviah, [d. Dea. Nath[anie]ll & Mary], b. June 25, 1730 | TPR | 109 |
| ----, d. [Aaron & Eunice], b. Dec. [ ], 1742; d. Dec. [ ], 1742 | 1 | 127 |
| ----, m. Huldah **RILEY**, May 3, 1792 | 2 | 13 |
| **SLAYTON**, Adaline C., of Woodstock, Vt., m. J. Lyman **BRADLEY**, M. D., of Manchester, Conn., Nov. 28, 1850, by Rev. Albert F. Park | 3 | 47 |
| **SMITH**, Abby Lovisa, d. [Denison & Lovisa], b. Jan. 17, 1819; d. Aug. 25, 1845, ae 27 | 2 | 84 |
| Abigail, d. [Policarpus & Dorothy], b. Apr. 17, 1765 | 1 | 113 |
| Abigail, d. [Bartholomew & Hannah], b. Aug. 14, 1792 | 2 | 110 |
| Ann, m. John **JOHNSON**, Sept. 6, 1764 | 1 | 131 |
| Ann Melora, d. [George & Ann Eliza], b. July 25, 1838 | 2 | 272 |
| Anne, [d. David & Betty], b. May 27, 1768 | 1 | 79 |
| Asenath, d. [Policarpus & Dorothy], b. Oct. 1, 1762 | 1 | 113 |
| Bartholomew, b. May 5, 1763, in Groton; m. Hannah [ ], Sept. 8, 1791; d. Apr. 29, 1848, ae 85, in Colchester | 2 | 110 |
| Betty, d. [Policarpus & Dorothy], b. Dec. 29, 1758 | 1 | 113 |
| Caroline, d. [Denison & Lovisa], b. Sept. 8, 1821; d. Nov. 4, 1849, ae 28 | 2 | 84 |
| Charles, s. [John], b. Mar. 19, 1749 | 1 | 103 |
| Charles, of Ellington, m. Caroline C. **ARMSTRONG**, May 15, 1850, by Rev. George W. Pendleton | 3 | 3 |
| Charles Denison, s. [Denison & Lovisa], b. Aug. 30, 1828; d. Sept. 12, 1846, ae 18 y. 12 d. | 2 | 84 |
| Charlotte, d. [Bartholomew & Hannah], b. Nov. 30, 1795 | 2 | 110 |
| Dan[iel], m. Deborah **SPARROW**, May 15, 1806 | 2 | 136 |
| Daniel, s. [Policarpus & Dorothy], b. May 6, 1760 | 1 | 113 |
| David, s. [John], b. July 20, 1744 | 1 | 103 |
| David, m. Betty **STARK**, Aug. 15, 1765 | 1 | 79 |
| Deborah, w. Elijah, d. Mar. [ ], 1773 | 2 | 2 |
| Deborah Gales, d. [Capt. Elijah & Deborah], b. Feb. 28, 1773 | 2 | 2 |
| Denison, s. [Frederick & Abigail], b. Mar. 19, 1790 | 2 | 68 |
| Denison, m. Lovisa **OTIS**, Nov. 8, 1815, by Salmon Cone | 2 | 84 |
| Eliza J., of Salem, m. William **SHEPERD**, of Colchester, Mar. 23, 1835, by Rev. Lyman Strong | 2 | 275 |

| | Vol. | Page |
|---|---|---|
| **SMITH**, (cont.) | | |
| Elizabeth, d. [Joshua & Elizabeth], b. Apr. 12, 1752 | 1 | 132 |
| Ellen Maria, twin with Richard William, d. [Dan[iel] & Deborah], b. Aug. 30, 1809 | 2 | 136 |
| Fanny, d. [Bartholomew & Hannah], b. May 28, 1797 | 2 | 110 |
| Fanny, of Colchester, m. Walter **HALE**, of Glastonbury, Nov. 14, 1836, by Rev. Andrew M. Smith | 2 | 292 |
| Frederick, b. Aug. 22, 1762; m. Abigail **PAYNE**, Mar. 28, 1789; d. July 20, 1850, ae 58 | 2 | 68 |
| Frederick, of Chatham, m. Elizabeth Margery **WILLIAMS**, of Colchester, May 3, 1770 | 1 | 85 |
| George, s. [Bartholomew & Hannah], b. Nov. 9, 1801 | 2 | 110 |
| George, m. Ann Eliza **BULKELEY**, b. of Colchester, Nov. 16, 1834, by Rev. Lyman Strong | 2 | 272 |
| George, m. Elizabeth **GROT**, b. of Colchester, June 5, 1854, by Erastus Dickinson | 3 | 62 |
| Hannah, w. Bartholomew, b. June 20, 1764, in Groton; d. Jan. 16, 1845, ae 80 y. 6 m. 26 d., in Colchester | 2 | 110 |
| Hannah M., m. Erastus C. **BROWN**, June 6, 1847, by Rev. A. Gleason | 3 | 32 |
| Harriet, d. [Bartholomew & Hannah], b. Nov. 17, 1803 | 2 | 110 |
| Harriet, b. Nov. 17, 1803; m. Joseph D. **PACKWOOD**, Sept. 1, 1829, by Salmon Cone, V. D. M. | 2 | 214 |
| Henry, m. Rhoda **NILES**, Aug. 19, 1820 | 2 | 152 |
| Hiram, of Margaretta, Ohio, m. Rachel C. **KELLOGG**, of Colchester, Oct. 17, 1838, by Rev. Joel R. Arnold | 2 | 118 |
| Isaac, [s. Frederick & Margery], b. Oct. 7, 1771 | 1 | 85 |
| John, s. [Joshua & Elizabeth], b. Mar. 21, 1754 | 1 | 132 |
| John, of Somers, m. Mary Ann **MILLER**, of Colchester, May 10, 1843, by Rev. Joel R. Arnold | 3 | 4 |
| Joseph, m. Mary **FULLER**, Nov. 1, 1750 | 1 | 104 |
| Joseph, s. [Bartholomew & Hannah][, b. June 24, 1794 | 2 | 110 |
| Joseph, of Colchester, m. Almira **FOX**, of East Haddam, Mar. 29, 1824, by Salmon Cone, V. D. M. | 2 | 165 |
| Joshua, m. Elizabeth **PUMERY**, Jan. 11, 1750 | 1 | 132 |
| Julius T., of Middle Haddam, m. Margaret T. **HILLS**, of Colchester, Sept. 27, 1846, by Rev. P. Brockett | 3 | 28 |
| Martha, m. James **MUN**, Jr., Nov. 23, 1738 | 1 | 136 |
| Mary, d. [Joseph & Mary], b. Aug. 26, 1751 | 1 | 104 |
| Mary, d. [Joshua & Elizabeth], b. Mar. 6, 1756 | 1 | 132 |
| Mary, d. [Bartholomew & Hannah], b. Dec. 16, 1805 | 2 | 110 |
| Nathan, [s. David & Betty], b. Jan. 10, 1766 | 1 | 79 |
| Nehemiah, of Colchester, m. Abigail **AVERY**, of Groton, May 3, 1758 | 1 | 39 |
| Noah, s. [Thomas & Lydia], b. Nov. 9, 1782 | 2 | 35 |
| Olive, d. [John], b. Feb. 12, 1753 | 1 | 103 |
| Olive, m. James **TREADWAY**, Jr., Apr. 21, 1768 | 1 | 83 |
| Patience, d. [Policarpus & Dorothy], b. Jan. 27, 1767 | 1 | 113 |

| | Vol. | Page |
|---|---|---|
| **SMITH**, (cont.) | | |
| Policarpus, m. Dorothy **SKINNER**, Jan. 4, 1758 | 1 | 113 |
| Richard William, twin with Ellen Maria, s. [Dan[ie]] & Deborah], b. Aug. 30, 1809 | 2 | 136 |
| Roswell, s. [John], b. Feb. 19, 1741/2 | 1 | 103 |
| Ros[w]el[l], of Colchester, m. Abigail **HOLMS**, of Stonington, Mar. 11, 1762 | 1 | 57 |
| Ruth, m. Newhall **TAINTOR**, Jan. [ ], 1809 | 2 | 144 |
| Sally, d. [Frederick & Abigail], b. July 10, 1793 | 2 | 68 |
| Shubael, s. John, b. Dec. 7, 1737 | 1 | 103 |
| Shubael, of Colchester, m. Hannah **WATERMAN**, of Norwich, June 11, 1760 | 1 | 163 |
| Shubael, s. [Bartholomew & Hannah], b. May 2, 1800 | 2 | 110 |
| Susan Ann, d. [Dan[iel] & Deborah], b. May 20, 1807 | 2 | 136 |
| Temperance, d. [John], b. Dec. 7, 1746 | 1 | 103 |
| Temperance, d. [Joshua & Elizabeth], b. Mar. 21, 1758 | 1 | 132 |
| Temperance, wid. of Capt. John, m. James **TREADWAY**, Dec. 10, 1761 | 1 | 125 |
| Thomas, s. Thomas & Lydia, b. May 21, 1780 | 2 | 35 |
| Violett C., of Woodstock, m. Charles L. **PALMER**, Nov. 1, 1853, by Rev. Anthony Palmer | 3 | 60 |
| Zimmi L., of Norwich, m. Eliza L. **WELLS**, of Colchester, Mar. 20, 1823, by Rev. William Palmer | 2 | 136 |
| -----, child of [Joshua & Elizabeth], b. Aug. 29, 1750; d. Sept. 6, 1750 | 1 | 132 |
| -----, infant of [Bartholomew & Hannah], b. Mar. 13, 1799; d. Mar. 23, 1799 | 2 | 110 |
| **SNOBO**, Judith had d. Amelia **SWAN**, alias **WILLIAMS**, b. Jan. 24, 1810 (Perhaps "Judith **SWAN**") | 2 | 77 |
| **SNOW**, Hiram, m. Jane M. **HOLCOMB**, b. of Colchester, Sept. 10, 1834, by Rev. Augustus Bolles | 3 | 63 |
| John C., of Chatham, m. Phebe E. **EMMONS**, of Colchester, Dec. 27, 1825, by Jacob Seales, V. D. M., at the house of Dyar Emmons | 2 | 183 |
| Joseph, m. Laura A. **MITCHELL**, b. of Colchester, Jan. 8, 1854, by Rev. Anthony Palmer | 3 | 59 |
| Oliver, of Suffield, m. Laura Esther **CLARK**, of Colchester, Feb. 5, 1832, by Rev. Lyman Strong | 2 | 236 |
| Rebeckah, m. John **GATES**, Jr., Jan. 22, 1755 | 1 | 41 |
| **SOLES**, Gilbert, of Lebanon, m. Samentha **FRANCES**, of Colchester, Apr. 1, 1842, by Rev. Rob[er]t C. Mills | 2 | 192 |
| **SOUTHWORTH**, Gardiner, of Natchez, m. Sarah T. **ISHAM**, of Colchester, July 28, 1829, by Salmon Cone, V. D. M. | 2 | 214 |
| Gardiner, d. Nov. 9, 1851, ae 58, in Colchester | 2 | 214 |
| Roger, of Mansfield, m. Louisa **RANSOM**, of Colchester, Jan. 21, 1834, by Rev. Lyman Strong | 2 | 262 |
| **SPAF[F]ORD**, Mary, of Lebanon, m. Elisha **PRATT**, of Colchester, May 3, 1758 | 1 | 155 |

| | Vol. | Page |
|---|---|---|
| **SPALDING**, Harriet G., of Colchester, m. Samuel F. **BENNETT**, of Hampton, Apr. 12, 1841, by Rev. Daniel G. Sprague | 2 | 212 |
| **SPARROW**, Ardelia E., of Colchester, m. Edwin T. **CRAGIN**, of New York, May 31, 1853, by Rev. Erastus Dickinson | 3 | 56 |
| Deborah, m. Dan[iel] **SMITH**, May 15, 1806 | 2 | 136 |
| **SPENCER**, Alfred, of Sheffield, Conn., m. Frances C. **BUELL**, of Colchester, Mar. 26, 1846, by Rev. Joel R. Arnold | 3 | 27 |
| Betty, m. Niles **TAYLOR**, July 12, 1764 | 1 | 90 |
| Caleb, [s. Samuell], b. June 28, 1718 | L-1 | 450 |
| Edward, [s. Samuell], b. Apr. 29, 1711 | L-1 | 450 |
| Elijah, of Lyme, m. Mary **BIGELOW**, of Colchester, Sept. 12, 1824, by Rev. Simeon Dickinson | 2 | 169 |
| Emily B., of Colchester, m. Daniel A. **BURR**, of Haddam, Oct. 15, 1849, by Rev. Albert F. Park | 3 | 42 |
| Frances L., of Colchester, m. Charles D. **MUCKET**, of East Haddam, Feb. 17, 1847, by Rev. P. Brockett | 3 | 31 |
| Hannah, m. Joseph **WHAY**, Jan. 5, 1763 | 1 | 84 |
| Hepsibah, d. Samuell, b. Dec. 8, 1701 | L-1 | 450 |
| Joseph W., of East Haddam, m. Phebe L. **BROTHERHOOD**, of Colchester, Sept. 28, 1828, by Rev. Joseph Harvey | 2 | 207 |
| Phebe L., m. William M. **CARRIER**, May 12, 1850, by D. Trumbull | 3 | 3 |
| Sally, of East Haddam, m. Nathaniel P. **RANSOM**, of Colchester, Dec. 12, 1799 | 2 | 73 |
| Samuell, [s. Samuell], b. Mar. 8, 1704 | L-1 | 450 |
| Sarah, [d. Samuell], b. Sept. 14, 1714 | L-1 | 450 |
| Temperance, of Saybrook, m. John **BIGELOW**, Jr., Sept. 29, 1791 | 2 | 62 |
| Temperance, m. John **BIGELOW**, Jr., Sept. 29,. 1791 | 2 | 143 |
| William, [s. Samuell], b. Aug. 9, 1708 | L-1 | 450 |
| **SPERRY**, Ann Eliza, d. [David & Ann], b. Mar. 23, 1817 | 2 | 134 |
| David, m. Ann **WHITTLESEY**, Sept. [ ], 1811 | 2 | 134 |
| Orlando, s. [David & Ann], b. Sept. 23, 1819 | 2 | 134 |
| **SPICER**, Lois L., of Lebanon, m. Leonard T. **ARMSTRONG**, of Bozrah, Sept. 30, 1822, by Rev. William Palmer, at the house of [Rev. William Palmer] | 2 | 155 |
| **SPRAGUE**, Daniel Henry, s. [James L. & Juliett], b. June 8, 1840 | 3 | 8 |
| Edward Payson, s. [Daniel G. & Caroline W.], b. Oct. 18, 1843 | 3 | 9 |
| **STANDISH**, George G., s. [Lucius G. & Mary], b. Apr. 6, 1846 | 2 | 159 |
| George W., of Bozrah, m. Lucinda A. **HARVEY**, of Colchester, Feb. 14, 1850, by Rev. Albert F. Park | 3 | 12 |
| Julia F., d. [Lucius G. & Mary], b. Nov. 27, 1843 | 2 | 159 |
| Lucius G., b. Sept. 7, 1812, in Preston; m. Mary **BALCH**, Sept. 7, 1834, by Rev. Lyman Strong | 2 | 159 |
| Lucius G., of Bozrah, m. Mary **BALCH**, of Colchester, Sept. 7, 1834, by Rev. Lyman Strong | 2 | 269 |
| Mary P., d. [Lucius G. & Mary], b. Mar. 20, 1840, | | |

| | Vol. | Page |
|---|---|---|
| **STANDISH**, (cont.) | | |
| in Stafford, Conn. | 2 | 159 |
| **STANNARD**, Alanson B., m. Rebecca **RICHARDS**, b. of Colchester, Nov. 14, 1821, by Salmon Cone, V. D. M. | 2 | 149 |
| Henry Butler, s. [Alanson B. & Rebecca], b. Jan. 1, 1823 | 2 | 149 |
| Rebeckah R., of Colchester, m. Frederick W. **LEE**, of Guilford, Dec. 9, 1832, by Rev. Lyman Strong | 2 | 240 |
| **STANTON**, James M., m. Sophia **GILBERT**, b. of Hebron, Apr. 23, 1835, by Rev. Lyman Strong | 2 | 277 |
| **STAPLES**, Amia, [d. Elijah & Hannah], b. Apr. 20, 1747; d. May 30, 1747 | 1 | 95 |
| Benjamin, [s. Elijah & Hannah], b. July 23, 1751 | 1 | 95 |
| Dolly Irene, d. [Joseph & Susannah], b. July 15, 1821; d. Sept. 17, 1831 | 2 | 114 |
| Dorothy, m. Talcott Loveland **BUELL**, b. of Colchester (Westchester), June 26, 1838, by Rev. Joel R. Arnold | 2 | 276 |
| Dorothy R., m. Ralph H. **SKINNER**, Sept. 15, 1850, by Rev. S. D. Jewett | 3 | 2 |
| Dorothy Roxana, d. [Oren & Dorothy], b. Apr. 15, 1826 | 2 | 249 |
| Elijah, m. Hannah **DERBY**, Oct. 20, 1744 | 1 | 95 |
| Elijah, [s. Elijah & Hannah], b. Nov. 30, 1755 | 1 | 95 |
| Elijah, Jr., m. Hannah **BIGELOW**, b. of Colchester, Sept. 22, 1778 | 2 | 23 |
| Elizabeth, [d. Elijah & Hannah], b. Oct. 7, 1746 | 1 | 95 |
| Hannah Bigelow, d. [Elijah, Jr. & Hannah], b. Dec. 27, 1778(?) | 2 | 23 |
| Jane Elizabeth, d. [William O. & Abby Jane], b. Jan. 10, 1850 | 2 | 249 |
| Jerusha Kellogg, d. [Joseph & Susannah], b. Jan. 24, 1828 | 2 | 114 |
| John, [s. Elijah & Hannah], b. Feb. 14, 1753 | 1 | 95 |
| John, m. Rhoda **DAY**, Mar. 9, 1783; d. Nov. 7, 1832 | 2 | 44 |
| John Brainard, s. [Joseph & Susannah], b. July 22, 1814 | 2 | 114 |
| Joseph, s. [John & Rhoda], b. Apr. 23, 1784 | 2 | 44 |
| Joseph, m. Susannah **BRAINARD**, Dec. 8, 1808 | 2 | 114 |
| Joseph Oren, s. [Joseph & Susannah], b. July 30, 1826; d. Mar. 31, 1827 | 2 | 114 |
| Laura, of Colchester, m. John **AUSTIN**, of Canterbury, Oct. 21, 1832, by Rev. Lyman Strong | 2 | 239 |
| Lucy B., m. Nathaniel F. **BRAINARD**, b. of Colchester, Mar. 25, 1834, by Rev. Joseph Harvey | 2 | 264 |
| Lucy Brainard, d. [Joseph & Susannah], b. May 24, 1811 | 2 | 114 |
| Lucy Roxanna, d. [Oren & Dorothy], b. June 13, 1824; d. June 4, 1826 | 2 | 249 |
| Mary, m. William **REXFORD**, May 30, 1830, by Rev. Peter Griffing | 2 | 223 |
| Oren, s. [John & Rhoda], b. Feb. 28, 1788; d. Aug. 9, 1806 | 2 | 44 |
| Oren, m. Dorothy **BRAINARD**, Dec. 1, 1819; d. Aug. 9, 1826, ae 38 | 2 | 249 |
| Rhoda Day, d. [Joseph & Susannah], b. Nov. 18, 1809 | 2 | 114 |

| | Vol. | Page |
|---|---|---|
| **STAPLES**, (cont.) | | |
| Roxy Eliza, d. [Joseph & Susannah], b. Dec. 15, 1824 | 2 | 114 |
| Sally Maria, d. [Joseph & Susannah], b. Jan. 25, 1813; d. Sept. 24, 1831 | 2 | 114 |
| Sarah, [d. Elijah & Hannah], b. May 12, 1748, d. Nov. 18, 1749 | 1 | 95 |
| Susannah, d. [Joseph & Susannah], b. May 4, 1816 | 2 | 114 |
| Susannah, w. Joseph, d. Apr. 21, 1848, ae 60 | 2 | 114 |
| William O., m. Abby Jane **CARRIER**, Apr. 8, 1844 | 2 | 249 |
| William O., s. [William O. & Abby Jane], b. June 27, 1845 | 2 | 249 |
| William Oren, s. [Oren & Dorothy], b. Dec. 1, 1821 | 2 | 249 |
| **STARK**, Abraham, [s. Stephen & Eunice], b. Apr. 12, 1755 | 1 | 24 |
| Asahel, [s. Stephen & Eunice], b. Apr. 20, 1772 | 1 | 24 |
| Betty, m. David **SMITH**, Aug. 15, 1765 | 1 | 79 |
| Cata, [d. Stephen & Eunice], b. Sept. 10, 1760 | 1 | 24 |
| Charles, [s. Stephen & Eunice], b. Apr. 2, 1774 | 1 | 24 |
| Clarissa, of Colchester, m. Ralph **SKINNER**, of Marlborough, May 28, 1823, by Salmon Cone, V. D. M. | 2 | 136 |
| David, [s. Stephen & Eunice], b. Feb. 16, 1776 | 1 | 24 |
| Dema, [d. Stephen & Eunice], b. Oct. 15, 1762 | 1 | 24 |
| Ebenezer, [s. Stephen & Eunice], b. Feb. 20, 1768 | 1 | 24 |
| Elizabeth, d. [Samuel & Elizabeth], b. Aug. 13, 1743 | 1 | 147 |
| Emily, of Colchester, m. Edwin B. **GARDINER**, of Norwich, Apr. 16, 1848, by Rev. P. Brockett | 3 | 35 |
| Hanna[h], [d. Stephen & Eunice], b. Sept. 10, 1758 | 1 | 24 |
| James F., b. Feb. 25, 1806. Certified by Ruth Stark | 2 | 118 |
| James F., m. Clarissa A. **WORTHINGTON**, June 10, 1828, by Rev. Peter G. Clarke, of East Haddam | 2 | 204 |
| James F., m. Clarissa A. **WORTHINGTON**, b. of Colchester, June 10, 1828, by Rev. Peter G. Clarke, of East Haddam | 2 | 204 |
| Lucy E., of Colchester, m. George **WELLS**, of Richford, N. Y., June 10, 1833, by Rev. Lyman Strong | 2 | 255 |
| Mary, m. Israel **WELLS**, Sept. 15, 1823, by Salmon Cone, V. D. M. | 2 | 159 |
| Mary Maria, m. Henry **WATROUS**, Nov. 27, 1842, by Rev. Rob[er]t C. Mills | 2 | 275 |
| Olive, [d. Stephen & Eunice], b. Aug. 25, 1757 | 1 | 24 |
| Pardon, [s. Stephen & Eunice], b. Feb. 29, 1764 | 1 | 24 |
| Ruth, certified that James F. **STARK**, was b. Feb. 25, 1806 | 2 | 118 |
| Samuel, m. Elizabeth **JOYNER**, Oct. 7, 1742 | 1 | 147 |
| Stephen, m. Eunice **THOMAS**, Jan. 10, 1755 | 1 | 24 |
| Stephen, [s. Stephen & Eunice], b. Jan. 20, 1766 | 1 | 24 |
| Susanna, [d. Samuel & Elizabeth], b. Apr. 17, 1745 | 1 | 147 |
| Thomas, [s. Stephen & Eunice], b. Apr. 25, 1770 | 1 | 24 |
| William, m. Sally **BEEBE**, Feb. 16, 1793 | 2 | 55 |
| **STARR**, Ebenezer, m. Sally L. **SKINNER**, b. of Colchester, Oct. 20, 1845, by Rev. S. D. Jewett | 3 | 25 |
| **STEPHENS**, [see also **STEVENS**], Jonathan D., m. Rossetta | | |

| | Vol. | Page |
|---|---|---|
| **STEPHENS**, (cont.) | | |
| **BANNING**, Oct. 30, 1842, by Giles Shattuck, J. P. | 2 | 281 |
| **STERLING**, Abigail, m. Samuel **KELLOGG**, Jan. 8, 1735/6 | L-3 | 451 |
| Elizabeth, m. Noah **PUMORY**, Dec. 16, 1724 | L-1 | 444 |
| Esther, of Lyme, m. Daniel **YEOMANS**, of Colchester, May 10, 1770 | 1 | 88 |
| **STEVENS**, [see also **STEPHENS**], Abel D., m. Sophia **BOGUE**, b. of Colchester, Sept. 21, 1834, by Rev. Joseph Harvey | 2 | 271 |
| Hannah, m. Ezra **GATES**, June 23, 1756 | 1 | 47 |
| **STEWART**, Daniel, s. [Micael & Margarett], b. Apr. 2, 1745 | 1 | 132 |
| James, s. [Micael & Margarett], b. Feb. 27, 1742/3 | 1 | 132 |
| Mary, d. [Micael & Margarett], b. Mar. 1, 1738 | 1 | 132 |
| **STILES**, Eunice, d. Job, b. Jan. 28, 1754 | 1 | 152 |
| Eunice, d. [Job], b. Jan. 28, 1754; d. Jan. 31, 1756 | 1 | 144 |
| Grace, d. [Job], b. Nov. 3, 1755 | 1 | 144 |
| Hephzibah, [d. Job, Jr. & Lydia], b. June 17, 1759 | 1 | 22 |
| Jemima, d. Job, b. Jan. 10, 1746 | 1 | 144 |
| Job, Jr., of Colchester, m. Lydia **PHELPS**, of Hebron, Mar. 30, 1758 | 1 | 22 |
| John, s. [Job], b. Oct. 6, 1745 | 1 | 144 |
| Levinne, d. [Job], b. Apr. 3, 1749 | 1 | 144 |
| Samuel, s. Job, b. Aug. 25, 1751 | 1 | 152 |
| Samuel, s. [Job], b. Aug. 25, 1751; d. Oct. 26, 1757 | 1 | 144 |
| Samuel, s. [Job], b. Jan. 1, 1758 | 1 | 144 |
| **STILLMAN**, Statura Y., m. Daniel C. **CONE**, b. of East Haddam, Sept. 28, 1845, by Rev. M. P. Alderman | 3 | 25 |
| **STODDARD**, Eliza, of Ithaca, N. Y., m. Henry **BROWN**, of Colchester, July 7, 1852 | 3 | 51 |
| Hannah, m. Asaph **HURLBUTT**, June 18, 1809, at Groton | 2 | 111 |
| **STORES**, Aaron, s. [Lemuel & Hannah], b. Aug. 2, 1751 | 1 | 149 |
| Hannah, d. [Lemuel & Hannah], b. June 10, 1750; d. Sept. 30, [1750] | 1 | 149 |
| Hannah, d. [Lemuel & Hannah], b. Mar. [ ], 1755 | 1 | 149 |
| Hannah, w. Lemuel, d. June 29, 1759, ae 30 | 1 | 149 |
| Lemuel, m. Hannah **GILLETT**, June 11, 1749 | 1 | 149 |
| Lemuel, s. [Lemuel & Hannah], b. Apr. 26, 1753 | 1 | 149 |
| Martha, m. Nehemiah **GILLETT**, Jan. 22, 1761 | 1 | 55 |
| Roger, 2d, s. [Lemuel & Hannah], b. Apr. 12, 1759 | 1 | 149 |
| **STOWEL**, Ebenezer, of Windham, m. Betsey **LOOMIS**, of Colchester, Feb. 24, 1822, by Rev. Jacob Seales | 2 | 113 |
| **STRANAHAN**, James, of East Haddam, m. Sophia **WILLIAMS**, of Salem, June 21, 1831, by Rev. Lyman Strong | 2 | 232 |
| **STRICKLAND**, Ann D., of New London, m. George A. **MORGAN**, of Colchester, Jan. 8, 1851, by Rev. Albert F. Park | 2 | 69 |
| William, of New York, m. Abby Jane **BROWN**, of Colchester, Aug. 20, 1851, by Rev. George W. Pendleton | 2 | 58 |
| **STRONG**, Abigail H., [w. Edward H.], d. Feb. 20, 1843, ae 21 | | |

| | Vol. | Page |
|---|---|---|
| **STRONG**, (cont.) | | |
| (In the marriage the name is "Abigail M.") | 2 | 280 |
| Adonijah, s. [Asa & Bettras], b. May 21, 1749 | 1 | 133 |
| Ambrose, s. [Asa & Bettras], b. Nov. 1, 1750 | 1 | 133 |
| Ambrose, m. Lydia **HOLDREDGE**, Oct. 4, 1770 | 2 | 62 |
| Ann, m. George **STRONG**, b. of Colchester, Jan. 2, 1821, by Salmon Cone, V. D. M. | 2 | 103 |
| Anna, [d. Josiah & Hannah], b. Feb. 11, 1735 | 1 | 46 |
| Anson Young, s. [Zenas & Polly], b. Dec. 19, 1792 | 2 | 54 |
| Asa, m. Bettras **CROUCH**, June 7, 1744 | 1 | 133 |
| Asahell, [s. Josiah], b. June 22, 1725 | L-3 | 195 |
| Asahel, s. Josiah, b. June 22, 1725 | TM-1 | 195 |
| Asahel, s. [Asa & Bettras], b. Mar. 29, 1747; d. Apr. 13, 1748 | 1 | 133 |
| Asahel, 2d, s. [Asa & Bettras], b. Oct. 17, 1760 | 1 | 133 |
| Asenath, [d. Ezra & Temperance], b. Aug. 3, 1760 | 1 | 49 |
| Benjamin, [s. Josiah & Hannah], b. Feb. 15, 1759 | 1 | 46 |
| Bette, d. [Asa & Bettras], b. Nov. 3, 1755 | 1 | 133 |
| Caleb, [s. Josiah], b. Feb. 20, 1713/14 | L-3 | 194 |
| Caleb, s. Josiah, b. Feb. 20, 1713 | TM-1 | 194 |
| Caleb, [s. Josiah & Hannah], b. June 20, 1749 | 1 | 46 |
| Charles, s. [Ambrose & Lydia], b. Aug. 27, 1777 | 2 | 62 |
| Clarissa, of Colchester, m. Levi **MANN**, of Hebron, Jan. 8, 1832, by Rev. Lyman Strong | 2 | 235 |
| Clarissa M., of Colchester, m. Rev. Jason **ATWATER**, of Middlebury, May 4, 1837, by Rev. Lyman Strong | 2 | 106 |
| Content, [d. Josiah & Hannah], b. Apr. 20, 1754 | 1 | 46 |
| Daniel, m. Clarissa S. **BROWN**, b. of Colchester, Feb. 26, 1834, by Rev. Lyman Strong | 2 | 263 |
| Darkis, [d. John & Abijah], b. Feb. 10, 1729/30 | L-1 | 446 |
| David, [s. Ezra], b. June 6, 1751 | 1 | 146 |
| Dimis, of Colchester, m. Israel **KENYON**, of Onondaga, N. Y., Feb. 5, 1821, by Salmon Cone, V. D. M. | 2 | 123 |
| Dorothy, [d. Josiah], b. May 25, 1718 | L-3 | 194 |
| Eastus, of Hebron, m. Mary **STRONG**, of Colchester, Dec. 6, 1829, by Salmon Cone, V. D. M. | 2 | 216 |
| Edward H., m. Abigail M. **UTTLEY**, Apr. 12, 1842, by Rev. Joel R. Arnold | 2 | 280 |
| Eleazer, m. Harriet **WYLES**, Mar. 31, 1830, by Salmon Cone, V. D. M. | 2 | 221 |
| Elijah, twin with Elisha, s. [Ambrose & Lydia], b. June 26, 1771 | 2 | 62 |
| Elisha, twin with Elijah, s. [Ambrose & Lydia], b. June 26, 1771 | 2 | 62 |
| Elizabeth, d. Josiah, b. Oct. 21, 1705 | L-3 | 194 |
| Elizabeth, d. Josiah, b. Oct. 21, 1705 | TM-1 | 194 |
| Elizabeth W., of Colchester, m. Roger L. **PHELPS**, of Hebron, May 29, 1834, by Rev. Lyman Strong | 2 | 267 |
| [E]uniss, [d. Josiah], b. Nov. 19, 1711 | L-3 | 194 |

| | Vol. | Page |
|---|---|---|
| **STRONG**, (cont.) | | |
| Eunice, d. Josiah, b. Nov. 19, 1711 | TM-1 | 194 |
| [E]unice, m. Ebenezer **THOMAS**, Dec. 7, 1730 | L-3 | 8 |
| Eunice, [d. John & Eunice], b. Aug. 23, 1767 | 1 | 76 |
| Ezra, [s. Ezra & Temperance], b. Aug. 4, 1763 | 1 | 49 |
| Ezra, d. Mar. 7, 1785 | 2 | 38 |
| Freedom, [d. Ezra], b. Nov. 13, 1745 | 1 | 146 |
| George, m. Ann **STRONG**, b. of Colchester, Jan. 2, 1821, by Salmon Cone, V. D. M. | 2 | 103 |
| Gibbert, [s. John & Rachel], b. Mar. 2, 1770 | 1 | 75 |
| Hannah, [d. Josiah & Hannah], b. June 8, 1734 | 1 | 46 |
| Hannah, m. Ezra **BIGELOW**, Sept. 1, 1755 | 1 | 12 |
| Henry, s. [Zenas & Polly], b. Oct. 30, 1790 | 2 | 54 |
| Irena, [d. Josiah], b. Oct. 20, 1722 | L-3 | 195 |
| Irena, d. Josiah, b. Oct. 20, 1722 | TM-1 | 195 |
| Irene, d. [Asa & Bettras], b. May 20, 1745 | 1 | 133 |
| James Levi, s. James, of Bolton, Ct., b. June 8, 1852, in Colchester | 2 | 286 |
| Jamin, of Bolton, Conn., m. Lucy A. **GILLETT**, of Colchester, Sept. 20, 1848, by Rev. F. W. Bill | 3 | 37 |
| Jemima, [d. Josiah & Hannah], b. Apr. 7, 1738 | 1 | 46 |
| Jemima, m. Amasa **BIGELOW**, Dec. 13, 1754 | 1 | 11 |
| Joanna, d. [Asa & Bettras], b. Dec. 10, 1753 | 1 | 133 |
| Johana, m. Benjamin **WARNER**, Mar. 17, 1719 | L-1 | 449 |
| John, m. Abijah **CHAPELL**, Feb. 5, 1723/4 | L-1 | 446 |
| John, [s. John & Abijah], b. Feb. 8, 1724/5 | L-1 | 446 |
| John, [s. Ezra], b. Dec. 7, 1743 | 1 | 146 |
| John, of Colchester, m. Eunice **BALDWIN**, of Norwich, Nov. 7, 1764 | 1 | 76 |
| John, m. Rachel **CURTIS**, Sept. 26, 1765 | 1 | 75 |
| John, [s. John & Rachel], b. Apr. 26, 1766 | 1 | 75 |
| Joshua, s. Josiah, b. July 20, 1720 | L-3 | 195 |
| Joshua, s. Josiah, b. July 20, 1720 | TM-1 | 195 |
| Joshua, [s. Josiah & Hannah], b. Apr. 24, 1743 | 1 | 46 |
| Josiah, [s. Josiah], b. Sept. 9, 1709 | L-3 | 194 |
| Josiah, s. Josiah, b. Sept. 9, 1709 | TM-1 | 194 |
| Josiah, m. Hannah **FULLER**, Nov. 1, 1733 | 1 | 46 |
| Josiah, [s. Josiah & Hannah], b. Jan. 28, 1740 | 1 | 46 |
| Kettern, d. [Ambrose & Lydia], b. Jan. 27, 1773 (Perhaps "Betterm" or Rettern") | 2 | 62 |
| Loes, [d. John & Abijah], b. Nov. 22, 1728; d. Jan. 14, 1729 | L-1 | 446 |
| Lucy, [d. Ezra], b. Oct. 4, 1748 | 1 | 146 |
| Lyman, Rev., b. Sept 12, 1781, in South Hampton, Mass. | 2 | 83 |
| Mary, [d. Josiah], b. Sept. 19, 1707 | L-3 | 194 |
| Mary, d. Josiah, b. Sept. 19, 1707 | TM-1 | 194 |
| Mary, [d. Josiah & Hannah], b. Oct. 10, 1746 | 1 | 46 |
| Mary, of Colchester, m. Eastus **STRONG**, of Hebron, Dec. 6, 1829, by Salmon Cone, V. D. M. | 2 | 216 |

| | Vol. | Page |
|---|---|---|
| **STRONG**, (cont.) | | |
| Nathaniel, m. Ann E. **BIGELOW**, b. of Colchester, Dec. 31, 1844, by Rev. Robert C. Mills | 3 | 18 |
| Patience, [d. Josiah & Hannah], b. Apr. 25, 1752; d. Jan. 15, 1753 | 1 | 46 |
| Rachell, [d. Josiah], b. Apr. 21, 1716 | L-3 | 194 |
| Rachel, d. Josiah, b. Apr. 21, 1716 | TM-1 | 194 |
| Rachel, [d. John & Rachel], b. June 18, 1768 | 1 | 75 |
| Rebecca, of Colchester, m. Hazael* **GOTT**, of Hebron, Mar. 20, 1821, by Rev. Salmon Cone (* Correction handwritten in margin of original manuscript.) | 2 | 154 |
| Rettern, [see under Kettern] | | |
| Roxanna, d. [Ambrose & Lydia], b. Apr. 13, 1775; d. Mar. 13, 1776 | 2 | 62 |
| Ruben, s. John & Abijah, b. May 8, 1733 | TPR | 110 |
| Solomon, [s. Ezra & Temperance], b. Aug. 19, 1765 | 1 | 49 |
| Susannah, [d. John & Eunice], b. Sept. 4, 1765 | 1 | 76 |
| Temperance, [d. Ezra & Temperance], b. Jan. 15, 1758 | 1 | 49 |
| Vesta, d. [Zenas & Polly], b. Apr. 13, 1789, in Amena Dutchers County, N. Y. | 2 | 54 |
| Zebalon, [s. John & Abijah], b. Dec. 11, 1726 | L-1 | 446 |
| Zenas, m. Polly **YOUNGS**, [ ], in N. Y. State | 2 | 54 |
| -----, m. Caleb **LOOMIS**, Jr., Aug. 31, 1755 | 1 | 40 |
| -----, d. [David], b. Mar. 27, 1775 | 2 | 38 |
| **STUKLEY**, Sarah, [m.] Ephraim **DAY**, [ ] | 1 | 12 |
| **SULLARD**, Maria, m. Sherman **WILLIAMS**, b. of Lebanon, Jan. 30, 1839, by Rev. Lyman Strong | 2 | 98 |
| **SWAN**, Abigail Marvin, d. [Asa & Ann], b. Aug. 21, 1772 | 2 | 5 |
| Amelia, alias **WILLIAMS**, d. Judith **SNOBO** (?), b. Jan. 24, 1810 | 2 | 77 |
| Anne, d. [Asa & Ann], b. Aug. 13, 1774 | 2 | 5 |
| Asa, m. Ann **BULKELEY**, May 29, 1771 | 2 | 5 |
| Asa, s. [Asa & Anna], b. May 16, 1779 | 2 | 52 |
| Benjamin, Jr., of Woodstock, Vt., m. Ann **ISHAM**, of Colchester, July 3, 1834, by Rev. Lyman Strong | 2 | 268 |
| Elias, s. [Asa & Anna], b. Mar. 31, 1781 | 2 | 52 |
| Lois, d. [Asa & Anna], b. Mar. 20, 1777 | 2 | 52 |
| Mary, of Stonington, m. John **CAVERLEY**, of Colchester, Mar. 15, 1753 | 1 | 100 |
| Nabby Marvin, d. [Asa & Anna], b. Aug. 21, 1771 | 2 | 52 |
| Nancy, d. [Asa & Anna], b. Aug. 13, 1774 | 2 | 52 |
| Nancy, m. Dudley **WORTHINGTON**, Oct. 5, 1793; d. Jan. 27, 1814 | 2 | 74 |
| Sally, d. [Asa & Anna], b. July 14, 1784 | 2 | 52 |
| Thomas J., of Franklin, m. Elizabeth C. **WAY**, of Colchester, Oct. 29, 1834, by Rev. Christopher Leffingwell | 3 | 64 |
| **SWEET**, Ama, [d. Joseph & Freelove], b. Aug. 17, 1746 | 1 | 147 |
| Anna, d. [Joseph & Freelove], b. Mar. 16, 1754 | 1 | 147 |

| | Vol. | Page |
|---|---|---|
| **SWEET**, (cont.) | | |
| Eben[eze]r, [s. Joseph & Freelove], b. Apr. 5, 1743 | 1 | 147 |
| Freelove, d. [Joseph & Freelove], b. Dec. 22, 1738 | 1 | 147 |
| Freelove Tennant, [s. Joseph], d. [ ], 1790, in Deerfield, Mass., ae 80 | 1 | 147 |
| Joseph, m. Freelove **TENNANT**, Mar. 16, 1738 | 1 | 147 |
| Joseph, s. [Joseph & Freelove], b. Aug. 4, 1741 | 1 | 147 |
| Sarah, d. [Joseph & Freelove], b. Mar. 17, 1756 | 1 | 147 |
| **SWETLAND**, Sarah, w. John, formerly Wid. **TREADWAY**, d. Feb. 28, 1753, O. S. | L-1 | 654 |
| **SWIFT**, Catharine Esther, d. [Charles A. & Henrietta], b. Aug. 8, 1841; d. Apr. 28, 1842, ae 2 | 2 | 195 |
| Charity, w. [Nathan], d. [ ], in Lebanon, ae [ ] | 2 | 195 |
| Charity E., of Colchester, m. Welcome K. **ADAMS**, of Canterbury, Mar. 16, 1841, by Rev. Joel R. Arnold | 2 | 231 |
| Charles A., of Windham, m. Henrietta **BENJAMIN**, of Colchester, Apr. 17, 1838, by Rev. Andrew M. Smith | 2 | 195 |
| Charles A., d. Jan. 18, 1851, ae 38 | 2 | 195 |
| Harriet, of Colchester, m. Isaac D. **CHAPPELL**, of Lyme, Mar. 27, 1839, by Rev. Joel R. Arnold | 2 | 169 |
| Henrietta Benjamin, d. [Charles A. & Henrietta], b. Feb. 6, 1840 | 2 | 195 |
| Mary, m. Daniell **PRATT**, Oct. [ ], 1733 | 1 | 136 |
| Nathan, d. Apr. 30, 1843, ae 65 | 2 | 195 |
| **TABER**, Gurdon, m. Zemiah **MORGAN**, Jan. 23, 1839, by Benj[amin] Trumbull, J. P. | 2 | 97 |
| **TAINTOR**, Abigail B., of Colchester, m. Eli S. **CORBIN**, of Chenango Co., n. Y., June 5, 1843, by Rev. Joel R. Arnold | 3 | 6 |
| Abigail Brainard, d. [Newhall & Ruth], b. Mar. 13, 1820 | 2 | 144 |
| Addison Copp, s. [Newhall & Ruth], b. Sept. 2, 1835 | 2 | 144 |
| Ann, [d. Micaiell & Vniss], b. Oct. 21, 1734; d. Jan. 31, 1755 | L-1 | 451 |
| Anne, [d. Charles & Mary], b. July 13, 1767 | 1 | 95 |
| Belle, d. [John & Esther], b. May 9, 1752 | 1 | 182 |
| Charles, s. [Newhall & Ruth], b. Feb. 26, 1818; d. July 25, 1840, at Harrisonburgh, La. | 2 | 144 |
| Charles, [s. Micaiell & Vniss], b. Feb. 8, 1722/3 | L-1 | 451 |
| Charles, s. [John & Sarah], b. Dec. 17, 1762 | 1 | 182 |
| Charles, m. Mary **WELLS**, Aug. 20, 1766 | 1 | 95 |
| Charles, [s. Charles & Mary], b. Jan. 1, 1769 | 1 | 95 |
| Charles, Capt., d. Mar. 16, 1807 | 1 | 95 |
| Charlotte, d. [Newhall & Ruth], b. Apr. 13, 1822 | 2 | 144 |
| Clarissa, d. [Roger & Nabby], b. Sept. 19. 1790 | 2 | 60 |
| Edward Morton, s. [Morton & Mary Angelina], b. Aug. 17, 1834, in Buffalo, N. Y.; d. Feb. 27, 1837, in Colchester | 2 | 257 |
| Esther, d. [John & Esther], b. Jan. 10, 1754; d. Apr. 12, 1755 | 1 | 182 |
| Esther, 2d, d. [John & Esther], b. Apr. 26, 1756 | 1 | 182 |
| Esther, w. [John], d. Sept. 19, 1756 | 1 | 182 |

| | Vol. | Page |
|---|---|---|
| **TAINTOR**, (cont.) | | |
| Esther, m. Joseph **ISHAM**, Jr., May 18, 1774 | 1 | 144 |
| Vniss (Eunice], [d. Micaiell & Vniss], b. Apr. 13, 1717 | L-1 | 451 |
| Eunice, m. Aaron **SKINNER**, Aug. 4, 1737 | 1 | 127 |
| Eunice, m. Aaron **SKINNER**, Aug. 4, 1737 | TPR | 112 |
| Eunice, d. [John & Sarah], b. June 23, 1759; d. July 28, 1759 | 1 | 182 |
| [E]unice, [d. Charles & Mary], b. Dec. 27, 1777 | 1 | 95 |
| Garshom, s. [John & Sarah], b. May 17, 1765 | 1 | 182 |
| Harriet Newell, d. [Newhall & Ruth], b. Sept. 15, 1815 | 2 | 144 |
| Jesse F., of Venice, Ohio, m. Eunice S. **PIERCE**, of Colchester, July 28, 1834, by Rev. Lyman Strong | 2 | 268 |
| John, [s. Micaiell & Vniss], b. July 23, 1725 | L-1 | 451 |
| John, m. Esther **CLARK**, [ ], 1751 | 1 | 182 |
| John, m. Sarah **BULKELEY**, Nov. 23, 1758 | 1 | 182 |
| John, s. [John & Sarah], b. Sept. 23, 1760 | 1 | 182 |
| John Edward, s. [Morton & Mary Angelina], b. Dec. 31, 1836 | 2 | 257 |
| Lydia, [d. Micael, Jr. & Lydia], b. Jan. 8, 1768 | 1 | 25 |
| Mary, [d. Micaiell & Vniss], b. Nov. 6, 1727 | L-1 | 451 |
| Mary, m. David **WELLS**, Jan. 19, 1748/9 | 1 | 151 |
| Mary Skinner, d. [Newhall & Ruth], b. Apr. 14, 1810 | 2 | 144 |
| Micaiell, m. Vniss **FOOT**, Dec. 3, 1712 | L-1 | 451 |
| Micaiell [& Vniss], b. Dec. 31, 1719 | L-1 | 451 |
| Micaiell, d. Feb. 19, 1730/31 | L-3 | 456 |
| Michael, [s. Michael, Jr.], b. Mar. 14, 1748 | 1 | 102 |
| Michael, Jr., d. Nov. 20, 1748 | 1 | 102 |
| Mic[h[ael, Jr., m. Lydia **LO[O]MIS**, Apr. 2, 1767 | 1 | 25 |
| Mic[h]ael, [s. Micael, Jr. & Lydia], b. Apr. 7, 1770 | 1 | 25 |
| Morton, m. Mary Angelina **AVERY**, Sept. 19, 1833, by Rev. Lyman Strong | 2 | 257 |
| Morton Avery, s. [Morton & Mary Angelina], b. Apr. 10, 1841, at Natchez, Miss. | 2 | 257 |
| Newhall, m. Ruth **SMITH**, Jan. [ ], 1809 | 2 | 144 |
| Prudence, [d. Micaiell & Vniss], b. Dec. 9, 1729 | L-1 | 451 |
| Prudence, m. John **OTIS**, Dec. 20, 1750 | 1 | 153 |
| Ralph Smith, s. [Newhall & Ruth], b. Nov. 13, 1811 | 2 | 144 |
| Roger, s. [John & Sarah], b. Dec. 22, 1767 | 1 | 182 |
| Roger, m. Nabby **BULKELEY**, Dec. 6, 1789 | 2 | 60 |
| Roger, s. [Newhall & Ruth], b. Aug. 16, 1824 | 2 | 144 |
| Ruth Caroline, d. [Newhall & Ruth], b. Dec. 28, 1830 | 2 | 144 |
| Sarah, m. Noah **CLARK**, June 10, 1719 | L-1 | 447 |
| Sarah, [d. Micaiell & Vniss], b. Apr. 3, 1731 | L-1 | 451 |
| Sarah, [d. Michael, Jr.], b. Dec. 30, 1745 | 1 | 102 |
| Sarah, m. John **WATROUS**, [ ], 1751 | 1 | 118 |
| Sarah, [d. Micael, Jr. & Lydia], b. Dec. 23, 1771 | 1 | 25 |
| Sarah, m. Joshua Robbins **BULKELEY**, Sept. 7, 1793 | 2 | 68 |
| Sarah Bulkeley, d. [John & Sarah], b. Aug. 22, 1773 (handwritten in original manuscript) | 1 | 182 |
| Solomon, s. [John & Sarah], b. Oct. 7, 1769 | 1 | 182 |

| | Vol. | Page |
|---|---|---|
| **TAINTOR**, (cont.) | | |
| Solomon, s. [Newhall & Ruth], b. Apr. 4, 1828 | 2 | 144 |
| Sophia Deming, d. [Newhall & Ruth], b. Sept. 20, 1813 | 2 | 144 |
| **TALBOT, TALBOTT**, Ann, wid. Benj[am]in, d. Oct. 18, 1864, at Iowa City | 2 | 41 |
| Benjamin, of Murfreesburg, N. C., m. Anne **WATROUS**, of Colchester, Sept. 30, 1817; d. July 14, 1834, at Marietta, Ohio | 2 | 147 |
| Benjamin, s. [Benjamin & Anne], b. May 22, 1827, at Brooklyn, N. Y. | 2 | 147 |
| Caroline, d. [Benjamin & Anne], b. Apr. 12, 1821, at Murfreesburg, N. C.; d. Aug. 23, 1827, at Colchester | 2 | 147 |
| Mary Anne Wetmore, d. [Benjamin & Anne], b. Aug. 25, 1830, at Brooklyn; d. May 22, 1832, at Brooklyn, N. Y. | 2 | 147 |
| Rebecca, d. [Benjamin & Anne], b. May 4, 1819, at Murfreesburg, N. C.; d. June 6, 1824, in Brooklyn, N Y. | 2 | 147 |
| **TALCOTT**, Harvey, of Coventry, m. Sarah **KELLOGG**, of Colchester, Apr. 17, 1822, by Solomon Cone, V. D. M. | 2 | 83 |
| **TARBELL**, Margaret, m. Zebulon **BILLINGS**, Aug. 9, 1798 | 2 | 129 |
| **TATTOON**, Anthony, m. Mary Ann [ ] | 2 | 108 |
| Austin, s. [Anthony & Mary Ann], b. Jan. 14, 1826 | 2 | 108 |
| **TAYLOR, TAYLER**, Amanda A., of Colchester, m. David **HAYNES**, of Lebanon, Nov. 29, 1849, by Rev. John Avery, of Exeter | 3 | 44 |
| Annee, [d. Ebenezer & Phebe], b. Aug. 5, 1747, in Barnstable | 1 | 49 |
| Benjamin, twin with Joseph, [s. Ebenezer & Phebe], b. Nov. 13, 1753 | 1 | 49 |
| Bennett, [s. Niles & Betty], b. June 24, 1767 | 1 | 90 |
| Bethia, [d. James], b. Nov. 12, 1709 | L-1 | 799 |
| Bettey, m. Joseph **INGRAHAM**, Nov. 24, 1773 | 1 | 139 |
| Caroline B., of Colchester, m. David **FOOTE**, of Marlborough, Apr. 17, 1831, by Rev. Lyman Strong | 1 2 | 230 |
| Charles, [s. Josiah & Sibbel], b. Nov. 29, 1763 | 1 | 52 |
| Charles, of Great Barrington, Mass., m. Emily A. **JUDD**, of Colchester, June 3, 1823, by Salmon Crane, V. D. M. | 2 | 146 |
| Charles Gustavus, of New York, m. Elizabeth Frances **OSBORN**, of Colchester, Sept. 11, 1844, by Rev. Joel R. Arnold | 3 | 16 |
| Clarissa, [d. Josiah & Sibbel], b. Apr. 1, 1775 | 1 | 52 |
| Daniel, [s. Josiah & Sibbel], b. Oct. 5, 1765 | 1 | 52 |
| Daniel, m. Margaret **FOOT**, Oct. 28, 1792; d. May 11, 1812, ae 46 | 2 | 90 |
| Daniel, s. [Daniel & Margaret], b. Oct. 17, 1796 | 2 | 90 |
| Ebenezer, [s. Ebenezer & Phebe], b. Dec. 1, 1751 | 1 | 49 |
| Edward, [s. Ebenezer & Phebe], b. Nov. 11, 1755 | 1 | 49 |
| Esther, m. Charles **FOOT**, b. of Colchester, Nov. 22, 1820, by Salmon Cone, V. D. M. | 2 | 97 |
| George, m. Frances Caroline **CONE**, b. of Colchester, Feb. | | |

| | Vol. | Page |
|---|---|---|
| **TAYLOR, TAYLER,** (cont.) | | |
| 2, 1832, by Salmon Cone, V. D. M. | 2 | 236 |
| George W., of New London, m. Mary S. **BURNHAM**, of Colchester, Aug. 17, 1845, by Rev. Lyman Strong | 3 | 23 |
| Hannah, m. Jacob **LO[O]MIS**, Mar. 22, 1716 | L-1 | 447 |
| Hannah P., m. Alvenus **CONE**, Nov. 29, 1824, by Salmon Cone, V. D. M. | 2 | 173 |
| Harriet, of Colchester, m. James **TEW**, of Lebanon, Nov. 19, 1840, by Rev. Lyman Strong | 2 | 98 |
| Henry, of Colchester, m. Laura C. **COON**, of East Haddam, Mar. 9, 1843, by Rev. Rob[er]t C. Mills | 3 | 2 |
| Jakkens, [s. Niles & Betty], b. Apr. 11, 1769 | 1 | 90 |
| James, [s. James], b. Aug. 16, 1707 | L-1 | 799 |
| Jerusha, m. Jeremiah **FOOT**, Oct. 16, 1791 | 2 | 93 |
| Jerusha, see under Joshua | | |
| John, of Lebanon, m. Clarissa **BUTTON**, of Colchester, Apr. 1, 1850, by Griswold E. Morgan, J. P. | 3 | 40 |
| Joseph, twin with Benjamin, [s. Ebenezer & Phebe], b. Nov. 13, 1753 | 1 | 49 |
| Joseph, [s. Josiah & Sibbel], b. Aug. 22, 1768 | 1 | 52 |
| Joshua*, [s. Josiah & Sibbel], b. Nov. 25, 1771 (*Jerusha) | 1 | 52 |
| Josiah, m. Sibbel **NORTHAM**, Nov. 4, 1761 | 1 | 52 |
| Laura, d. [Daniel & Margaret], b. Dec. 1, 1806 | 2 | 90 |
| Leuie, [Levi}, [s. James], b. Mar. 17, 1713 | L-1 | 799 |
| Louisa, alias **FREEMAN**, m. Samuel **FREEMAN**, b. of Colchester (colored), Dec. 17, 1829, by Samuel A. Peters, J. P. | 2 | 217 |
| Lucy, [d. Niles & Betty], b. Sept. 10, 1773 | 1 | 90 |
| Margaret, d. [Daniel & Margaret], b. June 23, 1794 | 2 | 90 |
| Margaret, [w. Daniel], d. Nov. 6, 1843, ae 68 | 2 | 90 |
| Margaret, see under Margaret **AVERY** | 2 | 90 |
| Martha, [d. James], b. Nov. 29, 1704 | L-1 | 799 |
| Martha, [d. Ebenezer & Phebe], b. May 5, 1750; d. Feb. 16, 1751 | 1 | 49 |
| Martha, 2d, [d. Ebenezer & Phebe], b. Apr. 14, 1763 | 1 | 49 |
| Mary, d. James, b. Nov. 9, 1701 | L-1 | 799 |
| Mary, m. William E. **BULKELEY**, June 8, 1826, by Salmon Cone, V. D. M. | 2 | 187 |
| Nancy, m. James **HANDCOX**, b. of Colchester, June 2, 1850, by Griswold E. Morgan, J. P. | 3 | 2 |
| Nancy M., of Colchester, m. Edward **JOHNSTON**, of Lebanon, Nov. 26, 1846, by Rev. Joel R. Arnold | 3 | 30 |
| Nath[anie]ll, s. Joseph & Deliverance, b. Apr. 20, 1743 | 1 | 31 |
| Niles, m. Betty **SPENCER**, July 12, 1764 | 1 | 90 |
| Niles, [s. Niles & Betty], b. Feb. 14, 1771 | 1 | 90 |
| Olive, twin with Oliver, [d. Ebenezer & Phebe], b. Nov. 29, 1760 | 1 | 49 |
| Oliver, twin with Olive, [s. Ebenezer & Phebe], b. Nov. | | |

| | Vol. | Page |
|---|---|---|
| **TAYLOR, TAYLER,** (cont,) | | |
| 29, 1760 | 1 | 49 |
| Sarah, m. Ebenezer **SKIN[N]ER**, Mar. 17, 1725 | L-1 | 450 |
| Sarah, [d. Ebenezer & Phebe], b. July 8, 1757 | 1 | 49 |
| Sophia, d. [Daniel & Margaret], b. July 11, 1800 | 2 | 90 |
| Spencer, [s. Niles & Betty], b. Apr. 10, 1765 | 1 | 90 |
| Stephen, d. Jan. 3, 1718/19 | L-1 | 447 |
| Susannah, m. Moses **FULLER**, Dec. 12, 1782 | 2 | 6 |
| Susannah, m. Moses **FULLER**, Dec. 12, 1782 | 2 | 22 |
| **TENNANT**, Abigail, m. Joshua **WELCH**, Apr. 17, 1735 | 1 | 107 |
| Anna, m. John **RATHBUN**, Mar. 30, 1737 | 1 | 108 |
| Ellis, d. [John & Mary], b. Jan. 11, 1761 | 1 | 179 |
| Freelove, m. Joseph **SWEET**, Mar. 16, 1738 | 1 | 147 |
| Hannah, m. Silas **CLARKE**, b. of Colchester, Nov. 21, 1823, by Daniel Waldo | 2 | 159 |
| John, m. Mary **RANDALL**, Feb. 28, 1760 | 1 | 179 |
| John, s. [John & Mary], b. Aug. 4, 1762 | 1 | 179 |
| Mary, [d. Samuel & Sarah], b. Oct. 7, 1754 | 1 | 45 |
| Samuel, of Colchester, m. Sarah **CARTER**, of Stonington, June 8, 1753 | 1 | 45 |
| Sarah, m. Joshua **RATHBUN**, Dec. 4, 1745 | 1 | 108 |
| Sarah, [d. Samuel & Sarah], b. Jan. 20, 1757 | 1 | 45 |
| **TEW**, James, of Lebanon, m. Harriet **TAYLOR**, of Colchester, Nov. 19, 1840, by Rev. Lyman Strong | 2 | 98 |
| William, m. Sybel **CARDWELL**, b. of Salem, Mar. 14, 1833, by Rev. Lyman Strong | 2 | 242 |
| **THATCHER**, Nancy, m. Jared **BROWN**, Mar. 20, 1828, by Avery Morgan, J. P. | 2 | 202 |
| **THOMAS**, Abigail, m. John **WOODWORTH**, Dec. 6, 1753 | 1 | 21 |
| Almeda, of Colchester, m. George **RANDALL**, of Salem, Jan. 30, 1853, by Rev. G. W. Pendleton | 3 | 54 |
| Ann, [d. Ebenezer & Eunice], b. Mar. 28, 1743; d. Jan. 9, 1748 | 1 | 54 |
| David, [s. Ebenezer & Eunice], b. Jan. 8, 1750 | 1 | 54 |
| Ebenezer, m. [E]unice **STRONG**, Dec. 7, 1730 | L-3 | 8 |
| Ebenezer, [s. Ebenezer & Eunice], b. Mar. 14, 1745 | 1 | 54 |
| Ebenezer, d. Aug. 30, 1752 | 1 | 54 |
| Edward Y., m. Eunice **WELLS**, Feb. 21, 1828, by Salmon Cone, V. D. M. | 2 | 200 |
| Eunice, w. Capt. E. Y., d. Sept. 30, 1842, ae 37 | 2 | 147 |
| Eunice, m. Stephen **STARK**, Jan. 10, 1755 | 1 | 24 |
| Hannah, m. Edward **BROWN**, Feb. 7, 1745 | 1 | 149 |
| Israel, [s. Ebenezer & Eunice], b. May 9, 1741 | 1 | 54 |
| Josiah, see under Josiah **LOMAS** | 1 | 128 |
| Julius, of Lebanon, m. Harriet R. **WAY**, of Colchester, Dec. 30, 1837, by Rev. Lyman Strong | 2 | 295 |
| Lucy, [d. Ebenezer & Eunice], b. July 26, 1747 | 1 | 54 |
| Lucy, of Lebanon, m. John **PALMER**, of Colchester, Feb. 10, | 2 | 66 |

| | Vol. | Page |
|---|---|---|
| **THOMAS**, (cont.) | | |
| 1791 | 2 | 66 |
| Mary, m. Joseph **PEPOON**, Jan. 13, 1725 | L-1 | 453 |
| Sarah, see under Sarah **LOMAS** | 1 | 128 |
| Sarah Y., ae 22, m. Henry W. **BURR**, ae 23, b. of Colchester, June 21, 1853, by Rev. J. A. Copp | 3 | 59 |
| Zilpha Ann, [d. Ebenezer & Eunice], b. Feb. 26, 1750 | 1 | 54 |
| Zilpha Ann, [d. Ebenezer & Eunice], b. Feb. 26, 1752. Re-entered at the desire of her mother | 1 | 54 |
| **THOMPSON, TOMSON, TOMESON, TOMSEON**, Benjamin, s. Henry, b. June 19, 1709 | L-3 | 197 |
| Benjamin, s. Henry, b. June 19, 1709 | TM-1 | 197 |
| Cornelia, m. Joseph P. **CHICK**, b. of Colchester, Feb. 17, 1851, by Rev. Lyman Strong | 3 | 1 |
| Debett, of Colchester, m. Charles W. **BROWN**, of East Haddam, Jan. 4, 1843, by Rev. Abraham Holway | 3 | 5 |
| Dinah, d. Henry, b. Feb. 18, 1718/19 | L-3 | 197 |
| Dinah, d. Henry, b. Feb. 18, 1718/19 | TM-1 | 197 |
| Isaac, [s. Henry], b. Apr. 20, 1711 | L-3 | 197 |
| Isaac, s. Henry, b. Apr. 20, 1711 | TM-1 | 197 |
| Lucy Ann, of Windham, m. George W. **FREEMAN**, of Colchester, Nov. 23, 1841, by Rev. Joel R. Arnold | 2 | 121 |
| Lydia, m. Elijah **NEWTON**, Nov. 30, 1807, at Columbia, d. June 27, 1827 | 2 | 115 |
| Mary, of Belerica, m. Rev. Thomas **SKINNER**, of Colchester, Oct. 2, 1746 | 1 | 138 |
| Mary Ann, of Newark, N. Y., m. William **EVANS**, of Colchester, Aug. 23, 1843, by Rev. Joel R. Arnold | 3 | 6 |
| Thankfull, [s. Henry], b. Apr. 17, 1713 | L-3 | 197 |
| Thankfull, d. Henry, b. Apr. 17, 1713 | TM-1 | 197 |
| William C., of Mansfield, Conn., m. Fanny H. **WEST**, of Colchester, Apr. 3, 1844, by Rev. A. B. Wheeler | 3 | 12 |
| **[TIFFANY], TIFFENEY, TIFFINE**, Abi, m. Isaiah **MUN**, Jan. 18, 1767 | 1 | 95 |
| Sarah, m. Ebenezer **DAY**, Feb. 3, 1717/18 | L-1 | 446 |
| **TILDEN**, Arine, m. Samuel **HACKLEY**, Nov. 8, 1764 | 1 | 83 |
| Joseph W., of Lebanon, m. Clarissa E. **FULLER**, of Colchester, Nov. 25, 1841, by Rev. Daniel G. Sprague, West Chester | 2 | 141 |
| Judeth, d. Isaac, b. Apr. 30, 1749 | 1 | 136 |
| Judith, m. Oliver **BUEL**, Dec. 15, 1768 | 1 | 83 |
| **TILLOTSON**, Warren, m. Emeline **FISH**, b. of Colchester, Sept. 2, 1838, by Rev. Andrew M. Smith | 2 | 180 |
| **TINKER**, Avery Morgan, s. [Joshua & Mary F.], b. Jan. 7, 1811 | 2 | 134 |
| Joshua, m. Mary F. **ROGERS**, Apr. 15, 1810 | 2 | 134 |
| Sabra, b. Feb. 8, 1774, in Montville; m. John **TURNER**, Jan. 7, 1796; d. Dec. 2, 1851, ae 78 | 2 | 123 |
| **TISDALE**, Eliphalet, d. Oct. 16, 1828, ae 42 | 2 | 127 |

| | Vol. | Page |
|---|---|---|
| **TISDALE**, (cont.) | | |
| Polly, wid. Eliphalet, d. Oct. 21, 1831, ae 46 | 2 | 127 |
| **TOWNSEND**, Mary, d. [William & Rachel], b. May 1, 1785; d. Sept. 1, 1786 | 2 | 56 |
| William, m. Rachel **SKINNER**, Oct. [ ], 1784 | 2 | 56 |
| **TOZER**, Mary, m. Nathaniel **HARRIS**, Feb. 1, 1764 | 2 | 64 |
| **TRACY**, Daniel, & w. Eunice moved from East Haddam to Colchester | 2 | 57 |
| Eliphaz, s. [Daniel & Eunice], b. May 29, 1790 | 2 | 57 |
| George Leonard, s. [Nehemiah & Caroline M.], b. May 6, 1834 | 2 | 247 |
| Jerusha C., m. Asahel **SKINNER**, Jan. 15, 1817; d. Feb. 15, 1851, ae 57 | 2 | 105 |
| John, s. [Judah S. & Teresa E.], b. June 2, 1843 | 2 | 293 |
| Judah Lewis, s. [Robbins], b. Mar. 24, 1821 | 2 | 247 |
| Judah S., of Colchester (Westchester), m. Teresa E. **PALMER**, of East Haddam, May 9, 1842, by Rev. Lyman Strong | 2 | 293 |
| Lew Arnold, s. [Nehemiah & Caroline M.], b. Sept. 20, 1839 | 2 | 247 |
| Lydia, m. Amasa **FOOT**, Mar. 5, 1820 | 2 | 252 |
| Mary L., d. [Judah S. & Teresa E.], b. Oct. 29, 1846 | 2 | 293 |
| Nehemiah, of Colchester, m. Caroline M. **BUELL**, of Chatham, May 5, 1833 | 2 | 247 |
| Robbins, d. Sept. 12, 1853, ae 56 y. 4 m. | 2 | 293 |
| Sarah, d. [Daniel & Eunice], b. May 18, 1792 | 2 | 57 |
| Sarah Emeline, d. [Nehemiah & Caroline M.], b. May 18, 1843 | 2 | 247 |
| Stephen, of Franklin, m. Sarah A. **FOOTE**, of Colchester, Feb. 25, 1824, by Rev. William Palmer, at the house of Solomon Scoville | 2 | 162 |
| Susan C., m. Harvey **HUTCHINSON**, Nov. 4, 1830, by Rev. Joseph Harvey | 2 | 226 |
| William E., m. Elizabeth **DAY**, b. of Colchester, Nov. 3, 1836, by Rev. Samuel J. Curtiss | 2 | 297 |
| **TREADWAY, TREDWAY**, Abigaiel, [d. James & Sarah], b. May 29, 1726 | L-1 | 453 |
| Alfred, s. [Elijah & Deborah], b. Sept. 1, 1781 | 2 | 124 |
| Alpheas, [s. Josiah & Eunice], b. Aug. 14, 1750 | 1 | 94 |
| Alpheas, m. Phebe **GATES**, [ ] | 2 | 142 |
| Alpheas Harvey, s. [Alpheas & Phebe], b. Oct. 29, 1806 | 2 | 142 |
| Amos, [s. Josiah & Eunice], b. Feb. 19, 1738 | 1 | 94 |
| Anne, [d. James & Sarah], b. Mar. 9, 1724 | L-1 | 453 |
| Anne, twin with Bethiah, [d. John & Winefred], b. July 3, 1768 | 1 | 86 |
| Anne, [d. Asa & Mabel], b. July 23, 1778 | 1 | 82 |
| Anne, d. [Asa & Mabel], b. July 23, 1778 | 2 | 53 |
| Asa, s. [James & Sarah], b. Apr. 13, 1736 | 1 | 125 |
| Asa, [m. Mabel **ROBERTS**, Dec. 27, 1759 | 1 | 82 |

| | Vol. | Page |
|---|---|---|
| **TREADWAY, TREDWAY**, (cont.) | | |
| Asa, [s. Asa & Mabel], b. Sept. 17, 1760; d. Aug. 16, 1772 | 1 | 82 |
| Asa, s. [Asa & Mabel], d. Aug. 16, 1772 | 2 | 53 |
| Asa, 2d, [s. Asa & Mabel], b. Dec. 20, 1773 | 1 | 82 |
| Asa, 2d, s. [Asa & Mabel], b. Dec. 20, 1773 | 2 | 53 |
| Asa, m. Mabel **ROBERTS**, [ ] | 2 | 53 |
| Bethiah, d. [James & Sarah], b. Dec. 9, 1740 | 1 | 125 |
| Bethiah, twin with Anne, [d. John & Winefred], b. July 3, 1768 | 1 | 86 |
| Betsey, d. [David & Sarah], b. Dec. 18, 1782 | 2 | 79 |
| Betsey, [d. David & Sarah], b. Feb. 9, 1784 | 1 | 79 |
| Butler, [s. Asa & Mabel], b. Nov. 13, 1775 | 1 | 82 |
| Butler, s. [Asa & Mebel], b. Nov. 15, 1775 | 2 | 53 |
| Charles, [s. Josiah & Eunice], b. June 21, 1747 | 1 | 94 |
| Daniel, [s. David & Sarah], b. Feb. 16, 1787 | 1 | 79 |
| Daniel, s. [David & Sarah], b. Feb. 19, 1787 | 2 | 79 |
| Dan[iel], s. [David & Sarah], b. Feb. 16, 1791 | 2 | 79 |
| David, [s. Josiah & Eunice], b. Apr. 25, 1743 | 1 | 94 |
| David, m. Sarah **GUSTIN**, Oct. 12, 1765 | 2 | 79 |
| David, m. Sarah **GRIFFIN**, May 8, 1766 | 1 | 79 |
| David, [s. David & Sarah], b. Mar. 5, 1769 | 1 | 79 |
| David, s. [David & Sarah], b. Mar. 5, 1769 | 2 | 79 |
| Dyar, s. [Eliphalet & Abigail], b. Dec. 24, 1778 | 2 | 88 |
| Dyer, m. Jerusha [ ] | 2 | 111 |
| Elijah, [s. James & Sarah], b. Apr. 8, 1722 | L-1 | 453 |
| Elijah, [s. Josiah & Eunice], b. July 5, 1753 | 1 | 94 |
| Elijah, m. Deborah **HARRIS**, [ ] | 2 | 124 |
| Elijah Waterman, s. [Elijah & Deborah], b. Dec. 26, 1793 | 2 | 124 |
| Eliphalet, [s. Josiah & Eunice], b. Apr. 3, 1739 | 1 | 94 |
| Eliphalet, m. Abigail **WISE**, May 29, 1766 | 1 | 85 |
| Eliphalet, [s. Eliphalet & Abigail], b. Feb. 14, 1768 | 1 | 85 |
| Eliphalet, s. [Eliphalet & Abigail], b. Apr. 27, 1787 | 2 | 88 |
| Eliphalet, m. Wid. Abigail [ ] | 2 | 88 |
| Elizabeth, [d. John & Windfred], b. May 12, 1766 | 1 | 86 |
| Eunice, [d. James & Sarah], b. Nov. 4, 1717 | L-1 | 453 |
| Eunice, [d. Josiah & Eunice], b. July 4, 1740 | 1 | 94 |
| Eunice, [d. Eliphalet & Abigail], b. Sept. 1, 1766 | 1 | 85 |
| Eunice, d. [Elijah & Deborah], b. Jan. 26, 1780 | 2 | 124 |
| Ezekiel, [s. Asa & Mabel], b. June 19, 1762 | 1 | 82 |
| Ezra, twin with Nancy, s. [David & Sarah], b. May 4, 1776 | 2 | 79 |
| Ezra, twin with Nancy, [s. David & Sarah], b. May 14, 1776 | 1 | 79 |
| Fanny, d. [Elijah & Deborah], b. Nov. 2, 1790 | 2 | 124 |
| George W., m. Rhoda S. **BILLINGS**, b. of Salem, Ct., Apr. 19, 1840, by Rev. Joel R. Arnold | 2 | 228 |
| Hannah, d. [James & Sarah], b. Aug. 31, 1748 | 1 | 125 |
| Hannah, [d. David & Sarah], b. May 14, 1771 | 1 | 79 |
| Hannah, d. [David & Sarah], b. July 24, 1771 | 2 | 79 |
| James, d. May 26, 1728, in 52d y. of his age | L-1 | 453 |

| | Vol. | Page |
|---|---|---|
| **TREADWAY, TREDWAY**, (cont.) | | |
| James, m. Sarah **MUN[N]**, June 4, 1729 | L-3 | 8 |
| James, s. James & Sarah, b. May 12, 1730 | 1 | 125 |
| James, s. [Josiah & Eunice], b. Dec. 19, 1748 | 1 | 94 |
| James, m. Temperance **SMITH**, wid. of Capt. John, Dec. 10, 1761 | 1 | 125 |
| James, Jr., m. Olive **SMITH**, Apr. 21, 1768 | 1 | 83 |
| James, d. July 2, 1780 | 1 | 125 |
| James, Sr., d. July 2, 1780 | 2 | 57 |
| Jerusha, d. [Elijah & Deborah], b. Apr. 4, 1778 | 2 | 124 |
| John, s. [James & Sarah], b. Apr. 16, 1733 | 1 | 125 |
| John, [s. Josiah & Eunice], b. May 11, 1755 | 1 | 94 |
| John, m. Winefred **WISE**, Jan. 11, 1764 | 1 | 86 |
| John, s. [Elijah & Deborah], b. July 28, 1783 | 2 | 124 |
| John, 2d, m. Nancy **WORTHINGTON**, Feb. 8, 1808 | 2 | 125 |
| John, s. [John, 2d, & Nancy], b. Dec. 5, 1808 | 2 | 125 |
| John, d. Jan. [ ], 1814, ae 81 | 1 | 86 |
| Josiah, m. Eunice **FOOT**, May 13, 1735 | 1 | 94 |
| Josiah, [s. Josiah & Eunice], b. June 20, 1736 | 1 | 94 |
| Lois, [d. James & Sarah], b. Feb. 2, 1720 | L-1 | 453 |
| Lois, m. Israel **NEWTON**, June 7, 1750 | 1 | 50 |
| Lovice, [d. Asa & Mabel], b. Nov. 17, 1769; d. Mar. 21, 1792 | 1 | 82 |
| Lovice, d. [Asa & Mabel], b. Nov. 17, 1769 | 2 | 53 |
| Lydia, [d. James & Sarah], b. Jan. 16, 1714 | L-1 | 453 |
| Lydia, d. [James & Sarah], b. May 14, 1738 | 1 | 125 |
| Lydia, m. Amos **WELLS**, Nov. 23, 1758 | 1 | 104 |
| Lydia, d. [Elijah & Deborah], b. Aug. 1, 1785 | 2 | 124 |
| Lydia Marvin, d. [Alpheas & Phebe], b. Apr. 28, 1804 | 2 | 142 |
| Mabel, [d. Asa & Mabel], b. Mar. 27, 1765 | 1 | 82 |
| Mary, d. James & Sarah, b. July 15, 1709 | L-1 | 453 |
| Mary, [d. Josiah & Eunice], b. June 19, 1745 | 1 | 94 |
| Mary, d. [James & Sarah], b. Jan. 12, 1745/6; d. June 27, 1750 | 1 | 125 |
| Mary, d. [James & Sarah], b. Feb. 26, 1751 | 1 | 125 |
| Mary Ann, d. [Alpheas & Phebe], b. Feb. 19, 1803 | 2 | 142 |
| Nancy, twin with Ezra, d. [David & Sarah], b. May 4, 1776 | 2 | 79 |
| Nancy, twin with Ezra, [d. David & Sarah], b. May 14, 1776 | 1 | 79 |
| Nancy, d. [Elijah & Deborah], b. Jan. 13, 1788 | 2 | 124 |
| Philothetee, d. [David & Sarah], b. Feb. 12, 1779 | 2 | 79 |
| Philotheta, [d. David & Sarah], b. Feb. 12, 1782 | 1 | 79 |
| Prudence, [d. Asa & Mabel], b. Nov. 6, 1767 | 1 | 82 |
| Rhoda Backus, d. [Dyer & Jerusha], b. Oct. 17, 1806 | 2 | 111 |
| Sally, m. Butler **KELLOGG**, Jan. 9, 1788 | 2 | 57 |
| Sarah, [d. James & Sarah], b. Apr. 15, 1711 | L-1 | 453 |
| Sarah, m. James **RANSOM**, May 22, 1735 | 1 | 51 |
| Sarah, [d. Josiah & Eunice], b. Mar. 31, 1742 | 1 | 94 |
| Sarah, d. [James & Sarah], b. Mar. 20, 1743 | 1 | 125 |
| Sarah, wid. James, d. Jan. 28, 1753 | 1 | 83 |

| | Vol. | Page |
|---|---|---|
| **TREADWAY, TREDWAY,** (cont.) | | |
| Sarah, w. James, d. Jan. 8, 1761 | 1 | 125 |
| Sarah, m. Martin **KELLOGG,** Feb. 4, 1762 | 1 | 36 |
| Sarah, m. Asa **JONES,** [ ], 1762 | 1 | 110 |
| Sarah, [d. John & Winefred], b. Nov. 3, 1764 | 1 | 86 |
| Sarah, [d. David & Sarah], b. Oct. 12, 1766 | 1 | 79 |
| Sarah, d. [David & Sarah], b. Oct. 12, 1766 | 2 | 79 |
| Winefred, [w. John], d. Feb. [ [, 1821, ae [ ] | 1 | 86 |
| ----, s. [James & Sarah], b. Apr. 7, 1732; d. same day | 1 | 125 |
| **TREAT,** John T. P., m. Susan E. **BENJAMIN,** Sept. 18, 1854, by Rev. Selah B. Treat | 3 | 64 |
| **TROWBRIDGE,** John, of Chatham, m. Margary **SHIPMAN,** of Colchester, May 9, 1826, by Salmon Cone, V. D. M. | 2 | 186 |
| **TRUMBULL, TRUMBLE,** Anna Heywood, m. Ralph Henry **ISHAM,** b. of Colchester, June 12, 1838, by Rev. Joel R. Arnold | 2 | 264 |
| Benjamin, of Colchester, m. Elizabeth **MATHER,** of Saybrook, Mar. 15, 1800 | 2 | 85 |
| Benjamin, Hon., d. June 14, 1850, in Backson County, Mich., ae 81 | 2 | 85 |
| Benjamin Mather, s. [Benjamin & Elizabeth], b. May 17, 1801 | 2 | 85 |
| Catharine, m. Benjamin **BURNHAM,** "about 13 or 14 y. ago", by Epaphras Lord, J. P. Dated Jan. 5, 1784 | 2 | 36 |
| David Daggett, s. [Benjamin & Elizabeth], b. June 29, 1811 | 2 | 85 |
| Elizabeth, d. Oct. 20, 1828, ae 46 | 2 | 85 |
| Erastus, s. [Benjamin & Elizabeth], b. May 11, 1809 | 2 | 85 |
| George, s. [Benjamin & Elizabeth], b. June 4, 1818 | 2 | 85 |
| Jane, d. [Benjamin & Elizabeth], b. Aug. 12, 1822; d. June 4, 1839, ae 16 | 2 | 85 |
| John, s. [Benjamin & Elizabeth], b. Dec. 23, 1804; d. Sept. 11, 1806 | 2 | 85 |
| John Selden, s. [Benjamin & Elizabeth], b. Mar. 3, 1807 | 2 | 85 |
| Julia, d. [Benjamin & Elizabeth], b. Feb. 3, 1803; d. Oct. 7, 1806 | 2 | 85 |
| Julia Elizabeth, d. [Benjamin & Elizabeth], b. Mar. 28, 1816; d. Apr. 17, 1851, ae 35, in Jackson County, Mich. | 2 | 85 |
| Lyman, s. [Benjamin & Elizabeth], b. Oct. 12, 1813 | 2 | 85 |
| Sally Maria, d. [Benjamin & Elizabeth], b. May 11, 1820 | 2 | 85 |
| **TUBBS,** Daniel, m. Alethea **VALLETT,** Jan. 30, 1809 | 2 | 96 |
| David, s. [Simon & Sarah], b. Mar. 8, 1752 | 1 | 128 |
| John, s. [Simon & Sarah], b. Apr. 21, 1748 | 1 | 128 |
| Joseph, s. Joseph & Martha, b. May 13, 1744 | 1 | 87 |
| Joseph, s. [Simon & Sarah], b. Mar. 6, 1750 | 1 | 128 |
| Joseph, m. Hannah **MORGAN,** Apr. 31 (?), 1767 | 1 | 87 |
| Joseph, [s. Joseph & Hannah], b. Aug. 9, 1768 | 1 | 87 |
| Mary, d. [Simon & Sarah], b. Jan. 6, 1743 | 1 | 105 |
| Nathan, s. Simon & sarah], b. Mar. 20, 1738 | 1 | 128 |
| Nathan, s. Simon [& Sarah], b. Mar. 20, 1738 | 1 | 105 |

| | Vol. | Page |
|---|---|---|
| **TUBBS**, (cont.) | | |
| Phebe, d. [Simon & Sarah], b. Mar. 19, 1742 | 1 | 105 |
| Sarah, d. Simon [& Sarah], b. Jan. 1, 1740 | 1 | 105 |
| Simeon, s. Simeon, b. Apr. 9, 1746 | 1 | 104 |
| Simon, m. Sarah **WATE**, of Lyme, Dec. 7, 1736 | 1 | 105 |
| Simon, m. Sarah **WAIT**, Dec. 27, 1736 | 1 | 105 |
| Simon, s. [Simon & Sarah], b. Apr. 19, 1746 | 1 | 105 |
| **TUBELL**, Abner Chapman, s. [William & Ann], b. Aug. 4, 1791 | 2 | 83 |
| Ann, d. [William & Ann], b. Sept. [ ], 1776; d. Apr. [ ], 1777 | 2 | 83 |
| Charlotte Butler, d. [William & Ann], b. Dec. 18, 1793 | 2 | 83 |
| Etheldred, s. [William & Ann], b. Dec. 6, 1774 | 2 | 83 |
| Henry, s. [William & Ann], b. Mar. 16, 1789 | 2 | 83 |
| Iantha, d. [William & Ann], b. Jan. 3, 1773; d. Mar. [ ], 1774 | 2 | 83 |
| Margaret, d. [William & Ann], b. Feb. 14, 1778 | 2 | 83 |
| Mary Ann, d. [William & Ann], b. Apr. 14, 1782 | 2 | 83 |
| Minerva, d. [William & Ann], b. Mar. 4, 1780 | 2 | 83 |
| Sarah, d. [William & Ann], b. June 22, 1784 | 2 | 83 |
| William, m. Ann **CHAPMAN**, Mar. [ ], 1772 | 2 | 83 |
| William, s. [William & Ann], b. Sept. 1, 1787 | 2 | 83 |
| **TUCK**, Mary, of Hebron, m. William **DAYTON**, of Colchester, Apr. 7, 1833, by Amherst Scoville, J. P. (Perhaps "**BUCK**"?) | 2 | 242 |
| **TUCKER**, Hardein, m. Sabra **CLARK**, b. of Bozrah, Dec. 15, 1822, by Rev. William Palmer, at the house of [William Palmer] | 2 | 158 |
| **TURNER**, Ann Eliza, m. Daniel **SAFFORD**, June 25, 1833 | 2 | 78 |
| Ann Eliza, m. Daniel **SAFFORD**, of Boston, Mass., June 25, 1833 | 2 | 187 |
| Aurelia L., m. Joshua B. **WHEELER**, b. of Colchester, May 9, 1827, by Lyman Strong | 2 | 196 |
| Aurelia Lucy, d. [John & Sabra], b. Jan. 10, 1805 | 2 | 123 |
| Eliza, of Colchester, m. Rev. John W. **SALTER**, of Bozrah, Mar. 1, 1842, by Rev. Joel R. Arnold | 2 | 218 |
| Emeline Smith, d. [John & Sabra], b. June 16, 1808; d. Mar. 22, 1825 | 2 | 123 |
| Harriet, m. Israel **NEWTON**, Jan. 14, 1819 | 2 | 165 |
| John, b. Jan. 19, 1771, in Montville; m. Sabra **TINKER**, Jan. 7, 1796 | 2 | 123 |
| Sabra, [w. John], d. Dec. 2, 1851, ae 78 | 2 | 123 |
| Sally, of Montville, m. Ransom **BECKWITH**, of Colchester, Apr. 6, 1824, by Salmon Cone, V. D. M. | 2 | 165 |
| William T., m. Ann Eliza **BIGELOW**, May 24, 1826, by Salmon Cone, V. D. M.; d. Oct. 19, 1832, ae 32 | 2 | 187 |
| William Tinker, s. [John & Sabra], b. Feb. 27, 1801; d. Oct. 19, 1832 | 2 | 123 |
| **UNDERWOOD**, Thomas, m. Abby Jane **SHAILOR**, b. of Colchester, Aug. 15, 1839, by Rev. Joel R. Andrews | 2 | 103 |

| | Vol. | Page |
|---|---|---|
| **USHER**, Abby M., of Chatham, m. David S. **BIGELOW**, of Colchester, Nov. 9, 1852, by Rev. S. D. Jewett | 3 | 54 |
| Abby Mandana, d. [Revilo & Mandana], b. June 7, 1833 | 2 | 194 |
| Amatus Revilo, s. [Revilo & Mandana], b. Oct. 3, 1834; d. Aug. 21, 1838 | 2 | 194 |
| Catherine Meroa, d. [Revilo C. & Mandana], b. Dec. 26, 1827 | 2 | 122 |
| Catharine Merva, d. [Revilo & Mandana], b. Dec. 26, 1827 | 2 | 194 |
| James Chauncey, s. [Revilo & Mandana], b. Sept. 2, 1837 | 2 | 194 |
| Jonathan, [s. Robert & Susannah], b. July 4, 1768; d. Sept. 22, 1769 | 1 | 11 |
| Jonathan, 2d, [s. Robert & Susannah], b. Nov. 7, 1770 | 1 | 11 |
| Oliver, [s. Robert & Susannah], b. Sept. 16, 1766 | 1 | 11 |
| Revilo C., m. Mandana **ROBBINS**, Apr. 4, 1827 | 2 | 122 |
| Revilo C., of Chatham, m. Mandana **ROBBINS**, of Colchester, Apr. 4, 1827, by Rev. Joseph Harvey | 2 | 194 |
| Robert, m. Susannah **GALES**, May 23, 1765 **(GATES?)** | 1 | 11 |
| Robert Bela, s. [Revils C. & Mandana], b. Sept. 28, 1831 | 2 | 122 |
| Robert Bela, s. [Revilo & Mandana], b. Sept. 28, 1831 | 2 | 194 |
| **UTTLEY**, Abigail M., m. Edward H. **STRONG**, Apr. 12, 1842, by Rev. Joel R. Arnold; d. Feb. 20, 1843, ae 21 | 2 | 280 |
| Harriet A., m. Israel E. **HARVEY**, b. of Colchester, Mar. 19, 1844, by Rev. Joel R. Arnold | 3 | 11 |
| **VALLETT**, Alethea, m. Daniel **TUBBS**, Jan. 30, 1809 | 2 | 96 |
| **VENNER**, Mary, m. Jonathan **DODGE**, Jr., July 13, 1769 | 1 | 42 |
| **WADHAM, WADHAMS**, Caleb, of Pittsfield, Mass., m. Sally **CRANE**,. of Colchester, Mar. 20, 1825, by Benjamin Trumbull, J. P. | 2 | 176 |
| Norman T., of Goshen, m. Mary **GILLET**, of Colchester, Nov. 6, 1838, by Rev. Lyman Strong | 2 | 109 |
| **WAITE, WAIT, WATE**, Sarah, of Lyme, m. Simon **TUBBS**, Dec. 7, 1736 | 1 | 105 |
| Sarah, m. Simon **TUBBS**, Dec. 27, 1736 | 1 | 105 |
| Sarah Ann, m. Guy **BIGELOW**, Mar. 8, 1827 | 2 | 78 |
| Sarah Ann, m. Guy **BIGELOW**, Mar. 8, 1827 | 2 | 125 |
| **WAKEFIELD**, Lucius Henry, s. Isabel, b. Aug. 28, 1825 | 2 | 138 |
| **WALBRIDGE, WALLBRIDGE**, Susan T., m. John A. **POTTER**, b. of Bozrah, Apr. 4, 1852, by Rev. George W. Pendleton | 3 | 50 |
| W[illia]m, of Portland, m. Susan L. **CHAPMAN**, of Westchester, Sept. 21, 1845, by Rev. S. D. Jewett | 3 | 24 |
| William, d. Oct. 27, 1850, ae 33 | 2 | 67 |
| **WALCH**, [see also **WELCH**], Anne, m. William **DODGE**, June 30, 1757 | 1 | 30 |
| **WALLER**, Hannah, [d. John & Susannah], b. [ ] | 1 | 28 |
| John, m. Susannah **CORPS**, b. of Colchester, Dec. [ ], 1759 | 1 | 28 |
| John, d. Sept. [ ], 1761 | 1 | 28 |
| Susannah, Wid., m. Alexander **DODGE**, Jr., Jan. 2, 1764 | 1 | 28 |
| **WANTON, WATON**, Betsey, of Colchester, m. Dennis | | |

| | Vol. | Page |
|---|---|---|
| **WANTON, WATON**, (cont.) | | |
| **BROOKS**, of Chatham, Mar. 18, 1832, at her dwelling house in Colchester, by John Bigelow, J. P. | 2 | 237 |
| Emeline, of Colchester, m. Anson W. **JACKSON**, of East Haddam, Nov. 26, 1834, by Rev. Joseph Harvey | 2 | 273 |
| Mary, m. Thomas **CARRIER**, July 21, 1762 | 1 | 80 |
| **WARD**, Mary, d. Rev. John, 1st min. of Haverhill, Mass., & gd. d. Rev. Nathaniel **WARD**, 1st min. of Ipswich, b. June 24, 1649. She was mother of Rev. Samuel **WOODBRIDGE** | 2 | 310 |
| Nathaniel, Rev., 1st min. of Ipswich & author of "The Simple Cobler of Aggawam" had s. Rev. John **WARD**, 1st min. of Haverhille, Mass., & gd. d. Mary **WARD** | 2 | 310 |
| **WARNER**, Benjamin, m. Johan[n]a **STRONG**, Mar. 17, 1719 | L-1 | 449 |
| C[h]loe, [d. Nathan & Mary], b. Sept. 16, 1760 | 1 | 80 |
| Collins, s. [Oliver & Rachel], b. Feb. 3, 1787 | 2 | 73 |
| Dorothy, [s. Nathan & Mary], b. Aug. 10, 1758; d. Sept. 8, 1758 | 1 | 80 |
| Elihu, [s. Nathan & Mary], b. Oct. 6, 1761 | 1 | 80 |
| Hannah, [d. Nathan & Mary], b. Mar. 9, 1767; d. Mar. 15, 1767 | 1 | 80 |
| Mary, [d. Nathan & Mary], b. Nov. 16, 1752 | 1 | 80 |
| Mary, 2d, m. Jonathan **DODGE**, Jr., July 13, 1769 | 2 | 65 |
| Mary, Jr., m. Jonathan **DODGE**, Jr., July 13, 1770 | 1 | 82 |
| Mary, w. Nathan, d. Aug. 9, 1788 | 2 | 81 |
| Matthew Griswold, m. Lucretia Hubbard **LOOMIS**, Nov. 30, 1825, by Jacob Seales, V. D. M., at the house of David Loomis | 2 | 182 |
| Matthew Griswold, s. [Matthew Griswold & Lucretia Hubbard], b. Jan. 1, 1827 | 2 | 182 |
| Nathan, m. Mary **OWEN**, Mar. 21, 1751 | 1 | 80 |
| Nathan, [s. Nathan & Mary], b. Mar. 9, 1756; d. Aug. 9, 1758 | 1 | 80 |
| Nathan, s. [Oliver & Rachel], b. Apr. 3, 1788 | 2 | 73 |
| Olcott, s. [Oliver & Rachel], b. Sept. 17, 1792 | 2 | 73 |
| Oliver, [s. Nathan & Mary], b. Sept. 18, 1763 | 1 | 80 |
| Oliver, m. Rachel **LOOMIS**, Dec. 8, 1786 | 2 | 73 |
| Owen, s. [Oliver & Rachel], b. Mar. 6, 1790 | 2 | 73 |
| **WATERMAN**, Bildad, m. Lucy **BUDENTON**, Apr. 18, 1765 | 1 | 81 |
| Bildad, m. [ ], 1765 | 1 | 85 |
| Charles, [s. Ezra & Lydia], b. Dec. 2, 1762 | 1 | 40 |
| Elijah, s. [Zebulon & Sarah], b. Mar. 19, 1789; d. Nov. 28, 1791 | 2 | 75 |
| Elizabeth, m. Samuel **GATES**, Jan. 5, 1757 | 1 | 145 |
| Ezra, m. Lydia [ ], Nov. 29, 1761 | 1 | 40 |
| Ezra, [s. Ezra & Lydia], b. July 15, 1765 | 1 | 40 |
| Gurdon, s. [Zebulon & Sarah], b. Feb. 26, 1787 | 2 | 75 |
| Hannah, of Norwich, m. Shubael **SMITH**, of Colchester, June 11, 1760 | 1 | 163 |
| Hannah, of Bozrah, m. Stephen **FOOT**, of Colchester, | | |

| | Vol. | Page |
|---|---|---|
| **WATERMAN**, (cont.) | | |
| Nov. 16, 1786; d. Jan. 20, 1848, ae 82 | 2 | 56 |
| Henry, s. [Zebulon & Sarah], b. Nov. 9, 1782 | 2 | 75 |
| Lydia, m. Elisha **CHAPMAN**, May 29, 1760 | 1 | 56 |
| Lydia, w. Ezra, d. June 21, 1768 | 1 | 40 |
| Lydia, d. [Zebulon & Sarah], b. June 10, 1785 | 2 | 75 |
| Mary, m. Jabez **JONES**, Jr., Feb. 24, 1757 | 1 | 44 |
| Sarah, d. [Zebulon & Sarah], b. Oct. 11, 1779 | 2 | 75 |
| Walter, [s. Bildad & Lucy], b. June 24, 1769 | 1 | 81 |
| Warren, s. [Zebulon & Sarah], b. July 25, 1791 | 2 | 75 |
| William, [s. Bildad & Lucy], b. June 22, 1766 | 1 | 81 |
| Zebulon, m. Sarah **HAMILTON**, Oct. 14, 1776 | 2 | 75 |
| -----, s. [Zebulon & Sarah], b. Nov. 3, 1781; d. Nov. 10, 1781 | 2 | 75 |
| **WATERS**, Alice, m. Gideon **QUAS**, [ ] | 2 | 47 |
| Assenath, [d. Samuel & Hopestill], b. Aug. 26, 1760 | 1 | 24 |
| *Benjamin, b. Feb. 28, 1744; Pension record no. 3634, m. Beulah **HOLLISTER**, Ellisburgh, N. Y. Mar. 18, 1853. Pen. rec. *(handwritten in on original manuscript) | | |
| Catharine, m. Aaron **CHAMBERLAIN**, Sept. 8, 1785; d. Apr. 22, 1786 | 2 | 40 |
| Elles, [d. Samuel & Hopestill], b. Mar. 27, 1756 | 1 | 24 |
| John, s. [Timothy & Sarah], b. Sept. 23, 1780 | 2 | 61 |
| Joseph, [s. William & Margeret], b. June 2, 1726 | L-1 | 449 |
| Lazarus, m. Lois **LO[O]MIS**, Dec. 11, 1760 | 1 | 44 |
| Lois, [d. Lazarus & Lois], b. Apr. 27, 1761 | 1 | 44 |
| Lydia, [d. Lazarus & Lois], b. Feb. 5, 1763 | 1 | 44 |
| Lydia, d. [Timothy & Sarah], b. Apr. 11, 1791 | 2 | 61 |
| Margaret, [d. Samuel & Hopestill], b. Feb. 9, 1753 | 1 | 24 |
| Mary, m. Richard **MENTOR**, Sept. 29, 1757 | 1 | 33 |
| Mary, [d. William, Jr. & Mary], b. Aug. 12, 1760 | 1 | 43 |
| Mary, of Hebron, m. Ephraim **BIGELOW**, of Colchester, Feb. 23, 1769 | 2 | 4 |
| Mary, m. Elijah **PRATT**, Oct. 22, 1778 | 2 | 22 |
| Patty, m. Ralph **CARRIER**, Aug. 30, 1819 | 2 | 130 |
| Reuben, s. [Timothy & Sarah], b. [ ] 24, 1788 | 2 | 61 |
| Russel[l], s. [Timothy & Sarah], b. Mar. 4, 1786 | 2 | 61 |
| Samuel, m. Hopestill **HAMBLIN**, Nov. 6, 1751 | 1 | 24 |
| Sarah had slaves Harry, s. Rose, b. Nov. 14, 1784; York, s. Rose, b. Sept. 2, 1786; Hope, d. Rose, b. Sept. [ ], 1789 | 2 | 47 |
| Temperance, of Hebron, m. Joseph **HILLS**, of Colchester, Oct. 6, 1791 | 2 | 74 |
| Timothy, m. Sarah **SKINNER**, Feb. 24, 1779; d. July 9, 1804 | 2 | 61 |
| Timothy, s. [Timothy & Sarah], b. Dec. 29, 1782 | 2 | 61 |
| Vilaty, [d. Samuel & Hopestill], b. Dec. 18, 1762 | 1 | 24 |
| William, m. Margeret **HILLS**, Jan. 13, 1725 | L-1 | 449 |
| William, Jr., s. William & Margaret, b. Feb. 17, 1734 | 1 | 119 |

| | Vol. | Page |
|---|---|---|
| **WATERS**, (cont.) | | |
| William, Jr., of Colchester, m. Mary **JURDEN**, of Middletown, June 21, 1759 | 1 | 43 |
| **WATON**, [see under **WANTON**] | | |
| **WATROUS**, Anne, d. [John Richard & Lydia], b. Feb. 8, 1790 | 2 | 41 |
| Anne, of Colchester, m. Benjamin **TALBOTT**, of Murfreesburg, N. C., Sept. 30, 1817 | 2 | 147 |
| Bradford, s. [Timothy & Julia], b. Nov. 6, 1831 | 2 | 246 |
| Caroline, d. [John Richard & Lydia], b. June 29, 1797 | 2 | 41 |
| Caroline, d. [Reuben & Lydia], b. May 7, 1820 | 2 | 117 |
| Caroline, m. Frederick **MORGAN**, May 20, 1823, by Salmon Cone, V. D. M. | 2 | 148 |
| Caroline, m. Reuben P. **DOUGLASS**, b. of Colchester, Apr. 26, 1852, by Geo[rge] W. Pendleton | 3 | 51 |
| Caroline, m. Reuben P. **DOUGLASS**, b. of Colchester, Apr. 26, 1852, by Geo[rge] W. Pendleton | 3 | 52 |
| Charles, s. [John & Jerusha], b. Apr. 25, 1769 | 1 | 118 |
| Charles, m. Lucy M. **BUELL**, b. of Colchester, Nov. 1, 1821, by Rev. Jacob Seales | 2 | 147 |
| Chauncey, s. [Reuben & Lydia], b. Sept. 1, 1822; d. May 27, 1827 | 2 | 117 |
| Clarissa, d. [John & Nancy], b. Jan. 18, 1810 | 2 | 245 |
| Clarissa, m. Joseph D. **WILLIAMS**, b. of Colchester, Mar. 28, 1839, by Rev. Andrew M. Smith | 2 | 31 |
| Daniel, s. [John & Jerusha], b. May 23, 1761 | 1 | 118 |
| Daniel, m. Lydia Ann **BULKELEY**, [ ]; d. June 6, 1828 | 2 | 100 |
| Daniel Ellsworth, s. [Daniel & Lydia Ann], b. June 22, 1792 | 2 | 100 |
| Elijah, s. [Reuben & Lydia], b. Mar. 12, 1818 | 2 | 117 |
| Erastus, s. [John & Jerusha], b. Mar. 4, 1774 | 1 | 118 |
| Erastus, s. [Reuben & Lydia], b. Nov. 3, 1829 | 2 | 117 |
| Eunice, d. [John & Jerusha], b. June 29, 1766 | 1 | 118 |
| Eunice, m. Charles **BULKELEY**, [ ] | 2 | 78 |
| Frances A., of Colchester, m. William F. **CLARK**, of Chatham, Sept. 14, 1851, by Rev. S. D. Jewitt | 2 | 139 |
| Frances Augusta, d. [John R. & Louisa], b. Apr. 4, 1807 | 2 | 41 |
| Frances Augusta, of Colchester, m. Parsons **ROSE**, of New York, June 14, 1826, by Nath[anie]l T. Wheaton | 2 | 188 |
| Frederick A., m. Maria F. **WHEELER**, Jan. 5, 1825, by Salmon Cone, V. D. M. | 2 | 174 |
| Frederick Augustus, s. [Daniel & Lydia Ann], b. Nov. 25, 1794 | 2 | 100 |
| Harriet, d. [Reuben & Lydia], b. Nov. 21, 1831 | 2 | 117 |
| Harriet, of Colchester, m. Ransiel N. **HUTCHINS**, of Bolton, Apr. 10, 1834, by Rev. Lyman Strong | 2 | 266 |
| Harriet A., of Colchester, m. Daniel G. **FILLEY**, of New York, [Sept.] 13, 1854, by Rev. S. D. Jewett | 3 | 63 |
| Henry, m. Mary Maria **STARK**, Nov. 27, 1842, by Rev. Rob[er]t C. Mills | 2 | 275 |

| | Vol. | Page |
|---|---|---|
| **WATROUS**, (cont.) | | |
| Henry C., s. [Reuben & Lydia], b. Feb. 8, 1824; d. May 27, 1827 | 2 | 117 |
| Jared D., s. [John & Nancy], b. Sept. 19, 1812 | 2 | 245 |
| Jerah, m. Sarah Ann **YOUNG**, b. of Colchester, [June] 9, 1844, by Rev. S. D. Jewett | 3 | 15 |
| Jerusha, d. [John & Jerusha], b. Apr. 27, 1763 | 1 | 118 |
| Jerusha, w. John, d. Apr. 25, 1804 | 1 | 118 |
| John, m. Sarah **TAINTOR**, [ ], 1751 | 1 | 118 |
| John, m. Jerusha **HUNTINGTON**, May 28, 1760 | 1 | 118 |
| John, m. Nancy **BIGELOW**, Mar. 30, 1809 | 2 | 245 |
| John, d. Jan. 11, 1817 | 1 | 118 |
| John Charles, s. [Daniel & Lydia Ann], b. July 30, 1800; d. Aug. 4, 1800 | 2 | 100 |
| John Charles, 2d, s. [Daniel & Lydia Ann], b. Aug. 1, 1801 | 2 | 100 |
| John D., m. Susan D. **WILLIAMS**, b. of Colchester, May 7, 1845, by Rev. Robert Allyn | 3 | 21 |
| John L., m. Laura E. **ISHAM**, Oct. 20, 1824, by Salmon Cone, V. D. M. | 2 | 170 |
| John Lucian, s. [John R. & Louisa], b. Mar. 1, 1801 | 2 | 41 |
| John R., m. Louisa **WOODBRIDGE**, Wid. of Nath[anie]ll S., of Lyme, Mar. 29, 1798 | 2 | 41 |
| John R., m. Lucretia W. **RANSOM**, Mar. 30, 1829; d. Dec. 13, 1842 | 2 | 41 |
| John Richard, s. [John & Sarah], b. Mar. 16, 1754 | 1 | 118 |
| John Richard, m. Lydia **WRIGHT**, June 10, 1783 | 2 | 41 |
| John Richard, s. [John L. & Laura E.], b. June 27, 1820 | 2 | 170 |
| Josiah, s. [John & Nancy], b. Sept. 16, 1815 | 2 | 245 |
| Lois, d. [Reuben & Lydia], b. Aug. 7, 1827 | 2 | 117 |
| Louisa, w. John R., d. Feb. 15, 1823, ae 67 | 2 | 41 |
| Lucretia, m. Richard W. **CARRIER**, b. of Colchester, June 30, 1844, by Rev. Lyman Strong | 3 | 14 |
| Lydia, w. John Richard, d. July 30, 1797 | 2 | 41 |
| Lydia, m. David Olcott **SHATTUCK**, Mar. 1, 1824, at the house of Rev. Jacob Seales, in West Chester, by Rev. Jacob Seales | 2 | 126 |
| Maria, of Colchester, m. George W. **BRUMLEY**, of Bozrah, Sept. 7, 1845, by Rev. M. P. Alderman | 3 | 24 |
| Mary Ann, d. [Timothy & Julia], b. May 17, 1829 | 2 | 246 |
| Mary Ann, m. John C. **SHEPERD**, b. of Colchester, Mar. 30, 1853, by Rev. S. D. Jewett | 3 | 55 |
| Mary J., m. Solomon L. **GILLETT**, July 24, 1826, by Salmon Cone, V. D. M. | 2 | 188 |
| Mary Jerusha, d. [Daniel & Lydia Ann], b. Aug. 9, 1803 | 2 | 100 |
| Nancy, of Colchester, m. Maltby **COVELL**, of Hartford, Oct. 9, 1833, by Rev. Lyman Strong | 2 | 258 |
| Nancy Bulkeley, d. [Daniel & Lydia Ann], b. Apr. 16, 1797 | 2 | 100 |
| Nathaniel Huntington, s. [Daniel & Lydia Ann], b. Feb. 13, | | |

| | Vol. | Page |
|---|---|---|
| **WATROUS**, (cont.) | | |
| 1808 | 2 | 100 |
| Reuben, m. Lydia **BROWN**, Jan. 1, 1812 | 2 | 117 |
| Richard Henry, s. [John Richard & Lydia], b. Apr. 12, 1784; d, Feb. 25, 1786 | 2 | 41 |
| Richard Henry, 2d, s. [John Richard & Lydia], b. Apr. 24, 1787; d. Mar. 2, 1795 | 2 | 41 |
| Sarah, w. John, d. Jan. 3, 1755 | 1 | 118 |
| Sarah, d. [Reuben & Lydia], b. Jan. 3, 1813 | 2 | 117 |
| Sarah, m. Noah D. **NILES**, b. of Colchester, Mar. 5, 1840, by Rev. Lyman Strong | 2 | 76 |
| Sarah Anna, d. [John & Sarah], b. Aug. 14, 1752 | 1 | 118 |
| Sarah Isham, w. Erastus, d. of Stephen [& Hannah] **FOOT**, d. July 4, 1831, ae 40 y. 2 m. in Montpelier, Vt. | 2 | 56 |
| Theodore, m. Lydia **ACKLEY**, Apr. 1, 1827, by Samuel A. Peters, J. P. | 2 | 194 |
| Timothy, m. Julia **CARRIER**, Dec. 25, 1826 | 2 | 246 |
| William, s. [Reuben & Lydia], b. Jan. 5, 1815 | 2 | 117 |
| William, m. Laura E. **WILLIAMS**, b. of Colchester, Nov. 22, 1840, by Rev. Lyman Strong | 2 | 113 |
| Zerviah, d. [John & Jerusha], b. Oct. 14, 1771; d. June 4, 1775 | 1 | 118 |
| -----, s. [John Richard & Lydia], b. Feb. 20, 1786; d. Feb. 20, 1786 | 2 | 41 |
| -----, d. [Daniel & Lydia Ann], b. Jan. 11, 1794; d. same day | 2 | 100 |
| -----, child of [Timothy & Julia], b. Sept. 17, 1827; d. Oct. 13, 1827 | 2 | 246 |
| **WAY, WHAY**, Albert C., s. [George & Esther W.], b. June 6, 1821; d. May 15, 1826, ae 5 | 2 | 84 |
| Caroline, m. Asel **WOODWORTH**, of Montville, Nov. 20, 1828, at the house of Thomas Way, in Colchester, by Asa Wilcox, Elder | 2 | 210 |
| Clarissa, d. [William & Dimmis], b. Jan. 4, 1811; d. Feb. 19, 1815 | 2 | 151 |
| Clarissa, d. [William & Dimmis], b. Mar. 28, 1817 | 2 | 151 |
| Dimmis, [w. William], d. Feb. 13, 1850, ae 70 | 2 | 151 |
| Elizabeth, [d. John, Jr. & Bathsheba], b. Oct. 20, 1760 | 1 | 24 |
| Elizabeth C., of Colchester, m. Thomas J. **SWAN**, of Franklin, Oct. 29, 1834, by Rev. Christopher Leffingwell | 3 | 64 |
| Elizabeth M., of Colchester, m. Isaac **BRAGAW**, of Newark, N. J. May 12, 1841, by Rev. Joel R. Arnold | 2 | 205 |
| Ezra, [s. Joseph & Hannah], b. Mar. 3, 1767 | 1 | 84 |
| George, b. Nov. 4, 1786, in Lyme; m. Esther W. **CHAPMAN**, Aug. 14, 1820; d. Sept. 7, 1851, ae 65 | 2 | 84 |
| George, s. [William & Dimmis], b. Nov. 5, 1808 | 2 | 151 |
| Hannah, [d. Joseph & Hannah], b. Aug. 25, 1763 | 1 | 84 |
| Harriet,, d. [William & Dimmis], b. Sept. 26, 1803 | 2 | 151 |
| Harriet, of Colchester, m. Frederick P. **RAND**, of Hartford, | | |

| | Vol. | Page |
|---|---|---|
| **WAY, WHAY**, (cont.) | | |
| Sept. 30, 1833, by Rev. Lyman Strong | 2 | 258 |
| Harriet R., of Colchester, m. Julius **THOMAS**, of Lebanon, Dec. 30, 1837, by Rev. Lyman Strong | 2 | 295 |
| Jabez, [s. Joseph & Hannah], b. Feb. 8, 1765 | 1 | 84 |
| John, Jr., m. Bathsheba **GARDINER**, Jan. 15, 1756 | 1 | 24 |
| John, [s. John, Jr. & Bathsheba], b. Nov. 28, 1758 | 1 | 24 |
| John, d. Feb. 14, 1768 | 1 | 84 |
| John, m. Clarissa W. **LEE**, Feb. 1, 1829, by Salmon Cone, V. D. M. | 2 | 209 |
| John C., s. [George & Esther W.], b. Feb. 7, 1826 | 2 | 84 |
| Joseph, m. Hannah **SPENCER**, Jan. 5, 1763 | 1 | 84 |
| Joshua, [s. John, Jr. & Bathsheba], b. Mar. 14, 1757 | 1 | 24 |
| Laura, d. [William & Dimmis], b. Jan. 4, 1806 | 2 | 151 |
| Laura, of Colchester, m. Robert **BUELL**, of Hartford, Sept. 27, 1830, by Rev. Lyman Strong | 2 | 225 |
| Levi, [s. John, Jr. & Bathsheba], b. Aug. 9, 1767 | 1 | 24 |
| Lucy, d. [William & Dimmis], b. Mar. 9, 1813; d. May 26, 1839, ae 26 | 2 | 151 |
| Mary, of Colchester, m. Churchill **BLACKMAN**, of Coventry, Dec. 5, 1830, by Rev. Lyman Strong | 2 | 227 |
| Polly, d. [William & Dimmis], b. July 28, 1801 | 2 | 151 |
| Russel[l], m. Sophia Ann **RANSOM**, b. of Colchester, Oct. 5, 1841, by Rev. Joel R. Arnold | 2 | 176 |
| Samuel, [s. John, Jr. & Bathsheba], b. May 16, 1763 | 1 | 24 |
| William, s. [William & Dimmis], b. Aug. 9, 1815 | 2 | 151 |
| William, m. Dimmis **PACKWOOD**, [ ]; d. Feb. 20, 1835, ae 64 | 2 | 151 |
| **WEBSTER**, Emily E., m. John N. **PEASE**, b. of Colchester, Apr. 14, 1835, by Rev. Lyman Strong | 2 | 276 |
| Levi, s. [Stephen & Delilah], b. Apr. 29, 1791 | 2 | 26 |
| Levi, m. Anna **JONES**, b. of Colchester, [Mar.] 30, 1851, by Rev. S. D. Jewett | 2 | 73 |
| Lucy A., m. Horace **FOOT**, b. of Colchester, Oct. 10, 1849, by Rev. G. W. Pendleton | 3 | 42 |
| Mabel, m. Jonathan **LESTER**, Apr. 11, 1789 | 2 | 80 |
| Sarah, m. Josiah C. **NEWTON**, b. of Colchester, June 18, 1837, by Rev. Andrew M. Smith | 2 | 154 |
| Stephen, m. Delilah **SHAW**, Aug. 3, 1790 | 2 | 26 |
| Stephen, m. Hannah **BULKELEY**, Feb. 1, 1829, by Rev. Joseph Harvey, of Westchester | 2 | 210 |
| **WEDGE**, Sarah, m. Peter **GRAVES**, July 1, 1742 | 1 | 95 |
| **WELCH, WECH**, [see also **WALCH**], Alfred, s. [Daniel, Jr. & Nancy], b. Dec. 10, 1789 | 2 | 65 |
| Anna, d. [Joshua & Abigail], b. Jan. 3, 1736 | 1 | 107 |
| Anne, twin with William, [d. William], b. July 2, 1767 | 1 | 86 |
| Caleb, s. [Joshua & Abigail], b. July 2, 1745 | 1 | 107 |
| Daniel, Jr., m. Nancy **BROWN**, Aug. 24, 1788 | 2 | 65 |

| | Vol. | Page |
|---|---|---|
| **WELCH, WECH**, (cont.) | | |
| Elizabeth, d. [Joshua & Abigail], b. Aug. 22, 1740 | 1 | 107 |
| Joshua, m. Abigail **TENNANT**, Apr. 17, 1735 | 1 | 107 |
| Joshua, s. [Joshua & Abigail], b. Apr. 19, 1743 | 1 | 107 |
| Mary, d. [Joshua & Abigail], b. Feb. 17, 1738 | 1 | 107 |
| Mary, m. Edward **LOVERIDGE**, June 31(?), 1762 | 1 | 81 |
| Mary, m. Ezra or Asa **MARRINER**, Apr. 17, 1770 | 2 | 3 |
| Mary Ann, m. Ananias **DATHICK**, Feb. 14, 1771 | 1 | 163 |
| Matilda, d. [Daniel, Jr. & Nancy], b. Jan. 26, 1793 | 2 | 65 |
| Mehetable, m. John **FOX**, Dec. 9, 1777 | 2 | 58 |
| Nancy, d. [Daniel, Jr. & Nancy], b. May 26, 1791 | 2 | 65 |
| Sarah, m. Amos **MORGAN**, Nov. 9, 1769 | 1 | 91 |
| William, twin with Anne, [s. William], b. July 2, 1767 | 1 | 86 |
| William, Jr., of Colchester, m. Deborah **JEWETT**, of East Haddam, July 7, 1775 | 2 | 11 |
| **WELD**, Abby R., m. James **LAMB**, b. of Colchester, Mar. 27, 1851, by Rev. George W. Pendleton | 2 | 270 |
| Cornelius d., of New York, m. Abby R. **ROGERS**, of Colchester, Aug. 28, 1834, by Rev. Alpheas Geer, of Hebron | 2 | 270 |
| **WELLES, WELLS, WELES**, Abigaiell, m. William **MARINER**, Jan. 27, 1721/22 | L-1 | 448 |
| Abigail, [d. Ephraim, Jr. & Lydia], b. Feb. 2, 1729/30 | 1 | 135 |
| Abigail, w. Ensign Ephraim, d. Nov. 16, 1731 | L-3 | 458 |
| Alice, [d. James & Hannah], b. Nov. 29, 1772 | 1 | 32 |
| Amanda, d. [Ephraim & Ursula], b. Oct. 6, 1803 | 2 | 103 |
| Amasa, [s. James & Hannah], b. May 29, 1765 | 1 | 32 |
| Amos, [s. Noah & Sarah], b. Feb. 28, 1735 | L-3 | 452 |
| Amos, m. Lydia **TREADWAY**, Nov. 23, 1758 | 1 | 104 |
| Amos, s. [Amos & Lydia], b. Oct. 10, 1760 | 1 | 104 |
| Ann, d. [Levi & Jerusha], b. May 31, 1770; d. Aug. 10, 1770 | 1 | 140 |
| Ann, wid. John, d. Jan. 29, 1798, ae 80 | 2 | 81 |
| Ann R., of Colchester, m. Uzziel **BRIDGES**, of Genesee, N. Y., Nov. 24, 1845, by Rev. Joel R. Arnold | 3 | 26 |
| Anna, m. Preserved **GARDINER**, May 19, 1763 | 1 | 56 |
| Anna, d. [Martin & Larana], b. Mar. 14, 1777 | 2 | 59 |
| Asa, s. [Amos & Lydia], b. July 26, 1764 | 1 | 104 |
| Asa, [s. Levi & Jerusha], b. Aug. 6, 1774 | 1 | 140 |
| Benjamin, s. [John & Sarah], b. Apr. 17, 1784 | 2 | 82 |
| Betsey, m. Jason **COLEMAN**, Aug. 28, 1780, by Ichabod Allyn | 2 | 5 |
| Bettey, [d. James & Hannah], b. Apr. 15, 1757 | 1 | 32 |
| Charles, s. [Levi & Jerusha], b. May 31, 1772 | 1 | 140 |
| Charles, s. [Martin & Larana], b. Jan. 21, 1775; d. Mar. 17, 1776 | 2 | 59 |
| Charles, 2d, s. [Martin & Larana], b. Sept. 6, 1787 | 2 | 59 |
| Charlotte, d. [Levi & Jerusha], b. Feb. 4, 1762 | 1 | 140 |
| Cyrus, [s. James & Hannah], b. May 23, 1768 | 1 | 32 |

| | Vol. | Page |
|---|---|---|
| **WELLES, WELLS, WELES**, (cont.) | | |
| Dauid, [s. Noah & Sarah], b. Sept. 10, 1723 | L-1 | 799 |
| David, [s. Noah & Sarah], b. Sept. 10, 1723 | L-3 | 452 |
| David, m. Mary **TAINTOR**, Jan. 19, 1748/9 | 1 | 151 |
| David, s. [David & Mary], b. Apr. 22, 1750 | 1 | 151 |
| David, s. [Martin & Larana], b. Jan. 5, 1790 | 2 | 59 |
| Dudley, s. [Martin & Larana], b. Jan. 4, 1781; d. July 9, 1781 | 2 | 59 |
| Eliab, s. [Amos & Lydia], b. Sept. 26, 1762 | 1 | 104 |
| Eliphalet, s. [Martin & Larana], b. May 2, 1771; d. Feb. 16, 1776 | 2 | 59 |
| Eliphalet, s. [John & Sarah], b. Sept. 19, 1779 | 2 | 82 |
| Elisha, [s. Elisha], b. May 16, 1749 | 1 | 145 |
| Elisha [Sr.], d. Aug. 31, 1751 | 1 | 145 |
| Elishabee, [s. Elisha], b. Sept. 5, 1751 | 1 | 145 |
| Eliza, of Colchester, m. George **PERRY**, of Lebanon, June 24, 1844, by Rev. Charles William Bradley | 3 | 16 |
| Eliza L., of Colchester, m. Zimmi L. **SMITH**, of Norwich, Mar. 20, 1823, by Rev. William Palmer | 2 | 136 |
| Elizabeth, m. George **BROWN**, Apr. 12, 1730 | 1 | 56 |
| Elizabeth, [d. Ephraim, Jr. & Lydia], b. May 4, 1740 | 1 | 135 |
| Elizabeth, m. Samuel **WORTHINGTON**, Dec. 26, 1749 | 1 | 121 |
| Elizabeth, m. Daniel **KELLOGG**, Jan. 14, 1778; d. May 23, 1815 | 2 | 80 |
| Emily, m. Edwin **BANNING**, Aug. 28, 1828, by Rev. Tubal Wakefield | 2 | 205 |
| Enos, Capt., d. Feb. 10, 1846, ae 65 | 2 | 69 |
| Ephraim, Jr., m. Lydia **CHAPMAN**, Feb. 2, 1726/7 | 1 | 135 |
| Ephraim, [s. Ephraim, Jr. & Lydia], b. Aug. 26, 1731 | 1 | 135 |
| Ephraim, m. Sarah **GATES**, Feb. 10, 1763 | 1 | 127 |
| Ephraim, s. [Ephraim & Sarah], b. June 16, 1770 | 1 | 127 |
| Ephraim, Sr., d. Sept. [ ], 1786 | 1 | 135 |
| Ephraim, d. July 18, 1799 | 1 | 127 |
| Ephraim, m. Ursula **GRISWOLD**, Mar. 3, 1800 | 2 | 103 |
| Ephraim, s. [Ephraim & Ursula], b. Dec. 19, 1800; d. Apr. 14, 1801 | 2 | 103 |
| Ephraim Thomas, s. [Ephraim & Ursula], b. Apr. 5, 1805 | 2 | 103 |
| Eunice, [d. David & Mary], b. May [ ], 1764 | 1 | 151 |
| Eunice, d. [John, 3d, & Eunice], b. June 11, 1805 | 2 | 147 |
| Eunice, m. Edward Y. **THOMAS**, Feb. 21, 1828, by Salmon Cone, V. D. M. | 2 | 200 |
| Eunice, [w. John, 3d], d. Dec. 11, 1843, ae 65 | 2 | 147 |
| Eunice M., of Marlboro, m. Edwin **BOGUE**, of Colchester, Jan. 11, 1852, by Octavus Emmons, J. P. | 3 | 49 |
| Ezekiel, s. [Ephraim, Jr. & Lydia], b. July 8, 1748 | 1 | 135 |
| George, s. [Ephraim & Ursula], b. Dec. 8, 1806 | 2 | 103 |
| George, of Richford, N. Y., m. Lucy E. **STARK**, of Colchester, June 10, 1833, by Rev. Lyman Strong | 2 | 255 |
| Gidion, [s. Noah & Sarah], b. Jan. 22, 1728/9 | L-1 | 799 |

| | Vol. | Page |
|---|---|---|
| **WELLES, WELLS, WELES**, (cont.) | | |
| Gideon, [s. Noah & Sarah], b. Jan. 22, 1728/9 | L-3 | 452 |
| Guy, [s. James & Hannah], b. Aug. 22, 1766 | 1 | 32 |
| Hannah, d. Ephream, b. Jan. 2, 1709/10 | L-3 | 195 |
| Hannah, d. Ephraim, b. Jan. 2, 1709/10 | TM-1 | 195 |
| Hannah, m. Isaac **JONES**, July 11, 1717 | L-1 | 453 |
| Hannah, [d. Ephraim, Jr. & Lydia], b. Oct. 7, 1734 | 1 | 135 |
| Hannah, [d. James & Hannah], b. May 13, 1756; d. May 21, 1758 | 1 | 32 |
| Hannah, d. [Ephraim & Sarah], b. Jan. 17, 1767 | 1 | 127 |
| Hannah, m. W[illia]m **BAKER**, Jan. 31, 1782 | 2 | 32 |
| Harriet, d. [John, 3d, & Eunice], b. Feb. 10, 1810 | 2 | 147 |
| Harriet, of Colchester, m. Dan[iel] **HUNTINGTON**, of Lebanon, Oct. 28, 1830, by Rev. Lyman Strong | 2 | 225 |
| Henry, of New Haven, m. Frances Jane **BULKELEY**, of Colchester, Apr. 15, 1841, by Rev. Augustus Bolles | 2 | 191 |
| Hubbell, of Colchester, m. Zerviah **CHANDLER**, of Lebanon, May 20, 1754 | 1 | 140 |
| Hubbell, twin with Mabel, s. [Hubbell & Zerviah], b. Oct. 26, 1770 | 1 | 140 |
| Irene, [d. Jonathan & Mary], b. May 4, 1729 | L-1 | 452 |
| Ireney, d. [Hubbell & Zerviah], b. Oct. 21, 1756 | 1 | 140 |
| Israel, s. [David & Mary], b. Mar. 15, 1761 | 1 | 151 |
| Israel, m. Mary **STARK**, Sept. 15, 1823, by Salmon Cone, V. D. M. | 2 | 159 |
| Israel Wyat[t], s. Noah & Sarah], b. Dec. 17, 1714 | L-1 | 799 |
| Israell Wyatt, [s. Noah & Sarah], b. Dec. 17, 1714 | L-3 | 452 |
| James, m. Hannah **LO[O]MIS**, Mar, 28, 1754 | 1 | 32 |
| James, m. Esther **WITTER**, Sept. 1, 1816 | 2 | 109 |
| Jerusha, [d. Noah & Sarah], b. Jan. 6, 1716; d. Dec. 17, 1717 | L-1 | 799 |
| Jerusha, [d. Noah & Sarah], b. Jan. 6, 1716/17; d. Dec. 17, 1717 | L-3 | 452 |
| Jerusha, [d. Noah & Sarah], b. Jan. 28, 1733/4 | L-3 | 452 |
| Jerusha, d. [Levi & Jerusha], b. Dec. 26, 1759 | 1 | 140 |
| John, m. Elizabeth **CHAMBERLIN**, Sept. 8, 1715 | L-1 | 450 |
| John, [s. John & Elizabeth], b. Nov. 24, 1718 | L-1 | 450 |
| John, m. Sarah **CHAMBERLAIN**, Oct. 1, 1770 | 2 | 82 |
| John, s. [John & Sarah], b. July 4, 1773 | 2 | 82 |
| John, s. [Martin & Larana], b. Feb. 14, 1779 | 2 | 59 |
| John, 3d, d. Feb. 24, 1842, ae 63 | 2 | 147 |
| John, 3d, m. Eunice **BULKELEY**, [ ] | 2 | 147 |
| Jonathan, m. Mary **NEWTON**, July 11, 1717 | L-1 | 452 |
| Jonathan, [s. Jonathan & Mary], b. Apr. 13, 1718 | L-1 | 452 |
| Jonathan, s. [Hubbell & Zerviah], b. Sept. 25, 1765 | 1 | 140 |
| Joseph, [s. Ephraim, Jr. & Lydia], b. Jan. 2, 1743/4 | 1 | 135 |
| Joseph, s. [John & Sarah], b. Sept. 27, 1781 | 2 | 82 |
| Joshua, [s. Ephraim, Jr. & Lydia], b. May 18, 1738 | 1 | 125 |

| | Vol. | Page |
|---|---|---|
| **WELLES, WELLS, WELES**, (cont.) | | |
| Larana, w. Martin, d. May 12, 1818, ae 66 | 2 | 59 |
| Larana, see also Lurana | | |
| Levi, m. Jerusha **CLARK**, May 3, 1759 | 1 | 140 |
| Levi, s. [Levi & Jerusha], b. Aug. 3, 1764 | 1 | 140 |
| Lewis Bulkeley, [s. John, 3d, & Eunice], b. Sept. 9, 1807 | 2 | 147 |
| Lois, s. [John & Sarah], b. May 22, 1775 | 2 | 82 |
| Lovina, d. [Ephraim & Sarah], b. Apr. 21, 1765 | 1 | 127 |
| Lucinda, d. [David & Mary], b. Feb. 10, 1758 | 1 | 151 |
| Lucretia, [d. Ephraim, Jr. & Lydia], b. Feb. 24, 1732/3 | 1 | 135 |
| Lucy, d. [Hubbell & Zerviah], b. May 8, 1761 | 1 | 140 |
| Lucy B., m. Joshua B. **ROGERS**, Feb. 27, 1833, by Salmon Cone, V. D. M. | 2 | 241 |
| Lurana, d. [Martin & Larana], b. Feb. 3, 1768; d. Feb. 14, 1776 | 2 | 59 |
| Lurana, see also Larana | | |
| Lidiah, [d. Ephream], b. Jan. 18, 1711/12 | L-3 | 195 |
| Lydia, d. Ephraim, b. Jan. 18, 1711/12 | TM-1 | 195 |
| Lydia, d. [Ephraim, Jr. & Lydia], b. May 24, 1728 | 1 | 135 |
| Lidia, m. Elnathan **ROWLEY**, Oct. 3, 1736 | L-3 | 456 |
| Lydia, m. John **CHAMBERLAIN**, Jr., Mar. 16, 1758 | 1 | 147 |
| Lydia, m. David **KILLBORN**, Jr., Mar. 13, 1793 | 2 | 79 |
| Lynde Griswold, d. [Ephraim & Ursula], b. Feb. 22, 1802 | 2 | 103 |
| Mabel, twin with Hubbell, d. [Hubbell & Zerviah], b. Oct. 26, 1770 | 1 | 140 |
| Martin, m. Larana **PUMROY**, [ ], 1767; d. May 13, 1819, ae 77 | 2 | 59 |
| Martin, s. [Martin & Larana], b. July 29, 1769; d. Feb. 18, 1776 | 2 | 59 |
| Martin, 2d, s. [Martin & Larana], b. June 24, 1782 | 2 | 59 |
| Mary, [d. John & Elizabeth], b. July 15, 1716 | L-1 | 450 |
| Mary, [d. Jonathan & Mary], b. Sept. 14, 1724 | L-1 | 452 |
| Mary, m. Thomas **DAY**, Feb. 2, 1727 | 1 | 140 |
| Mary, m. Elijah **WORTHINGTON**, Oct. 4, 1733 | 1 | 151 |
| Mary, [d. Ephraim, Jr. & Lydia], b. Mar. 28, 1742 | 1 | 135 |
| Mary, [d.Elisha], b. Oct. 29, 1746 | 1 | 145 |
| Mary, d. [David & Mary], b. Dec. 22, 1754 | 1 | 151 |
| Mary, m. David **MORGAN**, Dec. 17, 1757 | 1 | 164 |
| Mary, m. Charles **TAINTOR**, Aug. 20, 1766 | 1 | 95 |
| Mary, d. [Hubbell & Zerviah], b. May 24, 1768 | 1 | 140 |
| Molly, [d. James & Hannah], b. July 2, 1776 | 1 | 32 |
| Moses, [d. Noah & Sarah], b. Oct. 3, 1725 | L-1 | 799 |
| Moses, [s. Noah & Sarah], b. Oct. 3, 1725 | L-3 | 452 |
| Noah, m. Sarah **WYAT[T]**, Apr. 15, 1714 | L-1 | 799 |
| Noah, m. Sarah **WYATT**, Apr. 15, 1714 | L-3 | 452 |
| Noah, [s. Noah & Sarah], b. Sept. 25, 1718 | L-1 | 799 |
| Noah, [s. Noah & Sarah], b. Sept. 25, 1718 | L-3 | 452 |
| Noah, s. [David & Mary], b. Oct. 5, 1753 | 1 | 151 |

| | Vol. | Page |
|---|---|---|
| **WELLES, WELLS, WELES**, (cont.) | | |
| Noah, s. [Martin & Larana], b. Mar. 14, 1773 | 2 | 59 |
| Olive, [d. James & Hannah], b. [ ], 1755; d. May 15, 1758 | 1 | 32 |
| Olive, 2d, [d. James & Hannah], b. Sept. 18, 1758 | 1 | 32 |
| Orrin Matthew, s. [Ephraim & Ursula], b. Aug. 10, 1808 | 2 | 103 |
| Paoli, [s. Levi & Jerusha], b. Jan. 22, 1769 | 1 | 140 |
| Patience, d. [David & Mary], b. Aug. 13, 1752 | 1 | 151 |
| Ralph, s. [Martin & Larana], b. Sept. 27, 1786; d. Oct. 19, 1786 | 2 | 59 |
| Rebeckah, [d. Ephream], b. Sept. 1, 1715 | L-3 | 195 |
| Rebeckah, d. Ephraim, b. Sept. 1, 1715 | TM-1 | 195 |
| Rhoda, m. Noah **POMROY**, Jr., Jan. 12, 1780 | 2 | 96 |
| Rhoda, d. [Martin & Larana], b. Oct. 22, 1794 | 2 | 59 |
| Rhodolphus, [s. Levi & Jerusha], b. Sept. 12, 1767; d. Sept. 28, 1775 | 1 | 140 |
| Rocksa, d. [Martin & Larana], b. Nov. 11, 1784 | 2 | 59 |
| Rowenay, d. [Levi & Jerusha], b. Feb. 9, 1766 | 1 | 140 |
| Roxana, d.[Martin & Larana], d. June 7, 1812;, ae 27 y. 7 m. (see also Rocksa) | 2 | 59 |
| Roxana, d. [John, 3d, & Eunice], b. Mar. 20, 1813 | 2 | 147 |
| Rubin, [s. Jonathan & Mary], b. May 23, 1722 | L-1 | 452 |
| Ruby, d. [Hubbell & Zerviah], b. June 1, 1763 | 1 | 140 |
| Ruby, d. [Ephraim & Sarah], b. Apr. 25, 1772 | 1 | 127 |
| Samuel, s. [Martin & Larana], b. Aug. 3, 1792 | 2 | 59 |
| Sarah, [d. Noah & Sarah], b. Jan. 12, 1720/21 | L-1 | 799 |
| Sarah, [d. Noah & Sarah], b. Jan. 12, 1721/2 | L-3 | 452 |
| Sarah, d. [Ephraim, Jr. & Lydia], b. Apr. 28, 1746 | 1 | 135 |
| Sarah, d. [Ephraim & Sarah], b. Jan. 26, 1764 | 1 | 127 |
| Sarah, d. [Amos & Lydia], b. July 6, 1768 | 1 | 104 |
| Sarah, m. William **WORTHINGTON**, b. of Colchester, July 5, 1770 | 1 | 53 |
| Sarah, m. William **WORTHINGTON**, b. of Colchester, July 5, 1770 | 2 | 53 |
| Sarah, d. [John & Sarah], b. June 20, 1771 | 2 | 82 |
| Sarah, w. Lieut. Noah, was d. of Lt. Israel **WYATT** | 1 | 141 |
| Sarah, d. Lt. Noah & Sarah (**WYATT**), m. Oliver **BULKELEY**, [ ] | 1 | 141 |
| Silas, [s. Noah & Sarah], b. July 8, 1730 | L-3 | 452 |
| Silas, s. [Amos & Lydia], b. Feb. 13, 1759 | 1 | 104 |
| Simion, [s. Jonathan & Mary], b. June 17, 1720 | L-1 | 452 |
| Sophia, d. [John, 3d, & Eunice], b. Jan. 22, 1816 | 2 | 147 |
| Sophia, m. Olcott **WORTHINGTON**, May 19, 1836, by Rev. Joel R. Arnold | 2 | 286 |
| Theodosia, [d. James & Hannah], b. Oct. 8, 1770 | 1 | 32 |
| Thomas, [s. Ephraim, Jr. & Lydia], b. June 28, 1736 | 1 | 135 |
| Thomas, m. Sarah **KILLBORN**, Sept. 18, 1740 | 1 | 145 |
| Thomas,s. Ephraim & Sarah],b. Dec. 22, 1768;d. Jan. 23, 1769 | 1 | 127 |
| Thomas, d. Dec. [ ], 1780 | 2 | 73 |

| | Vol. | Page |
|---|---|---|
| **WELLES, WELLS, WELES**, (cont.) | | |
| Ursula Griswold, d. [Ephraim & Ursula], b. May 21, 1810 | 2 | 103 |
| Walter, [s. David & Mary], b. Apr. [ ], 1770 | 1 | 151 |
| Walter, s. [John & Sarah], b. Apr. 16, 1776 | 2 | 82 |
| William, [s. David & Mary], b. Jan. [ ], 1767 | 1 | 151 |
| Zerviah, d. [Hubbell & Zerviah], b. Jan. 8, 1759 | 1 | 140 |
| ----, s. [Amos & Lydia], b. Mar. 20, 1770; d. Mar. 25, 1770 | 1 | 104 |
| **WENTWORTH, WINTWORTH**, Katharine, m. Daniel **CHAPMAN**, Mar. 22, 1713 | TPR | 112 |
| Ketem, m. Daniell **CHAPMAN**, Mar. 22, 1713 | L-1 | 399 |
| **WEST**, Caroline Nancy, d. [Jabez & Fanny], b. Feb. 23, 1833 | 2 | 250 |
| Ellen E., of Colchester, m. Ezra M. **CASE**, of Hartford, Sept. 25, 1850, by Rev. Lyman Strong | 2 | 111 |
| Enos, Capt., d. Feb. 10, 1846, ae 65 | 2 | 69 |
| Fanny H., of Colchester, m. William C. **THOMPSON**, of Mansfield, Conn., Apr. 3, 1844, by Rev. A. B. Wheeler | 3 | 12 |
| Fanny Witter, d. [Jabez & Fanny], b. Apr. 3, 1827 | 2 | 250 |
| Jabez, b. Feb. 22, 1799; m. Fanny **BALCH**, Feb. 19, 1824 | 2 | 250 |
| John, of Colchester, m. Maria Matilda **HURD**, of East Haddam, Sept. 2, 1834, by Rev. Lyman Strong | 2 | 269 |
| Julia A., of Colchester, m. Brutus **BARROWS**, of Groton, Sept. 21, 1836, by Rev. Andrew M. Smith | 2 | 290 |
| Lusina, of Colchester, m. George W. **KELLOGG**, of Belchertown, Mass., Dec. 1, 1845, by Rev. Joel R. Arnold | 3 | 26 |
| Mary Elizabeth, d. [Jabez & Fanny], b. Feb. 19, 1825 | 2 | 250 |
| Mercy Aurelia, d. [Jabez & Fanny], b. Nov. 28, 1828 | 2 | 250 |
| Seth B., of Marlborough, Conn., m. Cynthia **LAMPHERE**, of Colchester, June 28, 1852, by Geo[rge], W. Pendleton | 3 | 52 |
| Susan Maria, d. [Jabez & Fanny], b. Apr. 29, 1831 | 2 | 250 |
| Warren, of Chatham, m. Tabitha **DAY**, of Colchester, Apr. 30, 1821, by Rev. Jacob Seales | 2 | 125 |
| -----, of Lebanon, m. William **CHAMBERLAIN**, [ ] | 2 | 3 |
| **WESTCOTT**, Ann J., of New Haven, m. Lucius E. **FORD**, of Colchester, Apr. 6, 1849, by Rev. G. W. Pendleton | 3 | 39 |
| **WHAY**, [see under **WAY**] | | |
| **WHEELER**, Emeline Turner, d. [Joshua B. & Aurelia L.], b. Mar. 30, 1834 | 2 | 196 |
| Esther, m. Rev. Augustus **BOLLES**, b. of Colchester, Feb. 27, 1842, by Rev. J. R. Arnold | 2 | 231 |
| Fanny B., of Colchester, m. Asahel O. **COMSTOCK**, of La Roy, N. Y., May 8, 1836, by Rev. Lyman Strong | 2 | 285 |
| Fanny Sabra, d. [Joshua B. & Aurelia L. ], b. Nov. 30, 1839 | 2 | 196 |
| Frederic A., of Columbia, m. Pattis P. **BLY**, of Ludlow, Mass., Mar. 14, 1841, at the house of Rev. J. R. Arnold, by Rev. Hiram Bell, in Colchester | 2 | 229 |
| Gardiner, of Tolland, m. Tabitha **CHAMBERLAIN**, Sept. 10, 1837, by Rev. Joel R. Arnold | 2 | 113 |

| | Vol. | Page |
|---|---|---|
| **WHEELER**, (cont._ | | |
| John Turner, s. [Joshua B. & Aurelia L.], b. Oct. 18, 1836; d. Feb. 15, 1837 | 2 | 196 |
| Joshua B., m. Aurelia L. **TURNER**, b. of Colchester, May 9, 1827, by Lyman Strong | 2 | 196 |
| Leonard, of Avon, m. Emma D. **COMSTOCK**, of Colchester, Aug. 31, 1836, by Rev. Andrew M. Smith | 2 | 290 |
| Maria F., m. Frederick A. **WATROUS**, Jan. 5, 1825, by Salmon Cone, V. D. M. | 2 | 174 |
| William Turner, s. [Joshua B. & Aurelia L.], b. Mar. 12, 1838 | 2 | 196 |
| **WHIPPLE**, Fanny, m. David **FLOWER**, Nov. 23, 1825, by Salmon Cone, V. D. M. | 2 | 180 |
| Otis, m. Emily **PIERCE**, of Utica, N. Y., Mar. 13, 1827, by Salmon Cone, V. D. M. | 2 | 193 |
| **WHITCOMB, WHITCOM**, Anna, [d. Job & Anna], b. Feb. 2, 1763 | 1 | 38 |
| Hiram, [s. Job & Anna], b. Feb. 28, 1758 | 1 | 38 |
| Isaac, [s.John & Mahitable], b. Aug. 24, 1728 | L-1 | 444 |
| Israell, [s. John & Mahitable], b. Mar. 13, 1733 | L-1 | 444 |
| Jemima, [d. John & Mahitable], b. Feb. 24, 1716/17 | L-1 | 444 |
| Job, [s. John & Mahitable], b. May 8, 1724 | L-1 | 444 |
| Job, m. Anna **SKINNER**, Mar. 10, 1757 | 1 | 38 |
| Job, [s. Job & Anna], b. Sept. 21, 1768; d. Nov. 20, 1768 | 1 | 38 |
| John, m. Mahitable **DUNHAM**, Feb. 15, 1715/16 | L-1 | 444 |
| John, [s. John & Mahitable], b. Jan. 13, 1718/19 | L-1 | 444 |
| John, [s. Job & Anna], b. June 10, 1766 | 1 | 38 |
| Mary, [d. John & Mahitable], b. Sept. 15, 1726 | L-1 | 444 |
| Mary, m. Benjamin **ADDAMS**, [ ] | 1 | 55 |
| Mahitable, [d. John & Mahitable], b. Apr. 9, 1722 | L-1 | 444 |
| Solomon, [s. Job & Anna], b. Sept. 3, 1760 | 1 | 38 |
| **WHITE**, Abigail, wid., m. Daniel **PRATT**, July [ ], 1776 | 1 | 136 |
| Anna, of Hebron, m. John **NORTHAM**, of Colchester, Nov. 10, 1757 | 1 | 27 |
| George C., of Bolton, m. Elizabeth B. **MORGAN**, of Colchester, Sept. 23, 1841, by Rev. Joel R. Arnold | 2 | 243 |
| Nancy S., of Chatham, m. Amasa **CLARK**, of East Haddam, Sept. 26, 1847, by Rev. J. R. Arnold | 3 | 33 |
| Sally, b. Sept. 25, 1795; m. Charles **GRAVES**, Oct. 6, 1811 | 2 | 55 |
| Sarah, d. [Joseph **GILLET**, Jr. & Sarah **GILLET**], d. July 26, 1851, ae 59 | 2 | 76 |
| **WHITMAN**, Margaret, of Norwich, m. Rufus **RANDALL**, of Colchester, Dec. 6, 1757 | 1 | 32 |
| **WHITNEY**, Hannah, m. Latham H. **CHAMPLAIN**, b. of Colchester, Jan. 4, 1853, by Rev. G. W. Pendleton | 3 | 54 |
| **WHITTLESEY**, Ann, m. David **SPERRY**, Sept. [ ], 1811 | 2 | 134 |
| **WICKWIRE, WICKWARE**, Abby E., of Colchester, m. Joseph A. **BUCKINGHAM**, of New London, Sept. 24, 1848, by Rev. P. Brockett | 3 | 36 |

| | Vol. | Page |
|---|---|---|
| **WICKWIRE, WICKWARE,** (cont.) | | |
| Anne, m. James **BROWN**, Oct. 14, 1714 | L-1 | 799 |
| Phebe, m. Andrew **CARRIER**, Feb. 24, 1792 | 2 | 76 |
| **WILCOX, WILLCOX**, Asa, m. Mercy **RATHBUN**, Nov. 28, 1791; d. Jan. 4, 1834, in Salem, Ct. ae 69 | 2 | 135 |
| Asa, s. [Asa & Mercy], b. July 9, 1801 | 2 | 135 |
| Elizabeth, d. [Asa & Mercy], b. July 19, 1794 | 2 | 135 |
| Francis, s. [Asa & Mercy], b. June 4, 1809 | 2 | 135 |
| Isaiah, s. [Asa & Mercy], b. June 16, 1805 | 2 | 135 |
| Jeremiah, of Lebanon, m. Susannah D. **WILLIAMS**, of Colchester, Sept. 6, 1840, by Augustus Bolles, V. D. M. | 2 | 158 |
| Mercy, d. [Asa & Mercy], b. Jan. 13, 1793; d. Feb. 13, 1810 | 2 | 135 |
| Mercy, [s. Asa], d. Mar. 28, 1837, in Salem, Ct. | 2 | 135 |
| Prudence, d. [Asa & Mercy], b. July 22, 1798; d. Feb. 28, 1799 | 2 | 135 |
| Rebecca, d. [Asa & Mercy], b. Dec. 6, 1799; d. Sept. 23, 1804 | 2 | 135 |
| Sarah, d. [Asa & Mercy], b. Oct. 9, 1796; d. Jan. 9, 1848, ae 51 | 2 | 135 |
| **WILDE**, David, s. [Jonas & Mary], b. Jan. 19, 1754 | 1 | 152 |
| Job, s. [Jonas & Mary], b. Aug. 29, 1752 | 1 | 152 |
| John, s. [Jonas & Mary], b. Mar. 27, 1749 | 1 | 152 |
| Jonas, m. Mary **FOOT**, Oct. 10, 1748 | 1 | 152 |
| Russel[l], s. [Jonas & Mary], b. July 9, 1763 | 1 | 152 |
| **WILLEY**, Jabez, s. Thomas, d. May 9, 1742 | 1 | 140 |
| **WILLIAMS**, Abigail, [d. John & Abigail], b. Sept. 30, 1749 | 1 | 52 |
| Abraham, [s. Nathan & Elizabeth], b. July 21, 1726 | L-3 | 8 |
| Alanson, s. [Elijah, Jr. & Editha], b. June 16, 1779 | 2 | 77 |
| Alanson, m. Sally B. **SKINNER**, Nov. 22, 1805 | 2 | 150 |
| Amelia, alias **SWAN**, d. Judith **SNOBO**(?), b. Jan. 24, 1810 | 2 | 77 |
| Ann, [d. Nathan & Eliza], [b.] Apr. 24, 1739 | 1 | 142 |
| Ann, [d. John & Abigail], b. Mar. 22, 1753 | 1 | 52 |
| Ann Asenath, d. [Justus W. & Almira], b. June 13, 1841 | 2 | 240 |
| Anna Mack, m. Jonathan **NORTHAM**, Jr., Apr. 1, 1754 | 1 | 99 |
| Asa, s. [Daniel & Asenath], b. Apr. 28, 1786; d. Feb. 15, 1810 | 2 | 46 |
| Asenath, d. [Daniel & Asenath], b. Apr. 10, 1791 | 2 | 46 |
| Asenath, Mrs., d. Apr. 27, 1841, ae 82 | 2 | 46 |
| Asenath, see also Sena | | |
| Augustin, s. [Elijah, Jr. & Editha], b. Mar. 29, 1781 | 2 | 77 |
| Bethiah, d. [William & Deborah], b. Apr. 20, 1740; d. Oct. 20, 1740 | 1 | 102 |
| Bethiah, 2d, d. [William & Deborah], b. June 20, 1742 | 1 | 102 |
| Caroline L., m. Loren W. **LOOMIS**, b. of Colchester, Nov. 19, 1834, by Rev. Joseph Harvey | 2 | 273 |
| Charles, m. Rachel [     ], Nov. 22, 1746 | 1 | 124 |
| Charles, s. [Charles & Rachel], b. Dec. 16, 1749; d. Jan. 1, 1768 | 1 | 124 |
| Charles, [s. John & Freelove], b. Nov. 18, 1768 | 1 | 79 |
| Charlotte F., m. Samuel N. **BRAINARD**, b. of Colchester, | | |

| | Vol. | Page |
|---|---|---|
| **WILLIAMS**, (cont.) | | |
| June 9, 1853, by Rev. S. D. Jewett, Westchester | 3 | 56 |
| Chauncey, s. [Jonathan & Tabitha], b. Apr. 5, 1825 | 2 | 69 |
| Clarissa, d. [Elijah, Jr. & Editha], b. May 7, 1776 | 2 | 77 |
| Clarissa A., d. [Joseph D. & Clarissa], b. Aug. 17, 1843 | 2 | 31 |
| Daniel, s. [Weeks & Joanna], b. Nov. 1, 1757 | 1 | 142 |
| Daniel, m. Asenath **DAY**, Dec. 14, 1780 | 2 | 46 |
| Daniel, s. [Daniel & Asenath], b. Apr. 26, 1789 | 2 | 46 |
| Daniel, Jr., of Colchester, m. Alice **BLISH**, of East Haddam, May 9, 1834, by Amhurst D. Scoville, J. P. | 2 | 265 |
| Daniel, d. May 21, 1844, ae 86 | 2 | 46 |
| Daniel Asa, s. [Jonathan & Tabitha], b. Nov. 13, 1818 | 2 | 69 |
| Daniel W., s. [Joseph D. & Clarissa], b. Nov. 30, 1845 | 2 | 31 |
| David, [s. John & Abigail], b. Nov. 19, 1747 | 1 | 52 |
| David, s. [Weeks & Joanna], b. Feb. 10, 1765 | 1 | 142 |
| David B., of East Haddam, m. Nancy T. **EMERSON**, of Westchester, July 4, 1850, in Westchester, by Rev. Stephen F. Lopee, of Hadlyme | 2 | 96 |
| David Brainard, s. [Jonathan & Tabitha], b. Feb. 14, 1821 | 2 | 69 |
| Deborah, d. [William & Deborah], b. Apr. 1, 1750 | 1 | 102 |
| Dorothy, m. Simeon **CROCKER**, Mar. 7, 1751 | 1 | 112 |
| Dudley, s. [Weeks & Joanna], b. Mar. 27, 1762; d. May 14, 1764 | 1 | 142 |
| Dudley, s. [Weeks & Joanna], b. Apr. 22, 1767 | 1 | 142 |
| Edwin P., m. Martha Ann **CHAMPLAIN**, June 28, 1840, by Rev. Augustus Bolles | 2 | 104 |
| Eleanor, of Lebanon, m. David **KELLOGG**, [ ], 1766 | 1 | 121 |
| Eli, s. [Daniel & Asenath], b. Sept. 23, 1781 | 2 | 46 |
| Eli, m. Olive **CONE**, Dec. 9, 1823, by Salmon Cone, V.D.M. | 2 | 139 |
| Elias L., m. Caroline M. **BILL**, b. of Lebanon, Mar. 17, 1846, by Rev. Lyman Strong | 3 | 27 |
| Elijah, m. Elizabeth **ADAMS**, Dec. 20, 1750 | 1 | 134 |
| Elijah, s. [Elijah & Elizabeth], b. Aug. 19, 1751 | 1 | 134 |
| Elijah, s. [Elijah], b. Feb. 6, 1752 | 1 | 101 |
| Elijah, Jr., m. Editha **DAY**, June 27, 1775 | 2 | 77 |
| Elisha Kellogg, s. [Jonathan & Tabitha], b. Dec. 14, 1808 | 2 | 69 |
| Elizabeth, d. Charles, b. Feb. 13, 1702 | L-3 | 193 |
| Elizabeth, d. Charles, b. Feb. 13, 1702 | TM-1 | 193 |
| Elizabeth, d. Charles & Elizabeth, b. Feb. 18, 1702/3 | TM-1 | 194 |
| Elizabeth, [d. William & Dorothy], b. Mar. 13, 1716 | L-1 | 451 |
| Elizabeth, m. Nathaniell **KELLOGG**, July 1, 1725 | L-3 | 9 |
| Elizabeth, m. Nathaniel **KELLOGG**, July [ ], 1725 | L-3 | 9 |
| Elisabeth, w. Charles, d. Sept. 13, 1725 | TPR | 110 |
| Elizabeth, [d. Nathan & Elizabeth], b. Mar. 30, 1729 | L-3 | 8 |
| Elizabeth, m. Joseph **SKINNER**, Nov. [ ], 1733 | 1 | 116 |
| Elizabeth, of Cochester, m. H. D. **BARROWS**, of Ohio City, Ohio, Jan. 1, 1840, by Rev. Joel R. Arnold | 2 | 118 |
| Elizabeth, d. [Elijah], b. June 29, 1753 | 1 | 101 |

| | Vol. | Page |
|---|---|---|
| **WILLIAMS**, (cont.) | | |
| Elizabeth, d. [Elijah & Elizabeth], b. June 29, 1753 | 1 | 134 |
| Elizabeth, d. [William & Deborah], b. Mar. 31, 1759 | 1 | 102 |
| Elizabeth M., b. Feb. 2, 1820, in Ledyard, Ct.; m. John **PATTEN**, Feb. 3, 1846, in Salem, Ct. | 2 | 156 |
| Elizabeth Margery, [s. Isaac & Lucy], b. Mar. 16, 1754 | 1 | 35 |
| Enos, m. Ruby **LOOMIS**, Dec. 8, 1785 | 2 | 67 |
| Esther, d. [Daniel & Asenath], b. Jan. 10, 1795 | 2 | 46 |
| Esther, m. Asa **FULLER**, Feb. 16, 1823, by Rev. Simeon Dickenson, at the house of Mr. Daniel Williams | 2 | 82 |
| Francis A., of East Haddam, m. Asenath **DANIELS**, of Colchester, May 12, 1844, by Rev. Robe[r]t C. Mills | 3 | 13 |
| Frederick W., d. May 19, 1829, ae 69 | 2 | 69 |
| Griswold, s. [Enos & Ruby], b. Feb. 4, 1791 | 2 | 67 |
| Hannah, d. Nathan & Eliza, b. Nov. 6, 1733 | 1 | 142 |
| Hannah, d. [Elijah & Elizabeth], b. Sept. 20, 1757 | 1 | 134 |
| Hannah, m. Simeon **CROCKER**, Nov. 26, 1779 | 2 | 70 |
| Hannah, d. [Daniel & Asenath], b. Aug. 22, 1784 | 2 | 46 |
| Henry G., of East Haddam, m. Joanna **DANIELS**, of Colchester, Feb. 28, 1847, by Rev. P. Brockett | 3 | 31 |
| Henry Skinner, s. [Alanson & Sally B.], b. Feb. 19, 1817 | 2 | 150 |
| Hezekiah, s. [Enos & Ruby], b. Oct. 19, 1798 | 2 | 67 |
| Isaac, [s. William & Dorothy], b. July 16, 1728 | L-1 | 451 |
| Isaac, s. [Charles & Rachel], b. July 20, 1751; d. Jan. 15, 1768 | 1 | 124 |
| Isaac, m. Lucy **FULLER**, June 22, 1752 | 1 | 35 |
| Isaac, d. June 12, 1754 | 1 | 35 |
| James, [s. John & Freelove], b. July 15, 1766 | 1 | 79 |
| James, of Hebron, m. Asenena **FREEMAN**, of Colchester, Jan. 1, 1824, by Salmon Cone, V. D. M. | 2 | 161 |
| Jira, s. [Enos & Ruby], b. May 8, 1787 | 2 | 67 |
| Joanna, d. [Weeks & Joanna], b. Feb. 8, 1770 | 1 | 142 |
| Joanna, d. Apr. 21, 1804 | 2 | 46 |
| John, [s. William & Dorothy], b. July 22, 1718 | L-1 | 451 |
| John, m. Abigail **CROCKER**, Feb. 25, 1744 | 1 | 52 |
| John, [s. John & Abigail], b. Apr. 20, 1745 | 1 | 52 |
| John, d. June 17, 1754 | 1 | 52 |
| John, s. [Charles & Rachel], b. Jan. 1, 1758 | 1 | 124 |
| John, m. Freelove **HAMILTON**, of Colchester, June 3, 1764 | 1 | 79 |
| John, [s. John & Freelove], b. Nov. 17, 1764 | 1 | 79 |
| John M., d. Feb. 12, 1851, ae 70 | 2 | 161 |
| Jonathan, s. [Daniel & Asenath], b. Feb. 16, 1783 | 2 | 46 |
| Jonathan, m. Tabitha **KELLOGG**, Feb. 16, 1808 | 2 | 69 |
| Jonathan, s. [Jonathan & Tabitha], b. Mar. 23, 1827 | 2 | 69 |
| Jonathan, d. June 10, 1904 | 2 | 69 |
| Jonathan C., m. Mary A. **SKINNER**, Nov. 9, 1840, by Rev. Daniel G. Sprague, West Chester | 2 | 272 |
| Joseph, s. [Elijah & Elizabeth], b. Feb. 14, 1759; | | |

| | Vol. | Page |
|---|---|---|
| **WILLIAMS**, (cont.) | | |
| d. Mar. 21, 1775 | 1 | 134 |
| Joseph, s. [Elijah, Jr. & Editha], b. Mar. 16, 1787 | 2 | 77 |
| Joseph D., m. Clarissa **WATROUS**, b. of Colchester, Mar. 28, 1839, by Rev. Andrew M. Smith | 2 | 31 |
| Joseph Day, s. [Daniel & Asenath], b. Apr. 12, 1799 | 2 | 46 |
| Joseph H., s. [Joseph D. & Clarissa], b. Feb. 20, 1840 | 2 | 31 |
| Judah, s. [Nathan & Eliza], b. Dec. 14, 1741 | 1 | 142 |
| Justin, s. [Enos & Ruby], b. Oct. 28, 1792 | 2 | 67 |
| Justin Newton, s. [Jonathan & Tabitha], b. Jan. 24, 1829; d. June 10, 1903 | 2 | 69 |
| Justus Dorrance, s. [Justus W. & Almira], b. Jan. 3, 1836 | 2 | 240 |
| Justus W., m. Almira **LEFFINGWELL**, b. of Colchester, Jan. 1, 1833, by Rev. Benjamin G. Goff | 2 | 240 |
| Justus Weeks, s. [Daniel & Asenath], b. May 15, 1801 | 2 | 46 |
| Laura, d. [Enos & Ruby], b. Feb. 16, 1803 | 2 | 67 |
| Laura, m. Charles A. **CHASE**, Sept. 2, 1827, by Salmon Cone, V. D. M. | 2 | 198 |
| Laura E., m. William **WATROUS**, b. of Colchester, Nov. 22, 1840, by Rev. Lyman Strong | 2 | 113 |
| Laura Esther, d. [Jonathan & Tabitha], b. Nov. 22, 1812 | 2 | 69 |
| Lavine, d. [Elijah, Jr. & Editha], b. Mar. 1, 1783 | 2 | 77 |
| Looring, twin with Warren, s. [Elijah, Jr. & Editha], b. Feb. 14, 1780 | 2 | 77 |
| Loren Alanson, s. [Alanson & Sally B.], b. Sept. 10, 1806 | 2 | 150 |
| Lydia, d. [Enos & Ruby], b. Dec. 7, 1788 | 2 | 67 |
| Lydia, m. Erastus **CHESTER**, Mar. 29, 1812 | 2 | 139 |
| Margaret, d. [Elijah, Jr & Editha], b. Oct. 16, 1784 | 2 | 77 |
| Margery, [d. William & Dorothy], b. July 5, 1720 | L-1 | 451 |
| Margery, [d. Nathan & Eliza], b. Sept. 27, 1736 | 1 | 142 |
| Margery, m. David **ADAMS**, Feb. 1, 1738/9 | 1 | 134 |
| Margery, of Colchester, m. Frederick **SMITH**, of Chatham, May 3, 1770 | 1 | 85 |
| Margary, w. Capt. Peleg, d. Jan. 9, 1801, ae 48 | 2 | 161 |
| Margery, m. Henry **DART**, b. of Colchester, Apr. 2, 1822, by Rev. William Palmer, at Mr. E. Williams | 2 | 99 |
| Maria R., of Colchester, m. Joseph D. **HURD**, of East Haddam, Mar. 17, 1850, by Rev. S. D. Jewett, at Westchester | 3 | 3 |
| Marshall Selden, s. [Alanson & Sally B.], b. May 18, 1826 | 2 | 150 |
| Mary, d. [William & Deborah], b. Nov. 29, 1747 | 1 | 102 |
| Mary, d. [Elijah & Elizabeth], b. Dec. 4, 1767 | 1 | 134 |
| Mary, d. [Enos & Ruby], b. June 7, 1801 | 2 | 67 |
| Mary, m. Ely H. **GILLETT**, b. of Colchester, Sept. 11, 1821, by Salmon Cone, V. D. M. | 2 | 143 |
| Mary, m. Asa **RANDALL**, Jr., b. of Colchester, Dec. 25, 1836, by Rev. Andrew M. Smith | 2 | 292 |
| Mary, Wid. of [Frederick W.], d. Aug. 16, 1837, ae 74 | 2 | 69 |

| | Vol. | Page |
|---|---|---|
| **WILLIAMS**, (cont.) | | |
| Mary, m. Benjamin **ADAMS**, Jr. [ ] | 2 | 15 |
| Mary Ann, b. Apr. 23, 1808 | 2 | 220 |
| Mary Ann,, b. Apr. 23, 1808; m. William **KEENEY**, Mar. 7, 1830, by Salmon Cone, V. D. M. | 2 | 220 |
| Mary Ellen, d. [Justus W. & Almira], b. Apr. 16, 1838 | 2 | 240 |
| Mehetable, d. [Elijah & Elizabeth], b. June 21, 1755 | 1 | 134 |
| Mercy, of New London, m. Jonathan **DODGE**, of Colchester, Nov. 7, 1744 | 1 | 37 |
| Mercy, m. Jonathan **DODGE**, Nov. 7, 1744 | 1 | 140 |
| Nathan, m. Elizabeth **LEWIS**, Sept. 16, 1725 | L-3 | 8 |
| Nathan, s. [William & Deborah], b. Apr. or Mar. [ ], 1754 | 1 | 102 |
| Nathan, of East Haddam, m. Francis **BROWN**, of Colchester, Apr. 30, 1838, by Joshua B. Rodges, J. P. | 2 | 259 |
| Peleg, Capt., d. Sept. 15, 1823, ae 70 | 2 | 161 |
| Rachel, d. [Elijah & Elizabeth], b. Oct. 7, 1764 | 1 | 134 |
| Rachel, m. David **ADAMS**, Feb. 24, 1790; d. Jan. 10, 1841 | 2 | 116 |
| Ralph Tracy, s. [Alanson & Sally B.], b. May 5, 1823 | 2 | 150 |
| Rhoda, m. Timothy **BIGELOW**, Dec. 2, 1762 | 1 | 111 |
| Rhoda, d. [Daniel & Asenath], b. Dec. 18, 1797 | 2 | 46 |
| Robbins Noyes, s. [Alanson & Sally B.], b. Oct. 4, 1811 | 2 | 150 |
| Ruth, d. [Elijah & Elizabeth], b. Dec. 26, 1761 | 1 | 134 |
| Ruth, w. Capt. Peleg, d. Mar. 13, 1849 | 2 | 161 |
| Sally Maria, d. [Alanson & Sally B.], b. Nov. 21, 1820 | 2 | 150 |
| Samuel, s. [Weeks], b. Feb. 26, 1753 | 1 | 101 |
| Samuel, s. [Weeks & Joanna], b. Feb. 26, 1753 | 1 | 142 |
| Samuel Sylvester, s. [Alanson & Sally B.], b. May 12, 1809 | 2 | 150 |
| Sarah, m. Oliver **DODGE**, Mar. 19, 1767 | 1 | 77 |
| Sarah E., b. June 10, 1816; m. Isaac Henry **DAY**, Oct. 10, 1842, Chatham, Ct. | 2 | 126 |
| Sarah Jane, d. [Justus W. & Almira], b. July 9, 1834 | 2 | 240 |
| Sena, m. Hiram **DANIELS**, [ ]; d. Apr. 17, 1835, ae 44 | 2 | 67 |
| Sena, see also Asenath | | |
| Sherman, m. Maria **SULLARD**, b. of Lebanon, Jan. 30, 1839, by Rev. Lyman Strong | 2 | 98 |
| Silvester, s. [Elijah, Jr. & Editha], b. Jan. 11, 1778 | 2 | 77 |
| Sophia, of Salem, m. James **STRANAHAN**, of East Haddam, June 21, 1831, by Rev. Lyman Strong | 2 | 232 |
| Susan D., m. John D. **WATROUS**, b. of Colchester, May 7, 1845, by Rev. Robert Allyn | 3 | 21 |
| Susannah, [d. John & Abigail], b. Sept. 28, 1751 | 1 | 52 |
| Susannah, d. [Daniel & Asenath], b. June 1, 1793 | 2 | 46 |
| Susanna, d. [Jonathan & Tabitha], b. Dec. 4, 1814 | 2 | 69 |
| Susannah D., of Colchester, m. Jeremiah **WILLCOX**, of Lebanon, Sept. 6, 1840, by Augustus Bolles, V. D. M. | 2 | 158 |
| Warren, twin with Looring, s. [Elijah, Jr. & Editha], b. Feb. 14, 1780 | 2 | 77 |
| Warren S., of Chatham, m. Mary B. **ARNOLD**, of Haddam, | | |

| | Vol. | Page |
|---|---|---|
| **WILLIAMS**, (cont.) | | |
| Oct. 18, 1842, by Rev. Joel R. Arnold | 2 | 206 |
| Warren Wadsworth, s. [Alanson & Sally B.], b. July 11, 1814 | 2 | 150 |
| Weeks, m. Joanna **LO[O]MIS**, Dec. 20, 1750 | 1 | 142 |
| Weeks, s. [Weeks & Joanna], b. Mar. 2, 1755 | 1 | 142 |
| Weeks, d. Aug. 1, 1793 | 2 | 38 |
| William, m. Dorothy **JO[H]NSON**, Oct. 21, 1713 | L-1 | 451 |
| William, [s. William & Dorothy], b. Oct. 13, 1714 | L-1 | 451 |
| William, of Colchester, m. Deborah **CONE**, of East Haddam, Feb. 16, 1738 | 1 | 102 |
| William, s. [William & Deborah], b. Oct. 20, 1745 | 1 | 102 |
| W[illia]m A., m. Elizabeth L. **PARKHURST**, b. of Colchester, Apr. 3, 1843, by Rev. Daniel G. Sprague | 3 | 4 |
| -----, d. Weeks [& Joanna], b. Jan. 26, 1752; d. same day | 1 | 142 |
| **WILSON, WILLSON**, Sarah, m. Nic[h]olas **ACKLEY**, [ ] | 1 | 115 |
| Seth Abram, of Killingly, m. Ellen Maria **LEE**, of Colchester, Sept. 21, 1853, by Rev. Erastus Dickinson | 3 | 58 |
| **WINTWORTH**, [see under **WENTWORTH**] | | |
| **WISE**, Abigail, m. Eliphalet **TREADWAY**, May 29, 1766 | 1 | 85 |
| Benjamin, d. Sept. 28, 1760 | 1 | 54 |
| Jemima, m. George **DODGE**, Jan. 29, 1761 | 1 | 153 |
| Margaret, [d. Benjamin & Winefred], b. July 19, 1760 | 1 | 11 |
| William, m. Abigail **DODGE**, Oct. 23, 1760 | 1 | 54 |
| Winefred, m. John **TREADWAY**, Jan. 11, 1764 | 1 | 86 |
| -----, [d. Benjamin & Winefred], b. July 8, 1758; d. Aug. 12, 1758 | 1 | 11 |
| **WITHERELL**, Hannah, m. Daniel **LO[O]MIS**, Oct. 7, 1731 | L-3 | 456 |
| **WITTER**, Esther, m. James **WELLS**, Sept. 1, 1816 | 2 | 109 |
| **WOOD**, Ezra, m. Eliza **FULLER**, b. of Colchester, Jan. 12, 1834, by Artemas Worthington, J. P. | 2 | 262 |
| **WOODARD**, Sophronia Tyler, of Glastonbury, m. Elijah **OSBORNE**, of Savannah, Ga., Sept. 19, 1830, by Salmon Cone, V. D. M. | 2 | 224 |
| **WOODBRIDGE**, Elizabeth, m. Rev. Ephraim **LITTLE**, Dec. 8, 1737 | 1 | 122 |
| Elizabeth, d. Rev. Samuel **WOODBRIDGE**, 1st minister at East Hartford, Conn., m. Rev. Ephraim **LITTLE**, of Colchester, Dec. 8, 1737; d. Nov. 13, 1754, ae 40 | 2 | 310 |
| Louisa, wid. of Nath[anie]ll S., of Lyme, m. John R. **WATROUS**, Mar. 29, 1798; d. Feb. 15, 1823, ae 67 | 2 | 41 |
| Mary, see under Mary **WARD** | 2 | 311 |
| Nathaniel S., d. Nov. 24, 1822 | 2 | 41 |
| Samuel, Rev., 1st min. of East Hartford, b. [ ], 1683, s. Rev. Benjamin **HOLDRIDGE** (sic), sometime min. at Bristol, Me., & in 1668 of Kittery, Me.; gd. s. of Rev. John **WOODBRIDGE**, 1st min. of Andover, Mass.; nephew of Rev. John **WOODBRIDGE**, of Killingworth & Wethersfield; nephew of Rev. Timothy | | |

| | Vol. | Page |
|---|---|---|
| **WOODBRIDGE**, (cont.) | | |
| Woodbridge, 6th min. of First Church, Hartford | 2 | 310 |
| Samuel, Rev., m. Mabel **HUBBARD**, wid. of Rev. John, of Jamaica, L. I., Dec. 9, 1707 | 2 | 310 |
| Timothy, d. Feb. 16, 1829 | 2 | 44 |
| **WOODWARD**, [see under **WOODARD**] | | |
| **WOODWELL**, Sarah, m. Ezekiel **LORD**, Sept. 16, 1798 | 2 | 114 |
| **WOODWORTH**, Asel, of Montville, m. Caroline **WAY**, Nov. 20, 1828, at the house of Thomas Way, in Colchester, by Asa Wilcox, Elder | 2 | 210 |
| Boliver, m. Jane **HARRINGTON**, b. of Norwich, Apr. 20, 1846, by Rev. Pierpoint Brockett | 3 | 27 |
| John, m. Abigail **THOMAS**, Dec. 6, 1753 | 1 | 21 |
| John, m. Sarah **NILES**, [ ], 1776 | 2 | 17 |
| John, s. [John & Sarah], b. Aug. 27, 1784 | 2 | 17 |
| Ruth, w. John, d. Feb. [ ], 177[ ] | 2 | 17 |
| Sarah, d. [John & Sarah], b. Feb. 18, 1781 | 2 | 17 |
| **WORDEN**, Ruth, m. Daniel **DODGE**, Apr. 11, 1756 | 1 | 85 |
| **WORTHINGTON**, Abigail, [d. Daniel & Elizabeth], b. Mar. 10, 1740 | L-3 | 448 |
| Abigail, [m.] Capt. Benjamin **MATHER**, Mar. 14, 1763 | 1 | 61 |
| Almy, [d. Daniel & Elizabeth], b. Apr. 12, 1741 | L-3 | 448 |
| Ama, m. Noah **SAXTON**, Apr. 7, 1762 | 1 | 88 |
| Amasai, [s. Daniel & Elizabeth], b. Apr. 16, 1746 | L-3 | 448 |
| Anne, [d. Elijah & Anna], b. Jan. 24, 1775 | 1 | 45 |
| Anne, m. Charles **DAY**, Jan. 17, 1796 | 2 | 120 |
| Artemus, [s. Elijah & Anna], b. Dec. 11, 1777 | 1 | 45 |
| Artemus, m. Clarissa **WORTHINGTON**, Nov. 24, 1800 | 2 | 85 |
| Asa, [s. Daniell & Elizabeth], b. June 16, 1724 | L-1 | 448 |
| Asa, s. Dan[ie]ll, d. Sept. 9, 1751 | 1 | 151 |
| Asa, s. [Samuel & Elizabeth], b. June 23, 1752; d. Aug. 18, 1754 | 1 | 121 |
| Augustus, s. [Henry & Sophia], b. Apr. 11, 1808; d. Apr. 30, 1832, ae 24 | 2 | 172 |
| Betsey, d. [Dan & Louis], b. Apr. 14, 1782 | 2 | 7 |
| Billy, [s. William & Sarah], b. July 24, 1784 | 1 | 53 |
| Billy, s. [William & Sarah], b. July 24, 1784 | 2 | 53 |
| Caroline, of Colchester, m. Seth E. **LATHROP**, of Salem, Sept. 28, 1824, by Rev. William Jarvis | 2 | 168 |
| Charles, [s. Elias, Jr. & Anne], b. Aug. 15, 1777 | 1 | 84 |
| Charles, s. [Dan & Louis], b. Aug. 27, 1778 | 2 | 7 |
| Charles, m. Margaret **BRIDGES**, Apr. 23, 1797 | 2 | 248 |
| Charles, m. Diadama **COMSTOCK**, b. of Colchester, Mar. 9, 1834, by Rev. Lyman Strong | 2 | 248 |
| Clarissa, d. [Joel & Eunice], b. Jan. 30, 1778 | 2 | 34 |
| Clarissa, m. Artemus **WORTHINGTON**, Nov. 24, 1800; d. Aug. 27, 1849, ae 71 | 2 | 85 |
| Clarissa, d. [Dudley & Nancy], b. Apr. 1, 1808 | 2 | 74 |

| | Vol. | Page |
|---|---|---|
| **WORTHINGTON**, (cont.) | | |
| Clarissa, w. Artemus, d. Aug. 27, 1849 | 2 | 34 |
| Dan, twin with Gad, s. [Elijah & Mary], b. June 11, 1747 | 1 | 151 |
| Dan, m. Louis **FOOT**, [ ], 1772 | 2 | 7 |
| Dan, s. [Dan & Louis], b. Sept. 22, 1774 | 2 | 7 |
| Daniell, m. Elizabeth **LO[O]MIS**, Jan. 3, 1720/21 | L-1 | 448 |
| Daniel, [s. Daniell & Elizabeth], b. Aug. 18, 1734 | L-1 | 448 |
| Daniel, s. [Samuel & Elizabeth], b. May 19, 1750 | 1 | 121 |
| Daniel, s. [Elias & Rhoda], b. Feb. 9, 1766 | 1 | 102 |
| Daniel, Sr., d. Mar. 1, 1784 | 2 | 53 |
| David, s. [Samuel & Elizabeth], d. July 29, 1754 | 1 | 121 |
| David, 2d, s. [Samuel & Elizaabeth], b. July 19, 1755 | 1 | 121 |
| Dennis, s. Eliphalet & Sally, negro, b. Mar. 1, 1788 | 2 | 325 |
| Dudley, s. [John & Abigail], b. Aug. 18, 1770 | 1 | 110 |
| Dudley, m. Nancy **SWAN**, Oct. 5, 1793 | 2 | 74 |
| Dudley, m. Bettey **REID**, Oct. 12, 1814 | 2 | 74 |
| Dudley Wright, s. [Dudley & Nancy], b. Aug. 19, 1795 | 2 | 74 |
| Elias, [s. Daniell & Elizabeth], b. Oct. 31, 1722 | L-1 | 448 |
| Elias, m. Rhoda **CHAMBERLAIN**, Sept. 19, 1744 | 1 | 102 |
| Elias, s. [Elias & Rhoda], b. Dec. 25, 1749 | 1 | 102 |
| Elias, Jr., m. Anne **MORGAN**, Oct. 24, 1771 | 1 | 84 |
| Elias, s. [Joel & Eunice], b. June 24, 1788; d. Oct. 1, 1849, ae 61 | 2 | 34 |
| Elias, Col., d. Sept. 23, 1811, in his 90th y. | 1 | 102 |
| Elias M., of Colchester, m. Emily **PIERCE**, of Lebanon, Nov. 8, 1832 | 2 | 272 |
| Elias M., m. Emily **PIERCE**, Nov. 8, 1832 | 2 | 283 |
| Elias Morgan, s. [Charles & Margaret], b. June 11, 1799 | 2 | 248 |
| Elijah, m. Mary **WELLS**, Oct. 4, 1733 | 1 | 151 |
| Elijah, s. [Elijah & Mary], b. Jan. 1, 1735/6 | 1 | 151 |
| Elijah, m. Anna **LAVIT**, Apr. 29, 1756 | 1 | 45 |
| Elijah, Capt., d. Oct. 13, 1764, ae 55 | 1 | 151 |
| Elijah, [s. Elijah & Anna], b. Dec. 6, 1765 | 1 | 45 |
| Elijah, Jr., m. Sarah B. **LEWIS**, Sept. 8, 1791 | 2 | 63 |
| Elijah, Sr., d. July 15, 1797 | 1 | 45 |
| Eliphalet, s. [Joseph & Polly], b. Sept. 1, 1797 | 2 | 63 |
| Elizabeth, [d. Daniell & Elizabeth], b. July 24, 1721 | L-1 | 448 |
| Elizabeth, m. Nehemiah **DANIELS**, Jan. [ ], 1744 | 1 | 57 |
| Elizabeth, [d. Elijah & Anna], b. Jan. 15, 1757 | 1 | 45 |
| Elizabeth, d. Dec. 3, 1789 | 2 | 53 |
| Enoch, s. [Gershom B. & Lucy A.], b. Dec. 17, 1836 | 2 | 233 |
| Eratus, [s. Elijah & Anna], b. May 8, 1761 | 1 | 45 |
| Eunice, w. Joel, d. Aug. 16, 1846, ae 90 | 2 | 34 |
| Frank, [s. William & Sarah], b. Nov. 29, 1787 | 1 | 53 |
| Frank, s. [William & Sarah], b. Nov. 29, 1787 | 2 | 53 |
| Gad, twin with Dan, s. [Elijah & Mary], b. June 11, 1747 | 1 | 151 |
| Gad, m. Rebeckah **ROB[B]INS**, Sept. 25, 1774 | 2 | 7 |
| Gad, s. Dan & Louis], b. May 28, 1786 | 2 | 7 |

| | Vol. | Page |
|---|---|---|
| **WORTHINGTON**, (cont.) | | |
| Gershom B., m. Lucy A. **RATHBUN**, b. of Colchester, Sept. 18, 1831, by Rev. Lyman Strong | 2 | 233 |
| Gaishom Bulkeley, s. [Dudley & Nancy], b. May 19, 1798; d. May 7, 1801 | 2 | 74 |
| Gars[h]om Bulkeley, 2d, s. [Dudley & Nancy], b. Aug. 1, 1805 | 2 | 74 |
| Guy, s. [Dan & Louis], b. Apr. 5, 1788 | 2 | 7 |
| Harriet, twin with an unnamed boy, d. [Elijah, Jr. & Sarah B.], b. July 25, 1793 | 2 | 63 |
| Harriet, 1st, d. [Charles & Margaret], b. Mar. 29, 1805 | 2 | 248 |
| Harriet, 2d, d. [Charles & Margaret], b. Dec. 9, 1806 | 2 | 248 |
| Harriet, m. Alfred B. **PIERCE**, b. of Colchester, May 25, 1831, by Rev. Lyman Strong | 2 | 231 |
| Henry, [s. William & Sarah], b. May 27, 1773; d. Feb. 20, 1777 | 1 | 53 |
| Henry, s. [William & Sarah], b. May 27, 1773; d. Feb. 20, 1777 | 2 | 53 |
| Henry, s. [Joel & Eunice], b. Sept. 3, 1780; d. Sept. 15, 1849, ae 69 | 2 | 34 |
| Henry, m. Sophia **RANSOM**, Jan. 6, 1806, by Salmon Cone; d. Sept. 15, 1849, ae 69 | 2 | 172 |
| Israel, [s. William & Sarah], b. Mar. 20, 1771; d. Feb. 9, 1775 | 1 | 53 |
| Israel, s. [William & Sarah], b. Mar. 20, 1771; d. Feb. 9, 1775 | 2 | 53 |
| Israel N., s. [Joel & Eunice], b. May 22, 1782; d. Dec. 16, 1819, ae 37 | 2 | 34 |
| Jacob, s. Daniel & Elizabeth, b. Feb. 2, 1735/6 | L-1 | 447 |
| Jacob, of Colchester, m. Phebe **BURCHARD**, of Norwich, May 29, 1760 | 1 | 113 |
| Jacob, d. Sept. 25, 1763 | 1 | 113 |
| Jerusha, d. [Dan & Louis], b. June 26, 1776 | 2 | 7 |
| Joel, s. [Elias & Rhoda], b. Apr. 21, 1753 | 1 | 102 |
| Joel, m. Eunice **NEWTON**, Jan. 23, 1777; d. June 24, 1817, ae 64 | 2 | 34 |
| Joel, d. Jan. 29, 1817, in his 64th year | 1 | 102 |
| John, s. [Elijah & Mary], b. Feb. 17, 1743/4 | 1 | 151 |
| John, m. Abigail **WRIGHT**, Jan. 4, 1770 | 1 | 110 |
| John, s. [Dan & Louis], b. May 2, 1784 | 2 | 7 |
| John had slave Jinne, who had Mille, b. Mar. 4, 1789; Daniel b. Dec. 25, 1786; James Pattison, b. Apr. 10, 1795; Richard Lyman, b. Oct. 4, 1803 | 2 | 48 |
| John Henry, m. Augusta E. **GATES**, b. of East Hampton, [Oct.] 11, 1834, by Rev. S. D. Jewett, at Colchester | 3 | 65 |
| John J., of East Haddam, m. Sally M. **DAY**, of Colchester, May 6, 1830, by Rev. Joseph Harvey | 2 | 222 |
| Joseph, m. Polly **BULKELEY**, Sept. 10, 1791 | 2 | 63 |
| Joseph, s. [Joseph & Polly], b. Sept. 6, 1795 | 2 | 63 |
| Joseph, [s. Elijah & Anna], b. [ ] | 1 | 45 |

| | Vol. | Page |
|---|---|---|
| **WORTHINGTON**, (cont.) | | |
| Joshua, s. [Gad & Rebeckah], b. Aug. 20, 1745 (1775?) | 2 | 7 |
| Judeth, d. [Elijah & Mary], b. Jan. 22, 1742 | 1 | 151 |
| Judeth, m. John **BULKELEY**, Jan. 11, 1759 | 1 | 115 |
| Judeth, d. [Dan & Louis], b. June 30, 1780 | 2 | 7 |
| Judith, m. Elias W. **NEWTON**, Apr. 25, 1803 | 2 | 104 |
| Justin, [s. Elijah & Anna], b. [ ] | 1 | 45 |
| Laura, d. [Dan & Louis], b. Aug. 14, 1793 | 2 | 7 |
| Laura, b. Jan. 20, 1786; m. Ralph **ISHAM**, Mar. 29, 1804; d. June 7, 1847, ae 61 | 2 | 105 |
| Laura, d. [Henry & Sophia], b. Dec. 19, 1809; d. Jan. 25, 1812, ae 2 y. 1 m. 6 d. | 2 | 172 |
| Lois, d. [Joel & Eunice], b. Oct. 1, 1785 | 2 | 34 |
| Lois, m. Benjamin R. **BULKELEY**, [ ] | 2 | 149 |
| Louisa, d. [Dan & Louis], b. Dec. 9, 1795 | 2 | 7 |
| Lydia, d. [Elias & Rhoda], b. Apr. 15, 1745; d. June 8, 1758 | 1 | 102 |
| Lydia, 2d, d. [Elias & Rhoda], b. Oct. 22, 1760 | 1 | 102 |
| Lydia, [d. William & Sarah], b. Jan. 29, 1775 | 1 | 53 |
| Lydia, d. [William & Sarah], b. Jan. 29, 1775 | 2 | 53 |
| Lydia, m. Asa **NEWTON**, b. of Colchester, Jan. 23, 1777 | 2 | 88 |
| Margaret, w. Charles, d. May 2, 1832 | 2 | 248 |
| Margaret Eliza, d. [Elias M. & Emily], b. Sept. 16, 1834 | 2 | 272 |
| Margaret Eliza, d. [Elias M. & Emily], b. Sept. 16, 1834 | 2 | 283 |
| Maria, d. [Joseph & Polly], b. Feb. 28, 1800 | 2 | 63 |
| Mary, m. Daniell **JONES**, Oct. 13, 1720 | L-1 | 446 |
| Mary, d. Daniel & Elizabeth, b. Aug. 2, 1737 | L-3 | 448 |
| Mary, d. [Elijah & Mary], b. June 19, 1739 | 1 | 151 |
| Mary, m. John **HOPSON**, Apr. 19, 1759 | 1 | 119 |
| Mary Ann, d. [Charles & Margaret], b. June 14, 1802; d. June [ ], 1842, ae 40 | 2 | 248 |
| Mary Jane, d. [Gershom B. & Lucy A.], b. Feb. 15, 1833 | 2 | 233 |
| Mehitabell, [d. Daniell & Elizabeth], b. Feb. 10, 1731/2 | L-1 | 448 |
| Mehitabel, [d. Daniel & Elizabeth], b. June 27, 1742; d. July 1, 1742 | L-3 | 448 |
| Mehetable, m. Aaron **SKINNER**, Apr. 12, 1764 | 1 | 148 |
| Melanthon, s. [Henry & Sophia], b. Jan. 16, 1812; d. Mar. 1, 1826, ae 14 | 2 | 172 |
| Molle, [d. Elijah & Anna], b. Oct. 16, 1758; d. Nov. 10, 1758 | 1 | 45 |
| Molle, d. [Jacob & Phebe], b. July 10, 1761 | 1 | 113 |
| Molly, d. [Dan & Louis], b. Dec. 10, 1772 | 2 | 7 |
| Nancy, d. [Joseph & Polly], b. July 1, 1792 | 2 | 63 |
| Nancy, m. John **TREADWAY**, 2d, Feb. 8, 1808 | 2 | 125 |
| Nancy, [w. Dudley], d. Jan. 27, 1814 | 2 | 74 |
| Nancy S., of Colchester, m. Reuben **BRADLEY**, of Russell, Mass., Apr. 13, 1823, by Salmon Cone, V. D. M. | 2 | 137 |
| Nancy Swan, d. [Dudley & Nancy], b. Dec. 30, 1800 | 2 | 74 |
| Olcot[t], [s. Elias, Jr. & Anne], b. Mar. 28, 1780; d. July 20, 1834 | 1 | 84 |

| | Vol. | Page |
|---|---|---|
| **WORTHINGTON**, (cont.) | | |
| Olcott, s. [Charles & Margaret], b. Aug. 21, 1809 | 2 | 248 |
| Olcott, m. Sophia **WELLS**, May 19, 1836, by Rev. Joel R. Arnold | 2 | 286 |
| Orra, [d. William & Sarah], b. June 24, 1790 | 1 | 53 |
| Orra, d. [William & Sarah], b. June 24, 1790 | 2 | 53 |
| Rebecca, w. Gad, d. Sept. 21, 1821 | 2 | 7 |
| Rhoda, [d. Daniell & Elizabeth], b. Sept. 25, 1730 | L-1 | 448 |
| Rhoda, [d. Elias, Jr. & Anne], b. Aug. 21, 1775 | 1 | 84 |
| Rhode, d. [Elias & Rhoda], b. Nov. 7, 1751; d. June 12, 1758 | 1 | 102 |
| Robert, s. [Dan & Louis], b. Sept. 29, 1791 | 2 | 7 |
| Sally Reid, d. [Dudley & Bettey], b. June 25, 1816 | 2 | 74 |
| Samuel, [s. Daniell & Elizabeth], b. Feb. 16, 1728/9 | L-1 | 448 |
| Samuel, m. Elizabeth **WELLS**, Dec. 26, 1749 | 1 | 121 |
| Sarah, [d. Daniel & Elizabeth], b. Nov. 27, 1734 | L-1 | 447 |
| Sarah, [d. William & Sarah], b. Dec. 2, 1776 | 1 | 53 |
| Sarah, d. [William & Sarah], b. Dec. 2, 1776 | 2 | 53 |
| Sarah R., of Colchester, m. Simon **HUNTINGTON**, of Griswold, Sept. 22, 1833, by Rev. Lyman Strong | 2 | 257 |
| Selena, [d. William & Sarah], b. Sept. 14, 1779 | 1 | 53 |
| Selina, d. [William & Sarah], b. Sept. 14, 1779 | 2 | 53 |
| Sibil, [d. Daniell & Elizabeth], b. Apr. 19, 1727 | L-1 | 448 |
| Sophia, w. Olcott, d. Dec. 15, 1864 | 2 | 147 |
| Sophia Emily, d. [Dudley & Nancy], b. July 15, 1803 | 2 | 74 |
| Sophia Jane, d. [Henry & Sophia], b. Feb. 26, 1807 | 2 | 172 |
| Sophia Jane, m. Alfred **OTIS**, Sept. 17, 1832, by Rev. Lyman Strong | 2 | 238 |
| Sybil, see under Sibil | | |
| Tabitha, m. John **SKINNER**, Nov. 9, 1758 | 1 | 38 |
| Telitha, [d. Daniel & Elizabeth], b. Nov. 25, 1738 | L-3 | 448 |
| Temperance, d. [Samuel & Elizabeth], b. Nov. 1, 1756 | 1 | 121 |
| Theodosia, [d. William & Sarah], b. Oct. 13, 1781 | 1 | 53 |
| Theodosia, d. [William & Sarah], b. Oct. 13, 1781 | 2 | 53 |
| William, [s. Daniel & Elizabeth], b. Oct. 20, 1743; d. Mar. 4, 1744 | L-3 | 448 |
| William, [s. Daniel & Elizabeth], b. Jan. 29, 1744/5 | L-3 | 448 |
| William, m. Sarah **WELLS**, b. of Colchester, July 5, 1770 | 1 | 53 |
| William, m. Sarah **WELLS**, b. of Colchester, July 5, 1770 | 2 | 53 |
| ------, twin with Harriet, s. [Elijah, Jr. & Sarah B.], b. July 25, 1793; d. 2 days after | 2 | 63 |
| **WRIGHT**, Abigail, d. [Dudley & Dimmis], b. July 25, 1746 | 1 | 132 |
| Abigail, m. John **WORTHINGTON**, Jan. 4, 1770 | 1 | 110 |
| Amasa, s. [John & Lucy], b. Jan. 6, 1787 | 2 | 25 |
| Ann, [d. Joseph], b. Aug. 3, 1707 | L-1 | 799 |
| Ann, d. [Timothy & Mehetable], b. Apr. 24, 1747 | 1 | 120 |
| Anna Sears, d. [John & Lucy], b. Feb. 15, 1782; d. Sept. 14, 1814, ae 33 | 2 | 25 |
| Azariah, s. [Dudley & Dimmis], b. June 28, 1749 | 1 | 132 |

| | Vol. | Page |
|---|---|---|
| **WRIGHT**, (cont.) | | |
| Azariah, d. Sept. 28, 1828 | 2 | 67 |
| Dimmis, d. [Dudley & Dimmis], b. Jan. 17, 1757 | 1 | 132 |
| Dimmis, w. Dudley, d. Feb. 20, 1793 | 1 | 132 |
| Dimis, m. Reuben **BLISH**, Sept. [ ], 1800 | 2 | 106 |
| Dudley, [s. Joseph], b. Apr. 6, 1717 | L-1 | 799 |
| Dudley, m. Dimmis **LO[O]MIS**, Sept. 9, 1744 | 1 | 132 |
| Dudley, s. [Dudley & Dimmis], b. Jan. 1, 1753 | 1 | 132 |
| Dudley, Capt. had slave Zilpha who had s. Ira, b. Mar. 16, 1785 | 2 | 48 |
| Dudley, Capt., had Ira, s. Zilpha, negro slave, b. Mar. [ ], 1785 | 2 | 94 |
| Dudley, d. June 11, 1806 | 1 | 132 |
| George Washington, s. [Azariah, Jr. & Dorcas], b. July 8, 1815 | 2 | 155 |
| James Orlando, s. [Azariah, Jr. & Dorcas], b. Nov. 26, 1820 | 2 | 155 |
| John, [s. Joseph], b. Jan. 2, 1715 | L-1 | 799 |
| John, [s. Joseph], d. Oct. 25, 1718 | L-1 | 799 |
| John, 2d, s. Joseph, b. Jan. 12, 1724/5 | L-1 | 799 |
| John, s. [Timothy & Mehetable], b. May 27, 1745 | 1 | 120 |
| John, of Colchester, m. Lucy **SEARS**, of East Haddam, Nov. 22, 1776; d. June 6, 1826, ae 82 | 2 | 25 |
| John, s. [John & Lucy], b. Nov. 25, 1783; d. [ ] | 2 | 25 |
| John Henry, s. [Azariah, Jr. & Dorcas], b. Jan. 11, 1819 | 2 | 155 |
| Joseph, [s. Joseph], b. Oct. 15, 1704 | L-1 | 799 |
| Joseph, s. [Timothy & Mehetable], b. June 13, 1736 | 1 | 120 |
| Joseph, Capt., d. Sept. 10, 1756 | 1 | 120 |
| Lo[o]mis, s. [Dudley & Dimmis], b. June 12, 1745; d. Nov. 7, 1745 | 1 | 132 |
| Lucy, d. [John & Lucy], b. Sept. 4, 1777; d. Mar. 22, 1803 | 2 | 25 |
| Lucy, [w. John], d. Sept. 15, 1829, ae 77 | 2 | 25 |
| Lucy Ann, d. Amasa & Nancy, d. Feb. [ ], 1816, ae 11 m. | 2 | 25 |
| Lucy Ann, 2d, d. [Amasa & Nancy], & w. Rollin **SANFORD**, of Brooklyn, N. Y., d. Apr. 20, 1843, ae 27 | 2 | 25 |
| Lydia, d. [Dudley & Dimmis], b. May 30, 1761 | 1 | 132 |
| Lydia, m. John Richard **WATROUS**, June 10, 1783; d. July 30, 1797 | 2 | 41 |
| Marcy Emeline, d. [Azariah, Jr. & Dorcas], b. Mar. 7, 1807 | 2 | 155 |
| Mary, [d. Joseph], b. Nov. 15, 1719 | L-1 | 799 |
| Mary, d. [Timothy & Mehetable], b. July 6, 1742 | 1 | 120 |
| Mary, w. Capt. Joseph, d. Nov. 28, 1755 | 1 | 120 |
| Mary Ann, d. [Azariah, Jr. & Dorcas], b. Mar. 29, 1813 | 2 | 155 |
| Mehetable, d. [Timothy & Mehetable], b. Jan. 4, 1738/9; d. May 27, 1756 | 1 | 120 |
| Mercy, m. Noah **COLEMAN**, Mar. 5, 1730 | L-3 | 6 |
| Miles, s. [Timothy & Mehetable], b. July 9, 1737 | 1 | 120 |
| Sarah, [d. Joseph], b. Apr. 5, 1710; d. Aug. 17, 1710 | L-1 | 799 |
| Sophia, d. [Dudley & Dimmis]. b. Sept. 9, 1765 | 1 | 132 |

| | Vol. | Page |
|---|---|---|
| **WRIGHT**, (cont.) | | |
| Susan A., m. Henry **PACKER**, b. of Colchester, Apr. 1, 1835, by Rev. Lyman Strong | 2 | 275 |
| Susan Areline, d. [Azariah, Jr. & Dorcas], b. Nov. 19, 1808 | 2 | 155 |
| Timothy, [s. Joseph], b. Mar. 5, 1712 | L-1 | 799 |
| Timothy, of Colchester, m. Mehetable **BRAINARD**, of East Haddam, July 3, 1735 | 1 | 120 |
| Timothy, Maj., d. Oct. 24, 1756 | 1 | 120 |
| Timothy, s. [John & Lucy], b. Nov. 18, 1779; d. Apr. 3, 1846, ae 66 y. 4 m. 15 d. | 2 | 25 |
| -----, s. [Joseph], b. Jan. 17, 1702; d. Jan. 28, 1702 | L-1 | 799 |
| **WYATT, WYAT**, Dinah, d. Isreal & Sarah (**PRATT**), b. Jan. 27, 1706/7 | L-1 | 448 |
| Hannah, m. Benjamin **CHAMBERLIN**, Dec. 14, 1731 | L-3 | 455 |
| Isreall, [s. Isreal & Sarah (**PRATT**), d. June 25, 1712, in the 12th y. of his age | L-1 | 448 |
| Jerusiah, [d. Isreal & Sarah (**PRATT**), b. Nov. 25, 1711; d. Dec. 2, 1711 | L-1 | 448 |
| Mary, [d. Isreal & Sarah (**PRATT**), b. Nov. 19, 1716 | L-1 | 448 |
| Sarah, m. Noah **WEL[L]ES**, Apr. 15, 1714 | L-1 | 799 |
| Sarah, m. Noah **WELLS**, Apr. 15, 1714 | L-3 | 452 |
| Sarah, d. Lt. Israel, m. Lt. Noah **WELLS**, & had d. Sarah who m. Oliver **BULKELEY**, (no dates given) | 1 | 141 |
| Susan[n]ah, m. James **NEWTON**, May 31, 1716 | L-1 | 399 |
| **WYLES**, Asa, s. [David & Eleaner], b. Nov. 20, 1775 | 2 | 68 |
| David, m. Eleanor **RANDALL**, June [ ], 1775 | 2 | 68 |
| Harriet, m. Eleazer **STRONG**, Mar. 31, 1830, by Salmon Cone, V. D. M. | 2 | 221 |
| Henry, s. [David & Eleanor], b. Jan. 30, 1779 | 2 | 68 |
| John, s. [David & Eleanor], b. Nov. 19, 1790 | 2 | 68 |
| Orral, d. [David & Eleanor], b. Feb. 14, 1777 | 2 | 68 |
| Orrel, b. Feb. 14, 1777; m. Samuel A. **PETERS**, Jan. 17, 1799; d. May 20, 1836, ae 58 | 2 | 86 |
| Polly, d. [David & Eleanor], b. June 6, 1783 | 2 | 68 |
| Russel[l], s. [David & Eleanor], b. Mar. 10, 1785 | 2 | 68 |
| Sarah, d. [David & Eleanor], b. Apr. 8, 1781 | 2 | 68 |
| Sophia, d. [David & Eleanor], b. Feb. 19, 1787 | 2 | 68 |
| **WYLLYS**, Mehetable, d. Samuel, of Hartford, & Ruth (**HAYNES**) **WYLLYS**; m. Rev. Daniel **BISSELL**, of Charlestown, Mass. [ ] | 2 | 310 |
| **YEAPON**, Amanda, of Colchester, m. William **FOSTER**, of New Milford, Conn., July 8, 1849, by Augustus W. Lord, J. P. | 3 | 41 |
| **YEMMONS**, George, of Columbia, Conn., m. Lydia A. **BILL**, of Colchester, Apr. 25, 1852, by Rev. George W. Pendleton | 3 | 51 |
| **YEOMAN, YEOMANS, YEAMAN**,Anna, d. [David & Irene],b. Aug. 20, 1785 (Laura handwritten in original manuscript ) | 2 | 16 |
| Asa, s. [Moses & Sarah], b. Apr. 1, 1746; d. May 6, 1766 | 1 | 139 |
| Asa, s. [David & Irene], b. Nov. 17, 1793 | 2 | 16 |

| | Vol. | Page |
|---|---|---|
| **YEOMAN, YEOMANS, YEAMAN**, (cont.) | | |
| Cata*, d. David & Irene], b. June 18, 1783 (* Electa handwritten in original manuscript) | 2 | 16 |
| Dan Augustus, s. [David & Irene], b. Nov. 3, 1800; d. Oct. 18, 1803 | 2 | 16 |
| Daniel, s. [Moses & Sarah], b. Sept. 17, 1749 | 1 | 139 |
| Daniel, of Colchester, m. Esther **STERLING**, of Lyme, May 10, 1770 | 1 | 88 |
| David, s. [Moses & Sarah], b. Feb. 25, 1751/2 | 1 | 139 |
| David, m. Irene **DAY**, b. of Colchester, Jan. 7, 1774 | 2 | 16 |
| David, s. [David & Irene], b. Apr. 11, 1778 | 2 | 16 |
| Elisha*, s. [David & Irene], b. Feb. 17, 1780 (* Ralph handwritten in original manuscript) | 2 | 16 |
| Fred*, s. [David & Irene], b. Oct. 10, 1781 (* Alfred handwritten in original manuscript) | 2 | 16 |
| Gene*, d. [David & Irene], b. July 7, 1789 (*Irene handwritten in original manuscript) | 2 | 16 |
| George, of Columbia, m. Lydia A. **BILL**, of Colchester, Apr. 25, 1852, by Geo[rge] W. Pendleton | 3 | 52 |
| Horace, s. [David & Irene], b. Sept. 27, 1787 | 2 | 16 |
| Lydia, d. [Moses & Sarah], b. Dec. 14, 1755 | 1 | 139 |
| Moses, m. Sarah **PRATT**, June 11, 1738 | 1 | 139 |
| Moses, s. [Moses & Sarah], b. Oct. 3, 1740; d. July 11, 1761 | 1 | 139 |
| Moses, s. [David & Irene], b. Dec. 2, 1774 | 2 | 16 |
| Moses, d. Mar. 16, 1778 | 1 | 139 |
| Moses, d. Mar. 16, 1778 | 2 | 16 |
| Oliver Gustavus, s. [David & Irene], b. Oct. 27, 1798 | 2 | 16 |
| Philena, d. [David & Irene], b. Apr. 12, 1796 | 2 | 16 |
| Rebecca, m. David **DODGE**, May 15, 1717 | 1 | 145 |
| Ruth, d. [Moses & Sarah], b. Apr. 20, 1743; d. July 19, 1748 | 1 | 139 |
| Sal* Pratt, d. [David & Irene], b. July 20, 1776 (*Sophia handwritten in original manuscript) | 2 | 16 |
| Sally, d. [David & Irene], b. Aug. 22, 1791 | 2 | 16 |
| Sarah, d. [Moses & Sarah], b. Sept. 14, 1739; d. July 17, 1748 | 1 | 139 |
| Sarah, d. [Moses & Sarah], b. July 6, 1758 | 1 | 139 |
| Sophia, m. Noah B. **FOOT**, [ ] | 2 | 102 |
| **YOUNG, YOUNGS**, Polly, m. Zenas **STRONG**, [ ], in N. Y. State | 2 | 54 |
| Sarah Ann, m. Jerah **WATROUS**, b. of Colchester, [June] 9, 1844, by Rev. S. D. Jewett | 3 | 15 |
| **NO SURNAME**, | | |
| Abigail, wid., m. Eliphalet **TREADWAY**, [ ] | 2 | 88 |
| Hannah, m. Bartholomew **SMITH**, Sept. 8, 1791 | 2 | 110 |
| Lydia, m. Ezra **WATERMAN**, Nov. 29, 1761 | 1 | 40 |
| Mary, m. Elknah **INGRAHAM**, Mar. 2, 1780 | 2 | 28 |
| Rachel, m. Charles **WILLIAMS**, Nov. 22, 1746 | 1 | 124 |
| Sybel, m. Ned **CARTER**, Feb. 9, 1769, by Ichabod Allyn | 1 | 27 |

## COLEBROOK VITAL RECORDS
## 1779 - 1810

| | Page |
|---|---|
| **ALDERMAN**, Phebe, m. Daniel C. **PHELPS**, b. of Colebrook, Sept. 16, 1804 | 49 |
| **ALLIN**, [see also **ALLYN**], John, m. Hannah **WEST**, b. of Winchester, Dec. 16, 1796 | 44-5 |
| Lydia, of Winchester, m. Elihu **ROCKWELL**, of Colebrook, Feb. 14, 1788 | 32 |
| Polly, m. Lewis **MILLER**, b. of Winchester, Aug. 25, 1789 | 34-5 |
| Sharhel, m. Jonathan **DUGLAS**, b. of Winchester, Oct. 2, 1798 | 46 |
| **ALLYN** [see also **ALLIN**], Aaron, m. Amelia **DARROW**, b. of Barkhemsted, Feb. 20, 1785 | 25 |
| Lydia, m. Samuel **CLINTON**, b. of Berkhemsted, Nov. 3, 1785 | 26 |
| **ANDRUS**, Ira, m. Clarisey **CLINTON**, b. of Barkhemsted, Feb. 18, 1799 | 47 |
| Mary, m. Daniel **DeWOLF**, b. of Winchester, Oct. 11, 1787 | 31 |
| Rebecca, m. John **PITKIN**, b. of Colebrook, Feb. 4, 1790 | 35 |
| **AUSTIN**, Ruth, of Winchester, m. Josiah **MILLER**, of Torrington, Nov. 10, 1790 | 35 |
| **BABCOCK**, Rufus, s. Rev. Rufus & Zeruah, b. Sept. 18, 1798 | 121 |
| Rufus, Rev., m. Marcy **BRINMADE**, of Salisbury, Nov. 19, 1812 | 146 |
| **BACON**, Anne, m. Martin **WOODRUFF**, b. of Barkhamsted, Feb. 5, 1796 | 43 |
| **BALCOM**, Mary, of Winchester, m. Noadiah Branard **GATES**, of Berkhemsted,June 4, 1787 | 31 |
| **BARNES**, Charles, of New Hartford, m. Rebecca **FOX**, of Winchester, Apr. 29, 1798 | 45-6 |
| **BASS**, Anne, m. Daniel **EGLESTON**, Jr., b. of Colebrook, May 11, 1786 | 29 |
| Nathan, m. Linde **MILLS**, b. of Colebrook, Apr. 22, 1787 | 30-1 |
| Sally, alias Nelson, of Colebrook, m. Isaac **BENEDICT**, of Norfolk, Nov. 29, 1796 | 44 |
| **BAXTER**, John, of Sandersfield, Mass., m. Anne **GOWDY**, of Colebrook, Jan. 12, 1785 | 24 |
| **BEACH**, Candice, of Hartland, m. Paules **MOORE**, of Berkhemsted, Jan. 22, 1792 | 39 |
| Laman, of Colebrook, m. Lydia Mason **WRIGHT**, of Winchester, May 5, 1796 | 44 |
| **BEEBE**, Ezra, m. Lois **FLETCHER**, b. of Colebrook, Sept. 20, 1809 | 48 |
| **BENEDICT**, Isaac, of Norfolk, m. Sally **BASS**, alias **NELSON**, of Colebrook, Nov. 29, 1796 | 44 |
| **BENHAM**, Martha, m. Abraham **CATLIN**, b. of Berkhemsted, Feb. 21, 1786 | 28 |
| **BETTES, BETTIS**, Lenard, m. Susannah **COUCH**, b. of Sandisfield, Dec. 27, 1796 | 45 |
| Sarah, m. Zacheus **HOLCOMB**, b. of Sandisfield, May 1, 1788 | 33 |
| **BIDWELL**, Eleazer, a grand juror brought action on Oct. 13, 1783 for | |

Page

**BIDWELL**, (cont.)
breach of peace vs. Moses **WILLCOX**, of Colebrook, his w. Hannah & his d. Hannah & in Mar. 1784 the defendants appealed. Elijah Rockwell, J. P. 22
**BLAKESLEE, BLAKSSLEE, BLAKSLEE**, Asenath, d. Samuel & Phebe, b. June 4, 1785 121
Federal, s. Samuel & Phebe, b. Jan. 25, 1792 121
Gad, s. Samuel & Phebe, b. June 13, 1794 121
Joel, s. Samuel & Phebee, b. Aug. 13, 1787 121
Lois Ives, d. Samuel & Phebe, b. Oct. 13, 1796 121
Lois Ives, d. Samuel & Phebe, d. Mar. 21, 1797 156
Phebee, d. Samuel & Phebee, b. Oct. 30, 1789 121
Samuel, 2nd, s. Samuel & Phebee, b. Nov. 17, 1783 121
**BOGUE**, Chauncy, s. Daniel & Lois, b. Feb. 23, 1795 121
Francis, s. Daniel & Lois, b. Oct. 3, 1780 121
Henry, s. Daniel & Lois, b. June 23, 1791 121
John, s. Daniel & Lois, b. Feb. 24, 1782 121
**BOWDEN**, Elijah, of New York State, m. Mary **HALL**, now of Colebrook, Aug. 29, 1791 37
**[BRAINERD], BRANARD**, Seeby, m. Anne **PARDEE**, b. of Berkhemsted, Dec. 28, 1786 30
**BRINMADE**, Marcy, of Salisbury, m. Rev. Rufus **BABCOCK**, Nov. 19, 1812 146
**BROCKER**, Sally, of Colebrook, m. Asher **SCOVEL**, of Harwinton, Mar. 23, 1795 42
**BUCKINGHAM**, Abigail, Mrs. of Saybrook, b. Apr. 29, 1751, O. S.; m. John **ROCKWELL**, Oct. 3, 1779 137
**BURR**, Ada, d. John & Joel, b. Apr. 10, 1795 121
Horasha, late of Colebrook, m. Lette **GRINNELL**, of Winchester, Feb. 10, 1801 48
**CARTER**, Benjamin, m. Sarah Anne **WILLCOXSON**, b. of Winchester, Dec. 12, 1790 36
**CASE**, Nathan, m. Rachel **MUNGER**, b. of Norfolk, Feb. 16, 1785 24
William, m. [ ] **MOORE**, b. of Barkhemsted, May 13, 1795 43
**CATLIN**, Abraham, m. Martha **BENHAM**, b. of Berkhemsted, Feb. 21, 1786 28
**CHADWICK**, Polly, m. Osias **SPENCER**, b. of Winchester, Oct. 5, 1801 48
**CHAPPAL**, Sarah, of Mountville, m. Appleton **STILMAN**, of Colebrook, Jan. 31, 1788 31-2
**CLARK**, Calvin, of Sharon, m. Ruth **HOSKINS**, of Colebrook, Nov. 14, 1786 29-30
Ichobad, of Colebrook, m. Leucy **TANNER**, of Winchester, Jan. 6, 1791 36
Isaiah, of Colebrook, m. Charlotte **MOORE**, of Barkhemsted, Nov. 6, 1799 47
Marcy, of Farmington, m. Arial **SPALDEN**, of Canaan, Sept. 25, 1785 25-6
Timothy, m. Jemima **HUBBART**, b. of Colebrook, Feb. 24, 1805 49
**CLINTON**, Clarisey, m. Ira **ANDRUS**, b. of Barkhemsted, Feb. 18, 1799 47
Henry, Jr., m. Elenor **DARROW**, b. of Berkhemsted, Oct. 19, 1786 29
Samuel, m. Lydia **ALLYN**, b. of Berkhemsted, Nov. 3, 1785 26
Shelden, m. Peter **HARINGTON**, b. of Berkhemsted, Sept. 30, 1792 40
**COLLINS**, Angustus, s. David & Jerusha, b. July 31, 1804 123

Page

**COLLINS**, (cont.)
David, s. David & Jerusha, b. Mar. 1, 1799 123
James Pierpoint, s. David & Jerusha, b. Jan. 7, 1801 123
Jerusha, d. David & Jerusha, b. Jan. 1, 1809 123
Laura Levina, d. David & Jerusha, b. Jan. 17, 1812 123
William Sheriden, s. David & Jerusha, b. Feb. 15, 1806 123
**CONE**, Noah, of Sandisfield, m. Huldah **PRATT**, of Colebrook, Feb. 19, 1789 34
**COOK**, Joseph, of Lowden, m. Abigail **WRIGHT**, of Colebrook, Nov. 27, 1783 22
**COUCH**, Susannah, m. Lenard **BETTIS**, b. of Sandisfield, Dec. 27, 1796 45
**CRISSEY, CRISSEE**, Abigail, m. Silvenus **SIMONS**, b. of Colebrook, Jan. 17, 1792 39
Eunice, m. Philip **SIMONS**, b. of Colebrook, Jan. 12, 1792 38
Israel, m. Elsie **WOODRUFF**, b. of Winchester, Feb. 7, 1788 32
Mary, of Winchester, m. Joseph **LOOMIS**, of New Hartford, Jan. 10, 1786 27
Naomi, m. Daniel **POTTER**, b. of Winchester, Dec. 8, 1785 26
**CROW**, Deborah, m. Zerah **PHELPS**, b. of Berkhemsted, Sept. 24, 1789 35
**CURTIS, CURTICE**, Lorane, m. Benjamin **HALE**, b. of Colebrook, June 9, 1791 37
Lorane, m. Benjamin **HALE**, b. of Colebrook, June 9, 1791, by Elijah Rockwell, J. P. 149
**DARROW**, Amelia, m. Aaron **ALLYN**, b. of Barkhemsted, Feb. 20, 1785 25
Elenor, m. Henry **CLINTON**, Jr., b. of Berkhemsted, Oct. 19, 1786 29
**DAVIS**, Marcy, m. Nathan **ROSE**, b. of Winchester, Feb. 26, 1794 42
**DeWOLF**, Daniel, m. Mary **ANDRUS**, b. of Winchester, Oct. 11, 1787 31
**DOOLITTLE**, Jesse, Jr., m. Hannah **JOY**, b. of Winchester, Nov. 15, 1787 31
Ruth, m. Chancy **MILLS**, b. of Winchester, Sept. 27, 1784 23
Sarah, of Winchester, m. John **MILLER**, of Glastonbury, Jan. 29, 1795 42
**[DOUGLASS], DUGLAS**, Jonathan, m. Sharhel **ALLIN**, b. of Winchester, Oct. 2, 1798 46
**DUNHAM**, Elias, of Winchester, m. Jerusha **LEWIS**, of Berkhemsted, Mar. 10, 1791 37
Jonathan, m. Susanna **KELLOGG**, b. of Winchester, Nov. 24, 1791 38
**[EGGLESTON], EGLESTON, EGCLATON, EGILSTON**, Daniel, Jr., m. Anne **BASS**, b. of Colebrook, May 11, 1786 29
Harriot, d. Daniel, Jr. & Anne, b. Sept. 10, 1786 125
Harris, m. Rhoda **WOODRUFF**, b. of Colebrook, May 8, 1794 42
Isaac, of Windsor, m. Elisabeth **ROCKWELL**, of Colebrook, Jan. 31, 1788 32
Sarah, of Winchester, m. Hezekiah **WOODRUFF**, Jr., of Colebrook, Jan. 14, 1801 47
**FIELD**, Martin, m. Marthy **MINER**, b. of Colebrook, July 12, 1792 40
**FILLEY**, Mary, m. Adam **NOTT**, b. of Winchester, Feb. 14, 1786 27-8
Polley, m. John **MANNING**, b. of Winchester, Mar. 21, 1803 48
Roger, of Colebrook, m. Abiah **HALE**, of Chatham, May 21, 1792 39
**FLETCHER**, Hannah, of Colebrook, m. Russell **LOOMIS**, of Coventry, Apr. 1, 1796 43

Page

**FLETCHER**, (cont.)
Lois, m. Ezra **BEEBE**, b. of Colebrook, Sept. 20, 1809 48
**FOWLER**, Hannah, of Torrington, m. Paul **ROBERTS**, of Berkhemsted, May 11, 1788 33
**FOX**, Meriam, m. Lemuel **WHITE**, b. of Colebrook, May 7, 1789 34
Rebecca, of Winchester, m. Charles **BARNES**, of New Hartford, Apr. 29, 1798 45-6
**GATES**, Noadiah Branard, of Berkhemsted, m. Mary **BALCOM**, of Winchester, June 4, 1787 31
**GOWDY**, Anne, of Colebrook, m. John **BAXTER**, of Sandersfield, Mass., Jan. 12, 1785 24
Benett, s. Samuel & Elice, b. Dec. 31, 1793 127
Betsey, d. Samuel & Elice, b. Sept. 16, 1788 127
Biel, s. Samuel & Elice, b. May 6, 1791 127
Samuel, s. Samuel & Elice, b. May 28, 1786 127
**GRINNELL, GRINEL**, Betsey, m. Eli **MARSHEL**, b. of Winchester, Dec. 12, 1802 48
Lette, of Winchester, m. Horasha **BURR**, late of Colebrook, Feb. 10, 1801 48
Rufus, of Wincester, m. Anne **MARSHEL**, of Colebrook, Nov. 9, 1797 45
**HALE**, [see also **HALL**], Abiah, of Chatham, m. Roger **FILLEY**, of Colebrook, May 21, 1792 39
Benjamin, m. Lorane **CURTICE**, b. of Colebrook, June 9, 1791 37
Benjamin, m. Lorane **CURTIS**, b. of Colebrook, June 9, 1791, by Elijah Rockwell, J. P. 149
Josiah Curtis, s. Benjamin & Lorane, b. Jan. 8, 1792 128
**HALL**, [see also **HALE**], Easther, m. Thomas **POST**, b. of Colebrook, Jan. 5, 1794 41
Mary, now of Colebrook, m. Elijah **BOWDEN**, of New York State, Aug. 29, 1791 37
**HANMER**, Joseph Wilcox, [s. Joseph & Sibyl], b. Sept. 9, 1831 128
Samuel Francis, [s. Joseph & Sibyl], b. June 5, 1835 128
**[HARRINGTON], HARINGTON**, Peter, m. Shelden **CLINTON**, b. of Berkhemsted, Sept. 30, 1792 40
**HART**, Stephen, m. [E]unice **LYMAN**, b. of Colebrook, Sept. 9, [probably 1790] 35
**HAYDEN**, Nathaniel, of Torrington, m. Sally **RANSOM**, of Barkhemsted, Apr. 4, 1799 47
Seth, m. Huldah **SOPER**, b. of Barkhemsted, Dec. 2, 1804 49
**HAYES**, Welthy, of Granby, m. David **KNIGHT**, of Colebrook, May 10, 1793 40-1
**HENDEE**, Clemons, m. Abigail **MORRISS**, b. of Colebrook, Mar. 5, 1786 28
Lucy, of Colebrook, m. Zebulon **THOMSON**, of Winchester, Aug. 30, 1784 23
**[HEWITT], HEWIT**, Anne, w. Joshua, b. Apr. 19, 1766 128
Anne, d. Joshua & Anne, b. Feb. 27, 1791 128
Joshua, b. Jan. 15, 1765 128
Joshua, s. Joshua & Anne, b. May 7, 1791 128

Page

**HOLCOMB**, Zacheus, m. Sarah **BETTES**, b. of Sandisfield, May 1, 1788 33
**HOLLESTER**, Isaac, m. Elizabeth **LEAVENS**, b. of Colebrook, Mar. 7, 1786 28-9
**HORTON**, Abigail, w. Benjamin, d. Apr. 18, 1798, ae 76 159
**HOSKINS**, Eunice, m. Nathaniel **KINNE**, b. of Colebrook, Oct. 14, 1795 43
John, of Colebrook, m. Lewcy **MALLARY**, of Winchester, Mar. 10, 1791 36
Ruth, of Colebrook, m. Calvin **CLARK**, of Sharon, Nov. 14, 1786 29-30
**HUBBART**, Jemima, m. Timothy **CLARK**, b. of Colebrook, Feb. 24, 1805 49
**HUNGERFORD**, Jane, m. David **MILLS**, b. of Winchester, May 8, 1788 33
**HUNTLEY**, Asher, m. Betty **TIFFENY**, b. of Hartland, Nov. 14, 1792 40
**HURD**, Edee, d. Seth & Thankfull, b. Dec. 17, 1786 128
Easther, d. Seth & Thankfull, b. Jan. 28, 1785 128
Seth, of Killingworth, m. Thankful **RAY**, of Haddam, Jan. 2, 1782, by Eleazar May 149
Smith, eldest s. Seth & Thankfull, b. Jan. 5, 1783 128
**INEIZM**(?), Peter, of New York State, m. Margerit **PHILLIPS**, of Colebrook, Apr. 13, 1794 41
**IVES**, Rhoda, d. Joseph, b. Oct.14, 1781 129
Truman, s. Joseph, b. Jan. 8, 1784 129
**JONES**, Godfrey, of Colebrook, m. Sally **WALTER**, of Winchester, Oct. 27, 1791 38
**JOPP**, Betey, of Winchester, m. Roger **OLMSTED**, of New Hartford, Dec. 11, 1788 34
**JOY**, Hannah, m. Jesse **DOOLITTLE**, Jr., b. of Winchester, Nov. 15, 1787 31
**KELLOGG**, Lurannah, of Barkhemsted, m. Aaron **WEST**, of Winchester, Nov. 4, 1784 23
Susanna, m. Jonathan **DUNHAM**, b. of Winchester, Nov. 24, 1791 38
**KINNE**, Nathaniel, m. Eunice **HOSKINS**, b. of Colebrook, Oct. 14, 1795 43
**KNEELAND**, Clara, d. Isaac, Jr. & Keziah, b. Nov. 7, 1790 130
Wyllys, s. Isaac, Jr. & Keziah, b. Sept. 10, 1794 130
**KNIGHT**, David, of Colebrook, m. Welthy **HAYES**, of Granby, May 10, 1793 40-1
**[KNOWLTON], NOLTON**, Lovinah, of Winchester, m. Cornelius **PHELPS**, of Heebron, Jan. 21, 1784 22-3
**LEAVENS**, Elizabeth, m. Isaac **HOLLESTER**, b. of Colebrook, Mar. 7, 1786 28-9
**LEWIS**, Jerusha, of Berkhemsted, m. Elias **DUNHAM**, of Winchester, Mar. 10, 1791 37
**LOOMIS**, Joseph, of New Hartford, m. Mary **CRISSEE**, of Winchester, Jan. 10, 1786 27
Mina, m. Asahel **WELLS**, b. of Winchester, Jan. 27, 1799 46
Russell, of Coventry, m. Hannah **FLETCHER**, of Colebrook, Apr. 1, 1796 43
**LYMAN**, [E]unice, m. Stephen **HART**, b. of Colebrook, Sept. 9, [probably 1790] 35
**[MALLORY], MALLARY, MALLERY, MELLERY**, Amasa, m. Saloma **SMITH**, b. of Winchester, Jan. 7, 1789 34
Lewcy, of Winchester, m. John **HOSKINS**, of Colebrook, Mar. 10, 1791 36
Loly, m. Benjamin **WHEELER**, b. of Winchester, May 4, 1785 25

Page

**MANLY**, Russell, of Windsor, m. Rebecca **WOODRUFF**, of Colebrook, June 30, 1796 44
**MANNING**, John, m. Polley **FILLEY**, b. of Colebrook, Mar. 21, 1803 48
[**MARSHALL**], **MARSHEL**, Anne, of Colebrook, m. Rufus **GRINNELL**, of Winchester, Nov. 9, 1797 45
Eli, m. Betsey **GRINEL**, b. of Winchester, Dec. 12, 1802 48
**MARTIN**, Andrew, s. Asahel & Mary, b. Dec. 28, 1780 132
Asahel, m. Mary **ROBERTS**, May 24, 1780 150
Asahel, s. Asahel & Mary, b. May 28, 1782 132
[E]unice, eldest d. Asahel & Mary, b. Mar. 26, 1786 132
Isaac, s. Asahel & Mary, b. Mar. 16, 1784 132
Judah, s. Asahel & Mary, b. Feb. 9, 1790 132
Mary, d. Asahel & Mary, b. Jan. 30, 1788 132
**MERRIMAN**, William, of Berkhemsted, m. Lydia **WRIGHT**, of Winchester, Aug. 8, 1793 41
**MILLER**, John, of Glastonbury, m. Sarah **DOOLITTLE**, of Winchester, Jan. 29, 1795 42
Josiah, of Torrington, m. Ruth **AUSTIN**, of Winchester, Nov. 10, 1790 35
Lewis, m. Polly **ALLIN**, b. of Winchester, Aug. 25, 1789 34-5
**MILLS**, Chancy, m. Ruth **DOOLITTLE**, b. of Winchester, Sept. 27, 1784 23
David, m. Jane **HUNGERFORD**, b. of Winchester, May 8, 1788 33
Gardner, m. Mary **SKINNER**, b. of Colebrook, Apr. 12, 1796 43-4
Linde, m. Nathan **BASS**, b. of Colebrook, Apr. 22, 1787 30-1
Pheeby, made affidavit Nov. 16, 1784 before Elijah Rockwell, J. P. that "the child she was now the mother of was David **SMITH**, late of Barkhempsted" 24
Phebe, of Winchester, m. David **SMITH**, of Sandersfield, Apr. 22, 1785 25
**MINER**, Marthy, m. Martin **FIELD**, b. of Colebrook, July 12, 1792 40
**MOORE**, Charlotte, of Barkhemsted, m. Isaiah **CLARK**, of Colebrook, Nov. 6, 1799 47
Cullen, s. Aaron & Polly, b. Dec. 22, 1797 132
Paules, of Berkhemstsed, m. Candice **BEACH**, of Hartland, Jan. 22, 1792 39
-----, m. William **CASE**, b. of Barkhemested, May 13, 1795 43
**MOOT**, Jonathan, m. Submit **WEEB**, b. of New York State, Nov. 24, 1786 30
**MORRISS**, Abigail, m. Clemons **HENDEE**, b. of Colebrook, Mar. 5, 1786 28
**MUNGER**, Rachel, m. Nathan **CASE**, b. of Norfolk, Feb. 16, 1785 24
**NELSON**, Sally, see Sally **BASS** 44
**NOLTON**, [see under **KNOWLTON**]
**NORTH**, Eben, s. Rufus & Esther, b. Mar. 2, 1790 133
Joel, s. Rufus & Esther, b. June 10, 1795 133
Lester, s. Rufus & Esther, b. July 5, 1797 133
Martin, s. Rufus & Esther, b. Nov. 5, 1804 133
**NORTON**, Levi, of Norfolk, m. Rhoda **PALMER**, of Winchester, Feb. 5, 1786 27
**NOTT**, Adam, m. Mary **FILLEY**, b. of Winchester, Feb. 14, 1786 27-8
**OLMSTED**, Roger, of New Hartford, m. Betey **JOPP**, of Winchester, Dec. 11, 1788 34
**PALMER**, Enoch, of Winchester, m. Elisabeth **SOPER**, of Torrington, 36

Page

**PALMER**, (cont.)
Nov. 23, 1790
Rhoda, of Winchester, m. Levi **NORTON**, of Norfolk, Feb. 5, 1786 27
**PARDEE**, Anne, m. Seeby **BRANARD**, b. of Berkhemsted, Dec. 28, 1786 30
**PHELPS**, Cornelius, of Heebron, m. Lovinah **NOLTON**, of Winchester, Jan. 21, 1784 22-3
Daniel C., m. Phebe **ALDERMAN**, b. of Colebrook, Sept. 16, 1804 49
Zerah, m. Deborah **CROW**, b. of Berkhemsted, Sept. 24, 1789 35
**PHILLIPS, PHILLIP**, Betsey, m. Benoni **WEBB**, b. of Colebrook, Aug. 12, 1798 46
Margerit, of Colebrook, m. Peter **INEIZM**(?), of New York State, Apr. 13, 1794 41
**PITKIN**, John, m. Rebecca **ANDRUS**, b. of Colebrook, Feb. 4, 1790 35
**PLUMLEY**, Joseph, s. Samuel & Silva, b. Dec. 5, 1803 135
Lodice, d. Samuel & Silva, b. May 13, 1806 135
**POST**, Thomas, m. Easther **HALL**, b. of Colebrook, Jan. 5, 1794 41
**POTTER**, Daniel, m. Naomi **CRISSEE**, b. of Winchester, Dec. 8, 1785 26
**PRATT**, Huldah, of Colebrook, m. Noah **CONE**, of Sandisfield, Feb. 19, 1789 34
**PRESTON**, Abraham, m. Eunice **WILKENSON**, b. of Winchester, Nov. 20, 1792 40
**RANSOM**, Sally, of Barkhemsted, m. Nathaniel **HAYDEN**, of Torrington, Apr. 4, 1799 47
**RAY**, Thankful, of Haddam, m. Seth **HURD**, of Killingworth, Jan. 2, 1782, by Eleazar May 149
**ROBERTS**, Judah, m. Thankfull **WRIGHT**, b. of Colebrook, Mar. 7, 1786 28
Mary, m. Asahel **MARTIN**, May 24, 1780 150
Paul, of Berkhemsted, m. Hannah **FOWLER**, of Torrington, May 11, 1788 33
**ROCKWELL**, Anne, d. Elijah & Lucy, b. Oct. 9, 1783 137
Betey, d. Elijah & Lucy, b. Feb. 18, 1789 137
Elihu, of Colebrook, m. Lydia **ALLIN**, of Winchester, Feb. 14, 1788 32
Elijah, s. Joseph & Anne, b. Nov. 14, 1744 137
Elijah, m. Lucy **WRIGHT**, Jan. 19, 1775 152
Elijah, s. Elijah & Lucy, b. Nov. 9, 1777 137
Elisabeth, of Colebrook, m. Isaac **EGLESTON**, of Windsor, Jan. 31, 1788 32
Hannah, m. Samuel **SEYMOUR**, b. of Colebrook, Nov. 24, 1791 38
John, b. Aug. 25, O. S. 1743, at East Windsor; m. Mrs. Abigail **BUCKINGHAM**, of Saybrook, Oct. 3, 1779 137
John, s. John & Abigail, b. Sept. 27, 1782 137
Lovisa, d. John & Abigail, b. Feb. 15, 1791 137
Lucy, w. Elijah, b. Oct. 7, 1756 137
Lucy, d. Elijah & Lucy, b. June 8, 1776 137
Lucy, 1st, d. Elijah & Lucy, d. Apr. 2, 1778 164
Lucy, d. Elijah & Lucy, b. Jan. 8, 1779 137
Nabby, d. John & Abigail, b. Jan. 20, 1787 137
Theron, s. Elijah & Lucy, b. June 5, 1782 137
Uzal, s. John & Abigail, b. May 29, 1785 137

Page
**ROSE**, Nathan, m. Marcy **DAVIS**, b. of Winchester, Feb. 26, 1794 42
**RUSSELL**, Elizur, s. Stephen & Elinor, b. Mar. 1, 1776 138
Elizur, s. Stephen & Elinor, d. Oct. 19, 1778 164
Elizur, 2nd, s. Stephen & Elinor, b. Nov. 23, 1779 138
John Hough, s. Stephen, & Elinor, b. Dec. 21, 1773 138
Lucy, d. Stephen & Elinor, b. Feb. 3, 1778 138
Meracha, d. Stephen & Elinor, b. Jan. 14, 1782 138
Phalarcus, s. Stephen & Elinor, b. Aug. 24, 1786 138
Roswell, s. Stephen & Elinor, b. Mar. 24, 1772 138
Samuel, s. Stephen & Elinor, b. Aug. 25, 1786 138
**SAXTON**, Anne, d. Jonathan & Prudence, b. Apr. 21, 1802 139
Milo, s. Jonatha&n Prudence, b. May 22, 1804 139
**SCOVEL**, Asher, of Harwinton, m. Sally **BROCKER**, of Colebrook, Mar. 23, 1795 42
**SEYMOUR**, Samuel, m. Hannah **ROCKWELL**, b. of Colebrook, Nov. 24, 1791 38
**SHEPARD**, Alpha, s. Ebenezer & Mercy, b. Mar. 11, 1789 139
Caroline, d. Ebenezer & Marcy, b. July 26, 1773 139
Ebenezer, s. Ebenezer & Mercy, b. Feb. 13, 1775 139
Ebenezer, 2nd, s. Ebenezer & Marcy, b. Sept. 19, 1777 139
Mercy, d. Ebenezer & Mercy, b. Nov. 24, 1787 139
Prudence, d. Ebenezer & Marcy, b. June 8, 1771 139
Prudence, 3rd d. Ebenezer & Mercy, b. Apr. 4, 1783 139
Truman, s. Ebenezer & Mercy, b. Feb. 5, 1781 139
William, s. Ebenezer & Mercy, b. Apr. 7, 1779 139
**SIMONS**, Lydia, of Colebrook, m. Benjamin **WATTERS***, of Granby, June 23, 1791 ***(WALTERS?)** 37
Philip, m. Eunice **CRISSEY**, Jan. 12, 1792 38
Silvenus, m. Abigail **CRISSSEY**, b. of Colebrook, Jan. 17, 1792 39
**SKINNER**, Mary, m. Gardner **MILLS**, b. of Colebrook, Apr. 12, 1796 43-4
**SMITH**, Benjamin, m. Onnor **SMITH**, b. of Winchester, Dec. 29, 1796 45
David, late of Barkhemsted. Pheeby **MILLS**, made affidavit Nov. 16, 1784 before Elijah Rockwell, Jr. P., that "the child she was now the mother of was David **SMITH**, late of Barkhemsted" 24
David, late of Sandersfield, m. Phebe **MILLS**, of Winchester, Apr. 22, 1785 25
Francis B., s. Elisha & Lovis, b. Mar. 13, 1837 139
Onnor, m. Benjamin **SMITH**, b. of Winchester, Dec. 29, 1796 45
Saloma, m. Amasa **MALLERY**, b. of Winchester, Jan. 7, 1789 34
**SOPER**, Elisabeth, of Torrington, m. Enoch **PALMER**, of Winchester, Nov. 23, 1790 36
Huldah, m. Seth **HAYDEN**, b. of Barkhemsted, Dec. 2, 1804 49
**SPALDEN**, Arial, of Canaan, m. Marcy **CLARK**, of Farmington, Sept. 25, 1785 25-6
**SPENCER**, Osias, m. Polly **CHADWICK**, b. of Winchester, Oct. 5, 1801 48
**STILLMAN, STILMAN**, Appleton, of Colebrook, m. Sarah **CHAPPAL**, of Mountville, Jan. 31, 1788 31
Elijah, s. John & Susannah, b. June 3, 1779 139

Page

**STILLMAN, STILMAN**, (cont.)
George, s. John & Susannah, b. July 10, 1784 139
Huldah, d. John & Susannah, b. Feb. 11, 1782 139
Linda, d. William & Sarah, b. Mar. 6, 1803 139
Robens, s. John & Susannah, b. Apr. 5, 1786 139
**TANNER**, Leucy, of Winchester, m. Ichobad **CLARK**, of Colebrook, Jan. 6, 1791 36
**THOMSON**, Zebulon, of Winchester, m. Lucy **HENDEE**, of Colebrook, Aug. 30, 1784 23
**TIFFENY**, Betty, m. Asher **HUNTLEY**, b. of Hartland, Nov. 14, 1792 40
**TODD**, Mary, m. Judah **WEST**, b. of Winchester, Dec. 26, 1785 26-7
**UNDERWOOD**, Elizabeth, d. John & Elisabeth, b. Nov. 7, 1794 142
John, s. John & Elisabeth, b. Feb. 14, 1796 142
**VIETS**, Benjamin, s. David & Mary, b. Oct. 17, 1783 143
**WAKEFIELD**, Emily Chloe, d. Hezekiah & Hariet, b. Jan. 25, 1809 145
Walter, s. Hezekiah & Hariot, b. Dec. 1, 1811 145
**WALTER**, Sally, of Winchester, m. Godfrey **JONES**, of Colebrook, Oct. 27, 1791 38
**WATTERS**, Benjamin, of Granby, m. Lydia **SIMONS**, of Colebrook, June 23, 1791 37
**WEBB, WEEB**, Benoni, m. Betsey **PHILLIP**, b. of Colebrook, Aug. 12, 1798 46
Submit, m. Jonathan **MOOT**, b. of New York, State, Nov. 24, 1786 30
**WELLS**, Asahel, m. Mina **LOOMIS**, b. of Winchester, Jan. 27, 1799 46
**WEST**, Aaron, of Winchester, m. Lurannah **KELLOGG**, of Barkhemsted, Nov. 4, 1784 23
Hannah, m. John **ALLIN**, b. of Winchester, Dec. 16, 1796 44-5
Judah, m. Mary **TODD**, b. of Winchester, Dec. 26, 1785 26-7
**WHEELER**, Benjamin, m. Loly **MELLERY**, b. of Winchester, May 4, 1785 25
**WHITE**, Anne, d. Lemuel & Miriam, b. Mar. 21, 1801 145
Henry King, s. Henry & Easther, b. Oct. 18, 1807 145
Lemuel, m. Meriam **FOX**,, b. of Colebrook, May 7, 1789 34
Lidia, d. Lemuel & Miriam, b. June 11, 1794 145
Miriam, d. Lemuel & Miriam, b. Feb. 16, 1790 145
**WHITING, WHITEING**, Aaron, s. John & Sylvey, b. Aug. 22, 1796 144
Ammetine, d. Seth & Tryphena, b. Sept. 28, 1808 144
Aurillia, d. John & Sylvey, b. July 6, 1798 144
Caroline, d. Seth & Tryphena, b. Feb. 7, 1811 144
Harvy, s. John & Silvah, b. Jan. 14, 1788 144
John, s. John & Silvah, b. Aug. 24, 1790 144
Loomis, s. Seth & Tryphena, b. Feb. 14, 1797 144
Nancy, d. Seth & Tryphena, b. Dec. 2, 1791 144
Ralph Bradley, s. Willard & Elvira, b. June 16, 1824 144
Roxsy, d. John & Selviah, b. Aug. 13, 1782 144
Roxsy, d. John & Selviah, b. Aug. 13, 1782* *(Line drawn through entry) 167
Roxsy, d. John & Selviah, b. Oct. 11, 1785 144
Samuel, s. John & Silvah, b. Feb. 7, 1792 144

Page

**WHITING, WHITEING**, (cont.)
Sarah, d. Seth & Tryphena, b. July 18, 1798 144
Seth Grant, s. Seth & Tryphena, b. May 18, 1801 144
Susan, d. John & Sylvey, b. Sept. 16, 1800 144
Sylvay, d. John & Sylvay, b. May 31, 1794 144
Thomas Foster, s. John & Sylvey, b. Aug. 17, 1802 144
Trasey, s. Seth & Tryphena, b. Jan. 29, 1799 144
Tryphena, d. John & Selviah, b. Feb. 5, 1784 144
Willard, s. Seth & Tryphena, b. Nov. 8, 1794 144
William Franklin, s. John & Sylvey, b. Apr. 30, 1806 144
**[WILCOX], WILLCOX**, Hannah, see Moses **WILLCOX** 22
Moses, of Colebrook, his w. Hannah & his d. Hannah, appealed Mar. [ ], 1784 from court's decision on action brought by Eleazer **BIDWELL** a grand juror. Elijah Rockwell, J. P. 22
**WILLCOXSON**, Sarah Anne, m. Benjamin **CARTER**, b. of Winchester, Dec. 12, 1790 36
**WILKENSON**, Eunice, m. Abraham **PRESTON**, b. of Winchester, Nov. 20, 1792 40
**WILLSON**, Abijah, m. Lucy **WRIGHT**, b. of Winchester, [ ] 13, 1798 46
**WOLCOTT**, John Hitchcock, m. Mary **WRIGHT**, b. of Colebrook, Apr. 25, 1792 39
**WOODRUFF**, Daniel E., s. [Hezekiah & Sarah], b. May 1, 1810 144
Elsie, m. Israel **CRISSEE**, b. of Winchester, Feb. 7, 1788 32
Hezekiah, Jr., of Colebrook, m. Sarah **EGELSTON**, of Winchester, Jan. 14, 1801 47
Hezekiah, Jr., s. Hezekiah & Sarah, b. Mar. 4, 1815 144
Lemuel, s. [Hezekiah, Jr. & Sarah], b. Aug. 29, 1804 144
Martin, m. Anne **BACON**, b. of Barkhemsted, Feb. 5, 1796 43
Mary, d. Hezekiah & Sarah, b. Aug. 30, 1817 144
Orra, d. Hezekiah & Sarah, b. May 15, 1808 144
Rebecca, of Colebrook, m. Russell **MANLY**, of Windsor, June 30, 1796 44
Rhoda, m. Harris **EGCLATON**, b. of Colebrook, May 8, 1794 42
Sarah M., d. Hezekiah & Sarah, b. Aug. 19, 1812 144
Wyllys, s. Hezekiah, Jr. & Sarah, b. July 3, 1801 144
**WRIGHT**, Abigail, of Colebrook, m. Joseph **COOK**, of Lowden, Nov. 27, 1783 22
Lucy, m. Elijah **ROCKWELL**, Jan. 19, 1775 152
Lucy, m. Abijah **WILLSON**, b. of Winchester, [ ] 13, 1798 46
Lydia, of Winchester, m. William **MERRIMAN**, of Berkhemsted, Aug. 8, 1793 41
Lydia Mason, of Winchester, m. Laman **BEACH**, of Colebrook, May 5, 1796 44
Mary, m. John Hitchcock **WOLCOTT**, b. of Colebrook, Apr. 25, 1792 39
Thankfull, m. Judah **ROBERTS**, b. of Colebrook, Mar. 7, 1786 28

## COLUMBIA VITAL RECORDS
## 1804 - 1852

Page

**ABBOTT**, Phebe D., of Columbia, m. Daniel **CHAPMAN**, of Tolland, Nov. 28, 1833, by David Dickinson 54

**ABEL, ABELL**, Henry W., m. Sarah E. **HOLBROOK**, b. of Columbia, Nov. 28, 1833, by David Dickinson 54

John N., of Columbia, m. Mrs. Eliza A. **PALMER**, of East Haddam, [Feb. ] 4, [1849], by Rev. H. Merrell 25

Solomon N., m. Emily A. **HUNT**, Nov. 28, 1839, by C. Kittredge 43

**ALDEN**, Gideon A., of Enfield, Conn., m. Eliza D. **LITTLE**, of Columbia, Feb. 20, 1842, by Francis L. Robinson, of Enfield, Conn. 37

**ALLEN**, Elizabeth Ann, of Lima, m. John **ROGERS**, of Columbia, Mar. 5, 1822, by Rev. William Palmer, of Colchester, in the house of Martin Webber 76

Horace, of East Haddam, m. Lavina **HOLISTER**, of Columbia, Mar. 1, 1829, by David Dickinson 61

Meriam, m. Nathan **CLARK**, Mar. 7, 1782 67

Royal J., of Manchester, m. Ursula R. **WHEELER**, of Columbia, Nov. 29, 1849, by Rev. James W. Woodward 27

**ALMSBURY**, Ralph, m. Maria **WEBBER**, Dec. 17, 1825, by Amhurst Scoville, J. P. 83

**ANDREWS**, Ruth, of Hebron, m. Ambrose **FULLER**, of Columbia, May 7, 1825, by David Dickinson 82

**ANTHNAN** (?), George, s. Frances & Eunice, b. July 8, 1793. Recorded Oct. 11, 1811 1

George, s. Francis & Eunice, b. July 10, 1793. Recorded Jan. 1812 1

**ARMSTRONG**, John, of Freeport, Me., m. Lucina C. **RICHARDSON**, of Columbia, Jan. 9, 1849, by Rev. James W. Woodword 25

**AVERY**, Dudley B., m. Lucretia **BESTER**, b. of Columbia, Aug. 22, 1844, by Rev. James W. Woodworth 13

**BABCOCK**, Ann, of Lebanon, m. David **DIXON**, of Manchester, Oct. 26, 1846, by Rev. Ebenezer Robinson 20

Thankful, m. Samuel **BUCKINGHAM**, b. of Columbia, Dec. 30, 1821, by David Dickinson 75

**BAILEY**, Lucretia, m. Joshua **PORTER**, b. of Columbia, Dec. 31, 1829, by David Dickinson 87

**BARKER**, Thomas, of Hinsdale, Mass., m. Wid. Ruby **FULLER**, of Columbia, Aug. 28, 1837, by Alpheas Kingsley, J. P. 51

**BARSTOW**, Betsey, m. Charles **WRIGHT**, July 4, 1782 68

Celinda S., of Columbia, m. Jared S. **MANLEY**, of Columbia, Dec. 21, 1841, by James W. Woodword 40

Hubbard, of Columbia, m. Sophia **MORGAN**, of Columbia, June 8,

Page

**BARSTOW**, (cont.)
1842, by James W. Woodword 38
**BEAUMONT**, Prince, m. Esther **UNCAS**, May 14, 1837, by Amhurst Scoville, J. P. 50
**BECKWITH**, Louisa, m. Sam[ue]l **BLIVEN**, Oct. [ ], 1826, by Sam[ue]l Little, J. P. 71
**BEEBE**, James M., m. Salena **FORD**, Mar. 18, 1851, by H. G. Willard, Willimantic 31
**BENNETT**, Emily L., of Windham, m. Benjamin F. **SNOW**, of Providence, R. I., June 10, 1849, by William Osborn, J. P. 26
Lucina, m. James **PINNEO**, Dec. 23, 1832, by Rev. Charles Nichols 58
**BESTER**, Lucretia, m. Dudley B. **AVERY**, b. of Columbia, Aug. 22, 1844, by Rev. James W. Woodworth 13
**BILL**, Cynthia, m. Aaron **YEOMANS**, b. of Columbia, Mar. 21, 1827, by Rev. Esek Brown, of Lebanon 72
George W., m. Harriet R. **TICKNOR**, b. of Columbia, Mar. 24, 1844, by Rev. James W. Woodworth. Int. pub. 10
Lucy A., m. Charles A. **POST**, Oct. 23, 1850, by Rev. Fred[eric]k D. Avery, at the house of Chester Bill 30
**BLACKMAN**, George F., of Coventry, m. Emily A. **NEWELL**, of Columbia, [Apr], 10, 1837, by Rev. Alpha Miller 50
**BLISH**, [see also **BLISS**], Mary Ann, of Columbia, m. Leonard H. **PERKINS**, of Andover, Sept. 22, 1850, by Rev. Roswell C. Lamb, at her father's residence 31
**BLISS**, [see also **BLISH**], Charles, m. Polly **WEBSTER**, of Columbia, Oct. 30, 1825, by David Dickinson 82
Chester A., of Albany, N. Y., m. Hannah C. **HILL**, of Columbia, Aug. 21, 1843, by Rev. Ebenezer Robinson 12
Elias, of Hudson, N. Y., m. Mary M. **HILLS**, of Columbia, Dec. 4, 1837, by Levi Meech, Elder 50
Ruby, m. Samuel **WEST**, Jr., May 10, 1822, by David Dickinson 76
Sally, of Columbia, m. Flavel **CLARK**, of Herkimer, N. Y., Sept. 13, 1834, by David Dickinson (Written "Sally **BISS**") 55
Samuel, Jr., m. Betsey **DORRANCE**, Oct. 12, 1820, by David Dickinson 72
**BLIVEN**, Sam[ue]l, m. Louisa **BECKWITH**, Oct. [ ], 1826, by Sam[ue]l Little, J. P. 71
**BLY**, William A., of Springfield, Mass., m. Betsey P. **SNOW**, of Columbia, July 5, 1835, by David Dickinson 62
**BOLLES**, Abigail, of Columbia, m. Horatio **LIESTER**, of Coventry, Apr. 10, 1839, by Sylvester Selden, Hebron 44
Almira, of Columbia, m. Isaac N. **SILL**, of Andover, May 5, 1846, by Rev. James W. Woodward 18
Clarriss, of Columbia, m. Allen B. **SMITH**, of Montville, June 27, 1837, by Sylvester Selden, Hebron 51
Mary, of Columbia, m. Calvin **ROBINSON**, of Windham, Jan. 8, 1839, by Sylvester Selden 46
**BON[N]ER(?)**, Mary Ann, m. Emory **LIVERMORE**, b. of Brimfield, Mass., Feb. 15, 1854, by Rev. Fred[erick] D. Avery, at the Parsonage

Page

**BON[N]ER**(?), (cont.)
in Columbia (Perhaps "**BOWEN**"?) 7
**BOYNTON**, Norman, of Coventry, m. Rachel **POTTER**, of Columbia, Oct. 7, 1844, by Rev. James W. Woodward 14
**BREWSTER**, Alvin, m. Lavina **NEWCOMB**, Nov. 29, 1820, by Amhurst Scoville, J. P. 73
**BRIDGMAN**, Letetia, m. Chester **LINCOLN**, b. of Columbia, Jan. 19, 1825, by Rev. Esek Brown, of Lebanon 81
**BROWN**, Almira, of Columbia, m. Bradford L. **COOK**, of Palmer, Mass., July 29, 1838, by Daniel Holbrook, J. P. 47
Chauncey E., m. Mary E. **DOWNER**, Apr. 2, 1851, by Rev. F. D. Avery 31
Elizabeth, m. Andrew B. **UTLEY**, of Pomfret, Mar. 31, 1850, by Rev. J. R. Arnold 28
Horace, m. Phebe A. **CHAPMAN**, b. of Columbia, Feb. 25, 1838, by Daniel Holbrook, J. P. 47
Lydia, m. Ephraim **MINOR**, Apr. 28, 1822, by David Dickinson 76
Mary, of Columbia, m. Chester F. **WINSLEY**, of Hebron, June 20, 1834, by David Dickinson 55
Percy, m. Abel **FRANKLIN**, b. of Columbia, Sept. 23, 1833, by David Dickinson. Int. pub. 58
Robert, m. Harty M. **POTTER**, b. of Columbia, Oct. 7, 1844, by Rev. James W. Woodward 14
Sally M., m. Carlos **COLLINS**, Oct. 28, 1849, by Rev. Henry Bromley 27
**BUCKINGHAM**, Martha, m. Simon **LOOMIS**, Nov. [ ], 1777, by Joseph Huntington, D. D., at Lebanon 70
Samuel, m. Thankful **BABCOCK**, b. of Columbia, Dec. 30, 1821, by David Dickinson 75
**BURCHARD**, Anna, of Norwich, m. Cary **CLARK**, of Columbia, Jan. 6, 1825, by David Dickinson 81
**BUTTON**, Lydia, m. Oliver **FOX**, b. of Columbia, Sept. 11, 1842, by Rev. James W. Woodword 38
**BYRNE**, Samuel G., of Windham, m. Nancy A. **LITTLE**, of Columbia, Apr. 29, 1844, by Rev. James W. Woodworth 11
**CARVER**, Adaline S., m. Augustus **THOMPSON**, b. of Columbia, Dec. 3, 1829, by Rev. Esek Brown, of Lebanon 86
Matilda Ann, d. [Willia]m & Cynthia, b. Jan. 21, 1811 2
Matilda Ann, of Columbia, m. William A. **MEAD**, of S. Coventry, Oct. 23, 1837, by [Rev.] Alpha Miller 49
**CASWELL**, Eunice, of Columbia, m. George **YOUNG**, of Windham, Dec. 9, 1824, by Rev. Esek Brown, of Lebanon 80
**CHAMBERLAIN**, Joel, m. Lovina **NEWCOMB**, Jan. 20, 1780, by Rev. Thomas Brockway 67
Rufus, of Mansfield, m. Amanda M. **THOMAS**, of Columbia, Dec. 21, 1841, by C. Kittredge 42
**CHAMPLAIN**, Christopher G., of Columbia, m. Hannah S. **HYDE**, of Lebanon, Oct. 22, 1843, by Rev. Ebenezer Robinson 12
**CHAPIN**, Frances E., of Springfield, Mass., m. Henry B. **GATES**, of Willimantic, Nov. 24, 1853, by Rev. Fred[eric]k D. Avery,

Page

**CHAPIN**, (cont.)
at the house of Mrs. Tabitha Collins, in Columbia 6
**CHAPMAN**, Daniel, of Tolland, m. Phebe D. **ABBOTT**, of Columbia, Nov. 28, 1833, by David Dickinson 54
Phebe A., m. Horace **BROWN**, b. of Columbia, Feb. 25, 1838, by Daniel Holbrook, J. P. 47
Sally S., m. Seth **COLLINS**, Nov. 25, 1792, by Thomas Brockway. Witnesses; Charles Woodword, Joshua Woodword. Recorded Nov. 2, 1806 62
**CHEESBRO**, Reuben M., m. Laura A. **PIERCE**, Nov. 14, 1847, by Rev. F. P. Coe 22
**CHESTER**, Sumner R., of Chaplin, m. Lucy L. **INGRAHAM**, of Columbia, May 23, [1841], b. Rev. James W. Woodword, at the house of Mr. Bill 40
**CLARK**, Alinda, d. of Chester, m. Nelson F. **DANIELS**, of Barre, N. Y., Oct. 13, 1845, by Rev. James W. Woodward 17
Belden, m. Harriet **KINGSLEY**, b. of Lebanon, Apr. 7, 1831, by David Dickinson 56
Betsey, m. Thaddeus **HUNT**, b. of Columbia, Dec. 12, 1820, by David Dickinson 74
Cary, of Columbia, m. Anna **BURCHARD**, of Norwich, Jan. 6, 1825, by David Dickinson 81
Charles H., of Columbia, m. Caroline O. **PALMER**, of Willimantic, Oct. 17, 1852, by Rev. Fred[eric]k D. Avery 32
Ellen Strong, b. May 7, 1807 2
Fanny Charlotte, of Columbia, m. Sam[ue]l Edson **LYMAN**, of Barre, N. Y. Oct. 20, 1841, by Cha[rle]s Kittredge 39
Flavel, m. Rhoda **HARTSHORN**, Nov. 15, 1787, by Asahel Clark, J. P. [Witnesses:] Bela Wood and Asa Kingsley. Recorded Nov. 7, 1806 64
Flavel, of Herkimer, N. Y., m. Sally **BISS***, of Columbia, Sept. 13, 1834, by David Dickinson (***BLISS?**) 55
Gideon, m. Jemima **NEWCOMB**, Apr. 10, 1788 68
Henry C., m. Paulina **MANLEY**, b. of Columbia, Oct. 14, 1847, by Rev. James W. Woodword 21
Hetty Ann, m. James B. **JOHNSON**, b. of Columbia, Nov. 28, 1844, by Rev. James W. Woodword 16
Jane Rebeckah, b. May 4, 1807 2
Lyman C., m. Cynthia **YEOMENS**, b. of Columbia, Nov. 1, 1838, by Rev. Philo Judson, of Willimantic 45
Mary A., m. Shubael P. **ISHAM**, b. of Columbia, Sept. 8, 1852, by Rev. Fred[eric]k D. Avery 32
Mary E., m. Justin **HOLBROOK**, b. of Columbia, May 9, 1849, by Rev. James W. Woodword 25
Nancy Hooker, b. July 31, 1805 2
Nathan, m. Meriam **ALLEN**, Mar. 7, 1782 67
**COGGESHALL**, Julia A., of Columbia, m. George C. **RIXFORD**, of Mansfield, Sept. 4, 1849, by Rev. James W. Woodword 26

Page

COLE, Isabell, m. Eleazer C. **WOODWORD**, Sept. 24, 1794, by Thomas Brockway. Witnesses; Eleazer Woodword, Mary Woodword 63

**COLLINS**, Albert G., m. Mary **WOODWORTH**, b. of Columbia, Nov. 29, 1827, by David Dickinson 59

Ambrose, father of Geo[rge] W., d. July 11, 1840 34

Azel D., m. Pamelia **WOODWORTH**, May 6, 1828, by Silas Fuller, J. P. 59

Carlos, m. Sally M. **BROWN**, of Columbia, Oct. 28, 1849, by Rev. Henry Bromley 27

Esther Ann, [d. Rufus], b. Dec. 11, 1831 2

Esther Ann, [d. Rufus], d. June 3, 1832 2

Mary Adelaide, d. Geo[rge], W. & Mary Ann, b. Aug. 7, 1840 34

Mary W., of Columbia, m. Dan **SPRAGUE**, of Covington, N. Y., May 15, 1834, by David Dickinson 55

Nancy A., m. Warren A. **FULLER**, b. of Columbia, May 16, 1826, by David Dickinson 84

Nancy A., Mrs., of Columbia, m. Dr. Asa W. **FULLER**, of Warwick, R. I., June 30, 1839, by Rev. Chauncey Booth, of Coventry 45

Nancy Adeline, [d. Rufus], b. Dec. 20, 1835 2

Olive M., m. John J. **PERRY**, b. of Columbia, June 7, 1854, by Rev. Fred[eric]k D. Avery 5

Olivia Maria, [d. Rufus], b. Oct. 26, 1833 2

Samuel Ambrose, s. Geo[rge] W., b. Nov. 2, 1841 35

Seth, m. Sally S. **CHAPMAN**, Nov. 25, 1792, by Thomas Brockway. Witnesses: Charles Woodword, Joshua Woodword. Recorded Nov. 2, 1806 62

**COOK**, Bradford L., of Palmer, Mass., m. Almira **BROWN**, of Columbia, July 29, 1838, by Daniel Holbrook, J. P. 47

Henry C., of Portland, m. Abigail J. **ROOT**, of Columbia, Oct. 31, 1847, by Rev. Henry Baylies, of Hebron, at the bride's residence. Int. pub. 21

Maryanna M., of Columbia, m. Norton B. **LOOMIS**, of Lebanon, Nov. 18, 1845, by Rev. Fredirick P. Coe 18

**COTTRELL**, Betsey, m. Gordon J. **WILLIAMS**, b. of Columbia, Feb. 19, 1821, by David Dickinson 74

**COVELL**, Eliza Ann M., m. Frederick A. **WHEELER**, Jan. 7, 1844, by Rev. James W. Woodworth. Int. pub. 9

**CURTIS**, Sarah, m. Solomon **CUSHMAN**, May 26, 1768, by Eleazer Wheelock 67

**CUSHMAN**, Solomon, m. Sarah **CURTIS**, May 26, 1768, by Eleazer Wheelock 67

**DANIELS**, Nelson F., of Barre, N. Y., m. Alinda **CLARK**, d. of Chester, Oct. 13, 1845, by Rev. James W. Woodward 17

**DAVIDSON**, William, of Hartwick, N. Y., m. Mary **TICKNOR**, of Columbia, Sept. 8, 1831, by David Dickinson. Int. pub. 89

**DEWEY**, Asahel, m. Sophia **LOOMIS**, Sept. 24, 1840, by Rev. Alpha Miller 42

Elmore G., m. Elizabeth C. **LYMAN**, Sept. 25, 1834, by David Dickinson 52

Page

**DEWEY**, (cont.)
Harriet R., m. William A. **YEOMANS**, Aug. 19, 1839, by Charles Kittredge 91
Helen A., of Columbia, m. Levi E. **SMITH**, of Hartford, [Oct.] 15, [1854], by Rev. Fred[eric]k D. Avery 5
Lydia A., m. Samuel E. **LYMAN**, Sept. 24, 1837, by Rev. Philo Judson, of Willimantic 49
Mary L., of Columbia, m. Alanson H. **FULLER**, of Lebanon, Sept. 25, 1844, by Rev. James W. Woodword 13
**DICKINSON**, Lilliee, m. Freeman **SMITH**, Sept. 22, 1824, by David Dickinson 79
Louisa, m. Earl **LOOMIS**, b. of Columbia, Sept. 22, 1824, by David Dickinson 80
**DIXON**, David, of Manchester, m. Ann **BABCOCK**, of Lebanon, Oct. 26, 1846, by Rev. Ebenezer Robinson 20
**DORRANCE**, Betsey, m. Samuel **BLISS**, Jr., Oct. 12, 1820, by David Dickinson 72
**DOUBLEDAY**, Amos G., of Columbia, m. Elizabeth L. **SNOW**, of Lebanon, Oct. 8, 1837, by Dexter Bullard, Minister 48
**DOWNER**, Amanda M., of Columbia, m. John **TICKNOR**, of Brimfield, Apr. 9, 1829, by David Dickinson 56
Eliza Ann, m. Benjamin **HARTSON**, b. of Columbia, Jan. 19, 1825, by David Dickinson 81
Maria, m. George **WRIGHT**, b. of Columbia, May 12, 1824, by David Dickinson 79
Mary E., m. Chauncey E. **BROWN**, Apr. 2, 1851, by Rev. F. D. Avery 31
William, m. Marianne **LITTLE**, Apr. 2, 1839, by Cha[rle]s Kettridge 44
**DURGIN**, Joseph H., of Willimantic, m. Lydia **FORD**, of Columbia, Feb. 3, 1850, by Rev. James W. Woodword 28
**DYER, DYRE**, Edwin, of Spring Prairie, Wis., m. Cynthia **LITTLE**, of Columbia, "last evening", [Oct. 29, 1848], by Rev. James W. Woodword 24
George W., of Willimantic, m. Martha E. **WEBBER**, of Columbia, Oct. 9, 1842, by Rev. James W. Woodword 35
**EDDY**, Benjamin J., of Providence, R. I., m. Harriet **HOLOWAY**, of Taunton, Mass., Sept. 6, 1849, by John S. Yeomans, J. P. 26
**EDWARDS**, Betsey, m. Aaron **ROGERS**, b. of Norwich, Oct. 1, 1821, by David Dickinson 75
**FOOT**, Hiram S., m. Emily **MACK**, b. of Columbia, Nov. 8, 1829, by David Dickinson 86
**FORD**, Ardelia, m. Daniel A. **PIERCE**, b. of Columbia, Jan. 13, 1842, by Rev. Ebenezer Robinson 12
Lydia, of Columbia, m. Joseph H. **DURGIN**, of Willimantic, Feb. 3, 1850, by Rev. James W. Woodword 28
Salena, m. James M. **BEEBE**, Mar. 18, 1851, by H. G. Willard, Willimantic 31
**FOX**, Oliver, m. Lydia **BUTTON**, b. of Columbia, Sept. 11, 1842, by Rev. James W. Woodword 38

Page

**FRANKLIN**, Abel, m. Percy **BROWN**, b. of Columbia, Sept. 23, 1833, by David Dickinson. Int. Pub. 58

Levina, m. Henry H. **MAYNARD**, b. of Columbia, June 7, 1840, by Sylvester Selden, Hebron 41

Lucinda, of Columbia, m. James H. **TOWNSEND**, of Falls Township, O., Oct. 17, 1844, by Rev. Edgar J. Doolittle 14

**FRISBIE**, Sarah A., of Columbia, m. Samuel L. **GRAY**, of New London, Aug. 26, 1838, by Alphus Kingsley, J. P. 48

**FULLER**, Alanson H., of Lebanon, m. Mary L. **DEWEY**, of Columbia, Sept. 25, 1844, by Rev. James W. Woodword 13

Ambrose, of Columbia, m. Ruth **ANDREWS**, of Hebron, May 7, 1825, by David Dickinson 82

Asa W., Dr., of Warwick, R. I., m. Mrs. Nancy A. **COLLINS**, of Columbia, June 30, 1839, by Rev. Chauncey Booth, of Coventry 45

Elizabeth H., of Lebanon, m. Oliver D. **GRAVES**, of Hebron, June 19, 1843, by Rev. James W. Woodworth 7

Esther, m. John **PORTER**, June 19, 1805, by Rev. Nehemiah Dodge 69

Ferdinand, of Lebanon, m. Martha E. **HUTCHINSON**, of Columbia, Mar. 29, 1843, by James W. Woodword 36-7

Jonathan C., m. Nancy A. **HOLBROOK**, b. of Columbia, Nov. 28, 1833, by David Dickinson 54

Nancy C., of Columbia, m. Samuel J. **WATKINZ**, of Peru, Mass., Oct. 30, 1842, by Rev. Israel D. Otis 36

Nancy J., of Lebanon, m. Charles A. Goodrich, of Portland, Jan. 1, 1850, by Rev. James W. Woodword 27

Ruby, wid., of Columbia, m. Thomas **BARKER**, of Hinsdale, Mass., Aug. 28, 1837, by Alpheas Kingsley, J. P. 51

Samuel B., m. Lamira **LITTLE**, b. of Columbia, July 13, 1837, by Sylvester Selden, Hebron 51

Warren A., m. Nancy A. **COLLINS**, b. of Columbia, May 16, 1826, by David Dickinson 84

**GAREY**, Polly, m. Amos **PORTER**, Jan. 24, 1815, by Rev. Thomas Rich 84

**GATES**, E. H., of Vernon, m. Lucinda **WHEELER**, of Columbia, Dec. 4, 1848, by Rev. James W. Woodword, at the house of the bride's father 24

Henry B., of Willimantic, m. Frances E. **CHAPIN**, of Springfield, Mass., Nov. 24, 1853, by Rev. Fred[eric]k D. Avery, at the house of Mrs. Tabitha Collins, Columbia 6

**GAY**, George, of Lebanon, m. Abbey M. **PORTER**, of Columbia, Sept. 17, 1833, by David Dickinson 54

**GODFREY**, William H., of Coventry, m. Sally **LINCOLN**, of Columbia, Aug. 29, 1829, by Rev. Josiah R. Clark 85

**GOODRICH**, Charles A., of Portland, m. Nancy J. **FULLER**, of Lebanon, Jan. 1, 1850, by Rev. James W. Woodword 27

Mary, m. David L. **ROGERS**, b. of Wethersfield, Aug. 5, 1838, by Asahel Clark, J. P. 46

**GOODWIN**, James B., of Burlington, Ia., m. Maria **HOLBROOK**, of Columbia, Apr. 19, 1848, by Rev. James W. Woodword, at the

Page

**GOODWIN**, (cont.)
house of Dia Holbrock 22

**GOULD**, Silas, m. Harmony **JONES**, Apr. 27, 1835, by Alpheas Kingsley, J. P. 53

**GRAVES**, Oliver D., of Hebron, m. Elizabeth H. **FULLER**, of Lebanon, June 19, 1843, by Rev. James W. Woodworth 7

**GRAY**, Samuel L., of New London, m. Sarah A. **FRISBIE**, of Columbia, Aug. 26, 1838, by Alphus Kingsley, J. P. 48

**GRIFFING**, Mary, m. Asahel **HUNT**, Aug. 30, 1841, by Alpheas Kingsley, J. P. 41

**HALL**, Dimmis, of Columbia, m. Henry **HINKLEY**, of Hebron, Dec. 21, 1820, by David Dickinson 74

Fanny M., of Columbia, m. James **PILKINGTON**, of Manchester, Apr. 8, 1830, by D. Dickinson 87

Mary M., of Columbia, m. James **PILKINGTON**, of Manchester, Apr. 15, 1832, by David Dickinson. Int. pub. 58

Russell, m. [E]unice **SQUEIRS**, Mar. 14, 1830, by Siles Fuller, J. P. 87

**HANLEY**, Susan A., of Columbia, m. Willard B. **LOOMIS**, of Andover Soc. Oct. 5, 1834, by David Dickinson 52

**HARTSHORN, HARTSON**, Benjamin, m. Eliza Ann **DOWNER**, b. of Columbia, Jan. 19, 1825, by David Dickinson 81

Hezekiah, m. Mary **WOOD**, Nov. 26, 1788 68

Lucy W., of Columbia, m. Eliphalet **WELCH**, of County Oswego, N. Y., Nov. 9, 1828, by Rev. Esek Brown, of Lebanon 61

Lurana, m. Asa **KINGSBURY**, Jan. 30, 1783, by Thomas Brockway. Witnesses: Bela Wood, Rhoda Clark 66

Polly, m. Asahel **NEWCOMB**, b. of Columbia, Mar. [ ], 1823, by David Dickinson 73

Rhoda, m. Flavel **CLARK**, Nov. 15, 1787, by Asahel Clark, J. P. [Witnesses], Bela Wood, Asa Kingsley. Recorded Nov. 7, 1806 64

Roxellana, m. Bela **WOOD**, Feb. 19, 1786, by Rev. Thomas Brockway. [Witnesses], Asa Kingsbury, Rhoda Clark. Recorded Nov. 10, 1806 64

**HAYWARD**, Elisha H., of Buffaloe, N. Y., m. Fanny L. **SCOVILLE**, of Columbia, Oct. 11, 1827, by Rev. Esek Brown, of Lebanon 59

**HAZARD**, Elizabeth D., of Columbia, m. John M. **SMITH**, of Andover, Apr. 13, 1843, by John M. Hunt 36

**HERRIN**, Robert O., m. Nancy **McLEEN**, Dec. 17, 1826, by David Dickinson 72

**HILLS, HILL**, Emma, of Columbia, m. Russell **WILCOX**, of Lebanon, May 11, 1836, by Levi Meech, Elder 63

Hannah C., of Columbia, m. Chester A. **BLISS**, of Albany, N. Y., Aug. 21, 1843, by Rev. Ebenezer Robinson 12

Mary M., of Columbia, m. Elias **BLISS**, of Hudson, N. Y., Dec. 4, 1837, by Levi Meech, Elder 50

**HINKLEY**, Henry, of Hebron, m. Dimmis **HALL**, of Columbia, Dec. 21, 1820, by David Dickinson 74

**HITCHCOCK**, Samuel, m. Mary A. **HUNT**, Nov. 15, 1850, by Rev. Fred[eric]k D. Avery, at the Cong. Meeting House 29

Page

**HOLBROOK**, Abby Jane, [d. Dan[ie]l & E[mily], b. Sept. 21, 1830; d. July 1, 1831 4
Caroline, [d. Dan[ie]l & E[mily], b. Jan. 9, 1827; d. July 1, 1842 4
Charlotte L., of Columbia, m. Benjamin F. **STRONG**, of Mass., Jan. 2, 1844, by Rev. James W. Woodworth 9
Daniel, m. Emily **KINNE**, Feb. 22, 1814 4
Daniel, m. Nancy **WILLIAMS**, b. of Columbia, Nov. 1, 1843, by Rev. James Woodworth 8
Emily, [d. Dan[ie]l & E[mily], b. Sept. 15, 1817; m. Geo[rge] O. **LITTLE**, Oct. 27, 1841 4
Emily, w. Daniel, d. Jan. 13, 1841 4
Emily, m. George O. **LITTLE**, Oct. 27, 1841, by James W. Woodword. Int. pub. 39
Justin, m. Mary E. **CLARK**, b. of Columbia, May 9, 1849, by Rev. James W. Woodword 25
Maria, of Columbia, m. James B. **GOODWIN**, of Burlington, Ia., Apr. 19, 1848, by Rev. James W. Woodword, at the house of Dia Holbrock 22
Mary A., m. Septimus **LOOMIS**, b. of Columbia, Mar. 18, 1844, by Rev. James W. Woodworth. Int. pub. 10
Maryanne Almantha, [d. Dan[ie]l & E[mily], b. July 5, 1834 4
Melvina A., of Columbia, m. Hiram B. **WARE**, of Hartford, Apr. 5, 1840, by Cha[rle]s Kittredge 43
Nancy A., m. Jonathan C. **FULLER**, b. of Columbia, Nov. 28, 1833, by David Dickinson 54
Nancy Aurelia, [d. Dan[ie]l & E[mily], b. May 22, 1820; d. Oct. 2, 1842 4
Nathan H., of Columbia, m. Jane **PORTER**, July 4, 1836, by Rev. David Dickinson 90
Nathan K., s. Dan[ie]l & E[mily], b. Sept. 29, 1815; m. Jane R. **PORTER**, July 4, 1836 4
Nathan K., ae 20 y. 7 m. 5 d. m. Jane R. **PORTER**, July 4, 1836 4
Olivia, [d. Dan[ie]l & E[mily], b. Apr. 6, 1824 4
Sarah E., m. Henry W. **ABEL**, b. of Columbia, Nov. 28, 1833, by David Dickinson 54
Silas A., m. Elizabeth P. **WRIGHT**, b. of Columbia, Apr. 10, 1850, by Rev. John Avery, of Exeter 28

**[HOLLISTER], HOLISTER**, Lavina, of Columbia, m. Horace **ALLEN**, of East Haddam, Mar. 1, 1829, by David Dickinson 61

**[HOLLOWAY], HOLOWAY**, Harriet, of Taunton, Mass., m. Benjamin J. **EDDY**, of Providence, R. I., Sept. 6, 1849, by John S. Yeomens, J. P. 26

**HOUSE**, Benjamin, of Coventry, m. Submit **WEST**, of Columbia, June 29, 1826, by Joel West, of Chatham 84
Harriet, m. Asahel **WOODWORD**, Mar. 24, 1806, by Royal Taylor. Witnesses: Eleazer C. Woodword, Charles Woodword 65
Lovina, m. William **WILLSON**, Oct. 22, 1777 68

**HULL**, James, of South Kingstown, R. I., m. Mary **POTTER**, of Columbia, Mar. 25, 1821, by David Dickinson 78

Page

**HUNT**, Anson, m. Betsey **RICHARDSON**, b. of Columbia, May 29, 1839, by Charles Kittridge 44
Anson, m. Betsey A. **MANLEY**, b. of Columbia, [ 1846?], by Rev. James W. Woodward 19
Asahel, m. Mary **GRIFFING**, Aug. 30, 1841, by Alpheas Kingsley, J. P. 41
Daniel, Rev., of Pomfret, m. Mary **PORTER**, of Columbia, May 29, 1839, by Charles Kittridge 44
Eliza Jane, m. Edward **NYE**, Sept. 29, 1850, by Rev. Fred[eric]k D. Avery, at the house of Asa Hunt 30
Emily A., m. Solomon N. **ABELL**, Nov. 28, 1839, by C. Kittredge 43
Mary A., m. Samuel **HITCHCOCK**, Nov. 15, 1850, by Rev. Fred[eric]k D. Avery, at the Cong. Meeting House 29
Thaddeus, m. Betsey **CLARK**, b. of Columbia, Dec. 12, 1820, by David Dickinson 74
**HURLBURT**, George R., m. Cina O. **PERKINS**, b. of Andover, May 3, 1847, by Rev. James W. Woodword 20
**HUTCHINSON**, David E., of Hebron, m. Laura L. **LITTLE**, of Columbia, Sept. 13, 1848, by Rev. James W. Woodword 23
Elisha, of Bolton, m. Hannah **WOODWORD**, of Columbia, Jan. "about the 15th", 1823, by David Dickinson 78
Martha E., of Columbia, m. Ferdinand **FULLER**, of Lebanon, Mar. 29, 1843, by James E. Woodword 36-7
**HYDE**, Hannah S., of Lebanon, m. Christopher G. **CHAMPLAIN**, of Columbia, Oct. 22, 1843, by Rev. Ebenezer Robinson 12
**INGRAHAM**, Lucy L, of Columbia, m. Sumner R. **CHESTER**, of Chaplin, May 23, [1841], by Rev. James W. Woodword, at the house of Mr. Bill 40
**ISHAM**, Girdon, of Tolland, m. Abigail **STRONG**, of Columbia, Dec. 18, 1823, by David Dickinson 77
Shubael P., m. Mary A. **CLARK**, b. of Columbia, Sept. 8, 1852, by Rev. Fred[eric]k D. Avery 32
**JACKSON**, Horace W., of Norwich, m. Levina **WRIGHT**, of Columbia, Nov. 28, 1844, by Rev. James W. Woodward 15
**JOHNSON**, James B., m. Hetty Ann **CLARK**, b. of Columbia, Nov. 28, 1844, by Rev. James W. Woodword 16
**JONES**, Alfred, of Hebron, m. Polly **KINGSLEY**, Apr. 25, 1829, by Henry Brown 56
Harmony, m. Silas **GOULD**, Apr. 27, 1835, by Alpheas Kingsley, J. P. 53
Polly, m. Charles **WOODWORD**, June 24, 1800, by Thomas Brockway. Witnesses; Asahel Woodword, Eleazer C. Woodword 65
**JUD[D]**, Elias, of Coventry, m. Jerusha **THOMPSON**, of Columbia, May 22, 1831, by Amhurst Scoville, J. P. 57
**KINGSBURY**, Asa, m. Lurana **HARTSHORN**, Jan. 30, 1783, by Thomas Brockway. Witnesses; Bela Wood, Rhoda Clark 66
Asa, Jr., [s. Asa & Lurana], b. Jan. 10, 1794 66
Charles, [s. Asa & Lurana], b. Sept. 22, 1802 67
Clara, [d. Asa & Lurana], b. Dec. 2, 1783; d. Mar. 10, 1790 66
Eleazer, [s. Asa & Lurana], b. June 27, 1801; d. June 30, 1801 66

Page

**KINGSBURY**, (cont.)
Flavel, [s. Asa & Lurana], b. Mar. 31, 1791 66
Hezekiah, [s. Asa & Lurana], b. June 2, 1788 66
Hezekiah, of Hebron, m. Delia **RICHARDSON**, of Columbia, Oct. 26, 1824, by Rev. Augustus B. Collins, of Andover 79
John, [s. Asa & Lurana], b. May 11, 1799 66
John, of Coventry, m. Mrs. Edith **TICKNOR**, of Columbia, Jan. 26, 1826, by David Dickinson 83
Joseph, [s. Asa & Lurana], b. May 8, 1785 66
Lurana, [d. Asa & Lurana], b. Oct. 30, 1796 66
W[illia]m, [s. Asa & Lurana], b. Aug. 19, 1804 67

**KINGSLEY**, Darius, m. Elizabeth **SCOVILLE**, b. of Columbia, Jan. 29, 1824, by David Dickinson 78
Elizabeth A., b. Sept. 17, 1822 3
Harriet, m. Belden **CLARK**, b. of Lebanon, Apr. 7, 1831, by David Dickinson 56
James Monroe, of Lebanon, m. Lucinda D. **KINGSLEY**, of Columbia, Oct. 12, 1845, by Rev. James W. Woodward, at the house of the bride's father. Int. pub. 17
Lucinda D., of Columbia, m. James Monroe **KINGSLEY**, of Lebanon, Oct. 12, 1845, by Rev. James W. Woodward, at the house of the bride's father. Int. pub. 17
Mary P., b. Mar. 22, 1829 3
Naomi, of Columbia, m. Joseph **YOUNG**, of Lebanon, May 14, 1828, by Rev. Esek Brown, of Lebanon 60
Polly, m. Alfred **JONES**, of Hebron, Apr. 25, 1829, by Henry Brown 56
Shubael W., m. Mary **LOOMIS**, b. of Columbia, May 8, 1831, by David Dickinson. Int. pub. 57
William A., b. Dec. 31, 1824 3

**KINNE**, Emily, m. Daniel **HOLBROOK**, Feb. 22, 1814 4

**KIRKLIN**, Thomas, of Springfield, Mass., m. Polly **MANLEY**, of Columbia, Jan. 17, 1822, by David Dickinson 75

**LESTER**, [see under **LIESTER**]

**LEWIS**, Martha, of Columbia, m. John R. **PROUD**, of Lisbon, Jan. 28, 1838, by Rev. Philo Judson, of Willimantic 91

**LIESTER**, Horatio, of Coventry, m. Abigail **BOLLES**, of Columbia, Apr. 10, 1839, by Sylvester Selden, Hebron 44

**LINCOLN**, Chester, m. Letetia **BRIDGMAN**, b. of Columbia, Jan. 19, 1825, by Rev. Esek Brown, of Lebanon 81
Gilbert, of Columbia, m. Betsey S. **WHEELER**, of Coventry, Dec. 6, 1846, by Rev. James W. Woodward 19
Phelina A., of Columbia, m. George A. **POLK**, of Stafford, Nov. 25, 1841, by James W. Woodword 39
Sally, of Columbia, m. William H. **GODFREY**, of Coventry, Aug. 29, 1829, by Rev. Josiah R. Clark 85
Violatia, m. Joseph P. **LOOMER**, Nov. 10, 1823, by David Dickinson 77

**LITTLE**, Agnes P., m. Abraham A. **PORTER**, b. of Columbia, Mar. 4, 1844, by Rev. Alpha Miller, of Andover 11

| | Page |
|---|---|
| **LITTLE**, (cont.) | |
| Alanson, of Columbia, m. Lavinia **YEOMANS**, of Middletown, Jan. 1, 1845, by Rev. James W. Woodword | 16 |
| Amanda C., m. Giles **LITTLE**, b. of Columbia, Nov. 21, 1850, by Rev. N. S. Hunt, of Preston | 29 |
| Anson, b. June 20, 1806 | 30 |
| Charles, b. Sept. 26, 1818 | 30 |
| Charles D., of Saginaw, Mich., m. Cynthia P. **WEBSTER**, of Columbia, Nov. 29, 1853, by Rev. Fred[eric]k D. Avery, at the Parsonage | 6 |
| Cynthia, of Columbia, m. Edwin **DYRE**, of Spring Prairie, Wis., "last evening" [Oct. 29, 1848], by Rev. James W. Woodword | 24 |
| David D., m. Maria J. **LOOMIS**, b. of Columbia, Apr. 26, 1853, by Rev. Fred[eric]k D. Avery | 33 |
| Edwin H., m. Elizabeth **WEST**, b. of Columbia, Apr. 24, 1844, by Rev. James W. Woodworth | 11 |
| Eliza D., of Columbia, Conn., m. Gideon A. **ALDEN**, of Enfield, Conn., Feb. 20, 1842, by Francis L. Robinson, of Enfield, Conn. | 37 |
| Emily, b. Apr. 27, 1809 | 30 |
| Emily, d. Sam[ue]l & Jerusha, b. June 14, 1830 | 32 |
| Geo[rge] O., m. Emily **HOLBROOK**, Oct. 27, 1841 | 4 |
| George O., m. Emily **HOLBROOK**, of Columbia, Oct. 27, 1841, by James W. Woodword. Int. pub. | 39 |
| Giles, m. Amanda C. **LITTLE**, b. of Columbia, Nov. 21, 1850, by Rev. N. S. Hunt, of Preston | 29 |
| Henry B., m. Cynthia A. **YEOMANS**, b. of Columbia, June 1, 1848, by Rev. James W. Woodword | 23 |
| Lamira, m. Samuel B. **FULLER**, b. of Columbia, July 13, 1837, by Sylvester Selden, Hebron | 51 |
| Laura L., of Columbia, m. David E. **HUTCHINSON**, of Hebron, Sept 13, 1848, by Rev. James W. Woodword | 23 |
| Levi, m. Matilda **WRIGHT**, b. of Columbia, Feb. 5, 1826, by David Dickinson | 83 |
| Levina, b. May 11, 1802 | 30 |
| Levina, d. Samuel & Levina, d. May 24, 1807 | 32 |
| Levina, w. Samuel, d. June 16, 1807 | 32 |
| Marianne, m. William **DOWNER**, Apr. 2, 1839, by Cha[rle]s Kittredge | 44 |
| Nancy A., of Columbia, m. Samuel G. **BYRNE**, of Windham, Apr. 29, 1844, by Rev. James W. Woodworth | 11 |
| Sally, m. Amhurst **SCOVILLE**, Oct. 9, 1798. Witnesses: Consider Little, Rebeckah Little | 67 |
| Samuel, Jr., b. Mar. 6, 1804 | 30 |
| Samuel, Jr., m. Amey **PINNEO**, b. of Columbia, Dec. 17, 1829, by David Dickinson | 86 |
| Samuel, Jr., m. Clarissa **PINNEO**, May 3, 1840, by Cha[rle]s Kittredge | 41 |
| Saxton Bailey, b. Apr. 19, 1813 | 30 |
| Sexton B., m. Sarah M. **TRACY**, b. of Columbia, Aug. 21, 1836, by Rev. Jesse Fisher, of Windham | 90 |
| Silas F., s. Joseph P. & Violota, b. Sept. 19, 1824 | 34 |

Page

**LITTLE**, (cont.)
William Buckingham, b. June 6, 1815 30
William G., m. Pamelia S. **WOODWORD**, b. of Columbia, May 4, 1842, by James W. Woodword 37

**LIVERMORE**, Emory, m. Mary Ann **BON[N]ER**(?)*, b. of Brimfield, Mass., Feb. 15, 1854, by Rev. Fred[eric]k D. Avery, at the Parsonage, Columbia (***BOWEN** or **BOWER**?) 7

**LOOMER**, Joseph P., m. Violatia **LINCOLN**, Nov. 10, 1823, by David Dickinson 77
Septimus, m. Emily **POST**, b. of Columbia, Nov. 20, 1831, by Rev. Alpheas Gear, of Hebron 57

**LOOMIS**, Charlotte E., d. Septimus & Emily L., b. Oct. 1, 1832 1
Charlotte E., of Columbia, m. George **POMEROY**, of Coventry, Jan. 11, 1854, by Rev. Fred[eric]k D. Avery, at the house of Septimus Loomis 6
Charlotte W., wid. George, d. Feb. [ ], 1851 82
Earl, m. Louisa **DICKINSON**, b. of Columbia, Sept. 22, 1824, by David Dickinson 80
Maria J., m. David D. **LITTLE**, b. of Columbia, Apr. 26, 1853, by Rev. Fred[eric]k D. Avery 33
Martha L., d. Septimus & Emily L., b. Nov. 6, 1835 1
Mary, m. Shubael W. **KINGSLEY**, b. of Columbia, May 8, 1831, by David Dickinson. Int. pub. 57
Nelson B., of Lebanon, m. Harriet M. **POST**, of Columbia, Jan. 1, 1838, by Sylvester Selden, Hebron 46
Norton B., of Lebanon, m. Maryanna M. **COOK**, of Columbia, Nov. 18, 1845, by Rev. Fredirick P. Coe 18
Septimus, m. Mary A. **HOLBROOK**, b. of Columbia, Mar. 18, 1844, by Rev. James W. Woodworth. Int. pub. 10
Silas F., m. Pamelia M. **WHITE**, b. of Columbia, Nov. 4, 1846, by Rev. James W. Woodward 19
Simon, m. Martha **BUCKINGHAM**, Nov. [ ], 1777, by Joseph Huntington, D. D., at Lebanon 70
Sophia, m. Asahel **DEWEY**, Sept. 24, 1840, by Rev. Alpha Miller 42
Willard B., of Andover Soc., m. Susan A. **HANLEY**, of Columbia, Oct. 5, 1834, by David Dickinson 52

**LORD**, Elisha, of Hebron, m. C[h]loe **MANLEY**, of Columbia, Dec. 29, 1824, by David Dickinson 80

**LORING**, Nathani[e]l S., of Lebanon, m. Jane E. **NEWCOMB**, of Columbia, Feb. 28, 1841, by Rev. Ebenezer Robinson 40

**LYMAN**, Chester W., m. Cornelia E. **PORTER**, b. of Columbia, Nov. 13, 1831, by David Dickinson 89
Elizabeth C., m. Elmore G. **DEWEY**, Sept. 25, 1834, by David Dickinson 52
George W., of Columbia, m. Eunice M. **ROBERTSON**, of Coventry, Oct. 20, 1839, by Charles Kittredge 42
Samuel E., m. Lydia A. **DEWEY**, Sept. 24, 1837, by Rev. Philo Judson, of Williamantic 49

Page

LYMAN, (cont.)
Sam[ue]l Edson, of Barre, N. Y., m. Fanny Charlotte **CLARK**, of Columbia, Oct. 20, 1841, by Cha[rle]s Kittredge 39
Sophia C., m. John S. **YEOMANS**, b. of Columbia, Oct. 14, 1830, by David Dickinson 88

**MACK**, Emily, m. Hiram S. **FOOT**, b. of Columbia, Nov. 8, 1829, by David Dickinson 86

**MAIN**, Cynthia, of North Stonington, m. Alfred **TURNER**, of Groton, Oct. 1, 1829, by Asahel Clark, J. P. 56

**MAINARD**, [see under **MAYNARD**]

**MANLEY, MANLY**, Asa, m. Rosanna **TRACY**, b. of Columbia, Jan. 28, 1830, by David Dickinson 87
Betsey A., m. Anson **HUNT**, b. of Columbia, [ 1846], by Rev. James W. Woodward 19
C[h]loe, of Columbia, m. Elisha **LORD**, of Hebron, Dec. 29, 1824, by David Dickinson 80
Harriet A., of Columbia, m. Elizer F. **ROOT**, of Rockville, June 2, 1850, by Rev. John Avery, of Exeter 29
Jared S., of Columbia, m. Celinda S. **BARSTOW**, of Columbia, Dec. 21, 1841, by James W. Woodword 40
Paulina, m. Henry C. **CLARK**, b. of Columbia, Oct. 14, 1847, by Rev. James W. Woodword 24
Polly, of Columbia, m. Thomas **KIRKLIN**, of Springfield, Mass., Jan. 17, 1822, by David Dickinson 75

**MAYNARD, MAINARD**, Henry H., m. Levina **FRANKLIN**, b. of Columbia, June 7, 1840, by Sylvester Selden, Hebron 41
Martha, m. Reuben **WELLER***, Mar. 14, 1821, by Silas Fuller, J. P. (*Perhaps "**WELLES**"?) 74

**McLEEN**, Nancy, m. Robert O. **HERRIN**, Dec. 17, 1826, by David Dickinson (Perhaps "Robert **O'HERRIN**") 72

**MEAD**, Adelaide Gertrude, d. William A. & Matilda Ann, b. Mar. 4, 1838 3
William A., of S. Coventry, m. Matilda Ann **CARVER**, of Columbia, Oct. 23, 1837, by [Rev.] Alpha Miller 49

**MERCHANT**, Stephen G., of Sunderland, Mass., m. Mary A. **SPARROW**, of Tolland, Mar. 31, 1845, by Rev. Alpha Doolittle, of Andover 16

**MERRIFIELD**, Marcelia, m. Artemas **WOODWORD**, July 2, 1800, by Thomas Brockway. Witnesses, Asahel Loomis, Esther Loomis 70
Martha, m. Artemus **WOODWORD**, July 2, 1800 1

**METZZAR**, Andrew, of Greenville, Norwich, m. Emily Ann **WEBBER**, of Columbia, "last evening", [Oct. 14, 1844], b. Rev. James W. Woodward 15

**MINOR, MINER**, Ephraim, m. Lydia **BROWN**, Apr. 28, 1822, by David Dickinson 76
Hannah, w. Ephraim, d. Sept. 23, 1821, in her 33rd y. 3

**[MOREY]**, [see under **MORY**]

**MORGAN**, Sophia, m. Hubbard **BARSTOW**, b. of Columbia, June 8, 1842, by James W. Woodword 38

**MORTON**, Lucius, of Hartford, m. Nancy C. **RICHARDSON**, of Columbia,

Page

MORTON, (cont.)
May 31, 1848, by Rev. James W. Woodword 23
MORY, Lucinda, of Manchester, m. James **SNOW**, of Columbia, Nov. 5, 1848, by Ambrose Fuller 24
**NEWCOMB**, Asahel, m. Polly **HARTSHORN**, b. of Columbia, Mar. [ ], 1823, by David Dickinson 73
Jane E., of Columbia, m. Nathan[ie]l S. **LORING**, of Lebanon, Feb. 28, 1841, by Rev. Ebenezer Robinson 40
Jemima, m. Gideon **CLARK**, Apr. 10, 1788 68
Lovina, m. Joel **CHAMBERLAIN**, Jan. 20, 1780, by Rev. Thomas Brockway 67
Lavina, m. Alvin **BREWSTER**, Nov. 29, 1820, by Amhurst Scoville, J. P. 73
**NEWELL**, Emily A., of Columbia, m. George F. **BLACKMAN**, of Coventry, [Apr.] 10, 1837, by Rev. Alpha Miller 50
Gratia, m. Edward **YEOMANS**, Oct. 10, 1827, by Rev. Joseph Ireson 91
Lewis P., of Pomfret, m. Caroline **WEBBER**, of Columbia, May 7, 1825, by David Dickinson 82
**NOICE**, Mary J., of Ashford, m. Sam[ue]l Harlow **SNOW**, Dec. 20, 1834, by Daniel Holbrook, J. P. 62
**NYE**, Edward, m. Eliza Jane **HUNT**, Sept. 29, 1850, by Rev. Fred[eric]k D. Avery, at the house of Asa Hunt 30
**O'HERRIN***, Robert, m. Nancy **McLEEN**, Dec. 17, 1826, by David Dickinson (*Perhaps "Robert O. **HERRIN**") 72
**PALMER**, Caroline O., of Willimantic, m. Charles H. **CLARK**, of Columbia, Oct. 17, 1852, by Rev. Fred[eric]k D. Avery 32
Eliza A., Mrs., of East Haddam, m. John N. **ABEL**, of Columbia, [Feb] 4, [1849], by Rev. H. Merrell 25
**PARKER**, Ephraim, of Vernon, m. Abby Ann **WHEELER**, of Columbia, Aug. 31, 1828, by Rev. Chauncey Booth, of Coventry 60
**PENHALLOW**, Daniel, of Columbia, m. Ruth **SKINNER**, of Hebron, Apr. 1, 1823, by David Dickinson 77
**PERKINS**, Cina O., m. George R. **HURLBURT**, b. of Andover, May 3, 1847, by Rev. James W. Woodword 20
Leonard H., of Andover, m. Mary Ann **BLISH**, of Columbia, Sept. 22, 1850, by Rev. Roswell C. Lamb, at her father's residence 31
**PERRY**, John, s. James & Sally, b. June 1, 1824 3
John J., m. Olive M. **COLLINS**, b. of Columbia, June 7, 1854, by Rev. Fred[eric]k D. Avery 5
Susan, d. James & Sally, b. Aug. 18, 1827 3
**PIDGE**, Alma C., m. Hezekiah **THOMPSON**, b. of Windham, Sept. 3, 1843, by Rev. James W. Woodworth 8
**PIERCE**, Daniel A., m. Ardelia **FORD**, b. of Columbia, Jan. 13, 1842, by Rev. Ebenezer Robinson 12
Laura A., m. Reuben M. **CHEESBRO**, Nov. 14, 1847, by Rev. F. P. Coe 22
**PILKINGTON**, James, of Manchester, m. Fanny M. **HALL**, of Columbia, Apr. 8, 1830, by D. Dickinson 87
James, of Manchester, m. Mary M. **HALL**, of Columbia, Apr. 15, 1832,

Page

**PILKINGTON**, (cont.)
by David Dickinson. Int. pub. 58
**PINNEO, PENNEO**, Amey, m. Samuel **LITTLE**, Jr., b. of Columbia, Dec. 17, 1829, by David Dickinson 86
Clarrissa, m. Samuel **LITTLE**, Jr., May 3, 1840, by Cha[rle]s Kittredge 41
James, m. Lucina **BENNETT**, Dec. 23, 1832, by Rev. Charles Nichols 58
Joseph, m. Azuba **WRIGHT**, Jan. 17, 1787, by Rev. Thomas Brockway 69
**POLK**, George A., of Stafford, m. Phelina A. **LINCOLN**, of Columbia, Nov. 25, 1841, by James W. Woodword 39
**POMEROY**, George, of Coventry, m. Charlotte E. **LOOMIS**, of Columbia, Jan. 11, 1854, by Rev. Fred[eric]k D. Avery, at the house of Septimus Loomis 6
**PORTER**, Abbey M., of Columbia, m. George **GAY**, of Lebanon, Sept. 17, 1833, by David Dickinson 54
Abraham A., m. Agnes P. **LITTLE**, b. of Columbia, Mar. 4, 1844, by Rev. Alpha Miller, of Andover 11
Amos, m. Polly **GAREY**, Jan. 24, 1815, by Rev. Thomas Rich 84
Caroline R., of Columbia, m. Andrew H. **ROCKWELL**, of Lebanon, Sept. 28, 1837, by Sylvester Selden 52
Charlotte, of Columbia, m. Samuel F. **WEST**, of Deleware, O., Sept. 28, 1837, by Sylvester Selden 52
Corintha N., of Columbia, m. Lewis H. **TAYLOR**, of Chatham, Apr. 1, 1835, by David Dickinson. Int. Pub. 53
Cornelia E., m. Chester W. **LYMAN**, b. of Columbia, Nov. 13, 1831, by David Dickinson 89
Jane, m. Nathan H. **HOLBROOK**, July 4, 1836, by Rev. David Dickinson 90
Jane R., m. Nathan K. **HOLBROOK**, ae 20 y. 7 m. 5 d., July 4, 1836 4
John, m. Esther **FULLER**, June 19, 1805, by Rev. Nehemiah Dodge 69
Joshua, m. Lucretia **BAILEY**, b. of Columbia, Dec. 31, 1829, by David Dickinson 87
Louisa C., m. Asahel O. **WRIGHT**, May 9, 1837, by Rev. Daniel Dickinson 35
Mary, of Columbia, m. Daniel **HUNT**, Minister, of Pomfret, May 29, 1839, by Charles Kittridge 44
Sally, m. Capt. Samuel **WEST**, Nov. 14, 1820, by David Dickinson 73
**POST**, Charles A., m. Lucy A. **BILL**, Oct. 23, 1850, by Rev. Fred[eric]k D. Avery, at the house of Chester Bill 30
Emily, m. Septimus **LOOMER**, b. of Columbia, Nov. 20, 1831, by Rev. Alpheas Geer, of Hebron 57
Harriet M., of Columbia, m. Nelson B. **LOOMIS**, of Lebanon, Jan. 1, 1838, by Sylvester Selden, Hebron 46
Sybel R., m. Gurdon Y. **ROBINSON**, b. of Columbia, Nov. 30, 1843, by Rev. Ebenezer Robinson 13
**POTTER**, Harty M., m. Robert **BROWN**, b. of Columbia, Oct. 7, 1844, by Rev. James W. Woodward 14
Martha, m. Holder **SLOCUM**, b. of Lebanon, June 2, 1830, by David Dickinson 88

Page

**POTTER**, (cont.)

Mary, of Columbia, m. James **HULL**, of South Kingstown, R. I., Mar. 25, 1821, by David Dickinson 78

Rachel, of Columbia, m. Norman **BOYNTON**, of Coventry, Oct. 7, 1844, by Rev. James W. Woodward 14

**PROUD**, John R., of Lisbon, m. Martha **LEWIS**, of Columbia, June 28, 1838, by Rev. Philo Judson, of Willimantic 91

**RICHARD**, Albert G., of Springfield, N. Y., m. Sophia **WRIGHT**, of Columbia, Sept. 7, 1831, by David Dickinson. Int. pub. 88

**RICHARDSON**, Betsey, m. Anson **HUNT**, b. of Columbia, May 29, 1839, by Charles Kittridge 44

Delia, of Columbia, m. Hezekiah **KINGSBURY**, of Hebron, Oct. 26, 1824, by Rev. Augustus B. Collins, of Andover 79

Lucina C., of Columbia, m. John **ARMSTRONG**, of Freeport, Me., Jan. 9, 1849, by Rev. James W. Woodword 25

Nancy C., of Columbia, m. Lucius **MORTON**, of Hartford, May 31, 1848, by Rev. James W. Woodword 23

**RIXFORD**, George C., of Mansfield, m. Julia A. **COGGESHALL**, of Columbia, Sept. 4, 1849, by Rev. James W. Woodword 26

**ROBERTSON**, Eunice M., of Coventry, m. George W. **LYMAN**, of Columbia, Oct. 20, 1839, by Charles Kittredge 42

**ROBINSON**, Calvin, of Windham, m. Mary **BOLLES**, of Columbia, Jan. 8, 1839, by Sylvester Selden 46

Gurdon Y., m. Sybel R. **POST**, b. of Columbia, Nov. 30, 1843, by Rev. Ebenezer Robinson 13

**ROCKWELL**, Andrew H., of Lebanon, m. Caroline R. **PORTER**, of Columbia, Sept. 28, 1837, by Sylvester Selden 52

**ROGERS**, Aaron, m. Betsey **EDWARDS**, b. of Norwich, Oct. 1, 1821, by David Dickinson 75

David L., m. Mary **GOODRICH**, b. of Wethersfield, Aug. 5, 1838, by Asahel Clark, J. P. 46

John, of Columbia, m. Elizabeth Ann **ALLEN**, of Lima, Mar. 5, 1822, by Rev. William Palmer, of Colchester, in the house of Martin Webber 76

**ROOT**, Abigail J., of Columbia, m. Henry C. **COOK**, of Portland, Oct. 31, 1847, by Rev. Henry Baylies, of Hebron, at the bride's residence. Int. pub. 21

Elizer F., of Rockville, m. Harriet A. **MANLY**, of Columbia, June 2, 1850, by Rev. John Avery, of Exeter 29

**SCOVILLE**, Amhurst, m. Sally **LITTLE**, Oct. 9, 1798. Witnesses: Consider Little, Rebeckah Little 67

Amhurst, [s. Amhurst & Sally], b. May 9, 1800; d. Apr. 22, 1803 68

Charles Amhurst, [s. Amhurst & Sally], b. Mar. 23, 1804 68

Elizabeth, [twin with Sally], d. [Amhurst & Sally], b. Mar. 29, 1802 68

Elizabeth, m. Darius **KINGSLEY**, b. of Columbia, Jan. 29, 1824, by David Dickinson 78

Fanny L., of Columbia, m. Elisha H. **HAYWARD**, of Buffaloe, N. Y., Oct. 11, 1827, by Rev. Esek Brown, of Lebanon 59

Page

**SCOVILLE**, (cont.)
Fanny Little, [d. Amhurst & Sally], b. Mar. 22, 1806 68
Lydia L., m. Sanford **YOEMANS**, b. of Columbia, Feb. 20, 1838, by Rev. B. Cook, Jr., of Willimantic 47
Mary Ann, of Columbia, m. Daniel P. **SPRAGUE**, of Hebron, Andover Society, Dec. 26, 1831, by Rev. Esek Brown, of Lebanon 89
Sally, [twin with Elizabeth], d. [Amhurst & Sally], b. Mar. 29, 1802 68
**SILL**, Isaac N., of Andover, m. Almira **BOLLES**, of Columbia, May 5, 1846, by Rev. James W. Woodward 18
**SKINNER**, Ruth, of Hebron, m. Daniel **PENHALLOW**, of Columbia, Apr. 1, 1823, by David Dickinson 77
**SLOCUM**, Holder, m. Martha **POTTER**, b. of Lebanon, June 2, 1830, by David Dickinson 88
**SMITH**, Allen B., of Montville, m. Clarriss **BOLLES**, of Columbia, June 27, 1837, by Sylvester Selden, Hebron 51
Freeman, m. Lillie **DICKINSON**, Sept. 22, 1824, by David Dickinson 79
John M., of Andover, m. Elizabeth D. **HAZARD**, of Columbia, Apr. 13, 1843, by John M. Hunt 36
Levi E., of Hartford, m. Helen A. **DEWEY**, of Columbia, [Oct.] 15, [1854], by Rev. Fred[eric]k D. Avery 5
**SNOW**, Benjamin F., of Providence, R. I., m. Emily L. **BENNETT**, of Windham, June 10, 1849, by William Osborn, J. P. 26
Betsey P., of Columbia, m. William A. **BLY**, of Springfield, Mass., July 5, 1835, by David Dickinson 62
Daniel Pinney, s. Dudley, b. Jan. 7, 1825 33
Elizabeth L., of Lebanon, m. Amos G. **DOUBLEDAY**, of Columbia, Oct. 8, 1837, by Dexter Bullard, Minister 48
James, of Columbia, m. Lucinda **MORY**, of Manchester, Nov. 5, 1848, by Ambrose Fuller 24
Sam[ue]l Harlow, m. Mary J. **NOICE**, of Ashford, Dec. 20, 1834, by Daniel Holbrook, J. P. 62
Sophia, m. Richard **WHEELER**, b. of Columbia, July 16, 1826, by David Dickinson 71
**SPARROW**, Mary A., of Tolland, m. Stephen G. **MERCHANT**, of Sunderland, Mass., Mar. 31, 1845, by Rev. Alpha Doolittle, of Andover 16
**SPRAGUE**, Dan, of Covington, N. Y., m. Mary W. **COLLINS**, of Columbia, May 15, 1834, by David Dickinson 55
Daniel P., of Hebron, Andover Society, m. Mary Ann **SCOVILLE**, of Columbia, Dec. 26, 1831, by Rev. Esek Brown, of Lebanon 89
**SQUEIRS**, [E]unice, m. Russell **HALL**, Mar. 14, 1830, by Silas Fuller, J. P. 87
**STETSON**, Horace W., of Hartford, m. Jane V. **WOODWORTH**, of Columbia, Jan. 4, 1848, by Rev. Frederick P. Coe 22
**STRONG**, Abigail, of Columbia, m. Girdon **ISHAM**, of Tolland, Dec. 18, 1823, by David Dickinson 77
Benjamin F., of Mass., m. Charlotte L. **HOLBROOK**, of Columbia, Jan. 2, 1844, by Rev. James W. Woodworth 9
Lydia, of Hebron, m. Edward **WEBBER**, of Columbia, Mar. 31, 1835,

Page

**STRONG**, (cont.)
by David Dickinson. Int. pub. 53
**TANNER**, Albert Taylor, s. Nathan & Charlotte, b. Sept. 11, 1808 34
Frederic C., [s. Nathan & Charlotte], b. Sept. 27, 1810 34
**TAYLOR**, Lewis H., of Chatham, m. Corintha N. **PORTER**, of Columbia, Apr. 1, 1835, by David Dickinson. Int. pub. 53
**THOMAS**, Amanda M., of Columbia, m. Rufus **CHAMBERLAIN**, of Mansfield, Dec. 21, 1841, by C. Kittredge 42
**THOMPSON**, Augustus, [s. James & Hannah], b. Feb. 24, 1803 33
Augustus, m. Adaline S. **CARVER**, b. of Columbia, Dec. 3, 1829, by Rev. Esek Brown, of Lebanon 86
Caroline, m. Horace **THOMPSON**, Jr., Nov. 30, 1837, by Samuel Little, J. P. 49
Emily, [d. James & Hannah], b. May 30, 1807 33
George W., of Bristol, Vt., m. Lois J. **THOMPSON**, of Columbia, Sept. 12, 1838, by Rev. Ebenezer Robinson 45
Hezekiah, m. Alma C. **PIDGE**, b. of Windham, Sept. 3, 1843, by Rev. James W. Woodworth 8
Horace, Jr., m. Caroline **THOMPSON**, Nov. 30, 1837, by Samuel Little, J. P. 49
Jerusha, of Columbia, m. Elias **JUD[D]**, of Coventry, May 22, 1831, by Amhurst Scoville, J. P. 57
Laura, d. James & Hannah, b. Jan. 17, 1801 33
Leonard, [s. James & Hannah], b. Feb. 28, 1805 33
Lewis O., s. James & Hannah, b. Oct. 3, 1816 2
Lois J., of Columbia, m. George W. **THOMPSON**, of Bristol, Vt., Sept. 12, 1838, by Rev. Ebenezer Robinson 45
**TICKNOR**, Daniel, m. Lydia **YEOMANS**, b. of Columbia, Jan. 15, 1829, by Rev. Esek Brown, of Lebanon 61
Edith, Mrs., of Columbia, m. John **KINGSBURY**, of Coventry, Jan. 26, 1826, by David Dickinson 83
Harriet R., m. George W. **BILL**, b. of Columbia, Mar. 24, 1844, by Rev. James W. Woodworth. Int. pub. 10
John, of Brimfield, m. Amanda M. **DOWNER**, of Columbia, Apr. 9, 1829, by David Dickinson 56
Mary, of Columbia, m. William **DAVIDSON**, of Hartwick, N. Y., Sept. 8, 1831, by David Dickinson. Int. pub. 89
**TOWNSEND**, James H., of Falls Township, O., m. Lucinda **FRANKLIN**, of Columbia, Oct. 17, 1844, by Rev. Edgar J. Doolittle 14
**TRACY**, Rosanna, m. Asa **MANLEY**, b. of Columbia, Jan. 28, 1830, by David Dickinson 87
Sarah M., m. Sexton B. **LITTLE**, b. of Columbia, Aug. 21, 1836, by Rev. Jesse Fisher, of Windham 90
**TURNER**, Alfred, of Groton, m. Cynthia **MAIN**, of North Stonington, Oct. 1, 1829, by Asahel Clark, J. P. 56
**TUTTLE**, William W., m. Elizabeth A. **WOODWARD**, Nov. 27, 1845, by Rev. Alpha Miller, of Andover 18
**UNCAS**, Esther, m. Prince **BEAUMONT**, May 14, 1837, by Amhurst

Page

UNCAS, (cont.)
Scoville, J. P. 50
**UTLEY**, Andrew B., of Pomfret, m. Elizabeth **BROWN**, Mar. 31, 1850, by Rev. J. R. Arnold 28
**VARNUM**, John, b. Oct. 23, 1798 71
**WALKER**, A. A., of R. I., m. Harriet E. **WEBBER**, of Columbia, Jan. 28, 1840, by Daniel Holbrook, J. P. 43
**WARE**, Hiram R., of Hartford, m. Melvina A. **HOLBROOK**, of Columbia, Apr. 5, 1840, by Cha[rle]s Kittredge 43
**WATKINS**, Samuel Jarvis, of Peru, Mass., m. Nancy C. **FULLER**, of Columbia, Conn., Oct. 30, 1842, by Rev. Israel D. Otis 36
**WEBBER**, Caroline, of Columbia, m. Lewis P. **NEWELL**, of Pomfret, May 7, 1825, by David Dickinson 82
Edward, of Columbia, m. Lydia **STRONG**, of Hebron, Mar. 31, 1835, by David Dickinson. Int. pub. 53
Emily Ann, of Columbia, m. Andrew **METZZAR**, of Greenville, Norwich, "last evening" [Oct. 14, 1844], by James W. Woodward 15
Harriet E., of Columbia, m. A. A. **WALKER**, of R. I., Jan. 28, 1840, by Daniel Holbrook, J. P. 43
Maria, m. Ralph **ALMSBURY**, Dec. 17, 1825, by Amhurst Scoville, J. P. 83
Martha E., of Columbia, m. George W. **DYER**, of Willimantic, Oct. 9, 1842, by Rev. James W. Woodword 35
**WEBSTER**, Cynthia P., of Columbia, m. Charles D. **LITTLE**, of Saginaw, Mich., Nov. 29, 1853, by Rev. Fred[eric]k D. Avery, at the Parsonage 6
Jerusha, m. Monson **WOODWORTH**, b. of Columbia, May 29, 1828, by David Dickinson 60
Polly, m. Charles **BLISS**, Oct. 30, 1825, by David Dickinson 82
**WELCH**, Eliphalet, of County of Oswego, N. Y., m. Lucy W. **HARTSON**, of Columbia, Nov. 9, 1828, by Rev. Esek Brown, of Lebanon 61
**WELLER***, Reuben, m. Martha **MAINARD**, Mar. 14, 1821, by Silas Fuller, J. P. (*Perhaps "**WELLES**"?) 74
**WEST**, Elizabeth, m. Edwin H. **LITTLE**, b. of Columbia, Apr. 24, 1844, by Rev. James W. Woodworth 11
Harriet L, m. Madison **WOODWORD**, b. of Columbia, Apr. 5, 1838, by Sylvester Selden, Hebron 90
Samuel, Capt., m. Sally **PORTER**, Nov. 14, 1820, by David Dickinson 73
Samuel, Jr., m. Ruby **BLISS**, May 10, 1822, by David Dickinson 76
Samuel F., of Deleware, O., m. Charlotte **PORTER**, of Columbia, Sept. 28, 1837, by Sylvester Selden 52
Submit, of Columbia, m. Benjamin **HOUSE**, of Coventry, June 29, 1826, by Rev. Joel West, of Chatham 84
**WHEELER**, Abby Ann, of Columbia, m. Ephraim **PARKER**, of Vernon, Aug. 31, 1828, by Rev. Chauncey Booth, of Coventry 60
Betsey S., of Coventry, m. Gilbert **LINCOLN**, of Columbia, Dec. 6, 1846, by Rev. James W. Woodward 19
Frederick A., of Columbia, m. Eliza Ann M. **COVELL**, Jan. 7, 1844,

Page

**WHEELER**, (cont.)
by Rev. James W. Woodworth. Int. pub. 9
Lucinda, of Columbia, m. E. H. **GATES**, of Vernon, Dec. 4, 1848, by Rev. James W. Woodword, at the house of the bride's father 24
Richard, m. Sophia **SNOW**, b. of Columbia, July 16, 1826, by David Dickinson 71
Strickland, m. Almira **WILSON**, Aug. 28, 1836, by Daniel Holbrook, J. P. 85
Ursula R., of Columbia, m. Royal J. **ALLEN**, of Manchester, Nov. 29, 1849, by Rev. James W. Woodword 27
**WHITE**, Pamelia M., m. Silas F. **LOOMIS**, b. of Columbia, Nov. 4, 1846, by Rev. James W. Woodward 19
**WILCOX**, Russell, of Lebanon, m. Emma **HILLS**, of Columbia, May 11, 1836, by Levi Meech, Elder 63
**WILLIAMS**, Gordon J., m. Betsey **COTTRELL**, b. of Columbia, Feb. 19, 1821, by David Dickinson 74
Nancy, m. Daniel **HOLBROOK**, b. of Columbia, Nov. 1, 1843, by Rev. James Woodworth 8
**WILSON, WILLSON**, Almira, m. Strickland **WHEELER**, Aug. 28, 1836, by Daniel Holbrook, J. P. 85
William, m. Lovina **HOUSE**, Oct. 22, 1777 68
**WINSLEY**, Chester F., of Hebron, m. Mary **BROWN**, of Columbia, June 20, 1834, by David Dickinson 55
Chester F., d. Mar. 24, 1862, ae 48 (handwritten in original manuscript)
Veranus P. s. of Chester F. d. Aug. 17, 1856, ae 21 (handwritten in original manuscript)
**WOOD**, Bela, m. Roxellana **HARTSHORN**, Feb. 19, 1786, by Rev. Thomas Brockway. (Witnesses:] Asa Kingsbury, Rhoda Clark. Recorded Nov. 10, 1806 64
Mary, m. Hezekiah **HARTSHORN**, Nov. 26, 1788 68
**WOODWORD**, Amanda, [d. J----], b. Dec. 15, 1803 69
Artemus, m. Martha **MERRIFIELD**, July 2, 1800 1
Artemus, m. Marcelia **MERRIFIELD**, July 2, 1800, by Thomas Brockway. Witnesses: Asahel Loomis, Esther Loomis 70
Asahel, m. Harriet **HOUSE**, Mar. 24, 1806, by Royal Taylor. Witnesses: Eleazer C. Woodword, Charles Woodword 65
Caroline, [s. Charles & Polly], b. Nov. 21, 1805 65
Charles, m. Polly **JONES**, June 24, 1800, by Thomas Brockway. Witnesses: Asahel Woodword, Eleazer C. Woodword 65
Eleazer C., m. Isabell **COLE**, Sept. 24, 1794, by Thomas Brockway. Witnesses; Eleazer Woodword, Mary Woodword 63
Eliza, d. [Artemus & Martha], b. Oct. 29, 1804 34
Eliza, [d. Artemas & Marcelia], b. Oct. 29, 1804 70
Elizabeth A., m. William W. **TUTTLE**, Nov. 27, 1845, by Rev. Alpha Miller, of Andover 18
Emiline, [d. Artemus & Martha], b. Apr. 3, 1807 34
Emeline, [d. Artemas & Marcelia], b. Apr. 3, 1807 70

**WOODWORD**, (cont.)
George, s. Artemus & Martha, b. Mar. 14, 1801 34
George, [s. Artemas & Marcelia], b. Mar. 14, 1801 70
Hannah, [d. Eleazer], b. May 28, 1796 71
Hannah, [d. J----], b. June 8, 1801 69
Hannah, of Columbia, m. Elisha **HUTCHINSON**, of Bolton, Jan. "about the 15th", 1823, by David Dickinson 78
Jasper, m. Amanda **WRIGHT**, Mar. 5, 1801 69
Lucy, [d. Charles & Polly], b. Sept. 30, 1802 65
Madison, m. Harriet L. **WEST**, b. of Columbia, Apr. 5, 1838, by Sylvester Selden, Hebron 90
Marcelia, [d. Artemus & Martha], b. Feb. 6, 1810 34
Marilla, w. Artemus, d. Feb. 19, 1810 48
Pamelia S., m. William G. **LITTLE**, b. of Columbia, May 4, 1842, by James W. Woodword 37
Ralph Jones, [s. Charles & Polly], b. Mar. 30, 1804 65
Seth, [s. Eleazer], d. Sept. 29, 1797 71
Seth, [s. Charles & Polly], b. Apr. 24, 1801 65
Sina, [d. Eleazer], b. Apr. 19, 1795 71
Sophia, [d. Eleazer], b. Apr. 25, 1791 71
W[illia]m, [s. J----], b. May 14, 1806 69

**WOODWORTH**, Jane V., of Columbia, m. Horace W. **STETSON**, of Hartford, Jan. 4, 1848, by Rev. Frederick P. Coe 22
Mary, m. Albert G. **COLLINS**, b. of Columbia, Nov. 29, 1827, by David Dickinson 59
Monson, m. Jerusha **WEBSTER**, b. of Columbia, May 29, 1828, by David Dickinson 60
Pamelia, m. Azel D. **COLLINS**, May 6, 1828, by Silas Fuller, J. P. 59

**WRIGHT**, Amanda, m. Jasper **WOODWORTH**, Mar. 5, 1801 69
Asahel O., m. Louisa C. **PORTER**, May 9, 1837, by Rev. Daniel Dickinson 35
Azuba, m. Joseph **PENNEO**, Jan. 17, 1787, by Rev. Thomas Brockway 69
Charles, m. Betsey **BARSTOW**, July 4, 1782 68
Elizabeth P., m. Silas A. **HOLBROOK**, b. of Columbia, Apr. 10, 1850, by Rev. John Avery, of Exeter 28
George, m. Maria **DOWNER**, b. of Columbia, May 12, 1824, by David Dickinson 79
Levina, of Columbia, m. Horace W. **JACKSON**, of Norwich, Nov. 28, 1844, by Rev. James W. Woodward 15
Matilda, m. Levi **LITTLE**, b. of Columbia, Feb. 5, 1826, by David Dickinson 83
Sophia, of Columbia, m. Albert G. **RICHARD**, of Springfield, N. Y., Sept. 7, 1831, by David Dickinson. Int. pub. 88

**YEOMANS**, Aaron, m. Cynthia **BILL**, b. of Columbia, Mar. 21, 1827, by Rev. Esek Brown, of Lebanon 72
Cynthia, m. Lyman C. **CLARK**, b. of Columbia, Nov. 1, 1838, by Rev. Philo Judson, of Willimantic 45
Cynthia A., m. Henry B. **LITTLE**, b. of Columbia, June 1, 1848,

Page

**YEOMANS**, (cont.)
by Rev. James W. Woodword 23
Edward, m. Gratia **NEWELL**, Oct. 10, 1827, by Rev. Joseph Ireson 91
John S., m. Sophia C. **LYMAN**, b. of Columbia, Oct. 14, 1830, by David Dickinson 88
Lavinia, of Middletown, m. Alanson **LITTLE**, of Columbia, Jan. 1, 1845, by Rev. James W. Woodword 16
Lydia, m. Daniel **TICKNOR**, b. of Columbia, Jan. 15, 1829, by Rev. Esek Brown, of Lebanon 61
Sanford, m. Lydia L. **SCOVILLE**, b. of Columbia, Feb. 20, 1838, by Rev. B. Cook, Jr., of Willimantic 47
William A., m. Harriet R. **DEWEY**, of Columbia, Aug. 19, 1839, by Charles Kittredge 91
**YOUNG**, George, of Windham, m. Eunice **CASWELL**, of Columbia, Dec. 9, 1824, by Rev. Esek Brown, of Lebanon 80
Joseph, of Lebanon, m. Naomi **KINGSLEY**, of Columbia, May 14, 1828, by Rev. Esek Brown, of Lebanon 60

# CORNWALL VITAL RECORDS
# 1740 - 1854

| | Vol. | Page |
|---|---|---|
| **ABBOTT, ABBIT, ABBOT**, Abel, m. Hannah **DIBBLE**, b. of Cornwall, Feb. 16, 1757, by Rev. Hezekiah Gold | 1 | 27 |
| Abel, s. Abel & Hannah, b. Dec. 26, 1765 | 1 | 66 |
| Amy, d. Abel & Hannah, b. July 20, 1760 | 1 | 38 |
| Anna, d. Abel & Hannah, b. Nov. 11, 1757 | 1 | 30 |
| Benjamin, s. Sela & Ann, b. July 12, 1762 | 1 | 47 |
| Benjamin Daley, s. Nathan & Mercy, b. Sept. 22, 1770 | 1 | 97 |
| Caleb, s. Sela & Ann, b. June 12, 1764 | 1 | 57 |
| Elizabeth, d. Nathan & Mercy, b. Mar. 19, 1758 | 1 | 31 |
| Esther, d. Nathan & Mercy, b. Aug. 23, 1768 | 1 | 79 |
| Esther, d. Abel & Hannah, b. May 22, 1775 | LR3 | 8 |
| Hannah, d. Namick & Sarah, b. Oct. 26, 1744 | 1 | 10 |
| Hannah, m. Daniel **SQUIER**, Feb. 19, 1761, by Rev. H. Gold | 1 | 48 |
| Hannah, d. Abel & Hannah, b. Jan. 17, 1764 | 1 | 54 |
| Irena, d. Nathan & Mercy, b. July 5, 1775 | LR3 | 14 |
| Jere D., m. Phebe H. **ALLYN**, Dec. 7, 1837, by Rev. Walter Smith, of the North Cong. Ch. | 3 | 53 |
| Mercy, d. Nathan & Mercy, b. Aug. 23, 1762 | 1 | 47 |
| Molly, d. Sela & Anna, b. Dec. 18, 1766 | 1 | 76 |
| Molly, d. Samuel & Hannah, b. July 26, 1776 | LR3 | 12 |
| Nathan, m. Mercy **DAY**, b. of Cornwall, Feb. 23, 1757, by Rev. Hezekiah Gold | 1 | 27 |
| Nathan, s. Nathan & Mercy, b. May 4, 1766 | 1 | 67 |
| Rebeckah, d. Abel & Hannah, b. May 21, 1770 | 1 | 95 |
| Rana*, d. Sele & Anna, b. Oct. 24, 1772; d. Oct. 31, 1772 *("Rena") | 1 | 106 |
| Rena, d. Sele & Anna, b. Feb. 7, 1774 | LR3 | 6 |
| Samuel, Jr., m. Hannah **BLEY**, May 2, 1769, by Rev. Hezekiah Gold | 1 | 88 |
| Samuel, s. Nathan & Mercy, b. Jan. 27, 1779 | LR3 | 13 |
| Sarah, d. Nathan & Mary, b. July 11, 1760 | 1 | 37 |
| Sarah, m. Jesse **JERRED***, Sept. 19, 1769, by Rev. Hezekiah Gold *("Gerard") | 1 | 94 |
| Sarah, d. Samuel & Hannah, b. May 8, 1774 | LR3 | 6 |
| Sarah, of Sharon, m. Ashbel **WALLER**, of Cornwall, Nov. 1, 1781, by Judah Kellogg, J. P. | 2 | 1 |
| Seely, m. Ann **JONES**, June 24, 1761, by Rev. H. Gold | 1 | 43 |
| Seth, s. Samuel, Jr. & Hannah, b. June 16, 1770 | 1 | 95 |
| Sinai, d. Sele & Ann, b. May 23, 1777 | LR3 | 14 |
| Theoda, s. Sele & Anna, b. July 15, 1770 | LR3 | 6 |
| **ACKERMAN**, John, m. Jerusha **STONE**, b. of Cornwall, May 29, | | |

| | Vol. | Page |
|---|---|---|
| **ACKERMAN**, (cont.) | | |
| 1839, by Rev. Samuel W. Smith | 3 | 58 |
| **ADAMS**, John, colored, had s. [ ], b. July [ ], 1851 | 3 | 114-15 |
| John Quincy, s. Samuel, b. Nov. 2, 1837 | 3 | 55 |
| Samuel Judson, s. Samuel, b. Aug. 23, 1836 | 3 | 51 |
| **AGUERG**, Felix, m. Anna **BEGLON**, b. Ireland, b. of Norfolk, Aug. 15, 1852, by Rev. John Smith | 3 | 122 |
| **ALLEN**, [see also **ALLING** & **ALLYN**], Abigail, d. Elisha & Abigail, b. May 31, 1768; d. Feb. 7, 1769 | 1 | 86 |
| Abigail, d. Elihu & Abigail, b. Mar. 2, 1770 | 1 | 93 |
| Adna, s. Daniel & Dorcas, b. Aug. 7, 1769 | 1 | 91 |
| Adna, m. Elizabeth **McNEAL**, Dec. 6, 1792, by Jacob Brush, Elder. Witnesses: Asaph Emmons & Philip Wayer | 3 | 20 |
| Alban, s. Daniel & Clarissa, b. May 22, 1802 | 3 | 5 |
| Ann, d. Elihu & Abigail, b. May 30, 1766 | 1 | 71 |
| Azuba, m. Ebenezer **SHERWOOD**, Apr. 10, 1769, by Rev. Hezekiah Gold | LR4 | 15 |
| Chester, s. Daniel & Clarissa, b. Apr. 18, 1804 | 3 | 5 |
| Clarinda, d. Daniel & Clarissa, b. Nov. 9, 1773 | 2 | 13 |
| Daniell, s. Daniell & Mary, b. June 19, 1744 | 1 | 5 |
| Daniel, m. Dorcas **DIBBLE**, b. of Cornwall, June 11, 1767, by Thomas Russell, J. P. | 1 | 76 |
| Daniel, d. Jan. 13, 1777 | LR3 | 7 |
| Daniel, s. Daniel, decd. & Dorcas, b. Mar. 22, 1777 | LR3 | 14 |
| Daniel, m. Clarissa **DEWEY**, b. of Cornwall, July 16, 1801, by Rev. Hecules Weston | 3 | 11 |
| Derinda, d. May 24, 1801 | 3 | 10 |
| Dorcas, m. Jethro **BONNEY**, May 11, 1780, by Judah Kellogg, J. P. | LR4 | 16 |
| Edward, s. Elihu & Abigail, b. June 26, 1762 | 1 | 48 |
| Elijah, s. Daniell, decd. & Mary, b. Jan. 28, 1747/8 | 1 | 7 |
| Elijah, of Cornwall, m. Sarah* **BISHOP**, of Stanford, Oct. 30, 1777, by Moses Mather, V. D. M. *("Mary" in Starr's Hist. of Cornwall) | LR3 | 16 |
| Elijah, d. Jan. 17, 1802, ae 54 | 3 | 10 |
| Elisha, s. Elihu & Abigail, b. Oct. 9, 1764 | 1 | 56 |
| Enos, s. Elihu & Abigail, b. June 23, 1774 | LR3 | 8 |
| Gabriell, s. Daniell & Mary, b. Dec. 12, 1742 | 1 | 5 |
| Gabriel, m Deborah **RUST**, Oct. 15, 1769, by Heman Swift, J. P. | 1 | 96 |
| Gabriel, d. July 26, 1776 | LR3 | 7 |
| Gabriel, s. Gabriel, decd., & Deborah, b. Dec. 19, 1776 | LR3 | 12 |
| Heber, 2nd, s. Joseph & Mary, b. Oct. 11, 1743 | 1 | 6 |
| Heman, s. Joseph & Mary, b. Oct. 15, 1740 | 1 | 6 |
| Horace, m. Rachel **GOLD**, b. of Cornwall, Oct. 21, 1828, by Rev. Silas Ambler | 2 | 64 |
| Ira, s. Joseph & Mary, b. Apr. 21, 1751 | 1 | 17 |
| Ira, s. Elijah & Sarah, b. Dec. 12, 1781 | 2 | 3 |

| | Vol. | Page |
|---|---|---|
| **ALLEN**, (cont.) | | |
| Josiah, s. Elihu & Abigail, b. Apr. 27, 1772 | 1 | 105 |
| Levi, s. Joseph & Mary, b. Jan. 16, 1745 | 1 | 6 |
| Lucinda, d. Gabriel & Deborah, b. June 4, 1770 | 1 | 96 |
| Lucy, d. Joseph & Mary, b. Apr. 2, 1747 | 1 | 6 |
| Lydia, d. Joseph & Mary, b. Apr. 6, 1742 | 1 | 6 |
| Martha, m. Elijah **DICKINSON**, July 21, 1768, by Hezekiah Gold | 1 | 83 |
| Mary, d. Daniel & Mary, b. Aug. 17, 1746 | 1 | 4 |
| Mary, d. Daniel & Mary, d. Oct. 10, 1746 (This entry is followed by the date "Jan. 23, 1746/7) | 1 | 2 |
| Orlo, s. Daniel & Dorcas, b. Oct. 18, 1771 | 1 | 99 |
| Philander, s. Elijah & Sarah, b. June 3, 1779 | LR3 | 16 |
| Samuel Seabury, s. Elijah & Sarah, b. Mar. 6, 1786 | 2 | 20 |
| Sarah, d. Elijah & Sarah, b. Apr. 19, 1784 | 2 | 9 |
| Sarah, d. Elijah & Sarah, d. Oct. 1, 1785 | 2 | 11 |
| Sarah, w. Elijah, d. Apr. 3, 1787 | 2 | 11 |
| Zeno, s. Elijah & Sarah, b. June 14, 1780 | LR4 | 16 |
| Zimri, s. Joseph & Mary, b. Dec. 10, 1748 | 1 | 10 |
| **ALLING**, [see also **ALLEN & ALLYN**], Betsey, m. Peter **BIERCE**, Oct. 8, 1818, by Rev. Timothy Stone | 2 | 48 |
| Elisha, m. Abigail **DEAN**, Jan. 9, 1759, by Solomon Palmer | 1 | 36 |
| John Mason, s. James & Maria F., b. July 28, 1816 | 2 | 42 |
| Joseph, d. Apr. 14, 1756 | 1 | 35 |
| Lewey, m. George **WHEATON**, b. of Cornwall, Nov. 16, 1815, by Rev. Pitkin Cowles, of Canaan | 2 | 37 |
| Mercy, Mrs., m. Sam[ue]ll **DEAN**, Aug. 21, 1757, by S. Palmer | 1 | 31 |
| Nathan, s. Elisha & Abigail, b. Mar. 13, 1760 | 1 | 36 |
| **ALLYN**, [see also **ALLEN & ALLING**], Lucy E., ae 22, b. Ledyard, res. Goshen, m. Samuel **DEAN**, farmer, ae 36, b. Cornwall, res. Sharon, Feb. 20, 1850, by Rev. LaValette Perrin | 3 | 112-13 |
| Phebe H., m. Jere D. **ABBOTT**, Dec. 7, 1837, by Rev. Walter Smith, of the North Cong. Ch. | 3 | 53 |
| Robert M., s. Anslin, farmer, ae 47 & Hannah, ae 35, res. Goshen, b. Sept. 28, 1848 | 3 | 98-9 |
| **ALVARD**, Asahel, m. Bette **MAY**, Sept. 19, 1765, by Rev. Hezekiah Gold | 1 | 63 |
| Asahel Gold, s. Asahel & Betty, b. Sept. 29, 1769 | 1 | 92 |
| Charles Henry, s. John & Phebe, b. July 6, 1833 | 3 | 39 |
| George Brown, s. [John & Phebe], b. Apr. 3, 1835 | 3 | 39 |
| **AMES**, Samuel, Jr., m. Temperance **POTTER**, b. of Cornwall, Nov. 29, 1827, by Horatio Smith, J. P. | 2 | 64 |
| **ANDREWS, ANDREW, ANDRUS**, Abigail, of Wallingford, m. John **SEDGWICK**, of Cornwall, Sept. 3, 1765, by James Dana | 1 | 70 |
| Benajah, s. Andrew & Mary, b. Oct. 18, 1783 | 2 | 7 |

| | Vol. | Page |
|---|---|---|
| **ANDREWS, ANDREW, ANDRUS**, (cont.) | | |
| Charles, s. Edward W., clergyman, ae 38, & Mary, ae 37, b. June 29, 1850 | 3 | 110-11 |
| Eli, d. Apr. 18, 1850, ae 74 | 3 | 112-13 |
| Elijah S., ae 26, of New Britain, m. Eliza S. **SCOVILL**, ae 17, of Cornwall, Nov. 26, 1854, by Rev. William M. Simons, of the Bap. Ch., Cornwall Hollow | 3 | 126 |
| Giles, s. Andrew & Mary, b. Mar. 6, 1788 | 2 | 19 |
| John T., m. Jane Ann **JONES**, Sept. 7, 1839, by N. M. Urmston | 3 | 58 |
| Major Andre, s. Andrew & Mary, b. July 8, 1792 | 3 | 24 |
| Margary, d. Andrew & Mary, b. Oct. 16, 1782 | 2 | 1 |
| Oreb, s. Andrew & Mary, b. Oct. 20, 1785 | 2 | 15 |
| Phebe, w. Caleb, d. July 25, 1793 | 2 | 26 |
| Sarah, of Wallingford, m. Elijah **STEELE**, of Cornwall, Aug. 4, 1773, by James Dana | LR3 | 5 |
| Sarah P., m. Araunah W. **HIDE**, Feb. 15, 1835, by Rev. William Andrews | 3 | 38 |
| Stephen, s. Andrew & Mary, b. Mar. 11, 1790 | 3 | 7 |
| Thomas, s. Rev. E. W., clergyman, ae 37, & Mary, ae 36, b. Sept. 20, 1848 | 3 | 98-9 |
| **ANSON**, Sarah, m. William **STONE**, Feb. 22, 1846, by Rev. K. K. Reynolds | 3 | 72 |
| **ANTHONY**, Cadence, m. William **WALLEY**, colored, Mar. 19, 1848, by Lewis Gunn | 3 | 90-1 |
| Candana, m. William **WALLEY**, b. of Cornwall, Mar. 19, 1848, by Rev. Lewis Gunn | 3 | 80 |
| **APPLY**, Hiram, of Goshen, m. Caroline **BEIRCE**, of Cornwall, Mar. 4, 1839, by Samuel W. Smith | 3 | 56 |
| John, of Goshen, m. Louisa **BEIRCE**, of Cornwall, Mar. 4, 1839, by Samuel W. Smith | 3 | 56 |
| **ARNOLD**, Lewis F., of Hudson, N. Y., m. Emily H. **BROWN**, of Cornwall, Feb. 25, 1840, by N. M. Urmston | 3 | 59 |
| **ATKINS**, William, m. Betsey **WALLY**, Apr. 19, 1833, by Rev. Levi Peck, of the Bap. Ch. | 3 | 36 |
| **AVERETT**, [see under **EVERETT & EVEREST**] | | |
| **AVERY**, Abel, m. Lucy **TROWBRIDGE**, Apr. 14, 1830, by Rev. Walter Smith, of the North Ch. | 3 | 46 |
| Betsey, m. James **BLAKE**, June 11, 1823, by Rev. Asa Tallmadge, of the Bapt. Ch. | 2 | 55 |
| Harriet, m. Wakeman Peirce **JOHNSON**, Jan. 14, 1847, by Rev. John R. Keep | 3 | 73 |
| Mary M., ae 15, b. Cornwall, res. Warren, m. Charles **CARTER**, farmer, ae 31, b. Warren, res. Warren, Dec. [ ], 1848, by John F. Wooster | 3 | 104-5 |
| **BABCOCK**, Sarah P., m. John W. **WILSON**, June 7, 1846, by R. K. Reynolds | 3 | 73 |
| **BACON**, Alanson, s. Ebenezer & Martha, b. Mar. 4, 1787 | 2 | 20 |

| | Vol. | Page |
|---|---|---|
| **BACON**, (cont.) | | |
| Benjamin, s. [Ebenezer & Martha], b. July 20, 1779 | 2 | 7 |
| Daniel, s. Ebenezer & Martha, b. Jan. 21, 1785 | 2 | 15 |
| James, s. [Ebenezer & Martha], b. Jan. 23, 1783 | 2 | 7 |
| Lucy, d. [Ebenezer & Martha], b. Apr. 18, 1781 | 2 | 7 |
| Sabre, d. Ebenezer & Martha, b. Mar. 11, 1777 | 2 | 7 |
| **BAILEY, BALEY**, Betsey Ann, m. Samuel **PRINDLE**, b. of Cornwall, Apr. 3, 1842, by James Wadsworth, J. P. | 3 | 64 |
| Emily, of Cornwall, m. William **RIDER**, of Dover, N. Y., May 6, 1827, by Rev. Walter Smith | 2 | 67 |
| Hannah, of Sharon, m. John **DIBBLE**, of Cornwall, Jan. 1, 1765, by Rev. Daniel Griswold, Jr. | 1 | 58 |
| Helen, d. William P. **SHOEMAKER**, ae 28 & Lucy, ae 24, b. Jan. 13, [1848] | 3 | 84-5 |
| Lindy, of Cornwall, m. Alpheas **HITCHCOCK**, of Lebanon, N. Y., Mar. 4, 1792, by Judah Kellogg, J. P. | 3 | 8 |
| Rachel*, m. Jethro **BONNEY**, Aug. 5, 1761, by Rev. H. Gold *(Arnold Copy has "Rachel **WALEY**") | 1 | 40 |
| Thomas, m. Elizabeth **FORD**, Oct. 5, 1820, by Benjamin Sedgwick, J. P. | 2 | 50 |
| William H., of Cornwall, m. Maria **DEAN**, of Canaan, Nov. 26, 1835, by Charles Prentice | 3 | 40 |
| **BAINS***, Thankfull, m. Stephen **LEE**, Sept. 8, 1743 *(Arnold Copy has "**BARNS**") | 1 | 3 |
| **BAKER**, Mary, b. Westport, res. Cornwall, d. Feb. 27, 1849 | 3 | 106-7 |
| **BALDWIN, BAULDWIN**, Abigail Harriet, d. [Jabez & Irena], b. June 19, 1820 | 3 | 51 |
| Ann, w. David, d. Apr. 7, 1749 | 1 | 42 |
| Anna, Mrs. of Goshen, m. Thomas **TANNER**, of Cornwall, Oct. 30, 1765, by Abel Newell | 1 | 80 |
| Anne, d. David & Ann, b. May 12, 1743 | 1 | 42 |
| Artemicia M., m. George A. **WHEATON**, b. of Cornwall, Feb. 20, 1842, by Rev. Lewis Gunn | 3 | 64 |
| Celia Maria, d. [Jabez & Irena], b. Jan. 11, 1822 | 3 | 51 |
| Charles F., m. Hannah M. **BRADBURY**, Oct. 8, 1845, at the house of Mr. Bradbury, by Rev. Joshua L. Maynard | 3 | 71 |
| Charles F., farmer, ae 28 & Hannah, ae 24, had d. [ ], b. Feb. 24, 1848 | 3 | 84-5 |
| David, s. David & Ann, b. June 8, 1746 | 1 | 42 |
| David, m. Joanna **PANGBORN**, Aug. 14, 1751, by Solomon Palmer | 1 | 15 |
| David, m. Joanna **PANGBORN**, b. of Cornwll, Aug. 14, 1751, by Solomon Palmer | 1 | 42 |
| David, Jr., m. Ruth **GIBBS**, b. of Cornwall, Aug. 9, 1769, by David Welch, J. P. | 1 | 96 |
| David, m. Ann **MITCHEL**, on or about Sept. 10, 1741, by Joseph Bird. Witnesses: John Catlin & Isaac Bissell | 1 | 42 |
| Eliza Jane, d. Jabez & Irena, b. Feb. 20, 1818 | 3 | 51 |

| | Vol. | Page |
|---|---|---|
| **BALDWIN, BAULDWIN**, (cont.) | | |
| Elizabeth, d. David & Joanna, b. Jan. 11, 1757 | 1 | 41 |
| Elizabeth, had s. Seth, b. Jan. 7, 1774 | LR3 | 6 |
| Eunice, d. David, Jr. & Ruth, b. Apr. 21, 1775 | LR3 | 10 |
| George, of New Milford, m. Anner **CURTISS**, of Cornwall, Mar. 10, 1844, by Rev. Daniel Baldwin | 3 | 70 |
| Hannah, m. James D. **FORD**, June 2, 1814, by Oliver Burnham, J. P. Witnesses: Benjamin Catlin & Anson Rogers | 2 | 45 |
| Harriet Eliza, d. [Phinehas & Nancy], b. Jan. 30, 1821 | 3 | 62 |
| Harriet Elizabeth, d. Phineas & Nancy, d. Dec. 29, 1823 | 3 | 60 |
| Harvey, [d. Phinehas & Nancy], b. Jan. 13, 1828 | 3 | 62 |
| Isaac, s. David & Ann, b. May 12, 1741 | 1 | 42 |
| Isaac, s. [David, Jr. & Ruth], b. Aug. 30, 1782 | 2 | 3 |
| Jaba, m. Irene **REED**, July 10, 1816, by Rev. Samuel Cockrand | 2 | 62 |
| Jane, m. Smith **NICKERSON**, Feb. 18, 1846, by Rev. K. K. Reynolds | 3 | 72 |
| Joanna, d. David & Joanna, b. Oct. 6, 1754 | 1 | 41 |
| Johannah, m. Samuel **BROWNSON**, Mar. 16, 1775, by Rev. Hezekiah Gold | LR3 | 7 |
| John Franklin, s. [Phinehas & Nancy], b. Apr. 29, 1823 | 3 | 62 |
| Jonathan Reed, s. [Jabez & Irena], b. July 21, 1826 | 3 | 51 |
| Joseph, s. David & Johannah, b. June 27, 1765 | 1 | 63 |
| Lucy Irena, d. [Jabez & Irena], b. May 14, 1823 | 3 | 51 |
| Lydia M., m. Robert T. **MINER**, b. of Cornwall, Nov. 17, 1842, by Rev.Joshua L. Maynard,of the North Cong. Ch. | 3 | 65 |
| Lydia Mariah, d. [Phinehas & Nancy], b. Sept. 8, 1815 | 3 | 62 |
| Mabil, d. David & Joanna, b. June 8, 1767 | 1 | 79 |
| Mary, d. David & Joanna, b. Nov. 7, 1752 | 1 | 41 |
| Mary Ann, d. [Jabez & Irena], b. May 21, 1832 | 3 | 51 |
| Mary E., dressmaker, res. Cornwall, d. Sept. 24, 1848, ae 21 | 3 | 106-7 |
| Molly, d. David, Jr. & Ruth, b. Mar. 19, 1778 | 2 | 3 |
| Nancy, m. Edmund C. **BUTLER**, b. of Cornwall, [Apr. 5, 1835], by Rev. William W. Andrews | 3 | 38 |
| Nancy, w. Phinehas, d. May 5, 1849, ae 55 y. | 3 | 75 |
| Nancy, d. May 5, 1849, ae 45 | 3 | 106-7 |
| Nancy Abigail, d. [Phinehas & Nancy], b. Aug. 16, 1833 | 3 | 62 |
| Nancy R., d. Dec. 26, 1847, ae 31 | 3 | 92-3 |
| Phinehas, m. Nancy **REXFORD**, Sept. 7, 1809 | 3 | 63 |
| Phinehas & Nancy, had infant b. July 9, 1813; d. next day | 3 | 62 |
| Phinehas & Nancy, had infant b. Mar. 15, 1830; d. June 7, 1830 | 3 | 62 |
| Phinehas, m. Harriet **JUDSON**, b. of Cornwall, Sept. 25, 1850, by E. W. Andrews | 3 | 96 |
| Phinehas, farmer, ae 67, b. Milford, res. Cornwall, m. 2nd w. Harriet **JUDSON**, ae 57, b. Cornwall, res. Cornwall, Sept. 25, 1851, by E. W. Andrews | 3 | 118-19 |

| | Vol. | Page |
|---|---|---|
| **BALDWIN, BAULDWIN,** (cont.) | | |
| Phinehas Riley, s. [Phinehas & Nancy], b. June 19, 1818 | 3 | 62 |
| Samuel, s. David & Joanna, b. Dec. 31, 1758 | 1 | 41 |
| Samuel R., m. Amy J. **PEIRCE**, July 5, 1835, by Rev. William Andrews | 3 | 40 |
| Samuel Rexford, s. Phinehas & Nancy, b. Sept. 10, 1811 | 3 | 62 |
| Sarah, d. David & Ann, b. Mar. 28, 1749 | 1 | 42 |
| Sarah, m. James **BEARSE**, Jr., Oct. 5, 1769, by Rev. Hezekiah Gold | 1 | 91 |
| Sarah Elizabeth, d. [Phinehas & Nancy], b. Aug. 24, 1825 | 3 | 62 |
| Seth, s. Elizabeth, b. Jan. 7, 1774 | LR3 | 6 |
| Stephen, s. David & Joanna, b. July 4, 1761 | 1 | 41 |
| Thadeus Robert, s. [Phinehas & Nancy], b. June 10, 1836 | 3 | 62 |
| William, m. Julia **TRAFFORD**, b. of Cornwall, Oct. 22, 1823, by Rev. Walter Smith, of the 2nd Cong. Ch. | 2 | 57 |
| William W., m. Nancy R. **WHEATON**, b. of Cornwall, July 9, 1843, by Rev. Thomas Edwards, of the M. E. Ch. | 3 | 66 |
| **BALLARD**, [see also **BULLARD**], Ester*, m. Elijah **STEAL**, Jan. 18, 1759, by Rev. Timothy Baldwin *("Ester **BULLARD**"?) | 1 | 36 |
| Jonathan*, m. Susannah **CANFIELD**, May 19, 1779, by Rev. Hezekiah Gold *("Jonathan **BELL**"in Starr's book) | LR4 | 14 |
| Martha, d. Thomas & Martha, b. Jan. 7, 1741/2 | 1 | 10 |
| Roswell, s. Thomas & Martha, b. Mar. 14, 1747 | 1 | 10 |
| Rufus, s. Thomas & Martha, b. Apr. 9, 1749 | 1 | 10 |
| **BARBER**, Betsey S., m. Timothy C. **JOHNSON**, Sept. 21, 1836, by Rev. William Andrews | 3 | 41 |
| Edwin, m. Alvira **BENEDICT**, Aug. 5, 1822, by Asa Tallmadge, Elder, of the Bapt. Church | 2 | 53 |
| Elkanah, m. Electa **TUBS**, Oct. 28, 1838, by Rev. Walter Smith | 3 | 56 |
| Emma Jane, d. Nicholas, farmer, ae 29, & Mary H., ae 26, b. Feb. 21, 1851 | 3 | 114-15 |
| Herbert Walter, s. Nathaniel, farmer, lawyer, ae 28 & Mary A., ae 24, res. Cornwall Milton Soc., b. Jan. 3, 1849 | 3 | 100-1 |
| Nathaniel, m. Mary H. **CURTISS**, Nov. 7, 1843, by Rev. Thomas Edwards, of the M. E. Ch. | 3 | 67 |
| **BARCE**, [see under **BIERCE**] | | |
| **BARLEY**, Caroline, d. Charles, shoemaker, ae 28, & Julia Ann, ae 28, res. Sharon, b. Sept. 22, 1847 | 3 | 86-7 |
| David, of Kent, m. Julia M. **CATLIN**, of Cornwall, Dec. 6, 1845, at the house of Benjamin Catlin, by Rev. Joshua L. Maynard, of the North Cong. Ch. | 3 | 72 |
| **BARNES, BARNS**, Abigail, of Canaan, m. Abner **HOCKLIN**, of Cornwall, Dec. 7, 1797, by Rev. Daniel Farrand, of Canaan. Witnesses: Rozel & Oliver Hocklin | 3 | 9 |
| Betsey Anne, d. Amos C. & Hannah, b. Mar. 26, 1811 | 2 | 42 |

| | Vol. | Page |
|---|---|---|
| **BARNES, BARNS**, (cont.) | | |
| Charles, m. Hannah M. **DIBBLE**, Feb. 5, 1828, by Rev. Walter Smith | 2 | 68 |
| Clinton Amos, s. Amos C. & Hannah, b. Sept. 15, 1809 | 2 | 42 |
| Edward, of Goshen, m. Rebecca **BONNEY**, of Cornwall, Jan. 2, 1834, by Aaron S. Hill | 3 | 36 |
| Elizabeth, m. Elisha **DICKINSON**, Aug. 2, 1769, by Rev. Hezekiah Gold | 1 | 87 |
| Joel, s. Joel & Mary, b. Nov. 11, 1793 | 2 | 41 |
| Laura Ann, d. [Joel & Anna], b. Aug. 28, 1822 | 3 | 2 |
| Mary Sylviney, d. [Joel & Anna], b. Aug. 13, 1827 | 3 | 2 |
| Salvency, d. Joel & Mary (or Molly), b. May 11, 1787 | 2 | 19 |
| Sherman Dickerson, s. Joel & Anna, b. Oct. 12, 1819 | 3 | 2 |
| Thankfull*, m. Stephen **LEE**, Sept. 8, 1743 *("Thankfull **BAINS**" in Starr's book) | 1 | 3 |
| **BARNUM**, Harriet, d. Mary, b. Aug. 31, 1848 | 3 | 102-3 |
| Jennett, m. Samuel N. **SHOVE**, Apr. 15, 1849, by William McAlister | 3 | 77 |
| Jennett, ae 20, b. Warren, res. Cornwall, m. Samuel A. **SHOVE**, salesman, ae 23, b. Warren, res. Cornwall, May 30, 1849, by Rev. William McAlister | 3 | 104-5 |
| Lucretia M., m. Noah R. **HART**, b. of Cornwall, Nov. 22, 1843, by Rev. Joshua L. Maynard, of the North Cong. Ch. | 3 | 67 |
| Lydia, m. Martin **COLE**, b. of Cornwall, Dec. 9, 1821, by Rev. Walter Smith, of the 2nd Church | 2 | 51 |
| Mary, had d. Harriet, b. Aug. 31, 1848 | 3 | 120-3 |
| Mary E., of Cornwall, m. Lewis O. **CAIN**, of Sharon, May 9, 1847, by Rev. Alfred Gates | 3 | 74 |
| Matilda, m. Daniel T. **CLARK**, b. of Cornwall, June 18, 1854, by Rev. R. D. Kirby | 3 | 126 |
| Sylvester, m. Lucy Anna **STONE**, June 22, 1826, by Rev. Asa Tallmadge, of the Bap. Ch. | 2 | 65 |
| William, clerk, b. Cornwall, res. Meriden, d. Oct. 20, 1849, ae 21 | 3 | 112-13 |
| **BARRET[T], BARRIT**, Catharine, d. Eleazer, d. May 8, 1746 | 1 | 6 |
| Eleazer, of Cornwall, m. Hannah **BULKLEY**, June 6, 1748, by Rev. Stephen Heaton | 1 | 8 |
| Esther, d. Eleazer & Cataran, b. Nov. 12, 1743 | 1 | 4 |
| **BARSE**, [see under **BIERCE**] | | |
| **BARTHOLOMEW**, Esther, of Goshen, m. Jesse **GLEASON**, of Cornwall, Oct. 3, 1822, by Rev. Walter Smith, of the 2nd Ch. | 2 | 54 |
| **BARTON**, William, s. Nehemiah & Sarah, b. May 21, 1801 | 3 | 31 |
| **BASSETT**, Anna, m. Elijah **STEELE**, Jr., Feb. 13, 1786, by Rev. John Cornwell | 2 | 16 |
| Esther M., m. Chauncey **GOODYEAR**, Jr., Apr. 28, 1834, by Rev. William Andrews | 3 | 37 |

| | Vol. | Page |
|---|---|---|
| **BASSETT**, (cont.) | | |
| Samuel, had servant Nancy, d. Elsex & Dinah, b. Sept. 4, 1785 | 2 | 12 |
| **BASTO**, Silva, of Sharon, m. Consider **TANNER**, of Cornwall, Jan. 29, 1795, by Rev. Israel Holly | 3 | 21 |
| **BATES**, Belinda, d. Isaac & Submit, b. Sept. 25, 1797 | 2 | 23 |
| Betsey, d. John, b. Mar. 5, 1795 | 2 | 30 |
| Betsey, d. Isaac & Submit, b. July 18, 1795 | 2 | 23 |
| Buel, s. Isaac & Submit, b. Sept. 14, 1793 | 2 | 30 |
| Isaac, m. Jemima **CARTER**, Apr. 9, 1761, by Rev. H. Gold | 1 | 43 |
| Isaac, s. Isaac & Jemima, b. Apr. 5, 1768 | 1 | 82 |
| Isaac, d. Nov. 24, 1786 | 2 | 11 |
| Isaac, m. Mrs. Submit **DEAN**, Mar. 29, 1792, by Rev. Peter Starr | 3 | 8 |
| Ithniel* Carter, s. Isaac & Jemima, b. May 13, 1773 *("Nathaniel" in Starr's book) | 2 | 13 |
| Jemima, d. Isaac & Jemima, b. Jan. 13, 1765 | 1 | 60 |
| John, s. Isaac & Jemima, b. July 28, 1763 | 1 | 52 |
| John, of Cornwall, m. Mrs. Vestilly **SACKETT**, of Warren, Nov. 24, 1792, by Rev. Peter Starr | 3 | 8 |
| Jonathan, of Hartland, m. Pamela **SEDGWICK**, of Cornwall, Mar. 29, 1821, by Rev. Walter Smith, of the 2nd Church | 2 | 50 |
| Lovisa, d. Isaac & Jemima, b. Nov. 28, 1766 | 1 | 74 |
| Lovisee, d. Isaac & Jemima, d. Jan. 29, 1768 | 1 | 82 |
| Lucinda, d. John & Violette, b. June 17, 1793 | 3 | 19 |
| Nabby, d. Isaac & Jemima, b. Feb. 26, 1772 | 1 | 103 |
| **BAXTER**, Mary Ann, of Canaan, m. Riley **COXEL**, of Cornwall, Feb. 1, 1838, by James Wadsworth, J. P. | 3 | 53 |
| **BEACH**, Albert N., m. Sarah A. **TRAFFORD**, Apr. 24, 1844, by Rev. William Day | 3 | 70 |
| Anson B., m. Elizabeth **PERKINS**, Mar. 6, 1826, by Rev. Asa Tallmadge, of the Bap. Ch. | 2 | 65 |
| Benjamin, Rev., d. July 12, 1816, ae 79 | 2 | 39 |
| Daniel Lorenzo, s. [Smith & Lucia], b. Aug. 21, 1848 | 3 | 95 |
| Elizabeth, d. Linus & Elizabeth, b. July 26, 1779 | LR4 | 14 |
| Henry Osborn, s. [Smith & Lucia], b. Mar. 31, 1840 | 3 | 95 |
| Jerusha, m. Solomon **HART**, Jr., July 6, 1786, by Judah Kellogg, J. P. | 2 | 16 |
| Job Smith Nathan Benedict, s. Simeon & Mary, b. Apr. 10, 1809 | 2 | 34 |
| Julius, m. Betsey **HUMPHREY**, b. of Goshen, Sept. 24, 1820, by Smith Dayton, Elder | 2 | 48 |
| Lucy Almeda, d. Smith & Lucia, b. Sept. 10, 1837 | 3 | 95 |
| Sarah, m. Thoeophilus **PIERCE**, Dec. 7, 1780, by Rev. Hezekiah Gold | 2 | 1 |
| Sarah L., of Cornwall, m. Almon L. **JOHNSON**, of Litchfield, Sept. 29, 1852, by N. C. Lewis | 3 | 123 |
| Sarah Maria, d. [Smith & Lucia], b. July 8, 1845 | 3 | 95 |

| | Vol. | Page |
|---|---|---|
| **BEACH**, (cont.) | | |
| Smith, farmer, & Lucy, had child b. Aug. 21, 1848; d. [ ], ae 3 d. | 3 | 88-9 |
| **BEARDSLEY**, Julius, m. Louisa **REED**, b. of Cornwall, Mar. 29, 1830, by Rev. Bradley Selleck | 3 | 45 |
| Julius, farmer, ae 43 & Eliza L., ae 38, had s. [ ], b. June 19, 1851 | 3 | 114-15 |
| Laura L., m. Harmon **WILSON**, Mar. 22, 1838, by Rev. Walter Smith, of the 2nd Cong. Ch. | 3 | 53 |
| Martha Eliza, d. Julius, farmer, ae 41 & Eliza L., ae 39, b. May 27, 1849 | 3 | 88-9 |
| Mary, d. Julius, farmer ae 43 & Eliza B., ae 37, b. Jan. 8, 1850 | 3 | 110-11 |
| Nehemiah, d. Apr. 6, 1804 | 3 | 6 |
| Philomelia, of Goshen, m. John **WOODWORTH**,of Cornwall, Jan. 9, 1823, by Rev. Walter Smith, of the 2nd Ch. | 2 | 55 |
| Stiles, d. Feb. 23, 1836, ae 56 | 3 | 43 |
| **BECKWITH**, Ruth, of Lyme, m. Robert **LOGINS**, of Woodbury, Mar. 6, 1760, by Rev. George Beckwith, of Lyme | 1 | 39 |
| **[BEEBE]**, **BEBE**, Josephine, d. Harry, laborer, ae 35 & Julia, ae 27, b. Jan. 9, 1848 | 3 | 84-5 |
| **BEERS**, [see also **BIERCE & PIERCE**], Alpheas, m. Tabitha C. **LEWIS**, Sept. 14, 1826, by Rev. Timothy Stone, of the 1st Ch. | 2 | 65 |
| Curtiss, farmer, b. Stratford, res. Cornwall, d. Mar. 10, 1848, ae 59 | 3 | 92-3 |
| Henry L., s. Curtiss & Alice, b. May 9, 1823 | 3 | 39 |
| James Henry, s. Alpheas & Tabitha, b. Mar. 18, 1831 | 3 | 47 |
| Job Curtiss, s. Curtiss & Alice, b. July 9, 1818 | 2 | 47 |
| John Wells, s. Menzias & Laury, b. Jan. 15, 1822 | 2 | 52 |
| John William Alphonso, s. Alpheus & Tabitha, b. Apr. 7, 1829 | 3 | 47 |
| Menzies, m. Laura **PEIRCE**, Jan. 1, 1821, by Rev. Timothy Stone, of the 1st Church | 2 | 49 |
| Mira Ann, m. Joseph P. **CANFIELD**, Oct. 4, 1825, by Rev. Timothy Stone, of the 1st Ch. | 2 | 63 |
| Sarah E., of Cornwall, m. Hiram **PEIRCE**, of Plymouth, May 30, 1849, by Rev. E. B. Andrews. Int. pub. | 3 | 82 |
| Sarah Elizabeth, d. [Curtis & Alice], b. Oct. 25, 1825 | 3 | 39 |
| Silas Curtis, s. Menzies & Laura, b. Mar. 13, 1827 | 3 | 2 |
| Susan E., ae 23, res. Cornwall, m. Hiram **PEIRCE**, manufacturer, ae 48, b. Cornwall, res. Plymouth, May 30, 1849, by Rev. E. B. Andrews | 3 | 104-5 |
| Victory C., s. [Curtis & Alice], b. Sept. 25, 1832 | 3 | 39 |
| **BEGLON**, Anna, m. Felix **AGUERG**, b. in Ireland, b. of Norfolk, Aug. 15, 1852, by Rev. John Smith | 3 | 122 |
| **BELKNAP**, Henry C., student, b. New York City, res. Cornwall; d. Apr. 12, 1850, ae 9 | 3 | 112-13 |

| | Vol. | Page |
|---|---|---|
| **BELL**, Abigail, d. Ketchell & Sarah, b. Oct. 2, 1764 | 1 | 57 |
| Abigail, m. William **BIERCE**, Jan. 17, 1787, by Rev. Hezekiah Gold | 2 | 22 |
| Benjamin, s. Ketchell & Abigail, b. Jan. 14, 1767 | 1 | 78 |
| Elizabeth, d. Julius & Elizabeth, b. Mar. 30, 1829 | 3 | 2 |
| Elizabeth M., of Cornwall, m. John H. **WELCH**, M. D., of New Hartford, July 12, 1848, by Rev. Jno Pettebone, of Winsted | 3 | 80 |
| Elizabeth M., housekeeper, ae 19, res. Cornwall, m. John H. **WELCH**, physician, ae 21, b. Norfolk, res. New Hartford, July 12, 1848, by Rev. Asa Pettebone | 3 | 90-1 |
| Hannah, d. Ketchell & Abigail, b. Mar. 2, 1769 | 1 | 89 |
| Hannah, d. the late Ketchell & Abigail, d. May 5, 1789 | 2 | 26 |
| Jane, d. May 23, 1849, ae 75 | 3 | 106-7 |
| Jonathan, s. Ketchell & Sarah, b. Jan. 22, 1755 | 1 | 24 |
| Jonathan*, m. Susannah **CANFIELD**, May 19, 1779, by Rev. Hezekiah Gold *(Arnold Copy has "Jonathan **BALLARD**") | LR4 | 14 |
| Joseph, s. Ketchell & Sarah, b. Mar. 21, 1757 | 1 | 27 |
| Joseph, s. Ketchell & Sarah, d. Feb. 18, 1776 | LR3 | 7 |
| Ketchel, of Cornwall, m. Sarah **WHITING***, d. Joseph, of Stanford, Nov. 14, 1753, by Moses Mather, V. D. M. *("**WHITNEY**" in Starr's book) | 1 | 19 |
| Ketchel, s. Ketchel & Sarah, b. Mar. 23, 1759 | 1 | 33 |
| Ketchel, of Cornwall, m. Mrs. Abigail **WALLER**, of New Milford, Apr. 30, 1766, by Nathaniel Taylor | 1 | 72 |
| Ketchell, Jr., m. Ruth **BRISTOL**, b. of Cornwall, Oct. 22, 1772, by Rev. Hezekiah Gold. Witness: Judah Kellogg | LR3 | 15 |
| Ketchel, d. June 3, 1786 | 2 | 11 |
| Ketchell, 2nd, d. Feb. 28, 1787 | 2 | 11 |
| Milla, d. Ketchell, Jr. & Ruth, b. Feb. 2, 1779 | LR3 | 15 |
| Ruth, d. Ketchell, Jr. & Ruth, b. Jan. 31, 1781 | LR4 | 19 |
| Ruth, of Cornwall, m. Nehemiah **MARSH**, of Canaan, June 10, 1795, by Judah Kellogg, J. P. | 3 | 21 |
| Sarah, d. Ketchell & Sarah, b. Nov. 25, 1761 | 1 | 44 |
| Sarah, w. Kitchell, d. Oct. 2, 1764 | 1 | 57 |
| **BENEDICT**, Alvira, m. Edwin **BARBER**, Aug. 5, 1822, by Asa Tallmadge, Elder, of the Bap. Church | 2 | 53 |
| Betty, d. John & Elizabeth, b. Sept. 23, 1779 | LR3 | 16 |
| Cyrus F., manufacturer, ae 32, b. Salisbury, res. Salisbury, m. Sarah **EGGLESTON**, ae 30, b. Cornwall, res. Salisbury, Mar. 27, 1850, by Rev. William McAlister | 3 | 112-13 |
| Edwin, of Danbury, m. Polly S. **CARTER**, of Cornwall, May 3, 1832, by Rev. Timothy Stone, of the Cong. Ch. | 3 | 50 |
| Elcy, d. Moses & Lucy, b. Apr. 4, 1786 | 2 | 17 |
| Ethel Taylor, s. Moses & Lucy, b. July 23, 1788 | 2 | 25 |
| Giles, farmer, ae 30, b. Goshen, res. Goshen, m. Nancy **FORD**, ae 20, res. Cornwall, Apr. 23, 1848, by Joshua | | |

| | Vol. | Page |
|---|---|---|
| **BENEDICT**, (cont.) | | |
| L. Maynard | 3 | 90-1 |
| Jerusha, d. Silas & Mary, b. June 27, 1814 | 2 | 61 |
| Jerusha, m. Elenda **OSBORN**, Sept. 28, 1836, by Rev. William Andrews | 3 | 41 |
| John, s. John & Lydiah, b. July 11, 1750 | 1 | 83 |
| John, d. Aug. 9, 1750 | 1 | 12 |
| John, m. Elizabeth **PIERCE**, Jan. 30, 1772, by Thomas Russell, J. P. | 1 | 101 |
| John, s. John & Elizabeth, b. Nov. 6, 1773 | 2 | 13 |
| Julia, d. Silas & Mary, b. Mar. 28, 1816 | 2 | 61 |
| Julia, of Cornwall, m. James **LANDON**, 2nd, of Litchfield, May 13, 1835, by Rev. David G. Tomlinson, of the Epis, Ch. Milton | 3 | 40 |
| Lucy, d. John & Elizabeth, b. Feb. 4, 1775 | LR3 | 8 |
| Lucy, d. Moses & Lucy, b. Apr. 22, 1792 | 3 | 24 |
| Lydia, d. [Moses & Lucy], b. Nov. 3, 1784 | 2 | 10 |
| Mariah, m. William **SEELEY**, b. of Cornwall, Nov. 10, 1822, by Rev. A. Derthick, of the Bap. Ch. of Warren | 2 | 54 |
| Moses, of Cornwall, m. Lucy **PECK**, of Danbury, Nov. 8, 1780, by Thomas Brooks | 2 | 8 |
| Ozias, s. Silas & Mary, b. Mar. 24, 1820 | 2 | 61 |
| Rachel, m. Consider **TANNER**, Mar. 3, 1772, by Hezekiah Gold | 1 | 102 |
| Rachel, m. Daniel **PERKINS**, Jr., Apr. 17, 1806, by Judah Kellogg, J. P. | 3 | 11 |
| Rebeckah, d. Moses & Lucy, b. Mar. 11, 1782 | 2 | 10 |
| Rebecca, of Cornwall, m. Rachel(?) **PERRY**, of West Stockbridge, Oct. 6, 1834, by Daniel Baldwin, of New Milford | 3 | 38 |
| Samuel, d. June 18, 1750 | 1 | 12 |
| Samuel, s. John & Elizabeth, b. June 8, 1783 | 2 | 5 |
| Sarah, d. Ephraim & Betty, b. Sept. 20, 1787 | 2 | 20 |
| Sarah, m. Guy **DOOLITTLE**, b. of Cornwall, Jan. 20, 1821, by Rev. Asa Tallmadge | 2 | 49 |
| Silas, s. Silas & Mary, b. May 10, 1818 | 2 | 61 |
| Silas, Jr., of Goshen, m. Nancy R. **FORD**, of Cornwall, Apr. 23, 1848, at the house of James Ford, by Rev. Joshua L. Maynard, of the North Cong. Ch. | 3 | 79 |
| Silas, farmer, ae 30, & Nancy ae 20, Goshen, had d. [ ], b. Aug. 20, 1848 | 3 | 84-5 |
| William, s. John & Elizabeth, b. Mar. 21, 1777 | LR3 | 14 |
| **BENNETT, BENNET**, Abigail, of New Milford, m. Daniel **GRIFFIS**, of Cornwall, July 22, 1755, by Paul Welch, of New Milford | 1 | 28 |
| Amanda L., d. Aug. 3, 1849, ae 14 | 3 | 112-13 |
| Archibald, m. Augusta V. **KIMBERLEY**, Jan. 27, 1853, by Ralph Smith | 3 | 125 |

| | Vol. | Page |
|---|---|---|
| **BENNETT, BENNET**, (cont.) | | |
| Elizabeth Naomi, d. Marshall D. W. & Abigail, b. Feb. 13, 1823 | 2 | 52 |
| Horace Lucius, s. Marshall W. & Abigail, b. Apr. 7, 1821 | 2 | 47 |
| Jedediah, s. Jedediah, of Oblong, N. U., d. Feb. 20, 1760 | 1 | 37 |
| Marshall D. W., m. Abigail **HITCHCOCK**, of Cornwall, May 21, 1820, by Asa Tallmadge, Elder | 2 | 48 |
| **BENSON**(?), Thomas, m. Mary **PATTERSON**, Oct. 17, 1760, by Rev. H. Gold | 1 | 37 |
| **BENTLEY**, Joseph, of Goshen, m. Maria **BEIRCE**, of Cornwall, Jan, 2, 1831, by Rev. Silas Ambler | 3 | 48 |
| **BIERCE, BARCE, BEIRCE, BEARSE, BARSE**, [see also **PIERCE & BEERS**], Abiah, m. Lemuel **JENNINGS**, Jan. 20, 1773, by Rev. Hezekiah Gold | 1 | 107 |
| Abigail, d. Sylvester & Sally, b. Aug. 14, 1812 | 2 | 41 |
| Abigail, w. William, d. Sept. 25, 1815 | 2 | 39 |
| Abigail, m. Hiram **NEAL**, Sept. 16, 1832, by Rev. Silas Ambler | 3 | 50 |
| Allin, s. Austin & Mary, b. Oct. 28, 1769 | 2 | 13 |
| Ann, d. James & Mary, b. Feb. 20, 1761 | 1 | 41 |
| Betsey A., w. Peter, d. Nov. 4, 1835, ae 41 y. 6 d. | 3 | 43 |
| Caroline, d. [Silvester & Sally], b. Oct. 4, 1810 | 3 | 18 |
| Caroline, of Cornwall, m. Hiram **APPLY**, of Goshen, Mar. 4, 1839, by Samuel W. Smith | 3 | 56 |
| Edwin, s. Sylvester & Sarah, b. Jan. 6, 1823 | 2 | 52 |
| Eliza, m. George W. **RILEY**, b. of Goshen, Sept. 1, 1851, by F. C. Youngs | 3 | 122 |
| Elizabeth, m. John **GRIFFIN**, Dec. 30, 1806, by Judah Kellogg, J. P. | 3 | 3 |
| Elizabeth R.,d. Peter & Betsey, d. June 5, 1836, ae 16 y. 13 d. | 3 | 43 |
| Elizabeth Rebecca, d. Peter & Betsey, b. Aug. 22, 1819 | 2 | 47 |
| Erastus, s. Joseph & Elizabeth, b. Oct. 13, 1776 | LR3 | 14 |
| Erastus, s. Joseph & Elizabeth, b. Dec. 21, 1778 | LR4 | 14 |
| Flora, of Cornwall, m. Roswell **CLARK**, of Sharon, June 12, 1837, by Robert Travis | 3 | 53 |
| Hannah, d. [Austin & Mary], b. Jan. 18, 1774 | 2 | 12 |
| Hannah, d. [William & Abigail], b. Mar. 2, 1789 | 2 | 21 |
| Heman, s. Joseph & Elizabeth, b. Feb. 28, 1775 | LR3 | 8 |
| Hezekiah, s. Joseph & Elizabeth, b. July 2, 1769 | 1 | 94 |
| James, Jr., m. Sarah **BALDWIN**, Oct. 5, 1769, by Rev. Hezekiah Gold | 1 | 91 |
| Joseph, m. Elizabeth **EM[M]ONS**, Sept. 19, 1768, by Thomas Russell, J. P. | 1 | 82 |
| Joseph, s. Joseph & Elizabeth, b. Jan. 8, 1772 | 1 | 106 |
| Joseph, s. Joseph & Elizabeth, b. Sept. 25, 1773 | LR3 | 8 |
| Joseph, Capt., d. Jan. 8, 1816, ae 74 | 2 | 39 |
| Julia Anne, d. Sylvester & Sarah, b. Feb. 6, 1820 | 2 | 52 |
| Lewey Alling, d. Peter & Elizabeth, b. Oct. 13, 1823 | 2 | 52 |

| | Vol. | Page |
|---|---|---|
| **BIERCE, BARCE, BEIRCE, BEARSE, BARSE,** (cont.) | | |
| Loiza, twin with Loretta, d. [Sylvester & Sally], b. Oct. 17, 1814 | 2 | 41 |
| Loretta*, twin with Loiza, d. [Sylvester & Sally], b. Oct. 17, 1814 *("Louella"?) | 2 | 41 |
| Louella*, m. George **SCOVIL**, Mar. 15, 1837, by Rev. William Andrew *("Loretta"?) | 3 | 52 |
| Louisa, of Cornwall, m. John **APPLY**, of Goshen, Mar. 4, 1839, by Samuel W. Smith | 3 | 56 |
| Lucia, b. Cornwall **HOLLOW**, res. Cornwall, d. May 14, 1851, ae 2 | 3 | 120-1 |
| Lucinda, d. William & Abigail, b. Dec. 19, 1796 | 3 | 25 |
| Lucius Nerius, s. William & Abigail, b. Aug. 4, 1801 | 2 | 32 |
| Lucretia, d. William & Abigail, b. July 30, 1787 | 2 | 21 |
| Marcus Aurelius, 3rd s. William & Abigail, b. Aug. 16, 1799 | 2 | 23 |
| Maria, twin with Mary, d. [Silvester & Sally], b. Feb. 16, 1809 | 3 | 18 |
| Maria, of Cornwall, m. Joseph **BENTLEY**, of Goshen, Jan. 2, 1831, by Rev. Silas Ambler | 3 | 48 |
| Mary, twin with Maria, d. [Silvester & Sally], b. Feb. 14, 1809 | 3 | 18 |
| Mary, m. Hiram **NEAL**, Mar. 11, 1830, by Rev. Walter Smith, of the North Ch. | 3 | 45 |
| Mary Anne, m. Stephen **BONNEY**, b. of Cornwall, Nov. 17, 1802, by Judah Kellogg, J. P. | 3 | 32 |
| Peter, m. Betsey **ALLING**, Oct. 8, 1818, by Rev. Timothy Stone | 2 | 48 |
| Peter, m. Eliza **CARTER**, Apr. 27, 1837, by Rev. William Andrews | 3 | 52 |
| Rebeckah, m. Joel **TUTTLE**, Oct. 2, 1781, by Rev. Hezekiah Gold | 2 | 1 |
| Sarah Ann, m. William **HUMPHREY**, Apr. 16, 1834, by Rev. William Andrews | 3 | 37 |
| Sarah Anne, d. Sylvester & Sarah, b. Aug. 4, 1817 | 2 | 44 |
| Sarah Jane, of Cornwall, m. Albert **EGGLESTON**, of North East Dutchess Cty., N. Y., Feb. 28, 1841, by Rev. E. Washburn | 3 | 61 |
| Solomon, of Cornwall, m. Betsey Ann **ROBINSON**, of Weston, Oct. 21, 1844, by H. Day | 3 | 70 |
| Toma Columbus, s. William & Abigail, b. Mar. 8, 1791 | 3 | 7 |
| William, m. Abigail **BELL**, Jan. 17, 1787, by Rev. Hezekiah Gold | 2 | 22 |
| William Whiting, s. William & Abigail, b. Dec. 25, 1794 | 2 | 30 |
| Winslow, s. [Austin & Mary], b. Sept. 21, 1775 | 2 | 12 |
| Zebulon, s. [Austin & Mary], b. Sept. 5, 1772 | 2 | 13 |
| Zebulon, s. Austin & Mary, b. Sept. 5, 1772; d. Apr. 20, 1776 | 2 | 12 |
| **BIRCH**, Jeremiah, m. Laura **DIBBLE**, July 6, 1828, by Rev. William Andrews | 2 | 68 |

| | Vol. | Page |
|---|---|---|
| **BIRDSALL, BIRDSILL**, Charlotte, m. Daniel **WINCHELL**, b. of Cornwall, Jan. 10, 1843, by Rev. John K. Still, of the M. E. Ch. | 3 | 66 |
| Josiah, farmer, b. N. Y. State, res. Cornwall, d. Jan. 22, 1848, ae 77 | 3 | 92-3 |
| Louisa, d. Joseph, trader, ae 41 & Ruby, ae 36, b. Jan. 16, 1849 | 3 | 100-1 |
| **BIRDSEYE**, Charlotte, d. [Ebenezer & Sarah], b. Mar. 29, 1794 | 3 | 31 |
| Charlotte, m. Lucius C. **ROUSE**, Nov. 30, 1818, by Rev. Timothy Stone, of the 1st Ch. Witness: William Kellogg, T. C. | 2 | 59 |
| Ebenezer, twin with Ezra, s. [Ebenezer & Sarah], b. May 15, 1798 | 3 | 31 |
| Eunice, w. Ebenezer, d. Jan. 23, 1787 | 2 | 26 |
| Eunice, d. [Ebenezer & Sarah], b. Mar. 11, 1793 | 3 | 31 |
| Ezekiel, s. [Ebenezer & Sarah], b. Mar. 17, 1796 | 3 | 31 |
| Ezekial, m. Lucinda **PIERCE**, Oct. 5, 1826, by Rev. Timothy Stone, of the 1st Ch. | 2 | 65 |
| Ezekiel, m. Mary M. **STONE**, Feb. 5, 1834, by William Andrews | 3 | 37 |
| Ezra, twin with Ebenezer, s. Ebenezer & Sarah, b. May 15, 1798 | 3 | 31 |
| Hannah, d. [Ebenezer & Sarah], b. Sept. 29, 1791 | 3 | 31 |
| Hannah, m. Joshua B. **CHAFFEE**, Dec. 25, 1820, by Rev. Timothy Stone | 2 | 49 |
| Ketchell, s. Ebenezer & Sarah, b. Aug. 24, 1790 | 3 | 31 |
| Sarah, w. Ebenezer, d. Jan. 1, 1809 | 3 | 4 |
| **BIRGE**, Chester G., m. Mary M. **NORTH**, Sept. 26, 1827, by Rev. William Andrews | 2 | 67 |
| **BISBEY**, Submit, d. Joseph & Zebiah, b. Mar. 25, 1756 | 1 | 32 |
| **BISHOP**, Amos, s. Luane, b. Mar. 15, 1808 | 2 | 47 |
| Ann, d. Talney* & Lois, b. May 14, 1760; d. same month 24th day *("Talma[d]ge" in Starr's book) | 1 | 45 |
| Asa, s. John & Mary, b. Aug. 6, 1769 | 1 | 90 |
| Burr, s. Talney* & Lois, b. July 27, 1763 *("Talmadge") | 1 | 53 |
| Ebenezer, Dr., m. Lydia **SCOTT**, June 28, 1777, by Rev. Hezekiah Gold | 2 | 2 |
| Ebenezer, s. [Ebenezer & Lydia], b. Oct. 5, 1790 | 3 | 7 |
| Electa, d. Ebenezer & Lydia, b. Mar. 26, 1781 | 2 | 3 |
| Electa, d. Ebenezer & Lydia, d. Mar. 29, 1781 | 2 | 2 |
| Jemima, m. John **TANNER**, Sept. 14, 1758, by Rev. Hezekiah Gold | 1 | 32 |
| Joab, s. John & Mary, b. Aug. 22, 1764 | 1 | 59 |
| John, s. John & Mary, b. Dec. 13, 1766 | 1 | 73 |
| Lois, d. Talney* & Lois, b. May 29, 1761 *("Talmadge") | 1 | 45 |
| Lucina, [twin with Lucene, d. Ebenezer & Lydia], b. Dec. 26, 1784 | 3 | 7 |
| Lucene, [twin with Lucina, d. Ebenezer & Lydia], b. Dec. | 3 | 7 |

| | Vol. | Page |
|---|---|---|
| **BISHOP**, (cont.) | | |
| 26, 1784 | 3 | 7 |
| Lydia, d. [Ebenezer & Lydia], b. Apr. 10, 1779 | 2 | 3 |
| Lydia, d. [Ebenezer & Lydia], d. Apr. 30, 1781 | 2 | 2 |
| Mary, m. Neamiah **PIERCE**, Sept. 14, 1758, by Rev. H. Gold | 1 | 33 |
| Rebecca, d. Ebenezer & Lydia, b. May 16, 1782 | 3 | 7 |
| Samantha, ae 18, m. Leander **WHITNEY**, farmer, ae 24, b. Warren, res. Warren, July 6, 1848, by Rev. John T. Norton | 3 | 90-1 |
| Samantha, m. Leander **WHITNEY**, b. of Cornwall, July 16, 1848, by John T. Norton | 3 | 80 |
| Sarah, m. William **CAMP**, Mar. 10, 1759, by Rev. H. Gold | 1 | 33 |
| Sarah*, of Stanford, m. Elijah **ALLEN**, of Cornwall, Oct. 30, 1777, by Moses Mather, V. D. M. *("Mary" in Starr's Hist.) | LR3 | 16 |
| Tallmadge, m. Lois **BURR**, Sept. 23, 1758, by Rev. Hezekiah Gold | 1 | 32 |
| **BLACKMAN**, Cyrenus, s. Zachariah & Alice, b. Aug. 9, 1793 | 2 | 30 |
| **BLACKNEY**, William A., of Grand Rapids, Mich., m. Mary Ann **BONNEY**, of Cornwall, Feb. 24, 1846, by Rev. Hiram Day | 3 | 72 |
| **BLAKE**, Almira D., m. Amos **CLARK**, Oct. 13, 1839, by Rev. Eleazer Beecher, of the Bap. Ch. | 3 | 59 |
| Flora, of Cornwall, m. Theron **SACKETT**, of Stanford, N. Y., Dec. 16, 1828, by Rev. Silas Ambler | 3 | 1 |
| James, m. Betsey **AVERY**, June 11, 1823, by Rev. Asa Tallmadge, of the Bap. Ch. | 2 | 55 |
| Julius, m. Adelia **MOREHOUSE**, b. of Cornwall, Feb. 26, 1826, by Rev. Timothy Stone | 2 | 63 |
| **BLAKESLEY**, Adaline, of Prospect, m. Hiram **COLE**, of Cornwall, Apr. 16, 1849, by James Wadsworth, J. P. | 3 | 82 |
| **BLEY**, Hannah, m. Samuel **ABBOTT**, Jr., May 2, 1769, by Rev. Hezekiah Gold | 1 | 88 |
| **BLINN, BLIN**, Abigail, m. Benjamin **CATLIN**, Jan. 28, 1813, by Rev. Josiah Hawes. Witnesses: James D. Ford & Anson Rogers | 2 | 45 |
| Lydia, m. Joel **CATLIN**, b. of Cornwall, Nov. 18, 1807, by Rev. Josiah Hawes, of the 2nd Ch. Witnesses: Eber Harrison & Amos Catlin | 3 | 33 |
| Sturgis, of Sharon, m. Caroline **NETTLETON**, of Cornwall, Nov. 27, 1839, by Erastus Doty | 3 | 58 |
| **BLISS**, Hannah, b. Ireland, res. Bridgeport, d. May 16, 1851, ae 87 | 3 | 120-1 |
| **BONNEY**, Abigail, d. [Col. Stephen & Anne], b. Oct. 24, 1815 | 2 | 61 |
| Adelia, m. Silas P. **JUDSON**, b. of Cornwall, Apr. 15, 1846, by Hiram Day | 3 | 72 |
| Adeline Louisa, d. [Col. Stephen & Anne], b. Aug. 15, 1823 | 2 | 61 |
| Ann, d. Jethro & Rachel, b. July 20, 1769 | 1 | 92 |
| Anna, d. Titus & Anna, b. Nov. 18, 1774 | LR3 | 8 |

| | Vol. | Page |
|---|---|---|
| **BONNEY**, (cont.) | | |
| Anne, w. Col. Stephen, d. Oct. 18, 1824 | 2 | 56 |
| Benjamin, s. Peres & Priscilla, b. Feb. 20, 1782 | 2 | 4 |
| Caroline, of Cornwall, m. Lucius **JESSUP**, of Middletown, N. J., Oct. 29, 1851, by Rev. Ralph Smith, of the 1st Cong. Ch. | 3 | 97 |
| Charlotte, d. [Col. Stephen & Anne], b. Aug. [ ], 1818 | 2 | 61 |
| Chloe, d. Jethro & Rachel, b. Aug. 27, 1762 | 1 | 48 |
| Edward, s. Levi & Mary, b. June 24, 1765 | 1 | 61 |
| Emeline, d. [Col. Stephen & Anne], b. Feb. 24, 1812 | 2 | 61 |
| Hannah, d. [John & Orilla], b. June 13, 1810 | 3 | 28 |
| Heman, s. Jethro & Rachel, b. Feb. 13, 1767 | 1 | 76 |
| Heman, s. Jethro & Rachel, d. Oct. 27, 1783 | 2 | 6 |
| Herman, m. C. A. **CROSS**, Dec. 31, 1849, by Rev. William McAlister | 3 | 82 |
| Hezekiah, s. [John & Orilla], b. Sept. 23, 1803 | 3 | 28 |
| Ira, m. Abigail **PECK**, June 8, 1825, by Rev. Asa Tallmadge, of the Bap. Ch. | 2 | 65 |
| Jethro, m. Rachel **WALEY***, Aug. 5, 1761, by Rev. H. Gold *("**BAILEY**") in Starr's book) | 1 | 40 |
| Jethro, s. Levi & Mary, b. Mar. 15, 1771 | 1 | 98 |
| Jethro, m. Dorcas **ALLEN**, May 11, 1780, by Judah Kellogg, J. P. | LR4 | 16 |
| Joel, s. Perez & Prescilla, b. Aug. 15, 1786 | 2 | 21 |
| John, s. Titus & Anna, b. May 27, 1772 | 1 | 104 |
| John, s. [John & Orilla], b. Feb. 24, 1806 | 3 | 28 |
| John Bisbee, s. Levi & Mary, b. Mar. 13, 1777 | LR3 | 14 |
| Joshua, s. Peres & Prescilla, b. Dec. 10, 1772 | LR3 | 8 |
| Josiah, s. Perez & Priscilla, b. Feb. 12, 1784 | 2 | 10 |
| Jotham, s. Jethro & Rachel, b. Nov. 28, 1764 | 1 | 58 |
| Julius Peirce, s. Col. Stephen & Anne, b. Aug. 29, 1808 | 2 | 61 |
| Levi, m. Mary **MAY**, Oct. 4, 1764, by Rev. Hezekiah Gold | 1 | 58 |
| Levi, s. Jethro & Rachel, b. Sept. 10, 1774 | LR3 | 8 |
| Lois, m. Chauncey **MARVIN**, b. of Cornwall, Jan. 30, 1833, by Rev. Silas Ambler | 3 | 35 |
| Lucretia, d. Levi & Mary, b. Mar. 13, 1774 | LR3 | 6 |
| Lucy, d. Jethro & Rachel, b. Feb. 3, 1772 | 1 | 107 |
| Lucy, d. [Perez & Prescilla], b. Oct. 24, 1788 | 2 | 21 |
| Mariette, d. [Col. Stephen & Anne], b. Jan. 11, 1814 | 2 | 61 |
| Marette, of Cornwall, m. William J. **DEDRICK**, of Amenia, N. Y., Sept. 25, 1848, by Rev. Hiram Day | 3 | 81 |
| Marriett, ae 35, res. Cornwall, m. William **DEDRICK**, dentist, ae 37, b. Coxsackie, N. Y., res. Amenia, N. Y., Apr. 15, 1849, by Rev. Hiram Day | 3 | 104-5 |
| Mary, d. Levi & Mary, b. Apr. 28, 1779 | 2 | 6 |
| Mary A., m. Henry **FRINK**, Nov. 17, 1831, by Rev. William Andrews | 3 | 49 |
| Mary Ann, of Cornwall, m. William A. **BLACKNEY**, of | | |

| | Vol. | Page |
|---|---|---|
| **BONNEY**, (cont.) | | |
| Grand Rapids, Mich., Feb. 24, 1846, by Rev. Hiram Day | 3 | 72 |
| Mary Anne, d. [Col. Stephen & Anne], b. Mar. 5, 1810 | 2 | 61 |
| Mira, d. John & Orilla, b. Dec. 20, 1799 | 3 | 28 |
| Molly, d. Peres & Prescilla, b. Apr. 4, 1778 | LR3 | 15 |
| Nabby, d. Peres & Prescilla, b. Apr. 12, 1771 | 1 | 100 |
| Orpha, d. [John & Orilla], b. Nov. 10, 1801 | 3 | 28 |
| Rebecca, of Cornwall, m. Edward **BARNES**, of Goshen, Jan. 2, 1834, by Aaron S. Hill | 3 | 36 |
| Rezpah, d. [Levi & Mary], b. Apr. 13, 1782 | 2 | 6 |
| Ruth, d. Levi & Mary, b. Apr. 3, 1768 | 1 | 81 |
| Sal!y, d. Levi & Mary, b. Dec. 25, 1786 | 2 | 20 |
| Sally, d. Perez & Priscilla, b. Feb. 15, 1790 | 3 | 24 |
| Samuel Sherman, s. [John & Orilla], b. Feb. 28, 1812 | 3 | 28 |
| Seth, s. [Peres & Prescilla], b. Jan. 5, 1775 | LR3 | 8 |
| Stephen, s. Perez & Priscilla, b. Mar. 17, 1780 | LR4 | 15 |
| Stephen, m. Mary Anne **BARCE**, b. of Cornwall, Nov. 17, 1802, by Judah Kellogg, J. P. | 3 | 32 |
| Stephen, s. [Col. Stephen & Anne], b. Feb. 25, 1821 | 2 | 61 |
| Stephen, Col, m. Irene **ROUSE**, Mar. 2, 1825, by Rev. Timothy Stone, of the 1st Ch. | 2 | 62 |
| Thomas, s. Peres & Prisella, b. Jan. 11, 1769 | 1 | 90 |
| Titus, m. Anna **PIERCE**, Feb. 21, 1771, by Rev. Hezekiah Gold | 1 | 104 |
| William, m. Eliza **EVERETT**, Oct. 1, 1826, by Rev. Timothy Stone, of the 1st Ch. | 2 | 65 |
| William Bradford, s. [John & Orilla], b. Jan. 3, 1808 | 3 | 28 |
| **BOOTH**, Charles H., of New Milford, m. Celestia M. **CROSS**, of Cornwall, Feb. 14, 1847, by R. K, Reynolds | 3 | 74 |
| **BOSTWICK**, Betsey, m. Jason **CROSS**, b. of Cornwall, Nov. 2, 1828, by Rev. E. Washburn | 3 | 1 |
| **BOUDINET**, Elias, of the Cherokee Nation, m. Harriet **GOLD**, of Cornwall, Mar. 28, 1826, by Rev. Francis A. Case, of the Cong. Ch. Goshen | 2 | 63 |
| **BOYD**, John, of Waterbury, m. Margaret **KYLE**, of Cornwall, June 31, 1852, by J. L. Maynard | 3 | 122 |
| **BRADBURY**, Hannah M., m. Charles F. **BALDWIN**, Oct. 8, 1845, at the house of Mr. Bradbury, by Rev. Joshua L. Maynard, of the North Cong. Ch. | 3 | 71 |
| **BRADFORD**, Benjamin, of Cornwall, m. Catharine Rebecca **JACKSON**, of Sharon, Sept. 3, 1838, by N. M. Urmston | 3 | 54 |
| Charlotte, m. William H. **RUGG**, May 17, 1832, by Rev. Walter Smith, of the North Cong. Ch. | 3 | 49 |
| Eleanor, m. Joseph P. **HARRISON**, b. of Cornwall, Feb. 21, 1803, by Judah Kellogg, J. P. | 3 | 32 |
| Eleanor, m. John **HARRISON**, Mar. 13, 1833, by Rev. Walter Smith, of the North Cong. Ch. | 3 | 36 |
| Elisha, m. Lucy **ROSSETER**, of Cornwall, Aug. 10, 1786, by | | |

| | Vol. | Page |
|---|---|---|
| **BRADFORD**, (cont.) | | |
| Rev. Hezekiah Gold | 2 | 16 |
| Emeline, of Cornwall, m. William **MARSH**, of Goshen, Jan. 18, 1821, by Joseph Harvey | 2 | 49 |
| Hannah, m. Ebenezer **SHERWOOD**, Jan. 2, 1772, by Rev. Hezekiah Gold | LR4 | 15 |
| James F., m. wid. Hannah **HARRISON**, b. of Cornwall, May 29, 1831, by Silas Ambler | 3 | 48 |
| John, m. Lucinda* **HARRISON**, Sept. 14, 1829, by Rev. Walter Smith, of the North Ch. *("Lucretia" in Starr's book) | 3 | 44 |
| Rachel, Mrs., m. Shubael **LAWREE**, Dec. 5, 1792, by Judah Kellogg, J. P. | 3 | 20 |
| Sarah M., m. William H. **RUGG**, Nov. 28, 1837, by Rev. Walter Smith, of the North Cong. Ch. | 3 | 53 |
| **BRADLEY**, Esther A., of Cornwall, m. Erastus **HOWE**, of Canaan, Jan. 27, 1850, by Rev. Joshua L. **MAYNARD**, of the North Cong. Ch., at his house | 3 | 83 |
| Fanny E., of Cornwall, m. Erastus C. **HOLCOMB**, of Donnerville, N. J., Sept. 5, 1852, by Rev. Luther B. Hart | 3 | 123 |
| George, m. Eliza **STONE**, b. of Litchfield, Jan. 27, 1832, by Rev. Silas Ambler | 3 | 49 |
| Harriet, m. Lucius **KELLOGG**, M. D., Mar. 9, 1851, by George Wheaton, J. P. | 2 | 96 |
| Harriet, ae 29, b. Prospect, res. Dover, N. Y., m. Lucius **KELLOGG**, doctor, ae 69, b. Cornwall, res. Dover, N. Y., Mar. [ ], 1851, by George Wheaton | 3 | 118-19 |
| Ladan*, of Goshen, m. Jerusha **PALMER**, of Cornwall, Mar. 11, 1829, by Rev. Silas Ambler *("Leighton W." in Starr's book) | 3 | 1 |
| Sarah Elizabeth, d. James W., carpenter, ae 35 & Ellen W., ae 32, res. Cornwall Hallow, b. Oct. 6, 1848 | 3 | 98-9 |
| **BREWSTER**, George M., s. Jasper P., farmer, ae 32, & Susan, ae 28, b. Nov. 11, 1850 | 3 | 116-17 |
| Hydra M., d. Jasper, farmer, ae 30 & Susan, ae 25, b. Feb. 15, 1849 | 3 | 98-9 |
| Sarah, had s. Elijah **NELSON**, b. Jan. 1, 1799 | 3 | 15 |
| **BRINSMADE**, Daniel N., m. Lucy **MERWIN**, Mar. 19, 1806, by Rev. Timothy Stone | 3 | 3 |
| **BRISTOL**, Abel Lyman, s. [Nathan & Hannah], b. Jan. 10, 1787 | 2 | 17 |
| Anna, d. [Nathan & Hannah], b. July 23, 1783 | 2 | 17 |
| Charles, s. [Nathan & Hannah], b. June 1, 1781 | 2 | 17 |
| Daniel Merwin, s. Nathan & Hannah, b. Aug. 17, 1776 | 2 | 17 |
| Horace, s. [Nathan & Hannah], b. Feb. 6, 1778 | 2 | 17 |
| John, m. Margary **GIBBS**, Nov. 13, 1789, by Judah Kellogg, J. P. | 3 | 8 |
| John, m. Sally **ROGERS**, b. of Cornwall, June 23, 1795, by Judah Kellogg, J. P. | 3 | 21 |

| | Vol. | Page |
|---|---|---|
| **BRISTOL**, (cont.) | | |
| Margaret, w. John, d. Dec. 23, 1793 | 2 | 28 |
| Nicy, d. [Nathan & Hannah], b. Mar. 28, 1785 | 2 | 17 |
| Necy, m. Ezra **MALLORY**, b. of Cornwall, Sept. 22, 1803, by Rev. Henry Christie | 3 | 32 |
| Ruth, m. Ketchell **BELL**, Jr., b. of Cornwall, Oct. 22, 1772, by Rev. Hezekiah Gold. Witness: Judah Kellogg | LR3 | 15 |
| **BRONSON, BROWNSON**, Abbalana, d. Daniel & Rhoda, b. Aug. 15, 1805 | 3 | 17 |
| Anner, d. Timothy & Hannah, b. Feb. 17, 1768 | 1 | 79 |
| Anner, m. Rozel **HOCHKIN**, b. of Cornwall, Mar. 2, [1790], by Rev. Hezekiah Gold. Witnesses: Abraham Hochkin & Abraham Hochkin, Jr. | 2 | 22 |
| Bethesda, d. Daniel & Rhoda, b. Aug. 20, 1801 | 3 | 5 |
| Chloe, d. Daniel & Rhoda, b. Apr. 1, 1799 | 2 | 31 |
| Climena Amelia, d. [Daniel & Rhoda], b. May 5, 1809 | 3 | 17 |
| Daniel, s. Jacob, Jr. & Ruth, b. Apr. 17, 1776 | LR3 | 10 |
| Daniel, m. Rhoda **HOLCOMB**, b. of Cornwall, June 5, 1794, by Hercules Weston | 3 | 21 |
| Daniel, s. Daniel & Rhoda, b. Sept. 11, 1803 | 3 | 5 |
| Daniel, m. Marrilla **DEAN**, b. of Cornwall, June 26, 1828, by Rev. Silas Ambler | 2 | 68 |
| David How, s. Daniel & Rhoda, b. July 27, 1811 | 3 | 13 |
| Elias, s. Jacob, Jr. & Ruth, b. May 14, 1780 | LR4 | 15 |
| Elias, s. Jacob & Ruth, d. Aug. 31, 1807 | 3 | 4 |
| Jacob, Jr., m. Ruth **KENT***, Mar. 29, 1770, by Rev. Hezekiah Gold *("**HART**" in Starr's book) | 1 | 93 |
| Jacob, the elder, m. Mary **BURNHAM**, Dec. 6, 1779, by Rev. Hezekiah Gold | LR4 | 16 |
| Jacob, d. June 15, 1792 | 2 | 28 |
| Jacob, d. Apr. 2, 1833, ae [ ] | 3 | 43 |
| Malana, m. Lyman P. **BUDDINGTON**, Jan. 12, 1826, by Rev. Asa Tallmadge, of the Bap. Ch. | 2 | 65 |
| Naomi, d. Samuel & Chloe, b. May 14, 1765 | 1 | 64 |
| Rebeckah, w. Jacob, d. Aug. 8, 1779 | LR3 | 15 |
| Rhoda, m. Henry **WILMOTT**, Sept. 20, 1821, by Asa Tallmadge, Elder, of the Bap. Church | 2 | 53 |
| Roman Filer, s. [Daniel & Rhoda], b. May 1, 1807 | 3 | 17 |
| Ruth, d. Daniel & Rhoda, b. Mar. 30, 1795 | 3 | 22 |
| Salana, d. [Daniel & Rhoda], b. Dec. 12, 1796 | 3 | 22 |
| Samuel, m. Johannah **BALDWIN**, Mar. 16, 1775, by Rev. Hezekiah Gold | LR3 | 7 |
| Timothy, m. Hannah **DIBBLE**, b. of Cornwall, Sept. 25, [1765], by Thomas Russell, J. P. | 1 | 62 |
| Timothy, d. [Feb. 12, 1807], ae 72 y. | 3 | 4 |
| Timothy, d. Feb. 12, 1807 | 3 | 6 |
| **BROODER**, Bridget, m. Patrick **HALPIN**, Jan. 7, 1853, by Rev. Peter Kelley. Int. Pub. | 3 | 125 |

| | Vol. | Page |
|---|---|---|
| **BROOKS**, John, m. Caroline **MARVIN**, Sept. 20, 1837, by Rev. William W. Andrews, of Kent | 3 | 56 |
| **BROWN**, Azubah, m. Joseph **PANGBORN**, Dec. 28, 1752, by Solomon Palmer | 1 | 18 |
| Charlotte, of Cornwall, m. Albro A. **SABINS**, of North East, N. Y., Mar. 1, 1848, at the house of Mr. Brown, by Rev. Joshua L. Maynard, of North Cong. Ch. | 3 | 79 |
| Charlotte, ae 19, b. Goshen, res. Cornwall, m. Albro A. **SABINS**, carpenter, ae 26, b. North East, N. Y., res. Cornwall, Mar. 1, 1848, by Rev. Joshua L. Maynard | 3 | 90-1 |
| Emily H., of Cornwall, m. Lewis F. **ARNOLD**, of Hudson, N. Y., Feb. 25, 1840, by N. M. Urmston | 3 | 59 |
| Harriet L., m. Henry **REED**, b. of Cornwall, May 1st sabbath, 1847, by J. W. Andrews | 3 | 76 |
| Joseph, of Goshen, m. Lucretia D. **PENDLETON**, of Cornwall, Feb. 22, 1846, by Rev. Alfred Gates | 3 | 72 |
| Lucy Ann, m. John E. **SEDGWICK**, b. of Cornwall, Dec. 27, 1835, by Rev. Thomas Sparks | 3 | 41 |
| Mary L., m. Philip C. **LUDDINGTON**, b. of Cornwall, Oct. 17, 1820, by Rev. Timothy Stone | 2 | 48 |
| Mercy, m. Isaac **SPALDING**, b. of Cornwall, Dec. 10, 1754, by George Halloway, J. P. | 1 | 22 |
| Mercy, wid., d. Dec. 22, 1761 | 1 | 69 |
| Palmer, m. Jerusha **HART**, Dec. 25, 1833, by Rev. Walter Smith, of the North Cong. Ch. | 3 | 37 |
| Rosetta, see Rosetta **HOW** | 2 | 67 |
| Sally, farming, d. Apr. [ ], 1851, ae 55 | 3 | 120-1 |
| Samuell, d. Dec. 16, 1750 | 1 | 16 |
| Sophia L., m. Samuel S. **REED**, b. of Cornwall, Oct. 22, 1848, by Rev. Hiram Day | 3 | 81 |
| Sophia L., ae 23, res. Cornwall, m. Samuel S. **REED**, farmer, ae 27, res. Cornwall, Oct. 22, 1848, by Rev. Hiram Day | 3 | 104-5 |
| **BROWNSON**, [see under **BRONSON**] | | |
| **BRUSH**, Austain, of New Fairfield, m. Harriet Lucetta **ROGERS**, of Cornwall, May 22, 1848, by Rev. Hiram Day | 3 | 80 |
| Austin, merchant, ae 24, b. New Fairfield, res. Cornwall, m. Harriet L. **ROGERS**, ae 26, b. Cornwall, May 22, 1848, by Rev. H. Day | 3 | 90-1 |
| **BRYANT**, Elizabeth, m. Reuben **SQUIRE**, May 19, [1761], by Rev. Nathaniel Bartlet, of Reading | 1 | 71 |
| Socrates, of Sheffield, Mass., m. Jerusha **TYRELL**, of Cornwall, Nov. 9, 1826, by Rev. Walter Smith | 2 | 65 |
| **BUCKINGHAM**, Benjamin, had negro Edward, or Ned, s. James & Patience, b. Mar. 9, 1789, at New Milford (now the property of Heman Swift) | 3 | 24 |
| **BUCKLEY**, [see under **BULKLEY**] | | |
| **BUDDALL**, Nancy, m. William **SAWYER**, Nov. 29, 1837, by | | |

| | Vol. | Page |
|---|---|---|
| **BUDDALL**, (cont.) | | |
| Rev. Robert Travis | 3 | 53 |
| **BUDDINGTON**, Lyman P., m. Malana **BROWNSON**, Jan. 12, 1826, by Rev. Asa Tallmadge, of the Bap. Ch. | 2 | 65 |
| **BUDSALL**, Mary Ann, m. Philo **SEELEY**, b. of Cornwall, Oct. 20, 1842, by Rev. Thomas Edwards | 3 | 65 |
| **BUEL, BUELL**, George, of Litchfield, m. Mary **SMITH**, of Cornwall, Nov, 28, 1836, by Rev. Thomas Benedict, of Torrington | 3 | 42 |
| Jesse, Capt. of Cornwall, m. Mrs. Lucy **ROGERS**, of Montville, Sept. 5, 1790, by Judah Kellogg, J. P. | 2 | 22 |
| Munson, s. Jesse & Lydia, b. Sept. 10, 1770 | 1 | 102 |
| Paulina, m. Philo **CARTER**, June 26, 1788, by Peter Starr | 3 | 8 |
| **BULKLEY, BUCKLEY**, Fanny, d. Peter & Dorothy, b. [ ] 8, 1795 | 3 | 22 |
| Hannah, m. Eleazer **BARRET**, of Cornwall, June 6, 1748, by Rev. Stephen Heaton | 1 | 8 |
| Hannah, d. [Peter & Dorothy], b. Nov. 5, 1796 | 3 | 22 |
| Julia, d. Cornelius, laborer, ae 38 & Sarah, ae 40, res. Sharon, b. Aug. 27, 1850 | 3 | 116-17 |
| William C., s. Cornelius, laborer & Sarah A., res. Sharon, b. May 14, 1848 | 3 | 84-5 |
| **BULL**, Anna, d. Noah & Mary, b. Apr. 17, 1760 | 1 | 36 |
| Asenath, [d. Noah & Mary], b. Oct. 17, 1765 | 2 | 13 |
| Martin, s. Noah & Mary, b. Oct. 6, 1775 | LR3 | 10 |
| Mary, d. Noah & Mary, b. Nov. 10, 1761 | 1 | 44 |
| Noah, m. Mary **TEFFENY***, July 19, 1759, by Rev. Hezekiah Gold *("Hannah **JEFFERY**" in Starr's book) | 1 | 36 |
| Noah & Mary, had s. [ ], b. Oct. 4, 1772 | 2 | 13 |
| Noah Ashley, [s. Noah & Mary], b. June 15, 1770 | 2 | 13 |
| Sarah, [d. Noah & Mary], b. Mar. 28, 1768 | 2 | 13 |
| ---rary, [child of Noah & Mary], b. Nov. 29, 1763 | 2 | 13 |
| **BULLARD**, [see also **BALLARD**], Ester, m. Elijah **STEAL**, Jan. 18, 1759, by Rev. Timothy Baldwin | 1 | 36 |
| **BUNKER**, Benjamin, laborer, Indian, d. July 19, 1849, ae 40 | 3 | 106-7 |
| Eli, of Cornwall, m. Fanny Main* **WATSON**, of Glastonbury, Feb. 9, 1842, by Rev. Timothy Stone *("Maria"?) | 3 | 64 |
| **BUNNELL, BUNNEL**, Alfred F., of Plymouth, m. Harriet N. **JOHNSON**, of Cornwall, Sept. 3, 1839, by N. M. Urmston | 3 | 58 |
| Charles, s. Joel, charcoal maker & Fanny, res. Goshen, b. Dec. 10, 1847 | 3 | 86-7 |
| Polly, m. Harry **PEIRCE**, b. of Cornwall, Feb. 3, 1827, by Rev. John Lovejoy, of the M. E. Ch. | 2 | 66 |
| **BURNHAM**, Abner, s. Appleton & Mary, b. May 14, 1766 | 1 | 74 |
| Abner, s. Appleton & Maary, b. July 11, 1771 | 1 | 100 |
| Clarissa, d. Oliver & Sarah, b. June 7, 1788 | 3 | 7 |
| Emily J., m. John C. **HART**, June 12, 1834, by Rev. Walter | | |

| | Vol. | Page |
|---|---|---|
| **BURNHAM**, (cont.) | | |
| Smith, of the North Cong. Ch. | 3 | 37 |
| Mary, m. Jacob **BROWNSON**, Dec. 6, 1779, by Rev. Hezekiah Gold | LR4 | 16 |
| Mary H., m. Rev. Albert **JUDSON**, Dec. 3, 1829, by Rev. Walter Smith, of the North Ch. | 3 | 45 |
| Oliver, s. Appelton & Mary, b. Nov. 11, 1760 | 1 | 39 |
| Oliver, m. Sarah **ROGERS**, Oct. 17, 1787, by Rev. John Cornwell | 3 | 8 |
| Philomela, d. Appleton & Mary, b. May 1, 1764 | 1 | 57 |
| Philomela, m. Elias **HART**, b. of Cornwall, June 14, 1781, by Rev. Mr. Gold. Witnesses: Phinehas Hart & Solomon Hart | LR4 | 18 |
| Rhoda, m. James Marsh **DAWGLASS**, Feb. 8, 1774, by Rev. Hezekiah Gold | LR3 | 7 |
| Rhoda, d. [Oliver & Sarah], b. Oct. 30, 1789 | 3 | 7 |
| Rhoda, m. Victorianus **CLARK**, b. of Cornwall, Sept. 18, 1822, by Rev. Walter Smith, of the 2nd Cong. Ch. | 2 | 54 |
| Woolcott, s. Appleton & Mary, b. Apr. 19, 1762 | 1 | 50 |
| **BURR**, Lois, m. Tallmadge **BISHOP**, Sept. 23, 1758, by Rev. Hezekiah Gold | 1 | 32 |
| **BURREL**, Jannet, m. Elisha **CLARK**, b. of Cornwall, June 30, 1822, by Rev. Walter Smith, of the 2nd Church | 2 | 53 |
| **BURTON**, Nehemiah, m. Mrs. Sarah **NEWTON**, Oct. 31, 1799, by Henry Christie, Dea. | 2 | 24 |
| **BUTLER**, Amanda, m. Ranslear **HALL**, b. of Cornwall, June 28, 1827, by Rev. Silas Ambler | 2 | 67 |
| David, s. [Samuel, Jr. & Prudence], b. June 10, 1776 | LR3 | 12 |
| Edmund C., m. Nancy **BALDWIN**, b. of Cornwall, [Apr. 5, 1835], by Rev. William W. Andrews | 3 | 38 |
| Hannah, m. Ozias **HURLBURT**, Jan. 7, 1770, by Rev. Hezekiah Gold | LR3 | 5 |
| Lucretia A., of Cornwall, m. Myron **DOKIN**, of North East, Feb. 3, 1841, by Rev. Erastus Doty, of Colebrook | 3 | 61 |
| Mary Jane, of Cornwall, m. George D. **GOODWIN**, of Sharon, July 19, 1846, by Rev. Alfred Gates | 3 | 73 |
| Polly, d. Samuel, Jr. & Prudence, b. May 2, 1769 | LR3 | 12 |
| Ralph, m. Abigail **REED**, b. of Cornwall, Sept. 23, 1849, by Harley Goodwin | 3 | 123 |
| Sally B., of Cornwall, m. Augustus B. **GRAY**, of Sharon, Mar. 4, 1838, by Rev. Erastus Doty | 3 | 54 |
| Samuel, s. [Samuel, Jr. & Prudence], b. Apr. 26, 1771 | LR3 | 12 |
| Zachariah, s. [Samuel, Jr. & Prudence], b. Aug. 17, 1773 | LR3 | 12 |
| **CAIN**, [see under **O'CAIN**] | | |
| **CALHOUN**, Abby Jones, d. [Jedidiah & Jane], b. Dec. 17, 1811 | 2 | 47 |
| Charlotte E., m. Myron **HARRISON**, June 2, 1830, by Rev. William Andrews | 3 | 46 |
| Charlotte Elizabeth, d. [John & Sarah], b. Oct. 12, 1808 | 3 | 2 |

| | Vol. | Page |
|---|---|---|
| **CALHOUN**, (cont.) | | |
| David Patterson, s. Jedidiah & Jane, b. Dec. 27, 1808 | 2 | 47 |
| David Patterson, s. Jedediah & Jane, d. Apr. 3, 1809 | 2 | 46 |
| Frederick Jedidiah, s. [Jedidiah & Jane], b. June 27, 1820 | 2 | 47 |
| Harriet J., m. William L. **CLARK**, Oct. 12, 1836, by Rev. William Andrews | 3 | 42 |
| Harriet Jane, d. [John & Sarah], b. Dec. 4, 1814 | 3 | 2 |
| Jedidiah, m. Jane **PATTERSON**, b. of Cornwall, Feb. 24, 1808, by Rev. Timothy Stone, of 1st Church | 2 | 50 |
| John Benjamin, s. [John & Sarah], b. Sept. 8, 1822 | 3 | 2 |
| John C., m. Betsey **SWIFT**, b. of Cornwall, Oct. 9, 1822, by Rev. Timothy Stone, of the 1st Ch. | 2 | 54 |
| John Clark, s. [Jedidiah & Jane], b. May 18, 1814 | 2 | 47 |
| Joseph Fay, s. [John & Sarah], b. Aug. 23, 1819 | 3 | 2 |
| Mary L., of Cornwall, m. Charles **FORD**, of Washington, June 18, 1845, by Hiram Day | 3 | 71 |
| Mary Laura, d. [Jedidiah & Jane], b. Nov. 23, 1816, at Warren | 2 | 47 |
| Polly, m. Rufus **PAYNE**, Jr., Jan. 13, 1830, by Rev. William Andrews | 3 | 45 |
| Polly Swift, d. John & Polly, b. Oct. 4, 1801 | 3 | 2 |
| Ruth R., m. Frederick **KELLOGG**, Sept. 16, 1829, by Rev. William Andrews | 3 | 44 |
| Ruthy Robinson, d. [John & Sarah], b. Oct. 25, 1805 | 3 | 2 |
| Sarah F., m. Stephen J. **GOLD**, Nov. 15, 1826, by Rev. Timothy Stone, of the 1st Ch. | 2 | 66 |
| Sarah Fay, d. John & Sarah, b. Feb. 17, 1804 | 3 | 2 |
| **CALKINS**, George W., of Cornwall, m. Sarah J. **STONE**, of Litchfield, May 4, 1851, by F. C. Youngs | 3 | 97 |
| George W., farmer, ae 19, b. Cornwall, res. Cornwall, m. Sarah J. **STONE**, ae 24, b. Litchfield, res. Cornwall, May 14, 1851, by Rev. Mr. Youngs | 3 | 118-19 |
| George W., of Cornwall, m. Rhoda T. **GIBBS**, of Kent, Oct. 3, 1852, by Rev. Henry Burton, of Sharon | 3 | 124 |
| George Wilbur, s. William R., carpenter, ae 31, & Laura, ae 32, b. Mar. 23, 1849 | 3 | 102-3 |
| Marriet, m. William A. **HOLCOMB**, b. of Cornwall, July 9, 1843, by Rev. Joshua L. Maynard, of the North Cong. Ch. | 3 | 67 |
| Orra, m. James **NEWTON**, Dec. 23, 1837, by Rev. Walter Smith, of the North Cong. Ch. | 3 | 53 |
| Philip, m. Hannah A. **FORD**, b. of Cornwall, Jan. 5, 1842, by Rev. Lewis Gunn | 3 | 63 |
| Sarah, m. Henry **DUNBAR**, Nov. 28, 1832, by Rev. Walter Smith, of the North Cong. Ch. | 3 | 35 |
| **CAMBRIDGE**, Charles, laborer, colored, ae 26, b. Milford, res. Cornwall, m. Caroline **STARR**, colored, ae 18, b. Sharon, res. Cornwall, Oct. 26, 1847, by Rev. Lewis Gunn | 3 | 90-1 |

| | Vol. | Page |
|---|---|---|
| **CAMBRIDGE**, (cont.) | | |
| Julia, colored, ae 23, b. Sharon, res. Cornwall, m. David **PATCHAM**, laborer, ae 31, colored, b. Sharon, res. Cornwall, Oct. 26, 1847, by Rev. Lewis Gunn | 3 | 90-1 |
| William Henry, s. Charles, farmer, colored, ae 27, & Caroline, ae 18, colored, b. Nov. 25, 1849 | 3 | 100-1 |
| **CAMP**, Amos, m. Jemima **HART**, June 26, 1782, by Rev. Hezekiah Gold | 2 | 8 |
| Amos, s. Amos & Jemima, b. Mar. 9, 1786 | 2 | 19 |
| Esther, d. [Amos & Jemima], b. Dec. 4, 1787 | 2 | 19 |
| Phebe, d. Amos & Jemima, b. Apr. [ ], 1784 | 2 | 12 |
| Phebe, d. Amos & Jemima, d. June 23, 1788 | 2 | 11 |
| William, m. Sarah **BISHOP**, Mar. 10, 1759, by Rev. H. Gold | 1 | 33 |
| **CANFIELD**, Andrew, s. Edward, laborer, ae 20, & Hannah, ae 18, b. June 5, 1851 | 3 | 116-17 |
| Joseph P., m. Mira Ann **BEERS**, Oct. 4, 1825, by Rev. Timothy Stone, of the 1st Ch. | 2 | 63 |
| Saba, m. Solomon **EMMONS**, May 22, 1778, by Rev. Hezekiah Gold | LR4 | 14 |
| Susannah, m. Jonathan **BALLARD***, May 19, 1779, by Rev. Hezekiah Gold *("**BELL**") in Starr's book) | LR4 | 14 |
| **CARROLL**, Daniel, s. Daniel, res. Sharon, b. Sept. 2, 1848 | 3 | 102-3 |
| John, s. Daniel, laborer, ae 40, & Mary L., ae 28, b. Feb. 21, 1851 | 3 | 116-17 |
| **CARTER**, Abel C., m. Minerva **SACKETT**, Dec. 10, 1795, by Peter Starr | 3 | 3 |
| Abel C. & Minerva, had s. [ ], b. Oct. 15, 1799; d. 20th of the same month | 3 | 13 |
| Abel C., Dea., m. Sarah Ann **JOHNSON**, June 17, 1827, by Rev. Timothy Stone | 2 | 67 |
| Abel C., of Cornwall, m. Sarah **WOODRUFF**, of Watertown, Aug. 26, 1838, by Rev. N. M. Urmston, of the 1st Cong. Ch. | 3 | 54 |
| Abel Curtiss, s. Abel C. & Minerva, b. May 23, 1797 | 3 | 13 |
| Anne, m. Noah **HARRISON**, July 21, 1785, by Rev. John Cornwall | 2 | 8 |
| Benjamin L., of Branford, m. Flora F. **HART**, of Cornwall, July 2, 1850, at the house of Elias Hart, by Rev. Joshua L. Maynard, of the North Cong. Ch. | 3 | 96 |
| Charles, farmer, ae 31, b. Warren, res. Warren, m. Mary M. **AVERY**, ae 15, b. Cornwall, res. Warren, Dec. [ ], 1848, by John F. Wooster | 3 | 104-5 |
| Chloe M., m. Martin **COLE**, b. of Cornwall, June 18, 1849, by Rev. E. B. Andrews | 3 | 83 |
| Eliza, m. Peter **BIERCE**, Apr. 27, 1837, by Rev. William Andrews | 3 | 52 |
| Elizur*, d. [Abel C. & Minerva], b. Sept. 4, 1800 *("Eliza") | 3 | 13 |

| | Vol. | Page |
|---|---|---|
| **CARTER**, (cont.) | | |
| Erastus, laborer, ae 41 & Rebecca, ae 39, had child b. July 9, 1850 | 3 | 108-9 |
| Jemima, m. Isaac **BATES**, Apr. 9, 1761, by Rev. H. Gold | 1 | 43 |
| Lydia*, of Sharon, m. Oliver **FOORD**, of Cornwall, Nov. 23, 1774, by Colton M. Smith *(Arnold Copy has "Lydia **CURTICE**") | LR3 | 7 |
| Lydia, d. [Abel C. & Minerva], b. Apr. 26, 1802 | 3 | 13 |
| Lydia, m. John P. **STONE**, Oct. 1, 1837, by Rev. William Andrews | 3 | 53 |
| Martha, m. Thomas **DEAN**, Oct. 23, 1753, by Rev. Thomas Halstead, of Fishkill | 1 | 33 |
| Mary, d. Nathaniel, d. Nov. 4, 1759 | 1 | 34 |
| Mary, d. Nathaniel & Sarah, d. Nov. 5, 1759 | 1 | 35 |
| Minerva, m. Silas* **JUDSON**, Oct. 13, 1830, by William Andrews *("Silas Patterson **JUDSON**" in Starr's book) | 3 | 46 |
| Minerva Sacket, d. [Abel C. & Minerva], b. July 12, 1808 | 3 | 13 |
| Norval, s. Salmon & Alice, b. May 16, 1794 | 2 | 30 |
| Patty M., m. Julius **PERRY**, Nov. 13, 1836, by Rev. William Andrews | 3 | 52 |
| Paulina, d. Philo & Paulina, b. Sept. 12, 1790 | 3 | 24 |
| Philo, m. Paulina **BUELL**, June 26, 1788, by Peter Starr | 3 | 8 |
| Philo, s. Philo & Paulina, b. July 28, 1792 | 3 | 19 |
| Polly S., of Cornwall, m. Edwin **BENEDICT**, of Danbury, May 3, 1832, by Rev. Timothy Stone, of the Cong. Ch. | 3 | 50 |
| Polly Swift, d. [Abel C. & Minerva], b. May 3, 1810 | 3 | 13 |
| Salmon, m. Alice **HUBBEL**, Apr. 15, 1793, by Jedidiah Hubbel, J. P. | 3 | 21 |
| Sarah, m. Barzillai **DUDLEY**, Mar. 6, 1750, by Solomon Palmer | 1 | 13 |
| Sarah, d. Philo & Polina, b. Apr. 10, 1789 | 2 | 25 |
| Theron, s. John & Mary, b. Jan. 11, 1782 | 2 | 23 |
| Thomas*, m. Abigail **HOW**, June 22, 1756, by Rev. H. Gold *("Thomas **PORTER**" in Starr's book) | 1 | 35 |
| Zacariah*, s. Thomas & Abigail, b. May 30, 1759 *("Zachariah Howe **PORTER**" in Starr's book) | 1 | 35 |
| Zenas, s. John & Mary, b. Jan. 1, 1778 | 2 | 23 |
| **CARTWRIGHT**, Austin, of Sharon, m. Betsey A. **TAYLOR**, of Cornwall, Mar. 28, 1844, by Rev. Thomas Edwards | 3 | 68 |
| **CASE**, Ann, see Ann **FITZGERALD** | 3 | 125 |
| **CATLIN, CATLING**, Benjamin, m. Abigail **BLIN**, Jan. 28, 1813, by Rev. Josiah Hawes. Witnesses: James D. Ford & Anson Rogers | 2 | 45 |
| Benjamin Franklin, s. [Benjamin & Abigail], b. Oct. 5, 1821 | 2 | 64 |
| Bradley, s. Joel & Lydia, b. Aug. 27, 1813 | 2 | 35 |
| Bradley, d. Nov. 1, 1821, ae 63 | 2 | 46 |
| Clarissa, d. [Theron & Elizabeth], b. July 27, 1805 | 2 | 35 |
| David Clark, s. [Theron & Elizabeth], b. Aug. 5, 1807 | 2 | 35 |

| | Vol. | Page |
|---|---|---|
| **CATLIN, CATLING**, (cont.) | | |
| Eli, s. [Theron & Elizabeth], b. Sept. 15, 1801 | 2 | 35 |
| Eliza, d. [Theron & Elizabeth], b. Nov. 11, 1803 | 2 | 35 |
| Isaac Blinn, s. [Benjamin & Abigail], b. July 13, 1823 | 2 | 64 |
| Joel, m. Lydia **BLINN**, b. of Cornwall, Nov. 18, 1807, by Rev. Josiah Hawes, of the 2nd Ch. Witnesses: Eber Harrison & Amos Catlin | 3 | 33 |
| John Belden, s. [Theron & Elizabeth], b. Nov. 27, 1811 | 2 | 35 |
| Julia M., of Cornwall, m. David **BARLEY**, of Kent, Dec. 6, 1845, at the house of Benjamin Catlin, by Rev. Joshua L. Maynard, of the North Cong. Ch. | 3 | 72 |
| Julia Maria, d. [Benjamin & Abigail], b. Aug. 19, 1825 | 2 | 64 |
| Mary, d. Roger & Elizabeth, b. Nov. 9, 1774 | LR3 | 12 |
| Mary A., m. William H. **HUMISON**, b. of Cornwall, Jan. 23, 1840, by Rev. S. W. Smith | 3 | 59 |
| Mary Amelia, d. Benjamin & Abigail, b. Jan. 12, 1814 | 2 | 44 |
| Mary Elizabeth, d. [Theron & Elizabeth], b. Dec. 26, 1813 | 2 | 35 |
| Nancy, d. Theron & Elizabeth, b. Apr. 25, 1799 | 2 | 35 |
| Nancy Cornelia, d. Benjamin & Abigail, b. June 7, 1819 | 2 | 64 |
| Olive, d. John, farmer, ae 30, & Clarissa Maria, ae 28, b. Aug. 1, 1851 | 3 | 114-15 |
| Roger, s. Roger & Elizabeth, b. Apr. 10, 1766 | 1 | 68 |
| Samuel, s. Bradley, d. Dec. 5, 1813, ae 18 y. | 2 | 33 |
| Samuel, s. [Benjamin & Abigail], b. May 16, 1815 | 2 | 44 |
| Samuel B., s. John, laborer, ae 29 & Clarissa, ae 28, b. June 9, 1849 | 3 | 100-1 |
| Theron, m. Elizabeth **CLARKE**, b. of Cornwall, June 14, 1798, by Rev. Asahel Hooker, of Goshen. Witnesses: Mary Kellogg & Demis Kellogg | 2 | 36 |
| Theron Wells, s. [Theron & Elizabeth], b. Mar. 3, 1810 | 2 | 35 |
| Warring, s. Roger & Elizabeth, b. May 25, 1768 | 1 | 94 |
| William, s. William H., stone cutter, ae 31 & Lucy A., ae 27, b. June 27, 1848 | 3 | 84-5 |
| William H., of Cornwall, m. Lucy A. **NEWEL**, of Goshen, Nov. 19, 1843, by Rev. Joshua L. Maynard, of the N. Cong. Ch. | 3 | 67 |
| William Henry, s. [Benjamin & Abigail], b. Aug. 27, 1817 | 2 | 44 |
| **CHAFFEE**, Joshua B., m. Hannah **BIRDSEYE**, Dec. 25, 1820, by Rev. Timothy Stone | 2 | 49 |
| **CHAMBERLAIN**, Samuel, m. Delia **ROEBUCK**, Jan. 5, 1836, by Rev. William Andrews | 3 | 41 |
| Sarah E., d. Willis, laborer & Jennet, b. June 16, 1851 | 3 | 116-17 |
| **CHANDLER**, Abnah, m. Sarah **HILL**, Dec. 12, 1759, by Rev. Able Nowel | 1 | 35 |
| Abner, s. Abner & Sarah, b. Apr. 10, 1763 | 1 | 51 |
| Amy, twin with Anna, d. Jonathan & Sarah, b. Apr. 27, 1765 | 1 | 60 |
| Anna, twin with Amy, d. Jonathan & Sarah, b. Apr. 27, 1765 | 1 | 60 |
| Anna, d. Benjamin & Elizabeth, b. Sept. 6, 1769; d. Oct. | | |

| | Vol. | Page |
|---|---|---|
| **CHANDLER**, (cont.) | | |
| 30, 1769 | 1 | 92 |
| Anne, d. Benjamin & Elizabeth, b. Aug. 22, 1770 | 1 | 95 |
| Asaph, s. Benjamin & Elizabeth, b. July 18, 1774 | LR3 | 8 |
| Ashbel, s. Jonathan & Sarah, b. Apr. 11, 1773 | 1 | 110 |
| Benjamin, m. Elizabeth **CHANDLER**, Oct. 3, 1752, by Solomon Palmer | 1 | 18 |
| Benjamin, s. Benjamin & Elizabeth, b. Jan. 22, 1761 | 1 | 39 |
| Benjamin, s. Benjamin & Elizabeth, d. Apr. 30, 1770, in the 10th y. of his age | 1 | 95 |
| Benjamin, s. Benjamin & Elizabeth, b. Aug. 26, 1772 | 1 | 105 |
| Betty, m. Noah **FOURD**, b. of Cornwall, Sept. 2, 1754, by George Halloway, J. P. | 1 | 21 |
| Betty, d. Abner & Sarah, b. Jan. 8, 1772 | 1 | 102 |
| Chloe, d. Jonathan & Sarah, b. Oct. 3, 1760 | 1 | 39 |
| Deborah, m. Hezekiah **FORD**, Dec. 7, 1757, by Rev. Hezekiah Gold | 1 | 31 |
| Elizabeth, m. Benjamin **CHANDLER**, Oct. 3, 1752, by Solomon Palmer | 1 | 18 |
| Elizabeth, d. Benj[ami]n & Elizabeth, b. Feb. 12, 1763 | 1 | 50 |
| Hill, s. Abner & Sarah, b. May 14, 1761 | 1 | 40 |
| Huldah, d. Benjamin & Elizabeth, b. Feb. 14, 1759 | 1 | 34 |
| Jesse, s. Benjamin & Elizabeth, b. Nov. 5, 1764 | 1 | 58 |
| John, s. Benjamin & Elizabeth, b. Apr. 28, 1757 | 1 | 28 |
| Jonathan, m. Sarah **PIERCE**, Apr. 13, 1758, by Rev. Hezekiah Gold | 1 | 33 |
| Jonathan, s. Jonathan & Sarah, b. July 26, 1767 | 1 | 77 |
| Joseph, s. Joseph, d. May 27, 1750 | 1 | 12 |
| Joseph, s. Benjamin & Elizabeth, b. Sept. 10, 1753 | 1 | 19 |
| Lucina, d. Abner & Sarah, b. Aug. 12, 1769 | 1 | 91 |
| Liddia, d. Jonathan & Sarah, b. June 1, 1759 | 1 | 35 |
| Mary, d. Jonathan & Sarah, b. July 5, 1762 | 1 | 47 |
| Nabby, d. Jonathan & Sarah, b. Feb. 1, 1775 | LR3 | 8 |
| Olive, d. Abner & Sarah, b. Jan. 29, 1774 | 2 | 13 |
| Philo, s. Abner & Sarah, b. Feb. 11, 1765 | 1 | 60 |
| Prudence, d. Benjamin & Elizabeth, b. Sept. 18, 1766 | 1 | 72 |
| Sarah, d. Benjamin & Elizabeth, b. Oct. 14, 1755 | 1 | 24 |
| Sarah, d. Jonathan & Sarah, b. Jan. 17, 1771 | 1 | 100 |
| Seth, s. Benjamin & Elizabeth, b. Feb. 10, 1768 | 1 | 81 |
| Seth, s. Jonathan & Sarah, b. Apr. 27, 1769 | 1 | 89 |
| Simeon, m. Eunice **ROBARDS**, Apr. 5, 1750, by Solomon Palmer | 1 | 12 |
| Uri, s. Abner & Sarah, b. Feb. 15, 1767 | 1 | 74 |
| **CHANLEY**, Andrew, moulder, had s. [ ], b. [ ] | 3 | 108-9 |
| **CHASE**, Aaron B., of Welton, N. Y., m. Harriet S. Rexford, of Cornwall, Mar. 3, 1852, at the house of Riley M. Rexford, by Rev. J. L. Maynard, of the North Cong. Ch. | 3 | 122 |
| Timothy C., m. Lucy J. **HOW**, Dec. 31, 1832, by Rev. Walter | | |

| | Vol. | Page |
|---|---|---|
| **CHASE**, (cont.) | | |
| Smith, of the North Cong. Ch. | 3 | 35 |
| **CHATTERSON**, Rebecca, m. Philip A. **RHODES**, Mar. 10, 1844, by Myron Harrison, J. P. | 3 | 68 |
| **[CHICHESTER], CHIDDESTER**, Jonathan, s. William & Eunice, d. Mar. 31, 1744, in the 12th y. of his age | 1 | 11 |
| Mary, d. William & Eunice, d. May 2, 1750, in the 20th y. of her age | 1 | 11 |
| **CHIPMAN**, Ann A., m. Joseph **CLARK**, b. of Cornwall, Apr. 14, 1844, by Rev. Thomas Edwards, of the M. E. Ch. | 3 | 70 |
| **CHITTENDEN**, Denison, m. Annette A. **COON**, Sept. 29, 1831, by Rev. William Andrews | 3 | 48 |
| Truxton, of Westmoreland, N. Y., m. Maria Jane **HUMISTON**, of Cornwall, Oct. 2, 1839, by N. M. Urmston | 3 | 58 |
| **CHRISTIE**, Asbury, s. Henry & Elizabeth, b. Jan. 27, 1792 | 2 | 35 |
| Asbury, s. Henry, d. Feb. 23, 1792 | 2 | 33 |
| Asbury, s. [Henry & Elizabeth], b. Mar. 8, 1795 | 2 | 35 |
| Betsey, [twin with Henry, d. Henry & Elizabeth], b. Feb. 9, 1793 | 2 | 35 |
| Betsey, d. Henry, d. Oct. 2, 1795 | 2 | 33 |
| Betsey, d. [Henry & Elizabeth], b. Apr. 15, 1797 | 2 | 35 |
| Edward Rogers, s. [Henry & Elizabeth], b. Mar. 7, 1799 | 2 | 35 |
| Henry, m. Elizabeth **ROGERS**, Mar. 20, 1791, by [ ]. Witnesses: Cynthia White & Hannah Sedgwick | 2 | 36 |
| Henry, [twin with Betsey, s. Henry & Elizabeth], b. Feb. 9, 1793 | 2 | 35 |
| John Fletcher, s. [Henry & Elizabeth], b. Mar. 14, 1801 | 2 | 35 |
| Peggy, d. [Henry & Elizabeth], b. Mar. 1, 1803 | 2 | 35 |
| **CLARK, CLARKE, CLERK**, Abigail, d. [Hezekiah & Sylvia], b. Nov. 28, 1782 | 2 | 27 |
| Abigail, m. John **HART**, b. of Cornwall, Oct. 6, [1799], by Rev. John Cornwell, of Amenia, N. Y. Witnesses: Birdseye Clark & Lucius Kellogg | 3 | 9 |
| Amos, m. Almira D. **BLAKE**, Oct. 13, 1839, by Rev. Eleazer Beecher, of the Bap. Ch. | 3 | 59 |
| Andrew, s. [George & Lydia], b. Aug. 1, 1796, in Oxford | 2 | 42 |
| Anna, d. [David & Elizabeth], b. May 25, 1793 | 3 | 18 |
| Anne, m. Luman **HOPKINS**, Sept. 1, 1813, by Rev. Timothy Stone | 2 | 37 |
| Betsey Delania, d. [Lyman & Alvira], b. May 4, 1827 | 3 | 62 |
| Calvin, s. [Hezekiah & Sylvia], b. Mar. 23, 1791 | 2 | 27 |
| Caroline Alvina, d. Jaleel & Susan, b. May 27, 1825 | 3 | 57 |
| Caroline Alvena, d. Jaliel, d. Jan. 25, 1831 | 3 | 55 |
| Catharine, d. [David & Elizabeth], b. Sept. 16, 1791 | 3 | 18 |
| Catharine, m. Noah **ROGERS**, Jr., Sept. 14, 1829, by Rev. Walter Smith, of the North Ch. | 3 | 44 |
| Catharine Rebeckah, d. William & Rebeckah, b. Apr. 2, 1809 | 2 | 40 |

| | Vol. | Page |
|---|---|---|
| **CLARK, CLARKE, CLERK**, (cont.) | | |
| Charlotte, d. [David & Elizabeth], b. Sept. 5, 1795 | 3 | 18 |
| Clarissa, ae 22, res. Cornwall, m. George **NICHOLS**, farmer, ae 28, res. Hamilton, N. Y., Feb. 26, 1849, by Joshua L. Maynard | 3 | 104-5 |
| Clarissa A., of Cornwall, m. Rev. Frederick **MUNSON**, of Greenwich, June 28, 1848, at the house of William Clark, by Rev. Joshua L. Maynard, of the North Cong. Ch. | 3 | 81 |
| Clarissa A., ae 27, b. Cornwall, m. Frederick **MONSON**, clergyman, ae 28, b. Bethlem, res. Greenwich, June 28, 1848, by Joshua L. Maynard | 3 | 90-1 |
| Clarisse Anne, d. [William & Rebecca], b. Mar. 10, 1821 | 2 | 47 |
| Clarissa Anne, d. [William & Rebeckah], b. Mar. 10, 1821 | 3 | 2 |
| Clarissa Augusta, d. [Victorianus & Rhoda], b. Sept. 12, 1827 | 3 | 47 |
| Clarrena A., of Cornwall, m. Hanford **NICHOLS**, of Georgetown, N. Y., Feb. 26, 1849, at the house of O. B. Clark, by Rev. Joshua L. Maynard, of the North Cong. Ch. | 3 | 81 |
| Daniel T., m. Matilda **BARNUM**, b. of Cornwall, June 18, 1854, by Rev. R. D. Kirby | 3 | 126 |
| David, s. David & Elizabeth, b. May 13, 1777 | 3 | 18 |
| David, d. May 17, 1811 | 3 | 4 |
| David, s. [William & Rebeckah], b. Dec. 26, 1812 | 2 | 40 |
| Dorothy, d. [David & Elizabeth], b. Aug. 20, 1782 | 3 | 18 |
| Dorothy, m. Hudson **JENNINGS**, b. of Cornwall, Oct. 7, 1804, by Judah Kellogg, J. P. | 3 | 11 |
| Edmund Rogers, s. Pierce J. & Grace, b. Jan. 4, 1834 | 3 | 39 |
| Edward Elliot, [twin with Ellen Elizabeth], s. Joseph & Ann A., b. Dec. 26, 1846 | 3 | 77 |
| Elisha, s. [George & Lydia], b. Feb. 22, 1799, in Oxford | 2 | 42 |
| Elisha, m. Jannet **BURREL**, b. of Cornwall, June 30, 1822, by Rev. Walter Smith, of the 2nd Church | 2 | 53 |
| Elizabeth, d. [David & Elizabeth], b. June 22, 1779 | 3 | 18 |
| Elizabeth, m. Theron **CATLIN**, b. of Cornwall, June 14, 1798, by Rev. Asahel Hooker, of Goshen. Witnesses: Mary Kellogg & Demis Kellogg | 2 | 36 |
| Ellen Elizabeth, [twin with Edward Elliot], d. Joseph & Ann A., b. Dec. 26, 1846 | 3 | 77 |
| Ephraim, s. [Hezekiah & Sylvia], b. Nov. 15, 1789 | 2 | 27 |
| Ephraim, s. Hezekiah & Sylvia, d. Dec. 6, 1789 | 2 | 28 |
| Esther, d. Hezekiah & Sylvia, b. Jan. 26, 1801 | 3 | 31 |
| Flora Ann, m. Judson **WELLS**, b. of Cornwall, Dec. 24, 1843, by Rev. Thomas Edwards, of the M. E. Ch. | 3 | 68 |
| Frances, d. George C. & Caroline, res. Goshen, b. May 3, 1851 | 3 | 114-15 |
| Frederick Dwigh[t], s. William & Rebecca, b. July 30, 1816 | 2 | 43 |
| George, d. Nov. 21, 1841, ae 89 | 3 | 60 |

| | Vol. | Page |
|---|---|---|
| **CLARK, CLARKE, CLERK,** (cont.) | | |
| Hannah, d. [David & Elizabeth], b. Dec. 13, 1786 | 3 | 18 |
| Harriet Ann, d. Peirce J. & Grace, b. May 30, 1831 | 3 | 47 |
| Harriet C., m. Harvey **WHEEDON**, Aug. 16, 1837, by Rev. Walter Smith, of the 2nd Cong. Ch. | 3 | 52 |
| Harriet Eliza, d. [William & Rebeckah], b. Oct. 10, 1814 | 2 | 40 |
| Harriet Emeline, d. [Willia]m L. & Harriet Jane, b. June 15, 1838 | 3 | 95 |
| Heman Daggett, s. Peirce, J. & Grace, b. Apr. 11, 1836 | 3 | 51 |
| Henry, s. Jaliel & Susan, b. Oct. 18, 1818 | 3 | 57 |
| Hezekiah, s. [Hezekiah & Sylvia], b. Apr. 22, 1787 | 2 | 27 |
| Hiram Northrop, s. [William & Rebeckah], b. Aug. 22, 1823 | 3 | 2 |
| Jaleel, s. [George & Lydia], b. Dec. 14, 1785, in Oxford | 2 | 42 |
| Jonathan, s. George & Lydia, b. Oct. 14, 1783, in Oxford | 2 | 42 |
| Joseph, s. Lyman & Alvira, b. Dec. 25, 1814 | 3 | 62 |
| Joseph, m. Ann A. **CHIPMAN**, b. of Cornwall, Apr. 14, 1844, by Rev. Thomas Edwards, of the M. E. Ch. | 3 | 70 |
| Julia Harriet, d. [Victorianus & Rhoda], b. Apr. 4, 1831 | 3 | 47 |
| L. Jane, m. Jonathan T. **NORTON**, May 11, 1852, at the U. S. Hotel, West Cornwall, by Rev. J. L. Maynard | 3 | 122 |
| Laura, d. [George & Lydia], b. Aug. 8, 1794, in Oxford | 2 | 42 |
| Laura Ann, d. [Lyman & Alvira], b. May 18, 1817 | 3 | 62 |
| Laura Jane, d. [Victorianus & Rhoda], b. May 9, 1829 | 3 | 47 |
| Leavit Walter, s. William L. & Emeline, b. Oct. 18, 1833 | 3 | 95 |
| Leman, twin with Lyman, s. [George & Lydia], b. Apr. 15, 1789, in Oxford | 2 | 42 |
| Lorain, d. Nehemiah & Lorain, b. Oct. 20, 1793 | 2 | 29 |
| Lydia, w. George, d. July 22, 1841, ae 84 | 3 | 60 |
| Lydia Ann, d. [Jaliel & Susan], b. Feb. 8, 1820 | 3 | 57 |
| Lydia Clarissa, d. [William L. & Harriet Jane], b. Nov. 8, 1846 | 3 | 95 |
| Lyman, twin with Leman, s. [George & Lydia], b. Apr. 15, 1789, in Oxford | 2 | 42 |
| Mary, d. [William & Rebeckah], b. May 20, 1828 | 3 | 2 |
| Mary Ann, d. [Jaliel & Susan], b. Jan. 25, 1823 | 3 | 57 |
| Mary Frost, d. David & Mary, b. Sept. 10, 1775 | 3 | 18 |
| Milton, s. Hezekiah & Sylvia, b. July 29, 1795 | 3 | 26 |
| Nancy, d. [David & Elizabeth], b. Feb. 5, 1781 | 3 | 18 |
| Nancy, d. William & Rebecca, b. June 15, 1818 | 2 | 47 |
| Nancy, d. William & Rebeckah, b. June 15, 1818 | 3 | 2 |
| Nancy, m. Henry L. **ROGERS**, b. of Cornwall, Feb. 16, 1842, by Joshua L. Maynard | 3 | 64 |
| Nehemiah, m. Lorain **PEIRCE**, May 1, 1788, by Rev. Hezekiah Gold | 2 | 16 |
| Nelson, s. [Lyman & Alvira], b. Apr. 17, 1819 | 3 | 62 |
| Nelson Ives, s. William & Rebecca, b. Sept. 3, 1831 | 3 | 51 |
| Oliver Franklin, s. Victorianus & Rhoda, b. Nov. 2, 1823 | 3 | 47 |
| Peirce J., m. Grace **HINDMAN**, Oct. 22, 1829, by Rev. | | |

| | Vol. | Page |
|---|---|---|
| **CLARK, CLARKE, CLERK**, (cont.) | | |
| William Andrews | 3 | 45 |
| Peirce Johnson, s. Nehemiah & Lorain, b. Apr. 16, 1806 | 3 | 16 |
| Polly, d. [Hezekiah & Sylvia], b. Sept. 25, 1780 | 2 | 27 |
| Polly, m. John **KELLOGG**, Aug. 26, 1799, by Israel Holly | 2 | 24 |
| Rebecca, w. William, d. Apr. 27, 1832, ae 42 | 3 | 43 |
| Roswell, m. Agnes E. **HOPKINS**, Oct. 10, 1835, by Rev. William Andrews | 3 | 40 |
| Roswell, of Sharon, m. Flora **BIERCE**, of Cornwall, June 12, 1837, by Robert Travis | 3 | 53 |
| Samuel, s. [William & Rebeckah], b. May 16, 1826 | 3 | 2 |
| Sarah, d. Hezekiah & Sylvia, b. Dec. 4, 1776 | 2 | 27 |
| Sarah Alvina, d. Sheldon, farmer, ae 28 & Melissa, ae 32, res. Goshen, b. Jan. 19, 1850 | 3 | 110-11 |
| Sarah Anne, d. Nehemiah & Lorain, b. Feb. 18, 1791 | 3 | 19 |
| Sarah Ann, m. Hanford **NICHOLS**, July 5, 1832, by Rev. William Andrews | 3 | 50 |
| Sarah Frances, d. William & Patience, b. June 3, 1834 | 3 | 51 |
| Sarah Rebecca, d. [William L. & Harriet Jane], b. Feb. 1, 1840 | 3 | 95 |
| Sheldon, s. [Lyman & Alvira], b. Jan. 8, 1822 | 3 | 62 |
| Sheldon, m. Melissa **COOK**, b. of Cornwall, Feb. 22, 1843, by Myron Harrison, J. P. | 3 | 66 |
| Sheldon, farmer & Milissa, res. Goshen, had child b. Aug. 7, 1848; d. [ ], ae 17 d. | 3 | 88-9 |
| Socrates, laborer, ae 45 & Mariah, ae 42, had child, b. Nov. 10, 1848 | 3 | 98-9 |
| Sylvia, d. [Hezekiah & Sylvia], b. Apr. 8, 1785 | 2 | 27 |
| Sylvia, m. Nathan **HART**, of Cornwall, Feb. 8, 1804, by Oliver Burnham, J. P. Witness: William Kellogg, T. C. | 3 | 33 |
| Tabitha, d. [David & Elizabeth], b. Apr. 3, 1784 | 3 | 18 |
| Uri, s. [Hezekiah & Sylvia], b. Oct. 25, 1778 | 2 | 27 |
| Uri, m. Hannah **HYATT**, b. of Cornwall, Oct. 6, [1799], by Rev. John Cornwell, of Amenia, N. Y. Witnesses: Birdseye Clark & Louisa Kellogg | 3 | 9 |
| Victorianus, s. Nehemiah & Lorain, b. July 18, 1789 | 2 | 21 |
| Victorianus, m. Rhoda **BURNHAM**, b. of Cornwall, Sept. 18, 1822, by Rev. Walter Smith, of the 2nd Cong. Ch. | 2 | 54 |
| Wells, m. Polly **RUSSELL**, b. of Cornwall, July 19, 1795, by Judah Kellogg, J. P. | 3 | 21 |
| William, s. [David & Elizabeth], b. Sept. 23, 1788 | 3 | 18 |
| William, m. Rebeckah **NORTHROP**, Oct. 16, 1807, by Rev. Timothy Stone | 2 | 37 |
| William, m. Patience **HOLLISTER**, Jan. 1, 1833, by Rev. William Andrews | 3 | 35 |
| William L., m. Emeline **HOW**, Nov. 29, 1832, by Rev. Walter Smith, of the North Cong. Ch. | 3 | 35 |
| William L., m. Harriet J. **CALHOUN**, Oct. 12, 1836, by Rev. | | |

| | Vol. | Page |
|---|---|---|
| **CLARK, CLARKE, CLERK**, (cont.) | | |
| William Andrews | 3 | 42 |
| William Leavet, s. [William & Rebeckah], b. Feb. 4, 1811 | 2 | 40 |
| **CLEMENS**, Daniel, of Litchfield, m. Jane **DEAN**, of Canaan, July 16, 1801, by Judah Kellogg, J. P. | 2 | 24 |
| **CLEVELAND**, Daniel, of Madison, N. Y., m. Julia R. **GOLD**, of Cornwall, Nov. 14, 1821, by Rev. Walter Smith, of the 2nd Church | 2 | 51 |
| **CODMAN**, Margarette, d. James, grocer, b. Mar. [ ], 1851 | 3 | 114-15 |
| **COE**, David, m. Esther **WRIGHT**, Nov. 27, 1823, by Elder Daniel Brayton, of the M. E. Ch. | 2 | 57 |
| Henry, s. John D., farmer, ae 42 & Urusla, ae 37, b. Feb. 24, 1848 | 3 | 84-5 |
| **COGSWELL**, Emily, of Cornwall, m. A. L. **ROGERS**, of New Milford, Nov. 29, 1849, by Rev. Joshua L. Maynard, of the North Cong. Ch. at his house | 3 | 83 |
| **COLE**, [see also **COWLES**], Abigail W., of Cornwall, m. John **GRISWOLD**, of Guilford, Apr. 10, 1845, at the house of Irad Cole, by Rev. Joshua L. Maynard, of the North Cong. Ch. | 3 | 71 |
| Abigail Wood, d. [Irad & Abigail], b. Jan. 4, 1827 | 3 | 47 |
| Adaline, ae 22, b. New Haven, res. Cornwall, m. 2nd h. Hiram **COLE**, basket maker, ae 50, b. Sharon, res. Cornwall, Apr. 10, 1849, by James Wadsworth | 3 | 104-5 |
| Adaline, b. New York State, res. Cornwall, d. Sept. 8, 1850, ae 26 | 3 | 120-1 |
| Benjamin, s. [Seth & Abigail], b. Nov. 20, 1799 | 2 | 23 |
| Benjamin, m. Adaline M. **HAGOR**, Mar. 31, 1847, at the house of Mr. Coe, by Rev. Joshua L. Maynard, of North Cong. Ch. | 3 | 74 |
| Chloe G., d. Benjamin, laborer, ae 28 & Adaline, ae 26, b. Sept. 7, 1850 | 3 | 116-17 |
| Eben, s. James & Annah, b. Mar. 4, 1783 | 2 | 4 |
| Edmund, m. Almira **MARVIN**, b. of Cornwall, May 29, 1822, by Rev. Walter Smith, of the 2nd Church | 2 | 53 |
| Edmund Field, s. Irad & Abigail, b. Mar. 24, 1834 | 3 | 39 |
| Elma, [twin with Frances M.], d. Hiram, laborer, ae 60 & Linne, ae 21, res. Sharon, b. [ ] | 3 | 114-15 |
| Frances M., [twin with Elma], d. Hiram, laborer, ae 60 & Linne, ae 21, res. Sharon, b. [ ] | 3 | 114-15 |
| Fred Rexford, s. Benjamin, farmer, ae [ ] & Adaline, b. Feb. 9, 1848 | 3 | 88-9 |
| Hannah, d. Seth & Abigail, b. Aug. 23, 1786 | 2 | 17 |
| Hiram, s. Seth & Abigail, b. Aug. 15, 1792 | 3 | 22 |
| Hiram, basket maker, ae 50, b. Sharon, res. Cornwall, m. 2nd w. Adaline **COLE**, ae 22, b. New Haven, res. Cornwall, Apr. 10, 1849, by James Wadsworth | 3 | 104-5 |
| Hiram, of Cornwall, m. Adaline **BLAKESLEY**, of | | |

| | Vol. | Page |
|---|---|---|
| **COLE**, (cont.) | | |
| Prospect, Apr. 16, 1849, by James Wadsworth, J. P. | 3 | 82 |
| Ichabod, d. Oct. 22, 1801, ae 88 y. | 3 | 10 |
| James, s. Timothy & Rebeckah, b. June 18, 1761 | 1 | 40 |
| James, m. Annah **STILSON**, July 25, 1782, by Rev. Hezekiah Gold | 2 | 5 |
| John, s. Timothy & Rebeckah, b. Nov. 18, 1757 | 1 | 30 |
| John, s. Seth & Abigail, b. Nov. 13, 1788 | 2 | 25 |
| John Henry, s. [Irad & Abigail], b. Jan. 14, 1829 | 3 | 47 |
| Joseph, s. Seth & Abigail, b. Oct. 1, 1796 | 2 | 23 |
| Levi, m. Mary Ann **DAVIDSON**, b. of Cornwall, Feb. 17, 1851, by Rev. J. L. Maynard, of the North Cong. Ch. | 3 | 97 |
| Levi, laborer, ae 21, res. Cornwall, m. Mary **DAVIDSON**, ae 23, b. Sharon, res. Cornwall, Mar. 1, 1851, by Rev. J. L. Maynard | 3 | 118-19 |
| Lucinda S., of Cornwall, m. Sidney H. **MARSHALL**, of Salisbury, Sept. 14, 1847, at the house of Irad Cole, by Rev. Joshua L. Maynard, of the North Cong. Ch. | 3 | 76 |
| Lucinda Sophronia, d. Irad & Abigail, b. May 17, 1825 | 3 | 47 |
| Martin, m. Lydia **BARNUM**, b. of Cornwall, Dec. 9, 1821, by Rev. Walter Smith, of the 2nd Church | 2 | 51 |
| Martin, m. Chloe M. **CARTER**, b. of Cornwall, June 18, 1849, by Rev. E. B. Andrews | 3 | 83 |
| Ruth, Mrs. of New Milford, m. George **DIBBLE**, of Cornwall, July 14, 1779, by Nathaniel Taylor | LR3 | 13 |
| Sabra S., of Cornwall, m. Walter **STERLING**, of Bridgeport, Mar. 10, 1852, at the house of Irad Cole, by Rev. J. L. Maynard | 3 | 122 |
| Sabra Smith, d. [Irad & Abigail], b. July 30, 1830 | 3 | 47 |
| Samuel, s. Seth & Abigail, b. Dec. 20, 1784 | 2 | 9 |
| Sarah, of Wilton, m. Benjamin **DIBBLE**, of Cornwall, Dec. 4, 1754, by Rev. William Gaylord, of Wilton | 1 | 22 |
| Seth, s. Timothy & Rebeckah, b. July 30, 1764 | 1 | 57 |
| Seth, m. Abigail **EMMONS**, Feb. 26, 1784, by Rev. Hezekiah Gold | 2 | 5 |
| Timothy, d. Feb. 18, 1783 | 2 | 2 |
| Timothy, s. James & Annah, b. Mar. 18, 1785 | 2 | 10 |
| Timothy, s. Seth & Abigail, b. Oct. 1, 1790 | 3 | 23 |
| Truman, s. [Seth & Abigail], b. May 6, 1794 | 3 | 22 |
| **COLLINS**, Bridget, ae 25, b. Ireland, res. Cornwall, m. John **COLLINS**, farmer, ae 23, b. Ireland, res. Cornwall, Jan. 1, 1849, by John Brady | 3 | 104-5 |
| John, farmer, ae 23, b. Ireland, res. Cornwall, m. Bridget **COLLINS**, ae 25, b. Ireland, res. Cornwall, Jan. 1, 1849, by John Brady | 3 | 104-5 |
| Susan, m. Seth **PIERCE**, 3rd, Apr. 12, 1826, by Rev. Timothy Stone, of the 1st Ch. | 2 | 63 |
| **COLTON**, Charles H., of Harwinton, m. Sarah **DIBBLE**, of | | |

| | Vol. | Page |
|---|---|---|
| **COLTON**, (cont.) | | |
| Cornwall, Nov. 8, 1846, by Rev. Joshua L. Maynard, of North Cong. Ch., at his house | 3 | 73 |
| **CONLEY**, Catharine, d. Andrew, laborer, b. Feb. 17, [1851] | 3 | 114-15 |
| **COOK**, John, of Cornwall, m. Polly **CURTISS**, of Warren, Sept. 11, 1854, by Rev. R. D. Kirby | 3 | 126 |
| Melissa, m. Sheldon **CLARK**, b. of Cornwall, Feb. 22, 1843, by Myron Harrison, J. P. | 3 | 66 |
| **COON**, Annette A., m. Denison **CHITTENDEN**, Sept. 29, 1831, by Rev. William Andrews | 3 | 48 |
| Catharine, m. Merrill **PENDLETON**, Sept. 11, 1831, by Rev. Walter Smith, of the North Ch. | 3 | 48 |
| **CORBIN, CORBAN**, Emeline, m. Eli B. **SMITH**, b. of Plymouth, Nov. 29, 1838, by N. M. Urmston | 3 | 56 |
| Julia E., d. Josiah B., farmer, ae 29 & Lydia A., ae 25, b. Sept. 24, 1847 | 3 | 86-7 |
| Mary B., of Philadelphia, Pa., m. Samuel **JEFFERS**, of Cornwall, Dec. 23, 1846, at the house of Titus L. Hart, by Rev. Joshua L. Maynard, of the North Cong. Ch. | 3 | 73 |
| **CORNELL**, Peter, m. Abigail M. **HARRISON**, Oct. 14, 1830, by Rev. Walter Smith, of the Cong. Ch. | 3 | 46 |
| Lydia, m. Noah **ROGERS**, Jr., b. of Cornwall, Oct. 27, 1789, by Judah Kellogg, J. P. | 2 | 22 |
| **COTTER**, Eliza, m. George **WHEATON**, Sept. 5, 1824, by Rev. Walter Smith, of the 2nd Ch. | 2 | 58 |
| Franklin A., s. James P., farmer, ae [ ] & Mary, b. Feb. 6, 1850 | 3 | 114-15 |
| Harriet N., of Cornwall, m. John S. **SHERWOOD**, of New York City, Mar. 26, 1844, by Rev. Joshua L. Maynard, of the North Cong. Ch. | 3 | 70 |
| Mary E., m. Russell R. **PRATT**, b. of Cornwall, Oct. 20, 1840, by Rev. J. Atwater | 3 | 59 |
| Samuel Andrew, s. Ambrose L. & Mary A., b. Sept. 25, 1822 | 2 | 52 |
| **COWLES**, [see also **COLE**], Lucia, d. Jason & Thankful, b. Jan. 25, 1799 | 2 | 31 |
| Maria, d. Jason & Thankful, b. Mar. 20, 1805 | 3 | 30 |
| **COXEL**, Riley, of Cornwall, m. Mary Ann **BAXTER**, of Canaan, Feb. 1, 1838, by James Wadsworth, J. P. | 3 | 53 |
| **COY**, Justin, of Springfield, Mass., m. Alma **PICKET**, of Cornwall, Apr. 18, 1830, by Rev. Eleazer Beecher, of the Bap. Ch. in New Milford | 3 | 46 |
| **CRANDALL**, Coddington, m. Lucy **HARRISON**, Nov. 30, 1820, by Benjamin Sedgwick, J. P. | 2 | 48 |
| John H., farmer, ae 28, res. Cornwall, m. Wealthy **O'CAIN**, ae 20, res. Cornwall, Dec. [ ], 1849, in New York State | 3 | 112-13 |
| **CRANE**, J. W., tinner, had chilld, b. [ ] | 3 | 108-9 |
| **CROCKER**, Alice, d. Jonathan & Rachel, b. Mar. 27, 1764 | 1 | 61 |
| Alice, d. Jonathan & Rachel, d. Dec. 24, 1767 | 1 | 107 |

| | Vol. | Page |
|---|---|---|
| **CROCKER**, (cont.) | | |
| Ephraim, s. Jonathan & Rachel, b. Mar. 28, 1769 | 1 | 108 |
| Heman, s. [Jonathan & Rachel], b. Oct. 21, 1772 | 1 | 108 |
| John, s. Jonathan & Rachel, b. Nov. 5, 1765 | 1 | 73 |
| John, s. [Jonathan & Rachel], d. Dec. 30, 1767 | 1 | 107 |
| Levi, s. Levi & Freelove, b. Dec. 19, 1753 | 1 | 21 |
| Rachel, d. Jonathan & Rachel, b. June 29, 1767 | 1 | 108 |
| **CROCKWELL**, James, laborer, ae 34, had child b. June 6, 1848 | 3 | 88-9 |
| **CRONER**, Diana, m. Seth **DIBBLE**, Dec. 19, 1805, by Rev. Josiah Hawes | 3 | 11 |
| **CROSS**, Andrew Jason, s. Alban G. & Abigail, b. Oct. 18, 1819 | 2 | 60 |
| C. A., m. Herman **BONNEY**, Dec. 31, 1849, by Rev. William McAlister | 3 | 82 |
| Celestia M., of Cornwall, m. Charles H. **BOOTH**, of New Milford, Feb. 14, 1847, by R. K. Reynolds | 3 | 74 |
| Hiram Augustus, s. [Alban G & Abigail], b. Jan. 8, 1821 | 2 | 60 |
| Jason, m. Betsey **BOSTWICK**, b. of Cornwall, Nov. 2, 1828, by Rev. E. Washburn | 3 | 1 |
| Jonathan Dibble, s. Alban & Abigail, b. July 21, 1817 | 2 | 43 |
| Lucretia, d. Uriah & William (?)*, b. Apr. 20, 1777 *("Millison" in Starr's book) | 2 | 20 |
| **CRUMB**, William, of New York, m. Phebe Ann **ROBINSON**, of Goshen, Jan. 13, 1850, by E. N. Jenckes | 3 | 83 |
| **CULBY**, Michael, d. June 22, 1851, ae [ ] | 3 | 120-1 |
| **CUMMINGS**, Philip C., m. Lucetta J. **WHEATON**, b. of Cornwall, June 8, 1852, at the house of George Wheaton, by Rev. Joshua L. Maynard | 3 | 122 |
| **CUNNINGHAM**, Ann, of Cornwall, m. Lawrence **McGAY**, of Dover, N. Y., Oct. 30, 1853, by Rev. Henry Burton, of Sharon | 3 | 124 |
| **CURRAN**, John, laborer, ae 26 & Ellen, ae 22, b. July 15, 1849 | 3 | 100-1 |
| **CURTIS, CURTICE, CURTISS**, Anner, of Cornwall, m. George **BALDWIN**, of New Milford, Mar. 10, 1844, by Rev. Daniel Baldwin | 3 | 70 |
| Charles E., s. Eber, farmer, ae 30 & Jerusha, ae 24, b. Nov. 26, 1849 | 3 | 108-9 |
| Eber E., m. Jerusha **HOADLEY**, Nov. 7, 1843, by Rev. Thomas Edwards, of the M. E. Ch. | 3 | 67 |
| Eber E., farmer & Jerusha, had d. [ ], b. [ ] | 3 | 114-15 |
| Lucy, d. Martin & An[n]er, b. Nov. 21, 1781, at Warren | 2 | 45 |
| Lydia*, of Sharon, m. Oliver **FOORD**, of Cornwall, Nov. 23, 1774, by Colton M. Smith *("Lydia **CARTER**" in Starr's Book) | LR3 | 7 |
| Mary H., m. Nathaniel **BARBER**, Nov. 7, 1843, by Rev. Thomas Edwards, of the M. E. Ch. | 3 | 67 |
| Polly, of Warren, m. John **COOK**, of Cornwall, Sept. 11, 1854, by Rev. R. D. Kirby | 3 | 126 |
| Sarah A., m. Allen **WILLIAMS**, b. of Cornwall, Mar. 28, | | |

| | Vol. | Page |
|---|---|---|
| **CURTIS, CURTICE, CURTISS,** (cont.) | | |
| 1852, by F. C. Youngs | 3 | 122 |
| Willis, m. Prudence **TROWBRIDGE**, Mar. 12, 1829, by Rev. Walter Smith, of the North Ch. | 3 | 1 |
| **DAKIN, DOKIN**, Myron, of North East, m. Lucretia A. **BUTLER**, of Cornwall, Feb. 3, 1841, by Rev. Erastus Doty, of Colebrook | 3 | 61 |
| William, m. Aurelia **NICKERSON**, Feb. 6, 1853, by Ralph Smith | 3 | 125 |
| **DAVIS, DAVIES**, Joseph, had s. [ ], b. Jan. 19, 1849 | 3 | 102-3 |
| Joseph, d. Jan. 19, 1849 | 3 | 106-7 |
| **DAVISON, DAVIDSON**, Asa, Jr., laborer, ae 44 & Catharine, ae 37, had child b. July 10, 1848 | 3 | 84-5 |
| Charles E., s. Asa, laborer, ae 47 & Catherine, ae 41, b. Aug. 22, 1850 | 3 | 116-17 |
| Charles Moor, carpenter, d. Jan. 26, 1851, ae 22 | 3 | 120-1 |
| Clarissa, m. Ebenezer B. **DURAND**, b. of Cornwall, July 22, 1832, by Rev. Aaron S. Hill. Int. Pub. | 3 | 50 |
| Lydia E., of Cornwall, m. Ebenezer W. **WOOSTER**, of Goshen, Dec. 30, 1847, by Rev. M. Bydenburgh | 3 | 78 |
| Mary, ae 23, b. Sharon, res. Cornwall, m. Levi **COLE**, laborer, ae 21, res. Cornwall, Mar. 1, 1851, by Rev. J. L. Maynard | 3 | 118-19 |
| Mary Ann, m. Levi **COLE**, b. of Cornwall, Feb. 17, 1851, by Rev. J. L. Maynard, of the North Cong. Ch. | 3 | 97 |
| **DAY**, Arthur Hiram, s. [Hiram & Emily L.], b. June 7, 1847 | 3 | 77 |
| Harriet Foster, d. Hiram & Emily L., b. Mar. 5, 1845 | 3 | 77 |
| Martha, m. Chester **MARKHAM**, Nov. 22, 1828, by Rev. Walter Smith, of the North Ch. | 3 | 1 |
| Mercy, m. Nathan **ABBOT**, b. of Cornwall, Feb. 23, 1757, by Rev. Hezekiah Gold | 1 | 27 |
| **DEAN, DIENE**, Aaron, s. Thomas & Martha, b. May 1, 1768 | 1 | 79 |
| Abigail, m. Elisha **ALLING**, Jan. 9, 1759, by Solomon | 1 | 36 |
| Palmer | | |
| Addison, of Canaan, m. Weltha S. **DEAN**, of Cornwall, Oct. | 3 | 96 |
| 6, 1850, by E. W. Andrews | | |
| Addison, founder, b. Canaan, res. Canaan, m. Wealthy **DEAN**, | 3 | 118-19 |
| b. Canaan, res. Canaan, Oct. 6, 1850, by E. W. Andrews | 1 | 51 |
| Ashbel, s. Moses & Hannah, b. May 18, 1763 | 1 | 38 |
| Benjamin, s. Moses & Hannah, b. Nov. 29, 1760 | 1 | 48 |
| Benjamin, m. Ruth **TANNER**, Oct. 14, 1762, by Rev. H. Gold | 2 | 64 |
| Clarinda, d. [Daniel A. & Clarinda], b. Feb. 28, 1818 | 3 | 5 |
| Cyrus, s. John & Martha, b. June 8, 1788 | 1 | 63 |
| Daniel, s. Benjamin & Ruth, b. Mar. 31, 1765 | 2 | 64 |
| Daniel, s. [Daniel A. & Clarinda], b. Nov. 5, 1820 | LR4 | 19 |
| Daniel Allen, s. Samuel & Mercy, b. Sept. 1, 1771 | 3 | 90-1 |
| Delia, m. Alva **PALMER**, farmer, [ ], by Joshua L. Maynard | | |
| Delia A., m. Alvin B. **PALMER**, b. of Cornwall, Nov. 10, | | |

| | Vol. | Page |
|---|---|---|
| **DEAN, DIENE**, (cont.) | | |
| Maynard, of the North Cong. Ch. | 3 | 76 |
| Denis, s. [Samuel & Mercy], b. Jan. 15, 1775 | LR4 | 19 |
| Ebenezer, s. Thomas & Martha, b. Mar. 24, 1764 | 1 | 68 |
| Ebenezer, [s. Reuben & Lucretia], b. June 24, 1808; d. Mar. 8, 1833 | 3 | 55 |
| Elizabeth, m. Zachariah **DIBBLE**, b. of Cornwall, Feb. 2, 1748/9, by Solomon Palmer | 1 | 10 |
| Elizabeth, d. Mary, b. Sept. 10, 1759 | 1 | 39 |
| Ezra, s. Moses & Hannah, b. Jan. 3, 1758 | 1 | 31 |
| Hiram, s. William & Parthena, b. Apr. 30, 1799 | 2 | 31 |
| Hiram G., farmer, ae 27, res. Cornwall, m. Maria P. **HOLMES**, ae 21, res. Cornwall, Nov. 25, 1850, by Rev. Salmon Gale | 3 | 118-19 |
| Ira, s. Daniel A. & Clarinda, b. Oct. 31, 1815 | 2 | 64 |
| James, s. Benjamin & Ruth, b. Oct. 17, 1768 | 1 | 85 |
| Jane, of Canaan, m. Daniel **CLEMENS**, of Litchfield, July 16, 1801, by Judah Kellogg, J. P. | 2 | 24 |
| Jennett, of Cornwall, m. John O. **CAIN**, of Sharon, Feb. 17, 1841, by Rev. John W. Salter | 3 | 61 |
| Jeresiah, s. [John & Martha], b. Oct. 25, 1784 | 2 | 10 |
| Jerijah, s. [John & Martha], b. Oct. 29, 1782 | 2 | 10 |
| John, s. Samuel & Mercy, b. Aug. 8, 1758 | 1 | 32 |
| John, m. Martha **SCOTT**, Oct. 12, 1780, by Rev. Hezekiah Gold | LR4 | 16 |
| Joseph, s. Benjamin & Ruth, b. June 8, 1779 | LR4 | 14 |
| Joseph How, s. Daniel Allen & Clarissa, b. May 21, 1807 | 2 | 38 |
| Josiah, s. Thomas & Martha, b. Mar. 22, 1766 | 1 | 68 |
| Josiah, s. Reuben & Lucretia, b. Jan. 3, 1783(?)* *("1785"?) | 3 | 55 |
| Josiah, s. Reuben, 2nd & Lucretia, b. Jan. 3, 1785 | 2 | 17 |
| Ketchell, s. [John & Martha], b. June 3, 1803 | 3 | 5 |
| Lucinda, d. Reuben & Lucretia, b. Sept. 21, 1790 | 3 | 23 |
| Lucinda, d. [Reuben & Lucretia], b. Sept. 22, 1790 | 3 | 55 |
| Lucretia, d. [Reuben & Lucretia], b. July 14, 1797 | 3 | 55 |
| Malacia, [d. Reuben & Lucretia], b. May 24, 1799 | 3 | 55 |
| Maria, of Canaan, m. William H. **BAILEY**, of Cornwall, Nov. 26, 1835, by Charles Prentice | 3 | 40 |
| Marrilla, m. Daniel **BRONSON**, b. of Cornwall, June 26, 1828, by Rev. Silas Ambler | 2 | 68 |
| Martha, m. Elisha **DICKINSON**, Dec. 9, 1756, by Rev. Judah Champion, of Litchfield | 1 | 31 |
| Martha, d. Thomas & Martha, b. Sept. 9, 1759 | 1 | 35 |
| Martha, d. Benjamin & Ruth, b. Dec. 17, 1770 | 1 | 99 |
| Mary, d. John & Lucy, b. Jan. 13, 1759 | 1 | 33 |
| Mary, had d. Elizabeth, b. Sept. 10, 1759 | 1 | 39 |
| Mary, m. Thomas **FLEMING**, Aug. 14, 1762, by Rev. Hezekiah Gold | LR4 | 17 |
| Mary R., m. Barbarina **EGLESTON**, b. of Cornwall, | | |

| | Vol. | Page |
|---|---|---|
| **DEAN, DIENE**, (cont.) | | |
| May 14, 1827, by Rev. Silas Ambler | 2 | 67 |
| Melissa, of Cornwall, m. Orion **HUTCHINSON**, of Sharon, Feb. 6, 1839, by N. M. Urmston | 3 | 56 |
| Mercy, w. Samuel, d. Jan. 29, 1781 | LR4 | 19 |
| Molly, d. John & Martha, b. Apr. 16, 1781 | 2 | 10 |
| Moses, m. Hannah **TANNER**, b. of Cornwall, Apr. 29, 1757, by Rev. Hezekiah Gold | 1 | 28 |
| Orphea, d. William & Parthena, b. July 7, 1797 | 2 | 31 |
| Peirce, s. [Reuben & Lucretia], b. Dec. 20, 1804 | 3 | 55 |
| Percis, m. John L. **JOHNSON**, Nov. 25, 1830, by Rev. William Andrews | 3 | 46 |
| Porter, s. [Reuben & Lucretia], b. Dec. 28, 1793 | 3 | 55 |
| Porter, of Cornwall, m. Lycy **SCOFFIELD**, of Oxford, Feb. 27, 1822, by Rev. Timothy Stone, of 1st Church | 2 | 51 |
| Rachel, d. Benjamin & Ruth, b. Feb. 2, 1767 | 1 | 85 |
| Reuben, s. Thomas & Martha, b. Aug. 29, 1757 | 1 | 31 |
| Reuben, b. Aug. 29, 1757; m. Lucretia **FRANCIS**, Dec. 11, 1783 | 3 | 55 |
| Reuben, d. Apr. 8, 1831 | 3 | 55 |
| Rhoda, d. Thomas & Olive, b. Feb. 24, 1777 | LR3 | 14 |
| Ruth, d. Benjamin & Ruth, b. July 6, 1763 | 1 | 53 |
| Sam[ue]ll, m. Mrs. Mercy **ALLING**, Aug. 21, 1757, by S. Palmer | 1 | 31 |
| Samuel, s. Thomas & Martha, b. Nov. 2, 1761 | 1 | 68 |
| Samuel, d. Dec. 5, 1807 | 2 | 39 |
| Samuel, s. [Daniel Allen & Clarissa], b. Dec. 17, 1812 | 2 | 38 |
| Samuel, farmer, ae 36, b. Cornwall, res. Sharon, m. 2nd w. Lucy E., **ALLYN**, ae 32, b. Ledyard, res. Goshen, Feb. 20, 1850, by Rev. LaValette Perrin | 3 | 112-13 |
| Stephen, s. Reuben & Lucretia, b. May 3, 1788 | 2 | 25 |
| Stephen, s. [Reuben & Lucretia], b. May 3, 1788 | 3 | 55 |
| Stephen, [s. Reuben & Lucretia], d. Oct. 22, 1838, ae 50 y. | 3 | 55 |
| Submit, d. Samuel & Mercy, b. Mar. 15, 1769 | 1 | 91 |
| Submit, Mrs., m. Isaac **BATES**, Mar. 29, 1792, by Rev. Peter Starr | 3 | 8 |
| Thankfull, d. Samuel & Mercy, b. Feb. 3, 1764 | 1 | 54 |
| Thankfull, d. Samuel & Mercy, d. Sept. 15, 1781 | LR4 | 19 |
| Thomas, m. Martha **CARTER**, Oct. 23, 1753, by Rev. Thomas Halstead, of Fishkill | 1 | 33 |
| Thomas, s. Thomas & Martha, b. June 23, 1754 | 1 | 31 |
| Thomas, m. Olive **WILLOUGHBY**, Apr. 23, 1776, by Rev. Hezekiah Gold | LR3 | 9 |
| Thomas, s. Thomas & Olive, b. Apr. 11, 1779 | LR3 | 16 |
| Thomas, d. Mar. 1, 1804, ae 78 | 3 | 6 |
| Thomas, of New Milford, Penn., m. Jerusha **LEWIS**, of Cornwall, Feb. 20, 1848, by Rev. M. Bydenburgh | 3 | 78 |
| Thomas, farmer, ae 68, b. Cornwall, res. N. Milford, m. 2nd | | |

| | Vol. | Page |
|---|---|---|
| **DEAN, DIENE**, (cont.) | | |
| w. Jerusha **LEWIS**, ae 66, b. Waterbury, res. Cornwall, Feb. 20, 1848, by Rev. Moses Blydenburgh | 3 | 90-1 |
| Wealthy, b. Canaan, res. Canaan, m. Addison **DEAN**, founder, b. Canaan, res. Canaan, Oct. 6, 1850, by E. W. Andrews | 3 | 118-19 |
| Weltha S., of Cornwall, m. Addison **DEAN**, of Canaan, Oct. 6, 1850, by E. W. Andrews | 3 | 96 |
| Willard, s. [John & Martha], b. July 30, 1794 | 3 | 5 |
| William, s. Samuel & Mercy, b. May 20, 1766 | 1 | 67 |
| William, s. Benjamin & Ruth, b. May 30, 1774 | LR3 | 6 |
| William, s. [John & Martha], b. May 17, 1798 | 3 | 5 |
| Zera, s. [John & Martha], b. Aug. 31, 1791 | 3 | 5 |
| **DEDRICK**, William, dentist, ae 37, b. Coxsackie, N. Y., res. Amenia, N. Y., m. Marriett **BONNEY**, ae 35, res. Cornwall, Apr. 15, 1849, by Rev. Hiram Day | 3 | 104-5 |
| William J., of Amenia, N. Y., m. Marette **BONNEY**, of Cornwall, Sept. 25, 1848, by Rev. Hiram Day | 3 | 81 |
| **DELANY, DELANE**, Daniel, m. Jennet **WILSON**, Oct. 23, 1824, by Rev. Asa Tallmadge, of the Bap. Ch. | 2 | 65 |
| Patrick, m. Ann **FITZGERALD**, alias **CASE**, b. of Cornwall, Dec. 7, 1852, by Rev. John Smith | 3 | 125 |
| **DEMUS**, Polly, houseworker, d. Mar. 23, 1848, old age | 3 | 92-3 |
| **DENNOCH***, Olive, d. James & Margaret, b. May 15, 1761 *("**PINNOCK**" in Starr's book) | 1 | 45 |
| **DEWEY**, Clarissa, m. Daniel **ALLEN**, b. of Cornwall, July 16, 1801, by Rev. Hecules Weston | 3 | 11 |
| **DEXTER**, Elizabeth, d. Thomas & Elizabeth, b. Feb. 6, 1779 | LR3 | 16 |
| Elizabeth, w. Thomas, d. Apr. 1, 1779 | LR3 | 16 |
| Thomas, m. Elizabeth **GARNSEY**, Sept. 17, 1778, by Rev. Hezekiah Gold | LR3 | 16 |
| **DIBBLE, DIBLE**, Abigail, d. Ebenezer & Elizabeth, b. Aug. 17, 1757 | 1 | 29 |
| Abigail, d. Ebenezer & Elizabeth, d. Apr. 25, 1762 | 1 | 46 |
| Abigail, d. John, 2nd & Rebeckah, b. May 16, 1769 | 1 | 87 |
| Abigail, d. John, d. June 27, 1791 | 2 | 26 |
| Adah, d. Benjamin & Sarah, b. July 16, 1759 | 1 | 34 |
| Adah, d. Benjamin & Sarah, d. Apr. 25, 1780 | LR4 | 14 |
| Almira, d. Truman & Ruth, b. June 3, 1846 | 3 | 95 |
| Amy, d. Zachariah & Elizabeth, b. Apr. 3, 1763 | 1 | 65 |
| Ama, d. [Israel & Elizabeth], d. Oct. 29, 1777 | LR4 | 14 |
| Amy, d. Israel & Elizabeth, b. May 16, 1769 | 1 | 88 |
| Anne, d. Clemons & Rhoda, b. Mar. 20, 1765 | 1 | 59 |
| Augustus Norton, s. [Seth & Diania], b. Feb. 26, 1812 | 3 | 13 |
| Benajah, s. [Israel & Elizabeth], b. Feb. 22, 1779; d. Apr. 11, 1779 | LR4 | 14 |
| Benjamin, Jr., of Cornwall, m. Lydia **MILLER**, of Sharon, Mar. 8, 1753, by Solomon Palmer | 1 | 19 |
| Benjamin, of Cornwall, m. Sarah **COLE**, of [Wilton], Dec. | | |

| | Vol. | Page |
|---|---|---|
| **DIBBLE, DIBLE,** | | |
| 4, 1754, by Rev. William Gaylord, of Wilton | 1 | 22 |
| Benjamin, s. Israel & Elizabeth, b. Dec. 13, 1763 | 1 | 52 |
| Benjamin, 2nd, of Cornwall, m. Chloe **DRINKWATER**, of New Milford, Mar. 24, 1791, by Judah Kellogg, J. P. | 2 | 22 |
| Benjamin, d. May 1, 1798 | 3 | 10 |
| Betsey, d. George & Ruth, b. Apr. 7, 1799 | 3 | 31 |
| Betsey, m. James H. **JARVIS**, of Salem, N. Y., Oct. 8, 1827, by Rev. Silas Ambler | 2 | 68 |
| Charity, d. Clemens & Rhoda, b. May 2, 1768 | 1 | 81 |
| Chloe, m. William **RUSSELL**, Oct. 10, 1821, by Annarius Derthick, of Warren | 2 | 51 |
| Cinderilla, d. Benjamin & Chloe, b. Feb. 3, 1800 | 2 | 23 |
| Cinderilla, m. Elkanah **MEAD**, b. of Cornwall, Jan. 7, 1828, by Rev. Silas Ambler, of the Bapt. Ch. | 2 | 68 |
| Clement, s. John & Hannah, b. Mar. 4, 1741 | 1 | 14 |
| Clement, m. Rhoda **DIBBLE**, Mar. 18, 1762, by Rev. H. Gold | 1 | 46 |
| Clinton, farmer, d. Dec. 16, 1848, ae 34 | 3 | 106-7 |
| Daniel, s. John, 3rd & Esther, b. Feb. 4, 1765 | 1 | 59 |
| David, s. Ebenezer & Elizabeth, b. Sept. 30, 1751 | 1 | 15 |
| David, m. Mabal **GARNSEY**, Oct. 28, 177[ ], by Rev. Hezekiah Gold | 2 | 14 |
| Dolly, d. Israel & Elizabeth, b. Aug. 22, 1774 | LR3 | 6 |
| Dorcas, w. Benj[ami]n, d. Oct. 10, 1742 | 1 | 9 |
| Dorcas, d. Benjamin & Dorcas, b. May 31, 1746 | 1 | 2 |
| Dorcas, d. Israel & Elizabeth, b. Jan. 3, 1766 | 1 | 66 |
| Dorcas, m. Daniel **ALLEN**, b. of Cornwall, June 11, 1767, by Thomas Russell, J. P. | 1 | 76 |
| Ebenezer, s. David & Mable, b. July 21, 1773 | 2 | 14 |
| Ebenezer, m. Mary **PIERCE**, b. of Cornwall, May 12, 1776, by Thomas Swift. J. P. | LR3 | 9 |
| Ebenezer, Lieut., d. Feb. 29, 1784 | 2 | 6 |
| Elisha, s. Silas & Eunice, b. May 25, 1770 | 1 | 96 |
| Elizabeth, d. [Israel & Elizabeth], b. Sept. 15, 1772 | 1 | 109 |
| Elizabeth, w. Lieut. Ebenezer, d. Oct. 9, 1775 | LR3 | 7 |
| Elizabeth, d. Israel & Elizabeth, d. Mar. 25, 1796 | 2 | 28 |
| Ellen, d. Truman & Eunice, b. Dec. 15, 1836 | 3 | 62 |
| Emily, d. Seth & Diania, b. June 21, 1808 | 3 | 13 |
| Emily, m. Willard **KIMBERLY**, May 4, 1831, by Rev. William Andrews | 3 | 48 |
| Esther, d. John & Hannah, b. Apr. 29, 1744; d. Nov. 21, 1746 | 1 | 15 |
| Esther, d. Clement & Rhoda, b. July 18, 1763 | 1 | 51 |
| Eunice, d. John, 3rd & Esther, b. June 23, 1772 | 1 | 104 |
| Eunice, d. Silas & Eunice, b. Sept. 15, 1777 | LR3 | 14 |
| George, s. Benjamin & Sarah, b. Nov. 23, 1755 | 1 | 23 |
| George, of Cornwall, m. Mrs. Ruth **COLE**, of New Milford, July 14, 1779, by Nathaniel Taylor | LR3 | 13 |
| George, m. Olive **HICKINSON**, Mar. 15, 1810, by Rev. | | |

| | Vol. | Page |
|---|---|---|
| **DIBBLE, DIBLE**, (cont.) | | |
| Henry Christie | 3 | 3 |
| George, s. [Truman & Ruth], b. Mar. 17, 1833 | 3 | 51 |
| Hannah, d. John & Hannah, b. Mar. 2, 1739 | 1 | 14 |
| Hannah, d. Benjamin & Dorcas, b. Oct. [ ], 1740 | 1 | 2 |
| Hannah, m. Abel **ABBOT**, b. of Cornwall, Feb. 16, 1757, by Rev. Hezekiah Gold | 1 | 27 |
| Hannah, m. Timothy **BROWNSON**, b. of Cornwall, Sept. 25, [1765], by Thomas Russell, J. P. | 1 | 62 |
| Hannah, d. John, 3rd & Esther, b. May 15, 1767 | 1 | 77 |
| Hannah, d. Israel & Elizabeth, b. Oct. 18, 1776 | LR3 | 12 |
| Hannah, d. Israel & Elizabeth, b. Oct. 18, 1776 | LR4 | 14 |
| Hannah, wid. John, Sr., d. Dec. 19, 1792 | 2 | 28 |
| Hannah M., m. Charles **BARNS**, Feb. 5, 1828, by Rev. Walter Smith | 2 | 68 |
| Hannah Maria, d. Benjamin & Cloe, b. Dec. 14, 1809 | 3 | 17 |
| Huldah, d. Benjamin & Sarah, b. July 8, 1757 | 1 | 28 |
| Huldah, m. Joshua **HARTSTON**, Oct. 29, 1775, by Rev. Hezekiah Gold | LR3 | 5 |
| Ire, s. Silas & [E]unice, b. Feb. 4, 1768 | 1 | 79 |
| Ire, s. [Silas & Eunice], d. Aug. 23, 1770 | 1 | 96 |
| Isaac, s. Silas & Eunice, b. Aug. 27, 1772 | 2 | 17 |
| Israel, s. Benjamin & Dorcas, b. Dec. 7, 1742 | 1 | 2 |
| Israel, m. Elizabeth **MILLARD**, Mar. 3, 1763, by Rev. H. Gold | 1 | 50 |
| Israel, s. Israel & Elizabeth, b. Dec. 19, 1770 | 1 | 109 |
| Israel, Jr., d. May 26, 1802 | 3 | 10 |
| Israel, d. Oct. 9, 1824, ae 82 y. | 2 | 56 |
| James, s. John & Hannah, b. Dec. 21, 1747 | 1 | 15 |
| Jane, d. Ebenezer & Elizabeth, b. Oct. 23, 1749 | 1 | 15 |
| Jemimi, d. Benjamin & Dorcas, b. May 1, 1744 | 1 | 4 |
| Jemima, m. Timothy **ROWLEY**, Mar. 9, 1769, by Rev. H. Gold | 1 | 86 |
| Jethro, s. John, 3rd & Esther, b. July 18, 1762 | 1 | 50 |
| John, late of Norwalk, now of Cornwall, m. 2nd w. Hennah **LEWSEE***, May 30, 1732, by Rev. Mr. Sturgeon, of Welton Parish. Witnesses: John Dunning & Hannah Dunning *("**LEWIS**, in Starr's book) | 1 | 14 |
| John, late of Norwalk, now of Cornwall, m. 2nd w. Hannah **LEWSEE**, May 30, 1732, by Rev. Mr. Sturgion, of Wilton Parish. Witnesses: John Dunning & Hannah Dunning. Sworn to May 5, 1750, before Thomas Benedict, J. P. | 1 | 20 |
| John, s. John & Hannah, b. Oct. 4, 1736 | 1 | 14 |
| John, m. Rebeccah **MERRET**, of Stamford, Dec. 18, 1753, by Rev. Noah Wells, of Stamford | 1 | 20 |
| John, m. Esther **MAGUIRER***, Apr. 30, 1759, by Rev. H. Gold *("**MACKQUAVER**" in Starr's book) | 1 | 34 |
| John, of Cornwall, m. Hannah **BALEY**, of Sharon, Jan. 1, | | |

| | Vol. | Page |
|---|---|---|
| **DIBBLE, DIBLE,** (cont.) | | |
| 1765, by Rev. Daniel Griswold, Jr. | 1 | 58 |
| John, 3rd & Esther, had d. [ ], b. June 22, 1774 | 2 | 13 |
| John, s. Silas & Eunice, b. Mar. 21, 1775 | LR3 | 8 |
| John, Jr., d. Jan. 26, 1782, in the 82nd y. of his age | 2 | 1 |
| John, d. Nov. 7, 1791 | 2 | 26 |
| Jonah, s. Israel & Elizabeth, b. Nov. 3, 1782 | 2 | 4 |
| Jonathan, s. John, 2nd & Rebecca, b. Jan. 19, 1756 | 1 | 24 |
| Jonathan, m. Rachel **ROSSETER**, July 3, 1781, by Judah Kellogg, J. P. | LR4 | 18 |
| Jonathan, d. Aug. 10, 1820, ae 64 | 2 | 46 |
| Julia, m. Orson **NICKERSON**, b. of Cornwall, Jan. 17, 1847, by Rev. Hiram Day | 3 | 74 |
| Laura, m. Jeremiah **BIRCH**, July 6, 1828, by Rev. William Andrews | 2 | 68 |
| Loary, d. Benjamin & Cloe, b. July 3, 1806 | 3 | 16 |
| Lucina, d. Benjamin, 2nd & Chloe, b. Aug. 11, 1797 | 3 | 25 |
| Lucy, d. George & Ruth, b. Oct. 15, 1787 | 2 | 18 |
| Marinda, d. [Truman & Eunice], b. Nov. 23, 1839 | 3 | 62 |
| Marshall, m. Jennett **KELLOGG**, b. of Cornwall, Dec. 9, 1843, by Rev. Joshua L. Maynard, of the North Cong. Ch. | 3 | 68 |
| Mary, d. Seth & Diantha, b. Oct. 9, 1806 | 3 | 16 |
| Mary, d. Truman & Ruth, b. Feb. 15, 1829 | 3 | 51 |
| Mary, of Cornwall, m. Augustus **MILES**, of Albany, N. Y., Nov. 8, 1829, by Rev. Silas Ambler | 3 | 45 |
| Mary, of Cornwall, m. Zena **HOTCHKISS**, of New Haven, Mar. 16, 1845, by Hiram Day | 3 | 71 |
| Matthew, s. Clement & Rhoda, b. June 12, 1780 | LR3 | 15 |
| Mindwell, d. George & Ruth, b. Feb. 21, 1782 | 2 | 3 |
| Mindwell, d. George & Ruth, d. June 6, 1784 | 2 | 6 |
| Minerva, d. Benjamin & Cloe, b. Nov. 3, 1795 | 3 | 22 |
| Minerva, m. David **MEAD**, Apr. 3, 1824, by Rev. Asa Tallmadge, of the Bap. Ch. | 2 | 65 |
| Molly, d. John, 3rd & Esther, b. Dec. 22, 1760 | 1 | 38 |
| Noah, s. Israel & Elizabeth, b. Mar. 28, 1780 | LR4 | 15 |
| Norman Bradford, s. [Seth & Diania], b. May 15, 1810 | 3 | 13 |
| Norman F., m. Eunice L. **STONE**, Apr. 6, 1837, by Rev. William Andrews | 3 | 52 |
| Orphea, d. Benjamin & Chloe, b. Mar. 16, 1794 | 2 | 29 |
| Rachel, Mrs., m. Dea. Josiah **HOPKINS**, [ ], by Rev. Timothy Stone, of 1st Soc. [Recorded Oct. 20, 1821] | 2 | 50 |
| Rebecca, d. John & Hannah, b. Mar. 22, 1733 | 1 | 14 |
| Rebeckah, d. Israel & Elizabeth, b. Oct. 4, 1767 | 1 | 77 |
| Rebecca, w. John, d. Nov. 7, 1785 | 2 | 11 |
| Reuben, s. Clemens & Rhoda, b. Aug. 2, 1771 | 1 | 100 |
| Rhoda, m. Clement **DIBBLE**, Mar. 18, 1762, by Rev. H. Gold | 1 | 46 |
| Rosetta, m. Robert **HOXLY**, Mar. 16, 1841, by Rev. Timothy Stone | 3 | 63 |

| | Vol. | Page |
|---|---|---|
| **DIBBLE, DIBLE,** (cont.) | | |
| Ruth, d. John, 2nd & Rebecah, b. Dec. 24, 1757 | 1 | 30 |
| Ruth, m. Ebenezer **GARNSEY**, Sept. 30, 1778, by Rev. Hezekiah Gold | LR3 | 13 |
| Ruth, w. George, d. June 28, 1803 | 3 | 6 |
| Ruth, d. Truman & Eunice B., b. May 3, 1824 | 2 | 60 |
| Ruth, m. William Henry **WELLS**, July 23, 1838, by Rev. Walter Smith | 3 | 54 |
| Sally, d. George & Ruth, b. June 4, 1780 | LR4 | 15 |
| Sarah, w. Benjamin, d. Aug. 15, 1792 | 2 | 26 |
| Sarah, d. Truman & Eunice, b. Mar. 2, 1827 | 2 | 60 |
| Sarah, of Cornwall, m. Charles H. **COLTON**, of Harwinton, Nov. 8, 1846, by Rev. Joshua L. Maynard, of the North Cong. Ch., at his house | 3 | 73 |
| Seth, s. Zachariah & Rachel, b. Apr. 6, 1747 | 1 | 46 |
| Seth, s. Israel & Elizabeth, b. Jan. 31, 1785 | 2 | 9 |
| Seth, m. Diana **CRONER**, Dec. 19, 1805, by Rev. Josiah Hawes | 3 | 11 |
| Silas, s. John & Hannah, b. July 10, 1749 | 1 | 15 |
| Silas, m. Eunice **WEDGE**, Mar. 26, 1767, by Thomas Russell, J. P. | 1 | 75 |
| Silas, s. Silas & Eunice, b. Aug. 5, 1780 | LR4 | 16 |
| Susa, d. Clemens & Rhoda, b. Apr. 27, 1785 | 2 | 15 |
| Sylvanus, s. Ens. Ebenezer & Elizabeth, b. Jan. 15, 1762 | 1 | 44 |
| Sylvanus, s. Lieut. Ebenezer & Elizabeth, d. Nov. 16, 1783 | 2 | 6 |
| Thankful, d. Benjamin & Chloe, b. Sept. 4, 1803 | 3 | 12 |
| Thomas, s. Ebenezer & Elizabeth, b. Jan. 30, 1760 | 1 | 35 |
| Thomas, s. Ens. Ebenezer, d. July 11, 1760 | 1 | 37 |
| Thomas, s. David & Mabal, b. Mar. 9, 1777 | LR3 | 12 |
| Truman, s. George & Ruth, b. Jan. 23, 1796 | 3 | 26 |
| Truman, m. Eunice **PECK**, Nov. 5, 1823, by Rev. Timothy Stone, of the 1st Ch. | 2 | 57 |
| Wakeman P., m. Jane **NICKERSON**, b. of Cornwall, Dec. 31, 1843, by Rev. Joshua L. Maynard, of the North Cong. Ch. | 3 | 68 |
| Wakeman S., mechanic & Jane, had s. [ ], b. May 9, 1849 | 3 | 100-1 |
| Zachariah, m. Elizabeth **DEAN**, b. of Cornwall, Feb. 2, 1748/9, by Solomon Palmer | 1 | 10 |
| Zachariah, s. Zachariah & Elizabeth, b. Nov. 4, 1749 | 1 | 10 |
| Zachariah, s. Clemons & Rhoda, b. Sept. 16, 1777 | LR3 | 14 |
| **DICKINSON, DICKENSON,** [see also **HICKENSON**], Amanda, m. Aaron C. **STONE**, Oct. 19, 1826, by Rev. Asa Tallmadge, of the Bap. Ch. | 2 | 66 |
| Amos, m. Abby **TRAFFORD**, Sept. 15, 1850, at Cornwall Bridge, by Rev. William McAlister | 3 | 96 |
| Asahel, s. Elisha & Martha, b. Jan. 9, 1762 | 1 | 64 |
| Ebenezer, s. Elisha & Martha, b. May 19, 1767 | 1 | 89 |
| Elijah, m. Rachel **HARRIS**, b. of Cornwall, June 15, 1758, by John Patterson, J. P. | 1 | 64 |

| | Vol. | Page |
|---|---|---|
| **DICKINSON, DICKENSON**, (cont.) | | |
| Elijah, s. Elijah & Rachel, b. Sept. 10, 1766 | 1 | 73 |
| Elijah, m. Martha **ALLEN**, July 21, 1768, by Hezekiah Gold | 1 | 83 |
| Elisha, m. Martha **DEAN**, Dec. 9, 1756, by Rev. Judah Champion, of Litchfield | 1 | 31 |
| Elisha, m. Elizabeth **BARNES**, Aug. 2, 1769, by Rev. Mr. Hezekiah Gold | 1 | 87 |
| Enos, mechanic, ae 61, b. Litchfield, res. Sharon, m. 2nd w. Abby **TRAFFORD**, ae 45, b. Canaan, res. Sharon, Sept. 15, 1851, by Rev. William McAlister | 3 | 118-19 |
| Friend, s. Elisha & Martha, b. Dec. 19, 1757 | 1 | 31 |
| Hannah, d. Elisha & Martha, b. July 27, 1763 | 1 | 64 |
| Martha, w. Elisha, d. Apr. 15, 1769 | 1 | 88 |
| Martha, w. Elijah, d. Apr. 18, 1789, in the 65th y. of her age | 2 | 11 |
| Mary Ann, of Cornwall, m. Sylvester C. **GRISWOLD**, of Litchfield, Apr. 3, 1850, by Rev. Joshua L. Maynard, of the North Cong. Ch., at his house | 3 | 83 |
| Milo, m. Amanda **JOHNSON**, Jan. 17, 1836, by Rev. T. Atwater | 3 | 41 |
| Nathaniel, s. Elisha & Elizabeth, b. Mar. 25, 1772 | 1 | 108 |
| Pacience, d. Elijah & Rachel, b. Dec. 19, 1759 | 1 | 64 |
| Philip, s. Elisha & Elizabeth, b. May 22, 1770 | 1 | 98 |
| Prudence, d. Elijah & Rachel, b. July 12, 1762 | 1 | 64 |
| Rachel, w. Elijah, d. Feb. 21, 1768 | 1 | 81 |
| Reny, d. Elisha & Martha, b. July 17, 1765 | 1 | 64 |
| Wallace, b. Sharon, res. Sharon, d. Sept. 2, 1847, ae 3 w. | 3 | 92-3 |
| Wallace, s. William, laborer, ae 28, & Caroline, ae 28, res. Sharon, b. Aug. 12, 1848 | 3 | 84-5 |
| **DIENE**, [see under **DEAN**] | | |
| **DILLON**, Michael, m. Bridget **KEERNANN**, Jan. 7, 1853, by Rev. Peter Kelley. Int. Pub. | 3 | 125 |
| **DOOLITTLE**, Benjamin, s. [Benjamin & Harriet], b. Feb. 14, 1803 | 2 | 43 |
| Bird, s. [Benjamin & Harriet], b. May 24, 1813 | 2 | 43 |
| Birdseye, farmer, ae 37, res. Cornwall, m. Emeline **PEET**, ae 23, res. Cornwall, Feb. [ ], 1849 | 3 | 104-5 |
| Erastus W., s. [Benjamin & Harriet], b. Mar. 21, 1810; d. Oct. 22, 1813 | 2 | 43 |
| Erastus W., s. Benjamin, d. Oct. 12, 1813 | 2 | 39 |
| Guy, m. Sarah **BENEDICT**, b. of Cornwall, Jan. 20, 1821, by Rev. Asa Tallmadge | 2 | 49 |
| Guy Fenn, s. [Benjamin & Harriet], b. Apr. 18, 1798 | 2 | 43 |
| Harriet, d. [Benjamin & Harriet], b. July 22, 1805 | 2 | 43 |
| Lucius, s. [Benjamin & Harriet], b. Feb. 24, 1815 | 2 | 43 |
| Samuel, s. Benjamin & Harriet, b. June 27, 1796 | 2 | 43 |
| **[DOUGLASS], DAWGLASS**, Abia, d. William & Martha, b. Mar. 25, 1768 | 1 | 83 |
| Elias, s. James Marsh & Rhoda, b. Feb. 28, 1775 | LR3 | 8 |
| Hannah, d. James & Rachel, b. July 2, 1738 | 1 | 11 |

| | Vol. | Page |
|---|---|---|
| **[DOUGLASS], DAGLASS**, (cont.) | | |
| Hannah, d. James & Rachel, b. July 2, 1738 | ! | 13 |
| James Marsh, s. James & Rachel, b. Mar. 18, 1747 | 1 | 11 |
| James Marsh, s. James & Rachel, b. Mar. 18, 1747 | 1 | 13 |
| James Marsh, m. Rhoda **BURNHAM**, Feb. 8, 1774, by Rev. Hezekiah Gold | LR3 | 7 |
| John, s. James & Rachel, b. June 14, 1749 | 1 | 11 |
| John, s. James & Rachel, b. June 14, 1749 | 1 | 13 |
| Olive, d. James & Rachel, b. Apr. 2, 1745 | 1 | 11 |
| Olive, d. James & Rachel, b. Apr. 2, 1745 | 1 | 13 |
| Rachel, d. James & Rachel, b. May 2, 1740 | 1 | 11 |
| Rachel, d. [James], & Rachel, b. May 2, 1740 | 1 | 13 |
| Sarah, d. James & Rachel, b. Sept. 8, 1743 | 1 | 11 |
| Sarah, d. James & Rachel, b. Sept. 8, 1743 | 1 | 13 |
| Susanna, d. William & Martha, b. Aug. 29, 1766 | 1 | 83 |
| **DOWNING**(?)*, Liveras, of Brookfield, m. Sarah M. **WINCHELL**, of Cornwall, Mar. 23, 1851, by F. C. Youngs *("**DUNNING**"?) | 3 | 96 |
| **DRIGGS**, Joseph, of Berkshire Cty., Mass., m. Cornelia **PIERSON**, of Cornwall, May 14, 1826, by Rev. Timothy Stone, of the 1st Ch. | 2 | 65 |
| **DRINKWATER**, Chloe, of New Milford, m. Benjamin **DIBBLE**, 2nd, of Cornwall, Mar. 24, 1791, by Judah Kellogg, J. P. | 2 | 22 |
| **DUDLEY**, Abigail, [d. Gideon & Elizabeth], b. May 10, 1754 | 1 | 30 |
| Anna, d. Gideon & Elizabeth, b. Nov. 17, 1745 | 1 | 30 |
| Anna, m. Martin **DUDLEY**, June 21, 1763, by Rev. Hezekiah Gold | 1 | 53 |
| Barzillai, m. Sarah **CARTER**, Mar. 6, 1750, by Solomon Palmer | 1 | 13 |
| Elizabeth, [d. Gideon & Elizabeth], b. Feb. 15, 1752 | 1 | 30 |
| Elizabeth, w. Gideon, d. May 21, 1765 | 1 | 61 |
| Elizabeth, d. Gideon, d. Oct. 15, 1766 | 1 | 73 |
| Gideon, [s. Gideon & Elizabeth], b. Feb. 2, 1749; d. Dec. 28, 1751 | 1 | 30 |
| Gideon, s. Martin & Ann, b. Feb. 12, 1765 | 1 | 59 |
| Isaac, s. Martin & Anna, b. Feb. 9, 1764; d. Mar. 9, 1764 | 1 | 56 |
| Joseph, [s. Gideon & Elizabeth], b. Nov. 14, 1755 | 1 | 30 |
| Joseph, s. Gideon, d. Nov. 20, 1766 | 1 | 73 |
| Louisa, [d. Gideon & Elizabeth], b. Nov. 15, 1747 | 1 | 30 |
| Lovisa, d. Gideon, d. Jan. 5, 1767 | 1 | 73 |
| Martin, m. Anna **DUDLEY**, June 21, 1763, by Rev. Hezekiah Gold | 1 | 53 |
| Mary, d. Gideon & Elizabeth, b. Jan. 9, 1760 | 1 | 61 |
| Sarah, d. Barzillai & Sarah, b. Feb. 1, 1752 | 1 | 26 |
| Sibe, d. Barzillai & Sarah, b. May 16, 1750 | 1 | 14 |
| **DUNBAR**, Henry, s. Sarah **CALKINS**, Nov. 28, 1832, by Rev. Walter Smith, of the North Cong. Ch. | 3 | 35 |
| **DUNHAM**, Hiram, m. Palina **JENNINGS**, Jan. 11, 1821, by Rev. | | |

| | Vol. | Page |
|---|---|---|
| **DUNHAM**, (cont.) | | |
| Asa Blair, of the 1st Soc. in Kent | 2 | 49 |
| **DUNNING***, Liveras, of Brookfield, m. Sarah M. **WINCHELL**, of Cornwall, Mar. 23, 1851, by F. C. Youngs *("**DOWNING**"(?) ) | 3 | 96 |
| **DURAND**, Ebenezer b., m. Clarissa **DAVISON**, b. of Cornwall, July 22, 1832, by Rev. Aaron S. Hill. Int. Pub. | 3 | 50 |
| Sarah, of Oxford, m. John **PAYNE**, of Cornwall, Dec. 13, 1815, in Oxford, by Rev. Aaron Humphrey, of Oxford | 2 | 45 |
| **EDDY**, George M., hatter, ae 25, b. Salisbury, res. Providence, m. 2nd w. Jane E. **HILL**, ae 23, b. Newtown, res. Providence, Apr. 16, 1851, by Rev. Mr. Youngs | 3 | 118-19 |
| George N., of Providence, m. Jane C. **HILL**, of Cornwall, Apr. 16, 1851, by F. C. Youngs | 3 | 97 |
| **EDSON**, Clarissa Isabella, m. William S. **LUDDINGTON**, Jan. 9, 1821, by Rev. Walter Smith, of the 2nd Church | 2 | 49 |
| **EGGLESTON, EGLESTON**, Albert, of North East Dutchess Cty., N. Y., m. Sarah Jane **BIERCE**, of Cornwall, Feb. 28, 1841, by Rev. E. Washburn | 3 | 61 |
| Barbarina, m. Mary R. **DEAN**, b. of Cornwall, May 14, 1827, by Rev. Silas Ambler | 2 | 67 |
| Jeremiah, sash & blind maker, ae 20, b. Sharon, res. W. Cornwall; m. Abigail **PALMER**, ae 17, May 10, 1848, by Hiram Day | 3 | 90-1 |
| Jeremiah D., m. Abigail S. **PALMER**, b. of Cornwall, May 10, 1848, by Rev. Hiram Day | 3 | 79 |
| Sarah, ae 30, b. Cornwall, res. Salisbury, m. 2nd h. Cyrus F. **BENEDICT**, manufacturer, ae 32, b. Salisbury, res. Salisbury, Mar. 27, 1850, by Rev. William McAlister | 3 | 112-13 |
| **ELLIS**, Darwin, of Waterbury, m. Phebe Ann **MAIZE**, of Cornwall, Sept. 16, 1849, by Rev. Lewis Gunn | 3 | 82 |
| **ELY**, James, m. Louisa **EVEREST**, July 30, 1822, by Rev. Timothy Stone, of the 1st Church | 2 | 53 |
| **EMMONS, EMONS**, Abigail, d. Samuel & Hamar, b. Mar. 10, 1766 | 1 | 70 |
| Abigail, m. Seth **COLE**, Feb. 26, 1784, by Rev. Hezekiah Gold | 2 | 5 |
| Adonijah, s. Solomon & Saba, b. Mar. 14, 1785 | 2 | 10 |
| Amanday, d. [Asa & Hannah], b. Aug. 3, 1786 | 2 | 18 |
| Asa, s. Woodruff & Esther, b. July 12, 1756 | 1 | 24 |
| Asa, s. Salmon & Hannah, b. Sept. 9, 1775 | LR3 | 10 |
| Asaph, m. Nancy **SELEY**, Aug. 11, 1784, by Rev. Hezekiah Gold | 2 | 8 |
| Asbel, s. Simeon & Mary, b. Oct. 21, 1784 | 2 | 21 |
| Betty, d. Salmon & Hannah, b. Aug. 3, 1773 | LR3 | 6 |
| Bildad, s. [Solomon & Saba], b. June 2, 1791 | 3 | 23 |
| Charles P., s. Luther & Elizabeth, b. Nov. 14, 1817 | 2 | 60 |
| Charlotte, d. Asa & Hannah, b. Oct. 17, 1795 | 3 | 22 |
| Chauncey, s. Asa & Hannah, b. Apr. 1, 1784 | 2 | 18 |

| | Vol. | Page |
|---|---|---|
| **EMMONS, EMONS**, (cont.) | | |
| Elizabeth, d. Woodruff & Esther, b. Sept. 29, 1745 | 1 | 5 |
| Elizabeth, d. Woodruff & Esther, d. June 16, 1748 | 1 | 8 |
| Elizabeth, d. Woodruff & Esther, b. May 5, 1749 | 1 | 8 |
| Elizabeth, m. Joseph **BEARSE**, Sept. 19, 1768, by Thomas Russell, J. P. | 1 | 82 |
| Elvira, ae 22, b. Sharon, res. Sharon, m. Russell **MILLARD**, Jr., blacksmith, ae 22, b. Cornwall, res. Sharon, Oct. 10, 1847, by Rev. Samuel Weeks | 3 | 90-1 |
| Elvira H., m. Russell **MILLARD**, b. of Sharon, Oct. 10, 1847, by Samuel Weeks | 3 | 74 |
| Esther, d. Asa & Hannah, b. Aug. 6, 1779 | 2 | 3 |
| Francis Brown, s. Solomon & Saba, b. Apr. 24, 1787 | 2 | 19 |
| Hannah, d. Samuel & Ruhamah, b. June 3, 1768 | 1 | 81 |
| Harvey C., s. [Luther & Elizabeth], b. Nov. 30, 1819 | 2 | 60 |
| Horace, s. Solomon & Sabe, b. Sept. 30, 1778 | LR3 | 15 |
| Ira, s. Salmon & Hannah, b. Apr. 13, 1782 | 2 | 7 |
| John, s. Samuel & Hanner, b. Jan. 15, 1772 | 1 | 102 |
| Lewis, s. Asaph & Nancy, b. May 14, 1785 | 2 | 12 |
| Lewis, s. Luther & Elizabeth, b. Feb. 9, 1828 | 2 | 69 |
| Lucretia, d. Salmon & Hannah, b. May 15, 1780 | LR4 | 16 |
| Lucy E., d. [Luther & Elizabeth], b. Oct. 3, 1822 | 2 | 60 |
| Luther, s. Asa & Hannah, b. May 18, 1780 | 3 | 23 |
| Luther, m. Elizabeth **JOHNSON**, Nov. 26, 1816, by Rev. Timothy Stone, of the 1st Ch. | 2 | 58 |
| Lydia, d. Solomon & Saba, b. Apr. 26, 1789 | 3 | 23 |
| Maria, d. Luther & Elizabeth, b. June 9, 1825 | 2 | 69 |
| Maria J., m. William W. **PENDLETON**, Feb. 26, 1845, at the house of Luther Emmons, by Rev. Joshua L. Maynard, of the North Cong. Ch. | 3 | 71 |
| Mary, d. Solomon & Saba, b. Nov. 15, 1780 | LR4 | 16 |
| Mary Anne, d. Timothy & Mary, b. Feb. 20, 1780 | 2 | 1 |
| Polly, d. Asa & Hannah, b. June 25, 1793 | 2 | 27 |
| Ralph, s. [Asa & Hannah], b. Sept. 5, 1781 | 2 | 3 |
| Ruhamah, m. Jacob **SCHOVILL**, Oct. 18, 1778, by Rev. Hezekiah Gold | LR3 | 13 |
| Salmon, m. Hannah **JEFFREY**, Nov. 5, 1772, by Rev. H. Gold | LR3 | 5 |
| Salmon, s. [Salmon & Hannah], b. Mar. 4, 1784 | 2 | 7 |
| Samuell, s. Woodruff & Esther, b. Feb. 20, 1743/4 | 1 | 5 |
| Samuel, m. Hannah* **JENNINGS***, June 12, 1765, by Rev. Hezekiah Gold *("Hamar" in Starr's book) | 1 | 62 |
| Samuel, s. Asaph & Nancy, b. Feb. 16, 1787 | 2 | 18 |
| Sarah, d. Woodruff & Esther, b. Feb. 7, 1750/1 | 1 | 14 |
| Sarah, d. Solomon & Saba, b. Oct. 20, 1782 | 2 | 5 |
| Simeon, s. Woodruff & Esther, b. Sept. 3, 1747 | 1 | 5 |
| Simeon, m. Mary **ROBERTS**, June 21, 1775, by Ebenezer Knibloe | LR3 | 5 |
| Simeon Smithson, s. Simeon & Mary, b. Aug. 2, 1782 | 2 | 4 |

| | Vol. | Page |
|---|---|---|
| **EMMONS, EMONS**, (cont.) | | |
| Solomon, s. Woodruff & Ester, b. Nov. 27, 1752 | 1 | 20 |
| Solomon, s. Woodruff & Ester, b. July 19, 1754 | 1 | 22 |
| Solomon, m. Saba **CANFIELD**, May 22, 1778, by Rev. Hezekiah Gold | LR4 | 14 |
| Woodruff, m. Esther **PRENTISS**, Mar. 10, 1743, by Joseph Miner, J. P. | 1 | 6 |
| **EVEREST**, [see also **EVERETT**], Asahel Moss, s. Daniel & Eunice, b. Jan. 21, 1782 | 2 | 19 |
| Cornelius Bradford, s. [Daniel & Eunice], b. Mar. 14, 1789 | 3 | 19 |
| Daniel, m. Eunice **PATTERSON**, Nov. 27, 1774, by Rev. Hezekiah Gold | LR3 | 7 |
| Daniel, twin with Eunice, s. Daniel & Eunice, b. July 6, 1784 | 2 | 15 |
| Eunice, twin with Daniel, d. Daniel & Eunice, b. July 6, 1784 | 2 | 15 |
| Isaac, s. Daniel & Eunice, b. Oct. 10, 1777 | LR3 | 11 |
| Lois, d. Daniel & Eunice, b. Sept. 8, 1792 | 3 | 19 |
| Louisa, m. James **ELY**, July 30, 1822, by Rev. Timothy Stone, of the 1st Church | 2 | 53 |
| Nancy, d. Daniel & Eunice, b. Aug. 26, 1786 | 2 | 20 |
| Nancy, m. William **TUTTLE**, Aug. 30, 1823, by Rev. Timothy Stone, of the 1st Ch. | 2 | 57 |
| Sherman, s. Daniel & Eunice, b. Mar. 25, 1775 | LR3 | 10 |
| **EVERETT, AVERETT, EVERITT**, [see also **EVEREST**], Abigail, d. Daniel & Lydiah, b. July 25, 1759 | 1 | 83 |
| Anna, d. Benjamin & Esther, b. July 28, 1747 | 1 | 13 |
| Asa, of Ellsworth, m. Mary **KELLOGG**, of Cornwall, June 2, 1851, at the house of Mr. Payne, by Rev. J. L. Maynard, of the North Cong. Ch. | 3 | 97 |
| Asa, farmer, ae 71, b. Litchfield, res. Sharon, m. 2nd w. Mary **KELLOGG**, ae 47, res. Cornwall, June 2, 1851, by Rev. J. L. Maynard | 3 | 118-19 |
| Asael, s. Daniel & Lidia, b. Dec. 8, 1754 | 1 | 23 |
| Asahel*, s. Daniel & Lydia, d. May 7, 1757 *("Asahel **EVEREST**"?) | 1 | 28 |
| Charles, Rev. of Warren, m. Nancy **WEEDEN**, of Cornwall, Oct. 27, 1831, by Rev. Luther Mead | 3 | 49 |
| Daniel, s. Daniel & Lydia, b. Apr. 16, 1752 | 1 | 18 |
| Daniel, d. July 2, 1825 | 1 | 18 |
| Eliza, m. William **BONNEY**, Oct. 1, 1826, by Rev. Timothy Stone, of the 1st Ch. | 2 | 65 |
| Esther, d. Jan. 11, 1849, ae 73 | 3 | 106-7 |
| Hulda, d. Benjamin & Esther, b. Dec. 28, 1749 | 1 | 13 |
| Israel, s. Daniel & Lydiah, b. June 1, 1761 | 1 | 84 |
| Josiah, s. Daniel & Lidia, d. Feb. 9, 1754 | 1 | 22 |
| Liddia*, d. Daniel & Lyddia, b. Jan. 12, 1757 *("Liddia **EVEREST**"?) | 1 | 29 |
| **FELCH**, Nathan, of Royaltown, Cty. of Worcester, now of Cornwall, m. Rebecca **SHEPARD**, of Cornwall, May 14, | | |

| | Vol. | Page |
|---|---|---|
| **FELCH**, (cont.) | | |
| 1805, by Judah Kellogg, J. P. | 3 | 11 |
| **FENN**, William D., of Sharon, m. Minerva **PRATT**, of Cornwall, Jan. 1, 1827, by Rev. Walter Smith | 2 | 66 |
| **FERRIS**, Andrew Benjamin, s. [James & Bitsey], b. Jan. 1, 1831 | 3 | 39 |
| George Dibble, s. James & Bitsey, b. Oct. 1, 1828 | 3 | 39 |
| James H., m. Sophia **PECK**, Feb. 18, 1836, by Rev. Timothy Stone | 3 | 41 |
| **[FINDLEY], FINDLA**, Agnes, m. Rufus **PAYNE**, Feb. 17, 1774, by Rev. Hezekiah Gold | 2 | 14 |
| **FITCH**, Henry, m. Jerusha M. **HART**, b. of Cornwall, Sept. 1, 1852, by Rev. Ralph Smith | 3 | 123 |
| **FITZGERALD**, Ann, alias **CASE**, m. Patrick **DELANY**, b. of Cornwall, Dec. 7, 1852, by Rev. John Smith | 3 | 125 |
| Margary, d. John, laborer, ae 30 & Ann, ae 23, b. Sept. 13, 1848 | 3 | 98-9 |
| **FLEMING, FLEMMING**, Benoni, s. Thomas & Mary, b. Feb. 18, 1765 | 1 | 67 |
| Mary Ann, d. Thomas & Mary, b. Sept. 25, 1770 | LR3 | 14 |
| Thomas, m. Mary **DEAN**, Aug. 14, 1762, by Rev. Hezekiah Gold | LR4 | 17 |
| **FORD, FOORD, FOURD**, Abigail, d. Amos & Sarah, b. June 28, 1758 | 1 | 71 |
| Amanda, m. Artemis **SCOVIL**, Oct. 30, 1836, by James Wadsworth, J. P. | 3 | 42 |
| Amos, s. Amos & Sarah, d. Jan. 12, 1760 | 1 | 53 |
| Amos, d. Dec. 5, 1762 | 1 | 53 |
| Amos, s. Hezekiah & Deborah, b. May 17, 1768 | 1 | 98 |
| Amos, m. Rachel **PARMELY**, Feb. 17, 1837, by James Wadsworth, J. P. | 3 | 42 |
| Betty, d. Noah & Betty, b. July 1, 1755 | 1 | 24 |
| Caroline, d. Hezekiah & Deborah, b. May 19, 1766 | 1 | 72 |
| Charles, of Washington, m. Mary L. **CALHOUN**, of Cornwall, June 18, 1845, by Hiram Day | 3 | 71 |
| Chauncey, [twin with Chester, s. James D. & Hannah], b. Aug. 10, 1816 | 2 | 14 |
| Chester, [twin with Chauncey, s. James D. & Hannah], b. Aug. 10, 1816 | 2 | 44 |
| Deborah, d. Hezekiah & Deborah, b. July 19, 1764 | 1 | 58 |
| Dianthe, d. [Hezekiah & Deborah], b. May 24, 1770 | 1 | 98 |
| Edmond, s. Oliver, d. Dec. 5, 1813, ae 16 y. | 2 | 33 |
| Edmund C., s. James D. & Hannah, b. Feb. 26, 1815 | 2 | 44 |
| Edmund C., s. James D., d. Dec. 21, 1816 | 2 | 46 |
| Elisha, m. Julia Ann **NICKERSON**, Dec. 31, 1843, by Rev. Joshua L. Maynard, of the North Cong. Ch. | 3 | 68 |
| Elizabeth, m. Thomas **BAILEY**, Oct. 5, 1820, by Benjamin Sedgwick, J. P. | 2 | 50 |
| Hannah A., m. Philip **CALKINS**, b. of Cornwall, Jan. 5, | | |

| | Vol. | Page |
|---|---|---|
| **FORD, FOORD, FOURD**, (cont.) | | |
| 1842, by Rev. Lewis Gunn | 3 | 63 |
| Hezekiah, m. Deborah **CHANDLER**, Dec. 7, 1757, by Rev. Hezekiah Gold | 1 | 31 |
| James, s. Oliver & Lydia, b. Nov. 6, 1791 | 2 | 27 |
| James D., m. Hannah **BALDWIN**, June 2, 1814, by Oliver Burnham, J. P. Witnesses: Benjamin Catlin & Anson Rogers | 2 | 45 |
| Jemimi, d. Oliver & Lydia, b. Mar. 18, 1784 | 2 | 7 |
| John, s. [James D. & Hannah], b. June 23, 1818 | 2 | 44 |
| John Grannis, s. Oliver & Lydia, b. June 1, 1777 | LR3 | 14 |
| Joseph, s. Hezekiah & Deborah, b. Aug. 27, 1760 | 1 | 37 |
| Liddey, d. Amos & Sarah, b. May 17, 1756 | 1 | 25 |
| Lydia, d. Oliver & Lydia, b. Apr. 20, 1782 | 2 | 6 |
| Lydia J., m. Almond E. **TODD**, b. of Cornwall, Mar. 24, 1844, by Rev. Thomas Edwards | 3 | 68 |
| Nancy, ae 20, res. Cornwall, m. Giles **BENEDICT**, farmer, ae 30, b. Goshen, res. Goshen, Apr. 23, 1848, by Joshua L. Maynard | 3 | 90-1 |
| Nancy R., of Cornwall, m. Silas **BENEDICT**, Jr., of Goshen, Apr. 23, 1848, at the house of James Ford, by Rev. Joshua L. Maynard, of the North Cong. Ch. | 3 | 79 |
| Noah, m. Betty **CHANDLER**, b. of Cornwall, Sept. 2, 1754, by George Halloway, J. P. | 1 | 21 |
| Noah, s. Hezekiah & Deborah, b. July 28, 1774 | LR3 | 8 |
| Oliver, of Cornwall, m. Lydia **CURTICE***, of Sharon, Nov. 23, 1774, by Colton M. Smith *("**CARTER**" in Starr's book) | LR3 | 7 |
| Oliver, s. Oliver & Lydia, b. June 10, 1789 | 3 | 23 |
| Paul Bissbee, s. Oliver & Lydia, b. June 22, 1787 | 2 | 20 |
| Polly, d. Thaddeus & Sarah, b. Oct. 22, 1779 | LR4 | 17 |
| Rebeckah, d. Hezekiah & Deborah, b. Apr. 16, 1762 | 1 | 47 |
| Revilo, s. Oliver & Lydia, b. May 22, 1780 | LR4 | 16 |
| Rume, d. Timothy & Thankful, b. Sept. 25, 1766 | 1 | 76 |
| Samuel Wadsworth, s. Oliver & Lydia, b. Apr. 22, 1794 | 2 | 30 |
| Sarah, d. Amos & Sarah, b. Apr. 4, 1754 | 1 | 25 |
| Sarah, d. Hezekiah & Deborah, b. Apr. 24, 1772 | LR3 | 8 |
| Sarah E., of Cornwall, m. Luther S. **JOHNSON**, of Litchfield, Nov. 6, 1854, by Rev. Ira Pettibone | 3 | 125 |
| Submit, d. Amos, decd. & Sarah, b. Dec. 8, 1762 | 1 | 33 |
| Submit, d. Amos, decd. & Sarah, b. Dec. 8, 1762 | 1 | 53 |
| Submit, d. Oliver & Lydia, b. Sept. 27, 1775 | LR3 | 10 |
| Tabathy, d. Amos & Sarah, b. June 8, 1760 | 1 | 52 |
| Tabitha, d. Thaddeus & Sarah, b. Sept. 3, 1782 | 2 | 9 |
| William Church, s. Hezekiah & Deborah, b. Mar. 19, 1776 | LR3 | 10 |
| Zera*, s. Thaddeus & Sarah, b. Sept. 8, 1777 *("Levi"? in Starr's Hist. of Cornwall) | LR3 | 11 |
| **FOSTER**, Stephen J., of Morristown, N. J., m. Helen A. | | |

| | Vol. | Page |
|---|---|---|
| **FOSTER**, (cont.) | | |
| **PRATT**, of Cornwall, Sept. 1, 1841, by Rev. J. L. Maynard, of the North Cong. Ch. | 3 | 63 |
| **FOX**, Ansel, s. Reuben & Hannah, b. Aug. 8, 1778 | 2 | 2 |
| Charles, s. Reuben & Hannah, b. May 20, 1783 | 3 | 24 |
| Charlotte M., m. Robert **WILCOX**, b. of Cornwall, Feb. 16, 1853, by Rev. Harley Goodwin, of South Canaan | 3 | 124 |
| Hannah, d. Reuben & Hannah, b. Feb. 9, 1776 | LR3 | 12 |
| Helan, d. [Reuben & Hannah], b. Jan. 3, 1781 | 2 | 2 |
| Huldah, d. [Reuben & Hannah], b. Jan. 31, 1786 | 3 | 24 |
| Levina, d. Reuben & Hannah, b. Oct. 4, 1773 | LR3 | 12 |
| Sophronia, m. Miles **ROUSE**, Oct. 23, 1821, by Rev. Timothy Stone, of the 1st Soc. | 2 | 50 |
| **FRANCIS**, Lucretia, b. Apr. 22, 1764; m. Reuben **DEAN**, Dec. 11, 1783 | 3 | 55 |
| **FREEMAN**, Juliett, ae 19, colored, b. Sharon, res. Cornwall, m. John **GOLDEN**, laborer, colored, ae 23, b. Sharon, res. Cornwall, May 2, 1851, by Myron Harrison | 3 | 118-19 |
| Luman, m. Sarah Ann **WESTON**, Oct. 23, 1831, by Horatio Smith, J. P. | 3 | 49 |
| Luman, m. Chloe Ann **WESTON**, b. of Cornwall, Dec. 16, 1847, by Rev. Lewis Gunn | 3 | 81 |
| **FRINK**, Abbey, m. Samuel F. **WINTON**, b. of Cornwall, Dec. 16, 1847, by H. Day | 3 | 76 |
| Abby, ae 26, res. Cornwall, m. Samuel S. **NEWTON**, peddler, ae 27, res. Cornwall, Dec. 16, 1847, by Rev. Hiram Day | 3 | 90-1 |
| Abby, b. Wallingford, res. Cornwall, d. Apr. 29, 1848, ae 71 | 3 | 92-3 |
| Henry, m. Mary A. **BONNEY**, Nov. 17, 1831, by Rev. William Andrews | 3 | 49 |
| Henry, laborer, ae 43 & Mary, ae 35, had child b. May 12, 1850 | 3 | 108-9 |
| Jane, m. Jonathan B. **SHEPARD**, Feb. 1, 1838, by William W. Andrews | 3 | 56 |
| Lucy P., m. Philo **SWIFT**, 2nd, Mar. 4, 1835, by Rev. William Andrews | 3 | 38 |
| Mariah, m. Elizur **WILSON**, Nov. 30, 1826, by Rev. Timothy Stone, of the 1st Ch. | 2 | 66 |
| **FRY**, Caty, d. James, millright, ae 27 & Catharine, ae 22, b. Mar. [ ], 1848 | 3 | 84-5 |
| **FULLER**, Amie, m. Ezra **SQUIRE**, Sept. 3, 1751, by Solomon Palmer | 1 | 16 |
| Ashbel, of Kent, m. Olive C. **SEDGWICK**, of Cornwall, Apr. 12, 1842, by Rev. J. L. Maynard, of the North Cong. Ch. | 3 | 64 |
| Ephraim, s. Aaron & Ruth, b. Mar. 3, 1752 | 1 | 17 |
| Freelove, d. Aaron & Ruth, b. Apr. 30, 1760 | 1 | 36 |
| Gershom, s. Aaron & Ruth, b. Jan. 20, 1749/50 | 1 | 10 |
| Israel, of Cornwall, m. Joanna **WAIT**, of Lime, Nov. 15, 1763, by Samuel Pettebone, J. P. | 1 | 52 |

| | Vol. | Page |
|---|---|---|
| **FULLER**, (cont.) | | |
| Mary, d. Aaron & Ruth, b. July 22, 1757 | 1 | 29 |
| Mathew, s. Aaron & Ruth, b. Mar. 27, 1754 | 1 | 21 |
| Roswell, m. Mary **SAWYER**, Aug. 10, 1764,by Daniel Farrand | 1 | 55 |
| **GARDINER**, [see also **GARNER**], John Marshall, m. Eliza M. **JOHNSON**, b. of Cornwall, Apr. 14, 1851, by F. C. Youngs | 3 | 97 |
| Lydia, ae 18, b. Cornwall, res. West Cornwall, m. Edward **SANFORD**, druggist, ae 24, b. Cornwall, res. West Cornwall, Apr. 15, 1851, by Rev. Mr. Youngs | 3 | 118-19 |
| Marshall, carpenter, ae 21, b. Norwich, res. Cornwall, m. E. M. **JOHNSON**, ae 17, res. Cornwall, Apr. 15, 1851, by Rev. Mr. Youngs | 3 | 118-19 |
| Viletta C., m. Edward **SANFORD**, Apr. 14, 1851, by F. C. Youngs | 3 | 97 |
| **GARNER**, [see also **GARDINER**], Ellen, d. Lorenzo, b. Mar. 21, 1845 | 3 | 95 |
| **GARNSEY**, [see under **GUERNSEY**] | | |
| **GARRISON**, Jacob, Jr., d. June 10, 1848, ae 4 y. | 3 | 92-3 |
| Jacob, s. Jacob, teamster, ae 49 & Nancy, ae 36, res. West Cornwall, b. July 1, 1848 | 3 | 86-7 |
| Jacob, b. Cornwall, res. West Cornwall, d. [ ], ae 1 | 3 | 112-13 |
| **GARSON** (?), Hannah, see under Hannah **GAWSON** | | |
| **GAWSON** (?)*, Hannah, m. Samuel **WESTON**, Aug. 23, 1831, by Horatio Smith, J. P. *("**LAWSON**"? or "**GARSON**"?) | 3 | 48 |
| **GAY**, Adolphus, m. Sarah B. **SWIFT**, Jan. 23, 1843, by John W. Beecher | 3 | 66 |
| **GAYLORD**, Jay, of Warren, m. Elizabeth A. **JOHNSON**, of Cornwall, Mar. 25, 1839, by N. M. Urmston | 3 | 56 |
| **[GERARD]**, [see under **JERRED**] | | |
| **GIBBS**, Margary, m. John **BRISTOL**, Nov. 13, 1789, by Judah Kellogg, J. P. | 3 | 8 |
| Rhoda T., of Kent, m. George W. **CALKINS**, of Cornwall, Oct. 3, 1852, by Rev. Henry Burton, of Sharon | 3 | 124 |
| Ruth, m. David **BALDWIN**, Jr., b. of Cornwall, Aug. 9, 1769, by David Welch, J. P. | 1 | 96 |
| **GIBSON, GYPSON**, Martha, d. Jonathan & Mary, b. Aug. 26, 1752 | 1 | 18 |
| Onnuel B., m. Betsey Jane **STONE**, b. of Warren, July 28, 1839, by Rev. Samuel W. Smith, of the M. E. Ch. | 3 | 58 |
| **GILBERT**, Abigail Maria, d. Orrin & Mary, b. Oct. 1, 1823 | 2 | 61 |
| Joseph Lyman, s. Orrin & Mary, b. June 29, 1825 | 2 | 61 |
| Loiza Ann, d. Orrin & Mary, b. Mar. 9, 1827 | 2 | 69 |
| Rachel, d. Joel & Ruth, b. Apr. 4, 1780 | LR4 | 17 |
| **[GIRARD]**, [see uner **JERRED**] | | |
| **GLEASON**, Jesse, of Cornwall, m. Esther **BARTHOLOMEW**, of Goshen, Oct. 3, 1822, by Rev. Walter Smith, of the 2nd Ch. | 2 | 54 |
| **GOLD**, [see also **GOULD**], Benjamin, m. Eleanor **JOHNSON**, b. of | | |

| | Vol. | Page |
|---|---|---|
| **GOLD**, (cont.) | | |
| Cornwall, Nov. 25, 1784, by [ ]. Witnesses: Mrs. Eleanor Swift & Joshua Peerce, 3rd | 2 | 16 |
| Benjamin, Capt. & Eleanor, had d. [ ], b. Mar. 21, 1786 | 2 | 29 |
| Benjamin, Capt. & Eleanor, had, [ ], d. Mar. 25, 1786, ae 4 d. | 2 | 28 |
| Benjamin Franklin, s. [Capt. Benjamin & Eleanor], b. May 29, 1792 | 2 | 29 |
| Caroline(?) *Melissa, of Cornwall, m. John **LOVEL**, of Sharon, Dec. 25, 1825, by Rev. Timothy Stone *(Written "Carorine") | 2 | 63 |
| Eleanor P., d. Col. Benjamin & Eleanor, d. Feb. 27, 1809 | 3 | 4 |
| Eleanor Pierce, d. [Capt. Benjamin & Eleanor], b. June 14, 1790 | 2 | 29 |
| Flora, of Cornwall, m. Herman L. **VAILL**, of Litchfield, Jan. 22, 1823, by Rev. Joseph Harvey, of the 1st Cong. Ch. in Goshen | 2 | 55 |
| Harriet, of Cornwall, m. Elias **BOUDINET**, of the Cherokee Nation, Mar. 28, 1826, by Rev. Francis A. Case, of the Cong. Ch. Goshen | 2 | 63 |
| Hezekiah, Rev., m. Mrs. Sarah **SEDGWICK**, Nov. 22, 1758, by Rev. Nathaniel Shepherd, of New Milford | 1 | 32 |
| Hezekiah, s. Hezekiah & Sarah, b. May 4, 1761 | 1 | 40 |
| Hezekiah, Rev., d. May 31, 1790 | 2 | 26 |
| Hezekiah S., m. Chloe Ann **PEET**, Sept. 6, 1836, by Rev. William Andrews | 3 | 41 |
| Julia L., of Cornwall, m. Frederick **LYMAN**, of Goshen, Sept. 14, 1843, by Rev. Ephraim Lyman | 3 | 67 |
| Julia R., of Cornwall, m. Daniel **CLEVELAND**, of Madison, N. Y., Nov. 14, 1821, by Rev. Walter Smith, of the 2nd Church | 2 | 51 |
| Laura S., m. William F. **STEPHENS**, Jan. 1, 1828, by Rev. Walter Smith, of the 2nd Soc. | 2 | 68 |
| Polly, d. [Capt. Benjamin & Eleanor], b. Mar. 8, 1794 | 2 | 29 |
| Rachel, m. Horace **ALLEN**, b. of Cornwall, Oct. 21, 1828, by Rev. Silas Ambler | 2 | 64 |
| Rebecca C., d. Theodore S., farmer, ae 33 & Caroline, ae 30, b. July 29, 1851 | 3 | 114-15 |
| Sally M., m. Edward **ROGERS**, b. of Cornwall, Mar. 4, 1810, by Rev. Josiah Hawes, of Canaan | 2 | 37 |
| Sarah Ann, m. Samuel **HOPKINS**, Sept. 24, 1805, by Rev. Timothy Stone, of the 1st Ch. | 3 | 3 |
| Sarah Anne, d. [Benjamin & Eleanor], b. Dec. 29, 1788 | 2 | 25 |
| Stephen J., m. Sarah F. **CALHOUN**, Nov. 15, 1826, by Rev. Timothy Stone, of the 1st Ch. | 2 | 66 |
| Thomas, s. Rev. Hezekiah & Sarah, b. Nov. 23, 1759 | 1 | 34 |
| Thomas Ruggles, s. Benjamin & Eleanor, b. Mar. 25, 1787 | 2 | 25 |
| **GOLDEN**, John, laborer, colored, ae 23, b. Sharon, res. Cornwall, m. Juliett **FREEMAN**, ae 19, colored, b. Sharon, res. | | |

| | Vol. | Page |
|---|---|---|
| **GOLDEN**, (cont.) | | |
| Cornwall, May 2, 1851, by Myron Harrison | 3 | 118-19 |
| **GOODSELL**, Maria, d. David & Louisa, b. Sept. 10, 1808 | 3 | 30 |
| **GOODWIN**, George D., of Sharon, m. Mary Jane **BUTLER**, of Cornwall, July 19, 1846, by Rev. Alfred Gates | 3 | 73 |
| **GOODYEAR**, Bethiah, of Cornwall, m. Ira **NICHOLS**, of Trumbull, Jan. 14, 1823, by Stephen Mason | 2 | 55 |
| Chauncey, Jr., m. Esther M. **BASSETT**, Apr. 28, 1834, by Rev. William Andrews | 3 | 37 |
| **GOULD**, [see also **GOLD**], Nathan, tailor, ae 28, b. Greenfield, res. Bridgeport, m. Mary **SAWYER**, ae 22, b. Cornwall, res. Sharon, Feb. 20, 1848, by Rev. Moses B. Blydenburgh | 3 | 90-1 |
| **GRAY**, Augustus B., of Sharon, m. Sally B. **BUTLER**, of Cornwall, Mar. 4, 1838, by Rev. Erastus Doty | 3 | 54 |
| **GREEN**, Daniel, s. Nathaniel, d. Jan. 22, 1754 | 1 | 20 |
| Nathaniell, d. May 16, 1850 | 1 | 16 |
| Theron, farmer & Margaret, had child, b. Feb. 4, 1848 | 3 | 86-7 |
| **GRIFFIN**, [see also **GRIFFIS**], John, m. Elizabeth **BIERCE**, Dec. 30, 1806, by Judah Kellogg, J. P. | 3 | 3 |
| **GRIFFIS**, [see also **GRIFFIN**], Daniel, of Cornwall, m. Abigail **BENNET**, of New Milford, July 22, 1755, by Paul Welch, of New Milford | 1 | 28 |
| David, s. Thomas & Sarah, d. Apr. 21, 1750 | 1 | 17 |
| David, s. Daniel & Abigail, b. Feb. 17, 1758 | 1 | 32 |
| Isabel, m. Elisha **HATCH**, Nov. 13, 1746, by Solomon Palmer | 1 | 8 |
| James, m. Hannah **SIMMONS**, Oct. 22, 1767, by Rev. Hezekiah Gold | 1 | 84 |
| James, s. James & Hannah, b. May 30, 1773 | 1 | 110 |
| Lucy, d. Daniel & Abigail, b. Nov. 20, 1756 | 1 | 29 |
| Mary, m. Ezra **TYLER**, Mar. 8, 1750, by Solomon Palmer | 1 | 13 |
| Sarah, m. Ebenezer **TYLER**, Nov, 25, 1742, by Solonon Palmer | 1 | 9 |
| Sarah Bordon, d. James & Hannah, b. July 19, 1777 | LR3 | 9 |
| Thomas, d. Sept. 5, 1758 | 1 | 32 |
| **GRISWOLD**, Henry, of Litchfield, m. Nancy **PERKINS**, of Cornwall, Mar. 12, 1829, by Rev. Silas Ambler | 3 | 44 |
| John, of Guilford, m. Abigail W. **COLE**, of Cornwall, Apr. 10, 1845, at the house of Irad Cole, by Rev. Joshua L. Maynard, of the North Cong. Ch. | 3 | 71 |
| Lyman, of Litchfield, m. Rachel **PRINDLE**(?), of Cornwall, Mar. 18, 1844, by Rev. Joshua L. Maynard, of the North Cong. Ch. | 3 | 70 |
| Sylvester C., of Litchfield, m. Mary Ann **DICKINSON**, of Cornwall, Apr. 3, 1850, by Rev. Joshua L. Maynard, of the North Cong. Ch., at his house | 3 | 83 |
| **GUERNSEY, GARNSEY**, Ebenezer, m. Ruth **DIBBLE**, Sept. 30, 1778, by Rev. Hezekiah Gold | LR3 | 13 |

| | Vol. | Page |
|---|---|---|
| **GUERNSEY, GARNSEY**, (cont.) | | |
| Ebenezer, d. Feb. 6, 1781 | LR4 | 18 |
| Elizabeth, m. Thomas **DEXTER**, Sept. 17, 1778, by Rev. Hezekiah Gold | LR3 | 16 |
| Elizabeth, d. Ebenezer & Ruth, b. Feb. 2, 1780 | LR4 | 16 |
| Mabal, m. David **DIBBLE**, Oct. 28, 177[ ], by Rev. Hezekiah Gold | 2 | 14 |
| **GUILD**, Alfred Truman, s. Truman, farmer, ae 43 & Lamisa, ae 40, res. Warren, Milton Soc., b. June 20, 1849 | 3 | 100-1 |
| Lucinda, m. Josiah **JENNINGS**, June 16, 1822, by Asa Tallmadg, Elder, of the Bap. Church | 2 | 53 |
| Lucinda, farmer's wid., b. Coventry, res. Warren, d. Feb. 22, 1849, ae 80 | 3 | 106-7 |
| **GYPSON**, [see under **GIBSON**] | | |
| **HACKETT**, Martha, m. Solomon **HOWLAND**, Nov. 16, 1800, by Judah Kellogg | 2 | 24 |
| **HAGOR**, Adaline M., m. Benjamin **COLE**, Mar. 31, 1847, at the house of Mr. Coe, by Rev. Joshua L. Maynard, of the North Cong. Ch. | 3 | 74 |
| **HALL**, Charles, s. [John & Sarah Ann], b. June 18, 1832 | 3 | 47 |
| Edward, s. John & Sarah Ann, b. Sept. 6, 1830 | 3 | 47 |
| Elizabeth, of Cornwall, m. Franklin **JEWEL**, of Brookfield, Apr. 9, 1848, by Rev. M. Bydenburgh | 3 | 78 |
| Elizabeth, ae 19, b. Kent, res. N. Milford, m. Franklin **JEWEL**, ae 29, b. Fishkill, N. Y., res. N. Milford, Apr. 9, 1848, by Rev. Moses B. Blydenburgh | 3 | 90-1 |
| Joel, m. Sarah Ann **JOHNSON**, Nov. 14, 1832, by Rev. Walter Smith, of the North Cong. Ch. | 3 | 35 |
| Levi, s. Hezekiah & Susanna, b. Apr. 11, 1791 | 3 | 23 |
| Lorinda, ae 18, res. Cornwall, m. Noah F. **PENDLETON**, carpenter, ae 24, res. Cornwall, Jan. 19, 1851, by Rev. Salmon Gale | 3 | 118-19 |
| Ranslear, m. Amanda **BUTLER**, b. of Cornwall, June 28, 1827, by Rev. Silas Ambler | 2 | 67 |
| Sarah, d. Judson, mechanic, ae 44 & Sarah, ae 33, b. Apr. 9, 1849 | 3 | 100-1 |
| Sergant E., of Perryville, N. Y., m. Sarah A. **NICKERSON**, of West Cornwall, July 2, 1854, by R. M. S. Pease. Int.Pub. | 3 | 126 |
| Simeon, of Armenia, m. Theodosia **KELLOGG**, of Cornwall, Apr. 3, 1827, by Rev. John Lovejoy, of the M. E. Ch. | 2 | 66 |
| **HALLOCK**, Daniel, farmer & Maria, had child b. Apr. [ ], 1850 | 3 | 108-9 |
| **HALLOWAY**, George, Capt., d. July 13, 1756 | 1 | 23 |
| **HALPIN**, Patrick, m. Bridget **BROODER**, Jan. 7, 1853, by Rev. Peter Kelley. Int. Pub. | 3 | 125 |
| **HAMILTON, HAMBLETON**, [see also **HAMLIN**], Christian, m. John **MILLARD**, Jr., May 21, 1761, by Rev. H. Gold | 1 | 40 |
| Jane, ae 34, b. Cornwall, res. West Cornwall, m. William R. **WHITE**, shoemaker, ae 30, b. Cornwall, res. West | | |

| | Vol. | Page |
|---|---|---|
| **HAMILTON, HAMBLETON**, (cont.) | | |
| Cornwall, Dec. 11, 1849, by Rev. William McAlister | 3 | 112-13 |
| Jane, m. William **WHITE**, Dec. 12, 1849, by Rev. William McAlister | 3 | 77 |
| **HAMLIN**, [see also **HAMILTON**], Eleazer, m. Mary Ann **SCOVILL**, May 31, 1837, by Rev. Walter Smith, of the North Cong. Ch. | 3 | 52 |
| **HAMMOND**, Samuel, m. Lydia **HIDE**, Oct. 28, 1834, by Rev. Walter Smith, of the North Cong. Ch. | 3 | 38 |
| **HAMSON**, William E., m. Tammy E. **WINANS**, b. of Cornwall, Dec. 11, 1842, by Rev. Joshua L. Maynard, of the N. Cong. Ch. | 3 | 66 |
| **HANCHETT, HANCHET**, Caroline E., m. Lyman **PRINDLE**, Apr. 22, 1849, by W[illia]m McAlister | 3 | 77 |
| Caroline E., milliner & dressmaker, ae 19, res. Cornwall, m. Lyman B. **PRINDLE**, miller, ae 24, b. Canaan, res. Lee, Mass., Apr. 22, 1849, by Rev. William McAlister | 3 | 104-5 |
| **HARD**, Cyrenus, of New York, m. Emma, E. **PEIRCE**, of Cornwall, Sept. 12, 1854, by Rev. Ira Pettibone | 3 | 125 |
| **HARDING**, Asa W., of Newton, m. Julia M. **STODDARD**, of Cornwall, Sept. 30, 1851, at the house of William Stoddard, by Rev. Joshua L. Maynard, of the North Cong. Ch. | 3 | 96 |
| **HARRIS**, David, s. Thomas & Sarah, b. Apr. 7, 1764 | 1 | 58 |
| Elizabeth, d. Joshua & Ruth, b. May 7, 1765 | 1 | 62 |
| Elizabeth, d. Rev. Reuben & Betsey, b. July 13, 1810 | 3 | 28 |
| Hannah, d. Joshua & Ruth, b. Apr. 5, 1770 | 1 | 95 |
| Israel, s. John & Rachel, b. Feb. 16, 1746/7 | 1 | 7 |
| Joshua, m. Ruth **SYMMONS**, Sept. 17, 1760, by Samuel Pettebone, J. P. | 1 | 37 |
| Joshua, s. Joshua & Ruth, b. Apr. 9, 1761 | 1 | 43 |
| Lucretia, d. Joshua & Ruth, b. July 31, 1767 | 1 | 78 |
| Rachel, d. John & Rachel, b. Feb. 2, 1749 | 1 | 9 |
| Rachel, m. Elijah **DICKINSON**, b. of Cornwall, June 15, 1758, by John Patterson, J. P. | 1 | 64 |
| Ruth, d. Thomas & Sarah, b. Oct. 23, 1762 | 1 | 51 |
| Ruth, d. Joshua & Ruth, b. Apr. 26, 1763 | 1 | 22 |
| **HARRISON**, Abigail M., m. Peter **CORNELL**, Oct. 14, 1830, by Rev. Walter Smith, of the Cong. Ch. | 3 | 46 |
| Amanda, d. Noah & Hannah, d. Nov. 16, 1775 | LR3 | 7 |
| Amanda, d. Noah & Anna, b. Mar. 20, 1789 | 2 | 25 |
| Chandler, s. [Edmund & Ruth], b. Jan. 30, 1803 | 3 | 34 |
| Chandler, s. Edmund, d. Mar. 9, 1829, ae 26 y. | 3 | 43 |
| Daniel, Jr., m. Sarah **PARKER**, Sept. 13, 1781, by Judah Kellogg, J. P. | LR4 | 18 |
| Eber, s. [Daniel, Jr. & Sarah], b. July 19, 1786 | 2 | 17 |
| Edmond, s. Noah & Hannah, b. May 1, 1768 | 1 | 86 |
| Edmund, of Cornwall, m. Ruth **HOPKINS**, of Warren, Feb. 19, | | |

| | Vol. | Page |
|---|---|---|
| **HARRISON**, (cont.) | | |
| 1795, by Justus Sackett, J. P. | 2 | 36 |
| Hannah, w. Daniel, Jr., d. June 12, 1779 | LR3 | 15 |
| Hannah, w. Noah, d. Feb. 18, 1785 | 2 | 11 |
| Hannah, d. Noah & Anne, b. Dec. 10, 1786 | 2 | 17 |
| Hannah, d. Daniel, Jr. & Sarah, b. Oct. 5, 1789 | 3 | 19 |
| Hannah, d. [Edmund & Ruth], b. Feb. 13, 1810 | 3 | 34 |
| Hannah, wid., m. James F. **BRADFORD**, b. of Cornwall, May 29, 1831, by Silas Ambler | 3 | 48 |
| Heman, s. Noah & Hannah, b. Nov. 13, 1769 | 1 | 92 |
| Heman, d. Mar. 23, 1829, ae 59 y. | 3 | 43 |
| John, m. Eleanor **BRADFORD**, Mar. 13, 1833, by Rev. Walter Smith, of the North Cong. Ch. | 3 | 36 |
| John B., s. John R., farmer, ae 41 & Eleanor, ae 40, res. Sharon, b. Nov. 4, 1848 | 3 | 100-1 |
| John R., s. [Edmund & Ruth], b. Sept. 23, 1807 | 3 | 34 |
| Joseph, s. Daniel & Hannah, d. Dec. 2, 1776 ("A prisoner in New York City") | LR3 | 11 |
| Joseph P., m. Eleanor **BRADFORD**, b. of Cornwall, Feb. 21, 1803, by Judah Kellogg, J. P. | 3 | 32 |
| Joseph Page, s. Daniel, Jr. & Hannah, b. June 12, 1779 | LR3 | 15 |
| Julius B., m. Alura A. **MINER**, b. of Cornwall, June 4, 1843, by Rev. Adam Reed | 3 | 66 |
| Lucinda*, m. John **BRADFORD**, Sept. 14, 1829, by Rev. Walter Smith, of the North Ch. *("Lucretia" in Starr's book) | 3 | 44 |
| Lucretia, d. [Edmund & Ruth], b. Sept. 9, 1805 | 3 | 34 |
| Lucy, m. Coddington **CRANDALL**, Nov. 30, 1820, by Benjamin Sedgwick, J. P. | 2 | 48 |
| Luman, s. Noah & Hannah, b. May 28, 1776 | LR3 | 10 |
| Luther B., m. Mary E. **SCOFIELD**, Dec. 30, 1828, by Rev. Walter Smith, of North Cong. Ch. | 3 | 1 |
| Martha, d. William H., charcoal maker, ae 35 & Mary., ae 34, b. Mar. 18, 1848 | 3 | 84-5 |
| Mary E., d. July 15, 1848, ae 21 m. | 3 | 92-3 |
| Mary E., d. William H., farmer, ae 37 & Mary A., ae 35, b. Feb. 22, 1850 | 3 | 110-11 |
| Mervin Frederick, s. Heman, farmer, ae 35 & Mary, ae 23, res. Cornwall Hollow, b. Aug. 31, 1848 | 3 | 98-9 |
| Miron, s. [Edmund & Ruth], b. Sept. 25, 1800 | 3 | 34 |
| Miron, s. [Eber & Laury], b. June 15, 1812 | 2 | 34 |
| Myron, m. Charlotte E. **CALHOUN**, June 2, 1830, by Rev. William Andrews | 3 | 46 |
| Noah, m. Hannah **ROGERS**, June 3, 1767, by Rev. Hezekiah Gold | 1 | 86 |
| Noah, m. Anne **CARTER**, July 21, 1785, by Rev. John Cornwall | 2 | 8 |
| Noah, s. [Edmund & Ruth], b. Feb. 27, 1798 | 3 | 34 |

| | Vol. | Page |
|---|---|---|
| **HARRISON**, (cont.) | | |
| Rufus, s. Edmund & Ruth, b. Apr. 12, 1796 | 3 | 34 |
| Sylvester, s. Daniel, Jr. & Sarah, b. Nov. 7, 1782 | 2 | 17 |
| Sylvester, s. Daniel, Jr. & Sarah, d. Sept. 22, 1786 | 2 | 11 |
| Sylvester Hart, s. Eber & Laury, b. Jan. 3, 1810 | 2 | 34 |
| William Hopkins, s. Edmund & Ruth, b. Oct. 13, 1813 | 3 | 34 |
| [ ]anday, d. Noah & Hannah, b. May 19, 1773 | 2 | 13 |
| **HART**, Abigail Amelia, d. [Nathan & Sylvia], b. Oct. 11, 1808 | 2 | 34 |
| Albert B., res. Cornwall, m. Julia **HITCHCOCK**, tailoress, b. N. Milford, res. Cornwall, Sept. 29, 1848, by Joseph L. Maynard | 3 | 104-5 |
| Albert B., m. Julia **HITCHCOCK**, b. of Cornwall, Jan. 15, 1849, by Rev. Joshua L. Maynard, of the North Cong. Ch. | 3 | 81 |
| Alfred, m. Cynthia L. **NETTLETON**, Oct. 29, 1833, by Rev. Walter Smith, of the North Cong. Ch. | 3 | 36 |
| Alice, d. Silas* & Phile, b. Feb. 4, 1789 *("Elias" in Starr's book) | 2 | 21 |
| Alvan, m. Harriet M. **NODINE**, b. of Cornwall, May 12, 1851, by Harley Goodwin | 3 | 123 |
| Alvin Nelson*, s. [Capt. Elias & Philomela], b. Feb. 11, 1804 *(Arnold Copy had "Nelson") | 2 | 38 |
| Amanda, d. Solomon, Jr. & Jerusha, b. Dec. 28, 1788 | 2 | 21 |
| Amy, m. Seth **PEERCE**, b. of Cornwall, June 18, 1772, by Rev. Hezekiah Gold | 1 | 105 |
| Amy, d. Silas & Amey, b. Mar. 15, 1784 | 2 | 15 |
| Amy, s. Silas, d. July 22, 1787 | 2 | 26 |
| Charlotte M., d. Elias N., farmer, ae 30 & Caroline, ae 26, b. Aug. 31, 1848 | 3 | 98-9 |
| Clarisse, d. Rufus & Esther, b. May 6, 1796 | 2 | 32 |
| Clarissa, of Cornwall, m. Robert C. **NODINE**, of Springfield, N. Y., Sept. 11, 1839, by Rev. J. C. Hart, of Springfield | 3 | 58 |
| Elias, m. Philomela **BURNHAM**, b. of Cornwall, June 14, 1781, by Rev. Mr. Gold. Witnesses: Phinehas Hart & Solomon Hart | LR4 | 18 |
| Elias, s. Elias & Philomele, b. Nov. 5, 1784 | 2 | 9 |
| Elias N., m. Caroline **HITCHCOCK**, Dec. 1, 1835, by Rev. Walter Smith, of the North Cong. Ch. | 3 | 40 |
| Elisha, s. Lot & Elizabeth, b. June 27, 1801 | 2 | 32 |
| Enos, s. Elias & Philomela, b. May 9, 1782 | 2 | 3 |
| Enos, s. Elias & Philomela, d. Dec. 27, 1783 | 2 | 6 |
| Esther M., of Cornwall, m. Sheldon **WHITTLESEY**, of New Preston, Mar. 13, 1844, by Rev. Joshua L. Maynard, of the North Cong. Ch. | 3 | 70 |
| Flora F., of Cornwall, m. Benjamin L. **CARTER**, of Branford, July 2, 1850, at the house of Elias Hart, by Rev. Joshua L. Maynard, of the North Cong. Ch. | 3 | 96 |
| George Washington, s. [Rufus & Esther], b. Dec. 11, 1800 | 2 | 32 |
| Harriet, d. [Capt. Elias & Philomela], b. Mar. 9, 1798 | 2 | 38 |

| | Vol. | Page |
|---|---|---|
| **HART**, (cont.) | | |
| Harriet, m. Gideon P. **PANGMAN**, b. of Cornwall, Apr. 18, 1827, by Rev. Walter Smith | 2 | 67 |
| H. Milton, farmer, ae 38 & Eunice J., ae 33, had s. [ ], b. Aug. 5, 1849 | 3 | 98-9 |
| Hezekiah Hilton, s. [Nathan & Sylvia], b. Aug. 21, 1810 | 2 | 34 |
| Jemima, m. Amos **CAMP**, June 26, 1782, by Rev. Hezekiah Gold | 2 | 8 |
| Jerusha, d. [Capt. Elias & Philomela], b. Apr. 15, 1801 | 2 | 38 |
| Jerusha, m. Palmer **BROWN**, Dec. 25, 1833, by Rev. Walter Smith, of the North Cong. Ch. | 3 | 37 |
| Jerusha, m. Henry **FITCH**, b. of Cornwall, Sept. 1, 1852, by Rev. Ralph Smith | 3 | 123 |
| John, Lieut., d. Dec. 18, 1773 | LR3 | 5 |
| John, s. Titus & Esther, b. Apr. 24, 1779 | LR3 | 11 |
| John, m. Abigail **CLARK**, b. of Cornwall, Oct. 6, [1799], by Rev. John Cornwell, of Amenia, N. Y. Witnesses: Birdseye Clark & Lucius Kellogg | 3 | 9 |
| John, s. Titus, d. June 29, 1801, ae 22 | 3 | 10 |
| John, m. Mary **WINANS**, b. of Cornwall, Dec. 8, 1840, by Rev. John W. Salter | 3 | 61 |
| John C., m. Emily J. **BURNHAM**, June 12, 1834, by Rev. Walter Smith, of the North Cong. Ch. | 3 | 37 |
| John Clark, s. Nathan & Sylvia, b. Dec. 10, 1804 | 3 | 12 |
| John Cotter, s. [Rufus & Esther], b. Apr. 17, 1798 | 2 | 32 |
| Juliaette, m. Horace **HITCHCOCK**, b. of Cornwall, Aug. 3, 1846, at the house of Elias Hart, by Rev. Joshua L. Maynard, of the North Cong. Ch. | 3 | 73 |
| Julius, s. [Capt. Elias & Philomela], b. Feb. 29, 1796 | 2 | 38 |
| Laury, d. Capt. Elias & Philomela, b. Mar. 28, 1790 | 2 | 38 |
| Laura, m. Eber **HUMISON**, b. of Cornwall, Oct. 6, 1808, by Rev. Josiah Hawes, of the 2nd Ch. Witnesses: Joel Catlin & Amos Catlin | 3 | 33 |
| Lucy, d. Lot & Elizabeth, b. Apr. 4, 1795 | 2 | 30 |
| Maria, m. Elisha **WINAAT**, b. of Cornwall, Dec. 9, 1840, by Rev. John W. Salter | 3 | 61 |
| Milan, m. Paulina **NETTLETON**, May 1, 1832, by Rev. Walter Smith, of the North Cong. Ch. | 3 | 49 |
| Nathan, s. Titus & Esther, b. June 12, 1776 | LR3 | 12 |
| Nathan, m. Sylvia **CLARK**, b. of Cornwall, Feb. 8, 1804, by Oliver Burnham, J. P. Witness: William Kellogg, T. C. | 3 | 33 |
| Nathan, Jr., farmer, ae 26, res. Cornwall, m. S. Amelia **WHITTLESEY**, ae 20, b. Washington, res. Washington, Sept. 4, 1847, by Hollis Read | 3 | 90-1 |
| Nelson*, s. [Capt. Elias & Philomela], b. Feb. 11, 1804 *("Alvin **NELSON**" in Starr's book) | 2 | 38 |
| Noah R., m.Lucretia M.**BARNUM**,b.of Cornwall,Nov. 22,1843, 1843, by Rev. Joshua L. Maynard, of the N. Cong Ch. | 3 | 67 |

| | Vol. | Page |
|---|---|---|
| **HART**, (cont.) | | |
| Noah R., ae 29 & Lucretia, ae 24, had child b. July 25, 1848 | 3 | 98-9 |
| Oliver Burnham, s. Elias & Philomela, b. Aug. 25, 1787 | 2 | 20 |
| Philomela, d. [Capt. Elias & Philomela], b. June 17, 1793 | 2 | 38 |
| Philomelia, m. Anson **ROGERS**, Oct. 20, 1814, by John Sedgwick, J. P. Witnesses: James D. Ford & Benjamin Catlin | 2 | 45 |
| Phinehas, m. Betsey **WICKWIRE**, Mar. 18, 1784, by Judah Kellogg, J. P. | 2 | 8 |
| Polly, d. Phinehas & Betsey, b. Mar. 3, 1785 | 2 | 17 |
| Reuben, s. Solomon, Jr. & Jerusha, b. May 30, 1787 | 2 | 20 |
| Rufus, s. John & Martha, b. Mar. 15, 1773 | 2 | 13 |
| Ruth*, m. Jacob **BROWNSON**, Jr., Mar. 29, 1770, by Rev. Hezekiah Gold *(Arnold Copy has "Ruth **KENT**") | 1 | 93 |
| Silas, m. Amy **PEIRCE**, Apr. 17, 1783, by Rev. Hezekiah Gold | 2 | 16 |
| Solomon, Jr., m. Jerusha **BEACH**, July 6, 1786, by Judah Kellogg, J. P. | 2 | 16 |
| Solomon, s. [Nathan & Sylvia], b. Sept. 17, 1812 | 2 | 34 |
| Stephen, s. [Silas & Amey], b. June 4, 1785 | 2 | 15 |
| Titus Leavett, s. Nathan & Sylvia, b. Apr. 26, 1811 | 2 | 34 |
| **HARTSHORN**, Adah, d. Joshua & Huldah, b. Dec. 23, 1777 | LR3 | 9 |
| Anner, d. Joshua & Huldah, b. May 7, 1781 | LR4 | 18 |
| Aner, d. Joshua & Huldah, d. Aug. 19, 1798 | 3 | 10 |
| Clarissa, d. Joshua & Huldah, b. Feb. 27, 1801 | 2 | 32 |
| David, s. Joshua & Huldah, b. Jan. 6, 1787 | 2 | 17 |
| Jemima, d. Joshua & Huldah, b. June 13, 1789 | 2 | 25 |
| Jemima, m. Dr. Abram **PALMER**, b. of Cornwall, Nov. 13, 1823, by Rev. Walter Smith, of the 2nd Cong. Ch. | 2 | 57 |
| Joshua, m. Huldah **DIBBLE**, Oct. 29, 1775, by Rev. Hezekiah Gold | LR3 | 5 |
| Josiah, s. Joshua & Huldah, b. Feb. 10, 1776 | LR3 | 12 |
| Josiah, s. Joshua & Huldah, d. Sept. 29, 1777 | LR3 | 9 |
| **HATCH**, Elisha, m. Isabel **GRIFFIS**, Nov. 13, 1746, by Solomon Palmer | 1 | 8 |
| Elisha, s. Elisha & Isabel, b. Aug. 20, 1747; d. same day | 1 | 8 |
| Isabel, d. Elisha & Isabel, b. Nov. 24, 1748 | 1 | 8 |
| Levi P., tailor, had d. [ ], b. [ ] | 3 | 108-9 |
| Lucinda, d. Henry S., mason, ae 36 & Sarah A., ae 32, Sharon, b. Sept. 8, 1847 | 3 | 84-5 |
| Sarah E., d. Henry, mechanic, ae 37 & Sarah A., ae 36, res. Sharon, b. Mar. 13, 1851 | 3 | 116-17 |
| **HAWKINS**, Benjamin P., of East Windsor, m. Mary M. **TROWBRIDGE**, of Cornwall, Apr. 5, 1835, by Rev. William W. Andrews | 3 | 38 |
| **HAYDEN**, John O., of Middletown, m. Betsey **SPELLMAN**, of Cornwall, Sept. 26, 1824, by Rev. Walter Smith, of the 2nd Ch. | 2 | 58 |

| | Vol. | Page |
|---|---|---|
| **HAYES**, Ezekiel, of New Haven, m. Martha A. **KELLOGG**, of Cornwall, July 2, 1848, by Rev. Hiram Day | 3 | 80 |
| Ezekiel, printer, b. Cornwall, res. New Haven, m. Martha A. **KELLEY**, res. Cornwall, July 2, 1848, by Rev. Hiram Day | 3 | 90-1 |
| **HECTOR**, David, laborer, ae 18, colored & Julia, ae 18, colored, had d. [ ], b. Mar. 28, 1849 | 3 | 100-1 |
| **HENRY**, Hannah, d. Ebenezer & Hannah, b. Nov. 6, 1770 | 1 | 98 |
| **HENSHAM**, William, of Baltimore, Md., m. Jane E. **PANGMAN**, of Cornwall, Nov. 1, 1852, by Rev. Henry Burton, of Sharon | 3 | 124 |
| **HICKINSON**, [see also **DICKINSON & NICKERSON**), Olive, m. George **DIBBLE**, Mar. 15, 1810, by Rev. Henry Christie | 3 | 3 |
| **HICKOK**, Jacob, m. Mary **WHEELER**, of Canaan, May 29, 1838, by James Wadsworth, J. P. | 3 | 54 |
| **HIDE**, Araunah W., m. Sarah P. **ANDREWS**, Feb. 15, 1835, by Rev. William Andrews | 3 | 38 |
| Lydia, m. Samuel **HAMMOND**, Oct. 28, 1834, by Rev. Walter Smith, of the North Cong. Ch. | 3 | 38 |
| **HILL**, Aaron S., Rev. of Goshen, m. Abiah Ann **JUDSON**, of Cornwall, Apr. 22, 1833, by Rev. Aaron Hunt | 3 | 36 |
| Jane C., of Cornwall, m. George N. **EDDY**, of Providence, Apr. 16, 1851, by F. C. Youngs | 3 | 97 |
| Jane E., ae 23, b. Newtown, res. Providence, m. George M. **EDDY**, hatter, ae 25, b. Salisbury, res. Providence, Apr. 16, 1851, by Rev. Mr. Youngs | 3 | 118-19 |
| Mary A., of Cornwall, m. Stephen R. **YOUNG**, of Kent, Oct. 28, 1839, by Rev. Samuel W. Smith | 3 | 58 |
| Sarah, m. Abnah **CHANDLER**, Dec. 12, 1759, by Rev. Able Nowel | 1 | 35 |
| **HINDMAN**, Grace, m. Peirce J. **CLARK**, Oct. 22, 1829, by Rev. William Andrews | 3 | 45 |
| Harriet, of Cornwall, m. Whiting W. **PIERCE**, of Ohio, Sept. 1, 1824, by Rev. Timothy Stone | 2 | 58 |
| John, s. Patrick & Agniss, b. Jan. 20, 1767 | 1 | 80 |
| Patrick, m. Agnes **SHAW**, b. of Cornwall, Sept. 16, [1764], by Thomas Russell, J. P. | 1 | 59 |
| William, s. Patrick & Agnas, b. June 24, 1765 | 1 | 69 |
| William, m. Laura **PATTERSON**, [ ], by Rev. Timothy Stone, of the 1st Ch. Recorded Mar. 26, 1825 | 2 | 62 |
| **HITCHCOCK**, Abigail, m. Marshall D. W. **BENNETT**, May 21, 1820, by Asa Tallmadge, Elder | 2 | 48 |
| Alpheas, of Lebanon, N. Y., m. Lindy **BAILEY**, of Cornwall, Mar. 4, 1792, by Judah Kellogg, J. P. | 3 | 8 |
| Caroline, m. Elias N. **HART**, Dec. 1, 1835, by Rev. Waiter Smith, of the North Cong. Ch. | 3 | 40 |

| | Vol. | Page |
|---|---|---|
| **HITCHCOCK**, (cont.) | | |
| Horace, m. Juliaette **HART**, b. of Cornwall, Aug. 3, 1846, at the house of Elias Hart, by Rev. Joshua L. Maynard, of the North Cong. Ch. | 3 | 73 |
| Julia, tailoress, b. N. Milford, res. Cornwall, m. Albert B. **HART**, res. Cornwall, Sept. 29, 1848, by Joseph L. Maynard | 3 | 104-5 |
| Julia, m. Albert B. **HART**, b. of Cornwall, Jan. 15, 1849, by Rev. Joshua L. Maynard, of the North Cong. Ch. | 3 | 81 |
| **HOADLEY**, Benjamin, of Saybrook, m. Sarah **TANNER**, of Cornwall, May 15, 1823, by David Miller | 2 | 55 |
| Charles William, of Winchester, m. Lois **THOMPSON**, of Cornwall, Nov. 24, 1831, by Benjamin Sedgwick, J. P. | 3 | 49 |
| Jerusha, m. Eber E. **CURTISS**, Nov. 7, 1843, by Rev. Thomas Edwards, of the M. E. Ch. | 3 | 67 |
| **HOCHKIN**, [see under **HOTCHKISS**] | | |
| **HOCKLIN**, Abner, of Cornwall, m. Abigail **BARNES**, of Canaan, Dec. 7, 1797, by Rev. Daniel Farrand, of Canaan. Witnesses: Rozel & Oliver Hocklin | 3 | 9 |
| **HOLCOMB, HOLECOMB**, Erastus C., of Donnerville, N. J., m. Fanny E. **BRADLEY**, of Cornwall, Sept. 5, 1852, by Rev. Luther B. Hart | 3 | 123 |
| John, s. John & Rhoda, b. Oct. 1, 1772 | 1 | 110 |
| Rhoda, m. Daniel **BROWNSON**, b. of Cornwall, June 5, 1794, by Hercules Weston | 3 | 21 |
| William A., m. Marriet **CALKINS**, b. of Cornwall, July 9, 1843, by Rev. Joshua L. Maynard, of the North Cong. Ch. | 3 | 67 |
| **HOLLEY**, [see under **HOLLY**] | | |
| **HOLLISTER**, David A., m. Celia M. **TRAFFORD**, b. of Cornwall, Mar. 26, 1837, by Rev. E. Washburn | 3 | 42 |
| Lyman, m. Charlotte **SWIFT**, Feb. 27, 1833, by William Andrews | 3 | 35 |
| Patience, m. William **CLARK**, Jan. 1, 1833, by Rev. William Andrews | 3 | 35 |
| **HOLLY, HOLLEY**, Delia M., m. Stephen **MILES**, Nov. 19, 1829, by Rev. Walter Smith, of the North Ch. | 3 | 45 |
| Lydia, m. Elijah **STEELE**, Jr., Aug. 5, 1798, by Rev. Israel Holly | 3 | 9 |
| Olive, m. Augustus **WELCH**, Aug. 11, 1822, by Asa Tallmadge, Elder of the Bap. Church | 2 | 53 |
| **HOLMES**, Julia E., m. Walie **ROOT**, b. of Cornwall, Dec. 12, 1841, by Rev. Joshua L. Maynard, of the North Cong. Ch. | 3 | 64 |
| Maria P., ae 21, res. Cornwall, m. Hiram G. **DEAN**, farmer, ae 27, res. Cornwall, Nov. 25, 1850, by Rev. Salmon Gale | 3 | 118-19 |
| **HOPKINS**, Agnes, d. [Josiah, Jr. & Sarah P.], b. Jan. 19, 1815 | 2 | 41 |

| | Vol. | Page |
|---|---|---|
| **HOPKINS**, (cont.) | | |
| Agnes E., m. Roswell **CLARK**, Oct. 19, 1835, by Rev. William Andrews | 3 | 40 |
| Ann Pierce, d. Samuel & Sarah Ann, b. July 2, 1806 | 3 | 17 |
| Anna, d. Luman & Anna, b. Nov. 10, 1818 | 2 | 43 |
| Anne, w. Dea. Josiah, d. Mar. 22, 1820 | 2 | 46 |
| Anne P., m. John C. **LEWIS**, Sept. 15, 1824, by Rev. Thomothy Stone | 2 | 58 |
| Azuba Ann, m. Obadiah **McILVAINE**, Jan. 24, 1832, by Rev. William Andrews | 3 | 49 |
| Azuba Anne, d. Josiah, Jr. & Sarah P., b. Feb. 13, 1809 | 2 | 41 |
| Benjamin Gold, s. Capt. James & Sarah Anne, b. Mar. 4, 1811 | 3 | 13 |
| Betsey Anne Peirce, d. [John & Betsey], b. Nov. 4, 1814 | 2 | 40 |
| Catharine Emily, d. [Luman & Anna], b. July 22, 1816 | 2 | 43 |
| Eleanor, d. Samuel, d. Feb. 24, 1830, ae 21 y. | 3 | 43 |
| Eleanor Johnson, d. [Samuel & Sarah], b. Mar. 5, 1808 | 3 | 17 |
| Francis Gold, s. Benjamin G. & Mary B., b. Mar. 7, 1834 | 3 | 39 |
| Freeman, s. Josiah & Anna, b. Dec. 29, 1782 | 2 | 4 |
| Harriet Elizabeth, d. Luman & Anna, b. Oct. 11, 1814 | 2 | 43 |
| Heman, s. Josiah & Anne, b. Apr. 7, 1788 | 2 | 19 |
| Hezekiah Palmer, s. Josiah & Anna, b. Apr. 2, 1796 | 3 | 25 |
| John, s. Josiah & Anne, b. Oct. 25, 1785 | 2 | 15 |
| Johne Pierce, s. Josiah & Anna, b. July 24, 1800 | 2 | 31 |
| Josiah, m. Anna **PIERCE**, Aug. 8, 1776, by Rev. Hezekiah Gold | LR3 | 13 |
| Josiah, s. Josiah & Anna, b. Feb. 17, 1778 | LR3 | 13 |
| Josiah, Jr., m. Sarah P. **PAYNE**, Jan. 12, 1808, by Rev. Timothy Stone | 2 | 37 |
| Josiah, Dea., m. Mrs. Rachel **DIBBLE**, [ ], by Rev. Timothy Stone, of 1st Soc. (Recorded Oct. 20, 1821) | 2 | 50 |
| Lucy, d. Daniel & Sarah, d. Apr. 20, 1780 | 2 | 1 |
| Luman, s. Josiah & Anne, b. Sept. 30, 1791 | 3 | 19 |
| Luman, m. Anne **CLARK**, Sept. 1, 1813, by Rev. Timothy Stone | 2 | 37 |
| Marshall, s. [Josiah, Jr. & Sarah P.], b. July 24, 1810 | 2 | 41 |
| Mary Anne Nodine, d. [John & Betsey], b. June 9, 1812 | 2 | 40 |
| Mary Elizabeth, d. Benjamin G. & Mary, b. Jan. 4, 1836 | 3 | 39 |
| Rosseter, s. Josiah & Anne, b. Apr. 28, 1794 | 2 | 30 |
| Rosseter, farmer, ae 36 & Adelia, ae 33, had d. [ ], b. Aug. 4, 1849 | 3 | 98-9 |
| Rossetter B., s. [Josiah, Jr. & Sarah P.], b. Mar. 2, 1813 | 2 | 41 |
| Ruth, of Warren, m. Edmund **HARRISON**, of Cornwall, Feb. 19, 1795, by Justus Sackett, J. P. | 2 | 36 |
| Samuel, s. Josiah & Anne, b. Nov. 3, 1780 | LR4 | 17 |
| Samuel, m. Sarah Ann **GOLD**, Sept. 24, 1805, by Rev. Timothy Stone, of the 1st Ch. | 3 | 3 |
| Samuel, d. Oct. 14, 1834, ae 54 y. | 3 | 43 |
| Samuel Josiah, s. Benjamin Gold & Mary B., b. June 26, 1832 | 3 | 47 |

| | Vol. | Page |
|---|---|---|
| **HOPKINS**, (cont.) | | |
| Sarah A., ae 25, res. Cornwall, m. Hopkins T. S. **JOHNSON**, farmer, ae 27, res. Cornwall, Oct. 7, 1849, by Rev. H. E. Vaill | 3 | 112-13 |
| Sarah A., m. Hopkins T. S. **JOHNSON**, b. of Cornwall, Oct. 17, 1849, by Rev. Herman L. Vaill | 3 | 82 |
| Sarah Anne, d. Samuel & Sarah Anne, b. Mar. 16, 1824 | 2 | 60 |
| Sarah Anne Russell, d. John & Betsey, b. Nov. 6, 1809 | 2 | 40 |
| **HOSFORD, HORSFORD**, Esther, d. Samuel & Mary, b. Aug. 19, 1753 | 1 | 18 |
| Mary, d. Samuell & Mary, b. Oct. 27, 1751 | 1 | 16 |
| Samuell, s. Samuell & Mary, b. Mar. 8, 1749/50 | 1 | 10 |
| Samuel, d. Sept. 6, 1757 | 1 | 29 |
| Samuel, d. Sept. 6, 1757 | 1 | 36 |
| **HOSKINS, HOSKIN**, John, s. Daniel & Sarah, b. Apr. 20, 1781 | 2 | 1 |
| Oliver, s. Abraham & Sarah, b. Oct. 16, 1774 | LR3 | 10 |
| **HOTCHKISS, HOCHKIN**, Abraham, Jr., m. Lettis **MINER**, Mar. 14, 1793, by Judah Kellogg, J. P. | 3 | 20 |
| Anne, d. Rozel & An[n]er, b. Aug. 8, 1791 | 3 | 19 |
| George, s. David D., farmer, ae 35 & Mary, ae 21, b. Oct. 19, 1849 | 3 | 108-9 |
| Hannah, d. Rozel & Anner, b. Feb. 19, 1800 | 3 | 15 |
| Henry S., m. Hannah A. **TROWBRIDGE**, Sept. 30, 1832, by Rev. Walter Smith, of the North Cong. Ch. | 3 | 50 |
| Herman, s. Oliver & Cynthia, b. Aug. 27, 1799 | 2 | 31 |
| James Hervey, s. Beriah & Thankfull, b. Feb. 23, 1781 | LR4 | 18 |
| Lettice, b. New London, res. Cornwall, d. Feb. 27, 1849, ae [ ] | 3 | 106-7 |
| Oliver, m. Cynthia **JACKSON**, Oct. 4, 1798, by Rev. Israel Holly | 3 | 20 |
| Rozel, m. Anner **BROWNSON**, b. of Cornwall, Mar. 2, [1790], by Rev. Hezekiah Gold. Witnesses: Abraham Hochkin & Abraham Hochkin, Jr. | 2 | 22 |
| William S., of New Haven, m. Cynthia **PECK**, of Cornwall, Sept. 16, 1838, by Rev. N. M. Urmston, of the 1st Ch. | 3 | 54 |
| Zena, of New Haven, m. Mary **DIBBLE**, of Cornwall, Mar. 16, 1845, by Hiram Day | 3 | 71 |
| **HOWE, HOW**, Abigail, m. Thomas **CARTER***, June 22, 1756, by Rev. H. Gold *("**PORTER**" in Starr's book) | 1 | 35 |
| Adeline, m. Melo A. **JEWEL**, b. of Cornwall, Jan. 18, 1842, by Joshua L. Maynard | 3 | 64 |
| Elisha, carpenter, ae 25, res. Cornwall, m. Elizabeth **SIMONS**, ae 27, b. Goshen, res. Cornwall, Sept. 18, 1851, by Rev. Mr. Yates | 3 | 118-19 |
| Emeline, m. William L. **CLARK**, Nov. 29, 1832, by Rev. Walter Smith, of the North Cong. Ch. | 3 | 35 |
| Erastus, of Canaan, m. Esther A. **BRADLEY**, of Cornwall, Jan. 27, 1850, by Rev. Joshua L. Maynard, of the | | |

| | Vol. | Page |
|---|---|---|
| **HOWE, HOW**, (cont.) | | |
| North Cong. Ch., at his house | 3 | 83 |
| Henry L., carpenter, ae 22, b. Canaan, res. Goshen, m. Mary A. **MERWIN**, ae 21, b. Oswell, Rutland Co., Ct., res, Goshen, Nov. 28, 1850, by Rev. J. L. Maynard | 3 | 118-19 |
| Henry L., of Canaan, m. Mary A. **MERWIN**, of Cornwall, Nov. 28, 1850, at the house of Edwin Merwin, by Rev. Joshua L. Maynard, of the North Cong. Ch. | 3 | 96 |
| Irene, d. Lyman F., farmer, ae 39 & Harriet A., ae 32, res. Cornwall Hollow, b. May 31, 1849 | 3 | 98-9 |
| Lucy, m. John **STONE***, Aug. 31, 1758, by Rev. Hezekiah Gold *("**PIERCE**" in Starr's Hist. of Cornwall) | 1 | 32 |
| Lucy J., m. Timothy C. **CHASE**, Dec. 31, 1832, by Rev. Walter Smith, of the North Cong. Ch. | 3 | 35 |
| Melvina A., d. Dier S., farmer, ae 24 & Em[ma] Jane, ae 23, b. Dec. 1, 1847 | 3 | 86-7 |
| Malvina Manesta, d. Dier, farmer & Jane, b. Dec. 2, 1847 | 3 | 86-7 |
| Mary, m. William **JOHNSON**, May 31, 1759, by Rev. H. Gold | 1 | 34 |
| Rosetta, alias **BROWN**, m. Isaac A. **NORTON**, May 3, 1827, by Rev. Asa Tallmadge, of the Bap. Ch. | 2 | 67 |
| Samuel W., farmer, res. Cornwall, d. Dec. 15, 1850, ae 40 | 3 | 120-1 |
| Theisa, m. Samuel **WHEELER**, b. of Cornwall, June 29, 1842, by Rev. J. L. Maynard, of the North Cong. Ch. | 3 | 65 |
| **[HOWELL], HOWEL**, Edward, of Sharon, m. Jemima **ROWLEY**, of Cornwall, Aug. 27, 1794, by Rev. Israel Holly, of Cornwall | 3 | 21 |
| Jemima, d. Dec. 19, 1798 | 3 | 10 |
| **HOWLAND**, Mary, m. Capt. John **JEFFREY**, July 24, 1760, by Rev. H. Gold | 1 | 44 |
| Solomon, m. Martha **HACKETT**, Nov. 16, 1800, by Judah Kellogg, J. P. | 2 | 24 |
| **HOXLY**, Robert, m. Rosetta **DIBBLE**, Mar. 16, 1841, by Rev. Timothy Stone | 3 | 63 |
| **[HOYT], HOIT**, Molly, d. June 16, 1794 | 2 | 28 |
| **HUBBARD**, Francis J., s. Solon, physician, ae 30 & Lucretia, ae 18, b. Feb. 23, 1848 | 3 | 86-7 |
| Solon, Dr., m. Lucinda A. **WILLIS**, Feb. 1, 1846, by Rev. K. K. Reynolds | 3 | 72 |
| Washington I., s. Solon, physician, ae 37 & Lucinda, ae 22, b. Oct. 1, 1850 | 3 | 116-17 |
| **HUBBEL[L], HUBBEL**, Alice, m. Salmon **CARTER**, Apr. 15, 1793, by Jedidiah Hubbel, J. P. | 3 | 21 |
| Caroline, of Kent, m. Lyman J. **TAYLOR**, of Cornwall, Nov. 10, 1840, by Rev. John W. Salter | 3 | 59 |
| **HULL**, Flora, of Cornwall, m. Timothy **JOURDAN**, of Sharon, Nov. 29, 1849, by E. N. Jenckes | 3 | 82 |
| **HUMISTON, HUMISON**, Eber, m. Laura **HART**, b. of Cornwall, | | |

| | Vol. | Page |
|---|---|---|
| **HUMISTON, HUMISON**, (cont.) | | |
| Oct. 6, 1808, by Rev. Josiah Hawes, of the 2nd Ch. Witnesses: Joel Catlin & Amos Catlin | 3 | 33 |
| Maria Jane, of Cornwall, m. Truxton **CHITTENDEN**, of Westmoreland, N. Y., Oct. 2, 1839, by N. M. Urmston | 3 | 58 |
| William H., m. Mary A. **CATLIN**, b. of Cornwall, Jan. 23, 1840, by Rev. S. W. Smith | 3 | 59 |
| **HUMPHREY**, Betsey, m. Julius **BEACH**, b. of Goshen, Sept. 24, 1820, by Smith Dayton, Elder | 2 | 48 |
| Elizabeth, d. Tho[ma]s & Elizabeth, b. Nov. 22, 1768 | 1 | 103 |
| Rufus, s. [Thomas & Elizabeth], b. Feb. 24, 1771 | 1 | 103 |
| William, m. Sarah Ann **BIERCE**, Apr. 16, 1834, by Rev. William Andrews | 3 | 37 |
| **HUNT**, Caroline, of Cornwall, m. Nelson **THOMAS**, of Roxbury, Sept*. 31, 1840, by Rev. Ebenezer Washburn *("Aug.") | 3 | 59 |
| **HURLBURT, HURLBUT**, Heart, s. Jonathan & Sarah, d. Sept. 29, 1751 | 1 | 15 |
| Jonathan, of Cornwall, m. Lydia **MERRIT***, of Hartford, Jan. 1, [1754], by Thomas Hosmer, J. P. *(**MERRIL[L]**" in Starr's book) | 1 | 21 |
| Jonathan, s. Jonathan & Sarah, d. Dec. 11, 1756 | 1 | 25 |
| Jonathan, physician, b. Cornwall, res. Utica, N. Y., d. Aug. 10, 1848, ae 59 | 3 | 106-7 |
| Minerva, had s. James K. **POLK**, b. Dec. 2, 1845 | 3 | 69 |
| Ozias, m. Hannah **BUTLER**, Jan. 7, 1770, by Rev. Hezekiah Gold | LR3 | 5 |
| Sarah, w. Jonathan, d. Oct. 7, 1751 | 2 | 26 |
| Sarah, w. Jonathan, d. Oct. 10, 1751 | 1 | 15 |
| Ulyses, s. Ozias & Hannah, b. July 21, 1770 | LR3 | 8 |
| **HUTCHINSON**, Orion, of Sharon, m. Melissa **DEAN**, of Cornwall, Feb. 6, 1839, by N. M. Urmston | 3 | 56 |
| **HYATT**, Hannah, m. Uri **CLARK**, b. of Cornwall, Oct. 6, [1799], by Rev. John Cornwell, of Amenia, N. Y. Witnesses: Birdseye Clark & Louisa Kellogg | 3 | 9 |
| **HYLA**, Benjamin, agriculturist, ae [ ] & Harriet, had s. [ ], b. Mar. 16, 1851 | 3 | 114-15 |
| **IVES**, Theodore R., m. Mary E. **ROGERS**, b. of Cornwall, May 14, 1845, at the house of Daniel L. Rogers, by Rev. Joshua L. Maynard, of the North Cong. Ch. | 3 | 71 |
| **JACKSON**, Catharine Rebecca, of Sharon, m. Benjamin **BRADFORD**, of Cornwall, Sept. 3, 1838, by N. M. Urmston | 3 | 54 |
| Cynthia, m. Oliver **HOCHKIN**, Oct. 4, 1798, by Rev. Israel Holly | 3 | 20 |
| Hannah, m. Edward **ROGERS**, July 18, 1773, by Rev. H. Gold | LR3 | 5 |
| Huldah, m. Tryal **TANNER**, May 12, 1777, by Rev. Hezekiah Gold | 2 | 16 |

| | Vol. | Page |
|---|---|---|
| **JAKINS**, William, blacksmith, colored & Ann, had s. [ ], b. May [ ] | 3 | 114-15 |
| **JARVIS**, James H., of Salem, N. Y., m. Betsey **DIBBLE**, Oct. 8, 1827, by Rev. Silas Ambler | 2 | 68 |
| **JEFFERS**, [see also **JEFFREY**], Ebenezer, d. Oct. 18, 1804 | 3 | 27 |
| Hannah, d. [Ebenezer & Mary], b. Aug. 24, 1803 | 3 | 28 |
| Harriet, d. [Ebenezer & Mary], b. Mar. 4, 1799 | 3 | 28 |
| John, Capt., d. May 9, 1812, ae 51 (Of the U. S. Army) | 3 | 27 |
| Mary, dairy woman, d. Jan. 1, 1849, ae 73 | 3 | 106-7 |
| Sally, m. Samuel **WADSWORTH**, b. of Cornwall, Sept. 14, 1825, by Rev. Walter Smith, of the 2nd Ch. | 2 | 62 |
| Samuel, s. [Ebenezer & Mary], b. Nov. 5, 1796 | 3 | 28 |
| Samuel, of Cornwall, m. Mrs. Mary B. **CORBAN**, of Philadelphia, Pa., Dec. 23, 1846, at the house of Titus L. Hart, by Rev. Joshua L. Maynard, of North Cong. Ch. | 3 | 73 |
| Sarah, d. Ebenezer & Mary, b. Jan. 17, 1795 | 3 | 28 |
| William, s. [Ebenezer & Mary], b. July 6, 1801 | 3 | 28 |
| **JEFFREY**, [see also **JEFFERS**], Abraham, s. Capt. John & Mary, b. Apr. 5, 1771; d. May 6, 1771 | 1 | 101 |
| Abraham, s. John & Mary, b. Feb. 15, 1773 | 1 | 107 |
| Ebenezer, s. Capt. John & Mary, b. Apr. 26, 1764 | 1 | 55 |
| Hannah*, m. Noah **BULL**, July 19, 1759, by Rev. Hezekiah Gold *(Arnold Copy has "Mary **TEFFENY**") | 1 | 36 |
| Hannah, m. Salmon **EMONS**, Nov. 5, 1772, by Rev. H. Gold | LR3 | 5 |
| Isaac, w. Capt. John & Mary, b. Oct. 27, 1774 | LR3 | 16 |
| John, Capt., m. Mary **HOWLAND**, July 24, 1760, by Rev. H. Gold | 1 | 44 |
| John, s. Capt. John & Mary, b. June 5, 1761 | 1 | 44 |
| Salome, d. Capt. John & Mary, b. July 16, 1762 | 1 | 47 |
| Samuel Bishop, s. Capt. John & Mary, b. Mar. 29, 1769 | 1 | 89 |
| Sarah, d. John & Mary, b. Apr. 5, 1771 | 1 | 101 |
| Thomas, s. Capt. John & Mary, b. Apr. 21, 1766 | 1 | 68 |
| **JENCKES**, Edward A., Rev., ae 27, b. Springfield, Mass., res. Cornwall, m. 2nd w. Sarah A. **NETTLETON**, ae 24, res. Cornwall, Jan. 14, 1849, by Alfred Gates | 3 | 104-5 |
| **JENNINGS**, Benjamin, s. Lemuel & Abiah, b. May 7, 1774 | LR3 | 6 |
| Charles, s. Seth R., laborer, ae 28 & Sarah M., ae 24, b. Feb. 20, 1848 | 3 | 86-7 |
| David T., farmer, b. Warren, res. Warren, d. Sept. 9, 1848, ae 18 | 3 | 106-7 |
| Hannah*, m. Samuel **EMONS**, June 12, 1765, by Rev. Hezekiah Gold *("Hamar" in Starr's book) | 1 | 62 |
| Hudson, s. Lemuel & Abia, b. Apr. 16, 1784 | 2 | 7 |
| Hudson, m. Dorothy **CLARK**, b. of Cornwall, Oct. 7, 1804, by Judah Kellogg, J. P. | 3 | 11 |
| Josiah, m. Lucinda **GUILD**, June 16, 1822, by Asa Tallmadge, Elder of the Bap. Church | 2 | 53 |
| Lemuel, m. Abiah **BEARCE**, Jan. 20, 1773, by Rev. Hezekiah | | |

| | Page | Page |
|---|---|---|
| **JENNINGS**, (cont.) | | |
| Gold | 1 | 107 |
| Mary, d. Lemuel & Abiah, b. Mar. 29, 1776 | LR3 | 10 |
| Palina, m. Hiram **DUNHAM**, Jan. 11, 1821, by Rev. Asa Blair, of the 1st Soc. in Kent | 2 | 49 |
| Sally, single, d. Aug. 22, 1848, ae 45 | 3 | 92-3 |
| Sally, laborer, d. Aug. 22, 1848, ae 45 | 3 | 106-7 |
| Sarah, b. Kent, res. Cornwall, d. Dec. 18, 1849, ae 25 | 3 | 106-7 |
| Wealthy, d. Lemuel & Abiah, b. Feb. 16, 1778 | LR3 | 9 |
| **JEROME**, Ruth, m. James F. **WADSWORTH**, Sept. 18, 1837, by Rev. Walter Smith, of the 2nd Cong. Ch. | 3 | 52 |
| **JERRED**, Jesse, m. Sarah **ABBOTT**, Sept. 19, 1769, by Rev. Hezekiah Gold | 1 | 94 |
| **JESSUP**, Lucius, of Middletown, N. J., m. Caroline **BONNEY**, of Cornwall, Oct. 29, 1851, by Rev. Ralph Smith, of the 1st Cong. Ch. | 3 | 97 |
| **JEWELL, JEWEL**, Adaline, d. Aug. 28, 1850, ae 28* "old age" *(82?) | 3 | 120-1 |
| Albi*, d. Joshua & Mary, b. July [ ], 1745 *("Abi" in Starr's book) | 1 | 7 |
| Anna, d. Joshua & Mary, b. May 25, 1747 | 1 | 7 |
| Christian, d. David & Christian, b. Oct. 23, 1742 | 1 | 3 |
| David, m. Christian **LUMMIS**, Nov. 5, 1741 | 1 | 3 |
| David, s. Nathaniell & Sarah, b. Jan. 1, 1741/2 | 1 | 4 |
| David, s. David & Christian, b. Dec. 2, 1746 | 1 | 5 |
| Eliphalet, s. Joshua & Mary, b. Nov. 22, 1736 | 1 | 7 |
| Franklin, of Brookfield, m. Elizabeth **HALL**, of Cornwall, Apr. 9, 1848, by Rev. M. Bydenburgh | 3 | 78 |
| Franklin, ae 29, b. Fishkill, N. Y., res. N. Milford, m. Elizabeth **HALL**, ae 19, b. Kent, res. N. Milford, Apr. 9, 1848, by Rev. Moses B. Blydenburgh | 3 | 90-1 |
| Hannah, d. David & Christian, b. Jan. 19, 1744/5 | 1 | 5 |
| Joseph, s. Nathaniell & Sarah, b. June 18, 1744 | 1 | 4 |
| Joshua, s. Joshua & Mary, b. May 14, 1741 | 1 | 7 |
| Martha, of Cornwall, m. Peter M. **MILLS**, of Chester, N. H., Aug. 18, 1833, by Rev. Levi Peck, of the Bap. Ch. | 3 | 36 |
| Mary, d. Joshua & Mary, b. July 12, 1743 | 1 | 7 |
| Melo A., m. Adeline **HOWE**, b. of Cornwall, Jan. 18, 1842, by Joshua L. Maynard | 3 | 64 |
| Mirra, of Cornwall, m. Lucas **LANE**, of Plymouth, Mar. 25, 1822, by Rev. Walter Smith, of the 2nd Church | 2 | 51 |
| Oliver, s. Joshua & Mary, b. Mar. 19, 1738/9 | 1 | 7 |
| Sarah, d. Joshua & Mary, b. Aug. 19, 1734 | 1 | 7 |
| William G., d. Aug. 4, 1850, ae 7 | 3 | 120-1 |
| **JOHNSON**, Alanson, s. [Charles & Rhoda], b. Oct. 25, 1791 | 3 | 12 |
| Almon L., of Litchfield, m. Sarah L. **BEACH**, of Cornwall, Sept. 29, 1852, by N. C. Lewis | 3 | 123 |
| Amanda, d. Timothy & Sarah, b. Mar. 8, 1795 | 3 | 26 |

| | Vol. | Page |
|---|---|---|
| **JOHNSON**, (cont.) | | |
| Amanda, m. Milo **DICKINSON**, Jan. 17, 1836, by Rev. T. Atwater | 3 | 41 |
| Amasa, s. Amasa & Phebe, b. Jan. 19, 1760 | 1 | 35 |
| Amos, Jr., m. Elizabeth **PIERCE**, b. of Cornwall, Sept. 11, 1755, by George Kellogg, J. P. Witnesses: John Pierce & Nehemiah Pierce | 1 | 23 |
| Amos, s. Amos, Jr. & Elizabeth, b. May 2, 1757 | 1 | 29 |
| Amos, Capt., d. May 8, 1766 | 1 | 68 |
| Amos Mallory, s. Timothy & Sarah, b. Jan. 28, 1801 | 2 | 32 |
| Amy, m. Joshuah **PIERCE**, Jr., b. of Cornwall, Sept. 11, 1754, by George Kellogg, J. P. Sworn to Aug. 9, 1756, before Gideon Thompson, J. P., by John Pierce, Nehemiah Pierce | 1 | 23 |
| Anna, d. Amos, Jr. & Elizabeth, b. Feb. 1, 1764 | 1 | 56 |
| Anna, spinner, d. Apr. 3, 1848, ae 84 | 3 | 92-3 |
| Anna B., d. Timothy C., farmer, ae 37 & Betsey J., ae 33, res. Goshen Milton Soc. b. May 24, 1849 | 3 | 100-1 |
| Anna Charlotte, d. Buckley & Abigail, b. Oct. 2, 1814 | 2 | 41 |
| Anne, d. Nathaniel & Mary, b. Mar. 25, 1760 | 1 | 37 |
| Anne, 2nd d. [Philemon & Philomela], b. Apr. 23, 1790 | 3 | 22 |
| Benjamin P., m. Mary A. **MINER**, b. of Cornwall, Sept. 3, 1839, by N. M. Urmston | 3 | 58 |
| Benjamin Palmer, s. Bulkley & Abigail, b. Nov. 2, 1802 | 3 | 5 |
| Bulkley, s. Amos & Elizabeth, b. Aug. 15, 1771 | 1 | 99 |
| Charles, s. [Charles & Rhoda], b. May 29, 1794 | 3 | 12 |
| Collis Spencer, s. [Saymour & Julia Ann], b. Oct. 3, 1840 | 3 | 69 |
| Collis Spencer, s. Seymour & Julia Ann, d. Feb. 13, 1841 | 3 | 75 |
| David, s. Solomon & Eleanor, b. Mar. 28, 1774 | LR3 | 6 |
| David Frank, s. Buckley & Abigail, b. Aug. 13, 1807 | 3 | 29 |
| Dorothy Wood, d. Palmer & Selah, b. Feb. 22, 1807 | 3 | 16 |
| E. M., ae 17, res. Cornwall, m. Marshall **GARDINER**, carpenter, ae 21, b. Norwich, res. Cornwall, Apr. 15, 1851, by Rev. Mr. Youngs | 3 | 118-19 |
| Earl, s. Timothy & Sarah, b. May 14, 1799 | 2 | 23 |
| Eber J., m. Huldah **MALTBY**, b. of Cornwall, Nov. 7, 1838, by N. M. Urmston | 3 | 54 |
| Eber J., of Cornwall, m. Adalia E. **LEWIS**, of Norfolk, Dec. 1, 1842, by Rev. Joshua L. Maynard, of the North Cong. Ch. | 3 | 66 |
| Eber J., farmer, d. Oct. 6, 1848, ae 35 | 3 | 106-7 |
| Eber Ives, s. Samuel P. & Mariam, b. Jan. 2, 1813 | 3 | 34 |
| Eleanor, m. Benjamin **GOLD**, b. of Cornwall, Nov. 25, 1784. Witnesses: Mrs. Eleanor Swift & Joshua Peerce, 3rd | 2 | 16 |
| Eliza A., m. Senaca **SLOCOM**, Nov. 4, 1852, by Ralph Smith | 3 | 125 |
| Eliza J., d. wid. Eliza, farmer, ae 30, b. Mar. 21, 1849 | 3 | 100-1 |
| Eliza M., m. John Marshall **GARDINER**, b. of Cornwall, Apr. 14, 1851, by F. C. Youngs | 3 | 97 |

| | Vol. | Page |
|---|---|---|
| **JOHNSON**, (cont.) | | |
| Eliza Melvina, d. Earl & Lucia Ann, b. Oct. 16, 1833 | 3 | 39 |
| Elizabeth, d. Amos & Elizabeth, b. Jan. 28, 1759 | 1 | 33 |
| Elizabeth, d. Amos & Elizabeth, d. Feb. 27, 1759 | 1 | 33 |
| Elizabeth, d. Amos & Elizabeth, b. Feb. 29, 1760 | 1 | 35 |
| Elizabeth, d. Timothy & Sarah, b. Jan. 8, 1793 | 2 | 29 |
| Elizabeth, m. Luther **EMMONS**, Nov. 26, 1816, by Rev. Timothy Stone, of the 1st Ch. | 2 | 58 |
| Elizabeth A., of Cornwall, m. Jay **GAYLORD**, of Warren, Mar. 25, 1839, by N. M. Urmston | 3 | 56 |
| Erastus, s. [Charles & Rhoda], b. Oct. 28, 1787 | 3 | 12 |
| Eunice, d. Charles & Rhoda, b. Sept. 1, 1785 | 3 | 12 |
| Harriet A., d. Timothy C. & Betsey, b. July 31, 1837 | 3 | 62 |
| Harriet N., of Cornwall, m. Alfred F. **BUNNELL**, of Plymouth, Sept. 3, 1839, by N. M. Urmston | 3 | 58 |
| Harriet Newell, d. Benjamin P., farmer, ae 48 & Mary Ann **MINNA**, ae 34, b. Nov. 19, 1850 | 3 | 114-15 |
| Hopkins T. S., farmer, ae 27, res. Cornwall, m. Sarah A. **HOPKINS**, ae 25, res. Cornwall, Oct. 7, 1849, by Rev. H. E. Vaill | 3 | 112-13 |
| Hopkins T. S., m. Sarah A. **HOPKINS**, b. of Cornwall, Oct. 17, 1849, by Rev. Herman L. Vaill | 3 | 82 |
| Jeremiah Sanford, s. Seymour & Julia Ann, b. Aug. 11, 1836 | 3 | 69 |
| Jesse Gilbert, s. Samuel P. & Mariam, b. Jan. 16, 1809 | 3 | 30 |
| John L., m. Percis **DEAN**, Nov. 25, 1830, by Rev. William Andrews | 3 | 46 |
| John Lyman, s. Bulkly & Abigail, b. July 6, 1800 | 3 | 31 |
| Laura, d. Bulkley & Abigail, b. Oct. 29, 1798 | 2 | 23 |
| Laura, d. Feb. 21, 1849, ae [ ] | 3 | 106-7 |
| Lewis Palmer, s. Palmer & Selah, b. May 20, 1817 | 2 | 43 |
| Lucy, d. Amasa & Elizabeth, b. Aug. 24, 1769 | 1 | 92 |
| Lucy, d. Solomon & Eleanor, b. Feb. 8, 1771 | 1 | 98 |
| Lucy, d. Timothy & Sarah, b. Feb. 21, 1803 | 3 | 16 |
| Luther S., of Litchfield, m. Sarah E. **FORD**, of Cornwall, Nov. 6, 1854, by Rev. Ira Pettibone | 3 | 125 |
| Mana M., m. Philomela **VAIL**, Sept. 27, 1829, by Rev. William Andrews | 3 | 44 |
| Maria, of Cornwall, m. David **MALLORY**, of Warren, Nov. 22, 1824, by Rev. Timothy Stone | 2 | 59 |
| Marietta, d. Samuel P. & Mira, b. Aug. 12, 1801 | 3 | 31 |
| Marietta, m. Frederick M. **PECK**, June 1, 1834, by Rev. William Andrews | 3 | 37 |
| Mary E., d. Benjamin P., laborer, ae 46 & Mary, ae 33, b. Dec. 4, 1848 | 3 | 100-1 |
| Myra C., of Cornwall, m. Samuel **PECK**, of Watertown, Feb. 28, 1836, by Rev. Heman L. Noell | 3 | 41 |
| Mira Caroline, d. Samuel P. & Merian, b. Aug. 13, 1806 | 3 | 16 |
| Olive, Mrs., m. Eliakim **MALLORY**, Dec. 20, 1785, by Rev. | | |

| | Vol. | Page |
|---|---|---|
| **JOHNSON**, (cont.) | | |
| John Cornwell | 2 | 16 |
| Patty Louisa, d. Samuel P. & Mira, b. July 6, 1803 | 3 | 5 |
| Philomela, 3rd d. [Philemon & Philomela], b. Jan. 17, 1796 | 3 | 22 |
| Philomon, 2nd, s. [Philemon & Philomela], b. Feb. 6, 1793 | 3 | 22 |
| Philus Blake, s. Eber J. & Huldah, b. Dec. 14, 1839 | 3 | 57 |
| Rhoda, d. [Charles & Rhoda], b. Aug. 26, 1796 | 3 | 12 |
| Samuel Hopkins, s. Hopkins T. S. & Sarah A., b. Oct. 30, 1850 | 3 | 95 |
| Samuel Hopkins, s. H. T. S., farmer, ae 29 & Sarah A., ae 26, b. Oct. 30, 1850 | 3 | 114-15 |
| Samuel Joseph Barnett, s. Samuel P. & Marann, b. Aug. 22, 1816 | 2 | 44 |
| Samuel Joseph Barnett, s. Samuel P. & Marrann, b. Aug. 22, 1816 | 2 | 45 |
| Samuel P., farmer, d. Jan. 26, 1849, ae 82 | 3 | 106-7 |
| Samuel Pierce, s. Amos & Elizabeth, b. Sept. 11, 1767 | 1 | 80 |
| Sarah, d. Philemon & Philomela, b. Apr. 7, 1789 | 3 | 22 |
| Sarah, d. [Timothy & Sarah], b. Oct. 8, 1797 | 3 | 26 |
| Sarah, d. Timothy & Sarah, d. Dec. 6, 1799 | 3 | 6 |
| Sarah, w. Timothy, d. Oct. 2, 1805 | 3 | 6 |
| Sarah A., of Cornwall, m. Andrew J. **SPURR**, of Sheffield, Mass., Sept. 2, 1850, by E. W. Andrews | 3 | 83 |
| Sarah Ann, d. [Timothy & Sarah], b. Mar. 21, 1805 | 3 | 16 |
| Sarah Ann, m. Dea. Abel C. **CARTER**, June 17, 1827, by Rev. Timothy Stone | 2 | 67 |
| Sarah Ann, m. Joel **HALL**, Nov. 14, 1832, by Rev. Walter Smith, of the North Cong. Ch. | 3 | 35 |
| Seth, s. Solomon & Eleanor, b. Feb. 4, 1769 | 1 | 85 |
| Seymour, s. Palmer & Selah, b. Aug. 16, 1812 | 3 | 14 |
| Seymour, m. Julia A. **SANFORD**, Sept. 14, 1835, by Rev. William Andrews | 3 | 40 |
| Solomon, m. Eliner **PIERCE**, Sept. 28, 1758, by Rev. H. Gold | 1 | 33 |
| Solomon, s. Solomon & Eleanor, b. May 29, 1760 | 1 | 39 |
| Solomon, 3rd s. [Philemon & Philomela], b. July 14, 1794 | 3 | 22 |
| Solon Beaumont, s. [Seymour & Julia Ann], b. Aug. 4, 1838 | 3 | 69 |
| Sophronia, d. Palmer & Selah, b. Aug. 15, 1809 | 3 | 30 |
| Stephen, s. Solomon & Eleanor, b. Aug. 8, 1762 | 1 | 47 |
| Susan, m. Jacob **NEWPORT**, Nov. 18, 1820, by Rev. Timothy Stone | 2 | 48 |
| Thomas Stafford **HOPKINS**, s. Samuel P. & Mereann, b. Aug. 19, 1822 | 3 | 39 |
| Timothy, s. Amos, Jr. & Elizabeth, b. May 11, 1762 | 1 | 47 |
| Timothy C., m. Betsey S. **BARBER**, Sept. 21, 1836, by Rev. William Andrews | 3 | 41 |
| Timothy Chauncey, s. Buckley & Abigail, b. Sept. 5, 1811 | 2 | 41 |
| Urania Maria, d. Buckly & Abigail, b. Aug. 13, 1805 | 3 | 15 |

| | Vol. | Page |
|---|---|---|
| **JOHNSON**, (cont.) | | |
| Wakeman Peirce, s. Buckly, b. Aug. 23, 1809 | 3 | 30 |
| Wakeman Peirce, m. Harriet **AVERY**, Jan. 14, 1847, by Rev. John R. Keep | 3 | 73 |
| Walter Barber, s. Lewis P. & Rebecca, b. Aug. 13, 1852 | 3 | 95 |
| Welley, s. [Philemon & Philomela], b. Dec. 10, 1791 | 3 | 22 |
| Wilbier A., s. Lewis P. & Rebecca, b. July 1, 1844 | 3 | 95 |
| William, m. Mary **HOW**, May 31, 1759, by Rev. H. Gold | 1 | 34 |
| William, s. William & Mercy, b. May 18, 1762 | 1 | 47 |
| William, d. Nov. 12, 1767 | 1 | 98 |
| William W., s. [Timothy C. & Betsey], b. July 12, 1839 | 3 | 62 |
| **JONES**, Abigail, d. Zach[aria]h H. & Jane, b. Mar. 8, 1769 | 1 | 87 |
| Almond T., m. Lucia **WILCOX**, Sept. 27, 1837, by Rev. Walter Smith, of the 2nd Cong. Ch. | 3 | 52 |
| Ann, m. Seely **ABBOT**, June 24, 1761, by Rev. H. Gold | 1 | 43 |
| Caleb, s. Zachariah How & Jane, b. June 20, 1782 | 2 | 4 |
| Caleb, m. Harriet **SWIFT**, b. of Cornwall, Feb. 28, 1811, by Rev. Timothy Stone | 2 | 37 |
| Edmund, s. John & Isabella, b. Aug. 26, 1787 | 2 | 20 |
| Hannah, m. Matthew **PATTERSON**, b. of Cornwall, Apr. 13, 1772, by Thomas Russell, J. P. | 1 | 106 |
| Jane, w. Capt. Zachariah H., d. Mar. 12, 1813 | 3 | 27 |
| Jane, d. Caleb & Harriet, b. May 17, 1814 | 2 | 38 |
| Jane Ann, m. John T. **ANDREW**, Sept. 7, 1839, by N. M. Urmston | 3 | 58 |
| Jared, s. John & Isabella, b. Feb. 12, 1784 | 2 | 9 |
| John, s. Caleb & Mary, b. Oct. 14, 1757 | 1 | 48 |
| John, s. Caleb & Mary, b. Oct. 17, 1757 | 1 | 30 |
| Mary Frisbie, d. John & Isabella, b. Jan. 22, 1782 | 2 | 5 |
| Zachariah H., Capt. d. Aug. 1, 1817, ae [ ] | 2 | 39 |
| **JOURDAN**, Timothy, of Sharon, m. Flora **HULL**, of Cornwall, Nov. 29, 1849, by E. N. Jenckes | 3 | 82 |
| **JOYNER**, Asael, s. William & Sarah, b. June 22, 1748 | 1 | 7 |
| **JUDD**, Amanda, d. [Ephraim & Abigail], b. Sept. 22, 1811 | 2 | 40 |
| Amanda, d. [Ephraim & Abigail], d. Mar. 13, 1813 | 2 | 33 |
| Amzi Morris, s. [Ephraim & Abigail], b. May 8, 1814 | 2 | 40 |
| Edwin, s. [Ephraim & Abigail], b. Dec. 9, 1806 | 2 | 40 |
| Flora, d. Ephraim & Abigail, b. July 12, 1802 | 2 | 40 |
| Flora, m. Albert **NORTHROP**, b. of Cornwall, Jan. 30, 1825, by Rev. Timothy Stone, of the 1st Ch. | 2 | 59 |
| Lewis, s. [Ephraim & Abigail], b. Apr. 29, 1809 | 2 | 40 |
| Philip Morris, s. [Ephraim & Abigail], b. Aug. 5, 1804 | 2 | 40 |
| Philip Morris, s. Ephraim & Abigail, d. Apr. 5, 1811 | 2 | 33 |
| **JUDSON**, Abel, s. [Abel & Abigail], b. Dec. 29, 1784 | 3 | 14 |
| Abel Clark, s. Abel & Ruby, b. Dec. 4, 1808 | 3 | 14 |
| Abiah, d. [Samuel Agua & Abiah], b. Dec. 15, 1804 | 3 | 14 |
| Abiah Ann, of Cornwall, m. Rev. Aaron S. **HILL**, of Goshen, Apr. 22, 1833, by Rev. Aaron Hunt | 3 | 36 |

| | Vol. | Page |
|---|---|---|
| **JUDSON**, (cont.) | | |
| Albert, Rev., m. Mary H. **BURNHAM**, Dec. 3, 1829, by Rev. Walter Smith, of the North Ch. | 3 | 45 |
| Amey Curtiss, d. [Abel & Abigail], b.Mar. 29, 1780 | 3 | 14 |
| Amy Curtiss, d. Abel, d. Mar. 12, 1813, ae 33 | 3 | 27 |
| Charles S., d. Sept. 18, 1849, ae 2 | 3 | 112-13 |
| David, s. [Abel & Abigail], b. Apr. 2, 1771, at Stratford | 3 | 14 |
| Delia Sophia, d. [Abel & Ruby], b. Mar. 26, 1812 | 3 | 14 |
| Harriet, m. Phinehas **BALDWIN**, b. of Cornwall, Sept. 25, 1850, by E. W. Andrews | 3 | 96 |
| Harriet, ae 57, b. Cornwall, res. Cornwall, m. Phinehas **BALDWIN**, farmer, ae 67, b. Milford, res. Cornwall, Sept. 25, 1851, by E. W. Andrews | 3 | 118-19 |
| Joseph, s. Abel & Abigail, b. Feb. 22, 1770, at Stratford | 3 | 14 |
| Mary Anne, d. [Samuel Agua & Abiah], b. Nov. 6, 1797 | 3 | 14 |
| Phebe, d. [Samuel Agua & Abiah], b. Apr. 25, 1803 | 3 | 14 |
| Samuel Hall, s. [Samuel Agua & Abiah], b. Mar. 30, 1799 | 3 | 14 |
| Samuel Hull, s. Samuel Agur. d. June 8, 1802 | 3 | 27 |
| Samuel Wesley, s. [Samuel Agua & Abiah], b. Nov. 15, 1806 | 3 | 14 |
| Sarah, d. [Abel & Abigail, b. Apr. 25, 1775, at Stratford | 3 | 14 |
| Sarah, d. Samuel Agua & Abiah, b. Aug. 30, 1795, at Stratford | 3 | 14 |
| Sarah, see Sarah **PEIRCE** | 3 | 27 |
| Sarah Abiah, Mrs., m. Henry **READ**, Dec. 1, 1799, by Rev. Henry Christie | 2 | 24 |
| Silas*, m. Minerva **CARTER**, Oct. 13, 1830, by William Andrews *("Silas Patterson **JUDSON**" in Starr's book) | 3 | 46 |
| Silas P., m. Adelia **BONNEY**, b. of Cornwall, Apr. 15, 1846, by Hiram Day | 3 | 72 |
| **KEARNS**, Mary, d. James, laborer, ae 24 & Honor, ae 24, b. Feb. 28, 1850 | 3 | 98-9 |
| **KEELER**, Frederick A., of Albany, N. Y., m. Ruby Ann **PEET**, of Warren, Dec. 30, 1854, by Rev. J. F. Jones, of College St. Bap. Ch. | 3 | 126 |
| **KEERNANN**, Bridget, m. Michael **DILLON**, Jan. 7, 1853, by Rev. Peter Kelley. Int. Pub. | 3 | 125 |
| **KELLOGG**, Charles Calhoun, s. Frederick & R. R., b. June 27, 1833 | 3 | 57 |
| Charles William, s. William & Demis, b. Dec. 16, 1798 | 2 | 31 |
| Frederick, s. William & Demis, b. Sept. 5, 1801 | 3 | 14 |
| Frederick, m. Ruth R. **CALHOUN**, Sept. 16, 1829, by Rev. William Andrews | 3 | 44 |
| Gerret, s. William & Demis, b. Feb. 1, 1792; d. Dec. 3, 1794 | 2 | 27 |
| Gerret, s. William & Demis, b. July 30, 1796 | 3 | 25 |
| Hannah, d. [William & Demis], b. Aug. 7, 1811 | 3 | 14 |
| Hannah, m. John W. **REED**, Oct. 31, 1836, by Rev. William Andrews | 3 | 42 |
| Harriet, d. [William & Demia], b. Dec. 12, 1808 | 3 | 14 |

| | Vol. | Page |
|---|---|---|
| **KELLOGG**, (cont.) | | |
| Jennet, d. William & Demis, b. Jan. 10, 1817 | 2 | 43 |
| Jennett, m. Marshall **DIBBLE**, b. of Cornwall, Dec. 9, 1843, by Rev. Joshua L. Maynard, of the North Cong. Ch. | 3 | 68 |
| John, s. Judah & Mary, d. July 25, 1776 | LR3 | 7 |
| John, s. Jusah & Mary, b. Sept. 22, 1777 | LR3 | 9 |
| John, m. Polly **CLARK**, Aug. 26, 1799, by Israel Holly | 2 | 24 |
| Judah, d. Apr. 20, 1819, ae 80 y. | 2 | 46 |
| Lucius, s. Judah & Mary, b. May 3, 1781 | LR4 | 17 |
| Lucius, M. D., m. Harriet **BRADLEY**, Mar. 9, 1851, by George Wheaton, J. P. | 3 | 96 |
| Lucius, doctor, ae 69, b. Cornwall, res. Dover, N. Y., m. 2nd w. Harriet **BRADLEY**, ae 29, b. Prospect, res. Dover, N. Y., Mar. [ ], 1851, by George Wheaton | 3 | 118-19 |
| Lucretia, d. Charles & Delia M., b. Mar. 20, 1819, in Stockbridge | 3 | 57 |
| Martha A., of Cornwall, m. Ezekiel **HAYES**, of New Haven, July 2, 1848, by Rev. Hiram Day | 3 | 80 |
| Mary, d. Judah & Mary, b. July 6, 1783 | 2 | 5 |
| Mary, d. [William & Demis], b. Jan. 10, 1804 | 3 | 14 |
| Mary, 2d, m. Eliphalet H. **SHEPARD**, July 7, 1813, by Rev. Timothy Stone, of the 1st Ch. Witness: William Kellogg, T. C. | 3 | 33 |
| Mary, wid. Judah, d. Aug. 24, 1836, ae 91 | 3 | 43 |
| Mary, of Cornwall, m. Asa **EVERETT**, of Ellsworth, June 2, 1851, at the house of Mr. Payne, by Rev. J. L. Maynard, of the North Cong. Ch. | 3 | 97 |
| Mary, ae 47, res. Cornwall, m. Asa **EVERETT**, farmer, ae 71, b. Litchfield, res. Sharon, June 2, 1851, by Rev. J. L. Maynard | 3 | 118-19 |
| Mary Jane, d. [Frederick & R. R.], b. Sept. 28, 1838 | 3 | 57 |
| Miles, s. John & Polly, b. Aug. 29, 1801 | 2 | 42 |
| Philo, s. William & Demis, b. Mar. 1, 1794 | 2 | 30 |
| Sarah Fay, d. [Frederick & R. R.], b. May 20, 1836 | 3 | 57 |
| Theodosia, of Cornwall, m. Simeon **HALL**, of Armenia, Apr. 3, 1827, by Rev. John Lovejoy, of the M. E. Ch. | 2 | 66 |
| William, m. Demis **SWIFT**, Nov. 11, 1790, b. Peter Starr | 3 | 20 |
| William, d. May 28, 1829, ae 60 | 3 | 43 |
| William Frederick, s. Frederick & Ruth, b. Nov. 17, 1830 | 3 | 47 |
| **[KELLY], KELLEY**, Catharine, w. of laborer, b. Ireland, res. Cornwall, d. July 30, 1850, ae 29 | 3 | 112-13 |
| Martha A., res. Cornwall, m. Ezekiel **HAYES**, printer, b. Cornwall, res. New Haven, July 2, 1848, by Rev. Hiram Day | 3 | 90-1 |
| Michael, s. William, b. Oct. 24, 1848 | 3 | 102-3 |
| William, clergyman, ae 31 & Catharine, ae 29, had child s. b. July 30, 1850 | 3 | 108-9 |

| | Vol. | Page |
|---|---|---|
| **KENNEY**, Joseph, of Courtlandville, N. Y., m. Mary **WICKWIRE**, of Cornwall, Sept. 16, 1841, by Rev. Lewis Gunn | 3 | 63 |
| **KENT***, Ruth, m. Jacob **BROWNSON**, Jr., Mar. 29, 1770, by Rev. Hezekiah Gold *("**HART**" in Starr's book) | 1 | 93 |
| **KILBOURNE**, Benjamin, m. Amanda **MILLARD**, July 1, 1821, by Rev. Walter Smith, of the 2nd Church | 2 | 50 |
| **KIMBERLY, KIMBERLEY**, Augusta V., m. Archibald **BENNETT**, Jan. 27, 1853, by Ralph Smith | 3 | 125 |
| Willard, m. Emily **DIBBLE**, May 4, 1831, by Rev. William Andrews | 3 | 48 |
| **KNICKERBOCKER**, Solomon, m. Clarissa **ROOT**, Oct. 16, 1832, by Rev. Walter Smith, of the North Cong. Ch. | 3 | 35 |
| **KYLE**, Margaret, of Cornwall, m. John **BOYD**, of Waterbury, June 31, 1852, by J. L. Maynard | 3 | 122 |
| **LAMMENT**, John, wood sawer, had d. [ ], b. [ ] | 3 | 108-9 |
| **LAMONT**, Daniel, m. Mary **TERRILL**, b. of Cornwall, Aug. 23, 1852, by Rev. Ralph Smith | 3 | 123 |
| **LAMTON**, Benjamin, of Goshen, m. Mrs. Jane E. **NETTLETON**, of Cornwall, Jan. 20, 1848, by Rev. Alfred Yates | 3 | 78 |
| **LANDON**, James, 2nd, of Litchfield, m. Julia **BENEDICT**, of Cornwall, May 13, 1835, by Rev. David G. Tomlinson, of the Epis. Ch. Milton | 3 | 40 |
| **LANE**, Eri L., of Cornwall, m. Catharine R. **SMITH**, of New Haven, July 11, 1852, by Harley Goodwin | 3 | 123 |
| Lucas, of Plymouth, m. Mirra **JEWEL**, of Cornwall, Mar. 25, 1822, by Rev. Walter Smith, of the 2nd Church | 2 | 51 |
| **LATHROP**, Frederick, of New Milford, m. Lorenda E. **PALMER**, of Cornwall, Sept. 4, 1853, by Ralph Smith | 3 | 125 |
| **LAWREE**, [see under **LOWRY**] | | |
| **LAWRENCE**, Julia A., m. Edward **PEIRCE**, b. of Cornwall, Jan. 19, 1844, by Amos D. Watrous | 3 | 68 |
| **LAWSON**, (?), Hannah, see under Hannah **GAWSON** | | |
| **LAWTON**, Benjamin, farmer, ae 22, b. Goshen, res. Goshen, m. Jane T. **NETTLETON**, ae 22, res. Cornwall, Jan. 12, 1848, by Alfred Gates | 3 | 90-1 |
| **LEACH**, Theodore, of Torrington, m. Lucy **WRIGHT**, of Cornwall, Aug. 27, 1835, by Rev. Charles Chittenden, of Litchfield. Witnesses: Lewis Gunn & Carrington Todd | 3 | 40 |
| **LEE**, Jane C., m. Smith **PERRY**, b. of Cornwall, Feb. 3, 1833, by Peter Bierce, J. P. | 3 | 35 |
| Stephen, m. Thankfull **BARNS***, Sept. 8, 1743 *("**BAINS**" in Starr's book) | 1 | 3 |
| **LEETE**, Rhoda, of Guilford, m. Noah **ROGERS**, of Cornwall, Oct. 23, 1765, at Guilford, by James Sproutt | 1 | 67 |
| **LEFFINGWELL**, William, of Sheffield, Mass., m. Matilda **PARMELEE**, of Cornwall, Oct. 3, 1841, by James Wadsworth, J. P. | 3 | 63 |

| | Vol. | Page |
|---|---|---|
| **LEONARD**, Eunice, m. Richard **WICKWIRE**, 2nd, b. of Canaan, [ ], by Judah Kellogg, J. P. (Recorded Sept. 19, 1801) | 2 | 24 |
| Marcus W., s. Marcus & Ruth, b. Aug. 3, 1839 | 3 | 57 |
| **LEWIS, LEWSEE**, Adalia E., of Norfolk m. Eber J. **JOHNSON**, of Cornwall, Dec. 1, 1842, by Rev. Joshua L. Maynard, of the North Cong. Ch. | 3 | 66 |
| Elam, of Stonington, m. Rhoda **TODD**, of Warren, Jan. 5, 1832, by Rev. Luther Mead | 3 | 49 |
| Eloiza, d. Cleor & Sarah, b. July 2, 1793 | 3 | 25 |
| Hannah*, m. John **DIBBLE**, late of Norwalk, now of Cornwall, May 30, 1732, by Rev. Mr. Sturgeon, of Welton Parish. Witnesses: John & Hannah Dunning *(Written "Hannah **LEWSEE**") | 1 | 14 |
| Hannah, m. John **DIBBLE**, late of Norwalk, now of Cornwall, May 30, 1732, by Rev. Mr. Sturgion, of Wilton Parish. Witnesses: John & Hannah Dunning. Sworn to May 5, 1750, before Thomas Benedict. J. P. | 1 | 20 |
| Jerusha, of Cornwall, m. Thomas **DEAN**, of New Milford, Penn., Feb. 20, 1848, by Rev. M. Bydenburgh | 3 | 78 |
| Jerusha, ae 66, b. Waterbury, res. Cornwall, m. 2nd h. Thomas **DEAN**, farmer, ae 68, b. Cornwall, res. N. Milford, Feb. 20, 1848, by Rev. Moses B. Blydenburgh | 3 | 90-1 |
| John C., m. Anne P. **HOPKINS**, Sept. 15, 1824, by Rev. Timothy Stone | 2 | 58 |
| Silva, d. [Cleor & Sarah], b. Jan. 23, 1796 | 3 | 25 |
| Tabitha C., m. Alpheas **BEERS**, Sept. 14, 1826, by Rev. Timothy Stone, of the 1st Ch. | 2 | 65 |
| **LEWSEE**, [see under **LEWIS**] | | |
| **LINDSLEY, LINDSLY**, Polly, d. Ephraim & Molly, b. July 25, 1788 | 3 | 7 |
| William, s. [Ephraim & Molly], b. May 16, 1790 | 3 | 7 |
| **LOCKMAN**, Orrilla, d. Charles, farmer, ae 22 & Ann Sophia, ae 19, b. July 17, 1851 | 3 | 114-15 |
| **LOCKWOOD**, Hannah, of Danbury, m. Joshua **PIERCE**, of Cornwall, Apr. 6, 1786, by Rev. Joseph Peck | 2 | 8 |
| **LOGINS**, Robert, of Woodbury, m. Ruth **BECKWITH**, of Lyme, Mar. 6, 1760, by Rev. George Beckwith, of Lyme | 1 | 39 |
| **LOOMIS, LUMMIS**, Christian, m. David **JEWELL**, Nov. 5, 1741 | 1 | 3 |
| David Edward, s. Edward R. & Sarah, b. June 17, 1838 | 3 | 57 |
| Lucinda Jane, d. [Edward R. & Sarah B.], b. Jan. 22, 1836 | 3 | 51 |
| Sarah Elvira, d. Edward R. & Sarah B., b. June 21, 1834 | 3 | 51 |
| **LOVEL**, John, of Sharon, m. Caroline *Melissa **GOLD**, of Cornwall, Dec. 25, 1825, by Rev. Timothy Stone. *(Written "Carorine") | 2 | 63 |
| **LOWRY, LOWREE**, Gad, s. Nathaniel & Jerusha, b. Apr. 14, 1766 | 1 | 67 |
| Shubael, s. Nathaniel & Jerusha, b. Apr. 9, 1764 | 1 | 56 |
| Shubael, m. Mrs. Rachel **BRADFORD**, Dec. 5, 1792, by | 3 | 20 |

| | Vol. | Page |
|---|---|---|
| **LOWRY, LOWREE,** (cont.) | | |
| Judah Kellogg, J. P. | 3 | 20 |
| **LUDDINGTON**, Philip C., m. Mary L. **BROWN**, b. of Cornwall, Oct. 17, 1820, by Rev. Timothy Stone | 2 | 48 |
| William S., m. Clarissa Isabella **EDSON**, of Cornwall, Jan. 9, 1821, by Rev. Walter Smith, of the 2nd Church | 2 | 49 |
| **LYMAN**, Frederick, of Goshen, m. Julia L. **GOLD**, of Cornwall, Sept. 14, 1843, by Rev. Ephraim Lyman | 3 | 67 |
| **McALISTER**, Jane, d. William, farmer, ae 28 & Elizabeth, ae 27, res. Sharon, b. May 2, 1850 | 3 | 108-9 |
| **MacALPINE**, Elizabeth, m. Levi **PIERCE**, Aug. 8, 1764, by Rev. Hezekiah Gold | 1 | 97 |
| **McCORMICK, MacCORMICK**, John, b. Canaan, res. Cornwall, d. Aug. 20, 1850, ae 2 1/2 | 3 | 112-13 |
| John, s. John, laborer & Bridget, b. Jan. 24, 1851 | 3 | 116-17 |
| Mary, had, d. [ ], b. Feb. 1, 1851 | 3 | 116-17 |
| Mary Ann, d. John, b. May 12, 1849 | 3 | 102-3 |
| **McFARLAND**, James, m. May **MANSFIELD**, Apr. 11, 1853, by Ralph Smith | 3 | 125 |
| **McGAY**, Lawrence, of Dover, N. Y., m. Ann **CUNNINGHAM**, of Cornwall,Oct. 30, 1853,by Rev. Henry Burton, of Sharon | 3 | 124 |
| **McHOOD**, William, s. Joseph & Mary, b. July 6, 1785 | 3 | 24 |
| **McILVAINE**, Obadiah, m. Azuba Ann **HOPKINS**, Jan. 24, 1832, by Rev. William Andrews | 3 | 49 |
| **McMINTRY**, Orra Jane, d. Nov. 6, 1851, ae 11 | 3 | 120-1 |
| **McMULLEN**, Michael, laborer, b. Cornwall, Hollow, res, Cornwall, d. July 3, 1851 | 3 | 120-1 |
| **McNEAL**, Elizabeth, m. Adna **ALLEN**, Dec. 6, 1792, by Jacob Brush, Elder. Witnesses: Asaph Emmons & Philip Wayer | 3 | 20 |
| **MACQUAVER***, Easter, m. John **DIBBLE**, Apr. 30, 1759, by Rev. H. Gold *(Arnold copy has **MAGUIRER**") | 1 | 34 |
| **McSWENEY**, Thomas, m. Caroline S. **PRITCHARD**, July 10, 1842, by Harley Goodwin | 3 | 65 |
| **MAGUIRER***, Easter, m. John **DIBBLE**, Apr. 30, 1759, by Rev. H. Gold. *("**MACQUAVER**" in Starr's Book) | 1 | 34 |
| **MAIN**, Alfred, s. Colvin, b. May 4, 1849 | 3 | 102-3 |
| **MAIZE**, Phebe Ann, of Cornwall, m. Darwin **ELLIS**, of Waterbury, Sept. 16, 1849, by Rev. Lewis Gunn | 3 | 82 |
| **MALLORY**, Almon Caton, s. Elisha Bradley & Tabiatha, b. Oct. 8, 1807 | 3 | 17 |
| David, of Warren, m. Maria **JOHNSON**, of Cornwall, Nov. 22, 1824, by Rev. Timothy Stone | 2 | 59 |
| David, d. June 1, 1841, ae 87 y. | 3 | 60 |
| David Clark, s. [Elisha Bradley & Tabitha], b. Aug. 16, 1809 | 3 | 17 |
| Edwin, s. Ezra & Nicy, b. July 31, 1804 | 3 | 15 |
| Eliakim, m. Mrs. Olive **JOHNSON**, Dec. 20, 1785, by Rev. John Cornwell | 2 | 16 |
| | 2 | 19 |

| | Vol. | Page |
|---|---|---|
| **MALLORY**, (cont.) | | |
| Elisha Bradley, s. Eliakim & Olive, b. Nov. 15, 1786 | 2 | 19 |
| Elisha Bradley, m. Mrs. Tabitha **WADSWORTH**, Sept. 25, 1806, by Rev. Josiah Hawes, of the 2nd Ch. | 3 | 3 |
| Ezra, m. Necy **BRISTOL**, b. of Cornwall, Sept. 22, 1803, by Rev. Henry Christie | 3 | 32 |
| Hannah, of Stratford, m. Reuben **SQUIERES**, of Fairfield, May [ ], 1738, by Rev. Jedediah Mills, of Stratford | 1 | 27 |
| Harriet Elizabeth, d. Elisha Bradley & Tabitha, b. Sept. 20, 1812 | 3 | 34 |
| Olive, d. Eliakim & Olive, b. Jan. 23, 1789 | 2 | 25 |
| Sarah, w. Eliakim, d. June 22, 1785 | 2 | 11 |
| **MALTBY**, Huldah, m. Eber J. **JOHNSON**, b. of Cornwall, Nov. 7, 1838, by N. M. Urmstom | 3 | 54 |
| **MANSFIELD**, Charles, of Canaan, m. Mary Ann **PRINDLE**, of Cornwall, Jan. 1, 1837, by Charles Prentice | 3 | 42 |
| Mary, m. James **McFARLAND**, Apr. 11, 1853, by Ralph Smith | 3 | 125 |
| Punderson, farmer, ae 31 & Sela, ae 27, had s. [ ], b. Apr. 8, 1851 | 3 | 114-15 |
| **MAPLES**, Abigail, m. James **STERLING**, Jr., Feb. 6, 1803, by Judah Kellogg, J. P. | 3 | 32 |
| **MAREMAN**, [see under **MERRIMAN**] | | |
| **MARKHAM**, Chester, m. Martha **DAY**, Nov. 22, 1828, by Rev. Walter Smith, of the North Ch. | 3 | 1 |
| **MARSH**, Abigail, d. [Dr. Isaac & Polly], b. Apr. 29, 1815; d. June 2, 1832, in the 18th y. of her age | 3 | 60 |
| Almira, d. [Dr. Isaac & Polly], b. Dec. 9, 1812; d. Apr. 11, 1837, in the 25th y. of her age | 3 | 60 |
| Anne, d. [Dr. Isaac & Polly], b. June 16, 1805; d. Nov. 18, 1829, in the 25th y. of her age | 3 | 60 |
| Isaac, Dr., b. Feb. 18, 1777; d. Sept. 1, 1829, in the 53rd y. of his age | 3 | 60 |
| Laura, d. [Dr. Isaac & Polly], b. Aug. 1, 1807; d. Jan. 11, 1829 in the 22nd y. of her age | 3 | 60 |
| Mary, d. [Dr. Isaac & Polly], b. Oct. 11, 1810; d. May 19, 1930, in the 20th y. of her age | 3 | 60 |
| Nehemiah, of Canaan, m. Ruth **BELL**, of Cornwall, June 10, 1795, by Judah Kellogg, J. P. | 3 | 21 |
| Polly, w. [Dr. Isaac], b. Nov. 4, 1781; d. Mar. 19, 1843, in the 62nd y. of her age | 3 | 60 |
| William, of Goshen, m. Emeline **BRADFORD**, of Cornwall, Jan. 18, 1821, by Joseph Harvey | 2 | 49 |
| **MARSHALL**, Sidney H., of Salisbury, m. Lucinda S. **COLE**, of Cornwall, Sept. 14, 1847, at the house of Irad Cole, by Rev. Joshua L. Maynard, of the North Cong. Ch. | 3 | 76 |
| **MARVIN**, Almira, m. Edmund **COLE**, b. of Cornwall, May 29, 1822, by Rev. Walter Smith, of the 2nd Church | 2 | 53 |

| | Vol. | Page |
|---|---|---|
| **MARVIN**, (cont.) | | |
| Caroline, m. John **BROOKS**, Sept. 20, 1837, by Rev. William W. Andrews, of Kent | 3 | 56 |
| Chauncey, m. Lois **BONNEY**, b. of Cornwall, Jan. 30, 1833, by Rev. Silas Ambler | 3 | 35 |
| Cynthia L., m. Franklin **MARVIN**, Dec. 5, 1853, by T. S. Gold, J. P. | 3 | 124 |
| Cynthia Louisa, d. [Cyrus L. & Clemena A.], b. May 6, 1834 | 3 | 51 |
| Franklin, m. Cynthia L. **MARVIN**, Dec. 5, 1853, by T. S. Gold, J. P. | 3 | 124 |
| Henry Porter, s. Cyrus L. & Clemena A., b. May 8, 1833 | 3 | 51 |
| Lovicey, m. Ezra **PHILLIPS**, July 9, 1825, by Rev. Asa Tallmadge, of the Bapt. Ch. | 2 | 65 |
| Sarah, of Cornwall, m. Cyrus H. **NORCUTT**, of Johnson, O., Mar. 15, 1848, by Rev. Hiram Day | 3 | 78 |
| **MATHER**, Abner, s. Joseph & Anne, b. Jan. 10, 1752 | 1 | 25 |
| Elisha, s. Joseph & Anne, b. Dec. 7, 1757 | 1 | 25 |
| Jerusha, d. Joseph & Ann, b. Nov. 3, 1755 | 1 | 25 |
| Joseph, s. Joseph & Anne, b. Nov. 5, 1750 | 1 | 25 |
| **MAY**, Bette, m. Asahel **ALVARD**, Sept. 19, 1765, by Rev. Hezekiah Gold | 1 | 63 |
| Hannah, m. James **STERLING**, June 28, 1767, by Thomas Russell, J. P. | 1 | 78 |
| Mary, m. Levi **BONNEY**, Oct. 4, 1764, by Rev. Hezekiah Gold | 1 | 58 |
| **MAYNARD**, Amelia C., d. Joshua L. H. & Abigail U. B., b. June 7, 1842 | 3 | 69 |
| Francis A., s. [Joshua L. H. & Abigail U. B.], b. June 27, 1843 | 3 | 69 |
| Jane R., of Norwich, m. Theodore D. **WHALEY**, of Montville, Jan. 25, 1847, by Rev. Joshua L. Maynard, of the North Cong. Ch., at his house | 3 | 74 |
| Joshua L., Rev. m. Thankful S. **ROGERS**, of Underhill, Vt., Oct. 20, 1847, by Harley Goodwin | 3 | 76 |
| Robert Leland, s. Joshua L., b. Oct. 20, 1846 | 3 | 95 |
| **MEACHAM**, Joseph E., m. Frances J. **STANTON**, Oct. 14, 1834, by Rev. William Andrews | 3 | 38 |
| **MEAD**, Benjamin F., s. David & Minerva, b. May 27, 1826 | 2 | 64 |
| David, m. Minerva **DIBBLE**, Apr. 3, 1824, by Rev. Asa Tallmadge, of the Bap. Ch. | 2 | 65 |
| Elkanah, m. Cinderilla **DIBBLE**, b. of Cornwall, Jan. 7, 1828, by Rev. Silas Ambler, of the Bap. Ch. | 2 | 68 |
| Mary, of Sharon, m. William H. **PARISH**, of Cornwall, Aug. 8, 1852, by Rev. Henry Burton, of Sharon | 3 | 124 |
| **MERCER**, Cycel, laborer, b. France, res. Cornwall, d. Jan. 23, 1849, ae 27 | 3 | 106-7 |
| **[MERRILL], MERRIL**, Lydia*, of Hartford, m. Jonathan **HURLBURT**, of Cornwall, Jan. 1, [1754], by Thomas | | |

| | Vol. | Page |
|---|---|---|
| **[MERRILL], MERRIL**, (cont.) | | |
| Hosmer, J. P. *(Arnold Copy has "Lydia **MERRIT**") | 1 | 21 |
| **[MERRIMAN], MAREMAN, MORREMAN, MOREMAN**, | | |
| Miles, of Sharon, m. Milleseneth **SEELEY**, of Cornwall, Jan. 22, 1825, by Rev. John Lovejoy, of the M. E. Ch. | 2 | 63 |
| Nathan, s. Titus & Sarah, b. Oct. 20, 1769 | 1 | 92 |
| Titus, m. Sarah **SIMMONS**, Nov. 13, 1768, by Rev. Hezekiah Gold | 1 | 88 |
| **MERRIT, MERRET**, Lydia*, of Hartford, m. Jonathan **HURLBURT**, of Cornwall, Jan. 1, [1754], by Thomas Hosmer, J. P. *("Lydia **MERRIL**" in Starr's book) | 1 | 21 |
| Rebeccah, of Stamford, m. John **DIBBLE**, Dec. 18, 1753, by Rev. Noah Wells, of Stamford | 1 | 20 |
| **MERRY**, Hannah, m. Matthew **MILLARD**, Aug. 22, 1765, by Joel Bordwell | 1 | 65 |
| **MERWIN**, Emily Elizabeth, d. Edwin A., farmer, ae 43 & Betsey, ae 42, res. Cornwall Hollow, b. Jan. 25, 1849 | 3 | 98-9 |
| Lucy, m. Daniel N. **BRINSMADE**, Mar. 19, 1806, by Rev. Timothy Stone | 3 | 3 |
| Mary, m. Rev. Timothy **STONE**, b. of Cornwall, Jan. 26, 1804, by E. Porter | 3 | 32 |
| Mary A., of Cornwall, m. Henry L. **HOW**, of Canaan, Nov. 28, 1850, at the house of Edwin Merwin, by Rev. Joshua L. Maynard, of the North Cong. Ch. | 3 | 96 |
| Mary A., ae 21, b. Oswell, Rutland Co., Vt., res. Goshen, m. Henry L. **HOWE**, carpenter, ae 22, b. Canaan, res. Goshen, Nov. 28, 1850, by Rev. J. L. Maynard | 3 | 118-19 |
| **MESSENGER, MESSINGER**, Andrew, twin with Roderick, s. Samuell & Mabell, b. Mar. 11, 1741/2 | 1 | 2 |
| Roderick, twin with Andrew, s. Samuell & Mabell, b. Mar. 11, 1741/2 | 1 | 2 |
| Samuell & Mabell, had s. [ ], b. Mar. 18, 1739/40 | 1 | 2 |
| **METCALF**, Lorenzo, of South Adams, Mass., m. Olive **SCOVILL**, of Cornwall, Sept. 22, 1844, by Rev. Joshua L. Maynard, of the North Cong. Ch. | 3 | 70 |
| **MILES**, Augustus, of Albany, N. Y., m. Mary **DIBBLE**, of Cornwall, Nov. 8, 1829, by Rev. Silas Ambler | 3 | 45 |
| Patty, d. Capt. John, d. July 26, [1837], ae 40 | 3 | 43 |
| Patty, see also Polly | | |
| Polly, d. [John & Eunice], b. July 3, 1797 | 3 | 26 |
| Polly, see also Patty | | |
| Sharlot*, d. John & Eunice, b. Oct. 7, 1795 *(This spelling by particular directions of her parents) | 3 | 26 |
| Stephen, m. Delia M. **HOLLY**, Nov. 19, 1829, by Rev. Walter Smith, of the North Ch. | 3 | 45 |
| **MILLARD**, [see also **MILLER**], Adelia, of Cornwall, m. Nathan **SKIFF**, of Kent, Nov. 18, 1828, by Rev. L. P. Hickok, of the Cong. Ch. in Kent | 3 | 1 |

| | Vol. | Page |
|---|---|---|
| **MILLARD**, (cont.) | | |
| Amanda, m. Benjamin **KILBOURNE**, July 1, 1821, by Rev. Walter Smith, of the 2nd Church | 2 | 50 |
| Asa, m. Aurilla **WILSON**, b. of Cornwall, [Nov.] 27, [1822], by Rev. A. Derthick | 2 | 54 |
| Azuba, w. Joel, d. Jan. 5, 1814, ae 42 | 2 | 39 |
| Benajah, of Cornwall, m. Rebeckah **ROBERDS**, of Sharon, June 7, 1765, by John Ransom, J. P. | 1 | 70 |
| Benajah, s. [Benajah & Rebeccah], b. Apr. 3, 1773 | 1 | 109 |
| Benajah, d. Apr. 3, 1776 | LR3 | 7 |
| Charles, s. John, Jr. & Christiana, b. Feb. 19, 1762 | 1 | 46 |
| Charlotte L., of Cornwall, m. Rollin S. **WOOSTER**, of Litchfield, Jan. 30, 1854, by Rev. Henry Burton, of Sharon | 3 | 124 |
| Chloe, d. [Nathan & Submit], b. Apr. 21, 1764 | 1 | 84 |
| C[h]loe, d. [Nathan & Submit], b. Apr. 21, 1764 | 2 | 9 |
| Chloe, d. John, Jr. & Christiania, b. Jan. 10, 1776 | LR3 | 10 |
| Dianthe, d. John & Christiania, b. Mar. 30, 1778 | LR4 | 17 |
| Edmund, s. Matthew & Hannah, b. Feb. 14, 1768 | 1 | 79 |
| Elizabeth, m. Israel **DIBBLE**, Mar. 3, 1763, by Rev. H. Gold | 1 | 50 |
| Harvey, s. [Rufus & Rachel], b. Oct. 19, 1793 | 2 | 27 |
| Heman, s. Benajah & Rebeckah, b. June 16, 1765 | 1 | 70 |
| Ira, s. [John & Christiania], b. Nov. 12, 1780 | LR4 | 17 |
| Ira, s. John, Jr. & Christiania, b. [ ] | 2 | 10 |
| Jason, s. Mathew & Hannah, b. May 17, 1766 | 1 | 74 |
| Jerusha, d. John, Jr. & Christiania, b. Feb. 24, 1773 | 1 | 109 |
| Joel, s. Joshua & Lydia, b. Aug. 11, 1765 | 1 | 66 |
| Joel, s. [Nathan & Submit], b. Feb. 23, 1767 | 1 | 84 |
| Joel, s. [Nathan & Submit], b. Feb. 23, 1767 | 2 | 9 |
| John, Jr., m. Christian **HAMBLETON**, May 21, 1761, by Rev. H. Gold | 1 | 40 |
| John, s. Benajah & Rebeccah, b. Jan. 12, 1771 | 1 | 109 |
| Joshua, of Cornwall, m. Mrs. Lydiah **YOUNG**, of Sharon, Mar. 6, 1765, by Daniel Griswold, J. P. | 1 | 63 |
| Lawrany, d. Benajah & Rebeccah, b. June 21, 1767 | 1 | 108 |
| Lydia, d. [Nathan & Submit], b. Dec. 13, 1770 | 2 | 9 |
| Lydia, m. Samuel **REXFORD**, b. of Cornwall, Nov. 6, 1788, by Rev. Hezekiah Gold | 2 | 36 |
| Lydia, of Cornwall, m. Ethel **NORTH**, of Torrington, Dec. 8, 1824, by Rev. Walter Smith, of the 2nd Cong. Ch. | 2 | 59 |
| Matthew, d. Sept. 24, 1749 | 1 | 9 |
| Matthew, m. Hannah **MERRY**, Aug. 22, 1765, by Joel Bordwell | 1 | 65 |
| Nathan, m. Submit **RILEY**, June 24, 1761, by Rev. Hezekiah Gold | 1 | 85 |
| Philo, s. John, Jr. & Christiania, b. Apr. 27, 1768 | 1 | 85 |
| Roswell, s. John, Jr. & Christiania, b. Mar. 22, 1766 | 1 | 71 |
| Roswell, s. Rufus & Rachel, b. Apr. 9, 1791 | 2 | 27 |

| | Vol. | Page |
|---|---|---|
| **MILLARD**, (cont.) | | |
| Rufus, s. John & Catharine, b. Feb. 12, 1764 | 1 | 54 |
| Russell, s. [John, Jr. & Christiania], b. Apr. 15, 1785 | 2 | 10 |
| Russell, m. Elvira H. **EMMONS**, b. of Sharon, Oct. 10, 1847, by Samuel Weeks | 3 | 74 |
| Russell, Jr., blacksmith, ae 22, b. Cornwall, res. Sharon, m. Elvira **EMMONS**, ae 22, b. Sharon, res. Sharon, Oct. 10, 1847, by Rev. Samuel Weeks | 3 | 90-1 |
| Sarah, d. John, Jr. & Christiania, b. Apr. 19, 1770 | 1 | 93 |
| Submit, d. Nathan & Submit, b. June 5, 1762 | 1 | 84 |
| Submit, d. Nathan & Submit, b. June 5, 1762 | 2 | 9 |
| **MILLER**, [see also **MILLARD**], Ebenezer, s. Matthew & Mary, d. July 27, 17[ ] | 1 | 2 |
| Ebenezer, s. Matthew & Mary, b. July 26, 1745 | 1 | 2 |
| Esther, d. Matthew & Mary, b. Oct. 11, 1742 | 1 | 5 |
| James, s. Henry & Elizabeth, b. Mar. 15, 1771 | 1 | 98 |
| Lydia, of Sharon, m. Benjamin **DIBBLE**, Jr., of Cornwall, Mar. 8, 1753, by Solomon Palmer | 1 | 19 |
| Mary, d. Matthew & Mary, b. June 14, 1744; d. same day | 1 | 2 |
| Matthew, s. Matthew & Phebe, d. July 20, 1743 | 1 | 5 |
| Mehetable, m. Benoni **PECK**, Apr. 7, 1757, by Hezekiah Gold | 1 | 30 |
| **MILLET***, Philena, Mrs., m. Seymour **MURRY**, Mar. 8, 1781, by Jonathan Huntington, J. P. *("**WILLET**" in Starr's book) | 2 | 2 |
| **MILLS**, Peter M., of Chester, N. H., m. Martha **JEWEL**, of Cornwall, Aug. 18, 1833, by Rev. Levi Peck, of the Bap. Ch. | 3 | 36 |
| **MINER**, Alura A., m. Julius B. **HARRISON**, b. of Cornwall, June 4, 1843, by Rev. Adam Reed | 3 | 66 |
| Angenette, of Cornwall, m. Joseph B. **PALMER**, of Goshen, July 3, 1844, at the house of Darius Miner, by Rev. Joshua L. Maynard | 3 | 70 |
| Charles, s. [Darius & Patty], b. Oct. 3, 1822 | 2 | 52 |
| Darius, of Salisbury, m. Armirel **SANDERS**, of Cornwall, Sept. 27, 1792, by Judah Kellogg, J. P. | 3 | 8 |
| Darius, s. [Darius & Patty], b. Sept. 15, 1820 | 2 | 52 |
| Darius D., m. Nancy E. **WADSWORTH**, b. of Cornwall, Oct. 10, 1842, by Rev. Joshua L. Maynard, of the North Cong. Ch. | 3 | 65 |
| Harriet, d. [Darius & Patty], b. Oct. 24, 1818 | 2 | 52 |
| Harriet A., m. Sidney A. **WASHBURN**, Sept. 8, 1836, by Rev. Walter Smith, of the 2nd Cong. Ch. | 3 | 42 |
| John, s. Juther, Jr., farmer, ae 32 & Ellen, ae 25, b. Nov. 30, 1849 | 3 | 110-11 |
| Lettis, m. Abraham **HOCHKIN**, Jr., Mar. 14, 1793, by Judah Kellogg, J. P. | 3 | 20 |
| Luther, Jr., m. Ellen **TODD**, Apr. 8, 1846, by R. K. Reynolds | 3 | 72 |
| Luther, Jr., farmer, ae 20 & Ellen J., ae 23, had child b. Feb. | | |

| | Vol. | Page |
|---|---|---|
| **MINER**, (cont.) | | |
| 19, 1848 | 3 | 88-9 |
| Mary A., m. Benjamin P. **JOHNSON**, b. of Cornwall, Sept. 3, 1839, by N. M. Urmston | 3 | 58 |
| Mary Anne, d. [Darius & Patty], b. Apr. 27, 1816 | 2 | 52 |
| Mary E., m. Joseph **NORTHROP**, b. of Cornwall, Sept. 4, 1841, by Rev. J. L. Maynard, of the North Cong. Ch. | 3 | 63 |
| Patty, d. Darius & Patty, b. Mar. 22, 1814 | 2 | 52 |
| Robert T., m. Lydia M. **BALDWIN**, b. of Cornwall, Nov. 17, 1842, by Rev. Joshua L. Maynard, of the North Cong. Ch. | 3 | 65 |
| **MITCHELL**, [see also **WITCHELL**], Ann, m. David **BALDWIN**, on or about Sept. 10, 1741, by Joseph Bird. Witnesses: John Catlin & Isaac Bissell | 1 | 42 |
| **MONROE**, Charles, m. Lois **WELCH**, b. of Warren, July 28, [1823], by Joshua Williams | 2 | 57 |
| **MOORE**, John, s. Robert, laborer, ae 23 & Anna, ae 23, b. Dec. 14, 1850 | 3 | 114-15 |
| **MOREHOUSE**, Adelia, m. Julius **BLAKE**, b. of Cornwall, Feb. 26, 1826, by Rev. Timothy Stone | 2 | 63 |
| **MOREMAN**, [see under **MERRIMAN**] | | |
| **MOREY, MORY, MORRY**, [see also **MURRY**], John, s. [Asa & Elizabeth], b. Aug. 29, 1772 | 1 | 110 |
| Sarah, d. Asa & Elizabeth, b. Apr. 11, 1771 | 1 | 110 |
| **MORREMAN**, [see under **MERRIMAN**] | | |
| **MORRIS**, Azubah, of Goshen, m. Samuel **SEELEY**, of Cornwall, Sept. 24, 1843, by Rev. Thomas Edwards, of the M. E. Ch. | 3 | 67 |
| Lanson Lewis, s. Lanson & Lucy, b. Dec. 3, 1814 | 2 | 40 |
| Sally, m. Ezra **TAYLOR**, b. of Cornwall, Nov. 17, 1822, by Rev. David Miller, of the M. E. Ch. | 2 | 54 |
| **MORSE**, [see also **MOSS**], Milo, m. Sophia **MORSE**, Apr. 14, 1827, by Rev. Timothy Stone, of the 1st Ch. | 2 | 66 |
| Sophia, m. Milo **MORSE**, Apr. 14, 1827, by Rev. Timothy Stone, of the 1st Ch. | 2 | 66 |
| **MORY**, [see under **MOREY**] | | |
| **MOSS**, [see also **MORSE**, Anna, d. Isaac & Anna, b. Feb. 13, 1748/9 | 1 | 7 |
| Asahel, d. Aug. 11, 1763 | 1 | 59 |
| Israel, s. Israel & Lydia, d. Sept. 21, 1750, in the 19th y. of his age | 1 | 11 |
| Israel, d. Apr. 15, 1757 | 1 | 28 |
| Susanna, d. Isaac & Anna, b. May 10, 1751 | 1 | 14 |
| **MUNGER**,Rhoda,of Litchfield, m. Warren **PRINDLE**,of Cornwall, Dec. 10, 1837,by Thomas Benedict, of Torrington | 3 | 53 |
| **MUNSON, MONSON**, Frederick, Rev. of Greenwich, m. Clarissa A. **CLARK**, of Cornwall, June 28, 1848, at the house of William Clark, by Rev. Joshua L. Maynard, of the | | |

| | Vol. | Page |
|---|---|---|
| **MUNSON, MONSON**, (cont.) North Cong. Ch. | 3 | 81 |
| Frederick, clergyman, ae 28, b. Bethlem, res. Greenwich, m. Clarissa A. **CLARK**, ae 27, b. Cornwall, June 28, 1848, by Joshua L. Maynard | 3 | 90-1 |
| **MURPHY**, Hugh, wood sawer, had child, b. [ ] | 3 | 108-9 |
| **MURRY**, [see also **MOREY**], John, s. Seymour & Philena, b. Mar. 9, 1782 | 2 | 3 |
| Seymour, m. Mrs. Philena **MILLET**, Mar. 8, 1781, by Jonathan Huntington, J. P. | 2 | 2 |
| **NAIL**, [see also **NEAL**], Egbert B., of Unionvill, Dutchess Cty., N. Y., m. Anna **WRIGHT**, of Cornwall, Aug. 27, 1833, by Daniel Coe | 3 | 36 |
| **NEAL**, [see also **NAIL**], Hiram, m. Mary **BIERCE**, Mar. 11, 1830, by Rev. Walter Smith, of the North Ch. | 3 | 45 |
| Hiram, m. Abigail **BEIRCE**, Sept. 16, 1832, by Rev. Silas Ambler | 3 | 50 |
| **NELSON**, Elijah, s. Sarah **BREWSTER**, b. Jan. 1, 1799 | 3 | 15 |
| **NETTLETON**, Caroline, of Cornwall, m. Sturgis **BLINN**, of Sharon, Nov. 27, 1839, by Erastus Doty | 3 | 58 |
| Cynthia L., m. Alfred **HART**, Oct. 29, 1833, by Rev. Walter Smith, of the North Cong. Ch. | 3 | 36 |
| Emily, of Cornwall, m. John C. **NORTON**, of New Marlborough, Mass., Sept. 24, 1842, by Rev. Joshua L. Maynard, of the North Cong. Ch. | 3 | 65 |
| Jane E., Mrs. of Cornwall, m. Benjamin **LAMTON**, of Goshen, Jan. 20, 1848, by Rev. Alfred Yates | 3 | 78 |
| Jane T., ae 22, res. Cornwall, m. Benjamin **LAWTON**, farmer, ae 22, b. Goshen, res. Goshen, Jan. 12, 1848, by Alfred Gates | 3 | 90-1 |
| Jehersa, of Cornwall, m. Fowler **SPERRY**, of Bethany, Oct. 24, 1843, by Rev. Joshua L. Maynard, of the North Cong. Ch. | 3 | 67 |
| Paulina, m. Milan **HART**, May 1, 1832, by Rev. Walter Smith, of the North Cong. Ch. | 3 | 49 |
| Rosalinda, m. Thomas F. **WHITING**, [ ], by Rev. C. P. Wilson, of the Bap. Ch., in Amenia, N. Y. (Recorded June 23, 1827) | 2 | 67 |
| Sarah A., of Cornwall, m. Rev. E. J. **SMITH**, of Springfield, Mass., Jan. 14, 1849, by Rev. Alfred Gates | 3 | 82 |
| Sarah A., ae 24, res. Cornwall, m. Rev. Edward A. **JENCKES**, ae 27, b. Springfield, Mass., res. Cornwall, Jan. 14, 1849, by Alfred Gates | 3 | 104-5 |
| **NEWBURY**, Amasa S., m. Cornelia **PANGMAN**, Jan. 15, 1829, by Rev. William Andrews | 3 | 1 |
| **NEWCOMB**, Hannah, of Kent, m. William **TANNER**, of Cornwall, Mar. 23, 1749, by Rev. Cyrus Marsh, of Kent | 1 | 9 |

| | Vol. | Page |
|---|---|---|
| **NEWCOMB**, (cont.) | | |
| Oliver, s. Benjamin & Hannah, b. Apr. 13, 1750 | 1 | 16 |
| **NEWEL[L]**, Lucy A., of Goshen, m. William H. **CATLIN**, of Cornwall, Nov. 19, 1843, by Rev. Joshua L. Maynard, of the North Cong. Ch. | 3 | 67 |
| **NEWPORT**, Jacob, m. Susan **JOHNSON**, Nov. 18, 1820, by Rev. Timothy Stone | 2 | 48 |
| **NEWTON**, Frederick, s. James, farmer & Orra, res. Gt. Hill, Cornwall, b. Feb. 24, 1848 | 3 | 86-7 |
| James, m. Orra **CALKINS**, Dec. 23, 1837, by Rev. Walter Smith, of the North Cong. Ch. | 3 | 53 |
| Jane Bell, d. Samuel S., clergyman, ae 29 & Abigail, ae 28, res. Sharon, now N. Milford, b. May 27, 1850 | 3 | 108-9 |
| Nancy, d. James, farmer, ae 42 & Orra, ae 32, b. Oct. 24, 1849 | 3 | 110-11 |
| Samuel S., peddler, ae 27, res. Cornwall, m. Abby **FRINK**, ae 26, Dec. 16, 1847, by Rev. Hiram Day | 3 | 90-1 |
| Sarah, Mrs., m. Nehemiah **BURTON**, Oct. 31, 1799, by Henry Christie, Dea. | 2 | 24 |
| Sarah, d. Samuel S., farmer, ae 28 & Abby, ae 27, b. Jan. 23, 1849 | 3 | 100-1 |
| **NICHOLS**, George, farmer, ae 28, res. Hamilton, N. Y., m. Clarissa **CLARK**, ae 22, res. Cornwall, Feb. 26, 1849, by Joshua L. Maynard | 3 | 104-5 |
| Hanford, m. Sarah Ann **CLARK**, July 5, 1832, by Rev. William Andrews | 3 | 50 |
| Hanford, of Georgetown, N. Y., m. Clarrena A. **CLARK**, of Cornwall, Feb. 26, 1849, at the house of O. B. Clark, by Rev. Joshua L. Maynard, of the North Cong. Ch. | 3 | 81 |
| Ira, of Trumbull, m. Bethiah **GOODYEAR**, of Cornwall, Jan. 14, 1823, by Stephen Mason | 2 | 55 |
| **NICKERSON**, [see also **HICKINSON**], Aurelia, m. William **DAKIN**, Feb. 6, 1853, by Ralph Smith | 3 | 125 |
| Charlotte, ae 17, res. Cornwall, m. Giles **PALMER**, carpenter, ae 20, res. Cornwall, May 21, 1848, by Hiram Day | 3 | 90-1 |
| Charlotte Lorinda, m. Silas A. **PALMER**, b. of Cornwall, May 24, 1848, by Rev. Hiram Day | 3 | 79 |
| Helen, d. Orson, farmer, ae [ ] & Julia, b. Apr. 20, 1849 | 3 | 100-1 |
| Jane, m. Wakeman P. **DIBBLE**, of Cornwall, Dec. 31, 1843, by Rev. Joshua L. Maynard, of the North Cong. Ch. | 3 | 68 |
| Julia Ann, m. Elisha **FORD**, Dec. 31, 1843, by Rev. Joshua L. Maynard, of the North Cong. Ch. | 3 | 68 |
| Orson, m. Julia **DIBBLE**, b. of Cornwall, Jan. 17, 1847, by Rev. Hiram Day | 3 | 74 |
| Sarah A., of West Cornwall, m. Sergant E. **HALL**, of Perryville, N. Y., July 2, 1854, by R. M. S. Pease. Int. Pub. | 3 | 126 |
| Smith, m. Jane **BALDWIN**, Feb. 18, 1846, by Rev. K. K. | | |

| | Vol. | Page |
|---|---|---|
| **NICKERSON**, (cont.) | | |
| Reynolds | 3 | 72 |
| **NODINE**, Harriet M., m. Alvan **HART**, b. of Cornwall, May 12, 1851, by Harley Goodwin | 3 | 123 |
| Robert C., of Springfield, N. J., m. Clarissa **HART**, of Cornwall, Sept. 11, 1839, by Rev. J. C. Hart, of Springfield | 3 | 58 |
| **NORCUTT**, Cyrus H., of Johnson, O., m. Sarah **MARVIN**, of Cornwall, Mar. 15, 1848, by Rev. Hiram Day | 3 | 78 |
| **NORTH**, Burritt B., m. Maria L. **PEIRCE**, May 31, 1832, by Rev. William Andrews | 3 | 50 |
| Ethel, of Torrington, m. Lydia **MILLARD**, of Cornwall, Dec. 8, 1824, by Rev. Walter Smith, of the 2nd Cong. Ch. | 2 | 59 |
| George P., s. Barrett B. & Maria, b. Apr. 13, 1833 | 3 | 47 |
| Joseph, physician, b. Goshen, res. Cornwall, d. Sept. 23, 1848, ae 74 | 3 | 106-7 |
| Mary M., m. Chester G. **BIRGE**, Sept. 26, 1827, by Rev. William Andrews | 2 | 67 |
| Morilla, d. Dr. Joseph & Abigail, d. Jan. 28, 1802, ae 4 | 3 | 10 |
| Pascal, s. Barritt B. & Mana, b. Mar. 7, 1836 | 3 | 57 |
| Rowland J., s. Barrett B., physician, ae 42 & Maria L., ae 39, b. Mar. 17, 1848 | 3 | 84-5 |
| Thomas L., s. Joseph, farmer, ae 39 & Mary T., ae 24, b. Feb. 23, 1848 | 3 | 88-9 |
| William B., s. Burrit B. & Maria, b. June 22, 1834 | 3 | 39 |
| **NORTHROP**, Albert, m. Flora **JUDD**, b. of Cornwall, Jan. 30, 1825, by Rev. Timothy Stone, of the 1st Ch. | 2 | 59 |
| Amanda, d. [Joseph & Charity], b. Jan. 6, 1801 | 2 | 34 |
| Amanda, d. Joseph, d. June 9, 1809 | 2 | 33 |
| Eliza, d. Joseph & Charity, b. Oct. 27, 1798 | 2 | 34 |
| Hiram B., m. Julia M. **SMITH**, b. of Cornwall, May 2, 1841, by Rev. Brown Emerson | 3 | 61 |
| Hiram Bishop, s. Drake, b. Mar. 4, 1804 | 2 | 47 |
| Joseph, m. Mary E. **MINER**, b. of Cornwall, Sept. 4, 1841, by Rev. J. L. Maynard, of North Cong. Ch. | 3 | 63 |
| Mary Ann, d. [Joseph & Charity], b. Aug. 29, 1808 | 2 | 34 |
| Morris, s. [Joseph & Charity], b. Mar. 16, 1803 | 2 | 34 |
| Naomi, w. Dea. [ ], d. June 30, 1840, ae 78 | 3 | 60 |
| Rebeckah, m. William **CLARK**, Oct. 16, 1807, by Rev. Timothy Stone | 2 | 37 |
| Sally B., m. John **RIDGE**, of the Cherokee Nation, Jan. 27, 1824, by Rev. Walter Smith, of the 2nd Cong. Ch. | 2 | 58 |
| **NORTON**, [see also **ORTON**], Augustus F., m. Eliza M. **ROGERS**, Nov. 12, 1834, by Rev. Walter Smith, of the North Cong. Ch. | 3 | 38 |
| Elisha B., m. Almira **TUPPER**, b. of Cornwall, Mar. 16, 1829, by Rev. Silas Ambler | 3 | 44 |

| | Vol. | Page |
|---|---|---|
| **NORTON**, (cont.) | | |
| Hiram, of Fabius, N. Y., m. Eliza **PECK**, of Cornwall, Jan. 10, 1828, by Rev. L. P. Hickok, of the 1st Soc. of Kent | 2 | 68 |
| Isaac A., m. Rosetta **HOW** alias **BROWN**, May 3, 1827, by Rev. Asa Tallmadge, of the Bap. Ch. | 2 | 67 |
| John C., of New Marlborough, Mass., m. Emily **NETTLETON**, of Cornwall, Sept. 24, 1842, by Rev. Joshua L. Maynard, of the North Cong. Ch. | 3 | 65 |
| Jonathan T., m. L. Jane **CLARK**, May 11, 1852, at the U. S. Hotel, West Cornwall, by Rev. J. L. Maynard | 3 | 122 |
| Laura, m. Comfort **WHITE**, Dec. 3, 1827, by Rev. Walter Smith, of the North Ch. | 2 | 68 |
| **NOYCE**, Milton, m. Mary Ann **SEDGWICK**, Dec. 11, 1828, by Rev. Walter Smith, of the North Ch. | 3 | 1 |
| **O'CAIN**, John, of Sharon, m. Jennett **DEAN**, of Cornwall, Feb. 17, 1841, by Rev. John W. Salter | 3 | 61 |
| John, farmer, ae 32 & Jennett, ae 29, had child, b. May 3, 1848 | 3 | 86-7 |
| Lewis, of Sharon, m. Mary E. **BARNUM**, of Cornwall, May 9, 1847, by Rev. Alfred Gates | 3 | 74 |
| Rocelia Jeraldine, d. Dennis, farmer & Elizabeth, b. Mar. 6, 1848 | 3 | 86-7 |
| Wealthy, ae 20, res. Cornwall, m. John H. **CRANDALL**, farmer, ae 28, res. Cornwall, Dec. [ ], 1849, in York State | 3 | 112-13 |
| **O'HARA**, Margaret, of Cornwall, m. Nathan **PAYNE**, of Kent, Oct. 17, 1853, by Obadiah Bierce, J. P. | 3 | 123 |
| **ORTON**, [see also **NORTON**], David, s. Thomas & Hephzibah, b. Jan. 3, 1748/9 | 1 | 7 |
| Roger, s. Thomas & Hephzibah, b. Aug. 5, 1745 | 1 | 4 |
| Thomas, s. Thomas & Hephzibah, b. Feb. [ ], 1746/7 | 1 | 6 |
| **OSBORN**, Elbert, of Fairfield, m. Sarah **WRIGHT**, of Cromwell, Sept. 22, 1825, by Rev. John Lovejoy, of the M. E. Ch. | 2 | 62 |
| Elenda, m. Jerusha **BENEDICT**, Sept. 28, 1836, by Rev. William Andrews | 3 | 41 |
| **PACK**, [see under **PECK**] | | |
| **PAGE**, Albert, of Penyan Yates Cty., N. Y., m. Lucy **PERKINS**, of Cornwall, Feb. 19, 1838, by Rev. Daniel Baldwin | 3 | 54 |
| Lucy, m. Augustus **WHITCOMB**, b. of Cornwall, Oct. 20, 1852, by Rev. Luther B. Hart | 3 | 124 |
| **PALMER**, Abigail, d. Solomon & Abigail, b. Nov. [ ], 1742 | 1 | 17 |
| Abigail, ae 17, m. Jeremiah **EGGLESTON**, sash & blind maker, ae 20, b. Sharon, res. W. Cornwall, May 10, 1848, by Hiram Day | 3 | 90-1 |
| Abigail S., m. Jeremiah D. **EGLESTON**, b. of Cornwall, May 10, 1848, by Rev. Hiram Day | 3 | 79 |
| Abram, Dr., m. Jemima **HARTSHORN**, b. of Cornwall, Nov. | | |

| | Vol. | Page |
|---|---|---|
| **PALMER**, (cont.) | | |
| 13, 1823, by Rev. Walter Smith, of the 2nd Cong. Ch. | 2 | 57 |
| Alva, farmer, m. Delia **DEAN**, [ ], by Joshua L. Maynard | 3 | 90-1 |
| Alvin B., m. Delia A. **DEAN**, b. of Cornwall, Nov. 10, 1847, at the house of Betsey Dean, by Rev. Joshua L. Maynard, of the North Cong. Ch. | 3 | 76 |
| Amey, d. Solomon & Abigail, b. May 18, 1750 | 1 | 17 |
| Anna, d. Solomon & Abigail, b. Mar. 15, 1746 | 1 | 17 |
| Chiliab, s. Solomon & Abigail, b. Nov. 28, 1744; d. Apr. 28, 1745 | 1 | 17 |
| Edgar, s. Silas, farmer, ae 23 & Charlotte, ae 19, b. May 9, 1850 | 3 | 108-9 |
| Giles, carpenter, ae 20, res. Cornwall, m. Charlotte **NICKERSON**, ae 17, res. Cornwall, May 21, 1848, by Hiram Day | 3 | 90-1 |
| Irene, m. James **WADSWORTH**, b. of Cornwall, Feb. 16, 1774, at Canaan, by Rev. Daniel Farrand | LR3 | 7 |
| Jerusha, of Cornwall, m. Ladan* **BRADLEY**, of Goshen, Mar. 11, 1829, by Rev. Silas Ambler *("Leighton W." in Starr's book) | 3 | 1 |
| Joseph B., of Goshen, m. Angenette **MINER**, of Cornwall, July 3, 1844, by Rev. Joshua L. Maynard, at the house of Darius Miner | 3 | 70 |
| Julius Harvey, s. [Benjamin, Jr. & Betsey], b. May 30, 1812 | 3 | 28 |
| Lorenda E., of Cornwall, m. Frederick **LATHROP**, of New Milford, Sept. 4, 1853, by Ralph Smith | 3 | 125 |
| Sarah, d. Solomon & Abigail, b. May 15, 1748 | 1 | 17 |
| Silas A., m. Charlotte Lorinda **NICKERSON**, b. of Cornwall, May 24, 1848, by Rev. Hiram Day | 3 | 79 |
| Solomon, s. Solomon & Abigail, b. Nov. 1, 1740 | 1 | 17 |
| William Walden, s. Benjamin, Jr. & Betsey, b. Jan. 2, 1809 | 3 | 28 |
| **PANGBORN, PAGBORN**, [see also **PANGMAN**], Elizabeth, d. Joanna, b. June 5, 1750 | 1 | 15 |
| Hannah, d. Timothy & Deborah, b. Dec. 22, 1743 | 1 | 4 |
| Joanna, had d. Elizabeth, b. June 5, 1750 | 1 | 15 |
| Joanna, m. David **BALDWIN**, Aug. 14, 1751, by Solomon Palmer | 1 | 15 |
| Joanna, m. David **BALDWIN**, b. of Cornwall, Aug. 14, 1751, by Solomon Palmer | 1 | 42 |
| John, m. Sarah **WOOD**, Nov. 5, 1761, by Rev. H. Gold | 1 | 48 |
| Joseph, m. Azubah **BROWN**, Dec. 28, 1752, by Solomon Palmer | 1 | 18 |
| Lydia, d. John, m. Samuel **PAGBORN**, s. Joseph, Jr., July 18, 1784, by Judah Kellogg, J. P. | 2 | 5 |
| Prudence, d. Joseph, Jr. & Ashuba, b. Mar. 10, 1759 | 1 | 36 |
| Samuel, s. Joseph, Jr. & Ashuba, b. Mar. 25, 1757 | 1 | 36 |
| Samuel, s. Joseph, Jr., m. Lydia **PANGBORN**, d. John, July 18, 1784, by Judah Kellogg, J. P. | 2 | 5 |

| | Vol. | Page |
|---|---|---|
| **PANGBORN, PAGBORN**, (cont.) | | |
| Timothy, m. Deborah **YOUNG**, [Oct.] 15, 1742, by Samuell Lewis, J. P. | 1 | 3 |
| Timothy, s. Joseph & Mary, b. Apr. 20, 1746 | 1 | 4 |
| **PANGMAN**, [see also **PANGBORN**], Antoinette, of Cornwall, m. Oscar M. **SHERMAN**, of Lee, Mass., Nov. 17, 1852, by Ralph Smith | 3 | 125 |
| Cornelia, m. Amasa S. **NEWBURY**, Jan. 15, 1829, by Rev. William Andrews | 3 | 1 |
| Gideon P., m. Harriet **HART**, b. of Cornwall, Apr. 18, 1827, by Rev. Walter Smith | 2 | 67 |
| Gideon P., farmer, d. Nov. 4, 1849, ae 56 | 3 | 112-13 |
| Jane E., of Cornwall, m. William **HENSHAM**, of Baltimore, Md., Nov. 1, 1852, by Rev. Henry Burton, of Sharon | 3 | 124 |
| Susannah, d. Joseph, Jr. & Asube, b. Oct. 6, 1754 | 1 | 36 |
| **PARKER**, Sarah, m. Daniel **HARRISON**, Jr., Sept. 13, 1781, by Judah Kellogg, J. P. | LR4 | 18 |
| **PARMELEE, PARMALEE, PARMELEY, PARMELY**, Eliza, m. Sullivan M. N. **TUTTLE**, Sept. 4, 1830, by Rev. William Andrews | 3 | 46 |
| Joshua, d. June 2, 1780 | 2 | 1 |
| Joshua, s. Joshua & Rebecca, b. June 2, 1780 | 2 | 1 |
| Julian, m. Francis J. **YALE**, Oct. 7, 1831, by Rev. William Andrews | 3 | 48 |
| Matilda, of Cornwall, m. William **LEFFINGWELL**, of Sheffield, Mass., Oct. 3, 1841, by James Wadsworth, J. P. | 3 | 63 |
| Phebe H., of Cornwall, m. Lucius C. **STONE**, of Litchfield, Mar. 21, 1839, by N. M. Urmston | 3 | 56 |
| Rachel, m. Amos **FORD**, Feb. 17, 1837, by James Wadsworth, J. P. | 3 | 42 |
| **[PARRISH], PARISH**, William H., of Cornwall, m. Mary **MEAD**, of Sharon, Aug. 8, 1852, by Rev. Henry Burton, of Sharon | 3 | 124 |
| **PATCHAM**, Charlotte J., d. David, laborer, colored, ae 39 & Julia, ae 23, b. Aug. 8, 1848 | 3 | 84-5 |
| David, laborer, ae 31, colored, b. Sharon, res. Cornwall, m. Julia **CAMBRIDGE**, colored, ae 23, b. Sharon, res. Cornwall, Oct. 26, 1847, by Rev. Lewis Gunn | 3 | 90-1 |
| **PATTERSON**, Ashbel, s. John & Mary, d. June 30, 1756 | 1 | 23 |
| Ashbel, s. Matthew & Hannah, b. Feb. 1, 1778 | LR3 | 9 |
| Burton Clark, s. [Sherman & Polly], b. Sept. 10, 1839 | 3 | 62 |
| David, d. Mar. 26, 1823 | 2 | 46 |
| David Wells, s. Josiah & Phebe, b. Aug. 20, 1771 | 1 | 101 |
| Eunice, m. Daniel **EVEREST**, Nov. 27, 1774, by Rev. Hezekiah Gold | LR3 | 7 |
| Henry Sherman, s. [Sherman & Polly], b. Jan. 28, 1842 | 3 | 62 |
| Jane*, d. Matthew & Hannah, b. July 9, 1773 *("Irene" | | |

| | Vol. | Page |
|---|---|---|
| **PATTERSON**, (cont.) | | |
| in Starr's book) | LR3 | 9 |
| Jane, m. Jedidiah **CALHOUN**, b. of Cornwall, Feb. 24, 1808, by Rev. Timothy Stone, of 1st Church | 2 | 50 |
| John, s. Josiah & Phebe, b. Oct. 27, 1756 | 1 | 25 |
| Josiah, s. [Josiah & Phebe], b. Apr. 22, 1767 | 1 | 94 |
| Laura, m. William **HINDMAN**, [ ], by Rev. Timothy Stone, of the 1st Ch. Recorded Mar. 26, 1825 | 2 | 62 |
| Martin, d. Feb. 12, 1807, ae 62 y. | 3 | 4 |
| Mary, m. Thomas **BENSON**(?), Oct. 17, 1760, by Rev. H. Gold | 1 | 37 |
| Mary, d. Josiah & Phebe, b. Oct. 14, 1762 | 1 | 94 |
| Matthew, m. Hannah **JONES**, b. of Cornwall, Apr. 13, 1772, by Thomas Russell, J. P. | 1 | 106 |
| Parthenia, d. Josiah & Phebe, b. Aug. 29, 1754 | 1 | 25 |
| Silas Gilbert, s. Sherman & Polly, b. Mar. 11, 1838 | 3 | 62 |
| **PAYNE**, Agnes, w. Rufus, b. [ ]in Scotland; came to America, in 1767; d. Aug. 21, 1825, ae 74 | 2 | 56 |
| Betsey, m. Joshua **PIERCE**, June 26, 1805, by Judah Kellogg, J. P. | 3 | 11 |
| Charlotte Elizabeth, d. [Rufus & Polly], b. Aug. 23, 1838 | 3 | 69 |
| Elihu, s. Rufus & Agnis, b. Mar. 24, 1780 | LR4 | 14 |
| Elizabeth Wells, d. Rufus & Agnes, b. Oct. 16, 1777 | 2 | 14 |
| George C., s. Rufus, laborer, ae 59 & Mary S., ae 47, b. July 24, 1849 | 3 | 98-9 |
| George Silliman, s. John & Sarah, b. Nov. 3, 1816 | 2 | 44 |
| Hannah, d. Seeley, b. Feb. 18, 1849 | 3 | 102-3 |
| Harriet S., of Cornwall, m. Allen G. **STUDLEY**, of Ellsworth, Sept. 6, 1840, by Rev. John W. Salter | 3 | 59 |
| Jennet, d. [John & Sarah], b. Sept. 9, 1818 | 2 | 44 |
| John, of Cornwall, m. Sarah **DURAND**, of Oxford, Dec. 13, 1815, in Oxford, by Rev. Aaron Humphrey, of Oxford | 2 | 45 |
| John C., d. Feb. 27, 1849, ae 14 | 3 | 106-7 |
| John Calhoun, s. [Rufus & Polly], b. Oct. 7, 1834 | 3 | 69 |
| Joseph Benjamin, s. [Rufus & Polly], b. Apr. 4, 1841 | 3 | 69 |
| Mary Swift, d. Rufus & Polly, b. Dec. 24, 1830 | 3 | 69 |
| Nancy, d. Rufus & Agnis, b. Apr. 22, 1793 | 2 | 27 |
| Nathan, m. Lucretia **PECK**, b. of Cornwall, Mar. 16, 1851, by F. C. Youngs | 3 | 96 |
| Nathan, of Kent, m. Margaret **O'HARA**, of Cornwall, Oct. 17, 1853, by Obadiah Bierce, J. P. | 3 | 123 |
| Polly, d. [Rufus & Agnis], b. July 27, 1788 | 2 | 19 |
| Rufus, m. Agnes **FINDLA**, Feb. 17, 1774, by Rev. Hezekiah Gold | 2 | 14 |
| Rufus, s. Rufus & Agnis, b. Oct. 8, 1790 | 3 | 23 |
| Rufus, Jr., m. Polly **CALHOUN**, Jan. 13, 1830, by Rev. William Andrews | 3 | 45 |
| Sarah F., of Cornwall, m. Enoch B. **STUDLEY**, of Sharon, | | |

| | Vol. | Page |
|---|---|---|
| **PAYNE**, (cont.) | | |
| (Ellsworth Soc.), Nov. 30, 1842, by Rev. Joshua L. Maynard, of the North Cong. Ch. | 3 | 65 |
| Sarah P., m. Josiah **HOPKINS**, Jr., Jan. 12, 1808, by Rev. Timothy Stone | 2 | 37 |
| Sarah Parmelee, d. [Rufus & Agnis], b. Mar. 24, 1786 | 2 | 19 |
| Solomon, s. Rufus & Agnis, b. Feb. 16, 1784 | 2 | 19 |
| William Rufus, s. [Rufus & Polly], b. Mar. 16, 1832 | 3 | 69 |
| **PECK, PACK**, Abigail, m. Ira **BONNEY**, June 8, 1825, by Rev. Asa Tallmadge, of the Bap. Ch. | 2 | 65 |
| Alice, d. Benoni & Mehitable, b. Oct. 4, 1765 | 1 | 65 |
| Alice, d. Benoni, d. Oct. 19, 1767 | 1 | 78 |
| Benoni, m. Mehetable **MILLER**, Apr. 7, 1757, by Hezekiah Gold | 1 | 30 |
| Benoni, s. Benoni & Mehetable, b. May 11, 1775 | LR3 | 12 |
| Chloe, d. Benoni & Mehetable, b. Jan. 14, 1761 | 1 | 50 |
| Cynthia, of Cornwall, m. William S. **HOTCHKISS**, of New Haven, Sept. 16, 1838, by Rev. N. M. Urmston, of the 1st Ch. | 3 | 54 |
| Elisha, s. Elisha, farmer & Harriet, b. Feb. [ ], 1850 | 3 | 108-9 |
| Elisha R., m. Harriet **WELLS**, b. of Cornwall, Sept. 26, 1832, by Rev. Timothy Stone | 3 | 50 |
| Eliza, of Cornwall, m. Hiram **NORTON**, of Fabins, N. Y., Jan. 10, 1828, by Rev. L. P. Hickok, of the 1st Soc. of Kent | 2 | 68 |
| Eunice, d. Benoni & Mehettabel, b. Mar. 4, 1770 | 1 | 96 |
| Eunice, m. Truman **DIBBLE**, Nov. 5, 1823, by Rev. Timothy Stone, of the 1st Ch. | 2 | 57 |
| Fidelia Emerence, adopted d. Frederick M., b. Dec. 25, 1836 | 3 | 51 |
| Frederick M., m. Marietta **JOHNSON**, June 1, 1834, by Rev. William Andrews | 3 | 37 |
| Jane, d. Benoni & Mehitable, b. Jan. 14, 1764 | 1 | 56 |
| Joseph, d. Nov. 16, 1749 | 1 | 10 |
| Joseph, s. Benoni & Mehetable, b. Jan. 16, 1779 | LR3 | 13 |
| Joseph, s. Benoni & Mehetable, d. Apr. 7, 1782 | 2 | 2 |
| Lucretia, m. Nathan **PAYNE**, b. of Cornwall, Mar. 16, 1851, by F. C. Youngs | 3 | 96 |
| Lucy, of Danbury, m. Moses **BENEDICT**, of Cornwall, Nov. 8, 1780, by Thomas Brooks | 2 | 8 |
| Margaret, d. Benoni & Mehetable, b. July 30, 1771 | 1 | 99 |
| Mehetable, d. Benony & Mehetable, b. Jan. 17, 1759 | 1 | 33 |
| Rhoda, d. Benoni & Mehetable, b. Sept. 27, 1762 | 1 | 50 |
| Ruth, d. Benoni & Mehitable, b. Feb. 15, 1767 | 1 | 78 |
| Samuel, of Watertown, m. Myra C. **JOHNSON**, of Cornwall, Feb. 28, 1836, by Rev. Heman L. Noell | 3 | 41 |
| Silas, s. Ens. Benoni & Mehetable, b. Sept. 6, 1768 | 1 | 84 |
| Sophia, m. James H. **FERRIS**, Feb. 18, 1836, by Rev. Timothy Stone | 3 | 41 |

| | Vol. | Page |
|---|---|---|
| **PECK, PACK**, (cont.) | | |
| Sible, d. Benony & Mehetable, b. Dec. 12, 1757 | 1 | 30 |
| Sybel, d. Benoni & Mehetable, d. Nov. 16, 1783 | 2 | 6 |
| William K.*, of Norfolk, m. Hannah R. **WEBB**, Jan. 8, 1850, by Rev. E. B. Andrews. Int. Pub. *("William K. **PEET**"?) | 3 | 77 |
| **PEET**, Abijah, s. Ethel & Chloe, b. July 10, 1782, at Warren | 2 | 45 |
| Chloe Ann, m. Hezekiah S. **GOLD**, Sept. 6, 1836, by Rev. William Andrews | 3 | 41 |
| Chloe Anne, d. [Abijah & Lucy], b. Apr. 26, 1812 | 2 | 45 |
| Emeline, ae 23, res. Cornwall, m. Birdseye **DOOLITTLE**, farmer, ae 37, res. Cornwall | 3 | 104-5 |
| Ethel Curtiss, s. [Abijah & Lucy], b. Feb. 26, 1814 | 2 | 45 |
| Fanny Abiah, d. Abijah & Lucy, b. May 12, 1806 | 2 | 45 |
| Fanny Abijah, d. Abijah & Lucy, d. Feb. 3, 1811, at Warren | 2 | 46 |
| Martin Luther, s. [Abijah & Lucy], b. Dec. 19, 1815 | 2 | 45 |
| Miron Dayton, s. Abijah & Lucy, b. Feb. 8, 1820 | 2 | 47 |
| Ruby Ann, of Warren, m. Frederick A. **KEELER**, of Albany, N. Y., Dec. 30, 1854, by Rev. J. F. Jones, of College St. Bap. Ch. | 3 | 126 |
| William R., attorney, ae 26, b. Salisbury, res. Norfolk, m. Hannah R. **WEBB**, ae 24, b. Warren, res. Norfolk, Jan. 8, 1850, by Rev. E. B. Andrews *("William R. **PECK**"?) | 3 | 112-13 |
| **PENDLETON**, Lucretia D., of Cornwall, m. Joseph **BROWN**, of Goshen, Feb. 22, 1846, by Rev. Alfred Gates | 3 | 72 |
| Merrill, m. Catharine **COON**, Sept. 11, 1831, by Rev. Walter Smith, of the North Ch. | 3 | 48 |
| Noah F., carpenter, ae 24, res. Cornwall, m. Lorinda **HALL**, ae 18, res. Cornwall, Jan. 19, 1851, by Rev. Salmon Gale | 3 | 118-19 |
| William, farmer, b. Guilford, res. Cornwall, d. Aug. 23, 1850, ae 81 | 3 | 120-1 |
| William W., m. Maria J. **EMMONS**, Feb. 26, 1845, at the house of Luther Emmons, by Rev. Joshua L. Maynard, of the North Cong. Ch. | 3 | 71 |
| **PERKINS**, Beecher, s. [Daniel, Jr. & Rachel], b. May 3, 1811 | 2 | 64 |
| Daniel, Jr., m. Rachel **BENEDICT**, Apr. 17, 1806, by Judah Kellogg, J. P. | 3 | 11 |
| Daniel B., b. Goshen, res. Cornwall, d. Oct. 4, 1849, ae 2 | 3 | 112-13 |
| Daniel Orlando, s. [Daniel, Jr. & Rachel], b. Jan. 15, 1825 | 2 | 64 |
| Eli, s. [Daniel, Jr. & Rachel], b. Feb. 26, 1817 | 2 | 64 |
| Elizabeth, d. Daniel, Jr. & Rachel, b. Feb. 20, 1807 | 2 | 64 |
| Elizabeth, m. Anson B. **BEACH**, Mar. 6, 1826, by Rev. Asa Tallmadge, of the Bap. Ch. | 2 | 65 |
| Lucy, d. [Daniel, Jr. & Rachel], b. Dec. 9, 1812 | 2 | 64 |
| Lucy, of Cornwall, m. Albert **PAGE**, of Penyan Yates Cty., N. Y., Feb. 19, 1838, by Rev. Daniel Baldwin | 3 | 54 |

| | Vol. | Page |
|---|---|---|
| **PERKINS**, (cont.) | | |
| Nancy, d. [Daniel, Jr. & Rachel], b. Dec. 20, 1809 | 2 | 64 |
| Nancy, of Cornwall, m. Henry **GRISWOLD**, of Litchfield, Mar. 12, 1829, by Rev. Silas Ambler | 3 | 44 |
| **PERRY**, Julius, m. Patty M. **CARTER**, Nov. 13, 1836, by Rev. William Andrews | 3 | 52 |
| Lurenia, d. E. G., carpenter & Jolina W., b. June 11, 1850 | 3 | 108-9 |
| Rachel(?), of West Stockbridge, m. Rebecca **BENEDICT**, of Cornwall, Oct. 6, 1834, by Daniel Baldwin, of New Milford | 3 | 38 |
| Smith, m. Jane C. **LEE**, b. of Cornwall, Feb. 3, 1833, by Peter Bierce, J. P. | 3 | 35 |
| **PHALAN**, Joseph, laborer, ae 22 & Mariah, ae 18, had s. [ ], b. Dec. 3, 1850 | 3 | 116-17 |
| **PHILLIPS**, Daniel B. Jr., s. Daniel B., carpenter, ae 25 & Mary, ae 26, b. Apr. 23, 1848 | 3 | 86-7 |
| Ezra, m. Lovicey **MARVIN**, July 9, 1825, by Rev. Asa Tallmadge, of the Bap. Ch. | 2 | 65 |
| **PICKET**, Alma, of Cornwall, m. Justin **COY**, of Springfield, Mass., Apr. 18, 1830, by Rev. Eleazer Beecher, of the Bap. Ch. in New Milford | 3 | 46 |
| **PIERCE, PEERCE**, [see also **BIERCE**], Agnus, d. Levi & Elizabeth, b. May 27, 1776 | LR3 | 12 |
| Alpine, s. [Levi & Elizabeth], b. July 6, 1770 | 1 | 97 |
| Ame, d. Joshua & Ame, b. Sept. 16, 1759 | 1 | 34 |
| Amy, d. Capt. Seth & Amy, b. July 18, 1781 | 2 | 3 |
| Amy, m. Silas **HART**, Apr. 17, 1783, by Rev. Hezekiah Gold | 2 | 16 |
| Amy J., m. Samuel R. **BALDWIN**, July 5, 1835, by Rev. William Andrews | 3 | 40 |
| Anna, d. Joshua & Hopestill, b. Feb. 20, 1749/50 | 1 | 13 |
| Anna, d. Joshua, Jr. & Amy, b. Dec. 5, 1756 | 1 | 26 |
| Anna, m. Titus **BONNEY**, Feb. 21, 1771, by Rev. Hezekiah Gold | 1 | 104 |
| Anna, m. Josiah **HOPKINS**, Aug. 8, 1776, by Rev. Hezekiah Gold | LR3 | 13 |
| Benjamin, s. William & Sarah, b. Feb. 6, 1761 | 1 | 39 |
| Benjamin, s. [Isaac & Betty], b. Aug. 18, 1790 | 3 | 15 |
| Betsey, d. [Isaac & Betty], b. Apr. 2, 1783 | 3 | 15 |
| Billy, s. [Isaac & Betty], b. Dec. 10, 1795 | 3 | 15 |
| Charles Edward, s. Seth, 3rd & Susan M., b. Dec. 13, 1830 | 3 | 47 |
| Dwight Wellington, s. [Joshua & Betsey W.], b. July 5, 1816 | 2 | 60 |
| Edward, m. Julia A. **LAWRENCE**, Jan. 19, 1844, by Amos D. Watrous | 3 | 68 |
| Eleanor, d. Joshua & Hopestill, b. Apr. 28, 1739 | 1 | 12 |
| Eliner, m. Solomon **JOHNSON**, Sept. 28, 1758, by Rev. H. Gold | 1 | 33 |
| Elizabeth, d. Joshua & Hopestill, b. Jan. 25, 1832/3 | 1 | 12 |
| Elizabeth, m. Amos **JOHNSON**, Jr., b. of Cornwall, Sept. | | |

| | Vol. | Page |
|---|---|---|
| **PIERCE, PEERCE,** (cont.) | | |
| 11, 1755, by George Kellogg, J. P. Witnesses: John Pierce & Nehemiah Pierce | 1 | 23 |
| Elizabeth, m. John **BENEDICT**, Jan. 30, 1772, by Thomas Russell, J. P. | 1 | 101 |
| Emma E., of Cornwall, m. Cyrenus **HARD**, of New York, Sept. 12, 1854, by Rev. Ira Pettibone | 3 | 125 |
| Emma Elizabeth, d. Seth, 2nd & Susan, b. Dec. 13, 1832 | 3 | 77 |
| Fayette Washington, s. [Joshua & Betsey W.], b. June 28, 1813 | 2 | 60 |
| Frederick Joshua, s. [Mills J. & Eunicy], b. Nov. 4, 1837 | 3 | 57 |
| Hannah, d. William & Sarah, b. Jan. 29, 1770 | 1 | 97 |
| Hannah, d. [Isaac & Betty], b. May 26, 1788 | 3 | 15 |
| Harry, m. Polly **BUNNELL**, b. of Cornwall, Feb. 3, 1827, by Rev. John Lovejoy, of the M. E. Ch. | 2 | 66 |
| Hiram, of Plymouth, m. Sarah E. **BEERS**, of Cornwall, May 30, 1849, by Rev. E. B. Andrews. Int. Pub. | 3 | 82 |
| Hiram, manufacturer, ae 48, b. Cornwall, res. Plymouth, m. 2nd w. Susan E. **BEERS**, ae 23, res. Cornwall, May 30, 1849, by Rev. E. B. Andrews | 3 | 104-5 |
| Hiram Wellington, s. Mills J. & Eunicy, b. Dec. 7, 1834 | 3 | 57 |
| Huldah Gold, d. Seth & Amy, b. July 6, 1773 | LR3 | 5 |
| Huldah Gold, d. Seth & Amy, b. July 6, 1773 | 2 | 13 |
| Irene, d. Capt. Seth, d. Feb. 15, 1814 | 2 | 39 |
| Isaac Smith, s. [Isaac & Betty], b. May 1, 1797 | 3 | 15 |
| Isabella, d. [Peter & Betsey A.], b. Feb. 3, 1831 | 3 | 51 |
| James A., s. Peter & Betsey A., b. Nov. 4, 1825 | 3 | 51 |
| Joel, s. [Levi & Elizabeth], b. July 4, 1768 | 1 | 97 |
| John, s. Joshua & Hopestill, b. Nov. 10, 1734 | 1 | 12 |
| John *, m. Lucy **HOW**, Aug. 31, 1758, by Rev. Hezekiah Gold *(Arnold Copy has " John **STONE**") | 1 | 32 |
| John, s. Levi & Elizabeth, b. Oct. 24, 1766 | 1 | 97 |
| John, s. Joshua, Jr. & Amy, b. May 15, 1774 | LR3 | 6 |
| John Hart, s. Seth & Amey, b. Oct. 15, 1777; d. Jan. 1, 1777 | LR3 | 11 |
| John Hart, Col., d. Aug. 10, 1825, in the 48th y. of his age | 2 | 56 |
| Joshua, s. Joshua & Hopestill, b. Nov. 8, 1730 | 1 | 12 |
| Joshuah, Jr., m. Amy **JOHNSON**, b. of Cornwall, Sept. 11, 1754, by George Kellogg, J. P. Sworn to Aug. 9, 1756, before Gideon Thompson, J. P., by John Pierce & Nehemiah Pierce | 1 | 23 |
| Joshua, s. Joshua, Jr. & Amey, b. Sept. 16, 1762 | 1 | 48 |
| Joshua, of Cornwall, m. Hannah **LOCKWOOD**, of Danbury, Apr. 6, 1786, by Rev. Joseph Peck | 2 | 8 |
| Joshua, Capt., d. Jan. 22, 1793 | 2 | 26 |
| Joshua, d. Mar. 13, 1794, in the 89th y. of his age | 2 | 28 |
| Joshua, m. Betsey **PAYNE**, June 26, 1805, by Judah Kellogg, J. P. | 3 | 11 |
| Laura, m. Menzies **BEERS**, Jan. 1, 1821, by Rev. Timothy | | |

| | Vol. | Page |
|---|---|---|
| **PIERCE, PEERCE**, (cont.) | | |
| Stone, of the 1st Church | 2 | 49 |
| Levi, m. Elizabeth **MacALPINE**, Aug. 8, 1764, by Rev. Hezekiah Gold | 1 | 97 |
| Low Rain*, d. Joshua, Jr. & Amy, b. Mar. 23, 1766 *("Lorain") | 1 | 69 |
| Lorain, m. Nehemiah **CLARK**, May 1, 1788, by Rev. Hezekiah Gold | 2 | 16 |
| Lucia E., d. Edwin, farmer, ae 25 & Almeda, ae 21, b. Nov. 5, 1848 | 3 | 100-1 |
| Lucinda, m. Ezekiel **BIRDSEYE**, Oct. 5, 1826, by Rev. Timothy Stone, of the 1st Ch. | 2 | 65 |
| Lucy, d. John & Lucy, b. Oct. 28, 1760 | 1 | 37 |
| Lucy, w. John, d. Jan. 13, 1809 | 3 | 4 |
| Margaret, d. Levi & Elizabeth, b. Sept. 29, 1779 | LR4 | 16 |
| Maria L., m. Burritt B. **NORTH**, May 31, 1832, by Rev. William Andrews | 3 | 50 |
| Maria Louisa, d. [Joshua & Betsey W.], b. July 4, 1809 | 2 | 60 |
| Mary, d. John & Lucy, d. Sept. 12, 1760 | 1 | 37 |
| Mary, d. Nehemiah & Mary, b. Sept. 14, 1760 | 1 | 39 |
| Mary, m. Ebenezer **DIBBLE**, b. of Cornwall, May 12, 1776, by Thomas Swift, J. P. | LR3 | 9 |
| Mary, m. Edward Adams **SQUIER**, Nov. 9, 1778, by Rev. Hezekiah Gold | LR3 | 13 |
| Mary C., d. Seth, 3rd & Susan, b. Jan. 1, 1829 | 3 | 2 |
| Mills, of Cornwall, m. Eunice **TICKNER**, of Sharon, Oct. 18, 1832, by Rev. Aaron S. Hill | 3 | 50 |
| Mills Johnson, of Joshua & Betsey W., b. Oct. 27, 1806 | 2 | 60 |
| Molly, d. William & Sarah, b. Mar. 1, 1767 | 1 | 75 |
| Neamiah, m. Mary **BISHOP**, Sept. 14, 1758, by Rev. H. Gold | 1 | 33 |
| Nehemiah, d. Sept. 7, 1776 | LR3 | 9 |
| Nehemiah, s. Isaac & Betty, b. Apr. 29, 1781 | 2 | 4 |
| Nehemiah, s. Isaac & Betty, b. Apr. 29, 1781 | 3 | 15 |
| Paul, d. May 30, 1825, ae Revolutionary Soldier | 2 | 56 |
| Presilla, d. Joshua & Hopestill, b. Oct. 28, 1745 | 1 | 13 |
| Rhene, d. Seth & Amy, b. Apr. 24, 1775 | LR3 | 10 |
| Sally, d. William & Sarah, b. Oct. 11, 1762 | 1 | 48 |
| Samuel Johnson, s. Joshua, Jr. & Amy, b. Dec. 27, 1769 | 1 | 94 |
| Sarah, d. Joshua & Hopestill, b. Dec. 4, 1736 | 1 | 12 |
| Sarah, m. Jonathan **CHANDLER**, Apr. 13, 1758, by Rev. Hezekiah Gold | 1 | 33 |
| Sarah, wid. William, d. Mar. 9, 1777 | LR3 | 9 |
| Sarah, w. Capt. John, d. of Abel **JUDSON**, d. Mar. 13, 1813, ae 38 | 3 | 27 |
| Seth, s. Joshua & Hopestill, b. Oct. 28, 1742 | 1 | 12 |
| Seth, m. Amy **HART**, b. of Cornwall, June 18, 1772, by Rev. Hezekiah Gold | 1 | 105 |
| Seth, s. [Isaac & Betty], b. Aug. 7, 1799 | 3 | 15 |

| | Vol. | Page |
|---|---|---|
| **PIERCE, PEERCE,** (cont.) | | |
| Seth, 3rd, m. Susan **COLLINS**, Apr. 12, 1826, by Rev. Timothy Stone, of the 1st Ch. | 2 | 63 |
| Seth, Capt., d. Aug. 29, 1833, ae 90 y. 10 m. | 3 | 43 |
| Theophilus, s. William & Sarah, b. Dec. 4, 1759 | 1 | 35 |
| Theophilus, m. Sarah **BEACH**, Dec. 7, 1780, by Rev. Hezekiah Gold | 2 | 1 |
| Whiting W., of Ohio, m. Harriet **HINDMAN**, of Cornwall, Sept. 1, 1824, by Rev. Timothy Stone | 2 | 58 |
| William, s. Levi & Elizabeth, b. Sept. 2, 1765 | 1 | 97 |
| William, s. Rufus & Agnes, b. June 3, 1775 | LR3 | 10 |
| William, s. William & Sarah, b. June 23, 1775 | LR3 | 14 |
| William, d. Feb. 21, 1777 | LR3 | 9 |
| William, s. Theophilus & Sarah, b. Mar. 31, 1782 | 2 | 3 |
| **PIERSON**, Cornelia, of Cornwall, m. Joseph **DRIGGS**, of Berkshire, Cty., Mass., May 14, 1826, by Rev. Timothy Stone, of the 1st Ch. | 2 | 65 |
| Polly, m. John **STEAD**, b. of Cornwall, Dec. 10, [1820], by Rev. A. Derthick, of Bap. Soc. in Warren | 2 | 49 |
| **PINNOCK***, Olive, d. James & Margaret, b. May 15, 1761 *(Arnold Copy has "**DENNOCH**") | 1 | 45 |
| **PITCHER**, Maria, of Amenia, m. Lyman **TYLER**, of Broo[k]lin(?), Aug. 19, 1828, by Rev. Silas Ambler | 2 | 68 |
| **PLANT**, Naomi, of Cornwall, m. Peter **RICHARDS**, of Goshen, Apr. 29, 1827, by Rev. Walter Smith | 2 | 67 |
| Reuben, m. Charlotte **SMITH**, Nov. 7, 1830, by Rev. William Andrews | 3 | 46 |
| **POHAMUS**,(?), Roland, of Canaan, m. Sarah **REABY**, of Cornwall, [colored], Jan. 3, 1841, by Rev. Ebenezer Washburn | 3 | 61 |
| **POLK**, James K., s. Minerva **HURLBURT**, b. Dec. 2, 1845 | 3 | 69 |
| **PORTER**, Abigail, d. Thomas & Abigail, b. May 2, 1765 | 1 | 78 |
| Anna, d. Thomas & Abigail, b. Nov. 30, 1761 | 1 | 44 |
| Catherine M., d. W. S., tavern keeper, ae 36, & Martha R., ae 34, b. Sept. 14, 1847 | 3 | 86-7 |
| Jane, b. Farmington, res. Cornwall, d. Apr. 27, 1848, ae 5 m. | 3 | 92-3 |
| Thomas*, m. Abigail **HOW**, June 22, 1756, by Rev. H. Gold *("Thomas **CARTER**" in Arnold Copy) | 1 | 35 |
| Thomas, s. Thomas & Abigail, b. May 11, 1767 | 1 | 78 |
| Zachariah **HOWE***, s. Thomas & Abigail, b. May 30, 1759, *(Arnold Copy has Zacariah **CARTER**") | 1 | 35 |
| **POTTER**, Richard, m. Ursula **WICKWIRE**, Apr. 17, 1835, by James Wadsworth, J. P. | 3 | 38 |
| Temperance, m. Samuel **AMES**, Jr., b. of Cornwall, Nov. 29, 1827, by Horatio Smith, J. P. | 2 | 64 |
| **PRATT**, Almon B., Rev., m. Amanda **ROGERS**, b. of Cornwall, Aug. 11, 1841, by Rev. Joshua L. Maynard, of the Cong. Ch. | 1 | 63 |

| | Vol. | Page |
|---|---|---|
| **PRATT**, (cont.) | | |
| Eliakim M., m. Abigail **ROGERS**, Sept. 14, 1829, by Rev. Walter Smith, of the North Ch. | 3 | 44 |
| Helen A., of Cornwall, m. Stephen J. **FOSTER**, of Morristown, N. J., Sept. 1, 1841, by Rev. J. L. Maynard, of the North Cong. Ch. | 3 | 63 |
| Lydia, m. Matthew Millard **STEELE**, Jan. 8, 1784, by Rev. Hezekiah Gold | 2 | 8 |
| Lydia A., res. Cornwall, d. Sept. 11, 1848, ae 2 | 3 | 106-7 |
| Mary A., b. Hamden, res. Cornwall, d. Oct. 12, 1848, ae 73 | 3 | 106-7 |
| Mary Aurelia, d. Ezra D., farmer, ae 37 & Ann Aurilia, ae 28, b. May 22, 1848 | 3 | 84-5 |
| Minerva, of Cornwall, m. William D. **FENN**, of Sharon, Jan. 1, 1827, by Rev. Watler Smith | 2 | 66 |
| Noah Rogers, s. Almon B., farmer, ae 37 & Amanda, ae 32, b. Jan. 24, 1849 | 3 | 98-9 |
| Russell R., m. Mary E. **COTTER**, b. of Cornwall, Oct. 20, 1840, by Rev. J. Atwater | 3 | 59 |
| **PRENTISS**, Esther, m. Woodruff **EMMONS**, Mar. 10, 1743, by Joseph Miner, J. P. | 1 | 6 |
| **PRESTON**, Alanson, m. Eliza C. **REED**, b. of Cornwall, Apr. 16, 1848, by Rev. Joshua L. Maynard, of the North Cong. Ch. | 3 | 79 |
| Alanson, farmer, ae 31, b. Sharon, res. Cornwall, m. Eliza C. **REED**, ae 18, b. Cornwall, Apr. 16, 1848, by Joshua L. Maynard | 3 | 90-1 |
| Sarah, m. Franklin **REED**, b. of Cornwall, May 17, 1853, by Rev. Harley Goodwin, of Canaan | 3 | 124 |
| **PRINDLE**, Lyman, m. Caroline E. **HANCHET**, Apr. 22, 1849, by W[illia]m McAlister | 3 | 77 |
| Lyman B., miller, ae 24, b. Canaan, res. Lee, Mass., m. Caroline E. **HANCHETT**, milliner & dessmaker, ae 19, res. Cornwall, Apr. 22, 1849, by Rev. William McAlister | 3 | 104-5 |
| Mary Ann, of Cornwall, m. Charles **MANSFIELD**, of Canaan, Jan. 1, 1837, by Charles Prentice | 3 | 42 |
| Rachel(?), of Cornwall, m. Lyman **GRISWOLD**, of Litchfield, Mar. 18, 1844, by Rev. Joshua L. Maynard, of the North Cong. Ch. | 3 | 70 |
| Samuel, m. Betsey Ann **BAILEY**, b. of Cornwall, Apr. 3, 1842, by James Wadsworth, J. P. | 3 | 64 |
| Warren, of Cornwall, m. Rhoda **MUNGER**, of Litchfield, Dec. 10, 1837, by Thomas Benedict, of Torrington | 3 | 53 |
| **PRITCHARD**, Adaline, m. Henry **WRIGHT**, Feb. 16, 1846, by Rev. K. K. Reynolds | 3 | 72 |
| Caroline S., m. Thomas **McSWENEY**, July 10, 1842, by Harley Goodwin | 3 | 65 |
| Jane, of Cornwall, m. Henry **WRIGHT**, of Litchfield, Dec. | | |

| | Vol. | Page |
|---|---|---|
| **PRITCHARD**, (cont.) | | |
| 22, 1844, by Myron Harrison, J. P. | 3 | 71 |
| **PUNDERSON, PONDERSON**, Samuel, Dr. of N[ew] Haven, m. Caroline **SWIFT**, of Cornwall, May 21, [1823], by Rev. Timothy Stone | 2 | 55 |
| **REABY**, Sarah, of Cornwall, m. Roland **POHANUS**, of Canaan (colored), Jan. 3, 1841, by Rev. Ebnezer Washburn | 3 | 61 |
| **READ, REED**, Abigail, m. Ralph **BUTLER**, b. of Cornwall, Sept. 23, 1849, by Harley Goodwin | 3 | 123 |
| Allesha, d. Henry & Sarah Abiah, b. Oct. 29, 1800 | 3 | 29 |
| Betsey, d. [Henry & Sarah Abiah], b. Oct. 3, 1802 | 3 | 29 |
| Daniel, farmer, ae 28 & Jane, ae 20, had s. [ ], b. July [ ] | 3 | 116-17 |
| Elias, s. John & Susanna, b. Mar. 20, 1794 | 2 | 30 |
| Eliza C., m. Alanson **PRESTON**, b. of Cornwall, Apr. 16, 1848, by Rev. Joshua L. Maynard, of the North Cong. Ch. | 3 | 79 |
| Eliza C., ae 18, b. Cornwall, m. Alanson **PRESTON**, farmer, ae 31, b. Sharon, res. Cornwall, Apr. 16, 1848, by Joshua L. Maynard | 3 | 90-1 |
| Elizabeth, of Cornwall, m. Ebenezer **WING**, of Sharon, Dec. 26, 1833, by Aaron S. Hill | 3 | 36 |
| Franklin, m. Sarah **PRESTON**, b. of Cornwall, May 17, 1853, by Rev. Harley Goodwin, of Canaan | 3 | 124 |
| George, s. Samuel S., farmer, ae 29 & Sophia L., ae 24, b. Nov. 2, 1850 | 3 | 110-11 |
| Henry, m. Mrs. Sarah Abiah **JUDSON**, Dec. 1, 1799, by Rev. Henry Christie | 2 | 24 |
| Henry, m. Harriet L. **BROWN**, b. of Cornwall, May 1st sabbath, 1847, by J. W. Andrews | 3 | 76 |
| Henry, laborer & Harriet, had s. [ ], b. July 7, 1849 | 3 | 100-1 |
| Henry Franklin, s. Geo[rge] **DANIEL**, farmer, ae 21, & Eliza, ae 21, b. Mar. 25, 1848 | 3 | 84-5 |
| Irene, m. Jaba **BALDWIN**, July 10, 1816, by Rev. Samuel Cockrand | 2 | 62 |
| James, farmer, ae 58 & Rhoda, ae 48, had s. [ ], b. Sept. 20, 1850 | 3 | 114-15 |
| James, s. Henry, carpenter, ae 31 & Harriet, ae 29, b. Jan. 16, 1851 | 3 | 116-17 |
| James H., m. Rhoda **WICKWIRE**, b. of Cornwall, Sept. 4, 1825, by Rev. John Lovejoy, of the M. E. Ch. | 2 | 62 |
| John Rollin, s. John W., shoemaker, ae 36 & Hannah, ae 35, b. Nov. 26, 1848 | 3 | 102-3 |
| John W., m. Hannah **KELLOGG**, Oct. 31, 1836, by Rev. William Andrews | 3 | 42 |
| Louisa, m. Julius **BEARDSLEY**, b. of Cornwall, Mar. 29, 1830, by Rev. Bradley Selleck | 3 | 45 |
| Mary, of Cornwall, m. Warren **STEARNES**, of Killingly, Jan. 29, 1823, by Rev. David Miller | 2 | 55 |

| | Vol. | Page |
|---|---|---|
| **READ, REED**, (cont.) | | |
| Samuel S., m. Sophia L. **BROWN**, b. of Cornwall, Oct. 22, 1848, by Rev. Hiram Day | 3 | 81 |
| Samuel S., farmer, ae 27, res. Cornwall, m. Sophia L. **BROWN**, ae 23, res. Cornwall, Oct. 22, 1848, by Rev. Hiram Day | 3 | 104-5 |
| Sarah Abia Caroline, d. Henry & Sarah Abia, b. Dec. 10, 1808 | 3 | 17 |
| Sarah Abiah Caroline, d. Henry, d. July 26, 1820 | 2 | 46 |
| **REXFORD**, Harriet S., of Cornwall, m. Aaron B. **CHASE**, of Welton, N . Y., Mar. 3, 1852, at the h ouse of Riley M. Rexford, by Rev. J. L. Maynard, of the North Cong. Ch. | 3 | 122 |
| Mary, d. Daniel & Hannah, b. Apr. 19, 1778 | 2 | 5 |
| Nancy, d. Samuel & Lydia, b. Oct. 6, 1793 | 2 | 38 |
| Nancy, m. Phinehas **BALDWIN**, Sept. 7, 1809 | 3 | 63 |
| Riley M., m. Sarah **SCOVEL**, b. of Cornwall, Oct. 24, 1824, by Rev. Walter Smith, of the 2nd Ch. | 2 | 59 |
| Riley Millard, s. [Samuel & Lydia], b. June 6, 1805 | 2 | 38 |
| Roswell, s. [Daniel & Hannah], b. Dec. 4, 1780 | 2 | 5 |
| Samuel, m. Lydia **MILLARD**, b. of Cornwall, Nov. 6, 1788, by Rev. Hezekiah Gold | 2 | 36 |
| **RHODES**, Philip A., m. Rebecca **CHATTERSON**, Mar. 10, 1844, by Myron Harrison, J. P. | 3 | 68 |
| **RICHARDS**, Peter, of Goshen, m. Naomi **PLANT**, of Cornwall, Apr. 29, 1827, by Rev. Walter Smith | 2 | 67 |
| Ruth, b. Goshen, res. Goshen, married, d. Mar. 23, 1848, ae 38 | 3 | 92-3 |
| William P., of Woodbury, m. Calista M. **WHEELER**, of Cornwall, Sept. 26, 1824, by Rev. Walter Smith, of the 2nd Ch. | 2 | 58 |
| **RIDER**, William, of Dover, N. Y., m. Emily **BAILEY**, of Cornwall, May 6, 1827, by Rev. Walter Smith | 2 | 67 |
| **RIDGE**, John, of the Cherokee Nation, m. Sally B. **NORTHROP**, Jan. 27, 1824, by Rev. Walter Smith, of the 2nd Cong. Ch. | 2 | 58 |
| **RIGGS**, Ella Gertrude, d. Clark, tailor, b. Sept. 2, 1850 | 3 | 114-15 |
| **RILEY**, George W., of Goshen, m. Eliza **BIERCE**, of Goshen, Sept. 1, 1851, by F. C. Youngs | 3 | 122 |
| Submit, m. Nathan **MILLARD**, June 24, 1761, by Rev. Hezekiah Gold | 1 | 85 |
| **RIPNER**, Thankful, d. Samuel & Mary, b. Jan. 16, 1778 | LR3 | 15 |
| **ROBERTS, ROBARDS, ROBERDS, ROBBERT**, Esther A., of Cornwall, m. Frederick **YALE**, of Canaan, Mar. 3, 1850, by E. N. Jenckes | 3 | 83 |
| Eunice, m. Simeon **CHANDLER**, Apr. 5, 1750, by Solomon Palmer | 1 | 12 |
| Frederick, of Goshen, m. Hannah **SPELLMAN**, of Cornwall, Jan. 23, 1825, by Rev. Charles Prentice, of Canaan | 2 | 59 |
| Mary, m. Sineon **EMONS**, June 21, 1775, by Ebenezer | LR3 | 5 |

| | Vol. | Page |
|---|---|---|
| **ROBERTS, ROBARDS, ROBERDS, ROBBERT,** (cont.) Knibloe | LR3 | 5 |
| Rebeckah, of Sharon, m. Benajah **MILLARD**, of Cornwall, June 7, 1765, by John Ransom, J. P. | 1 | 70 |
| Sally, d. Feb. 10, 1850, ae 81 | 3 | 112-13 |
| **ROBINSON**, Betsey Ann, of Weston, m. Solomon **BIERCE**, of Cornwall, Oct. 21, 1844, by H. Day | 3 | 70 |
| Phebe Ann, of Goshen, m. William **CRUMB**, of New York, Jan. 13, 1850, by E. N. Jenckes | 3 | 83 |
| **ROCKEFELLER**, Francis, s. Jacob, blacksmith, b. Nov. 27, 1849 | 3 | 108-9 |
| **ROEBUCK**, Delia, m. Samuel **CHAMBLERLAIN**, Jan. 5, 1836, by Rev. William Andrews | 3 | 41 |
| **ROGERS**, A. L., of New Milford, m. Emily **COGSWELL**, of Cornwall, Nov. 29, 1849, by Rev. Joshua L. Maynard, of the North Cong. Ch., at his house | 3 | 83 |
| Abigail, d. [Noah, Jr. & Lydia], b. June 11, 1793 | 3 | 29 |
| Abigail, d. Noah, Jr. & Lydia, d. July 22, 1799 | 3 | 4 |
| Abigail, 4th d. [Noah, Jr. & Lydia], b. Aug. 29, 1805 | 3 | 29 |
| Abigail, m. Eliakim M. **PRATT**, Sept. 14, 1829, by Rev. Walter Smith, of the North Ch. | 3 | 44 |
| Amanda, m. Rev. Almon B. **PRATT**, b. of Cornwall, Aug. 11, 1841, by Rev. Joshua L. Maynard, of the Cong. Ch. | 3 | 63 |
| Anson, s. [Edward & Hannah], b. Apr. 2, 1792 | 3 | 26 |
| Anson, m. Philomelia **HART**, Oct. 20, 1814, by John Sedgwick, J. P. Witnesses: James D. Ford & Benjamin Catlin | 2 | 45 |
| Artimesia, d. [Edward & Hannah], b. Sept. 12, 1789 | 3 | 26 |
| Artemesia, d. [Edward & Hannah], d. Oct. 6, 1794 | 3 | 10 |
| Clarissa, d. Noah & Rhoda, b. June 30, 1776 | LR3 | 10 |
| Clarissa, d. Noah & Rhoda, d. [ ] | LR4 | 18 |
| Clarissa Irene, d. [Noah & Rhoda], b. May 2, 1779 | LR4 | 18 |
| Cynthia, d. [Capt. Edward & Hannah], b. Apr. 4, 1779 | LR3 | 11 |
| Cynthia, d. [Edward & Hannah], b. Dec. 8, 1782 | 3 | 26 |
| Cynthia, Mrs., m. Elias **WHITE**, Jan. 2, 1800, by Rev. Henry Christie | 2 | 24 |
| Cynthia Amelia, d. Anson & Philomelia, b. July 30, 1816 | 2 | 44 |
| Daniel Leete*, s. Noah, Jr. & Lydia, b. Feb. 13, 1791 *(Arnold Copy has "Leete **ROGERS**") | 3 | 29 |
| Edward, m. Hannah **JACKSON**, July 18, 1773, by Rev. H. Gold | LR3 | 5 |
| Edward, s. Edward & Hannah, b. Nov. 19, 1780 | 3 | 26 |
| Edward, s. Edward & Hannah, d. June 4, 1781 | 3 | 10 |
| Edward, 2nd, s. [Edward & Hannah], b. May 30, 1787 | 3 | 26 |
| Edward, m. Sally M. **GOLD**, b. of Cornwall, Mar. 4, 1810, by Rev. Josiah Hawes, of Canaan | 2 | 37 |
| Edward, d. July 24, 1813, ae 78 | 3 | 27 |
| Eliza M., m. Augustus F. **NORTON**, Nov. 12, 1834, by Rev. Walter Smith, of the North Cong. Ch. | 3 | 38 |

| | Vol. | Page |
|---|---|---|
| **ROGERS**, (cont.) | | |
| Elizabeth, m. Henry **CHRISTIE**, Mar. 20, 1791, by [ ]. Witnesses: Cynthia White & Hannah Sedgwick | 2 | 36 |
| Elizabeth Wheeler, d. Capt. Edward & Hannah, b. June 23, 1774 | LR3 | 11 |
| Hannah, m. Noah **HARRISON**, June 3, 1767, by Rev. Hezekiah Gold | 1 | 86 |
| Hannah, d. [Capt. Edward & Hannah], b. May 29, 1776 | LR3 | 11 |
| Harriet L., ae 26, b. Cornwall, m. Austin **BRUSH**, merchant, ae 24, b. New Fairfield, res. Cornwall, May 22, 1848, by Rev. H. Day | 3 | 90-1 |
| Harriet Lucetta, of Cornwall, m. Austain **BRUSH**, of New Fairfield, May 22, 1848, by Rev. Hiram Day | 3 | 80 |
| Henry L., m. Nancy **CLARK**, b. of Cornwall, Feb. 16, 1842, by Joshua L. Maynard | 3 | 64 |
| Hezekiah Gold, s. Edward & Sarah Maria, b. Feb. 24, 1811 | 2 | 38 |
| John, 2nd s. [Noah, Jr. & Lydia], b. Jan. 28, 1801 | 3 | 29 |
| John Beach, s. Dr. Timothy & Eunice, b. Aug. 14, 1786 | 2 | 20 |
| Leete*, s. Noah, Jr. & Lydia, b. Feb. 13, 1791 *("Daniel Leete **ROGERS**") | 3 | 29 |
| Lucretia, d. [Edward & Hannah], b. Mar. 17, 1785 | 3 | 26 |
| Lucretia, m. John **WARD**, b. of Cornwall, June 23, 1803, by Rev. Henry Christie | 2 | 36 |
| Lucy, Mrs. of Montville, m. Capt. Jesse **BUELL**, of Cornwall, Sept. 5, 1790, by Judah Kellogg, J. P. | 2 | 22 |
| Lydia, d. Timothy & Eunice, b. Dec. 9, 1781 | 2 | 7 |
| Lydia, 2nd d. [Noah, Jr. & Lydia], b. Nov. 18, 1795 | 3 | 29 |
| Lydia, w. Noah, Jr., d. Apr. 27, 1808 | 3 | 4 |
| Mary E., m. Theodore R. **IVES**, b. of Cornwall, May 14, 1845, at the house of Daniel L. Rogers, by Rev. Joshua L. Maynard, of the North Cong. Ch. | 3 | 71 |
| Medad, s. [Timothy & Eunice], b. Oct. 26, 1783 | 2 | 7 |
| Noah, of Cornwall, m. Rhoda **LEETE**, of Guilford, Oct. 23, 1765, at Guilford, by James Sproutt | 1 | 67 |
| Noah, s. Noah & Rhoda, b. Oct. 13, 1766 | 1 | 77 |
| Noah, Jr., m. Lydia **CORNWELL**, b. of Cornwall, Oct. 27, 1789, by Judah Kellogg, J. P. | 2 | 22 |
| Noah, 3rd, s. [Noah, Jr. & Lydia], b. May 12, 1803 | 3 | 29 |
| Noah, Jr. & Lydia, had child, d. Apr. 27, 1808 | 3 | 4 |
| Noah, d. Oct. 17, 1810, ae 79 | 2 | 39 |
| Noah, Jr., m. Catharine **CLARK**, Sept. 14, 1829, by Rev. Walter Smith, of the North Ch. | 3 | 44 |
| Rhoda, d. Noah & Rhoda, b. Sept. 15, 1770 | 1 | 97 |
| Rhoda, 3rd, d. [Noah, Jr. & Lydia], b. June 9, 1798 | 3 | 29 |
| Sally, m. John **BRISTOL**, b. of Cornwall, June 23, 1795, by Judah Kellogg, J. P. | 3 | 21 |
| Sarah, d. Noah & Rhoda, b. June 24, 1768 | 1 | 82 |
| Sarah, m. Oliver **BURNHAM**, Oct. 17, 1787, by Rev. John | | |

| | Vol. | Page |
|---|---|---|
| **ROGERS**, (cont.) | | |
| Cornwell | 3 | 8 |
| Seeley, s. Noah, Jr. & Lydia, b. Feb. 13, 1791 | 3 | 4 |
| Thankfull S., of Underhill, Vt., m. Rev. Joshua L. **MAYNARD**, Oct. 20, 1847, by Harley Goodwin | 3 | 76 |
| William C., m. Martha E. **SCOVIL**, b. of Cornwall, Apr. 13, 1853, by Rev. Frederick Manson, of N. Greenwich | 3 | 124 |
| **ROOT**, Almira Ann, m. Andrew P. **SMITH**, Aug. 14, 1830, by Rev. William Andrews | 3 | 46 |
| Clarissa, m. Solomon **KNICKERBOCKER**, Oct. 16, 1832, by Rev. Walter Smith, of the North Cong. Ch. | 3 | 35 |
| Hiram, m. Mary **WHEELER**, Dec. 2, 1821, by Asa Tallmadge, Elder, of the Bap. Church | 2 | 53 |
| Walie, m. Julia E. **HOLMES**, b. of Cornwall, Dec. 12, 1841, by Rev. Joshua L. Maynard, of the North Cong. Ch. | 3 | 64 |
| **ROSSETER**, Lucy, of Cornwall, m. Elisha **BRADFORD**, Aug. 10, 1786, by Rev. Hezekiah Gold | 2 | 16 |
| Rachel, m. Jonathan **DIBBLE**, July 3, 1781, by Judah Kellogg, J. P. | LR4 | 18 |
| **ROUSE**, [see also **RUSS**], Albion C., s. Albion C., farmer, ae 50 & Martha, ae 36, b. Sept. 14, 1848 | 3 | 98-9 |
| Birdseye Whiting, s. Lucius C. & Charlotte, b. Sept. 18, 1819 | 2 | 60 |
| Charlotte Emily, d. [Lucius C. & Charlotte], b. Nov. 20, 1820 | 2 | 60 |
| Irene, m. Col. Stephen **BONNEY**, Mar. 2, 1825, by Rev. Timothy Stone, of the 1st Ch. | 2 | 62 |
| Lucius C., m. Charlotte **BIRDSEYE**, Nov. 30, 1818, by Rev. Timothy Stone, of the 1st Ch. Witness: William Kellogg, T. C. | 2 | 59 |
| Lucius Cary, s. Whiting & Deborah, b. June 25, 1796 | 3 | 25 |
| Miles, m. Sophronia **FOX**, Oct. 23, 1821, by Rev. Timothy Stone, of the 1st Soc. | 2 | 50 |
| **ROWLEY**, Jemima, of Cornwall, m. Edward **HOWEL**, of Sharon, Aug. 27, 1794, by Rev. Israel Holly, of Cornwall | 3 | 21 |
| Timothy, m. Jemima **DIBBLE**, Mar. 9, 1769, by Rev. H. Gold | 1 | 86 |
| **[ROYCE], ROYS**, Abigail, d. Stpehen & Mary, b. Nov. 30, 1766 | LR3 | 11 |
| Caleb, s. Stephen & Mary, b. Nov. 16, 1774 | LR3 | 11 |
| Irena, d. Stephen & Mary, b. Feb. 22, 1762 | 1 | 48 |
| Levina*, d. Stephen & Mary, b. Apr. 5, 1756 *(Arnold Copy had "Lucina") | 1 | 23 |
| Lucina*, d. Stephen & Mary, b. Apr. 5, 1756 *("Levina" in Starr's book) | 1 | 23 |
| Lucy, d. Stephen & Mary, b. Aug. 7, 1757 | 1 | 30 |
| Mary, d. Stephen & Mary, b. Dec. 7, 1760 | 1 | 37 |
| Samuel, s. Stephen & Mary, b. July 3, 1754 | 1 | 22 |
| Sarah, d. Stephen & Mary, b. June 2, 1769 | LR3 | 11 |
| Stephen, s. Stephen & Mary, b. July 8, 1764 | 1 | 66 |
| Zachariah How, s. Stephen & Mary, b. Jan. 21, 1771 | LR3 | 11 |
| Zachariah How, s. Stephen & Mary, b. Jan. 21, 1771 | 1 | 101 |

| | Vol. | Page |
|---|---|---|
| **RUGG**, William H., m. Charlotte **BRADFORD**, May 17, 1832, by Rev. Walter Smith, of the North Cong. Ch. | 3 | 49 |
| William H., m. Sarah M. **BRADFORD**, Nov. 28, 1837, by Rev, Walter Smith, of the North Cong. Ch. | 3 | 53 |
| **RUSS, RUS**, [see also **ROUSE & RUST**], Lemuel, s. Jonathan & Mary, b. June 24, 1765; d. same day | 1 | 62 |
| Lucena, d. Jonathan & Mary, b. Dec. 29, 1763 | 1 | 54 |
| Nathan, s. Jonathan & Mary, b. Nov. 25, 1761 | 1 | 46 |
| Submit, d. Jonathan & Mary, b. Mar. 11, 1769; d. same day | 1 | 86 |
| **RUSSELL**, Cynthia, d. Thomas & Mary, b. Mar. 14, 1769 | 1 | 90 |
| Lucretia, d. Thomas & Mary, b. June 16, 1763 | 1 | 51 |
| Polly, m. Wells **CLARK**, b. of Cornwall, July 19, 1795, by Judah Kellogg, J. P. | 3 | 21 |
| Samuel Smithson, s. Thomas & Mary, b. Dec. 21, 1766 | 1 | 75 |
| Thomas, s. Thomas & Mary, b. Nov. 27, 1761 | 1 | 43 |
| William, m. Chloe **DIBBLE**, of Cornwall, Oct. 10, 1821, by Annarius Derthick, of Warren | 2 | 51 |
| William, d. Feb. 26, 1826 (A Revulutionary Soldier) | 2 | 56 |
| **RUST**, [see also **RUSS & ROUSE**], Deborah, m. Gabriel **ALLEN**, Oct. 15, 1769, by Heman Swift, J. P. | 1 | 96 |
| **RYAN**, Eleanor, d. Patric, tailor, ae 33 & Eleanor, ae 31, b. Aug. 28, 1849 | 3 | 108-9 |
| **SABINS**, Albro A., of North East, N. Y., m. Charlotte **BROWN**, of Cornwall, Mar. 1, 1848, by Rev. Joshua L. Maynard, of the North Cong. Ch., at the house of Mr. Brown | 3 | 79 |
| Albro A., carpenter, ae 26, b. North East, N. Y., res. Cornwall, m. Charlotte **BROWN**, ae 19, b. Goshen, res. Cornwall, Mar. 1, 1848, by Rev. Joshua L. Maynard | 3 | 90-1 |
| **SACKETT, SACKET**, Huldah Henriette, d. Moses & Cordelia L., b. Dec. 5, 1816 | 2 | 42 |
| Minerva, m. Abel C. **CARTER**, Dec. 10, 1795, by Peter Starr | 3 | 3 |
| Theron, of Stanford, N. Y., m. Flora **BLAKE**, of Cornwall, Dec. 16, 1828, by Rev. Silas Ambler | 3 | 1 |
| Vestilly, Mrs., of Warren, m. John **BATES**, of Cornwall, Nov. 24, 1792, by Rev. Peter Starr | 3 | 8 |
| **SANDERS**, Armirel, of Cornwall, m. Darius **MINER**, of Salisbury, Sept. 27, 1792, by Judah Kellogg, J. P. | 3 | 8 |
| **SANFORD**, Caroline, m. Billings **SMITH**, June 9, 1822, by Asa Tallmadge, Elder, of the Bap. Church | 2 | 53 |
| Edward, m. Viletta C. **GARDINER**, Apr. 14, 1851, by F. C. Youngs | 3 | 97 |
| Edward, druggist, ae 24, b. Cornwall, res. West Cornwall, m. Lydia **GARDINER**, ae 18, b. Cornwall, res. West Cornwall, Apr. 15, 1851, by Rev. Mr. Youngs | 3 | 118-19 |
| Julia A., m. Seymour **JOHNSON**, Sept. 14, 1835, by Rev. William Andrews | 3 | 40 |
| Lydia Ann, d. Isaac, carpenter, ae [ ] & Louisa, b. Mar. 6, 1850 | 3 | 108-9 |

| | Vol. | Page |
|---|---|---|
| **SANFORD**, (cont.) | | |
| Nancy M., of Goshen, m. L. M. **WADLEIGH**, of Springfield, Mass., Apr. 17, 1848, at the house of Harlow G. Buel, by Rev. Joshua L. Maynard, of the North Cong. Ch. | 3 | 79 |
| Nancy M., b. Goshen, res. Goshen, m. Lorenzo M. **WADLEIGH**, carpenter, res. Springield, Mass., Apr. 17, 1848, by Joshua L. Maynard | 3 | 90-1 |
| **SAWYER**, Amy, d. Nathan & Molly, b. Feb. 13, 1771 | 1 | 103 |
| Elizabeth, d. Samuel & Mary, b. Nov. 8, 1777 | LR3 | 14 |
| Elizabeth, d. Samuel & Mary, b. Nov. 8, 1777 | 2 | 7 |
| Ira, s. [Nathan], b. July 10, 1774 | 2 | 4 |
| Mary, m. Boswell **FULLER**, Aug. 10, 1764, by Daniel Farrand | 1 | 55 |
| Mary, d. [Samuel & Mary], b. Apr. 20, 1774 | LR3 | 12 |
| Mary, ae 22, b. Cornwall, res. Sharon, m. Nathan **GOULD**, tailor, ae 28, b. Greenfield, res. Bridgeport, Feb. 20, 1848, by Rev. Moses B. Blydenburgh | 3 | 90-1 |
| Matilda, d. Samuel & Mary, b. Sept. 18, 1786 | 2 | 18 |
| Nathan, s. [Samuel & Mary], b. Nov. 8, 1783 | 2 | 7 |
| Nathan, farmer, d. Feb. [ ], 1851, ae 67 | 3 | 120-1 |
| Rhoda, d. Samuel & Mary, b. June 18, 1789 | 2 | 31 |
| Salmon, s. Nathan, b. Apr. 27, 1773 | 2 | 4 |
| Samuel, s. Samuel & Mary, b. Jan. 3, 1771 | LR3 | 12 |
| Samuel, d. Aug. 25, 1813 | 3 | 27 |
| Sarah, d. [Nathan], b. July 7, 1776 | 2 | 4 |
| Stephen, s. [Nathan], b. Sept. 23, 1778 | 2 | 4 |
| Violette, d. [Samuel & Mary], b. Jan. 18, 1781 | 2 | 7 |
| William, m. Nancy **BUDDALL**, of Cornwall, Nov. 29, 1837, by Rev. Robert Travis | 3 | 53 |
| **SCOFIELD, SCOFFIELD**, [see under **SCOVILLE**] | | |
| **SCOTT**, Lydia, m. Dr. Ebenezer **BISHOP**, June 28, 1777, by Rev. Hezekiah Gold | 2 | 2 |
| Martha, m. John **DEAN**, Oct. 12, 1780, by Rev. Hezekiah Gold | LR4 | 16 |
| **SCOVILLE, SCHOPHEL, SCHOVILL, SCOFFIELD, SCOFIELD, SCOPHEL, SCOVEL, SCOVIL, SCOVILL,** | | |
| Artemis, m. Amanda **FORD**, Oct. 30, 1836, by James Wadsworth, J. P. | 3 | 42 |
| Eliza S., ae 17, of Cornwall, m. Elijah S. **ANDREWS**, ae 26, of New Britain, Nov. 26, 1854, by Rev. William M. Simons, of the Bap. Ch., Cornwall Hollow | 3 | 126 |
| George, m. Louella **BEIRCE**, Mar. 15, 1837, by Rev. William Andrews | 3 | 52 |
| Ithamer, s. Timothy & Thankful, b. Aug. 7, 1764 | 1 | 65 |
| Jacob, s. Sam[ue]l & Ruth, b. Nov. 6, 1756 | 1 | 30 |
| Jacob, m. Ruhamah **EMMONS**, Oct. 18, 1778, by Rev. Hezekiah Gold | LR3 | 13 |
| Jonathan, farmer, d. Sept. 29, 1850, ae 76 | 3 | 120-1 |

| | Vol. | Page |
|---|---|---|
| **SCOVILLE, SCHOPHEL, SCHOVILL, SCOFFIELD, SCOFIELD, SCOPHEL, SCOVEL, SCOVIL, SCOVILL,** (cont.) | | |
| Lucy Elizabeth, d. Charles & Armenia A., b. Jan. 21, 1844 | 3 | 69 |
| Lycy, of Oxford, m. Porter **DEAN**, of Cornwall, Feb. 27, 1822, by Rev. Timothy Stone, of the 1st Church | 2 | 51 |
| Martha E., m. William C. **ROGERS**, b. of Cornwall, Apr. 13, 1853, by Rev. Frederick Manson, of N. Greenwich | 3 | 124 |
| Mary Ann, m. Eleazer **HAMLIN**, May 31, 1837, by Rev. Walter Smith, of the North Cong. Ch. | 3 | 52 |
| Mary Anne, d. Samuel & Sarah, b. Sept. 26, 1816 | 2 | 44 |
| Mary E., m. Luther B. **HARRISON**, Dec. 30, 1828, by Rev. Walter Smith, of North Cong. Ch. | 3 | 1 |
| Olive, of Cornwall, m. Lorenzo **METCALF**, of South Adams, Mass., Sept. 22, 1844, by Rev. Joshua L. Maynard, of the North Cong. Ch. | 3 | 70 |
| Ruth, d. Timothy & Thankfull, d. Feb. 16, 1764 | 1 | 65 |
| Sam[ue]l, s. Samuel & Ruth, b. Nov. 8, 1758 | 1 | 33 |
| Samuel M., s. Samuel & Sarah, b. Oct. 17, 1810 | 2 | 34 |
| Sarah, m. Riley M. **REXFORD**, b. of Cornwall, Oct. 24, 1824, by Rev. Walter Smith, of the 2nd Ch. | 2 | 59 |
| Seymour J., s. [Samuel & Sarah], b. July 27, 1812 | 2 | 34 |
| Sylvester M., m. Harriet **WINANS**, May 27, 1834, by Rev. Walter Smith, of the North Cong. Ch. | 3 | 37 |
| Timothy, s. Timothy & Thankfull, b. Sept. 13, 1762 | 1 | 65 |
| **SEATON**, Horace, of Hartford, m. Minerva **STODDARD**, of Cornwall, Aug. 9, 1840, by John C. Hart | 3 | 59 |
| **SEDGWICK**, Abigail, twin with Stephen, d. Maj. John & Abigail b. Mar. 1, 1783; d. Apr. 25, 1783 | 2 | 5 |
| Abigail, d. [John A. & Nancy], b. Jan. 25, 1797 | 3 | 15 |
| Abigail, d. John & Nancy, d. Aug. 8, 1800 | 3 | 6 |
| Albert, s. [John A. & Nancy], b. May 20, 1801 | 3 | 15 |
| Amanda, d. [Col. John A. & Nancy], b. Mar. 12, 1809 | 3 | 30 |
| Anne, d. Major John & Abigail, b. Apr. 6, 1775 | LR3 | 15 |
| Benjamin, s. Maj. John & Abigail, b. Jan. 25, 1781 | LR4 | 17 |
| Charles F., s. John A. & Nancy, b. Sept. 1, 1795 | 3 | 15 |
| Elizabeth, d. [Major John & Abigail], b. Oct. 9, 1777; d. Jan. 4, 1778 | LR3 | 15 |
| Emily, d. Thoedore S., farmer, ae 30 & Caroline L., ae 24, b. Jan. 31, 1849 | 3 | 98-9 |
| Henry, s. John & Abigail, b. Sept. 13, 1767 | 1 | 80 |
| John, of Cornwall, m. Abigail **ANDRUS**, of Wallingford, Feb. 3, 1765, by James Dana | 1 | 70 |
| John, s. Benjamin & Olive, d. Sept. 13, 1813 | 2 | 38 |
| John, Gen., d. Aug. 28, 1820, ae 79 (A Revolutionary Officer) | 2 | 46 |
| John Andrus, s. John & Abigail, b. Mar. 8, 1764 | 1 | 70 |
| John E., m. Lucy Ann **BROWN**, b. of Cornwall, Dec. 27, 1835, by Rev. Thomas Sparks | 3 | 41 |
| | 3 | 16 |

| | Vol. | Page |
|---|---|---|
| **SEDGWICK**, (cont.) | | |
| Mary Ann, d. Benjamin, b. July 29, 1749 | 1 | 16 |
| Mary Ann, d. Col. John A. & Nancy, b. Oct. 20, 1806 | 3 | 30 |
| Mary Ann, m. Milton **NOYCE**, Dec. 11, 1828, by Rev. Walter Smith, of the North Ch. | 3 | 1 |
| Olive C., of Cornwall, m. Ashbel **FULLER**, of Kent, Apr. 12, 1842, by Rev. J. L. Maynard, of the North Cong. Ch. | 3 | 64 |
| Olive Collins, d. Benjamin & Olive, b. Jan. 15, 1817 | 2 | 43 |
| Pamelia, d. [Major John & Abigail], b. Dec. 21, 1798 | LR3 | 15 |
| Pamela, of Cornwall, m. Jonathan **BATES**, of Hartland, Mar. 29, 1821, by Rev. Walter Smith, of the 2nd Church | 2 | 50 |
| Parnel, d. John & Abigail, b. Oct. 4, 1771 | 1 | 103 |
| Philo Collins, s. Benjamin & Olive, b. July 18, 1810 | 3 | 28 |
| Roderick, s. John & Abigail, b. Mar. 3, 1770 | 1 | 94 |
| Roderic, s. Col. John & Abigail, b. Jan. 21, 1785 | 2 | 10 |
| Sarah, Mrs., m. Rev. Hezekiah **GOLD**, Nov. 23, 1758, by Rev. Nathaniel Shepherd, of New Milford | 1 | 32 |
| Sarah, d. John & Abigail, b. Dec. 27, 1765 | 1 | 70 |
| Sarah, d. Gen. John, d. Oct. 5, 1815 | 2 | 33 |
| Stephen, twin with Abigail, s. Maj. John & Abigail, b. Mar. 1, 1783 | 2 | 5 |
| **SEELEY, SELEY**, Arthur Wellington, s. Luman & Polly, b. Oct. 9, 1815 | 2 | 40 |
| Elvira, d. [Luman & Polly], b. Aug. 31, 1805 | 3 | 12 |
| Harriet J., d. Samuel S., farmer, ae 23 & Huldah E., ae 26, b. May 30, 1848 | 3 | 86-7 |
| Harvey Hamilton, s. Luman & Polly, b. June 17, 1812 | 3 | 34 |
| Justus Bradley, s. Luman & Polly, b. Oct. 31, 1809 | 3 | 18 |
| Lenora, b. Sharon, res. Cornwall, d. Aug. 7, 1850, ae 3 | 3 | 120-1 |
| Luman, m. Polly **TRALL**, b. of Cornwall, Nov. 4, 1801, by Judah Kellogg, J. P. | 3 | 32 |
| Milleseneth, of Cornwall, m. Miles **MORREMAN**, of Sharon, Jan. 22, 1825, by Rev. Jaohn Lovejoy, of the M. E. Ch. | 2 | 63 |
| Nancy, m. Asaph **EMMONS**, Aug. 11, 1784, by Rev. Hezekiah Gold | 2 | 8 |
| Philo, m. Mary Ann **BUDSALL**, b. of Cornwall, Oct. 20, 1842, by Rev. Thomas Edwards | 3 | 65 |
| Samuel, s. Luman & Polly, b. Oct. 11, 1802 | 3 | 12 |
| Samuel, of Cornwall, m. Azubah **MORRIS**, of Goshen, Sept. 24, 1843, by Rev. Thomas Edwards, of the M. E. Ch. | 3 | 67 |
| Samuel, farmer, d. Dec. [ ], 1848, ae [ ] | 3 | 106-7 |
| William, m. Mariah **BENEDICT**, b. of Cornwall, Nov. 10, 1822, by Rev. A. Derthick, of the Bap. Ch. of Warren | 2 | 54 |
| **SEWARD**, Amos, s. [Capt. Nathan & Martha], b. Feb. 20, 1786 | 2 | 18 |
| Lucinda, d. Capt. Nathan & Martha, b. Jan. 6, 1784 | 2 | 18 |
| **SEYMOUR**, Lois E., d. Caleb, b. July 23, 1849 | 3 | 102-3 |
| **SHAW**, Agnes, m. Patrick **HINDMAN**, b. of Cornwall, Sept. 16, [1764], by Thomas Russell, J. P. | 1 | 59 |

| | Vol. | Page |
|---|---|---|
| **SHEFFIELD**, James, d. Sept. 10, 1848 | 3 | 106-7 |
| **SHEPARD**, Anna, d. Ebenezer & Ruth, b. Nov. 9, 1790 | 3 | 23 |
| Annah, w. Allen, d. Jan. 6, 1826, ae 59 | 2 | 56 |
| Elbert, m. Cynthia **WHEATON**, May 31, 1846, by R. K. Reynolds | 3 | 73 |
| Eliphalet H., m. Mary **KELLOGG**, 2nd, July 7, 1813, by Rev. Timothy Stone, of the 1st Ch. Witness: William Kellogg, T. C. | 3 | 33 |
| Eliphalet Hull, s. [Allen & Anner], b. May 23, 1789 | 2 | 41 |
| Esther Anne, d. [Allen & Anner], b. Sept. 7, 1796 | 2 | 41 |
| Fredus. s. [Allen & Anner], b. Sept. 6, 1806 | 2 | 41 |
| Fredus, s. Allen, d. Jan. 4, 1826, ae 19 y. | 2 | 56 |
| George Hull, s. [Eliphalet H. & Mary], b. July 24, 1815 | 2 | 41 |
| Harriet, d. [Allen & Anner], b. July 23, 1794 | 2 | 41 |
| Harriet, m. Carrington **TODD**, b. of Cornwall, Oct. 31, 1832, by Rev. Aaron S. Hill | 3 | 50 |
| Jonathan B., m. Jane **FRINK**, Feb. 1, 1838, by William W. Andrews | 3 | 56 |
| Mary Anne, d. Eliphalet H. & Mary, b. Apr. 1. 1814 | 2 | 41 |
| Mary Anne, d. Eliphalet H. & Mary, d. Oct. 6, 1817 | 2 | 39 |
| Rebeckah, d. Allen & Anner, b. Dec. 18, 1786 | 2 | 41 |
| Rebecca, of Cornwall, m. Nathan **FELCH**, late of Royaltown, Cty. of Worcester, now of Cornwall, May 14, 1805, by Judah Kellogg, J. P. | 3 | 11 |
| **SHERALIER**, William, m. Mary Ann **TUTTLE**, Mar. 23, 1831, by Rev. Walter Smith, of the North Cong. Ch. | 3 | 48 |
| **SHERMAN**, George H., s. Oscar, mechanic, ae 27 & Jane, ae 24, b. Sept. 8, 1850 | 3 | 116-17 |
| George H., d. May 13, 1851, ae 8 m. | 3 | 120-1 |
| Margaret, d. Sept. 13, 1847, ae 1 | 3 | 92-3 |
| Oscar M., of Lee, Mass., m. Antionette **PANGMAN**, of Cornwall, Nov. 17, 1852, by Ralph Smith | 3 | 125 |
| **SHERWOOD**, Azubah, d. Ebenezer & Azubah, b. Feb. 28, 1771 | LR4 | 15 |
| Azubah, w. Ebenezer, d. Mar. 16, 1771 | LR4 | 15 |
| Ebenezer, m. Azuba **ALLEN**, Apr. 10, 1769, by Rev. Hezekiah Gold | LR4 | 15 |
| Ebenezer, m. Hannah **BRADFORD**, Jan. 2, 1772, by Rev. Hezekiah Gold | LR4 | 15 |
| Ebenezer, s. Ebenezer & Hannah, b. Jan. 28, 1779 | LR4 | 15 |
| Ebenezer, d. Jan. 24, 1785 | 2 | 11 |
| Hannah, d. [Ebenezer & Hannah], b. Sept. 5, 1782 | 2 | 12 |
| John, s. Ebenezer & Hannah, b. Sept. 25, 1773 | LR4 | 15 |
| John S., of New York, m. Harriet N. **COTTER**, of Cornwall, Mar. 26, 1844, by Rev. Joshua L. Maynard, of the North Cong. Ch. | 3 | 70 |
| Joshua Bradford, s. Ebenezer & Hannah, b. May 19, 1772 | LR4 | 15 |
| Molly, d. Ebenezer & Hannah, b. Mar. 2, 1777 | LR4 | 15 |
| Orvilla, d. Ebenezer & Hannah, b. Nov. 10, 1780 | 2 | 12 |

| | Vol. | Page |
|---|---|---|
| **SHERWOOD**, (cont.) | | |
| Sarah, d. [Ebenezer & Hannah], b. Mar. 2, 1784 | 2 | 12 |
| **SHOVE**, Samuel A., salesman, ae 23, b. Warren, res. Cornwall, m. Jennett **BARNUM**, ae 20, b. Warren, res. Cornwall, May 30, 1849, by Rev. William McAlister | 3 | 104-5 |
| Samuel N., m. Jennett **BARNUM**, Apr. 15, 1849, by William McAlister | 3 | 77 |
| **SIMMONS, SYMMONS**, [see also **SIMONS**], David, s. Ebenezer & Mary, b. Feb. 26, 1769 | 1 | 87 |
| Hannah, m. James **GRIFFIS**, Oct. 22, 1767, by Rev. Hezekiah Gold | 1 | 84 |
| John, s. Job & Abigail, b. Jan. 17, 1761 | 1 | 44 |
| Mary, d. Job & Abigail, b. May 7, 1764 | 1 | 60 |
| Rufus, s. Job & Abigail, b. Oct. 1, 1768 | 1 | 86 |
| Ruth, m. Joshua **HARRIS**, Sept. 17, 1760, by Samuel Pettebone, J. P. | 1 | 37 |
| Sarah, m. Titus **MOREMAN**, Nov. 13, 1768, by Rev. Hezekiah Gold | 1 | 88 |
| Solomon, s. Job & Abigail, b. Aug. 24, 1766 | 1 | 73 |
| Silve, d. Job & Abigail, b. Dec. 12, 1762 | 1 | 48 |
| **SIMONS**, [see also **SIMMONS**], Elizabeth, ae 27, b. Goshen, res. Cornwall, m. Elisha **HOWE**, carpenter, ae 25, res. Cornwall, Sept. 18, 1851, by Rev. Mr. Yates | 3 | 118-19 |
| **SKIFF**, Nathan, of Kent, m. Adelia **MILLARD**, of Cornwall, Nov. 18, 1828, by Rev. L. P. Hickok, of the Cong. Ch. in Kent | 3 | 1 |
| **SLADE**, Florilla M., of Kent, m. James J. **WEBB**, of Santa Fe., Feb. 1, 1853, by Ralph Smith | 3 | 125 |
| **SLOCOMB, SLOCOM**, Major Howard, s. Seneca, butcher, ae 42 & Eunice, ae 42, b. Oct. 4, 1848 | 3 | 98-9 |
| Senaca, m. Eliza A. **JOHNSON**, Nov. 4, 1852, by Ralph Smith | 3 | 125 |
| **SMALLEY**, Liddia, d. Samuell & Hannah, b. Feb. 27, 1757 | 1 | 27 |
| **SMITH**, Ambrose, moulder, had child, b. [ ] | 3 | 108-9 |
| Andrew P., m. Almira Ann **ROOT**, Aug. 14, 1830, by Rev. William Andrew | 3 | 46 |
| Aurilia F., twin with Cornelia A., d. Archibald, blacksmith, ae 46, & Oby, ae 37, b. Nov. 13, 1847 | 3 | 84-5 |
| Billings, m. Caroline **SANFORD**, June 9, 1822, by Asa Tallmadge, Elder, of the Bap. Church | 2 | 53 |
| Catharine R., of New Haven, m. Eri L. **LANE**, of Cornwall, July 11, 1852, by Harley Goodwin | 3 | 123 |
| Charlotte, m. Reuben **PLATT**, Nov. 7, 1830, by Rev. William Andrews | 3 | 46 |
| Cornelia A., twin with Aurilia F., d. Archibald, blacksmith, ae 46, & Oby, ae 37, b. Nov. 13, 1847 | 3 | 84-5 |
| E. J., of Springfiled, Mass., m. Sarah A. **NETTLETON**, of Cornwall, Jan. 14, 1849, by Rev. Alfred Gates | 3 | 82 |

| | Vol. | Page |
|---|---|---|
| **SMITH**, (cont.) | | |
| Eli B., of Plymouth, m. Emeline **CORBIN**, of Plymouth, Nov. 29, 1838, by N. M. Urmston | 3 | 56 |
| Gad, of Sharon, m. Polly **TRAFFORD**, of Cornwall, Sept. 7, 1834, by Rev. Chester William Turner, of the M. E. Ch. | 3 | 37 |
| James M., of Sharon, m. Delia M. **TRAFFORD**, of Cornwall, Mar. 26, 1837, by Rev. E. Washburn | 3 | 42 |
| Julia M., m. Hiram B. **NORTHROP**, b. of Cornwall, May 2, 1841, by Rev. Brown Emerson | 3 | 61 |
| Mary, of Cornwall, m. George **BUEL**, of Litchfield, Nov. 28, 1836, by Rev. Thomas Benedict, of Torrington | 3 | 42 |
| William, teacher, ae 26 & Nancy, ae 34, dressmaker, had child, b. July 12, 1848 | 3 | 88-9 |
| **SPAULDING, SPALDING, SPAULDON**, Amasa, s. Isaac & Mercy, b. June 7, 1759 | 1 | 34 |
| Ashel, s. Thomas & Sarah, b. June 22, 1760 | 1 | 37 |
| Edward, s. Isaac & Mercy, b. June 13, 1761 | 1 | 43 |
| George, s. Phinehas & Sarah, b. Nov. 27, 1761 | 1 | 45 |
| Isaac, d. Sept. 29, 1754 | 1 | 21 |
| Isaac, m. Mercy **BROWN**, b. of Cornwall, Dec. 10, 1754, by George Halloway, J. P. | 1 | 22 |
| Mary, d. Isaac & Mercy, b. May 22, 1763 | 1 | 52 |
| Mehetabel, d. Phinehas & Sarah, b. June 17, 1746/7 | 1 | 6 |
| Nathan, s. Phinehas & Sarah, b. Mar. 3, 1752 | 1 | 17 |
| Nehemiah, s. Isaac & Mercy, b. Aug. 9, 1757 | 1 | 29 |
| Philip, s. Phinehas & Sarah, b. June 23, 1754 | 1 | 27 |
| Phinehas, s. Phinehas & Sarah, b. Dec. 25, 1749 | 1 | 10 |
| Sam[ue]ll, s. Isaac & Mercy, b. Feb. 16, 1756 | 1 | 24 |
| Sarah, d. Phinehas & Sarah, b. Jan. 29, 1757 | 1 | 25 |
| Sarah, d. Phineas & Sarah, d. Sept. 19, 1759 | 1 | 34 |
| Sarah, w. Timothy, d. Dec. 9, 1766 | 1 | 74 |
| Timothy, m. Sarah **SQUIERS**, Jan. 25, 1764, by Rev. Hezekiah Gold | 1 | 60 |
| **SPELLMAN**, Betsey, of Cornwall, m. John O. **HAYDEN**, of Middletown, Sept. 26, 1824, by Rev. Walter Smith, of the 2nd Ch. | 2 | 58 |
| Hannah, of Cornwall, m. Frederick **ROBERTS**, of Goshen, Jan. 23, 1825, by Rev. Charles Prentice, of Canaan | 2 | 59 |
| Maria, m. John **WHITLOCK**, of Ridgfield, Feb. 12, 1822, by Rev. Walter Smith, of the 2nd Church | 2 | 51 |
| **SPENCER**, Burrall, s. Zachariah & Nancy, b. Sept. 8, 1812 | 3 | 14 |
| Sylvia Anne, d. Zachariah & Nancy, b. July 3, 1810 | 3 | 13 |
| Zachariah, d. Aug. 2, 1812 | 3 | 27 |
| **SPERRY**, Fowler, of Bethany, m. Jehersa **NETTLETON**, of Cornwall, Oct. 24, 1843, by Rev. Joshua L. Maynard, of the North Cong. Ch. | 3 | 67 |
| **SPURR**, Andrew J., of Sheffield, Mass., m. Sarah A. **JOHNSON**, | | |

| | Vol. | Page |
|---|---|---|
| **SPURR**, (cont.) | | |
| of Cornwall, Sept. 2, 1850, by E. W. Andrews | 3 | 83 |
| **SQUIRE, SQUIER, SQUIRES**, Bettey, d. Reuben & Hannah, b. Mar. 13, 1752 | 1 | 26 |
| Crandall Holley, s. Augustus & Hope, b. Nov. 21, 1824 | 2 | 64 |
| Daniel, s. Reuben & Hannah, b. Dec. 26, 1738 | 1 | 26 |
| Daniel, m. Hannah **ABBOTT**, Feb. 19, 1761, by Rev. H. Gold | 1 | 48 |
| Ebenezer, s. Reuben & Hannah, b. May 17, 1758 | 1 | 34 |
| Edward Adams, m. Mary **PIERCE**, Nov. 9, 1778, by Rev. Hezekiah Gold | LR3 | 13 |
| Eli, s. Daniel & Hannah, b. July 11, 1764 | 1 | 60 |
| Ezra, m. Amie **FULLER**, Sept. 3, 1751, by Solomon Palmer | 1 | 16 |
| Hannah, w. Reuben, d. Jan. 13, 1761 | 1 | 71 |
| Hannah, d. Daniel & Hannah, b. Jan. 19, 1762 | 1 | 50 |
| Hannah, d. Daniel & Hannah, b. Oct. 15, 1766 | 1 | 74 |
| Ichabod, s. Reuben & Hannah, b. June 22, 1745* *("1741" in Starr's book) | 1 | 26 |
| John, s. Reuben & Hannah, b. May 5, 1755 | 1 | 27 |
| Leah, d. Edward Adam & Mary, b. Apr. 14, 1781 | LR4 | 17 |
| Nabbe, d. Edward A., & Mary, b. June 28, 1783 | 2 | 5 |
| Reuben, of Fairfield, m. Hannah **MALLORY**, of Stratford, May [ ], 1738, by Rev. Jedediah Mills, of Stratford | 1 | 27 |
| Reuben, m. Elizabeth **BRYANT**, May 19, [1761], by Rev. Nathaniel Bartlet, of Reading | 1 | 71 |
| Samuel Norton, s. Augustus & Hope, b. Aug. 12, 1822 | 2 | 64 |
| Sarah, d. Reuben & Hannah, b. Dec. 27, 1745 | 1 | 26 |
| Sarah, d. Reuben & Hannah, b. Sept. 22, 1747 | 1 | 26 |
| Sarah, m. Timothy **SPAULDING**, Jan. 25, 1764, by Rev. Hezekiah Gold | 1 | 60 |
| Sarah, d. Edward Adam & Mary, b. July 13, 1779 | LR4 | 14 |
| Washington Adams, s. [Augustus & Hope], b. Mar. 5, 1820 | 2 | 52 |
| William Kingdom, s. Augustus & Hope, b. Dec. 18, 1817 | 2 | 52 |
| **STANTON**, Frances J., m. Joseph E. **MEACHAM**, Oct. 14, 1834, by Rev. William Andrews | 3 | 38 |
| **STARKE, STARK**, Hannah, d. Samuell & Elizabeth, b. Dec. 19, 1749 | 1 | 26 |
| Samuel, his w. [ ], d. Dec. 31, 1749 | 1 | 16 |
| Samuell, d. Jan. 25, 1749/50 | 1 | 16 |
| **STARR**, Caroline, colored, ae 18, b. Sharon, res. Cornwall, m. Charles **CAMBRIDGE**, laborer, colored, ae 26, b. Milford, res. Cornwall, Oct. 26, 1847, by Rev. Lewis Gunn | 3 | 90-1 |
| **STEAD**, John, m. Polly **PIERSON**, b. of Cornwall, Dec. 10, [1820], by Rev. A. Derthick, of Bap. Soc. in Warren | 2 | 49 |
| **STEARNES**, Warren, of Killingly, m. Mary **REED**, of Cornwall, Jan. 29, 1823, by Rev. David Miller | 2 | 55 |
| **STEELE, STEAL**, Alsop, s. Matthew & Lydia, b. Oct. 27, 1789 | 2 | 21 |
| Clarissa, d. Elijah, Jr. & Anne, b. Oct. 6, 1786 | 2 | 19 |

| | Vol. | Page |
|---|---|---|
| **STEELE, STEAL**, (cont.) | | |
| Elijah, m. Ester **BULLARD**, Jan. 18, 1759, by Rev. Timothy Baldwin | 1 | 36 |
| Elijah, s. Elijah & Esther, b. Feb. 6, 1764 | 1 | 54 |
| Elijah, s. Elijah & Esther, b. Feb. 6, 1764 | 1 | 87 |
| Elijah, of Cornwall, m. Sarah **ANDREWS**, of Wallingford, Aug. 4, 1773, by James Dana | LR3 | 5 |
| Elijah, Jr., m. Anna **BASSETT**, Feb. 13, 1786, by Rev. John Cornwell | 2 | 16 |
| Elijah, Jr., m. Lydia **HOLLY**, Aug. 5, 1798, by Rev. Israel Holly | 3 | 9 |
| Eliphalet Mosefield*, s. [Elijah & Esther], b. Jan. 20, 1766 *("Marshfield" in Starr's book) | 1 | 87 |
| Elma, d. Matthew M. & Lydia, b. Nov. 30, 1787 | 2 | 20 |
| Esther, w. Elijah, d. Apr. 20, 1771 | 1 | 105 |
| Esther, d. Matthew Millard & Lydia, b. Aug. 18, 1784 | 2 | 9 |
| Guli, d. Matthew Millard & Lydia, b. Dec. 3, 1785 | 2 | 15 |
| Jerusha, d. [Eliphalet & Hannah], b. Feb. 24, 1793 | 2 | 32 |
| Lucy, d. Matthew & Lydia, b. Nov. 19, 1791 | 3 | 24 |
| Matthew, s. Elijah & Esther, b. Mar. 23, 1760; d. Mar. 29, 1760 | 1 | 36 |
| Matthew Millard, s. Elijah & Esther, b. Nov. 10, 1761 | 1 | 44 |
| Matthew Millard, m. Lydia **PRATT**, Jan. 8, 1784, by Rev. Hezekiah Gold | 2 | 8 |
| Orlo, s. [Elijah & Esther], b. Feb. 21, 1768; d. Mar. 22, 1768 | 1 | 87 |
| Orlo, s. Eliphalet & Hannah, b. May 14, 1791 | 2 | 32 |
| Sally, d. [Elijah, Jr. & Anne], b. Apr. 13, 1788 | 2 | 19 |
| **STEPHENS**, [see under **STEVENS**] | | |
| **STERLING**, Amy, d. James & Hannah, b. May 19, 1771 | 1 | 99 |
| Anne, d. James & Hannah, b. Mar. 23, 1785 | 2 | 10 |
| Daniel, s. James & Hannah, b. May 3, 1769 | 1 | 90 |
| Hannah, d. James & Hannah, b. Jan. 7, 1783 | 2 | 4 |
| Heman B., m. Harriet **WELLS**, b. of Cornwall, Feb. 20, 1842, by Philo Kellogg, J. P. | 3 | 64 |
| Heman Bradley, s. Isaac & Urania, b. Feb. 19, 1802 | 3 | 12 |
| Isaac, s. James & Hannah, b. June 20, 1773 | 2 | 13 |
| Isaac Hilliard, s. Isaac & Urania, b. May 28, 1799 | 2 | 23 |
| James, s. Hannah **MAY**, June 28, 1767, by Thomas Russell, J. P. | 1 | 78 |
| James, s. James & Hannah, b. Sept. 10, 1781 | LR4 | 17 |
| James, Jr., m. Abigail **MAPLES**, Feb. 6, 1803, by Judah Kellogg, J. P. | 3 | 32 |
| Johne Rosseter, s. Isaac & Melissent, b. Oct. 25, 1809 | 3 | 17 |
| Nathaniel, s. James & Hannah, b. Nov. 1, 1775 | LR3 | 10 |
| Rachel, d. James & Hannah, b. Jan. 15, 1778 | LR3 | 15 |
| Samuel, s. James & Hannah, b. Apr. 1, 1793 | 2 | 29 |
| Sarah, d. James & Hannah, b. Dec. 1, 1786 | 2 | 18 |
| Thomas, s. James & Hannah, b. Dec. 6, 1767 | 1 | 69 |

| | Vol. | Page |
|---|---|---|
| **STERLING**, (cont.) | | |
| Urania, w. Isaac, d. Sept. 19, 1804 | 3 | 6 |
| Urena Johnson, d. Isaac & Urania, b. June 2, 1804 | 3 | 12 |
| Walter, of Bridgeport, m. Sabra S. **COLE**, of Cornwall, Mar. 10, 1852, at the house of Irad cole, by Rev. J. L. Maynard | 3 | 122 |
| **STEVENS, STEPHENS**, Harvey, m. Mehetable **THOMAS**, Apr. 30, 1810, by Rev. Reuben Harris, of the M. E. Ch. | 3 | 33 |
| Susan, colored, b. Milford, res. Cornwall, d. Mar. 31, 1848, ae 33 | 3 | 92-3 |
| William F., m. Laura S. **GOLD**, Jan. 1, 1828, by Rev. Walter Smith, of the 2nd Soc. | 2 | 68 |
| **STEWART**, Bradley Seeley, s. [Stephen & Hannah], b. Aug. 27, 1784 | 2 | 18 |
| Elizabeth, m. Samuel Wood, Apr. 7, 1788, by Rev. Hezekiah Gold | 2 | 22 |
| Eunice, d. Daniel & Zervia, b. Aug. 5, 1786 | 3 | 23 |
| Ira, s. Daniel & Zerviah, b. Aug. 18, 1784 | 2 | 9 |
| Jared Shaw, s. Stephen & Hannah, b. Oct. 13, 1781 | 2 | 18 |
| Juliana, d. [Stephen & Hannah], b. July 29, 1786 | 2 | 18 |
| Lydiah, d. Daniel & Phebe, b. May 10, 1770 | LR3 | 6 |
| Olive, d. [Daniel & Zeriah], b. July 11, 1779 | LR3 | 16 |
| Phebe, w. Daniel, d. Jan. 20, 1775 | LR3 | 15 |
| Rachel, d. [Daniel & Zervia], b. Sept. 21, 1790 | 3 | 23 |
| Zeriah, d. Daniel & Zeriah, b. Aug. 12, 1777 | LR3 | 16 |
| **STILSON**, Annah, m. James **COLE**, July 25, 1782, by Rev. Hezekiah Gold | 2 | 5 |
| **STODDARD**, Julia M., of Cornwall, m. Asa W. **HARDING**, of Newton, Sept. 30, 1851, at the house of William Stoddard, by Rev. Joshua L. Maynard, of the North Cong. Ch. | 3 | 96 |
| Minerva, m. John P. **WADSWORTH**, Mar. 10, 1829, by Rev. Walter Smith, of North Ch. | 3 | 44 |
| Minerva, of Cornwall, m. Horace **SEATON**, of Hartford, Aug. 9, 1840, by John C. Hart | 3 | 59 |
| **STONE**, Aaron C., m. Amanda **DICKENSON**, Oct. 19, 1826, by Rev. Asa Tallmadge, of Bap. Ch. | 2 | 66 |
| Betsey Jane, m. Onnuel B. **GIBSON**, b. of Warren, July 28, 1839, by Rev. Samuel W. Smith, of the M. E. Ch. | 3 | 58 |
| Eliza, m. George **BRADLEY**, b. of Litchfield, Jan. 27, 1832, by Rev. Silas Ambler | 3 | 49 |
| Eunice L., m. Norman F. **DIBBLE**, Apr. 6, 1837, by Rev. William Andrews | 3 | 52 |
| Eunice Lucy Irene, d. [Rev. Timothy & Mary], b. July 19, 1814 | 2 | 40 |
| Jerusha, m. John **ACKERMAN**, b. of Cornwall, May 29, 1839, by Rev. Samuel W. Smith | 3 | 58 |
| John*, m. Lucy **HOW**, Aug. 31, 1758, by Rev. Hezekiah | | |

| | Vol. | Page |
|---|---|---|
| **STONE**, (cont.) | | |
| Gold *("John **PIERCE**" in Starr's book) | 1 | 32 |
| John P., m. Lydia **CARTER**, Oct. 1, 1837, by Rev. William Andrews | 3 | 53 |
| John Peirce, s. Rev. Timothy & Mary, b. Jan. 17, 1805 | 3 | 5 |
| Lucius C., of Litchfield, m. Phebe H. **PARMELEY**, of Cornwall, Mar. 21, 1839, by N. M. Urmston | 3 | 56 |
| Lucy Anna, m. Sylvester **BARNUM**, June 22, 1826, by Rev. Asa Tallmadge, of the Bap. Ch. | 2 | 65 |
| Mary M., m. Ezekiel **BIRDSEYE**, Feb. 5, 1834, by William Andrews | 3 | 37 |
| Mary Merwin, d. Rev. Timothy & Mary, b. Feb. 15, 1807 | 3 | 16 |
| Sarah J., of Litchfield, m. George W. **CALKINS**, of Cornwall, May 4, 1851, by F. C. Youngs | 3 | 97 |
| Sarah J., ae 24, b. Litchfield, res. Cornwall, m. George W. **CALKINS**, farmer, ae 19, b. Cornwall, res. Cornwall, May 14, 1851, by Rev. Mr. Youngs | 3 | 118-19 |
| Timothy, Rev., m. Mary **MERWIN**, b. of Cornwall, Jan. 26, 1804, by E. Porter | 3 | 32 |
| Timothy Dwight Porter, s. Rev. Timothy & Mary, b. July 27, 1811 | 2 | 40 |
| William, m. Sarah **ANSON**, Feb. 22, 1846, by Rev. K. K. Reynolds | 3 | 72 |
| **STUDLEY**, Allen G., of Ellsworth, m. Harriet S. **PAYNE**, of Cornwall, Sept. 6, 1840, by Rev. John W. Salter | 3 | 59 |
| Enoch B., of Sharon, m. Sarah F. **PAYNE**, of Cornwall, Nov. 30, 1842, by Rev. Joshua L. Maynard, of the North Cong. Ch. | 3 | 65 |
| **SWEATLAND**, Sibble, d. David & Eunice, b. Mar. 23, 1774 | LR3 | 6 |
| **SWEENEY**, James, s. Robert, b. July 30, 1849 | 3 | 102-3 |
| **SWIFT**, Abiah, d. Isaac & Patience, b. Sept. 15, 1778 | LR4 | 15 |
| Abiah, d. Isaac & Patience, b. Sept. 15, 1778 | 2 | 12 |
| Betsey, m. John C. **CALHOUN**, b. of Cornwall, Oct. 9, 1822, by Rev. Timothy Stone, of the 1st Ch. | 2 | 54 |
| Caroline, of Cornwall, m. Dr. Samuel **PONDERSON**, of N[ew] Haven, May 21, [1823], by Rev. Timothy Stone | 2 | 55 |
| Charlotte, d. [Ira & Grace], b. Mar. 19, 1804 | 3 | 34 |
| Charlotte, m. Lyman **HOLLISTER**, Feb. 27, 1833, by William Andrews | 3 | 35 |
| Demis, m. William **KELLOGG**, Nov. 11, 1790, by Peter Starr | 3 | 20 |
| Edmund Rogers, s. [Ira & Grace], b. Jan. 22, 1813 | 3 | 34 |
| Elisha, s. Lieut. Heman & Mary, b. Aug. 10, 1764 | 1 | 61 |
| Elisha, s. Ira & Grace, b. Nov. 21, 1801 | 3 | 34 |
| Elizabeth M., m. Joseph L. **WHITNEY**, Sept. 12, 1849, by Rev. William McAlister | 3 | 77 |
| Eunice, w. Philo, d. June 7, 1823, ae 52, y. | 2 | 46 |
| George, farmer, ae 28 & Susan, ae 26, had d. [ ], b. May | | |

| | Vol. | Page |
|---|---|---|
| **SWIFT**, (cont.) | | |
| 16, 1848 | 3 | 86-7 |
| Harriet, m. Caleb **JONES**, b. of Cornwall, Feb. 28, 1811, by Rev. Timothy Stone | 2 | 37 |
| Heman, Gen., b. Oct. 14, O. S., 1733, at Sandwich, Mass., d. Nov. 12, 1814, ae 81. "Served as Col. during the Rev. War; was twelve years a member of the Council of Conn." | 2 | 33 |
| Heman, twin with [ ], s. Heman & Mary, b. Sept. 23, 1768 | 1 | 93 |
| Heman, had negro Peony, d. James & Patience, b. Oct. 6, 1791 | 3 | 24 |
| Heman, had negro Lottis, d. Patience, b. Oct. 22, 1795 | 3 | 22 |
| Heman, m. Caroline **WHITCOMB**, Jan. 4, 1830, by Rev. William Andrews | 3 | 45 |
| Heman S., m. Jane E. **TRAFFORD**, Sept. 10, 1835, by Rev. William Andrews | 3 | 40 |
| Heman Seth, s. [Ira & Grace], b. July 2, 1808 | 3 | 34 |
| Jabez, s. Heman & Mary, b. Sept. 11, 1766 | 1 | 72 |
| Laura Rogers, d. [Ira & Grace], b. Apr. 17, 1806 | 3 | 34 |
| Mariette, d. Jan. 13, 1849, ae 52 | 3 | 106-7 |
| Mary, w. Gen. Heman, d. Mar. 13, 1788 | 2 | 11 |
| Mary, of Cornwall, m. W[illia]m J. **WARNER**, of Preble, N. Y., June 1, 1845, by Rev. Hiram Day | 3 | 71 |
| Patience, d. [Isaac & Patience], b. Mar. 13, 1784 | 2 | 12 |
| Philo, s. Heman & Mary, b. Nov. 10, 1762 | 1 | 65 |
| Philo, s. [Ira & Grace], b. July 24, 1810 | 3 | 34 |
| Philo, 2nd, m. Lucy P. **FRINK**, Mar. 4, 1835, by Rev. William Andrews | 3 | 38 |
| Rebecca M., farming, b. Canaan, res. Cornwall, d. May 28, 1851, ae 55 | 3 | 120-1 |
| Samantha, m. John M. **WARNER**, Sept. 1, 1835, by Rev. William Andrews | 3 | 40 |
| Sarah, w. Hon. Heman, d. Apr. 17, 1804 | 3 | 6 |
| Sarah, b. Southbury, res. Cornwall, d. Nov. 9, 1847, ae 84 | 3 | 92-3 |
| Sarah B., m. Adolphus **GAY**, Jan. 23, 1843, by John W. Beecher | 3 | 66 |
| Susan, b. Sharon, res. Cornwall, d. May 22, 1849, ae 29 | 3 | 106-7 |
| -----, twin with Heman, s. Heman & Mary, b. Sept. 23, 1768; d. Sept. 30, 1768 | 1 | 93 |
| **TANNER, TENNER**, Amy, d. John & Jemima, b. Apr. 12, 1764 | 1 | 66 |
| Anna, d. Thomas & Anna, b. Jan. 2, 1777 | LR3 | 14 |
| Archibald, s. [Tryal & Huldah], b. Feb. 3, 1786 | 2 | 15 |
| Asenath, d. [Consider & Rachel], b. Jan. 11, 1775 | 2 | 29 |
| Benjamin, s. [Consider & Rachel], b. Aug. 30, 1779 | 2 | 29 |
| Bridget, d. Tryal & Huldah, b. Apr. 15, 1797 | 2 | 32 |
| Consider, m. Rachel **BENEDICT**, Mar. 3, 1772, by Hezekiah Gold | 1 | 102 |
| Consider, of Cornwall, m. Silva **BASTO**, of Sharon, Jan. | | |

| | Vol. | Page |
|---|---|---|
| **TANNER, TENNER**, (cont.) | | |
| 29, 1795, by Rev. Israel Holly | 3 | 21 |
| Ebenezer, s. William & Hannah, b. Jan. 20, 1757 | 1 | 28 |
| Ebenezer, s. [Consider & Rachel], b. Mar. 4, 1788 | 2 | 29 |
| Ebenezer Garnsey, s. William & Milleson, b. Aug. 3, 1785 | 2 | 18 |
| Ephraim, s. William & Hannah, b. June 17, 1754 | 1 | 28 |
| Frederic, s. [Consider & Rachel], b. Dec. 15, 1781 | 2 | 29 |
| Hannah, m. Moses **DEAN**, b. of Cornwall, Apr. 29, 1757, by Rev. Hezekiah Gold | 1 | 28 |
| Hannah, d. Consider & Rachel, b. Feb. 10, 1773 | 2 | 29 |
| Ira, s. Thomas & Anna, b. June 12, 1767 | 1 | 77 |
| Isaac, s. Thomas & Anna, b. Sept. 8, 1773 | LR3 | 6 |
| John, m. Jemima **BISHOP**, Sept. 14, 1758, by Rev. Hezekiah Gold | 1 | 32 |
| Julius, s. Tryal & Huldah, b. July 30, 1790 | 3 | 25 |
| Laura, d. [Tryal & Huldah], b. Feb. 23, 1784 | 2 | 15 |
| Margaret, d. [Tryal & Huldah], b. June 17, 1782 | 2 | 15 |
| Mehetable, d. Thomas & Martha, d. July 17, 1749 | 1 | 8 |
| Nancy, d. Tryal & Huldah, b. Nov. 10, 1779 | 2 | 15 |
| Olive, d. [Consider & Rachel], b. Nov. 18, 1784 | 2 | 29 |
| Panthea, d. Tryal & Huldah, b. Jan. 10, 1795 | 3 | 25 |
| Panthea, d. [Tryal & Huldah], b. Jan. 10, 1795 | 3 | 25 |
| Prior, s. Tryal & Huldah, b. Feb. 22, 1788 | 2 | 21 |
| Prudence, d. John & Jemima, b. Apr. 9, 1761 | 1 | 41 |
| Rachel, d. [Consider & Rachel], b. Jan. 12, 1794 | 2 | 29 |
| Rachel, w. Consider, d. Feb. 4, 1794 | 2 | 28 |
| Ruth, m. Benjamin **DEAN**, Oct. 14, 1762, by Rev. H. Gold | 1 | 48 |
| Samuel Benedict, s. [Consider & Rachel], b. Mar. 24, 1791 | 2 | 29 |
| Sarah, d. John & Jamima, b. Sept. 3, 1762 | 1 | 48 |
| Sarah, d. William & Milla, b. Dec. 25, 1783 | 2 | 7 |
| Sarah, of Cornwall, m. Benjamin **HOADLEY**, of Saybrook, May 15, 1823, by David Miller | 2 | 55 |
| Submit, d. Mehetable, b. July 15, 1749; d. same month 18th day | 1 | 8 |
| Sylvia, d. Consider & Sylvia, b. Feb. 25, 1796 | 3 | 22 |
| Tommas, s. Tommas & Martha, b. June 30, 1743 | 1 | 3 |
| Thomas, of Cornwall, m. Mrs. Anna **BALDWIN**, of Goshen, Oct. 30, 1765, by Abel Newell | 1 | 80 |
| Thomas, s. Thomas & Anna, b. Apr. 7, 1769 | 1 | 89 |
| Tryal, s. William & Hannah, b. Dec. 20, 1751 | 1 | 16 |
| Tryal, m. Huldah **JACKSON**, May 12, 1777, by Rev. Hezekiah Gold | 2 | 16 |
| William, of Cornwall, m. Hannah **NEWCOMB**, of Kent, Mar. 23, 1749, by Rev. Cyrus Marsh, of Kent | 1 | 9 |
| William, s. William & Hannah, b. Jan. 28, 1762 | 1 | 45 |
| William, s. [Consider & Rachel], b. Feb. 27, 1777 | 2 | 29 |
| William, s. Capt. Thomas & Anne, b. Oct. 2, 1782 | 2 | 6 |
| **TAYLOR**, Almeda L., d. Jan. 14, 1850, ae 3 | 3 | 112-13 |

| | Vol. | Page |
|---|---|---|
| **TAYLOR**, (cont.) | | |
| Amos, m. Flora **VAILL**, Apr. 10, 1836, by C. Chittenden | 3 | 41 |
| Benjamin, m. Harriet **TAYLOR**, Jan. 1, 1843, by George Wheaton, J. P. | 3 | 66 |
| Benjamin, farmer & Harriet, had child, b. Feb. 25, 1848 | 3 | 86-7 |
| Betsey A., of Cornwall, m. Austin **CARTWRIGHT**, of Sharon, Mar. 28, 1844, by Rev. Thomas Edwards | 3 | 68 |
| Ezra, m. Sally **MORRIS**, b. of Cornwall, Nov. 17, 1822, by Rev. David Miller, of the M. E. Ch. | 2 | 54 |
| Harriet, m. Benjamin **TAYLOR**, Jan. 1, 1843, by George Wheaton, J. P. | 3 | 66 |
| Helen, L., d. Henry, farmer, ae [ ] & Lucie, b. Aug. 30, 1848 | 3 | 102-3 |
| Henry, m. Lucia **VIALL**, b. of Cornwall, Jan. [ ], 1835, by Rev. Chester William Turner, of the M. E. Ch. | 3 | 38 |
| James, m. Eunice **WADSWORTH**, Oct. 3, 1826, by Rev. Asa Tallmadge, of the Bap. Ch. | 2 | 66 |
| Lyman J., of Cornwall, m. Caroline **HUBBEL**, of Kent, Nov. 10, 1840, by Rev. John W. Salter | 3 | 59 |
| Rhoda, of Danbury, m. Phinehas **WALLER**, of Cornwall, Apr. 19, 1749, by E. White | 1 | 8 |
| Sally, b. Milford, res. Cornwall, d. Mar. 8, 1850, ae 68 | 3 | 112-13 |
| **TEFFENY***, Mary, m. Noah **BULL**, July 19, 1759, by Rev. Hezekiah Gold *("Hannah **JEFFERY**" in Starr's book) | 1 | 36 |
| **TERRILL, TERREL, TYRELL**, Jerusha, of Cornwall, m. Socrates **BRYANT**, of Sheffield, Mass., Nov. 9, 1826, by Rev. Walter Smith | 2 | 65 |
| Joseph, of Kent, m. Ann **TUCKER**, of Cornwall, Oct. 28, 1829, by Rev. Bradley Selleck | 3 | 44 |
| Mary, m. Daniel **LAMONT**, b. of Cornwall, Aug. 23, 1852, by Rev. Ralph Smith | 3 | 123 |
| **THOMAS**, Mehetable, m. Harvey **STEPHENS**, Apr. 30, 1810, by Rev. Reuben Harris, of the M. E. Ch. | 3 | 33 |
| Nelson, of Roxbury, m. Caroline **HUNT**, of Cornwall, Sept.* 31, 1840, by Rev. Ebenezer Washburn *("Aug.") | 3 | 59 |
| **THOMPSON, THOMSON**, Betsey, of Cornwall, m. Eber **THOMPSON**, of Torrington, July 17, 1831, by Benjamin Sedgwick, J. P. | 3 | 48 |
| Eber, of Torrington, m. Betsey **THOMSON**, of Cornwall, July 17, 1831, by Benjamin Sedgwick, J. P. | 3 | 48 |
| Lois, of Cornwall, m. Charles William **HOADLEY**, of Winchester, Nov. 24, 1831, by Benjamin Sedgwick, J. P. | 3 | 49 |
| **THORP**, Abel, s. [Abel & Hannah], b. Feb. 25, 1790 | 3 | 7 |
| Abigail, d. Abel & Hannah, b. Feb. 15, 1788 | 3 | 7 |
| Almeda, d. Titus & Phebe, b. Apr. 3, 1799 | 2 | 31 |
| Hannah, d. Abel & Hannah, b. June 9, 1783 | 2 | 15 |
| Hercules Weston, s. Abel & Hannah, b. June 22, 1792 | 3 | 19 |
| Levi, s. [Abel & Hannah], b. July 28, 1785 | 2 | 15 |
| **TICKNER**, Eunice, of Sharon, m. Mills **PIERCE**, of Cornwall, | | |

| | Vol. | Page |
|---|---|---|
| **TICKNER**, (cont.) | | |
| Oct. 18, 1832, by Rev. Aaron S. Hill | 3 | 50 |
| [**TIFFANY**], [see under **TEFFENY**] | | |
| **TODD**, Almond E., m. Lydia J. **FORD**, b. of Cornwall, Mar. 24, 1844, by Rev. Thomas Edwards | 3 | 68 |
| Almond Edward, s. [Carrington & Betsey], b. Nov. 20, 1820 | 2 | 61 |
| Carrington, m. Harriet **SHEPARD**, b. of Cornwall, Oct. 31, 1832, by Rev. Aaron S. Hill | 3 | 50 |
| Cynthia J., d. Almond E., farmer, ae 29 & Lydia J., ae 23, b. Sept. 21, 1847 | 3 | 86-7 |
| Edward J., s. Almond E. & Lydia, b. Mar. 25, 1845 | 3 | 69 |
| Ellen, m. Luther **MINER**, Jr., Apr. 8, 1846, by R. K. Reynolds | 3 | 72 |
| Ellen Elizabeth, d. Almond E. & Lydia, b. Mar. 25, 1846 | 3 | 69 |
| Ellen Jerusha, d. Carrington & Betsey, b. Jan. 4, 1825 | 2 | 61 |
| Harriet, d. Jonathan & Rhoda, b. [ ] 24, 1806 | 3 | 30 |
| Lewis How, s. Carrington & Betsey, b. Feb. 4, 1819 | 2 | 61 |
| Rhoda, d. [Jonathan & Rhoda], b. Nov. 2, 1808 | 3 | 30 |
| Rhoda, of Warren, m. Elam **LEWIS**, of Stonington, Jan. 5, 1832, by Rev. Luther Mead | 3 | 49 |
| **TOWNSEND**, Anna, d. Amasa & Thela, b. Dec. 16, 1757 | 1 | 26 |
| Martin, s. Martin & Rhoda, b. Dec. 11, 1756 | 1 | 26 |
| Nathan, s. Martin & Rhoda, b. Oct. 2, 1764 | 1 | 69 |
| Phebe, d. Amasa & Phebe, b. July 3, 1762 | 1 | 48 |
| Warring, s. Amasa & Phebe, b. May 13, 1764 | 1 | 55 |
| **TRAFFORD**, Abby, m. Amos **DICKINSON**, Sept. 15, 1850, at Cornwall Bridge, by Rev. William McAlister | 3 | 96 |
| Abby, ae 45, b. Canaan, res. Sharon, m. Enos **DICKINSON**, mechanic, ae 61, b. Litchfield, res. Sharon, Sept. 15, 1851, by Rev. William McAlister | 3 | 118-19 |
| Celia M., m. David A. **HOLLISTER**, b. of Cornwall, Mar. 26, 1837, by Rev. E. Washburn | 3 | 42 |
| Delia M., of Cornwall, m. James M. **SMITH**, of Sharon, Mar. 26, 1837, by Rev. E. Washburn | 3 | 42 |
| Jane E., m. Heman S. **SWIFT**, Sept. 10, 1835, by Rev. William Andrews | 3 | 40 |
| Julia, m. William **BALDWIN**, b. of Cornwall, Oct. 22, 1823, by Rev. Walter Smith, of the 2nd Cong. Ch. | 2 | 57 |
| Polly, of Cornwall, m. Gad **SMITH**, of Sharon, Sept. 7, 1834, by Rev. Chester William Turner, of the M. E. Ch. | 3 | 37 |
| Sarah A., m. Albert N. **BEACH**, Apr. 24, 1844, by Rev. William Day | 3 | 70 |
| **TRALL**, Polly, m. Luman **SEELEY**, b. of Cornwall, Nov. 4, 1801, by Judah Kellogg, J. P. | 3 | 32 |
| **TROWBRIDGE**, Hannah A., m. Henry S. **HOTCHKISS**, Sept. 30, 1832, by Rev. Walter Smith, of the North Cong. Ch. | 3 | 50 |
| Lucy, m. Abel **AVERY**, Apr. 14, 1830, by Rev. Walter Smith, of the North Ch. | 3 | 46 |

| | Vol. | Page |
|---|---|---|
| **TROWBRIDGE**, (cont.) | | |
| Mary M., of Cornwall, m. Benjamin P. **HAWKINS**, of East Windsor, Apr. 5, 1835, by Rev. William W. Andrews | 3 | 38 |
| Prudence, m. Willis **CURTISS**, Mar. 12, 1829, by Rev. Walter Smith, of the North Ch. | 3 | 1 |
| **TROY**, Margaret, d. Roger, laborer & Mary, b. Nov. 1, 1847 | 3 | 84-5 |
| Mary, d. Roger, laborer, ae 40 & Mary, ae 30, b. Oct. 6, 1849 | 3 | 108-9 |
| **TUBS**, Electa, m. Elkanah **BARBER**, Oct. 28, 1838, by Rev. Walter Smith | 3 | 56 |
| **TUCKER**, Ann, of Cornwall, m. Joseph **TERREL**, of Kent, Oct. 28, 1829, by Rev. Bradley Selleck | 3 | 44 |
| **TULLY**, Michael Kenney, s. John, b. Sept. 14, 1848 | 3 | 102-3 |
| **TUPPER**, Almira, m. Elisha B. **NORTON**, b. of Cornwall, Mar. 16, 1829, by Rev. Silas Ambler | 3 | 44 |
| **TUTTLE**, Alvin, s. Joel & Rebecca, b. Sept. 15, 1784 | 2 | 12 |
| [E]unice, d. Joel & Rebecca, b. Dec. 9, 1782 | 2 | 4 |
| Joel, m. Rebeckah **BARCE**, Oct. 2, 1781, by Rev. Hezekiah Gold | 2 | 1 |
| Mary Ann, m. William **SHERALIER**, Mar. 23, 1831, by Rev. Walter Smith, of the North Cong. Ch. | 3 | 48 |
| Sullivan M. N., m. Eliza **PARMALEE**, Sept. 4, 1830, by Rev. William Andrews | 3 | 46 |
| William, m. Nancy **EVEREST**, Aug. 30, 1823, by Rev. Timothy Stone, of the 1st Ch. | 2 | 57 |
| **TYLER, TILER**, Ebenezer, m. Sarah **GRIFFIS**, Nov. 25, 1742, by Solomon Palmer | 1 | 9 |
| Ebenezer, s. Ebenezer & Sarah, b. July 15, 1744; d. Oct. 22, 1744 | 1 | 9 |
| Ebenezer, s. Ebenezer & Sarah, b. Dec. 17, 1746 | 1 | 9 |
| Ezra, m. Mary **GRIFFIS**, Mar. 8, 1750, by Solomon Palmer | 1 | 13 |
| Ezra, s. Ezra & Mary, b. Jan. 15, 1753 | 1 | 20 |
| Lyman, of Broo[k]lin(?), m. Maria **PITCHER**, of Amenia, Aug. 19, 1828, by Rev. Silas Ambler | 2 | 68 |
| Mary, d. Ezra & Mary, b. June 20, 1757 | 1 | 31 |
| Nathaniel, s. Eben & Sarah, b. Feb. 10, 1750/1 | 1 | 14 |
| Solomon, s. Ebenezer & Sarah, b. Oct. 9, 1752 | 1 | 19 |
| **TYRELL**, [see under **TERRILL**] | | |
| **VAILL, VIALL, VAIL, VAILE**, Flora, m. Amos **TAYLOR**, Apr. 10, 1836, by C. Chittenden | 3 | 41 |
| Herman L., of Litchfield, m. Flora **GOLD**, of Cornwall, Jan. 22, 1823, by Rev. Joseph Harvey, of the 1st Cong. Ch. in Goshen | 2 | 55 |
| Lucia, m. Henry **TAYLOR**, b. of Cornwall, Jan. [ ], 1835, by Rev. Chester William Turner, of the M. E. Ch. | 3 | 38 |
| Mary Ellen, d. William, wagon maker, ae [ ] & Mary, b. Mar. 23, 1849 | 3 | 102-3 |
| Mary Jane, d. Philander, shoemaker, ae 44 & Urena M., ae 43, b. Aug. 29, 1848 | 3 | 86-7 |

| | Vol. | Page |
|---|---|---|
| **VAILL, VIALL, VAIL, VAILE,** (cont.) | | |
| Philomela, m. Mana M. **JOHNSON**, Sept. 27, 1829, by Rev. William Andrews | 3 | 44 |
| **VANDIKE**, Benjamin, of Hide Park, N. Y., m. Hannah **WHITCOMB**, of Cornwall, Apr. 4, 1830, by Horatio Smith, J. P. | 3 | 45 |
| **WADLEIGH**, L. M., of Springfield, Mass., m. Nancy M. **SANFORD**, of Goshen, Apr. 17, 1848, at the house of Harlow G. Buel, by Rev. Joshua L. Maynard, of the North Cong. Ch. | 3 | 79 |
| Lcrenzo M., carpenter, res. Springfield, Mass., m. Nancy M. **SANFORD**, b. Goshen, res. Goshen, Apr. 17, 1848, by Joshua L. Maynard | 3 | 90-1 |
| **WADSWORTH, WADWORTH**, Eunice, m. James **TAYLOR**, Oct. 3, 1826, by Rev. Asa Tallmadge, of the Bap. Ch. | 2 | 66 |
| James, m. Irene **PALMER**, b. of Cornwall, Feb. 16, 1774, at Canaan, by Rev. Daniel Farrand | LR3 | 7 |
| James, d. July 7, 1821, ae 71 | 2 | 46 |
| James F., m. Ruth **JEROME**, Sept. 18, 1837, by Rev. Walter Smith, of the 2nd Cong. Ch. | 3 | 52 |
| John P., m. Minerva **STODDARD**, Mar. 10, 1829, by Rev. Walter Smith, of North Ch. | 3 | 44 |
| Mary, d. Samuel & Sarah, b. July 22, 1768 | 1 | 83 |
| Mary E., d. Samuel & Sarah, b. Sept. 12, 1828 | 3 | 2 |
| Nancy E., m. Darius D. **MINER**, b. of Cornwall, Oct. 10, 1842, by Rev. Joshua L. Maynard, of the North Cong. Ch. | 3 | 65 |
| Samuel, m. Sally **JEFFERS**, b. of Cornwall, Sept. 14, 1825, by Rev. Walter Smith, of the 2nd Ch. | 2 | 62 |
| Tabitha, Mrs., m. Elisha Bradley **MALLORY**, Sept. 25, 1806, by Rev. Josiah Hawes, of the 2nd Ch. | 3 | 3 |
| William C., s. Samuel & Sarah, b. Oct. 18, 1826 | 2 | 69 |
| **WAIT**, Joanna, of Lime, m. Israel **FULLER**, of Cornwall, Nov. 15, 1763, by Samuel Pettebone, J. P. | 1 | 52 |
| **WALLER, WALLERS**, [see also **WALLEY**], Abigail, Mrs. of New Milford, m. Ketchel **BELL**, of Cornwall, Apr. 30, 1766, by Nathaniel Taylor | 1 | 72 |
| Ashble, s. Phinehas & Phebe, b. Oct. 18, 1759 | 1 | 35 |
| Ashbel, of Cornwall, m. Sarah **ABBOTT**, of Sharon, Nov. 1, 1781, by Judah Kellogg, J. P. | 2 | 1 |
| Daniel, s. Dea. Phinehas & Rhoda, b. Mar. 17, 1760 | 1 | 69 |
| Eliad Rockwell, s. [Nathan & Elizabeth], b. May 28, 1776 | 2 | 2 |
| Esther, d. Phinehas & Rhodah, b. Mar. 21, 1768 | 1 | 91 |
| Gideon*, d. Dea. Phinehas & Rhoda, b. May 10, 1756 *("Lydia" in Starr's book) | 1 | 24 |
| Hannah, d. Dea. Phinehas & Rhoda, b. Jan. 6, 1762 | 1 | 55 |
| Joseph, s. Dea. Phinehas & Rhoda, b. Feb. 4, 1764 | 1 | 55 |
| Levi, s. Phinehas & Phebe, b. Mar. 17, 1758 | 1 | 35 |

| | Vol. | Page |
|---|---|---|
| **WALLER, WALLERS**, (cont) | | |
| Lucy, d. [Nathan & Elizabeth], b. June 17, 1781 | 2 | 2 |
| Lydia*, d. Dea. Phinehas & Rhoda, b. May 10, 1756 *(Arnold Copy has "Gideon") | 1 | 24 |
| Lydia, d. [Nathan & Elizabeth], b. Oct. 21, 1778 | 2 | 2 |
| Mercy, d. Phinehas & Rhoda. b. Oct. 9, 1751 | 1 | 16 |
| Nathan, s. Dea. Phineas & Rhoda, b. Mar. 7, 1753 | 1 | 24 |
| Phinehas, of Cornwall, m. Rhoda **TAYLOR**, of Danbury, Apr. 19, 1749, by E. White | 1 | 8 |
| Phinehas, s. Nathan & Elizabeth, b. Jan. 31, 1774 | 2 | 2 |
| Rhoda, d. Phinehas & Rhoda, b. July 21, 1750 | 1 | 12 |
| **WALLEY**, [see also **WALLER**], Batsey, m. William **ATKINS**, Apr. 19, 1833, by Rev. Levi Peck, of the Bap. Ch. | 3 | 36 |
| Rachel*, m. Jethro **BONNEY**, Aug. 5, 1761, by Rev. H. Gold *("Rachel **BAILEY**" in Starr's book) | 1 | 40 |
| William, m. Candana **ANTHONY**, b. of Cornwall, Mar. 19, 1848, by Rev. Lewis Gunn | 3 | 80 |
| William, colored, m. Cadence **ANTHONY**, Mar. 19, 1848, by Lewis Gunn | 3 | 90-1 |
| **WALTER**, John, s. Pierce & Martha, b. Jan. 14, 1754 | 1 | 24 |
| Mary, d. Pierce & Martha, b. Oct. 19, 1756 | 1 | 24 |
| Mary, d. Pierce & Martha, d. Mar. 20, 1757 | 1 | 27 |
| Sarah, d. Parce & Martha, b. Feb. 24, 1752 | 1 | 19 |
| **WARD**, Artemecia, d. John & Lucretia, b. Aug. 21, 1804 | 2 | 35 |
| Clarissa, d. [John & Lucretia], b. Nov. 2, 1809 | 2 | 35 |
| Esther, d. [John & Lucretia], b. Dec. 24, 1813 | 2 | 35 |
| Hannah, d. [John & Lucretia], b. Nov. 30, 1805 | 2 | 35 |
| John, m. Lucretia **ROGERS**, b. of Cornwall, June 23, 1803, by Rev. Henry Christie | 2 | 36 |
| John Rogers, s. [John & Lucretia], b. Nov. 21, 1811 | 2 | 35 |
| Nancy, d. [John & Lucretia], b. Nov. 20, 1807 | 2 | 35 |
| **WARNER**, John M., m. Samantha **SWIFT**, Sept. 1, 1835, by Rev. William Andrews | 3 | 40 |
| W[illia]m J., of Preble, N. Y., m. Mary **SWIFT**, of Cornwall, June 1, 1845, by Rev. Hiram Day | 3 | 71 |
| **WASHBURN**, Sidney A., m. Harriet A. **MINER**, Sept. 8, 1836, by Rev. Walter Smith, of the 2nd Cong. Ch. | 3 | 42 |
| **WATSON**, Fanny Main*, of Glastonbury, m. Eli **BUNKER**, of Cornwall, Feb. 9, 1842, by Rev. Timothy Stone *("Maria"?) | 3 | 64 |
| **WEBB**, Hannah R., m. William K, **PECK***, of Norfolk, Jan. 8, 1850, by Rev. E. B. Andrews. Int. Pub. *("**PEET**"?) | 3 | 77 |
| Hannah R., ae 24, b. Warren, res. Norfolk, m. William R. **PEET***, attorney, ae 26, b. Salisbury, res. Norfolk, Jan. 8, 1850, by Rev. E. B. Andrews *("**PECK**"?) | 3 | 112-13 |
| James J., of Santa Fe, m. Florilla M. **SLADE**, of Kent, Dec. 1, 1853, by Ralph Smith | 3 | 125 |
| **WEDGE**, Amasa, s. Stephen & Temperance, b. Aug. 12, 1782 | 2 | 9 |

| | Vol. | Page |
|---|---|---|
| **WEDGE**, (cont.) | | |
| Eunice, m. Silas **DIBBLE**, Mar. 26, 1767, by Thomas Russell, J. P. | 1 | 75 |
| **WEEDEN**, [see also **WHEATON & WHEEDON**], Nancy, of Cornwall, m. Charles **EVERETT** (Rev.), of Warren, Oct. 27, 1831, by Rev. Luther Mead | 3 | 49 |
| **WELCH**, Augustus, m. Olive **HOLLEY**, Aug. 11, 1822, by Asa Tallmadge, Elder of the Bap. Church | 2 | 53 |
| Elizabeth B., d. John H., physician & Elizabeth, ae 22, res. Salisbury, b. Mar. 13, 1851 | 3 | 114-15 |
| John H., M. D. of New Hartford, m. Elizabeth M. **BELL**, of Cornwall, July 12, 1848, by Rev. Jno. Pettebone, of Winsted | 3 | 80 |
| John H., physician, ae 21, b. Norfolk, res. New Hartford, m. Elizabeth M. **BELL**, housekeeper, ae 19, res. Cornwall, July 12, 1848, by Rev. Asa Pettebone | 3 | 90-1 |
| Lois, m. Charles **MONROE**, b. of Warren, July 28, [1823], by Joshua Williams | 2 | 57 |
| **WELLS**. Egbert, d. Jan. 21, 1849 | 3 | 106-7 |
| Harriet, m. Elisha R. **PECK**, b. of Cornwall, Sept. 26, 1832, by Rev. Timothy Stone | 3 | 50 |
| Harriet, m. Heman B. **STERLING**, b. of Cornwall, Feb. 20, 1842, by Philo Kellogg, J. P. | 3 | 64 |
| Hester, d. George, peddler, ae 30 & Mary, ae 20, b. Dec. 24, 1849 | 3 | 108-9 |
| Judson, m. Flora Ann **CLARK**, b. of Cornwall, Dec. 24, 1843, by Rev. Thomas Edwards, of the M. E. Ch. | 3 | 68 |
| Judson, farmer, ae [ ] & Olive, had s. [ ], b. June 18, 1851 | 3 | 116-17 |
| Wilbur, s. Franklin, b. Mar. 22, 1849 | 3 | 102-3 |
| William Henry, m. Ruth **DIBBLE**, July 23, 1838, by Rev. Walter Smith | 3 | 54 |
| **WESTON**, Chloe Ann, Luman **FREEMAN**, b. of Cornwall, Dec. 16, 1847, by Rev. Lewis Gunn | 3 | 81 |
| Samuel, m. Hannah **GAWSON***, Aug. 23, 1831, by Horatio Smith, J. P. *("**LAWSON** or **GARSON**") | 3 | 48 |
| Sarah Ann, m. Luman **FREEMAN**, Oct. 23, 1831, by Horatio Smith, J. P. | 3 | 49 |
| **WHALEY**, Theodore D., of Montville, m. Jane R. **MAYNARD**, of Norwich, Jan. 25, 1847, by Rev. Joshua L. Maynard, of the North Cong. Ch., at his house | 3 | 74 |
| **WHEATON**, [see also **WHEEDON & WEEDEN**], Cynthia, m. Elbert **SHEPARD**, May 31, 1846, by R. K. Reynolds | 3 | 73 |
| Cynthia Love, d. George & Love, b. Jan. 6, 1819 | 2 | 43 |
| George, m. Lewey **ALLING**, b. of Cornwall, Nov. 16, 1815, by Rev. Pitkin Cowles, of Canaan | 2 | 37 |
| George, m. Eliza **COTTER**, Sept. 5, 1824, by Rev. Walter Smith, of the 2nd Ch. | 2 | 58 |
| George A., m. Artemicia M. **BALDWIN**, b. of Cornwall, Feb. | | |

| | Vol. | Page |
|---|---|---|
| **WHEATON**, (cont.) | | |
| 20, 1842, by Rev. Lewis Gunn | 3 | 64 |
| George Allen, s. George & Lewey, b. July 30, 1821 | 2 | 47 |
| Harriet N., d. George A., farmer, ae [ ] & Artemissa, b. Oct. 16, 1848 | 3 | 100-1 |
| Lewey, w. George, d. July 26, 1823, ae 26 y. | 2 | 56 |
| Lucetta Irene, d. George & Elizabeth Rhoda, b. Feb. 9, 1827 | 2 | 61 |
| Lucetta J., m. Philip C. **CUMMINGS**, b. of Cornwall, June 8, 1852, at the house of George Wheaton, by Rev. Joshua L. Maynard | 3 | 122 |
| Nancy R., m. William W. **BALDWIN**, b. of Cornwall, July 9, 1843, by Rev. Thomas Edwards, of the M. E. Ch. | 3 | 66 |
| Nancy Rebecca, d. George & Lewey, b. Oct. 26, 1816 | 2 | 42 |
| **WEEDON, WHEDON**, [see also **WHEATON**], Harvey, m. Harriet C. **CLARK**, Aug. 16, 1837, by Rev. Walter Smith, of the 2nd Cong. Ch. | 3 | 52 |
| Laura, m. Edwin **WHITE**, Sept. 13, 1837, by Rev. Walter Smith, of the 2nd Cong. Ch. | 3 | 52 |
| **WHEELER**, Calista M., of Cornwall, m. William P. **RICHARDS**, of Woodbury, Sept. 26, 1824, by Rev. Walter Smith, of the 2nd Ch. | 2 | 58 |
| Mary, m. Hiram **ROOT**, Dec. 2, 1821, by Asa Tallmadge, Elder, of the Bap. Church | 2 | 53 |
| Mary, of Canaan, m. Jacob **HICKOK**, May 29, 1838, by James Wadsworth, J. P. | 3 | 54 |
| Samuel, m. Theisa **HOWE**, b. of Cornwall, June 29, 1842, by Rev. J. L. Maynard, of the North Cong. Ch. | 3 | 65 |
| **WHINNEGAR**, Solomon, s. Henry & Mercy, b. Oct. 5, 1771 | 1 | 105 |
| **WHITCOMB**, Augustus, m. Lucy **PAGE**, b. of Cornwall, Oct. 20, 1852, by Rev. Luther B. Hart | 3 | 124 |
| Caroline, m. Heman **SWIFT**, Jan. 4, 1830, by Rev. William Andrews | 3 | 45 |
| Hannah, of Cornwall, m. Benjamin **VANDIKE**, of Hide Park, N. Y., Apr. 4, 1830, by Horatio Smith, J. P. | 3 | 45 |
| Leonard, farmer, ae 24, res. Cornwall, m. Sarah **BUCKLEY**, ae 26, res. Cornwall (No date on original manuscript) | 3 | 104-5 |
| Royal E., s. Augustus, farmer, ae 30 & Chloe, ae 31, b. Nov. 14, 1847 | 3 | 84-5 |
| **WHITE**, Betty, d. John & Elizabeth, b. Dec. 20, 1761 | 1 | 43 |
| Comfort, s. Elias & Cynthia, b. Jan. 3, 1802 | 3 | 31 |
| Comfort, m. Laura **NORTON**, Dec. 3, 1827, by Rev. Walter Smith, of the North Ch. | 2 | 68 |
| Diana, d. John & Elizabeth, b. Mar. 14, 1755 | 1 | 31 |
| Edward Rogers, s. Elias & Cynthia, b. Feb. 14, 1804 | 3 | 12 |
| Edwin, s. Elias & Cynthia, b. Sept. 21, 1806 | 3 | 16 |
| Edwin, m. Laura **WHEDON**, Sept. 13, 1837, by Rev. Walter Smith, of the 2nd Cong. Ch. | 3 | 52 |
| Elias, m. Mrs. Cynthia **ROGERS**, Jan. 2, 1800, by Rev. | | |

| | Vol. | Page |
|---|---|---|
| **WHITE**, (cont.) | | |
| Gideon, farmer, ae 41 & Laura, ae 30, had child b. May 21, 1848 | 3 | 86-7 |
| Ruana, d. John & Elizabeth, b. Jan. 25, 1754; d. Jan. 30, 1754 | 1 | 31 |
| Ruth, d. John & Elizabeth, b. Sept. 1, 1757 | 1 | 31 |
| Thomas, s. John & Elizabeth, b. Jan. 19, 1752 | 1 | 17 |
| William, m. Jane **HAMILTON**, Dec. 12, 1849, by Rev. William McAlister | 3 | 77 |
| William R., shoemaker, ae 30, b. Cornell, res. West Cornwll, m. Jane **HAMILTON**, ae 34, b. Cornwall, res. West Cornwall, Dec. 11, 1849, by Rev. William McAlister | 3 | 112-13 |
| **WHITING***, Sarah, d. Joseph, of Stanford, m. Ketchel **BELL**, of Cornwall, Nov. 14, 1753, by Moses Mather, V. D. M. *("**WHITNEY**" in Starr's book) | 1 | 19 |
| Thomas F., m. Rosalinda **NETTLETON**, [ ], by Rev. C. P. Wilson, of the Bap. Ch., in Amenia, N. Y. (Recorded June 23, 1827) | 2 | 67 |
| **WHITLOCK**, John, of Ridgfield, m. Maria **SPELLMAN**, Feb. 12, 1822, by Rev. Walter Smith, of 2nd Church | 3 | 51 |
| **WHITMORE**, Roswell, s. Samuel, b. Sept. 22, 1768 | 1 | 89 |
| Samuel Park, s. Samuel & Deliverance, b. Sept. 9, 1770 | 1 | 100 |
| **WHITNEY**, Abigail, d. July 31, 1781 | LR4 | 18 |
| Asa, d. June [ ], 1776 | LR3 | 11 |
| Benjamin, s. Asa & Abigail, b. July 29, 1776 | LR3 | 12 |
| Elizabeth, d. J. L., laborer, ae [ ] & Elizabeth, b. Mar. 24, 1851 | 3 | 114-15 |
| Joseph L., m. Elizabeth M. **SWIFT**, Sept. 12, 1849, by Rev. William McAlister | 3 | 77 |
| Leander, farmer, ae 24, b. Warren, res. Warren, m. Samantha **BISHOP**, ae 18, July 6, 1848, by Rev. John T. Norton | 3 | 90-1 |
| Leander, m. Samantha **BISHOP**, b. of Cornwall, July 16, 1848, by John T. Norton | 3 | 80 |
| Rebecca Smith, d. Asa & Abigail, b. Oct. 8, 1773 | 2 | 13 |
| Sarah*, d. Joseph of Stanford, m. Ketchel **BELL**, of Cornwall, Nov. 14, 1753, by Moses Mather, V. D. M. *("Sarah **WHITING**" in Arnold Copy) | 1 | 19 |
| William, s. Leander, collier, ae 27 & Samantha, ae 21, b. Sept. 5, 1850 | 3 | 114-15 |
| **WHITTLESEY**, S. Amelia, ae 20, b. Washington, res. Washington, m. Nathan **HART**, Jr., farmer, ae 26, res. Cornwall, Sept. 4, 1847, by Hollis Read | 3 | 90-1 |
| Sheldon, of New Preston, m. Esther M. **HART**, of Cornwall, Mar. 13, 1844, by Rev. Joshua L. Maynard, of the North Cong. Ch. | 3 | 70 |
| **WICKWIRE**, Betsey, m. Phinehas **HART**, Mar. 18, 1784, by Judah Kellogg, J. P. | 2 | 8 |

| | Vol. | Page |
|---|---|---|
| **WICKWIRE**, (cont.) | | |
| Charles, farmer, ae 38 & Mary Ann, ae 31, had child b. May 20, 1848 | 3 | 84-5 |
| Mary, of Cornwall, m. Joseph **KENNEY**, of Courtlandville, N. Y., Sept. 16, 1841, by Rev. Lewis Gunn | 3 | 63 |
| Rhoda, m. James H. **REED**, b. of Cornwall, Sept. 4, 1825, by Rev. John Lovejoy, of the M. E. Ch. | 2 | 62 |
| Richard, 2nd, m. Eunice **LEONARD**, b. of Canaan, [ ], by Judah Kellogg, J. P. (Recorded Sept. 19, 1801) | 2 | 24 |
| Ursula, m. Richard **POTTER**, Apr. 17, 1835, by James Wadsworth, J. P. | 3 | 38 |
| **WILCOX, WILLCOX, WILLCOCKS**, Caroline, d. Samuel & Phebe, b. Mar. 16, 1774 | LR3 | 10 |
| Clarissa, d. [Zadock & Lois], b. May 17, 1791 | 3 | 26 |
| Fanny M., m. Russel H. **WILLCOX**, May 27, 1834, by Rev. Walter Smith, of the North Cong. Ch. | 3 | 37 |
| Harriet, d. [Zadock & Lois], b. Aug. 16, 1793 | 3 | 26 |
| John Flavel, s. Samuel & Phebe, b. Nov. 25, 1775 | LR3 | 10 |
| Lovisa, d. Zadock & Lois, b. Mar. 15, 1779 | 3 | 26 |
| Lucia, m. Almond T. **JONES**, Sept. 27, 1837, by Rev. Walter Smith, of the 2nd Cong. Ch. | 3 | 52 |
| Reuben, s. [Zadock & Lois], b. Dec. 14, 1780 | 3 | 26 |
| Robert, m. Charlotte M. **FOX**, b. of Cornwall, Feb. 16, 1853, by Rev. Harley Goodwin, of South Canaan | 3 | 124 |
| Ruloff, s. [Zadock & Lois], b. Sept. 9, 1785 | 3 | 26 |
| Ruluff, s. Zadock & Lois, d. Apr. 7, 1788 | 3 | 10 |
| Russel H., m. Fanny M. **WILCOX**, May 27, 1834, by Rev. Walter Smith, of the North Cong. Ch. | 3 | 37 |
| **WILLET***, Philena, Mrs., m. Seymour **MURRY**, Mar. 8, 1781, by Jonathan Huntington, J. P. (*Arnold copy has "**MILLET**") | 2 | 2 |
| **WILLEY**, Abel, s. Abel & Mary, b. Jan. 25, 1748/9 | 1 | 8 |
| **WILLIAMS**, Allen, m. Sarah A. **CURTICE**, b. of Cornwall, Mar. 28, 1852, by F. C. Youngs | 3 | 122 |
| Eben Sturgis, s. Sturgis & Deborah, b. Apr. 18, 1808 | 3 | 30 |
| Harvey Hatch, s. [Sturgis & Deborah], b. Jan. 30, 1806 | 3 | 29 |
| Huldah Merinda, d. [Sturgis & Deborah], b. Feb. 18, 1800 | 3 | 29 |
| John, farmer & Mary, had s. [ ], b. June 3, 1849 | 3 | 100-1 |
| Nelson, s. Sturgis & Deborah, b. May 26, 1798 | 3 | 29 |
| Norman, s. [Sturgis & Deborah], b. Aug. 18, 1802 | 3 | 29 |
| Reuben Sackett, s. [Sturgis & Deborah], b. Mar. 14, 1804 | 3 | 29 |
| **WILLIS**, Lucinda A., m. Dr. Solon **HUBBARD**, Feb. 1, 1846, by Rev. K. K. Reynolds | 3 | 72 |
| **WILLOUGHBY**, DeGrasse, s. Solomon* & Salome, b. May 3, 1789 *("Salmon" in Starr's book) | 2 | 25 |
| Dianthe, d. Salmon & Salome, b. June 27, 1790 | 3 | 7 |
| Harriet, d. Salmon & Salome, b. May 29, 1793 | 3 | 19 |
| Olive, m. Thomas **DEAN**, Apr. 23, 1776, by Rev. Hezekiah | | |

| | Vol. | Page |
|---|---|---|
| **WILLOUGHBY**, (cont.) | | |
| Gold | LR3 | 9 |
| Oliver, s. Salmon & Salome, b. Feb. 19, 1786 | 2 | 10 |
| **WILMOTT**, Henry, m. Rhoda **BROWNSON**, Sept. 20, 1821, by Asa Tallmadge, Elder, of the Bap. Church | 2 | 53 |
| **WILSON**, Aurilla, m. Asa **MILLARD**, b. of Cornwall, [Nov.] 27, [1822], by Rev. A. Derthick | 2 | 54 |
| Elizur, m. Mariah **FRINK**, Nov. 30, 1826, by Rev. Timothy Stone, of the 1st Ch. | 2 | 66 |
| Harmon, m. Laura L. **BEARDSLEY**, Mar. 22, 1838, by Rev. Walter Smith, of the 2nd Cong. Ch. | 3 | 53 |
| Icilda Francis, child of John, farmer & Sarah, res. Gt. Hill, Cornwall, b. Jan. 1, 1848 | 3 | 86-7 |
| Jennet, m. Daniel **DELANE**, Oct. 23, 1824, by Rev. Asa Tallmadge, of the Bap. Ch. | 2 | 65 |
| John, farmer, d. Jan. 20, 1849, ae 86 | 3 | 106-7 |
| John W., m. Sarah P. **BABCOCK**, June 7, 1846, by R. K. Reynolds | 3 | 73 |
| **WINAAT**, Elisha, m. Maria **HART**, b. of Cornwall, Dec. 9, 1840, by Rev. John W. Salter | 3 | 61 |
| **WINANS**, Harriet, m. Sylvester M. **SCOVIL**, May 27, 1834, by Rev. Walter Smith, of the North Cong. Ch. | 3 | 37 |
| Mary, m. John **HART**, b. of Cornwall, Dec. 8, 1840, by Rev. John W. Salter | 3 | 61 |
| Tammy E., m. William E. **HANSON**, b. of Cornwall, Dec. 11, 1842, by Rev. Joshua L. Maynard, of the North Cong. Ch. | 3 | 66 |
| **WINCHELL**, Daniel, m. Charlotte **BIRDSALL**, b. of Cornwall, Jan. 10, 1843, by Rev. John K. Still, of the M. E. Ch. | 3 | 66 |
| Sarah M., of Cornwall, m. Liveras **DUNNING**(?), of Brookfield, Mar. 23, 1851, by F. C. Youngs | 3 | 96 |
| **WING**, Ebenezer, of Sharon, m. Elizabeth **REED**, of Cornwall, Dec. 26, 1833, by Aaron S. Hill | 3 | 36 |
| **WINTON**, Samuel F., m. Abbey **FRINK**, b. of Cornwall, Dec. 16, 1847, by H. Day | 3 | 76 |
| **WITCHELL**, [see also **MITCHELL**], Morris E., s. Elisha, laborer, colored & Polly, ae 27, b. Sept. 24, 1850 | 3 | 116-17 |
| **WIX**, Anna, d. Zephaniah & Lydia, b. Nov. 28, 1761 | 1 | 45 |
| Anna, d. Zephaniah & Lidiah, d. Mar. 17, 1762 | 1 | 46 |
| Betty, d. Zephaniah & Lydia, b. July 20, 1757 | 1 | 38 |
| Deborah, d. Zephaniah & Lydia, b. Apr. 5, 1767 | 1 | 82 |
| Deborah, d. Zephaniah & Lydiah, b. Apr. 6, 1767 | 1 | 75 |
| Ezekiel, s. Zephaniah & Lydiah, b. Jan. 15, 1750 | 1 | 38 |
| Ezekiel, s. [Zepheniah & Lidiah], d. Apr. 30, 1762 | 1 | 46 |
| Joseph, s. Zephaniah & Lydiah, b. Mar. 7, 1774 | LR3 | 6 |
| Lucy, d. Zephaniah & Lydia, b. Jan. 25, 1759 | 1 | 38 |
| Lydiah, d. Zephaniah & Lydiah, b. Aug. 18, 1763 | 1 | 51 |
| Mary, d. Zephaniah & Lydia, b. Feb. 9, 1769 | 1 | 84 |

| | Vol. | Page |
|---|---|---|
| **WIX**, (cont.) | | |
| Shubael, s. Zephaniah & Lydia, b. Apr. 27, 1772 | 1 | 106 |
| Uriah, s. Zephaniah & Lydia, b. Oct. 17, 1753 | 1 | 38 |
| Zadock, s. Zephaniah & Lydiah, b. June 14, 1765 | 1 | 62 |
| **WOLF**, Rebecca, b. New York State, res. Cornwall, d. Jan. 22, 1851, ae 59 | 3 | 120-1 |
| **WOOD**, Samuel, m. Elizabeth **STEWART**, Apr. 7, 1788, by Rev. Hezekiah Gold | 2 | 22 |
| Sarah, m. John **PANGBORN**, Nov. 5, 1761, by Rev. H. Gold | 1 | 48 |
| **WOODRUFF**, Sarah, of Watertown, m. Abel C. **CARTER**, of Cornwall, Aug. 26, 1838, by Rev. N. M. Urmston, of the 1st Cong. Ch. | 3 | 54 |
| **WOODWORTH**, James, s. William, carpenter, ae 27 & Matilda, ae 28, b. Jan. 26, 1848 | 3 | 86-7 |
| John, of Cornwall, m. Philomelia **BEARDSLEY**, of Goshen, Jan. 9, 1823, by Rev. Walter Smith, of the 2nd Ch. | 2 | 55 |
| **WOOSTER**, Ebenezer W., of Goshen, m. Lydia E. **DAVISON**, of Cornwall, Dec. 30, 1847, by Rev. M. Bydenburgh | 3 | 78 |
| Rollin S., of Litchfield, m. Charlotte L. **MILLARD**, of Cornwall, Jan. 30, 1854, by Rev. Henry Burton, of Sharon | 3 | 124 |
| **WRIGHT**, Anna, of Cornwall, m. Egbert B. **NAIL**, of Unionvill, Dutchess Cty., N. Y., Aug. 27, 1833, by Daniel Coe | 3 | 36 |
| Esther, m. David **COE**, Nov. 27, 1823, by Elder Daniel **BRAYTON**, of the M. E. Ch. | 2 | 57 |
| Henry, of Litchfield, m. Jane **PRITCHARD**, of Cornwall, Dec. 22, 1844, by Myron Harrison, J. P. | 3 | 71 |
| Henry, m. Adaline **PRITCHARD**, Feb. 16, 1846, by Rev. K. K. Reynolds | 3 | 72 |
| Lucy, of Cornwall, m. Thoedore **LEACH**, of Torrington, Aug. 27, 1835, by Rev. Charles Chittenden, of Litchfield. Witnesses: Lewis Gunn & Carrington Todd | 3 | 40 |
| Sarah, of Cromwell, m. Elbert **OSBORN**, of Fairfield, Sept. 22, 1825, by Rev. John Lovejoy, of the M. E. Ch. | 2 | 62 |
| **YALE**, Francis J., m. Julian **PARMELEE**, Oct. 7, 1831, by Rev. William Andrews | 3 | 48 |
| Frederick, of Canaan, m. Esther A. **ROBERTS**, of Cornwall, Mar. 3, 1850, by E. N. Jenckes | 3 | 83 |
| **YOUNG**, Deborah, m. Timothy **PANGBORN**, [Oct.] 15, 1742, by Samuell Lewis, J. P. | 1 | 3 |
| Lydiah, Mrs. of Sharon, m. Joshua **MILLARD**, of Cornwall, Mar. 6, 1765, by Daniel Griswold, J. P. | 1 | 63 |
| Naomi Abigail, d. Israel & Mary, b. Nov. 19, 1794 | 3 | 25 |
| Ralph Love, s. [Israel & Mary], b. July 26, 1797 | 3 | 25 |
| Stephen R., of Kent, m. Mary A. **HILL**, of Cornwall, Oct. 28, 1839, by Rev. Samuel W. Smith | 3 | 58 |
| **NO SURNAME**, | | |
| Amos, s. Elsex & Dinah (negro servants), b. July 15, 1787 | 2 | 21 |

| | Vol. | Page |
|---|---|---|
| **NO SURNAME**, (cont.) | | |
| Benjamin, s. William & Parthena, b. June 6, 1807 | 3 | 18 |
| Oısenas, s. William & Parthene, b. Aug. 11, 1801 | 3 | 18 |
| Rachel, d. [Elsex & Dinah] (negro servants), b. Sept. 14, 1789 | 2 | 21 |
| William Bayley, s. [William & Parthena], b. May 7, 1810 | 3 | 18 |
| ----, b. May 10, 1773 | 2 | 13 |

www.ingramcontent.com/pod-product-compliance
Lightning Source LLC
Chambersburg PA
CBHW072059040426
42334CB00041B/1359

* 9 7 8 0 8 0 6 3 1 5 2 1 8 *